Perl Module Reference

Perl Module Reference
Volume 1

Ellen Siever and David Futato

O'REILLY™

Cambridge · Köln · Paris · Sebastopol · Tokyo

Perl Module Reference, Volume 1
compiled and edited by Ellen Siever and David Futato

Compilation Copyright © 1997 O'Reilly & Associates, Inc. All rights reserved.
Printed in the United States of America.
Copyright for individual modules and associated documentation appears in the text.

Published by O'Reilly & Associates, Inc., 101 Morris Street, Sebastopol, CA 95472.

Editor: Susan B. Peck

Production Editors: Nicole Gipson Arigo and Nancy Wolfe Kotary

Printing History:

November 1997:   First Edition.

Table of Contents

Preface

The modules available on CPAN (Comprehensive Perl Archive Network) are an invaluable resource for the Perl programmer. The functionality covered by modules on CPAN range from the seemingly trivial to the absolutely essential, from tiny modules that simplify a tedious task to extensive packages that push the envelope of Perl's capabilities.

The documentation for these modules is embedded into the code itself, using a markup language called *pod*, for Plain Old Documentation. pod makes it easy for module developers to document their module as they go along, and update the documentation as needed.

While the pod infrastructure makes the documentation for a single module easy to access, this book (and its companion volume) mark the first time that the pod for the majority of the CPAN modules has been published in print. Although we do not cover every module on CPAN, we tried to include the ones that we determined to be most stable or most essential. If one of your favorite modules is missing from these volumes, however, it's not necessarily because we didn't think they were "good enough"; we were also restricted by what was available at the time of compilation, and whether the author(s) gave us permission to include their modules in the book.

Please note that while we made every effort to include only modules that are stable and that work as advertised, we were not able to test them ourselves and neither we nor O'Reilly & Associates can accept any responsibility for them.

About the Perl Resource Kit

Until now, Perl has been something that was accessible only to an "in crowd"— much as the Internet itself was a few years ago. Perl is widely available on the

Net, but it hasn't had any kind of standard packaged distribution. This has limited its availability both to new users and to many corporate users who must have a supported distribution before they can adopt a product. The Perl Resource Kit addresses this need, while providing valuable resources, technical knowledge, and software tools to those member of the in-crowd who already use Perl on a regular basis.

The Perl Resource Kit, UNIX Edition, is a definitive Perl distribution, complete with essential documentation, for all Perl users. It contains a collection of Perl software and over 1500 pages of documentation, including the first printed documentation for more than 600 widely used Perl modules. The Kit is for programmers, webmasters, system administrators, and others who use—or want to use—Perl.

The modules documented in the Perl Resource Kit were created by members of the Perl freeware community. O'Reilly actively supports the Perl freeware community and has since the publication of our first Perl book, *Programming Perl*. With the Perl Resource Kit and our Perl books, Perl conferences, and other efforts, we seek to extend the visibility of Perl and help ensure the healthy growth of Perl and its community.

The Perl Resource Kit contains:

- *Programming with Perl Modules*, an introduction to programming with some of the most important Perl modules

- *Perl Module Reference* (two volumes), a comprehensive reference for significant Perl modules

- *Perl Utilities Guide*, documentation for Perl software tools contained in the Kit

- Perl Resource Kit Software (on CD-ROM). This includes a Java/Perl tool (JPL) written by Larry Wall, which allows programmers to write Java classes with Perl implementations; a snapshot of the freeware Perl tools on CPAN (Comprehensive Perl Archives Network), with an install program, a search tool, and a web-aware interface for identifying more recent online CPAN tools; and many bits of example code and sample programs.

- The Autumn 1997 issue of *The Perl Journal*, a quarterly magazine devoted to the Perl language

Conventions Used in This Book

This section lists the conventions we used. We've applied them as consistently as possible, but given the number of authors, who of course used their own conventions, we have not always been successful.

Italic

> is used for URLs, filenames, and email addresses, as well as for emphasis.

`Constant width`

> is used for functions, methods, and other fragments of Perl code in regular text, as well as for blocks of code examples.

`Constant width italic`

> is used for arguments of functions and methods, to be replaced with a user-supplied value (or expression).

Horizontal rules separate each module's documentation from the next.

Contacting Technical Support

If you've thoroughly investigated other sources for help (see Chapter 1 of the *Perl Utilities Guide* for suggestions) and still need assistance, technical support is available for the Perl Resource Kit. Before contacting technical support, make sure you have registered your copy of the Resource Kit online at *http://perl.oreilly.com/register.html*. Registering your copy helps us provide better service and keep you up-to-date on what is happening with Perl at O'Reilly.

Support for the Perl Resource Kit comes in three flavors:

- Once you register your Resource Kit, you have up to 30 days of free initial installation support on Solaris 2.5.* and higher and Linux 2.0.* and higher for the software included on the CD-ROM. This support is available by phone at (707) 829-0515 from 7:00 a.m. to 5:00 p.m. (Pacific Time, U.S.A.), Monday through Friday.

- After the 30 days or for software problems beyond installation, technical support is available for a fee through the Perl Clinic, which you can reach in several ways:
  - — on the Web at *http://www.perlclinic.com/*
  - — by email at *info@perlclinic.com*
  - — by phone in the United States and Canada at (604) 606-4611
  - — by phone in Europe and elsewhere at 44 (0) 1483 424424.

- For help and information on the books included in the Resource Kit, technical support is available by email at *perltech@oreilly.com*. Please use this email address to ask questions about and/or report errors in the books.

Acknowledgments

First and foremost, we want to thank all the module authors and maintainers who graciously gave us permission to include their documentation in this book and without whom there would be no Perl Module Reference. We wish we could list them all, but there are too many. In most cases, they are credited in the documentation for their modules.

Thanks also to the many people here at O'Reilly, without whom this book would never have gotten done. Thanks to our editor, Susan Peck, for her advice and support; to Linda Mui, for additional editorial support; to Gina Blaber, who oversaw everything, managed the process of getting the permissions, and provided chocolates; to the rest of the Resource Kit team for support, encouragement, and the answers to many questions; and to Laura Schmier and Trina Jackson for managing the task of organizing and maintaining lists of modules, authors, and permissions.

Thanks to our production editors, Nicole Gipson Arigo and Nancy Wolfe Kotary, who did an incredible job of pulling everything together on an unbelievably short schedule and also did quality control. Thanks to Sheryl Avruch for production management and quality control, Robert Romano for the figures, Ted Meister for the cover design, Nancy Priest and Edie Freedman for the interior design, Mike Sierra for FrameMaker support, and Madeleine Newell for production assistance. Kristin Barendsen and Lunaea Hougland proofread, and Elissa Haney and Kathleen Faughnan helped with FrameMaker formatting.

Ellen would like to thank Stephen and Michael for their support and patience while she spent most of her time glued to the computer, and David for being so easy to work with.

David would like to thank his partner Ron for his patience, his friends Scott and Hilary for their understanding, and his parents for their support. And thanks also to his co-conspirator, Ellen, for working with his insane hours.

1

Introduction

New with the release of Perl 5, modules are chunks of reusable Perl code that can be easily imported into other Perl programs. This portability has led to an explosion of modules on CPAN, the Comprehensive Perl Archive Network, where (including those distributed individually and in bundles) there are now well over 600 modules available for free download.

This book documents many, but certainly not all, of those modules. We have tried to include as many as possible, but there are omissions for various reasons. Some modules on CPAN are not yet in a stable release, and some had little if any documentation included. There were a number of authors who were unreachable, and a few who did not wish their modules to be included in a printed book. See the section "CPAN: The Comprehensive Perl Archive Network" for information about finding the CPAN site nearest you to locate modules not included in this book, or use the CPAN Graphical Setup tool included on the CD-ROM of this kit.

As mentioned in the Preface, we have not tested the modules ourselves and assume no responsibility for them.

How This Book Is Organized

The book is divided into two volumes, with pages numbered sequentially between them. These two volumes have been divided into sections that parallel the CPAN categorization structure; Volume 1 contains this introduction and CPAN categories 02 through 07, while Volume 2 contains the remaining CPAN categories (08 through 23) and an alphabetical index of both volumes sorted by the simple module name, such as Peek, Zlib, or Folder. Within each chapter, modules are listed alphabetically by their fully qualified namespace, such as Devel::Peek, Convert::Zlib, or Mail::Folder.

See Chapter 1, *Introduction to Perl Modules and CPAN*, in *Programming with Perl Modules* for an introduction to modules and their namespaces, and to the structure and categories of CPAN itself.

CPAN: The Comprehensive Perl Archive Network

The Comprehensive Perl Archive Network, or CPAN, is a massive collection of Perl resources, which includes:

- distributions of Perl

- a complete listing of, and source code for, Perl modules

- documentation for both Perl and Perl modules

- information about Perl and module authors

- hints for Perl programming

- guidelines for writing your own modules for submission to CPAN

and more. CPAN is mirrored on Internet sites on six continents; to find the site nearest you, point your web browser at *http://www.perl.com/CPAN* (do *not* include a trailing slash). Chapter 13, *Contributing to CPAN*, in *Programming with Perl Modules* also lists the registered CPAN sites, and gives a detailed set of guidelines for developing your own modules to contribute to CPAN.

2

Perl Core Modules

This section documents the core Perl modules, many of which are included as part of the Perl distribution. This section also includes documentation of the pod modules, which describe Perl's internal document format.

Alias—declare symbolic aliases for Perl data

Synopsis

```
use Alias qw(alias const attr);
alias TEN => $ten, Ten => \$ten, Ten => \&ten,
     Ten => \@ten, Ten => \%ten, TeN => \*ten;
{
   local @Ten;
   my $ten = [1..10];
   alias Ten => $ten;    # local @Ten
}
const pi => 3.14, ten => 10;
package Foo;
use Alias;
sub new { bless {foo => 1, _bar => [2, 3]}, $_[0] }
sub a_method {
   my $s = attr shift;
   # $foo, @_bar are now local aliases for
   # $_[0]{foo}, @{$_[0]{_bar}} etc.
}
sub b_method {
  local $Alias::KeyFilter = "_";
  local $Alias::AttrPrefix = "main::";
  my $s = attr shift;
  # local @::_bar is now available, ($foo, $::foo are not)
}
sub c_method {
  local $Alias::KeyFilter = sub { $_ = shift; return (/^_/ ? 1 : 0) };
```

```
      local $Alias::AttrPrefix = sub {
                                  $_ = shift;
                                  s/^_(.+)$/main::$1/;
                                  return $_
                               };
      my $s = attr shift;
      # local @::bar is now available, ($foo, $::foo are not)
  }
```

Description

This module provides general mechanisms for aliasing Perl data for convenient access.

It works by putting values on the symbol table with user-supplied names. Values that are references will get dereferenced to their base types. This means that a value of [1,2,3] with a name of foo will be made available as @foo, not $foo.

The exception to this rule is the default behavior of the attr function, which will not dereference values which are blessed references (e.g., objects). See $Alias::Deref for how to change this default behavior.

Functions

alias

> Given a list of name => value pairs, alias declares aliases in the caller's namespace. If the value supplied is a reference, the alias is created for the underlying value instead of the reference itself (there is no need to use this module to alias references—they are automatically "aliased" on assignment). This allows the user to alias most of the basic types.
>
> If the value supplied is a scalar compile-time constant, the alias becomes read-only. Any attempt to write to it will fail with a run-time error.
>
> Aliases can be dynamically scoped by predeclaring the target variable as local. Using attr for this purpose is more convenient, and recommended.

attr

> Given a hash reference, attr aliases the values of the hash to the names that correspond to the keys. It always returns the supplied value. The aliases are local to the enclosing block. If any of the values are unblessed references, they are available as their dereferenced types. Thus, the action is similar to saying:
>
> ```
> alias %{$_[0]}
> ```
>
> but, in addition, also localizes the aliases, and does not dereference objects. Dereferencing of objects can be forced by setting the Deref option. See $Alias::Deref.
>
> This can be used for convenient access to hash values and hash-based object attributes.
>
> Note that this makes available the semantics of local subroutines and methods, which opens up a number of possibilities. We could make truly private methods by putting anonymous subroutines within an object. These subroutines would be available within methods where we use attr, but would not be visible to the outside world as normal methods. We could forbid recursion in methods by always putting an empty subroutine in the object hash with the same key as the method name. This would be useful where a method has to run code from other modules, but cannot be certain whether that module will call it back again.

The default behavior is to create aliases for all the entries in the hash in the `caller`'s namespace. This can be controlled by setting a few options. See "Config-uration Variables" for details.

const

> This is simply a function alias for **alias**, described above. It is provided on demand at **use** time, since it reads better for constant declarations. Note that hashes and arrays cannot be constrained with **const**.

Configuration Variables

The following configuration variables can be used to control the behavior of the **attr** function. They are typically set after the **use Alias;** statement. Another typical usage is to localize them in a block so that their values are effective only within that block.

$Alias::KeyFilter

> This constant specifies the key prefix used for determining which hash entries will be interned by **attr**. It can be a CODE reference, in which case it will be called with the key, and the Boolean return value determines whether that hash entry is a candidate attribute.

$Alias::AttrPrefix

> This specifies a prefix to prepend to the names of localized attributes created by **attr**. It can be a CODE reference, in which case it will be called with the key, and the result will determine the full name of the attribute. The value can have embedded package delimiters (`::` or `'`), which cause the attributes to be interned in that namespace instead of the **caller**'s own namespace. For example, setting it to **main::** makes **use strict 'vars';** somewhat more palatable (since we can refer to the attributes as $::foo, etc., without actually declaring the attributes).

$Alias::Deref

> Controls the implicit dereferencing behavior of **attr**. If it is set to `""` or 0, **attr** will not dereference blessed references. If it is a true value (anything but `""`, 0, or a CODE reference), all references will be made available as their dereferenced types, including values that may be objects. The default is `""`.
>
> This option can be used as a filter if it is set to a CODE reference, in which case it will be called with the key and the value (whenever the value happens to be a reference), and the boolean return value determines whether that particular refer-ence must be dereferenced.

Exports

```
alias
attr
```

Examples

Run these code snippets and observe the results to become more familiar with the features of this module.

```
use Alias qw(alias const attr);
$ten = 10;
alias TEN => $ten, Ten => \$ten, Ten => \&ten,
      Ten => \@ten, Ten => \%ten;
alias TeN => \*ten;   # same as *TeN = *ten
```

```
# aliasing basic types
$ten = 20;
print "$TEN|$Ten|$ten\n";    # should print "20|20|20"
sub ten { print "10\n"; }
@ten = (1..10);
%ten = (a..j);
&Ten;                        # should print "10"
print @Ten, "|", %Ten, "\n";
# this will fail at run time
const _TEN_ => 10;
eval { $_TEN_ = 20 };
print $@ if $@;
# dynamically scoped aliases
@DYNAMIC = qw(m n o);
{
   my $tmp = [ qw(a b c d) ];
   local @DYNAMIC;
   alias DYNAMIC => $tmp, PERM => $tmp;
   $DYNAMIC[2] = 'zzz';
   # prints "abzzzd|abzzzd|abzzzd"
   print @$tmp, "|", @DYNAMIC, "|", @PERM, "\n";
   @DYNAMIC = qw(p q r);
   # prints "pqr|pqr|pqr"
   print @$tmp, "|", @DYNAMIC, "|", @PERM, "\n";
}
# prints "mno|pqr"
print @DYNAMIC, "|", @PERM, "\n";
# named closures
my($lex) = 'abcd';
$closure = sub { print $lex, "\n" };
alias NAMEDCLOSURE => \&$closure;
NAMEDCLOSURE();              # prints "abcd"
$lex = 'pqrs';
NAMEDCLOSURE();              # prints "pqrs"
# hash/object attributes
package Foo;
use Alias;
sub new {
  bless
    { foo => 1,
      bar => [2,3],
      buz => { a => 4},
      privmeth => sub { "private" },
      easymeth => sub { die "to recurse or to die, is the question" },
    }, $_[0];
}
sub easymeth {
  my $s = attr shift;    # localizes $foo, @bar, %buz etc with values
  eval { $s->easymeth }; # should fail
  print $@ if $@;
  # prints "1|2|3|a|4|private|"
  print join '|', $foo, @bar, %buz, $s->privmeth, "\n";
}
$foo = 6;
```

```
@bar = (7,8);
%buz = (b => 9);
Foo->new->easymeth;        # this will not recurse endlessly
# prints "6|7|8|b|9|"
print join '|', $foo, @bar, %buz, "\n";
# this should fail at run-time
eval { Foo->new->privmeth };
print $@ if $@;
```

Notes

It is worth repeating that the aliases created by **alias** and **const** will be created in the **caller**'s namespace (although we can use the **AttrPrefix** option to specify a different namespace for **attr**). If that namespace happens to be localized, the aliases created will be local to that block. **attr** localizes the aliases for us.

Remember that references will be available as their dereferenced types.

Aliases cannot be lexical, since, by neccessity, they live on the symbol table. However, lexicals can be aliased. Note that this provides a means of reversing the action of anonymous type generators \, [] and {}. This allows us to anonymously construct data or code and give it a symbol-table presence when we choose.

Any occurrence of :: or ' in names will be treated as package qualifiers, and the value will be interned in that namespace.

Remember that aliases are very much like references, only we don't have to dereference them as often (which means we won't have to pound on the dollar signs so much). Using this module will dramatically reduce noise characters in object-oriented Perl code.

We can dynamically make subroutines and named closures with this scheme. It is also possible to alias packages, but that might be construed as abuse.

Bugs

use strict 'vars'; is not very usable, since we depend so much on the symbol table. You can declare the attributes with **use vars** to avoid warnings. Setting $Alias::AttrPrefix to **main::** is one way to avoid **use vars** and frustration.

Tied variables cannot as of yet be aliased properly.

Author

Gurusamy Sarathy, *gsar@umich.edu*

Copyright

Copyright © 1995–97 Gurusamy Sarathy. All rights reserved. This program is free software; you can redistribute it and/or modify it under the same terms as Perl itself.

See Also

perl(1)

AutoLoader—load functions only on demand

Synopsis

```
package GoodStuff;
use Exporter;
use AutoLoader;
@ISA = qw(Exporter AutoLoader);
```

Description

The AutoLoader module provides a standard mechanism for delayed loading of functions stored in separate files on disk. Each file has the same name as the function (plus a *.al*), and comes from a directory named after the package (with the *auto* directory). For example, the function named `GoodStuff::whatever()` would be loaded from the file *auto/GoodStuff/whatever.al.*

A module using the AutoLoader should have the special marker __END__ prior to the actual subroutine declarations. All code before this marker is loaded and compiled when the module is used. At the marker, Perl stops parsing the file.

When a subroutine not yet in memory is called, the AUTOLOAD function attempts to locate it in a directory relative to the location of the module file itself. As an example, assume *POSIX.pm* is located in */usr/local/lib/perl5/POSIX.pm*. The AutoLoader will look for the corresponding subroutines for this package in */usr/ local/lib/perl5/auto/POSIX/*.al.*

Lexicals declared with `my` in the main block of a package using the AutoLoader will not be visible to autoloaded functions, because the given lexical scope ends at the __END__ marker. A module using such variables as file-scoped globals will not work properly under the AutoLoader. Package globals must be used instead. When running under `use strict`, the `use vars` pragma may be employed in such situations as an alternative to explicitly qualifying all globals with the package name. Package variables predeclared with this pragma will be accessible to any autoloaded routines, but of course will not be invisible outside the module file.

The AutoLoader is a counterpart to the SelfLoader module. Both delay the loading of subroutines, but the SelfLoader accomplishes this by storing the subroutines right there in the module file rather than in separate files elsewhere. While this avoids the use of a hierarchy of disk files and the associated I/O for each routine loaded, the SelfLoader suffers a disadvantage in the one-time parsing of the lines after __DATA__, after which routines are cached. The SelfLoader can also handle multiple packages in a file.

AutoLoader, on the other hand, reads code only as it is requested, and in many cases should be faster. But it requires a mechanism like AutoSplit to create the individual files.

On systems with restrictions on filename length, the file corresponding to a subroutine may have a shorter name than the routine itself. This can lead to conflicting filenames. The AutoSplit module will warn of these potential conflicts when used to split a module.

Author

Perl5 Porters, *perl5-porters@perl.org*

Carp—generate error messages

Synopsis

```
use Carp;
carp "Be careful!";       # warn of errors (from perspective of caller)
croak "We're outta here!"; # die of errors (from perspective of caller)
confess "Bye!";           # die of errors with stack backtrace
```

Description

carp() and croak() behave like **warn** and **die**, respectively, except that they report the error as occurring not at the line of code where they are invoked, but at a line in one of the calling routines. Suppose, for example, that you have a routine goo() containing an invocation of carp(). In that case—and assuming that the current stack shows no callers from a package other than the current one—carp() will report the error as occurring where goo() was called. If, on the other hand, callers from different packages are found on the stack, then the error is reported as occurring in the package immediately preceding the package in which the carp() invocation occurs. The intent is to let library modules act a little more like built-in functions, which always report errors where you call them from.

confess() is like **die** except that it prints out a stack backtrace. The error is reported at the line where confess() is invoked, not at a line in one of the calling routines.

Author

Perl5 Porters, *perl5-porters@perl.org*

Config—access Perl configuration information

Synopsis

```
use Config;
if ($Config{cc} =~ /gcc/) {
    print "built by gcc

}

use Config qw(myconfig config_sh config_vars);
print myconfig();
print config_sh();
config_vars(qw(osname archname));
```

Description

The Config module contains all the information that the *Configure* script had to figure out at Perl build time (over 450 values).*

Shell variables from the *config.sh* file (written by *Configure*) are stored in a read-only hash, %Config, indexed by their names. Values set to the string undef in *config.sh* are returned

---

* Perl was written in C, not because it's a portable language, but because it's a ubiquitous language. A bare C program is about as portable as Chuck Yeager on foot.

as undefined values. The **Perl exists** function should be used to check whether a named variable exists.

myconfig
> Returns a textual summary of the major Perl configuration values.

config_sh
> Returns the entire Perl configuration information in the form of the original *config.sh* shell variable assignment script.

config_vars(@names)
> Prints to STDOUT the values of the named configuration variables. Each is printed on a separate line in the form:

> ```
> name='value';
> ```

> Names that are unknown are output as name='UNKNOWN';.

Here's a more sophisticated example using %Config:

```
use Config;

defined $Config{sig_name} or die "No sigs?";
foreach $name (split(' ', $Config{sig_name})) {
    $signo{$name} = $i;
    $signame[$i] = $name;
    $i++;
}

print "signal #17 = $signame[17]

if ($signo{ALRM}) {
    print "SIGALRM is $signo{ALRM}
}
```

Because configuration information is not stored within the Perl executable itself, it is possible (but unlikely) that the information might not relate to the actual Perl binary that is being used to access it. The Config module checks the Perl version number when loaded to try to prevent gross mismatches, but can't detect subsequent rebuilds of the same version.

Author

Perl5 Porters, *perl5-porters@perl.org*

---

constant—Perl pragma to declare constants

Synopsis

```
use constant BUFFER_SIZE    => 4096;
use constant ONE_YEAR       => 365.2425 * 24 * 60 * 60;
use constant PI             => 4 * atan2 1, 1;
use constant DEBUGGING      => 0;
use constant ORACLE         => 'oracle@cs.indiana.edu';
use constant USERNAME       => scalar getpwuid($<);
use constant USERINFO       => getpwuid($<);
```

```
sub deg2rad { PI * $_[0] / 180 }
print "This line does nothing"                unless DEBUGGING;
```

Description

This will declare a symbol to be a constant with the given scalar or list value.

When you declare a constant such as pi using the method shown above, each machine your program runs upon can have as many digits of accuracy as it can use. Also, your program will be easier to read and more likely to be maintained, and maintained correctly (and far less likely to send a space probe to the wrong planet because nobody noticed the one equation in which you wrote 3.14195).

Notes

The value or values are evaluated in a list context. You may override this with **scalar**, as shown previously.

These constants do not directly interpolate into double-quoted strings, although you may use references to do so. See the *perlref* manpage for details about how this works.

```
print "The value of PI is ${\( PI )}.\n";         # scalar
print "Your USERINFO is @{[ USERINFO ]}.\n";      # list
```

Multiple values are returned as lists, not as arrays.

```
$homedir = USERINFO[7];            # WRONG
$homedir = (USERINFO)[7];          # Right
@homedir = USERINFO;               # Get the whole list
```

The use of all caps for constant names is merely a convention, although it is recommended in order to make constants stand out, and to help avoid collisions with other barewords, keywords, and subroutine names. Constant names must begin with a letter.

Symbols are package-scoped. That is, you can refer to a constant CONST in package Other as Other::CONST.

Omitting the value for a symbol gives it the value of **undef** in a scalar context or the empty list, (), in a list context. This isn't as nice as it may sound, because in this case you must either quote the symbol name or use a big arrow (=>) with nothing to point to. It is probably best to declare these explicitly.

```
use constant UNICORNS      => ();
use constant LOGFILE       => undef;
```

The result from evaluating a list constant in a scalar context is not documented, and is *not* guaranteed to be any particular value in the future. In particular, you should not rely upon it being the number of elements in the list, especially since it is not that value in the current implementation.

Technical Note

In the current implementation, scalar constants are actually inlinable subroutines. As of version 5.004 of Perl, the appropriate scalar constant is inserted directly in place of some subroutine calls, thereby saving the overhead of a subroutine call. See "Constant Functions" for details about how and when this happens.

Bugs

In the current version of Perl, list constants are not inlined, some symbols may be redefined without generating a warning, and **defined** works reliably only upon scalar constants. Also, in the current implementation, scalar constants and elements of list constants must be either **undef**, numbers, or strings. References are stringified, so they aren't especially useful. Magical values (such as $!) are also stringified, so they lose their magic.

It is not possible to have a subroutine or keyword with the same name as a constant. (This is probably a good thing.)

Unlike constants in some other languages, these Perl constants cannot be overridden on the command line or via environment variables.

Author

Tom Phoenix, *rootbeer@teleport.com*

Copyright

Copyright © 1997 Tom Phoenix

This module is free software; you can redistribute it or modify it under the same terms as Perl itself.

DynaLoader—automatic dynamic loading of Perl modules

Synopsis

```
package YourModule;
require DynaLoader;
@ISA = qw(... DynaLoader ...);

bootstrap YourModule;
```

Description

This module defines the standard Perl interface to the dynamic linking mechanisms available on many platforms. A common theme throughout the module system is that *using* a module should be easy, even if the module itself (or the installation of the module) is more complicated as a result. This applies particularly to the DynaLoader. To use it in your own module, all you need are the incantations listed above in the synopsis. This will work whether YourModule is statically or dynamically linked into Perl. (This is a *Configure* option for each module.) The **bootstrap()** method will either call YourModule's bootstrap routine directly if YourModule is statically linked into Perl, or if not, YourModule will inherit the **bootstrap()** method from DynaLoader, which will do everything necessary to load in your module, and then call YourModule's **bootstrap()** method for you, as if it were there all the time and you called it yourself. Piece of cake, of the have-it-and-eat-it-too variety.

The rest of this description talks about the DynaLoader from the viewpoint of someone who wants to extend the DynaLoader module to a new architecture. The *Configure* process selects which kind of dynamic loading to use by choosing to link in one of several C implementations, which must be linked into Perl statically. (This is unlike other C extensions, which provide a single implementation that may be linked in either statically or dynamically.)

The DynaLoader is designed to be a very simple, high-level interface that is sufficiently general to cover the requirements of SunOS, HP-UX, NeXT, Linux, VMS, Win-32, and other platforms. By itself, though, DynaLoader is practically useless for accessing non-Perl libraries because it provides almost no Perl-to-C "glue". There is, for example, no mechanism for calling a C library function or supplying its arguments in any sort of portable form. This job is delegated to the other extension modules that you may load in by using DynaLoader.

Internal Interface Summary

Variables:

```
@dl_library_path
@dl_resolve_using
@dl_require_symbols
$dl_debug
```

Subroutines:

```
bootstrap($modulename);
@filepaths = dl_findfile(@names);
$filepath = dl_expandspec($spec);
$libref   = dl_load_file($filename);
$symref   = dl_find_symbol($libref, $symbol);
@symbols = dl_undef_symbols();
dl_install_xsub($name, $symref [, $filename]);
$message = dl_error;
```

The **bootstrap()** and **dl_findfile()** routines are standard across all platforms, and so are defined in *DynaLoader.pm*. The rest of the functions are supplied by the particular *.xs* file that supplies the implementation for the platform. (You can examine the existing implementations in the *ext/DynaLoader/*.xs* files in the Perl source directory. You should also read *DynaLoader.pm*, of course.) These implementations may also tweak the default values of the variables listed below.

Variables

@dl_library_path

The default list of directories in which dl_findfile() will search for libraries. Directories are searched in the order they are given in this array variable, beginning with subscript 0. @dl_library_path is initialized to hold the list of "normal" directories (*/usr/lib* and so on) determined by the Perl installation script, *Configure*, and given by $Config{'libpth'}. This is to ensure portability across a wide range of platforms. @dl_library_ path should also be initialized with any other directories that can be determined from the environment at run-time (such as LD_LIBRARY_PATH for SunOS). After initialization, @dl_library_path can be manipulated by an application using push and unshift before calling dl_findfile(). unshift can be used to add directories to the front of the search order either to save search time or to override standard libraries with the same name. The load function that dl_load_file() calls might require an absolute pathname. The dl_findfile() function and @dl_library_path can be used to search for and return the absolute pathname for the library/object that you wish to load.

@dl_resolve_using

A list of additional libraries or other shared objects that can be used to resolve any undefined symbols that might be generated by a later call to **dl_load_file()**. This is required only on some platforms that do not handle dependent libraries automatically. For example, the Socket extension shared library (*auto/Socket/Socket.so*) contains references to many socket functions that need to be resolved when it's loaded. Most platforms will automatically know where to find the "dependent" library (for example, */usr/lib/libsocket.so*). A few platforms need to be told the location of the dependent library explicitly. Use **@dl_resolve_using** for this. Example:

```
@dl_resolve_using = dl_findfile('-lsocket');
```

@dl_require_symbols

A list of one or more symbol names that are in the library/object file to be dynamically loaded. This is required only on some platforms.

dl_error

Error message text from the last failed DynaLoader function.

```
$message = dl_error();
```

Note that, similar to **errno** in UNIX, a successful function call does not reset this message. Implementations should detect the error as soon as it occurs in any of the other functions and save the corresponding message for later retrieval. This will avoid problems on some platforms (such as SunOS) where the error message is very temporary (see, for example, *dlerror*(3)).

$dl_debug

Internal debugging messages are enabled when **$dl_debug** is set true. Currently, setting **$dl_debug** affects only the Perl side of the DynaLoader. These messages should help an application developer to resolve any DynaLoader usage problems. **$dl_debug** is set to $ENV{'PERL_DL_DEBUG'} if defined. For the DynaLoader developer and porter there is a similar debugging variable added to the C code (see *dlutils.c*) and enabled if Perl was built with the -DDEBUGGING flag. This can also be set via the PERL_DL_DEBUG environment variable. Set to 1 for minimal information or higher for more.

dl_findfile

Determines the full paths (including file suffix) of one or more loadable files, given their generic names and optionally one or more directories. Searches directories in **@dl_library_path** by default and returns an empty list if no files were found.

```
@filepaths = dl_findfile(@names)
```

Names can be specified in a variety of platform-independent forms. Any names in the form **-lname** are converted into *libname.**, where *.** is an appropriate suffix for the platform. If a name does not already have a suitable prefix or suffix, then the corresponding file will be sought by trying prefix and suffix combinations appropriate to the platform: *$name.o, lib$name.** and *$name*. If any directories are included in **@names**, they are searched before **@dl_library_path**. Directories may be specified as **-Ldir**. Any other names are treated as filenames to be searched for. Using arguments of the form **-Ldir** and **-lname** is recommended. Example:

```
@dl_resolve_using = dl_findfile(qw(-L/usr/5lib -lposix));
```

dl_expandspec

Some unusual systems such as VMS require special filename handling in order to deal with symbolic names for files (that is, VMS's Logical Names). To support these systems, either a **dl_expandspec()** function can be implemented in the *dl_*.xs* file or code can be added to the autoloadable **dl_ expandspec()** function in *DynaLoader.pm*.

```
$filepath = dl_expandspec($spec)
```

dl_load_file

Dynamically load **$filename**, which must be the path to a shared object or library. An opaque "library reference" is returned as a handle for the loaded object.

```
$libref = dl_load_file($filename)
```

dl_load_file() returns the undefined value on error. (On systems that provide a handle for the loaded object such as SunOS and HP-UX, the returned handle will be **$libref**. On other systems **$libref** will typically be **$filename** or a pointer to a buffer containing **$filename**. The application should not examine or alter **$libref** in any way.) Below are some of the functions that do the real work. Such functions should use the current values of **@dl_require_symbols** and **@dl_resolve_using** if required.

```
SunOS:  dlopen($filename)
HP-UX:  shl_load($filename)
Linux:  dld_create_reference(@dl_require_symbols);
        dld_link($filename)
NeXT:   rld_load($filename, @dl_resolve_using)
VMS:    lib$find_image_symbol($filename,
                              $dl_require_symbols[0])
```

dl_find_symbol

Returns the address of the symbol **$symbol**, or the undefined value if not found.

```
$symref = dl_find_symbol($libref, $symbol)
```

If the target system has separate functions to search for symbols of different types, then **dl_find_symbol()** should search for function symbols first and then search for other types. The exact manner in which the address is returned in **$symref** is not currently defined. The only initial requirement is that **$symref** can be passed to, and understood by, **dl_install_xsub()**. Here are some current implementations:

```
SunOS:  dlsym($libref, $symbol)
HP-UX:  shl_findsym($libref, $symbol)
Linux:  dld_get_func($symbol) and/or dld_get_symbol($symbol)
NeXT:   rld_lookup("_$symbol")
VMS:    lib$find_image_symbol($libref, $symbol)
```

dl_undef_symbols

Returns a list of symbol names which remain undefined after **dl_load_ file()**.

```
@symbols = dl_undef_symbols()
```

It returns () if these names are not known. Don't worry if your platform does not provide a mechanism for this. Most platforms do not need it and hence do not provide it; they just return an empty list.

dl_install_xsub

Creates a new Perl external subroutine named $perl_name using $symref as a pointer to the function that implements the routine.

    dl_install_xsub($perl_name, $symref [, $filename])

This is simply a direct call to newXSUB(). It returns a reference to the installed function. The $filename parameter is used by Perl to identify the source file for the function if required by die, caller, or the debugger. If $filename is not defined, then *DynaLoader* will be used.

bootstrap()

This is the normal entry point for automatic dynamic loading in Perl.

    bootstrap($module);

It performs the following actions:

- Locates an *auto/$module* directory by searching @INC
- Uses dl_findfile() to determine the filename to load
- Sets @dl_require_symbols to (boot_$module)
- Executes an *auto/$module/$module.bs* file if it exists (typically used to add to @dl_resolve_using any files that are required to load the module on the current platform)
- Calls dl_load_file() to load the file
- Calls dl_undef_symbols() and warns if any symbols are undefined
- Calls dl_find_symbol() for "boot_$module"
- Calls dl_install_xsub() to install it as ${module}::bootstrap
- Calls &{"${module}::bootstrap"} to bootstrap the module (actually it uses the function reference returned by dl_install_xsub() for speed)

Author

Perl5 Porters, *perl5-porters@perl.org*

English—use English or awk names for punctuation variables

Synopsis

    use English;
    ...
    if ($ERRNO =~ /denied/) { ... }

Description

This module provides aliases for the built-in "punctuation" variables. Variables with side effects that get triggered merely by accessing them (like $0) will still have the same effects under the aliases.

For those variables that have an *awk*(1) version, both long and short English alternatives are provided. For example, the $/ variable can be referred to either as $RS or as $INPUT_RECORD_SEPARATOR if you are using the English module.

Here is the list of variables along with their English alternatives:

Perl	English		Perl	English
@_	@ARG		$?	$CHILD_ERROR
$_	$ARG		$!	$OS_ERROR
$&	$MATCH		$!	$ERRNO
$`	$PREMATCH		$@	$EVAL_ERROR
$'	$POSTMATCH		$$	$PROCESS_ID
$+	$LAST_PAREN_MATCH		$$	$PID
$.	$INPUT_LINE_NUMBER		$<	$REAL_USER_ID
$.	$NR		$<	$UID
$/	$INPUT_RECORD_SEPARATOR		$>	$EFFECTIVE_USER_ID
$/	$RS		$>	$EUID
$|	$OUTPUT_AUTOFLUSH		$(	$REAL_GROUP_ID
$,	$OUTPUT_FIELD_SEPARATOR		$(	$GID
$,	$OFS		$)	$EFFECTIVE_GROUP_ID

Author

Perl5 Porters, *perl5-porters@perl.org*

Exporter—default import method for modules

Synopsis

```
# in module YourModule.pm:
package YourModule;
use Exporter ();
@ISA = qw(Exporter);

@EXPORT = qw(...);             # Symbols to export by default.
@EXPORT_OK = qw(...);         # Symbols to export on request.
%EXPORT_TAGS = (tag => [...]); # Define names for sets of symbols.

# in other files that wish to use YourModule:
use YourModule;               # Import default symbols into my package.
use YourModule qw(...);       # Import listed symbols into my package.
use YourModule ();            # Do not import any symbols!
```

Description

Any module may define a class method called **import()**. Perl automatically calls a module's **import()** method when processing the use statement for the module. The module itself doesn't have to define the **import()** method, though. The Exporter module implements a default `import()` method that many modules choose to inherit instead. The Exporter module supplies the customary import semantics, and any other `import()` methods will tend to deviate from the normal import semantics in various (hopefully documented) ways. Now we'll talk about the normal import semantics.

Specialized Import Lists

Ignoring the class name, which is always the first argument to a class method, the arguments that are passed into the `import()` method are known as an *import list*. Usually the import list is nothing more than a list of subroutine or variable names, but occasionally you may want to get fancy. If the first entry in an import list begins with !, :, or /, the list is treated as a series of specifications that either add to or delete from the list of names to import. They are processed left to right. Specifications are in the form:

Symbol	Meaning
[!]*name*	This *name* only
[!]:DEFAULT	All names in @EXPORT
[!]:*tag*	All names in $EXPORT_TAGS (*tag*) anonymous list
[!]/*pattern*/	All names in @EXPORT and @EXPORT_OK that match *pattern*

A leading ! indicates that matching names should be deleted from the list of names to import. If the first specification is a deletion, it is treated as though preceded by :DEFAULT. If you just want to import extra names in addition to the default set, you will still need to include :DEFAULT explicitly.

For example, suppose that *YourModule.pm* says:

```
@EXPORT      = qw(A1 A2 A3 A4 A5);
@EXPORT_OK   = qw(B1 B2 B3 B4 B5);
%EXPORT_TAGS = (
    T1 => [qw(A1 A2 B1 B2)],
    T2 => [qw(A1 A2 B3 B4)]
);
```

Individual names in EXPORT_TAGS must also appear in @EXPORT or @EXPORT_OK. Note that you cannot use the tags directly within either @EXPORT or @EXPORT_OK (though you could preprocess tags into either of those arrays, and in fact, the **export_tags()** and **export_ok_tags()** functions below do precisely that).

An application using YourModule can then say something like this:

```
use YourModule qw(:DEFAULT :T2 !B3 A3);
```

The :DEFAULT adds in A1, A2, A3, A4, and A5. The :T2 adds in only B3 and B4, since A1 and A2 were already added. The !B3 then deletes B3, and the A3 does nothing because A3 was already included. Other examples include:

```
use Socket qw(!/^[AP]F_/ !SOMAXCONN !SOL_SOCKET);
use POSIX  qw(:errno_h :termios_h !TCSADRAIN !/^EXIT/);
```

Remember that most patterns (using //) will need to be anchored with a leading ^, for example, /^EXIT/ rather than /EXIT/.

You can say:

```
BEGIN { $Exporter::Verbose=1 }
```

in order to see how the specifications are being processed and what is actually being imported into modules.

Module Version Checking

The Exporter module will convert an attempt to import a number from a module into a call to $module_name->require_version($value). This can be used to validate that the version of the module being used is greater than or equal to the required version. The Exporter module also supplies a default require_version() method, which checks the value of $VERSION in the exporting module.

Since the default require_version() method treats the $VERSION number as a simple numeric value, it will regard version 1.10 as lower than 1.9. For this reason it is strongly recommended that the module developer use numbers with at least two decimal places; for example, 1.09.

Prior to release 5.004 or so of Perl, this worked only with modules that use the Exporter module; in particular, this means that you can't check the version of a class module that doesn't require the Exporter module.

Managing Unknown Symbols

In some situations you may want to prevent certain symbols from being exported. Typically this applies to extensions with functions or constants that may not exist on some systems.

The names of any symbols that cannot be exported should be listed in the @EXPORT_ FAIL array.

If a module attempts to import any of these symbols, the Exporter will give the module an opportunity to handle the situation before generating an error. The Exporter will call an export_fail() method with a list of the failed symbols:

```
@failed_symbols = $module_name->export_fail(@failed_symbols);
```

If the export_fail() method returns an empty list, then no error is recorded and all requested symbols are exported. If the returned list is not empty, then an error is generated for each symbol and the export fails. The Exporter provides a default export_fail() method that simply returns the list unchanged.

Uses for the export_fail() method include giving better error messages for some symbols and performing lazy architectural checks. Put more symbols into @EXPORT_ FAIL by default and then take them out if someone actually tries to use them and an expensive check shows that they are usable on that platform.

Tag Handling Utility Functions

Since the symbols listed within %EXPORT_TAGS must also appear in either @EXPORT or @EXPORT_OK, two utility functions are provided that allow you to easily add tagged sets of symbols to @EXPORT or @EXPORT_OK:

```
%EXPORT_TAGS = (Bactrian => [qw(aa bb cc)],
                Dromedary => [qw(aa cc dd)]);
Exporter::export_tags('Bactrian');    # add aa bb cc to @EXPORT
Exporter::export_ok_tags('Dromedary'); # add aa cc dd to @EXPORT_OK
```

Any names that are not tags are added to @EXPORT or @EXPORT_OK unchanged, but will trigger a warning (with –w) to avoid misspelled tag names being silently added to @EXPORT or @EXPORT_OK. Future versions may regard this as a fatal error.

Author

Perl5 Porters, *perl5-porters@perl.org*

Filter::cpp—cpp source filter

Synopsis

```
use Filter::cpp;
```

Description

This source filter pipes the current source file through the C preprocessor (cpp) if it is available.

As with all source filters, its scope is limited to the current source file only. Every file you want to be processed by the filter must have the line:

```
use Filter::cpp ;
```

near the top.

Here is an example script that uses the filter:

```
use Filter::cpp ;
#define FRED 1
$a = 2 + FRED ;
print "a = $a\n" ;
#ifdef FRED
print "Hello FRED\n" ;
#else
print "Where is FRED\n" ;
#endif
```

This is what it will output:

```
a = 3
Hello FRED
```

Author

Paul Marquess, *pmarquess@bfsec.bt.co.uk*

Filter::decrypt—template for a decrypt source filter

Synopsis

```
use Filter::decrypt;
```

Description

This is a sample decrypting source filter.

Although this is a fully functional source filter, which does implement a *very simple* decrypt algorithm, it is *not* intended to be used as it is supplied. Consider it as a template which you can combine with a proper decryption algorithm to develop your own decryption filter.

Warning

It is important to note that a decryption filter can *never* provide complete security against attack. At some point the parser within Perl needs to be able to scan the original decrypted source. This means that at some stage, fragments of the source will exist in a memory buffer.

The best you can hope to achieve by decrypting your Perl source using a source filter is to make it impractical to crack.

Given that proviso, there are a number of things you can do to make life more difficult for the prospective cracker.

- Strip the Perl binary to remove all symbols.
- Build the decrypt extension using static linking. If the extension is provided as a dynamic module, there is nothing to stop someone from linking it at run time with a modified Perl binary.
- Do not build Perl with –DDEBUGGING. If you do, your source can be retrieved with the **–Dp** command-line option. (The sample filter contains logic to detect the DEBUGGING option.)
- Do not build Perl with C debugging support enabled.
- Do not implement the decryption filter as a subprocess (like the **cpp** source filter). It is possible to peek into the pipe that connects to the subprocess.
- Do not use the decrypt filter as-is. The algorithm used in this filter has been purposefully left simple.

If you feel that the source filtering mechanism is still not secure enough, you could try using the **unexec/undump** method. See the Perl FAQ for further details.

Author

Paul Marquess, *pmarquess@bfsec.bt.co.uk*

Filter::exec—exec source filter

Synopsis

```
use Filter::exec qw(command parameters) ;
```

Description

This filter pipes the current source file through the program that corresponds to the given *command* (with possible *parameters*).

As with all source filters, its scope is limited to the current source file only. Every file you want to be processed by the filter must have the line:

```
use Filter::exec qw(command) ;
```

near the top.

Here is an example script which uses the filter:

```
use Filter::exec qw(tr XYZ PQR) ;
$a = 1 ;
print "XYZ a = $a\n" ;
```

This is the output:

```
PQR = 1
```

Warning

You should be *very* careful when using this filter. Because of the way the filter is implemented it is possible to end up with deadlock. Be especially careful when stacking multiple instances of the filter in a single source file.

Author

Paul Marquess, *pmarquess@bfsec.bt.co.uk*

Filter::sh—sh source filter

Synopsis

```
use Filter::sh 'command' ;
```

Description

This filter pipes the current source file through the program that corresponds to the *command* parameter using the Bourne shell.

As with all source filters, its scope is limited to the current source file only. Every file you want to be processed by the filter must have this line near the top:

```
use Filter::sh 'command' ;
```

Here is an example script that uses the filter:

```
use Filter::sh 'tr XYZ PQR' ;
$a = 1 ;
print "XYZ a = $a\n" ;
```

This is what it will output:

```
PQR = 1
```

Warning

You should be *very* careful when using this filter. Because of the way the filter is implemented it is possible to end up with deadlock. Be especially careful when stacking multiple instances of the filter in a single source file.

Author

Paul Marquess, *pmarquess@bfsec.bt.co.uk*

Filter::tee—tee source filter

Synopsis

```
use Filter::tee 'filename' ;
use Filter::tee '>filename' ;
use Filter::tee '>>filename' ;
```

Description

This filter copies all text from the line after the use in the current source file to the file specified by the parameter *filename*.

By default (and when the filename is prefixed with a >), the output file will be emptied first if it already exists.

If the output filename is prefixed with >>, it will be opened for appending.

This filter is useful as a debugging aid when developing other source filters.

Author

Paul Marquess, *pmarquess@bfsec.bt.co.uk*

Filter::Util::Call—Perl Source Filter Utility Module

Synopsis

Method filter:

```
package MyFilter ;

use Filter::Util::Call ;
sub import
{
    my($type, @arguments) = @_ ;
    filter_add([]) ;
}

sub filter
{
    my($self) = @_ ;
    my($status) ;

    $status = filter_read() ;
    $status ;
}

1 ;
```

Closure filter:

```
package MyFilter ;

use Filter::Util::Call ;
sub import
{
    my($type, @arguments) = @_ ;

    filter_add(
        sub
        {
            my($status) ;
            $status = filter_read() ;
            $status ;
```

```
            } )
    }

    1 ;
```

Description

This module provides you with the framework to write source filters in Perl.

A Perl *source filter* is implemented as a Perl module. The structure of the module can take one of two broadly similar formats (as shown previously in the Synopsis). To distinguish between them, the first will be referred to as a *method filter* and the second as a *closure filter*.

To make use of either of the two filter modules, place the line shown here in a Perl source file:

```
    use MyFilter;
```

The skeleton modules shown above are fully functional source filters, albeit fairly useless ones. As they stand, all they do is pass the source stream through, without modifying it at all.

As you can see, both modules have a broadly similar structure. They both make use of the Filter::Util::Call module and both have an `import` method. The difference between them is that the method filter requires a `filter` method, whereas the closure filter gets the equivalent of a `filter` method with the anonymous subroutine passed to `filter_add`.

To make proper use of the closure filter shown above you need to have a good understanding of the concept of a *closure*. See the *perlref* manpage for more details on the mechanics of closures.

Methods

The following methods are included in Filter::Util::Call:

`import()`

>The `import` method is used to create an instance of the filter. It is called indirectly by Perl when it encounters the `use MyFilter` line in a source file (See *import* for more details on `import`).

>It will always have at least one parameter automatically passed by Perl corresponding to the name of the package. In the example above it will be `MyFilter`.

>Apart from the first parameter, `import` can accept an optional list of parameters. These can be used to pass parameters to the filter. For example:

>```
>    use MyFilter qw(a b c);
>```

>will result in the `@_` array having the following values:

>```
>    @_ [0] => "MyFilter"
>    @_ [1] => "a"
>    @_ [2] => "b"
>    @_ [3] => "c"
>```

>Before terminating, the `import` function must explicitly install the filter by calling `filter_add`.

`filter()` *(or anonymous* sub*)*

>Either the `filter` method (used with a method filter) or the anonymous `sub` (used with a closure filter) is where the main processing for the filter is done.

The difference between the two types of filters is that the method filter uses the object passed to the method to store any context data, whereas the closure filter uses the lexical variables that are maintained by the closure.

Note that the single parameter passed to the method filter, $self, is the same reference that was passed to filter_add and blessed into the filter's package. See the example filters later on for details of using $self.

Here is a list of the common features of the anonymous sub and the filter() method.

$_

> Although $_ doesn't actually appear explicitly in the sample filters shown earlier, it is implicitly used in a number of places.
>
> First, when either filter or the anonymous sub are called, a local copy of $_ will automatically be created. It will always contain the empty string at this point.
>
> Next, both filter_read and filter_read_exact will append any source data that is read to the end of $_.
>
> Finally, when filter or the anonymous sub are finished processing, they are expected to return the filtered source using $_.
>
> This implicit use of $_ greatly simplifies the filter.

$status

> The status value, which is returned by the user's filter method or anonymous sub, and the filter_read and filter_read_exact functions take the same set of values, namely:
>
> < 0   Error
> = 0   EOF
> > 0   OK

filter_read, filter_read_exact, *and* filter_del

> These functions are common to both types of filters. See the description under "Functions."

Functions

Filter::Util::Call provides the following functions:

filter_add()

> The function, filter_add, actually installs the filter. It takes one parameter, which should be a reference. The kind of reference used will dictate which of the two filter types will be used.
>
> If a CODE reference is used, a closure filter will be assumed.
>
> If a CODE reference is not used, a method filter will be assumed. In a method filter, the reference can be used to store context information. The reference will be blessed into the package by filter_add.
>
> See the filters at the end of this document for examples of using context information using both method filters and closure filters.

filter_read() *and* filter_read_exact()

> These functions are used by the filter to obtain either a line or block from the next filter in the chain, or the actual source file if there aren't any other filters.

The function `filter_read` takes two forms:

```
$status = filter_read() ;
$status = filter_read($size) ;
```

The first form is used to request a *line*, while the second requests a *block*.

In line mode, `filter_read` will append the next source line to the end of the `$_` scalar.

In block mode, `filter_read` will append a block of data that is `<= $size` to the end of the `$_` scalar. It is important to emphasise the that `filter_read` will not necessarily read a block of precisely `$size` bytes.

If you need to be able to read a block that has an exact size, you can use the function `filter_read_exact`. It works identically to `filter_read` in block mode, except it will try to read a block of exactly `$size` bytes in length. The only circumstances in which it will not return a block of `$size` bytes long is on EOF or error.

It is very important to check the value of `$status` after *every* call to `filter_read` or `filter_read_exact`.

`filter_del()`

The function `filter_del` is used to disable the current filter. It does not affect the running of the filter. All it does is tell Perl not to call the filter anymore.

See "Example 4: Using filter_del" for details.

Exports

The following functions are exported by `Filter::Util::Call`:

```
filter_add()
filter_read()
filter_read_exact()
filter_del()
```

Examples

Here are a few examples which simply illustrate the key concepts, as most of them (in their current form) are of little practical use.

The *examples* subdirectory has copies of all these filters implemented both as method filters and as closure filters.

Example 1: A simple filter

Below is a method filter which is hard-wired to replace all occurrences of the string `Joe` with `Jim`.

```
package Joe2Jim ;

use Filter::Util::Call ;
sub import
{
    my($type) = @_ ;

    filter_add(bless []) ;
}

sub filter
```

```
    {
        my($self) = @_ ;
        my($status) ;

        s/Joe/Jim/g
            if ($status = filter_read()) > 0 ;
        $status ;
    }

    1 ;
```

Here is an example of using the filter:

```
use Joe2Jim ;
print "Where is Joe?\n" ;
```

This is what the script above will print:

```
Where is Jim?
```

Example 2: Using the context

To make the previous example more usuable in real-world scenarios, we make use of the context data and allow arbitrary *from* and *to* strings to be used. This time we will use a closure filter. To reflect its enhanced role, the filter is called Subst:

```
package Subst ;

use Filter::Util::Call ;
use Carp ;

sub import
{
    croak("usage: use Subst qw(from to)")
        unless @_ == 3 ;
    my ($self, $from, $to) = @_ ;
    filter_add(
        sub
        {
            my ($status) ;
            s/$from/$to/
                if ($status = filter_read()) > 0 ;
            $status ;
        })
}
1 ;
```

and is used like this:

```
use Subst qw(Joe Jim) ;
print "Where is Joe?\n" ;
```

Example 3: Using the context within the filter

Here is a filter that is a variation of the Joe2Jim filter. As well as substituting all occurrences of Joe to Jim, it keeps a count of the number of substitutions made in the context object.

Once EOF is detected ($status is zero) the filter will insert an extra line into the source stream. When this extra line is executed it will print a count of the number of substitutions actually made. Note that $status is set to 1 in this case.

```
package Count ;

use Filter::Util::Call ;

sub filter
{
    my ($self) = @_ ;
    my ($status) ;

    if (($status = filter_read()) > 0 ) {
        s/Joe/Jim/g ;
        ++ $$self ;
    }
    elsif ($$self >= 0) { # EOF
        $_ = "print q[Made ${$self} substitutions\n]" ;
        $status = 1 ;
        $$self = -1 ;
    }
    $status ;
}

sub import
{
    my ($self) = @_ ;
    my ($count) = 0 ;
    filter_add(\$count) ;
}

1 ;
```

Here is a script which uses this filter:

```
use Count ;
print "Hello Joe\n" ;
print "Where is Joe\n" ;
```

It outputs:

```
Hello Jim
Where is Jim
Made 2 substitutions
```

Example 4: Using filter_del

Another variation on a theme, this filter modifies the Subst filter to allow a starting and stopping pattern to be specified as well as the *from* and *to* patterns. If you know the *vi* editor, it is equivalent to this command:

```
:/start/,/stop/s/from/to/
```

When used as a filter we want to invoke it like this:

```
use NewSubst qw(start stop from to) ;
```

Here is the module:

```
package NewSubst ;

use Filter::Util::Call ;
use Carp ;

sub import
{
    my ($self, $start, $stop, $from, $to) = @_ ;
    my ($found) = 0 ;
    croak("usage: use Subst qw(start stop from to)")
        unless @_ == 5 ;

    filter_add(
        sub
        {
            my ($status) ;

            if (($status = filter_read()) > 0) {

                $found = 1
                    if $found == 0 and /$start/ ;

                if ($found) {
                    s/$from/$to/ ;
                    filter_del() if /$stop/ ;
                }

            }
            $status ;
        } )

}

1 ;
```

Author

Paul Marquess, *pmarquess@bfsec.bt.co.uk*

Filter::Util::Exec — exec source filter

Description

This module is provides the interface to allow the creation of source filters that use a UNIX coprocess.

See Filter::exec, Filter::cpp and Filter::sh for examples of the use of this module.

Author

Paul Marquess, *pmarquess@bfsec.bt.co.uk*

perlpod—plain old documentation

Description

A pod-to-whatever translator reads a pod file paragraph by paragraph and translates it to the appropriate output format. There are three kinds of paragraphs:

- A verbatim paragraph, distinguished by being indented (that is, it starts with space or tab). It should be reproduced exactly, with tabs assumed to be on eight-column boundaries. There are no special formatting escapes, so you can't italicize or anything like that. A \ means \, and nothing else.

- A command. All command paragraphs start with =, followed by an identifier, followed by arbitrary text that the command can use however it pleases. Currently recognized commands are:

```
=head1 heading
=head2 heading
=item text
=over N
=back
=cut
=pod
=for X
=begin X
=end X
```

The =pod directive does nothing beyond telling the compiler to lay off parsing code through the next =cut. It's useful for adding another paragraph to the doc if you're mixing up code and pod a lot.

head1 and head2 produce first- and second-level headings, with the text in the same paragraph as the =head*n* directive forming the heading description.

item, over, and back require a little more explanation: =over starts a section specifically for the generation of a list using =item commands. At the end of your list, use =back to end it. You will probably want to use 4 as the number to =over (i.e., =over 4), as some formatters use this for indentation. This should probably be a default. Note also that there are some basic rules to using =item:

- Don't use it outside an =over/=back block

- Use at least one inside an =over/=back block

- You don't *have* to include the =back if the list just runs off the document

- Perhaps most important, keep the items consistent: either use =item * for all of them, to produce bullets, or use =item 1., =item 2., etc., to produce numbered lists, or use =item foo, =item bar, etc., (i.e., things that look nothing like bullets or numbers). If you start with bullets or numbers, stick with them, as many formatters use the first =item type to decide how to format the list.

for, begin, and end let you include sections that are not interpreted as pod text, but are passed directly to particular formatters. A formatter that can utilize that format will use the section, otherwise it will completely ignore it. The directive =for specifies that the entire next paragraph is in the format indicated by the first word after =for, like this:

```
=for html <br>
<p> This is a raw HTML paragraph </p>
```

The paired commands =begin and =end work very similarly to =for, but instead of only accepting a single paragraph, all text from =begin to a paragraph with a matching =end are treated as a particular format.

Here are some examples of how to use these:

```
=begin html

<br>Figure 1.<IMG SRC="figure1.png"><br>

=end html

=begin text

     ----------------
    |   foo        |
    |          bar  |
     ----------------

^^^^ Figure 1.  ^^^^

=end text
```

Some format names that formatters currently are known to accept include roff, man, latex, tex, text, and html. (Some formatters treat some of these as synonyms.)

And don't forget, when using any command, that the command lasts until the end of the *paragraph*, not the line. Hence in the examples below, you can see the empty line after each command to end its paragraph.

Some examples of lists include:

```
=over 4

=item *

First item

=item *

Second item

=back

=over 4

=item Foo()

Description of Foo function

=item Bar()

Description of Bar function

=back
```

- An ordinary block of text. It is filled, and maybe even justified. Certain interior sequences are recognized, both here and in commands:

```
I<text>      Italicize text, used for emphasis or variables
B<text>      Embolden text, used for switches and programs
S<text>      Text contains non-breaking spaces
C<code>      Literal code
L<name>      A link (cross-reference) to name
             L<name>              Manual page
             L<name/ident>        Item in manual page
             L<name/"sec">        Section in other manual page
             L<"sec">             Section in this manual page
                                  (the quotes are optional)
             L</"sec">            Ditto
F<file>      A filename
X<index>     An index entry
Z<>          A zero-width character
E<escape>    A named character (very similar to HTML escapes)
             E<lt>                A literal <
             E<gt>                A literal >
             (These are optional, except in other interior
             sequences and when preceded by a capital letter)
             E<n>                 Character number n (probably ASCII)
             E<html>              Some non-numeric HTML entity, such
                                  as E<Agrave>
```

That's it. The intent is simplicity, not power. I wanted paragraphs to look like paragraphs (block format), so that they stand out visually, and so that I could run them through fmt easily to reformat them (that's F7 in my version of vi). I wanted the translator (and not me) to worry about whether " or ′ is a left quote or a right quote within filled text, and I wanted it to leave the quotes alone, dammit, in verbatim mode, so I could slurp in a working program, shift it over four spaces, and have it print out, er, verbatim. And presumably in a constant-width font.

In particular, you can leave things like this verbatim in your text:

- Perl
- FILEHANDLE
- $variable
- function()
- manpage(3r)

Doubtless a few other commands or sequences will need to be added along the way, but I've gotten along surprisingly well with just these.

Note that I'm not at all claiming this to be sufficient for producing a book. I'm just trying to make an idiot-proof common source for nroff, TeX, and other markup languages, as used for online documentation. Translators exist for pod2man (that's for nroff(1) and troff(1)), pod2html, pod2latex, and pod2fm.

Embedding Pods in Perl Modules

You can embed pod documentation in your Perl scripts. Start your documentation with =head1 at the beginning and end it with =cut. Perl ignores the pod text. See any of the supplied library modules for examples. If you're going to put your pods at the end of the file, and you're using an __END__ or __DATA__ cut mark, make sure to put an empty line there before the first pod directive.

```
__END__

=head1 NAME

modern - I am a modern module
```

If you had not had that empty line there, then the translators wouldn't have seen the pod.

Common Pod Pitfalls

- Pod translators usually require paragraphs to be separated by completely empty lines. If you have an apparently empty line with some spaces on it, this can cause odd formatting.

- Translators mostly add wording around an L<> link, so that L<foo(1)> becomes "the foo(1) manpage", for example (see pod2man for details). Thus, you shouldn't write things like "the L<foo> manpage", if you want the translated document to read sensibly.

- The script *pod/checkpods.PL* in the Perl source distribution provides skeletal checking for lines that look empty but aren't, but it is there only as a placeholder until someone writes Pod::Checker. The best way to check your pod is to pass it through one or more translators and proofread the result, or print out the result and proofread that. Some of the problems found may be bugs in the translators, which you may or may not wish to work around.

Author

Larry Wall

See Also

pod2man, PODs: Embedded Documentation

Pod::Text—a class for converting pod data to formatted ASCII text

Synopsis

```
use Pod::Text;
pod2text("perlfunc.pod");
```

or:

```
use Pod::Text;
package MyParser;
@ISA = qw(Pod::Text);
sub new {
    ## constructor code ...
}
## implementation of appropriate subclass methods ...
package main;
$parser = new MyParser;
@ARGV = ('-')  unless (@ARGV > 0);
```

```
for (@ARGV) {
    $parser->parse_from_file($_);
}
```

Description

Pod::Text is a module that can convert documentation in the pod format (such as can be found throughout the Perl distribution) into formatted ASCII. Termcap is optionally supported for boldface/underline and can be enabled via `$Pod::Text::termcap=1`. If termcap has not been enabled, then backspaces are used to simulate bold and underlined text.

A separate `pod2text` program is included, which is primarily a wrapper for Pod::Text::pod2text().

The single function `pod2text()` can take one or two arguments. The first should be the name of a file to read the pod from, or <&STDIN to read from STDIN. The second argument, if provided, should be a filehandle glob where output should be sent.

Author

Tom Christiansen, *tchrist@mox.perl.com*

Modified to derive from Pod::Parser by Brad Appleton, *Brad_Appleton-GBDA001@email.mot.com*

See Also

Pod::Parser

---

pod2fm — convert pod format to FrameMaker documents and book file

Synopsis

```
pod2fm [-mmlonly |
        -nodoc [-lock]
        [-book [book_name] [-noopen]
            [-template document [-format types]... [-toc] [-index]
        ]
    ]
```

Description

This program parses all files a with *.pod* extension and creates FrameMaker documents. You can control what is generated by arguments given on the command line. `pod2fm` can:

• Generate Frame MML, MIF, and binary formats

• Generate hypertext links to a group of documents

• Create a Frame "book" that includes all of the documents from a run

• Create Table of Contents and Index documents

• Create documents that can be used with FrameViewer for online docs

Options

-mmlonly
-nommlonly

> This switch tells `pod2fm` if it should stop execution after it has generated the MML version of the document. The document is written into a file with the *.mml* extension.

> If **-mmlonly** is specified, it has to be the only command-line switch.

> The default is **-nommlonly**.

-nodoc
-doc

> The switch instructs `pod2fm` to use the FrameMaker tool `fmbatch` to convert the *.doc* file, which is in MIF format, to the binary FrameMaker format.

> The default is **-doc**.

-lock
-nolock

> Pod2fm generates hypertext markers so that if you to click on a marked word in a document, Frame will take you to the spot in a document that the marker is pointing to. To be able to use this feature, you need to save the documents as locked or read-only. The **-lock** option causes `pod2fm` to generate locked versions of the documents.

> The **-lock** option only works if you are generating binary documents. (See the **-doc** option.)

> The default is **-nolock**.

-book [*book_name*]

> This switch allows `pod2fm` to create a FrameMaker book file that contains all the documents that are on the command line. A book is a way to organize a group of related documents so they can be operated on at the same time. A book file allows you to apply a common format to all the documents and to print them at the same time.

> *book_name* is an optional argument to **-book**. It allows you to specify a name for the book file. If *book_name* is not specified, it defaults to `perl`. In any case, the filename extension is *.book*.

-noopen
-open

> If this option is on the command line, `pod2fm` tries to open the book it created in FrameMaker. Because this options works on the book file, you must be generating a book with the **-book** option.

> The default is **-open**.

-template *document*

> Pod2fm generates a minimal format for the documents it produces. You can use the **-template** option to specify a template document that `pod2fm` can copy the format from so that you can control the format. You can control which format in the template document to use with the **-format** option. The *document* name is a required argument to **-template** and specifies the path to the document template.

-format *type*

> The option **-format** allows you to control which format to copy from the template document specified with the **-template** option. You can specify one or

more arguments to each **-format** option by providing a comma-separated list of format *type*s, like this:

```
-format Page,Paragraph,Character
```

You can also have more than one **-format** option on the command line.

The legal format *type*s are:

all
  All *type*s are specified (the default)

Character
  Character formats

Paragraph
  Paragraph formats

Page
  Master page layouts

Reference
  Reference page layouts

Table
  Table formats

Variables
  Variable definitions

Math
  Math definitions

Cross
  Cross-reference definitions

Color
  Color definitions

Conditional
  Conditional text definitions

There are two additional *type*s that can be included as an argument to control how the other *type*s are used:

Break
  Preserve page breaks

Other
  Preserve other format changes

-toc
-notoc
-index
-noindex
  When you are generating a book from a template with **pod2fm**, you can generate a Table of Contents and an Index by specifying the **-toc** and the **-index** options. See the "Table of Contents" and "Index" subsections of the "TEMPLATES" section of this manpage, for more information.

  The defaults are **-notoc** and **-noindex**.

Templates

By using the `-template` command-line option when you are generating a book using the `-book` option, you can override the default formats that pod2fm produces.

A template is a FrameMaker document, in binary form or MIF, that has formats you want already applied to it. With this version of pod2fm, you can override the Master Page and Reference Page layouts, and paragraph formats. There are other formats that you can specify, like character formats and color definitions, but this version of pod2fm does not do anything with them.

Paragraph Formats

There are several paragraph formats that pod2fm uses, and there is a mapping from the pod command to the paragraph format that is produced. The exception to the mapping is the =over and =back commands: they modify the paragraph format by shifting its left edge by .1" times the amount in the =over command. You need to take this into account when you are changing the paragraph format. If you drop the size of the font in the format, you do not get a smaller shift. An =over 5 always gives an indent of .5".

The paragraph formats that pod2fm uses are:

pod_TITLE

> Paragraphs marked with this format contain the name of the pod. The name is automatically added to the start of each document, and this format is only used here.

> You can use the `pod_TITLE` tag to generate a header or footer with the name of the pod in it by changing the Master Page layout. If you are generating a book, this format is exported so that you can create a Table of Contents by changing the Reference Page.

pod_Body

> This format marks a standard paragraph. The left edge moves with each =over n and =back. The edge moves by *n* times .1".

pod_head1

> This format is used for section headers. The command is used like:

> > =head1 *text*

> where *text* is printed in this format. The =over and =back commands do not change this format.

> If you are generating a book, this format is exported so that you can create a Table of Contents by changing the Reference Page. Also, a marker is placed on the text so that it can be placed in an Index.

pod_head2

> This format is used for sub-section headers. The command is used like:

> > =head2 *text*

> where *text* is printed in this format. The =over and =back commands do not change this format.

> If you are generating a book, this format is exported so that you can create a Table of Contents by changing the Reference Page. Also, a marker is placed on the text so that it can be placed in an Index.

pod_ol

This format is used on ordered (numbered) lists. If the indent command is in this form:

```
=item n[.]
```

where *n* is any number followed by an optional period, the next paragraph is marked with this format and prints as a hanging indent that starts with an automatically generated number and a period. The start of the paragraph is shifted by the amount in the =over command. Any paragraphs that come after the first are marked with **pod_Body** and the left edge is shifted by the amount from the =over command.

pod_ul

This format is used on unordered lists. If the indent command is in this form:

```
=item *
```

the next paragraph is marked with this format and prints as a hanging indent that starts with a bullet. The start of the paragraph is shifted by the amount in the =over command. Any paragraphs that come after the first are marked with **pod_Body** and the left edge is shifted by the amount from the =over command.

pod_dl

This format is used on description lists. If the indent command is in this form:

```
=item * text
```

the *text* is printed after a bullet, on a line by itself. Any paragraphs that come after the first are marked with **pod_Body** and the left edge is shifted by the amount from the =over command.

pod_hi

This format is used on hanging indent lists. If the indent command is in this form:

```
=item text
```

the *text* is printed as a hanging indent. The next paragraph is marked with this format and prints with the start of the paragraph shifted by the amount in the =over command. Any paragraphs that come after the first are marked with **pod_Body** and the left edge is shifted by the amount from the =over command.

pod_il

This format is used on implied lists. If the first line of a paragraph is in this form:

```
____hang_____text
  |             |
  +- spaces  +- tabs
      or
     tabs
```

the *hang* is printed as a hanging indent and the *text* is printed with the left edge shifted to 2.5" from the current **pod_Body** left edge. The rest of the lines in the paragraph are treated the same, i.e., each line in the pod's paragraph is converted to a FrameMaker paragraph that is marked with **pod_il**. Any paragraphs that come after the first are marked with **pod_Body** and the left edge is shifted by the amount from the =over command.

pod_pre

This format is used on verbatim paragraphs. If the first line of a paragraph is in this form:

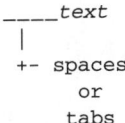

```
_____text
|
+- spaces
     or
   tabs
```

the *text*, including the leading whitespace, is printed with the left edge shifted to the current **pod_Body** left edge. The rest of the lines in the paragraph are treated the same, i.e., each line in the pod's paragraph is converted to a FrameMaker paragraph that is marked with **pod_pre**. Any paragraphs that come after the first are marked with **pod_Body**, and the left edge is shifted by the amount from the **=over** command.

Table of Contents

If you are producing a book, and you have a **-template** command-line option, and you are importing the Master Page Layout (**-format** Page or the default), you can produce a Table of Contents by adding the **-toc** option. **pod2fm** automatically adds a generated document called *book_nameTOC.doc* to the book file, where *book_name* is the optional argument to the **-book** command-line option. If no argument is give on the **-book**, you get a document called *perlTOC.doc*.

To specify the format of the Table of Contents, you need to go to the reference pages of the template document and create a flow called TOC. Within the flow, create a picture of what the Table of Contents will look like. You can add building blocks to the picture that allow you to control what is printed, e.g., the page number and text for the TOC entry. See the FrameMaker On-Line Help or *Using FrameMaker* printed manual for a complete description of how to set up a TOC Reference page.

The TOC entry is derived from paragraphs in the documents in the book that are marked with specific paragraph formats. **pod2fm** uses the paragraph formats **pod_TITLE**, **pod_head1**, and **pod_head2** to mark the TOC entries.

To make a TOC entry show, you need to create a new paragraph format that tracks the format used in the documents. The new paragraph has the form:

*format_name*TOC

where *format_name* is the format name used in the document. Here is an example of a TOC specification:

```
Paragraph tagged     Specifies
----------------     ---------
pod_TITLE            <$paratext><$nopage>
pod_head1               <$paratext>\t<$pagenum>
pod_head2                  <$paratext>\t<$pagenum>
```

which prints something like this:

```
POD2FM
    NAME                                    1
    SYNOPSIS                                1
    DESCRIPTION                             1
    OPTIONS                                 1
    TEMPLATES                               3
        Paragraph Formats                   3
        Table of Contents                   5
        Index                               6
```

Index

An Index document is much the same as a Table of Contents document: you must be generating a book and importing Reference Page Layouts from a template, and have a `-index` command-line option.

The format for the Index is also specified on a Reference Page in a flow called IX, and it has its own set of building blocks. Please see the FrameMaker documentation for more details on how to create the Index Reference Page.

`pod2fm` generates the index from any Index markers that have been placed in the documents. The markers are generated on any `=head` or `=item` command and any interior sequences (like `I\<\>`, `B\<\>`, and `L\<\>`) that refer to an `=head` or `=item.`

Bugs

`fmbatch` dies when it tries to work on a Table of Contents or an Index. This happens both in ImportFormats and Update. To get around this, just open the book file in **maker** and do the Import Formats and Update there.

You can't change the amount of indent using a template file (yet...).

Authors

Based on `pod2html`. Extended by Mark Pease, *Mark_Pease-RXYE0@email.mot.com,* for MML. `fmbatch` and book support added by Tim Bunce, *Tim.Bunce@ig.co.uk.*

Please send bug reports to Mark Pease.

SelfLoader—load functions only on demand

Synopsis

```
package GoodStuff;
use SelfLoader;

[initializing code]
__DATA__
sub {...};
```

Description

This module is used for delayed loading of Perl functions that (unlike AutoLoader functions) are packaged within your script file. This gives the *appearance* of faster loading.

In the example above, SelfLoader tells its user (GoodStuff) that functions in the GoodStuff package are to be autoloaded from after the __DATA__ token.

The __DATA__ token tells Perl that the code for compilation is finished. Everything after the __DATA__ token is available for reading via the filehandle GoodStuff::DATA, where GoodStuff is the name of the current package when the __DATA__ token is reached. This token works just the same as __END__ does in the package main, except that the data after __END__ is retrievable only in package main, whereas data after __DATA__ is retrievable in whatever the current package is.

Note that it is possible to have __DATA__ tokens in the same package in multiple files, and that the last __DATA__ token in a given package that is encountered by the compiler is the one accessible by the filehandle. That is, whenever the __DATA__ token is parsed, any DATA filehandle previously open in the current package (opened in a different file, presumably) is closed so that the new one can be opened. (This also applies to __END__ and the main::DATA filehandle: main::DATA is reopened whenever __END__ is encountered, so any former association is lost.)

SelfLoader Autoloading

The SelfLoader will read from the GoodStuff::DATA filehandle to get definitions for functions placed after __DATA__, and then evaluate the requested subroutine the first time it's called. The costs are the one-time parsing of the data after __DATA__, and a load delay for the first call of any autoloaded function. The benefits are a speeded up compilation phase, with no need to load functions that are never used.

You can use __END__ after __DATA__. The SelfLoader will stop reading from DATA if it encounters the __END__ token, just as you might expect. If the __END__ token is present, and is followed by the token DATA, then the SelfLoader leaves the Good-Stuff::DATA filehandle open on the line after that token.

The SelfLoader exports the AUTOLOAD subroutine to the package using the Self-Loader, and this triggers the automatic loading of an undefined subroutine out of its DATA portion the first time that subroutine is called.

There is no advantage to putting subroutines that will always be called after the __DATA__ token.

Autoloading and File-Scoped Lexicals

A `my $pack_lexical` statement makes the variable `$pack_lexical` visible *only* up to the __DATA__ token. That means that subroutines declared elsewhere cannot see lexical variables. Specifically, autoloaded functions cannot see such lexicals (this applies to both the SelfLoader and the AutoLoader). The `use vars` pragma (see later in this chapter) provides a way to declare package-level globals that will be visible to autoloaded routines.

SelfLoader and AutoLoader

The SelfLoader can replace the AutoLoader—just change `use AutoLoader` to use `SelfLoader`* and the __END__ token to __DATA__.

There is no need to inherit from the SelfLoader.

The SelfLoader works similarly to the AutoLoader, but picks up the subroutine definitions from after the __DATA__ instead of in the *lib/auto/* directory. SelfLoader needs less maintenance at the time the module is installed, since there's no need to run AutoSplit. And it can run faster at load time because it doesn't need to keep opening and closing files to load subroutines. On the other hand, it can run slower because it needs to parse the code after the __DATA__. Details of the AutoLoader and another view of these distinctions can be found in that module's documentation.

---

* Be aware, however, that the SelfLoader exports a function into your package. But if you have your own function and are using the AutoLoader too, you probably know what you're doing.

How to Read DATA from Your Perl Program

(This section is relevant only if you want to use the GoodStuff::DATA together with the SelfLoader.)

The SelfLoader reads from wherever the current position of the GoodStuff::DATA filehandle is, until EOF or the __END__ token. This means that if you want to use that filehandle (and *only* if you want to), you should either

- Put all your subroutine declarations immediately after the __DATA__ token and put your own data after those declarations, using the __END__ token to mark the end of subroutine declarations. You must also ensure that the SelfLoader first reads its stubs by calling `SelfLoader->load_stubs();`, or by using a function which is selfloaded; or

- You should read the GoodStuff::DATA filehandle first, leaving the handle open and positioned at the first line of subroutine declarations.

You could even conceivably do both.

Classes and Inherited Methods

This section is only relevant if your module is a class, and has methods that could be inherited.

A subroutine stub (or forward declaration) looks like:

```
sub stub;
```

That is, it is a subroutine declaration without the body of the subroutine. For modules that aren't classes, there is no real need for stubs as far as autoloading is concerned.

For modules that *are* classes, and need to handle inherited methods, stubs are needed to ensure that the method inheritance mechanism works properly. You can load the stubs into the module at require time, by adding the statement `SelfLoader->load_stubs();` to the module to do this.

The alternative is to put the stubs in before the __DATA__ token before releasing the module, and for this purpose the Devel::SelfStubber module is available. However this does require the extra step of ensuring that the stubs are in the module. If you do this, we strongly recommended that you do it before releasing the module and *not* at install time.

Multiple Packages and Fully Qualified Subroutine Names

Subroutines in multiple packages within the same file are supported—but you should note that this requires exporting SelfLoader::AUTOLOAD to every package which requires it. This is done automatically by the SelfLoader when it first loads the subs into the cache, but you should really specify it in the initialization before __DATA__ by putting a `use SelfLoader` statement in each package.

Fully qualified subroutine names are also supported. For example:

```
__DATA__
sub foo::bar {23}
package baz;
sub dob {32}
```

will all be loaded correctly by the SelfLoader, and the SelfLoader will ensure that the packages "foo" and "baz" correctly have the SelfLoader::AUTOLOAD method when the data after __DATA__ is first parsed.

Author

Jack Shirazi, *js@biu.icnet.uk*

Copyright

Copyright © 1995 Jack Shirazi. All rights reserved. This program is free software; you can redistribute it and/or modify it under the same terms as Perl itself.

See Also

AutoLoader

UNIVERSAL — default general behavior for all objects

Synopsis

```
require UNIVERSAL;

$class = $any_object->class();
$bool = $any_object->is_instance();
```

Description

UNIVERSAL provides general default methods that any object can call.

Methods

`->class()`

> This method returns the class of its object.

`->is_instance()`

> This method returns true if its object is an instance of some class, false if its object is the class (package) itself (i.e., if "A" is a package, then `A->is_instance()` is false, but `$a = bless [],A; $a->is_instance()` is true).

Example

The following illustrates the methods, and can be executed using `perl -x UNIVERSAL.pm`:

```
#!perl


    require UNIVERSAL;
    package C;
    sub new {bless []}

    package main;
    sub test {
       my($obj,$meth,@args) = @_;
       print $obj,'->',$meth,'(',@args,") gives '",
             join(',',$obj->$meth(@args)),"'\n"
    }
```

```
        test(C,'is_instance');                #C->is_instance()
        test(C->new(),'is_instance');         #C->new()->is_instance()

        test(C,'class');                      #C->class()
        test(C->new(),'class');               #C->new()->class()   "foo"

    __END__
```

Author

Jack Shirazi, *js@biu.icnet.uk*

Copyright

Copyright © 1995 Jack Shirazi. All rights reserved. This program is free software; you can redistribute it and/or modify it under the same terms as Perl itself.

3

Development Support

In this section we cover the modules for software development, including debugging tools, code profiling utilities, and performance benchmarking. Also included in this section are installation and diagnostic utilities.

Devel::CallerItem——an object representing a function call from the stack of function calls

Synopsis

```
require Devel::CallerItem;

$call = Devel::CallerItem->from_depth($depth) || return;
$passed_arguments_ref = $call->argument_list_ref();
$callpack = $call->pack();
$callfile = $call->file();
$callline = $call->line();
$callsub = $call->subroutine();
$bool = $call->has_args();
$bool = $call->wants_array();
($arg_ref,@caller) = $call->as_array();
$call_string = $call->as_string($print_level);
$passed_arguments_string = $call->arguments_as_string();

$printable_arg = Devel::CallerItem->printable_arg($arg,$print_level);
```

Description

Devel::CallerItem objects hold all the information about a specific function call on the stack. The information is that obtained from `caller` and @DB::args, packaged into an object. This module also includes some useful methods to print the object as a formatted string.

Methods

->from_depth(*DEPTH*)

This method is the constructor for the class. *DEPTH* is a number, corresponding to the stack level as used by `caller`. The following two calls are equivalent in terms of what gets put into @caller:

```
@caller = caller($DEPTH);
($arg_ref,@caller) = Devel::CallerItem->from_depth($DEPTH)
                                        ->as_array();
```

->argument_list_ref()

Returns a reference to an array. This array holds the arguments passed to the function call on the stack.

If the function was called as &func;, this array is not empty; it holds the array that was passed down to the function func.

->pack()

The package from which the function was called.

->file()

The file from which the function was called.

->line()

The line from which the function was called.

->subroutine()

The fully qualified package name of the function that was called.

->has_args()

A Boolean indicating whether the function was called with arguments.

->wants_array()

A Boolean indicating the context in which the function was called.

->as_array()

Equivalent to the following:

```
($call->argument_list_ref(),$call->pack(),$call->file(),
    $call->line(),$call->subroutine(),$call->has_args(),
    $call->wants_array());
```

->as_string(*PRINT_LEVEL*)

Returns the object in string format suitable for printing. It displays a fully informative message about the function call, like one of the following:

```
$ = func(args) called from FILE line LINE;
$ = &func called from FILE line LINE;
@ = func(args) called from FILE line LINE;
@ = &func called from FILE line LINE;
```

This gives the context (scalar: $, array: @) and whether it was called with arguments or without (&). *PRINT_LEVEL* determines the level of detail printed about the arguments to the function (see `printable_arg` below).

->arguments_as_string(*PRINT_LEVEL*)

Returns a string representing the arguments held in the **argument_list_ref**. This is equivalent to calling **printable_arg** for each argument and joining them with commas.

```
->printable_arg(ARG, PRINT_LEVEL)
```
Renders *ARG* printable. *PRINT_LEVEL* affects the detail of what is printed. There are three levels: 0, 1, and 2. (Currently, any value outside this range is treated as "2", but this may change in future versions of this module, as more print levels are added. To ensure compatibility, be sure to use one of the supported values.)

Level 0 makes strings printable, but scalars that return references are just stringified—i.e., an argument such as [33,{'g' => 55}] would appear as something like "ARRAY(0x9882c)". This is the default.

At level 1, an argument such as [33,{'g' => 55}] would be fully expanded to [33,{'g' => 55}], but any scalar that is repeated in the arguments (e.g., a recursive object) is stringified to something like "ARRAY(0x9882c)". For example, if you had [$a = bless [],A;$b=[$a];$a->[0]=$b], which is a recursive object, then $a would be printed as "[[A=ARRAY(0x83038)]]".

Finally, at level 2, arguments are printed with an associated variable and bless statement if needed, so with $a above, $a is printed as "($v1 = bless [($v2 = [$v1])], A)". Note that this does not actually rebuild $a in Perl code; Perl parses this as $v1 being empty in an internal array, and it is assigned to only after the outer anonymous array is built. This nomenclature is used purely to make explicit any recursive arguments or arguments passed multiple times; while this level of detail is needed on occasion, there is a clear cost in clarity.

Note that the format of items printed out (dependent on *PRINT_LEVEL*) is likely to change in future versions, once a standardized module for printing variables is released.

Example

The following is a simple example, illustrating the three levels of detail available using the PRINT_LEVEL settings, and can be executed using **perl -x Devel/CallerItem.pm**.

```perl
#!perl

require Devel::CallerItem;

$a="pp";
$c = bless [], A;
$d = [$c];
$c->[0] = $d;
sub level0 {
    print Devel::CallerItem->from_depth(0)->as_string(0),"\n"
}
sub level1 {
    print Devel::CallerItem->from_depth(0)->as_string(1),"\n"
}
sub level2 {
    print Devel::CallerItem->from_depth(0)->as_string(2),"\n"
}

level0('hi',21,[44,[66,{"q","hi"},\$a],$c]);
level1('hi',21,[44,[66,{"q","hi"},\$a],$c]);
level2('hi',21,[44,[66,{"q","hi"},\$a],$c]);

__END__
```

Author

Jack Shirazi, *js@biu.icnet.uk*

Copyright

Copyright © 1995 Jack Shirazi. All rights reserved. This program is free software; you can redistribute it and/or modify it under the same terms as Perl itself.

Portions of this code are modified pieces of the `sigtrap` module.

Devel::CoreStack—try to generate a stack dump from a core file

Synopsis

```
perl -MDevel::CoreStack -e 'stack'
perl -MDevel::CoreStack -e 'stack("../myperl", "./mycore", "debugger")'
```

Description

This module attempts to generate a stack dump from a core file by locating the best available debugger (if any) and running it with the appropriate arguments and command script.

Author

Alligator Descartes, *descarte@hermetica.com*

Devel::DProf—a Perl code profiler

Synopsis

```
perl5 -d:DProf test.pl
```

Description

The Devel::DProf package is a Perl code profiler, which collects information on the execution time of a Perl script and of the subs in that script. This information can be used to determine which subroutines are using the most time and which subroutines are being called most often, or to create an execution graph of the script, showing subroutine relationships.

To profile a Perl script, run the Perl interpreter with the –d debugging switch. The profiler uses the debugging hooks. For example, to profile script *test.pl* the following command should be used:

```
perl5 -d:DProf test.pl
```

When the script terminates, the profiler will dump the profile information to a file called *tmon.out*. A tool like **dprofpp** can be used to interpret the information in that profile. The following command will print the top 15 subroutines that used the most time:

```
dprofpp
```

To print an execution graph of the subroutines in the script, use the following command:

```
dprofpp -T
```

Consult the *dprofpp* manpage for other options.

Profile Format

The profile is a text file that looks like this:

```
#fOrTyTwO
$hz=100;
$XS_VERSION='DProf 19970606';
# All values are given in HZ
$rrun_utime=2; $rrun_stime=0; $rrun_rtime=7
PART2
+ 26 28 566822884 DynaLoader::import
- 26 28 566822884 DynaLoader::import
+ 27 28 566822885 main::bar
- 27 28 566822886 main::bar
+ 27 28 566822886 main::baz
+ 27 28 566822887 main::bar
- 27 28 566822888 main::bar
[....]
```

The first line is the magic number. The second line is the hertz value, or clock ticks, of the machine where the profile was collected. The third line is the name and version identifier of the tool that created the profile. The fourth line is a comment. The fifth line contains three variables holding the user time, system time, and real time of the process while it was being profiled. The sixth line indicates the beginning of the sub entry/exit profile section.

The columns in PART2 are:

- sub entry(+)/exit(-) mark
- app's user time at sub entry/exit mark, in ticks
- app's system time at sub entry/exit mark, in ticks
- app's realtime at sub entry/exit mark, in ticks
- fully qualified sub name, when possible

Autoload

When Devel::DProf finds a call to an &AUTOLOAD subroutine it looks at the $AUTO-LOAD variable to find the real name of the sub being called.

Bugs

XSUBs, built-in functions, and destructors cannot be measured by Devel::DProf.

Mail bug reports and feature requests to the Perl5 Porters mailing list at *perl5-porters@africa.nicoh.com*.

Author

Dean Roehrich, *roehrich@cray.com*

See Also

perl, dprofpp, times(2)

Devel::DumpStack—access to the current stack of subroutine calls, and dumping the stack in a readable form

Synopsis

```
use Devel::DumpStack ...;

dump_stack($depth,$indent,$print_level); #Prints to STDERR
$stack = stack_as_string($depth,$indent,$print_level);
$call_string = call_at_depth($depth,$print_level);
($args,$pack,$file,$line,$sub,$has_args,$wantarray) = caller2($depth);

$printable_arg = printable_arg($arg,$print_level);

dump_on_die($print_level); #dumps stack to STDERR on a 'die'
```

Description

Provides functions to access and dump the current stack of subroutine calls.

Functions

dump_stack(*DEPTH, INDENT, PRINT_LEVEL*)
dump_stack(*DEPTH, INDENT*)
dump_stack(*DEPTH*)
dump_stack()

> Prints the current functions stack to STDERR. *DEPTH* is the depth of the stack to print from—equivalent to the depth in **caller()**. Note that you can use negative numbers for *DEPTH* if you want to include the **dump_stack** call and calls under it on the stack print.
>
> *PRINT_LEVEL* is 0, 1, or 2, depending on the level of detail you want printed out for arguments. For a description of *PRINT_LEVEL*, see Devel::CallerItem.
>
> The lines printed are in one of the appropriate formats:

```
$ = func(args) called from FILE line LINE;
$ = &func called from FILE line LINE;
@ = func(args) called from FILE line LINE;
@ = &func called from FILE line LINE;
```

> which gives the context (scalar: $, array: @), and whether it was called with arguments or without (&).
>
> *INDENT* is a string is appended to the beginning of each line printed out.

stack_as_string(*DEPTH, INDENT, PRINT_LEVEL*)
stack_as_string(*DEPTH, INDENT*)
stack_as_string(*DEPTH*)
stack_as_string()

> Produces the same results as **dump_stack**, but instead of printing to STDERR, it returns the stack as a string.

dump_on_die(*PRINT_LEVEL*)
dump_on_die()

> Inserts a handler for any **die** calls, so that when a **die** is called, the current stack is first printed to STDERR before exiting the process. (You probably don't want to do this if you are **die**-ing in an **eval**.) *PRINT_LEVEL* is as above.

```
printable_arg(ANYTHING, PRINT_LEVEL)
printable_arg(ANYTHING)
```
   Renders its argument printable. *PRINT_LEVEL* is as above.

```
caller2(DEPTH)
caller2()
```
   Returns exactly what `caller` returns, except that the reference to the argument
   array for the call at the specified depth is prepended to the array—i.e., the first
   element of the returned array is a reference to the argument array of the function
   called at *DEPTH*, and the subsequent elements are the elements returned by
   `caller`, in the same order. Returns `undef` if there is no call at *DEPTH*.

```
call_at_depth(DEPTH, PRINT_LEVEL)
call_at_depth(DEPTH)
call_at_depth()
```
   Returns a string in the format as given in `dump_stack` above, but just for the
   single function call at the given *DEPTH*. *PRINT_LEVEL* is as above.

Example

The following is a simple example, and can be executed using `perl  -x  Devel/DumpStack.pm`:

```
#!perl
    use Devel::DumpStack qw(dump_stack);

    $a='pp';
    $c = bless [], A;
    $d = [$c];
    $c->[0] = $d;
    sub a { dump_stack(0,'    ',1); print STDERR "\n";}
    sub c { $scalar_context =   a(@_)}
    sub b { c([44,[66,{'q','hi'},\$a],$c])}
    @arr_context = &b;


    __END__
```

Author

Jack Shirazi, *js@biu.icnet.uk*

Copyright

Devel::Peek—a data debugging tool for the XS programmer

Synopsis

```
use Devel::Peek 'Dump';
Dump( $a );
Dump( $a, 5 );
```

Description

Devel::Peek contains functions that allow raw Perl datatypes to be manipulated from a Perl script. This module is used by those who do XS programming to check that the data they are sending from C to Perl looks as they think it should look. The trick, then, is to know what the raw datatype is supposed to look like when it gets to Perl. This document offers some tips and hints to describe good and bad raw data.

It is very possible that this document will fall far short of being useful to the casual reader, who is expected to understand the material in the first sections of the *perlguts* manpage.

Devel::Peek supplies a `Dump()` function that can dump a raw Perl datatype. It also supplies `SvREFCNT()`, `SvREFCNT_inc()`, and `SvREFCNT_dec()`, which can query, increment, and decrement reference counts on SVs. This document will take a passive, and safe, approach to data debugging and for that it will describe only the `Dump()` function.

Examples

The following examples don't attempt to show everything, as that would be a monumental task, and, frankly, we don't want this manpage to be an internals document for Perl. The examples do demonstrate some basics of the raw Perl datatypes, and should suffice to get most determined people on their way. There are no guidewires or safety nets, nor blazed trails, so be prepared to travel alone from this point on and, if at all possible, don't fall into the quicksand (it's bad for business).

Oh, one final bit of advice: take the *perlguts* manpage with you. When you return we expect to see it well-thumbed.

A Simple Scalar String

Let's begin by looking at a simple scalar that is holding a string.

```
use Devel::Peek 'Dump';
$a = "hello";
Dump $a;
```

The output:

```
SV = PVIV(0xbc288)
  REFCNT = 1
  FLAGS = (POK,pPOK)
  IV = 0
  PV = 0xb2048 "hello"
  CUR = 5
  LEN = 6
```

This says $a is an SV, a scalar. The scalar is a PVIV, a string. Its reference count is 1. It has the POK flag set, meaning it is currently being evaluated as a string. Because POK is set, we look at the PV item to see what is in the scalar. If the FLAGS had been IOK we would look at the IV item. CUR indicates the number of characters in the PV. LEN indicates the number of bytes in the PV (one more than CUR, in this case, because LEN includes an extra byte for the end-of-string marker).

A Simple Scalar Number

If the scalar contains a number, the raw SV will be leaner.

```
use Devel::Peek 'Dump';
$a = 42;
Dump $a;
```

The output:

```
SV = IV(0xbc818)
  REFCNT = 1
  FLAGS = (IOK,pIOK)
  IV = 42
```

This says $a is an SV, a scalar. The scalar is an IV, a number. Its reference count is 1. It has the IOK flag set, meaning it is currently being evaluated as a number. Because IOK is set we look at the IV item to see what is in the scalar.

A Simple Scalar with an Extra Reference

If the scalar from the previous example had an extra reference:

```
use Devel::Peek 'Dump';
$a = 42;
$b = \$a;
Dump $a;
```

The output:

```
SV = IV(0xbe860)
  REFCNT = 2
  FLAGS = (IOK,pIOK)
  IV = 42
```

Notice that this example differs from the previous example only in its reference count. Compare this to the next example, where we dump $b instead of $a.

A Reference to a Simple Scalar

This shows what a reference looks like when it references a simple scalar.

```
use Devel::Peek 'Dump';
$a = 42;
$b = \$a;
Dump $b;
```

The output:

```
SV = RV(0xf041c)
  REFCNT = 1
  FLAGS = (ROK)
  RV = 0xbab08
SV = IV(0xbe860)
  REFCNT = 2
  FLAGS = (IOK,pIOK)
  IV = 42
```

Starting from the top, this says $b is an SV. The scalar is an RV, a reference. It has the ROK flag set, meaning it is a reference. Because ROK is set we have an RV item rather than an IV or PV. Notice that Dump follows the reference and shows us what $b was referencing. We see the same $a that we found in the previous example.

A Reference to an Array

This shows what a reference to an array looks like.

```
use Devel::Peek 'Dump';
$a = [42];
Dump $a;
```

The output:

```
SV = RV(0xf041c)
  REFCNT = 1
  FLAGS = (ROK)
  RV = 0xb2850
SV = PVAV(0xbd448)
  REFCNT = 1
  FLAGS = ()
  IV = 0
  NV = 0
  ARRAY = 0xb2048
  ALLOC = 0xb2048
  FILL = 0
  MAX = 0
  ARYLEN = 0x0
  FLAGS = (REAL)
Elt No. 0
SV = IV(0xbe860)
  REFCNT = 1
  FLAGS = (IOK,pIOK)
  IV = 42
```

This says that $a is an SV and an RV. That RV points to another SV, which is a PVAV, an array. The array has one element, element zero, which is another SV.

If $a pointed to an array of two elements, we would see the following:

```
use Devel::Peek 'Dump';
$a = [42,24];
Dump $a;
```

The output:

```
SV = RV(0xf041c)
  REFCNT = 1
  FLAGS = (ROK)
  RV = 0xb2850
SV = PVAV(0xbd448)
  REFCNT = 1
  FLAGS = ()
  IV = 0
  NV = 0
  ARRAY = 0xb2048
  ALLOC = 0xb2048
  FILL = 0
  MAX = 0
  ARYLEN = 0x0
  FLAGS = (REAL)
Elt No. 0
SV = IV(0xbe860)
  REFCNT = 1
  FLAGS = (IOK,pIOK)
  IV = 42
Elt No. 1
SV = IV(0xbe818)
  REFCNT = 1
```

```
FLAGS = (IOK,pIOK)
IV = 24
```

A Reference to a Hash

The following shows the raw form of a reference to a hash.

```
use Devel::Peek 'Dump';
$a = {hello=>42};
Dump $a;
```

The output:

```
SV = RV(0xf041c)
  REFCNT = 1
  FLAGS = (ROK)
  RV = 0xb2850
SV = PVHV(0xbd448)
  REFCNT = 1
  FLAGS = ()
  IV = 1
  NV = 0
  ARRAY = 0xbd748
  KEYS = 1
  FILL = 1
  MAX = 7
  RITER = -1
  EITER = 0x0
Elt "hello" => 0xbaaf0
SV = IV(0xbe860)
  REFCNT = 1
  FLAGS = (IOK,pIOK)
  IV = 42
```

This shows that $a is a reference pointing to an SV, and that SV is a PVHV, a hash.

Dumping a Large Array or Hash

The Dump() function, by default, dumps up to 4 elements from an array or hash. This number can be increased by supplying a second argument to the function.

```
use Devel::Peek 'Dump';
$a = [10,11,12,13,14];
Dump $a;
```

Notice that Dump() prints only elements 10 through 13 in the above code. The following code will print all of the elements.

```
use Devel::Peek 'Dump';
$a = [10,11,12,13,14];
Dump $a, 5;
```

A Reference to an SV That Holds a C Pointer

This is what you really need to know as an XS programmer, of course. When an XSUB returns a pointer to a C structure, that pointer is stored in an SV and a reference to that SV is placed on the XSUB stack. So the output from an XSUB which uses something like the T_PTROBJ map might look something like this:

```
SV = RV(0xf381c)
  REFCNT = 1
```

```
      FLAGS = (ROK)
      RV = 0xb8ad8
   SV = PVMG(0xbb3c8)
      REFCNT = 1
      FLAGS = (OBJECT,IOK,pIOK)
      IV = 729160
      NV = 0
      PV = 0
      STASH = 0xc1d10        "CookBookB::Opaque"
```

This shows that we have an SV which is an RV. That RV points at another SV. In this
case, the second SV is a PVMG, a blessed scalar. Because it is blessed it has the
OBJECT flag set. Note that an SV that holds a C pointer also has the IOK flag set. The
STASH is set to the package name which this SV was blessed into.

The output from an XSUB that uses something like the T_PTRREF map, which doesn't
bless the object, might look something like this:

```
   SV = RV(0xf381c)
      REFCNT = 1
      FLAGS = (ROK)
      RV = 0xb8ad8
   SV = PVMG(0xbb3c8)
      REFCNT = 1
      FLAGS = (IOK,pIOK)
      IV = 729160
      NV = 0
      PV = 0
```

Bugs

Readers have been known to skip important parts of the *perlguts* manpage, causing much
frustration for all.

See Also

The *perlguts* manpage, and the *perlguts* manpage, again.

Devel::Symdump—dump symbol names or the symbol table

Synopsis

```
# Constructor
require Devel::Symdump;
@packs = qw(some_package another_package);
$obj = Devel::Symdump->new(@packs);            # no recursion
$obj = Devel::Symdump->rnew(@packs);           # with recursion

# Methods
@array = $obj->packages;
@array = $obj->scalars;
@array = $obj->arrays;
@array = $obj->hashs;
@array = $obj->functions;
@array = $obj->filehandles;  # deprecated, use ios instead
```

```
@array = $obj->dirhandles;    # deprecated, use ios instead
@array = $obj->ios;
@array = $obj->unknowns;

$string = $obj->as_string;
$string = $obj->as_HTML;
$string = $obj1->diff($obj2);
$string = Devel::Symdump->isa_tree;    # or $obj->isa_tree
$string = Devel::Symdump->inh_tree;    # or $obj->inh_tree
# Methods with autogenerated objects
# all of those call new(@packs) internally
@array = Devel::Symdump->packages(@packs);
@array = Devel::Symdump->scalars(@packs);
@array = Devel::Symdump->arrays(@packs);
@array = Devel::Symdump->hashes(@packs);
@array = Devel::Symdump->functions(@packs);
@array = Devel::Symdump->ios(@packs);
@array = Devel::Symdump->unknowns(@packs);
```

Description

This little package serves to access the symbol table of Perl.

Methods

Devel::Symdump->rnew(@packages)

> returns a symbol table object for all subtrees below @packages. Nested modules are analyzed recursively. If no package is given as argument, it defaults to main. Therefore, to get the whole symbol table, just do a rnew without arguments.

Devel::Symdump->new(@packages)

> does not go into recursion and analyzes only the packages that are given as arguments.

The methods packages(), scalars(), arrays(), hashes(), functions(), ios(), and unknowns() each return an array of fully qualified symbols of the specified type in all packages that are held within a Devel::Symdump object, but without the leading $, @, or %. In a scalar context, they will return the number of such symbols. Unknown symbols are usually either formats or variables that haven't yet gotten a defined value.

as_string() returns a simple string, while as_HTML() returns HTML representations of the object.

diff() prints the difference between two Devel::Symdump objects in human-readable form. The format is similar to the one used by the as_string method.

isa_tree() and inh_tree() both return a simple string representation of the current inheritance tree. The difference between the two methods is the direction from which the tree is viewed: top-down or bottom-up. As I'm sure many users will have different expectation about what is top and what is bottom, I'll provide an example of what happens when the Socket module is loaded.

The inh_tree method shows a package name on the left-hand side and, indented to the right, the packages that use the name:

```
% print Devel::Symdump->inh_tree
AutoLoader
        DynaLoader
                Socket
```

```
DynaLoader
        Socket
Exporter
        Carp
        Config
        Socket
```

The `isa_tree` method displays ISA relationships from left to right, so Socket IS A DynaLoader and DynaLoader IS A AutoLoader (at least at the time this manpage was written):

```
% print Devel::Symdump->isa_tree
Carp
        Exporter
Config
        Exporter
DynaLoader
        AutoLoader
Socket
        Exporter
        DynaLoader
                AutoLoader
```

You may call both methods, `isa_tree()` and `inh_tree()`, with an object. If you do that, the object will store the output and retrieve it when you call the same method again later. The typical usage would be to use them as class methods directly, however.

Subclassing

The design of this package is intentionally primitive and allows it to be subclassed easily. An example of a (possibly) useful subclass is Devel::Symdump::Export, a package which exports all methods of the Devel::Symdump package and turns them into functions.

Incompatibility Alert

Perl 5.003 already offered the opportunity to test for the individual slots of a GLOB with the *GLOB{XXX} notation. Devel::Symdump version 2.00 uses this method internally which means that the type of undefined values is recognized in general. Previous versions couldn't determine the type of undefined values, so the slot *unknowns* was invented. From version 2.00, this slot is still present but will usually not contain any elements.

The interface has changed slightly between the Perl versions 5.003 and 5.004. To be precise, from Perl 5.003_11 the names of the members of a GLOB have changed. IO is the internal name for all kinds of input-output handles while FILEHANDLE and DIRHANDLE are deprecated.

Devel::Symdump accordingly introduces the new method `ios()`, which returns filehandles *and* directory handles. The old methods `filehandles()` and `dirhandles()` are still supported for a transitional period. They will probably have to go in future versions.

Authors

Andreas Koenig, *koenig@franz.ww.TU-Berlin.de*, and Tom Christiansen, *tchrist@perl.com*. Based on the old *dumpvar.pl* by Larry Wall.

ExtUtils::Command—utilities to replace common UNIX commands in Makefiles

Synopsis

```
perl -MExtUtils::command -e cat files... > destination
perl -MExtUtils::command -e mv source... destination
perl -MExtUtils::command -e cp source... destination
perl -MExtUtils::command -e touch files...
perl -MExtUtils::command -e rm_f file...
perl -MExtUtils::command -e rm_rf directories...
perl -MExtUtils::command -e mkpath directories...
perl -MExtUtils::command -e eqtime source destination
perl -MExtUtils::command -e chmod mode files...
perl -MExtUtils::command -e test_f file
```

Description

The module is used in Win32 port to replace common UNIX commands. Most commands are wrappers on generic modules File::Path and File::Basename.

cat
> Concatenates all files mentioned on command line to STDOUT.

eqtime *src dst*
> Sets modified time of *dst* to that of *src*.

rm_rf *directories ...*
> Removes *directories* recursively (even if read-only).

rm_f *files ...*
> Removes *files* (even if read-only).

touch *files ...*
> Makes *files* exist, with current timestamp.

mv *source ... destination*
> Moves *source* to *destination*. Multiple sources are allowed if destination is an existing directory.

cp *source ... destination*
> Copies *source* to *destination*. Multiple sources are allowed if destination is an existing directory.

chmod *mode files ...*
> Sets UNIX-like permissions *mode* on *files*.

mkpath *directory ...*
> Creates *directory*, including any parent directories.

test_f *file*
> Tests if *file* exists.

Bugs

Should probably be Auto/Self loaded.

Author

Nick Ing-Simmons, *nick@ni-s.u-net.com*

See Also

ExtUtils::MakeMaker, ExtUtils::MM_Unix, ExtUtils::MM_Win32

ExtUtils::F77 — simple interface to F77 libs

Synopsis

```
use ExtUtils::F77;              # Automatic guess
use ExtUtils::F77 qw(sunos);    # Specify system
use ExtUtils::F77 qw(linux g77); # Specify system and compiler
```

Description

This is a simple interface to F77 libraries based on rule-of-thumb knowledge of various UNIX systems.

It includes a simple self-documenting Perl database of knowledge/code for figuring out how to link for various combinations of operating systems and compilers. Updates for the database entries may be sent to *kgb@aaoepp.aao.gov.au*; input on systems not already in the database is welcome.

Methods

runtime()
>   Returns list of F77 runtime libraries.

runtimeok()
>   Returns true only if runtime libraries have been found successfully.

trail_()
>   Returns true if F77 names have trailing underscores.

compiler()
>   Returns command to execute the compiler (e.g. "f77").

cflags()
>   Returns compiler flags.

testcompiler
>   Tests to see if compiler actually works.

Author

Karl Glazebrook, *KGB@aaoepp2.aao.gov.au*

ExtUtils::Install — install files from here to there

Synopsis

```
use ExtUtils::Install;
install($hashref,$verbose,$nonono);
uninstall($packlistfile,$verbose,$nonono);
pm_to_blib($hashref);
```

Description

Both `install()` and `uninstall()` are specific to the way ExtUtils::MakeMaker handles the installation and deinstallation of Perl modules. They are not designed as general-purpose tools.

`install()` takes three arguments: a reference to a hash, a verbose switch, and a don't-really-do-it switch. The hash ref contains a mapping of directories: each key/value pair is a combination of directories to be copied. Key is a directory to copy from, while value is a directory to copy to. The whole tree below the "from" directory will be copied preserving timestamps and permissions.

There are two keys with a special meaning in the hash: "read" and "write". After the copying is done, install will write the list of target files to the file named by `$hashref->{write}`. If there is another file named by `$hashref->{read}`, the contents of this file will be merged into the written file. The read and the written file may be identical, but on AFS it is quite likely that people are installing to a different directory than the one where the files later appear.

`uninstall()` takes as first argument a file containing filenames to be unlinked. The second argument is a verbose switch, the third is a no-don't-really-do-it-now switch.

`pm_to_blib()` takes a hashref as the first argument and copies all keys of the hash to the corresponding values efficiently. Filenames with the extension *.pm* are autosplit. Second argument is the autosplit directory.

ExtUtils::Liblist—determine libraries to use and how to use them

Synopsis

```
require ExtUtils::Liblist;
ExtUtils::Liblist::ext($potential_libs, $Verbose);
```

Description

This utility takes a list of libraries in the form `-llib1 -llib2 -llib3` and prints out lines suitable for inclusion in an extension Makefile. Extra library paths may be included with the form `-L/another/path`; this will affect the searches for all subsequent libraries.

It returns an array of four scalar values: EXTRALIBS, BSLOADLIBS, LDLOADLIBS, and LD_RUN_PATH.

Dependent libraries can be linked in one of three ways:

For static extensions

By the `ld` command when the Perl binary is linked with the extension library. EXTRALIBS gives a list of libraries that need to be linked with when linking a Perl binary that includes this extension. Only those libraries that actually exist are included. These are written to a file and used when linking Perl.

For dynamic extensions

By the `ld` command when the shared object is built/linked. LDLOADLIBS gives a list of those libraries that can or must be linked into the shared library when created using `ld`. These may be static or dynamic libraries. LD_RUN_PATH is a colon-separated list of the directories in LDLOADLIBS. It is passed as an environment variable to the process that links the shared library.

For dynamic extensions

By the DynaLoader when the shared object is loaded. BSLOADLIBS gives a list of those libraries that are needed but can be linked in dynamically at run time on this platform. SunOS/Solaris does not need this because `ld` records the information (from LDLOADLIBS) into the object file. This list is used to create a *.bs* (bootstrap) file.

Portability

This module deals with a lot of system dependencies and has quite a few architecture-specific `if`s in the code.

VMS implementation

The version of `ext()` that is executed under VMS differs from the UNIX or OS/2 version in several respects:

- Input library and path specifications are accepted with or without the `-l` and `-L` prefixes used by UNIX linkers. If neither prefix is present, a token is considered a directory to search if it is in fact a directory, and a library to search if it is not a directory. Authors who wish their extensions to be portable to UNIX or OS/2 should use the UNIX prefixes, since the UNIX or OS/2 version of `ext()` requires them.

- Wherever possible, shareable images are preferred to object libraries, and object libraries to plain object files. In accordance with VMS naming conventions, `ext()` looks for files named *libshr* and *librtl*; it also looks for *liblib* and *liblib* to accomodate UNIX conventions used in some ported software.

- For each library that is found, an appropriate directive for a linker options file is generated. The return values are space-separated strings of these directives, rather than elements used on the linker command line.

- LDLOADLIBS and EXTRALIBS are always identical under VMS, and BSLOADLIBS and LD_RIN_PATH are always empty.

In addition, an attempt is made to recognize several common UNIX library names, and filter them out or convert them to their VMS equivalents, as appropriate.

In general, the VMS version of `ext()` should properly handle input from extensions originally designed for a UNIX or VMS environment. If you encounter problems, or discover cases where the search could be improved, please let us know.

See Also

ExtUtils::MakeMaker

ExtUtils::MakeMaker—create an extension Makefile

Synopsis

```
use ExtUtils::MakeMaker;
WriteMakefile( ATTRIBUTE => VALUE [, ...] );
```

which is really:

```
MM->new(\%att)->flush;
```

Description

This utility is designed to write a Makefile for an extension module from a *Makefile.PL*. It is based on the *Makefile.sh* model provided by Andy Dougherty and the Perl5 Porters.

It splits the task of generating the Makefile into several subroutines that can be individually overridden. Each subroutine returns the text it wishes to have written to the Makefile.

MakeMaker is object-oriented. Each directory below the current directory that contains a *Makefile.PL* is treated as a separate object. This makes it possible to write an unlimited number of Makefiles with a single invocation of `WriteMakefile()`.

How to Write a Makefile.PL

The short answer is: Don't.

Always begin with h2xs, even if you're not building around a header file, and even if you don't have an XS component. I can't stress that enough: always begin with **h2xs**.

Run **h2xs**(1) before you start thinking about writing a module. For so called pm-only modules that consist of **.pm* files only, **h2xs** has the **-X** switch. This will generate dummy files of all kinds that are useful for the module developer.

The medium answer is:

```
use ExtUtils::MakeMaker;
WriteMakefile( NAME => "Foo::Bar" );
```

The long answer is the rest of this document.

Default Makefile Behavior

The generated Makefile enables the user of the extension to invoke:

```
perl Makefile.PL # optionally "perl Makefile.PL verbose"
make
make test        # optionally set TEST_VERBOSE=1
make install     # See below
```

The Makefile to be produced may be altered by adding arguments of the form KEY=VALUE, e.g.:

```
perl Makefile.PL PREFIX=/tmp/myperl5
```

Other interesting targets in the generated Makefile are:

```
make config      # to check if the Makefile is up-to-date
make clean       # delete local temp files (Makefile gets renamed)
make realclean   # delete derived files (including ./blib)
make ci          # check in all the files in the MANIFEST file
make dist        # see below the Distribution Support section
```

make test

MakeMaker checks for the existence of a file named *test.pl* in the current directory and, if it exists, adds commands to the test target of the generated Makefile that will execute the script with the proper set of Perl **-I** options.

MakeMaker also checks for any files matching glob("t/*.t"). It will add commands to the test target of the generated Makefile that execute all matching files via the Test::Harness module with the -I switches set correctly.

make testdb

A useful variation of the above is the target testdb. It runs the test under the Perl debugger (see the *perldebug* manpage). If the file *test.pl* exists in the current directory, it is used for the test.

If you want to debug some other testfile, set TEST_FILE variable like this:

```
make testdb TEST_FILE=t/mytest.t
```

By default the debugger is called using -d option to Perl. If you want to specify some other option, set TESTDB_SW variable:

```
make testdb TESTDB_SW=-Dx
```

make install

make alone puts all relevant files into directories that are named by the macros INST_LIB, INST_ARCHLIB, INST_SCRIPT, INST_MAN1DIR, and INST_MAN3DIR. All these default to something below *./blib* if you are *not* building below the Perl source directory. If you *are* building below the Perl source, INST_LIB and INST_ARCHLIB default to *../../lib*, and INST_SCRIPT is not defined.

The *install* target of the generated Makefile copies the files found below each of the INST_* directories to their INSTALL* counterparts. Which counterparts are chosen depends on the setting of INSTALLDIRS according to the following table:

| | INSTALLDIRS set to: | |
	perl	site
INST_ARCHLIB	INSTALLARCHLIB	INSTALLSITEARCH
INST_LIB	INSTALLPRIVLIB	INSTALLSITELIB
INST_BIN	INSTALLBIN	
INST_SCRIPT	INSTALLSCRIPT	
INST_MAN1DIR	INSTALLMAN1DIR	
INST_MAN3DIR	INSTALLMAN3DIR	

The INSTALL... macros in turn default to their %Config ($Config{installprivlib}, $Config{installarchlib}, etc.) counterparts.

You can check the values of these variables on your system with:

```
perl '-V:install.*'
```

And to check the sequence in which the library directories are searched by Perl, run:

```
perl -le 'print join $/, @INC'
```

PREFIX and LIB attribute

PREFIX and LIB can be used to set several INSTALL* attributes in one go. The quickest way to install a module in a non-standard place might be:

```
perl Makefile.PL LIB=~/lib
```

This will install the module's architecture-independent files into ~/lib, and the architecture-dependent files into ~/lib/$archname/auto.

Another way to specify many INSTALL directories with a single parameter is PREFIX:

```
perl Makefile.PL PREFIX=~
```

This will replace the string specified by $Config{prefix} in all of the $Config{install*} values.

Note that in both cases the tilde expansion is done by MakeMaker, not by Perl by default, nor by **make**.

If the user has superuser privileges, and is not working on AFS (Andrew File System) or relatives, then the defaults for INSTALLPRIVLIB, INSTALLARCHLIB, INSTALLSCRIPT, etc. will be appropriate, and this incantation will be best:

```
perl Makefile.PL; make; make test
make install
```

By default, **make install** writes some documentation of what has been done into the file *$(INSTALLARCHLIB)/perllocal.pod*. This feature can be bypassed by calling **make pure_install**.

AFS Users

AFS users will have to specify the installation directories, as these most probably have changed since Perl itself has been installed. They will have to do this by calling:

```
perl Makefile.PL INSTALLSITELIB=/afs/here/today \
    INSTALLSCRIPT=/afs/there/now INSTALLMAN3DIR=/afs/for/manpages
make
```

Be careful to repeat this procedure every time you recompile an extension, unless you are sure the AFS installation directories are still valid.

Static Linking of a New Perl Binary

An extension that is built with the above steps is ready to use on systems supporting dynamic loading. On systems that do not support dynamic loading, any newly created extension has to be linked together with the available resources. MakeMaker supports the linking process by creating appropriate targets in the Makefile whenever an extension is built. You can invoke the corresponding section of the makefile with:

```
make perl
```

This produces a new Perl binary in the current directory with all extensions linked in that can be found in INST_ARCHLIB, SITELIBEXP, and PERL_ARCHLIB. To do that, MakeMaker writes a new Makefile; on UNIX, this is called *Makefile.aperl* (may be system-dependent). If you want to force the creation of a new Perl, it is recommended that you delete this *Makefile.aperl*, so the directories are searched through for linkable libraries again.

The binary can be installed into the directory where Perl normally resides on your machine with:

```
make inst_perl
```

To produce a Perl binary with a different name than **perl**, either say:

```
perl Makefile.PL MAP_TARGET=myperl
make myperl
make inst_perl
```

or say:

```
perl Makefile.PL
make myperl MAP_TARGET=myperl
make inst_perl MAP_TARGET=myperl
```

In any case, you will be prompted with the correct invocation of the `inst_perl` target that installs the new binary into INSTALLBIN.

`make inst_perl` per default writes some documentation of what has been done into the file *$(INSTALLARCHLIB)/perllocal.pod*. This can be bypassed by calling `make pure_inst_perl`.

Warning

The `inst_perl` target will most probably overwrite your existing Perl binary. Use with care!

Sometimes you might want to build a statically linked Perl, even though your system supports dynamic loading. In this case, you may explicitly set the linktype with the invocation of the *Makefile.PL*, or make:

```
perl Makefile.PL LINKTYPE=static    # recommended
```

or:

```
make LINKTYPE=static                # works on most systems
```

Determination of Perl Library and Installation Locations

MakeMaker needs to know, or to guess, where certain things are located. Especially INST_LIB and INST_ARCHLIB (where to put the files during the *make*(1) run), PERL_LIB and PERL_ARCHLIB (where to read existing modules from), and PERL_INC (header files and *libperl*.**).

Extensions may be built either using the contents of the Perl source directory tree or from the installed Perl library. The recommended way is to build extensions after you have run `make install` on Perl itself. You can do that in any directory on your hard disk that is not below the Perl source tree. The support for extensions below the *ext* directory of the Perl distribution is good only for the standard extensions that come with Perl.

If an extension is being built below the *ext* directory of the Perl source, MakeMaker will set PERL_SRC automatically (e.g., *../..*). If PERL_SRC is defined and the extension is recognized as a standard extension, then other variables default to the following:

```
PERL_INC     = PERL_SRC
PERL_LIB     = PERL_SRC/lib
PERL_ARCHLIB = PERL_SRC/lib
INST_LIB     = PERL_LIB
INST_ARCHLIB = PERL_ARCHLIB
```

If an extension is being built away from the Perl source then MakeMaker will leave PERL_SRC undefined and default to using the installed copy of the Perl library. The other variables default to the following:

```
PERL_INC     = $archlibexp/CORE
PERL_LIB     = $privlibexp
PERL_ARCHLIB = $archlibexp
INST_LIB     = ./blib/lib
INST_ARCHLIB = ./blib/arch
```

If Perl has not yet been installed, PERL_SRC can be defined on the command line as shown in the previous section.

Which Architecture-Dependent Directory?

If you don't want to keep the defaults for the INSTALL* macros, MakeMaker helps you minimize the typing needed: the usual relationship between INSTALLPRIVLIB and INSTALLARCHLIB is determined by Configure at Perl compilation time. MakeMaker supports the user who sets INSTALLPRIVLIB. If INSTALLPRIVLIB is set, but INSTALL-ARCHLIB is not, then MakeMaker defaults the latter to be the same subdirectory of INSTALLPRIVLIB as Configure decided for the counterparts in %Config; otherwise it defaults to INSTALLPRIVLIB. The same relationship holds for INSTALLSITELIB and INSTALLSITEARCH.

MakeMaker gives you much more freedom than you need to configure internal variables and get different results. It is worth mentioning that *make*(1) also lets you configure most of the variables that are used in the Makefile, but in the majority of situations this will not be necessary. It should be done only if the author of a package recommends it (or you know what you're doing).

Using Attributes and Parameters

The following attributes can be specified as arguments to WriteMakefile() or as NAME=VALUE pairs on the command line:

C

    Reference to array of *.c filenames. Initialized from a directory scan and the values portion of the XS attribute hash. This is not currently used by MakeMaker but may be handy in *Makefile.PLs*.

CONFIG

    Array reference (e.g., [qw(*archname manext*)]), defining *archname* and *manext* from *config.sh*. MakeMaker will add to CONFIG the following values anyway:

ar	dlext	ldflags	ranlib
cc	dlsrc	libc	sitearchexp
cccdlflags	ld	lib_ext	sitelibexp
ccdlflags	lddlflags	obj_ext	so

CONFIGURE

    CODE reference. The subroutine should return a hash reference. The hash may contain further attributes (e.g., {LIBS => ...}) that have to be determined by some evaluation method.

DEFINE

    Something like "-DHAVE_UNISTD_H".

DIR

    Reference to array of subdirectories containing *Makefile.PLs* (e.g., ['sdbm'] in *ext/SDBM_File*).

DISTNAME

    Your name for distributing the package (by tar file). This defaults to NAME above.

DL_FUNCS

Hashref of symbol names for routines to be made available as universal symbols. Each key/value pair consists of the package name and an array of routine names in that package. Used only under AIX (export lists) and VMS (linker options) at present. The routine names supplied will be expanded in the same way as XSUB names are expanded by the `XS()` macro. Defaults to:

```
{"$(NAME)" => ["boot_$(NAME)" ] }
```

e.g.:

```
{"RPC" => [qw( boot_rpcb rpcb_gettime getnetconfigent )],
 "NetconfigPtr" => [ 'DESTROY'] }
```

DL_VARS

Array of symbol names for variables to be made available as universal symbols (e.g., [qw(Foo_version Foo_numstreams Foo_tree)]). Used only under AIX (export lists) and VMS (linker options) at present. Defaults to [].

EXCLUDE_EXT

Array of extension names to exclude when doing a static build (e.g., [qw(Socket POSIX)]). This is ignored if INCLUDE_EXT is present. Consult INCLUDE_EXT for more details.

This attribute may be most useful when specified as a string on the command line:

```
perl Makefile.PL EXCLUDE_EXT='Socket Safe'
```

EXE_FILES

Reference to array of executable files. The files will be copied to the INST_SCRIPT directory. `make realclean` will delete them from there again.

NO_VC

In general, any generated Makefile checks for the current version of MakeMaker and the version the Makefile was built under. If NO_VC is set, the version check is neglected. Do not write this into your *Makefile.PL*; use it interactively instead.

FIRST_MAKEFILE

The name of the Makefile to be produced. Defaults to the contents of MAKEFILE, but can be overridden. This is used for the second Makefile that will be produced for the MAP_TARGET.

FULLPERL

Perl binary able to run this extension.

H

Reference to array of **.h* file names. Similar to C.

INC

Include file directories (e.g., `-I/usr/5include -I/path/to/inc`).

INCLUDE_EXT

Array of extension names to be included when doing a static build (e.g. [qw(Socket POSIX)]). MakeMaker will normally build with all of the installed extensions when doing a static build, and that is usually the desired behavior. If INCLUDE_EXT is present, MakeMaker will build only with those extensions which are explicitly mentioned.

It is not necessary to mention DynaLoader or the current extension when filling in INCLUDE_EXT. If the INCLUDE_EXT is mentioned but is empty, only DynaLoader and the current extension will be included in the build.

This attribute may be most useful when specified as a string on the command line:

```
perl Makefile.PL INCLUDE_EXT='POSIX Socket Devel::Peek'
```

INSTALLARCHLIB

Used by `make install`, which copies files from INST_ARCHLIB to this directory if INSTALLDIRS is set to Perl.

INSTALLBIN

Directory to install binary files (e.g. *tkperl*) into.

INSTALLDIRS

Determines which of the two sets of installation directories to choose: *install-privlib* and *installarchlib*, versus *installsitelib* and *installsitearch*. The first pair is chosen with INSTALLDIRS=`perl`, the second with INSTALLDIRS=`site`. Default is `site`.

INSTALLMAN1DIR

This directory gets the manpages at `make install` time. Defaults to `$Config{installman1dir}`.

INSTALLMAN3DIR

This directory gets the manpages at `make install` time. Defaults to `$Config{installman3dir}`.

INSTALLPRIVLIB

Used by `make install`, which copies files from INST_LIB to this directory if INSTALLDIRS is set to Perl.

INSTALLSCRIPT

Used by `make install`, which copies files from INST_SCRIPT to this directory.

INSTALLSITELIB

Used by `make install`, which copies files from INST_LIB to this directory if INSTALLDIRS is set to `site` (default).

INSTALLSITEARCH

Used by `make install`, which copies files from INST_ARCHLIB to this directory if INSTALLDIRS is set to `site` (default).

INST_ARCHLIB

Same as INST_LIB for architecture-dependent files.

INST_BIN

Directory into which, during `make`, you will put real binary files. These will be copied to INSTALLBIN during `make install`.

INST_EXE

Old name for INST_SCRIPT; deprecated. Please use INST_SCRIPT instead.

INST_LIB

Directory where we put library files of this extension while building it.

INST_MAN1DIR

Directory to hold the man pages at `make` time.

INST_MAN3DIR

Directory to hold the man pages at `make` time.

INST_SCRIPT
> The directory where executable files should be installed during make. Defaults to *./blib/bin*, just to have a dummy location during testing. make install will copy the files in INST_SCRIPT to INSTALLSCRIPT.

LDFROM
> Defaults to $(OBJECT) and is used in the ld command to specify what files to link/load from. (Also see dynamic_lib below for how to specify ld flags.)

LIBPERL_A
> The filename of the Perl library that will be used together with this extension. Defaults to *libperl.a*.

LIB
> LIB can be set only at perl Makefile.PL time. It has the effect of setting both INSTALLPRIVLIB and INSTALLSITELIB to that value regardless of any other variables.

LIBS
> An anonymous array of alternative library specifications to be searched for (in order) until at least one library is found, e.g.:
>
>   'LIBS' => ["-lgdbm", "-ldbm -lfoo", "-L/path -ldbm.nfs"]
>
> Note that any element of the array contains a complete set of arguments for the ld command, so do not specify:
>
>   'LIBS' => ["-ltcl", "-ltk", "-lX11"]
>
> See *ODBM_File/Makefile.PL* for an example where an array is needed. If you specify a scalar, as in:
>
>   'LIBS' => "-ltcl -ltk -lX11"
>
> MakeMaker will turn it into an array with one element.

LINKTYPE
> static or dynamic (default unless usedl=undef in *config.sh*). Should only be used to force static linking (also see linkext below).

MAKEAPERL
> Boolean that tells MakeMaker to include the rules to make a Perl. This is handled automatically as a switch by MakeMaker. The user normally does not need to set it.

MAKEFILE
> The name of the Makefile to be produced.

MAN1PODS
> Hashref of pod-containing files. MakeMaker will default this to all EXE_FILES files that include pod directives. The files listed here will be converted to manpages and installed as was requested at Configure time.

MAN3PODS
> Hashref of *.pm* and *.pod* files. MakeMaker will default this to all *.pod* and any *.pm* files that include pod directives. The files listed here will be converted to manpages and installed as was requested at Configure time.

MAP_TARGET
> If it is intended that a new Perl binary be produced, this variable may hold a name for that binary. Defaults to perl.

MYEXTLIB

> If the extension links to a library that it builds, set this to the name of the library (see **SDBM_File**).

NAME

> Perl module name for this extension (DBD::Oracle). This will default to the directory name but should be explicitly defined in the *Makefile.PL*.

NEEDS_LINKING

> MakeMaker will figure out whether an extension contains linkable code anywhere down the directory tree, and will set this variable accordingly. However, you can speed it up a bit if you define this boolean variable yourself.

NOECHO

> Defaults to @. By setting it to an empty string you can generate a Makefile that echos all commands. Mainly used in debugging MakeMaker itself.

NORECURS

> Boolean. Used to inhibit descending into subdirectories.

OBJECT

> List of object files. Defaults to $(BASEEXT)$(OBJ_EXT), but can be a long string containing all object files (e.g., `tkpBind.o tkpButton.o tkpCanvas.o`).

OPTIMIZE

> Defaults to −O. Set it to −g to turn debugging on. The flag is passed to subdirectory makes.

PERL

> Perl binary for tasks that can be done by *miniperl*.

PERLMAINCC

> The call to the program that is able to compile *perlmain.c*. Defaults to $(CC).

PERL_ARCHLIB

> Same as PERL_LIB for architecture-dependent files.

PERL_LIB

> Directory containing the Perl library to use.

PERL_SRC

> Directory containing the Perl source code (use of this should be avoided, as it may be undefined).

PL_FILES

> Reference to a hash of files to be processed as Perl programs. MakeMaker will default to any found *.PL* file (except *Makefile.PL*) being a key and the basename of the file being the value, e.g.:

```
{'foobar.PL' => 'foobar'}
```

> The *.PL* files are expected to produce output to the target files themselves.

PM

> Hashref of *.pm* files and *.PL* files to be installed, e.g.:

```
{'name_of_file.pm' => '$(INST_LIBDIR)/install_as.pm'}
```

> By default this will include **.pm* and **.PL*. If a *lib* directory exists and is not listed in DIR (above), any *.pm* and *.PL* files it contains will also be included by default. Defining PM in the *Makefile.PL* will override PMLIBDIRS.

PMLIBDIRS

Reference to array of subdirectories containing library files. Defaults to [`'lib'`, `$(BASEEXT)`]. The directories will be scanned and any files they contain will be installed in the corresponding location in the library. A `libscan()` method can be used to alter the behavior. Defining PM in the *Makefile.PL* will override PMLIBDIRS.

PREFIX

Can be used to set the three INSTALL* attributes in one go (except for probably INSTALLMAN1DIR, if it is not below PREFIX according to `%Config`). They will have PREFIX as a common directory node and will branch from that node into *lib*, *lib/ARCHNAME*, or whatever Configure decided at the build time of your Perl (unless you override one of them, of course).

PREREQ_PM

Hashref including names of modules that need to be available to run this extension (e.g., `Fcntl` for `SDBM_File`) as the keys of the hash and the desired versions as the values. If the required version number is 0, we check only if any version is installed already.

SKIP

Array reference (e.g., [`qw(name1 name2)`]). Skip (do not write) sections of the Makefile.

Warning

Do not use the SKIP attribute for the neglectible speedup. It may seriously damage the resulting Makefile. Only use it if you really need it.

TYPEMAPS

Reference to array of typemap filenames. Use this when the typemaps are in some directory other than the current directory or when they are not named *typemap*. The last typemap in the list takes precedence. A typemap in the current directory has highest precedence, even if it isn't listed in TYPEMAPS. The default system typemap has lowest precedence.

VERSION

Your version number for distributing the package. This defaults to 0.1.

VERSION_FROM

Instead of specifying the VERSION in the *Makefile.PL*, you can let MakeMaker parse a file to determine the version number. The parsing routine requires that the file named by VERSION_FROM contains one single line to compute the version number. The first line in the file that contains the regular expression:

```
/\$((([\w\:\']*)\bVERSION)\b.*\=/
```

will be evaluated with `eval()`, and the value of the named variable *after* the `eval()` will be assigned to the VERSION attribute of the MakeMaker object. The following lines will be parsed correctly:

```
$VERSION = '1.00';
( $VERSION ) = '$Revision: 1.1 $ ' =~ /\$Revision:\s+([^\s]+)/;
$FOO::VERSION = '1.10';
```

but these will fail:

```
my $VERSION = '1.01';
local $VERSION = '1.02';
local $FOO::VERSION = '1.30';
```

The file named in VERSION_FROM is added as a dependency to Makefile to guarantee that the Makefile contains the correct VERSION macro after a change of the file.

XS

Hashref of *.xs* files. MakeMaker will default this to:

```
{'name_of_file.xs' => 'name_of_file.c'}
```

The *.c* files will automatically be included in the list of files deleted by a **make clean**.

XSOPT

String of options to pass to *xsubpp*. This might include **-C++** or **-extern**. Do not include typemaps here; the TYPEMAP parameter exists for that purpose.

XSPROTOARG

May be set to an empty string, which is identical to **-prototypes**, or **-noprototypes**. See the *xsubpp* documentation for details. MakeMaker defaults to the empty string.

XS_VERSION

Your version number for the *.xs* file of this package. This defaults to the value of the VERSION attribute.

Additional Lowercase Attributes

These additional attributes can be used to pass parameters to the methods which implement that part of the Makefile.

clean

```
{FILES => "*.xyz foo"}
```

depend

```
{ANY_TARGET => ANY_DEPENDECY, ...}
```

dist

If you specify COMPRESS, then SUFFIX should also be altered, as it is needed to tell **make** the target file of the compression. Setting DIST_CP to **ln** can be useful, if you need to preserve the timestamps on your files. DIST_CP can take the values **cp**, which copies the file; **ln**, which links the file; and **best**, which copies symbolic links and links the rest. The default is **best**.

```
{TARFLAGS => 'cvfF', COMPRESS => 'gzip', SUFFIX => 'gz',
SHAR => 'shar -m', DIST_CP => 'ln', ZIP => '/bin/zip',
ZIPFLAGS => '-rl', DIST_DEFAULT => 'private tardist' }
```

dynamic_lib

```
{ARMAYBE => 'ar', OTHERLDFLAGS => '...', INST_DYNAMIC_DEP => '...'}
```

installpm

Deprecated as of MakeMaker 5.23. See **pm_to_blib** in the ExtUtils::MM_Unix module.

linkext

Specifies the LINKTYPE. Note that with Pre-5.0 MakeMakers, this must be set to the empty string if there is nothing to be linked. Since version 5.00 of MakeMaker, such a line can be deleted safely, as MakeMaker now recognizes when there's nothing to be linked.

```
{LINKTYPE => 'static', 'dynamic' or ''}
```

```
macro
    {ANY_MACRO => ANY_VALUE, ...}
realclean
    {FILES => '$(INST_ARCHAUTODIR)/*.xyz'}
tool_autosplit
    {MAXLEN => 8}
```

Overriding MakeMaker Methods

If you cannot achieve the desired Makefile behavior by specifying attributes you may define private subroutines in the `Makefile.PL`. Each subroutine returns the text it wishes to have written to the Makefile. To override a section of the Makefile you can either say:

```
sub MY::c_o { "new literal text" }
```

or you can edit the default by saying something like:

```
sub MY::c_o {
        package MY; # so that "SUPER" works right
        my $inherited = shift->SUPER::c_o(@_);
        $inherited =~ s/old text/new text/;
        $inherited;
}
```

If you are running experiments with embedding Perl as a library into other applications, you might find MakeMaker not sufficient. You'd better have a look at ExtUtils::embed, which is a collection of utilities for embedding.

If you still need a different solution, try to develop another subroutine that fits your needs and submit the diffs to *perl5-porters@nicoh.com* or *comp.lang.perl.misc* as appropriate. For a complete description of all MakeMaker methods, see ExtUtils::MM_ Unix.

Here is a simple example of how to add a new target to the generated Makefile:

```
sub MY::postamble {
    '
$(MYEXTLIB): sdbm/Makefile
        cd sdbm && $(MAKE) all
';
}
```

Hintsfile Support

MakeMaker.pm uses the architecture-specific information from *Config.pm*. In addition, it evaluates architecture-specific hints files in a *hints* directory. The hints files are expected to be named like their counterparts in *PERL_SRC/hints*, but with a *.pl* filename extension (e.g., *next_3_2.pl*). They are simply **evaled** by MakeMaker within the `WriteMakefile()` subroutine, and can be used to execute commands as well as to include special variables. The rules by which *hintsfile* is chosen are the same as in Configure.

The *hintsfile* is **evaled** immediately after the arguments given to `WriteMakefile` are stuffed into a hash reference `$self`, but before this reference becomes blessed. If you want to do the equivalent to override or create an attribute, you would say something like:

```
$self->{LIBS} = ['-ldbm -lucb -lc'];
```

Distribution Support

For authors of extensions, MakeMaker provides several Makefile targets. Most of the support comes from the ExtUtils::Manifest module, where additional documentation can be found.

make distcheck

> Reports which files are below the build directory but not in the MANIFEST file and vice versa. (See `fullcheck()` in the ExtUtils::Manifest module for details.)

make skipcheck

> Reports which files are skipped due to the entries in the *MANIFEST.SKIP* file. (See `skipcheck()` in the ExtUtils::Manifest module for details.)

make distclean

> Does a `realclean` first and then the `distcheck`. Note that this is not needed to build a new distribution as long as you are sure that the MANIFEST file is okay.

make manifest

> Rewrites the MANIFEST file, adding all remaining files found. (See `mkmanifest()` in the ExtUtils::Manifest module for details.)

make distdir

> Copies all the files that are in the MANIFEST file to a newly created directory with the name $(DISTNAME)-$(VERSION). If that directory exists, it will be removed first.

make disttest

> Makes a `distdir` first, and runs a `perl Makefile.PL`, a `make`, and a `make test` in that directory.

make tardist

> First does a `distdir`, then a command $(PREOP) which defaults to a null command. This is followed by $(TOUNIX), which defaults to a null command under UNIX, and will convert files in the distribution directory to UNIX format otherwise. Next it runs `tar` on that directory to compress it into a tarfile, and deletes the directory. Finishes with a command $(POSTOP), which defaults to a null command.

make dist

> Defaults to $(DIST_DEFAULT), which in turn defaults to `tardist`.

make uutardist

> Runs a `tardist` first and uuencodes the tarfile.

make shdist

> First does a `distdir`, then a command $(PREOP), which defaults to a null command. Next it runs `shar` on that directory to compress it into a sharfile, and deletes the intermediate directory again. Finishes with a command $(POSTOP), which defaults to a null command. Note that for `shdist` to work properly a `shar` program that can handle directories is mandatory.

make zipdist

> First does a `distdir`, then a command $(PREOP), which defaults to a null command. Runs $(ZIP) $(ZIPFLAGS) on that directory to compress it into a zipfile, then deletes that directory. Finishes with a command $(POSTOP), which defaults to a null command.

make ci

> Does a $(CI) and a $(RCS_LABEL) on all files in the MANIFEST file.

Customization of the `dist` targets can be done by specifying a hash reference to the `dist` attribute of the `WriteMakefile` call. The following parameters are recognized:

```
CI              ('ci -u')
COMPRESS        ('compress')
POSTOP          ('@ :')
PREOP           ('@ :')
TO_UNIX         (depends on the system)
RCS_LABEL       ('rcs -q -Nv$(VERSION_SYM):')
SHAR            ('shar')
SUFFIX          ('Z')
TAR             ('tar')
TARFLAGS        ('cvf')
ZIP             ('zip')
ZIPFLAGS        ('-r')
```

An example:

```
WriteMakefile( 'dist' => { COMPRESS=>"gzip", SUFFIX=>"gz" })
```

Authors

Andy Dougherty, *doughera@lafcol.lafayette.edu*; Andreas Koenig, *koenig@franz.ww.TU-Berlin.de*; Tim Bunce, *Tim.Bunce@ig.co.uk*

VMS support by Charles Bailey (*bailey@genetics.upenn.edu*). OS/2 support by Ilya Zakharevich (*ilya@math.ohio-state.edu*). Contact the MakeMaker mailing list via email at *makemaker@franz.ww.tu-berlin.de* if you have any questions.

See Also

ExtUtils::MM_Unix, ExtUtils::Manifest, ExtUtils::testlib, ExtUtils::Install, ExtUtils::embed

---

ExtUtils::Manifest—utilities to write and check a MANIFEST file

Synopsis

```
require ExtUtils::Manifest;
ExtUtils::Manifest::mkmanifest;
ExtUtils::Manifest::manicheck;
ExtUtils::Manifest::filecheck;
ExtUtils::Manifest::fullcheck;
ExtUtils::Manifest::skipcheck;
ExtUtild::Manifest::manifind();
ExtUtils::Manifest::maniread($file);
ExtUtils::Manifest::manicopy($read,$target,$how);
```

Description

`mkmanifest()` writes all files in and below the current directory to a file named in the global variable $ExtUtils::Manifest::MANIFEST (which defaults to MANIFEST) in the current directory. It works similar to:

```
find . -print
```

but in doing so checks each line in an existing MANIFEST file and includes any comments that are found in the existing MANIFEST file in the new one. Anything between white space and an end of line within a MANIFEST file is considered to be a comment. Filenames and comments are separated by one or more TAB characters in the output. All files that match any regular expression in a file *MANIFEST.SKIP* (if such a file exists) are ignored.

`manicheck()` checks whether all the files within a MANIFEST in the current directory really do exist. It only reports discrepancies and exits silently if MANIFEST and the tree below the current directory are in sync.

`filecheck()` finds files below the current directory that are not mentioned in the MANIFEST file. An optional file *MANIFEST.SKIP* will be consulted. Any file matching a regular expression in such a file will not be reported as missing in the MANIFEST file.

`fullcheck()` does both a `manicheck()` and a `filecheck()`.

`skipcheck()` lists all the files that are skipped due to your *MANIFEST.SKIP* file.

`manifind()` returns a hash reference. The keys of the hash are the files found below the current directory.

`maniread($file)` reads a named MANIFEST file (defaults to MANIFEST in the current directory) and returns a HASH reference with files being the keys and comments being the values of the HASH. Blank lines and lines starting with # in the MANIFEST file are discarded.

`manicopy($read, $target, $how)` copies the files that are the keys in the HASH %$read to the named *$target* directory. The HASH reference *$read* is typically returned by the `maniread()` function. This function is useful for producing a directory tree identical to the intended distribution tree. The third parameter, *$how*, can be used to specify a different methods of "copying". Valid values are `cp`, which actually copies the files; `ln`, which creates hard links; and `best`, which mostly links the files but copies any symbolic link to make a tree without any symbolic link. `best` is the default.

MANIFEST.SKIP

The file *MANIFEST.SKIP* may contain regular expressions of files that should be ignored by `mkmanifest()` and `filecheck()`. The regular expressions should appear one on each line. Blank lines and lines starting with # are skipped. Use \# if you need a regular expression to start with a sharp character. A typical example:

```
\bRCS\b
^MANIFEST\.
^Makefile$
~$
\.html$
\.old$
^blib/
^MakeMaker-\d
```

Variables

$ExtUtils::Manifest::MANIFEST defaults to MANIFEST. Changing it results in both a different MANIFEST and a different *MANIFEST.SKIP* file. This is useful if you want to maintain different distributions for different audiences (such a user version and a developer version including RCS).

$ExtUtils::Manifest::Quiet defaults to 0. If it is set to a true value, all functions act silently.

Exports

&mkmanifest, &manicheck, &filecheck, &fullcheck, &maniread, and &manicopy are exportable.

Diagnostics

All diagnostic output is sent to STDERR.

Not in MANIFEST: *file*
> is reported if a file is found that is missing in the MANIFEST file and is excluded by a regular expression in the file *MANIFEST.SKIP*.

No such file: *file*
> is reported if a file mentioned in a MANIFEST file does not exist.

MANIFEST: $!
> is reported if MANIFEST could not be opened.

Added to MANIFEST: *file*
> is reported by mkmanifest() if $Verbose is set and a file is added to MANI-FEST. $Verbose is set to 1 by default.

See Also

ExtUtils::MakeMaker, which has handy targets for most of the functionality.

Author

Andreas Koenig, *koenig@franz.ww.TU-Berlin.de*

ExtUtils::Mkbootstrap —make a bootstrap file for use by DynaLoader

Synopsis

```
mkbootstrap
```

Description

Mkbootstrap typically gets called from an extension Makefile.

No *.bs* file is supplied with the extension. Instead, there is a *_BS* file which has code for the special cases, like Posix for Berkeley DB on the NeXT.

This file will get parsed, and produce a maybe empty @DynaLoader::dl_resolve_using array for the current architecture. That will be extended by $BSLOADLIBS, which was computed by ExtUtils::Liblist::ext(). If this array still is empty, we do nothing, or we write a *.bs* file with an @DynaLoader::dl_resolve_using array.

The *_BS* file can put some code into the generated *.bs* file by placing it in $bscode. This is a handy escape mechanism that may prove useful in complex situations.

If @DynaLoader::dl_resolve_using contains -L* or -l* entries then Mkbootstrap will auto-matically add a dl_findfile() call to the generated *.bs* file.

ExtUtils::Mksymlists — write linker options files for dynamic extension

Synopsis

```
use ExtUtils::Mksymlists;
Mksymlists({ NAME    => $name ,
             DL_VARS  => [ $var1, $var2, $var3 ],
             DL_FUNCS => { $pkg1 => [ $func1, $func2 ],
                           $pkg2 => [ $func3 ] });
```

Description

ExtUtils::Mksymlists produces files used by the linker under some OSs during the creation of shared libraries for dynamic extensions. It is normally called from a MakeMaker-generated Makefile when the extension is built. The linker option file is generated by calling the function **Mksymlists**, which is exported by default from ExtUtils::Mksymlists. It takes one argument, a list of key/value pairs, in which the following keys are recognized:

NAME

> This gives the name of the extension (e.g., Tk::Canvas) for which the linker option file will be produced.

DL_FUNCS

> This is identical to the DL_FUNCS attribute available via MakeMaker, from which it is usually taken. Its value is a reference to an associative array, in which each key is the name of a package, and each value is a reference to an array of function names which should be exported by the extension. For instance, one might say **DL_FUNCS => { Homer::Iliad => [qw(trojans greeks)], Homer::Odyssey => [qw(travellers family suitors)] }**. The function names should be identical to those in the XSUB code; Mksymlists will alter the names written to the linker option file to match the changes made by *xsubpp*. In addition, if none of the functions in a list begins with the string **boot_**, Mksymlists will add a bootstrap function for that package, just as *xsubpp* does. (If a **boot_***pkg* function is present in the list, it is passed through unchanged.) If DL_FUNCS is not specified, it defaults to the bootstrap function for the extension specified in NAME.

DL_VARS

> This is identical to the DL_VARS attribute available via MakeMaker, and, like DL_FUNCS, it is usually specified via MakeMaker. Its value is a reference to an array of variable names which should be exported by the extension.

FILE

> This key can be used to specify the name of the linker option file (minus the OS-specific extension), if for some reason you do not want to use the default value, which is the last word of the NAME attribute (e.g., for Tk::Canvas, FILE defaults to **Canvas**).

FUNCLIST

> This provides an alternate means to specify function names to be exported from the extension. Its value is a reference to an array of function names to be exported by the extension. These names are passed through unaltered to the linker options file.

DLBASE

> This item specifies the name by which the linker knows the extension, which may be different from the name of the extension itself (for instance, some linkers add an '_' to the name of the extension). If it is not specified, it is derived from the NAME attribute. It is presently used only by OS/2.

When calling Mksymlists, one should always specify the NAME attribute. In most cases, this is all that's necessary. In the case of unusual extensions, however, the other attributes can be used to provide additional information to the linker.

Author

Charles Bailey, *bailey@genetics.upenn.edu*

ExtUtils::MM_Unix — methods used by ExtUtils::MakeMaker

Synopsis

```
require ExtUtils::MM_Unix;
```

Description

The methods provided by this package are designed to be used in conjunction with ExtUtils::MakeMaker. When MakeMaker writes a Makefile, it creates one or more objects that inherit their methods from a package MM. MM itself doesn't provide any methods, but it is a ExtUtils::MM_Unix class. The inheritance tree of MM lets operating-specific packages take the responsibility for all the methods provided by MM_Unix. We are trying to reduce the number of necessary overrides by defining rather primitive operations within ExtUtils::MM_Unix.

If you are going to write a platform-specific MM package, please try to limit the necessary overrides to primitive methods; if it is not possible to do so, let's work out how to achieve that gain.

If you are overriding any of these methods in your *Makefile.PL* (in the MY class), please report that to the MakeMaker mailing list. We are trying to minimize the necessary method overrides and switch to data-driven *Makefile.PLs* wherever possible. In the long run, fewer methods will be overridable via the MY class.

Methods

The following description of methods is still under development. Please refer to the code for unsuitably documented sections and complain loudly to the makemaker mailing list.

Not all of the methods below are overridable in a *Makefile.PL*. Overridable methods are marked as (o). All methods are overridable by a platform specific *MM_*.pm* file (See ExtUtils::MM_VMS) and ExtUtils::MM_OS2).

Preloaded methods

canonpath
> No physical check on the filesystem, but a logical cleanup of a path. On UNIX, eliminate successive slashes and successive "/.".

catdir
> Concatenate two or more directory names to form a complete path ending with a directory. First, remove the trailing slash from the resulting string, because it doesn't look good, isn't necessary, and confuses OS/2. Of course, if this is the root directory, don't cut off the trailing slash.

`catfile`

>   Concatenates one or more directory names and a filename to form a complete path ending with a filename.

`curdir`

>   Returns a string representing the current directory ("." on UNIX).

`rootdir`

>   Returns a string representing the root directory ("/" on UNIX).

`updir`

>   Returns a string representing the parent directory (".." on UNIX).

SelfLoaded methods

`c_o` *(o)*

>   Defines the suffix rules to compile different flavors of C files to object files.

`cflags` *(o)*

>   Does very much the same as the `cflags` script in the Perl distribution. It doesn't return the whole compiler command line, but rather initializes all of its parts. The const_cccmd method actually returns the definition of the CCCMD macro which uses these parts.

`clean` *(o)*

>   Defines the clean target.

`const_cccmd` *(o)*

>   Returns the full compiler call for C programs and stores the definition in CONST_CCCMD.

`const_config` *(o)*

>   Defines a couple of constants in the Makefile that are imported from `%Config`.

`const_loadlibs` *(o)*

>   Defines EXTRALIBS, LDLOADLIBS, BSLOADLIBS, and LD_RUN_PATH. See ExtUtils::Liblist for details.

`constants` *(o)*

>   Initializes lots of constants and *.SUFFIXES* and *.PHONY*.

`depend` *(o)*

>   Same as the macro for the `depend` attribute.

`dir_target` *(o)*

>   Takes an array of directories that need to exist and returns a Makefile entry for a *.exists* file in these directories. Returns nothing if the entry has already been processed. We're helpless, though, if the same directory comes as $(FOO) and as "bar". Both of them get an entry; that's why we use "::".

`dist` *(o)*

>   Defines a lot of macros for distribution support.

`dist_basics` *(o)*

>   Defines the targets `distclean`, `distcheck`, `skipcheck`, and `manifest`.

`dist_ci` *(o)*

>   Defines a check-in target for RCS.

dist_core *(o)*

Defines the targets dist, tardist, zipdist, uutardist, and shdist.

dist_dir *(o)*

Defines the scratch directory target that will hold the distribution before tar-ing (or shar-ing).

dist_test *(o)*

Defines a target that produces the distribution in the scratch directory, and runs perl Makefile.PL; make; make test in that subdirectory.

dlsyms *(o)*

Used by AIX and VMS to define DL_FUNCS and DL_VARS and write the *.exp* files.

dynamic *(o)*

Defines the dynamic target.

dynamic_bs *(o)*

Defines targets for bootstrap files.

dynamic_lib *(o)*

Defines how to produce the *.so* (or equivalent) files.

exescan

Deprecated method. Use libscan instead.

extliblist

Called by init_others, and calls ext ExtUtils::Liblist. See ExtUtils::Liblist for details.

file_name_is_absolute

Takes as argument a path and returns true, if it is an absolute path.

find_perl

Finds the executables PERL and FULLPERL.

Methods to actually produce chunks of text for the Makefile

The methods here are called for each MakeMaker object in the order specified by @ExtUtils::MakeMaker::MM_Sections.

force *(o)*

Just writes FORCE:

guess_name

Guess the name of this package by examining the working directory's name. MakeMaker calls this only if the developer has not supplied a NAME attribute.

has_link_code

Returns true if C, XS, MYEXTLIB, or similar objects exist within this object that need a compiler. Does not descend into subdirectories as needs_ linking() does.

init_dirscan

Initializes DIR, XS, PM, C, O_FILES, H, PL_FILES, MAN*PODS, and EXE_FILES.

init_main

Initializes NAME, FULLEXT, BASEEXT, PARENT_NAME, DLBASE, PERL_SRC, PERL_LIB, PERL_ARCHLIB, PERL_INC, INSTALLDIRS, INST_*, INSTALL*, PREFIX, CONFIG, AR, AR_STATIC_ARGS, LD, OBJ_EXT, LIB_EXT, EXE_EXT,

MAP_TARGET, LIBPERL_A, VERSION_FROM, VERSION, DISTNAME, and VERSION_SYM.

init_others

Initializes EXTRALIBS, BSLOADLIBS, LDLOADLIBS, LIBS, LD_RUN_PATH, OBJECT, BOOTDEP, PERLMAINCC, LDFROM, LINKTYPE, NOOP, FIRST_MAKEFILE, MAKEFILE, NOECHO, RM_F, RM_RF, TEST_F, TOUCH, CP, MV, CHMOD, and UMASK_NULL.

install *(o)*

Defines the install target.

installbin *(o)*

Defines targets to install EXE_FILES.

libscan *(o)*

Takes a path to a file that is found by init_dirscan and returns false if we don't want to include this file in the library. Mainly used to exclude RCS, CVS, and SCCS directories from installation.

linkext *(o)*

Defines the linkext target, which in turn defines the LINKTYPE.

lsdir

Takes as arguments a directory name and a regular expression. Returns all entries in the directory that match the regular expression.

macro *(o)*

Simple subroutine to insert the macros defined by the macro attribute into the Makefile.

makeaperl *(o)*

Called by staticmake. Defines how to write the Makefile to produce a static new Perl.

By default the Makefile produced includes all the static extensions in the Perl library. (Purified versions of library files, e.g., *DynaLoader_pure_p1_c0_032.a*, are automatically ignored to avoid link errors.)

makefile *(o)*

Defines how to rewrite the Makefile.

manifypods *(o)*

Defines targets and routines to translate the pods into manpages and put them into the *INST_** directories.

maybe_command

Returns true if the argument is likely to be a command.

maybe_command_in_dirs

Method under development. Not yet used.

needs_linking *(o)*

Does this module need linking? Looks into subdirectory objects (see also has_link_code()).

nicetext

Misnamed method (to be changed in a later version). The **MM_Unix** method just returns the argument without further processing.

On VMS this used to ensure that colons marking targets are preceded by space—most UNIX Makes don't need this, but it's necessary under VMS to distinguish the target delimiter from a colon appearing as part of a filespec.

parse_version

Parses a file and returns the value $VERSION is set to.

pasthru *(o)*

Defines the string that is passed to recursive make calls in subdirectories.

path

Takes no argument; returns the environment variable PATH as an array.

perl_script

Takes one argument, a filename, and returns the filename if the argument is likely to be a Perl script. On MM_Unix this is true for any ordinary, readable file.

perldepend *(o)*

Defines the dependency from all *.h* files that come with the Perl distribution.

pm_to_blib

Defines target that copies all files in the hash PM to their destination and autosplits them. See the description of ExtUtils::Install.

post_constants *(o)*

Returns an empty string per default. Dedicated to overrides from within *Make-file.PL* after all constants have been defined.

post_initialize *(o)*

Returns an empty string per default. Used in *Makefile.PLs* to add some chunk of text to the Makefile after the object is initialized.

postamble *(o)*

Returns an empty string. Can be used in *Makefile.PLs* to write some text to the Makefile at the end.

prefixify

Checks a path variable in $self from %Config, if it contains a prefix, and replaces it with another one.

Takes as arguments an attribute name, a search prefix, and a replacement prefix. Changes the attribute in the object.

processPL *(o)*

Defines targets to run *.PL* files.

realclean *(o)*

Defines the realclean target.

replace_manpage_separator

Takes the name of a package, which may be a nested package, in the form *Foo/Bar* and replaces the slash with "::". Returns the replacement.

static *(o)*

Defines the static target.

static_lib *(o)*

Defines how to produce the *.a* (or equivalent) files.

staticmake *(o)*

Calls makeperl.

subdir_x *(o)*

Helper subroutine for subdirs.

subdirs *(o)*

Defines targets to process subdirectories.

test *(o)*

Defines the test targets.

test_via_harness *(o)*

Helper method to write the test targets.

test_via_script *(o)*

Other helper method for test.

tool_autosplit *(o)*

Defines a simple Perl call that runs autosplit. May be deprecated by pm_ to_blib soon.

tools_other *(o)*

Defines SHELL, LD, TOUCH, CP, MV, RM_F, RM_RF, CHMOD, and UMASK_ NULL in the Makefile. Also defines the Perl programs MKPATH, WARN_IF_ OLD_PACKLIST, MOD_INSTALL. DOC_INSTALL, and UNINSTALL.

tool_xsubpp *(o)*

Determines typemaps, *xsubpp* version, and prototype behavior.

top_targets *(o)*

Defines the targets all, subdirs, config, and O_FILES .

writedoc

Obsolete, depecated method. Not used since Version 5.21.

xs_c *(o)*

Defines the suffix rules to compile XS files to C.

xs_o *(o)*

Defines suffix rules to go from XS to object files directly. This is only intended for broken make implementations.

perl_archive

This is an internal method that returns the path to a *libperl.a* equivalent to be linked to dynamic extensions. UNIX does not have one, but OS/2 and Win32 do.

export_list

This is an internal method that returns the name of a file that is passed to a linker to define symbols to be exported. UNIX does not have one, but OS/2 and Win32 do.

See Also

ExtUtils::MakeMaker

ExtUtils::MM_Win32—methods to override UNIX behavior in ExtUtils::MakeMaker

Synopsis

```
use ExtUtils::MM_Win32;      # Done internally by
                             # ExtUtils::MakeMaker if needed
```

Description

See ExtUtils::MM_Unix for a documentation of the methods provided there. This package overrides the implementation of these methods, not the semantics. An (o) indicates a method that is overridable.

Methods

catfile

> Concatenate one or more directory names and a filename to form a complete path ending with a filename.

static_lib *(o)*

> Defines how to produce the **.a* (or equivalent) files.

dynamic_lib *(o)*

> Defines how to produce the **.so* (or equivalent) files.

canonpath

> No physical check on the filesystem, but a logical cleanup of a path. On UNIX, eliminate successive slashes and successive "/.".

perl_script

> Takes one argument, a filename, and returns the filename if the argument is likely to be a Perl script. On MM_Unix this is true for any ordinary, readable file.

pm_to_blib

> Defines a target that copies all files in the hash PM to their destination and autosplits them. See the description of ExtUtils::Install.

test_via_harness *(o)*

> Helper method to write the test targets.

tool_autosplit *(override)*

> Use Win32 quoting on command line.

tools_other *(o)*

> Win32 overrides.
>
> Defines SHELL, LD, TOUCH, CP, MV, RM_F, RM_RF, CHMOD, and UMASK_NULL in the Makefile. Also defines the perl programs MKPATH, WARN_IF_OLD_PACKLIST, MOD_INSTALL. DOC_INSTALL, and UNINSTALL.

manifypods *(o)*

> We don't want manpage process. pod2html support will most likely be implemented in a later version to create HTML help files from the pod documentation.

dist_ci *(o)*

> Same as MM_Unix version (changes command-line quoting).

dist_core *(o)*

> Same as MM_Unix version (changes command-line quoting).

pasthru *(o)*
>   Defines the string that is passed to recursive make calls in subdirectories.

FindBin——locate directory of original Perl script

Synopsis
```
use FindBin;
BEGIN { unshift(@INC,"$FindBin::Bin/../lib") }
```
or:
```
use FindBin qw($Bin);
BEGIN { unshift(@INC,"$Bin/../lib") }
```

Description

This module locates the full path to the script *bin* directory to allow the use of paths relative to the *bin* directory.

This allows a user to set up a directory tree for a piece of software with directories *<root>/bin* and *<root>/lib* and then allow the use of modules in the *lib* directory without knowing where the software tree is installed.

If Perl is invoked using the -e option or the Perl script is read from STDIN, then FindBin sets both $Bin and $RealBin to the current directory.

Variables

$Bin
>   Path to the bin directory from where the script was invoked.

$Script
>   Basename of the script from which Perl was invoked.

$RealBin
> $Bin with all links resolved.

$RealScript
> $Script with all links resolved.

Bugs

If Perl is invoked as:
```
perl filename
```
and *filename* does not have executable rights, and a program called *filename* exists in the user's $ENV{PATH} which satisfies both -x and -T, then FindBin assumes it was invoked via the $ENV{PATH}.

A workaround is to invoke Perl as:
```
perl ./filename
```

Authors

Graham Barr, *gbarr@pobox.com*, and Nick Ing-Simmons, *nik@tiuk.ti.com*

Copyright

Make—module for processing Makefiles

Synopsis

```
require Make;
my $make = Make->new(...);
$make->parse($file);
$make->Script(@ARGV)
$make->Make(@ARGV)
$make->Print(@ARGV)
my $targ = $make->Target($name);
$targ->colon([dependancy...],[command...]);
$targ->dolon([dependancy...],[command...]);
my @depends  = $targ->colon->depend;
my @commands = $targ->colon->command;
```

Description

make->new creates an object if new(Makefile => $file) is specified, then it is parsed. If not, the usual Makefile sequence is used. (If GNU => 1 is passed to new, GNU makefile is looked for first.)

$make->Make(target...) makes the target(s) specified (or the first real target in the makefile).

$make->Print can be used to print (to the currently selected stream) a form of the makefile with all variables expanded.

$make->Script(target...) can be used to print (to the currently selected stream) the equivalent Bourne shell script that a make would perform (i.e., the output of make -n).

There are other methods (used by parse) that can be used to add and manipulate targets and their dependants. There is a hierarchy of classes which is still evolving. These classes and their methods will be documented when they are more stable.

The accepted syntax of Makefile is reasonably generic. In addition to the traditional:

```
.c.o :
        $(CC) -c ...
```

GNU make's "pattern" rules, e.g.:

```
%.o : %.c
        $(CC) -c ...
```

are also accepted. Likewise, a subset of GNU make's $(function arg...) syntax is supported.

Bugs

At present new must always find a Makefile, and $make->parse($file) can be used only to augment that file.

The rules for matching "dot rules" (e.g., .c.o) and/or pattern rules (e.g., %.o : %.c) are suspect.

Variables are possibly substituted in different "phases" of the process than in make(1) (or even GNU make), so "clever" uses will probably not work.

UNIXisms abound.

See Also

pmake

Author

Nick Ing-Simmons, *nik@tiuk.ti.com*

Test::Harness—run Perl standard test scripts with statistics

Synopsis

```
use Test::Harness;
runtests(@tests);
```

Description

Perl test scripts print `ok` *N* to standard output for each single test, where *N* is an increasing sequence of integers. The first line output by a standard test script is `1..M`, with *M* being the number of tests that should be run within the test script.

`Test::Harness::runtests(@tests)` runs all the test scripts named as arguments and checks standard output for the expected `ok` *N* strings.

After all tests have been performed, `runtests()` prints performance statistics, which are computed by the Benchmark module.

The Test Script Output

Any output from the test script to standard error is ignored and bypassed, and will be seen by the user. Lines written to standard output containing `/^(not\s+)?ok\b/` are interpreted as feedback for `runtests()`. All other lines are discarded.

It is tolerated if the test numbers after `ok` are omitted. In this case Test::Harness maintains temporarily its own counter until the script supplies test numbers again. So the following test script:

```
print <<END;
1..6
not ok
ok
not ok
ok
ok
END
```

will generate:

```
FAILED tests 1, 3, 6
Failed 3/6 tests, 50.00% okay
```

The global variable $Test::Harness::verbose is exportable and can be used to let `runtests()` display the standard output of the script without altering the behavior otherwise.

Exports

&runtests is exported by Test::Harness per default.

Diagnostics

`All tests successful.\nFiles=%d, Tests=%d, %s`

If all tests are successful some statistics about the performance are printed.

`FAILED tests %s\n\tFailed %d/%d tests, %.2f%% okay.`

For any single script that has failing subtests, statistics like the above are printed.

`Test returned status %d (wstat %d)`

For scripts that return a non-zero exit status, both $? >> 8 and $? are printed in a message similar to the above.

`Failed 1 test, %.2f%% okay. %s`

`Failed %d/%d tests, %.2f%% okay. %s`

If not all tests were successful, the script dies with one of the above messages.

Bugs

Test::Harness uses $^X to determine the Perl binary to run the tests with. Test scripts running via the shebang (#!) line may not be portable because $^X is not consistent for shebang scripts across platforms. This is no problem when Test::Harness is run with an absolute path to the Perl binary or when $^X can be found in the path.

Author

Current maintainer is Andreas Koenig (*koenig@franz.ww.TU-Berlin.de*).

See Also

See Benchmark for the underlying timing routines.

4

Operating System Interfaces

This section contains various modules for interfacing with operating system components, such as environment variables, POSIX, and the shell.

BSD::Resource—BSD process resource limit and priority functions

Synopsis

```
use BSD::Resource;
#
# the process resource consumption so far
#
($usertime, $systemtime,
 $maxrss, $ixrss, $idrss, $isrss, $minflt, $majflt, $nswap,
 $inblock, $oublock, $msgsnd, $msgrcv,
 $nsignals, $nvcsw, $nivcsw) = getrusage($ru_who);
 $rusage = getrusage($ru_who);


#
# the process resource limits
#
($nowsoft, $nowhard) = getrlimit($resource);

$rlimit = getrlimit($resource);

$success = setrlimit($resource, $newsoft, $newhard);
#
# the process scheduling priority
#
$nowpriority = getpriority($pr_which, $pr_who);

$success = setpriority($pr_which, $pr_who, $priority);
# The following is not a BSD function.
```

```
# It is a Perlish utility for the users of BSD::Resource.
$rlimits = get_rlimits();
```

Description

Functions

getrusage

This function gets resource usage statistics.

```
($usertime, $systemtime,
 $maxrss, $ixrss, $idrss, $isrss, $minflt, $majflt, $nswap,
 $inblock, $oublock, $msgsnd, $msgrcv,
 $nsignals, $nvcsw, $nivcsw) = getrusage($ru_who);

$rusage = getrusage($ru_who);

# $ru_who argument is optional; it defaults to RUSAGE_SELF

$rusage = getrusage();
```

The $ru_who argument is either RUSAGE_SELF (the current process) or RUSAGE_CHILDREN (all the child processes of the current process) or it may be left out, in which case RUSAGE_SELF is used.

RUSAGE_CHILDREN is the total sum of all the *terminated* (either successfully or unsuccessfully) child processes; there is no way to find information about child processes still running.

On some systems (those supporting both getrusage() and POSIX threads), there is also RUSAGE_THREAD. The BSD::Resource supports RUSAGE_THREAD if it is present, but understands nothing more about the POSIX threads themselves.

In list context, getrusage() returns the current resource usages as a list. On failure, it returns an empty list.

The elements of the list are, in order:

Index	Name	Usual meaning (quite system-dependent)
0	utime	user time
1	stime	system time
2	maxrss	maximum shared memory
3	ixrss	integral shared memory
4	idrss	integral unshared data
5	isrss	integral unshared stack
6	minflt	page reclaims
7	majflt	page faults
8	nswap	swaps
9	inblock	block input operations
10	oublock	block output operations
11	msgsnd	messages sent
12	msgrcv	messaged received

Index	Name	Usual meaning (quite system-dependent)
13	nsignals	signals received
14	nvcsw	voluntary context switches
15	nivcsw	involuntary context switches

In scalar context, `getrusage()` returns the current resource usages as an object. The object can be queried via methods named exactly like the Name column in the above table.

```
$ru = getrusage();
print $ru->stime, "\n";

$total_context_switches = $ru->nvcsw + $ru->nivcsw;
```

For a detailed description of the values returned by `getrusage()`, please consult your usual C programming documentation about `getrusage()`, as well as the header file *sys/resource.h*. (In Solaris, this might be *sys/rusage.h*.)

Notes:

- Officially, HP-UX does not support `getrusage()` at all, but for the time being, it does seem to.

- Because not all kernels are BSD and also because of the sloppy support of `getrusage()` by many vendors, many of the values may not be updated. For example, Solaris 1 claims in *sys/rusage.h* that the `ixrss` and the `isrss` fields are always zero.

getrlimit

This function gets resource limit information.

```
($nowsoft, $nowhard) = getrlimit($resource);

$rlimit = getrlimit($resource);
```

The `$resource` argument can be one of:

$resource	Usual meaning	Usual unit
RLIMIT_CPU	CPU time	seconds
RLIMIT_FSIZE	file size	bytes
RLIMIT_DATA	data size	bytes
RLIMIT_STACK	stack size	bytes
RLIMIT_CORE	coredump size	bytes
RLIMIT_RSS	resident set size	bytes
RLIMIT_MEMLOCK	memory locked data size	bytes
RLIMIT_NPROC	number of processes	n/a
RLIMIT_NOFILE	number of open files	n/a
RLIMIT_OPEN_MAX	number of open files	n/a
RLIMIT_AS	(virtual) address space	bytes
RLIMIT_VMEM	virtual memory (space)	bytes

What limits are available depends on the operating system. See below for get_ rlimits() on how to find out which limits are available. The last two pairs (NO_ FILE, OPEN_MAX) and (AS, VMEM) are the same. The former are the BSD names and the latter are the SVR4 names.

Two meta-resource symbols might exist:

    RLIM_NLIMITS
    RLIM_INFINITY

RLIM_NLIMITS is the number of possible (but not necessarily fully supported) resource limits; see also the get_rlimits() call below. RLIM_INFINITY is useful in setrlimit(); RLIM_INFINITY is represented as –1.

In list context, getrlimit() returns the current soft and hard resource limits as a list. On failure, it returns an empty list.

Processes have soft and hard resource limits. On crossing the soft limit, they receive a signal (for example, XCPU or XFSZ, corresponding to RLIMIT_CPU and RLIMIT_FSIZE, respectively). The processes can trap and handle some of these signals; please see "Signals". After reaching the hard limit, the processes are ruthlessly killed by the KILL signal, which cannot be caught.

Note: the level of "support" for a resource varies. Not all the systems:

* Even recognize all the limits

* Really track the consumption of a resource

* Care (send the signals) if a resource limit is exceeded

Again, please consult your usual C programming documentation. One notable exception for the better: officially, HP-UX does not support getrlimit() at all, but for the time being, it does seem to.

In scalar context, getrlimit() returns the current soft and hard resource limits as an object. The object can be queried via methods **cur** and **max**, the current and maximum resource limits for the $resource, respectively.

getpriority

getpriority() returns the current priority. Note: getpriority() can return zero or negative values completely legally. On failure, getpriority() returns undef (and $! is set as usual).

```
$nowpriority = getpriority($pr_which, $pr_who);
# the default $pr_who is 0 (the current $pr_which)

$nowpriority = getpriority($pr_which);
# the default $pr_which is PRIO_PROCESS (the process
# priority)

$nowpriority = getpriority();
```

The priorities returned by getpriority() are in the (inclusive) range PRIO_ MIN...PRIO_MAX. The $pr_which argument can be any of PRIO_PROCESS (a process), PRIO_USER (a user), or PRIO_PGRP (a process group). The $pr_who argument specifies the process/user/process group, with 0 signifying the current one.

The usual values for PRIO_MIN and PRIO_MAX are -20 and 20. A negative value means a better priority (a more impolite process), while a positive value means a worse priority (a more polite process).

Note: In AIX, if the BSD-compatibility library is not installed or is not found by the installation procedure of BSD::Resource, PRIO_MIN is 0 (corresponding to -20) and PRIO_MAX is 39 (corresponding to 19; the BSD priority 20 is unreachable).

setrlimit
> setrlimit() returns true on success and undef on failure.
>
> ```
>     $success = setrlimit($resource, $newsoft, $newhard);
> ```

Note: A normal user process can only lower its resource limits. The soft or hard limit RLIM_INFINITY means "as much as possible"; the real hard limits are normally buried inside the kernel and are *very* system-dependent.

setpriority
> setpriority() is used to change the scheduling priority. A positive priority means a more polite process/process group/user; a negative priority means a more impolite process/process group/user. The priorities handled by setpriority() are PRIO_MIN and PRIO_MAX. A normal user process can only lower its priority (i.e., make it more positive).

```
    $success = setpriority($pr_which, $pr_who, $priority);

    # NOTE! If there are two arguments, the second one is
    # the new $priority (not $pr_who) and the $pr_who is
    # defaulted to 0 (the current $pr_which)

    $success = setpriority($pr_which, $priority);

    # The $pr_who defaults to 0 (the current $pr_which) and
    # the $priority defaults to half of the PRIO_MAX, usually
    # that amounts to 10 (being a nice $pr_which).

    $success = setpriority($pr_which);

    # The $pr_which defaults to PRIO_PROCESS,

    $success = setpriority();
```
Note: A successful call returns 1, a failed call returns 0.

get_rlimits
> ```
>     $rlimits = get_rlimits();
> ```
> get_rlimits() returns a reference to a hash that has the names of the available resource limits as keys and their indices (those which are needed as the first argument to getrlimit() and setrlimit()) as values. For example:
> ```
>     $r = get_rlimits();
>     print "ok.\n" if ($r->{'RLIM_STACK'} == RLIM_STACK);
> ```

Note: This is not a real BSD function. It is a convenience function.

Examples

```
# the user and system times so far by the process itself

($usertime, $systemtime) = getrusage();
```

```
# ditto in OO way

$ru = getrusage();

$usertime   = $ru->utime;
$systemtime = $ru->stime;

# get the current priority level of this process

$currprio = getpriority();
```

Version

Release 1.06, June 1997

Author

Jarkko Hietaniemi, *jhi@iki.fi*

Errno—system errno constants

Synopsis

```
use Errno qw(EINTR EIO);
```

Description

Errno defines and conditionally exports all the error constants defined in your system *errno.h* include file.

Author

Graham Barr, *gbarr@pobox.com*

Copyright

Copyright © 1997 Graham Barr. All rights reserved. This program is free software; you can redistribute it and/or modify it under the same terms as Perl itself.

Fcntl—load the C fcntl.h defines

Synopsis

```
use Fcntl;

$nonblock_flag = O_NDELAY();
$create_flag = O_CREAT();
$read_write_flag = O_RDWR();
```

Description

This module is just a translation of the C *fcntl.h* file. Unlike the old mechanism, which required a translated *fcntl.ph* file, *fcntl* uses the *h2xs* program (see the Perl source distribution) and your native C compiler. This means that it has a much better chance of getting the numbers right.

Note that only `#define` symbols get translated; you must still correctly pack up your own arguments to pass as arguments for locking functions, and so on.

The following routines are exported by default, and each routine returns the value of the `#define` that is the same as the routine name:

FD_CLOEXEC	F_DUPFD	F_GETFD	F_GETFL	F_GETLK	F_RDLCK
F_SETFD	F_SETFL	F_SETLK	F_SETLKW	F_UNLCK	F_WRLCK
O_APPEND	O_CREAT	O_EXCL	O_NDELAY	O_NOCTTY	
O_NONBLOCK	O_RDONLY	O_RDWR	O_TRUNC	O_WRONLY	

POSIX—Perl Interface to IEEE Std 1003.1

Synopsis
```
use POSIX;                      # import all symbols
use POSIX qw(setsid);           # import one symbol
use POSIX qw(:errno_h :fcntl_h); # import sets of symbols

printf "EINTR is %d\n", EINTR;

$sess_id = POSIX::setsid();

$fd = POSIX::open($path, O_CREAT|O_EXCL|O_WRONLY, 0644);
# note: $fd is a filedescriptor, *NOT* a filehandle
```

Description
The POSIX module permits you to access all (or nearly all) the standard POSIX 1003.1 identifiers. Many of these identifiers have been given Perl-ish interfaces.

This description gives a condensed list of the features available in the POSIX module. Consult your operating system's manpages for general information on most features. Consult the appropriate Perl built-in function whenever a POSIX routine is noted as being identical to the function.

The "Classes" section later in this chapter describes some classes for signal objects, TTY objects, and other miscellaneous objects. The "Functions" section later in this chapter describes POSIX functions from the 1003.1 specification. The remaining sections list various constants and macros in an organization that roughly follows IEEE Std 1003.1b-1993.

Warning
A few functions are not implemented because they are C-specific. If you attempt to call one of these functions, it will print a message telling you that it isn't implemented, and will suggest using the Perl equivalent, should one exist. For example, trying to access the `setjmp()` call will elicit the message: `setjmp() is C-specific: use eval {} instead.`

Furthermore, some vendors will claim 1003.1 compliance without passing the POSIX Compliance Test Suites (PCTS). For example, one vendor may not define EDEADLK, or may incorrectly define the semantics of the *errno* values set by *open*(2). Perl does not attempt to verify POSIX compliance. That means you can currently say **use POSIX** successfully, and then later in your program find that your vendor has been lax and there's no usable ICANON macro after all. This could be construed to be a bug. Whose bug, we won't venture to guess.

Classes

POSIX::SigAction

new

Creates a new POSIX::SigAction object that corresponds to the C **struct sigaction**. This object will be destroyed automatically when it is no longer needed. The first parameter is the fully qualified name of a subroutine which is a signal handler. The second parameter is a POSIX::SigSet object. The third parameter contains the **sa_flags**.

```
$sigset = POSIX::SigSet->new;
$sigaction = POSIX::SigAction->new('main::handler', $sigset,
              &POSIX::SA_NOCLDSTOP);
```

This POSIX::SigAction object should be used with the POSIX::sigaction() function.

POSIX::SigSet

new

Creates a new SigSet object. This object will be destroyed automatically when it is no longer needed. Arguments may be supplied to initialize the set. Create an empty set:

```
$sigset = POSIX::SigSet->new;
```

Create a set with **SIGUSR1**:

```
$sigset = POSIX::SigSet->new(&POSIX::SIGUSR1);
```

addset

Adds a signal to a SigSet object. Returns **undef** on failure.

```
$sigset->addset(&POSIX::SIGUSR2);
```

delset

Removes a signal from the SigSet object. Returns **undef** on failure.

```
$sigset->delset(&POSIX::SIGUSR2);
```

emptyset

Initializes the SigSet object to be empty. Returns **undef** on failure.

```
$sigset->emptyset();
```

fillset

Initializes the SigSet object to include all signals. Returns **undef** on failure.

```
$sigset->fillset();
```

ismember

Tests the SigSet object to see whether it contains a specific signal.

```
if ($sigset->ismember(&POSIX::SIGUSR1 ) ){
    print "contains SIGUSR1\n";

}
```

POSIX::Termios

new
> Creates a new Termios object. This object will be destroyed automatically when it is no longer needed.
>
> $termios = POSIX::Termios->new;

getattr
> Gets terminal control attributes for a given *fd*, 0 by default. Returns **undef** on failure. Obtain the attributes for standard input:
>
> $termios->getattr()
>
> Obtain the attributes for standard output:
>
> $termios->getattr(1)

getcc
> Retrieves a value from the c_cc field of a Termios object. The c_cc field is an array, so an index must be specified.
>
> $c_cc[1] = $termios->getcc(&POSIX::VEOF);

getcflag
> Retrieves the c_cflag field of a Termios object.
>
> $c_cflag = $termios->getcflag;

getiflag
> Retrieves the c_iflag field of a Termios object.
>
> $c_iflag = $termios->getiflag;

getispeed
> Retrieves the input baud rate.
>
> $ispeed = $termios->getispeed;

getlflag
> Retrieves the c_lflag field of a Termios object.
>
> $c_lflag = $termios->getlflag;

getoflag
> Retrieves the c_oflag field of a Termios object.
>
> $c_oflag = $termios->getoflag;

getospeed
> Retrieves the output baud rate.
>
> $ospeed = $termios->getospeed;

setattr
> Sets terminal control attributes for a given *fd*. Returns **undef** on failure. The following sets attributes immediately for standard output.
>
> $termios->setattr(1, &POSIX::TCSANOW);

setcc
> Sets a value in the c_cc field of a Termios object. The c_cc field is an array, so an index must be specified.
>
> $termios->setcc(&POSIX::VEOF, 4);

setcflag
> Sets the c_cflag field of a Termios object.
>
> $termios->setcflag(&POSIX::CLOCAL);

setiflag
> Sets the c_iflag field of a Termios object.
>
> ```
> $termios->setiflag(&POSIX::BRKINT);
> ```

setispeed
> Sets the input baud rate. Returns **undef** on failure.
>
> ```
> $termios->setispeed(&POSIX::B9600);
> ```

setlflag
> Sets the c_lflag field of a Termios object.
>
> ```
> $termios->setlflag(&POSIX::ECHO);
> ```

setoflag
> Set the c_oflag field of a Termios object.
>
> ```
> $termios->setoflag(&POSIX::OPOST);
> ```

setospeed
> Sets the output baud rate. Returns **undef** on failure.
>
> ```
> $termios->setospeed(&POSIX::B9600);
> ```

Baud rate values
> B0 B50 B75 B110 B134 B150 B200 B300 B600 B1200 B1800 B2400 B4800 B9600 B19200 B38400

Terminal interface values
> TCSADRAIN TCSANOW TCOON TCIOFLUSH TCOFLUSH TCION TCIFLUSH TCSAFLUSH TCIOFF TCOOFF

c_cc *index values*
> VEOF VEOL VERASE VINTR VKILL VQUIT VSUSP VSTART VSTOP VMIN VTIME NCCS

c_cflag *field values*
> CLOCAL CREAD CSIZE CS5 CS6 CS7 CS8 CSTOPB HUPCL PARENB PARODD

c_iflag *field values*
> BRKINT ICRNL IGNBRK IGNCR IGNPAR INLCR INPCK ISTRIP IXOFF IXON PARMRK

c_lflag *field values*
> ECHO ECHOE ECHOK ECHONL ICANON IEXTEN ISIG NOFLSH TOSTOP

c_oflag *field values*
> OPOST

While these constants are associated with the Termios class, note that they are actually symbols in the POSIX package.

Here's an example of a complete program for getting unbuffered, single-character input on a POSIX system:

```
#!/usr/bin/perl -w
use strict;
$| = 1;
for (1..4) {
    my $got;
    print "gimme: ";
    $got = getone();
```

```
        print "--> $got\n";

    }
    exit;

    BEGIN {
        use POSIX qw(:termios_h);

        my ($term, $oterm, $echo, $noecho, $fd_stdin);

        $fd_stdin = fileno(STDIN);

        $term     = POSIX::Termios->new();
        $term->getattr($fd_stdin);
        $oterm    = $term->getlflag();

        $echo     = ECHO | ECHOK | ICANON;
        $noecho   = $oterm & ~$echo;

        sub cbreak {
            $term->setlflag($noecho);
            $term->setcc(VTIME, 1);
            $term->setattr($fd_stdin, TCSANOW);
        }

        sub cooked {
            $term->setlflag($oterm);
            $term->setcc(VTIME, 0);
            $term->setattr($fd_stdin, TCSANOW);
        }

        sub getone {
            my $key = "";
            cbreak();
            sysread(STDIN, $key, 1);
            cooked();
            return $key;
        }

    }

    END { cooked() }
```

Functions

Function Name	Definition
_exit	Identical to the C function _*exit*(2).
abort	Identical to the C function *abort*(3).
abs	Identical to Perl's built-in **abs** function.

access	Determines the accessibility of a file. Returns **undef** on failure.
	`if (POSIX::access("/", &POSIX::R_OK ) ){`
	`    print "have read permission\n";`
	`}`

Function Name	Definition
acos	Identical to the C function *acos*(3).
alarm	Identical to Perl's built-in `alarm` function.
asctime	Identical to the C function *asctime*(3).
asin	Identical to the C function *asin*(3).
assert	Similar to C macro *assert*(3).
atan	Identical to the C function *atan*(3).
atan2	Identical to Perl's built-in `atan2` function.
atexit	C-specific: use `END {}` instead.
atof	C-specific.
atoi	C-specific.
atol	C-specific.
bsearch	Not supplied. You should probably be using a hash anyway.
calloc	C-specific.
ceil	Identical to the C function *ceil*(3).
chdir	Identical to Perl's built-in `chdir` function.
chmod	Identical to Perl's built-in `chmod` function.
chown	Identical to Perl's built-in `chown` function.
clearerr	Use method `FileHandle::clearerr()` instead.
clock	Identical to the C function *clock*(3).
close	Closes a file. This uses file descriptors such as those obtained by calling `POSIX::open()`. Returns `undef` on failure. `$fd = POSIX::open("foo", &POSIX::O_RDONLY); POSIX::close($fd);`
closedir	Identical to Perl's built-in `closedir` function.
cos	Identical to Perl's built-in `cos` function.
cosh	Identical to the C function *cosh*(3).
creat	Creates a new file. This returns a file descriptor like the ones returned by `POSIX::open()`. Use `POSIX::close()` to close the file. `$fd = POSIX::creat("foo", 0611); POSIX::close($fd);`
ctermid	Generates the path name for the controlling terminal. `$path = POSIX::ctermid();`
ctime	Identical to the C function *ctime*(3)
cuserid	Gets the character login name of the user. `$name = POSIX::cuserid();`
difftime	Identical to the C function *difftime*(3).
div	C-specific.
dup	Similar to the C function *dup*(2). Uses file descriptors such as those obtained by calling `POSIX::open()`. Returns `undef` on failure.

Function Name	Definition
dup2	Similar to the C function *dup2*(2). Uses file descriptors such as those obtained by calling `POSIX::open()`. Returns undef on failure.
errno	Returns the value of *errno*. `$errno = POSIX::errno();`
execl	C-specific; use Perl's exec instead.
execle	C-specific; use Perl's exec instead.
execlp	C-specific; use Perl's exec instead.
execv	C-specific; use Perl's exec instead.
execve	C-specific; use Perl's exec instead.
execvp	C-specific; use Perl's exec instead.
exit	Identical to Perl's built-in exit function.
exp	Identical to Perl's built-in exp function.
fabs	Identical to Perl's built-in abs function.
fclose	Use method `FileHandle::close()` instead.
fcntl	Identical to Perl's built-in fcntl function.
fdopen	Use method `FileHandle::new_from_fd()` instead.
feof	Use method `FileHandle::eof()` instead.
ferror	Use method `FileHandle::error()` instead.
fflush	Use method `FileHandle::flush()` instead.
fgetc	Use method `FileHandle::getc()` instead.
fgetpos	Use method `FileHandle::getpos()` instead.
fgets	Use method `FileHandle::gets()` instead.
fileno	Use method `FileHandle::fileno()` instead.
floor	Identical to the C function *floor*(3).
fmod	Identical to the C function *fmod*(3).
fopen	Use method `FileHandle::open()` instead.
fork	Identical to Perl's built-in fork function.

fpathconf	Retrieves the value of a configurable limit on a file or directory. This uses file descriptors such as those obtained by calling `POSIX::open()`. Returns undef on failure. The following will determine the maximum length of the longest allowable pathname on the filesystem that holds */tmp/foo*.
	`$fd = POSIX::open("/tmp/foo", &POSIX::O_RDONLY);`
	`$path_max = POSIX::fpathconf($fd,`
	`                              &POSIX::_PC_PATH_MAX);`

fprintf	C-specific; use Perl's built-in printf function instead.
fputc	C-specific; use Perl's built-in print function instead.
fputs	C-specific; use Perl's built-in print function instead.
fread	C-specific; use Perl's built-in read function instead.

Function Name	Definition
free	C-specific
freopen	C-specific; use Perl's built-in `open` function instead.
frexp	Returns the mantissa and exponent of a floating-point number. `($mantissa, $exponent) = POSIX::frexp(3.14);`
fscanf	C-specific; use <> and regular expressions instead.
fseek	Use method `FileHandle::seek()` instead.
fsetpos	Use method `FileHandle::setpos()` instead.
fstat	Gets file status. This uses file descriptors such as those obtained by calling `POSIX::open()`. The data returned is identical to the data from Perl's built-in `stat` function. Odd how that happens… `$fd = POSIX::open("foo", &POSIX::O_RDONLY);` `@stats = POSIX::fstat($fd);`
ftell	Use method `FileHandle::tell()` instead.
fwrite	C-specific; use Perl's built-in `print` function instead.
getc	Identical to Perl's built-in `getc` function.
getchar	Returns one character from STDIN.
getcwd	Returns the name of the current working directory.
getegid	Returns the effective group ID (gid).
getenv	Returns the value of the specified environment variable.
geteuid	Returns the effective user ID (uid).
getgid	Returns the user's real group ID (gid).
getgrgid	Identical to Perl's built-in `getgrgid` function.
getgrnam	Identical to Perl's built-in `getgrnam` function.
getgroups	Returns the ids of the user's supplementary groups.
getlogin	Identical to Perl's built-in `getlogin` function.
getpgrp	Identical to Perl's built-in `getpgrp` function.
getpid	Returns the process's ID (pid).
getppid	Identical to Perl's built-in `getppid` function.
getpwnam	Identical to Perl's built-in `getpwnam` function.
getpwuid	Identical to Perl's built-in `getpwuid` function.
gets	Returns one line from STDIN.
getuid	Returns the user ID (uid).
gmtime	Identical to Perl's built-in `gmtime` function.
isalnum	Identical to the C function, except that it can apply to a single character or to a whole string. (If applied to a whole string, all characters must be of the indicated category.)
isalpha	Identical to the C function, except that it can apply to a single character or to a whole string.

Function Name	Definition
isatty	Returns a Boolean indicating whether the specified filehandle is connected to a TTY.
iscntrl	Identical to the C function, except that it can apply to a single character or to a whole string.
isdigit	Identical to the C function, except that it can apply to a single character or to a whole string.
isgraph	Identical to the C function, except that it can apply to a single character or to a whole string.
islower	Identical to the C function, except that it can apply to a single character or to a whole string.
isprint	Identical to the C function, except that it can apply to a single character or to a whole string.
ispunct	Identical to the C function, except that it can apply to a single character or to a whole string.
isspace	Identical to the C function, except that it can apply to a single character or to a whole string.
isupper	Identical to the C function, except that it can apply to a single character or to a whole string.
isxdigit	Identical to the C function, except that it can apply to a single character or to a whole string.
kill	Identical to Perl's built-in kill function.
labs	C-specific; use Perl's built-in abs function instead.
ldexp	Identical to the C function *ldexp*(3).
ldiv	C-specific; use the division operator / and Perl's built-in int function instead.
link	Identical to Perl's built-in link function.
localeconv	Gets numeric formatting information. Returns a reference to a hash containing the current locale formatting values. The database for the **de** (Deutsch or German) locale:

```
$loc = POSIX::setlocale(&POSIX::LC_ALL, "de");
print "Locale = $loc\n";
$lconv = POSIX::localeconv();
print "decimal_point    = ",
$lconv->{decimal_point}, "\n";
print "thousands_sep    = ",
$lconv->{thousands_sep}, "\n";
print "grouping         = ",
$lconv->{grouping}, "\n";
print "int_curr_symbol  = ",
$lconv->{int_curr_symbol}, "\n";
print "currency_symbol  = ",
$lconv->{currency_symbol}, "\n";
print "mon_decimal_point = ",
$lconv->{mon_decimal_point}, "\n";
```

Function Name	Definition
| | ```
print "mon_thousands_sep = ",
$lconv->{mon_thousands_sep}, "\n";
print "mon_grouping        = ",
$lconv->{mon_grouping}, "\n";
print "positive_sign       = ",
$lconv->{positive_sign}, "\n";
print "negative_sign       = ",
$lconv->{negative_sign}, "\n";
print "int_frac_digits     = ",
$lconv->{int_frac_digits}, "\n";
print "frac_digits         = ",
$lconv->{frac_digits}, "\n";
print "p_cs_precedes       = ",
$lconv->{p_cs_precedes}, "\n";
print "p_sep_by_space      = ",
$lconv->{p_sep_by_space}, "\n";
print "n_cs_precedes       = ",
$lconv->{n_cs_precedes}, "\n";
print "n_sep_by_space      = ",
$lconv->{n_sep_by_space}, "\n";
print "p_sign_posn         = ",
$lconv->{p_sign_posn}, "\n";
print "n_sign_posn         = ",
$lconv->{n_sign_posn}, "\n";
``` |
localtime	Identical to Perl's built-in `localtime` function.
log	Identical to Perl's built-in `log` function.
log10	Identical to the C function *log10*(3).
longjmp	C-specific; use Perl's built-in `die` function instead.
lseek	Moves the read/write file pointer. This uses file descriptors such as those obtained by calling `POSIX::open()`. `$fd = POSIX::open("foo", &POSIX::O_RDONLY);` `$off_t = POSIX::lseek($fd, 0, &POSIX::SEEK_SET);` Returns `undef` on failure.
malloc	C-specific.
mblen	Identical to the C function *mblen*(3).
mbstowcs	Identical to the C function *mbstowcs*(3).
mbtowc	Identical to the C function *mbtowc*(3).
memchr	C-specific; use Perl's built-in `index` instead.
memcmp	C-specific; use `eq` instead.
memcpy	C-specific; use = instead.
memmove	C-specific; use = instead.
memset	C-specific; use **x** instead.
mkdir	Identical to Perl's built-in `mkdir` function.
mkfifo	Similar to the C function *mkfifo*(2). Returns `undef` on failure.
```

Function Name	Definition
mktime	Converts date/time information to a calendar time. Returns **undef** on failure. Synopsis: mktime(*sec*, *min*, *hour*, *mday*, *mon*, *year*, *wday* = 0, *yday* = 0, *isdst* = 0) The month (*mon*), weekday (*wday*), and yearday (*yday*) begin at zero. That is, January is 0, not 1; Sunday is 0, not 1; January 1st is 0, not 1. The year (**year**) is given in years since 1900. That is, the year 1995 is 95; the year 2001 is 101. Consult your system's *mktime*(3) manpage for details about these and the other arguments. Calendar time for December 12, 1995, at 10:30 am. $time_t = POSIX::mktime(0, 30, 10, 12, 11, 95); print "Date = ", POSIX::ctime($time_t);
modf	Returns the integral and fractional parts of a floating-point number. ($fractional, $integral) = POSIX::modf(3.14);
nice	Similar to the C function *nice*(3). Returns **undef** on failure.
offsetof	C-specific.

open	Opens a file for reading or writing. This returns file descriptors, not Perl filehandles. Returns **undef** on failure. Use POSIX::close() to close the file. Open a file read-only:
	$fd = POSIX::open("foo");
	Open a file for reading and writing:
	$fd = POSIX::open("foo", &POSIX::O_RDWR);
	Open a file for writing, with truncation:
	$fd = POSIX::open("foo", &POSIX::O_WRONLY |
	                &POSIX::O_TRUNC);
	Create a new file with mode 0644; set up the file for writing:
	$fd = POSIX::open("foo", &POSIX::O_CREAT |
	                &POSIX::O_WRONLY, 0644);

opendir	Opens a directory for reading. Returns **undef** on failure. $dir = POSIX::opendir("/tmp"); @files = POSIX::readdir($dir); POSIX::closedir($dir);
pathconf	Retrieves the value of a configurable limit on a file or directory. Returns **undef** on failure. The following will determine the maximum length of the longest allowable pathname on the filesystem that holds */tmp*: $path_max = POSIX::pathconf("/tmp", &POSIX::_PC_PATH_MAX);
pause	Similar to the C function *pause*(3). Returns **undef** on failure.
perror	Identical to the C function *perror*(3).
pipe	Creates an interprocess channel. Returns file descriptors like those returned by POSIX::open(). ($fd0, $fd1) = POSIX::pipe(); POSIX::write($fd0, "hello", 5); POSIX::read($fd1, $buf, 5);

Function Name	Definition
pow	Computes $x raised to the power $exponent. `$ret = POSIX::pow($x, $exponent);`
printf	Prints the specified arguments to STDOUT.
putc	C-specific; use Perl's built-in print function instead.
putchar	C-specific; use Perl's built-in print function instead.
puts	C-specific; use Perl's built-in print function instead.
qsort	C-specific; use Perl's built-in sort function instead.
raise	Sends the specified signal to the current process.
rand	Non-portable; use Perl's built-in rand function instead.

read	Reads from a file. This uses file descriptors such as those obtained by calling POSIX::open(). If the buffer $buf is not large enough for the read, then Perl will extend it to make room for the request. Returns undef on failure.
	`$fd = POSIX::open("foo", &POSIX::O_RDONLY);`
	`$bytes = POSIX::read($fd, $buf, 3);`

readdir	Identical to Perl's built-in readdir function.
realloc	C-specific.
remove	Identical to Perl's built-in unlink function.
rename	Identical to Perl's built-in rename function.
rewind	Seeks to the beginning of the file.
rewinddir	Identical to Perl's built-in rewinddir function.
rmdir	Identical to Perl's built-in rmdir function.
scanf	C-specific; use <> and regular expressions instead.
setgid	Sets the real group id for this process, like assigning to the special variable $(.
setjmp	C-specific; use eval {} instead.
setlocale	Modifies and queries program's locale. The following will set the traditional UNIX system locale behavior. `$loc = POSIX::setlocale(&POSIX::LC_ALL, "C");`
setpgid	Similar to the C function *setpgid*(2). Returns undef on failure.
setsid	Identical to the C function *setsid*(8).
setuid	Sets the real user ID for this process, like assigning to the special variable $<.
sigaction	Detailed signal management. This uses POSIX::SigAction objects for the $action and $oldaction arguments. Consult your system's *sigaction*(3) manpage for details. Returns undef on failure. `POSIX::sigaction($sig, $action, $oldaction)`
siglongjmp	C-specific; use Perl's built-in die function instead.

Function Name	Definition
sigpending	Examines signals that are blocked and pending. This uses POSIX::SigSet objects for the $sigset argument. Consult your system's *sigpending*(2) manpage for details. Returns undef on failure. POSIX::sigpending($sigset)
sigprocmask	Changes and/or examines this process's signal mask. This uses POSIX::SigSet objects for the $sigset and $oldsigset arguments. Consult your system's *sigprocmask*(2) manpage for details. Returns undef on failure. POSIX::sigprocmask($how, $sigset, $oldsigset)
sigsetjmp	C-specific; use eval {} instead.
sigsuspend	Installs a signal mask and suspend process until signal arrives. This uses POSIX::SigSet objects for the $signal_mask argument. Consult your system's *sigsuspend*(2) manpage for details. Returns undef on failure. POSIX::sigsuspend($signal_mask)
sin	Identical to Perl's built-in sin function.
sinh	Identical to the C function *sinh*(3).
sleep	Identical to Perl's built-in sleep function.
sprintf	Identical to Perl's built-in sprintf function.
sqrt	Identical to Perl's built-in sqrt function.
srand	Identical to Perl's built-in srand function.
sscanf	C-specific; use regular expressions instead.
stat	Identical to Perl's built-in stat function.
strcat	C-specific; use .= instead.
strchr	C-specific; use index instead.
strcmp	C-specific; use eq instead.
strcoll	Identical to the C function *strcoll*(3).
strcpy	C-specific; use = instead.
strcspn	C-specific; use regular expressions instead.
strerror	Returns the error string for the specified *errno*.

strftime	Converts date and time information to string. Returns the string.
	strftime(*fmt, sec, min, hour, mday, mon, year,*
	          wday = 0, *yday* = 0, *isdst* = 0)
	The month (*mon*), weekday (*wday*), and yearday (*yday*) begin at zero. That is, January is 0, not 1; Sunday is 0, not 1; January 1st is 0, not 1. The year (*year*) is given in years since 1900. That is, the year 1995 is 95; the year 2001 is 101. Consult your system's *strftime*(3) manpage for details about these and the other arguments. The string for Tuesday, December 12, 1995:
	$str = POSIX::strftime("%A, %B %d, %Y", 0, 0, 0,
	                              12, 11, 95, 2);
	
	print $str, "\n";

Function Name	Definition
strlen	C-specific; use length instead.
strncat	C-specific; use .= and/or substr instead.
strncmp	C-specific; use eq and/or substr instead.
strncpy	C-specific; use = and/or substr instead.
strpbrk	C-specific.
strrchr	C-specific; use rindex and/or substr instead.
strspn	C-specific.
strstr	Identical to Perl's built-in index function.
strtod	C-specific.
strtok	C-specific.
strtol	C-specific.
strtoul	C-specific.
strxfrm	String transformation. Returns the transformed string. `$dst = POSIX::strxfrm($src);`

sysconf	Retrieves values of system configurable variables. Returns undef on failure. The following will get the machine's clock speed.
	`$clock_ticks =`
	`    POSIX::sysconf(&POSIX::_SC_CLK_TCK)`

system	Identical to Perl's built-in system function.
tan	Identical to the C function *tan*(3).
tanh	Identical to the C function *tanh*(3).
tcdrain	Similar to the C function *tcdrain*(3). Returns undef on failure.
tcflow	Similar to the C function *tcflow*(3). Returns undef on failure.
tcflush	Similar to the C function *tcflush*(3). Returns undef on failure.
tcgetpgrp	Identical to the C function *tcgetpgrp*(3).
tcsendbreak	Similar to the C function *tcsendbreak*(3). Returns undef on failure.
tcsetpgrp	Similar to the C function *tcsetpgrp*(3). Returns undef on failure.
time	Identical to Perl's built-in time function.

times	Returns elapsed realtime since some point in the past (such as system startup), user and system times for this process, and user and system times for child processes. All times are returned in clock ticks.
	`($realtime, $user, $system, $cuser, $csystem) =`
	`POSIX::times();`
	Note: Perl's built-in times function returns four values, measured in seconds.

tmpfile	Use method FileHandle::new_tmpfile() instead.
tmpnam	Returns a name for a temporary file. `$tmpfile = POSIX::tmpnam();`

Function Name	Definition
tolower	Identical to Perl's built-in lc function.
toupper	Identical to Perl's built-in uc function.
ttyname	Identical to the C function *ttyname(3)*.
tzname	Retrieves the time conversion information from the tzname variable. POSIX::tzset(); ($std, $dst) = POSIX::tzname();
tzset	Identical to the C function *tzset(3)*.
umask	Identical to Perl's built-in umask function.
uname	Gets name of current operating system. ($sysname, $nodename, $release, $version, $machine) = POSIX::uname();
ungetc	Use method FileHandle::ungetc() instead.
unlink	Identical to Perl's built-in unlink function.
utime	Identical to Perl's built-in utime function.
vfprintf	C-specific.
vprintf	C-specific.
vsprintf	C-specific.
wait	Identical to Perl's built-in wait function.
waitpid	Wait for a child process to change state. This is identical to Perl's built-in waitpid function. $pid = POSIX::waitpid(-1, &POSIX::WNOHANG); print "status = ", ($? / 256), "\n";
wcstombs	Identical to the C function *wcstombs(3)*.
wctomb	Identical to the C function *wctomb(3)*.
write	Writes to a file. Uses file descriptors such as those obtained by calling POSIX::open(). Returns undef on failure. $fd = POSIX::open("foo", &POSIX::O_WRONLY); $buf = "hello"; $bytes = POSIX::write($b, $buf, 5);

Pathname constants

_PC_CHOWN_RESTRICTED	_PC_LINK_MAX	_PC_MAX_CANON
_PC_MAX_INPUT	_PC_NAME_MAX	_PC_NO_TRUNC
_PC_PATH_MAX	_PC_PIPE_BUF	_PC_VDISABLE

POSIX constants

_POSIX_ARG_MAX	_POSIX_CHILD_MAX	_POSIX_CHOWN_RESTRICTED
_POSIX_JOB_CONTROL	_POSIX_LINK_MAX	_POSIX_MAX_CANON
_POSIX_MAX_INPUT	_POSIX_NAME_MAX	_POSIX_NGROUPS_MAX
_POSIX_NO_TRUNC	_POSIX_OPEN_MAX	_POSIX_PATH_MAX

_POSIX_PIPE_BUF	_POSIX_SAVED_IDS	_POSIX_SSIZE_MAX
_POSIX_STREAM_MAX	_POSIX_TZNAME_MAX	_POSIX_VDISABLE
_POSIX_VERSION		

System configuration

_SC_ARG_MAX	_SC_CHILD_MAX	_SC_CLK_TCK
_SC_JOB_CONTROL	_SC_NGROUPS_MAX	_SC_OPEN_MAX
_SC_SAVED_IDS	_SC_STREAM_MAX	_SC_TZNAME_MAX
_SC_VERSION		

Error constants

E2BIG	EACCES	EAGAIN
EBADF	EBUSY	ECHILD
EDEADLK	EDOM	EEXIST
EFAUL	EFBIG	EINTR
EINVAL	EIO	EISDIR
EMFILE	EMLINK	ENAMETOOLONG
ENFILE	ENODE	ENOENT
ENOEXEC	ENOLCK	ENOMEM
ENOSPC	ENOSYS	ENOTDIR
ENOTEMPTY	ENOTTY	ENXIO
EPERM	EPIPE	ERANGE
EROFS	ESPIPE	ESRCH
EXDEV		

File control constants

FD_CLOEXEC	F_DUPFD	F_GETFD
F_GETFL	F_GETLK	F_OK
F_RDLCK	F_SETFD	F_SETFL
F_SETLK	F_SETLKW	F_UNLCK
F_WRLCK	O_ACCMODE	O_APPEND
O_CREAT	O_EXCL	O_NOCTTY
O_NONBLOCK	O_RDONLY	O_RDWR
O_TRUNC	O_WRONLY	

Floating-point constants

DBL_DIG	DBL_EPSILON	DBL_MANT_DIG
DBL_MAX	DBL_MAX_10_EXP	DBL_MAX_EXP
DBL_MIN	DBL_MIN_10_EXP	DBL_MIN_EXP
FLT_DIG	FLT_EPSILON	FLT_MANT_DIG

FLT_MAX	FLT_MAX_10_EXP	FLT_MAX_EXP
FLT_MIN	FLT_MIN_10_EXP	FLT_MIN_EXP
FLT_RADIX	FLT_ROUNDS	LDBL_DIG
LDBL_EPSILON	LDBL_MANT_DIG	LDBL_MAX
LDBL_MAX_10_EXP	LDBL_MAX_EXP	LDBL_MIN
LDBL_MIN_10_EXP	LDBL_MIN_EXP	

Limit constants

ARG_MAX	CHAR_BIT	CHAR_MAX
CHAR_MIN	CHILD_MAX	INT_MAX
INT_MIN	LINK_MAX	LONG_MAX
LONG_MIN	MAX_CANON	MAX_INPUT
MB_LEN_MAX	NAME_MAX	NGROUPS_MAX
OPEN_MAX	PATH_MAX	PIPE_BUF
SCHAR_MAX	SCHAR_MIN	SHRT_MAX
SHRT_MIN	SSIZE_MAX	STREAM_MAX
TZNAME_MAX	UCHAR_MAX	UINT_MAX
ULONG_MAX USHRT_MAX		

Locale constants

LC_ALL	LC_COLLATE	LC_CTYPE
LC_MONETARY	LC_NUMERIC	LC_TIME

Math constants

HUGE_VAL

Signal constants

SA_NOCLDSTOP	SIGABRT	SIGALRM
SIGCHLD	SIGCONT	SIGFPE
SIGHUP	SIGILL	SIGINT
SIGKILL	SIGPIPE	SIGQUIT
SIGSEGV	SIGSTOP	SIGTERM
SIGTSTP	SIGTTIN	SIGTTOU
SIGUSR1	SIGUSR2	SIG_BLOCK
SIG_DFL	SIG_ERR	SIG_IGN
SIG_SETMASK	SIG_UNBLOCK	

Stat constants

S_IRGRP	S_IROTH	S_IRUSR
S_IRWXG	S_IRWXO	S_IRWXU
S_ISGID	S_ISUID	S_IWGRP

S_IWOTH	S_IWUSR	S_IXGRP
S_IXOTH	S_IXUSR	

Stat macros

S_ISBLK	S_ISCHR	S_ISDIR
S_ISFIFO	S_ISREG	

Stdlib constants

EXIT_FAILURE	EXIT_SUCCESS	MB_CUR_MAX
RAND_MAX		

Stdio constants

BUFSIZ	EOF	FILENAME_MAX
L_ctermid	L_cuserid	L_tmpname
TMP_MAX		

Time constants

CLK_TCK	CLOCKS_PER_SEC

Unistd constants

R_OK	SEEK_CUR	SEEK_END
SEEK_SET	STDIN_FILENO	STDOUT_FILENO
STRERR_FILENO	W_OK	X_OK

Wait constants

WNOHANG	WUNTRACED

Wait macros

WIFEXITED	WEXITSTATUS	WIFSIGNALED
WTERMSIG	WIFSTOPPED	WSTOPSIG

Proc::Forkfunc—fork off a function

Synopsis

```
use Proc::Forkfunc;
forkfunc(\&child_func,@child_args);
```

Description

Fork off a process. Call a function on the child process. The function should be passed in as a reference. The child function should not return.

Logic copied from somewhere, probably Larry Wall.

Author

David Muir Sharnoff, *muir@idiom.com*

Proc::Simple—launch and control background processes

Synopsis

```
use Proc::Simple;

$myproc = Proc::Simple->new();          # Create a new process object

$myproc->start("shell-command-line");   # Launch a shell process
$myproc->start(sub { ... });            # Launch a perl subroutine
$myproc->start(\&subroutine);           # Launch a perl subroutine

$running = $myproc->poll();             # Poll Running Process

$myproc->kill();                        # Kill Process (SIGTERM)

$myproc->kill("SIGUSR1");               # Send specified signal

Proc::Simple->debug($level);            # Turn debug on
```

Description

The Proc::Simple package provides objects that model real-life processes from a user's point of view. A new process object is created by:

```
$myproc = Proc::Simple->new();
```

Either shell-like command lines or references to Perl subroutines can be specified for launching a process in the background. A 10-second sleep process, for example, can be started via the shell as:

```
$myproc->start("sleep 10");
```

or as a Perl subroutine, with:

```
$myproc->start(sub { sleep(10); });
```

The **start** method returns immediately after starting the specified process in background, i.e. non-blocking, mode. It returns 1 if the process has been launched sucessfully and 0 if not.

The **poll** method checks whether the process is still running:

```
$running = $myproc->poll();
```

and returns 1 if it is, 0 if it's not. Finally:

```
$myproc->kill();
```

terminates the process by sending it the SIGTERM signal. As an option, another signal can be specified.

```
$myproc->kill("SIGUSR1");
```

sends the SIGUSR1 signal to the running process. **kill** returns 1 if it succeeds in sending the signal, 0 if it doesn't.

Note: Please keep in mind that there is no guarantee that the SIGTERM signal really terminates a process. Processes can have signal handlers defined that avoid a shutdown. If in doubt whether a process still exists, check it repeatedly with the `poll` routine after sending the signal.

Author

Michael Schilli, *schilli@tep.e-technik.tu-muenchen.de*

Quota—Perl interface to filesystem quotas

Synopsis

```
use Quota;
($block_curr, $block_soft, $block_hard, $block_timelimit,
 $inode_curr, $inode_soft, $inode_hard, $inode_timelimit) =
Quota::query($dev [,$uid]);
($block_curr, $block_soft, $block_hard, $block_timelimit,
 $inode_curr, $inode_soft, $inode_hard, $inode_timelimit) =
Quota::rpcquery($host, $path [,$uid]);
Quota::setqlim($dev, $uid, $block_soft, $block_hard,
               $inode_soft, $inode_hard [,$tlo]);
Quota::sync([$dev]);
$arg = Quota::getqcarg([$path]);
Quota::setmntent();
($dev, $path, $type, $opts) = Quota::getmntent();
Quota::endmntent();
```

Description

The Quota module provides access to filesystem quotas. The `quotactl` system call or `ioctl` is used to query or set quotas on the local host, or queries are submitted via RPC to a remote host. Mount tables can be parsed with `getmntent` and paths can be translated to device files (or whatever the actual `quotactl` implementation needs as an argument) of the according filesystem.

Functions

($bc,$bs,$bh,$bt, $ic,$is,$ih,$it) = Quota::query($dev, $uid)

Gets current usage and quota limits for a given filesystem and user. The user is specified by its numeric uid; defaults to the process' real uid.

The type of *$dev* varies from system to system. It's the argument that is used by the `quotactl` implementation to address a specific filesystem. It may be the path of a device file (e.g. */dev/sd0a*) or the path of the mount point or the quotas file at the top of the filesystem (e.g. */home.stand/quotas*). However, you do not have to worry about that; use Quota::getqcarg to automatically translate any path inside a filesystem to the required $dev argument.

$dev may also be in the form of `hostname:path`, which has the module transparently query the given host via a remote procedure call (RPC). In case you have NFS (or similar network mounts), this type of argument may also be produced by Quota::getqcarg. Note that RPC queries require `rquotad(1m)` to be running on the target system. If the daemon or host is down, the timeout is 12 seconds.

In $bc and $ic the current usage in blocks and inodes is returned. $bc and $is are the soft limits, $bh and $ih are the hard limits. If the soft limit is exceeded, writes by this user will fail for blocks or inodes after $bt or $it is reached. These times are expressed as usual, i.e., in elapsed seconds since 00:00 1/Jan/1970 GMT.

Quota::setqlim($dev, $uid, $bs,$bh, $is,$ih, $tlo)

Sets quota limits for the given user. Meanings of $dev, $uid, $bs, $bh, $is, and $ih are the same as in Quota::query.

$tlo decides how the time limits are initialized:

0

The time limits are set to NOT STARTED, i.e. the time limits are not initialized until the first write attempt by this user. This is the default.

1

The time limits are set to 7.0 days. No other alternatives (i.e. setting a specific time) are available in most implementations.

Note: If you want to set the quota of a particular user to zero (i.e., no write permission), you must not set all limits to zero, since that is equivalent to unlimited access. Instead, set only the hard limit to zero and the soft limit, for example, to 1.

Note also that you cannot set quotas via RPC.

Quota::sync($dev)

Causes the kernel to update the quota file on disk, or all quota files if no argument is given (the latter doesn't work on all systems, in particular on HP-UX 10.10).

The main purpose of this function is to check if quota is enabled in the kernel and for a particular filesystem. Read the quotaon(1m) manpage on how to enable quotas on a filesystem.

($bc,$bs,$bh,$bt,$ic,$is,$ih,$it) = Quota::rpcquery($host,$path,$uid)

This is equivalent to Quota::query("$host:$path",$uid), i.e., query quota for a given user on a given remote host via RPC. *$path* is the path of any file or directory inside the wanted filesystem on the remote host.

$arg = Quota::getqcarg($path)

Gets the required $dev argument for Quota::query and Quota::setqlim for the filesystem you want to operate on. $path is any path of an existing file or directory inside that filesystem. The path argument is optional and defaults to the current working directory.

The type of $dev varies between operating systems, i.e., for different implementations of the quotactl functionality. Hence it's important for compatibility to always use this module function and not really pass a device file to Quota::query (as returned by Quota::getdev). See also Quota::query above.

$dev = Quota::getdev($path)

Returns the device entry in the mount table for a particular filesystem, specified by any path of an existing file or directory inside it. $path defaults to the working directory. This device entry need not really be a device. For example, on network mounts (NFS) it's *host:mountpath*; with amd(1m), it may be something completely different.

Warning: *Never* use this to produce a `$dev` argument for other functions of this module, since it's not compatible. On some systems, `quotactl` does not work on devices, but works on the *quotas* file or some other kind of argument. Always use Quota::getqcarg.

`Quota::setmntent()`

Opens or resets the mount table. This is required before the first invocation of Quota::getmntent.

Note: On some systems, there is no equivalent function in the C library. But you still have to call this module procedure for initialization of module-internal variables.

`($dev, $path, $type, $opts) = Quota::getmntent()`

Returns the next entry in the system mount table. This table contains information about all currently mounted (local or remote) filesystems. The format and location of this table (e.g., */etc/mtab*) vary from system to system. This function is provided as a compatible way to parse the table. (On some systems, such as OSF/1, this table isn't accessible as a file at all; i.e., it's only available via Quota::getmntent.)

`Quota::endmntent()`

Closes the mount table. This should be called after the last use of Quota::getmntent to free possibly allocated file handles and memory. Always returns `undef`.

`Quota::strerr()`

Translates `$!` to a quota-specific error text. You should always use this function to output error messages, since the normal messages don't always make sense for quota errors (e.g., ESRCH: `No such process` is translated to `No quota for this user`).

Return Values

Functions that are supposed return lists or scalars return undef upon error. As usual, `$!` contains the error code (see Quota::strerr).

Quota::endmntent always returns `undef`. All other functions return undef only upon error.

Examples

An example for each function can be found in the test script *test/quotatest*. See also the *contrib* directory, which contains some longer scripts, kindly donated by users of the module.

Author

This module was written in 1995 by Tom Zoerner (*Tom.Zoerner@informatik.uni-erlangen.de*).

Additional testing and porting were done by David Lee (*T.D.Lee@durham.ac.uk*), Tobias Oetiker (*oetiker@ee.ethz.ch*), and Jim Hribnak (*hribnak@nucleus.com*).

See Also

perl(1), edquota(1m), quotactl(2) or quotactl(7I), mount(1m), mtab(4) or mnttab(4), quotaon(1m), setmntent(3), getmntent(3) or getmntinfo(3), endmntent(3), rpc(3), rquotad(1m)

SoftInstaller—Perl extension for generation of daughter packages for IBM's Software Installer

Synopsis

```
use OS2::SoftInstaller;
open PKG, '>my.pkg';
select PKG;
make_pkg toplevel => '.', zipfile => 'my.zip', packid => 'myzip',
  nozip => 0, exclude => undef, dirid => 'FILE', strip => 'emx/';
select STDOUT;
close PKG;
```

Description

Functions

`size_date_time_pkg(name)`

Takes file *name* and returns an array (*$size*, *$date*, *$time*) suitable for SoftInstaller SIZE, DATE, and TIME entries.

`make_pkg(...)`

The function `make_pkg()` takes a hash-like list of arguments. The recognized keys are:

`toplevel`

The top-level directory of the tree to duplicate.

`zipfile`

The name of the zipfile that corresponds to this directory in the distribution.

`packid`

The symbolic name for this zipfile, autogenerated if needed.

`nozip`

Do not generate the top-level description of the zipfile (this is useful if the same zipfile is used in multiple components).

`exclude`

If defined, this is a regexp for files to exclude from the generated package file.

`dirid`

The id of the directory to install to (e.g., FILE or AUX7).

`strip`

The prefix of all the files in the zipfile that should be removed. It is assumed that the default value for the directory to install to (eg, FILE or AUX7) already contains this prefix. (Useful for making the zipfile appropriate for manual install as well.)

We assume that `%unzip%` contains a value such as `unzip -oj`, `%unzip_d%` is something like `-d` (directory to extract), and the output of this script is included as follows into the parent package file.

```
FILE
  EXIT = 'setvar unzip=unzip -oj'
FILE
  EXIT = 'setvar unzip_d=-d'
```

```
INCLUDE
  NAME = 'my.pkg'
```

Author

Ilya Zakharevich, *ilya@math.ohio-state.edu*

See Also

perl(1)

Sys::AlarmCall—call to use the alarm handler

Synopsis

```
use Sys::AlarmCall;

$result = alarm_call($timeout1,$func1,@args1);
@result = alarm_call($timeout2,$func2,@args2);
```

Description

Sys::AlarmCall provides a straightforward function call to use the alarm handler. It also handles the logic that allows nested timeout calls if timeout calls are run through the `alarm_call()` functions.

The main advantages of Sys::AlarmCall are that:

- Simple calls, e.g.:

```
@result = &func(@args); #Normal function call with '&'
$result = func(@args);; #Normal function call
@result = &$code_reference(@args);
@result = $obj->func(@args); #Object method call
```

  become simple calls:

```
@result = alarm_call($timeout,'&func',@args);
$result = alarm_call($timeout,'func',@args);
@result = alarm_call($timeout,$code_reference,@args);
@result = alarm_call($timeout,'->func',$obj,@args);
```

  There's no need to deal with alarms and handlers or worry about where to intercept the timer or set globals.

- There's no need to worry if some subroutines within the call also set a timeout—this is handled logically by the Sys::AlarmCall package (as long as the subroutines also use the `alarm_call` function, of course. But if they don't, you're up the same creek anyway).

Function

Sys::AlarmCall exports one function:

alarm_call TIMEOUT, FUNCTION, ARGS

> TIMEOUT is a positive number; a fatal error occurs if TIMEOUT is not at least 1.

> FUNCTION is a string giving the function name (and an & if wanted, or preceded by -> (e.g. ->func) if using that; in that case, the calling object should be the first argument in ARGS).

ARGS is the list of arguments to the function.

Note: As a side effect of `alarm_call`, normally fatal errors in the FUNCTION call are caught and reported in the return.

In a scalar context, `alarm_call` returns the following:

* If the FUNCTION produces any sort of error (including fatal dies, which are trapped), it returns the error as a string, prepended by the value given by the variable $Sys::AlarmCall::SCALAR_ERROR (the default is ERROR).

* If the FUNCTION times out (i.e., if it doesn't return before TIMEOUT - 1), then it returns the value given by the variable $Sys::AlarmCall::TIMEOUT (the default is TIMEOUT).

* Otherwise, it returns the scalar that the FUNCTION returns.

In an array context, `alarm_call` returns the following:

* If the FUNCTION produces any sort of error (including fatal dies, which are trapped), it returns a two-element array. The first element is the value given by the variable $Sys::AlarmCall::ARRAY_ERROR (the default is ERROR), and the second element is the error string produced.

* If the FUNCTION times out (i.e., if it doesn't return before TIMEOUT - 1), then it returns a one-element array consisting of the value given by the variable $Sys::AlarmCall::TIMEOUT (the default is TIMEOUT).

* Otherwise, it returns the array that the FUNCTION returns.

Specific support for the `->` construct has been added to `alarm_call`, so that calling:

```
alarm_call($timeout,'->func',$obj,@args);
```

means that `alarm_call` translates this to:

```
$obj->func(@args);
```

Specific support for code references (e.g., $ref = sub {warn "this\n"}) has been added to `alarm_call`, so that calling:

```
alarm_call($timeout,$ref,@args);
```

means that `alarm_call` translates this to:

```
&{$ref}(@args);
```

Timers have resolutions of one second, but remember that a timeout value of 15 causes a timeout to occur at some point more than 14 seconds in the future. (See the `alarm()` function in the Perl manpage). Also, nested calls decrease the resolution (i.e., they make the uncertain interval larger) by one second per nesting depth. This is because an alarm call returns the time left, rounded up to the next second.

Examples

Example 1

```
use Sys::AlarmCall;
alarm_call(3,'select',undef,undef,undef,10);
```

This makes the `select()` system call, which should just block for ten seconds, but times it out after three seconds.

Example 2

```
use Sys::AlarmCall;
alarm_call(4,'read',STDIN,$r,5);
print $r;
```

This makes the read() system call, which should block until some characters are ready to be read from STDIN (after a return) and then should try to read up to five characters. However, the timeout of four seconds means that this call returns after four seconds if nothing has been read by then.

Example 3

```
use Sys::AlarmCall;
sub do1 {
    print "Hi, this is do1\n";
    select(undef,undef,undef,10);
    print "Bye from do1\n";
}
sub do2 {
    print "Hi, this is do2\n";
    alarm_call(5,'do1');
    print "Bye from do2\n";
}
sub do3 {
    print "Hi, this is do3\n";
    alarm_call(3,'do2');
    print "Bye from do3\n";
}
sub do4 {
    print "Hi, this is do4\n";
    alarm_call(8,'do2');
    print "Bye from do4\n";
}

foreach $test (('do1','do2','do3','do4')) {
    print "\n$test\n";
    $time = time;
    &$test;
    print "$test completed after ",
        time - $time ," seconds.\n";
}
```

In this example, when interrupts occur, you will see the "Hi" statement without the corresponding "Bye" statement.

do1 is a simple test that select() works correctly, delaying for 10 seconds. do2 is a simple test of alarm_call, testing that select() is interrupted after five seconds. The third and fourth "do"s are tests of nested calls to alarm_call. do3 should time out after three seconds, interrupting the call to do2 (so we should see no "bye" statement from do2). do4, on the other hand, has a timeout of eight seconds, so do2, which it calls and which is set to time out and return after five seconds, will complete, printing out its "bye" statement.

Warning: Using calls to alarm() in nested calls other than through the Sys::AlarmCall module may lead to inconsistencies. Calls to alarm *between* calls to alarm_call should be no problem. Any alarms pending are reset to the previous setting minus elapsed time (approximately) after a call to `alarm_call`. The alarm handler is also reset.

Bugs

Some Perl core calls (like `read` and `sysread`) don't cope when fed their arguments as an array. `alarm_call` explicitly specifies up to six arguments so that the Perl compiler reads them correctly. However, any core functions that take more than six arguments as a minimum are not accepted as valid by the compiler even if the correct number of arguments is passed. Consequently, if you want to time out on these specifically, you may need to wrap them in a subroutine.

Author

Jack Shirazi, *js@biu.icnet.uk*

Copyright

Copyright © 1995 Jack Shirazi. All rights reserved.

This program is free software; you can redistribute it and/or modify it under the same terms as Perl itself.

WaitStat—interpret and act on wait() status values

Synopsis

```
$description = waitstat $?;
exit waitstat_reuse $?;
waitstat_die $?, 'program-name';
close_die COMMAND, 'program-name';
```

Description

This module contains functions for interpreting and acting on wait status values. Nothing is exported by default.

Functions

waitstat *wait-status*

Returns a string representation of `wait()` status value *wait-status*. Returns values like 0, 64, and `killed` (SIGHUP).

This function is prototyped to take a single scalar argument.

waitstat_reuse *wait-status*

Turns *wait-status* into a value that can be passed to `exit`, converted in the same manner the shell uses. If *wait-status* indicates a normal exit, returns the exit value. If *wait-status* instead indicates death by signal, returns 128 plus the signal number.

This function is prototyped to take a single scalar argument.

waitstat_die *wait-status program-name*

`die()` if *wait-status* is non-zero (mentioning *program-name* as the source of the error).

This function is prototyped to take two scalar arguments.

close_die *filehandle name*

Close *filehandle*; if that fails, die() with an appropriate message that refers to *name*. This handles failed closings of both programs and files properly.

This function is prototyped to take a filehandle (actually, a glob ref) and a scalar.

Examples

```
close SENDMAIL;
exit if $? == 0;
log "sendmail failure: ", waitstat $?;
exit EX_TEMPFAIL;

$pid == waitpid $pid, 0 or croak "Failed to reap $pid: $!";
exit waitstat_reuse $?;

$output = 'some-program -with args';
waitstat_die $?, 'some-program';
print "Output from some-process:\n", $output;

open PROGRAM, '| post-processor' or die "Can't fork: $!";
while (<IN>) {
        print PROGRAM pre_process $_
            or die "Error writing to post-processor: $!";
}
# This handles both flush failures at close time and a non-zero exit
# from the subprocess.
close_die PROGRAM, 'post-processor';
```

Author

Roderick Schertler, *roderick@argon.org*

See Also

perl(1)

5

Networking, Devices, and InterProcess Communication

The modules in this section cover various networking protocols (such as TCP/IP, SNMP, and UDP) and network sockets. Also covered in this section are device controls, including controllers for modems, and modules working with shared memory.

DCE::ACL—Perl interface to DCE ACL client API

Synopsis

```
use DCE::ACL;
$aclh = DCE::ACL->bind($object);
```

Description

DCE::ACL provides a Perl interface to the **sec_acl_*** client API. As the **sec_acl_list_t** structure is rather complex, additional classes and methods are provided so that Perl scripts can deal with it in a reasonable fashion.

DCE::ACL::handle methods

DCE::ACL::handle->bind

See DCE::ACL-bind.

$aclh->num_acls

Returns the number of **acls** in the **sec_acl_list_t** structure.

```
$num = $aclh->num_acls
```

$aclh->get_manager_types

Equivalent to the **sec_acl_get_manager_types** function. **$manager_types** is an array reference.

```
($num_used, $num_types, $manager_types, $status) =
    $aclh->get_manager_types();
```

If called in a scalar context, only the $manager_types array reference is returned.

```
$manager = $aclh->get_manager_types->[0]; #first manager
```

$aclh->get_access

Equivalent to the sec_acl_get_access function.

```
($permset, $status) = $aclh->get_access($manager);
```

$aclh->get_printstring

Equivalent to the sec_acl_get_printstring function. $printstrings is an array reference of hash references.

```
($chain, $mgr_info, $tokenize, $total, $num, $printstrings,
$status) =
    $aclh->get_printstring($manager);
```

If called in a scalar context, only the $printstrings reference is returned.

```
$printstrings = $aclh->get_printstring($manager);
foreach $str (@$printstrings) {
    $permstr .=
        ($str->{permissions} & $entry->perms) ?
            $str->{printstring} : "-";
}
```

$aclh->test_access

Equivalent to the sec_acl_test_access function.

```
($ok, $status) = $aclh->test_access($manager, $perms);
```

$aclh->replace

Equivalent to the sec_acl_replace function.

```
$status = $aclh->replace($manager, $aclh->type_object, $list);
```

$aclh->lookup

Equivalent to the sec_acl_lookup function. $list is a reference to a sec_acl_list_t structure, blessed into the DCE::ACL::list class.

```
($list, $status) = $aclh->lookup($manager);
```

$aclh->new_list

This method does a lookup, deleting all entries and returning the empty list.

```
($list, $status) = $aclh->new_list($manager);
```

DCE::ACL::list methods

$list->acls

Returns a list of all acls if no index argument is given. When called in a scalar context, only the first acl is returned. Objects returned are references to sec_acl_t structures, blessed into the DCE::ACL class.

```
$acl = $list->acls;
```

DCE::ACL methods

DCE::ACL->bind

Equivalent to the sec_acl_bind function. Returns a reference to the sec_acl_list_t structure blessed into the DCE::ACL::handle class. The optional argument $bind_to_entry defaults to FALSE.

```
($aclh, $status) = DCE::ACL->bind($object, [$bind_to_entry]);
```

DCE::ACL->type
>   When given an integer argument, returns the string representation.
>
> $str = DCE::ACL->type(0); #returns 'user_obj'

DCE::ACL->type_*
>   A method is provided for each **sec_acl_type_t** type, returning an integer.
>
> $type = DCE::ACL->type_user;

$acl->num_entries
>   Returns the number of **sec_acl_entry_t** structures.
>
> $num = $acl->num_entries;

$acl->default_realm
>   Returns a hash reference with **uuid** and **name** keys.
>
> $name = $acl->default_realm->{name}; #/.../cell.foo.com

$acl->remove
>   Removes the specified entry from the **acl** structure, where entry is a reference to
>   sec_acl_entry_t structure, blessed into the DCE::ACL::entry class.
>
> $status = $acl->remove($entry);

$acl->delete
>   Removes all entries from the $acl, leaving only the **user_obj** entry, if present.

$acl->new_entry
>   Allocates memory needed for a new **sec_acl_entry_t** structure. Returns a reference to that structure, blessed into the DCE::ACL::entry class.
>
> $entry = $acl->new_entry;

$acl->add
>   Adds a **sec_acl_entry_t** structure to a **sec_acl_t** structure.
>
> $status = $acl->add($entry);

$acl->entries
>   Returns references to **sec_acl_entry_t** structures, blessed into the DCE::ACL::entry class. If an integer argument is given, only that entry is returned. Otherwise, a list of all entries is returned.
>
> $entry = $acl->entries(0); #return the first entry
>   foreach $entry ($acl->entries) { #return all entries
>   ...

DCE::ACL::entry methods

$entry->compare
>   Compares two **acl** entries. Returns **true** if they are the same and **false** otherwise.
>
> $match = $entry1->compare($entry2);

$entry->perms
>   Returns the permission bits for the specified entry, setting the bits if given an argument.
>
> $bits = $entry->perms;
>   for (qw(perm_read perm_control perm_insert)) {
> $bits |= DCE::ACL->$_();
>   }
> $e->perms($bits);

`$entry->entry_info`
> Returns a hash reference containing entry information, changing the information if given an argument.

```
$uuid = $entry->entry_info->{id}{uuid};
$entry->entry_info({
    entry_type => DCE::ACL->type_user,
    id => {
        uuid => $uuid,
    },
});
```

Author

Doug MacEachern, *dougm@osf.org*

See Also

perl(1), DCE::aclbase(3), DCE::Registry(3), DCE::UUID(3), DCE::Login(3), DCE::Status(3)

DCE::Login — Perl extension for interfacing to the DCE login API

Synopsis

```
use DCE::Login;
my($l, $status) = DCE::Login->get_current_context;
my $pwent = $l->get_pwent;
```

Description

Perl extension for interfacing to the DCE login API.

Author

Doug MacEachern, *dougm@osf.org*

See Also

perl(1), DCE::login_base(3), DCE::Registry(3)

DCE::login_base — constants from sec_login_*.h

Synopsis

```
use DCE::login_base;
```

Description

These constant methods are inherited by DCE::Login. A developer should not need to use this module and its methods directly.

Author

Doug MacEachern, *dougm@osf.org*

See Also

perl(1), DCE::Login(3), DCE::Registry(3)

DCE::Registry—Perl interface to DCE Registry API

Synopsis

```
use DCE::Registry;
my $rgy = DCE::Registry->site_open($site_name);
```

Description

This module provides an object-oriented Perl interface to the DCE Registry API. The `sec_` `rgy_` prefix has been dropped, and methods are invoked via a blessed `registry_` `context` object.

Author

Doug MacEachern, *dougm@osf.org*

See Also

perl(1), DCE::rgybase(3), DCE::Status(3), DCE::Login(3), DCE::UUID(3)

DCE::rgybase—constants from dce/rgybase.h

Synopsis

```
use DCE::rgybase;
```

Description

These constant methods are inherited by DCE::Registry. A developer should not need to use this module and its methods directly.

Here is a list of the available constants:

acct_admin_audit	acct_admin_client	acct_admin_flags_none
acct_admin_server	acct_admin_valid	acct_auth_dup_skey
acct_auth_flags_none	acct_auth_forwardable	acct_auth_post_dated
acct_auth_proxiable	acct_auth_renewable	acct_auth_tgt
acct_key_group	acct_key_last	acct_key_none
acct_key_org	acct_key_person	acct_user_flags_none
acct_user_passwd_valid	domain_group	domain_last
domain_org	domain_person	max_unix_passwd_len
name_max_len	name_t_size	no_override
no_resolve_pname	override	pgo_flags_none
pgo_is_an_alias	pgo_is_required	pgo_projlist_ok
plcy_pwd_flags_none	plcy_pwd_no_spaces	plcy_pwd_non_alpha

pname_max_len	pname_t_size	prop_auth_cert_ unbound
prop_embedded_unix_id	prop_readonly	prop_shadow_passwd
properties_none	quota_unlimited	resolve_pname
rgynbase_v0_0_included	status_ok	uxid_unknown
wildcard_name	wildcard_sid	

Author

Doug MacEachern, *dougm@osf.org*

See Also

perl(1), DCE::Registry(3), DCE::Login(3)

DCE::Status—make sense of DCE status codes

Synopsis

```
use DCE::Status;

$errstr = error_inq_text($status);
tie $status => DCE::Status;
```

Description

When a $scalar is tie'd to the DCE::Status class, it has a different value depending on the context it is evaluated in, similar to the magic $! variable. When evaluated in a numeric context, the numeric value is returned. Otherwise, the string value obtained from dce_error_inq_text is returned.

Exports

error_inq_text
   Equivalent to the dce_error_inq_text function.

```
$errstr = error_inq_text($status);
```

Author

Doug MacEachern, *dougm@osf.org*

See Also

perl(1), DCE::Registry(3), DCE::Login(3), DCE::ACL(3)

DCE::UUID—miscellaneous UUID functions

Synopsis

```
use DCE::UUID;
```

Description

DCE::UUID exports the following functions:

```
uuid_create()
        my($uuid, $status) = uuid_create();
uuid_hash()
        my($hash, $status) = uuid_hash($uuid);
```

Author

Doug MacEachern, *dougm@osf.org*

See Also

perl(1), DCE::Status(3), DCE::Registry(3), DCE::Login(3)

Net::Bind—load various Net::Bind modules

Synopsis

```
use Net::Bind;
```

Description

Net::Bind provides a simple mechanism to load all of the Net::Bind modules in one fell swoop.

Currently, this includes the following modules:

```
Net::Bind::Resolv
```

Futures releases will include:

```
Net::Bind::Boot
Net::Bind::Zone
Net::Bind::Dump
Net::Bind::Conf
```

Author

Kevin Johnson, *kjj@pobox.com*

Copyright

Copyright © 1997 Kevin Johnson, *kjj@pobox.com.*

Net::Bind::Resolv—a class to munge */etc/resolv.conf* data.

Synopsis

```
use Net::Bind::Resolv;
```

Description

This class provides an object-oriented Perl interface to */etc/resolv.conf* data.

Here is an example snippet of code:

```
use Net::Bind::Resolv;
my $res = new Net::Bind::Resolv('/etc/resolv.conf');
print $res->domain, "\n";
```

Or how about:

```
use Net::Bind::Resolv;
use IO::File;
my $res = new Net::Bind::Resolv;
$res->comment("Programmatically generated\nDo not edit by hand");
$res->domain('arf.fz');
$res->nameservers('0.0.0.0');
$res->options('debug');
print $res->as_string;
```

Methods

new([$filename])

> Returns a reference to a new Net::Bind::Resolv object. If $filename is given, then use that to pass the value to a call to read_from_file.

read_from_string($string)

> Populates the object with the parsed contents of $string. Returns 1 if no errors were encountered,; otherwise it returns 0.

> The following directives are understood:

domain DOMAIN
search SEARCHLIST...

> If a search directive and domain directive are found in the same file, the last one encountered is recorded and all previous ones are ignored.

nameserver IP_ADDR

> Each instance of a nameserver directive causes the given IP_ADDR to be remembered.

sortlist SORTLIST...
options OPTIONS...

> There are very few requirements placed on the data in $string. Multiple entries of certain directives, while technically incorrect, cause the last occurrence of the given directive to be the one remembered. If there is sufficient precedence for this to be otherwise, let me know.

> There is no requirement that the arguments to the directives be valid pieces of data. That job is delegated to local policy methods to be applied against the object.

read_from_file($filename)

> Populates the object with the parsed contents of $filename. This is really just a wrapper around read_from_string. Returns 0 if errors were encountered; otherwise it returns 1.

clear

> Zeros out the internal data in the object. This needs to be done if multiple read_from_string methods are called on a given Net::Bind::Resolv object and you do not want to retain the previous values in the object.

`domain([$domain])`

> Returns the value of the `domain` directive. If *$domain* is specified, then it sets the domain to the given value, and the `searchlist,` if defined in the object, is undefined.

`nameservers([@values])`

> Returns the list of nameserver entries in order. If called in an array context, it returns an array; otherwise it returns an array reference.

> If *@values* is specified, then it sets the nameserver list to the given values. Any items in *@values* that are list references are dereferenced as they are added.

`searchlist([@values])`

> Returns an array reference containing the items for the `search` directive. If called in an array context, it returns an array; otherwise it returns an array reference.

> If a list of values is specified, it sets the searchlist to those values, and the `domain,` if defined in the object, is undefined. Any items in *@values* that are list references are dereferenced as they are added.

`sortlist([@values])`

> Returns an array reference containing the items for the `sortlist` directive. If called in an array context, it returns an array; otherwise it returns an array reference.

> If a list of values is specified, then it sets the sortlist to those values. Any items in *@values* that are list references are dereferenced as they are added.

`options([@values])`

> Returns the items for the `options` directive. If called in an array context, it returns an array; otherwise it returns an array reference.

> If a list of values is specified, then sets the options to those values. Any items in *@values* that are list references are dereferenced as they are added.

`comments([@strings])`

> Returns the comments for the object. If called in an array context, it returns an array; otherwise it returns an array reference.

> If a list of strings is specified, then it sets the comments to those values after splitting the items on a NEWLINE boundary. This allows several combinations of arrays, array refs, or strings with embedded newlines to be specified. There is no need to prefix any of the comment lines with a comment character (`[;\#]`); the `as_string` automagically commentifies (:-) the comment strings.

> Any items in *@strings* that are list references are dereferenced as they are added.

`as_string`

> Returns a string representing the contents of the object. Technically, this string could be used to populate a *resolv.conf* file, but use `print` for that. The `print` method is a wrapper around this method. The data is generated in the following order:

```
comments
domain        (mutually exclusive with search)
search        (mutually exclusive with domain)
nameservers   (one line for each nameserver entry)
sortlist
options
```

print(*$fh*)

> A wrapper around **as_string** that prints a valid **resolver(5)** representation of the data in the object to the given filehandle.

check([*$policy*])

> Performs a policy/validity check of the data contained in the object using the given subroutine *&policy*. The given *$policy* routine is called as &$policy($self). If $policy is not given, it defaults to using **default_policy_check**. It returns the return status of the policy check routine.

default_policy_check

> A simple wrapper around various **check_*** methods.

check_domain

> Returns 1 if the domain member of the object is defined and is a valid RFC 1035 domain name; otherwise returns 0.

check_searchlist

> Returns 1 if the searchlist member of the object is defined and contains only valid RFC 1035 domain names; otherwise returns 0.

check_nameservers

> Returns 1 if the nameservers member of the object is defined and contains only IP addresses; otherwise returns 0.

> Uses **valid_ip** to do the real work.

check_sortlist

> Returns 1 if the sortlist member of the object is defined and contains only IP address/netmasks; otherwise returns 0.

> Uses **valid_netmask** to do the real work.

check_options

> Returns 1 if the options member of the object is empty or contains only valid options; otherwise returns 0.

> Currently recognized options are:

- debug
- ndots:N

qtynameservers

> Returns the quantity of nameserver entries present.

Caveats

The **read_from_{file|string}** methods and the **print** method are not isomorphic. Given an arbitrary file or string that is read in, the output of **print** is not guaranteed to be an exact duplicate of the original file. In the special case of files that are generated with this module, the results are isomorphic, assuming no modifications were made to the data between the time it was read in and when it was subsequently written back out.

Since Net::Bind::Resolv does not impose many requirements on the values of the various directives present in a */etc/resolv.conf* file, it is important to apply the appropriate policy methods against the object before writing it to a file that will be used by the resolver. Consider yourself warned!

Author

Kevin Johnson, *kjj@pobox.com*

Copyright

Copyright © 1997 Kevin Johnson, *kjj@pobox.com*.

Net::Bind::Utils—various routines common across Net::Bind packages.

Description

A catch-all place for various routines that are useful across most, if not all, of the Net::Bind interfaces.

This module is not designed to be subclassable.

Routines

valid_domain(*$domain*)

> Returns 1 if the given *$domain* string is defined and is a valid RFC 1035 domain name; otherwise returns 0.

valid_ip(*$ip*)

> Returns 1 if the given *$ip* string is defined and is an IP address; otherwise returns 0.

> The check for a valid IP address is currently very simple-minded. It merely checks for a dotted-quad consisting of all non-negative numbers with no number larger than 254.

valid_netmask(*$netmask*)

> Returns 1 if the given *$netmask* string is defined and is a netmask; otherwise returns 0.

> The check for a valid netmask is currently very simple-minded. It merely checks for a dotted-quad consisting of all non-negative numbers with no number larger than 255.

Author

Kevin Johnson, *kjj@pobox.com*

Copyright

Copyright © 1997 Kevin Johnson, *kjj@pobox.com*.

Net::Cmd—network command class (as used by FTP, SMTP, etc.)

Synopsis

```
use Net::Cmd;

@ISA = qw(Net::Cmd);
```

Description

Net::Cmd is a collection of methods that can be inherited by a subclass of IO::Handle. These methods implement the functionality required for a command-based protocol; for example, FTP and SMTP.

Methods

User

These methods provide a user interface to the Net::Cmd object:

debug(*VALUE*)

Sets the level of debug information for this object. If no argument is given, then the current state is returned. Otherwise, the state is changed to $value and the previous state is returned. Different packages may implement different levels of debug, but a non-zero value results in copies of all commands and responses also being sent to STDERR.

If *VALUE* is undef, then the debug level is set to the default debug level for the class.

This method can also be called as a static method to set or get the default debug level for a given class.

message()

Returns the text message returned from the last command.

code()

Returns the three-digit code from the last command. If a command is pending, then the value 0 is returned.

ok()

Returns non-zero if the last code value was greater than zero and less than 400. This holds true for most command servers. Servers where this does not hold may override this method.

status()

Returns the most significant digit of the current status code. If a command is pending, then CMD_PENDING is returned.

datasend(*DATA*)

Sends data to the remote server, converting LF to CRLF. Any line starting with a "." is prefixed with another ".". *DATA* may be an array or a reference to an array.

dataend()

Stops sending data to the remote server. This is done by ensuring that the data already sent ends with CRLF and then sending ".CRLF" to end the transmission. Once this data has been sent, **dataend** calls **response** and returns true if **response** returns CMD_OK.

Class

These methods are not intended to be called by the user, but are used or over-ridden by a subclass of Net::Cmd:

debug_print(*DIR, TEXT*)

> Prints debugging information. *DIR* denotes the direction, where *true* means that data is being sent to the server. Calls debug_text before printing to STDERR.

debug_text(*TEXT*)

> This method is called to print debugging information. *TEXT* is the text being sent. The method should return the text to be printed.

> This is primarily meant for the use of modules such as FTP, where passwords are sent but should not be displayed in the debugging information.

command(*CMD*[, *ARGS*, ...])

> Sends a command to the command server. All arguments are joined with a space character, CRLF is appended, and the resulting string is then sent to the command server.

> Returns undef upon failure.

unsupported()

> Sets the status code to 580 and the response text to "Unsupported command." Returns zero.

response()

> Obtains a response from the server. Upon success, the most significant digit of the status code is returned. Upon failure, such as a timeout, undef is returned.

parse_response(*TEXT*)

> This method is called by response as a method with one argument. It should return an array of two values: the three-digit status code and a flag that is true when this is part of a multi-line response and this line is not the last.

getline()

> Retrieves one line, delimited by CRLF, from the remote server. Returns undef upon failure.

> Note: If you use this method for any reason, please remember to add some debug_print calls to your method.

ungetline(*TEXT*)

> Ungets a line of text from the server.

read_until_dot()

> Reads data from the remote server until a line consisting of a single "." is received. Any lines starting with ".." has one "." removed.

> Returns a reference to a list containing the lines, or undef upon failure.

Exports

Net::Cmd exports six subroutines. Five of these (CMD_INFO, CMD_OK, CMD_MORE, CMD_REJECT and CMD_ERROR) correspond to possible results of response and status. The sixth is CMD_PENDING.

Author

Graham Barr, *gbarr@pobox.com*

Copyright

Net::DNS—Perl interface to the DNS resolver

Synopsis

```
use Net::DNS;
```

Description

Net::DNS is a collection of Perl modules to interface with the Domain Name System (DNS) resolver. It allows the programmer to perform queries that are beyond the capabilities of `gethostbyname` and `gethostbyaddr`.

Objects

Resolver Objects

> A resolver object is an instance of the Net::DNS::Resolver class. A program can have multiple resolver objects, each maintaining its own state information, such as the nameservers to be queried, whether recursion is desired, etc.

Packet Objects

> Net::DNS::Resolver queries return Net::DNS::Packet objects. Packet objects have five sections:

> - The header section, a Net::DNS::Header object
> - The question section, a list of Net::DNS::Question objects
> - The answer section, a list of Net::DNS::RR objects
> - The authority section, a list of Net::DNS::RR objects
> - The additional section, a list of Net::DNS::RR objects

Header Objects

> Net::DNS::Header objects represent the header section of a DNS packet.

Question Objects

> Net::DNS::Question objects represent the query section of a DNS packet.

RR Objects

> Net::DNS::RR is the base class for DNS resource record (RR) objects in the answer, authority, and additional sections of a DNS packet.

Methods

version

> Returns the version of Net::DNS.

> ```
> print Net::DNS->version;
> ```

See the manual pages listed above for class-specific methods.

Examples

The following examples show how to use the DNS modules. Please note that most of the examples are simple and expect a successful query and certain record types. See the demo scripts included with the source code for examples of more robust code.

```
#
# Look up a host's addresses.
#
use Net::DNS;
$res = new Net::DNS::Resolver;
$query = $res->search("foo.bar.com");
foreach $record ($query->answer) {
    print $record->address, "\n";
}


#
# Find the nameservers for a domain.
#
use Net::DNS;
$res = new Net::DNS::Resolver;
$query = $res->query("foo.com", "NS");
foreach $nameserver ($query->answer) {
    print $nameserver->nsdname, "\n";
}


#
# Find the MX records for a domain.
#
use Net::DNS;
$res = new Net::DNS::Resolver;
$query = $res->query("foo.com", "MX");
foreach $mxhost ($query->answer) {
    print $mxhost->preference, " ", $mxhost->exchange, "\n";
}


#
# Print a domain's SOA record in zone file format.
#
use Net::DNS;
$res = new Net::DNS::Resolver;
$query = $res->query("foo.com", "SOA");
($query->answer)[0]->print;


#
# Perform a zone transfer and print all the records.
#
use Net::DNS;
$res = new Net::DNS::Resolver;
$res->nameservers("ns.foo.com");
@zone = $res->axfr("foo.com");
foreach $rr (@zone) {
    $rr->print;
}
```

```
#
# Send a background query and do some other processing while
# waiting for the answer.
#
use Net::DNS;
$res = new Net::DNS::Resolver;
$socket = $res->bgsend("foo.bar.com");
until ($res->bgisready($socket)) {
    # do some work here
    # ...and some more here
}
$packet = $res->bgread($socket);
$packet->print;


#
# Send a background query and use select() to determine when the
#   answer has arrived.
#
use Net::DNS;
$res = new Net::DNS::Resolver;
$socket = $res->bgsend("foo.bar.com");
$rin = "";
vec($rin, $socket->fileno, 1) = 1;
# Add more descriptors to $rin if desired.
$timeout = 5;
$nfound = select($rout=$rin, undef, undef, $timeout);
if ($nfound < 1) {
    print "timed out after $timeout seconds\n";
}
elsif (vec($rout, $socket->fileno, 1) == 1) {
    $packet = $res->bgread($socket);
    $packet->print;
}
else {
    # Check for the other descriptors.
}
```

Copyright

Copyright © 1997 Michael Fuhr. All rights reserved. This program is free software; you can redistribute it and/or modify it under the same terms as Perl itself.

See Also

perl(1), Net::DNS::Resolver, Net::DNS::Packet, Net::DNS::Header, Net::DNS::Question, Net::DNS::RR, RFC 1035

Net::DNS::Header—DNS packet header class

Synopsis

```
use Net::DNS::Header;
```

Description

A Net::DNS::Header object represents the header portion of a DNS packet.

Methods

new

> Without an argument, new creates a header object appropriate for making a DNS query.
>
> ```
>         $header = new Net::DNS::Header;
>         $header = new Net::DNS::Header(\$data);
> ```
> If new is passed a reference to a scalar containing DNS packet data, it creates a header object from that data.
>
> Returns undef if unable to create a header object (e.g., if the data is incomplete).

print

> Dumps the header data to the standard output.
>
> ```
>         $header->print;
> ```

id

> Gets or sets the query identification number.
>
> ```
>         print "query id = ", $header->id, "\n";
>         $header->id(1234);
> ```

qr

> Gets or sets the query response flag.
>
> ```
>         print "query response flag = ", $header->qr, "\n";
>         $header->qr(0);
> ```

opcode

> Gets or sets the query opcode (the purpose of the query).
>
> ```
>         print "query opcode = ", $header->opcode, "\n";
>         $header->opcode("UPDATE");
> ```

aa

> Gets or sets the authoritative answer flag.
>
> ```
>         print "answer is ", $header->aa ? "" : "non-",
>     "authoritative\n";
>         $header->aa(0);
> ```

tc

> Gets or sets the truncated packet flag.
>
> ```
>         print "packet is ", $header->tc ? "" : "not ", "truncated\n";
>         $header->tc(0);
> ```

rd

> Gets or sets the recursion desired flag.
>
> ```
>         print "recursion was ", $header->rd ? "" : "not ",
>     "desired\n";
>         $header->rd(0);
> ```

ra

> Gets or sets the recursion available flag.
>
> ```
>         print "recursion is ", $header->ra ? "" : "not ",
>     "available\n";
>         $header->ra(0);
> ```

rcode

Gets or sets the query response code (the status of the query).

```
print "query response code = ", $header->rcode, "\n";
$header->rcode("SERVFAIL");
```

qdcount, zocount

Gets or sets the number of records in the question section of the packet. In dynamic update packets, this field is known as zocount and refers to the number of RRs in the zone section.

```
print "# of question records: ", $header->qdcount, "\n";
$header->qdcount(2);
```

ancount, prcount

Gets or sets the number of records in the answer section of the packet. In dynamic update packets, this field is known as prcount and refers to the number of RRs in the prerequisite section.

```
print "# of answer records: ", $header->ancount, "\n";
$header->ancount(5);
```

nscount, upcount

Gets or sets the number of records in the authority section of the packet. In dynamic update packets, this field is known as upcount and refers to the number of RRs in the update section.

```
print "# of authority records: ", $header->nscount, "\n";
$header->nscount(2);
```

arcount, adcount

Gets or sets the number of records in the additional section of the packet. In dynamic update packets, this field is known as adcount.

```
print "# of additional records: ", $header->arcount, "\n";
$header->arcount(3);
```

data

Returns the header data in binary format, appropriate for use in a DNS query packet.

```
$hdata = $header->data;
```

Copyright

Copyright © 1997 Michael Fuhr. All rights reserved. This program is free software; you can redistribute it and/or modify it under the same terms as Perl itself.

See Also

perl(1), Net::DNS, Net::DNS::Resolver, Net::DNS::Packet, Net::DNS::Question, Net::DNS::RR, RFC 1035 Section 4.1.1

Net::DNS::Packet—DNS packet object class

Synopsis

```
use Net::DNS::Packet;
```

Description

A Net::DNS::Packet object represents a DNS packet.

Methods

new

> If new is passed a reference to a scalar containing DNS packet data, it creates a packet object from that data. A second argument can be passed to turn on debugging output for packet parsing.
>
> ```
> $packet = new Net::DNS::Packet(\$data);
> $packet = new Net::DNS::Packet(\$data, 1);  # set debugging
> $packet = new Net::DNS::Packet("foo.com", "MX", "IN");
> ```
>
> ```
> ($packet, $err) = new Net::DNS::Packet(\$data);
> ```
>
> If passed a domain, type, and class, new creates a packet object appropriate for making a DNS query for the requested information.
>
> If called in array context, new returns a packet object and an error string. The error string is defined only if the packet object is undefined (i.e., can't be created).
>
> Returns undef if it is unable to create a packet object (e.g., if the packet data is truncated).

data

> Returns the packet data in binary format, suitable for sending to a nameserver.
>
> ```
> $data = $packet->data;
> ```

header

> Returns a Net::DNS::Header object representing the header section of the packet.
>
> ```
> $header = $packet->header;
> ```

question, zone

> Returns a list of Net::DNS::Question objects representing the question section of the packet.
>
> ```
> @question = $packet->question;
> ```
>
> In dynamic update packets, this section is known as zone and specifies the zone to be updated.

answer, pre, prerequisite

> Returns a list of Net::DNS::RR objects representing the answer section of the packet.
>
> ```
> @answer = $packet->answer;
> ```
>
> In dynamic update packets, this section is known as pre or prerequisite and specifies the RRs or RRsets, which must (not) preexist.

authority, update

> Returns a list of Net::DNS::RR objects representing the authority section of the packet.
>
> ```
> @authority = $packet->authority;
> ```
>
> In dynamic update packets, this section is known as update and specifies the RRs or RRsets to be added or deleted.

additional
> Returns a list of Net::DNS::RR objects representing the additional section of the packet.
>
> ```
> @additional = $packet->additional;
> ```

print
> Prints the packet data on the standard output in an ASCII format similar to that used in DNS zone files.
>
> ```
> $packet->print;
> ```

dn_expand
> Expands the domain name stored at a particular location in a DNS packet. The first argument is a reference to a scalar containing the packet data. The second argument is the offset within the packet where the (possibly compressed) domain name is stored.
>
> ```
> ($name, $nextoffset) = dn_expand(\$data, $offset);
> ```
>
> Returns the domain name and the offset of the next location in the packet.
>
> Returns (undef, undef) if the domain name couldn't be expanded.

Copyright

Copyright © 1997 Michael Fuhr. All rights reserved. This program is free software; you can redistribute it and/or modify it under the same terms as Perl itself.

See Also

perl(1), Net::DNS, Net::DNS::Resolver, Net::DNS::Header, Net::DNS::Question, Net::DNS::RR, RFC 1035 Section 4.1

Net::DNS::Question — DNS question class

Synopsis

```
use Net::DNS::Question
```

Description

A Net::DNS::Question object represents a record in the question section of a DNS packet.

Methods

new
> Creates a question object from the domain, type, and class passed as arguments.
>
> ```
> $question = new Net::DNS::Question("foo.com", "MX", "IN");
> ```

qname, zname
> Returns the domain name. In dynamic update packets, this field is known as zname and refers to the zone name.
>
> ```
> print "qname = ", $question->qname, "\n";
> ```

qtype, ztype
> Returns the record type. In dymamic update packets, this field is known as ztype and refers to the zone type (must be SOA).
>
> ```
> print "qtype = ", $question->qtype, "\n";
> ```

qclass, zclass

> Returns the record class. In dynamic update packets, this field is known as zclass and refers to the zone's class.
>
> ```
> print "qclass = ", $question->qclass, "\n";
> ```

print

> Prints the question record on the standard output.
>
> ```
> $question->print;
> ```

data

> Returns the question record in binary format suitable for inclusion in a DNS packet.
>
> ```
> $qdata = $question->data;
> ```

Copyright

Copyright © 1997 Michael Fuhr. All rights reserved. This program is free software; you can redistribute it and/or modify it under the same terms as Perl itself.

See Also

perl(1), Net::DNS, Net::DNS::Resolver, Net::DNS::Packet, Net::DNS::Header, Net::DNS::RR, RFC 1035 Section 4.1.2

Net::DNS::Resolver—DNS resolver class

Synopsis

```
use Net::DNS::Resolver;
```

Description

Instances of the Net::DNS::Resolver class represent resolver objects. A program can have multiple resolver objects, each maintaining its own state information, such as the nameservers to be queried, whether recursion is desired, etc.

The resolver configuration is read from the following files, in the order indicated:

```
/etc/resolv.conf
$HOME/.resolv.conf
././.resolv.conf
```

The following keywords are recognized in resolver configuration files:

domain

> The default domain.

search

> A space-separated list of domains to put in the search list.

nameserver

> A space-separated list of nameservers to query.

Files, except for */etc/resolv.conf,* must be owned by the effective user ID running the program, or they won't be read. In addition, several environment variables can also contain configuration information; see the "Environment" section.

Methods

new

Creates a new DNS resolver object.

```
$res = new Net::DNS::Resolver;
```

print

Prints the resolver state on the standard output.

```
$res->print;
```

searchlist

Gets or sets the resolver search list.

```
@searchlist = $res->searchlist;
$res->searchlist("foo.com", "bar.com", "baz.org");
```

nameservers

Gets or sets the nameservers to be queried.

```
@nameservers = $res->nameservers;
$res->nameservers("192.168.1.1", "192.168.2.2",
                  "192.168.3.3");
```

port

Gets or sets the port to which we send queries. This can be useful for testing a nameserver running on a non-standard port. The default is port 53.

```
print "sending queries to port ", $res->port, "\n";
$res->port(9732);
```

search

Performs a DNS query for the given name, applying the search list, if appropriate.

```
$packet = $res->search("mailhost");
$packet = $res->search("mailhost.foo.com");
$packet = $res->search("192.168.1.1");
$packet = $res->search("foo.com", "MX");
$packet = $res->search("user.passwd.foo.com", "TXT", "HS");
```

The search algorithm is as follows:

1. If the name contains at least one dot, try it as is.

2. If the name doesn't end in a dot, then append each item in the search list to the name. This is done only if dnsrch is true.

3. If the name doesn't contain any dots, try it as is.

The record type and class can be omitted; they default to A and IN. If the name looks like an IP address (four dot-separated numbers), then an appropriate PTR query is performed.

Returns a Net::DNS::Packet object, or undef if no answers are found.

query

Performs a DNS query for the given name; the search list is not applied. If the name doesn't contain any dots and defnames is true, then the default domain is appended.

```
$packet = $res->query("mailhost");
$packet = $res->query("mailhost.foo.com");
$packet = $res->query("192.168.1.1");
$packet = $res->query("foo.com", "MX");
$packet = $res->query("user.passwd.foo.com", "TXT", "HS");
```

The record type and class can be omitted; they default to A and IN. If the name looks like an IP address (four dot-separated numbers), then an appropriate PTR query is performed.

Returns a Net::DNS::Packet object, or **undef** if no answers are found.

send

Performs a DNS query for the given name. Neither the search list nor the default domain is appended.

```
$packet = $res->send($packet_object);
$packet = $res->send("mailhost.foo.com");
$packet = $res->send("foo.com", "MX");
$packet = $res->send("user.passwd.foo.com", "TXT", "HS");
```

The argument list can be either a Net::DNS::Packet object or a list of strings. The record type and class can be omitted; they default to A and IN. If the name looks like an IP address (four dot-separated numbers), then an appropriate PTR query is performed.

Returns a Net::DNS::Packet object whether there were any answers or not. Use **$packet->header->ancount** or **$packet->answer** to find out if there were any records in the answer section. Returns undef if there was an error.

bgsend

Performs a background DNS query for the given name; i.e., sends a query packet to the first nameserver listed in **$res->nameservers** and returns immediately without waiting for a response. The program can then perform other tasks while waiting for a response from the nameserver.

```
$socket = $res->bgsend($packet_object);
$socket = $res->bgsend("mailhost.foo.com");
$socket = $res->bgsend("foo.com", "MX");
$socket = $res->bgsend("user.passwd.foo.com", "TXT", "HS");
```

The argument list can be either a Net::DNS::Packet object or a list of strings. The record type and class can be omitted; they default to A and IN. If the name looks like an IP address (four dot-separated numbers), then an appropriate PTR query is performed.

Returns an IO::Socket object. The program must determine when the socket is ready for reading and call **$res->bgread** to get the response packet. You can use **$res->bgisready** to find out if the socket is ready, or you can use **vec** and the socket's **fileno** method to add the socket's file descriptor to a bitmask for **select**.

bgread

Reads the answer from a background query (see **bgsend** above). The argument is an IO::Socket object returned by **bgsend**.

```
$packet = $res->bgread($socket);
```

Returns a Net::DNS::Packet object or **undef** on error.

bgisready

Determines whether a socket is ready for reading. The argument is an IO::Socket object returned by **$res->bgsend**.

```
$socket = $res->bgsend("foo.bar.com");
until ($res->bgisready($socket)) {
```

```
            # do some other processing
        }
        $packet = $res->bgread($socket);
```

Returns **true** if the socket is ready, **false** if not.

axfr

Performs a zone transfer from the first nameserver listed in **nameservers**. The record class can be omitted; it defaults to IN.

```
        @zone = $res->axfr("foo.com");
        @zone = $res->axfr("passwd.foo.com", "HS");
```

Returns a list of Net::DNS::RR objects, or **undef** if the zone transfer failed.

retrans

Gets or sets the retransmission interval. The default is 5.

```
        print "retrans interval", $res->retrans, "\n";
        $res->retrans(3);
```

retry

Gets or sets the number of times to try the query. The default is 4.

```
        print "number of tries: ", $res->retry, "\n";
        $res->retry(2);
```

recurse

Gets or sets the **recursion** flag. If this flag is true, nameservers are requested to perform a recursive query. The default is true.

```
        print "recursion flag: ", $res->recurse, "\n";
        $res->recurse(0);
```

defnames

Gets or sets the **defnames** flag. If this flag is true, calls to **query** append the default domain to names that contain no dots. The default is true.

```
        print "defnames flag: ", $res->defnames, "\n";
        $res->defnames(0);
```

dnsrch

Gets or sets the **dnsrch** flag. If this flag is true, calls to **search** apply the search list. The default is true.

```
        print "dnsrch flag: ", $res->dnsrch, "\n";
        $res->dnsrch(0);
```

debug

Gets or sets the **debug** flag. If set, calls to **search**, **query**, and **send** print debugging information on the standard output. The default is false.

```
        print "debug flag: ", $res->debug, "\n";
        $res->debug(1);
```

usevc (not yet implemented)

Gets or sets the **usevc** flag. If true, then queries are performed using virtual circuits (TCP) instead of datagrams (UDP). The default is false.

```
        print "usevc flag: ", $res->usevc, "\n";
        $res->usevc(1);
```

igntc (not yet implemented)

Gets or sets the **igntc** flag. If true, truncated packets are ignored. If false, truncated packets cause the query to be retried using TCP. The default is false.

```
print "igntc flag: ", $res->igntc, "\n";
$res->igntc(1);
```

errorstring

Returns a string containing the status of the most recent query.

```
print "query status: ", $res->errorstring, "\n";
```

Environment

The following environment variables can also be used to configure the resolver:

RES_NAMESERVERS

A space-separated list of nameservers to query.

```
# Bourne Shell
RES_NAMESERVERS="192.168.1.1 192.168.2.2 192.168.3.3"
export RES_NAMESERVERS

# C Shell
setenv RES_NAMESERVERS "192.168.1.1 192.168.2.2 192.168.3.3"
```

RES_SEARCHLIST

A space-separated list of domains to put in the search list.

```
# Bourne Shell
RES_SEARCHLIST="foo.com bar.com baz.org"
export RES_SEARCHLIST

# C Shell
setenv RES_SEARCHLIST "foo.com bar.com baz.org"
```

LOCALDOMAIN

The default domain.

```
# Bourne Shell
LOCALDOMAIN=foo.com
export LOCALDOMAIN

# C Shell
setenv LOCALDOMAIN foo.com
```

RES_OPTIONS

A space-separated list of resolver options to set. Options that take values are specified as *option:value*.

```
# Bourne Shell
RES_OPTIONS="retrans:3 retry:2 debug"
export RES_OPTIONS

# C Shell
setenv RES_OPTIONS "retrans:3 retry:2 debug"
```

Bugs

TCP queries are not yet implemented.

Error reporting needs to be improved.

Copyright

Copyright © 1997 Michael Fuhr. All rights reserved. This program is free software; you can redistribute it and/or modify it under the same terms as Perl itself.

See Also

perl(1), Net::DNS, Net::DNS::Packet, Net::DNS::Header, Net::DNS::Question, Net::DNS::RR, resolver(5), RFC 1035

Net::DNS::RR — DNS Resource Record class

Synopsis

```
use Net::DNS::RR
```

Description

Net::DNS::RR is the base class for DNS Resource Record (RR) objects. See also the manual pages for each RR type.

Methods

print

Prints the record to the standard output. Calls the **string** method to get the RR's string representation.

```
$rrobj->print;
```

string

Returns a string representation of the RR. Calls the **rdatastr** method to get the RR-specific data.

```
print $rrobj->string, "\n";
```

rdatastr

Returns a string containing RR-specific data. Subclasses need to implement this method.

```
$s = $rrobj->rdatastr;
```

name

Returns the record's domain name.

```
$name = $rrobj->name;
```

type

Returns the record's type.

```
$type = $rrobj->type;
```

class

Returns the record's class.

```
$class = $rrobj->class;
```

ttl

Returns the record's time-to-live (TTL).

```
$ttl = $rrobj->ttl;
```

Copyright

Copyright © 1997 Michael Fuhr. All rights reserved. This program is free software; you can redistribute it and/or modify it under the same terms as Perl itself.

See Also

perl(1), Net::DNS, Net::DNS::Resolver, Net::DNS::Packet, Net::DNS::Header, Net::DNS::Question, RFC 1035 Section 4.1.3

Net::DNS::RR::A——DNS A resource record

Synopsis

```
    use Net::DNS::RR;
```

Description

Class for DNS Address (A) resource records.

Methods

address
>   Returns the RR's **address** field.
>
> ```
>         print "address = ", $rr->address, "\n";
> ```

Copyright

Copyright © 1997 Michael Fuhr. All rights reserved. This program is free software; you can redistribute it and/or modify it under the same terms as Perl itself.

See Also

perl(1), Net::DNS, Net::DNS::Resolver, Net::DNS::Packet, Net::DNS::Header, Net::DNS::Question, Net::DNS::RR, RFC 1035 Section 3.4.1

Net::DNS::RR::AFSDB——DNS AFSDB resource record

Synopsis

```
    use Net::DNS::RR;
```

Description

Class for DNS AFS database (AFSDB) resource records.

Methods

subtype
>   Returns the RR's **subtype** field. Use of the **subtype** field is documented in RFC 1183.
>
> ```
>         print "subtype = ", $rr->subtype, "\n";
> ```

hostname
>   Returns the RR's **hostname** field. See RFC 1183.
>
> ```
>         print "hostname = ", $rr->hostname, "\n";
> ```

Copyright

See Also

perl(1), Net::DNS, Net::DNS::Resolver, Net::DNS::Packet, Net::DNS::Header, Net::DNS::Question, Net::DNS::RR, RFC 1183 Section 1

Net::DNS::RR::CNAME—DNS CNAME resource record

Synopsis

```
use Net::DNS::RR;
```

Description

Class for DNS Canonical Name (CNAME) resource records.

Method

cname

> Returns the RR's canonical name.
>
> ```
> print "cname = ", $rr->cname, "\n";
> ```

Copyright

See Also

perl(1), Net::DNS, Net::DNS::Resolver, Net::DNS::Packet, Net::DNS::Header, Net::DNS::Question, Net::DNS::RR, RFC 1035 Section 3.3.1

Net::DNS::RR::HINFO—DNS HINFO resource record

Synopsis

```
use Net::DNS::RR;
```

Description

Class for DNS Host Information (HINFO) resource records.

Methods

cpu

> Returns the CPU type for this RR.
>
> ```
> print "cpu = ", $rr->cpu, "\n";
> ```

os

> Returns the operating system type for this RR.
>
> ```
> print "os = ", $rr->os, "\n";
> ```

Author

Michael Fuhr

Copyright

Copyright © 1997 Michael Fuhr. All rights reserved. This program is free software; you can redistribute it and/or modify it under the same terms as Perl itself.

See Also

perl(1), Net::DNS, Net::DNS::Resolver, Net::DNS::Packet, Net::DNS::Header, Net::DNS::Question, Net::DNS::RR, RFC 1035 Section 3.3.2

Net::DNS::RR::ISDN—DNS ISDN resource record

Synopsis

```
use Net::DNS::RR;
```

Description

Class for DNS ISDN resource records.

Methods
address

Returns the RR's **address** field.

```
print "address = ", $rr->address, "\n";
```

sa

Returns the RR's **subaddress** field.

```
print "subaddress = ", $rr->sa, "\n";
```

Author

Michael Fuhr

Copyright

Copyright © 1997 Michael Fuhr. All rights reserved. This program is free software; you can redistribute it and/or modify it under the same terms as Perl itself.

See Also

perl(1), Net::DNS, Net::DNS::Resolver, Net::DNS::Packet, Net::DNS::Header, Net::DNS::Question, Net::DNS::RR, RFC 1183 Section 3.2

Net::DNS::RR::LOC—DNS LOC resource record

Synopsis

```
use Net::DNS::RR;
```

Description

Class for DNS Location (LOC) resource records. See RFC 1876 for details.

Methods

`version`

Returns the version number of the representation; programs should always check this. Net::DNS currently supports only version 0.

```
print "version = ", $rr->version, "\n";
```

`size`

Returns the diameter of a sphere enclosing the described entity, in centimeters.

```
print "size = ", $rr->size, "\n";
```

`horiz_pre`

Returns the horizontal precision of the data, in centimeters.

```
print "horiz_pre = ", $rr->horiz_pre, "\n";
```

`vert_pre`

Returns the vertical precision of the data, in centimeters.

```
print "vert_pre = ", $rr->vert_pre, "\n";
```

`latitude`

Returns the latitude of the center of the sphere described by the **size** method, in thousandths of a second of arc. $2^{**}31$ represents the equator; numbers above that are North latitude.

```
print "latitude = ", $rr->latitude, "\n";
```

`longitude`

Returns the longitude of the center of the sphere described by the **size** method, in thousandths of a second of arc. $2^{**}31$ represents the prime meridian; numbers above that are East longitude.

```
print "longitude = ", $rr->longitude, "\n";
```

`latlon`

Returns the latitude and longitude as floating-point degrees. Positive numbers represent North latitude or East longitude; negative numbers represent South latitude or West longitude.

```
($lat, $lon) = $rr->latlon;
system("xearth", "-pos", "fixed $lat $lon");
```

`altitude`

Returns the altitude of the center of the sphere described by the **size** method, in centimeters, from a base of 100,000m below the WGS 84 reference spheroid used by GPS.

```
print "altitude = ", $rr->altitude, "\n";
```

Author

Michael Fuhr

Copyright

See Also

perl(1), Net::DNS, Net::DNS::Resolver, Net::DNS::Packet, Net::DNS::Header, Net::DNS::Question, Net::DNS::RR, RFC 1876

Net::DNS::RR::MG—DNS MG resource record

Synopsis

```
use Net::DNS::RR;
```

Description

Class for DNS Mail Group (MG) resource records.

Methods

mgmname

> Returns the RR's mailbox field.

```
print "mgmname = ", $rr->mgmname, "\n";
```

Author

Michael Fuhr

Copyright

Copyright © 1997 Michael Fuhr. All rights reserved. This program is free software; you can redistribute it and/or modify it under the same terms as Perl itself.

See Also

perl(1), Net::DNS, Net::DNS::Resolver, Net::DNS::Packet, Net::DNS::Header, Net::DNS::Question, Net::DNS::RR, RFC 1035 Section 3.3.6

Net::DNS::RR::MINFO—DNS MINFO resource record

Synopsis

```
use Net::DNS::RR;
```

Description

Class for DNS Mailbox Information (MINFO) resource records.

Methods

rmailbx

> Returns the RR's responsible mailbox field. See RFC 1035.

```
print "rmailbx = ", $rr->rmailbx, "\n";
```

emailbx

> Returns the RR's error mailbox field.

```
print "emailbx = ", $rr->emailbx, "\n";
```

Author

Michael Fuhr

Copyright

Copyright © 1997 Michael Fuhr. All rights reserved. This program is free software; you can redistribute it and/or modify it under the same terms as Perl itself.

See Also

perl(1), Net::DNS, Net::DNS::Resolver, Net::DNS::Packet, Net::DNS::Header, Net::DNS::Question, Net::DNS::RR, RFC 1035 Section 3.3.7

Net::DNS::RR::MR— DNS MR resource record

Synopsis

```
use Net::DNS::RR;
```

Description

Class for DNS Mail Rename (MR) resource records.

Methods

newname

Returns the RR's **newname** field.

```
print "newname = ", $rr->newname, "\n";
```

Author

Michael Fuhr

Copyright

Copyright © 1997 Michael Fuhr. All rights reserved. This program is free software; you can redistribute it and/or modify it under the same terms as Perl itself.

See Also

perl(1), Net::DNS, Net::DNS::Resolver, Net::DNS::Packet, Net::DNS::Header, Net::DNS::Question, Net::DNS::RR, RFC 1035 Section 3.3.8

Net::DNS::RR::MX— DNS MX resource record

Synopsis

```
use Net::DNS::RR;
```

Description

Class for DNS Mail Exchanger (MX) resource records.

Methods

preference

> Returns the preference for this mail exchange.

```
print "preference = ", $rr->preference, "\n";
```

exchange

> Returns the name of this mail exchange.

```
print "exchange = ", $rr->exchange, "\n";
```

Author

Michael Fuhr

Copyright

Copyright © 1997 Michael Fuhr. All rights reserved. This program is free software; you can redistribute it and/or modify it under the same terms as Perl itself.

See Also

perl(1), Net::DNS, Net::DNS::Resolver, Net::DNS::Packet, Net::DNS::Header, Net::DNS::Question, Net::DNS::RR, RFC 1035 Section 3.3.9

Net::DNS::RR::NAPTR—DNS NAPTR resource record

Synopsis

```
use Net::DNS::RR;
```

Description

Class for DNS NAPTR resource records.

Methods

order

> Returns the order field.

```
print "order = ", $rr->order, "\n";
```

preference

> Returns the preference field.

```
print "preference = ", $rr->preference, "\n";
```

flags

> Returns the flags field.

```
print "flags = ", $rr->flags, "\n";
```

service

> Returns the service field.

```
print "service = ", $rr->service, "\n";
```

regexp

> Returns the regexp field.

```
print "regexp = ", $rr->regexp, "\n";
```

replacement
> Returns the `replacement` field.

            print "replacement = ", $rr->replacement, "\n";

Copyright

Copyright © 1997 Michael Fuhr. All rights reserved. This program is free software; you can redistribute it and/or modify it under the same terms as Perl itself.

Net::DNS::RR::NAPTR is based on code contributed by Ryan Moats.

See Also

perl(1), Net::DNS, Net::DNS::Resolver, Net::DNS::Packet, Net::DNS::Header, Net::DNS::Question, Net::DNS::RR, *draft-ietf-urn-naptr-xx.txt*

Net::DNS::RR::NS— DNS NS resource record

Synopsis

            use Net::DNS::RR;

Description

Class for DNS Name Server (NS) resource records.

Method

nsdname
> Returns the domain name of the nameserver.

            print "nsdname = ", $rr->nsdname, "\n";

Copyright

Copyright © 1997 Michael Fuhr. All rights reserved. This program is free software; you can redistribute it and/or modify it under the same terms as Perl itself.

See Also

perl(1), Net::DNS, Net::DNS::Resolver, Net::DNS::Packet, Net::DNS::Header, Net::DNS::Question, Net::DNS::RR, RFC 1035 Section 3.3.11

Net::DNS::RR::PTR— DNS PTR resource record

Synopsis

            use Net::DNS::RR;

Description

Class for DNS Pointer (PTR) resource records.

Method

ptrdname
> Returns the domain name associated with this record.

            print "ptrdname = ", $rr->ptrdname, "\n";

Copyright

Copyright © 1997 Michael Fuhr. All rights reserved. This program is free software; you can redistribute it and/or modify it under the same terms as Perl itself.

See Also

perl(1), Net::DNS, Net::DNS::Resolver, Net::DNS::Packet, Net::DNS::Header, Net::DNS::Question, Net::DNS::RR, RFC 1035 Section 3.3.12

Net::DNS::RR::RP—DNS RP resource record

Synopsis

```
use Net::DNS::RR;
```

Description

Class for DNS Responsible Person (RP) resource records.

Methods

mbox

Returns a domain name that specifies the mailbox for the responsible person.

```
print "mbox = ", $rr->mbox, "\n";
```

txtdname

Returns a domain name that specifies a TXT record containing further information about the responsible person.

```
print "txtdname = ", $rr->txtdname, "\n";
```

Copyright

Copyright © 1997 Michael Fuhr. All rights reserved. This program is free software; you can redistribute it and/or modify it under the same terms as Perl itself.

See Also

perl(1), Net::DNS, Net::DNS::Resolver, Net::DNS::Packet, Net::DNS::Header, Net::DNS::Question, Net::DNS::RR, RFC 1183 Section 2.2

Net::DNS::RR::RT—DNS RT resource record

Synopsis

```
use Net::DNS::RR;
```

Description

Class for DNS Route Through (RT) resource records.

Methods

preference

Returns the preference for this route.

```
print "preference = ", $rr->preference, "\n";
```

intermediate
> Returns the domain name of the intermediate host.
>
> ```
> print "intermediate = ", $rr->intermediate, "\n";
> ```

Copyright

Copyright © 1997 Michael Fuhr. All rights reserved. This program is free software; you can redistribute it and/or modify it under the same terms as Perl itself.

See Also

perl(1), Net::DNS, Net::DNS::Resolver, Net::DNS::Packet, Net::DNS::Header, Net::DNS::Question, Net::DNS::RR, RFC 1183 Section 3.3

Net::DNS::RR::SOA —DNS SOA resource record

Synopsis

```
use Net::DNS::RR;
```

Description

Class for DNS Start of Authority (SOA) resource records.

Methods

mname
> Returns the domain name of the original or primary nameserver for this zone.
>
> ```
> print "mname = ", $rr->mname, "\n";
> ```

rname
> Returns a domain name that specifies the mailbox for the person responsible for this zone.
>
> ```
> print "rname = ", $rr->rname, "\n";
> ```

serial
> Returns the zone's serial number.
>
> ```
> print "serial = ", $rr->serial, "\n";
> ```

refresh
> Returns the zone's refresh interval.
>
> ```
> print "refresh = ", $rr->refresh, "\n";
> ```

retry
> Returns the zone's retry interval.
>
> ```
> print "retry = ", $rr->retry, "\n";
> ```

expire
> Returns the zone's expire interval.
>
> ```
> print "expire = ", $rr->expire, "\n";
> ```

minimum
> Returns the minimum (default) TTL for records in this zone.
>
> ```
> print "minimum = ", $rr->minimum, "\n";
> ```

Copyright

Copyright © 1997 Michael Fuhr. All rights reserved. This program is free software; you can redistribute it and/or modify it under the same terms as Perl itself.

See Also

perl(1), Net::DNS, Net::DNS::Resolver, Net::DNS::Packet, Net::DNS::Header, Net::DNS::Question, Net::DNS::RR, RFC 1035 Section 3.3.13

Net::DNS::RR::SRV—DNS SRV resource record

Synopsis

```
use Net::DNS::RR;
```

Description

Class for DNS Service (SRV) resource records.

Methods

`priority`

> Returns the priority for this target host.

```
print "priority = ", $rr->priority, "\n";
```

`weight`

> Returns the weight for this target host.

```
print "weight = ", $rr->weight, "\n";
```

`port`

> Returns the port on this target host for the service.

```
print "port = ", $rr->port, "\n";
```

`target`

> Returns the target host.

```
print "target = ", $rr->target, "\n";
```

Copyright

Copyright © 1997 Michael Fuhr. All rights reserved. This program is free software; you can redistribute it and/or modify it under the same terms as Perl itself.

See Also

perl(1), Net::DNS, Net::DNS::Resolver, Net::DNS::Packet, Net::DNS::Header, Net::DNS::Question, Net::DNS::RR, RFC 2052

Net::DNS::RR::TXT—DNS TXT resource record

Synopsis

```
use Net::DNS::RR;
```

Description

Class for DNS Text (TXT) resource records.

Method

txtdata

> Returns the descriptive text.

```
print "txtdata = ", $rr->txtdata, "\n";
```

Copyright

Copyright © 1997 Michael Fuhr. All rights reserved. This program is free software; you can redistribute it and/or modify it under the same terms as Perl itself.

See Also

perl(1), Net::DNS, Net::DNS::Resolver, Net::DNS::Packet, Net::DNS::Header, Net::DNS::Question, Net::DNS::RR, RFC 1035 Section 3.3.14

Net::DNS::RR::X25 — DNS X25 resource record

Synopsis

```
use Net::DNS::RR;
```

Description

Class for DNS X25 resource records.

Method

psdn

> Returns the PSDN address.

```
print "psdn = ", $rr->psdn, "\n";
```

Copyright

Copyright © 1997 Michael Fuhr. All rights reserved. This program is free software; you can redistribute it and/or modify it under the same terms as Perl itself.

See Also

perl(1), Net::DNS, Net::DNS::Resolver, Net::DNS::Packet, Net::DNS::Header, Net::DNS::Question, Net::DNS::RR, RFC 1183 Section 3.1

Net::Domain — attempt to evaluate the current host's Internet name and domain

Synopsis

```
use Net::Domain qw(hostname hostfqdn hostdomain);
```

Description

Using various methods, attempt to find the fully qualified domain name (FQDN) of the current host. From this, determine the hostname and the host domain.

Each of the functions returns **undef** if the FQDN cannot be determined.

> `hostfqdn()`
>> Identifies and returns the FQDN of the current host.
>
> `hostname()`
>> Returns the smallest part of the FQDN that can be used to identify the host.
>
> `hostdomain()`
>> Returns the remainder of the FQDN after the hostname has been removed.

Author

Graham Barr, *gbarr@pobox.com*. Adapted from Sys::Hostname by David Sundstrom, *sunds@asictest.sc.ti.com*.

Copyright

Net::DummyInetd—a dummy inetd server

Synopsis

```
use Net::DummyInetd;
use Net::SMTP;

$inetd = new Net::DummyInetd qw(/usr/lib/sendmail -ba -bs);

$smtp  = Net::SMTP->new('localhost', Port => $inetd->port);
```

Description

Net::DummyInetd is just what its name says: a dummy inetd server. Creation of a Net::DummyInetd causes a child process to be spawned off that listens to a socket. When a connection arrives on this socket, the specified command is forked and *exec*ed with STDIN and STDOUT file descriptors duplicated to the new socket.

This package was added as an example of how to use Net::SMTP to connect to a **sendmail** process that is not the default via STDIN and STDOUT. A Net::Inetd package will be available in the next release of **libnet**.

Constructor

`new(CMD)`
> Create a new object and spawn a child process that listens to a socket. `CMD` is a list, which is passed to **exec** when a new process needs to be created.

Method

`port`
> Return the port number on which the `DummyInetd` object is listening.

Author

Graham Barr, *gbarr@pobox.com*

Copyright

Net::FTP—FTP client class

Synopsis

```
use Net::FTP;

$ftp = Net::FTP->new("some.host.name");
$ftp->login("anonymous","me@here.there");
$ftp->cwd("/pub");
$ftp->get("that.file");
$ftp->quit;
```

Description

Net::FTP is a class implementing a simple FTP client in Perl, as described in RFC 959. It provides wrappers for a subset of the RFC 959 commands.

Overview

FTP stands for File Transfer Protocol. It is a way of transferring files between networked machines. The protocol defines a client (whose commands are provided by this module) and a server (which is not implemented in this module). Communication is always initiated by the client, and the server responds with a message and a status code (and sometimes with data).

The FTP protocol allows files to be sent to or fetched from the server. Each transfer involves a local file (on the client) and a remote file (on the server). In this particular module, the same filename is used for both local and remote files if only one filename is specified. This means that in transferring a remote file, */path/to/file* tries to put that file in */path/to/file* locally, unless you specify a local filename.

The protocol also defines several standard translations that the file can undergo during transfer. The possible translations are ASCII, EBCDIC, binary, and byte. ASCII is the default translation type and indicates that the sender of the file will translate the ends of lines to a standard representation that the receiver will then translate back into its local representation. EBCDIC indicates that the file being transferred is in EBCDIC format. Binary (also known as image) format sends the data as a contiguous bitstream. Byte format transfers the data as bytes, the values of which remain the same regardless of differences in byte size between the two machines (in theory, that is; in practice, you should only use this if you really know what you're doing).

Constructor

new(*HOST*[, *OPTIONS*])

This is the constructor for a new Net::FTP object. *HOST* is the name of the remote host to which an FTP connection is required.

OPTIONS are passed in a hash-like fashion, using key and value pairs. Possible options are:

Firewall

> The name of a machine that acts as an FTP firewall. This can be overridden by the environment variable FTP_FIREWALL. If FTP_FIREWALL is specified and a direct connection cannot be made to the given host, then the connection is made to the firewall machine and the string *@hostname* is appended to the login identifier. This kind of setup is also referred to as an FTP proxy.

Port

> The port number to connect to on the remote machine for the FTP connection.

Timeout

> The timeout value (defaults to 120).

Debug

> The debug level (see the debug method in Net::Cmd).

Passive

> If set to true, then all data transfers are done using passive mode. This is required for some dumb servers and some firewall configurations. This can also be set by the environment variable FTP_PASSIVE.

Methods

Unless otherwise stated, all methods return either true or false, where true means that the operation was a success. When a method states that it returns a value, failure is returned as undef or as an empty list.

login([*LOGIN*[,*PASSWORD*[, *ACCOUNT*]]])

> Logs in to the remote FTP server with the given login information. If there are no arguments, then Net::FTP uses the Net::Netrc package to look up the login information for the connected host. If no information is found, then a login of *anonymous* is used. If no password is given and the login is *anonymous*, then the user's email address is used for a password.

> If the connection is via a firewall, then the **authorize** method is called with no arguments.

authorize([*AUTH*[, *RESP*]])

> This is a protocol used by some firewall FTP proxies to authorize the user to send data out. If both arguments are not specified, then **authorize** uses Net::Netrc to do a lookup.

type (*TYPE*[, *ARGS*])

> Sends the *TYPE* command to the remote FTP server to change the type of data transfer. The return value is the previous value.

ascii([*ARGS*]), binary([*ARGS*]), ebcdic([*ARGS*]), byte([*ARGS*])

> Synonyms for **type** with the first argument set correctly.

> Note: EBCDIC and byte are not fully supported.

rename(*OLDNAME*, *NEWNAME*)

> Renames a file on the remote FTP server from *OLDNAME* to *NEWNAME*. This is done by sending the RNFR and RNTO commands.

delete(*FILENAME*)

> Sends a request to the server to delete *FILENAME*.

cwd ([*DIR*])

> Attempts to change the directory to the directory given in $dir. If $dir is "..",
> the FTP CDUP command is used to attempt to move up one directory. If no direc-
> tory is given, then an attempt is made to change the directory to the root directory.

cdup ( )

> Changes directory to the parent of the current directory.

pwd ( )

> Returns the full pathname of the current directory.

rmdir (*DIR*)

> Removes the directory with the name *DIR*.

mkdir (*DIR*[, *RECURSE*])

> Creates a new directory with the name *DIR*. If *RECURSE* is *true*, then mkdir
> attempts to create all the directories in the given path.

> Returns the full pathname to the new directory.

ls ([*DIR*])

> Gets a directory listing of *DIR*, or the current directory.

> Returns a reference to a list of lines returned from the server.

dir ([*DIR*])

> Gets a directory listing of *DIR*, or the current directory in long format.

> Returns a reference to a list of lines returned from the server.

get (*REMOTE_FILE*[, *LOCAL_FILE*])

> Gets *REMOTE_FILE* from the server and stores it locally. *LOCAL_FILE* may be a
> filename or a filehandle. If *LOCAL_FILE* is not specified, the file is stored in the
> current directory with the same leafname as the remote file.

> If WHERE is specified, continues transfer of the remote file from that point.

> Returns *LOCAL_FILE*, or the generated local filename if *LOCAL_FILE* is not given.

put (*LOCAL_FILE*[, *REMOTE_FILE*])

> Puts a file on the remote server. *LOCAL_FILE* may be a name or a filehandle. If
> *LOCAL_FILE* is a filehandle, then *REMOTE_FILE* must be specified. If *REMOTE_*
> *FILE* is not specified, then the file is stored in the current directory with the same
> leafname as *LOCAL_FILE*.

> Returns *REMOTE_FILE*, or the generated remote filename if *REMOTE_FILE* is not
> given.

put_unique (*LOCAL_FILE*[, *REMOTE_FILE*])

> Same as put, but uses the STOU command.

> Returns the name of the file on the server.

append (*LOCAL_FILE*[, *REMOTE_FILE*])

> Same as put, but appends to the file on the remote server.

> Returns *REMOTE_FILE*, or the generated remote filename if *REMOTE_FILE* is not
> given.

unique_name ( )

> Returns the name of the last file stored on the server using the STOU command.

mdtm (*FILE*)

> Returns the modification time of the given file.

size (*FILE*)

> Returns the size in bytes of the given file.

The following methods can return different results depending on how they are called. If the user explicitly calls either of the **pasv** or **port** methods, then these methods return a true or false value. If the user does not call either of these methods, then the result is a reference to a Net::FTP::dataconn-based object.

nlst ([*DIR*])

> Sends an NLST command to the server, with an optional parameter.

list ([*DIR*])

> Same as **nlst**, but uses the LIST command.

retr (*FILE*)

> Begins the retrieval of a file called *FILE* from the remote server.

stor (*FILE*)

> Tells the server that you wish to store a file. *FILE* is the name of the new file that should be created.

stou (*FILE*)

> Same as **stor**, but uses the STOU command. The name of the unique file that was created on the server is available via the **unique_name** method after the data connection has been closed.

appe (*FILE*)

> Tells the server that we want to append some data to the end of a file called *FILE*. If this file does not exist, then **appe** creates it.

If for some reason you want to have complete control over the data connection, including generating it and calling the **response** method when required, then you can use the following methods to do so.

However, calling these methods affects the use of only the methods above that can return a data connection. It has no effect on methods **get**, **put**, **put_unique**, or those that do not require data connections.

port ([*PORT*])

> Sends a *PORT* command to the server. If *PORT* is specified, then it is sent to the server. If not, then a listen socket is created and the correct information is sent to the server.

pasv ()

> Tells the server to go into passive mode. Returns the text that represents the port on which the server is listening; this text is in a suitable form to send to another FTP server using the **port** method.

The following methods can be used to transfer files between two remote servers, providing that the two servers can connect directly to each other:

pasv_xfer (*SRC_FILE*, *DEST_SERVER*[, *DEST_FILE*])

> Transfers a file between two remote FTP servers. If *DEST_FILE* is omitted, then the leafname of *SRC_FILE* is used.

pasv_wait (*NON_PASV_SERVER*)

> Waits for a transfer to complete between a passive server and a non-passive server. This method should be called on the passive server with the Net::FTP object for the non-passive server passed as an argument.

`abort()`

> Aborts the current data transfer.

`quit()`

> Sends the QUIT command to the remote FTP server and closes the socket connection.

Methods for the Adventurous

Net::FTP inherits from Net::Cmd, so methods defined in Net::Cmd may be used to send commands to the remote FTP server.

`quot(CMD[, ARGS])`

> Sends a command that Net::FTP does not directly support to the remote server and waits for a response.
>
> Returns the most significant digit of the response code.
>
> Warning: This call should only be used on commands that do not require data connections. Misuse of this method can hang the connection.

The Dataconn Class

Some of the methods defined in Net::FTP return an object derived from the dataconn class. The dataconn class itself is derived from the IO::Socket::INET class, so any normal I/O operations can be performed. However, the following methods are defined in the dataconn class, and I/O should be performed using these:

`read(BUFFER, SIZE[, TIMEOUT])`

> Reads *SIZE* bytes of data from the server and places them into *BUFFER*, also performing any CRLF translation necessary. *TIMEOUT* is optional; if it is not given, the timeout value from the command connection is used.
>
> Returns the number of bytes read before any CRLF translation.

`write(BUFFER, SIZE[, TIMEOUT])`

> Writes *SIZE* bytes of data from *BUFFER* to the server, performing any CRLF translation necessary. *TIMEOUT* is optional; if it is not given, the timeout value from the command connection is used.
>
> Returns the number of bytes written before any CRLF translation.

`abort()`

> Aborts the current data transfer.

`close()`

> Closes the data connection and gets a response from the FTP server. Returns true if the connection was closed successfully and the first digit of the response from the server was a "2".

Unimplemented

The following RFC 959 commands have not been implemented:

ALLO

> Allocates storage for the file to be transferred.

SMNT

> Mounts a different filesystem structure without changing login or accounting information.

HELP

> Asks the server for "helpful information" (that's what the RFC says) on the commands it accepts.

MODE

> Specifies the transfer mode (stream, block, or compressed) for the file to be transferred.

SITE

> Requests remote server site parameters.

SYST

> Requests remote server system identification.

STAT

> Requests remote server status.

STRU

> Specifies the file structure for the file to be transferred.

REIN

> Reinitializes the connection, flushing all I/O and account information.

Bugs

When reporting bugs or problems, please include as much information as possible. It may be difficult for me to reproduce the problem, as almost every setup is different.

A small script that yields the problem will probably be of help. It would also be useful if this script were run with the extra options `Debug => 1` passed to the constructor and the output sent with the bug report. If you cannot include a small script, then please include a debug trace from a run of your program that does yield the problem.

Author

Graham Barr, *gbarr@pobox.com*

Acknowledgments

Henry Gabryjelski (*henryg@WPI.EDU*), for the suggestion of creating directories recursively.

Nathan Torkington (*gnat@frii.com*), for some input on the documentation.

Roderick Schertler (*roderick@gate.net*), for various inputs.

Copyright

See Also

Net::Netrc, Net::Cmd

ftp(1), ftpd(8), RFC 959 (*http://www.cis.ohio-state.edu/htbin/rfc/rfc959.html*)

Net::Gen — generic sockets interface handling

Synopsis

```
use Net::Gen;
```

Description

The Net::Gen module provides basic services for handling socket-based communications. It supports no particular protocol family directly, however, so it is of direct use primarily to implementors of other modules. To this end, several housekeeping functions are provided for the use of derived classes, as well as several inheritable methods.

Also provided in this distribution are Net::Inet, Net::TCP, Net::UDP, and Net::UNIX, which are layered atop Net::Gen.

Public Methods

new

> Returns a newly initialized object of the given class. If called for a class other than Net::Gen, no validation of the supplied parameters is performed. (This is so that the derived class can add the parameter validation it needs to the object before allowing validation.)
>
> ```
> $obj = Net::Gen->new($classname);
> $obj = Net::Gen->new($classname, \%parameters);
> ```

new_from_fh

> Returns a newly initialized object of the given class, open on a newly dup()ed copy of the given filehandle or file descriptor. As many of the standard object parameters as possible are determined from the passed filehandle. This is determined (in part) by calling the corresponding **new, init,** and **getsockinfo** methods for the new object.
>
> ```
> $obj = $classname->new_from_fh(*FH);
> $obj = $classname->new_from_fh(\*FH);
> $obj = $classname->new_from_fh(fileno($fh));
> ```
>
> Only real filehandles or file descriptor numbers are allowed as arguments. This method makes no attempt to resolve filehandle names.

init

> Verifies that all previous parameter assignments are valid (via **checkparams**). Returns the incoming object on success, and **undef** on failure. This method is normally called from the **new** method appropriate to the class of the created object.
>
> ```
> return undef unless $self->init;
> ```

checkparams

> Verifies that all previous parameter assignments are valid. This method is normally called only via the **init** method, rather than directly.
>
> ```
> $ok = $obj->checkparams;
> ```

setparams

> Sets new parameters from the given hashref, with validation. This is done in a loop over the *key, value* pairs from the **newparams** parameter. The precise nature of the validation depends on the $newonly and $checkup parameters (which are optional), but in all cases the keys to be set are checked against those registered

with the object. If the $newonly parameter is negative, the value from the hashref is set only if there is not already a defined value associated with that key, but skipping the setting of the value is silent. If the $newonly parameter is not negative or if there is no existing defined value (if the $checkup parameter is false), then the setting of the new value is skipped if the new value is identical to the old value. If those checks don't cause the setting of a new value to be skipped, and if the $newonly parameter is positive and there is already a defined value for the specified key, a warning is issued and the new value is not set.

If none of the above checks causes the setting of a new value to be skipped, but if the specified key has a validation routine, that routine is called with the given object, the current key, and the proposed new value as parameters. The validation routine is allowed to alter the new-value argument to change what will be set. (This is useful when changing a hostname to be in canonical form, for example.) If the validation routine returns a non-null string, that string is used to issue a warning, and the new value is not set. If the validation routine returns a null string (or if there is no validation routine), the new value (finally) gets set for the given key.

```
$ok = $obj->setparams(\%newparams, $newonly, $checkup);
$ok = $obj->setparams(\%newparams, $newonly);
$ok = $obj->setparams(\%newparams);
```

The **setparams** method returns 1 if all parameters were successfully set, and undef otherwise.

setparam

Sets a single new parameter. Uses the **setparams** method and has the same rules for the handling of the $newonly and $checkup parameters. Returns 1 if the set was successful, and undef otherwise.

```
$ok = $obj->setparam($key, $value, $newonly, $checkup);
$ok = $obj->setparam($key, $value, $newonly);
$ok = $obj->setparam($key, $value);
```

delparams

Removes the settings for the specified parameters. Uses the **setparams** method (with undef for the values) to validate that the removal is allowed by the owning object. If the invocation of **setparams** is successful, then the parameters in question are removed. Returns 1 if all the removals were successful, and undef otherwise.

```
$ok = $obj->delparams(\@keynames);
```

delparam

Sugar-coated call to the **delparams** method. Functions just like it.

```
$ok = $obj->delparam($keyname);
```

getparams

Returns a hash (*not* a reference) consisting of the key-value pairs corresponding to the specified keyname list. Only those keys that exist in the current parameter list of the object are returned.

```
%hash = $obj->getparams(\@keynames, $noundefs);
%hash = $obj->getparams(\@keynames);
```

If the $noundefs parameter is present and true, then existing keys with undefined values are suppressed like non-existent keys.

getparam

> Returns the current setting for the named parameter (in the current object), or the specified default value if the parameter is not in the object's current parameter list.

> ```
> $value = $obj->getparam($key, $defval, $def_if_undef);
> $value = $obj->getparam($key, $defval);
> $value = $obj->getparam($key);
> ```

> If the optional $def_if_undef parameter is true, then undefined values are treated like non-existent keys and thus return the supplied default value $defval.

open

> Makes a call to the socket() builtin, using the current object parameters to determine the desired protocol family, socket type, and protocol number. If the object was already open, its stopio method is called before socket() is called again. The object parameters consulted (and possibly updated) are PF, AF, proto, and type. Returns true if the socket() call results in an open filehandle, undef otherwise.

> ```
> $ok = $obj->open;
> ```

condition

> (Re-)establishes the condition of the associated filehandle after an open() or accept(). Sets the socket to be autoflushed and marks it binmode(). No useful value is returned.

> ```
> $obj->condition;
> ```

listen

> Makes a call to the listen() builtin on the filehandle associated with the object. Propagates the return value from listen().

> ```
> $ok = $obj->listen($maxqueue);
> $ok = $obj->listen;
> ```

> If the $maxqueue parameter is missing, the value defaults to the value of the object's maxq parameter or the value of SOMAXCONN. If the SOMAXCONN constant is not available in your configuration, the default value used for the listen method is 5. This method fails if the object is not bound and cannot be made bound by a simple call to its bind method.

bind

> Makes a call to the bind() builtin on the filehandle associated with the object.

> ```
> $ok = $obj->bind;
> ```

> The arguments to bind() are determined from the current parameters of the object. First, if the filehandle has previously been bound or connected, it is closed. Then, if it is not currently open, a call to the open method is made.

> If all that works (which may be a no-op), then the following list of possible values is tried for the bind() builtin: First, if the value of the srcaddrlist object parameter is an array reference, the elements of the array are tried in order until a bind() succeeds or the list is exhausted. Second, if the srcaddrlist parameter is not set to an array reference, and if the srcaddr parameter is a non-null string, that string is used. Finally, if neither srcaddrlist nor srcaddr is suitably set, the AF parameter is used to construct a sockaddr struct that is mostly zeroed, and the bind() is attempted with that. If the bind() fails, undef is returned at this point. Otherwise, a call to the getsockinfo method is made, and then the value from a call to the isbound method is returned.

If all that seems too confusing, don't worry. Most clients will never need to do an explicit **bind** call, anyway. If you're writing a server or a privileged client that does need to bind to a particular local port or address, and you didn't understand the foregoing discussion, you may be in trouble. Don't panic until you've checked the discussion of binding in the derived class you're using, however.

unbind

Removes any saved binding for the object. Unless the object is currently connected, this results in a call to its **close** method, in order to ensure that any previous binding is removed. Even if the object is connected, the **srcaddrlist** object parameter is removed (via the object's **delparams** method). The return value from this method is indeterminate.

```
$obj->unbind;
```

connect

Attempts to establish a connection for the object.

```
$ok = $obj->connect;
```

First, if the object is currently connected or has been connected since the last time it was opened, its **close** method is called. Then, if the object is not currently open, its **open** method is called. If it's not open after that, undef is returned. If it is open, and if either of its **srcaddrlist** or **srcaddr** parameters are set to indicate that a **bind()** is desired, and it is not currently bound, its **bind** method is called. If the **bind** method is called and fails, undef is returned. (Most of the foregoing is a no-op for simple clients, so don't panic.)

Next, if the **dstaddrlist** object parameter is set to an array reference, a call to **connect()** is made for each element of the list until a call succeeds or the list is exhausted. If the **dstaddrlist** parameter is not an array reference, a single attempt is made to call **connect()** with the **dstaddr** object parameter. If no **connect()** call succeeds, undef is returned. Finally, a call is made to the object's **getsockinfo** method, and then the value from a call to its **isconnected** method is returned.

Note that the derived classes tend to provide additional capabilities that make the **connect** method easier to use than the above description would indicate.

getsockinfo

Attempts to determine connection parameters associated with the object.

```
($localsockaddr, $peersockaddr) = $obj->getsockinfo;
$peersockaddr = $obj->getsockinfo;
```

If a **getsockname()** call on the associated filehandle succeeds, the **srcaddr** object parameter is set to that returned **sockaddr**. If a **getpeername()** call on the associated filehandle succeeds, the **dstaddr** parameter is set to that returned **sockaddr**. In a scalar context, if both socket addresses are found, the **getpeername()** value is returned; otherwise undef is returned. In a list context, the **getsockname()** and **getpeername()** values are returned, unless both are undefined.

Derived classes normally replace this method with one that provides friendlier return information appropriate to the derived class and that establishes more of the object parameters.

shutdown

>Calls the shutdown() builtin on the filehandle associated with the object. This method is a no-op, returning 1 if the filehandle is not connected.

>>$ok = $obj->shutdown($how);
>>$ok = $obj->shutdown;

>The $how parameter is the same as in the shutdown() builtin, which in turn should be as described in the shutdown(2) manpage. If the $how parameter is not present, it is assumed to be 2.

>Returns 1 if there is nothing to do; otherwise propagates the return from the shutdown() builtin.

stopio

>Calls the close() builtin on the filehandle associated with the object, unless that filehandle is already closed.

>>$ok = $obj->stopio;

>Returns 1 or the return value from the close() builtin. This method is primarily for the use of server modules that need to avoid shutdown calls at inappropriate times. This method calls the delparams method for the keys of srcaddr and dstaddr.

close

>The close method is like a call to the shutdown method followed by a call to the stopio method. It is the standard way to close down an object.

>>$ok = $obj->close;

send

>This method calls the three-argument form of the send() builtin.

>>$ok = $obj->send($buffer, $flags);
>>$ok = $obj->send($buffer);

>The $flags parameter defaults to 0 if not supplied. The return value from the send() builtin is returned. This method makes no attempt to trap SIGPIPE.

sendto

>This method calls the four-argument form of the send() builtin.

>>$ok = $obj->sendto($buffer, $destsockaddr, $flags);
>>$ok = $obj->sendto($buffer, $destsockaddr);

>The $flags parameter defaults to 0 if not supplied. The return value from the send() builtin is returned. This method makes no attempt to trap SIGPIPE.

SEND

>This method calls the three- or four-argument form of the send() builtin.

>>$ok = $obj->SEND($buffer, $flags, $destsockaddr);
>>$ok = $obj->SEND($buffer, $flags);
>>$ok = $obj->SEND($buffer);

>The $flags parameter defaults to 0 if not supplied. If the value is missing or undefined, the three-argument form of the send() builtin is used. A defined $destsockaddr results in a four-argument send() call. The return value from the send() builtin is returned. This method makes no attempt to trap SIGPIPE.

PRINT
put

> This method uses the `print()` builtin to send the @whatever arguments to the filehandle associated with the object.
>
> $ok = $obj->put(@whatever);
> $ok = put $obj @whatever;
>
> That filehandle is always marked for autoflushing by the **open** method, so the method is in effect equivalent to this:
>
> $ok = $obj->send(join($, , @whatever) . $\ , 0);
>
> However, since multiple `fwrite()` calls are sometimes involved in the actual use of `print()`, this method can be more efficient than the above code sample for large strings in the argument list. It's a bad idea, except on stream sockets (SOCK_STREAM) though, since the record boundaries are unpredictable through stdio. This method makes no attempt to trap SIGPIPE.

get
recv

> This method calls the `recv()` builtin, and returns a buffer (if one is received) or undef on eof or error.
>
> $record = $obj->recv($maxlen, $flags, $whence);
> $record = $obj->recv($maxlen, $flags);
> $record = $obj->recv($maxlen);
> $record = $obj->recv;
>
> If an eof on a stream socket is seen, $! is 0 on return. If the $whence argument is supplied, it is filled in with the sending socket address if possible. If the $flags argument is not supplied, it defaults to 0. If the $maxlen argument is not supplied, it defaults to the receive buffer size of the associated filehandle (if known), or the preferred blocksize of the associated filehandle (if known, which it usually won't be), or 8192.

RECV

> This method calls the `recv()` method with the arguments and return rearranged to match the `recv()` builtin. This is for (eventual) support of tied filehandles.
>
> $from = $obj->RECV($buffer, $maxlen, $flags);
> $from = $obj->RECV($buffer, $maxlen);
> $from = $obj->RECV($buffer);

READLINE
getline

> This is a simulation of `<$filehandle>` that doesn't let **stdio** confuse the get/recv method.

isopen

> Returns **true** if the object currently has a socket attached to its associated filehandle, and **false** otherwise. If this method has not been overridden by a derived class, the value is the saved return value of the call to the `socket()` builtin (if it was called).
>
> $ok = $obj->isopen;

isconnected

> Returns **true** if the object's **connect** method has been used successfully to establish a "session" and that session is still connected. If this method has not been

overridden by a derived class, the value is the saved return value of the call to the `connect()` builtin (if it was called).

```
$ok = $obj->isconnected;
```

isbound

Returns `true` if the object's `bind` method has been used successfully and the binding is still in effect. If this method has not been overridden by a derived class, the value is the saved return value of the call to the `bind()` builtin (if it was called).

```
$ok = $obj->isbound;
```

didlisten

Returns `true` if the object's `listen` method has been used successfully and the object is still bound. If this method has not been overridden by a derived class, the value is undef on failure and the `$maxqueue` value used for the `listen()` builtin on success.

```
$ok = $obj->didlisten;
```

accept

Returns a new object in the same class as the given object if an `accept()` call succeeds, and undef otherwise. If the `accept()` call succeeds, the new object is marked as being open, connected, and bound.

```
$newobj = $obj->accept;
```

getsopt

Returns the unpacked values from a call to the `getsockopt()` builtin. In order to do the unpacking, the socket option must have been registered with the object. See the discussion below in "Known Socket Options."

```
@optvals = $obj->getsopt($level, $option);
@optvals = $obj->getsopt($optname);
```

Since registered socket options are known by name as well as by their level and option values, it is possible to make calls using only option name. If the name is not registered with the object, the return value is the same as that for `getsopt $obj -1,-1`, which is an empty return array and `$!` set appropriately (it should be set to EINVAL).

Examples:

```
($sotype) = $obj->getsopt('SO_TYPE');
@malinger = $obj->getsopt(SOL_SOCKET, SO_LINGER);
($sodebug) = $obj->getsopt('SOL_SOCKET', 'SO_DEBUG');
```

getropt

Returns the raw value from a call to the `getsockopt()` builtin.

```
$optsetting = $obj->getropt($level, $option);
$optsetting = $obj->getropt($optname);
```

If both the `$level` and `$option` arguments are given as numbers, the `getsockopt()` call will be made even if the given socket option is not registered with the object. Otherwise, the return value for unregistered objects is undef, with the value of `$!` set as described above for the `getsopt` method.

setsopt

Returns the result from a call to the `setsockopt()` builtin.

```
$ok = $obj->setsopt($level, $option, @optvalues);
$ok = $obj->setsopt($optname, @optvalues);
```

In order to be able to pack the @optvalues, the option must be registered with the object, just as for the getsopt method, above.

setropt

Returns the result from a call to the setsockopt() builtin.

```
$ok = $obj->setropt($level, $option, $rawvalue);
$ok = $obj->setropt($optname, $rawvalue);
```

If the $level and $option arguments are both given as numbers, the setsockopt() call is made even if the option is not registered with the object. Otherwise, unregistered options fail as for the setsopt method, above.

fhvec

Returns a vector suitable as an argument to the 4-argument select() call. This is for use in doing selects with multiple I/O streams.

```
$vecstring = $obj->fhvec;
```

select

Issues a four-argument select() call for the associated I/O stream.

```
($nfound, $timeleft, $rbool, $wbool, $xbool) =
    $obj->select($doread, $dowrite, $doxcept, $timeout);
$nfound = $obj->select($doread, $dowrite, $doxcept,
  $timeout);
```

All arguments are optional. The $timeout argument is the same as the fourth argument to select(). The first three are booleans, used to determine whether the select() should include the object's I/O stream in the corresponding parameter to the select() call. The return in list context is the standard two values from select(), follwed by Booleans indicating whether the actual select() call found reading, writing, or exception to be true. In scalar context, returns only the count of the number of matching conditions. This is probably useful only when you're checking just one of the three possible conditions.

ioctl

Returns the result of an ioctl() call on the associated I/O stream.

```
$rval = $obj->ioctl($func, $value);
```

fcntl

Returns the result of an fcntl() call on the associated I/O stream.

```
$rval = $obj->fcntl($func, $value);
```

format_addr

Returns a formatted representation of the address. This is a method so that it can be overridden by derived classes. It is used to implement "pretty-printing" methods for source and destination addresses.

```
$string = $obj->format_addr($sockaddr);
$string = format_addr Module $sockaddr;
```

format_local_addr

Returns a formatted representation of the local socket address associated with the object.

```
$string = $obj->format_local_addr;
```

format_remote_addr

Returns a formatted representation of the remote socket address associated with the object.

```
$string = $obj->format_remote_addr;
```

Protected Methods

Yes, I know that Perl doesn't really have protected methods as such. However, these are the methods that are useful only for implementing derived classes and not for the general user.

initsockopts

Given a prototype optiondesc hash ref, updates it to include all the data needed for the values it can find, and deletes the ones it can't.

```
$classname->initsockopts($level, \%optiondesc);
```

For example, here's a single entry from such a prototype optiondesc:

```
'SO_LINGER' => ['II'],
```

Given this, the $level of SOL_SOCKET, and the incoming class name of Net::Gen, initsockopts attempts to evaluate SO_LINGER in package Net::Gen. If it succeeds, it fills out the rest of the information in the associated array ref and adds another key to the hash ref for the value of SO_LINGER (which is 128 on my system). If it can't evaluate that pseudo-constant, it simply deletes the entry from the referenced hash. Assuming a successful evaluation of this entry, the resulting entries would look like this:

```
'SO_LINGER' => ['II', SO_LINGER+0, SOL_SOCKET+0, 2],
SO_LINGER+0 => ['II', SO_LINGER+0, SOL_SOCKET+0, 2],
```

(All right, so the expressions would be known values, but maybe you get the idea.)

A completed optiondesc hash is a set of key-value pairs, where the value is an array ref with the following elements:

```
[pack template, option value, option level, pack array len]
```

Such a completed optiondesc is one of the required arguments to the registerOptions method (see below).

registerOptions
register_options

This method attaches the socket options specified by the given option descriptions hash ref and the given level (as text and as a number) to the object.

```
$obj->registerOptions($levelname, $level, \%optiondesc);
```

The registered set of socket options is, in fact, a hashref of hashrefs, where the keys are the level names and level numbers, and the values are the optiondesc hash refs that get registered.

Example:

```
$self->registerOptions('SOL_SOCKET', SOL_SOCKET+0,
\%sockopts);
```

registerParamKeys
register_param_keys

This method registers the referenced keynames as valid parameters for setparams and the like for this object.

```
$obj->registerParamKeys(\@keynames);
```

The new methods can store arbitrary parameter values, but the init method later ensures that all those keys eventually got registered. This out-of-order setup is allowed because of possible cross-dependencies between the various parameters, so that, in some cases, they have to be set before they can be validated.

`registerParamHandlers`
`register_param_handlers`

This method registers the referenced keynames (if they haven't already been registered), and establishes the referenced keyhandlers as validation routines for those keynames.

```
$obj->registerParamHandlers(\@keynames, \@keyhandlers);
$obj->registerParamHandlers(\%key_handler_pairs);
```

Each element of the keyhandlers array must be a code reference. When the `setparams` method invokes the handler, it is called with three arguments: the target object, the keyname in question, and the proposed new value (which may be undef, especially if it is being called from the `delparams` method). See the discussion of validation routines in the `setparams` method description, above.

`ckeof`

After a zero-length read in the `get()` routine, `get()` calls this method to determine whether such a zero-length read meant EOF.

```
$wasiteof = $obj->ckeof;
```

The default method supplied here checks for non-blocking sockets (if necessary), and for a SOCK_STREAM socket. If EOF_NONBLOCK is true, or if the VAL_O_ NONBLOCK flag was not set in the `fcntl()` flags for the socket, or if the error code was not VAL_EAGAIN, and the socket is of type SOCK_STREAM, then this method returns `true`. It returns a false value otherwise. This method is overridable for classes like Net::Dnet, which support SOCK_SEQPACKET and need to make a protocol-family-specific check to tell a zero-length packet from EOF.

`fileno`

Gets the embedded filehandle.

```
$fnum = $obj->fileno;
```

I've strongly resisted giving people direct access to the filehandle embedded in the object because of the problems of mixing stdio input calls and traditional socket-level I/O. However, if you're sure you can keep things straight, here are the rules under which it's safe to use the embedded filehandle:

- Don't use Perl's own `stdio` calls. Stick to `sysread()` and `recv()`.

- Don't use the object's `getline` method, since that stores a read-ahead buffer in the object that only the object's own `get/recv` and `getline` methods know to return to you. (The object's `select` method knows about the buffer enough to tell you that a read will succeed if there's saved data, though.)

- Please don't change the state of the socket behind my back. That means no `close()`, `shutdown()`, `connect()`, `bind()`, or `listen()` built-ins. Use the corresponding methods instead, or all bets are off.

Given that, you can get at the filehandle in the object this way:

```
$fh = $obj->getfh;
```

That is a glob ref, by the way, but that doesn't matter for calling the built-in I/O primitives.

Known Socket Options

These are the socket options known to the Net::Gen module itself:

> SO_ACCEPTCONN, SO_BROADCAST, SO_DEBUG, SO_DONTROUTE, SO_ERROR, SO_KEEPALIVE, SO_OOBINLINE, SO_REUSEADDR, SO_USELOOPBACK, SO_RCVBUF, SO_SNDBUF, SO_RCVTIMEO, SO_SNDTIMEO, SO_RCVLOWAT, SO_SNDLOWAT, SO_TYPE, SO_LINGER

Known Object Parameters

These are the object parameters registered by the Net::Gen module itself:

PF
> Protocol family for this object

AF
> Address family (defaults from PF, and vice versa)

type
> The socket type to create (SOCK_STREAM, SOCK_DGRAM, etc.)

proto
> The protocol to pass to the socket() call (often defaulted to 0)

dstaddr
> The result of getpeername(), or an ephemeral proposed connect() address

dstaddrlist
> A reference to an array of socket addresses to try for connect()

srcaddr
> The result of getsockname(), or an ephemeral proposed bind() address

srcaddrlist
> A reference to an array of socket addresses to try for bind()

maxqueue
> An override of the default maximum queue depth parameter for listen(). This is used if the $maxqueue argument to listen() is not supplied.

Non-Method Subroutines

pack_sockaddr
> Returns a packed struct sockaddr corresponding to the provided $family (which must be a number) and the address-family-specific $fam_addr (pre-packed).
>
> ```
> $connect_address = pack_sockaddr($family, $fam_addr);
> ```

unpack_sockaddr
> The inverse of pack_sockaddr().
>
> ```
> ($family, $fam_addr) = unpack_sockaddr($packed_address);
> ```

VAL_O_NONBLOCK
> Gives the value found by the Configure script for setting a filehandle non-blocking. The value available from the Config module is a string representing the value found ($Config::Config{'o_nonblock'}), whereas the value from VAL_O_NONBLOCK is an integer, suitable for passing to sysopen() or for eventual use in fcntl().

VAL_EAGAIN
> Gives the value of the error symbol found by the `Configure` script, which is set by a non-blocking filehandle when no data is available. This differs from the value available from the `Config` module (`$Config::Config{'eagain'}`) in that the latter is a string, typically "EAGAIN".

RD_NODATA
> Gives the integer return value found by the `Configure` script for a `read()` system call on a non-blocking socket that has no data available. This is similar to the string representation of the value available from the `Config` module as `$Config::Config{'rd_nodata'}`.

EOF_NONBLOCK
> Returns a boolean value depending on whether a read from a non-blocking socket can distinguish an end-of-file condition from a no-data-available condition. This corresponds to the value available from the `Config` module as `$Config::Config{'d_eofnblk'}`, except that EOF_NONBLOCK is always defined.

Exports

default
> None.

exportable
> VAL_O_NONBLOCK, VAL_EAGAIN, RD_NODATA, EOF_NONBLOCK, `pack_sockaddr`, `unpack_sockaddr`

tags

The following are available for grouping exported items together:

`:NonBlockVals`
> EOF_NONBLOCK, RD_NODATA, VAL_EAGAIN, VAL_O_NONBLOCK

`:routines`
> `pack_sockaddr unpack_sockaddr`

`:ALL`
> All of the above.

Author

Spider Boardman, *spider@Orb.Nashua.NH.US*

Net::Inet—Internet socket interface module

Synopsis

```
use Net::Gen;            # optional
use Net::Inet;
```

Description

The Net::Inet module provides basic services for handling socket-based communications for the Internet protocol family. It inherits from Net::Gen, and is a base for Net::TCP and Net::UDP.

Public Methods

new
>   Returns a newly initialized object of the given class. If **new** is called for a derived
>   class, no validation of the supplied parameters is performed. (This is so that the
>   derived class can set up the parameter validation it needs in the object before
>   allowing the validation.) Otherwise, it causes the parameters to be validated by
>   calling its **init** method. In particular, this means that if both a host and a service
>   are given, then an object is only returned if a **connect()** call was successful.

```
$obj = new Net::Inet;
$obj = new Net::Inet $host, $service;
$obj = new Net::Inet \%parameters;
$obj = new Net::Inet $host, $service, \%parameters;
```

init
>   Verifies that all previous parameter assignments are valid (via **checkparams**).
>   Returns the incoming object on success, and undef on failure. Usually called only
>   via a derived class's **init** method or its own **new** call.

```
return undef unless $self->init;
return undef unless $self->init(\%parameters);
return undef unless $self->init($host, $service);
return undef unless $self->init($host, $service,
                                     \%parameters);
```

bind
>   Sets up the **srcaddrlist** object parameter with the specified $host and
> $service arguments if supplied (via the **thishost** and **thisport** object parame-
>   ters), and then returns the value from the inherited **bind** method.

```
$ok = $obj->bind;
$ok = $obj->bind($host, $service);
$ok = $obj->bind($host, $service, \%parameters);
```

Changing of parameters is also allowed, mainly for setting debug status or
timeouts.

Example:

```
$ok = $obj->bind(0, 'echo(7)'); # attach to local TCP echo port
```

unbind
>   Deletes the **thishost** and **thisport** object parameters, and then (assuming that
>   succeeds, which it should) returns the value from the inherited **unbind** method.

```
$obj->unbind;
```

connect
>   Attempts to establish a connection for the object.

```
$ok = $obj->connect;
$ok = $obj->connect($host, $service);
$ok = $obj->connect($host, $service, \%parameters);
```

If the $host or $service arguments are specified, they are used to set the
desthost and **destservice/destport** object parameters, with the side effect of
setting up the **dstaddrlist** object parameter. Then, the result of a call to the
inherited **connect** method is returned. Changing of parameters is also allowed,
mainly for setting debug status or timeouts.

format_addr

> Returns a formatted representation of the address. This is a method so that it can be overridden by derived classes. It is used to implement "pretty-printing" methods for source and destination addresses.
>
> ```
> $string = $obj->format_addr($sockaddr);
> $string = $obj->format_addr($sockaddr, $numeric_only);
> $string = format_addr Module $sockaddr;
> $string = format_addr Module $sockaddr, $numeric_only;
> ```
>
> If the $numeric_only argument is true, the address and port number are used, even if they can be resolved to names. Otherwise, the resolved hostname and service name are used if possible.

format_local_addr

> Returns a formatted representation of the local socket address associated with the object. A sugar-coated way of calling the format_addr method for the srcaddr object parameter.
>
> ```
> $string = $obj->format_local_addr;
> $string = $obj->format_local_addr($numeric_only);
> ```

format_remote_addr

> Returns a formatted representation of the remote socket address associated with the object. A sugar-coated way of calling the format_addr method for the dstaddr object parameter.
>
> ```
> $string = $obj->format_remote_addr;
> ```

getsockinfo

> An augmented form of Net::Gen::getsockinfo. Aside from updating more object parameters, it behaves the same as the one in the base class. The additional object parameters that get set are lcladdr, lclhost, lclport, lclservice, remaddr, remhost, remport, and remservice. (They are described in "Known Object Parameters," below.)

Protected Methods

(See the note in "Net::Gen/Protected Methods" about my definition of protected methods in Perl.)

There are no protected methods.

Known Socket Options

These are the socket options known to the Net::Inet module itself:

> IP_HDRINCL, IP_RECVDSTADDR, IP_RECVOPTS, IP_RECVRETOPTS, IP_TOS, IP_TTL, IP_ADD_MEMBERSHIP, IP_DROP_MEMBERSHIP, IP_MULTICAST_IF, IP_MULTICAST_LOOP, IP_MULTICAST_TTL, IP_OPTIONS, IP_RETOPTS

Known Object Parameters

These are the object parameters registered by the Net::Inet module itself:

IPproto

> The name of the Internet protocol in use on the socket associated with the object. Set as a side effect of setting the proto object parameter, and vice versa.

proto

> Used the same way as with Net::Gen, but has a handler attached to keep it in sync with IPproto.

thishost

> The source hostname or address to use for the bind method. When used in conjunction with the thisservice or thisport object parameter, causes the srcaddrlist object parameter to be set; that is how it affects the bind() action. This parameter is validated, and must be either a valid Internet address or a hostname for which an address can be found. If a hostname is given, and multiple addresses are found for it, then each address is entered into the srcaddrlist array reference.

desthost

> The destination hostname or address to use for the connect method. When used in conjunction with the destservice or destport object parameter, causes the dstaddrlist object parameter to be set; that is how it affects the connect() action. This parameter is validated and must be either a valid Internet address or a hostname for which an address can be found. If a hostname is given, and multiple addresses are found for it, then each address is entered into the dstaddrlist array reference, in order. This allows the connect method to attempt a connection to each address, as per RFC 1123.

thisservice

> The source service name (or number) to use for the bind method. An attempt is made to translate the supplied service name with getservbyname(). If that succeeds, or if it fails but the supplied value was strictly numeric, the port number is set in the thisport object parameter. If the supplied value is not numeric and can't be translated, the attempt to set the value fails. Otherwise, the srcaddrlist object parameter is updated, in preparation for an invocation of the bind method (possibly implicitly from the connect method).

thisport

> The source service number (or name) to use for the bind method. An attempt is made to translate the supplied service name with getservbyname() if the value is not strictly numeric. If the translation succeeds, the given name is set in the thisservice parameter, and the resolved port number is set in the thisport object parameter. If the supplied value is strictly numeric, and a call to getservbyport can resolve a name for the service, the thisservice parameter is updated appropriately. If the supplied value is not numeric and can't be translated, the attempt to set the value fails. Otherwise, the srcaddrlist object parameter is updated in preparation for an invocation of the bind method (possibly implicitly from the connect method).

destservice

> The destination service name (or number) to use for the connect method. An attempt is made to translate the supplied service name with getservbyname(). If the translation succeeds, or if it fails but the supplied value was strictly numeric, the port number is set in the destport object parameter. If the supplied value is not numeric and can't be translated, the attempt to set the value fails. Otherwise, if the desthost parameter has a defined value, the dstaddrlist object parameter is updated in preparation for an invocation of the connect method.

destport

> The destination service number (or name) to use for the **connect** method. An attempt is made to translate the supplied service name with **getservbyname**() if the value is not strictly numeric. If that succeeds, the given name is set in the **destservice** parameter, and the resolved port number is set in the **destport** parameter. If the supplied value is strictly numeric, and a call to **getservbyport** can resolve a name for the service, the **destservice** parameter is updated appropriately. If the supplied value is not numeric and can't be translated, the attempt to set the value fails. Otherwise, if the **desthost** parameter has a defined value, the **dstaddrlist** object parameter is updated in preparation for an invocation of the **connect** method.

lcladdr

> The local IP address stashed by the **getsockinfo** method after a successful **bind**() or **connect**() call.

lclhost

> The local hostname stashed by the **getsockinfo** method after a successful **bind**() or **connect**(), as resolved from the **lcladdr** object parameter.

lclport

> The local port number stashed by the **getsockinfo** method after a successful **bind**() or **connect**() call.

lclservice

> The local service name stashed by the **getsockinfo** method after a successful **bind**() or **connect**(), as resolved from the **lclport** object parameter.

remaddr

> The remote IP address stashed by the **getsockinfo** method after a successful **bind**() or **connect**() call.

remhost

> The remote hostname stashed by the **getsockinfo** method after a successful **bind**() or **connect**(), as resolved from the **remaddr** object parameter.

remport

> The remote port number stashed by the **getsockinfo** method after a successful **bind**() or **connect**() call.

remservice

> The remote service name stashed by the **getsockinfo** method after a successful **bind**() or **connect**(), as resolved from the **remport** object parameter.

Non-Method Subroutines

inet_aton

> Returns the packed AF_INET address in network order, if it is validly formed, or undef on error. This used to be a separate implementation in this package, but is now inherited from the Socket module.

```
$in_addr = inet_aton('192.0.2.1');
```

inet_addr

> A synonym for **inet_aton**() (for old fogeys like me who forget about the new name). (Yes, I know it's different in C, but in Perl there's no need to propagate the old **inet_addr**() brain damage, so I didn't.)

inet_ntoa

> Returns the ASCII representation of the AF_INET address provided (if possible), or undef on error. This used to be a separate implementation in this package, but is now inherited from the Socket module.
>
> ```
> $addr_string = inet_ntoa($in_addr);
> ```

htonl
htons
ntohl
ntohs

> As you'd expect, I think.

pack_sockaddr_in

> Returns the packed struct sockaddr_in corresponding to the provided $family, $port, and $in_addr arguments.
>
> ```
> $connect_address =
>         pack_sockaddr_in($family, $port, $in_addr);
> $connect_address = pack_sockaddr_in($port, $in_addr);
> ```
>
> The $family and $port arguments must be numbers, and the $in_addr argument must be a packed struct in_addr, such as the trailing elements from Perl's gethostent() return list. This differs from the implementation in the Socket module in that the $family argument is available (though optional).

unpack_sockaddr_in

> Returns the address family, port, and packed struct in_addr from the supplied packed struct sockaddr_in.
>
> ```
> ($family, $port, $in_addr) =
>         unpack_sockaddr_in($connected_address);
> ```
>
> This is the inverse of pack_sockaddr_in(). This differs from the implementation in the Socket module in that the $family value from the socket address is returned.

INADDR_UNSPEC_GROUP
INADDR_ALLHOSTS_GROUP
INADDR_ALLRTRS_GROUP
INADDR_MAX_LOCAL_GROUP

> Constant routines returning the unspecified local, all hosts, all routers, or the maximum possible local IP multicast group address, respectively. These routines return results in the form of a packed struct inaddr much like the INADDR_ANY results described in Socket/INADDR_ANY.

IN_CLASSA
IN_CLASSB
IN_CLASSC
IN_CLASSD
IN_MULTICAST
IN_EXPERIMENTAL
IN_BADCLASS

> These routines return the *network class* information for the supplied IP address. Of these, only IN_BADCLASS() and IN_MULTICAST() are really useful for today's Internet, since the advent of CIDR (classless Internet domain routing). In particular, IN_EXPERIMENTAL() is at the mercy of your vendor's definition.
>
> ```
> $boolean = IN_EXPERIMENTAL(INADDR_ALLHOSTS_GROUP);
> $boolean = IN_CLASSA(0x7f000001);
> ```

The first example above is true only on older systems, which almost certainly don't support IP multicast anyway. The argument to any of these functions can be either a packed `struct` `inaddr` such as that returned by `inet_ntoa`() or `unpack_sockaddr_in`(), or an integer (or integer expression) giving an IP address in host-byte order.

IPOPT_CLASS
IPOPT_COPIED
IPOPT_NUMBER

These routines extract information from IP option numbers, as per the information on IP options in RFC 791.

```
$optnum = IPOPT_NUMBER($option);

...
```

Other constants that relate to parts of IP or ICMP headers or vendor-defined socket options, as listed in "Exports" below.

Exports

default

INADDR_ALLHOSTS_GROUP, INADDR_ALLRTRS_GROUP, INADDR_ANY, INADDR_BROADCAST, INADDR_LOOPBACK, INADDR_MAX_LOCAL_GROUP, INADDR_NONE, INADDR_UNSPEC_GROUP, IPPORT_RESERVED, IPPORT_USER-RESERVED, IPPROTO_EGP, IPPROTO_EON, IPPROTO_GGP, IPPROTO_HELLO, IPPROTO_ICMP, IPPROTO_IDP, IPPROTO_IGMP, IPPROTO_IP, IPPROTO_IPIP, IPPROTO_MAX, IPPROTO_PUP, IPPROTO_RAW, IPPROTO_RSVP, IPPROTO_TCP, IPPROTO_TP, IPPROTO_UDP, htonl, htons, inet_addr, inet_aton, inet_ntoa, ntohl, ntohs

exportable

DEFTTL, ICMP_ADVLENMIN, ICMP_ECHO, ICMP_ECHOREPLY, ICMP_INFO-TYPE, ICMP_IREQ, ICMP_IREQREPLY, ICMP_MASKLEN, ICMP_MASKREPLY, ICMP_MASKREQ, ICMP_MAXTYPE, ICMP_MINLEN, ICMP_PARAMPROB, ICMP_REDIRECT, ICMP_REDIRECT_HOST, ICMP_REDIRECT_NET, ICMP_REDIRECT_TOSHOST, ICMP_REDIRECT_TOSNET, ICMP_SOURCEQUENCH, ICMP_TIMX-CEED, ICMP_TIMXCEED_INTRANS, ICMP_TIMXCEED_REASS, ICMP_TSLEN, ICMP_TSTAMP, ICMP_TSTAMPREPLY, ICMP_UNREACH, ICMP_UNREACH_HOST, ICMP_UNREACH_NEEDFRAG, ICMP_UNREACH_NET, ICMP_UNREACH_PORT, ICMP_UNREACH_PROTOCOL, ICMP_UNREACH_SRCFAIL, IN_BADCLASS, IN_CLASSA, IN_CLASSA_HOST, IN_CLASSA_MAX, IN_CLASSA_NET, IN_CLASSA_NSHIFT, IN_CLASSA_SUBHOST, IN_CLASSA_SUBNET, IN_CLASSA_SUBNSHIFT, IN_CLASSB, IN_CLASSB_HOST, IN_CLASSB_MAX, IN_CLASSB_NET, IN_CLASSB_NSHIFT, IN_CLASSB_SUBHOST, IN_CLASSB_SUBNET, IN_CLASSB_SUBNSHIFT, IN_CLASSC, IN_CLASSC_HOST, IN_CLASSC_MAX, IN_CLASSC_NET, IN_CLASSC_NSHIFT, IN_CLASSD, IN_CLASSD_HOST, IN_CLASSD_NET, IN_CLASSD_NSHIFT, IN_EXPERIMENTAL, IN_LOOPBACKNET, IN_MULTICAST, IPFRAGTTL, IPOPT_CIPSO, IPOPT_CLASS, IPOPT_CONTROL, IPOPT_COPIED, IPOPT_DEBMEAS, IPOPT_EOL, IPOPT_LSRR, IPOPT_MINOFF, IPOPT_NOP, IPOPT_NUMBER, IPOPT_OFFSET, IPOPT_OLEN, IPOPT_OPTVAL, IPOPT_RESERVED1, IPOPT_RESERVED2, IPOPT_RIPSO_AUX, IPOPT_RR, IPOPT_SATID, IPOPT_SECURITY, IPOPT_SECUR_CONFID, IPOPT_SECUR_EFTO, IPOPT_SECUR_MMMM, IPOPT_SECUR_RESTR, IPOPT_SECUR_SECRET, IPOPT_SECUR_TOPSECRET, IPOPT_SECUR_UNCLASS, IPOPT_SSRR, IPOPT_TS, IPOPT_TS_PRESPEC, IPOPT_TS_TSAN-

DADDR, IPOPT_TS_TSONLY, IPPORT_TIMESERVER, IPTOS_LOWDELAY, IPTOS_PREC_CRITIC_ECP, IPTOS_PREC_FLASH, IPTOS_PREC_FLASHOVERRIDE, IPTOS_PREC_IMMEDIATE, IPTOS_PREC_INTERNETCONTROL, IPTOS_PREC_NETCONTROL, IPTOS_PREC_PRIORITY, IPTOS_PREC_ROUTINE, IPTOS_RELIABILITY, IPTOS_THROUGHPUT, IPTTLDEC, IPVERSION, IP_ADD_MEMBERSHIP, IP_DEFAULT_MULTICAST_LOOP, IP_DEFAULT_MULTICAST_TTL, IP_DF, IP_DROP_MEMBERSHIP, IP_HDRINCL, IP_MAXPACKET, IP_MAX_MEMBERSHIPS, IP_MF, IP_MSS, IP_MULTICAST_IF, IP_MULTICAST_LOOP, IP_MULTICAST_TTL, IP_OPTIONS, IP_RECVDSTADDR, IP_RECVOPTS, IP_RECVRETOPTS, IP_RETOPTS, IP_TOS, IP_TTL, MAXTTL, MAX_IPOPTLEN, MINTTL, SUBNETSHIFT, `pack_sockaddr_in`, `unpack_sockaddr_in`

tags

The following `:tags` are in %EXPORT_TAGS, with the associated exportable values as listed:

`:sockopts`

> IP_HDRINCL, IP_RECVDSTADDR, IP_RECVOPTS, IP_RECVRETOPTS, IP_TOS, IP_TTL, IP_ADD_MEMBERSHIP, IP_DROP_MEMBERSHIP, IP_MULTICAST_IF, IP_MULTICAST_LOOP, IP_MULTICAST_TTL, IP_OPTIONS, IP_RETOPTS

`:routines`

> `pack_sockaddr_in`, `unpack_sockaddr_in`, `inet_ntoa`, `inet_aton`, `inet_addr`, `htonl`, `ntohl`, `htons`, `ntohs`, ICMP_INFOTYPE, IN_BADCLASS, IN_EXPERIMENTAL, IN_MULTICAST, IPOPT_CLASS, IPOPT_COPIED, IPOPT_NUMBER

`:icmpvalues`

> ICMP_ADVLENMIN, ICMP_ECHO, ICMP_ECHOREPLY, ICMP_IREQ, ICMP_IREQREPLY, ICMP_MASKLEN, ICMP_MASKREPLY, ICMP_MASKREQ, ICMP_MAXTYPE, ICMP_MINLEN, ICMP_PARAMPROB, ICMP_REDIRECT, ICMP_REDIRECT_HOST, ICMP_REDIRECT_NET, ICMP_REDIRECT_TOSHOST, ICMP_REDIRECT_TOSNET, ICMP_SOURCEQUENCH, ICMP_TIMXCEED, ICMP_TIMXCEED_INTRANS, ICMP_TIMXCEED_REASS, ICMP_TSLEN, ICMP_TSTAMP, ICMP_TSTAMPREPLY, ICMP_UNREACH, ICMP_UNREACH_HOST, ICMP_UNREACH_NEEDFRAG, ICMP_UNREACH_NET, ICMP_UNREACH_PORT, ICMP_UNREACH_PROTOCOL, ICMP_UNREACH_SRCFAIL

`:ipoptions`

> IPOPT_CIPSO, IPOPT_CONTROL, IPOPT_DEBMEAS, IPOPT_EOL, IPOPT_LSRR, IPOPT_MINOFF, IPOPT_NOP, IPOPT_OFFSET, IPOPT_OLEN, IPOPT_OPTVAL, IPOPT_RESERVED1, IPOPT_RESERVED2, IPOPT_RIPSO_AUX, IPOPT_RR, IPOPT_SATID, IPOPT_SECURITY, IPOPT_SECUR_CONFID, IPOPT_SECUR_EFTO, IPOPT_SECUR_MMMM, IPOPT_SECUR_RESTR, IPOPT_SECUR_SECRET, IPOPT_SECUR_TOPSECRET, IPOPT_SECUR_UNCLASS, IPOPT_SSRR, IPOPT_TS, IPOPT_TS_PRESPEC, IPOPT_TS_TSANDADDR, IPOPT_TS_TSONLY, MAX_IPOPTLEN

`:iptosvalues`

> IPTOS_LOWDELAY, IPTOS_PREC_CRITIC_ECP, IPTOS_PREC_FLASH, IPTOS_PREC_FLASHOVERRIDE, IPTOS_PREC_IMMEDIATE, IPTOS_PREC_INTERNETCONTROL, IPTOS_PREC_NETCONTROL, IPTOS_PREC_PRIORITY, IPTOS_PREC_ROUTINE, IPTOS_RELIABILITY, IPTOS_THROUGHPUT

`:protocolvalues`
> DEFTTL, INADDR_ALLHOSTS_GROUP, INADDR_ALLRTRS_GROUP, INADDR_ANY, INADDR_BROADCAST, INADDR_LOOPBACK, INADDR_MAX_LOCAL_GROUP, INADDR_NONE, INADDR_UNSPEC_GROUP, IN_LOOPBACKNET, IPPORT_RESERVED, IPPORT_USERRESERVED, IPPROTO_EGP, IPPROTO_EON, IPPROTO_GGP, IPPROTO_HELLO, IPPROTO_ICMP, IPPROTO_IDP, IPPROTO_IGMP, IPPROTO_IP, IPPROTO_IPIP, IPPROTO_MAX, IPPROTO_PUP, IPPROTO_RAW, IPPROTO_RSVP, IPPROTO_TCP, IPPROTO_TP, IPPROTO_UDP, IPFRAGTTL, IPTTLDEC, IPVERSION, IP_DF, IP_MAXPACKET, IP_MF, IP_MSS, MAXTTL, MAX_IPOPTLEN, MINTTL

`:ipmulticast`
> IP_ADD_MEMBERSHIP, IP_DEFAULT_MULTICAST_LOOP, IP_DEFAULT_MULTICAST_TTL, IP_DROP_MEMBERSHIP, IP_MAX_MEMBERSHIPS, IP_MULTICAST_IF, IP_MULTICAST_LOOP, IP_MULTICAST_TTL

`:deprecated`
> IN_CLASSA_HOST, IN_CLASSA_MAX, IN_CLASSA_NET, IN_CLASSA_NSHIFT, IN_CLASSA_SUBHOST, IN_CLASSA_SUBNET, IN_CLASSA_SUBNSHIFT, IN_CLASSB_HOST, IN_CLASSB_MAX, IN_CLASSB_NET, IN_CLASSB_NSHIFT, IN_CLASSB_SUBHOST, IN_CLASSB_SUBNET, IN_CLASSB_SUBNSHIFT, IN_CLASSC_HOST, IN_CLASSC_MAX, IN_CLASSC_NET, IN_CLASSC_NSHIFT, IN_CLASSD_HOST, IN_CLASSD_NET, IN_CLASSD_NSHIFT, IN_CLASSA, IN_CLASSB, IN_CLASSC, IN_CLASSD, IPPORT_TIMESERVER, SUBNETSHIFT

`:ALL`
> All of the above exportable items.

Notes

Anywhere a service or port argument is used above, the allowed syntax is either a service name, a port number, or a service name with a caller-supplied default port number. Examples are `echo`, `7`, and `echo(7)`, respectively. For a service argument, a bare port number must be translatable into a service name with `getservbyport()` or an error results. A service name must be translatable into a port with `getservbyname()` or an error results. However, a service name with a default port number succeeds (by using the supplied default), even if the translation with `getservbyname()` fails.

Not Yet Implemented

There is still no way to pretty-print the connection information after a successful `connect()` or `accept()`. (That's not strictly still true, but the following still holds.) This is largely because I'm not satisfied with any of the obvious ways to do it. Now taking suggestions. Proposals so far:

```
($peerproto, $peername, $peeraddr, $peerport, $peerservice) =
    $obj->getsockinfo;
@conninfo = $obj->getsockinfo($sockaddr_in);
# the above pair are a single proposal
%conninfo = $obj->getsockinfo;
%conninfo = $obj->getsockinfo($sockaddr_in);
# for these, the keys would be qw(proto hostname address port
    service)
```

Of course, it's probably better to return references rather than actual arrays, but you get the idea.

Author

Spider Boardman, *spider@Orb.Nashua.NH.US*

Net::Netrc—object-oriented interface to users' *.netrc* file

Synopsis

```
use Net::Netrc;

$mach = Net::Netrc->lookup('some.machine');
$login = $mach->login;
($login, $password, $account) = $mach->lpa;
```

Description

Net::Netrc is a class implementing a simple interface to the *.netrc* file used as by the FTP program.

Net::Netrc also implements security checks just like the FTP program. Net::Netrc checks first to be sure that the *.netrc* file is owned by the user; second, it checks that the ownership permissions are such that only the owner has read and write access. If these conditions are not met then a warning is output and the *.netrc* file is not read.

The .netrc File

The *.netrc* file contains login and initialization information used by the autologin process. It resides in the user's home directory. The following tokens are recognized; they may be separated by spaces, tabs, or new lines:

machine name

>   Identifies a remote machine name. The autologin process searches the *.netrc* file for a machine token that matches the remote machine specified. Once a match is made, the subsequent *.netrc* tokens are processed, stopping when the end of the file is reached or another machine or a default token is encountered.

default

>   This is the same as **machine name** except that **default** matches any name. There can be only one **default** token, and it must be after all machine tokens. This is normally used as:

>   default login anonymous password user@site

>   thereby giving the user automatic anonymous login to machines not specified in *.netrc*.

login name

>   Identifies a user on the remote machine. If this token is present, the autologin process initiates a login using the specified name.

password string

>   Supplies a password. If this token is present, the autologin process supplies the specified string if the remote server requires a password as part of the login process.

`account string`

> Supplies an additional account password. If this token is present, the autologin process supplies the specified string if the remote server requires an additional account password.

`macdef name`

> Defines a macro. Net::Netrc only parses this field to be compatible with FTP.

Constructor

The constructor for a Net::Netrc object is not called new, as it does not really create a new object. Instead, it is called lookup, as this is essentially what it does.

`lookup ( MACHINE [, LOGIN ])`

> Looks up and returns a reference to the entry for *MACHINE*. If *LOGIN* is given, then the entry returned has the given login. If *LOGIN* is not given, then the first entry in the *.netrc* file for *MACHINE* is returned.

If a matching entry cannot be found, and a default entry exists, then a reference to the default entry is returned.

Methods

`login ()`

> Returns the login id for the *.netrc* entry.

`password ()`

> Returns the password for the *.netrc* entry.

`account ()`

> Returns the account information for the *.netrc* entry.

`lpa ()`

> Returns a list of login, password and account information for the *.netrc* entry.

Author

Graham Barr, *gbarr@pobox.com*

See Also

Net::Netrc, Net::Cmd

Copyright

Copyright © 1995–1997 Graham Barr. All rights reserved. This program is free software; you can redistribute it and/or modify it under the same terms as Perl itself.

Net::NNTP—NNTP Client class

Synopsis

```
use Net::NNTP;

$nntp = Net::NNTP->new("some.host.name");
$nntp->quit;
```

Description

Net::NNTP is a class implementing a simple NNTP client in Perl, as described in RFC 977. Net::NNTP inherits its communication methods from Net::Cmd.

Constructor

`new ( [ HOST ] [, OPTIONS ])`

> This is the constructor for a new Net::NNTP object. *HOST* is the name of the remote host to which an NNTP connection is required. If not given, the two environment variables NNTPSERVER and NEWSHOST are checked, then Net::Config is checked, and if a host is not found, then **news** is used.

> *OPTIONS* are passed in a hash-like fashion, using key value pairs. Possible options are:

> `Timeout`
>> Specifies the maximum time, in seconds, to wait for a response from the NNTP server; a value of zero causes all I/O operations to block. (The default is 120.)

> `Debug`
>> Enables the printing of debugging information to STDERR.

Methods

Unless otherwise stated, all methods return either a **true** or **false** value, with **true** meaning that the operation was a success. When a method states that it returns a value, failure is returned as undef or an empty list.

`article ( [ MSGID|MSGNUM ] )`

> Retrieves the header, a blank line, and the body (text) of the specified article.

> If no arguments are passed, the current article in the current newsgroup is returned.

> *MSGNUM* is the numeric id of an article in the current newsgroup, and it changes the current article pointer. *MSGID* is the message id of an article, as shown in that article's header. It is anticipated that the client will obtain the *MSGID* from a list provided by the **newnews** command, from references contained within another article, or from the message-id provided in the response to some other commands.

> Returns a reference to an array containing the article.

`body ( [ MSGID|MSGNUM ] )`

> Retrieves the body (text) of the specified article.

> Takes the same arguments as **article**.

> Returns a reference to an array containing the body of the article.

`head ( [ MSGID|MSGNUM ] )`

> Retrieves the header of the specified article.

> Takes the same arguments as **article**.

> Returns a reference to an array containing the header of the article.

`nntpstat ( [ MSGID|MSGNUM ] )`

> The nntpstat command is similar to the **article** command, except that no text is returned. When selecting by message number within a group, the nntpstat command serves to set the "current article pointer" without sending text.

Using the nntpstat command to select by message-id is valid, but of question-able value, since a selection by message-id does *not* alter the current article pointer.

Returns the message-id of the current article.

group ([*GROUP*])

Sets and/or gets the current group. If *GROUP* is not given, then information is returned on the current group.

In a scalar context, the command returns the group name.

In an array context, the return value is a list containing the number of articles in the group, the number of the first article, the number of the last article, and the group name.

ihave (*MSGID* [, *MESSAGE*])

The ihave command informs the server that the client has an article whose id is *MSGID*. If the server desires a copy of that article, and *MESSAGE* has been given, the article is sent.

Returns true if the server desires the article and *MESSAGE*, if specified, was successfully sent.

If *MESSAGE* is not specified, then the message must be sent using the datasend and dataend methods from Net::Cmd.

MESSAGE can be either an array of lines or a reference to an array.

last ()

Sets the current article pointer to the previous article in the current newsgroup.

Returns the message-id of the article.

date ()

Returns the date on the remote server, in a UNIX time format (seconds since 1970).

postok ()

postok returns true if the server's initial response indicated that it will allow posting.

authinfo (*USER*, *PASS*)
list ()

Obtains information about all the active newsgroups. The result is a reference to a hash where the key is a group name and each value is a reference to an array. The elements in this array are: the first article number in the group, the last article number in the group, and any information flags about the group.

newgroups (*SINCE* [, *DISTRIBUTIONS*])

SINCE is a time value and *DISTRIBUTIONS* is either a distribution pattern or a reference to a list of distribution patterns. The result is the same as list, but the groups returned are limited to those created after *SINCE* and in one of the distri-bution areas in *DISTRIBUTIONS*, if specified.

newnews (*SINCE* [, *GROUPS* [, *DISTRIBUTIONS*]])

Returns a reference to a list that contains the message-ids of all news posted after *SINCE*, which are in a group that matches *GROUPS* and a distribution that matches *DISTRIBUTIONS*.

SINCE is a time value. *GROUPS* is either a group pattern or a reference to a list of group patterns. *DISTRIBUTIONS* is either a distribution pattern or a reference to a list of distribution patterns.

next ()

Sets the current article pointer to the next article in the current newsgroup.

Returns the message-id of the article.

post ([*MESSAGE*])

Posts a new article to the news server. If *MESSAGE* is specified and posting is allowed, then the message is sent.

If *MESSAGE* is not specified, then the message must be sent using the **datasend** and **dataend** methods from Net::Cmd.

MESSAGE can be either an array of lines or a reference to an array.

slave ()

Tells the remote server that I am not a user client, but probably another news server.

quit ()

Quits the remote server and closes the socket connection.

Extension methods

These methods use commands that are not part of the RFC 977 documentation. Some servers may not support all of them.

newsgroups ([*PATTERN*])

Returns a reference to a hash where the keys are all the group names that match *PATTERN*, or all of the groups if no pattern is specified, and each value contains the description text for the group.

distributions ()

Returns a reference to a hash where the keys are all the possible distribution names and the values are the distribution descriptions.

subscriptions ()

Returns a reference to a list containing a list of groups that are recommended for a new user to subscribe to.

overview_fmt ()

Returns a reference to an array that contains the names of the fields returned by xover.

active_times ()

Returns a reference to a hash, where the keys are the group names and each value is a reference to an array containing the time the group was created and an identifier, possibly an email address, of the creator.

active ([*PATTERN*])

Similar to list, but only active groups that match the pattern are returned. *PATTERN* can be a group pattern.

xgtitle (*PATTERN*)

Returns a reference to a hash, where the keys are all the group names that match *PATTERN* and each value is the description text for the group.

xhdr (*HEADER, MESSAGE-SPEC*)

Obtains the header field *HEADER* for all the messages specified.

The return value is a reference to a hash, where the keys are the message numbers and each value contains the text of the requested header for that message.

xover (*MESSAGE-SPEC*)

The return value is a reference to a hash, where the keys are the message numbers and each value contains a reference to an array that contains the overview fields for that message.

The names of the fields can be obtained by calling overview_fmt.

xpath (*MESSAGE-ID*)

Returns the pathname to the file on the server that contains the specified message.

xpat (*HEADER, PATTERN, MESSAGE-SPEC*)

The result is the same as xhdr, except that it is restricted to headers where the text of the header matches *PATTERN.*

xrover

The XROVER command returns reference information for the article(s) specified.

Returns a reference to a hash, where the keys are the message numbers and the values are the References: lines from the articles.

listgroup ([*GROUP*])

Returns a reference to a list of all the active messages in *GROUP,* or the current group if *GROUP* is not specified.

reader

Tells the server that you are a reader and not another server.

This is required by some servers. For example, if you are connecting to an INN server and you have transfer permission, your connection will be connected to the transfer daemon, not the NNTP daemon. Issuing this command causes the transfer daemon to hand over control to the NNTP daemon.

Some servers do not understand this command, but issuing it and ignoring the response is harmless.

Unsupported

The following NNTP commands are unsupported by the package, and there are no plans to provide support:

- AUTHINFO GENERIC
- XTHREAD
- XSEARCH
- XINDEX

Definitions

MESSAGE-SPEC

MESSAGE-SPEC is either a single message-id, a single message number, or a reference to a list of two message numbers.

If MESSAGE-SPEC is a reference to a list of two message numbers and the second number in a range is less than or equal to the first, then the range represents all the messages in the group after the first message number.

Note: For compatibility with earlier versions of Net::NNTP, a message spec can be passed as a list of two numbers. This is deprecated, and a reference to the list should now be passed.

PATTERN

The NNTP protocol uses the WILDMAT format for patterns. The WILDMAT format was first developed by Rich Salz based on the format used in the UNIX find command to articulate filenames. It was developed to provide a uniform mechanism for matching patterns in the same manner that the UNIX shell matches filenames.

Patterns are implicitly anchored at the beginning and end of each string when testing for a match.

There are five pattern-matching operations other than a strict one-to-one match between the pattern and the source to be checked for a match.

The first is an asterisk (*) to match any sequence of zero or more characters.

The second is a question mark (?) to match any single character. The third specifies a specific set of characters.

The set is specified as a list of characters, or as a range of characters where the beginning and end of the range are separated by a minus (or dash) character, or as any combination of lists and ranges. The dash can also be included in the set as a character if it is the beginning or end of the set. This set is enclosed in square brackets. The close square bracket (]) may be used in a set if it is the first character in the set.

The fourth operation is the same as the logical not of the third operation and is specified the same way as the third, with the addition of a caret character (^) at the beginning of the test string, just inside the open square bracket.

The final operation uses the backslash character to invalidate the special meaning of the open square bracket ([), the asterisk, the backslash, or the question mark. Two backslashes in sequence result in the evaluation of the backslash as a character with no special meaning.

Examples

[^]-] matches any single character other than a close square bracket or a minus sign/dash.

*bdc matches any string that ends with the string "bdc", including the string "bdc" (without quotes).

[0-9a-zA-Z] matches any single printable alphanumeric ASCII character.

a??d matches any four-character string that begins with a and ends with d.

See Also

Net::Cmd

Author

Graham Barr, *gbarr@pobox.com*

Copyright

Net::PH—CCSO nameserver client class

Synopsis

```
use Net::PH;

$ph = Net::PH->new("some.host.name",
                   Port    => 105,
                   Timeout => 120,
                   Debug   => 0);
if($ph) {
    $q = $ph->query({ field1 => "value1" },
                    [qw(name address pobox)]);

    if($q) {
    }
}

# Alternative syntax

if($ph) {
    $q = $ph->query('field1=value1',
                    'name address pobox');

    if($q) {
    }
}
```

Description

Net::PH is a class implementing a simple nameserver/PH client in Perl as described in the CCSO nameserver—Server-Client Protocol. Like other modules in the Net:: family the Net::PH object inherits methods from Net::Cmd.

Constructor

new ([*HOST*] [, *OPTIONS*])

This is the constructor for a new Net::PH object. *HOST* is the name of the remote host to which a PH connection is required.

```
$ph = Net::PH->new("some.host.name",
                   Port    => 105,
                   Timeout => 120,
                   Debug   => 0
                   );
```

If *HOST* is not given, then the SNPP_Host specified in Net::Config is used.

OPTIONS is an optional list of named options that are passed in a hash-like fashion, using key and value pairs. Possible options are the following.

Port
> Port number to connect to on remote host.

Timeout
> Maximum time, in seconds, to wait for a response from the nameserver; a value of zero causes all I/O operations to block. (The default is 120.)

Debug
> Enables the printing of debugging information to STDERR.

Methods

Unless otherwise stated, all methods return either a `true` or `false` value, with `true` meaning that the operation was a success. When a method states that it returns a value, failure is returned as undef or as an empty list.

`query( SEARCH [, RETURN ] )`
> Searches the database and returns fields from all matching entries.

```
$q = $ph->query({ name => $myname },
                [qw(name email schedule)]);


foreach $handle (@{$q}) {
    foreach $field (keys %{$handle}) {
        $c = ${$handle}{$field}->code;
        $v = ${$handle}{$field}->value;
        $f = ${$handle}{$field}->field;
        $t = ${$handle}{$field}->text;
        print "field:[$field] [$c][$v][$f][$t]\n" ;
    }
}
```

> The *SEARCH* argument is a reference to a hash containing field/value pairs that are passed to the nameserver as the search criteria.
>
> *RETURN* is optional, but if given, it should be a reference to a list that contains field names to be returned.
>
> The alternative syntax is to pass strings instead of references, for example:

```
$q = $ph->query('name=myname',
                'name email schedule');
```

> The *SEARCH* argument is a string that is passed to the nameserver as the search criteria.
>
> *RETURN* is optional, but if given, it should be a string that will contain field names being returned.
>
> Each match from the server is returned as a hash, where the keys are the field names and the values are Net::PH:Result objects (`code`, `value`, `field`, `text`).
>
> Returns a reference to an array that contains references to hashs, one per match, from the server.

`change( SEARCH , MAKE )`
> Changes field values for matching entries.

```
$r = $ph->change({ email => "*.domain.name" },
                 { schedule => "busy");
```

> The *SEARCH* argument is a reference to a hash containing field/value pairs that are passed to the nameserver as the search criteria.

The *MAKE* argument is a reference to a hash containing field/value pairs that are passed to the nameserver to set new values to designated fields.

The alternative syntax is to pass strings instead of references, for example:

```
$r = $ph->change('email="*.domain.name"',
                 'schedule="busy"');
```

Using that syntax, the *SEARCH* argument is a string passed to the nameserver as the search criteria and the *MAKE* argument is a string passed to the nameserver that will set new values to designated fields.

Upon success, all entries that match the search criteria have the new field values given in the *MAKE* argument.

login(*USER, PASS* [, *ENCRYPT*])

Enter login mode using *USER* and *PASS*.

```
$r = $ph->login('username','password',1);
```

If *ENCRYPT* is given and is true, then the password is used to encrypt a challenge text string provided by the server, and the encrypted string is sent back to the server. If *ENCRYPT* is not given, or is false, then the password is sent in clear text (this is not recommended).

logout()

Exit login mode and return to anonymous mode.

```
$r = $ph->logout();
```

fields([*FIELD_LIST*])

Returns a reference to a hash.

```
$fields = $ph->fields();
foreach $field (keys %{$fields}) {
    $c = ${$fields}{$field}->code;
    $v = ${$fields}{$field}->value;
    $f = ${$fields}{$field}->field;
    $t = ${$fields}{$field}->text;
    print "field:[$field] [$c][$v][$f][$t]\n";
}
```

The keys of the hash are the field names and the values are Net::PH:Result objects (code, value, field, text).

FIELD_LIST is a string that lists the fields for which info is returned.

add(*FIELD_VALUES*)

This method is used to add new entries to the nameserver database. You must successfully call the *login* manpage before this method can be used.

```
$r = $ph->add( { name => $name, phone => $phone });
```

Note: This method adds new entries to the database. To modify an existing entry, use the *change* manpage.

FIELD_VALUES is a reference to a hash containing field/value pairs that are passed to the nameserver and used to initialize the new entry.

The alternative syntax is to pass a string instead of a reference, for example:

```
$r = $ph->add('name=myname phone=myphone');
```

In that case, *FIELD_VALUES* is a string consisting of field/value pairs that the new entry will contain.

delete(*FIELD_VALUES*)

> This method is used to delete existing entries from the nameserver database. You must successfully call the login manpage before this method can be used.

> ```
> $r = $ph->delete('name=myname phone=myphone');
> ```

> Note: This method deletes entries to the database. To modify an existing entry, use the change manpage .

> *FIELD_VALUES* is a string that serves as the search criteria for the records to be deleted. Any entry in the database that matches this search criteria is deleted.

id([*ID*])

> Sends *ID* to the nameserver, which enters it into its logs. If *ID* is not given, then the UID of the user running the process is sent.

> ```
> $r = $ph->id('709');
> ```

status()

> Returns the current status of the nameserver.

siteinfo()

> Returns a reference to a hash containing information about the server's site.

> ```
> $siteinfo = $ph->siteinfo();
> foreach $field (keys %{$siteinfo}) {
>     $c = ${$siteinfo}{$field}->code;
>     $v = ${$siteinfo}{$field}->value;
>     $f = ${$siteinfo}{$field}->field;
>     $t = ${$siteinfo}{$field}->text;
>     print "field:[$field] [$c][$v][$f][$t]\n";
> }
> ```

> The keys of the hash are the field names and the values are Net::PH:Result objects (code, value, field, text).

quit()

> Quits the connection.

> ```
> $r = $ph->quit();
> ```

Q&A

How do I get the values of a Net::PH::Result object?

```
foreach $handle (@{$q}) {
    foreach $field (keys %{$handle}) {
        $my_code  = ${$q}{$field}->code;
        $my_value = ${$q}{$field}->value;
        $my_field = ${$q}{$field}->field;
        $my_text  = ${$q}{$field}->text;
    }
}
```

How do I get a count of the returned matches to my query?

```
$my_count = scalar(@{$query_result});
```

How do I get the status code and message of the last $ph command?

```
$status_code    = $ph->code;
$status_message = $ph->message;
```

See Also

Net::Cmd

Authors

Graham Barr, *gbarr@pobox.com*; Alex Hristov, *hristov@slb.com*

Acknowledgments

Password encryption code ported to Perl by Broc Seib *(bseib@purdue.edu)*, Purdue University Computing Center.

Otis Gospodnetic *(otisg@panther.middlebury.edu)* suggested passing parameters as string constants. Some queries cannot be executed when passing parameters as string references.

Example:

```
query first_name last_name email="*.domain"
```

Copyright

The encryption code is based upon `cryptit.c`, copyright © 1988 by Steven Dorner and the University of Illinois Board of Trustees, and by CSNET.

All other code is copyright © 1996–1997 Graham Barr *(gbarr@pobox.com)* and Alex Hristov *(hristov@slb.com)*. All rights reserved. This program is free software; you can redistribute it and/or modify it under the same terms as Perl itself.

Net::Ping—check a remote host for reachability

Synopsis

```
use Net::Ping;
$p = Net::Ping->new();
print "$host is alive.\n" if $p->ping($host);
$p->close();
$p = Net::Ping->new("icmp");
foreach $host (@host_array)
{
    print "$host is ";
    print "NOT " unless $p->ping($host, 2);
    print "reachable.\n";
    sleep(1);
}
$p->close();

$p = Net::Ping->new("tcp", 2);
while ($stop_time > time())
{
    print "$host not reachable ", scalar(localtime()), "\n"
        unless $p->ping($host);
    sleep(300);
}
undef($p);

# For backward compatibility
print "$host is alive.\n" if pingecho($host);
```

Description

This module contains methods to test the reachability of remote hosts on a network. A ping object is first created with optional parameters; a variable number of hosts may be pinged multiple times, and then the connection is closed.

You may choose one of three different protocols to use for the ping. With the tcp protocol the ping() method attempts to establish a connection to the remote host's echo port. If the connection is successfully established, the remote host is considered reachable. No data is actually echoed. This protocol does not require any special privileges, but has higher overhead than the other two protocols.

Specifying the udp protocol causes the ping() method to send a udp packet to the remote host's echo port. If the echoed packet is received from the remote host and the received packet contains the same data as the packet that was sent, the remote host is considered reachable. This protocol does not require any special privileges.

If the icmp protocol is specified, the ping() method sends an icmp echo message to the remote host, which is what the UNIX ping program does. If the echoed message is received from the remote host and the echoed information is correct, the remote host is considered reachable. Specifying the icmp protocol requires that the program be run as root or that the program be setuid to root.

Functions

Net::Ping->new([$proto [, $def_timeout [, $bytes]]]);

> Creates a new ping object. All of the parameters are optional. *$proto* specifies the protocol to use when doing a ping. The current choices are tcp, udp, or icmp. The default is udp.
>
> If a default timeout (*$def_timeout*) in seconds is provided, it is used when a timeout is not given to the ping() method (below). The timeout must be greater than 0 and the default, if not specified, is 5 seconds.
>
> If the number of data bytes (*$bytes*) is given, that many data bytes are included in the ping packet sent to the remote host. The number of data bytes is ignored if the protocol is tcp. The minimum (and default) number of data bytes is 1 if the protocol is udp and 0 otherwise. The maximum number of data bytes that can be specified is 1024.

$p->ping($host [, $timeout]);

> Pings the remote host and waits for a response. *$host* can be either the hostname or the IP number of the remote host. The optional timeout must be greater than 0 seconds and defaults to whatever was specified when the ping object was created. If the hostname cannot be found, or if there is a problem with the IP number, undef is returned. Otherwise, 1 is returned if the host is reachable and 0 if it is not. For all practical purposes, undef and 0 can be treated as the same case.

$p->close();

> Close the network connection for this ping object. The network connection is also closed by undef $p. The network connection is automatically closed if the ping object goes out of scope (e.g., $p is local to a subroutine, and you leave the subroutine).

pingecho($host [, $timeout]);

> To provide backward compatibility with the previous version of Net::Ping, a pingecho() subroutine is available with the same functionality as before.

pingecho() uses the tcp protocol. The return values and parameters are the same as described for the ping() method. This subroutine is obsolete and may be removed in a future version of Net::Ping.

Warning

pingecho(), or a ping object with the tcp protocol, uses alarm() to implement the timeout. So, don't use alarm() in your program while you are using pingecho() or a ping object with the tcp protocol. The udp and icmp protocols do not use alarm() to implement the timeout.

Notes

There will be less network overhead (and some efficiency in your program) if you specify either the udp or the icmp protocol. The tcp protocol generates at least 2.5 times the traffic for each ping than either udp or icmp does. If many hosts are pinged frequently, you may wish to implement a small wait (e.g., 25 ms or more) between each ping to avoid flooding your network with packets.

The icmp protocol requires that the program be run as root or that it be setuid to root. The tcp and udp protocols do not require special privileges, but not all network devices implement the echo protocol for tcp or udp.

Local hosts should normally respond to pings within milliseconds. However, on a very congested network, it may take up to three seconds or longer to receive an echo packet from a remote host. If the timeout is set too low under these conditions, it will appear that the remote host is not reachable (which is almost the truth).

Reachability doesn't necessarily mean that the remote host is actually functioning, beyond its ability to echo packets.

Because of a lack of anything better, this module uses its own routines to pack and unpack ICMP packets. It would be better for a separate module to be written that understands all of the different kinds of ICMP packets.

Net::POP3 — Post Office Protocol 3 Client class (RFC 1081)

Synopsis

```
use Net::POP3;

# Constructors
$pop = Net::POP3->new('pop3host');
$pop = Net::POP3->new('pop3host', Timeout => 60);
```

Description

This module implements a client interface to the POP3 protocol, enabling a Perl application to talk to POP3 servers. This documentation assumes that you are familiar with the POP3 protocol described in RFC 1081.

A new Net::POP3 object must be created with the new method. Once this has been done, all POP3 commands are accessed via method calls on the object.

Constructor

`new ( [ HOST, ] [ OPTIONS ] )`

> This is the constructor for a new Net::POP3 object. *HOST* is the name of the remote host to which a POP3 connection is required.
>
> If *HOST* is not given, then the POP3_Host specified in Net::Config is used.
>
> *OPTIONS* are passed in a hash-like fashion, using key and value pairs. Possible options are:

> `Timeout`
>> Maximum time, in seconds, to wait for a response from the POP3 server (the default is 120).

> `Debug`
>> Enables debugging information.

Methods

Unless otherwise stated, all methods return either a `true` or `false` value, with `true` meaning that the operation was a success. When a method states that it returns a value, failure is returned as undef or an empty list.

`user ( USER )`

> Sends the *USER* command.

`pass ( PASS )`

> Sends the *PASS* command. Returns the number of messages in the mailbox.

`login ( [ USER [, PASS ]] )`

> Sends both the the *USER* and *PASS* commands. If *PASS* is not given, Net::POP3 uses Net::Netrc to lookup the password using the host and username. If the username is not specified, then the current username is used.
>
> Returns the number of messages in the mailbox.

`top ( MSGNUM [, NUMLINES ] )`

> Gets the header and the first *NUMLINES* of the body for the message *MSGNUM*. Returns a reference to an array that contains the lines of text read from the server.

`list ( [ MSGNUM ] )`

> If called with an argument, `list` returns the size of the message in octets.
>
> If called without arguments, a reference to a hash is returned. The keys are the *MSGNUM*s of all undeleted messages and the values are their size in octets.

`get ( MSGNUM )`

> Gets the message *MSGNUM* from the remote mailbox. Returns a reference to an array that contains the lines of text read from the server.

`last ()`

> Returns the highest *MSGNUM* of all the messages accessed.

`popstat ()`

> Returns an array of two elements: the number of undeleted elements and the size of the mailbox in octets.

`delete ( MSGNUM )`

> Marks message *MSGNUM* to be deleted from the remote mailbox. All messages that are marked to be deleted are removed from the remote mailbox when the server connection closed.

reset ()

Resets the status of the remote POP3 server. This includes resetting the status of all messages to not be deleted.

quit ()

Quits and closes the connection to the remote POP3 server. Any messages marked as deleted are deleted from the remote mailbox.

Note

If a Net::POP3 object goes out of scope before the **quit** method is called, then the **reset** method is called before the connection is closed. This means that any messages marked for deletion will not be deleted.

See Also

Net::Netrc, Net::Cmd

Author

Graham Barr, *gbarr@pobox.com*

Copyright

Copyright © 1995–1997 Graham Barr. All rights reserved. This program is free software; you can redistribute it and/or modify it under the same terms as Perl itself.

Net::SMTP—Simple Mail Transfer Protocol client

Synopsis

```
use Net::SMTP;

# Constructors
$smtp = Net::SMTP->new('mailhost');
$smtp = Net::SMTP->new('mailhost', Timeout => 60);
```

Description

This module implements a client interface to the SMTP and ESMTP protocol, enabling a Perl application to talk to SMTP servers. This documentation assumes that you are familiar with the concepts of the SMTP protocol described in RFC 821.

A new Net::SMTP object must be created with the **new** method. Once this has been done, all SMTP commands are accessed through this object. The Net::SMTP class is a subclass of Net::Cmd and IO::Socket::INET.

Examples

This example prints the mail domain name of the SMTP server known as mailhost:

```
#!/usr/local/bin/perl -w

use Net::SMTP;

$smtp = Net::SMTP->new('mailhost');
print $smtp->domain,"\n";
$smtp->quit;
```

This example sends a small message to the postmaster at the SMTP server known as mailhost:

```
#!/usr/local/bin/perl -w

use Net::SMTP;

$smtp = Net::SMTP->new('mailhost');

$smtp->mail($ENV{USER});
$smtp->to('postmaster');

$smtp->data();
$smtp->datasend("To: postmaster\n");
$smtp->datasend("\n");
$smtp->datasend("A simple test message\n");
$smtp->dataend();

$smtp->quit;
```

Constructor

new Net::SMTP [*HOST,*] [*OPTIONS*]

This is the constructor for a new Net::SMTP object. *HOST* is the name of the remote host to which an SMTP connection is required.

If *HOST* is not given, then the SMTP_Host specified in Net::Config is used.

OPTIONS are passed in a hash-like fashion, using key and value pairs. Possible options are:

Hello

SMTP requires that you identify yourself. This option specifies a string to pass as your mail domain. If not given, a guess will be taken.

Timeout

Maximum time, in seconds, to wait for a response from the SMTP server (default: 120).

Debug

Enables debugging information.

Example:

```
$smtp = Net::SMTP->new('mailhost',
                    Hello => 'my.mail.domain'
                    Timeout => 30,
                    Debug   => 1,
                   );
```

Methods

Unless otherwise stated, all methods return either a **true** or **false** value, with **true** meaning that the operation was a success. When a method states that it returns a value, failure is returned as undef or an empty list.

domain ()

Returns the domain that the remote SMTP server identified itself as during connection.

hello (*DOMAIN*)

Tells the remote server the mail domain that you are in, using the EHLO command (or HELO if EHLO fails). Since this method is invoked automatically when the Net::SMTP object is constructed, the user should normally not have to call it manually.

mail (*ADDRESS* [, *OPTIONS*])
send (*ADDRESS*)
send_or_mail (*ADDRESS*)
send_and_mail (*ADDRESS*)

Sends the appropriate command to the server: MAIL, SEND, SOML, or SAML. *ADDRESS* is the address of the sender. This initiates the sending of a message. The method `recipient` should be called for each address that the message is to be sent to.

The `mail` method can some additional ESMTP *OPTIONS*, which are passed in hash-like fashion, using key and value pairs. Possible options are:

```
Size        => <bytes>
Return      => <???>
Bits        => "7" | "8"
Transaction => <ADDRESS>
Envelope    => <ENVID>
```

reset ()

Resets the status of the server. This may be called after a message has been initiated, but before any data has been sent, to cancel the sending of the message.

recipient (*ADDRESS* [, *ADDRESS* [...]])

Notifies the server that the current message should be sent to all of the addresses given. Each address is sent as a separate command to the server. Should the sending of any address result in a failure, then the process is aborted and a `false` value is returned. It is up to the user to call `reset` if desired.

to (*ADDRESS* [, *ADDRESS* [...]])

A synonym for `recipient`.

data ([*DATA*])

Initiates the sending of the data from the current message.

DATA may be a reference to a list or a list. If this is specified, the contents of *DATA* and a termination string `.\r\n` is sent to the server. The result is true if the data is accepted.

If *DATA* is not specified, then the result indicates that the server wishes the data to be sent. The data must then be sent using the `datasend` and `dataend` methods described in Net::Cmd.

expand (*ADDRESS*)

Requests the server to expand the given address. Returns a reference to an array that contains the text read from the server.

verify (*ADDRESS*)

Verifies that *ADDRESS* is a legitimate mailing address.

help ([*$subject*])

Requests help text from the server. Returns the text or undef upon failure.

```
quit ()
```
>   Sends the QUIT command to the remote SMTP server and closes the socket
>   connection.

See Also

Net::Cmd

Author

Graham Barr, *gbarr@pobox.com*

Copyright

Copyright © 1995–1997 Graham Barr. All rights reserved. This program is free software;
you can redistribute it and/or modify it under the same terms as Perl itself.

Net::SNPP —Simple Network Pager Protocol Client

Synopsis

```
use Net::SNPP;

# Constructors
$snpp = Net::SNPP->new('snpphost');
$snpp = Net::SNPP->new('snpphost', Timeout => 60);
```

Description

This module implements a client interface to the SNPP protocol, enabling a Perl application
to talk to SNPP servers. This documentation assumes that you are familiar with the SNPP
protocol described in RFC 1861.

A new Net::SNPP object must be created with the new method. Once this has been done,
all SNPP commands are accessed through this object.

Examples

This example sends a pager message in one hour saying "Your lunch is ready".

```
#!/usr/local/bin/perl -w

use Net::SNPP;

$snpp = Net::SNPP->new('snpphost');

$snpp->send( Pager   => $some_pager_number,
             Message => "Your lunch is ready",
             Alert   => 1,
             Hold    => time + 3600, # lunch ready in 1 hour

           ) || die $snpp->message;

$snpp->quit;
```

Constructor

new ([*HOST,*] [*OPTIONS*])

> This is the constructor for a new Net::SNPP object. *HOST* is the name of the remote host to which an SNPP connection is required.
>
> If *HOST* is not given, then the SNPP_Host specified in Net::Config is used.
>
> *OPTIONS* are passed in a hash-like fashion, using key and value pairs. Possible options are:

Timeout

> Maximum time, in seconds, to wait for a response from the SNPP server (the default is 120).

Debug

> Enables debugging information.

> *Example:*
> ```
>         $snpp = Net::SNPP->new('snpphost',
>                                Debug => 1,
>                               );
> ```

Methods

Unless otherwise stated, all methods return either a **true** or **false** value, with **true** meaning that the operation was a success. When a method states that it returns a value, failure is returned as undef or an empty list.

reset ()
help ()

> Requests help text from the server. Returns the text, or undef upon failure.

quit ()

> Sends the QUIT command to the remote SNPP server and closes the socket connection.

Exports

Net::SNPP exports all that Net::CMD exports, plus three more subroutines that can be used to compare against the result of **status**. These are: CMD_2WAYERROR, CMD_2WAYOK, and CMD_2WAYQUEUED.

See Also

Net::Cmd, RFC 1861

Author

Graham Barr, *gbarr@pobox.com*

Copyright

Net::TCP—TCP sockets interface module

Synopsis

```
use Socket;              # optional
use Net::Gen;            # optional
use Net::Inet;           # optional
use Net::TCP;
```

Description

The Net::TCP module provides services for TCP communications over sockets. It is layered atop the Net::Inet and Net::Gen modules, which are part of the same distribution.

Public Methods

The following methods are provided by the Net::TCP module itself, rather than just being inherited from Net::Inet or Net::Gen.

new

Returns a newly initialized object of the given class. If called for a derived class, no validation of the supplied parameters is performed. (This is so that the derived class can add the parameter validation it needs to the object before allowing the validation.) Otherwise, it causes the parameters to be validated by calling its **init** method, which Net::TCP inherits from Net::Inet. In particular, this means that if both a host and a service are given, then an object is only returned if a **connect**() call was successful.

```
$obj = new Net::TCP;
$obj = new Net::TCP $host, $service;
$obj = new Net::TCP \%parameters;
$obj = new Net::TCP $host, $service, \%parameters;
```

Server::new

Returns a newly initialized object of the given class. This is much like the regular **new** method, except that it makes it easier to specify just a service name or port number, and it automatically does a **setsockopt**() call to set SO_REUSEADDR to make the **bind**() more likely to succeed.

```
$obj = new Net::TCP::Server $service;
$obj = new Net::TCP::Server $service, \%parameters;
$obj = new Net::TCP::Server $lcladdr, $service,
                                      \%parameters;
```

Here is a simple example for server setup:

```
$lh = new Net::TCP::Server 7788 or die;
while ($sh = $lh->accept) {
    defined($pid=fork) or die "fork: $!\n";
    if ($pid) {                # parent doesn't need client fh
        $sh->stopio;
        next;
    }
    # child doesn't need listener fh
    $lh->stopio;
    # do per-connection stuff here
    exit;
}
```

Note that signal handling for the child processes is not included in this example. A sample server will be included in the final kit that will show how to manage the subprocesses.

Protected Methods

None.

Known Socket Options

These are the socket options known to the Net::TCP module itself:

```
TCP_NODELAY
TCP_MAXSEG
TCP_RPTR2RXT
```

Known Object Parameters

There are no object parameters registered by the Net::TCP module itself.

TIESCALAR

Tieing of scalars to a TCP handle is supported by inheritance from the TIESCALAR method of Net::Gen. That method succeeds only if a call to a **new** method results in an object for which the **isconnected** method returns true. That is why it is mentioned in connection with this module.

Example:

```
tie $x,Net::TCP,0,'finger' or die;
$x = "-s\n";
print $y while defined($y = $x);
untie $x;
```

This is an expensive re-implementation of **finger -s** on many machines.

Each assignment to the tied scalar is really a call to the **put** method (via the STORE method), and each read from the tied scalar is really a call to the **getline** method (via the FETCH method).

Exports

default

None.

exportable

TCPOPT_EOL, TCPOPT_MAXSEG, TCPOPT_NOP, TCPOPT_WINDOW, TCP_ MAXSEG, TCP_MAXWIN, TCP_MAX_WINSHIFT, TCP_MSS, TCP_NODELAY, TCP_ RPTR2RXT, TH_ACK, TH_FIN, TH_PUSH, TH_RST, TH_SYN, TH_URG

Tags

The following are available for grouping related exportable items:

`:sockopts`

TCP_NODELAY, TCP_MAXSEG, TCP_RPTR2RXT

`:tcpoptions`

TCPOPT_EOL, TCPOPT_MAXSEG, TCPOPT_NOP, TCPOPT_WINDOW

`:protocolvalues`

TCP_MAXWIN, TCP_MAX_WINSHIFT, TCP_MSS, TH_ACK, TH_FIN, TH_PUSH, TH_RST, TH_SYN, TH_URG

```
:ALL
```
      All of the above exportable items.

Author

Spider Boardman, *spider@Orb.Nashua.NH.US*

Net::Telnet—interact with TELNET port or other TCP ports

Synopsis

```
use Net::Telnet ();
```
See "Methods" section below.

Description

Net::Telnet allows you to make client connections to a TCP port and to do network I/O, especially with a port using the TELNET protocol. Simple I/O methods such as **print**, **get**, and **getline** are provided. More sophisticated interactive features are also provided, because connecting to a TELNET port ultimately means communicating with a program designed for human interaction. Some interactive features include the ability to specify a timeout and to wait for patterns to appear in the input stream, such as the prompt from a command interpreter.

This example prints information about users who are logged on to the remote host sparky:

```
$sparky = new Net::Telnet (Host => "sparky",
                           Timeout => 10,
                           Prompt => '/[$%#>] $/');
$sparky->login($username, $passwd);
@lines = $sparky->cmd("/usr/bin/who");
print @lines;
$sparky->close;
```

The methods **login()** and **cmd()** use the prompt setting in the object to determine when a login or command is complete. If the prompt doesn't match, it's likely that those commands will time out.

Reasons to use this class other than strictly with a TELNET port are:

* You're not familiar with sockets and you want a simple way to make client connections to TCP services.

* You want to be able to specify your own timeout while connecting, reading, or writing.

* You're communicating with an interactive program at the other end of some socket or pipe and you want to wait for certain patterns to appear.

Note: There are some important differences from most other Perl I/O calls. All input is buffered, while all output is flushed. The output record separator for **print()** is set to \n by default, so there's no need to append a new line to all your commands. See **output_record_separator()** to change the default. In the input stream, each \r\n sequence is converted to \n. In the output stream, each occurrence of \n is converted to the sequence \r\n. See **binmode()** to change the default. TCP protocols typically use the ASCII sequence **carriage-return newline** to designate a new line.

You need to be running at least Perl version 5.002 to use this module. This module does not require any libraries that don't come with the standard Perl distribution. If you have the IO:: libraries, methods are inherited from the class IO::Socket::INET; otherwise, FileHandle is used as a base class.

Special methods are provided to handle errors. Normally, when an error or timeout is encountered using a TELNET object, the program dies with an error message printed to standard error. You may arrange for the methods to return with an undefined value instead by using errmode() or the errmode option to new(). See errmode() for other sophisticated error mode settings. The error message itself may be obtained using errmsg().

Note that eof is not considered an error, while timing-out is.

While debugging your program, use input_log() or dump_log() to see what's actually being received and sent.

Two different styles of named arguments are supported. This document only shows the IO:: style:

```
Net::Telnet->new(Timeout => 20);
```

However, the dash-option style is also allowed:

```
Net::Telnet->new(-timeout => 20);
```

For more help, see the "Examples" section below.

This is an alpha version, meaning that the interface may change in future versions. Contact me, Jay Rogers, *jay@rgrs.com*, if you find any bugs or have suggestions for improvement.

Methods

new

    Creates a new Net::Telnet object

```
$obj = Net::Telnet->new([Binmode      => $mode,]
                        [Dump_Log     => $filename,]
                        [Errmode      => $errmode,]
                        [Fhopen       => $filehandle,]
                        [Host         => $host,]
                        [Input_log    => $file,]
                        [Input_record_separator => $char,]
                        [Output_log => $file,]
                        [Output_record_separator => $char,]
                        [Port         => $port,]
                        [Prompt       => $matchop,]
                        [Telnetmode => $mode,]
                        [Timeout      => $secs,]);
```

This is the constructor for Net::Telnet objects. A new object is returned on success; the $errmode action is performed on failure—see errmode(). The arguments are shortcuts to methods of the same name.

If the $host argument is given, then the object is opened by connecting to TCP $port on $host. Also see open(). The new object returned is given the following defaults in the absence of corresponding named arguments:

- The default host is localhost.
- The default port is 23.
- The default prompt is '/[$%#>] $/'.

- The default `timeout` is 10.
- The default `errmode` is `'die'`.
- The default `output_record_separator` is \n.
- The default `input_record_separator` is \n.
- The default `binmode` is 0, which means do new line translations.

binmode

Turns off/on new line translation.

```
$prev = $obj->binmode($mode);
```

This method controls whether or not sequences of \r\n are translated. By default, they are translated (i.e. binmode is *off*).

If $mode is missing or 1, then binmode is *on* and new-line translation is not done.

If $mode is 0, then binmode is *off* and new-line translation is done. In the input stream, each sequence of \r\n is converted to \n and in the output stream, each occurrence of \n is converted to a sequence of \r\n.

Note that input is always buffered. Changing binmode doesn't affect what's already been read into the buffer. Output is not buffered and changing binmode has an immediate effect.

break

Sends TELNET break character.

```
$ok = $obj->break;
```

This method sends the TELNET break character. This character is provided because it's a signal outside the US-ASCII set that is currently given local meaning within many systems. It's intended to indicate that the Break key or the Attention key was hit.

close

Closes the object.

```
$ok = $obj->close;
```

This method closes the socket, file, or pipe associated with the object.

cmd

Issues a command and retrieves output.

```
$ok = $obj->cmd($string);
$ok = $obj->cmd(String    => $string,
                [Output   => $ref,]
                [Prompt   => $match,]
                [Timeout  => $secs,]);

@output = $obj->cmd($string);
@output = $obj->cmd(String   => $string,
                    [Output  => $ref,]
                    [Prompt  => $match,]
                    [Timeout => $secs,]);
```

This method sends the command in $string, and reads the characters sent back by the command, up to and including the matching prompt. It's assumed that the program to which you're sending is some kind of command-prompting interpreter such as a shell.

In a scalar context, the characters read are discarded and a boolean is returned, indicating the success or failure of sending the command string and reading the prompt. Note that in order to have an error returned, errmode() must not be set to die.

In an array context, only the output generated by the command is returned, one line per element. In other words, all the characters between the echoed-back command string and the prompt are returned. If the command happens to return no output, an array containing one element, the null string, is returned. This is so the array will indicate true in a boolean context.

Optional named arguments are provided to override the current settings of prompt and timeout.

The output named argument provides an alternative method of receiving command output. If you pass a scalar reference, the output is returned in the referenced scalar. If you pass an array or hash reference, the lines of output are returned in the referenced array or hash.

dump_log

Logs all I/O in dump format.

```
$fh = $obj->dump_log;

$fh = $obj->dump_log($fh);

$fh = $obj->dump_log($filename);
```

This method starts or stops dump format logging of all the object's input and output. The dump format shows the blocks read and written in a hexadecimal and printable character format. This method is useful when debugging; however, you might want to first try input_log(), as it's more readable.

If no argument is given, the current log filehandle is returned. A null string indicates logging is off.

To stop logging, use a null string as an argument.

If an open filehandle is given, it is used for logging and returned. Otherwise, the argument is assumed to be the name of a file, the file is opened, and a filehandle to it is returned.

eof

Indicates whether end-of-file has been read.

```
$eof = $obj->eof;
```

This method indicates whether end-of-file has been read. Because the input is buffered, this isn't the same thing as $obj being closed. In other words, $obj can be closed, but there can still be stuff in the buffer to be read. Under this condition, you can still read, but you won't be able to write.

errmode

Sets action to perform on error.

```
$mode = $obj->errmode;

$prev = $obj->errmode($mode);
```

This method gets or sets the action to be taken when errors are encountered using the object. The first calling sequence returns the current error mode. The second calling sequence sets it to $mode and returns the previous mode. Valid values for $mode are die (the default), return, a coderef, or an arrayref.

When mode is die, then when an error is encountered using the object, the program dies and an error message is printed on standard error.

When mode is return, the method generating the error places an error message in the object and returns undef value in a scalar context and a null list in list context. The error message may be obtained using errmsg().

When mode is a coderef, then when an error is encountered, coderef is called with the error message as its first argument. Using this mode, you may have your own subroutine handle errors. If coderef itself returns, then the method generating the error returns undef or a null list, depending on the context.

When mode is an arrayref, the first element of the array must be a coderef. Any elements that follow are the arguments to coderef. When an error is encountered, the coderef is called with its arguments. Using this mode, you may have your own subroutine handle errors. If the coderef itself returns, then the method generating the error returns undef or a null list depending on the context.

errmsg

Returns the most recent error message.

```
$msg = $obj->errmsg;

$prev = $obj->errmsg(@msgs);
```

The first calling sequence returns the error message associated with the object. The null string is returned if no error has been encountered yet. The second calling sequence sets the error message for the object to the concatenation of @msgs and returns the previous error message. Normally, error messages are set internally by a method when an error is encountered.

error

Performs the error mode action.

```
$obj->error(@msgs);
```

This method concatenates @msgs into a string and places it in the object as the error message. Also see errmsg(). It then performs the error mode. Also see errmode().

If the error mode doesn't cause the program to die, then undef or a null list is returned, depending on the context.

This method is primarily used by this class or a subclass to perform the user-requested action when an error is encountered.

fhopen

Uses an existing open filehandle.

```
$ok = $obj->fhopen($fh);
```

This method associates the open filehandle $fh with the object for further I/O.

This method provides a way to use this module with a filehandle that's already open. Suppose you want to use the features of the module to do I/O to something other than a TCP port. Instead of opening the object for I/O to a TCP port by passing a host arg to new() or invoking open(), call this method instead.

get

    Reads a block of data.

        `$data = $obj->get([Timeout => $secs,]);`

This method reads a block of data from the object and returns it along with any buffered data. If no buffered data is available to return, it waits for data to read, using the timeout specified in the object. You can override that timeout using `$secs`. Also see `timeout()`. If buffered data is available to return, it also checks for a block of data that can be immediately read.

On eof, undef value is returned. On timeout or other error, the error-mode action is performed.

getline

    Reads the next line.

        `$line = $obj->getline([Timeout => $secs,]);`

This method reads and returns the next line of data from the object. You can use `input_record_separator()` to change the notion of what separates a line. The default is \n.

If a line isn't immediately available, this method blocks waiting for a line or the timeout. You can override the object's timeout for this method using `$secs`. Also see `timeout()`.

On eof, undef value is returned. On timeout or other error, the error-mode action is performed.

getlines

    Reads the next lines.

        `@lines = $obj->getlines([Timeout => $secs,]);`

This method reads and returns the next available lines of data from the object. You can use `input_record_separator()` to change the notion of what separates a line. The default is \n.

If a line isn't immediately available, this method blocks waiting for one or more lines or the timeout. You can override the object's timeout for this method using `$secs`. Also see `timeout()`.

On eof, a null array is returned. On timeout or other error, the error mode action is performed.

host

    Sets the name of the remote host.

        `$host = $obj->host;`

        `$prev = $obj->host($host);`

This method designates the remote host. With no argument, this method returns the current hostname set in the object. With an argument, it sets the current hostname to `$host` and returns the previous hostname. You may indicate the remote host using either a hostname or an IP address.

input_log

    Logs all input.

        `$fh = $obj->input_log;`

```
$fh = $obj->input_log($fh);
```

```
$fh = $obj->input_log($filename);
```

This method starts or stops logging of input. This is useful when debugging. Also see dump_log(). Because most command interpreters echo back commands received, it's likely that all your output will also be in this log. Note that input logging occurs after new line translation. See binmode() for details on new line translation.

If no argument is given, the log filehandle is returned. A null string indicates logging is off.

To stop logging, use a null string as an argument.

If an open filehandle is given, it is used for logging and returned. Otherwise, the argument is assumed to be the name of a file, the file is opened for logging, and a filehandle to it is returned.

input_record_separator
>   Sets the input-line delimiter.

```
$rs = $obj->input_record_separator;
```

```
$prev = $obj->input_record_separator($rs);
```

This method designates the line delimiter for input. It's used with getline(), getlines(), and cmd() to determine lines in the input.

With no argument, this method returns the current input record separator set in the object. With an argument, it sets the input record separator to $rs and returns the previous value.

lastline
>   Saves the last line read.

```
$line = $obj->lastline;
```

```
$prev = $obj->lastline($line);
```

This method saves the last line read from the object. This may be a useful error message when the remote side abnormally closes the connection. Typically, the remote side prints an error message before closing.

With no argument, this method returns the last line read from the object. With an argument, it sets the last line read to $line and returns the previous value. Normally, only internal methods set the last line.

login
>   Performs a standard login.

```
$ok = $obj->login($username, $password);
```

```
$ok = $obj->login(Name     => $username,
                  Password => $password,
                  [Prompt  => $match,]
                  [Timeout => $secs,]);
```

This method performs a standard login by waiting for a login prompt and responding with $username, then waiting for the password prompt and responding with $password, and then waiting for the command interpreter prompt. If any of the prompts sent don't match what's expected, the method times out, unless timeout is turned off.

Login prompts must match either of the patterns:

```
/login[: ]*$/i
/username[: ]*$/i
```

Password prompts must match the pattern:

```
/password[: ]*$/i
```

The command interpreter prompt must match the current value of **prompt()**.

Optional named arguments are provided to override the current settings of prompt and timeout.

max_buffer_length

Sets the maximum size of the input buffer.

```
$len = $obj->max_buffer_length;

$prev = $obj->max_buffer_length($len);
```

This method designates the maximum size of the input buffer. An error is generated when a read causes the buffer to exceed this limit. The default value is 1,048,576 bytes (1MB). The input buffer can grow much larger than the blocksize when you read using **getline()** or **waitfor()** and the data stream contains no newlines or matching waitfor patterns.

With no argument, this method returns the current maximum buffer length set in the object. With an argument, it sets the maximum buffer length to **$len** and returns the previous value.

open

Connects to host and port.

```
$ok = $obj->open($host);

$ok = $obj->open([Host    => $host,]
                 [Port    => $port,]
                 [Timeout => $secs,]);
```

This method opens a TCP connection to **$port** on **$host**. If either argument is missing, then the current value of **host()** or **port()** is used.

An optional named argument is provided to override the current setting of timeout.

Timeouts don't work for this method on machines that don't implement SIGALRM. For those machines, an error is returned when the system reaches its own timeout while trying to connect.

A side effect of this method is to reset the alarm interval associated with SIGALRM.

output_field_separator

Sets the field separator for print.

```
$ofs = $obj->output_field_separator;

$prev = $obj->output_field_separator($ofs);
```

This method designates the output field separator for `print()`. Ordinarily, the print method simply prints out the comma-separated fields you specify. Set this to specify what's printed between fields.

With no argument, this method returns the current output field separator set in the object. With an argument, it sets the output field separator to `$ofs` and returns the previous value.

output_log

Logs all output.

```
$fh = $obj->output_log;

$fh = $obj->output_log($fh);

$fh = $obj->output_log($filename);
```

This method starts or stops logging of output. This is useful when debugging. Also see `dump_log()`. Because most command interpreters echo back commands received, it's likely that all your output will also be in an input log. See `input_log()`. Note that output logging occurs before new line translation. See `binmode()` for details on new line translation.

If no argument is given, the log filehandle is returned. A null string indicates logging is off.

To stop logging, use a null string as an argument.

If an open filehandle is given, it is used for logging and returned. Otherwise, the argument is assumed to be the name of a file, the file is opened for logging, and a filehandle to it is returned.

output_record_separator

Sets the output-line delimiter.

```
$ors = $obj->output_record_separator;

$prev = $obj->output_record_separator($ors);
```

This method designates the output record separator for `print()`. Ordinarily, the print operator simply prints out the comma-separated fields you specify, with no trailing new line or record separator assumed. Set this variable to specify what's printed at the end of the print.

Note: The output record separator is set to `\n` by default, so there's no need to append all your commands with a new line.

With no argument, this method returns the current output record separator set in the object. With an argument, it sets the output record separator to `$ors` and returns the previous value.

port

Sets the remote port.

```
$port = $obj->port;

$prev = $obj->port($port);
```

This method designates the remote TCP port. With no argument, this method returns the current port number. With an argument, it sets the current port number to `$port` and returns the previous port. If `$port` is a service name, then it's first converted to a port number using the Perl function `getservbyname()`.

print

Writes to object.

        $ok = $obj->print(@list);

This method prints a string or a comma-separated list of strings to the opened object and returns non-zero if all data was successfully written.

By default, the `output_record_separator()` is set to \n in order to have your commands automatically end with a new line. In most cases, your output is being read by a command interpreter, which won't accept a command until `newline` is read. This is similar to someone typing a command and hitting the Return key.

On failure, it's possible that some data has been written. If you choose to try and recover from a print timeout, use `print_length()` to determine how much was written before the timeout occurred.

print_length

Returns the number of bytes written by print.

        $num = $obj->print_length;

This returns the number of bytes successfully written by the most recent `print()`.

prompt

Sets the pattern to match a prompt.

        $matchop = $obj->prompt;

        $prev = $obj->prompt($matchop);

This method sets the pattern used to find a prompt in the input stream. It must be a string representing a valid Perl pattern-match operator. The methods `login()` and `cmd()` try to read until the prompt is matched. If the pattern chosen doesn't match what's sent, then it's likely those commands will time out.

With no argument, this method returns the prompt set in the object. With an argument, it sets the prompt to `$matchop` and returns the previous value.

The default prompt is `/[$%#>] $/`.

Always use single quotes to construct `$matchop` to avoid unintended backslash interpretation. Using single quotes, you only need to add extra backslashes to quote patterns containing \' or \\.

telnetmode

Turns off/on TELNET command interpretation.

        $prev = $obj->telnet($mode);

This method controls whether or not TELNET commands in the datastream are recognized and handled. The TELNET protocol uses certain character sequences sent in the datastream to control the session. If the port you're connecting to isn't using the TELNET protocol, then you should turn this mode off. The default is *on*.

If `$mode` is 0, then TELNET mode is off. If `$mode` is missing or 1, then TELNET mode is on.

timed_out

Indicates if there was a timeout.

        $boolean = $obj->timed_out;

        $prev = $obj->timed_out($boolean);

This method indicates if a previous read or write method timed out.

With no argument, this method returns `true` if a previous method timed out. With an argument, it sets the indicator. Generally this is used by internal methods to clear the indicator.

timeout

Sets the I/O timeout interval.

```
$secs = $obj->timeout;

$prev = $obj->timeout($secs);
```

This method sets the timeout interval that's used when performing I/O or connecting to a port. When a method doesn't complete within the timeout interval, then it's an error and the error mode action is performed.

The timeout may be expressed as a relative or absolute value. If `$secs` is greater than or equal to the time the program was started, as determined by `$^T`, then it's the absolute time when timeout occurs. Also see the Perl function `time()`. A relative timeout happens `$secs` from the time the I/O method begins.

If `$secs` is 0, then timeout occurs if the data cannot be immediately read or written. Use `undef` to turn timeouts off.

With no argument, this method returns the timeout set in the object. With an argument, it sets the timeout to `$secs` and returns the previous value.

watchfor

Waits for a pattern in the input.

```
$ok = $obj->waitfor($matchop);
$ok = $obj->waitfor([Match   => $matchop,]
                    [String  => $string,]
                    [Timeout => $secs,]);

($prematch, $match) = $obj->waitfor($matchop);
($prematch, $match) = $obj->waitfor([Match   => $matchop,]
                                    [String  => $string,]
                                    [Timeout => $secs,]);
```

This method reads until a pattern match or string is found in the input stream. All the characters before and including the match are removed from the input stream. On `eof`, `undef` is returned. On timeout or other error, the error mode action is performed.

In an array context, the characters before the match and the matched characters are returned in `$prematch` and `$match`.

You can specify more than one pattern or string by simply providing multiple `Match` and/or `String` named arguments. A `$matchop` must be a string representing a valid Perl pattern-match operator. The `$string` is just a substring to find in the input stream.

An optional named argument is provided to override the current timeout setting.

Always use single quotes to construct `$matchop` to avoid unintended backslash interpretation. Using single quotes, you only need to add extra backslashes to quote patterns containing \' or \\.

Examples

This example gets the current weather forecast for Brainerd, Minnesota:

```
use Net::Telnet ();
my($forecast, $t);

$t = new Net::Telnet (-host => "rainmaker.wunderground.com");

## Wait for first prompt and "hit return".
$t->waitfor('/continue:.*$/');
$t->print("");

## Wait for second prompt and respond with city code.
$t->waitfor('/city code:.*$/');
$t->print("BRD");

## Read and print the first page of forecast.
($forecast) = $t->waitfor('/[ \t]+press return to continue/i');
print $forecast;

exit;
```

This example checks a POP server to see if you have mail:

```
use Net::Telnet ();
my($hostname, $line, $passwd, $pop, $username);

$hostname = "your_destination_host_here";
$username = "your_username_here";
$passwd = "your_password_here";

$pop = new Net::Telnet (-host => $hostname,
                        -port => 110,
                        -telnetmode => '');

## Read connection message.
$line = $pop->getline;
die $line unless $line =~ /^\+OK/;

## Send user name.
$pop->print("user $username");
$line = $pop->getline;
die $line unless $line =~ /^\+OK/;

## Send password.
$pop->print("pass $passwd");
$line = $pop->getline;
die $line unless $line =~ /^\+OK/;

## Request status of messages.
$pop->print("list");
$line = $pop->getline;
print $line;

exit;
```

Here's an example you can use to download a file of any type. The file is read from the remote host's standard output using cat. To prevent any output processing, the remote host's standard output is put in raw mode using the Bourne shell. The Bourne shell is used because some shells, notably tcsh, prevent changing tty modes. Upon completion, FTP-style statistics are printed to stderr.

```perl
use Net::Telnet;
my($block, $filename, $host, $hostname, $k_per_sec, $line,
    $num_read, $passwd, $prevblock, $prompt, $size, $size_bsd,
    $size_sysv, $start_time, $total_time, $username);

$hostname = "your_destination_host_here";
$username = "your_username_here";
$passwd = "your_password_here";
$filename = "your_download_file_here";

## Connect and login.
$host = new Net::Telnet (Host => $hostname,
                         Timeout => 30,
                         Prompt => '/[%#>] $/');
$host->login($username, $passwd);

## Make sure prompt won't match anything in send data.
$prompt = '_funkyPrompt_';
$host->prompt("/$prompt\$/");
$host->cmd("set prompt = '$prompt'");

## Get size of file.
($line) = $host->cmd("/usr/bin/ls -l $filename");
($size_bsd, $size_sysv) = (split ' ', $line)[3,4];
if ($size_sysv =~ /^\d+$/) {
    $size = $size_sysv;
}
elsif ($size_bsd =~ /^\d+$/) {
    $size = $size_bsd;
}
else {
    die "$filename: no such file on $hostname";
}

## Start sending the file.
binmode STDOUT;
$host->binmode;
$host->print("/usr/bin/sh -c 'stty raw; cat $filename'");
$host->getline;     # discard echoed back line

## Read file a block at a time.
$num_read = 0;
$prevblock = '';
$start_time = time;
while (($block = $host->get) and ($block !~ /$prompt$/o)) {
    if (length $block >= length $prompt) {
        print $prevblock;
        $num_read += length $prevblock;
```

```
                $prevblock = $block;
        }
        else {
            $prevblock .= $block;
        }

}
$host->close;

## Print last block without trailing prompt.
$prevblock .= $block;
$prevblock =~ s/$prompt$//;
print $prevblock;
$num_read += length $prevblock;
die "error: expected size $size, received size $num_read\n"
    unless $num_read == $size;

## Print totals.
$total_time = (time - $start_time) || 1;
$k_per_sec = ($size / 1024) / $total_time;
$k_per_sec = sprintf "%3.1f", $k_per_sec;
warn("$num_read bytes received in $total_time seconds ",
     "($k_per_sec Kbytes/s)\n");

exit;
```

Here's an example that shows how to talk to a program that must communicate via a terminal. In this case, we're talking to the telnet program via a pseudo-terminal. We use the Comm package to start the telnet program and return a filehandle to the pseudo-terminal. This example sends some initial commands and then allows the user to type commands to the telnet session.

```
use Net::Telnet;
my($comm_pty, $host, $hostname, $passwd, $pty,
   $username, @lines);

$hostname = "your_host_here";
$username = "your_name_here";
$passwd = "your_passwd_here";

## Start the telnet program so we can talk to it via a
## pseudo-terminal.
{
    local $^W = 0;   # Comm.pl isn't warning clean

    require "Comm.pl";
    &Comm::init("close_it", "interact",
                "open_proc", "stty_raw", "stty_sane");
    $comm_pty = &open_proc("telnet $hostname")
        or die "open_proc failed";

    ## Unfortunately the Comm package doesn't
    ## return us a fully qualified filehandle.  We
    ## must keep the filehandle Comm returned for
    ## its use and we must build another filehandle
```

```
                    ## qualified with the current package for our
                    ## use.
                    $pty = "main::" . $comm_pty;
            }


            ## Obtain a new Net::Telnet object that does I/O to the
            ## pseudo-terminal attached to the running telnet
            ## program.  The "Telnetmode" is "off" because we're
            ## not talking directly to a telnet port as we normally
            ## do, we're talking to a pseudo-terminal.  The
            ## "Output_record_separator" is now a carriage-return
            ## because that's what you'd normally hit when you get
            ## done typing a line at a terminal.
            $host = new Net::Telnet (Fhopen => $pty,
                                     Timeout => 10,
                                     Prompt => '/[%#>] $/',
                                     Telnetmode => 0,
                                     Output_record_separator => "\r");

            ## Issue some commands.
            $host->login($username, $passwd);
            $host->cmd("setenv DISPLAY $ENV{DISPLAY}");
            print $host->cmd("who");

            ## Allow the user to interact with telnet program until
            ## they exit.
            {
                no strict 'subs';   # so we can refer to STDIN
                local $^W = 0;      # Comm.pl isn't warning clean
                &stty_raw(STDIN);
                &interact($comm_pty);
                &stty_sane(STDIN);
                &close_it($comm_pty);
            }

            print "Exited telnet\n";
            exit;
```

References

RFC 854 - *TELNET Protocol Specification*
RFC 1143 - *The Q Method of Implementing TELNET Option Negotiation*
TELNET Options

Author

Jay Rogers, *jay@rgrs.com*

Copyright

Copyright © 1997 Jay Rogers. All rights reserved.

This program is free software; you can redistribute it and/or modify it under the same terms as Perl itself.

Net::Time—time and daytime network client interface

Synopsis

```
use Net::Time qw(inet_time inet_daytime);

print inet_time();              # use default host from Net::Config
print inet_time('localhost');
print inet_time('localhost', 'tcp');

print inet_daytime();           # use default host from Net::Config
print inet_daytime('localhost');
print inet_daytime('localhost', 'tcp');
```

Description

Net::Time provides subroutines that obtain the time on a remote machine.

inet_time ([*HOST* [, *PROTOCOL* [, *TIMEOUT*]]])

Obtains the time on *HOST*, or some default host if *HOST* is not given or not defined, using the protocol as defined in RFC 868. The optional argument *PROTOCOL* should define the protocol to use, either **tcp** or **udp**. The result is a UNIX-like time value, or **undef** upon failure.

inet_daytime ([*HOST* [, *PROTOCOL* [, *TIMEOUT*]]])

Obtains the time on HOST, or some default host if *HOST* is not given or not defined, using the protocol as defined in RFC 867. The optional argument *PROTOCOL* should define the protocol to use, either **tcp** or **udp**. The result is an ASCII string, or **undef** upon failure.

Author

Graham Barr, *gbarr@pobox.com*

Copyright

Copyright © 1995–1997 Graham Barr. All rights reserved. This program is free software; you can redistribute it and/or modify it under the same terms as Perl itself.

Net::UDP—UDP sockets interface module

Synopsis

```
use Socket;                # optional
use Net::Gen;              # optional
use Net::Inet;             # optional
use Net::UDP;
```

Description

The Net::UDP module provides services for UDP communications over sockets. It is layered atop the Net::Inet and Net::Gen modules, which are part of the same distribution.

Public Methods

The following methods are provided by the Net::UDP module itself, rather than just being inherited from Net::Inet or Net::Gen.

new

Returns a newly initialized object of the given class.

```
$obj = new Net::UDP;
$obj = new Net::UDP $host, $service;
$obj = new Net::UDP \%parameters;
$obj = new Net::UDP $host, $service, \%parameters;
```

If called for a derived class, no validation of the supplied parameters is performed. (This is so that the derived class can add the parameter validation it needs to the object before allowing the validation.) Otherwise, it causes the parameters to be validated by calling its `init` method, which Net::UDP inherits from Net::Inet. In particular, this means that if both a host and a service are given, that an object is only returned if a connect() call was successful.

Protected Methods

None.

Known Socket Options

There are no object parameters registered by the Net::UDP module itself.

Known Object Parameters

There are no object parameters registered by the Net::UDP module itself.

TIESCALAR

Tieing of scalars to a UDP handle is supported by inheritance from the TIESCALAR method of Net::Gen. That method only succeeds if a call to a new method results in an object for which the isconnected method returns true, which is why it is mentioned in connection with this module.

Example:

```
tie $x,Net::UDP,0,'daytime' or die;
$x = "\n"; $x = "\n";
print $y if defined($y = $x);
untie $x;
```

This is an expensive re-implementation of date on many machines.

Each assignment to the tied scalar is really a call to the put method (via the STORE method), and each read from the tied scalar is really a call to the getline method (via the FETCH method).

Exports

None

Author

Spider Boardman, *spider@Orb.Nashua.NH.US*

Net::UNIX — UNIX-domain sockets interface module

Synopsis

```
use Socket;              # optional
use Net::Gen;            # optional
use Net::UNIX;
```

Description

The Net::UNIX module provides services for UNIX-domain socket communication. It is layered atop the Net::Gen module, which is part of the same distribution.

Public Methods

The following methods are provided by the Net::UNIX module itself, rather than just being inherited from Net::Gen.

new

Returns a newly initialized object of the given class.

```
$obj = new Net::UNIX;
$obj = new Net::UNIX $pathname;
$obj = new Net::UNIX \%parameters;
$obj = new Net::UNIX $pathname, \%parameters;
```

If called for a derived class, no validation of the supplied parameters is performed. (This is so that the derived class can add the parameter validation it needs to the object before allowing the validation.) Otherwise, it causes the parameters to be validated by calling its **init** method. In particular, this means that if a pathname is given, an object is returned only if a **connect()** call was successful.

Server::new

Returns a newly initialized object of the given class. This is much like the regular **new** method, except that it does a **bind** rather than a **connect**, and it does a **listen**.

```
$obj = new Net::UNIX::Server $pathname;
$obj = new Net::UNIX::Server $pathname, \%parameters;
```

init

Verifies that all previous parameter assignments are valid (via **checkparams**). Returns the incoming object on success, and undef on failure. Usually called only via a derived class's **init** method or its own **new** call.

```
return undef unless $self = $self->init;
return undef unless $self = $self->init(\%parameters);
return undef unless $self = $self->init($pathname);
return undef unless $self = $self->init($pathname,
                                        \%parameters);
```

bind

Updates the object with the new parameters (if supplied), then sets up the **srcaddrlist** object parameter with the specified **$pathname** argument (if supplied), and then returns the value from the inherited **bind** method.

```
$ok = $obj->bind;
$ok = $obj->bind($pathname);
$ok = $obj->bind($pathname,\%newparameters);
```

Example:

```
$ok = $obj->bind('/tmp/.fnord'); # start a service on
                                 # /tmp/.fnord
```

connect

Attempts to establish a connection for the object. If the **newparams** argument is specified, it is used to update the object parameters. Then, if the **$pathname** argument is specified, it is used to set the **dstaddrlist** object parameter. Finally, the result of a call to the inherited **connect** method is returned.

```
$ok = $obj->connect;
$ok = $obj->connect($pathname);
$ok = $obj->connect($pathname,\%newparameters);
```

format_addr

```
$string = $obj->format_addr($sockaddr);
$string = format_addr Module $sockaddr;
```

Returns a formatted representation of the socket address. This is normally just a pathname, or the constant string ' '.

Protected Methods

None.

(See the description in the "Protected Methods" section of Net::Gen for my definition of protected methods in Perl.)

Known Socket Options

There are no socket options known to the Net::UNIX module itself.

Known Object Parameters

There are no object parameters registered by the Net::UNIX module itself.

TIESCALAR

Tieing of scalars to a UNIX-domain handle is supported by inheritance from the TIE-SCALAR method of Net::Gen. That method only succeeds if a call to a **new** method results in an object for which the **isconnected** method returns a true result. Thus, for Net::UNIX, TIESCALAR does not succeed unless the pathname argument is given.

Each assignment to the tied scalar is really a call to the **put** method (via the STORE method), and each read from the tied scalar is really a call to the **getline** method (via the FETCH method).

Non-Method Subroutines

pack_sockaddr_un

Returns the packed **struct sockaddr_un** corresponding to the provided **$family** and **$pathname** arguments. The **$family** argument as assumed to be AF_UNIX if it is missing. This is otherwise the same as the **pack_sockaddr_un()** routine in the Socket module.

```
$connect_address = pack_sockaddr_un($family, $pathname);
$connect_address = pack_sockaddr_un($pathname);
```

unpack_sockaddr_un

Returns the address family and pathname (if known) from the supplied packed **struct sockaddr_un**. This is the inverse of **pack_sockaddr_un()**. It differs from the implementation in the Socket module in its return of the `$family` value and in that it trims the returned pathname at the first null character.

```
($family, $pathname) = unpack_sockaddr_un($connected_
    address);
        $pathname = unpack_sockaddr_un($connected_address);
```

Exports

default

> None.

exportable

> pack_sockaddr_un   unpack_sockaddr_un

tags

> The following *:tags* are available for grouping exportable items:
>
> :routines
>
> > pack_sockaddr_un, unpack_sockaddr_un
>
> :ALL
>
> > All of the above exportable items.

Author

Spider Boardman, *spider@Orb.Nashua.NH.US*

Net::Whois—get and parse "whois" data from InterNIC

Synopsis

```
my $w = new Net::Whois::Domain $dom
    or die "Can't find info on $dom\n";
#
# Note that all fields except "name" and "tag" may be undef
#   because "whois" information is erratically filled in.
#
print "Domain: ", $w->domain, "\n";
print "Name: ", $w->name, "\n";
print "Tag: ", $w->tag, "\n";
print "Address:\n", map { "      $_\n" } $w->address;
print "Country: ", $w->country, "\n";
print "Servers:\n", map { "     $$_[0] ($$_[1])\n" } @{$w->servers};
my ($c, $t);
if ($c = $w->contacts) {
    print "Contacts:\n";
    for $t (sort keys %$c) {
        print "    $t:\n";
        print map { "\t$_\n" } @{$$c{$t}};
    }
}
$cur_server = Net::Whois::server;
Net::Whois::server 'new.whois.server';  # optional
```

Description

Net::Whois::Domain new() attempts to retrieve and parse the given domain's "whois" information from the InterNIC. If the constructor returns a reference, that reference can be used to access the various attributes of the domains' whois entry.

Note that the Locale::Country module (part of the Locale-Codes distribution) is used to recognize spelled-out country names; if that module is not present, only two-letter country abbreviations are recognized.

The server consulted is *whois.internic.net*, unless this is changed by a call to Net::Whois::server().

Author

Originally written by Chip Salzenberg in April of 1997 for Idle Communications, Inc.

Copyright

This module is free software; you can redistribute it and/or modify it under the same terms as Perl itself.

Parallel::Pvm—Perl extension for the Parallel Virtual Machine (PVM) Message Passing System

Synopsis

```
use Parallel::Pvm;
```

Description

The PVM message-passing system enables a programmer to configure a group of (possibly heterogenous) computers connected by a network into a parallel virtual machine. The system was developed by the University of Tennessee, Oak Ridge National Laboratory, and Emory University.

Using PVM, applications can be developed that spawn parallel processes onto nodes in the virtual machine to perform specific tasks. These parallel tasks can also periodically exchange information using a set of message-passing functions developed for the system.

PVM applications have been developed mostly in the scientific and engineering fields. However applications for real-time and client/server systems can also be developed. PVM simply provides a convenient way for managing parallel tasks and communications without need for rexec or socket-level programming.

As a utility, PVM enables an organization to leverage on the computers already available for parallel processing. Parallel applications can be started during non-peak hours to utilize idle CPU cycles. Or dedicated workstation clusters connected via a high performance network like ATM can be used for high-performance computing.

It is recommended that you read the PVM manual pages and the book *PVM: Parallel Virtual Machine, A Users's Guide and Tutorial for Networked Parallel Computing*. Both the PVM system and the book can be obtained from *http://www.epm.ornl.gov/pvm*.

For the rest of this document, we will provide a tutorial introduction to developing PVM applications using Perl. The interface for some of the PVM functions have been changed, of course, to give it a more Perl-like feel.

Remember: Think Perl, think parallel! Good luck!

Environment Variables

After installing PVM on your computer, there are two mandatory environment variables that have to be set in your *.login* or *.cshrc* files: PVM_ROOT and PVM_ARCH. PVM_ROOT points to the base of the PVM installation directory, and PVM_ARCH specifies the architecture of the computer on which PVM is running. An example of how this can be set for **csh** is shown below:

```
setenv PVM_ROOT /usr/local/pvm3
setenv PVM_ARCH '$PVM_ROOT/lib/pvmgetarch'
```

Setting Up Your rsh Permission

In order for PVM applications to run, **rsh** permission has to be enabled. This involves creating an *.rhosts* file in your HOME directory containing, for each line, the host and account name you wish to allow remote execution privileges. An example *.rhosts* file to allow a PVM application to remotely execute on the hosts onyx and prata using the account edward is shown below:

```
onyx   edward
prata  edward
```

Configuring Your Parallel Virtual Machine

Parallel process management and communications is handled by a set of distributed daemons running on each of the nodes of the virtual machine. The daemon executable, **pvmd**, is started when a computer is added to the virtual machine. A computer can be added to the virtual machine either statically in a console program or using a hostfile, or dynamically within the application code itself.

The first method of configuring your virtual machine is to use the console program *$PVM_ROOT/lib/pvm*. Run it from the command prompt. The console program will first add the local host into the virtual machine and display the prompt:

```
pvm>
```

To add a host, e.g., *onyx*, as a node in your parallel virtual machine, simply type:

```
pvm> add onyx
```

To display the current virtual machine configuration, type:

```
pvm> conf
```

which displays node information pertaining to the hostname, host ID, host architecture, relative speed, and data format. The console program has a number of other commands, which can be viewed by typing **help**.

The second method of configuring your virtual machine is to use a hostfile. The hostfile is simply an ASCII text file specifing the hostnames of the computers to be added into your virtual machine.

Additional options may be also be defined for the nodes pertaining to the working directory, execution path, login name, alternative hostname etc. A simple example of a hostfile is shown below.

```
* wd=$HOME/work ep=$HOME/bin
onyx
prata.nsrc.nus.sg
laksa ep=$HOME/perl5/bin
```

In the above sample hostfile, we are adding the hosts *onyx, prata.nsrc.nus.sg,* and *laksa* into the virtual machine. We are also specifying the working directory, *wd*, in which we want our application to run, and the execution path, *ep*, in which we want PVM to look for executables.

The * in the first line defines a global option for all the hosts specified after it. We can, however, provide an option locally to override this global option. This is seen for the host laksa, where we have specified its execution path to be *$HOME/perl5/bin* instead of the *$HOME/bin*.

The third method of configuring your virtual machine is to call the functions Parallel::Pvm::addhosts or Parallel::Pvm::delhosts within your application. You must still start your master pvmd daemon first. This can be achieved by starting PVM and typing quit, or simply typing:

```
echo quit | pvm
```

The PVM application can then be started and we can add the hosts *prata* and *laksa* by calling:

```
Parallel::Pvm::addhosts("prata","laksa");
```

Or we can delete a host from our configuration by calling:

```
Parallel::Pvm::delhosts("laksa");
```

PVM also provides a function, Parallel::Pvm::conf, to query the configuration of the parallel virtual machine. An example of code to check the current configuration is shown below.

```
($info,@conf) = Parallel::Pvm::conf ;
if ( $info == PvmOk ){
  foreach $node (@conf){
    print "host id = $node->{'hi_tid'}\n";
    print "host name = $node->{'hi_name'}\n";
    print "host architecture = $node->{'hi_arch'}\n";
    print "host speed = $node->{'hi_speed'}\n";
  }
}
```

Enrolling a Task into PVM

A task has to explictly enroll into PVM in order for it to be known by other PVM tasks. This can often be done by the call:

```
$mytid = Parallel::Pvm::mytid ;
```

where $mytid is the task ID, TID, assigned by the PVM system to the calling process. Note, however, that calling any PVM function in a program also enrolls it into the system.

Spawning Parallel Tasks

A PVM application can spawn parallel tasks in your parallel virtual machine. Assuming there is an executable called client, we can spawn four client tasks in our virtual machine by calling:

```
($ntask,@tids) = Parallel::Pvm::spawn("client",4);
```

For each of the four spawned processes, the PVM system first allocates a host node and looks for the executable in the execution path of that host. If the executable is found, it is started.

The task that called the Parallel::Pvm::spawn is known as the *parent* task. The number of *children* tasks actually spawned by Parallel::Pvm::spawn is returned in the scalar $ntask. The @tids array returns the task ID, **TID**, of the spawned children tasks which will be useful later for communicating with them. A TID < 0 indicates a task failure to spawn and can be used to determine the nature of the problem:

```
foreach $tid (@tids){
    if ( $tid < 0 ){
        if ( $tid == PvmNoMem )
            warn "no memory ! \n";
        }else if ( $tid == PvmSysErr ){
            warn "pvmd not responding ! \n";
        } ...
    }
}
```

For more sophisticated users, Parallel::Pvm::spawn may be given additional argument parameters to control how and where you want a task to be spawned. For example, you can specifically spawn client in the Internet host *onyx.nsrc.nus.sg* by calling:

```
Parallel::Pvm::spawn("client",1,PvmTaskHost,"onyx.nsrc.nus.sg");
```

Or you can spawn client only on host nodes of a particular architecture, say RS6K workstations, by calling:

```
Parallel::Pvm::spawn("client",4,PvmTaskArch,"RS6K");
```

Also, if the spawned remote executable requires an argument, argv, you can supply it by calling:

```
Parallel::Pvm::spawn("client",4,PvmTaskArch,"RS6K",argv);
```

Note that tasks which have been spawned by using Parallel::Pvm::spawn do not need to be explicitly enrolled into the PVM system.

Exchanging Messages Between Tasks

Messages can be sent to a task enrolled into PVM by specifying the example code sequence:

```
Parallel::Pvm::initsend ;
Parallel::Pvm::pack(2.345,"hello dude");
Parallel::Pvm::pack(1234);
Parallel::Pvm::send($dtid,999);
```

In our example, we first call Parallel::Pvm::initsend to initialize the internal PVM send buffer. We then call Parallel::Pvm::buffer to fill this buffer with a double (2.345), , a string ("hello dude"), and an integer (1234). Having filled the send buffer with the data that is to be sent, we call Parallel::Pvm::send to do the actual send to the task identifed by the TID $dtid. We also label the sending message to disambiguate it with other messages with a tag. This is done with the 999 argument in Parallel::Pvm::send function.

For the destination task, we can receive the message sent by performing a blocking receive with the function Parallel::Pvm::recv. A code sequence for the above example on the recipent end is the following.

```
if ( Parallel::Pvm::recv >= 0 ){
   $int_t = Parallel::Pvm::unpack ;
   ($double_t,$str_t) = Parallel::Pvm::unpack ;
}
```

Note that we must unpack the message in the reverse order in which we packed it. In our example, Parallel::Pvm::recv will receive any message sent to it. In order to selectively receive a message, we could specify the **TID** of the source task and the message tag. For example:

```
$tag = 999;
Parallel::Pvm::recv($stid,$tag) ;
```

Other message passing functions that you may find useful are Parallel::Pvm::psend, Parallel::Pvm::trecv, Parallel::Pvm::nrecv, and Parallel::Pvm::precv.

Parallel I/O

Note that the file descriptors in a parent task are not inhereted in the spawned children tasks, unlike `fork`. By default, any file I/O is performed in the working directory specified in the `hostfile` if no absolute path is provided for the opened file. If no working directory is specified, the default is the `$HOME` directory. For directories that are not NFS mounted, this means that each task performs its own separate I/O.

In the case of `tty` output, tasks that are not started from the command prompt have their `stdout` and `stderr` directed to the file `pvml.<uid>`. This may be redirected to a **parent** task by calling:

```
Parallel::Pvm::catchout;
```

for `stdout` or:

```
Parallel::Pvm::catchout(stderr);
```

for `stderr`. You can direct the `stdout` or `stderr` output of a task to another TID, other then its parent, by calling:

```
Parallel::Pvm::setopt(PvmOutTid,$tid);
```

Incorporating Fault Tolerance

The function Parallel::Pvm::notify can be used to incorporate some fault tolerance into your PVM application. You may use it to ask the PVM to monitor the liveliness of a set of hosts or tasks during the execution of a PVM application. For example, you can instrument your application to monitor three tasks with the TIDs **$task1**, **$task2**, and **$task3**, by using the code segments:

```
@monitor = ($task1,$task2,$task3);
Parallel::Pvm::notify(PvmTaskExit,999,@monitor_task);
...
if ( Parallel::Pvm::probe(-1,999) ){
   $task = Parallel::Pvm::recv_notify ;
   print "Oops! task $task has failed ... \n" ;
}
```

If either **$task1**, **$task2**, or **$task3** fails, the notification takes the form of a single message with the tag **999**. The message content will inform you of the TID of the failed task.

A similar scheme may be employed for the notification of host failures in your parallel virtual machine.

Client/Server Example:

Client:

```
use Pvm;
use File::Basename;
...
# Look for server tid and assume
# server name is 'service_provider'
@task_list = Parallel::Pvm::tasks ;
foreach $task (@task_list){
    $a_out = $task->{'ti_a_out'} ;
    $base = basename $a_out ;
    if ( $base eq 'service_provider' )
        $serv_tid = $task->{'ti_tid'} ;
}
# This is just one way (not necessarily the
# best) of getting a server tid.
# You could do the same thing by reading
# the server tid posted in a file.
...

# send request for service
Parallel::Pvm::send($serv_tid,$REQUEST);
# receive service from server
Parallel::Pvm::recv(-1,$RESPONSE);
@service_packet = Parallel::Pvm::unpack ;
...
```

Server:

```
while(1){
    ...
    if ( Parallel::Pvm::probe(-1,$REQUEST) ){
        # a service request has arrived !
        $bufid = Parallel::Pvm::recv ;
        ($info,$bytes,$tag,$stid) = Parallel::Pvm::bufinfo($bufid) ;
        if ( fork == 0 ){
            # fork child process to handle service
            ...

            # provide service
            Parallel::Pvm::initsend ;
            Parallel::Pvm::pack(@service);
            Parallel::Pvm::send($stid,$RESPONSE);

            # exit child process
            exit ;
        }
    }
    ...

}
```

PVM groups

The PVM dynamic group functions have not been ported to Perl yet. These functions provide facilities for collecting processes under a single group label and applying aggregate operations onto them. Examples of these functions are Parallel::Pvm::barrier, Parallel::Pvm::reduce, Parallel::Pvm::bcast, etc. One of our concerns is that these group functions may be changed or augmented in the future releases of PVM 3.4*. A decision for porting the group functions will be made after PVM 3.4 has been released.

Functions

Parallel::Pvm::addhosts

   Adds one or more hostnames to a parallel virtual machine:

        $info = Parallel::Pvm::addhosts(@host_list) ;

Parallel::Pvm::bufinfo

   Returns information about the requested message buffer:

        ($info,$bytes,$tag,$tid) = Parallel::Pvm::bufinfo($bufid);

Parallel::Pvm::catchout

   Catches output from children tasks:

        # Parallel::Pvm::catchout(stdout);
        $bufid = Parallel::Pvm::catchout;

Parallel::Pvm::config

   Returns information about the present virtual machine configuration:

        ($info,@host_ref_list) = Parallel::Pvm::config ;

Parallel::Pvm::delhosts

   Deletes one or more hosts from the virtual machine:

        $info = Parallel::Pvm::delhosts(@host_list);

Parallel::Pvm::exit

   Tells the local PVM daemon that the process is leaving:

        $info = Parallel::Pvm::exit ;

Parallel::Pvm::freebuf

   Disposes of a message buffer:

        $info = Parallel::Pvm::freebuf($bufid);

Parallel::Pvm::getopt

   Shows various libpvm options:

        $val = Parallel::Pvm::getopt(PvmOutputTid);
        $val = Parallel::Pvm::getopt(PvmFragSize);

Parallel::Pvm::getrbuf

   Returns the message buffer identifier for the active receive buffer:

        $bufid = Parallel::Pvm::getrbuf ;

Parallel::Pvm::getsbuf

   Returns the message buffer identifier for the active send buffer:

        $bufid = Parallel::Pvm::getsbuf ;

Parallel::Pvm::halt

   Shuts down the entire PVM system:

        $info = Parallel::Pvm::halt ;

Parallel::Pvm::hostsync

Gets time-of-day clock from PVM host:

```
($info,$remote_clk,$delta) = Parallel::Pvm::hostsync($host) ;
```

where `delta` is the time-of-day equivalent to `local_clk - remote_clk`.

Parallel::Pvm::initsend

Clears default send buffer and specifies message encoding:

```
# Parallel::Pvm::initsend(PvmDataDefault) ;
$bufid = Parallel::Pvm::initsend
```

Parallel::Pvm::kill

Terminates a specified PVM process:

```
$info = Parallel::Pvm::kill($tid);
```

Parallel::Pvm::mcast

Multicasts the data in the active message buffer to a set of tasks:

```
$info = Parallel::Pvm::mcast(@tid_list,$tag);
```

Parallel::Pvm::mkbuf

Creates a new message buffer:

```
# Parallel::Pvm::mkbuf(PvmDataDefault);
$bufid = Parallel::Pvm::mkbuf ;
$bufid = Parallel::Pvm::mkbuf(PvmDataRaw);
```

Parallel::Pvm::mstat

Returns the status of a host in the virtual machine:

```
$status = Parallel::Pvm::mstat($host);
```

Parallel::Pvm::mytid

Returns the `tid` of the calling process:

```
$mytid = Parallel::Pvm::mytid ;
```

Parallel::Pvm::notify

Requests notification of PVM events:

```
$info = Parallel::Pvm::notify(PvmHostDelete,999,$host_list);
# turns on notification for new host
$info = Parallel::Pvm::notify(PvmHostAdd);
# turns off notification for new host
$info = Parallel::Pvm::notify(PvmHostAdd,0);
```

Parallel::Pvm::nrecv

Does a nonblocking receive:

```
# Parallel::Pvm::nrecv(-1,-1);
$bufid = Parallel::Pvm::nrecv ;
# Parallel::Pvm::nrecv($tid,-1);
$bufid = Parallel::Pvm::nrecv($tid) ;
$bufid = Parallel::Pvm::nrecv($tid,$tag) ;
```

Parallel::Pvm::pack

Packs active message buffer with data:

```
$info = Parallel::Pvm::pack(@data_list);
```

Parallel::Pvm::parent

Returns the `tid` of the process that spawned the calling process:

```
$tid = Parallel::Pvm::parent ;
```

Parallel::Pvm::perror

Prints the error status of the last PVM call:

```
$info = Parallel::Pvm::perror($msg);
```

Parallel::Pvm::precv

Receives a message directly into a buffer:

```
# Parallel::Pvm::precv(-1,-1);
@recv_buffer = Parallel::Pvm::precv ;
# Parallel::Pvm::precv($tid,-1);
@recv_buffer = Parallel::Pvm::precv($tid);
@recv_buffer = Parallel::Pvm::precv($tid,$tag);
```

Note that the current limit for the receive buffer is 100 KB.

Parallel::Pvm::probe

Checks whether a message has arrived:

```
# Parallel::Pvm::probe(-1,-1);
$bufid = Parallel::Pvm::probe ;
# Parallel::Pvm::probe($tid,-1);
$bufid = Parallel::Pvm::probe($tid);
$bufid = Parallel::Pvm::probe($tid,$tag);
```

Parallel::Pvm::psend

Packs and sends data in one call:

```
$info = Parallel::Pvm::psend($tid,$tag,@send_buffer);
```

Parallel::Pvm::pstat

Returns the status of the specified PVM process:

```
$status = Parallel::Pvm::pstat($tid);
```

Parallel::Pvm::recv

Receives a message:

```
# Parallel::Pvm::recv(-1,-1);
$bufid = Parallel::Pvm::recv ;
# Parallel::Pvm::recv($tid,-1);
$bufid = Parallel::Pvm::recv($tid) ;
$bufid = Parallel::Pvm::recv($tid,$tag);
```

Parallel::Pvm::recvf

Redefines the comparison function used to accept messages:

```
Parallel::Pvm::recvf(\&new_foo);
```

Parallel::Pvm::recv_notify

Receives the notification message initiated by Parallel::Pvm::notify. This should be preceded by a Parallel::Pvm::probe:

```
# for PvmTaskExit and PvmHostDelete notification
if ( Parallel::Pvm::probe(-1,$notify_tag) ){
$message = Parallel::Pvm::recv_notify(PvmTaskExit) ;
}
# for PvmHostAdd notification
@htid_list = Parallel::Pvm::recv_notify(PvmHostAdd);
```

Parallel::Pvm::recvf_old

Resets the comparison function for accepting messages to the previous method before a call to Parallel::Pvm::recf.

Parallel::Pvm::reg_hoster

Registers this task as responsible for adding new PVM hosts:

```
$info = Parallel::Pvm::reg_hoster ;
```

Parallel::Pvm::reg_rm

Registers this task as a PVM resource manager:

```
$info = Parallel::Pvm::reg_rm ;
```

Parallel::Pvm::reg_tasker

Registers this task as responsible for starting new PVM tasks:

```
$info = Parallel::Pvm::reg_tasker ;
```

Parallel::Pvm::send

Sends the data in the active message buffer:

```
# Parallel::Pvm::send(-1,-1);
$info = Parallel::Pvm::send ;
# Parallel::Pvm::send($tid,-1);
$info = Parallel::Pvm::send($tid);
$info = Parallel::Pvm::send($tid,$tag);
```

Parallel::Pvm::sendsig

Sends a signal to another PVM process:

```
use POSIX qw(:signal_h);
...
$info = Parallel::Pvm::sendsig($tid,SIGKILL);
```

Parallel::Pvm::setopt

Sets various **libpvm** options:

```
$oldval=Parallel::Pvm::setopt(PvmOutputTid,$val);
$oldval=Parallel::Pvm::setopt(PvmRoute,PvmRouteDirect);
```

Parallel::Pvm::setrbuf

Switches the active receive buffer and saves the previous buffer:

```
$oldbuf = Parallel::Pvm::setrbuf($bufid);
```

Parallel::Pvm::setsbuf

Switches the active send buffer:

```
$oldbuf = Parallel::Pvm::setsbuf($bufid);
```

Parallel::Pvm::spawn

Starts new PVM processes:

```
# Parallel::Pvm::spawn("compute.pl",4,PvmTaskDefault,"");
($ntask,@tid_list) = Parallel::Pvm::spawn("compute.pl",4);
($ntask,@tid_list) =
Parallel::Pvm::spawn("compute.pl",4,PvmTaskHost,"onyx");
($ntask,@tid_list) =
Parallel::Pvm::spawn("compute.pl",4,PvmTaskHost,"onyx",argv);
```

Parallel::Pvm::tasks

Returns information about the tasks running on the virtual machine:

```
# Parallel::Pvm::tasks(0); Returns all tasks
($info,@task_list) = Parallel::Pvm::tasks ;
# Returns only for task $tid
($info,@task_list) = Parallel::Pvm::tasks($tid) ;
```

Parallel::Pvm::tidtohost
> Returns the host ID on which the specified task is running:
>
> ```
> $dtid = Parallel::Pvm::tidtohost($tid);
> ```

Parallel::Pvm::trecv
> Receives with timeout:
>
> ```
> # Parallel::Pvm::trecv(-1,-1,1,0); time out after 1 sec
> $bufid = Parallel::Pvm::trecv ;
> # time out after 2*1000000 + 5000 usec
> $bufid = Parallel::Pvm::trecv($tid,$tag,2,5000);
> ```

Parallel::Pvm::unpack
> Unpacks the active receive message buffer:
>
> ```
> @recv_buffer = Parallel::Pvm::unpack ;
> ```

Author

Edward Walker, *edward@nsrc.nus.sg*, National Supercomputing Research Centre, Singapore

See Also

perl(1), pvm_intro(1PVM)

Socket, sockaddr_in, sockaddr_un, inet_aton, inet_ntoa — load the C *socket.h* defines and structure manipulators

Synopsis

```
use Socket;
$proto = getprotobyname('udp');
socket(Socket_Handle, PF_INET, SOCK_DGRAM, $proto);
$iaddr = gethostbyname('hishost.com');
$port = getservbyname('time', 'udp');
$sin = sockaddr_in($port, $iaddr);
send(Socket_Handle, 0, 0, $sin);
$proto = getprotobyname('tcp');
socket(Socket_Handle, PF_INET, SOCK_STREAM, $proto);
$port = getservbyname('smtp');
$sin = sockaddr_in($port,inet_aton("127.1"));
$sin = sockaddr_in(7,inet_aton("localhost"));
$sin = sockaddr_in(7,INADDR_LOOPBACK);
connect(Socket_Handle,$sin);
($port, $iaddr) = sockaddr_in(getpeername(Socket_Handle));
$peer_host = gethostbyaddr($iaddr, AF_INET);
$peer_addr = inet_ntoa($iaddr);
$proto = getprotobyname('tcp');
socket(Socket_Handle, PF_UNIX, SOCK_STREAM, $proto);
unlink('/tmp/usock');
$sun = sockaddr_un('/tmp/usock');
connect(Socket_Handle,$sun);
```

Description

This module is just a translation of the C *socket.h* file. Unlike the old mechanism of requiring a translated *socket.ph* file, this uses the **h2xs** program (see the Perl source distribution) and your native C compiler. This means that it has a far more likely chance of getting the numbers right. This includes all of the commonly used pound-defines like AF_INET, SOCK_STREAM, etc.

In addition, some structure manipulation functions are available.

Functions

`inet_aton` *HOSTNAME*

> Takes a string giving the name of a host and translates that to the four-byte string (structure). Takes arguments of both the `rtfm.mit.edu` type and `18.181.0.24`. If the hostname cannot be resolved, returns undef.

`inet_ntoa` *IP_ADDRESS*

> Takes a four-byte IP address (as returned by `inet_aton()`) and translates it into a string of the form `d.d.d.d` where the `d`'s are numbers less than 256 (the normal readable four-dotted number notation for Internet addresses).

`INADDR_ANY`

> Note: Does not return a number, but a packed string.

> Returns the four-byte wildcard IP address that specifies any of the hosts IP addresses. (A particular machine can have more than one IP address, each address corresponding to a particular network interface. This wildcard address allows you to bind to all of them simultaneously.) Normally equivalent to `inet_aton(0.0.0.0)`.

`INADDR_LOOPBACK`

> Note: Does not return a number.

> Returns the four-byte loopback address. Normally equivalent to `inet_aton(localhost)`.

`INADDR_NONE`

> Note: Does not return a number.

> Returns the four-byte invalid IP address. Normally equivalent to `inet_aton(255.255.255.255)`.

`sockaddr_in` *PORT, ADDRESS*
`sockaddr_in` *SOCKADDR_IN*

> In an array context, unpacks its *SOCKADDR_IN* argument and returns an array consisting of (*PORT, ADDRESS*). In a scalar context, packs its (*PORT, ADDRESS*) arguments as a *SOCKADDR_IN* and returns it. If this is confusing, use `pack_sockaddr_in()` and `unpack_sockaddr_in()` explicitly.

`pack_sockaddr_in` *PORT, IP_ADDRESS*

> Takes two arguments, a port number and a four-byte *IP_ADDRESS* (as returned by `inet_aton()`). Returns the `sockaddr_in` structure with those arguments packed in with AF_INET filled in. For Internet domain sockets, this structure is normally what you need for the arguments in `bind()`, `connect()`, and `send()`, and is also returned by `getpeername()`, `getsockname()`, and `recv()`.

`unpack_sockaddr_in` *SOCKADDR_IN*

> Takes a `sockaddr_in` structure (as returned by `pack_sockaddr_in()`) and returns an array of two elements: the port and the four-byte IP-address. Croaks if the structure does not have AF_INET in the right place.

`sockaddr_un` *PATHNAME*
`sockaddr_un` *SOCKADDR_UN*

> In an array context, unpacks its *SOCKADDR_UN* argument and returns an array consisting of (*PATHNAME*). In a scalar context, packs its *PATHNAME* arguments as a *SOCKADDR_UN* and returns it. If this is confusing, use `pack_sockaddr_un()` and `unpack_sockaddr_un()` explicitly. These are only supported if your system has *sys/un.h.*

`pack_sockaddr_un` *PATH*

> Takes one argument, a pathname. Returns the `sockaddr_un` structure with that path packed in with AF_UNIX filled in. For UNIX domain sockets, this structure is normally what you need for the arguments in `bind()`, `connect()`, and `send()`, and is also returned by `getpeername()`, `getsockname()`, and `recv()`.

`unpack_sockaddr_un` *SOCKADDR_UN*

> Takes a `sockaddr_un` structure (as returned by `pack_sockaddr_un()`) and returns the pathname. Croaks if the structure does not have AF_UNIX in the right place.

Data Types and Data Type Utilities

This section documents various data types and utilities for data manipulation, the largest of these being the Math group of modules. Also listed are date and time utilities, as well as modules for graphing and statistical calculations.

Bit::ShiftReg—bit shift registers with rotate/shift operations

Synopsis

Imports all (or some, by leaving some out) of the available operations and functions:

```
use Bit::ShiftReg qw( bits_of_byte bits_of_short bits_of_int
    bits_of_long  LSB_byte MSB_byte LSB_short MSB_short LSB_int
    MSB_int LSB_long MSB_long ROL_byte ROR_byte SHL_byte SHR_byte
    ROL_short ROR_short SHL_short SHR_short ROL_int ROR_int SHL_int
    SHR_int ROL_long ROR_long SHL_long SHR_long );
```

Imports all available operations and functions:

```
use Bit::ShiftReg qw(:all);
```

Returns the module's version number:

```
$version = Bit::ShiftReg::Version();
```

Returns the number of bits in a byte (unsigned **char**) on your machine:

```
$bits 0= bits_of_byte();
```

Returns the number of bits in an unsigned **short** on your machine:

```
$bits = bits_of_short();
```

Returns the number of bits in an unsigned **int** on your machine:

```
$bits = bits_of_int();
```

Returns the number of bits in an unsigned **long** on your machine:

```
$bits = bits_of_long();
```

Returns the least significant bit (LSB) of a byte (unsigned **char**):

```
$lsb = LSB_byte($value);
```

Returns the most significant bit (MSB) of a byte (unsigned **char**):

```
$msb = MSB_byte($value);
```

Returns the least significant bit (LSB) of an unsigned **short**:

```
$lsb = LSB_short($value);
```

Returns the most significant bit (MSB) of an unsigned **short**:

```
$msb = MSB_short($value);
```

Returns the least significant bit (LSB) of an unsigned **int**:

```
$lsb = LSB_int($value);
```

Returns the most significant bit (MSB) of an unsigned **int**:

```
$msb = MSB_int($value);
```

Returns the least significant bit (LSB) of an unsigned **long**:

```
$lsb = LSB_long($value);
```

Returns the most significant bit (MSB) of an unsigned **long**:

```
$msb = MSB_long($value);
```

```
$carry = ROL_byte($value);
$carry = ROR_byte($value);
$carry_out = SHL_byte($value,$carry_in);
$carry_out = SHR_byte($value,$carry_in);
$carry = ROL_short($value);
$carry = ROR_short($value);
$carry_out = SHL_short($value,$carry_in);
$carry_out = SHR_short($value,$carry_in);
$carry = ROL_int($value);
$carry = ROR_int($value);
$carry_out = SHL_int($value,$carry_in);
$carry_out = SHR_int($value,$carry_in);
$carry = ROL_long($value);
$carry = ROR_long($value);
$carry_out = SHL_long($value,$carry_in);
$carry_out = SHR_long($value,$carry_in);
```

Notes:

- $value must be a variable in the calls of the functions ROL, ROR, SHL, and SHR and the contents of this variable are altered *implicitly* by these functions.

- The **carry** input value is always truncated to the least significant bit, i.e., input values for **carry** must be either 0 or 1.

- The value returned by the functions LSB, MSB, ROL, ROR, SHL, and SHR is always either 0 or 1.

Description

This module implements rotate left, rotate right, shift left, and shift right operations with carry flag for all C integer types.

The results depend on the number of bits that the integer types unsigned `char`, unsigned `short`, unsigned `int`, and unsigned `long` have on your machine.

The module automatically determines the number of bits of each integer type and adjusts its internal constants accordingly.

Here's how the operations work:

ROL (Rotate Left):

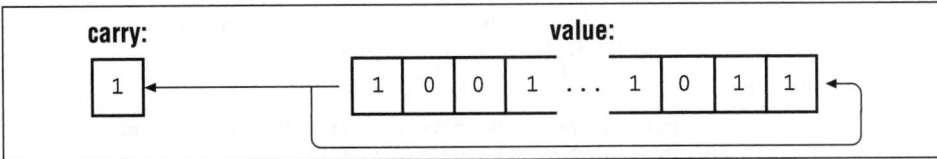

ROR (Rotate Right):

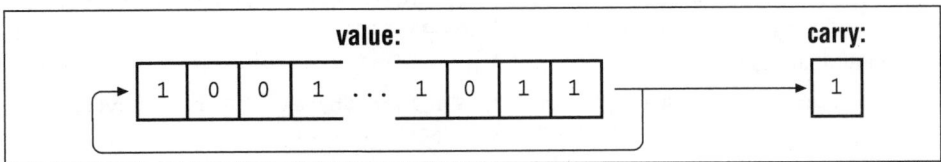

SHL (Shift Left:)

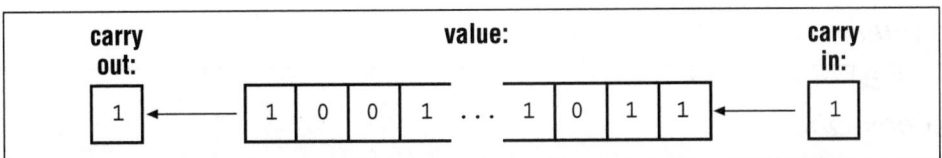

SHR (Shift Right):

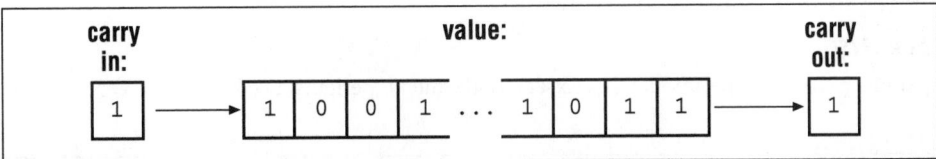

Example

Suppose you want to implement shift registers in a machine-independent way.

The only C integer type whose length in bits you can be pretty sure about is probably a byte, since the C standard only prescribes minimum lengths for `char`, `short`, `int`, and `long`, and that `sizeof(char)` `<=` `sizeof(short)` `<=` `sizeof(int)` `<=` `sizeof(long)`.

Here's how to implement a four-byte shift register and the four operations ROL, ROR, SHL, and SHR on it.

First, you need to define four byte registers:

```
$byte0 = 0;
$byte1 = 0;
$byte2 = 0;
$byte3 = 0;
```

Then proceed as follows:

ROL (Rotate left):

```
$carry = SHL_byte($byte3, SHL_byte($byte2, SHL_byte($byte1,
           SHL_byte($byte0, MSB_byte($byte3))))));
```

ROR (Rotate right):

```
$carry = SHR_byte($byte0, SHR_byte($byte1, SHR_byte($byte2,
           SHR_byte($byte3, LSB_byte($byte0))))));
```

SHL (Shift left):

```
$carry_out = SHL_byte($byte3, SHL_byte($byte2, SHL_byte($byte1,
               SHL_byte($byte0, $carry_in))));
```

SHR (Shift right):

```
$carry_out = SHR_byte($byte0, SHR_byte($byte1, SHR_byte($byte2,
               SHR_byte($byte3, $carry_in))));
```

Version

This manpage documents Bit::ShiftReg version 2.0.

Author

Steffen Beyer, *sb@sdm.de*

Copyright

Copyright © 1997 by Steffen Beyer. All rights reserved.

See Also

perl(1), perlsub(1), perlmod(1), perlxs(1), perlxstut(1), perlguts(1)

Bit::Vector—bit vectors of arbitrary length (base class)

Synopsis

Methods Implemented In C (Fastest)

Version

```
$version = Bit::Vector::Version(); # version of "Vector.xs"
```

new

```
$vector = new Bit::Vector($elements);
$vector = Bit::Vector->new($elements);
$vector = $any_vector->new($elements);
```

Resize
```
    $vector->Resize($elements);
```
Size
```
    $elements = $vector->Size();
```
Empty
```
    $vector->Empty();
```
Fill
```
    $vector->Fill();
```
Flip
```
    $vector->Flip();
```
Interval_Empty
```
    $vector->Interval_Empty($min,$max);
```
Interval_Fill
```
    $vector->Interval_Fill($min,$max);
```
Interval_Flip
```
    $vector->Interval_Flip($min,$max);
```
Interval_Scan_inc
```
    while (($min,$max) = $vector->Interval_Scan_inc($start))
```
Interval_Scan_dec
```
    while (($min,$max) = $vector->Interval_Scan_dec($start))
```
Bit_Off
```
    $vector->Bit_Off($index);
    $vector->Delete($index);            # (deprecated)
```
Bit_On
```
    $vector->Bit_On($index);
    $vector->Insert($index);            # (deprecated)
```
bit_flip
```
    $bit = $vector->bit_flip($index);
    if ($vector->bit_flip($index))
    $bit = $vector->flip($index);       # (deprecated)
    if ($vector->flip($index))          # (deprecated)
```
bit_test
```
    $bit = $vector->bit_test($index);
    if ($vector->bit_test($index))
    $bit = $vector->contains($index);
    if ($vector->contains($index))
    $bit = $vector->in($index);         # (deprecated)
    if ($vector->in($index))            # (deprecated)
```
equal
```
    if ($vector1->equal($vector2))
```
lexorder
```
    if ($vector1->lexorder($vector2))
```
Compare
```
    $cmp = $vector1->Compare($vector2);
```
Copy
```
    $vector1->Copy($vector2);
```

rotate_left
    $carry_out = $vector->rotate_left();

rotate_right
    $carry_out = $vector->rotate_right();

shift_left
    $carry_out = $vector->shift_left($carry_in);

shift_right
    $carry_out = $vector->shift_right($carry_in);

to_String
    $string = $vector->to_String();   # e.g., "A08A28AC"

from_string
    $ok = $vector->from_string($string);

Union
    $set1->Union($set2,$set3);   # in-place is possible!

Intersection
    $set1->Intersection($set2,$set3);   # in-place is possible!

Difference
    $set1->Difference($set2,$set3);   # in-place is possible!

ExclusiveOr
    $set1->ExclusiveOr($set2,$set3);   # in-place is possible!

Complement
    $set1->Complement($set2);   # in-place is possible!

subset
    if ($set1->subset($set2))
    if ($set1->inclusion($set2))   # (deprecated)

Norm
    $norm = $set->Norm();

Min
    $min = $set->Min();

Max
    $max = $set->Max();

Multiplication
    $matrix1->Multiplication($rows1,$cols1,
                             $matrix2,$rows2,$cols2,
                             $matrix3,$rows3,$cols3);

Closure
    $matrix->Closure($rows,$cols);

Methods Implemented in Perl

Version
    $version = $Bit::Vector::VERSION;   # version of "Vector.pm"

Shadow
    $other_vector = $some_vector->Shadow();

Clone
    $twin_vector = $some_vector->Clone();

new_from_String
```
eval { $vector = Bit::Vector->new_from_String($string); };
```
to_ASCII
```
$string = $vector->to_ASCII();        # e.g., "2,3,5-7,11,13-19"
```
from_ASCII
```
eval { $vector->from_ASCII($string); };
```

Overloaded Operators (Slowest)

```
# "$index" is a number or a Perl scalar variable containing a
# number which represents the set containing only that element:
```

Emptyness
```
if ($vector) # if not empty
if (! $vector) # if empty
unless ($vector) # if empty
```

Equality
```
if ($vector1 == $vector2)
if ($vector1 != $vector2)
if ($vector == $index)
if ($vector != $index)
```

Lexical Comparison
```
$cmp = $vector1 cmp $vector2;
if ($vector1 lt $vector2)
if ($vector1 le $vector2)
if ($vector1 gt $vector2)
if ($vector1 ge $vector2)
if ($vector1 eq $vector2)
if ($vector1 ne $vector2)
$cmp = $vector cmp $index;
if ($vector lt $index)
if ($vector le $index)
if ($vector gt $index)
if ($vector ge $index)
if ($vector eq $index)
if ($vector ne $index)
```

Shift Register
```
$carry_out = $vector << $carry_in;
$carry_out = $vector >> $carry_in;
$carry_out = $carry_in >> $vector;
$vector <<= $carry_in;
$vector >>= $carry_in;
```

Rotate Register
```
$carry_out = $vector << $vector->bit_test($vector->Size()-1);
$carry_out = $vector >> $vector->bit_test(0);
$carry_out = $vector->bit_test(0) >> $vector;
$vector <<= $vector->bit_test($vector->Size()-1);
$vector >>= $vector->bit_test(0);
```

String Conversion
```
$string = "$vector";
print "\$vector = '$vector'\n";
```

Union
```
$set1 = $set2 + $set3;
$set1 += $set2;
$set1 = $set2 | $set3;
$set1 |= $set2;
$vector1 = $vector2 + $index;
$vector += $index;
$vector1 = $vector2 | $index;
$vector |= $index;
```
Intersection
```
$set1 = $set2 * $set3;
$set1 *= $set2;
$set1 = $set2 & $set3;
$set1 &= $set2;
$vector1 = $vector2 * $index;
$vector *= $index;
$vector1 = $vector2 & $index;
$vector &= $index;
```
Difference
```
$set1 = $set2 - $set3;
$set1 -= $set2;
$set1 = $set2 - $set1;
$vector1 = $vector2 - $index;
$vector1 = $index - $vector2;
$vector -= $index;
```
ExclusiveOr
```
$set1 = $set2 ^ $set3;
$set1 ^= $set2;
$vector1 = $vector2 ^ $index;
$vector ^= $index;
```
Complement
```
$set1 = -$set2;
$set1 = ~$set2;
$set = -$set;
$set = ~$set;
```
Subset Relationship
```
if ($set1 <= $set2)
```
True Subset Relationship
```
if ($set1 < $set2)
```
Superset Relationship
```
if ($set1 >= $set2)
```
True Superset Relationship
```
if ($set1 > $set2)
```
Norm
```
$norm = abs($set);
```

Description

This class provides the following features.

- A versatile implementation of bit vectors of arbitrary length with efficient and easy-to-use methods for various applications, especially sets.
- A base class for all applications and classes using bit vectors as their underlying data type.
- Overloaded arithmetic and relational operators for maximum comfort.

The class allows you to create bit vectors and sets of arbitrary size (limited only by the size of a machine word and the amount of available memory on your system) with indices (= elements) in the range from zero to some positive integer, to dynamically change the size of such bit vectors or sets, and to perform a broad range of basic operations on them, such as:

- Padding or removing elements (setting and clearing single bits)
- Testing the presence of a certain element (testing a single bit)
- Setting or clearing contiguous ranges of bits
- Detecting contiguous ranges of set bits
- Copying bit vectors
- Converting a bit vector into either a compact (hexadecimal) or a human-readable string representation (allowing you to store bit vectors in a file, for instance)
- Reading in the contents of a bit vector from a string
- Comparing two bit vectors for equality and lexical order
- Performing bitwise shift and rotation operations
- Computing the union, intersection, difference, symmetric difference, or complement of sets
- Testing two sets for equality or inclusion (subset relationship)
- Computing the minimum, the maximum, and the norm (number of elements) of a set

and more. Note that it is very easy to implement sets of arbitrary intervals of integers using this module (negative indices are no obstacle), despite the fact that only intervals of positive integers, from zero to some positive integer, are supported directly.

Please refer to the Set::IntegerRange module (also contained in this distribution) and the Set::IntegerRange(3) manpage to see how this can be done.

The Bit::Vector module is mainly intended for mathematical or algorithmical computations. There are also a number of efficient algorithms that rely on sets (and bit vectors).

An example of such an efficient algorithm, which uses a different representation for sets, however, not bit vectors, is Kruskal's algorithm for minimal spanning trees in graphs.

(See the module Graph::Kruskal and the Graph::Kruskal(3) manpages.)

Another famous algorithm using bit vectors is the "Seave of Erathostenes" for calculating prime numbers, which is included in the distribution as a demo program (see the file *primes.pl*).

An important field of application is the computation of "first", "follow", and "look-ahead" character sets for the construction of LL, SLR, LR, and LALR parsers for compilers (or a compiler-compiler, like yacc, for instance).

(That's what the C library in this package was initially written for.)

See Aho, Hopcroft, Ullman, *The Design and Analysis of Computer Algorithms* for an excellent book on efficient algorithms and the famous "Dragon Book" on how to build compilers by Aho, Sethi, Ullman.

Therefore, this module is primarily designed for efficiency, which is the reason why most of its methods are implemented in C.

To increase execution speed, the module doesn't use bytes as its basic storage unit; rather, it uses machine words, assuming that a machine word is the most efficiently handled size of all scalar types on any machine (that's what the ANSI C standard proposes and assumes, anyway).

In order to achieve this, it automatically determines the number of bits in a machine word on your system and then adjusts its internal configuration constants accordingly.

The greater the size of this basic storage unit, the better the complexity (= execution speed) of the methods in this module (but also the greater the average waste of unused bits in the last word).

Note that the C library of this package (*BitVector.c*) is designed in such a way that it can be used independently from Perl and this Perl extension module.

For this, you can use the file *BitVector.o* exactly as it is produced when building this module. It contains no references to Perl, and it doesn't need any Perl header files in order to compile. It only needs *Definitions.h* and some system header files.

Note, however, that this C library does not perform any bounds checking whatsoever. Your application is responsible for bounds checking See the respective explanation in the file *BitVector.c* for more details and the file *Vector.xs* for an example of how this can be done.

In this module, all bounds and type checking, which should be absolutely foolproof, BTW, is done in the XSUB routines (in C).

For more details about the modules in the distribution, please refer to their respective manpages.

General Hints
Method naming convention
> Method names completely in lowercase indicate a boolean return value (except for method new(), of course).

Boolean return values
> Boolean return values in this class are always a numerical zero (0) for false and a numerical one (1) for true.

> This means that you may use the methods of this class with boolean return values as the conditional expression in if, unless, and while statements.

Version
> The function Bit::Vector::Version() (the version of the *Vector.xs* file) should always return the same version number as that contained in the variable $Bit::Vector::VERSION (the version of the *Vector.pm* file).

Methods Implemented in C
$vector = Bit::Vector->new($elements);
> This is the bit vector constructor method.

Call this method to create a new bit vector containing $elements bits (with indices from 0 to $elements - 1).

The method returns a reference to the new bit vector.

A new bit vector is always initialized so that all bits are cleared (turned off).

An exception is raised if the method is unable to allocate the necessary memory.

An exception is also raised if you try to create a bit vector with zero elements (i.e., with length zero).

Note that if you specify a negative number for $elements, it is interpreted as a large positive number due to its internal 2's complement binary representation.

In such a case, the bit vector constructor method obediently attempts to create a bit vector of that size, probably resulting in an exception, as explained above.

`$vector->Resize($elements);`

Changes the size of the given vector to the specified number of bits.

This method allows you to change the size of an existing bit vector or set, preserving as many bits from the old vector as will fit into the new one (i.e., all bits with indices smaller than the minimum of the sizes of the two vectors, old and new).

If the number of machine words needed to store the new vector is smaller than or equal to the number of words needed to store the old vector, the memory allocated for the old vector is reused for the new one, and only the relevant book-keeping information is adjusted accordingly.

This means that even if the number of bits increases, new memory is not necessarily being allocated (i.e., if the old and the new number of bits fit into the same number of machine words).

If the number of machine words needed to store the new vector is greater than the number of words needed to store the old vector, new memory is allocated for the new vector, the old vector is copied to the new one, the remaining bits in the new vector are cleared (turned off), and the old vector is deleted (i.e., the memory that was allocated for it is released).

This also means that if you decrease the size of a given vector so that it uses fewer machine words, and increase it again later so that it uses more words than before, but still less than the original vector, new memory is allocated anyway because the information about the size of the original vector is lost when you downsize it.

Note also that if you specify a negative number for $elements, it is interpreted as a large positive number due to its internal 2's complement binary representation.

In such a case, `Resize()` obediently attempts to create a bit vector of that size, probably resulting in an exception, as explained above (see method `new()`).

Finally, note that resizing a bit vector to a size of zero elements (length zero) is disallowed; an exception is raised if you try to do so.

`$elements = $vector->Size();`

Returns the size (number of bits) the given vector was created with or `Resize()`'d to.

`$vector->Empty();`

Clears all bits in the given vector.

`$vector->Fill();`

> Sets all bits in the given vector.

`$vector->Flip();`

> Flips (i.e., complements) all bits in the given vector.

`$vector->Interval_Empty($min,$max);`

> Clears all bits in the interval `[$min..$max]`, including both limits in the given vector.
>
> `$min` and `$max` may have the same value; this is the same as clearing a single bit with `Bit_Off()` (but less efficient).
>
> Note that `$vector->Interval_Empty(0,$vector->Size()-1);` is the same as `$vector->Empty();` (but less efficient).

`$vector->Interval_Fill($min,$max);`

> Sets all bits in the interval `[$min..$max]`, including both limits, in the given vector.
>
> `$min` and `$max` may have the same value; this is the same as setting a single bit with `Bit_On()` (but less efficient).
>
> Note that `$vector->Interval_Fill(0,$vector->Size()-1);` is the same as `$vector->Fill();` (but less efficient).

`$vector->Interval_Flip($min,$max);`

> Flips (i.e., complements) all bits in the interval `[$min..$max]`, including both limits, in the given vector.
>
> `$min` and `$max` may have the same value; this is the same as flipping a single bit with `bit_flip()` (but less efficient).
>
> Note that `$vector->Interval_Flip(0,$vector->Size()-1);` is the same as `$vector->Flip();` and `$vector->Complement($vector);` (but less efficient).

`($min,$max) = $vector->Interval_Scan_inc($start)`

> Returns the minimum and maximum indices of the next contiguous block of set bits (i.e., bits in the "on" state).
>
> The search starts at index `$start` (i.e., `$min >= $start`) and proceeds upwards (`$max >= $min`), thus repeatedly incrementing the search pointer `$start` internally.
>
> Note, though, that the contents of the variable (or scalar literal value) `$start` is not altered; i.e., you have to set the variable to the desired value yourself prior to each call to `Interval_Scan_inc()`. (See also the following example.)
>
> Actually, the bit vector is not searched bit by bit, but one machine word at a time, in order to speed up execution (this means that this method is quite efficient).
>
> An empty list is returned if no such block can be found.
>
> Note that a single set bit (surrounded by cleared bits) is a valid block by this definition. In that case, the return values for `$min` and `$max` are the same.
>
> Typical use:
>
> ```
> $start = 0;
> while (($start < $vector->Size()) &&
>     (($min,$max) = $vector->Interval_Scan_inc($start)))
> {
>     $start = $max + 2;
> ```

```
                 # do something with $min and $max
        }
```

($min, $max) = $vector->Interval_Scan_dec($start)

Returns the minimum and maximum indices of the next contiguous block of set bits (i.e., bits in the "on" state).

The search starts at index $start (i.e., $max <= $start) and proceeds downwards ($min <= $max), thus repeatedly decrementing the search pointer $start internally.

Note, though, that the contents of the variable (or scalar literal value) $start are not altered; i.e., you have to set the variable to the desired value yourself prior to each call to Interval_Scan_dec(). (See also the following example.)

Actually, the bit vector is not searched bit by bit, but one machine word at a time, in order to speed up execution (this means that this method is quite efficient).

An empty list is returned if no such block can be found.

Note that a single set bit (surrounded by cleared bits) is a valid block by this definition. In that case the return values for $min and $max are the same.

Typical use:

```
        $start = $vector->Size() - 1;
        while (($start >= 0) &&
            (($min,$max) = $vector->Interval_Scan_dec($start)))
        {
            $start = $min - 2;
            # do something with $min and $max
        }
```

$vector->Bit_Off($index);

Clears the bit with index $index in the given vector.

This is equivalent to removing the element $index from the given set.

Note that if you specify a negative number for $index, it is interpreted as a large positive number due to its internal 2's complement binary representation.

An exception is raised if $index lies outside the permitted range from 0 to $vector->Size()-1.

$vector->Bit_On($index);

Sets the bit with index $index in the given vector.

This is equivalent to adding the element $index to the given set.

Note that if you specify a negative number for $index, it is interpreted as a large positive number due to its internal 2's complement binary representation.

An exception is raised if $index lies outside the permitted range from 0 to $vector->Size()-1.

$vector->bit_flip($index)

Flips (i.e., complements) the bit with index $index in the given vector.

This is equivalent to adding the element $index to the given set if it is *not* contained yet and removing it if it is contained.

Also returns the *new* state of the specified bit, i.e., returns 0 if it is cleared (in the "off" state) or 1 if it is set (in the "on" state).

In other words, it returns **true** if the specified element is contained in the given set and **false** otherwise.

Note that if you specify a negative number for *$index*, it is interpreted as a large positive number due to its internal 2's complement binary representation.

An exception is raised if *$index* lies outside the permitted range from 0 to `$vector->Size()-1`.

`$vector->bit_test($index)`

Returns the current state of the bit with index *$index* in the given vector, i.e., returns 0 if it is cleared (in the "off" state) or 1 if it is set (in the "on" state).

In other words, it returns **true** if the specified element is contained in the given set and **false** otherwise.

Note that if you specify a negative number for *$index*, it is interpreted as a large positive number due to its internal 2's complement binary representation!

An exception is raised if *$index* lies outside the permitted range from 0 to `$vector->Size()-1`.

`$vector1->equal($vector2)`

Tests the two given bit vectors for equality.

Returns **true** (1) if the two bit vectors are exact copies of one another and **false** (0) otherwise.

An exception is raised if the two bit vectors have different sizes; in other words, if `$vector1->Size() != $vector2->Size()`.

`$vector1->lexorder($vector2)`

Tests the lexical order of the two given bit vectors.

That is, the two bit vectors are regarded as two large (positive) numbers in binary representation that are compared.

The least significant bit (LSB) of this binary number is the bit with index 0, the most significant bit (MSB) is the bit with index `$vector->Size()-1`.

Returns true (1) if the first bit vector is less than or equal to the second bit vector and false (0) otherwise.

An exception is raised if the two bit vectors have different sizes; in other words, if `$vector1->Size() != $vector2-Size()`.

`$vector1->Compare($vector2)`

Compares the two given bit vectors.

That is, the two bit vectors are regarded as two large (positive) numbers in binary representation that are compared.

The least significant bit (LSB) of this binary number is the bit with index 0, the most significant bit (MSB) is the bit with index `$vector->Size()-1`.

Returns −1 if the first bit vector is less than the second bit vector, 0 if the two bit vectors are exact copies of one another and 1 if the first bit vector is greater than the second bit vector.

An exception is raised if the two bit vectors have different sizes; in other words, if `$vector1->Size() != $vector2-Size()`.

`$vector1->Copy($vector2);`

Copies the contents of bit vector `$vector2` to bit vector `$vector1`.

The previous contents of bit vector $vector1 get overwritten, i.e., are lost.

Both vectors must exist beforehand, i.e., this method does not *create* any new bit vector object.

An exception is raised if the two bit vectors have different sizes; in other words, if $vector1->Size() != $vector2-Size().

$carry_out = $vector->rotate_left();

The least significant bit (LSB) is the bit with index 0; the most significant bit (MSB) is the bit with index $vector->Size()-1.

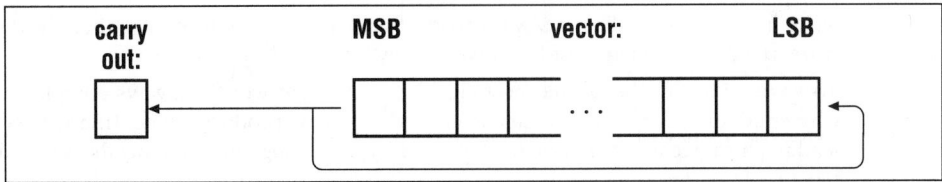

$carry_out = $vector->rotate_right();

The least significant bit (LSB) is the bit with index 0; the most significant bit (MSB) is the bit with index $vector->Size()-1.

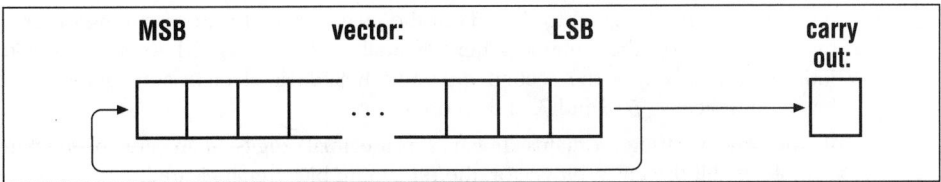

$carry_out = $vector->shift_left($carry_in);

The least significant bit (LSB) is the bit with index 0; the most significant bit (MSB) is the bit with index $vector->Size()-1.

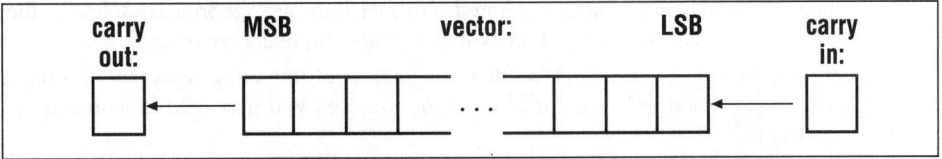

$carry_out = $vector->shift_right($carry_in);

The least significant bit (LSB) is the bit with index 0; the most significant bit (MSB) is the bit with index $vector->Size()-1.

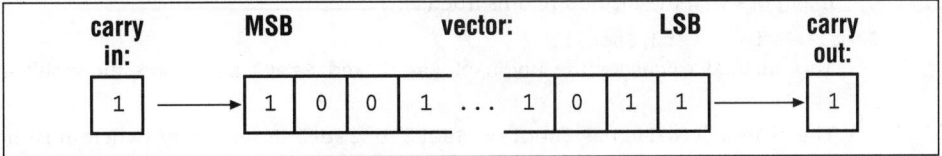

`$string = $vector->to_String();`

Returns a hexadecimal string representing the given bit vector.

Note that this representation is quite compact, in that it only needs twice the number of bytes needed to store the bit vector itself, internally!

The rightmost hexadecimal digit in this string represents the four least significant bits of the given bit vector (i.e., the bits with indices 3, 2, 1 and 0).

The leftmost hexadecimal digit(s) in the string represent(s) the most significant and/or unused bits—this is due to the fact that this class uses machine words as its basic storage unit (to increase efficiency).

Since a hexadecimal digit is always worth four bits, the length of the string always corresponds to a multiple of four bits anyway.

To spare extra overhead, the most significant machine word is always completely converted into hexadecimal characters, which may produce some (innocuous) leading hexadecimal zeros at the left end of the string representing the unused bits of that bit vector.

`$vector->from_string($string)`

Allows reading in the contents of a bit vector from a hexadecimal string, such as that returned by the method `to_String()` (described immediately previously).

The string is read from right to left (!), and the bits corresponding to each hexadecimal digit are assigned to the bits in the given bit vector in ascending order of their indices, i.e., the rightmost hexadecimal digit is assigned to the bits with indices 0, 1, 2 and 3, the second rightmost hexadecimal digit is assigned to the bits with indices 4, 5, 6 and 7, and so on.

If the given string contains fewer hexadecimal digits than are needed to completely fill the given bit vector, the remaining bits are all cleared.

In other words, even if the given string does not contain enough digits to completely fill the given bit vector, the previous contents of the bit vector are erased.

If the given string is longer than needed to fill the given bit vector, the superfluous characters are simply ignored. (In fact they are ignored completely; they are not even checked for proper syntax. See also immediately below.)

This behavior is intentional, so that you may read the string representing one bit vector into another bit vector of different size; i.e., you may read in as much of it as will fit.

If during the process of reading the given string, a character is encountered that is not a hexadecimal digit, an error ensues.

In such a case, the bit vector is filled with zeros starting at the point of the error, and the method returns false (0).

If all goes well the method returns true (1).

`$set1->Union($set2,$set3);`

This method calculates the union of `$set2` and `$set3` and stores the result in `$set1`.

This is usually written as `$set1 = $set2 u $set3` in set theory (where u is the "cup" operator).

On systems where the "cup" character is unavailable this operator is often denoted by a plus sign (+).

In-place calculation is also possible, i.e., $set1 may be identical with $set2 or $set3 or both.

An exception is raised if the sizes of the three sets do not match.

`$set1->Intersection($set2,$set3);`

This method calculates the intersection of $set2 and $set3 and stores the result in $set1.

This is usually written as $set1 = $set2 n $set3 in set theory (where n is the "cap" operator).

On systems where the "cap" character is unavailable this operator is often denoted by an asterisk (*).

In-place calculation is also possible, i.e., $set1 may be identical to $set2 or $set3 or both.

An exception is raised if the sizes of the three sets do not match.

`$set1->Difference($set2,$set3);`

This method calculates the difference of $set2 less $set3 and stores the result in $set1.

This is usually written as $set1 = $set2 \ $set3 in set theory (where \ is the "less" operator).

In-place calculation is also possible, i.e., $set1 may be identical to $set2 or $set3 or both.

An exception is raised if the sizes of the three sets do not match.

`$set1->ExclusiveOr($set2,$set3);`

This method calculates the symmetric difference of $set2 and $set3 and stores the result in $set1.

This can be written as ($vec2 u $vec3) \ ($vec2 n $vec3) in set theory (the union of the two sets less their intersection).

When sets are implemented as bit vectors, then the above formula is equivalent to the exclusive-or between corresponding bits of the two bit vectors (hence the name of this method).

Note that this method is also much more efficient than evaluating the above formula explicitly, since it uses a built-in machine language instruction internally.

In-place calculation is also possible, i.e., $set1 may be identical to $set2 or $set3 or both.

An exception is raised if the sizes of the three sets do not match.

`$set1->Complement($set2);`

This method calculates the complement of $set2 and stores the result in $set1.

In-place calculation is also possible, i.e., $set1 may be identical to $set2.

An exception is raised if the sizes of the two sets do not match.

`$set1->subset($set2)`

Returns true (1) if $set1 is a subset of $set2 (i.e., completely contained in $set2) and false (0) otherwise.

Note that by definition, if two sets are identical, they are also subsets (and also supersets) of each other.

An exception is raised if the sizes of the two sets do not match.

`$norm = $set->Norm();`

Returns the norm (number of bits that are set) of the given vector.

This is equivalent to the number of elements contained in the given set.

`$min = $set->Min();`

Returns the minimum of the given set.

If the set is empty, plus infinity (represented by the constant MAX_LONG on your system) is returned.

`$max = $set->Max();`

Returns the maximum of the given set.

If the set is empty, minus infinity (represented by the constant MIN_LONG on your system) is returned.

`$m1->Multiplication($r1,$c1,$m2,$r2,$c2,$m3,$r3,$c3,);`

This method multiplies two boolean matrices (stored as bit vectors), $m2 and $m3, and stores the result in matrix $m1.

An exception is raised if the product of the number of rows and columns of any of the three matrices differs from the size of the corresponding bit vector.

An exception is also raised if the numbers of rows and columns of the three matrices do not harmonize in the required manner:

```
rows1 == rows2
cols1 == cols3
cols2 == rows3
```

This method is used by the Math::MatrixBool application class (see also the Math::MatrixBool(3) manpage).

`$matrix->Closure($rows,$cols);`

This method calculates the reflexive transitive closure of the given boolean matrix (stored as a bit vector) using Kleene's algoritm.

(See the Math::Kleene(3) manpage for a brief introduction into the theory behind Kleene's algorithm.)

The reflexive transitive closure answers the question whether a path exists between any two vortices of a graph whose edges are given as a matrix:

- If a (directed) edge exists going from vortex i to vortex j, then the element in the matrix with coordinates (i,j) is set to 1 (otherwise it remains set to 0).

- If the edges are undirected, the resulting matrix is symmetric, i.e., elements (i,j) and (j,i) always contain the same value.

The matrix representing the edges of the graph only answers the question as to whether an *edge* exists between any two vortices of the graph, whereas the reflexive transitive closure answers the question whether a *path* (a series of adjacent edges) exists between any two vortices of the graph.

Note that the contents of the given matrix are modified by this method, so make a copy of the initial matrix if you are going to need it again later.

An exception is raised if the given matrix is not quadratic, i.e., if the number of rows and columns of the given matrix is not identical.

An exception is also raised if the product of the number of rows and columns of the given matrix differs from the size of its underlying bit vector.

This method is used by the Math::MatrixBool application class (see also the Math::MatrixBool(3) manpage).

Methods Implemented in Perl

`$other_vector = $some_vector->Shadow();`

Creates a new bit vector that has the same size as $some_vector bit is empty.

This is like a shadow that has the same shape as the object it originates from, but is flat and has no volume, i.e., contains nothing.

`$twin_vector = $some_vector->Clone();`

Creates a new bit vector of the same size as $some_vector and that is an exact copy of $some_vector.

`$vector = Bit::Vector->new_from_String($string);`

Creates a new bit vector of the size 4 * length($string) and tries to fill it with the contents of $string, which must consist entirely of hexadecimal characters.

Example:

```
$vector = Bit::Vector->new_from_
String("20208828828208A20A08A28AC");
```

(Fills $vector with all prime numbers below 100.)

The hexadecimal characters A through F may be lowercase or uppercase indiscriminately.

An exception is raised if the string contains other than hexadecimal characters.

An exception is also raised if the string is empty, because bit vectors of zero elements (length zero) are not permitted in this class.

Finally, an exception is also raised if the necessary memory for the bit vector cannot be allocated.

`$string = $vector->to_ASCII();`

Converts the given bit vector or set into an enumeration of single indices and ranges of indices (newsrc style), representing the bits that are set (i.e., in the "on" state) in the bit vector.

Example:

```
$vector = Bit::Vector->new(20);
$vector->Bit_On(2);
$vector->Bit_On(3);
$vector->Bit_On(11);
$vector->Interval_Fill(5,7);
$vector->Interval_Fill(13,19);
print $vector->to_ASCII(), "\n";
```

prints 2,3,5-7,11,13-19.

If the given bit vector is empty the resulting string is also empty.

```
$vector->from_ASCII($string);
```
First empties the given vector and then tries to set the bits and ranges of bits specified in the given string.

The string `$string` must contain positive integers or ranges separated by commas.

All other characters are disallowed (including white space).

An exception is raised if the string does not obey this syntax.

In each range the first integer must always be less than or equal to the second one, otherwise an exception is raised.

An exception is also raised if any of the integers exceeds the range of permitted indices in the given string, i.e., if any integer is greater than or equal to `$vector->Size()`.

Example:

```
eval { $vector->from_ASCII("2,3,5-7,11,13-19"); };
```
Note that the order of the indices and ranges is irrelevant, i.e.,

```
eval { $vector->from_ASCII("11,5-7,3,13-19,2"); };
```
results in the same vector as in the example above.

Ranges and indices may also overlap.

This is because each (single) index in the string is passed to the method `Bit_On()` and each range to the method `Interval_Fill()` internally.

So the resulting vector (or set) is just the union of all the specified elements and ranges.

Overloaded Operators

Emptyness

Note that the method for determining emptyness is quite efficient: the method stops searching the given bit vector as soon as it finds the first non-zero machine word.

(Actually, it uses the `Min()` method internally.)

Equality

The method for determining equality is also quite efficient:

It stops at the first differing machine word it finds.

Lexical Comparison

Using the overloaded operator `cmp` to compare two bit vectors, as in `$vector1 cmp $vector2`, is essentially the same as comparing the two corresponding hexadecimal strings returned by the `to_String()` method, i.e., `$vector1->to_String() cmp $vector2->to_String()`.

The result is exactly the same, provided that both bit vectors have the same size, but using the overloaded operator `cmp` is much more efficient since it avoids the additional overhead of converting both bit vectors into strings.

Moreover, with the overloaded operator `cmp`, the two bit vectors are compared one machine word (usually 32 or 64 bits) at a time, which is much faster than comparing one hexadecimal character (four bits worth) at a time in a string comparison.

This comparison ends as soon as two differing words are found, i.e., in many cases the operator doesn't even need to look at the entire bit vector.

Again, since the operator looks at more bits at a time, the search ends much earlier than in a string comparison.

Shift Register

You need to say:

```
$carry_out = $vector << $carry_in;
$carry_out = $vector >> $carry_in;
```

or:

```
$vector <<= $carry_in;
$vector >>= $carry_in;
```

in order to shift a bit vector in either direction using the overloaded operators << and >>.

Since both operators are implemented as being commutative (i.e., you may swap the two arguments without influencing the result), you can also say:

```
$carry_out = $carry_in >> $vector;
```

which is probably more intuitive.

Rotate Register

You need to say:

```
$carry_out = $vector << $vector->bit_test($vector->Size()-1);
$carry_out = $vector >> $vector->bit_test(0);
```

or:

```
$vector <<= $vector->bit_test($vector->Size()-1);
$vector >>= $vector->bit_test(0);
```

in order to rotate a bit vector in either direction using the overloaded operators << and >>.

Since both operators are implemented as being commutative (i.e., you may swap the two arguments without influencing the result), you can also say:

```
$carry_out = $vector->bit_test(0) >> $vector;
```

which is probably more intuitive.

String Conversion

Currently, conversion of a bit vector into a string using the overloaded operator "" is performed using the method to_ASCII() internally, which is probably the preferred behavior.

If you think that this operator should rather convert any given bit vector into a hexadecimal string using the method to_String(), then you should edit the file *Vector.pm* in this distribution as follows:

Locate the method "sub _string" and change the line

```
return( $object->to_ASCII() );
```

to

```
return( $object->to_String() );
```

Union

Since there is no "cup" character in the ASCII alphabet, the plus sign (+) is used here to denote the union operator from set theory.

The pipe symbol (or "vertical bar") (|) may be used as an alias for the plus sign (+).

Intersection

Since there is no "cap" character in the ASCII alphabet, the asterisk (*) is used here to denote the intersection operator from set theory.

The ampersand (&) may be used as an alias for the asterisk (*).

Difference

Since the backslash (\) is not an (overloadable) operator in Perl (and is a very special character anyway) the minus sign (–) is used here to denote the "less" operator from set theory.

ExclusiveOr

Since there is no widely accepted symbol to denote the symmetric difference in set theory (at least not to my knowledge—unless it is the dotted minus sign, which, alas, is also a character unavailable in the ASCII alphabet), the caret (^) (which is the exclusive-or operator anyway) is simply used here to express the symmetric difference of two sets.

Complement

The tilde (~) as well as the unary minus (-) are used interchangeably here to denote the complement of a set.

Subset Relationship

Since there is no "contained in or equal" sign in the ASCII alphabet, the usual operator <= is used instead to denote subset relationship.

True Subset Relationship

Since there is no "contained in" sign in the ASCII alphabet, the usual operator < is used instead to denote (true) subset relationship.

Superset Relationship

Since there is no "superset of or equal" sign in the ASCII alphabet, the usual operator >= is used instead to denote superset relationship.

True Superset Relationship

Since there is no "superset" of sign in the ASCII alphabet, the usual operator > is used instead to denote (true) superset relationship.

Norm

The function abs() can be used to return the number of elements in a given set.

Version

This manpage documents Bit::Vector version 4.0.

Author

Steffen Beyer, *sb@sdm.de*

Copyright

Copyright © 1995, 1996, 1997 by Steffen Beyer. All rights reserved.

See Also

Set::IntegerFast(3),   Set::IntegerRange(3),   Math::MatrixBool(3),   Math::MatrixReal(3), DFA::Kleene(3), Math::Kleene(3), Graph::Kruskal(3).

perl(1), perlsub(1), perlmod(1), perlref(1), perlobj(1), perlbot(1), perltoot(1), perlxs(1), perlxstut(1), perlguts(1), overload(3)

Data::Dumper—stringified Perl data structures, suitable for both printing and eval

Synopsis

```
use Data::Dumper;
# simple procedural interface
print Dumper($foo, $bar);
# extended usage with names
print Data::Dumper->Dump([$foo, $bar], [qw(foo *ary)]);
# configuration variables
{
  local $Data::Dump::Purity = 1;
  eval Data::Dumper->Dump([$foo, $bar], [qw(foo *ary)]);
}
# OO usage
$d = Data::Dumper->new([$foo, $bar], [qw(foo *ary)]);
   ...
print $d->Dump;
   ...
$d->Purity(1);
$d->Terse(1);
$d->Deepcopy(1);
eval $d->Dump;
```

Description

Given a list of scalars or reference variables, writes out their contents in Perl syntax. The references can also be objects. The contents of each variable is output in a single Perl statement.

The return value can be evaled to get back the original reference structure. Bear in mind that a reference so created does not preserve pointer equalities with the original reference.

Handles self-referential structures correctly. Any references that are the same as one of those passed in marked $VAR*n* (where *n* is a numeric suffix), and other duplicate references to substructures within $VAR*n* are appropriately labeled using arrow notation. You can specify names for individual values to be dumped if you use the Dump() method, or you can change the default $VAR prefix to something else. See $Data::Dumper::Varname and $Data::Dumper::Terse below.

The default output of self-referential structures can be evaled, but the nested references to $VAR*n* are undefined, since a recursive structure cannot be constructed using one Perl statement. You can set the Purity flag to 1 to get additional statements that correctly fill in these references.

In the extended usage form, the references to be dumped can be given user-specified names. If a name begins with an *, the output describes the dereferenced type of the supplied reference for hashes and arrays. Output of names is avoided where possible if the Terse flag is set.

Several styles of output are possible, all controlled by setting the Indent flag. See "Configuration Variables or Methods" below for details.

Methods

PACKAGE->new(ARRAYREF [, ARRAYREF])

Returns a newly created Data::Dumper object. The first argument is an anonymous array of values to be dumped. The optional second argument is an anonymous array of names for the values. The names need not have a leading $ sign, and must be comprised of alphanumeric characters. You can begin a name with a * to specify that the dereferenced type must be dumped instead of the reference itself, for array and hash references.

The prefix specified by $Data::Dumper::Varname is used with a numeric suffix if the name for a value is undefined.

Data::Dumper catalogs all references encountered while dumping the values. Cross-references (in the form of names of substructures in Perl syntax) are inserted at all possible points, preserving any structural interdependencies in the original set of values. Structure traversal is depth-first, and proceeds in order from the first supplied value to the last.

$OBJ->Dump *or* PACKAGE->Dump(ARRAYREF [, ARRAYREF])

Returns the stringified form of the values stored in the object (preserving the order in which they were supplied to new), subject to the configuration options below. In an array context, it returns a list of strings corresponding to the supplied values.

The second form, for convenience, simply calls the new method on its arguments before dumping the object immediately.

$OBJ->Dumpxs *or* PACKAGE->Dumpxs(ARRAYREF [, ARRAYREF])

This method is available if you were able to compile and install the XSUB extension to Data::Dumper. It is exactly identical to the Dump method above, only about four to five times faster, since it is written entirely in C.

$OBJ->Seen([HASHREF])

Queries or adds to the internal table of already encountered references. You must use Reset to explicitly clear the table if needed. Such references are not dumped; instead, their names are inserted wherever they are encountered subsequently.

Expects a anonymous hash of name => value pairs. The same rules apply for names as in new. If no argument is supplied, returns the "seen" list of name => value pairs, in an array context.

$OBJ->Values([ARRAYREF])

Queries or replaces the internal array of values that will be dumped.

$OBJ->Names([ARRAYREF])

Queries or replaces the internal array of user-supplied names for the values that will be dumped.

`$OBJ->Reset`

    Clears the internal table of "seen" references.

Functions

`Dumper(LIST)`

    Returns the stringified form of the values in the list, subject to the configuration options below. The values will be named `$VARn` in the output, where *n* is a numeric suffix. Returns a list of strings in an array context.

`DumperX(LIST)`

    Identical to the `Dumper()` function above, but this calls the XSUB implementation. Only available if you were able to compile and install the XSUB extensions in Data::Dumper.

Configuration Variables or Methods

Several configuration variables can be used to control the kind of output generated when using the procedural interface. These variables are usually `localized` in a block so that other parts of the code are not affected by the change.

These variables determine the default state of the object created by calling the **new** method, but cannot be used to alter the state of the object thereafter. The equivalent method names should be used instead to query or set the internal state of the object.

`$Data::Dumper::Indent` *or* `$OBJ->Indent([NEWVAL])`

    Controls the style of indentation. It can be set to 0, 1, 2, or 3. Style 0 spews output without any newlines, indentation, or spaces between list items. It is the most compact format possible that can still be called valid Perl. Style 1 outputs a readable form with newlines, but no fancy indentation (each level in the structure is simply indented by a fixed amount of whitespace). Style 2 (the default) outputs a very readable form that takes into account the length of hash keys (so the hash value lines up). Style 3 is like style 2, but also annotates the elements of arrays with their index (but the comment is on its own line, so array output consumes twice the number of lines). Style 2 is the default.

`$Data::Dumper::Purity` *or* `$OBJ->Purity([NEWVAL])`

    Controls the degree to which the output can be **evaled** to recreate the supplied reference structures. Setting it to 1 outputs additional Perl statements that correctly recreate nested references. The default is 0.

`$Data::Dumper::Pad` *or* `$OBJ->Pad([NEWVAL])`

    Specifies the string that will be prefixed to every line of the output. Empty string by default.

`$Data::Dumper::Varname` *or* `$OBJ->Varname([NEWVAL])`

    Contains the prefix to use for tagging variable names in the output. The default is VAR.

`$Data::Dumper::Useqq` *or* `$OBJ->Useqq([NEWVAL])`

    When set, enables the use of double quotes for representing string values. Whitespace other than space is represented as `[\n\t\r]`, "unsafe" characters are backslashed, and unprintable characters are output as quoted octal integers. Since setting this variable imposes a performance penalty, the default is 0. The `Dumpxs()` method does not honor this flag yet.

`$Data::Dumper::Terse` *or* `$OBJ->Terse([NEWVAL])`

When set, Data::Dumper emits single, non-self-referential values as atoms/terms rather than statements. This means that the `$VAR`*n* names will be avoided where possible, but be advised that such output may not always be parseable by `eval`.

`$Data::Dumper::Freezer` *or* `$OBJ->Freezer([NEWVAL])`

Can be set to a method name, or to an empty string to disable the feature. Data::Dumper invokes that method via the object before attempting to stringify it. This method can alter the contents of the object (if, for instance, it contains data allocated from C), and even rebless it in a different package. The client is responsible for making sure the specified method can be called via the object, and that the object ends up containing only Perl data types after the method has been called. Defaults to an empty string.

`$Data::Dumper::Toaster` *or* `$OBJ->Toaster([NEWVAL])`

Can be set to a method name, or to an empty string to disable the feature. Data::Dumper emits a method call for any objects that are to be dumped using the syntax `bless(DATA, CLASS)->METHOD()`. Note that this means that the method specified has to perform any modifications required on the object (like creating a new state within it, and/or reblessing it in a different package) and then return it. The client is responsible for making sure the method can be called via the object, and that it returns a valid object. Defaults to an empty string.

`$Data::Dumper::Deepcopy` *or* `$OBJ->Deepcopy([NEWVAL])`

Can be set to a boolean value to enable deep copies of structures. Cross-referencing is then done only when it's absolutely essential (i.e., to break reference cycles). Default is 0.

Exports

Dumper

Example

Run these code snippets to get a quick feel for the behavior of this module. When you are through with these examples, you may want to add or change the various configuration variables described above, to see their behavior. (See the test suite in the Data::Dumper distribution for more examples.)

```
use Data::Dumper;
package Foo;
sub new {bless {'a' => 1, 'b' => sub { return "foo" }}, $_[0]};
package Fuz;                      # a weird REF-REF-SCALAR object
sub new {bless \($_ = \ 'fu\'z'), $_[0]};
package main;
$foo = Foo->new;
$fuz = Fuz->new;
$boo = [ 1, [], "abcd", \*foo,
        {1 => 'a', 023 => 'b', 0x45 => 'c'},
        \\"p\q\'r", $foo, $fuz];

########
# simple usage
########
$bar = eval(Dumper($boo));
print($@) if $@;
```

```
print Dumper($boo), Dumper($bar);   # pretty print (no
                                    # array indices)
$Data::Dumper::Terse = 1;           # don't output names
                                    # where feasible
$Data::Dumper::Indent = 0;          # turn off all pretty print
print Dumper($boo), "\n";
$Data::Dumper::Indent = 1;          # mild pretty print
print Dumper($boo);
$Data::Dumper::Indent = 3;          # pretty print with
                                    # array indices

print Dumper($boo);
$Data::Dumper::Useqq = 1;           # print strings in double quotes
print Dumper($boo);


########
# recursive structures
########


@c = ('c');
$c = \@c;
$b = {};
$a = [1, $b, $c];
$b->{a} = $a;
$b->{b} = $a->[1];
$b->{c} = $a->[2];
print Data::Dumper->Dump([$a,$b,$c], [qw(a b c)]);


$Data::Dumper::Purity = 1;          # fill in the holes for eval
print Data::Dumper->Dump([$a, $b], [qw(*a b)]); # print as @a
print Data::Dumper->Dump([$b, $a], [qw(*b a)]); # print as %b


$Data::Dumper::Deepcopy = 1;        # avoid cross-refs
print Data::Dumper->Dump([$b, $a], [qw(*b a)]);


$Data::Dumper::Purity = 0;          # avoid cross-refs
print Data::Dumper->Dump([$b, $a], [qw(*b a)]);


########
# object-oriented usage
########


$d = Data::Dumper->new([$a,$b], [qw(a b)]);
$d->Seen({'*c' => $c});             # stash a ref without printing it
$d->Indent(3);
print $d->Dump;
$d->Reset;                          # empty the seen cache
```

```
    $d->Purity(0);
    print join "----\n", $d->Dump;


    ########
    # persistence
    ########


    package Foo;
    sub new { bless { state => 'awake' }, shift }
    sub Freeze {
        my $s = shift;
        print STDERR "preparing to sleep\n";
        $s->{state} = 'asleep';
        return bless $s, 'Foo::ZZZ';
    }

    package Foo::ZZZ;
    sub Thaw {
        my $s = shift;
        print STDERR "waking up\n";
        $s->{state} = 'awake';
        return bless $s, 'Foo';
    }

    package Foo;
    use Data::Dumper;
    my $a = Foo->new;
    my $b = Data::Dumper->new([$a], [L $b->Freezer('Freeze');
    $b->Toaster('Thaw');
    my $c = $b->Dump;
    print $c;
    my $d = eval $c;
    print Data::Dumper->Dump([$d], [M Bugs
```

Due to limitations of Perl subroutine-call semantics, you cannot pass an array or hash. Prepend it with a \ to pass its reference instead. This will be remedied in time, with the arrival of prototypes in later versions of Perl. For now, you need to use the extended usage form, and prepend the name with a * to output it as a hash or array.

Data::Dumper cheats with code references. If a code reference is encountered in the structure being processed, an anonymous subroutine that contains the string "DUMMY" is inserted in its place, and a warning is printed if Purity is set. You can eval the result, but bear in mind that the anonymous sub that gets created is just a placeholder. Someday, Perl will have a switch to cache on demand the string representation of a compiled piece of code, I hope.

The Useqq flag is not honored by Dumpxs() (it always outputs strings in single quotes).

Scalar objects have the weirdest-looking bless workaround.

Author

Gurusamy Sarathy, *gsar@umich.edu*

Version

Version 2.07 (7 December 1996)

See Also

perl(1)

Data::Flow—Perl extension for simple-minded recipe-controlled build of data

Synopsis

```
use Data::Flow;
$recipes = { path  => { default => './MANIFEST'},
              contents => { prerequisites => [J  <Char HardSpace ,
                            process =>
                            sub {
                              my $data = shift;
                              $data->{ shift() } = 'cat $data-
                                                      get('path')'
                                  x $data->get('x');
                            }
                          },
              };
$request = new Data::Flow $recipes;
$request->set( x => 1);
print $request->get('contents');
tie %request, Data::Flow, $recipes;
$request{x} = 1;
print $request{contents};
```

Description

The module Data::Flow provides its services via objects. The objects may be obtained by the usual paradigm:

```
$request = new Data::Flow $recipes;
```

The argument *$recipes* is a hash reference, which provides the rules for request processing. The objects support two methods, set() and get(). The first method is used to provide input data for processing, the second to obtain the output.

The unit of requested information is a *field*. The method set() takes a pair field => value; the method get() takes one argument: the field.

Every object is created without any fields filled in, but it knows how to *construct* fields based on other fields or some global into. This knowledge is provided in the argument *$recipe* of the new() function. This is a reference to a hash, keyed by fields. The values of this hash are hash references themselves, which describe how to acquire the field that is the corresponding key of the initial hash.

Keys

The internal hashes may have the following keys.

default

Describes the default value for the key, if none is provided by set(). The value becomes the value of the field of the object. No additional processing is performed. Example:

```
default => $Config{installdir}
```

prerequisites

Gives the fields that are needed for the construction of the given field. The corresponding value is an array reference. The array contains the *required* fields.

If defaults did not satisfy the request for a field, but $recipe->{field}{prerequisites} exists, the required fields are built before any further processing is done. Example:

```
prerequisites => [ qw(prefix arch) ]
```

process

Contains the rule to build the field. The value is a reference to a subroutine that takes two arguments: the object $request and the name of the required field. It is up to the subroutine to actually fill the corresponding field of $data, an error condition is raised if it does not. Example:

```
process => sub { my $data = shift;
                 $data->set( time => localtime(time) ) }
```

output

The corresponding value has the same meaning as for **process**, but the return value of the subroutine is used as the value of the field. Example:

```
output => sub { localtime(time) }
```

filter

Contains the rule to build the field based on other fields. The value is a reference to an array. The first element of the array is a reference to a subroutine, while the rest contains the names of the fields. When the subroutine is called, the arguments are the values of fields of the object $request that appear in the array (in the same order). The return value of the subroutine is used as the value of the field. Example:

```
filter => [ sub { shift + shift },
            'first_half', 'second_half' ]
```

Note that the mentioned field is automatically marked as **prerequisites**.

class_filter

This is similar to filter, but the first argument is the name of the method to call and the second one is the name of the package to use for the method invocation. The rest contains names of fields to provide as method arguments. Example:

```
class_filter => [ 'new', 'FileHandle', 'filename' ]
```

method_filter

This is similar to class_filter, but the second argument is the name of the field that is used to call the method upon. Example:

```
method_filter => [ 'show', 'widget_name', 'current_display' ]
```

Tied interface

The access to the same functionality is available via tied hash interface.

Author

Ilya Zakharevich, *ilya@math.ohio-state.edu*

See Also

perl(1), make(1).

Date::DateCalc—Gregorian calendar date calculations, in compliance with ISO/R 2015-1971 and DIN 1355 standards

Synopsis

```
use Date::DateCalc;
```

In this case, you must fully qualify every function with the name of this module. For example, `$flag = Date::DateCalc::leap($year)`.

Or:

```
use Date::DateCalc
qw( leap check_date compress uncompress check_compressed
compressed_to_short calc_days day_of_week dates_difference
calc_new_date date_time_difference calc_new_date_time
date_to_short date_to_string week_number first_in_week
weeks_in_year day_name_tab month_name_tab decode_day
decode_month decode_date days_in_month );
```

Or only portions thereof, whatever you need, or:

```
use DateCalc qw(:all);
```

which imports everything.

Description

Conventions

In the following discussion, `$year` stands for a "complete" year number (like 1995, for instance), whereas `$yy` may be either an abbreviated year number (like 95) or a complete year number.

Year numbers must be positive integers (greater than zero).

`$mm` stands for the number of a month (from 1 to 12), and `$dd` is the number of a day in a month (from 1 to 28, 29, 30, or 31, depending on the month and the year).

Hint: The functions that support abbreviated year numbers are the functions whose names contain the word "compress" and the function `decode_date()`.

Functions

`$flag = leap($year);`

This function returns a boolean value that is true (1) if the year `$year` is a leap year and false (0) otherwise.

No check is made to see if `$year` is in the valid range.

For years less than 1, the result is probably meaningless (it *is* almost meaningless, anyway, for years before 1582).

$flag = check_date($year, $mm, $dd);

This function returns a boolean value that is true (1) if the three numbers *$year*, *$mm*, and *$dd* represent a valid date, and false (0) otherwise.

When determining validity, leap years are taken into account; i.e., the 29th of February is rejected in non-leap years.

Year numbers must be greater than zero (negative values are interpreted as large positive numbers due to their internal 2's complement binary representation). A year number of zero is invalid.

$date = compress($yy, $mm, $dd);

This function encodes a date in 16 bits. The encoding scheme is as follows:

```
Bit-No.:        FEDCBA9 8765 43210
Contents:       yyyyyyy mmmm ddddd
```

If all bits are equal to zero, that is equivalent to <no date>.

Through this encoding scheme, it is possible to compare encoded dates for equality and *order* (less than/greater than) without any previous decoding.

Note, however, that contiguous dates do not necessarily have contiguous compressed representations.

That is, incrementing the compressed representation of a date may or may not yield a valid new date.

Note, also, that this function can only handle dates within one century.

This century can be biased at will by choosing a base century and year (also called an "epoch"). In this module, the base century is set to 1900 and the base year to 70 (standard on UNIX systems).

This allows the function to handle dates from 1970 up to 2069.

If the year *$yy* is equal to, say, 95, the function assumes you mean 1995. However, if you specify a year number that is smaller than 70, like 64, for instance, it assumes you mean 2064.

You are not confined to abbreviated year numbers (smaller than 100), however. The function also accepts complete year numbers, provided that they are in the supported range (that is, from 1970 to 2069).

If no valid date is specified, zero is returned.

($cc, $yy, $mm, $dd) = uncompress($date);

This function decodes dates that were encoded by compress(). It returns the century, year, month, and day of the date encoded in *$date* in the variables $cc, $yy, $mm, and $dd, respectively.

The expression $cc + $yy yields the complete year number (for example, 1900 + 95 = 1995).

If *$date* is zero or does not contain the compressed representation of a valid date, an empty list is returned.

$flag = check_compressed($date);

This function returns a boolean value that is true (1) if *$date* contains a valid encoded date, and false (0) otherwise.

When determining validity, leap years are taken into account, i.e., the 29th of February is rejected in non-leap years.

`$datestr = compressed_to_short($date);`

    This function converts the encoded date in *$date* to a string of the format "dd-mmm-yy", which is returned ("mmm" is the three-letter English abbreviation of the month's name).

    If the date in *$date* is invalid, the string <no date> is returned.

    Note that the string that is returned by this function is always exactly nine characters long.

`$days = calc_days($year, $mm, $dd);`

    This function returns the (theoretical) number of days between the first of January of the year one and the given date plus one.

    That is, the value returned for the first of January of the year one is 1, the value returned for the second of January of the year one is 2, and so on.

    This is because there is no year zero; the Christian calendar starts with the year one. Consequently, there is also no day zero; the calendar starts with the first day, i.e., day one.

    The function doesn't take into account the change in 1582 (or later, for some countries) from the Julian to the Gregorian calendar, which we use today. It simply extrapolates the Gregorian calendar backwards.

    This function is used internally to calculate the difference in days between two dates and to calculate the day of week.

    Use this function to compare dates for "less than" and "greater than," or to compare dates for equality more easily.

    Zero is returned if no valid date is specified. (This is another reason why `calc_days(1,1,1)` is equal to one and not to zero.)

`$weekday = day_of_week($year, $mm, $dd);`

    This function calculates the day of week for the given date (which must be a valid date).

    The return values have the following meaning:

0	=	Error
1	=	Monday
2	=	Tuesday
3	=	Wednesday
4	=	Thursday
5	=	Friday
6	=	Saturday
7	=	Sunday

    The value zero is returned if the date is not valid.

`$days = dates_difference($year1, $mm1, $dd1, $year2, $mm2, $dd2);`

    This function calculates the difference in days between the two given dates.

    The function calculates the difference `date 2 - date 1`; i.e., you normally specify the two dates in chronological order.

If date 1 is later than date 2, the result is negative, which allows you to use this function to compare dates.

If one of the two dates is invalid, the result degrades to the value of the function calc_days() for the other date, which may be negative. If both dates are invalid, the result is zero.

It is the user's responsibility to make sure that both dates are valid (use check_date() for this).

($year, $mm, $dd) = calc_new_date($year, $mm, $dd, $offset);
Starting from the given date, this function can calculate a new date that is $offset days away from the original date. $offset may be positive (for a date later than the original date) or negative (for a date earlier than the given date).

If the given date is invalid or the new date cannot be calculated (for instance, if the new date would be before the year one), an empty list is returned.

To calculate a new date with a year, month, and day offset, see the function year_month_day_offset() in the Date::DateCalcLib module.

($days, $hh, $mm, $ss) = date_time_difference($year1, $month1, $day1, $hh1, $mm1, $ss1, $year2, $month2, $day2, $hh2, $mm2, $ss2);
This function calculates the difference in days, hours, minutes, and seconds between the two given dates.

The function calculates the difference **date 2 - date 1**; i.e., you normally specify the two dates in chronological order.

If date 1 is later than date 2, each of the four values returned is negative, which allows you to use this function to compare dates and to feed its output into the next function, calc_new_date_time().

If one (or both) of the two date/time pairs is invalid, an empty list is returned.

A date/time pair is invalid either when the date is invalid or when the values for hour, minute, and second are outside the ranges 0–23, 0–59, and 0–59, respectively.

($year, $month, $day, $hh, $mm, $ss) = calc_new_date_time($year, $month, $day, $hh, $mm, $ss, $days_offset, $hh_offset, $mm_offset, $ss_offset);
Starting from the given date and time, a new date and time can be calculated with this function.

The new date is *$days_offset* days and *$hh_offset* hours, *$mm_offset* minutes and *$ss_offset* seconds away from the original date. The values of these four offsets may be positive or negative, independent of each other. This means that you can add, for instance, nine hours and subtract five minutes at the same time.

If the new date and time cannot be calculated (for instance, if the given date is invalid or the new date would be before the year one, or if the values for hour, minute and second are outside the ranges of 0–23, 0–59, and 0–59, respectively), an empty list is returned.

`$datestr = date_to_short($year, $mm, $dd);`

> This function converts the given date to a string of the format "www dd-mmm-yyyy", which is returned.
>
> "www" is a three-letter English abbreviation of the day of week, and "mmm" is a three-letter English abbreviation of the month.
>
> If the given date is invalid, the string **<no date>** is returned.

`$datestr = date_to_string($year, $mm, $dd);`

> This function converts the given date to a string of the format "wwwwwwwww, dd mmmmmmmmm yyyy", which is returned.
>
> "wwwwwwwww" is the day of week in English and "mmmmmmmmm" the name of the month, also in English.
>
> If the given date is invalid, the string **<no date>** is returned.

`($week, $year) = week_number($year, $mm, $dd);`

> This function calculates the number of the week in which the given date lies.
>
> This can occasionally be the last week of the previous year or the first week of the next year.
>
> If the given date is invalid, an empty list is returned.

`($year, $mm, $dd) = first_in_week($week, $year);`

> This function calculates the date of the first day (the Monday) of the given week in the given year.
>
> The return value **$year** is adjusted accordingly if the first day of the given week lies in the previous year.
>
> If the week number is invalid (less than one or greater than the number of weeks of the given year, as returned by the function **weeks_in_year**()), or if the year is invalid or the date cannot be calculated (for example, if the calculated date would be before the year one), an empty list is returned.
>
> With help of the expression:
>
> ```
> ($year,$mm,$dd) = first_in_week(week_number($year,$mm,$dd));
> ```
>
> it is possible to easily calculate the date of the Monday belonging to the week in which the given date lies.
>
> However, a fatal Perl error occurs if the given date is invalid.
>
> Alternatively, the expression:
>
> ```
> ($year,$mm,$dd) =
> calc_new_date($year,$mm,$dd,-day_of_week($year,$mm,$dd)+1);
> ```
>
> can be used to achieve the same effect.
>
> An empty list is returned if the given date is invalid.

`$weeks = weeks_in_year($year);`

> This function returns the number of weeks of the given year (52 or 53 weeks).
>
> No check is made to see if the year **$year** is in the valid range.
>
> For years less than 1, the result is probably meaningless.

`$day_name = day_name_tab($weekday);`

> This function accesses the internal table of the days of the week.

It returns the corresponding string for each numeric value of a day (as returned by the function `day_of_week()`).

The value of *$weekday* is taken modulo 8 internally to prevent out-of-range access to the internal array.

The following strings are returned:

0	=>	Error
1	=>	Monday
2	=>	Tuesday
3	=>	Wednesday
4	=>	Thursday
5	=>	Friday
6	=>	Saturday
7	=>	Sunday

`$month_name = month_name_tab($month);`

This function accesses the internal table of the month names.

It returns the corresponding string for each numeric value of a month.

The value of *$month* is taken modulo 13 internally to prevent out-of-range access to the internal array.

The strings that are returned are the following:

0	=>	Error
1	=>	January
2	=>	February
3	=>	March
4	=>	April
5	=>	May
6	=>	June
7	=>	July
8	=>	August
9	=>	September
10	=>	October
11	=>	November
12	=>	December

`$weekday = decode_day($buffer);`

This function provides the inverse of the function `day_name_tab()`.

Whereas `day_name_tab()` takes a number as its argument and returns a string, `decode_day()` takes a string (of any length), tries to find a match in the table of the names of days (Monday, Tuesday, and so on) and returns the corresponding number (1–7).

Only the first three characters are checked (in a case-insensitive manner) for a unique match. You may also provide only one or two characters if that is enough to uniquely identify the day.

Name of the day	Uniquely identified by	Value returned
Monday	M, Mo, Mon, ... Monday	1
Tuesday	Tu, Tue, ... Tuesday	2
Wednesday	W, We, Wed, ... Wednesday	3
Thursday	Th, Thu, ... Thursday	4
Friday	F, Fr, Fri, ... Friday	5
Saturday	Sa, Sat, ... Saturday	6
Sunday	Su, Sun, ... Sunday	7

If there is no match, zero is returned.

This function is roughly equivalent to this associative array:

```
%day_tab = ( 'Mon' => 1, 'Tue' => 2, 'Wed' => 3, 'Thu' => 4,
             'Fri' => 5, 'Sat' => 6, 'Sun' => 7);
$weekday = $day_tab{$buffer};
```

except for the capability to recognize abbreviations and to be case-independent.

$month = decode_month(*$buffer*);

This function provides the inverse of the function `month_name_tab()`.

While `month_name_tab` takes a number as its argument and returns a string, `decode_month` takes a string (of any length), tries to find a match in the table of the names of months (January, February, and so on), and returns the corresponding number (1–12).

Only the first three characters are checked (in a case-insensitive manner) for a unique match. You may also provide only one or two characters, if that uniquely identifies the month.

If there is no match, zero is returned.

Name of the month	Uniquely identified by	Value returned
January	Ja, Jan, ... January	1
February	F, Fe, Feb, ... February	2
March	Mar, ... March	3
April	Ap, Apr, ... April	4
May	May, ... May	5
June	Jun, ... June	6
July	Jul, ... July	7
August	Au, Aug, ... August	8
September	S, Se, Sep, ... September	9
October	O, Oc, Oct, ... October	10
November	N, No, Nov, ... November	11
December	D, De, Dec, ... December	12

This function is roughly equivalent to the associative array:

```
%month_tab = ( 'Jan' => 1, 'Feb' => 2, 'Mar' => 3, 'Apr' => 4,
               'May' => 5, 'Jun' => 6, 'Jul' => 7, 'Aug' => 8,
               'Sep' => 9, 'Oct' => 10, 'Nov' => 11, 'Dec' =>
               12);
$month = $month_tab{$buffer};
```

except for the capability to recognize abbreviations and to be case-independent.

($year, $mm, $dd) = decode_date($buffer);

Using this function, it is possible to parse dates in almost any format, provided the date is given as "day - month - year".

To decode dates in U.S. American format, i.e., dates given as "month - day - year", see the function **decode_date_us**() in the Date::DateCalcLib module.

The day and the year must be given as numbers, while the month may be specified either by a number or an abbreviation (up to three characters long) of the month's name in English (case is ignored).

If they uniquely identify the month, one or two letters are sufficient (e.g. "s" for September or "ja" for January).

The year may be abbreviated as well, for instance, 95 instead of 1995. (Year numbers below 100 are incremented by 1900.)

Any number of non-digits (i.e., all characters *not* in [0–9]) may precede the number of the day and follow the number of the year.

Any number of non-alphanumeric characters (i.e., all characters *not* in [A–Za–z0–9]) may separate the number of the day and the month, and the month and the number of the year.

If, after the preceding and trailing non-digit characters are removed, the string consists only of digits, it is automatically mapped to the day, month, and year, depending on its length, as intuitively as possible, as follows:

Length	Mapping
3	dmy
4	dmyy
5	dmmyy
6	ddmmyy
7	dmmyyyy
8	ddmmyyyy

Example

All of the following strings are recognized as "January 3 1964":

3.1.64

3 1 64

03.01.64

03/01/64

3. Jan 1964

3. Jan '64

03-Jan-64

3.Jan1964

3Jan64

3ja64

3164

If the function is unable to extract a valid date from its input, it returns an empty list.

$days = days_in_month($year, $mm);

This function accesses the internal table of the months' lengths and returns the length in days of the given month *$mm* in the given year *$year*.

It is necessary to specify the year *$year*, since the length of the month February is 29, instead of 28, in leap years.

This function is useful, for example, for calculating the last day of a month or the last working day (payday!) of a month.

This example finds the last working day of the month (not taking legal holidays into account):

```
$dd = days_in_month($year,$mm);
$dw = day_of_week($year,$mm,$dd) - 1;
if ($dw > 4)
{
    ($year,$mm,$dd) = calc_new_date($year,$mm,$dd,4-$dw);
}
```

This example calculates the last working day of the month (taking legal holidays into account). It assumes that the array **$holiday[$year][$mm][$dd] = 1;** contains all the legal holidays.

```
$dd = days_in_month($year,$mm);
while (1)
{
    while ($holiday[$year][$mm][$dd])
    {
        ($year,$mm,$dd) = calc_new_date($year,$mm,$dd,-1);
    }
    $dw = day_of_week($year,$mm,$dd) - 1;
    if ($dw > 4)
    {
        ($year,$mm,$dd) = calc_new_date($year,$mm,$dd,4-$dw);
    }
    else { last; }
}
```

The value of *$mm* is taken modulo 13 internally to prevent out-of-range access to the internal array.

The values the internal array contains are the following:

month	Normal year	Leap year
0	0	0
1	31	31

month	Normal year	Leap year
2	28	29
3	31	31
4	30	30
5	31	31
6	30	30
7	31	31
8	31	31
9	30	30
10	31	31
1	30	30
12	31	31

`$version = Date::DateCalc::Version();`

This function returns a string with the (numeric) version number of the **DateCalc** extension package.

Since this function is not exported, you always have to qualify it explicitly (i.e., `Date::DateCalc::Version()`), to avoid possible conflicts with version functions from other packages.

Example

```perl
#!perl -w
use strict;
no strict "vars";
use Date::DateCalc qw(decode_date date_to_short dates_difference);
print "\n";
$ok = 0;
while (! $ok)
{
    print "Please enter the date of your birthday (day-month-
year): ";
    $date = <STDIN>;
    print "\n";
    if (($yy1,$mm1,$dd1) = decode_date($date))
    {
        $datestr = date_to_short($yy1,$mm1,$dd1);
        print "Your date is: $datestr\n";
        print "\n";
        print "Is that correct? (Yes/No) ";
        $response = <STDIN>;
        print "\n";
        $ok = ($response =~ /^Y/i);
    }
}
print "Your birthday is: $datestr\n";
print "\n";
$ok = 0;
while (! $ok)
```

```
    {
        print "Please enter today's date (day-month-year): ";
        $date = <STDIN>;
        print "\n";
        if (($yy2,$mm2,$dd2) = decode_date($date))
        {
            $datestr = date_to_short($yy2,$mm2,$dd2);
            print "Your date is: $datestr\n";
            print "\n";
            print "Is that correct? (Yes/No) ";
            $response = <STDIN>;
            print "\n";
            $ok = ($response =~ /^Y/i);
        }
    }
    print "Today's date is: $datestr\n";
    print "\n";
    $days = dates_difference($yy1,$mm1,$dd1,$yy2,$mm2,$dd2);
    print "You are $days days old.\n";
    print "\n";
    __END__
```

Version

This manpage documents Date::DateCalc version 3.0.

Author

Steffen Beyer, *sb@sdm.de*

Copyright

Copyright © 1995, 1996, 1997 by Steffen Beyer. All rights reserved.

This package is free software; you can redistribute it and/or modify it under the same terms as Perl itself.

See Also

Date::DateCalcLib(3), perl(1), perlsub(1), perlmod(1), perlxs(1), perlxstut(1), perlguts(1)

Date::DateCalcLib—library of useful date calculation functions

Synopsis
```
use Date::DateCalcLib qw( nth_wday_of_month_year
decode_date_us decode_date_eu year_month_day_offset
parse_date easter_sunday );

use Date::DateCalcLib qw(:all);

($year,$mm,$dd) = nth_wday_of_month_year($nth,$wday,$month,$year);

($year,$mm,$dd) = decode_date_us($date);

($year,$mm,$dd) = decode_date_eu($date);
```

```
($year,$mm,$dd) = year_month_day_offset($year,$mm,$dd,$y_offs,
                                         $m_offs,$d_offs);

($year,$mm,$dd) = parse_date('/bin/date');

($year,$mm,$dd) = easter_sunday($year);
```

Description

This module expands the functionality of the Date::DateCalc module (see the Date::Date-Calc(3) manpage for more details), which is intended to be a rather basic set of tools, with functions for various special tasks like:

- Calculating the nth weekday for a given month and year

- Parsing dates in U.S. American and European format

- Calculating a new date with a year, month, and/or day offset

- Parsing the current date or the submission date of an email message

- Calculating Easter Sunday and all the related Christian feast days

Functions

Here is a detailed description of each function:

use Date::DateCalcLib qw(nth_wday_of_month_year decode_date_us decode_date_eu year_month_day_offset parse_date easter_sunday);
Use this statement to make the functions of this module available in your module or script.

You can also use any subset of the functions listed above by including only the names of the functions you actually need between the parentheses of the qw() operator above.

use Date::DateCalcLib qw(:all);
Alternate and simpler way of importing *all* the functions exported by this module into your module or script.

($year, $mm,$ dd) = nth_wday_of_month_year($nth, $wday, $month, $year);
This function calculates the *n*th weekday for a given month and year, for example the third Thursday of a given month and year.

$nth must be in the range 1 to 5 (for "the first" to "the fifth"), *$wday* must be in the range 1 to 7 (1 = Monday, 7 = Sunday), *$month* must (of course) be in the range 1 to 12, and *$year* must be greater than zero.

The function returns an empty list if any of its parameters is illegal or if the requested date cannot be calculated (for instance, if there is no fifth *$wday* in the given month and year).

Example

Suppose you have a meeting (of some user group, for instance) at regular intervals (let's say the first Friday of each month) and that you want to send mail to all members saying: "Remember: Tomorrow is our user group's meeting!" on the day before.

Given the current date, you go about this as follows:

- Convert the current date into days using the function `calc_days()` of the Date::DateCalc module. We'll refer to this number as "the number of days of the current date" below.

- Calculate the first Friday of the current month.

- Convert the resulting date into days using the function `calc_days()` of the Date::DateCalc module.

- See if the number of days of the current date + 1 is the same as the number of days of the first Friday of the current month.

- If so, send your mail.

- If not, calculate the first Friday of the *next* month (beware: if the month is equal to 12, you need to "wrap" it back to 1 and increment the year number).

  This is necessary because the first Friday of any given month could fall on the first day of that month, which means that the day before that (when you want to send your mail) is in the *previous* month.

- Convert the resulting date into days using the function `calc_days()` of the Date::DateCalc module.

- See if the number of days of the current date + 1 is the same as the number of days of the first Friday of the next month.

- If so, send your mail.

- If not, you're done for today.

(On a UNIX system, you would normally use a `cron` job running once every day to automatically carry out these calculations and to send the reminder mail.)

`($year,$mm,$dd) = decode_date_us($date);`

Using this function, you can parse dates in almost any format, provided the date is given as "month-day-year".

(To decode dates in European format, i.e., dates given as "day-month-year", see the function `decode_date_eu()` in this module or the function `decode_date()` in the Date::DateCalc module.)

The day and the year must be given as numbers, while the month may be specified either by a number or its name in English (however, only up to the first three characters are compared; any extra characters are ignored). The latter comparison is carried out in a case-insensitive manner.

If they uniquely identify the month, one or two letters are sufficient (e.g., "s" for September or "ja" for January).

The year may be abbreviated as well (for instance, 97 instead of 1997). Year numbers below 100 are incremented by 1900.

Note that leading zeros are ignored for all numeric values (i.e., contiguous strings of digits).

If the month given in the input string isn't numeric, any number of non-alphanumeric characters (i.e., all characters *not* in [A–Za–z0–9]) may precede and follow the month, and any number of non-digits (i.e., all characters *not* in [0–9]) may precede and follow the year.

If separating non-digits between the day and year are missing, the string of digits following the month is automatically mapped to the day and year depending on length of the string, as intuitively as possible, as follows:

Length	Mapping
2	dy
3	dyy
4	ddyy
5	dyyyy
6	ddyyyy

If the month given in the input string is numeric, any number of non-digits may precede the month, separate the month from the day and the day from the year, and follow the year.

If separating non-digits are missing, the string of digits contained in the input string is automatically mapped to the month, day, and year, depending on its length and as intuitively as possible, as follows:

Length	Mapping
3	mdy
4	mdyy
5	mddyy
6	mmddyy
7	mddyyyy
8	mmddyyyy

Example

All the following strings are recognized as "January 3rd 1964":

1 3 64

1.3.64

01.03.64

01/03/64

Jan 3 1964

January 3rd, 1964

Jan 3. '64

Jan-3-64

Jan3.1964

ja364

1364

If no valid date can be derived from the input string, the function returns an empty list.

```
($year,$mm,$dd) = decode_date_eu($date);
```

Using this function, you can parse dates in almost any format, provided the date is given as "day-month-year".

To decode dates in U.S. American format (i.e., dates given as "month-day-year") see the function **decode_date_us()** in this module.

The day and the year must be given as numbers, the month may be specified either by a number or its name in English (however, only up to the first three characters are compared; any extra characters are ignored). The latter comparison is carried out in a case-insensitive manner.

If they uniquely identify the month, one or two letters are sufficient (e.g., "s" for September or "ja" for January).

The year may be abbreviated as well (for instance 97 instead of 1997). Year numbers below 100 are incremented by 1900.

Note that this function is a little more flexible than the function **decode_date()** in the Date::DateCalc module, since it allows any number of leading zeros for numeric values and any number of letters for the name of the month.

If the month given in the input string isn't numeric, any number of non-alphanumeric characters (i.e., all characters *not* in [A–Za–z0–9]) may precede and follow the month (separating it from the day and the year), and any number of non-digits (i.e., all characters *not* in [0–9]) may precede the day and follow the year.

If the month given in the input string is numeric, any number of non-digits may precede the day, separate the day from the month and the month from the year, and follow the year.

In the latter case, if separating non-digits are missing, the string of digits contained in the input string is automatically mapped to the day, month, and year, depending on its length, as intuitively as possible, as follows:

Length	Mapping
3	dmy
4	dmyy
5	dmmyy
6	ddmmyy
7	dmmyyyy
8	ddmmyyyy

Example

All the following strings are recognized as "January 3rd 1964":

3.1.64

3 1 64

03.01.64

03/01/64

3. Jan 1964

3 January 1964

3. Jan '64

03-Jan-64

3.Jan1964

3Jan64

3ja64

3164

If no valid date can be derived from the input string, the function returns an empty list.

($year,$mm,$dd) = year_month_day_offset($year, $mm, $dd, $y_offs, $m_offs, $d_offs);

Many people have asked for a function to calculate a new date, starting with a given date and a year, month, and/or day offset. So here it is.

Note that all parameters must be integers.

The function ensures this by applying the int() function to every parameter.

An empty list is returned if the given date or any (intermediate or final) result is invalid.

Note that the day offset is added first using the calc_new_date() function of the Date::DateCalc module (see the Date::DateCalc(3) manpage).

Warning: an empty list is returned if this intermediate result is not a valid date.

After this, the month offset is added and finally the year offset (with a possible carry-over from the month) is added.

Note that all three offsets may have any (integer) value, provided that all (intermediate or final) results are valid dates, and they may have any sign (independent of each other).

If the final result happens to be the 29th of February in a non-leap year, the first of March is substituted.

Warning: Because the three offsets are always applied in the same order, and also because of the substitution mentioned above, the transformation calculated by this function is, in general, *not reversible*.

This is unlike the calc_new_date() function of the Date::DateCalc module.

Example:

```
($year,$mm,$dd) =
year_month_day_offset(
year_month_day_offset($year,$mm,$dd, $y_offs,$m_offs,$d_offs),
-$y_offs,-$m_offs,-$d_offs);
```

does not, in general, return the original date.

In the formula above, in order to reverse the effect of the first call to **year_month_day_offset()**, the offsets would not only need to have the opposite sign, but they also would need to be applied in reverse order in the second call to **year_month_day_offset()**.

($year,$mm,$dd) = parse_date($date);

This function is a (special) relative of the **decode_date_us()** and **decode_date_eu()** functions.

In contrast to the `decode_date_us()` and `decode_date_eu()` functions, however, the month is required to be a three-letter abbreviation of the month name (in English).

Moreover, the month name is required to be followed by the day number, separated from it by whitespace.

Another restriction is that year numbers must lie in the range 1900 to 2099. As compensation, the year number may come before or after the month/day pair.

This function is especially designed to parse dates returned by the UNIX **date** command.

Examples:

- Parse today's date:

  ```
  ($year,$mm,$dd) = parse_date('/bin/date');
  ```

- Parse the date of submission of an email:

  ```
  while (<MAIL>)
  {
      if (/^From \S/)
      {
          ($year,$mm,$dd) = parse_date($_);
          ...
      }
      ...
  }
  ```

The function returns an empty list if it can't extract a valid date from the input string.

`($year,$mm,$dd) = easter_sunday($year);`

Calculates the date of Easter Sunday for years in the range 1583 to 2299 using Gauss' Rule.

Returns an empty list for all arguments outside this range.

Other Christian feast days depend on Easter Sunday and can be calculated using the function `calc_new_date()` of the Date::DateCalc module (see the Date::Date-Calc(3) manpage for more info) as follows:

- Easter Sunday - 48

  ```
  ($year,$mm,$dd) = calc_new_date(easter_sunday($year),-48);
  Carnival Monday / Rosenmontag / Veille du Mardi Gras
  ```

- Easter Sunday - 47

  ```
  ($year,$mm,$dd) = calc_new_date(easter_sunday($year),-47);
  Mardi Gras / Faschingsdienstag, Karnevalsdienstag / Mardi Gras
  ```

- Easter Sunday - 46

  ```
  ($year,$mm,$dd) = calc_new_date(easter_sunday($year),-46);
  Ash Wednesday / Aschermittwoch / Mercredi des Cendres
  ```

- Easter Sunday - 7

  ```
  ($year,$mm,$dd) = calc_new_date(easter_sunday($year),-7);
  Palm Sunday / Palmsonntag / Dimanche des Rameaux
  ```

- Easter Sunday - 2

  ```
  ($year,$mm,$dd) = calc_new_date(easter_sunday($year),-2);
  Easter Friday / Karfreitag / Vendredi Saint
  ```

- Easter Sunday - 1

  ```
  ($year,$mm,$dd) = calc_new_date(easter_sunday($year),-1);
  Easter Saturday / Ostersamstag / Samedi de Paques
  ```

- Easter Sunday + 1

  ```
  ($year,$mm,$dd) = calc_new_date(easter_sunday($year),1);
  Easter Monday / Ostermontag / Lundi de Paques
  ```

- Easter Sunday + 39

  ```
  ($year,$mm,$dd) = calc_new_date(easter_sunday($year),39);
  Ascension of Christ / Christi Himmelfahrt / Ascension
  ```

- Easter Sunday + 49

  ```
  ($year,$mm,$dd) = calc_new_date(easter_sunday($year),49);
  Whitsunday / Pfingstsonntag / Dimanche de Pentecote
  ```

- Easter Sunday + 50

  ```
  ($year,$mm,$dd) = calc_new_date(easter_sunday($year),50);
  Whitmonday / Pfingstmontag / Lundi de Pentecote
  ```

- Easter Sunday + 60

  ```
  ($year,$mm,$dd) = calc_new_date(easter_sunday($year),60);
  Feast of Corpus Christi / Fronleichnam / Fete-Dieu
  ```

For more information about Easter Sunday and how to calculate it, see also, in the Usenet newsgroup *news.answers*, the following:

```
Calendar FAQ, v. 1.6 (modified 26 Dec 1996) Part 1/3
Calendar FAQ, v. 1.6 (modified 26 Dec 1996) Part 2/3
Calendar FAQ, v. 1.6 (modified 26 Dec 1996) Part 3/3
```

or:

http://www.math.uio.no/faq/calendars/faq.html

or:

http://www.pip.dknet.dk/~pip10160/calendar.html

All authored by Claus Tondering (*c-t@pip.dknet.dk*)

Version

This manpage documents Date::DateCalcLib version 1.0.

Author

Steffen Beyer, *sb@sdm.de*

Copyright

Copyright © 1997 by Steffen Beyer. All rights reserved.

This package is free software; you can redistribute it and/or modify it under the same terms as Perl itself.

See Also

Date::DateCalc(3)

Date::Format—date-formatting subroutines

Synopsis

```
use Date::Format;

@lt = timelocal(time);

print time2str($template, time);
print strftime($template, @lt);

print time2str($template, time, $zone);
print strftime($template, @lt, $zone);

print ctime(time);
print ascctime(@lt);

print ctime(time, $zone);
print asctime(@lt, $zone);
```

Description

This module provides routines to format dates into ASCII strings. The routines correspond to the C library routines strftime and ctime.

Routines

time2str(*TEMPLATE, TIME* [, *ZONE*])

time2str converts *TIME* into an ASCII string using the conversion specification given in *TEMPLATE*. *ZONE*, if given, specifies the zone that the output is required to be in; *ZONE* defaults to your current zone.

strftime(*TEMPLATE, TIME* [, *ZONE*])

strftime is similar to time2str with the exception that the time is passed as an array, such as the array returned by localtime.

ctime(*TIME* [, *ZONE*])

ctime calls time2str with the given arguments using the conversion specification %a %b %e %T %Y\n.

asctime(*TIME* [, *ZONE*])

asctime calls time2str with the given arguments using the conversion specification %a %b %e %T %Y\n.

Multi-language Support

Date::Format is capable of formatting into several languages: English, French, German, and Italian. Changing the language is done via a static method call. For example:

```
Date::Format->language('German');
```

changes the language into which all subsequent dates are formatted.

This is only a first pass. I am considering changing this to be:

```
$lang = Date::Language->new('German');
$lang->time2str("%a %b %e %T %Y\n", time);
```

I am open to suggestions on this.

Conversion Specification

Each conversion specification is replaced by the appropriate characters as described in the following list. The appropriate characters are determined by the LC_TIME category of the program's locale.

%%	PERCENT
%a	day of the week abbr
%A	day of the week
%b	month abbr
%B	month
%c	ctime format: Sat Nov 19 21:05:57 1994
%d	numeric day of the month
%e	DD
%D	MM/DD/YY
%h	month abbr
%H	hour, 24-hour clock, leading 0's
%I	hour, 12-hour clock, leading 0's
%j	day of the year
%k	hour
%l	hour, 12-hour clock
%m	month number, starting with 1
%M	minute, leading 0's
%n	NEWLINE
%o	ornate day of month— 1st, 2nd, 25th, etc.
%p	AM or PM
%r	time format: 09:05:57 PM
%R	time format: 21:05
%s	seconds since the epoch, UCT
%S	seconds, leading 0's
%t	TAB
%T	time format: 21:05:57
%U	week number, Sunday as first day of week
%w	day of the week, numerically, Sunday = 0

%W	week number, Monday as first day of week
%x	date format: 11/19/94
%X	time format: 21:05:57
%y	year (two digits)
%Y	year (four digits)
%Z	time zone in ASCII, e.g.: PST
%z	time zone in format −/ +0000

Author

Graham Barr, *gbarr@pobox.com*

Copyright

Date::Manip—date manipulation routines

Synopsis

```
use Date::Manip;

$date=&ParseDate(\@args)
$date=&ParseDate($string)
$date=&ParseDate(\$string)

@date=&UnixDate($date,@format)
$date=&UnixDate($date,@format)

$delta=&ParseDateDelta(\@args)
$delta=&ParseDateDelta($string)
$delta=&ParseDateDelta(\$string)

$d=&DateCalc($d1,$d2,$errref,$del)

$date=&Date_SetTime($date,$hr,$min,$sec)
$date=&Date_SetTime($date,$time)

$date=&Date_GetPrev($date,$dow,$today,$hr,$min,$sec)
$date=&Date_GetPrev($date,$dow,$today,$time)

$date=&Date_GetNext($date,$dow,$today,$hr,$min,$sec)
$date=&Date_GetNext($date,$dow,$today,$time)

&Date_Init()
&Date_Init("VAR=VAL",...)
```

```
$version=&DateManipVersion

$flag=&Date_IsWorkDay($date [,$flag]);

$date=&Date_NextWorkDay($date,$off [,$time]);
$date=&Date_PrevWorkDay($date,$off [,$time]);
```

The following routines are used by the above routines (though they can also be called directly). Make sure that $y is entered as the full four-digit year (it dies if a two-digit year is entered). Most (if not all) of the information below can be gotten from UnixDate, which is really the way I intended it to be gotten.

```
$day=&Date_DayOfWeek($m,$d,$y)
$secs=&Date_SecsSince1970($m,$d,$y,$h,$mn,$s)
$secs=&Date_SecsSince1970GMT($m,$d,$y,$h,$mn,$s)
$days=&Date_DaysSince999($m,$d,$y)
$day=&Date_DayOfYear($m,$d,$y)
$days=&Date_DaysInYear($y)
$wkno=&Date_WeekOfYear($m,$d,$y,$first)
$flag=&Date_LeapYear($y)
$day=&Date_DaySuffix($d)
$tz=&Date_TimeZone()
```

Description

This is a set of routines designed to make any common date/time manipulation easy to do. Operations such as comparing two times, calculating a time that is a given amount of time from another, or parsing international times are all easily done.

Date::Manip deals only with the Gregorian calendar (the one currently in use). The Julian calendar defined leap years as every fourth year. The Gregorian calendar improved on this by making every 100th year *not* a leap year, unless it was also the 400th year. The Gregorian calendar has been extrapolated back to the year 1000 AD and forward to the year 9999 AD. Note that in historical context, the Julian calendar was in use until 1582, when the Gregorian calendar was adopted by the Catholic church. Protestant countries did not accept it until later: Germany and the Netherlands in 1698, the British Empire in 1752, Russia in 1918. Note that the Gregorian calendar is itself imperfect. Each year is on average 26 seconds too long, which means that every 3,323 years, a day should be removed from the calendar. No attempt is made to correct for that.

Date::Manip is therefore not equipped to truly deal with historical dates, but should be able to perform (virtually) any operation dealing with a modern time and date.

Among other things, Date::Manip allows you to:

- Enter a date and be able to choose any convenient format

- Compare two dates, entered in different formats, to determine which is earlier

- Extract any information you want from *any* date using a format string similar to the UNIX date command

- Determine the amount of time between two dates

- Add a time offset to a date to get a second date (i.e. determine the date 132 days ago or two years and three months after Jan 2, 1992)

- Work with dates using international formats (foreign month names, 12-10-95 referring to October rather than December, etc.)

Each of these tasks is trivial (one or two lines at most) with this package. Although the word date is used extensively here, it is actually somewhat misleading. Date::Manip works with the full date *and* time (year, month, day, hour, minute, second).

In the documentation below, U.S. formats are used, but in most (if not all) cases, a non-English equivalent works equally well.

Examples

- Parse a date that is in any convenient format:

```
$date=&ParseDate("today");
$date=&ParseDate("1st thursday in June 1992");
$date=&ParseDate("05-10-93");
$date=&ParseDate("12:30 Dec 12th 1880");
$date=&ParseDate("8:00pm december tenth");
if (! $date) {
  # Error in the date
}
```

- Compare two dates:

```
$date1=&ParseDate($string1);
$date2=&ParseDate($string2);
if ($date1 lt $date2) {
  # date1 is earlier
} else {
  # date2 is earlier (or the two dates are identical)
}
```

- Extract information from a date:

```
print &UnixDate("today","The time is now %T on %b %e, %Y.");
=>  "The time is now 13:24:08 on Feb  3, 1996."
```

- Determine the amount of time between two dates:

```
$date1=&ParseDate($string1);
$date2=&ParseDate($string2);
$delta=&DateCalc($date1,$date2,\$err);
=> 0:0:DD:HH:MM:SS   the days, hours, minutes, and seconds
between the two
$delta=&DateCalc($date1,$date2,\$err,1);
=> YY:MM:DD:HH:MM:SS  the years, months, etc. between the two
```

Read the documentation below for an explanation of the difference.

- Determine a date a given offset from another:

```
$date=&DateCalc("today","+ 3hours 12minutes 6 seconds",\$err);
$date=&DateCalc("12 hours ago","12:30 6Jan90",\$err);
```

This even works with business days:

```
$date=&DateCalc("today","+ 3 business days",\$err);
```

- Work with dates in another language:

```
&Date_Init("Language=French","DateFormat=non-US");
$date=&ParseDate("1er decembre 1990");
```

Note: Some date forms do not work as well in languages other than English, but this is not because Date::Manip is incapable of handling them (almost nothing in this module is language-dependent). It is simply that I do not have the correct translation available for some words. If there is a date form that works in English, but does not work in a language you need, let me know, and if you can provide me the translation, I will fix Date::Manip.

Routines

ParseDate

This takes an array or a string containing a date and parses it.

```
$date=&ParseDate(\@args)
$date=&ParseDate($string)
$date=&ParseDate(\$string)
```

When the date is included as an array (for example, the arguments to a program), the array should contain a valid date in the first one or more elements (elements after a valid date are ignored). Elements containing a valid date are shifted from the array. The largest possible number of elements that can be correctly interpreted as a valid date is always used. If a string is entered rather than an array, that string is tested for a valid date. The string is unmodified, even if passed in by reference.

A date actually has two parts: date and time. A time must include hours and minutes and can optionally include seconds, fractional seconds, an am/pm-type string, and a time zone. For example:

```
HH:MN    [Zone]
HH:MN:SS   [Zone]
HH:MN am   [Zone]
HH:MN:SS am   [Zone]
HH:MN:SS:SSSS    [Zone]
HH:MN:SS.SSSS am [Zone]
```

Hours can be written using one or two digits when the time follows the date and is separated from the date with spaces or some other separator. Any time there is no space separating the time from a date and the part of the date immediately preceding the hour is a digit, two digits must be used for the hours.

Fractional seconds are also supported in parsing, but the fractional part is discarded.

Time zones always appear after the time and must be separated from all other parts of the time/date by spaces. For now, only rudimentary time-zone handling is done. When the date is parsed, it is converted to a specific time zone (which defaults to the time zone you are in, but this can be overridden using the `Date_Init` routine described later in this section). After that, the time zone is never used. Once converted, information about the time zone is no longer stored or used.

See the section "Time Zones" below for a list of all defined time-zone names.

Spaces in the date are almost always optional when there is absolutely no ambiguity if they are not present. Years can be entered as two or four digits, days and months as one or two digits. Both days and months must include two digits whenver they are immediately adjacent to another part of the date or time. Valid formats for a full date and time (and examples of how Dec 10, 1965 at 9:00 pm might appear) are:

```
DateTime
  Date=YYMMDD            1965121021:00:00
                         65121021:00
```

```
Date Time
Date%Time
   Date=mm%dd, mm%dd%YY      12/10/65 21:00
                             12 10 1965 9:00pm
      Date=mmm%dd, mmm%dd%YY  December-10-65-9:00:00pm
      Date=dd%mmm, dd%mmm%YY  10/December/65 9:00:00pm


   Date Time
      Date=mmmdd, mmmdd YY,   Dec10 65 9:00:00 pm
         mmmDDYY, mmm DDYY    December 10 1965 9:00pm
      Date=ddmmm, ddmmm YY, ddmmmYY, dd mmmYY
                             10Dec65 9:00:00 pm
                             10 December 1965 9:00pm


   TimeDate
   Time Date
   Time%Date
      Date=mm%dd, mm%dd%YY      9:00pm 12.10.65
                               21:00 12/10/1965
      Date=mmm%dd, mmm%dd%YY    9:00pm December/10/65
      Date=dd%mmm, dd%mmm%YY    9:00pm 10-December-65
                               21:00/10/Dec/65


   TimeDate
   Time Date
      Date=mmmdd, mmmdd YY, mmmDDYY
                          21:00:00DeCeMbEr10
      Date=ddmmm, ddmmm YY, ddmmmYY, dd mmmYY
                          21:00 10Dec95
```

Miscellaneous other allowed formats are:

```
which dofw in mmm [at time]
which dofw in mmm YY [at time]    "first sunday in june 1996
                                  at 14:00"


dofw week num [in YY] [at time]     "sunday week 22 in 1995"
which dofw [in YY] [at time]        "22nd sunday in 1996 at noon"
dofw which week [in YY] [at time]  "sunday 22nd week in 1996"
next/last dofw [at time]           "next friday at noon"
in num weeks [at time]             "in 3 weeks at 12:00"
num weeks ago [at time]            "3 weeks ago"
dofw in num week [at time]         "Friday in 2 weeks"
in num weeks on dofw [at time]     "in 2 weeks on friday"
dofw num week ago [at time]        "Friday 2 weeks ago"
num week ago dofw [at time]        "2 weeks ago friday"
```

In addition, the following strings are recognized:

```
today
now       (synonym for today)
yesterday (exactly 24 hours before now)
tomorrow  (exactly 24 hours from now)
noon      (12:00:00)
midnight  (00:00:00)
```

```
%        One of the valid date separators: - . / or whitespace
         (the same character must be used for all occurrences of
         a single date).
         For example, mm%dd%YY works for 1-1-95, 1 1 95, or
         1/1/95.
YY       Year, in two- or four-digit format
MM       Two-digit month (01 to 12)
mm       One- or two-digit month (1 to 12 or 01 to 12)
mmm      Month name or three-character abbreviation
DD       Two-digit day (01 to 31)
dd       One- or two-digit day (1 to 31 or 01 to 31)
HH       One- or two-digit hour in 12- or 24-hour mode (0 to 23
         or 00 to 23)
MN       Two-digit minutes (00 to 59)
SS       Two-digit seconds (00 to 59)
which    One of the strings (first-fifth, 1st-5th, or last)
dofw     Either the three-character abbreviation or full name of
         a day of the week
```

Some things to note:

- All strings are case-insensitive. "December" and "DEceMBer" both work.

- When no part of the date is given, defaults are used: the year defaults to the current year; hours, minutes, and seconds default to 00.

- In the above, the mm%dd formats can be switched to dd%mm by calling **Date_Init** and telling it to use a non-US date format.

- All **Date Time** and **DateTime** formats allow the word **at** in them (i.e., Jan 12 at 12:00) and **at** can replace the space. So the following are both acceptable: **Jan 12at12:00** and **Jan 12 at 12:00**.

- The time is usually entered in 24-hour mode. It can be followed by **am** or **pm** to force it to be read in 12-hour mode.

- The year may be entered as two or four digits. If entered as two digits, it is taken to be the year in the range CurrYear-89 to CurrYear+10. So, if the current year is 1996, the range is [1907 to 2006]. Thus, entering the year 00 refers to 2000, 05 to 2005, but 07 refers to 1907. Use four-digit years to avoid confusion!

- Any number of spaces or tabs can be used anywhere whitespace is appropriate.

- Dates are always checked to make sure they are valid.

- In all of the formats, the day of week ("Friday") can be entered anywhere in the date, and it is checked for accuracy. In other words:

```
Tue Jul 16 1996 13:17:00
```

works, but:

```
Jul 16 1996 Wednesday 13:17:00
```

does not work (because Jul 16, 1996 is Tuesday, not Wednesday). Note that depending on where the weekday comes, it may give unexpected results when used in array context. For example, the date ("Jun","25","Sun","1990") returns June 25 of the current year since Jun 25, 1990 is not Sunday.

- The times "12:00 am", "12:00 pm", and "midnight" are not well-defined. I use the following convention in Date::Manip:

```
midnight = 12:00am = 00:00:00
noon     = 12:00pm = 12:00:00
```

and the day goes from 00:00:00 to 23:59:59. In other words, midnight is the beginning of a day rather than the end of one. At midnight on July 5, July 5 has just begun. The time 24:00:00 is *not* allowed.

- The format of the date returned is YYYYMMDDHH:MM:SS. The advantage of this time format is that two times can be compared using simple string comparisons to find out which is later. Also, it is readily understood by a human. Alternate forms can be used if that is more convenient. See `Date_Init` below and the config variable Internal.

UnixDate

This takes a date and a list of strings containing formats roughly identical to the format strings used by the UNIX date(1) command. Each format is parsed, and an array of strings corresponding to each format is returned.

```
@date=&UnixDate($date,@format)
$date=&UnixDate($date,@format)
```

$date must be of the form produced by &ParseDate.

The format options are:

```
Year
    %y     year                      - 00 to 99
    %Y     year                      - 0001 to 9999

Month, week
    %m     month of year             - 01 to 12
    %f     month of year             - " 1" to "12"
    %b,%h  month abbreviation        - Jan to Dec
    %B     month name                - January to December
    %U     week of year, Sunday
           as first day of week      - 00 to 53
    %W     week of year, Monday
           as first day of week      - 00 to 53

Day
    %j     day of the year           - 001 to 366
    %d     day of month              - 01 to 31
    %e     day of month              - " 1" to "31"
    %v     weekday abbreviation      - " S"," M"," T",
                                       " W","Th"," F","Sa"
    %a     weekday abbreviation      - Sun to Sat
    %A     weekday name              - Sunday to Saturday
    %w     day of week               - 0 (Sunday) to 6
    %E     day of month with suffix  - 1st, 2nd, 3rd...

Hour
    %H     hour                      - 00 to 23
    %k     hour                      - " 0" to "23"
    %i     hour                      - " 1" to "12"
```

```
         %I    hour                      - 01 to 12
         %p    AM or PM

    Minute, second, time zone
         %M    minute                    - 00 to 59
         %S    second                    - 00 to 59
         %s    seconds from Jan 1, 1970 GMT
                                         - negative if before
                                           1/1/1970
         %o    seconds from Jan 1, 1970 in the current time zone
         %z,%Z timezone (3 characters)   - "EDT"

    Date, Time
         %c    %a %b %e %H:%M:%S %Y      - Fri Apr 28 17:23:15 1995
         %C,%u %a %b %e %H:%M:%S %z %Y   - Fri Apr 28 17:25:57
                                           EDT 1995
         %g    %a, %d %b %Y %H:%M:%S %z  - Fri, 28 Apr 1995
                                           17:23:15 EDT
         %D,%x %m/%d/%y                  - 04/28/95
         %l    date in ls(1) format
                  %b %e $H:$M            - Apr 28 17:23  (if within
                                           6 months)

                  %b %e  %Y             - Apr 28  1993  (otherwise)
         %r    %I:%M:%S %p               - 05:39:55 PM
         %R    %H:%M                     - 17:40
         %T,%X %H:%M:%S                  - 17:40:58
         %V    %m%d%H%M%y                - 0428174095
         %Q    %Y%m%d                    - 19961025
         %q    %Y%m%d%H%M%S              - 19961025174058
         %P    %Y%m%d%H%M%S              - 1996102517:40:58
         %F    %A, %B %e, %Y             - Sunday, January  1, 1996

    Other formats
         %n    insert a newline character
         %t    insert a tab character
         %%    insert a '%' character
         %+    insert a '+' character
```

The following formats are currently unused, but they may be used in the future:

```
    GJKLNO 1234567890 !@#$^&*()_|-=\'[];',./~{}:<>?
```

They currently insert the character following the %, but may (and probably will) change in the future as new formats are requested.

If a lone percent sign is the final character in a format, it is ignored.

Note that the ls format applies to dates within the past *or* future six months!

Note that the **%s** format was introduced in version 5.07. Prior to that, **%s** referred to the seconds since 1/1/70. This was moved to **%o** in 5.07.

This routine is loosely based on *date.pl* (version 3.2) by Terry McGonigal. None of his code was used, but most of his formats were.

ParseDateDelta

This takes an array and shifts a valid delta date (an amount of time) from the array.

```
$delta=&ParseDateDelta(\@args)
$delta=&ParseDateDelta($string)
$delta=&ParseDateDelta(\$string)
```

Recognized deltas are of the following forms:

- +Yy +Mm +Ww +Dd +Hh +MNmn +Ss

  Examples:

  ```
  +4 hours +3mn -2second
  + 4 hr 3 minutes -2
  4 hour + 3 min -2 s
  ```

- +Y:+M:+D:+H:+MN:+S

  Examples:

  ```
  0:0:0:4:3:-2
  +4:3:-2
  ```

- Mixed format

  Example:

  ```
  4 hour 3:-2
  ```

A field in the format +Yy is a sign, a number, and a string specifying the type of field. The sign is +, -, or absent (defaults to the next larger element). The valid strings specifying the field type are:

```
y:   y, yr, year, years
m:   m, mon, month, months
w:   w, wk, ws, wks, week, weeks
d:   d, day, days
h:   h, hr, hour, hours
mn:  mn, min, minute, minutes
s:   s, sec, second, seconds
```

Also, the s string may be omitted. The sign, number, and string may all be separated from each other by any amount of whitespace.

In the date, all fields must be given in the order: y m d h mn s. Any number of them may be omitted provided the rest remain in the correct order. In the second (colon) format, from two to six of the fields may be given. For example +D:+H:+MN:+S may be given to specify only four of the fields. In any case, both the mn and s field may be present. No spaces may be present in the colon format.

Deltas may also be given as a combination of the two formats. For example, the following is valid: +Yy +D:+H:+MN:+S. Again, all fields must be given in the correct order.

The word in may be prepended to the delta (in 5 years) and the word ago may be appended (6 months ago). The in is completely ignored. The ago has the affect of reversing all signs that appear in front of the components of the delta, i.e. -12 yr 6 mon ago is identical to "+12yr +6mon" (don't forget that there is an implied minus sign in front of the 6 because when no sign is explicitly given, the field carries the previously entered sign).

The week field does not occur in the colon-separated delta. This is to maintain backward compatibility with previous versions of Date::Manip. Parsing of weeks was not added until version 5.07. At that point, rather than change the internal format of the delta to Y:M:W:D:H:MN:S, I simply added the weeks to the days (1 week = 7 days) in order to be compatible with previous versions. So, they are not parsed in the colon format, only in the first format. Hopefully, this will not result in too much confusion.

One thing is worth noting. The year/month and day/hour/min/sec parts are returned in a "normalized" form. That is, the signs are adjusted so as to be all positive or all negative. For example, + 2 `day` - 2hour does not return 0:0:2:-2:0:0. It returns +0:0:1:22:0:0 (1 day 22 hours, which is equivalent). I find (and I think most others agree) that this is a more useful form.

Since the year/month and day/hour/min/sec parts must be normalized separately, there is the possibility that the sign of the two parts will be different. So, the delta + 2years -10 months - 2 `days` + 2 `hours` produces the delta +1:2:-1:22:0:0.

For backwards compatibility, it is possible to include a sign for all elements that are output. See the configuration variable `DeltaSigns` below.

DateCalc

This takes two dates, two deltas, or one of each and performs the appropriate calculation with them.

```
$d=&DateCalc($d1,$d2,\$err [,$mode])
```

Dates must be in the format given by `&ParseDate` and/or must be a string that can be parsed as a date. Deltas must be in the format returned by `&ParseDateDelta` or must be a string that can be parsed as a delta. Two deltas add together to form a third delta. A date and a delta return a second date. Two dates return a delta (the difference between the two dates).

Note that in many cases, it is somewhat ambiguous what the delta actually refers to. Although it is *always* known how many months there are in a year or hours in a day, etc., it is *not* known how many days form a month. As a result, the part of the delta containing month/year and the part with sec/min/hr/day must be treated separately. For example, `Mar 31, 12:00:00` plus a delta of `1month 2days` would yield `May 2 12:00:00`. The year/month is handled first, while the date is kept the same. Mar 31 plus one month is Apr 31 (but since April only has 30 days, it becomes Apr 30). Apr 30 + 2 days is May 2. As a result, in the case where two dates are entered, the resulting delta can take on two different forms. By default (`$mode=0`), an absolutely correct delta (ignoring daylight savings time) is returned in days, hours, minutes, and seconds.

If `$mode` is 1, the math is done using an approximate mode, where a delta is returned using years and months as well. The year and month part is calculated first, followed by the rest. For example, the two dates `Mar 12 1995` and `Apr 13 1995` have an exact delta of 31 `days`, but in the approximate mode, it is returned as 1 `month` 1 `day`. Also, `Mar 31` and `Apr 30` have deltas of 30 `days` or 1 `month` (since Apr 31 doesn't exist, it drops down to Apr 30). Approximate mode is a more human way of looking at things (you'd say 1 month and 2 days more often then 33 days), but it is less meaningful in terms of absolute time. In approximate mode, `$d1` and `$d2` must be dates. If either or both is a delta, the calculation is done in exact mode.

If `$mode` is 2, a business mode is used. That is, the calculation is done using business days, ignoring holidays, weekends, etc. In order to correctly use this mode, a `config` file must exist that contains the section defining holidays (see the documentation on the `config` file in the following section "Customizing Date::Manip"). The `config` file can also define the work week and the hours of the work day, so it is possible to have different config files for different businesses.

For example, if a `config` file defines the workday as 08:00 to 18:00, a work week as Mon-Sat, and the standard (American) holidays, then from Tuesday at 12:00 to the following Monday at 14:00 is 5 days and 2 hours. If the "end" of the day is reached in a calculation, it automatically switches to the next day. So, Tuesday at 12:00 plus 6 hours is Wednesday at 08:00 (provided Wednesday is not a holiday). Also, a date that does not fall on a workday automatically becomes the start of the next workday. So, Sunday 12:00 and Monday at 03:00 both automatically become Monday at 08:00 (provided Monday is not a holiday). In business mode, any combination of date and delta may be entered, but a delta should not contain a year or month field (weeks are fine, though).

See below for some additional comments about business-mode calculations.

Any other non-nil value of $mode is treated as $mode=1 (approximate mode).

The mode can be automatically set in the dates/deltas by including a keyword somewhere in it. For example, in English, if the word "approximately" is found in either of the date/delta arguments, approximate mode is forced. Likewise, if the word "business" or "exact" appears, business/exact mode is forced (and $mode is ignored). So, the following two examples are equivalent:

```
$date=&DateCalc("today","+ 2 business days",\$err);
$date=&DateCalc("today","+ 2 days",\$err,2);
```

Note that if the keyword method is used instead of passing in $mode, it is important that the keyword actually appear in the argument passed to `DateCalc`. The following do *not* work:

```
$delta=&ParseDateDelta("+ 2 business days");
$today=&ParseDate("today");
$date=&DateCalc($today,$delta,\$err);
```

because the mode keyword is removed from a date/delta by the parse routines, and the mode is reset each time a parse routine is called. Since DateCalc parses both of its arguments, whatever mode was previously set is ignored.

$err is set to:

- 1 if $d1 is not a delta or date
- 2 if $d2 is not a delta or date
- 3 if the date is outside the years 1000 to 9999

Nothing is returned if an error occurs.

When a delta is returned, the signs are set in such a way that the delta is strictly positive or strictly negative (1 **day** - 2 **hours** is never returned, for example). The only time when this cannot be enforced is when two deltas with a year/month component are entered. In that case, only the signs on the day/hour/min/sec part are standardized.

Date_SetTime

This takes a date and sets the time in that date.

```
$date=&Date_SetTime($date,$hr,$min,$sec)
$date=&Date_SetTime($date,$time)
```

For example, to get the time for 7:30 tomorrow, use the lines:

```
$date=&ParseDate("tomorrow")
$date=&Date_SetTime($date,"7:30")
```

Date_GetPrev

If $dow is defined, it is a day of the week (a string such as Fri or a number from 0 to 6). The date of the previous $dow is returned. If $date falls on this day of the week, the date returned is $date (if $curr is non-zero) or a week earlier (if $curr is 0). If a time is passed in (either as separate hours, minutes, and seconds or as a time in HH:MM:SS or HH:MM format), the time on this date is set to that time.

```
$date=&Date_GetPrev($date,$dow, $curr [,$hr,$min,$sec])
$date=&Date_GetPrev($date,$dow, $curr [,$time])
$date=&Date_GetPrev($date,undef,$curr,$hr,$min,$sec)
$date=&Date_GetPrev($date,undef,$curr,$time)
```

The following examples should illustrate the use of Date_GetPrev:

Date	Dow	Curr	Time	Returns
Fri Nov 22 18:15:00	Thu	0	12:30	Thu Nov 21 12:30:00
Fri Nov 22 18:15:00	Fri	0	12:30	Fri Nov 15 12:30:00
Fri Nov 22 18:15:00	Fri	1	12:30	Fri Nov 22 12:30:00

If $dow is undefined, then a time must be entered, and the date returned is the previous occurrence of this time. If $curr is non-zero, the current time is returned if it matches the criteria passed in. In other words, the time returned is the last time that a digital clock (in 24-hour mode) would have displayed the time you specified. If you define hours, then minutes and seconds default to 0, and you might jump back as much as an entire day. If hours are undefined, you are looking for the last time the minutes/seconds appeared on the digital clock, so at most, the time jumps back one hour.

Date	Curr	Hr	Min	Sec	Returns
Nov 22 18:15:00	0/1	18	undef	undef	Nov 22 18:00:00
Nov 22 18:15:00	0/1	18	30	0	Nov 21 18:30:00
Nov 22 18:15:00	0	18	15	undef	Nov 21 18:15:00
Nov 22 18:15:00	1	18	15	undef	Nov 22 18:15:00
Nov 22 18:15:00	0	undef	15	undef	Nov 22 17:15:00
Nov 22 18:15:00	1	undef	15	undef	Nov 22 18:15:00

Date_GetNext

Similar to Date_GetPrev.

```
$date=&Date_GetNext($date,$dow, $curr [,$hr,$min,$sec])
$date=&Date_GetNext($date,$dow, $curr [,$time])
$date=&Date_GetNext($date,undef,$curr,$hr,$min,$sec)
$date=&Date_GetNext($date,undef,$curr,$time)
```

Date_DayOfWeek

This returns the day of the week (0 for Sunday, 6 for Saturday). Dec 31, 0999 was Tuesday.

```
$day=&Date_DayOfWeek($m,$d,$y);
```

Date_SecsSince1970

This returns the number of seconds since Jan 1, 1970 00:00. The number returned is negative if you pass it a date earlier than that.

```
$secs=&Date_SecsSince1970($m,$d,$y,$h,$mn,$s)
```

Date_SecsSince1970GMT

This returns the number of seconds since Jan 1, 1970 00:00 GMT. The number is negative if you pass it a date earlier than that. If the value of CurrTZ is IGNORE, the number returned is identical to the number returned by Date_SecsSince1970 (i.e., the date is treated as being in GMT).

```
$secs=&Date_SecsSince1970GMT($m,$d,$y,$h,$mn,$s)
```

Date_DaysSince999

This returns the number of days since Dec 31, 0999.

```
$days=&Date_DaysSince999($m,$d,$y)
```

Date_DayOfYear

This returns the day of the year (001 to 366).

```
$day=&Date_DayOfYear($m,$d,$y);
```

Date_DaysInYear

This returns the number of days in the year (365 or 366).

```
$days=&Date_DaysInYear($y);
```

Date_WeekOfYear

This figures out the week number. $first is the first day of the week, which is usually 0 (Sunday) or 1 (Monday), but which can be any number between 0 and 6 in practice.

```
$wkno=&Date_WeekOfYear($m,$d,$y,$first);
```

Date_LeapYear

```
$flag=&Date_LeapYear($y);
```

This returns 1 if the argument is a leap year. Written by David Muir Sharnoff (*muir@idiom.com*)

Date_DaySuffix

This adds st, nd, rd, th to a date (i.e., 1st, 22nd, 29th). It works for international dates.

```
$day=&Date_DaySuffix($d);
```

Date_TimeZone

This returns a time zone.

```
$tz=&Date_TimeZone
```

It looks for the time zone in the following places, in order:

- $ENV{TZ}
- $main::TZ
- UNIX date command
- */etc/TIMEZONE*

If the time zone is not found in any of these places, an error occurs:

```
ERROR: Date::Manip unable to determine TimeZone.
```

Date_TimeZone can read zones of the format PST8PDT (see the following documentation on "Time Zones").

Date_ConvTZ

This converts a date (which MUST be in the format returned by ParseDate) from one time zone to another. The behavior of Date_ConvTZ depends on whether it is called with two or three arguments.

```
$date=&Date_ConvTZ($date,$from);
$date=&Date_ConvTZ($date,$from,$to);
```

If it is called with two arguments, $date is assumed to be in the time zone specified in $from, and it is converted to the time zone specified by the config variable ConvTZ. If ConvTZ is set to IGNORE, no conversion is done, and $date is returned unmodified (see the following documentation on ConvTZ). This form is most often used internally by the Date::Manip module. The three-argument form is of more use to most users.

If Date_ConvTZ is called with three arguments, the config variable ConvTZ is ignored; $date is specified in the time zone $from and is converted to the time zone $to. If $from is not given, it defaults to the working time zone.

Note: As in all the other cases, the $date returned from Date_ConvTZ has no time zone information included as part of it; to get the time zone that Date::Manip is working in, which is usually the local time zone, call UnixDate with the %z format.

For example, to convert 2/2/96 noon PST to CST (regardless of what time zone you are in, do the following:

```
$date=&ParseDate("2/2/96 noon");
$date=&Date_ConvTZ($date,"PST","CST");
```

Both time zones *must* be in one of the forms listed below in the section "Time Zones."

Date_Init

Normally, it is not necessary to explicitly call Date_Init. The first time any of the other routines is called, Date_Init is called to set everything up. If for some reason you want to change the configuration of Date::Manip, you can pass the appropriate string or strings to Date_Init to reinitialize the configuration.

```
$flag=&Date_Init();
$flag=&Date_Init("VAR=VAL","VAR=VAL",...);
```

The strings to pass in are of the form VAR=VAL. Any number of strings can be included, and they can come in any order. VAR may be any configuration variable. A list of all configuration variables is given in the section "Customizing Date::Manip" below. VAL is any allowed value for that variable. For example, to switch from English to French and use non-US format (so that 12/10 is Oct 12), do the following:

```
&Date_Init("Language=French","DateFormat=nonUS");
```

Note that the usage of Date_Init changed with version 5.07. The old calling convention is allowed, but is deprecated.

If you change time zones in the middle of using Date::Manip, comparing dates before the switch to dates after the switch produces incorrect results.

Date_IsWorkDay

This returns 1 if $date is a workday. If $flag is non-zero, the time is checked to see if it falls within work hours.

```
$flag=&Date_IsWorkDay($date [,$flag]);
```

Date_NextWorkDay

This finds the day $off workdays from now. If $time is specified, we must also take into account the time of day.

```
$date=&Date_NextWorkDay($date,$off [,$time]);
```

If $time is not specified, day 0 is today, if today is a workday, or the next workday if it isn't. In any case, the time of day is unaffected.

If $time is passed in, day 0 is now, if now is part of a workday, or the start of the next workday.

Date_PrevWorkDay

This is similar to Date_NextWorkDay.

```
$date=&Date_PrevWorkDay($date,$off [,$time]);
```

DateManipVersion

This returns the version of Date::Manip.

```
$version=&DateManipVersion
```

Time Zones

The following time-zone names are currently understood and can be used in parsing dates. These are zones that are defined in RFC822.

Universal:

GMT, UT

US zones:

EST, EDT, CST, CDT, MST, MDT, PST, PDT

Military:

A to Z (except J)

Other:

+HHMM or -HHMM

In addition, the following time-zone abbreviations are also accepted. In a few cases, the same abbreviation is used for two different time zones (for example, NST stands for Newfoundland Standard -0330 and North Sumatra +0630). In these cases, only one of the two is available. The one preceded by "#" is *not* available, but is documented here for completeness. This list of zones comes from the Time::Zone module by Graham Barr, David Muir Sharnoff, and Paul Foley.

IDLW	-1200	International Date Line West
NT	-1100	Nome
HST	-1000	Hawaii Standard
CAT	-1000	Central Alaska
AHST	-1000	Alaska-Hawaii Standard

YST	-0900	Yukon Standard
HDT	-0900	Hawaii Daylight
YDT	-0800	Yukon Daylight
PST	-0800	Pacific Standard
PDT	-0700	Pacific Daylight
MST	-0700	Mountain Standard
MDT	-0600	Mountain Daylight
CST	-0600	Central Standard
CDT	-0500	Central Daylight
EST	-0500	Eastern Standard
EDT	-0400	Eastern Daylight
AST	-0400	Atlantic Standard
#NST	-0330	Newfoundland Standard nst=North Sumatra +0630
NFT	-0330	Newfoundland
#GST	-0300	Greenland Standard gst=Guam Standard +1000
BST	-0300	Brazil Standard bst=British Summer +0100
ADT	-0300	Atlantic Daylight
NDT	-0230	Newfoundland Daylight
AT	-0200	Azores
WAT	-0100	West Africa
GMT	+0000	Greenwich Mean
UT	+0000	Universal (Coordinated)
UTC	+0000	Universal (Coordinated)
WET	+0000	Western European
CET	+0100	Central European
FWT	+0100	French Winter
MET	+0100	Middle European
EWT	+0100	Middle European Winter
SWT	+0100	Swedish Winter
#BST	+0100	British Summer bst=Brazil standard −0300
EET	+0200	Eastern Europe, USSR Zone 1
FST	+0200	French Summer
MEST	+0200	Middle European Summer
SST	+0200	Swedish Summer sst=South Sumatra +0700
BT	+0300	Baghdad, USSR Zone 2
IT	+0330	Iran
ZP4	+0400	USSR Zone 3
ZP5	+0500	USSR Zone 4

IST	+0530	Indian Standard
ZP6	+0600	USSR Zone 5
NST	+0630	North Sumatra nst=Newfoundland Std –0330
WAST	+0700	West Australian Standard
#SST	+0700	South Sumatra, USSR Zone 6 sst=Swedish Summer +0200
JT	+0730	Java (3pm in Cronusland!)
CCT	+0800	China Coast, USSR Zone 7
WADT	+0800	West Australian Daylight
JST	+0900	Japan Standard, USSR Zone 8
CAST	+0930	Central Australian Standard
EAST	+1000	Eastern Australian Standard
GST	+1000	Guam Standard, USSR Zone 9 gst=Greenland Std –0300
CADT	+1030	Central Australian Daylight
EADT	+1100	Eastern Australian Daylight
IDLE	+1200	International Date Line East
NZST	+1200	New Zealand Standard
NZT	+1200	New Zealand
NZDT	+1300	New Zealand Daylight

Other time zones can be added in the future upon request.

`DateManip` needs to be able to determine the local time zone. It can do this in various ways, such as looking at the TZ environment variable (see the `Date_TimeZone` documentation above) or using the TZ `config` variable (described in the following documentation). In either case, the time zone can be of the form STD#DST (for example, EST5EDT). Both the standard and daylight savings time abbreviations must be in the table above in order for this to work. Also, this form may *not* be used when parsing a date, as there is no way to determine whether the date is in daylight savings time or not. The following forms are also available and are treated like the STD#DST forms:

- US/Pacific
- US/Mountain
- US/Central
- US/Eastern

Business Mode

Anyone using business mode is going to notice a few quirks about it that should be explained. When I designed business mode, I had in mind what UPS tells me when they say two-day delivery, or what the local business that promises one business-day turnaround really means.

If you do a business-day calculation (with the workday set to 9:00–5:00), you get the following:

```
Saturday at noon + 1 business day = Tuesday at 9:00
Saturday at noon - 1 business day = Friday at 9:00
```

What does this mean?

Consider a business that works from 9:00 to 5:00. They have a drop box so I can drop things off over the weekend, and they promise one business-day turnaround. It doesn't matter if I drop something off Friday night, Saturday, or Sunday; they're going to get started on it Monday morning. It will be one business day to finish the job, so the earliest I can expect it to be done is around 17:00 Monday, or 9:00 Tuesday morning. Unfortunately, there is some ambiguity as to what day 17:00 really falls on, similar to the ambiguity that occurs when you ask what day midnight falls on. Although it's not the only answer, Date::Manip treats midnight as the beginning of a day rather than the end of one. In the same way, 17:00 is equivalent to 9:00 the next day and any time the date calculation encounters 17:00, it automatically converts it to 9:00 the next day. Although this introduces some quirks, I think it is justified. You just have to treat 9:00 as being ambiguous (in the same way you treat midnight as being ambiguous).

Equivalently, if I want a job to be finished on Saturday (despite the fact that I cannot pick it up, since the business is closed), I have to drop it off no later than Friday at 9:00. That gives them a full business day to finish it off. Of course, I could just as easily drop it off at 17:00 Thursday, or any time between then and 9:00 Friday. Again, it's a matter of treating 9:00 as ambiguous.

So, in case the business date calculations ever produce results that you find confusing, I believe the solution is to write a wrapper which, whenever it sees a date with a time of exactly 9:00, treats it specially, depending on what you want.

So Saturday + one business day = Tuesday at 9:00 (which means anything from Monday at 17:00 to Tuesday at 9:00), but Monday at 9:01 + one business day = Tuesday at 9:01, which is exact.

If this is not exactly what you have in mind, don't use the `DateCalc` routine. You can probably get whatever behavior you want using the routines `Date_IsWorkDay`, `Date_NextWorkDay`, and `Date_PrevWorkDay`, which are described previously.

Customizing Date::Manip

There are a number of variables that can be used to customize the way Date::Manip behaves. There are also several ways to set these variables.

At the top of the *Manip.pm* file, there is a section that contains all customization variables. These provide the default values.

The defaults can be overridden in a global config file (this file is optional). If the `GlobalCnf` variable is set in the *Manip.pm* file, it contains the full path to a `config` file. If the file exists, its values override those set in the *Manip.pm* file. A sample `config` file is included with the Date::Manip distribution. Modify it as appropriate, copy it to some suitable directory, and set the `GlobalCnf` variable in the *Manip.pm* file.

Each user can have a personal `config` file that is of the same form as the global `config` file. The variables `PersonalCnf` and `PersonalCnfPath` set the name and search path for the personal `config` file.

Finally, any variables passed in through `Date_Init` override all other values.

A `config` file can be composed of several sections (though only two of them are currently used). The first section sets configuration varibles. Lines in this section are of the form:

```
VARIABLE = VALUE
```

For example, to make the default language French, include the line:

```
Language = French
```

Only the variables described below may be used. Blank lines and lines beginning with a pound sign (#) are ignored. All spaces are optional and strings are case-insensitive.

A line that starts with an asterisk (*) designates a new section. The only additional section currently used is the holiday section. All lines in this section are of the form:

```
DATE = HOLIDAY
```

HOLIDAY is the name of the holiday. The name can be blank, but the day is still treated as a holiday. For example, the day after Thanksgiving or Christmas is often a work holiday, though neither are named.

DATE is a string that can be parsed to give a valid date in any year. It can be of the form:

```
Date
Date + Delta
Date - Delta
```

A valid holiday section would be:

```
*Holiday

1/1                               = New Year's Day
third Monday in Feb               = Presidents' Day
fourth Thu in Nov                 = Thanksgiving

# The Friday after Thanksgiving is an unnamed holiday most places
fourth Thu in Nov + 1 day         =
```

In a `Date + Delta` or `Date - Delta` string, you can use business mode by including the appropriate string (see the documentation on `DateCalc`) in the `Date` or `Delta`. So (in English), the first workday before Christmas could be defined as:

```
12/25 - 1 business day            =
```

The available Date::Manip variables are described in the following section:

IgnoreGlobalCnf

If this variable is used (any value is ignored), the global `config` file is not read. The variable must be present at the time of the initial call to `Date_Init` or the global `config` file is read.

EraseHolidays

If this variable is used (any value is ignored), the current list of defined holidays is erased. A new set will be created the next time a `config` file is read in.

PersonalCnf

This variable can be passed into `Date_Init` to read a different personal configuration file. It can also be included in the global `config` file to define where personal `config` files live.

PersonalCnfPath

> This is used in the same way as the **PersonalCnf** option. You can use tilde (~) expansions when defining the path.

Language

> Date::Manip can be used to parse dates in many different languages. Currently, it is configured to read English, Swedish, and French dates, but others can be added easily. Language is set to the language used to parse dates.

DateFormat

> Depending on what country you are in, you might see the date 12/10/96 as Dec 10 or as Oct 12. In the United States, the first is most common, but this certainly doesn't hold true for other countries. Setting **DateFormat** to **US** forces the first behavior (Dec 10). Setting **DateFormat** to anything else forces the second behavior (Oct 12).

TZ

> Date::Manip understands some time zones (others will be added in the future). At the very least, all the zones defined in RFC822 are supported. Currently supported zones are listed in the previous section "Time Zones" and all time zones should be entered as one of those values.

> Date::Manip must be able to determine the time zone the user is in. It does this by looking in the following places:

- The environment variable **TZ**
- The variable **$main::TZ**
- The file *eroo*
- The fifth element of the UNIX date command (not available on NT machines)

> At least one of these should contain a time zone in one of the supported forms. If it doesn't, the TZ variable must be set to contain the local time zone in the appropriate form.

> The TZ variable overrides the other methods of determining the time zone, so it should probably be left blank if any of the other methods works. Otherwise, you will have to modify the variable every time you switch to or from daylight savings time.

ConvTZ

> All date comparisons and calculations must be done in a single time zone in order for them to work correctly. So, when a date is parsed, it should be converted to a specific time zone. This allows dates to easily be compared and to be manipulated as if they are all in a single time zone.

> The **ConvTZ** variable determines which time zone should be used for storing dates. If it is left blank, all dates are converted to the local time zone (see the TZ variable above). If it is set to one of the time zones listed above, all dates are converted to this time zone. Finally, if it is set to the string **IGNORE**, all time zone information is ignored as the dates are read in (in this case, the two dates **1/1/96 12:00 GMT** and **1/1/96 12:00 EST** are treated as identical).

Internal

> When a date is parsed using **ParseDate**, that date is stored in an internal format that is understood by the Date::Manip routines **UnixDate** and **DateCalc**.

Originally, the format used to store the date internally was:

```
YYYYMMDDHH:MN:SS
```

It has been suggested that I remove the colons (:) to shorten this to:

```
YYYYMMDDHHMNSS
```

The main advantage of this is that some databases are colon-delimited, which makes storing the date from Date::Manip tedious.

In order to maintain backwards compatibility, the `Internal` variable was introduced. Set it to 0 to use the old format or to 1 to use the new format.

`FirstDay`

It is sometimes necessary to know what day of week is regarded as the first day. By default, this is Sunday, but many countries and people will prefer Monday (and in a few cases, a different day may be desired). Set the `FirstDay` variable to the first day of the week (0=Sunday to 6=Saturday). Incidentally, to be in complete accordance with ISO 8601, choose Monday as the default.

`WorkWeekBeg, WorkWeekEnd`

These specify the first and last days of the work week, which by default are Monday and Friday. `WorkWeekBeg` must come before `WorkWeekEnd` numerically. The days are numbered from 0 (Sunday) to 6 (Saturday). There is no way to handle an odd work week of, for example, Thursday to Monday.

`WorkDay24Hr`

If this is non-nil, a workday is treated as being 24 hours long. The `WorkDayBeg` and `WorkDayEnd` variables are ignored in this case.

`WorkDayBeg, WorkDayEnd`

The times when the workday starts and ends. `WorkDayBeg` must come before `WorkDayEnd` (i.e. there is no way to handle the night shift, where the work day starts one day and ends another). Also, the workday *must* be more than one hour long (of course, if this isn't the case, let me know . . . I want a job there!).

The time in both can be in any valid time format (including international formats), but seconds are ignored.

`DeltaSigns`

Prior to Date::Manip version 5.07, a negative delta put negative signs in front of every component (i.e., `0:0:-1:-3:0:-4`). By default, 5.07 changes this behavior to print only one or two signs in front of the year and day elements (even if these elements might be zero) and the sign for year/month and day/hour/minute/second are the same. Setting this variable to non-zero forces deltas to be stored with a sign in front of every element (including elements equal to zero).

Backwards Incompatibilities

For the most part, Date::Manip has remained backward-compatible at every release. There have been a few minor incompatibilities introduced at various stages.

Version 5.07 introduced two of these minor incompatibilities. In the UnixDate command, the `%s` format changed. In version 5.06, `%s` returned the number of seconds since Jan 1, 1970 in the current time zone. In 5.07, it returns the number of seconds since Jan 1, 1970 GMT. The `%o` format was added to return what `%s` previously returned.

Also in 5.07, the format for the deltas returned by ParseDateDelta changed. Previously, each element of a delta had a sign attached to it (+1:+2:+3:+4:+5:+6). The new format removes all unnecessary signs by default (+1:2:3:4:5:6). Also, because of the way deltas are normalized (see the documentation for `ParseDateDelta`), at most two signs are included. For backwards compatibility, the `config` variable `DeltaSigns` was added. If it is set to 1, all deltas include all six signs.

Finally, in 5.07 the format of the `Date_Init` calling arguments changed. The old method:

```
&Date_Init($language,$format,$tz,$convtz);
```

is still supported, but this support is likely to disappear in the future. Use the new calling format instead:

```
&Date_Init("var=val","var=val",...);
```

One more important incompatibility is projected for `ParseDate` in the next major release of Date::Manip, which will support full ISO 8601 date formats, including the format YY-MM-DD. The current version of `ParseDate` supports the format MM-DD-YY, which is commonly used in the U.S., but is not part of any standard. Unfortunately, there is no way to unambiguously look at a date of the format XX-XX-XX and determine whether it is YY-MM-DD or MM-DD-YY. As a result, the MM-DD-YY format will no longer be supported, in favor of the YY-MM-DD format. The MM/DD/YY and MM-DD-YYYY formats *will* still be supported!

Common Problems

Perhaps the most common problem occurs when you get the error:

```
Error: Date::Manip unable to determine TimeZone.
```

Date::Manip tries hard to determine the local time zone, but on some machines, it cannot do this (especially those without a UNIX date command; i.e., Microsoft Windows systems). To fix this, set the TZ variable, either at the top of the Manip.pm file or in the DateManip.cnf file. I suggest using the form **EST5EDT** so you don't have to change it every six months when going to or from daylight savings time.

Bugs

Daylight Savings Time

Date::Manip does not handle daylight savings time, though it does handle time zones to a certain extent. Converting from EST to PST works fine. Going from EST to PDT is unreliable.

The following examples are run in winter on the US East coast (i.e., in the EST timezone).

```
print UnixDate(ParseDate("6/1/97 noon"),"%u"),"\n";
=> Sun Jun  1 12:00:00 EST 1997
```

June 1 EST does not exist. June 1st falls during EDT. It should print:

```
=> Sun Jun  1 00:00:00 EDT 1997
```

Even explicitly adding the time zone doesn't fix things (if anything, it makes matters worse):

```
print UnixDate(ParseDate("6/1/97 noon EDT"),"%u"),"\n";
=> Sun Jun  1 11:00:00 EST 1997
```

Date::Manip converts everything to the current time zone (EST in this case).

Related problems occur when trying to do date calculations over a time zone change. These calculations may be off by an hour.

If you are running a script which uses Date::Manip over a period of time that starts in one time zone and ends in another (i.e., it switches from Daylight Savings Time to Standard Time or vice versa), many things may be wrong (especially elapsed time).

I hope to fix these problems in the next release so that it will convert everything to the current zones (e.g., EST or EDT).

Sorting Problems

If you use Date::Manip to sort a number of dates, you must call **Date_Init** either explicitly or by way of some other Date::Manip routine before it is used in the sort. For example, the following code fails:

```
use Date::Manip;
# &Date_Init;
sub sortDate {
    my($date1, $date2);
    $date1 = &ParseDate($a);
    $date2 = &ParseDate($b);
    return ($date1 cmp $date2);
}
@date = ("Fri 16 Aug 96",
         "Mon 19 Aug 96",
         "Thu 15 Aug 96");
@i=sort sortDate @dates;
```

but if you uncomment the **Date_Init** line, it works. The reason for this is that the first time you call **Date_Init**, it initializes a number of items used by Date::Manip. Some of these are sorted. It turns out that Perl 5.003 and earlier has a bug in it that does not allow a sort within a sort. The next version (5.004) may fix this. For now, the best thing to do is to call **Date_Init** explicitly.

Note: This is an extremely inefficient way to sort data. Instead, you should translate the dates to the Date::Manip internal format, sort them using a normal string comparison, and then convert them back to the desired format using **UnixDate**.

RCS Control

If you try to put Date::Manip under RCS control, you will have problems. Apparently, RCS replaces strings of the form **$Date...$** with the current date. This form occurs all over in Date::Manip. Since very few people will ever have a desire to do this (and I don't use RCS), I have not worried about it.

Author

Sullivan Beck, *beck@qtp.ufl.edu*

Date::Parse — parse date strings into time values

Synopsis

```
use Date::Parse;

$time = str2time($date);

($ss,$mm,$hh,$day,$month,$year,$zone) = strptime($date);
```

Description

Date::Parse provides two routines for parsing date strings into time values.

Parsing Routines

str2time(*DATE* [, *ZONE*])

> str2time parses *DATE* and returns a UNIX time value, or undef upon failure. *ZONE*, if given, specifies the time zone to assume when parsing if the date string does not specify a time zone.

strptime(*DATE* [, *ZONE*])

> strptime takes the same arguments as str2time but returns an array of values ($ss, $mm, $hh, $day, $month, $year, $zone). Elements are defined only if they can be extracted from the date string. The $zone element is the time zone offset in seconds from GMT. An empty array is returned upon failure.

Multi-Language Support

Date::Parse is capable of parsing dates in several languages: English, French, German, and Italian. Changing the language is done via a static method call. For example:

```
Date::Parse->language('German');
```

causes Date::Parse to attempt to parse any subsequent dates in German.

This is only a first pass. I am considering changing this to be:

```
$lang = Date::Language->new('German');
$lang->str2time("25 Jun 1996 21:09:55 +0100");
```

I am open to suggestions on this.

Author

Graham Barr, *gbarr@pobox.com*

Copyright

Copyright © 1995 Graham Barr. All rights reserved. This program is free software; you can redistribute it and/or modify it under the same terms as Perl itself.

DFA::Kleene—Kleene's Algorithm for Deterministic Finite Automata

Synopsis

```
use DFA::Kleene qw(initialize define_accepting_states
                   define_delta kleene example);
use DFA::Kleene qw(:all);
```

- Define the number of states (state #1 is the "start" state!) of your Deterministic Finite Automaton and the alphabet used (as a string containing all characters which are part of the alphabet):

  ```
  &initialize(6,"ab");
  ```

- Define which states are "accepting states" in your Deterministic Finite Automaton (list of state numbers):

  ```
  &define_accepting_states(2,3,4,5);
  ```

- Define the state transition function "delta" (arguments are: "from" state, character (or empty string!) read during the transition, "to" state):

  ```
  &define_delta(1,'a',4);
  ```

  You need several calls to this function in order to build a complete transition table describing your Deterministic Finite Automaton.

- Return a (sorted) list of regular expressions describing the language (= set of patterns) recognized ("accepted") by your Deterministic Finite Automaton:

  ```
  @language = &kleene();
  ```

- Calculate the language of a sample Deterministic Finite Automaton and print a (sorted) list of regular expressions:

  ```
  &example();
  ```

  The list that is printed should be equivalent to the following regular expression:

  ```
  (a(a)*b)*a(a)*(b)*
  ```

  This is the same as

  ```
  ((a+)b)*(a+)b*
  ```

Description

The routines in this module allow you to define a Deterministic Finite Automaton and to compute the "language" (set of "words" or "patterns") accepted (= recognized) by it.

Actually, a list of regular expressions is generated that describes the same language (set of patterns) as the one accepted by your Deterministic Finite Automaton.

The output generated by this module can easily be modified to produce Perl-style regular expressions that can actually be used to recognize words (= patterns) contained in the language defined by your Deterministic Finite Automaton.

Other modules in this series (variants of Kleene's algorithm):

- Math::MatrixBool (see `Kleene()`)
- Math::MatrixReal (see `kleene()`)

Version

This manpage documents DFA::Kleene version 1.0.

Author

Steffen Beyer, *sb@sdm.de*

Copyright

Copyright © 1996, 1997 by Steffen Beyer. All rights reserved.

This package is free software; you can redistribute it and/or modify it under the same terms as Perl itself.

See Also

Math::MatrixBool(3), Math::MatrixReal(3), Math::Kleene(3), Set::IntegerRange(3), Set::Integer-Fast(3), Bit::Vector(3)

See the Math::Kleene(3) manpage for the theory behind this algorithm!

FreezeThaw—converting Perl structures to strings and back

Synopsis

```
use FreezeThaw qw(freeze thaw cmpStr safeFreeze cmpStrHard);
$string = freeze $data1, $data2, $data3;
...
($olddata1, $olddata2, $olddata3) = thaw $string;
if (cmpStr($olddata2,$data2) == 0) {print "OK!"}
```

Description

Converts data to and from stringified form, appropriate for saving to or reading from permanent storage.

Deals with objects, circular lists, and the repeated appearence of the same refence. Does not deal with overloaded **stringify** operator yet.

Export

Default

> None.

Exportable

- freeze
- thaw
- cmpStr
- cmpStrHard
- safeFreeze

User API

cmpStr

> Analogue of cmp for data. Takes two arguments and compares them as separate entities.

cmpStrHard

> Analogue of cmp for data. Takes two arguments and compares them, considered as a group.

freeze

> Returns a string that encapsulates its arguments (considered as a group). thawing this string leads to a fatal error if arguments to **freeze** contained references to GLOBs and CODEs.

safeFreeze

> Returns a string that encapsulates its arguments (considered as a group). The result is thawable in the same process. thawing the result in a different process should result in a fatal error if arguments to **safeFreeze** contained references to GLOBs and CODEs.

thaw

> Takes one string argument and returns an array. The elements of the array are "equivalent" to arguments of the **freeze** command that created the string. Can result in a fatal error (see above).

Developer API

FreezeThaw freezes and thaws data blessed in some package by calling methods Freeze and Thaw in the package. The fallback methods are provided by FreezeThaw itself. The fallback Freeze freezes the "content" of blessed object (from Perl's point of view). The fallback Thaw blesses the thawed data back into the package.

So the package needs to define its own methods only if the fallback methods will fail (for example, in many cases, the "content" of an object is an address of some C data). The methods are called like:

```
$newcooky = $obj->Freeze($cooky);
$obj = Package->Thaw($content,$cooky);
```

To save and restore the data the following methods are applicable:

```
$cooky->FreezeScalar($data,$ignorePackage,$noduplicate);
```

during Freeze()ing, and:

```
$data = $cooky->ThawScalar;
```

There are two optional arguments, $ignorePackage and $noduplicate. $ignore-Package says that freezing should not call the methods even if $data is a reference to a blessed object, while $noduplicate says that the data should not be marked as seen already even if it has been seen. The default methods:

```
sub UNIVERSAL::Freeze {
   my ($obj, $cooky) = (shift, shift);
   $cooky->FreezeScalar($obj,1,1);
}
sub UNIVERSAL::Thaw {
   my ($package, $cooky) = (shift, shift);
   my $obj = $cooky->ThawScalar;
   bless $obj, $package;
}
```

call the FreezeScalar method of $cooky, since the freezing engine will see the data the second time during this call. Indeed, it is the freezing engine that calls UNIVERSAL::Freeze(), because it needs to freeze $obj. The above call to $cooky->FreezeScalar() handles the same data back to the engine, but because flags are different, the code does not cycle.

Freezing and thawing $cooky also allows the following additional method:

```
$cooky->isSafe;
```

to find out whether the current freeze was initiated by the **freeze** or the **safeFreeze** command. With the analogous method for **thaw**, $cooky returns information about whether the current **thaw** operation is considered safe (i.e., that it either does not contain data that is cached elsewhere, or that the data comes from the same application). You can use:

```
$cooky->makeSafe;
```

to prohibit the cacheing of data for the remainder of the freezing or thawing of the current object.

Two methods:

```
$value = $cooky->repeatedOK;
$cooky->noRepeated;              # Now repeated are prohibited
```

allow you to find out if repeated references are permitted and to change the current setting that allows or prohibits repeated references.

If you want to flush the cache of saved objects you can use:

```
FreezeThaw->flushCache;
```

However, this can invalidate some frozen strings, so that thawing them results in a fatal error.

Instantiating

Sometimes, when an object from a package is recreated in presence of repeated references, it is not safe to recreate the internal structure of an object in one step. In such a situation, recreation of an object is carried out in two steps: first the object is allocated and then it is instantiated.

The restriction is that during the allocation step, you cannot use any reference to any Perl object that can be referenced from any other place. This restriction is applied since that object may not yet exist.

Correspondingly, during the instantiation step, the previously allocated object should be filled, i.e., it can be changed in any way such that the references to this object remain valid.

The methods are called like this:

```
$pre_object_ref = Package->Allocate($pre_pre_object_ref);
    # Returns reference
Package->Instantiate($pre_object_ref,$cooky);
    # Converts into reference to blessed object
```

The reverse operations are

```
$object_ref->FreezeEmpty($cooky);
$object_ref->FreezeInstance($cooky);
```

During these calls, the object can freezeScalar some information (in a usual way) that will be used during Allocate and Instantiate calls (via thawScalar). Note that the return value of FreezeEmpty is cached during the phase of creation of uninialized objects. This *must* be used like this: the return value is the reference to the created object, so it is not destroyed until other objects are created; thus the frozen values of the different objects will not share the same references. Here is an example of a bad result:

```
$o1->FreezeEmpty($cooky);
```

This freezes {}, and $o2->FreezeEmpty($cooky) does the same. You cannot guarantee that these two copies of {} are different, unless a reference to the first one was preserved during the call to $o2->FreezeEmpty($cooky). If $o1->FreezeEmpty($cooky) returns the value of {} that it uses, that value is preserved by the engine.

The helper function FreezeThaw::copyContents is provided to simplify instantiation. The syntax is:

```
FreezeThaw::copyContents $to, $from;
```

The function copies the contents of the object $from to point to what the object $to points to (including the package for blessed references). Both arguments should be references.

The following default methods are provided:

FreezeEmpty
> Freezes an *empty* object of underlying type.

FreezeInstance
> Calls **Freeze**.

Allocate
> Thaws what was frozen by **FreezeEmpty**.

Instantiate
> Thaws what was frozen by **FreezeInstance**, uses **copyContents** to transfer this to the **$pre_object**.

Bugs/Features

A lot of objects are blessed in some obscure packages by XSUB typemaps. It is not clear how to (automatically) prevent the UNIVERSAL methods to be called for objects in these packages.

Graph::Edge—object class for an edge in a directed graph

Synopsis

```
use Graph::Node;
use Graph::Edge;

$parent = new Graph::Node('LABEL' => 'Parent Node');
$child  = new Graph::Node('LABEL' => 'Child Node');
$edge   = new Graph::Edge('FROM' => $parent,
                          'TO'   => $child);

$parent->save('simple.daVinci', 'daVinci');
```

Description

The Graph::Edge is a class implementing an edge, or arc, in a directed graph. A graph is constructed using **Node** and **Edge** objects, with nodes being defined with the Graph::Node class.

An Edge takes four standard attributes: ID, LABEL, FROM, and TO. In addition, you may also define any number of custom attributes. Attributes are manipulated using the **setAttribute** and **getAttribute** methods, which are defined in the base class, Graph::Element.

Constructor

```
$edge = new Graph::Edge( . . . );
```

This creates a new instance of the Graph::Edge object class, used in conjunction with the Graph::Node class to construct directed graphs.

You *must* specify the **FROM** and **TO** attributes of an edge when creating it:

```
$edge = new Graph::Edge('FROM'  => $parent,
                        'TO'    => $child,
                        'ID'    => 'identifier'
                       );
```

where the $parent and $child are Graph::Node objects. The ID attribute is optional, and must be a unique string identifying the edge. If you do not specify the ID attribute, the edge is assigned a unique identifier automatically.

Author

Neil Bowers, *neilb@cre.canon.co.uk*

Copyright

Copyright © 1997 Canon Research Centre Europe. All rights reserved. This module is free software; you can redistribute it and/or modify it under the same terms as Perl itself.

See Also

Graph::Node, for a description of the Node class

Graph::Element, for a description of the Base class, including the attribute methods

---

Graph::Element—base class for elements of a directed graph

Synopsis

```
$object->setAttribute('ATTR_NAME', $value);
$value = $object->getAttribute('ATTR_NAME');
```

Description

The Graph::Element module implements the base class for elements of a directed graph. It is subclassed by the Graph::Node and Graph::Edge modules. This module provides a constructor, and attribute setting mechanisms.

If you want to inherit this class, see the section below, "Inheriting This Class."

Constructor

`$edge = new Graph::Element( . . . );`

> This creates a new instance of the Graph::Element object class, which is the base class for Graph::Node and Graph::Edge.

> You can set attributes of the new object by passing arguments to the constructor:

```
$element = new Graph::Element('ATTR1'  => $value1,
                             'ATTR2'  => $value2
                             );
```

> If you do not set the ID attribute at creation time, a unique value is automatically assigned.

Methods

This module provide three methods, described in separate sections below:

- `setAttribute()`, which is used to change the value of one or more attribute.
- `getAttribute()`, which is used to get the value of exactly one attribute.
- `addAttributeCallback()`, which is used to associate a function with a particular object. The function is then invoked whenever the attribute is changed.

setAttribute

Changes an attribute of an object .

```
$object->setAttribute('ATTR_A' => $valueA,
                      'ATTR_B' => $valueB);
```

This method is used to set user-defined attributes on an object. These are different from the standard attributes, such as ID and LABEL.

getAttribute

Queries the value of an object's attribute.

```
$value = $object->getAttribute('ATTRIBUTE_NAME');
```

This method is used to get the value of a single attribute defined on an object. If the attribute name given has not been previously set on the object, undef is returned.

addAttributeCallback

Adds an attribute callback to an object.

```
$object->addAttributeCallback('ATTR_NAME', \&callback
                              function);

sub callback_function
{
    my $self       = shift;
    my $attr_name  = shift;    # name of attribute which changed
    my $attr_value = shift;    # new value of attribute

    # do some stuff here
}
```

This is used to add a callback function to an object, associated with a particular attribute. Whenever the attribute is changed, the callback function is invoked, with the attribute name and new value passed as arguments.

Virtual Methods for Accessing Attributes

In addition to the getAttribute and setAttribute methods, this class also supports virtual methods for accessing attributes.

For example, if you have set an attribute FOOBAR, then you can call method foobar() on the object:

```
$object->setAttribute('FOOBAR', $value);
$value = $object->foobar;
```

This capability assumes that all attribute names will be in UPPERCASE; the resulting method names will be all lowercase.

This feature is particularly useful for manipulating the ID, LABEL, FROM, and TO attributes:

```
$node->label('label for my node');
$id = $node->id;
$edge-to($node);
```

Note: this feature won't work if you use an attribute name which is the same as an existing method for your object class, such as new or DESTROY.

Inheriting This Class

If you want to provide attribute methods for your class, you just need the following lines in your module:

```
use Graph::Element;
@ISA = qw(Graph::Element);
```

This will give your objects the **getAttribute()**, **setAttribute()**, and **addAttributeCallback()** methods.

When subclassing Graph::Element you shouldn't need to override the constructor (**new()**), but should be able to get away with overriding the **initialise()** function.

Restrictions

This class assumes that the object instance for your class is a blessed hash (associative array) reference.

Author

Neil Bowers, *neilb@cre.canon.co.uk*

Copyright

Copyright © 1997 Canon Research Centre Europe. All rights reserved. This module is free software; you can redistribute it and/or modify it under the same terms as Perl itself.

See Also

Graph::Node, for a description of the Node class

Graph::Edge, for a description of the Edge class

Graph::Kruskal—Kruskal's Algorithm for Minimal Spanning Trees in graphs

Computes the Minimal Spanning Tree of a given graph according to some cost function defined on the edges of the graph.

Synopsis

```
use Graph::Kruskal qw(define_vortices define_edges heapify makeheap
heapsort find union kruskal example);
use Graph::Kruskal qw(:all);
```

* Defines a list of vortices (integers > 0):

```
&define_vortices(2,3,5,7,11,13,17,19,23,29,31);
```

* Defines (non-directed) edges on the vortices previously defined (always in triplets: "from" vortice, "to" vortice and cost of that edge):

```
&define_edges( 2,13,3, 3,13,2, 5,13,1, 3,5,2, 3,29,21 );
```

* Main subroutine for sorting the edges according to their costs:

```
&heapify($i,$n);
```

* Routine to initialize sorting of the edges:

```
&makeheap($n);
```

- The famous **heapsort** algorithm (not needed for Kruskal's algorithm as a whole but included here for the sake of completeness) for sorting the edges according to their costs:

  ```
  &heapsort($n);
  ```

- Disjoint (!) sets are stored as trees in an array in this algorithm:

  ```
  &find($i);
  &union($i,$j);
  ```

  Each element of some set (a cell in the array) contains a pointer to (the number of) another element, up to the root element that does not point anywhere, but contains the (negative) number of elements the set contains. The number of the root element is also used as an identifier for the set.

Example:

i :	1	2	3	4	5	6	7	8
parent[i] :	-4	-3	1	2	1	-1	3	4

This array contains the three sets S1, S2 and S6:

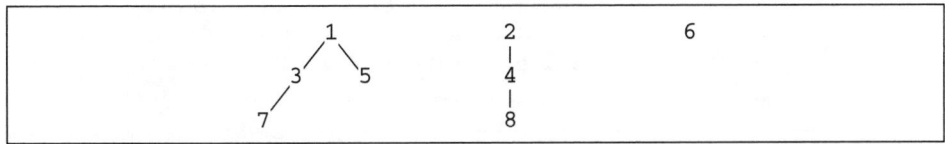

find returns the number of the root element (= the identifier of the set) of the tree in which the given element is contained:

```
find(a) := i  so that  a in Si
```

It also reduces the height of that tree by changing all the pointers from the given element up to the root element to point DIRECTLY to the root element.

Example:

i :	1	2	3	4	5	6	7	8
parent[i] :	-4	-3	1	2	1	-1	1	4

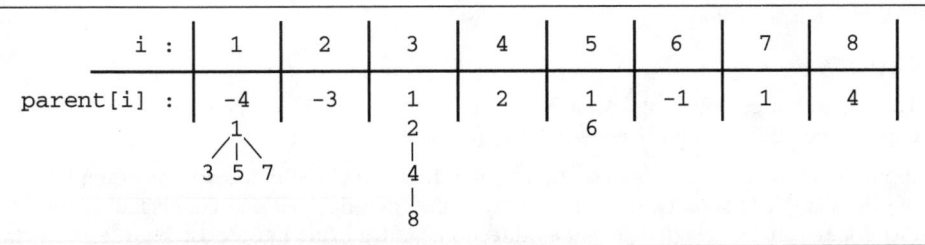

union takes the identifiers of two sets (= the numbers of their respective root elements) and merges the two sets by appending one of the two trees to the other. It always appends the *smaller* set to the *larger* one (to keep the height of the resulting tree as small as possible) and updates the number of elements contained in the resulting set which is stored in the root element's cell of the array.

Example:

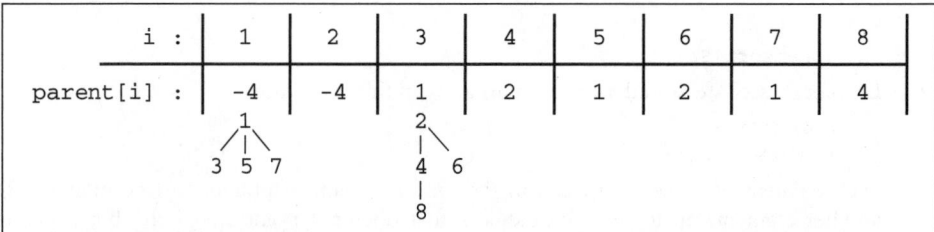

```
union(2,6) does the following:
complexity for O(n) "find" operations: O( G(n) n )
complexity for one "union" operation: O(1)
complexity for O(n) ( "find" + "union" ) operations: O( G(n) n )
where   G(n) := min{ j | F(j) >= n }
and     F(j) := 1           for j = 0
        F(j) := 2 ^ F(j-1)  for j > 0
also,   G(n) <= ld n        for all n
```

- This routine carries out the computations associated with Kruskal's algorithm.

    ```
    &kruskal();
    ```

    Returns an array of hashes (each hash containing the keys from, to and cost and the corresponding values) representing the minimal spanning tree of the graph previously defined by calls to define_vortices and define_edges.

    The result can also be found in @Graph::Kruskal::T.

    See the implementation of the subroutine example to see how to access this array directly (remember to fully qualify the name of this array in your program, i.e., use @Graph::Kruskal::T instead of just @T, since this array is not exported—or your program will not work!).

- Demonstrates how to use the various subroutines in this module.

    ```
    &example();
    ```

    Computes the minimal spanning tree of a sample graph.

    Just say use Graph::Kruskal qw(example); and &example(); in a little Perl script to see it "in action."

Description

This algorithm computes the Minimal Spanning Tree of a given graph according to some cost function defined on the edges of that graph.

Input: A set of vortices which constitute a graph (some cities on a map, for example); a set of edges (i.e., roads) between the vortices of the (non-directed and connected) graph (i.e., the edges can be traveled in either direction, and a path must exist between any two vortices); and the cost of each edge (for instance, the geographical distance).

Output: A set of edges forming a spanning tree (i.e., a set of edges linking all vortices, so that a path exists between any two vortices) which is free of circles (because it's a tree) and which is minimal in terms of the cost function defined on the set of edges.

See Aho, Hopcroft, Ullman, "The Design and Analysis of Computer Algorithms," for more details on the algorithm.

Version

This manpage documents Graph::Kruskal version 2.0.

Author

Steffen Beyer, *sb@sdm.de*

Copyright

Copyright © 1995, 1996, 1997 by Steffen Beyer. All rights reserved.

This package is free software; you can redistribute it and/or modify it under the same terms as Perl itself.

See Also

Math::MatrixBool(3), Math::MatrixReal(3), DFA::Kleene(3), Set::IntegerRange(3), Set::IntegerFast(3), Bit::Vector(3)

Graph::Node—object class for a node in a directed graph

Synopsis

```
use Graph::Node;
use Graph::Edge;
$parent = new Graph::Node('LABEL' => 'Parent Node');
$child  = new Graph::Node('LABEL' => 'Child Node');
$edge   = new Graph::Edge('FROM' => $parent,
                          'TO'   => $child);
$parent->save('simple.daVinci', 'daVinci');
```

Description

The Graph::Node module implements a *node* in a *directed graph*. A graph is constructed using Node and Edge objects; edges are defined with the Graph::Edge class.

Constructor

Create a new Node object. Returns a reference to a Graph::Node object:

```
$node = new Graph::Node('ID'    => 'identifier',
                        'LABEL' => 'text string'
                        );
```

The ID attribute is optional, and must be a unique string identifying the edge. If you do not specify the ID attribute, the edge will be assigned a unique identifier automatically.

The LABEL attribute is also optional, and specifies a text string which should be associated with the node. This should be used when drawing the Node, for example.

Methods

This class implements the following methods:

- setAttribute() sets the value of an attribute on the node
- getAttribute() gets the value of an attribute of the node
- save() saves the graph under the node in a specified file

The `save` method is described in the following paragraphs. The `setAttribute` and `getAttribute` methods are described in the documentation for the base class Graph::Element, where they are defined.

save—save directed graph to a file

`$filename`
> The name or full path of the file to save the directed graph into.

`$format`
> An optional string that specifies the format in which the graph should be saved. At the moment the only format supported is daVinci, which generates the file format used by the daVinci graph visualisation system.

The `save()` method is used to save a directed graph into a file. At the moment the graph is saved in the format used by the daVinci graph visualization system (daVinci v2.0).

The filename extension should be *.daVinci*, otherwise daVinci will complain.

Author

Neil Bowers, *neilb@cre.canon.co.uk*

Copyright

Copyright © 1997 Canon Research Centre Europe. All rights reserved. This module is free software; you can redistribute it and/or modify it under the same terms as Perl itself.

See Also

Graph::Node, for a description of the Node class

Graph::Element, for a description of the Base class, including the attribute methods

---

Kleene's Algorithm—a brief introduction to the theory behind it

Description

Semi-Rings

A Semi-Ring (`S, +, ., 0, 1`) is characterized by the following properties:

1. a) `(S, +, 0)` is a Semi-Group with neutral element `0`.

   b) `(S, ., 1)` is a Semi-Group with neutral element `1`.

   c) `0 . a = a . 0 = 0 for all a in S`.

2. `"+"` is commutative and *idempotent*, i.e., `a + a = a`.

3. Distributivity holds, i.e.,

   a) `a . ( b + c ) = a . b + a . c for all a,b,c in S`

   b) `( a + b ) . c = a . c + b . c for all a,b,c in S`

4. `SUM_{i=0}^{+infinity} ( a[i] )` exists, is well-defined and unique for all `a[i] in S`, and associativity, commutativity, and idempotency hold.

5. Distributivity for infinite series also holds, i.e.:

```
( SUM_{i=0}^{+infty} a[i] ) . ( SUM_{j=0}^{+infty} b[j] )
= SUM_{i=0}^{+infty} ( SUM_{j=0}^{+infty} ( a[i] . b[j] ) )
```

Examples

- `S1 = ({0,1}, |, &, 0, 1)`

  Boolean algebra. See also the *Math::MatrixBool(3)* manpage.

- `S2 = (pos. reals with 0 and +infty, min, +, +infty, 0)`

  Positive real numbers including zero and plus infinity. See also the Math::Matrix-Real(3) manpage.

- `S3 = (Pot(Sigma*), union, concat, {}, {''})`

  Formal languages over Sigma (= alphabet). See also the DFA::Kleene(3) manpage.

Operator '*'

Reflexive and transitive closure. Defines an operator called * as follows:

```
a in S   ==>   a* := SUM_{i=0}^{+infty} a^i
```

where:

```
a^0 = 1,   a^(i+1) = a . a^i
```

Then, also :

```
a* = 1 + a . a*,   0* = 1* = 1
```

holds.

Kleene's Algorithm

In its general form, Kleene's algorithm goes as follows:

```
for i := 1 to n do
    for j := 1 to n do
    begin
        C^0[i,j] := m(v[i],v[j]);
        if (i = j) then C^0[i,j] := C^0[i,j] + 1
    end
for k := 1 to n do
    for i := 1 to n do
        for j := 1 to n do
            C^k[i,j] := C^k-1[i,j] +
                        C^k-1[i,k] . ( C^k-1[k,k] )* . C^k-1[k,j]
for i := 1 to n do
    for j := 1 to n do
        c(v[i],v[j]) := C^n[i,j]
```

Kleene's Algorithm and Semi-Rings

Kleene's algorithm can be applied to any Semi-Ring having the properties listed previously.

Examples

- `S1 = ({0,1}, |, &, 0, 1)`

  `G(V,E)` is a graph with a set of vortices `V` and a set of edges `E`:

  ```
  m(v[i],v[j]) := ( (v[i],v[j]) in E ) ? 1 : 0
  ```

Kleene's algorithm then calculates:

```
c^{n}_{i,j} = ( path from v[i] to v[j] exists ) ? 1 : 0
```

using:

```
C^k[i,j] = C^k-1[i,j] | C^k-1[i,k] & C^k-1[k,j]
```

(Remember that 0* = 1* = 1.)

- S2 = (pos. reals with 0 and +infty, min, +, +infty, 0)

G(V,E) is a graph with a set of vortices V and a set of edges E, with costs m(v[i],v[j]) associated with each edge (v[i],v[j]) in E:

```
m(v[i],v[j]) := costs of (v[i],v[j])
for all (v[i],v[j]) in E
```

Set m(v[i],v[j]) := +infinity if an edge (v[i],v[j]) is not in E.

```
==> a* = 0 for all a in S2
==> C^k[i,j] = min( C^k-1[i,j] ,
    C^k-1[i,k] + C^k-1[k,j] )
```

Kleene's algorithm then calculates the costs of the "shortest" path from any v[i] to any other v[j]:

```
C^n[i,j] = costs of "shortest" path from v[i] to v[j]
```

- S3 = (Pot(Sigma*), union, concat, {}, {''})

M in DFA(Sigma) is a Deterministic Finite Automaton with a set of states Q, a subset F of Q of accepting states, and a transition function:

```
delta : Q x Sigma --> Q.
```

Define:

```
m(v[i],v[j]) :=
        { a in Sigma | delta( q[i] , a ) = q[j] }
```

and:

```
C^0[i,j] := m(v[i],v[j]);
if (i = j) then C^0[i,j] := C^0[i,j] union {''}
```

({''} is the set containing the empty string, whereas {} is the empty set.)

Then Kleene's algorithm calculates the language accepted by Deterministic Finite Automaton M using:

```
C^k[i,j] = C^k-1[i,j] union
    C^k-1[i,k] concat ( C^k-1[k,k] )* concat C^k-1[k,j]
```

and:

```
L(M) = UNION_{ q[j] in F } C^n[1,j]
```

(state q[1] is assumed to be the "start" state)

finally being the language recognized by Deterministic Finite Automaton M.

Note that instead of using Kleene's algorithm, you can also use the * operator on the associated matrix:

```
Define A[i,j] := m(v[i],v[j])
  ==> A*[i,j] = c(v[i],v[j])
```

Proof:

```
A* = SUM_{i=0}^{+infty} A^i
where A^0 = E_{n}
```

(Matrix with 1's in its main diagonal and 0's elsewhere.)

and:

```
A^(i+1) = A . A^i
```

Induction over k yields:

```
A^k[i,j] = c_{k}(v[i],v[j])
k = 0:   c_{0}(v[i],v[j]) = d_{i,j}
            with d_{i,j} := (i = j) ? 1 : 0
            and A^0 = E_{n} = [d_{i,j}]
k-1 -> k:
            c_{k}(v[i],v[j])
            = SUM_{l=1}^{n} m(v[i],v[l]) . c_{k-1}(v[l],v[j])
                = SUM_{l=1}^{n} ( a[i,l] . a[l,j] )
                = [a^{k}_{i,j}] = A^1 . A^(k-1) = A^k
```

qed.

In other words, the complexity of calculating the closure and doing matrix multiplications is of the same order $O(\ n^3\ )$ in Semi-Rings!

Author

This document is based on lecture notes and has been put into pod format by Steffen Beyer *(sb@sdm.de)*.

Copyright

Copyright © 1997 by Steffen Beyer. All rights reserved.

See Also

Math::MatrixBool(3), Math::MatrixReal(3), DFA::Kleene(3), which are all contained in the distribution of the Bit::Vector module, formerly named Set::IntegerFast.

Dijkstra's algorithm for shortest paths.

Math::Amoeba — multidimensional function minimization

Synopsis

```
use Math::Amoeba qw(ConstructVertices EvaluateVertices Amoeba
                                MinimiseND);
my ($vertice,$y)=MinimiseND(\@guess,\@scales,\&func,$tol,$itmax);
my @vertices=ConstructVertices(\@vector,\@offsets);
my @y=EvaluateVertices(\@vertices,\&func);
my ($vertice,$y)=Amoeba(\@vertices,\@y,\&func,$tol,$itmax);
```

Description

This is an implementation of the Downhill Simplex Method in Multidimensions (Nelder and Mead) for finding the (local) minimum of a function. Doing this in Perl makes it easy for that function to actually be the output of another program, such as a simulator.

Arrays and the function are passed by reference to the routines.

The simplest use is the `MinimiseND` function. This takes a reference to an array of guess values for the parameters at the function minimum, a reference to an array of scales for these parameters (sensible ranges around the guess in which to look), a reference to the function, and a convergence tolerance for the minimum and the maximum number of iterations to be taken. It returns an array consisting of a reference to the function parameters at the minimum and the value there.

The `Amoeba` function is the actual implementation of the Downhill Simplex Method in Multidimensions. It takes a reference to an array of references to arrays that are the initial n+1 vertices (where n is the number of function parameters), a reference to the function valuation at these vertices, a reference to the function, and a convergence tolerance for the minimum and the maximum number of iterations to be taken. It returns an array consisting of a reference to the function parameters at the minimum and the value there.

The `ConstructVertices` function is used by `MinimiseND` to construct the initial vertices for `Amoeba` as the initial guess plus the parameter scale parameters as vectors along the parameter axis.

The `EvaluateVertices` function takes these set of vertices, calling the function for each one and returning the vector of results.

Example

```
use Math::Amoeba qw(MinimiseND);
sub afunc {
  my ($a,$b)=@_;
  print "$a\t$b\n";
  return ($a-7)**2+($b+3)**2;
}
my @guess=(1,1);
my @scale=(1,1);
($p,$y)=MinimiseND(\@guess,\@scale,\&afunc,1e-7,100);
print "(",join(',',@{$p}),")=$y\n";
```

produces the output:

```
(6.99978191653352,-2.99981241563247)=1.00000008274829
```

Bugs

If the function value converges to exactly zero, then the condition for convergence fails and either the maximum iterations is exceeded or there is a divide by zero error. There is no obvious way to test for convergence in this case; however, adding 1 to the function value gives the expected behavior. That is, replace `\&afunc` with `sub { 1+afunc(@_); }` when calling the routines.

Let me know.

References

Numerical Recipes: The Art of Scientific Computing, by W.H. Press, B.P. Flannery, S.A. Teukolsky, W.T. Vetterling. Cambridge University Press. ISBN 0 521 30811 9.

Author

John A.R. Williams, *J.A.R.Williams@aston.ac.uk*

Math::Approx—approximate x,y values by a function

Description

Methods

new

The first argument after the class name must be a reference to a function that takes two arguments: the *degree* and the *x* value.

```
new Math::Approx (\&poly, 5, %x);
```

For interpolation with plain polynomials, *poly* can be defined as:

```
sub poly {
    my($n,$x) = @_;

    return $x ** $n;
}
```

The second argument is the maximum degree that should be used for interpolation. Degrees start with 0.

The rest of the arguments are treated as pairs of **x** and **y** samples that should be approximated.

The method returns a Math::Approx reference.

approx

The method returns the approximated **y** value for the **x** value given as the argument.

```
$approximation->approx(17);
```

fit

Returns the medim square error for the data points.

```
$approximation->fit;
```

plot

Prints all data pairs and the corresponding approximation pairs in a file whose filename is given as the argument. The file should be suitable for use with gnuplot(1).

```
$approximation->plot("tmp/app");
```

print

Prints information about the approximation on STDOUT.

```
$approximation->print;
```

Example

```
use Math::Approx;

sub poly {
    my($n,$x) = @_;

    return $x ** $n;
}

for (1..20) {
    $x{$_} = sin($_/10)*cos($_/30)+0.3*rand;
}
```

```
$a = new Math::Approx (\&poly, 5, %x);
$a->print;
$a->plot("mist");
print "Fit: ", $a->fit, "\n";
```

Author

Ulrich Pfeifer, *pfeifer@ls6.informatik.uni-dortmund.de*

See Also

gnuplot(1)

Math::Brent — one-dimensional function minimization

Synopsis

```
use Math::Brent qw(FindMinima BracketMinimum Brent Minimise1D);
my ($x,$y)=Minimise1D($guess,$scale,\&func,$tol,$itmax);
my ($ax,$bx,$cx,$fa,$fb,$fc)=BracketMinimum($ax,$bx,$cx,\&func);
my ($x,$y)=Brent($ax,$bx,$cx,\&func,$tol,$itmax);
```

Description

This is an implementation of **Brent**'s method for one-dimensional minimization of a function without using derivatives. This algorithm cleverly uses both the Golden Section Search and parabolic interpolation.

The main function, **Brent**, given a function reference \&func and a bracketing triplet of abscissas $ax, $bx, and $cx (such that $bx is between $ax and $cx and func($bx) is less than both func($ax) and func($cx)), isolates the minimum to a fractional precision of about $tol using Brent's method. A maximum number of iterations $itmax may be specified for this search—the maximum defaults to 100. An array is returned that consists of the abscissa of the minimum and the function value there.

The function **BracketMinimum**, given a function \&func and distinct initial points $ax and $bx, searches in the downhill direction (defined by the function as evaluated at the initial points) and returns an array of the three points $ax, $bx, and $cx that bracket the minimum of the function and the function values at those points.

The function **Minimise1D** provides a simple interface to the above two routines. Given a function \&func, an initial guess for its minimum, and its scaling ($guess,$scale) this routine isolates the minimum to a fractional precision of about $tol using Brent's method. A maximum number of iterations $itmax may be specified for this search—the maximum defaults to 100. The function returns an array consisting of the abscissa of the minimum and the function value there.

Example

```
use Math::Brent qw(Minimise1D);
sub func {
  my $x=shift ;
  return $x ? sin($x)/$x: 1;
}
```

```
my ($x,$y)=Minimise1D(1,1,\&func,1e-7);
print "Minimum is func($x)=$y\n";
```

produces the output:

```
Minimum is func(5.236068)=-.165388470697432
```

Bugs

Let me know of any problems.

Author

John A.R. Williams, *J.A.R.Williams@aston.ac.uk*

See Also

Numerical Recipes: The Art of Scientific Computing, by W.H. Press, B.P. Flannery, S.A. Teukolsky, W.T. Vetterling. Cambridge University Press. ISBN 0 521 30811 9.

Math::Derivative—first and second order differentiation of data

Synopsis

```
use Math::Derivative qw(Derivative1 Derivative2);
@dydx=Derivative1(\@x,\@y);
@d2ydx2=Derivative2(\@x,\@y);
@d2ydx2=Derivative2(\@x,\@y,$yp0,$ypn);
```

Description

This Perl package exports functions for performing numerical first-order (**Derivative1**) and second-order (**Derivative2**) differentiation on vectors of data. They both take references to two arrays containing the x and y ordinates of the data and return an array of the first or second derivative at the given x ordinates. **Derivative2** may optionally be given values to use for the first derivative at the start and end points of the data—otherwise "natural" values are used.

Bugs

Let me know.

Author

John A.R. Williams, *J.A.R.Williams@aston.ac.uk*

Math::Fortran—implements Fortran log10 and sign functions

Synopsis

```
use Math::Fortran qw(log10 sign);
$v=log10($x);
$v=sign($y);
$v=sign($x,$y);
```

Description

This module provides and exports some mathematical functions that are built into Fortran, but not Perl. Currently, there are only two functions included.

Functions

`log10`

> Log to the base of 10

`sign`

> *With 1 parameter*
> +1 if $y>=0, -1 otherwise.
>
> *With 2 parameters*
> +abs($x) if $y>=0, -abs($x) otherwise.

Bugs

I welcome other entries and bug reports for this module.

Author

John A.R. Williams, *J.A.R. Williams@aston.ac.uk*

Math::Matrix—multiply and invert matrices

Description

Methods

`new`

> Constructor arguments are a list of references to arrays of the same length. The arrays are copied. The method returns **undef** in case of error.
>
> ```
> $a = new Math::Matrix ([rand,rand,rand],
>                        [rand,rand,rand],
>                        [rand,rand,rand]);
> ```

`concat`

> Concatenates two matrices of the same row count. The result is a new matrix or **undef** in case of error.
>
> ```
> $b = new Math::Matrix ([rand],[rand],[rand]);
> $c = $a->concat($b);
> ```

`transpose`

> Returns the transposed matrix. This is the matrix where the columns and rows of the argument matrix are swapped.

`multiply`

> Multiplies two matrices where the length of the rows in the first matrix is the same as the length of the columns in the second matrix. Returns the product or **undef** in case of error.

`solve`

> Solves an equation system given by the matrix. The number of columns must be greater than the number of rows. If variables are dependent from each other, the second and all further of the dependent coefficients are 0. This lets the method

handle such systems. The method returns a matrix containing the solutions in its columns or **undef** in case of error.

print

> Prints the matrix on STDOUT. If the method has additional parameters, these are printed before the matrix is printed.

Example

```
use Math::Matrix;

srand(time);
$a = new Math::Matrix ([rand,rand,rand],
                       [rand,rand,rand],
                       [rand,rand,rand]);
$x = new Math::Matrix ([rand,rand,rand]);
$a->print("A\n");
$E = $a->concat($x->transpose);
$E->print("Equation system\n");
$s = $E->solve;
$s->print("Solutions s\n");
$a->multiply($s)->print("A*s\n");
```

Author

Ulrich Pfeifer, *pfeifer@ls6.informatik.uni-dortmund.de*

Math::MatrixBool—easy manipulation of matrices of booleans (boolean algebra)

Synopsis

```
use Math::MatrixBool;
```

• The matrix object constructor method:

```
$new_matrix = new Math::MatrixBool($rows,$columns);
```

An exception is raised if the necessary memory cannot be allocated.

• Alternate way of calling the matrix object constructor method:

```
$new_matrix = Math::MatrixBool->new($rows,$columns);
```

• Still another way of calling the matrix object constructor method (**$some_matrix** is not affected by this):

```
$new_matrix = $some_matrix->new($rows,$columns);
```

• This method allows you to read in a matrix from a string (for instance, from the keyboard, from a file, or from your code).

```
$new_matrix = Math::MatrixBool->new_from_string($string);
```

The syntax is simple: each row must start with " [" and end with "] \n" (where "\n" is the newline character and " " is a space or tab). In addition, it must contain one or more numbers, all separated from each other by spaces or tabs.

Additional spaces or tabs can be added at will, but no comments.

Numbers are either 0 or 1.

Examples:

```
$string = "[ 1 0 0 ]\n[ 1 1 0 ]\n[ 1 1 1 ]\n";
$matrix = Math::MatrixBool->new_from_string($string);
print "$matrix";
```

By the way, this prints:

```
[ 1 0 0 ]
[ 1 1 0 ]
[ 1 1 1 ]
```

But you can also do this in a much more comfortable way using the shell-like "here-document" syntax:

```
$matrix = Math::MatrixBool->new_from_string(<<'MATRIX');
[  1  0  0  0  0  0  1  ]
[  0  1  0  0  0  0  0  ]
[  0  0  1  0  0  0  0  ]
[  0  0  0  1  0  0  0  ]
[  0  0  0  0  1  0  0  ]
[  0  0  0  0  0  1  0  ]
[  1  0  0  0  0  0  1  ]
MATRIX
```

You can even use variables in the matrix:

```
$c1  =  $A1 * $x1 - $b1 >= 0  ?"1":"0";
$c2  =  $A2 * $x2 - $b2 >= 0  ?"1":"0";
$c3  =  $A3 * $x3 - $b3 >= 0  ?"1":"0";
$matrix = Math::MatrixBool->new_from_string(<<"MATRIX");
    [   1    0    0   ]
    [   0    1    0   ]
    [  $c1  $c2  $c3  ]
MATRIX
```

(Remember that you may use spaces and tabs to format the matrix to your taste.)

Note that this method uses exactly the same representation for a matrix as the **stringify** operator `""`. This means that you can convert any matrix into a string with `$string = "$matrix";` and read it back in later (for instance from a file).

If the string you supply (or someone else supplies) does not obey the syntax mentioned above, an exception is raised, which can be caught by **eval** as follows:

```
print "Please enter your matrix (in one line): ";
$string = <STDIN>;
$string =~ s/\\n/\n/g;
eval { $matrix = Math::MatrixBool->new_from_string($string); };
if ($@)
{
    print "$@";
    # ...
    # (error handling)
}
else
{
    # continue...
}
```

or as follows:

```
eval { $matrix = Math::MatrixBool->new_from_string(<<"MATRIX"); };
[   1    0    0   ]
[   0    1    0   ]
[  $c1  $c2  $c3  ]
MATRIX
if ($@)
# ...
```

Actually, the method shown above for reading a matrix from the keyboard is a little awkward, since you have to enter a lot of \n's for the newlines.

A better way is shown in this piece of code:

```
while (1)
{
  print "\nPlease enter your matrix ";
  print "(multiple lines, <ctrl-D> = done):\n";
  eval { $new_matrix =
      Math::MatrixBool->new_from_string(join('',<STDIN>)); };
  if ($@)
  {
      $@ =~ s/\s+at\b.*?$//;
      print "${@}Please try again.\n";
  }
  else { last; }
}
```

Possible error messages from the **new_from_string**() method are:

```
Math::MatrixBool::new_from_string(): syntax error in input string
Math::MatrixBool::new_from_string(): empty input string
```

If the input string has rows with varying numbers of columns, the following warning is printed to STDERR:

```
Math::MatrixBool::new_from_string(): missing elements will be set
to zero!
```

If everything is okay, the method returns an object reference to the (newly allocated) matrix containing the elements you specified.

- Returns the dimensions (the number of rows and columns) of the given matrix:

  ```
  ($rows,$columns) = $matrix->Dim();
  ```

- Sets all elements in the matrix to 0:

  ```
  $matrix->Empty();
  ```

- Sets all elements in the matrix to 1:

  ```
  $matrix->Fill();
  ```

- Flips (i.e., complements) all elements in the given matrix:

  ```
  $matrix->Flip();
  ```

- Sets all elements in the matrix to 0:

  ```
  $matrix->Zero();
  ```

- Fills the matrix with 1's in the main diagonal and 0's elsewhere:

  ```
  $matrix->One();
  ```

Note that multiplying this matrix with itself yields the same matrix again, provided it is quadratic.

- Sets a given element to 1:

      $matrix->Bit_On($row,$column);

- Alias for `Bit_On()`, deprecated:

      $matrix->Insert($row,$column);

- Sets a given element to 0:

      $matrix->Bit_Off($row,$column);

- Alias for `Bit_Off()`, deprecated:

      $matrix->Delete($row,$column);

- Flips (i.e., complements) a given element and returns its new value:

      $boolean = $matrix->bit_flip($row,$column);

- Alias for `bit_flip()`, deprecated:

      $boolean = $matrix->flip($row,$column);

- Tests whether a given element is set:

      $boolean = $matrix->bit_test($row,$column);

- Tests whether a given element is set (alias for `bit_test()`):

      $boolean = $matrix->contains($row,$column);

- Alias for `bit_test()`, deprecated:

      $boolean = $matrix->in($row,$column);

- Calculates the number of elements contained in the given matrix:

      $elements = $matrix->Number_of_elements();

- Calculates the "maximum"-norm of the given matrix:

      $norm_max = $matrix->Norm_max();

- Calculates the "1"-norm of the given matrix:

      $norm_one = $matrix->Norm_one();

- Calculates the sum of matrix2 and matrix3 and stores the result in matrix1 (in-place is also possible):

      $matrix1->Addition($matrix2,$matrix3);

- Calculates the product of matrix1 and matrix2 and returns an object reference to a new matrix where the result is stored:

      $product_matrix = $matrix1->Multiplication($matrix2);

- Computes the reflexive transitive closure of the given matrix and returns a new matrix containing the result. (The original matrix is not changed by this in any way.)

      $closure = $matrix->Kleene();

Uses a variant of Kleene's algorithm. See the *Math::Kleene(3)* manpage for more details about this algorithm.

This algorithm is mainly used in graph theory. Each position in the matrix corresponds to a (directed) possible connection ("edge") between two points ("vertices") of a graph. Each position in the matrix contains a 1 if the corresponding edge is part of the graph and a 0 if not.

Computing the closure of this matrix means finding out if there is a path (consisting of one or more edges) from any vortice of the graph to any other.

Note that there are more applications of Kleene's algorithm in other fields as well (see also Math::MatrixReal(3), DFA::Kleene(3), Math::Kleene(3)).

- Calculates the union of matrix2 and matrix3 and stores the result in matrix1 (in-place is also possible):

      $matrix1->Union($matrix2,$matrix3);

- Calculates the intersection of matrix2 and matrix3 and stores the result in matrix1 (in-place is also possible):

      $matrix1->Intersection($matrix2,$matrix3);

- Calculates matrix2 "minus" matrix3 (= **matrix2 \ matrix3**) and stores the result in matrix1 (in-place is also possible):

      $matrix1->Difference($matrix2,$matrix3);

  Note that this is set difference, not matrix difference. Matrix difference degenerates to (i.e., is the same as) matrix addition in a boolean algebra.

- Calculates the exclusive-or (which in the case of a boolean algebra happens to be the same as the addition) of matrix2 and matrix3 and stores the result in matrix1 (in-place is also possible):

      $matrix1->ExclusiveOr($matrix2,$matrix3);

- Calculates the complement of matrix2 and stores the result in matrix1 (in-place is also possible):

      $matrix1->Complement($matrix2);

- Tests if matrix1 is the same as matrix2:

      $boolean = $matrix1->equal($matrix2);

- Tests if matrix1 is a subset of matrix2:

      $boolean = $matrix1->subset($matrix2);

- Alias for **subset**(), deprecated:

      $boolean = $matrix1->inclusion($matrix2);

- Tests if matrix1 comes lexically before matrix2 (i.e., if (**matrix1 <= matrix2**) holds) as though the two bit vectors used to represent the two matrices were two large numbers in binary representation:

      $boolean = $matrix1->lexorder($matrix2);

  (Note that this is an *arbitrary* order relationship!)

- Lexically compares matrix1 and matrix2 and returns –1, 0, or 1 if (**matrix1 < matrix2**), (**matrix1 == matrix2**) or (**matrix1 > matrix2**) holds, respectively:

      $result = $matrix1->Compare($matrix2);

  (Again, the two bit vectors representing the two matrices are compared as though they were two large numbers in binary representation.)

- Copies the contents of matrix2 to an already existing matrix1:

      $matrix1->Copy($matrix2);

- Returns an object reference to a new, but empty, matrix of the same size as **some_matrix**:

      $new_matrix = $some_matrix->Shadow();

- Returns an object reference to a new matrix of the same size as **some_matrix**; the contents of **some_matrix** have already been copied to the new matrix:

```
$twin_matrix = $some_matrix->Clone();
```

Hint: Method names all in lowercase indicate a boolean return value (except for **new()** and **new_from_string()**, of course).

Please refer to "Overloaded Operators" below for ways of using overloaded operators instead of explicit method calls to facilitate calculations with matrices.

Description

This class lets you dynamically create boolean matrices of arbitrary size and perform all the basic operations for matrices on them, like:

- Setting or deleting elements
- Testing whether a certain element is set
- Computing the sum, difference, product, closure, and complement of matrices

  You can also compute the union, intersection, difference, and exclusive-or of the underlying bit vector.

- Copying matrices
- Testing two matrices for equality or inclusion (subset relationship)
- Computing the number of elements and the norm of a matrix

Please refer to "Overloaded Operators" below for ways of using overloaded operators instead of explicit method calls in order to facilitate calculations with matrices!

Overloaded Operators

Calculations with matrices can not only be performed with explicit method calls using this module, but also through "magical" overloaded arithmetic and relational operators.

For instance, instead of writing:

```
$matrix1 = Math::MatrixBool->new($rows,$columns);
$matrix2 = Math::MatrixBool->new($rows,$columns);
$matrix3 = Math::MatrixBool->new($rows,$columns);
[...]
$matrix3->Multiplication($matrix1,$matrix2);
```

you can just say:

```
$matrix1 = Math::MatrixBool->new($rows,$columns);
$matrix2 = Math::MatrixBool->new($rows,$columns);
[...]
$matrix3 = $matrix1 * $matrix2;
```

That's all!

Here is the list of all "magical" overloaded operators and their semantics (meaning):

Unary operators
    -, ~, abs, testing, !, ""

Binary (arithmetic) operators
    +, *, |, -, &, ^

Binary (relational) operators
    ==, !=, <, <=, >, >=

Binary (relational) operators

cmp, eq, ne, lt, le, gt, ge

Note that both arguments to a binary operator from the list above must be matrices; numbers or other types of data are not permitted as arguments and produce an error message.

—

Unary Minus ($matrix2 = -$matrix1;)

Same as "Complement," next item in list.

~

Complement ($matrix2 = ~$matrix1;)

The operator ~ (or unary -) computes the complement of the given matrix.

abs

Absolute value ($no_of_elem = abs($matrix);)

Here, the absolute value of a matrix has been defined as the number of elements the given matrix contains. This is *not* the same as the "norm" of a matrix!

test

Boolean test (if ($matrix) { ... })

You can actually test a matrix as though it were a boolean value.

No special operator is needed for this; Perl automatically calls the appropriate method in this package if $matrix is a blessed reference to an object of the Math::MatrixBool class or one of its derived classes.

This operation returns true (1) if the given matrix is not empty and false (") otherwise.

!

Negated boolean test (if (! $matrix) { ... })

You can also perform a negated test on a matrix as though it were a boolean value. For example:

```
if (! $matrix) { ... }
unless ($matrix) { ... }      #  internally, same as above!
```

This operation returns true (1) if the given matrix is empty and false (") otherwise.

" "

"Stringification" (print "$matrix";)

It is possible to get a string representation of a given matrix by just putting the matrix object reference between double quotes.

Note that in general, the string representation of a matrix spans over multiple lines (i.e., the string that is generated contains \n characters, one at the end of each row of the matrix).

Example:

```
$matrix = new Math::MatrixBool(5,6);
$matrix->One();
print "$matrix";
```

This will print:

```
[ 1 0 0 0 0 0 ]
[ 0 1 0 0 0 0 ]
[ 0 0 1 0 0 0 ]
[ 0 0 0 1 0 0 ]
[ 0 0 0 0 1 0 ]
```

+

Addition ($matrix3 = $matrix1 + $matrix2;)

The + operator calculates the sum of two matrices.

Examples:

```
$all   =  $odd + $even;
$all   += $odd;
$all   += $even;
```

Note that the '++' operator produces an error message if applied to an object of this class, because adding a number to a matrix makes no sense.

*

Multiplication ($matrix3 = $matrix1 * $matrix2;)

The * operator calculates the matrix product of two matrices.

Examples:

```
$test   =  $one * $one;
$test   *= $one;
$test   *= $test;
```

Note that you can use matrices of any size as long as their numbers of rows and columns correspond in the following way (example):

```
$matrix_3 = $matrix_1 * $matrix_2;
                    [ 2 2 ]
                    [ 2 2 ]
                    [ 2 2 ]
         [ 1 1 1 ]  [ 3 3 ]
         [ 1 1 1 ]  [ 3 3 ]
         [ 1 1 1 ]  [ 3 3 ]
         [ 1 1 1 ]  [ 3 3 ]
```

That is, the number of columns of **matrix1** is the same as the number of rows of **matrix2**, and the number of rows and columns of the resulting **matrix3** is determined by the number of rows of **matrix1** and the number of columns of **matrix2**, respectively.

This way you can also perform the multiplication of a matrix with a vector, since a vector is just a degenerated matrix with several rows but only one column, or just one row and several columns.

|

Union ($matrix3 = $matrix1 | $matrix2;)

The | operator is used to calculate the union of two matrices (of corresponding elements).

Examples:

```
$all   =  $odd | $even;
$all   |= $odd;
$all   |= $even;
```

−

Difference ($matrix3 = $matrix1 - $matrix2;)

The − operator calculates the (dotted) difference of two matrices, i.e.,

```
0 - 0 == 0
0 - 1 == 0
1 - 0 == 1
1 - 1 == 0
```

for each corresponding element.

Examples:

```
$odd  = $all  - $even;
$all  -= $even;
```

Note that the -- operator produces an error message if applied to an object of this class, because subtracting a number from a matrix makes no sense.

&

Intersection ($matrix3 = $matrix1 & $matrix2;)

The & operator is used to calculate the intersection of two matrices (of the corresponding elements).

Examples:

```
$rest = $all & $even;
$all  &= $even;
```

^

Exclusive-or ($matrix3 = $matrix1 ^ $matrix2;)

The ^ operator is used to calculate the exclusive-or of two matrices (i.e., of their corresponding elements).

In fact this operation is identical with the addition of two matrices in this case of a boolean algebra.

Examples:

```
$odd  = $all  ^ $even;
$all  ^= $even;
```

==

Test for equality (if ($matrix1 == $matrix2) { ... })

This operator tests two matrices for equality.

Note that without operator overloading, ($matrix1 == $matrix2) would test whether the two references pointed to the same object.

With operator overloading in effect, ($matrix1 == $matrix2) tests whether the two matrix objects contain exactly the same elements.

!=

Test for non-equality (if ($matrix1 != $matrix2) { ... })

This operator tests whether two matrices are different.

Note again that this tests whether the contents of the two matrices are not the same, and not whether the two references are different.

<

Test for true subset (if ($matrix1 < $matrix2) { ... })

This operator tests whether $matrix1 is a true subset of $matrix2, i.e., whether the elements contained in $matrix1 are also contained in $matrix2, but not all elements contained in $matrix2 are contained in $matrix1.

Example:

```
        [ 1 0 0 0 0 ]                            [ 1 0 0 0 1 ]
        [ 0 1 0 0 0 ]                            [ 0 1 0 0 0 ]
        [ 0 0 1 0 0 ]  is a true subset of       [ 0 0 1 0 0 ]
        [ 0 0 0 1 0 ]                            [ 0 0 0 1 0 ]
        [ 1 0 0 0 1 ]                            [ 1 0 0 0 1 ]
        [ 1 0 0 0 0 ]                            [ 1 0 0 0 1 ]
        [ 0 1 0 0 0 ]                            [ 0 1 0 0 0 ]
  but   [ 0 0 1 0 0 ]  is not a subset of        [ 0 0 1 0 0 ]
        [ 0 0 0 1 0 ]                            [ 0 0 0 1 0 ]
        [ 1 0 0 0 1 ]                            [ 0 0 0 0 1 ]
 (nor vice-versa!)
        [ 1 0 0 0 1 ]                            [ 1 0 0 0 1 ]
        [ 0 1 0 0 0 ]                            [ 0 1 0 0 0 ]
  and   [ 0 0 1 0 0 ]  is a subset of            [ 0 0 1 0 0 ]
        [ 0 0 0 1 0 ]                            [ 0 0 0 1 0 ]
        [ 1 0 0 0 1 ]                            [ 1 0 0 0 1 ]
```

but not a true subset. because the two matrices are identical.

<=

Test for subset (`if ($matrix1 <= $matrix2) { ... }`)

This operator tests whether $matrix1 is a subset of $matrix2, i.e.. whether all elements contained in $matrix1 are also contained in $matrix2.

This also evaluates to **true** when the two matrices are the same.

>

Test for true superset (`if ($matrix1 > $matrix2) { ... }`)

This operator tests whether $matrix1 is a true superset of $matrix2, i.e. whether all elements contained in $matrix2 are also contained in $matrix1, but not all elements contained in $matrix1 are contained in $matrix2.

Note that (`$matrix1 > $matrix2`) is exactly the same as (`$matrix2 < $matrix1`).

>=

Test for superset (`if ($matrix1 >= $matrix2) { ... }`)

This operator tests whether $matrix1 is a superset of $matrix2, i.e., whether all elements contained in $matrix2 are also contained in $matrix1.

It also evaluates to **true** when the two matrices are equal.

Note that (`$matrix1 >= $matrix2`) is exactly the same as (`$matrix2 <= $matrix1`).

cmp

Compare (`$result = $matrix1 cmp $matrix2;`)

This operator compares the two matrices lexically, i.e., it regards the two bit vectors representing the two matrices as two large (unsigned) numbers in binary representation and returns −1 if the number for $matrix1 is smaller than that for $matrix2, 0 if the two numbers are the same (i.e., when the two matrices are equal!) or 1 if the number representing $matrix1 is larger than the number representing $matrix2.

Note that this comparison has nothing whatsoever to do with algebra; it is just an arbitrary order relationship.

It is only intended to provide an (arbitrary) order by which (for example) an array of matrices can be sorted; for instance, to find out quickly (using binary search) if a specific matrix has already been produced in some matrix-producing process or not.

eq

Equal

ne

Not equal

lt

Less than

le

Less than or equal

gt

Greater than

ge

Greater than or equal

These are all operators derived from the `cmp` operator (see previous information).

They can be used instead of the `cmp` operator to make the intended type of comparison more obvious in your code.

For instance, (`$matrix1 le $matrix2`) is much more readable and clearer than ((`$matrix1 cmp $matrix2) <= 0`).

Version

This manpage documents Math::MatrixBool version 4.0.

Author

Steffen Beyer, *sb@sdm.de*

Copyright

Copyright © 1996, 1997 by Steffen Beyer. All rights reserved.

This package is free software; you can redistribute it and/or modify it under the same terms as Perl itself.

See Also

Bit::Vector(3), Math::MatrixReal(3), DFA::Kleene(3), Math::Kleene(3), Set::IntegerFast(3), Set::IntegerRange(3)

Math::MatrixReal—matrix of reals

Implements the data type "matrix of reals" (and consequently also "vector of reals").

Synopsis

* Make the methods and overloaded operators of this module available to your program:

  ```
  use Math::MatrixReal;
  ```

* Use one of these two variants to import (all) the functions which the module offers for export; currently these are **min()** and **max()**:

  ```
  use Math::MatrixReal qw(min max);
  use Math::MatrixReal qw(:all);
  ```

* The matrix object constructor method:

  ```
  $new_matrix = new Math::MatrixReal($rows,$columns);
  ```

  Note that this method is implicitly called by many of the other methods in this module!

* An alternate way of calling the matrix object constructor method:

  ```
  $new_matrix = Math::MatrixReal->new($rows,$columns);
  ```

* Still another way of calling the matrix object constructor method.

  ```
  $new_matrix = $some_matrix->new($rows,$columns);
  ```

  Matrix **$some_matrix** is not changed by this in any way.

* This method allows you to read in a matrix from a string (for instance, from the keyboard, from a file, or from your code):

  ```
  $new_matrix = Math::MatrixReal->new_from_string($string);
  ```

  The syntax is simple: each row must start with "[" and end with "]\n" (where "\n" is the newline character and " " is a space or tab) and must contain one or more numbers, all separated from each other by spaces or tabs.

  Additional spaces or tabs can be added at will, but no comments.

  Examples:

  ```
  $string = "[ 1 2 3 ]\n[ 2 2 -1 ]\n[ 1 1 1 ]\n";
  $matrix = Math::MatrixReal->new_from_string($string);
  print "$matrix";
  ```

  By the way, this prints:

  ```
  [  1.000000000000E+00  2.000000000000E+00  3.000000000000E+00 ]
  [  2.000000000000E+00  2.000000000000E+00 -1.000000000000E+00 ]
  [  1.000000000000E+00  1.000000000000E+00  1.000000000000E+00 ]
  ```

  But you can also do this in a much more comfortable way using the shell-like "here-document" syntax:

  ```
  $matrix = Math::MatrixReal->new_from_string(<<'MATRIX');
  [ 1 0 0 0 0 0  1 ]
  [ 0 1 0 0 0 0  0 ]
  [ 0 0 1 0 0 0  0 ]
  [ 0 0 0 1 0 0  0 ]
  [ 0 0 0 0 1 0  0 ]
  [ 0 0 0 0 0 1  0 ]
  [ 1 0 0 0 0 0 -1 ]
  MATRIX
  ```

  You can even use variables in the matrix:

  ```
  $c1 =   2 /  3;
  $c2 =  -2 /  5;
  $c3 =  26 /  9;
  ```

```
$matrix = Math::MatrixReal->new_from_string(<<"MATRIX");
  [   3    2    0   ]
  [   0    3    2   ]
  [  $c1  $c2  $c3  ]
MATRIX
```

(Remember that you may use spaces and tabs to format the matrix to your taste.)

Note that this method uses exactly the same representation for a matrix as the **string-ify** operator " ": this means that you can convert any matrix into a string with **$string = "$matrix"**; and read it back in later (for instance from a file).

Note, however, that you may suffer a precision loss in this process because only 13 digits are supported in the mantissa when printed!

If the string you supply (or someone else supplies) does not obey the syntax mentioned above, an exception is raised, which can be caught by **eval** as follows:

```
print "Please enter your matrix (in one line): ";
$string = <STDIN>;
$string =~ s/\\n/\n/g;
eval { $matrix = Math::MatrixReal->new_from_string($string); };
if ($@)
{
    print "$@";
    # ...
    # (error handling)
}
else
{
    # continue...
}
```

or as follows:

```
eval { $matrix = Math::MatrixReal->new_from_string(<<"MATRIX"); };
  [   3    2    0   ]
  [   0    3    2   ]
  [  $c1  $c2  $c3  ]
MATRIX
if ($@)
# ...
```

Actually, the method shown above for reading a matrix from the keyboard is a little awkward, since you have to enter a lot of \ns for the newlines.

A better way is shown in this piece of code:

```
while (1)
{
    print "\nPlease enter your matrix ";
    print "(multiple lines, <ctrl-D> = done):\n";
    eval { $new_matrix =
        Math::MatrixReal->new_from_string(join('',<STDIN>)); };
    if ($@)
    {
        $@ =~ s/\s+at\b.*?$//;
        print "${@}Please try again.\n";
    }
    else { last; }
}
```

Possible error messages of the **new_from_string()** method are:

```
Math::MatrixReal::new_from_string(): syntax error in input string
Math::MatrixReal::new_from_string(): empty input string
```

If the input string has rows with varying numbers of columns, the following warning is printed to STDERR:

```
Math::MatrixReal::new_from_string(): missing elements will be set
to zero!
```

If everything is okay, the method returns an object reference to the (newly allocated) matrix containing the elements you specified.

- Returns an object reference to a new, but empty, matrix (filled with 0's) of the same size as matrix **$some_matrix**.

  ```
  $new_matrix = $some_matrix->shadow();
  ```

  Matrix **$some_matrix** is not changed by this in any way.

- Copies the contents of matrix **$matrix2** to an already existing matrix **$matrix1**, which must have the same size as matrix **$matrix2**.

  ```
  $matrix1->copy($matrix2);
  ```

  Matrix **$matrix2** is not changed by this in any way.

- Returns an object reference to a new matrix of the same size as matrix **$some_matrix**. The contents of matrix **$some_matrix** have already been copied to the new matrix **$twin_matrix**.

  ```
  $twin_matrix = $some_matrix->clone();
  ```

  Matrix **$some_matrix** is not changed by this in any way.

- This is a projection method that returns an object reference to a new matrix (which in fact is a (row) vector since it has only one row) to which row number **$row** of matrix **$matrix** has already been copied.

  ```
  $row_vector = $matrix->row($row);
  ```

  Matrix **$matrix** is not changed by this in any way.

- This is a projection method which returns an object reference to a NEW matrix (which in fact is a (column) vector since it has only one column) to which column number **$column** of matrix **$matrix** has already been copied.

  ```
  $column_vector = $matrix->column($column);
  ```

  Matrix **$matrix** is not changed by this in any way.

- Assigns a zero to every element of the matrix **$matrix**, i.e., erases all values previously stored there, thereby effectively transforming the matrix into a zero matrix or null matrix, the neutral element of the addition operation in a Ring.

  ```
  $matrix->zero();
  ```

  (For instance, the [quadratic] matrices with n rows and columns and matrix addition and multiplication form a Ring. The most prominent characteristic of a Ring is that multiplication is not commutative, i.e., in general, **matrix1 * matrix2** is not the same as **matrix2 * matrix1**!)

- Assigns 1's to the elements on the main diagonal (elements (1,1), (2,2), (3,3) and so on) of matrix **$matrix** and 0's to all others, thereby erasing all values previously stored there and transforming the matrix into a one matrix, the neutral element of the multiplication operation in a Ring.

  ```
  $matrix->one();
  ```

(If the matrix is quadratic [which this method doesn't require], then multiplying the matrix with itself yields this same matrix again, and multiplying it with some other matrix leaves that other matrix unchanged.)

- Explicitly assigns a value $value to a single element of the matrix $matrix, located in row $row and column $column, thereby replacing the value previously stored there.

      $matrix->assign($row,$column,$value);

- Returns the value of a specific element of the matrix $matrix, located in row $row and column $column.

      $value = $matrix->element($row,$column);

- Returns a list of two items, representing the number of rows and columns the given matrix $matrix contains.

      ($rows,$columns) = $matrix->dim();

- Returns the "one" norm of the given matrix $matrix.

      $norm_one = $matrix->norm_one();

The "one" norm is defined as follows:

> For each column, the sum of the absolute values of the elements in the different rows of that column is calculated. Finally, the maximum of these sums is returned.

Note that the "one" norm and the maximum norm are mathematically equivalent, although for the same matrix they usually yield a different value.

Therefore, you should only compare values that have been calculated using the same norm.

Throughout this package, the "one" norm is (arbitrarily) used for all comparisons, for the sake of uniformity and comparability, except for the iterative methods solve_ GSM(), solve_SSM(), and solve_RM(), which use either norm depending on the matrix itself.

- Returns the maximum norm of the given matrix $matrix.

      $norm_max = $matrix->norm_max();

The maximum norm is defined as follows:

> For each row, the sum of the absolute values of the elements in the different columns of that row is calculated. Finally, the maximum of these sums is returned.

Note that the maximum norm and the "one" norm are mathematically equivalent, although for the same matrix they usually yield a different value.

Therefore, you should only compare values that have been calculated using the same norm!

Throughout this package, the "one" norm is (arbitrarily) used for all comparisons, for the sake of uniformity and comparability, except for the iterative methods solve_ GSM(), solve_SSM(), and solve_RM() which use either norm depending on the matrix itself.

- Calculates the negative of matrix $matrix2 (i.e., multiplies all elements with –1) and stores the result in matrix $matrix1 (which must already exist and have the same size as matrix $matrix2).

      $matrix1->negate($matrix2);

This operation can also be carried out in-place, i.e., input and output matrix may be identical.

- Calculates the transposed matrix of matrix $matrix2 and stores the result in matrix $matrix1 (which must already exist and have the same size as matrix $matrix2).

      $matrix1->transpose($matrix2);

This operation can also be carried out in-place, i.e., input and output matrix may be identical.

Transposition is a symmetry operation: imagine you rotate the matrix along the axis of its main diagonal (going through elements (1,1), (2,2), (3,3) and so on) by 180 degrees.

Another way of looking at it is to say that rows and columns are swapped. In fact the contents of element (i,j) are swapped with those of element (j,i).

Note that (especially for vectors) it makes a big difference if you have a row vector, like this:

      [-1 0 1]

or a column vector, like this:

      [-1]
      [0]
      [1]

the one vector being the transposed of the other.

This is especially true for the matrix product of two vectors:

```
                   [ -1 ]
    [ -1 0 1 ] * [  0 ]  =  [ 2 ] ,  whereas
                   [  1 ]

                              *        [ -1  0  1 ]
    [ -1 ]                                                      [  1  0 -1 ]
    [  0 ] * [ -1 0 1 ]  =  [ -1 ]   [  1  0 -1 ]  =  [  0  0  0 ]
    [  1 ]                     [  0 ]   [  0  0  0 ]     [ -1  0  1 ]
                              [  1 ]   [ -1  0  1 ]
```

So be careful about what you really mean.

Hint: Throughout this module, whenever a vector is explicitly required for input, a *column* vector is expected.

- Calculates the sum of matrix $matrix2 and matrix $matrix3 and stores the result in matrix $matrix1 (which must already exist and have the same size as matrix $matrix2 and matrix $matrix3).

      $matrix1->add($matrix2,$matrix3);

This operation can also be carried out in-place, i.e., the output and one (or both) of the input matrices may be identical.

- Calculates the difference of matrix $matrix2 minus matrix $matrix3 and stores the result in matrix $matrix1 (which must already exist and have the same size as matrix $matrix2 and matrix $matrix3).

      $matrix1->subtract($matrix2,$matrix3);

This operation can also be carried out in-place, i.e., the output and one (or both) of the input matrices may be identical.

Note that this operation is the same as $matrix1->add($matrix2,-$matrix3);, although the latter is a little less efficient.

- Calculates the product of matrix $matrix2 and the number $scalar (i.e., multiplies each element of matrix $matrix2 with the factor $scalar) and stores the result in matrix $matrix1 (which must already exist and have the same size as matrix $matrix2).

    ```
    $matrix1->multiply_scalar($matrix2,$scalar);
    ```

  This operation can also be carried out in-place, i.e., input and output matrix may be identical.

- Calculates the product of matrix $matrix1 and matrix $matrix2 and returns an object reference to a new matrix $product_matrix in which the result of this operation has been stored.

    ```
    $product_matrix = $matrix1->multiply($matrix2);
    ```

  Note that the dimensions of the two matrices $matrix1 and $matrix2 (i.e., their numbers of rows and columns) must harmonize in the following way (example):

    ```
                    [ 2  2 ]
                    [ 2  2 ]
                    [ 2  2 ]
    [ 1  1  1 ]     [ *  * ]
    [ 1  1  1 ]     [ *  * ]
    [ 1  1  1 ]     [ *  * ]
    [ 1  1  1 ]     [ *  * ]
    ```

  That is, the number of columns of matrix $matrix1 has to be the same as the number of rows of matrix $matrix2.

  The number of rows and columns of the resulting matrix $product_matrix is determined by the number of rows of matrix $matrix1 and the number of columns of matrix $matrix2, respectively.

- Returns the minimum of the two numbers, **number1** and **number2**.

    ```
    $minimum = Math::MatrixReal::min($number1,$number2);
    ```

- Returns the maximum of the two numbers, **number1** and **number2**.

    ```
    $minimum = Math::MatrixReal::max($number1,$number2);
    ```

- Copies the matrix $cost_matrix (which has to be quadratic) to a new matrix of the same size (i.e., it clones the input matrix) and applies Kleene's algorithm to it.

    ```
    $minimal_cost_matrix = $cost_matrix->kleene();
    ```

  See the Math::Kleene(3) manpage for more details about this algorithm!

  The method returns an object reference to the new matrix.

  Matrix $cost_matrix is not changed by this method in any way.

- This method is used to improve the numerical stability when solving linear equation systems.

    ```
    ($norm_matrix,$norm_vector) = $matrix->normalize($vector);
    ```

  Suppose you have a matrix A and a vector b and you want to find out a vector x so that A * x = b, i.e., the vector x which solves the equation system represented by the matrix A and the vector b.

  Applying this method to the pair (A,b) yields a pair (A´,b´) where each row has been divided by (the absolute value of) the greatest coefficient appearing in that row. So this coefficient becomes equal to 1 (or −1) in the new pair (A´,b´) (all others become smaller than 1 and greater than −1).

Note that this operation does not change the equation system itself because the same division is carried out on either side of the equation sign.

The method requires a quadratic (!) matrix $matrix and a vector $vector for input (the vector must be a column vector with the same number of rows as the input matrix) and returns a list of two items which are object references to a new matrix and a new vector, in this order.

The output matrix and vector are clones of the input matrix and vector to which the operation explained above has been applied.

The input matrix and vector are not changed by this in any way.

Example of how this method can affect the result of the methods to solve equation systems (explained immediately below following this method):

Consider the following little program:

```perl
#!perl -w
use Math::MatrixReal qw(new_from_string);
$A = Math::MatrixReal->new_from_string(<<"MATRIX");
[  1    2    3   ]
[  5    7   11   ]
[ 23   19   13   ]
MATRIX
$b = Math::MatrixReal->new_from_string(<<"MATRIX");
[   0   ]
[   1   ]
[  29   ]
MATRIX
$LR = $A->decompose_LR();
if (($dim,$x,$B) = $LR->solve_LR($b))
{
    $test = $A * $x;
    print "x = \n$x";
    print "A * x = \n$test";
}
($A_,$b_) = $A->normalize($b);
$LR = $A_->decompose_LR();
if (($dim,$x,$B) = $LR->solve_LR($b_))
{
    $test = $A * $x;
    print "x = \n$x";
    print "A * x = \n$test";
}
```

This prints:

```
x =
[   1.000000000000E+00  ]
[   1.000000000000E+00  ]
[  -1.000000000000E+00  ]
A * x =
[   4.440892098501E-16  ]
[   1.000000000000E+00  ]
[   2.900000000000E+01  ]
```

```
x =
[   1.000000000000E+00 ]
[   1.000000000000E+00 ]
[  -1.000000000000E+00 ]
A * x =
[   0.000000000000E+00 ]
[   1.000000000000E+00 ]
[   2.900000000000E+01 ]
```

You can see that in the second example (where normalize() has been used), the result is better, i.e., more accurate.

* This method is needed to solve linear equation systems.

```
$LR_matrix = $matrix->decompose_LR();
```

Suppose you have a matrix A and a vector b and you want to find out a vector x so that A * x = b, i.e., the vector x which solves the equation system represented by the matrix A and the vector b.

You might also have a matrix A and a whole bunch of different vectors b1..bk for which you need to find vectors x1..xk so that A * xi = bi, for i=1..k.

Using Gaussian transformations (multiplying a row or column with a factor, swapping two rows or two columns and adding a multiple of one row or column to another), it is possible to decompose any matrix A into two triangular matrices, called L and R (for Left and Right).

L has 1's on the main diagonal (the elements (1,1), (2,2), (3,3) and so so), non-zero values to the left and below of the main diagonal and all 0's in the upper right half of the matrix.

R has non-zero values on the main diagonal as well as to the right and above of the main diagonal and all 0's in the lower left half of the matrix, as follows:

```
      [ 1 0 0 0 0 ]       [ x x x x x ]
      [ x 1 0 0 0 ]       [ 0 x x x x ]
L =   [ x x 1 0 0 ]   R = [ 0 0 x x x ]
      [ x x x 1 0 ]       [ 0 0 0 x x ]
      [ x x x x 1 ]       [ 0 0 0 0 x ]
```

Note that L * R is equivalent to matrix A in the sense that L * R * x = b <==> A * x = b for all vectors x, leaving out of account permutations of the rows and columns (these are taken care of magically by this module) and numerical errors.

Trick:

Because we know that L has 1's on its main diagonal, we can store both matrices together in the same array without information loss, i.e.,

```
       [ R R R R R ]
       [ L R R R R ]
LR =   [ L L R R R ]
       [ L L L R R ]
       [ L L L L R ]
```

Beware, though, that LR and L * R are not the same!

Note also that for the same reason, you cannot apply the method normalize() to an LR decomposition matrix. Trying to do so will yield meaningless rubbish.

(You need to apply normalize() to each pair (Ai,bi) *before* decomposing the matrix Ai!)

Now how does all this help us in solving linear equation systems?

It helps us because a triangular matrix is the next best thing that can happen to us besides a diagonal matrix (a matrix that has non-zero values only on its main diagonal—in which case the solution is trivial, simply divide b[i] by A[i,i] to get x[i]).

To find the solution to our problem A * x = b, we divide this problem in parts: instead of solving A * x = b directly, we first decompose A into L and R and then solve L * y = b and finally R * x = y (motto: divide and rule).

From the illustration above it is clear that solving L * y = b and R * x = y is straightforward: we immediately know that y[1] = b[1]. We then deduce swiftly that:

```
y[2] = b[2] - L[2,1] * y[1]
```

(and we know y[1] by now!), that:

```
y[3] = b[3] - L[3,1] * y[1] - L[3,2] * y[2]
```

and so on.

Having effortlessly calculated the vector y, we now proceed to calculate the vector x in a similar fashion: we see immediately that x[n] = y[n] / R[n,n]. It follows that:

```
x[n-1] = ( y[n-1] - R[n-1,n] * x[n] ) / R[n-1,n-1]
```

and:

```
x[n-2] = ( y[n-2] - R[n-2,n-1] * x[n-1] - R[n-2,n] * x[n] )
         / R[n-2,n-2]
```

and so on.

You can see that—especially when you have many vectors b1..bk for which you are searching solutions to A * xi = bi—this scheme is much more efficient than a straightforward, brute force approach.

This method requires a quadratic matrix as its input matrix.

If you don't have that many equations, fill up with 0's (i.e., do nothing to fill the superfluous rows if it's a "fresh" matrix, i.e., a matrix that has been created with **new()** or **shadow()**).

The method returns an object reference to a new matrix containing the matrices L and R.

The input matrix is not changed by this method in any way.

Note that you can **copy()** or **clone()** the result of this method without losing its "magical" properties (for instance concerning the hidden permutations of its rows and columns).

However, as soon as you are applying any method that alters the contents of the matrix, its "magical" properties are stripped off, and the matrix immediately reverts to an "ordinary" matrix (with the values it just happens to contain at that moment, be they meaningful as an ordinary matrix or not!).

- Use this method to actually solve an equation system.

  ```
  ($dimension,$x_vector,$base_matrix) = $LR_matrix->solve_LR($b_
  vector);
  ```

Matrix **$LR_matrix** must be a (quadratic) matrix returned by the method **decompose_LR()**, the LR decomposition matrix of the matrix A of your equation system A * x = b.

The input vector `$b_vector` is the vector b in your equation system A * x = b, which must be a column vector and have the same number of rows as the input matrix `$LR_matrix`.

The method returns a list of three items if a solution exists or an empty list otherwise.

Therefore, you should always use this method like this:

```
if ( ($dim,$x_vec,$base) = $LR->solve_LR($b_vec) )
{
    # do something with the solution...
}
else
{
    # do something with the fact that there is no solution...
}
```

The three items returned are: the dimension `$dimension` of the solution space (which is 0 if only one solution exists, one if the solution is a straight line, 2 if the solution is a plane, and so on), the solution vector `$x_vector` (which is the vector x of your equation system A * x = b) and a matrix `$base_matrix` representing a base of the solution space (a set of vectors which put up the solution space like the spokes of an umbrella).

Only the first `$dimension` columns of this base matrix actually contain entries, the remaining columns are all zero.

Now what is all this stuff with that "base" good for?

The output vector x is *always* a solution of your equation system A * x = b.

But also any vector `$vector`:

```
$vector = $x_vector->clone();
$machine_infinity = 1E+99; # or something like that
for ( $i = 1; $i <= $dimension; $i++ )
{
    $vector += rand($machine_infinity) * $base_matrix->column($i);
}
```

is a solution to your problem A * x = b, i.e., if `$A_matrix` contains your matrix A, then:

```
print abs( $A_matrix * $vector - $b_vector ), "\n";
```

should print a number around 1E-16 or so.

By the way, note that you can actually calculate those vectors `$vector` a little more efficient as follows:

```
$rand_vector = $x_vector->shadow();
$machine_infinity = 1E+99; # or something like that
for ( $i = 1; $i <= $dimension; $i++ )
{
    $rand_vector->assign($i,1, rand($machine_infinity) );
}
$vector = $x_vector + ( $base_matrix * $rand_vector );
```

Note that the input matrix and vector are not changed by this method in any way.

- Use this method to calculate the inverse of a given matrix `$LR_matrix`, which must be a (quadratic) matrix returned by the method `decompose_LR()`:

```
$inverse_matrix = $LR_matrix->invert_LR();
```

The method returns an object reference to a new matrix of the same size as the input matrix containing the inverse of the matrix that you initially fed into `decompose_LR()` if the inverse exists, or an empty list otherwise.

Therefore, you should always use this method in the following way:

```
if ( $inverse_matrix = $LR->invert_LR() )
{
    # do something with the inverse matrix...
}
else
{
    # do something with the fact that there is no inverse matrix...
}
```

Note that by definition (disregarding numerical errors), the product of the initial matrix and its inverse (or vice versa) is always a matrix containing 1's on the main diagonal (elements (1,1), (2,2), (3,3) and so on) and 0's elsewhere.

The input matrix is not changed by this method in any way.

- `$condition = $matrix->condition($inverse_matrix);`

This method is just a shortcut for:

`abs($matrix) * abs($inverse_matrix)` Both input matrices must be quadratic and have the same size, and the result is meaningful only if one of them is the inverse of the other (for instance, as returned by the method `invert_LR()`).

The number returned is a measure of the condition of the given matrix `$matrix`, i.e., a measure of the numerical stability of the matrix.

This number is always positive. The smaller its value, the better the condition of the matrix (the better the stability of all subsequent computations carried out using this matrix).

Numerical stability means for example, if:

```
abs( $vec_correct - $vec_with_error ) < $epsilon
```

holds, there must be a `$delta` which doesn't depend on the vector `$vec_correct` (nor `$vec_with_error`, by the way) so that

```
abs( $matrix * $vec_correct - $matrix * $vec_with_error ) < $delta
```

also holds.

- Calculates the determinant of a matrix, whose LR decomposition matrix `$LR_matrix` must be given (which must be a (quadratic) matrix returned by the method `decompose_LR()`).

```
$determinant = $LR_matrix->det_LR();
```

In fact the determinant is a by-product of the LR decomposition: It is (in principle, that is, except for the sign) simply the product of the elements on the main diagonal (elements (1,1), (2,2), (3,3) and so on) of the LR decomposition matrix.

(The sign is taken care of "magically" by this module.)

- Calculates the order (called "Rang" in German) of a matrix, whose LR decomposition matrix `$LR_matrix` must be given (which must be a [quadratic] matrix returned by the method `decompose_LR()`).

```
$order = $LR_matrix->order_LR();
```

This number is a measure of the number of linear independent row and column vectors (= number of linear independent equations in the case of a matrix representing an equation system) of the matrix that was initially fed into decompose_LR().

If n is the number of rows and columns of the (quadratic) matrix, then n - order is the dimension of the solution space of the associated equation system.

- Returns the scalar product of vector $vector1 and vector $vector2.

    ```
    $scalar_product = $vector1->scalar_product($vector2);
    ```

Both vectors must be column vectors (i.e., a matrix having several rows but only one column).

This is a (more efficient) shortcut for:

```
$temp           = ~$vector1 * $vector2;
$scalar_product =  $temp->element(1,1);
```

or the sum i=1..n of the products vector1[i] * vector2[i].

Provided none of the two input vectors is the null vector, then the two vectors are orthogonal, i.e., have an angle of 90 degrees between them, exactly when their scalar product is 0, and vice versa.

- Returns the vector product of vector $vector1 and vector $vector2.

    ```
    $vector_product = $vector1->vector_product($vector2);
    ```

Both vectors must be column vectors (i.e., a matrix having several rows but only one column).

Currently, the vector product is only defined for 3 dimensions (i.e., vectors with 3 rows); all other vectors trigger an error message.

In 3 dimensions, the vector product of two vectors x and y is defined as:

```
              |  x[1]   y[1]   e[1]  |
determinant   |  x[2]   y[2]   e[2]  |
              |  x[3]   y[3]   e[3]  |
```

where the x[i] and y[i] are the components of the two vectors x and y, respectively, and the e[i] are unity vectors (i.e., vectors with a length equal to one) with a one in row i and 0's elsewhere (this means that you have numbers and vectors as elements in this matrix).

This determinant evaluates to the rather simple formula:

```
z[1] = x[2] * y[3] - x[3] * y[2]
z[2] = x[3] * y[1] - x[1] * y[3]
z[3] = x[1] * y[2] - x[2] * y[1]
```

A characteristic property of the vector product is that the resulting vector is orthogonal to both of the input vectors (if neither of both is the null vector; otherwise this is trivial), i.e., the scalar product of each of the input vectors with the resulting vector is always 0.

- ```
  $length = $vector->length();
  ```

This is actually a shortcut for:

```
$length = sqrt( $vector->scalar_product($vector) );
```

and returns the length of a given (column!) vector $vector.

Note that the length calculated by this method is in fact the "two" norm of a vector $vector.
```

The general definition for norms of vectors is the following:

```
sub vector_norm
{
    croak "Usage: \$norm = \$vector->vector_norm(\$n);"
      if (@_ != 2);
    my($vector,$n) = @_;
    my($rows,$cols) = ($vector->[1],$vector->[2]);
    my($k,$comp,$sum);
    croak "Math::MatrixReal::vector_norm(): vector is not a column
vector"
        unless ($cols == 1);
    croak "Math::MatrixReal::vector_norm(): norm index must be > 0"
      unless ($n > 0);
    croak "Math::MatrixReal::vector_norm(): norm index must be
integer"
        unless ($n == int($n));
    $sum = 0;
    for ( $k = 0; $k < $rows; $k++ )
    {
        $comp = abs( $vector->[0][$k][0] );
        $sum += $comp ** $n;
    }
    return( $sum ** (1 / $n) );
}
```

Note that the case n = 1 is the "one" norm for matrices applied to a vector, the case **n** = 2 is the euclidian norm or length of a vector, and if **n** goes to infinity, you have the "infinity" or "maximum" norm for matrices applied to a vector.

- In some cases it might not be practical or desirable to solve an equation system **A * x = b** using an analytical algorithm like the decompose_LR() and solve_LR() method pair.

```
$xn_vector = $matrix->solve_GSM($x0_vector,$b_vector,$epsilon);
$xn_vector = $matrix->solve_SSM($x0_vector,$b_vector,$epsilon);
$xn_vector = $matrix->solve_RM($x0_vector,$b_
vector,$weight,$epsilon);
```

In fact in some cases, due to the numerical properties (the condition) of the matrix A, the numerical error of the obtained result can be greater than by using an approximative (iterative) algorithm like one of the three implemented here.

All three methods, GSM (global step method or Gesamtschrittverfahren), SSM (single step method or Einzelschrittverfahren) and RM (relaxation method or Relaxationsverfahren), are fix-point iterations, that is, can be described by an iteration function **x(t+1) = Phi(x(t))** which has the property:

```
Phi(x)  =  x    <==>    A * x  =  b
```

We can define Phi(x) as follows:

```
Phi(x)  :=  ( En - A ) * x  +  b
```

where En is a matrix of the same size as A (n rows and columns) with 1's on its main diagonal and 0's elsewhere.

This function has the required property.

Proof:

```
            A * x         =    b
<==>     -( A * x )       =   -b
<==>     -( A * x ) + x   =   -b + x
<==>     -( A * x ) + x + b  =  x
<==>     x - ( A * x ) + b  =   x
<==>     ( En - A ) * x + b  =  x
```

This last step is true because:

```
x[i] - ( a[i,1] x[1] + ... + a[i,i] x[i] + ... + a[i,n] x[n] ) +
b[i]
```

is the same as:

```
( -a[i,1] x[1] + ... + (1 - a[i,i]) x[i] + ... + -a[i,n] x[n] ) +
b[i]
```

QED.

Note that actually solving the equation system **A** * **x** = **b** means to calculate:

```
         a[i,1] x[1] + ... + a[i,i] x[i] + ... + a[i,n] x[n]  =  b[i]
<==>     a[i,i] x[i]  =
         b[i]
         - ( a[i,1] x[1] + ... + a[i,i] x[i] + ... + a[i,n] x[n] )
         + a[i,i] x[i]
<==>     x[i]  =
         ( b[i]
            - ( a[i,1] x[1] + ... + a[i,i] x[i] + ... + a[i,n] x[n] )
            + a[i,i] x[i]
         ) / a[i,i]
<==>     x[i]  =
         ( b[i] -
            ( a[i,1] x[1] + ... + a[i,i-1] x[i-1] +
              a[i,i+1] x[i+1] + ... + a[i,n] x[n] )
         ) / a[i,i]
```

There is one major restriction, though: a fix-point iteration is guaranteed to converge only if the first derivative of the iteration function has an absolute value less than one in an area around the point **x(*)** for which `Phi( x(*) ) = x(*)` is to be true, and if the start vector **x(0)** lies within that area.

This is best verified grafically, which unfortunately is impossible to do in this textual documentation.

See literature on Numerical Analysis for details.

In our case, this restriction translates to the following three conditions.

There must exist a norm so that the norm of the matrix of the iteration function, (**En** - **A**), has a value less than one, the matrix A may not have any 0 value on its main diagonal and the initial vector **x(0)** must be "good enough", i.e., "close enough" to the solution **x(*)**.

(Remember school math: the first derivative of a straight line given by `y = a * x + b` is a.)

The three methods expect a (quadratic) matrix $matrix as their first argument, a start vector $x0_vector, a vector $b_vector (which is the vector b in your equation system A * x = b), in the case of the Relaxation Method (RM), a real number $weight best between zero and two, and finally an error limit (real number) $epsilon.

(Note that the weight $weight used by the Relaxation Method (RM) is *not* checked to lie within any reasonable range.)

The three methods first test the first two conditions of the three conditions listed above and return an empty list if these conditions are not fulfilled.

Therefore, you should always test their return value using some code like:

```
if ($xn_vector = $A_matrix->solve_GSM($x0_vector,$b_vector,1E-12) )
{
    # do something with the solution...
}
else
{
    # do something with the fact that there is no solution...
}
```

Otherwise, they iterate until abs(Phi(x) - x) < epsilon.

(Beware that theoretically, infinite loops might result if the starting vector is too far off the solution. In practice, this shouldn't be a problem. Anyway, you can always press Ctrl-C if you think that the iteration takes too long.)

The difference between the three methods is the following:

In the Global Step Method (GSM), the new vector x(t+1) (called y here) is calculated from the vector x(t) (called x here) according to the formula:

```
y[i] =
( b[i]
    - ( a[i,1] x[1] + ... + a[i,i-1] x[i-1] +
        a[i,i+1] x[i+1] + ... + a[i,n] x[n] )
) / a[i,i]
```

In the Single Step Method (SSM), the components of the vector x(t+1) which have already been calculated are used to calculate the remaining components, i.e.:

```
y[i] =
( b[i]
    - ( a[i,1] y[1] + ... + a[i,i-1] y[i-1] +   # note the "y[]"!
        a[i,i+1] x[i+1] + ... + a[i,n] x[n] )   # note the "x[]"!
) / a[i,i]
```

In the Relaxation Method (RM), the components of the vector x(t+1) are calculated by mixing old and new value (like cold and hot water), and the weight $weight determines the aperture of both the hot water tap as well as of the cold water tap, according to the formula:

```
y[i] =
( b[i]
    - ( a[i,1] y[1] + ... + a[i,i-1] y[i-1] +   # note the "y[]"!
        a[i,i+1] x[i+1] + ... + a[i,n] x[n] )   # note the "x[]"!
) / a[i,i]
y[i] = weight * y[i] + (1 - weight) * x[i]
```

Note that the weight $weight should be greater than 0 and less than 2(!).

The three methods are supposed to be of different efficiency. Experiment!

Remember that in most cases, it is probably advantageous to first **normalize()** your equation system prior to solving it.

Overloaded Operators

Unary operators
> -, ~, abs, test, !, "

Binary (arithmetic) operators
> +, -, *

Binary (relational) operators
> ==, !=, <, <=, >, =>
>
> eq, ne, lt, le, gt, ge

Note that the latter (eq, ne, . . .) are just synonyms of the former (==, !=, . . .), defined for convenience only.

Description

Unary minus (-)

Returns the negative of the given matrix, i.e., the matrix with all elements multiplied with the factor −1.

```
$matrix = -$matrix;
```

Transposition (~)

Returns the given matrix, transposed.

Examples:

```
$temp = ~$vector * $vector;
$length = sqrt( $temp->element(1,1) );
if (~$matrix == $matrix) { # matrix is symmetric ... }
```

Norm (abs)

Returns the "one" norm of the given matrix.

```
$error = abs( $A * $x - $b );
```

Boolean test (test)

Tests whether there is at least one non-zero element in the matrix.

```
if ($xn_vector) { # result of iteration is not zero ... }
```

Negated boolean test (!)

Tests whether the matrix contains only 0's.

Examples:

```
if (! $b_vector) { # heterogenous equation system ... }
else             { # homogenous equation system ... }
unless ($x_vector) { # not the null-vector! }
```

Stringify operator ("")

Converts the given matrix into a string.

Uses scientific representation to keep precision loss to a minimum in case you want to read this string back in again later with **new_from_string()**.

Uses a 13-digit mantissa and a 20-character field for each element so that lines will wrap nicely on an 80-column screen.

Examples:

```
$matrix = Math::MatrixReal->new_from_string(<<"MATRIX");
```

```
[ 1  0 ]
[ 0 -1 ]
MATRIX
print "$matrix";
[   1.000000000000E+00   0.000000000000E+00 ]
[   0.000000000000E+00  -1.000000000000E+00 ]
$string = "$matrix";
$test = Math::MatrixReal->new_from_string($string);
if $test == $matrix) { print ":-)\n"; } else { print ":-(\n"; }
```

Addition (+)

Returns the sum of the two given matrices.

Examples:

```
$matrix_S = $matrix_A + $matrix_B;
$matrix_A += $matrix_B;
```

Subtraction (–)

Returns the difference of the two given matrices.

Examples:

```
$matrix_D = $matrix_A - $matrix_B;
$matrix_A -= $matrix_B;
```

Note that this is the same as:

```
$matrix_S = $matrix_A + -$matrix_B;
$matrix_A += -$matrix_B;
```

(However, the latter are less efficient.)

Multiplication (*)

Returns the matrix product of the two given matrices or the product of the given matrix and scalar factor.

Examples:

```
$matrix_P = $matrix_A * $matrix_B;
$matrix_A *= $matrix_B;
$vector_b = $matrix_A * $vector_x;
$matrix_B = -1 * $matrix_A;
$matrix_B = $matrix_A * -1;
$matrix_A *= -1;
```

Equality (==)

Tests two matrices for equality.

```
if ( $A * $x == $b ) { print "EUREKA!\n"; }
```

Note that in most cases, due to numerical errors (because of the finite precision of computer arithmetics), it is a bad idea to compare two matrices or vectors this way.

Better use the norm of the difference of the two matrices you want to compare and compare that norm with a small number, like this:

```
if ( abs( $A * $x - $b ) < 1E-12 ) { print "BINGO!\n"; }
```

Inequality (!=)

Tests two matrices for inequality.

Example:

```
while ($x0_vector != $xn_vector) { # proceed with iteration...}
```

(Stops when the iteration becomes stationary.)

Note that (as with the == operator), it is usually a bad idea to compare matrices or vectors this way. Compare the norm of the difference of the two matrices with a small number instead.

Less than (<)

Examples:

```
if ( $matrix1 < $matrix2 ) { # ... }
if ( $vector < $epsilon ) { # ... }
if ( 1E-12 < $vector ) { # ... }
if ( $A * $x - $b < 1E-12 ) { # ... }
```

These are just shortcuts for saying:

```
if ( abs($matrix1) < abs($matrix2) ) { # ... }
if ( abs($vector) < abs($epsilon) ) { # ... }
if ( abs(1E-12) < abs($vector) ) { # ... }
if ( abs( $A * $x - $b ) < abs(1E-12) ) { # ... }
```

Uses the "one" norm for matrices and Perl's built-in **abs()** for scalars.

Less than or equal (<=)

As with the < operator, this is just a shortcut for the same expression with **abs()** around all arguments:

```
if ( $A * $x - $b <= 1E-12 ) { # ... }
```

which in fact is the same as:

```
if ( abs( $A * $x - $b ) <= abs(1E-12) ) { # ... }
```

Uses the "one" norm for matrices and Perl's built-in **abs()** for scalars.

Greater than (>)

As with the < and <= operator, this:

```
if ( $xn - $x0 > 1E-12 ) { # ... }
```

is just a shortcut for:

```
if ( abs( $xn - $x0 ) > abs(1E-12) ) { # ... }
```

Uses the "one" norm for matrices and Perl's built-in **abs()** for scalars.

Greater than or equal (>=)

As with the <, <=, and > operator, the following:

```
if ( $LR >= $A ) { # ... }
```

is simply a shortcut for:

```
if ( abs($LR) >= abs($A) ) { # ... }
```

Uses the "one" norm for matrices and Perl's built-in **abs()** for scalars.

Version

This manpage documents Math::MatrixReal version 1.2.

Author

Steffen Beyer, *sb@sdm.de*

Acknowledgments

Many thanks to Prof. Pahlings for stoking the fire of my enthusiasm for algebra and linear algebra at the university (RWTH Aachen, Germany), and to Prof. Esser and his assistant, Mr. Jarausch, for their fascinating lectures in numerical analysis.

Copyright

See Also

Math::MatrixBool(3),   DFA::Kleene(3),   Math::Kleene(3),   Set::IntegerRange(3), Set::IntegerFast(3)

Math::Spline—cubic spline interpolation of data

Synopsis

```
require Math::Spline;
$spline=new Math::Spline(\@x,\@y)
$y_interp=$spline->evaluate($x);

use Math::Spline qw(spline linsearch binsearch);
use Math::Derivative qw(Derivative2);
@y2=Derivative2(\@x,\@y);
$index=binsearch(\@x,$x);
$index=linsearch(\@x,$x,$index);
$y_interp=spline(\@x,\@y,\@y2,$index,$x);
```

Description

This package provides cubic spline interpolation of numeric data. The data is passed as references to two arrays containing the x and y ordinates. It may be used as an exporter of the numerical functions or, more easily, as a class module.

The Math::Spline class constructor **new** takes references to the arrays of x and y ordinates of the data. An interpolation is performed using the **evaluate** method, which, when given an x ordinate, returns the interpolated y ordinate at that value.

The **spline** function takes as arguments references to the x and y ordinate array, a reference to the second derivatives (calculated using **Derivative2**), the low index of the interval in which to interpolate, and the x ordinate in that interval. It returns the interpolated y ordinate. Two functions are provided to look up the appropriate index in the array of x data. For random calls, **binsearch** can be used; given a reference to the x ordinates and the x loopup value, it returns the low index of the interval in the data in which the value lies. Where the lookups are strictly in ascending sequence (e.g. if interpolating to produce a higher-resolution dataset to draw a curve), the **linsearch** function may more efficiently be used. It works like **binsearch**, but requires a third argument that is the previous index value, which is incremented if necessary.

Note: Requires the Math::Derivative module.

Example

```
require Math::Spline;
my @x=(1,3,8,10);
my @y=(1,2,3,4);
$spline=new Math::Spline(\@x,\@y);
print $spline->evaluate(5)."\n";
```

produces the output:

```
2.44
```

Bugs

Bug reports or constructive comments are welcome.

Author

John A.R. Williams, *J.A.R.Williams@aston.ac.uk*

See Also

Numerical Recipes: The Art of Scientific Computing, by W.H. Press, B.P. Flannery, S.A. Teukolsky, W.T. Vetterling. Cambridge University Press. ISBN 0 521 30811 9.

Math::Trig—inverse and hyperbolic trigonometric functions

Synopsis

```
use Math::Trig qw(tan sec csc cot asin acos atan asec acsc acot sinh
           cosh tanh sech csch coth asinh acosh atanh asech acsch acoth);
$v=tan($x);
$v=sec($x);
$v=csc($x);
$v=cot($x);
$v=asin($x);
$v=acos($x);
$v=atan($x);
$v=asec($x);
$v=acsc($x);
$v=acot($x);
$v=sinh($x);
$v=cosh($x);
$v=tanh($x);
$v=sech($x);
$v=csch($x);
$v=coth($x);
$v=asinh($x);
$v=acosh($x);
$v=atanh($x);
$v=asech($x);
$v=acsch($x);
$v=acoth($x);
```

Description

This module exports the missing inverse and hyperbolic trigonometric functions of real numbers. The inverse functions return values corresponding to the principal values. Specifying an argument outside of the domain of the function causes `undef` to be returned.

- `tan` returns the tangent of a real argument.
- `sec` returns the secant of a real argument.
- `csc` returns the cosecant of a real argument.
- `cot` returns the cotangent of a real argument.
- `asin` returns the inverse sine of a real argument.
- `acos` returns the inverse cosine of a real argument.
- `atan` returns the inverse tangent of a real argument.
- `asec` returns the inverse secant of a real argument.
- `acsc` returns the inverse cosecant of a real argument.
- `acot` returns the inverse cotangent of a real argument.
- `sinh` returns the hyperbolic sine of a real argument.
- `cosh` returns the hyperbolic cosine of a real argument.
- `tanh` returns the hyperbolic tangent of a real argument.
- `sech` returns the hyperbolic secant of a real argument.
- `csch` returns the hyperbolic cosecant of a real argument.
- `coth` returns the hyperbolic cotangent of a real argument.
- `asinh` returns the inverse hyperbolic sine of a real argument.
- `acosh` returns the inverse hyperbolic cosine of a real argument (positive value only).
- `atanh` returns the inverse hyperbolic tangent of a real argument.
- `asech` returns the inverse hyperbolic secant of a real argument (positive value only).
- `acsch` returns the inverse hyperbolic cosecant of a real argument.
- `acoth` returns the inverse hyperbolic cotangent of a real argument.

Bugs

Some functions may return `undef` even within their domain. This usually only occurs very close to a domain boundary or when evaluating a very large or small argument. It is usually caused by operations like internally adding 1 to 1e20 while evaluating the function with the other trigonometric and exponential functions.

Let me know about any others.

I welcome additions such as the inverse trigonometric functions and the complex versions of the functions to be included in this module.

Author

Initial version by John A.R. Williams, *J.A.R.Williams@aston.ac.uk*

Bug fixes and many additional functions by Jason Smith, *smithj4@rpi.edu*

Math::VecStat—some basic numeric stats on vectors

Synopsis

```
use Math::VecStat qw(max min maxabs minabs sum average);
$max=max(@vector);
$max=max(\@vector);
($max,$imax)=max(@vector);
($max,$imax)=max(\@vector);
$min=min(@vector);
$min=min(\@vector);
($max,$imin)=min(@vector);
($max,$imin)=min(\@vector);
$max=maxabs(@vector);
$max=maxabs(\@vector);
($max,$imax)=maxabs(@vector);
($max,$imax)=maxabs(\@vector);
$min=minabs(@vector);
$min=minabs(\@vector);
($max,$imin)=minabs(@vector);
($max,$imin)=minabs(\@vector);
$sum=sum($v1,$v2,...);
$sum=sum(@vector);
$sum=sum(\@vector);
$average=average($v1,$v2,...);
$av=average(@vector);
$av=average(\@vector);
```

Description

This package provides some basic statistics on numerical vectors. Each of the subroutines can take a copy of the vector, or preferably for efficiency, a reference to the vector to be operated on.

Subroutines

`max(@vector)`, `max(\@vector)`
> Returns the maximum value of the given values or vector. In an array context, returns the value and the index in the array where it occurs.

`min(@vector)`, `min(\@vector)`
> Returns the minimum value of the given values or vector. In an array context, returns the value and the index in the array where it occurs.

`maxabs(@vector)`, `maxabs(\@vector)`
> Returns the maximum value of the absolute of the given values or vector. In an array context, returns the value and the index in the array where it occurs.

`minabs(@vector)`, `minabs(\@vector)`
> Returns the minimum value of the absolute of the given values or vector. In an array context, returns the value and the index in the array where it occurs.

`sum($v1,$v2,...)`, `sum(@vector)`, `sum(\@vector)`
> Returns the sum of the given values or vector.

`average($v1,$v2,..)`, `average(@vector)`, `average(\@vector)`
> Returns the average of the given values or vector.

Bugs

Let me know. I welcome any appropriate additions for this package.

Author

John A.R. Williams, *J.A.R.Williams@aston.ac.uk*

PDL—Perl Data Language extension module

Description

The perlDL concept is to give standard Perl5 the ability to *compactly* store and *speedily* manipulate the large N-dimensional data sets that are the bread and butter of scientific computing. For example, $a=$b+$c can add two 2048x2048 images in only a fraction of a second.

It is hoped to eventually provide tons of useful functionality for scientific and numeric analysis.

The Perl Data Language project has a home page at *http://www.aao.gov.au/local/www/kgb/ perldl*. There you can find a Frequently Asked Questions List, contact information for the **perldl** mailing list, information about on-going development, and many other things.

Introduction

The fundamental Perl data structures are scalar variables (e.g., $x), which can hold numbers or strings, lists, or arrays of scalars (e.g., @x), and associative arrays/hashes of scalars (e.g., %x).

Perl v5 introduces data structures and objects to Perl. The simple scalar variable $x can now be a user-defined data type or a full-blown object.[*]

The fundamental idea behind perlDL is to allow $x to hold a whole 1D spectrum, or a 2D image, a 3D data cube, and so on, up to large N-dimensional data sets. These can be manipulated all at once. For example, $a = $b + 2 performs a vector operation on each value in the spectrum/image/etc.

You may well ask: "Why not just store a spectrum as a simple Perl @x-style list, with each pixel being a list item?" The two key answers to this are *memory* and *speed*. Because we know our spectrum consists of pure numbers, we can compactly store them in a single block of memory corresponding to a C-style numeric array. This takes up a *lot* less memory than the equivalent Perl list. It is then easy to pass this block of memory to a fast addition routine, or to any other C function that deals with arrays. As a result, perlDL is very fast—for example, one can multiply a 2048*2048 image in exactly the same time as it would take in C or FORTRAN (0.1 sec on my Sparc). A further advantage of this is that for simple operations (e.g., $x += 2), one can manipulate the whole array without caring about its dimensionality.

I find that when using perlDL, it is most useful to think of standard Perl @x variables as "lists" of generic "things" and PDL variables like $x as "arrays" that can be

---

[*] It actually holds a reference (a smart "pointer") to this but that is not relevant for ordinary use of perlDL.

contained in lists or hashes. Quite often in my perlDL scripts, I have @x contain a list of spectra or a list of images (or even a mix). Or perhaps you could have a hash (e.g., %x) of images...the only limit is memory.

perlDL variables support a range of data types—arrays can be bytes, short integers (signed or unsigned), long integers, floats, or double-precision floats.

Usage

perlDL is loaded into your Perl script using these commands:

```
use PDL;   # use the standard perlDL modules (Core Examples Io
           # Graphics::PG)

use PDL::Examples; # use only the Examples module (this will load
                   # internally whatever other modules it needs).

% perldl  # Invoke interactive shell from system command line.
```

The default is to import all the function names from a module. If you only want certain names imported, just say:

```
use PDL::Io qw(rfits rgrep) # Get only rfits() and rgrep from
                            # PDL::Io
```

Also, see the section below on "Object Orientation."

Create a New PDL Variable

Here are some ways of creating a PDL variable:

```
$a = pdl [1..10];              # 1D array
$a = pdl (1,2,3,4);            # Ditto
$b = pdl [[1,2,3],[4,5,6]];    # 2D 3x2 array
$b = pdl 42                    # 0-dimensional scalar
$c = pdl $a;                   # Make a new copy

$d = byte [1..10];             # See "Type conversion"
$e = zeroes(3,2,4);            # 3x2x4 zero-filled array

$c = rfits $file;              # Read FITS file

@x = ( pdl(42), zeroes(3,2,4), rfits($file) ); # Is a LIST of PDL
                                               # variables!
```

The pdl() function is used to initialize a PDL variable from a scalar, list, list reference, or another PDL variable.

In addition, all PDL functions automatically convert normal Perl scalars to PDL variables on the fly.

Also see the "Type Conversion" and "Input/Output" sections below.

Arithmetic

Here are some examples of arithmetic. You can also use other Perl operators and functions.

```
$a = $b + 2; $a++; $a = $b / $c; # Etc.

$c=sqrt($a); $d = log10($b+100); # Etc
```

```
$e = $a>42; # Vector condtional (like MATLAB) -
            # note I think this is much nicer than IDLs WHERE(),
e.g.:

$e = 42*($a>42) + $a*($a<=42); # Cap top

$a = $a / ( max($a) - min($a) );

print $a; # $a in string context prints it in a N-dimensional
          # format
```

Matrix Functions

perlDL hijacks x to use as the matrix multiplication operator (e.g., $c = $a x $b;).

perlDL is row-major, not column-major, so this is actually:

```
c(i,j) = sum_k a(k,j) b(i,k)
```

but when matrices are printed, the results look right. Just remember that the indices are reversed, e.g.:

```
$a = [                   $b = [
    [ 1  2  3  0]            [1 1]
    [ 1 -1  2  7]            [0 2]
    [ 1  0  0  1]            [0 2]
    ]                        [1 1]
                            ]
gives $c = [
         [ 1 11]
         [ 8 10]
         [ 2  2]
         ]
```

Note: transpose() does what it says and is a convenient way to turn row vectors into column vectors. It is bound to the unary operator ~ for convenience.

Writing a Simple Function

If you put the following in the file *dotproduct.pdl*, it will be autoloaded (see below).

```
sub dotproduct {
    my ($a,$b) = @_;
    return sum($a*$b) ;
}
1;
```

Type Conversion

The default for pdl() is double. Conversions are:

```
$a = float($b);
$c = long($d);    # "long" is 4 byte int
$d = byte($a);
```

Also double(), short(), ushort().

These routines also automatically convert Perl lists to allow a convenient shorthand, e.g.:

```
$a = byte [[1..10],[1..10]];  # Create 2D byte array
$a = float [1..1000];         # Create 1D float array
```

Here are the rules for automatic conversion during arithmetic:

```
If INT = any of byte/short/ushort/int and X is generic op
```

For VECTOR x SCALAR operations, these rules avoid over-promotion of vector types:

```
VECTOR INT   X SCALAR INT            Return is same type as VECTOR
VECTOR INT   X SCALAR float/double   Return float
VECTOR float X SCALAR float/double   Return float
```

For other VECTORxSCALAR and VECTORxVECTOR operations, the "higher" of two data types is returned, i.e., VECTOR double x float returns float, etc.

Printing

Printing automatically expands an array in N-dimensional format:

```
print $a;

$b = "Answer is = $a ";
```

Sections

perlDL betrays its Perl/C heritage in that arrays are zero-offset. Thus, a 100x100 image has indices 0..99,0..99.

Further, I adopt the convention that the center of the pixel (0,0) is at coordinate (0.0,0.0). Thus the above image ranges from −0.5..99.5, −0.5..99.5 in real space. All perlDL graphics functions conform to this defintion and hide the unit-offsetness of, for example, the PGPLOT FORTRAN library.

Again following the usual convention, coordinate (0,0) is at the bottom left when an image is displayed. It appears at the top right when using **"print $a"**, etc.

```
$b       = sec($a,   $x1, $x2, $y1, $y2, $z1, $z2, ... )
                                        #Take subsection
$newimage = ins($bigimage,$smallimage,$x,$y,$z...)
                                        # Insert at x,y,z
$c       = nelem ($a); # Number of pixels

$val = at($object, $x,$y,$z...)      # Pixel value at position
set($myimage, $x, $y, ... $value)   # Set value in image

$b = xvals($a);   # Fill array with X-coord values
                  # (also yvals(), zvals(), axisvals($x,$axis)
                  # and rvals() for radial distance from center).
```

Note: An experimental neat virtual slicing syntax is being worked on for PDL 2.0.

Input/Output

The PDL::Io module currently implements the following useful I/O functions:

```
$a   = rfits($file)  # Read a FITS file into a PDL variable
                     # (only IEEE float machines as yet)
wfits ($a, $file)    # Write FITS file

([$xaxis],$data) = rdsa($file)  # Read a STARLINK/FIGARO file using
                                # perl DSA module (available separately)
```

Read ASCII columns into $x, $y, etc.:

```
($x,$y,...) = rcols($file,[[$pattern],[$col1, $col2,] ...)
```

Read $1, $2, etc. pattern matches into $x, $y, etc.

```
($x,$y,...) = rgrep($file, $pattern)
```

For example:

```
($x,$y) = rcols $file, '/Mumble/', 2,3;
($a,$b) = rgrep $file, '/Foo (.*) Bar (.*) Mumble/';
```

Graphics

The philosophy behind perlDL is to make it work with a variety of existing graphics libraries, since no single package will satisfy all needs and all people, and this allows one to work with packages one already knows and likes. Obviously, there will be some overlaps in functionality and some lack of consistency and uniformity. This also saves the author from too much work in time he doesn't have!

PGPLOT

PGPLOT provdes a simple library for line graphics and image display.

There is an easy interface to this in the internal module PDL::Graphics::PG. (This calls routines in the separately available PGPLOT top-level Perl module, version 2.0 or higher.)

Current display commands:

```
imag      Display an image (uses pgimag()/pggray() as
          appropriate)
ctab      Load an image color table
line      Plot vector as connected points
points    Plot vector as points
errb      Plot error bars
cont      Display image as contour map
bin       Plot vector as histogram (e.g., bin(hist($data)))
hi2d      Plot image as 2D histogram (not very good IMHO...)
poly      Draw a polygon
vect      Display two images as a vector field
```

Device manipulation commands:

```
hold      Hold current plot window range--allows overlays, etc.
release   Release back to autoscaling of new plot window for
          each command
rel       Short alias for 'release'
env       Define a plot window, put on 'hold'
dev       Explicitly set a new PGPLOT graphics device
```

The actual PGPLOT module is loaded only when the first of these commands is executed, e.g:

```
perldl> $a = pdl [1..100]
perldl> $b = sqrt($a)
perldl> line $b
perldl> hold
Graphics on HOLD
perldl> $c = sin($a/10)*2 + 4
perldl> line $c
```

Notes: $transform for image, etc. is used in the same way as the TR() array in the underlying PGPLOT FORTRAN routine but is, fortunately, zero-offset.

It is also hoped to use other graphic libraries to enable more sophisticated plots then are possible with PGPLOT.

IIS

Many astronomers like to use SAOimage and Ximtool (or their derivations or clones). These are useful free widgets for inspection and visualization of images. (They are not provided with perlDL, but can easily be obtained from their official sites on the Net.)

The PDL::Graphics::IIS package allows one to display images using these tools (IIS is the name of an ancient item of image-display hardware whose protocols the tools conform to.)

The commands are:

```
iis          Display image
iiscur       Return a cursor position
iiscirc      Draw circles on image display
saoimage     Start SAOimage
ximtool      Start Ximtool
```

The variables are:

```
$stdimage    Frame buffer configuration
$iisframe    Frame buffer number to display in
```

The frame buffer configuration is set by the variable **$stdimage** (analogous to iraf) whose default is imt1024. System and user *imtoolrc* files are parsed, so if you understand them, you can do the same tricks as you can with IRAF.

Karma

To come?

Autoloading

If a PDL function, e.g., foo(), is currently undefined, a file *foo.pdl* is searched for in the current directory and any directories in the $PDLLIB, $PERL5LIB, and $PERLLIB environment variables, which contain colon-separated lists of directories.

If you want to change the path within **perldl**, simply change the lists @PDLLIB and @INC.

Note: *foo.pdl* is **required**, so it must return a true value (see the **require** Perl documentation).

Call External

This provides a simple way to pass the data arrays from PDL variables to external C routines. It uses Perl's built-in dynamic loader to load compiled C code.

The syntax is:

```
callext($file,$symbol, @pdl_list)
```

@pdl_list is a list of pdl variables. Numbers are converted automatically. The file must be dynamically loadable object code; the way the C compiler generates this is different from system to system, so see your man pages.

The C routine takes args (int nargs, pdl *args). The C type pdl is a simple data structure representing the Perl pdl variable. It is defined in the file *pdl.h*, which is included in the perlDL distribution and has no Perl dependencies. It is trivial to cast the data array (pdl.data) to (float), (double), etc., and to pass it to any other C routine.

This is all demonstrated in the files *demos/callext.** in the perlDL distribution.

Note: This is only intended as a quick and dirty prototyping interface for the scientist or hacker. perlDL developers should write a module along the lines of the example PDL::Examples. (Or better: join the *pdl-porters* mailing list and find out how to take advantage of the cool features coming up in PDL 2.0.)

perldl Shell

The program perldl (written in Perl) provides a simple command line for interactive use of PDL. See the perldl manpage for further information about its features.

You can also use PDL from the standard Perl debugger (e.g., by typing perl -MPDL -d -e 1).

Overload Operators

I have overloaded the following built-in Perl operators and functions in order that they work on PDL variables:

```
+ - * / > < >= <= << >> & | ^ == != <=> ** % ! ~
sin log abs atan2 sqrt cos exp
```

All the unary functions (sin, etc.) may be used with inplace(); see "Memory" below.

Object Orientation and perlDL

(Astronomers can ignore this bit. :-))

PDL variables such as $x are implemented via Perl objects. However, I have chosen to use an all-functional approach to perlDL syntax to be more astronomer-friendly.

Nevertheless, you can use perlDL in an object-oriented fashion. In fact if you say:

```
use PDL::OO;
```

It loads PDL functions as object-oriented methods in the PDL class. This means that you can say things like:

```
$a = PDL->rfits('m51.fits');
$b = PDL->new([1,2,2,1],[1,2,2,1],[1,2,2,1],[1,2,2,1]);
$smooth = $a->convolve($b);
$smooth->iis;
```

You can start the perldl shell in this mode with perldl -oo.

Note: As you can see from the above, all functions that create PDL variables are used with construct syntax in the OO mode. Finally, you can even use both forms by simply saying use PDL; use PDL::OO.

You can inherit from PDL methods (e.g. to a class Foo) by saying:

```
@Foo::ISA = ('PDL');               # Method path
%Foo::OVERLOAD = %PDL::OVERLOAD;   # Copy overload
```

Then PDL methods will work on Foo objects as long as you simply build on the existing PDL data-structure components (see below).

So it is possible to provide user-written modules to do really cool stuff for specific application areas, e.g., PDL::Spectrum might provide a $a that understands X-axes and error bars and +-/+ etc. might be overridden to do the Right Thing (tm). And writing the module would not be rocket science—just some cool Perl hacking.

And you would not have to even use method syntax. If $a came out of my hypothetical PDL::Spectrum, all the standard PDL functions (like `hist()`, to give a concrete example) would work on it in the standard way provided you simply built on the existing PDL data structure (which means simply containing a $$a{Data}, etc. PDL::Spectrum could even export it's own `hist()` function (which might do something more sophisticated using the X-axis, for example) to override the built-in.

If you were feeling really ambitious, you might do a PDL::Ir::Spectrum that understood about the gaps between the J, H, and K bands!

Important: This is an experimental feature. It may go away in PDL v2.0. It is not yet clear whether it is neat or a crock. :-) Comments welcome.

Memory Usage and References

A PDL variable such as $x is implemented as a "Perl reference." You can think of it as a pointer to a big block of memory holding the data and housekeeping information, i.e., *it does not copy the data*. Rather, you now have two names ($x and $y) for the same piece of data. To force an explicit data copy say:

```
$b = pdl $a; # Real copy
```

though this is rarely needed in practice.

Messing around with really huge data arrays may require some care. PDL provides facilities to let you perform operations on big arrays without generating extra copies, though this does require a bit more thought and care from the programmer.

Note: On some systems, it is better to configure Perl (during the build) to use the system `malloc()` function rather than Perl's built-in function. This is because Perl's function is optimized for speed rather than consumption of virtual memory; using the system `malloc()` can result in a factor-of-two improvement in the amount of memory storage you can use.

Simple arithmetic

If $a is a big image (e.g., occupying 10MB) and I say:

```
$a = $a + 1;
```

then the total `malloc()`'d memory usage grows to 20MB. This is because the expression $a+1 creates a temporary copy of $a to hold the result, then $a is assigned a reference to that. It is obviously done this way so $c=$a+1 works as expected. (Note that the old memory is reclaimed for further use, but one feature of UNIX dynamic memory allocation via `malloc()` is that the memory `malloced` by a process can never get smaller.)

Now if one says:

```
$b = $a;      # $b and $a now point to same data
$a = $a + 1;
```

Then $b and $a end up being different, as one naively expects, because a new reference is created to the result and $a is assigned to it.

However, if $a is a huge memory hog (e.g., a 3D volume), creating a copy of it may not be a good thing. One can avoid this memory overhead in the above example by saying:

```
$a++;
```

The operations ++, +=, --, -=, etc., all call a special "in-place" version of the arithmetic subroutine. This means that no more memory is needed; the downside is that if $b=$a, then $b is also incremented.

Functions

Most functions, e.g. log(), return a result that is a transformation of their argument. This makes for good programming practice. However, many operations can be done "in-place" and this may be required when large arrays are in use and memory is at a premium. For these circumstances, the operator inplace() is provided, which prevents the extra copy and allows the argument to be modified. For example:

```
$x = log($array);          # $array unaffected
log( inplace($bigarray) ); # $bigarray changed in situ
```

Warnings

- The usual caveats about duplicate references apply.

- When used with some functions that can not be applied *in situ* (e.g., con-volve()) unexpected effects may occur. I try to indicate inplace()-safe functions below.

- Type conversions (e.g., float()) may cause hidden copying.

Data Structure Guts

(For born fiddlers only.)

The data structure for $a is implemented by a hash (associative array), to which $a is a (blessed) reference.

PDL reserves for its own use:

```
$$a{Data} ; # The DATA (byte list)--can be passed directly to F77/C
            # subroutine if type matches. e.g., line() does a
            # float() and then calls PGPLOT::pgline_r (bypassing
            # packing)

$$a{Datatype}; # Holds numeric data type, $PDL_F, $PDL_D, etc...

$$a{Dims} ; # List reference holding dimensions,
            # e.g., @mydims = @{ $$a{Dims} };

$$a{Hdr}; # Optional extra hash reference holding header, e.g.
          # $airmass = $$a{Hdr}{'AIRMASS'}; %myhdr = %{ $$a{Hdr} };
          # rfits() populates this from the FITS header.

$$a{Inplace}; # Flag - inplace() sets this. Next time a copy is
              # attempted it does not occur and the flag is unset.
$$a{PDL};     # Pointer to cached C values of above. This allows
              # C routines to get at the data FAST.
```

Anything else stored in the structure is copied to new objects (e.g., by $b = $a + 1) automatically, as long as PDL knows how to copy it. (If it is a reference to another object, PDL tries the ->copy method.)

If your Perl routine manipulates the data structure guts directly, you don't want it to blow up in your face if you pass it a simple number rather than a PDL variable.

Simply call the function `topdl()` first to make it safe, e.g.:

```
sub myfiddle { my $pdl = topdl(shift); $$pdl{Data} = ... }
```

`topdl()` does *not* perform a copy if a PDL variable is passed; it just falls through, which is the desired behavior. The routine is not, of course, necessary in normal user-defined functions that do not care about internals.

Important: If you have changed the guts, you *must* call the method `$pdl->flush()` to update the C cache from the new Perl values, otherwise PDL gets very confused (Mnemonic: "flush the piddle after a fiddle").

Finally, there is no reason why the data structure should not contain another PDL variable.

Important: This structure was experimental and has already gone away in the latest development version of PDL 2.0. You have been warned. :-)

Complete List of Exported Functions

Defined in PDL::Core

```
byte short ushort long float double convert
                - Type conversions


pdl             - Create/copy a pdl
topdl           - Coerce to pdl if scalar
howbig          - Size of pdl datatype in bytes
nelem           - Number of elements
dims            - Return list of dimensions, e.g.,
                  @mydims = dims($x);
list            - Convert pdl to list - e.g. for (list $x) {..}
listindices     - Return list of index values (1D), e.g.,
                  for $i (listindices $x) {..}
log10*          - Take log base 10
min max sum     - Min/max/sum of pdl array
zeroes/ones     - Create zero/one-filled pdl array
sequence        - Create sequence-filled pdl array
reshape         - reshape the dimensions of a pdl array
sec             - subsection
ins* / set      - insertion/setting
at              - return pixel value at (x,y,z...)


axisvals* xvals* yvals* zvals* - Fill pdl with axis values


rvals           - Fill pdl with distance from it's center
callext         - Call external C routine in dynamically loadable
                  object
convolve        - convolve image with kernel (real space)
inplace         - Flag for inplace operation
hist            - histogram of data
stats           - return mean + standard deviation
transpose       - matrix transpose
qsort*          - Quick sort piddle
median          - median of piddle
oddmedian       - lower odd median of piddle
```

---

* Indicates `inplace()` is safe and useful with this function.

Defined in PDL::Examples

This section contains examples of how to add C functiions via XS, including use of the generic preprocessor (.g files are automatically converted to .c files with code automatically generated for each datatype).

```
fibonacci*    - Compute Fibonacci series (simple 1D example)
cc8compt*     - Connected 8-component labelling (2D example)
```

Defined in PDL::Io

See "Io" section above.

Defined in PDL::Graphics::*

See "Graphics" section above.

Complete List of PDL Methods

For convenience (the ->meth syntax looks more appropriate), some PDL routines are defined as methods:

```
$pdl->flush    - Update C cache from Perl values
$pdl->copy     - Copy a PDL
PDL->new       - Make a new PDL
```

PDL::FAQ—frequently asked questions about PDL

Description

This is version 0.2 of the PDL FAQ, a collection of frequently asked questions about PDL—the Perl Data Language.

This FAQ was generated on February 22, 1997.

Current maintainer: Christian Soeller (*csoelle@sghms.ac.uk*).

You can find the latest version of this document at *http://www.aao.gov.au/local/www/kgb/perldl/faq.html*. This FAQ will be posted monthly to the PDL mailing list, *perldl@jach.hawaii.edu*.

This is the first released version of the PDL FAQ. As such, it is almost certainly incomplete and may be unclear in parts. You are explicitly encouraged to let us know about questions that you think should be answered in this document but currently aren't. Similarly, if you think parts of this document are unclear, please let us know. Send your comments to the PDL mailing list at *perldl@jach.hawaii.edu* (preferably) or to the FAQ maintainer, Christian Soeller (*csoelle@sghms.ac.uk*).

Some questions and answers in this document are related to features of the current beta/alpha versions of PDL. To point this out, these sections are marked with the strings "[beta]" or "[alpha]".

General questions

What is PDL ?

PDL stands for Perl Data Language. To say it with the words of Karl Glazebrook, initiator of the PDL project:

The PDL concept is to give standard Perl5 the ability to *compactly* store and *speedily* manipulate the large N-dimensional data sets that are the bread and butter of scientific computing, e.g., $a=$b+$c can add two 2048x2048 images in only a fraction of a second.

It is hoped to eventually provide tons of useful functionality for scientific and numeric analysis.

For readers familiar with other scientific data evaluation packages, it may be helpful to add that PDL is in many respects similar to IDL, MATLAB, and similar packages. However, it tries to improve on a number of issues that were perceived (by the authors of PDL) as shortcomings of those existing packages.

Why yet another data language?

There are actually several reasons, and everyone should decide for himself which are the most important ones:

- PDL is "free software". The authors of PDL think that this concept has several advantages: everyone has access to the sources, which leads to better debugging, easily adaptable to your own needs, extensible for your purposes, etc.

- PDL is based on a powerful and well-designed scripting language: Perl. In contrast to other scientific/numeric data analysis languages, it has been designed using the language features of a proven language instead of having grown into existence from scratch, defining the control structures while features were added during development (leading to languages that often appear clumsy and badly planned for most existing packages with a similar scope as PDL).

- Using Perl as the basis, a PDL programmer has all the powerful features of Perl at hand right from the start. This includes regular expressions, associative arrays (hashes), well-designed interfaces to the operating system, network, etc. Experience has shown that even in numerically oriented programming, it is often extremely handy if you have easy access to powerful semi-numerical or completely non-numerical functionality as well. For example, you might want to offer the results of a complicated computation as a server process to other processes on the network, perhaps directly accepting input from other processes on the network. Using Perl and existing Perl extension packages, things like this are no problem at all (and it all fits into your "PDL script").

- Extremely easy extensibility and interoperability as PDL is a Perl extension; development support for Perl extensions is an integral part of Perl, and there are already numerous extensions to standard Perl freely available on the network.

- Integral language features of Perl (regular expressions, hashes, object modules), which immensely facilitate development and implementation of key concepts of PDL. One of the most striking examples of this is PDL::PP (see below), a code generator/parser/preprocessor that generates PDL functions from concise descriptions.

- None of the other existing DLs follow the Perl language rules, which the authors firmly believe in:

  - TIMTOWTDI: There is more than one way to do it. Minimalist languages are interesting for computer scientists, but for users, a little bit of redundancy makes things wildly easier to cope and allows for individual programming styles. For many people, this will undoubtedly be a reason to avoid PDL. ;-)

- Simple things are simple, complicated things possible: things that are often done should be easy to do in the language, whereas seldom-done things shouldn't be too cumbersome.

  All existing languages violate at least one of these rules.

- As a project for a future PDL, you should be able to use super-computer features, e.g., vector capabilities and parallel processing. This will probably be achieved by having PDL::PP ([alpha], see below) generate appropriate code on such architectures to exploit these features.

- Fill in your personal 111 favorite reasons here.

What is PDL good for?

Just in case you do not yet know what the main features of PDL are and what one can do with them, here is a (necessarily selective) list of key features:

PDL is well-suited for matrix computations, general handling of multidimensional data, image processing, general scientific computation, and numerical applications. It supports I/O for many popular image and data formats, 1D (line plots), 2D (images), and 3D (volume visualization, surface plots via OpenGL/MesaGL) graphics display capabilities, and it implements lots of numerical and semi-numerical algorithms.

[alpha] Some of these features (image I/O, 3D graphics (via OpenGL/MesaGL), matrix library) are currently in alpha testing.

What is the connection between PDL and Perl?

PDL is a Perl5 extension package. As such, it needs an existing Perl5 installation (see below) to run. Furthermore, much of PDL is written in Perl (plus some core functionality that is written in C). PDL programs are (syntactically) just Perl scripts that happen to use some of the functionality implemented by the package "PDL";

What do I need to run PDL on my machine?

Since PDL is just a Perl package, you need first of all an installation of Perl on your machine. As of this writing, PDL requires version 5 of Perl, version 5.003_11 or higher is recommended. More information on where and how to get a Perl installation can be found at the Perl home page (*http://www.perl.com*) and at many CPAN sites (if you do not know what CPAN is check the answer to the next question).

Furthermore, you need the PDL package, which will be installed as an extension within your PERL installation. See below for directions on how and where to get the latest PDL distribution.

Where do I get it?

PDL is available as source distribution in the *Comprehensive Perl Archive Network*, or CPAN. This archive contains not only the PDL distribution, but also just about everything else that is Perl-related. CPAN is mirrored by dozens of sites all over the world. The main site is *ftp://ftp.funet.fi/*. You can find a more local CPAN site by getting the file */pub/languages/perl/CPAN/MIRRORS/* from *ftp://ftp.funet.fi/*. Alternatively, you can point your Web browser at *http://www.perl.com/* and use its CPAN multiplex service. Within CPAN, you find the latest released version of PDL in the directory *CPAN/modules/by-module/PDL/*. Another site that has the latest PDL distribution and latest beta versions is *http://www.aao.gov.au/local/www/kgb/perldl/*. There are currently no other mirror sites in other parts of the world. This will hopefully change soon.

What machines does PDL run on, then?

Ideally, PDL should run on about every machine for which a port of Perl5 is available that supports Xsubs and the package Extutils::MakeMaker. In practice, you might run into problems if you try to compile PDL on some exotic platform it has never been tested on before. A list of platforms on which PDL has been successfully tested is available at *http://www.aao.gov.au/local/www/kgb/perldl/ports.html.* If you don't have a compiler, you can check if a binary distribution for your platform is available (we haven't yet got round to making binary versions/bundles available, but it is definitely on the TODO list) at the PDL home site located at *http://www.aao.gov.au/local/www/ kgb/perldl/.*

If you can (or cannot) get PDL working on a new (previously unsupported) platform, we would like to hear about it. Please report your success or failure to the PDL mailing list at *perldl@jach.hawaii.edu.* We will do our best to assist you in porting PDL to a new system.

What do I have to pay to get PDL?

We are delighted to be able to give you the nicest possible answer on a question like this: PDL is *free software* and all sources are publicly available. But still, there are some copyrights to comply with. So please, try to be as nice as we (the PDL authors) are and try to comply with them.

Oh, before you think it is *completely* free: you have to invest some time to pull the distribution from the net, compile and install it, and (maybe) read the manuals.

In the future, we hope to be able to supply bundles/binaries for a number of popular architectures. However, as of this writing you will have to find some means of how and where to compile the package yourself.

Are there other PDL information sources on the Internet?

First of all, for all purely Perl-related questions (see above why we often talk about Perl in the PDL FAQ) there are tons of sources on the net. A good starting-point is *http://www.perl.com/.*

The PDL home site can be accessed by pointing your web browser to *http:// www.aao.gov.au/local/www/kgb/perldl/.* It has tons of goodies for anyone interested in PDL:

- PDL distributions
- Online documentation
- Pointers to an HTML archive of the PDL mailing lists
- A list of platforms on which PDL has been successfully tested
- News about recently added features, ported libraries, etc.
- Name of the current pumpkin holders for the different PDL modules (if you want to know what that means you better had a look at the web pages)

If you are interested in PDL in general, you can join the PDL mailing list *perldl@jach.hawaii.edu.* This is a forum to discuss programming issues in PDL, report bugs, seek assistance with PDL-related problems, etc. To subscribe, send a message to *perldl-request@jach.hawaii.edu* containing a string in the following format:

```
subscribe me@my.email.address
```

where you should replace the string *me@my.email.address* with your email address. Past messages can be retrieved in digest format by anonymous ftp from *ftp:// ftp.jach.hawaii.edu/pub/ukirt/frossie/pdlp/*. A searchable archive and a hypertext version of the traffic on this list can be found at *http://www.rosat.mpe-garching.mpg.de/ mailing-lists/perldl/*.

If you are interested in all the technical details of the ongoing PDL development, you can join the PDL developers mailing list *pdl-porters@jach.hawaii.edu*. To subscribe, send a message to *pdl-porters-request@jach.hawaii.edu* containing a string in the following format:

```
subscribe me@my.email.address
```

where you should replace the string *me@my.email.address* with your email address. Past messages can be retrieved in digest format by anonymous ftp from *ftp:// ftp.jach.hawaii.edu/pub/ukirt/frossie/pdlp/*. A searchable archive and a hypertext version of the traffic on this list can be found at *http://www.rosat.mpe-garching.mpg.de/ mailing-lists/pdl-porters/*.

Crossposting between these lists should be avoided unless there is a *very* good reason for doing that.

What is the current version of PDL?

As of this writing (FAQ version 0.2 of February 22, 1997) the latest released version is 1.11. Currently in alpha test is 1.9_02. For those of you who are really audacious (and like to run into bugs), directions on how to get the current alpha versions of the latest "hot" PDL modules can be found at *http://www.aao.gov.au/local/www/kgb/perldl/ alpha.html*.

I am looking for a package to do XXX in PDL. Where shall I look for it?

A good place to start is again *http://www.aao.gov.au/local/www/kgb/perldl*. We hope to get round to compiling a list of packages that have already been or are in the process of being interfaced to PDL RSN (you know what that means...). This information will be accessible through the PDL home site.

Where can I get help with PDL-related problems (addiction...)?

Currently, the main PDL-related information source is the PDL mailing list at *perldl@jach.hawaii.edu* (But see also the question on *information sources*). It is devoted to information exchange about all general issues related to PDL. If you want to ask a development-related question, there is the PDL development mailing list *pdl-porters@jach.hawaii.edu*. Check the question about *information sources* for subscription directions and locations of archives of past/recent messages.

Before you post your questions to the list(s) make sure that

- Your problem has not already been dealt with in another section of this FAQ

- You have read the manual(s) (RTFM!)

- Your problem is not a general Perl programming question, in which case you'd better check the Perl FAQ (available at *http://www.perl.com/perl/faq/*) and/or ask the question in the relevant Perl newsgroups or mailing lists.

[alpha] There is this great XXX package on the Net. has it already been interfaced to pdl or how can I do it?

Check on PDL's home site (*http://www.aao.gov.au/local/www/kgb/perldl/*) to see if the package in question has already been ported or interfaced to PDL. The question on how to do the interfacing will probably be dealt with in the next version of the PDL::PP manpage (see below). Note that people willing to write interfaces for new packages should target them toward the upcoming beta versions, since the internals of PDL have changed *a lot* since the latest released version (1.11).

I want to contribute to the further development of PDL. How can I help?

If you have a certain project in mind, you should check if somebody else is already working on it, or if you could benefit from existing modules. Do so by posting your planned project to the PDL developers mailing list at *pdl-porters@jach.hawaii.edu*. To subscribe, send a message to *pdl-porters-request@jach.hawaii.edu* containing a string in the following format:

```
subscribe me@my.email.address
```

where you should replace the string *me@my.email.address* with your email address. You can also read past and current mail in the searchable hypertext version of the mailing list at *http://www.rosat.mpe-garching.mpg.de/mailing-lists/pdl-porters/*. We are always looking for people to write code and/or documentation. ;-)

I think I have found a bug in the current version of PDL. What shall I do?

First, make sure that the bug or problem you came across has not already been dealt with somewhere else in this FAQ. Second, you can check the searchable archive of the PDL mailing list to see whether this bug has already been discussed. If you still haven't found any explanation, you can post a bug report to *perldl@jach.hawaii.edu*.

Technical questions

What is perldl?

Sometimes `perldl` is used as a synonym for PDL. Strictly speaking, however, the name `perldl` is reserved for the little shell that comes with the PDL distribution and is supposed to be used for the interactive prototyping of PDL scripts. For details, check the `perldl` man page.

[alpha] How do I get online help for PDL?

This is currently a subject of ongoing development. We hope to be able to come up with an online help feature soon. A reference card and searchable index are planned as well. Support for these features will be built into the `perldl` shell.

[alpha] Oops, what is threading (is PDL a newsreader) ?

In the context of PDL, threading has a different meaning from what you normally associate with the term. Here, it denotes a feature of PDL that can be loosely defined as an implicit looping facility. For details, check the PDL::threading manpage.

[alpha] What on earth is this dataflow stuff ?

Dataflow is an experimental project that you don't need to concern yourself with (it should not interfere with your usual programming). However, if you want to know, look at the PDL::Dataflow file in the distribution. There are applications that will benefit from this feature.

[alpha] There is this strange pre-processor package (PDL::PP). Do I have to know about it?

PDL::PP is used to compile very concise definitions into XSUB routines implemented in C that can easily be called from PDL and that automatically support threading, data-flow, and other things without you having to worry about it.

For further details, see the PDL::PP documentation that is going to be in the distribution soon.

Sometimes I am getting these strange results when using inplace operations?

This question is related to the `inplace` function. From the documentation (PDL.pod):

> Most functions, e.g., `log()`, return a result that is a transformation of their argument. This makes for good programming practice. However, many operations can be done "in-place" and this may be required when large arrays are in use and memory is at a premium. For these circumstances, the operator `inplace()` is provided, which prevents the extra copy and allows the argument to be modified. e.g.:

```
$x = log($array);           # $array unaffected
log( inplace($bigarray) );  # $bigarray changed in situ
```

And also from the doc:

> Obviously, when used with some functions that can not be applied *in situ* (e.g., `convolve()`), unexpected effects may occur.

Check the list of PDL functions at the end of PDL.pod, which points out `inplace`-safe functions.

[alpha] What is this strange usage of the string concatenation operator .= in PDL scripts ?

See next question on assignment in PDL.

[alpha] Why are there two different kinds of assignment in PDL ?

This is caused by the fact that currently, the assignment operator = allows only restricted overloading. For some purposes of PDL (new indexing features, dataflow) it turned out to be necessary to have more control over the overloading of an assignment operator. Therefore, current alpha versions of PDL peruse the operator .= for certain types of assignments. For details, see the documentation about indexing/threading and dataflow that come with those versions of PDL.

What happens when I have several references to the same PDL object in different variables (cloning, etc?) ?

It's not clear yet.

Bugs

If you find any inaccuracies in this document (or disfunctional URLs), please report them to the `perldl` mailing list *perldl@jach.hawaii.edu* or to the current FAQ maintainer, Christian Soeller (*csoelle@sghms.ac.uk*).

Author and Copyright

This document emerged from a joint effort by several PDL developers to compile a list of the most frequently asked questions about PDL, with answers. Permission is granted for verbatim copying (and formatting) of this material as part of PDL. Permission is explicitly not granted for distribution in book or any corresponding form. Email the current FAQ maintainer, Christian Soeller (*csoelle@sghms.ac.uk*) or ask on the PDL mailing list *perldl@jach.hawaii.edu* if you are unclear.

Note: The PDL FAQ has been reprinted in the Perl Module Reference *with minor editing, by permission.*

PDL::NetCDF—interface NetCDF files to PDL objects

Perl extension that provides an interface to NetCDF portable binary gridded files via PDL objects.

Synopsis

```
# This is the 'traditional' interface for reading and writing NetCDF
# from/into PDLs:
use PDL;
use PDL::NetCDF qw(/^nc/ /^NC_/);
$ncid   = nccreate('file.nc', NC_CLOBBER);
$dim1id = ncdimdef($ncid, 'Dim1', 3);
$var1id = ncvardef($ncid, 'Var1', NC_FLOAT, [$dim1id]);
ncendef($ncid);
ncvarput($ncid, $var1id, [0], [3], float [0..2]);
ncclose($ncid);
...
$ncid  = ncopen('file.nc', NC_RDWR);
$dimid = ncdimid($ncid, 'Dim1');
$varid = ncvarid($ncid, 'Var1');
$p1    = ncvarget($ncid, $varid, [0], [3]);

print $p1; # This is a PDL object of type float
# yields [0, 1, 2]
# This is the object oriented interface (for reading only):
use PDL;
use PDL::NetCDF;
$obj = NetCDF::PDL->new ('file.nc');
$p1  = $obj->get('Var1');
print $p1;
# yields [0, 1, 2]
$dimsize = $obj->dimsize('dimname');
# This attribute will be a PDL or a string depending on its NetCDF
# type.
$attribute = $obj->getatt('attname', 'varname');
# One can also get global attributes using:
$global_attribute = $obj->getatt('attname');
```

For more information on NetCDF, see *http://www.unidata.ucar.edu/packages/netcdf/index.html*. Also see the test file *test.pl* in the distribution.

Description

This is the PDL interface to the Unidata NetCDF library. It is largely a copy of the original **netcdf-perl** (available through Unidata at *http://www.unidata.ucar.edu/packages/netcdf/index.html*).

The NetCDF standard allows N-dimensional binary data to be efficiently stored, annotated, and exchanged between many platforms.

The original interface has been left largely intact except for two functions (see the NetCDF *User's Guide*, available at the above URL, for more information. The manual documents the C interface, but the Perl interface is almost identical):

ncvarget
    get a hyperslab of data

ncvarput
    put a hyperslab of data

These two functions have been modified to receive and deliver PDL objects. (The originals returned one-dimensional Perl lists, which was quite inefficient for large data sets. The flattening of N-dimensional data was also irksome).

This version of the PDL interface also offers an object-oriented read-only interface to NetCDF. You must still write NetCDF files using the old-style interface, but reading NetCDF files is considerably simplified.

Use the function:

```
PDL::NetCDF->new ('file.nc')
```

to create a NetCDF file object. Then use:

```
$obj->get('varname') $obj->getatt ('attname', 'varname')
```

to get variables or attributes into PDLs.

Author

Doug Hunt (*dhunt@ucar.edu*) for the PDL version. Steve Emmerson (UCAR UniData) for the original version.

See Also

perl(1), netcdf(3)

---

print_cols—print elements in vertically sorted columns

Synopsis

```
use Array::PrintCols;
print_cols \@array;
print_cols \@I<array>, $colspec;
print_cols \@I<array>, $colspec, $total_width;
print_cols \@I<array>, $colspec, $total_width, $indent;
$Array::PrintCols::PreSorted = 0;
```

Description

The `print_cols` subroutine prints the items of `@array` in multiple alphabetically sorted vertical columns. One, two, or three optional arguments may be given to `print_cols` to control the width and number of the columns, the total width of the output, and the indentation. Reasonable defaults apply in the absence of the optional arguments (or when given as the empty string or zero). Generally, the minimum-width column is used when possible.

If $col_width is given as a non-negative number, it is treated as the minimum width of the column; the actual width will be the maximum of this value and the lengths of all array items.

If $col_width is given as a negative number, its absolute value is used to determine the total number of columns. However, that number cannot exceed the total number of columns possible based on the maximum length of all the array elements.

If a third argument is supplied, it is used as the total width of the output. The default for this value is the value of the environment variable $ENV{'COLUMNS'}, if defined, or 80.

If the fourth argument is given, it is used as the indent for all lines printed, which subtracts from the total width of the output. This value defaults to zero (ie: no indention of the output).

The variable $Array::PrintCols::PreSorted controls whether or not the print_cols subroutine expects its array argument to already be sorted. If this variable is nil or zero, print_cols causes a sorted *copy* of the input array to be printed.

Example

```
use Array::PrintCols;
@commands = sort qw( use list put get set quit help server );
# print in three columns with an indention of 1.
print_cols \@commands, -3, 0, 1;
```

Bugs

With Perl, you cannot default intervening arguments by leaving them empty; you must supply a zero or empty-string (").

Author

Copyright © 1995 Alan K. Stebbens, (*aks@hub.ucsb.edu*).

This program is free software; you can redistribute it and/or modify it under the terms of the GNU General Public License as published by the Free Software Foundation; either version 2 of the License, or (at your option) any later version.

This program is distributed in the hope that it will be useful, but WITHOUT ANY WARRANTY; without even the implied warranty of MERCHANTABILITY or FITNESS FOR A PARTICULAR PURPOSE. See the GNU General Public License for more details.

You should have received a copy of the GNU General Public License along with this program; if not, write to the Free Software Foundation, Inc., 675 Mass Ave, Cambridge, MA 02139, USA.

PRSG—Perl interface to pseudo-random sequence generator function

Synopsis

```
use Math::PRSG;
```

Description

This Perl extension implements a (159, 31, 0) LFSR, giving a period of 160 bits. This can then be used as an RNG if seeded well (i.e., with 160 bits of entropy) and if the output is fed through a message digest function (in order to prevent any prediction).

Functions

new

> Create a new PRSG object. A 160 bit (20-byte) **$seed** must be provided, which is used to seed the LFSR.
>
> ```
> my $prsg = new PRSG $seed;
> ```

seed

> Seed the LFSR with **$rnd**.
>
> ```
> $prsg->seed($rnd);
> ```

clock

> Clock the LFSR, returning the new register value as a 20-byte string.
>
> ```
> $value = $prsg->clock();
> ```

Copyright

Systemics Ltd., *http://www.systemics.com/*

Set::IntegerFast—sets of integers

Easy manipulation of sets of integers (intervals from zero to some positive integer)

Synopsis

Please refer to the Bit::Vector(3) manpage for an overview and description of the methods supplied by this module.

Description

This module is kept "alive" for backward compatibility only; it is strongly recommended that you use the Bit::Vector module in your application(s) instead.

You need to apply the following changes to your existing application(s):

```
"Set::IntegerFast"     -->     "Bit::Vector"          (required)
"Empty_Interval("      -->     "Interval_Empty("      (recommended)
"Fill_Interval("       -->     "Interval_Fill("       (recommended)
"Flip_Interval("       -->     "Interval_Flip("       (recommended)
"Delete("              -->     "Bit_On("              (recommended)
"Insert("              -->     "Bit_Off("             (recommended)
"flip("                -->     "bit_flip("            (recommended)
"in("                  -->     "bit_test("            (recommended)
"in("                  -->     "contains("            (alternative)
"inclusion("           -->     "subset("              (recommended)
```

Please refer to the file CHANGES in the Bit::Vector distribution for more details.

Version

This manpage documents Set::IntegerFast version 4.0.

Author

Steffen Beyer, *sb@sdm.de*

Copyright

Copyright © 1995, 1996, 1997 by Steffen Beyer. All rights reserved.

This package is free software; you can redistribute it and/or modify it under the same terms as Perl itself.

See Also

Bit::Vector(3), Set::IntegerRange(3), Math::MatrixBool(3), Math::MatrixReal(3), DFA::Kleene(3), Math::Kleene(3), Graph::Kruskal(3)

Set::IntegerRange—easy manipulation of sets of integers (arbitrary intervals)

Synopsis

Methods

Version
```
$version = $Set::IntegerRange::VERSION;
```

new
```
$set = new Set::IntegerRange($lower,$upper);
$set = Set::IntegerRange->new($lower,$upper);
$set = $any_set->new($lower,$upper);
```

Size
```
($lower,$upper) = $set->Size();
```

Empty
```
$set->Empty();
```

Fill
```
$set->Fill();
```

Flip
```
$set->Flip();
```

Interval_Empty
```
$set->Interval_Empty($lower,$upper);
$set->Empty_Interval($lower,$upper); # (deprecated)
```

Interval_Fill
```
$set->Interval_Fill($lower,$upper);
$set->Fill_Interval($lower,$upper);  # (deprecated)
```

Interval_Flip
```
$set->Interval_Flip($lower,$upper);
$set->Flip_Interval($lower,$upper);  # (deprecated)
```

Bit_Off
```
$set->Bit_Off($index);
$set->Delete($index);                # (deprecated)
```

Bit_On
```
$set->Bit_On($index);
$set->Insert($index);                # (deprecated)
```

bit_flip
```
$bit = $set->bit_flip($index);
if ($set->bit_flip($index))
```

```
      $bit = $set->flip($index);              # (deprecated)
      if ($set->flip($index))                 # (deprecated)
bit_test
      $bit = $set->bit_test($index);
      if ($set->bit_test($index))
      $bit = $set->contains($index);
      if ($set->contains($index))
      $bit = $set->in($index);                # (deprecated)
      if ($set->in($index))                   # (deprecated)
Norm
      $norm = $set->Norm();
Min
      $min = $set->Min();
Max
      $max = $set->Max();
Union
      $set1->Union($set2,$set3);              # in-place is possible!
Inersection
      $set1->Intersection($set2,$set3);       # in-place is possible!
Difference
      $set1->Difference($set2,$set3);         # in-place is possible!
ExclusiveOr
      $set1->ExclusiveOr($set2,$set3);        # in-place is possible!
Complement
      $set1->Complement($set2);               # in-place is possible!
equal
      if ($set1->equal($set2))
subset
      if ($set1->subset($set2))
      if ($set1->inclusion($set2))            # (deprecated)
lexorder
      if ($set1->lexorder($set2))
Compare
      $cmp = $set1->Compare($set2);
Copy
      $set1->Copy($set2);
Shadow
      $other_set = $some_set->Shadow();
Clone
      $twin_set = $some_set->Clone();
to_ASCII
      $string = $set->to_ASCII();             # e.g., "-8..-5,-1..2,4,6..9"
from_ASCII
      eval { $set->from_ASCII($string); };
to_String
      $string = $set->to_String();            # e.g., "0007AF1E"
```

from_String
```
eval { $set->from_String($string); };
```

Overloaded Operators

```
# "$index" is a number or a Perl scalar variable containing a
# number which represents the set containing only that element:
```

Emptyness
```
if ($set) # if not empty
if (! $set) # if empty
unless ($set) # if empty
```

Equality
```
if ($set1 == $set2)
if ($set1 != $set2)
if ($set == $index)
if ($set != $index)
```

Lexical Comparison
```
$cmp = $set1 cmp $set2;
if ($set1 lt $set2)
if ($set1 le $set2)
if ($set1 gt $set2)
if ($set1 ge $set2)
if ($set1 eq $set2)
if ($set1 ne $set2)
$cmp = $set cmp $index;
if ($set lt $index)
if ($set le $index)
if ($set gt $index)
if ($set ge $index)
if ($set eq $index)
if ($set ne $index)
```

String Conversion
```
$string = "$set";
print "\$set = '$set'\n";
```

Union
```
$set1 = $set2 + $set3;
$set1 += $set2;
$set1 = $set2 | $set3;
$set1 |= $set2;
$set1 = $set2 + $index;
$set += $index;
$set1 = $set2 | $index;
$set |= $index;
```

Intersection
```
$set1 = $set2 * $set3;
$set1 *= $set2;
$set1 = $set2 & $set3;
$set1 &= $set2;
$set1 = $set2 * $index;
$set *= $index;
$set1 = $set2 & $index;
$set &= $index;
```

Difference
```
$set1 = $set2 - $set3;
$set1 -= $set2;
$set1 = $set2 - $set1;
$set1 = $set2 - $index;
$set1 = $index - $set2;
$set -= $index;
```
ExclusiveOr
```
$set1 = $set2 ^ $set3;
$set1 ^= $set2;
$set1 = $set2 ^ $index;
$set ^= $index;
```
Complement
```
$set1 = -$set2;
$set1 = ~$set2;
$set = -$set;
$set = ~$set;
```
Subset Relationship
```
if ($set1 <= $set2)
```
True Subset Relationship
```
if ($set1 < $set2)
```
Superset Relationship
```
if ($set1 >= $set2)
```
True Superset Relationship
```
if ($set1 > $set2)
```
Norm
```
$norm = abs($set);
```

Description

This class lets you dynamically create sets of arbitrary intervals of integers and perform all the basic operations for sets on them (for a list of available methods and operators, see above).

See the Bit::Vector(3) manpage for more details.

Version

This manpage documents Set::IntegerRange version 4.0.

Author

Steffen Beyer, *sb@sdm.de*

Copyright

Copyright © 1996, 1997 by Steffen Beyer. All rights reserved.

This package is free software; you can redistribute it and/or modify it under the same terms as Perl itself.

See Also

Bit::Vector(3), Set::IntegerFast(3), Math::MatrixBool(3), Math::MatrixReal(3), DFA::Kleene(3), Math::Kleene(3), Graph::Kruskal(3)

Set::IntSpan—manage sets of integers

Synopsis

```
use Set::IntSpan;
$Set::IntSpan::Empty_String = $string;
$set    = new   Set::IntSpan $set_spec;
$valid  = valid Set::IntSpan $run_list;
copy $set $set_spec;

$run_list   = run_list $set;
@elements   = elements $set;

$u_set = union      $set $set_spec;
$i_set = intersect  $set $set_spec;
$x_set = xor        $set $set_spec;
$d_set = diff       $set $set_spec;
$c_set = complement $set;

equal       $set $set_spec;
equivalent  $set $set_spec;
superset    $set $set_spec;
subset      $set $set_spec;

$n = cardinality $set;
empty       $set;
finite      $set;
neg_inf     $set;
pos_inf     $set;
infinite    $set;
universal   $set;

member      $set $n;
insert      $set $n;
remove      $set $n;
$min = min  $set;
$max = max  $set;
```

Requires

Perl 5.002, Exporter

Exports

None

Description

Set::IntSpan manages sets of integers. It is optimized for sets that have long runs of consecutive integers. These arise, for example, in *.newsrc* files, which maintain lists of articles:

```
alt.foo: 1-21,28,31
alt.bar: 1-14192,14194,14196-14221
```

Sets are stored internally in a run-length coded form. This provides for both compact storage and efficient computation. In particular, set operations can be performed directly on the encoded representation.

Set::IntSpan is designed to manage finite sets. However, it can also represent some simple infinite sets, such as {x | x>n}. This allows operations involving complements to be carried out consistently, without having to worry about the actual value of MAXINT on your machine.

Set Specifications

Many of the methods take a *set specification*. There are four kinds of set specifications:

Empty

> If a set specification is omitted, then the empty set is assumed. Thus,
>
> ```
> $set = new Set::IntSpan;
> ```
>
> creates a new, empty, set. Similarly,
>
> ```
> copy $set;
> ```
>
> removes all elements from $set.

Object reference

> If an object reference is given, it is taken to be a Set::IntSpan object.

Array reference

> If an array reference is given, then the elements of the array are taken to be the elements of the set. The array may contain duplicate elements. The elements of the array may be in any order.

Run list

> If a string is given, it is taken to be a *run list*. A run list specifies a set using a syntax similar to that in *.newsrc* files.
>
> A run list is a comma-separated list of *runs*. Each run specifies a set of consecutive integers. The set is the union of all the runs.
>
> Runs may be written in any of several forms:

Finite forms

```
n        { n }
a-b      {x | a<=x && x<=b}
```

Infinite forms

```
(-n      {x | x<=n}
n-)      {x | x>=n}
(-)      The set of all integers
```

Empty forms

> The empty set is consistently written as ' ' (the null string). It is also denoted by the special form – (a single dash).

Restrictions

- The runs in a run list must be disjoint and must be listed in increasing order.
- Valid characters in a run list are 0–9, (,), –, and ,. Whitespace and underscore (_) are ignored. Other characters are not allowed.

Examples

-	{ }
1	{ 1 }
1-2	{ 1, 2 }
-5--1	{ -5, -4, -3, -2, -1 }
(-)	the integers
(--1	the negative integers
1-3, 4, 18-21	{ 1, 2, 3, 4, 18, 19, 20, 21 }

Methods

Creation

`new Set::IntSpan $set_spec;`

Creates and returns a new set. The initial contents of the set are given by *$set_spec*.

`valid Set::IntSpan $run_list;`

Returns `true` if *$run_list* is a valid run list. Otherwise, returns false and leaves an error message in $@.

`copy $set $set_spec;`

Copies *$set_spec* into *$set*. The previous contents of *$set* are lost. For convenience, `copy()` returns *$set*.

`$run_list = run_list $set`

Returns a run list that represents *$set*. The run list will not contain white space. *$set* is not affected.

By default, the empty set is formatted as '-'; a different string may be specified in $Set::IntSpan::Empty_String.

`@elements = elements $set;`

Returns an array containing the elements of *$set*. The elements will be sorted in numerical order. In scalar context, returns an array reference. *$set* is not affected.

Set operations

`$u_set = union $set $set_spec;`

Returns the set of integers in either *$set* or *$set_spec*

`$i_set = intersect $set $set_spec;`

Returns the set of integers in both *$set* and *$set_spec*

`$x_set = xor $set $set_spec;`

Returns the set of integers in *$set* or *$set_spec*, but not both

`$d_set = diff $set $set_spec;`

Returns the set of integers in *$set* but not in *$set_spec*

`$c_set = complement $set;`

Returns the complement of *$set*.

For all set operations, a new Set::IntSpan object is created and returned. The operands are not affected.

Comparison

`equal $set $set_spec;`

    Returns true if $set and $set_spec contain the same elements.

`equivalent $set $set_spec;`

    Returns true if $set and $set_spec contain the same number of elements. All infinite sets are equivalent.

`superset $set $set_spec`

    Returns true if $set is a superset of $set_spec.

`subset $set $set_spec`

    Returns true if $set is a subset of $set_spec.

Cardinality

`$n = cardinality $set`

    Returns the number of elements in $set. Returns -1 for infinite sets.

`empty $set;`

    Returns true if $set is empty.

`finite $set`

    Returns true if $set is finite.

`neg_inf $set`

    Returns true if $set contains {x | x<n} for some n.

`pos_inf $set`

    Returns true if $set contains {x | x>n} for some n.

`infinite $set`

    Returns true if $set is infinite.

`universal $set`

    Returns true if $set contains all integers.

Membership

`member $set $n`

    Returns true if the integer $n is a member of $set.

`insert $set $n`

    Inserts the integer $n into $set. Does nothing if $n is already a member of $set.

`remove $set $n`

    Removes the integer $n from $set. Does nothing if $n is not a member of $set.

Extrema

`min $set`

    Returns the smallest element of $set, or undef if there is none.

`max $set`

    Returns the largest element of $set, or undef if there is none.

Class Variables

`$Set::IntSpan::Empty_String`

    $Set::IntSpan::Empty_String contains the string that is returned when run_list() is called on the empty set. $Empty_String is initially –; alternatively, it may be set to ' '. Other values should be avoided to ensure that `run_list()` always returns a valid run list.

`run_list()` accesses `$Empty_String` through a reference stored in `$set->{empty_string}`. Subclasses that wish to override the value of `$Empty_String` can reassign this reference.

Diagnostics

Any method (except `valid()`) will `die()` if it is passed an invalid run list. Possible messages are:

Bad syntax

> `$run_list` has bad syntax.

Bad order

> `$run_list` has overlapping runs or runs that are out of order.

`elements $set` will `die()` if `$set` is infinite. `elements $set` can generate an "Out of memory!" message on sufficiently large finite sets.

Notes

Traps

Beware of forms like:

```
union $set [1..5];
```

This passes an element of `@set` to `union`, which is probably not what you want. To force interpretation of `$set` and [1..5] as separate arguments, use forms like

```
union $set +[1..5];
```

or:

```
$set->union([1..5]);
```

Error handling

There are two common approaches to error handling: exceptions and return codes. There seems to be some religion on the topic, so Set::IntSpan provides support for both.

To catch exceptions, protect method calls with an **eval**:

```
$run_list = <STDIN>;
eval { $set = new Set::IntSpan $run_list };
$@ and print "$@: try again\n";
```

To check return codes, use an appropriate method call to validate arguments:

```
$run_list = <STDIN>;
if (valid Set::IntSpan $run_list)
    { $set = new Set::IntSpan $run_list }
else
    { print "$@ try again\n" }
```

Similarly, use `finite()` to protect calls to `elements()`:

```
finite $set and @elements = elements $set;
```

Calling `elements()` on a large, finite set can generate an "Out of memory!" message, which cannot be trapped.

Applications that must retain control after an error can use `intersect()` to protect calls to `elements()`:

```
@elements = elements { intersect $set "-1_000_000 - 1_000_000"
   };
```

or check the size of `$set` first:

```
finite $set and cardinality $set < 2_000_000 and @elements =
        elements $set;
```

Limitations

Although Set::IntSpan can represent some infinite sets, it does *not* perform infinite-precision arithmetic. Therefore, finite elements are restricted to the range of integers on your machine.

Roots

The sets implemented here are based on Macintosh data structures called "regions." See *Inside Macintosh* for more information.

Author

Steven McDougall, *swm@cric.com*

Copyright

Copyright © 1996 Steven McDougall. All rights reserved. This module is free software; you can redistribute it and/or modify it under the same terms as Perl itself.

Set::Scalar—the basic set operations for Perl scalar/reference data

Synopsis

```
    use Set::Scalar;
```

or

```
    use Set::Scalar qw(union intersection);
```

to import, for example, `union` and `intersection` to the current namespace. By default, nothing is imported; the exportable routines are: `as_string`, `union`, `intersection`, `symmetric_difference`, `difference`, `in`, `compare`, `equal`, `disjoint`, `proper_subset`, `proper_superset`, `subset`, `superset`.

Please see below for further documentation.

Description

Sets are created with `new`. Lists as arguments for `new` give normal sets; hash references (please see `perlref`) give *valued sets*. The special sets, `null set` or the *none (empty)*, set, and the `universal set` *all* are created with `null` and `universal`.

```
    $a = Set::Scalar->new('a', 'b', 'c', 'd');   # set members
    $b = Set::Scalar->new('c', 'd', 'e', 'f');   # set members
    $c = Set::Scalar->new(qw(d e));              # set members
    $d = Set::Scalar->new({'f', 12, 'g', 34});   # 'valued' set
    $e = Set::Scalar->new($a, 'h', 'i');         # sets are recursive
    $n = Set::Scalar->null;                      # the empty set
    $u = Set::Scalar->universal;                 # the 'all' set
```

Valued sets are "added value" sets: normal sets have only their members, but valued sets have one scalar/ref value for each member. See the discussion about **values** and **valued_ members** for how to retrieve the values.

Set inversion or the *not* set is done with **inverse** or the overloaded prefix operator, −:

```
$i = $a->inverse;                # the 'not' set
$i = -$a;                        # or with the overloaded -
```

Displaying sets is done with **as_string** or, more commonly, with the overloaded stringification operator, "".

```
print "a = ", $a->as_string, "\n";
print "b = $b\n";                # or with the overloaded "
print "c = $c\n";
print "d = $d\n";
print "e = ", $e, "\n";
print "i = $i\n";
print "n = $n\n";
print "u = $u\n";
```

Note: Please do not try to display circular sets. Yes, circular sets can be built. Yes, trying to display them will cause infinite recursion.

The usual set operations are done with **union**, **intersection**, **symmetric_difference**, and **difference**, or with their overloaded infix operator counterparts, +, *, %, and −:

```
print "union(a,b) = ", Set::Scalar->union($a, $b), "\n";
print "a + b = ", $a + $b, "\n";   # or with the overloaded +
print "intersection(a,b) = ", Set::Scalar->intersection($a, $b), "\n";
print "a * b = ", $a * $b, "\n";   # or with the overloaded *
print "symmdiff(a,b) = ",
      Set::Scalar->symmetric_difference($a, $b), "\n";
print "a % b = ", $a % $b, "\n";   # or with the overloaded %
print "difference(a,b) = ", Set::Scalar->difference($a, $b), "\n";
print "a - b = ", $a - $b, "\n";   # or with the overloaded -
```

Note: The distributive laws (please see LAWS or *t/laws.t* in the Set::Scalar distribution) cannot always be satisfied. This is because in set algebra *the whole universe* (all the possible members of all the possible sets) is supposed to be defined beforehand *but* the set operations see only two sets at a time. This can cause the distributive laws:

```
X + (Y * Z) == (X + Y) * (X + Z)
X * (Y + Z) == (X * Y) + (X * Z)
```

to fail because the + and * do not necessarily "see" all the members of the X, Y, Z in time. Beware of this effect, especially when having simultaneously any two of the X, Y, Z, being identical in members except the other being inverted, or one the X, Y, Z, being the null set.

Modifying sets **in-place** is done with **insert** and **delete** or their overload counterparts += and −=. Testing for membership is done with **in**.

```
print "a  = $a\n";
$a->insert('x');
print "a' = $a\n";
print 'x is', $a->in('x') ? '' : ' not', " in a\n";
$a->delete('x');
print "a  = $a\n";
print 'x is', $a->in('x') ? '' : ' not', " in a\n";
```

Note: Set copying by = is shallow. Sets are objects and = copies only the topmost level. That is, the copy is a *reference* to the original set.

```
$x = $a;
print "a  = $a, x = $x, e = $e\n";
$a->insert('x');
print "a' = $a, x = $x, e = $e\n";  # also the 'copy' of a changes
$a->delete('x');
print "a' = $a, x = $x, e = $e\n";
```

For deep ("real") copying use `copy` (or `->new($set)`).

```
$y = $e->copy;
print "a  = $a, y = $y, e = $e\n";
$a->insert('y');
# the (real, deep) copy does not change
print "a' = $a, y = $y, e = $e\n";
$a->delete('y');
print "a' = $a, y = $y, e = $e\n";
```

Testing sets is done with `is_null`, `is_universal`, `is_inverted`, and `is_valued`.

```
print 'a is', $a->is_null      ? '' : ' not', " null\n";
print 'a is', $a->is_universal ? '' : ' not', " universal\n";
print 'a is', $a->is_inverted  ? '' : ' not', " inverted\n";
print 'a is', $a->is_valued    ? '' : ' not', " valued\n";
print 'd is', $d->is_null      ? '' : ' not', " null\n";
print 'd is', $d->is_universal ? '' : ' not', " universal\n";
print 'd is', $a->is_inverted  ? '' : ' not', " inverted\n";
print 'd is', $d->is_valued    ? '' : ' not', " valued\n";
print 'i is', $i->is_null      ? '' : ' not', " null\n";
print 'i is', $i->is_universal ? '' : ' not', " universal\n";
print 'i is', $i->is_inverted  ? '' : ' not', " inverted\n";
print 'i is', $i->is_valued    ? '' : ' not', " valued\n";
print 'n is', $n->is_null      ? '' : ' not', " null\n";
print 'n is', $n->is_universal ? '' : ' not', " universal\n";
print 'n is', $n->is_inverted  ? '' : ' not', " inverted\n";
print 'n is', $n->is_valued    ? '' : ' not', " valued\n";
print 'u is', $u->is_null      ? '' : ' not', " null\n";
print 'u is', $u->is_universal ? '' : ' not', " universal\n";
print 'u is', $u->is_inverted  ? '' : ' not', " inverted\n";
print 'u is', $u->is_valued    ? '' : ' not', " valued\n";
```

Comparing sets is done with:

```
compare
equal
disjoint
intersect
proper_subset
proper_superset
subset
superset
```

or, more commonly, with their overloaded infix operator counterparts:

```
<=>
==
!=
```

```
<>
<
>
<=
=>
```

Note: **compare** is a multivalued relational operator, not a binary (two-valued) one. It returns a *string* that is one of:

```
==
!=
<>
<
>
<=
=>
```

The **equal**, **disjoint**, **intersect**, **proper_subset**, **proper_superset**, **subset**, and **superset**, *are* binary (true or false) relational operators.

The difference between **disjoint** and **intersect** is that the former means completely disjoint (no common members at all), and the latter means partly disjoint (some common members, some not).

```
print "a <=> a = '", $a <=> $a, "'\n";
print "a == c\n" if ($a == $c);
print "b <=> c = '", $b <=> $c, "'\n";
print "c <=> b = '", $c <=> $b, "'\n";
print "b >= c\n" if ($b >= $c);
print "c <  b\n" if ($c <  $b);
print "a <=> c = '", $a <=> $c, "'\n";
print "a <=> d = '", $a <=> $d, "'\n";
```

Note: Please do not try to "sort" sets based on the **subset** and **superset** relational operators. This does not work in the general case because sets can have circular relationships. Circular sets cause infinite recursion.

The set members can be accessed with **members**. For the valued sets either the values can be accessed with **values** as a list or both the members and the values with **valued_members** as a hash. *None of these returns the items in any particular order;* the sets of Set::Scalar are unordered.

```
for $i ($a->members) {              print "a: $i\n"; }
for $i (Set::Scalar->values($d)) {  print "d: $i\n"; }
%d = $d->valued_members;
while (($k, $v) = each %d) {         print "d: $k $v\n"; }
```

Sets can be **grepped** and **mapped**.

```
%g = $a->grep(sub { $_[0] eq 'b' });
$g = Set::Scalar->new(keys %g);
print "g = $g\n";
%m = $d->map(sub { my ($k, $v, $d) = @_;
                   $k =~ tr/a-z/A-Z/;
                   $v *= $v;
                   $d = $k ne 'G';
                   ($k, $v, $d); });
$m = Set::Scalar->new({ %m });
print "m = $m\n";
```

The power set (the set of all the possible subsets of a set) is generated with **power_set**:

```
$p = $a->power_set;
print "p = $p\n";
```

Displaying sets can be fine-tuned either per set or by changing the global default display attributes using the `display_attr` with two arguments. The display attributes can be examined using the `display_attr` with one argument.

The display attributes are:

format
> A string which should contain magic sequences **%s** which marks the place of the *sign-edness* (normal or inverted) of set, and **%m**, which marks the place of the members of the set. The default is **%s(%m)**.

inverse
> A string that tells how to mark an inverted set (the **%s** in `format`). The default is **–**.

exists
> A string that tells how to mark an "existing" set. An "existing" set is a set that is not inverted, that is, a set that is "not not" (the **%s** in `format`). The default is ".

member_separator
> A string that tells how to separate the members of the set, (the **%m** in `format`). The default is ' '.

value_style
> A string that tells how to display valued sets. Only two styles are defined: **parallel** (the default) or **serial**. The former means that the order is:

```
m1 v1 m2 v2 ...
```

> and the latter means that the order is:

```
m1 m2 ... v1 v2 ...
```

value_indicator
> A string that tells how to separate the members from the values in the case of valued sets. In the **parallel** style there are as many **value_indicators** shown as there are members (or values), in the **serial** style only one **value_indicator** is shown.

value_separator
> A string that tells how to separate the members and the values in case of **serial** display of valued sets, (the **%m** in `format`). The default is ' '.

sort
> A name of a subroutine that tells how to order the members of the set. The default name is _DISPLAY_SORT, which sorts the members alphabetically. This is why the displayed form is something like this

```
(a b c d)
```

> and not anything random (to be exact, in hash order). Sets do not have any particular order per se (please see the members discussion).

```
print "format(a) = ", $a->display_attr('format'), "\n";
print "memsep(a) = ", $a->display_attr('member_separator'), "\n";
print "format(b) = ", $b->display_attr('format'), "\n";
print "memsep(b) = ", $b->display_attr('member_separator'), "\n";
# changing the per-set display attributes
$a->display_attr('format', '%s{%m}');
```

```
$a->display_attr('member_separator', ',');
print "a = $a, b = $b\n";
print "format(a) = ", $a->display_attr('format'), "\n";
print "memsep(a) = ", $a->display_attr('member_separator'), "\n";
print "format(b) = ", $b->display_attr('format'), "\n";
print "memsep(b) = ", $b->display_attr('member_separator'), "\n";
# changing the default display attributes
print "memsep = '", Set::Scalar->display_attr('member_separator'),
"'\n";
Set::Scalar->display_attr('member_separator', ':');
print "memsep = '", Set::Scalar->display_attr('member_separator'),
"'\n";
print "a = $a, b = $b\n";
Set::Scalar->display_attr('member_separator', ' ');
```

Author

Jarkko Hietaniemi, *Jarkko.Hietaniemi@iki.fi*

Set::Window—manages an interval on the integer line

Synopsis

```
use Set::Window;

$window  = new_lr Set::Window $left, $right;
$window  = new_ll Set::Window $left, $length;
$window  = empty  Set::Window;

$left    = $window->left;
$right   = $window->right;
$size    = $window->size;
@bounds  = $window->bounds;
@elements = $window->elements;

empty     $window;
eqivalent $window1 $window2;
equal     $window1 $window2;

$window = copy       $window
$window = offset     $window $offset
$window = inset      $window $inset
$window = cover      $window @windows
$window = intersect  $window @windows

@windows = $window->series($length);
```

Requires

Perl 5.003, Exporter

Exports

Nothing

Description

A Set::Window object represents a window on the integer line; that is, a finite set of consecutive integers.

Methods are provided for creating and modifying windows, for obtaining information about windows, and for performing some simple set operations on windows.

The Empty Window

The empty window represents the empty set. Like the empty set, the empty window is unique.

Methods

Creation

`new_lr Set::Window $left, $right`
> Creates and returns a new Set::Window object. `$left` and `$right` specify the first and last integers in the window.
>
> If `$right` is less than `$left`, returns the empty window.

`new_ll Set::Window $left, $length`
> Creates and returns a new Set::Window object. `$left` is the first integer in the interval, and `$length` is the number of integers in the interval
>
> If `$length` is less than one, returns the empty window.

`empty Set::Window`
> Creates and returns an empty `Set::Window` object.

Access

`$window->left`
> Returns the first integer in the window, or `undef` if `$window` is empty.

`$window->right`
> Returns the last integer in the window, or `undef` if `$window` is empty.

`$window->size`
> Returns the number of integers in the window.
>
> The identity `$window->size == $window->right - $window->left + 1` holds for all non-empty windows.

`$window->bounds`
> Returns a list of the first and last integers in `$window`, or `undef` if `$window` is empty. In scalar context, returns an array reference.

`$window->elements`
> Returns a list of the integers in `$window`, in order. In scalar context, returns an array reference.

Predicates

`empty $window`
> Returns true if `$window` is empty.

`equal $window1 $window2`
> Returns true if `$window1` and `$window2` are the same.
>
> All empty windows are `equal`.

equivalent $window1 $window2

>   Returns true if $window1 and $window2 are the same size.

Modification

These methods implement copy semantics: modifications are made to a copy of the original window. The original window is unaltered, and the new window is returned.

copy $window

>   Creates and returns a (deep) copy of $window.

offset $window $offset

>   Makes a copy of $window, and then shifts it by $offset. Positive values of $offset move the window to the right; negative values move it to the left. Returns the new window.

>   If offset is called on the empty window, it returns the empty window.

inset $window $inset

>   Makes a copy of $window, and then shrinks it by $inset at each end. If $inset is negative, the window expands. Returns the new window.

>   If inset is called on the empty window, it returns the empty window.

cover $window @windows

>   Creates and returns the smallest window that covers (i.e. contains) $window and all the @windows.

intersect $window @windows

>   Creates and returns the largest window that is contained by $window and all the @windows. This may be the empty window.

Utility

$window->series($length)

>   Returns a list of all the windows of $length that are contained in $window, ordered from left to right. In scalar context, returns an array reference.

>   If $length is greater than $window->length, the list will be empty. If $length is less than 1, returns undef.

Diagnostics

None.

Notes

Why?

Believe it or not, I actually needed this structure in a program. Maybe someone else will need it, too.

Weight

Set::Window objects are designed to be lightweight. If you need more functionality, consider using Set::IntSpan.

Error handling

Set::Window does not issue any diganostics; in particular, none of the methods can die.

Calling `elements` on a large window can lead to an **out of memory!** message, which cannot be trapped (as of Perl 5.003). Applications that must retain control can protect calls to `elements` with an `intersect`:

```
$limit = new_lr Set::Window -1_000_000, 1_000_000;
@elements = $window->intersect($limit)->elements;
```

or check the size of `$window` first:

```
length $window < 2_000_000 and @elements = elements $window;
```

Operations involving the empty window are handled consistently. They return valid results if they make sense, and `undef` otherwise. Thus:

```
Set::Window->empty->elements
```

returns an empty list, because the empty window has no elements, while:

```
Set::Windows->empty->bounds
```

returns `undef`, because the empty window has no first or last element.

Author

Steven McDougall, *swmcd@world.std.com*

Copyright

Copyright © 1996, 1997 Steven McDougall. All rights reserved. This module is free software; you can redistribute it and/or modify it under the same terms as Perl itself.

See Also

perl(1), Set::IntSpan

Sort::PolySort—general rules-based sorting of lists

Synopsis

```
use Sort::PolySort;
$s=new Sort::PolySort;                    # defaults to 'name'
@people=('John Doe','Jane Doll','John Quasimodo Doe');
print join(", ",$s->sort(@people),"\n";

use Sort::PolySort;
$s=new Sort::PolySort('dateus');          # sets internal
@dates=$s->sort(@dates);                  # uses internal
$s->by('email');                          # sets internal
@names=$s->sortby('name',@names);         # overrides internal
@emails=$s->sort(@emails);                # internal is still 'email'
```

Description

This module provides methods to sort a list of strings based on parsing the strings according to a configurable set of specifications.

Methods

The following methods are available:

new

    Creates a new polysort object. Takes optional argument of initial named spec set (defaults to name).

by

    Configures for the named set of sorting specs. Argument is name of spec set.

sort

    Sorts by the previously set (by **new** or **by**) specs. Argument is a list of items to sort. Returns the sorted list, leaving the original unchanged.

sortby

    Sorts by the given (named) set of specs. The specs are changed only for this particular sort, so future calls to **sort** will use whatever specs were in effect before the **sortby** call. First argument is name of spec set, second argument is a list of items to sort. Returns the sorted list, leaving the original unchanged.

get

    Returns an associative array of the current sort specs. See "Notes."

set

    Sets the current sort specs to the given associative array. Specs not appearing in the passed array retain their previous values, so this method can be used along with get to keep state during a subroutine call or to alter particular specs to get new sorting results. Argument is an associative array. See "Notes."

Specs

    The following specifications are local to each Sort::PolySort object:

    GLOBTOP

        Lump last two levels together?

    LEVELS

        Number of levels to consider (0=all)

    R2L

        Count fields right to left?

    NUMERIC

        Do numerical sort?

    CASE

        Do case-sensitive sort?

    DELIM1

        Primary element delimiter (must not be null).

    DELIM2

        Secondary element delimiter (can be null).

Parsing Scheme

    The following order is followed to determine the keys used to sort the given array:

    1. DELIM2 (if given)

        Remove up to leftmost (rightmost if R2L is true) occurrence of DELIM2 (will be brought back later).

    2. DELIM1

        Split remainder at all occurrences of DELIM1.

3. GLOBTOP (if true)

Rejoin left (right if R2L is true) two elements (always joined left-to-right, regardless of R2L).

4. R2L (if true)

Reverse list of elements.

5. LEVELS

Store first LEVELS (all if =0) elements (last two considered as a single element if GLOBTOP is true).

6. DELIM2 (if true)

Store string from left of DELIM2 as next element.

7. LEVELS (unless 0)

Rejoin remaining elements (in original order, regardless of R2L) and store as next element.

Named Specs

The following (case-sensitive) names are used by new, by, and sortby to represent predefined sets of specs:

datebr
> By European (dd/mm/yy) date

dateus
> By US-style (mm/dd/yy) date

email
> By user for each machine (all parts of FQDN)

email2
> By user for each top-level domain (last two atoms)

emaild
> By user for each domain-name (next-to-last atom)

ip
> By numerical (aaa.bbb.ccc.ddd) IP address

name
> By last name/first name/middle name or initials

Errors

The following errors may occur:

- No specname given
- by or sortby wasn't passed a specname.
- Never heard of specname "foo"
- new, by, or sortby was passed a name that was not in the list of known specnames.

Notes

The whole parsing method is pretty perverse, but honestly was the first thing that came to mind. It works, but is not very fast or extensible. Enough interested folks mailed me that I wanted to get this out now, but it's dyin' for a rewrite. So this is just a beta. The main interface will remain the same, but the parser will be rewritten and the spec variables changed. Accessor methods will change as a result (using %s=$s-get; ... ;$s->set(%s) will probably still work to save state, though). And accessor methods wll be added so that new names spec sets can be added at runtime or known ones modified. And new named spec sets will be added. And on and on and on...

Author

Daniel Macks, *dmacks@netspace.org*

Copyright

Copyright © 1996 by Daniel Macks. All rights reserved. This module is free software; you may redistribute it and/or modify it under the same terms as Perl itself.

Sort::Versions—a Perl 5 module for sorting of revision-like numbers

Synopsis

```
use Sort::Versions;
@l = sort versions qw( 1.2 1.2.0 1.2a.0 1.2.a 1.a 02.a );
...
use Sort::Versions;
print "lower" if versioncmp("1.2","1.2a")==-1;


...


use Sort::Versions;
%h = (1 => "d", 2 => "c", 3 => "b", 4 => "a");
@h = sort {versioncmp $h{$a}, $h{$b}} keys %h;
```

Description

Sort::Versions allows easy sorting of mixed non-numeric and numeric strings, like the "version numbers" that many shared library systems and revision control packages use. This is quite useful if you are trying to deal with shared libraries. It can also be applied to applications that intersperse variable-width numeric fields within text. Other applications can undoubtedly be found.

For an explanation of the algorithm, it's simplest to look at these examples:

```
1.1   <  1.2
1.1a  <  1.2
1.1   <  1.1.1
1.1   <  1.1a
1.1.a <  1.1a
1     <  a
a     <  b
1     <  2
1     <  0002
1.5   <  1.06
```

More precisely (but less comprehensibly), the two strings are treated as subunits delimited by periods. Each subunit can contain any number of groups of digits or non-digits. If digit groups are being compared on both sides, a numeric comparison is used, otherwise ASCII ordering is used. A group or subgroup with more units will win if all comparisons are equal.

One important thing to note is that if a numeric comparison is made, then leading zeros are ignored. Thus 1.5 sorts before 1.06, since two separate comparisons are being made: 1 == 1, and 5 < 6. This is *not* the same as if(1.5 < 1.06) {...}.

Usage

Sort::Versions exports **versions** and **versioncmp**. The former is a function suitable for handing directly to **sort**. The second function, **versioncmp**, takes two arguments and returns a cmp-style comparison value. This is handy in indirect comparisons, as shown above.

Author

Kenneth J. Albanowski, *kjahds@kjahds.com*

Copyright © 1996, Kenneth J. Albanowski. All rights reserved. This program is free software; you can redistribute it and/or modify it under the same terms as Perl itself.

Statistics::ChiSquare—how random is your data?

Synopsis

```
use Statistics::ChiSquare;
print chisquare(@actual_occurrences);
print chisquare_nonuniform([actual_occurrences],
                           [expected_occurrences]);
```

The Statistics::ChiSquare module is available at a CPAN site near you.

Description

Suppose you flip a coin 100 times, and it turns up heads 70 times. *Is the coin fair?*

Suppose you roll a die 100 times, and it shows 30 sixes. *Is the die loaded?*

In statistics, the *chi-square* test calculates "how random" a series of numbers is. But it doesn't simply say "random" or "not random." Instead, it gives you a *confidence interval*, which sets upper and lower bounds on the likelihood that the variation in your data is due to chance. See the examples below.

If you've ever studied elementary genetics, you've probably heard about Gregor Mendel. He was a wacky Austrian botanist who discovered (in 1865) that traits could be inherited in a predictable fashion. He performed lots of experiments with cross-fertilizing peas: green peas, yellow peas, smooth peas, wrinkled peas. A veritable Brave New World of legumes.

How many fertilizations are needed to be sure that the variations in the results aren't due to chance? Well, you can never be entirely sure. But the chi-square test tells you *how sure you should be.*

(As it turns out, Mendel faked his data. A statistician by the name of R.A. Fisher used the chi-square test again, in a slightly more sophisticated way, to show that Mendel was either very very lucky or a little dishonest.)

There are two functions in this module: **chisquare()** and **chisquare_nonuniform()**. **chisquare()** expects an array of occurrences: if you flip a coin seven times, yielding three heads and four tails, that array is (3, 4). `chisquare_nonuniform()` is a bit trickier—more about it later.

Instead of returning the bounds on the confidence interval in a tidy little two-element array, these functions return an English string. This was a deliberate design choice—many people misinterpret chi-square results; the text helps clarify the meaning. Both `chisquare()` and `chisquare_nonuniform()` return undef if the arguments aren't "proper."

Upon success, the string returned by `chisquare()` always matches one of these patterns:

```
There's a >\d+% chance, and a <\d+% chance, that this data is random.
```

or:

```
There's a <\d+% chance that this data is random.
```

unless there's an error. Here's one error you should know about:

```
(I can't handle \d+ choices without a better table.)
```

That deserves an explanation. The "modern" chi-square test uses a table of values (based on Pearson's approximation) to avoid expensive calculations. Thanks to the table, the `chisquare()` calculation is quite fast, but there are some collections of data it can't handle, including any collection with more than 21 slots. So you can't calculate the randomness of a 30-sided die.

`chisquare_nonuniform()` expects *two* arguments: a reference to an array of actual occurrences, followed by a reference to an array of expected occurrences.

`chisquare_nonuniform()` is used when you expect a nonuniform distribution of your data; for instance, if you expect twice as many heads as tails and want to see if your coin lives up to that hypothesis. With such a coin, you'd expect 40 heads and 20 tails in 60 flips; if you actually observed 42 heads and 18 tails, you'd call:

```
chisquare_nonuniform([42, 18], [40, 20])
```

The strings returned by `chisquare_nonuniform()` look like this:

```
There's a >\d+% chance, and a <\d+% chance,
    that this data is distributed as you expect.
```

Examples

Imagine a coin flipped 1000 times. The most likely outcome is 500 heads and 500 tails:

```
@coin = (500, 500);
print chisquare(@coin);
```

which prints:

```
There's a >99% chance, and a <100% chance,
    that this data is evenly distributed.
```

Imagine a die rolled 60 times that shows sixes just a wee bit too often:

```
@die1 = (9, 8, 10, 9, 9, 15);
print chisquare(@die1);
```

which prints:

```
There's a >50% chance, and a <70% chance,
    that this data is evenly distributed.
```

Imagine a die rolled 600 times that shows sixes *way* too often:

```
@die2  = (80, 70, 90, 80, 80, 200);
print chisquare(@die2);
```

which prints:

```
There's a <1% chance that this data is evenly distributed.
```

How random is `rand()`?

```
srand(time ^ $$);
@rands = ();
for ($i = 0; $i < 60000; $i++) {
    $slot = int(rand(6));
    $rands[$slot]++;
}
print "@rands\n";
print chisquare(@rands);
```

which prints (on my machine):

```
9987 10111 10036 9975 9984 9907
There's a >70% chance, and a <90% chance,
    that this data is evenly distributed.
```

(So much for pseudorandom number generation.)

All the above examples assume that you're testing a uniform distribution—testing whether the coin is fair (i.e. a 1:1 distribution), or whether the die is fair (i.e. a 1:1:1:1:1:1 distribution). That's why `chisquare()` could be used instead of `chisquare_nonuniform()`.

Suppose a mother with blood type AB and a father with blood type Ai (that is, blood type A, but heterozygous) have one hundred children. You'd expect 50 kids to have blood type A, 25 to have blood type AB, and 25 to have blood type B. Plain old `chisquare()` isn't good enough when you expect a nonuniform distribution like 2:1:1.

Let's say that couple has 40 kids with blood type A, 30 with blood type AB, and 30 with blood type B. Here's how you'd settle any nagging questions of paternity:

```
@data = (40, 30, 30);
@dist = (50, 25, 25);
print chisquare_nonuniform(\@data, \@dist);
```

which prints:

```
There's a >10% chance, and a <30% chance,
    that this data is distributed as you expect.
```

Author

Jon Orwant, MIT Media Lab, *orwant@media.mit.edu*

Statistics::Descriptive — basic descriptive statistical functions

Synopsis

```
use Statistics::Descriptive;
$stat = new Statistics::Descriptive;
```

```
$stat->AddData(1,2,3,4);
$mean = $stat->Mean();
$var  = $stat->Variance();
$tm   = $stat->TrimmedMean(.25);
```

Description

This module provides basic functions used in descriptive statistics. It has an object-oriented design and supports two different modes of data storage and calculation: sparse and full. With the sparse method, none of the data is stored and only a few statistical measures are available. Using the full method, the entire data set is retained and additional functions are available.

Functions

Sparse

sparse

> Creates a new sparse statistics variable.

AddData

> Adds data to the statistics variable. The cached statistical values are updated automatically.

Count

> Returns the number of data items.

Mean

> Returns the mean of the data.

Sum

> Returns the sum of the data.

Variance

> Returns the variance of the data. Division by n-1 is used.

StandardDeviation

> Returns the standard deviation of the data. Division by n-1 is used.

Full

new

> Creates a new statistics element. All the data is retained and all defined functions are available.

full

> Synonymous with **new**.

AddData

> Adds data to the statistics variable. The only variables that are automatically updated and recached are Count, Mean, Sum, Variance, and StandardDeviation. All other previously cached results are deleted, since with the addition of new data they are no longer valid.

Other

In addition to the functions mentioned in the sparse section, the following functions are also available when using full variables:

GetData

> Returns a copy of the data.

Max
>Returns the maximum value in the data set.

Min
>Returns the minimum value in the data set.

SampleRange
>Returns the sample range of the data.

Median
>Returns the median value of the data.

HarmonicMean
>Returns the harmonic mean of the data.

GeometricMean
>Returns the geometric mean of the data.

Mode
>Returns the mode of the data.

TrimmedMean
>TrimmedMean(trim) returns the mean with a fraction trim of entries at each end dropped. TrimmedMean(ltrim,utrim) returns the mean after a fraction ltrim has been removed from the lower end of the data and a fraction utrim has been removed from the upper end of the data.

FrequencyDistribution
>FrequencyDistribution(partitions) slices the data into partition sets and counts the number of items that fall into each partition. It returns an associative array, where the keys are the numerical values of the partitions used. The minimum value of the data set is not a key, and the maximum value of the data set is always a key. The number of entries for a particular partition key is the number of items that are greater than the previous partition key and less than or equal to the current partition key. For example:

```
$stat->AddData(1,1.5,2,2.5,3,3.5,4);
%f = $stat->FrequencyDistribution(2);
for (sort {$a <=> $b} keys %f) {
    print "key = $_, count = $f{$_}\n";
}
```

prints:

```
key = 2.5, count = 4
key = 4, count = 3
```

since there are four items less than or equal to 2.5, and three items greater than 2.5 and less than 4.

LeastSquaresFit
>LeastSquaresFit() performs a least squares fit on the data, assuming a domain of 1,2,3.... It returns an array of two elements; the value in the zero position is the constant (x^0) term and the value in the first position is the coefficient of the x^1 term. LeastSquaresFit(@x) uses the values in @x as the domain.

References

The Art of Computer Programming, Volume 2, Donald Knuth.

Handbook of Mathematica Functions, Milton Abramowitz and Irene Stegun.

Probability and Statistics for Engineering and the Sciences, Jay Devore.

Copyright

Copyright © 1994,1995 Jason Kastner (*jason@wagner.com*). All rights reserved.

This program is free software; you can redistribute it and/or modify it under the same terms as Perl itself.

Statistics::LTU—an implementation of Linear Threshold Units

Synopsis

```
use Statistics::LTU;

my $acr_ltu = new Statistics::LTU::ACR(3, 1);    # 3 attributes, scaled

$ltu->train([1,3,2],   $LTU_PLUS);
$ltu->train([-1,3,0], $LTU_MINUS);
...
print "LTU looks like this:\n";
$ltu->print;

print "[1,5,2] is in class ";
if ($ltu->test([1,5,2]) > $LTU_THRESHOLD) { print "PLUS" }
                                     else { print "MINUS" };

$ltu->save("ACR.saved") or die "Save failed!";
$ltu2 = restore Statistics::LTU("ACR.saved");
```

Description

Statistics::LTU defines methods for creating, destroying, training, and testing linear threshold units. A linear threshold unit is a one-layer neural network, also called a perceptron. LTUs are used to learn classifications from examples.

An LTU learns to distinguish between two classes based on the data given to it. After training on a number of examples, the LTU can then be used to classify new (unseen) examples. Technically, LTUs learn to distinguish two classes by fitting a hyperplane between examples; if the examples have n features, the hyperplane has n dimensions. In general, the weights of LTUs converge to define the separating hyperplane.

The *LTU.pm* file defines an uninstantiable base class (LTU) and four other instantiable classes built on top of LTU. The four individual classes differ in the training rules used are:

ACR
Absolute Correction Rule

TACR
Thermal Absolute Correction Rule (thermal annealing)

LMS
Least Mean Squares rule

RLS
Recursive Least Squares rule

Each of these training rules behaves somewhat differently. Exact details of how these work are beyond the scope of this document; see the additional documentation file (*ltu.doc*) for discussion.

Methods

Each LTU has the following methods:

new *TYPE*(*n_features, scaling*)

Creates an LTU of the given *TYPE*. *TYPE* must be one of:

- Statistics::LTU::ACR
- Statistics::LTU::TACR
- Statistics::LTU::LMS
- Statistics::LTU::RLS

n_features sets the number of attributes in the examples. If *scaling* is 1, the LTU automatically scales the input features to the range (-1, +1). For example:

```
$ACR_ltu = new Statistics::LTU::ACR(5, 1);
```

creates an LTU that trains using the absolute correction rule. It has five variables and scales features automatically.

copy

Copies the LTU and returns the copy.

destroy

Destroys the LTU (undefines its substructures). This method is kept for compatibility; it's probably sufficient simply to call `undef($ltu)`.

print

Prints a human-readable description of the LTU, including the weights.

save(*filename*)

Saves the LTU to the file *filename*. All the weights and necessary permanent data are saved. Returns 1 if the LTU was saved successfully; otherwise 0.

restore LTU(*filename*)

Static method. Creates and returns a new LTU from *filename*. The new LTU is of the same type.

test(*instance*)

Tests the LTU on *instance*, the instance vector, which must be a reference to an array. Returns the raw (non-thresholded) result. A typical use of this is:

```
if ($ltu->test($instance) >= $LTU_PLUS) {
    # instance is in class 1
} else {
    # instance is in class 2
}
```

correctly_classifies(*instance, realclass*)

Tests the LTU against an instance vector *instance*, which must be a reference to an array. *realclass* must be a number. Returns 1 if the LTU classifies *instance* in the same class as *realclass*. Technically, it returns 1 if *instance* is on the *realclass* side of the LTU's hyperplane.

weights

Returns a reference to a copy of the LTU's weights.

`set_origin_restriction(orig)`
>   Sets the LTU's origin restriction to *orig*, which should be 1 or 0. If an LTU is origin-restricted, its hyperplane must pass through the origin (so its intercept is 0). This is usually used for preference predicates, whose classifications must be symmetrical.

`is_cycling(n)`
>   Returns 1 if the LTU's weights seem to be cycling. This is a heuristic test, based on whether the LTU's weights have been pushed out in the past *n* training instances. See comments with the code.

`version`
>   Returns the version of the LTU implementation.

In addition to the methods above, each of the four classes of LTU defines a **train** method. The **train** method "trains" the LTU that an instance belongs in a particular class. For each **train** method, **instance** must be a reference to an array of numbers, and **value** must be a number. For convenience, two constants are defined: $LTU_PLUS and $LTU_MINUS, set to +1 and –1 respectively. These can be given as arguments to the **train** method. A typical **train** call looks like:

```
$ltu->train([1,3,-5], $Statistics_LTU_PLUS);
```

which trains the LTU that the instance vector (1,3,-5) should be in the PLUS class.

ACR: `train(instance, value)`
>   Returns 1 if the LTU already classified the instance correctly; otherwise 0.

RLS: `train(instance, value)`
>   Returns undef.

LMS: `train(instance, value, rho)`
>   Returns 1 if the LTU already classified the *instance* correctly, else 0. *rho* determines how much the weights are adjusted on each training instance. It must be a positive number.

TACR: `train(instance, value, temperature, rate)`
>   Uses the thermal perceptron (absolute correction) rule to train the specified linear threshold unit on a particular *instance*. The *instance* is a vector of numbers; each number is one attribute. The *value* should be either $LTU_PLUS (for positive instances) or $LTU_MINUS (for negative instances). The *temperature* and *rate* must be floating-point numbers.
>
>   This method returns 1 if the linear threshold unit already classified the instance correctly, otherwise it returns 0. The TACR rule only trains on instances that it does not already classify correctly.

Exports

For readability, LTU.pm exports three scalar constants: $LTU_PLUS (+1), $LTU_MINUS (–1) and $LTU_THRESHOLD (0).

Scalars

$LTU_PLUS and $LTU_MINUS (+1 and –1, respectively) may be passed to the **train** method. $LTU_THRESHOLD (set to zero) may be used to compare values returned from the **test** method.

Bugs

None known. This Perl module has been moderately exercised, but I don't guarantee anything.

Author

Tom Fawcett, *fawcett@nynexst.com*

LTU.pm is based on a C implementation by James Callan at the University of Massachusetts. His version has been in use for a long time, is stable, and seems to be bug-free. This Perl module was created by Tom Fawcett, and any bugs you find were probably introduced in translation. Send bugs, comments, and suggestions to *fawcett@nynexst.com*.

Storable — persistency for Perl data structures

Synopsis

```
use Storable;
store \%table, 'file';
$hashref = retrieve('file');
```

Description

The Storable package brings you persistency for your Perl data structures containing SCALAR, ARRAY, HASH, or REF objects, i.e., anything that can be conveniently stored to disk and retrieved at a later time.

It can be used in the regular procedural way by calling `store` with a reference to the object to store, and providing a filename. The routine returns `undef` for I/O problems or other internal error, a true value otherwise. Serious errors are propagated as a `die` exception.

To retrieve data stored to disk, you use `retrieve` with a filename, the objects stored into that file are recreated into memory for you, and a `reference` to the root object is returned. If an I/O error occurs while reading, undef is returned instead. Other serious errors are propagated via `die`.

Since storage is performed recursively, you might want to stuff references to objects that share a lot of common data into a single array or hash table, and then store that object. That way, when you retrieve back the whole thing, the objects will continue to share what they originally shared.

At the cost of slight header overhead, you may store to an already opened file descriptor using the `store_fd` routine, and retrieve from a file via `retrieve_fd`. Those names aren't imported by default, so you will have to do that explicitly if you need those routines. The file descriptor name you supply must be fully qualified.

You can also store data in network order to allow easy sharing across multiple platforms, or when storing on a socket known to be remotely connected. The routines to call have an initial n prefix for `network`, as in `nstore` and `nstore_fd`. At retrieval time, your data will be correctly restored, so you don't have to know whether you're restoring from native or network ordered data.

When using `retrieve_fd`, objects are retrieved in sequence, one object (i.e. one recursive tree) per associated `store_fd`.

If you're more from the object-oriented camp, you can inherit from Storable and directly store your objects by invoking `store` as a method. The fact that the root of the to-be-stored tree is a blessed reference (i.e. an object) is special-cased so that the retrieve does not provide a reference to that object, but rather the blessed object reference itself. (Otherwise, you'd get a reference to that blessed object).

Memory Store

The Storable engine can also store data into a Perl scalar instead, to later retrieve them. This is mainly used to freeze a complex structure in some safe compact memory place (where it can possibly be sent to another process via some IPC, since freezing the structure also serializes it, in effect). Later on, and maybe somewhere else, you can thaw the Perl scalar out and recreate the original complex structure in memory.

Surprisingly, the routines to be called are named **freeze** and **thaw**. If you wish to send out the frozen scalar to another machine, use **nfreeze** instead to get a portable image.

Note that freezing an object structure and immediately thawing it actually achieves a deep cloning of that structure. Storable provides you with a **dclone** interface which does not create that intermediary scalar, but instead freezes the structure in some internal memory space and then immediatly thaws it out.

Speed

The heart of Storable is written in C for decent speed. Extra low-level optimizations have been made when manipulating Perl internals, to sacrifice encapsulation for the benefit of greater speed.

Storage is usually faster than retrieval, since the latter has to allocate the objects from memory and perform the relevant I/O, while the former mainly performs I/O.

On my HP 9000/712 machine running HPUX 9.03 and with Perl 5.004, I can store 0.8 Mbyte/s, and I can retrieve at 0.72 Mbytes/s, approximatively (CPU + system time). This was measured with Benchmark and the *Magic: The Gathering* database from Tom Christiansen (1.9 MB).

Examples

Here are some code samples showing a possible usage of Storable:

```
use Storable qw(store retrieve freeze thaw dclone);
%color = ('Blue' => 0.1, 'Red' => 0.8, 'Black' => 0, 'White' => 1);
store(\%color, '/tmp/colors') or die "Can't store %a in /tmp/
colors!\n";
$colref = retrieve('/tmp/colors');
die "Unable to retrieve from /tmp/colors!\n" unless defined
$colref;
printf "Blue is still %lf\n", $colref->{'Blue'};
$colref2 = dclone(\%color);
$str = freeze(\%color);
printf "Serialization of %%color is %d bytes long.\n",
length($str);
$colref3 = thaw($str);
```

which prints (on my machine):

```
Blue is still 0.100000
Serialization of %color is 102 bytes long.
```

Warning

If you're using references as keys within your hash tables, you're bound to be disapointed when retrieving your data. Indeed, Perl stringifies references used as hash-table keys. If you later wish to access the items via another reference stringification (i.e. using the same reference that was used for the key originally to record the value into the hash table), it will work, because both references stringify to the same string.

It won't work across `store` and `retrieve` operations, however, because the addresses in the retrieved objects, which are part of the stringified references, will probably differ from the original addresses. The topology of your structure is preserved, but not hidden semantics like those.

Bugs

You can't store GLOB, CODE, FORMLINE, etc. If you can define semantics for those operations, feel free to enhance Storable so that it can deal with those.

The store functions `croak` if they run into such references unless you set `$Storable::forgive_me` to some `TRUE` value. In this case, the fatal message is turned in a warning and some meaningless string is stored instead.

Due to the aforementioned optimizations, Storable is at the mercy of Perl's internal redesign or structure changes. If that bothers you, you can try convincing Larry that what is used in Storable should be documented and consistently kept in future revisions. As I said, you may try.

Author

Raphael Manfredi, *Raphael_Manfredi@grenoble.hp.com*

Tie::Dir—class definition for reading directories via a tied hash

Synopsis

```
use Tie::Dir qw(DIR_UNLINK);

# Both of these produce identical results
#(ie %hash is tied)
tie %hash, Tie::Dir, ".", DIR_UNLINK;
new Tie::Dir \%hash, ".", DIR_UNLINK;

# This creates a reference to a hash, which is tied.
$hash = new Tie::Dir ".";

# All these examples assume that %hash is tied (ie one of the
# first two tie methods was used

# itterate through the directory
foreach $file ( keys %hash ) {
    ...
}

# Set the access and modification times (touch :-)
$hash{SomeFile} = time;
```

```
# Obtain stat information of a file
@stat = @{$hash{SomeFile}};

# Check if entry exists
if(exists $hash{SomeFile}) {
    ...
}

# Delete an entry, only if DIR_UNLINK specified
delete $hash{SomeFile};
```

Description

This module provides a method of reading directories using a hash.

The keys of the hash are the directory entries and the values are a reference to an array that holds the result of **stat** being called on the entry.

The access and modification times of an entry can be changed by assigning to an element of the hash. If a single number is assigned, then the access and modification times are both set to the same value; alternatively, the access and modification times may be set separately by passing a reference to an array with two entries. The first entry is the access time and the second is the modification time.

new [hashref,] dirname [, options]

This method ties the hash referenced by **hashref** to the directory **dirname**. If **hashref** is omitted then **new** returns a reference to a hash which has been tied; otherwise it returns the result of **tie**.

The possible options are:

DIR_UNLINK

Delete operations on the hash cause **unlink** to be called on the corresponding file.

Author

Graham Barr (*gbarr@pobox.com*), from a quick hack posted by Kenneth Albanowski (*kjahds@kjahds.com*) to the Perl5 Porters mailing list, based on a neat idea by Ilya Zakharevich.

Tie::IxHash—ordered associative arrays for Perl

Synopsis

```
# simple usage
use Tie::IxHash;
tie HASHVARIABLE, Tie::IxHash [, LIST];

# OO interface with more powerful features
use Tie::IxHash;
TIEOBJECT = Tie::IxHash->new( [LIST] );
TIEOBJECT->Splice( OFFSET [, LENGTH [, LIST]] );
TIEOBJECT->Push( LIST );
TIEOBJECT->Pop;
TIEOBJECT->Shift;
```

```
TIEOBJECT->Unshift( LIST );
TIEOBJECT->Keys( [LIST] );
TIEOBJECT->Values( [LIST] );
TIEOBJECT->Indices( LIST );
TIEOBJECT->Delete( [LIST] );
TIEOBJECT->Replace( OFFSET, VALUE, [KEY] );
TIEOBJECT->Reorder( LIST );
TIEOBJECT->SortByKey;
TIEOBJECT->SortByValue;
TIEOBJECT->Length;
```

Description

This Perl module implements Perl hashes that preserve the order in which the hash elements were added. The order is not affected when values corresponding to existing keys in the IxHash are changed. The elements can also be set to any arbitrary supplied order. The familiar Perl array operations can also be performed on the IxHash.

Standard TIEHASH Interface

The standard TIEHASH mechanism is available. This interface is recommended for simple uses, since the usage is exactly the same as regular Perl hashes after the tie is declared.

Object Interface

This module also provides an extended object-oriented interface that can be used for more powerful operations with the IxHash. The following methods are available:

FETCH, STORE, DELETE, EXISTS
> These standard TIEHASH methods mandated by Perl can be used directly. See the tie entry in perlfunc(1) for details.

Push, Pop, Shift, Unshift, Splice
> These additional methods resembling Perl functions are available for operating on key-value pairs in the IxHash. The behavior is the same as the corresponding Perl functions, except when a supplied hash key already exists in the hash. In that case, the existing value is updated, but its order is not affected. To unconditionally alter the order of a supplied key-value pair, first DELETE the IxHash element.

Keys
> Returns a list of IxHash element keys corresponding to the list of supplied indices. Returns all the keys if called without arguments.

Values
> Returns a list of IxHash element values corresponding to the list of supplied indices. Returns all the values if called without arguments.

Indices
> Returns the indices corresponding to the supplied list of keys.

Delete
> Removes elements with the keys supplied from the IxHash.

Replace
> Substitutes the IxHash element at the specified index with the supplied key-value pair. If a key is not supplied, simply substitutes the value at index with the

supplied value. If an element with the supplied key already exists, it is removed from the IxHash first.

Reorder

This method can be used to manipulate the internal order of the IxHash elements by supplying a list of keys in the desired order. Note, however, that any IxHash elements whose keys are not in the list are removed from the IxHash.

Length

Returns the number of IxHash elements.

SortByKey

Reorders the IxHash elements by textual comparison of the keys.

SortByValue

Reorders the IxHash elements by textual comparison of the values.

Example

```
use Tie::IxHash;
# simple interface
$t = tie(%myhash, Tie::IxHash, 'a' => 1, 'b' => 2);
%myhash = (first => 1, second => 2, third => 3);
$myhash{fourth} = 4;
@keys = keys %myhash;
@values = values %myhash;
print("y") if exists $myhash{third};

# OO interface
$t = Tie::IxHash->new(first => 1, second => 2, third => 3);
$t->Push(fourth => 4); # same as $myhash{'fourth'} = 4;
($k, $v) = $t->Pop;     # $k is 'fourth', $v is 4
$t->Unshift(neg => -1, zeroth => 0);
($k, $v) = $t->Shift;   # $k is 'neg', $v is -1
@oneandtwo = $t->Splice(1, 2, foo => 100, bar => 101);

@keys = $t->Keys;
@values = $t->Values;
@indices = $t->Indices('foo', 'zeroth');
@itemkeys = $t->Keys(@indices);
@itemvals = $t->Values(@indices);
$t->Replace(2, 0.3, 'other');
$t->Delete('second', 'zeroth');
$len = $t->Length;      # number of key-value pairs
$t->Reorder(reverse @keys);
$t->SortByKey;
$t->SortByValue;
```

Bugs

You cannot specify a negative length to Splice. Negative indexes are OK, though.

Indexing always begins at 0 (despite the current $[setting) for all the functions.

To do

Addition of elements with keys that already exist to the end of the IxHash must be controlled by a switch.

Provide TIEARRAY interface when it stabilizes in Perl.

Rewrite using XSUBs for efficiency.

Author

Gurusamy Sarathy, *gsar@umich.edu*

Copyright © 1995 Gurusamy Sarathy. All rights reserved. This program is free software; you can redistribute it and/or modify it under the same terms as Perl itself.

Version

Version 1.2 17 Feb 1997

See Also

perl(1)

Tie::Watch—place watchpoints on Perl variables

Synopsis

```
use Tie::Watch;
$watch = Tie::Watch->new(
    -variable => \$frog,
    -debug    => 1,
    -fetch    => [\&fetch, 'arg1', 'arg2', ..., 'argn'],
    -store    => \&store,
    -destroy  => sub {print "Final value=$frog.\n"},
}
%vinfo = $watch->Info;
$args  = $watch->Args(-fetch);
$val   = $watch->Fetch;
print "val=", $watch->Say($val), ".\n";
$watch->Store('Hello');
$watch->Delete;
```

Description

This class module binds subroutine(s) of your devising to a Perl variable. All variables can have FETCH, STORE and DESTROY callbacks. Additionally, hashes can define CLEAR, DELETE, EXISTS, FIRSTKEY, and NEXTKEY callbacks. With Tie::Watch you can:

- Alter a variable's value

- Prevent a variable's value from being changed

- Invoke a Perl/Tk callback when a variable changes

- Trace references to a variable

Callback format is patterned after the Perl/Tk scheme: either supply a code reference or supply an array reference and pass the callback code reference in the first element of the array, followed by callback arguments. (See examples in the "Synopsis," previously.)

Tie::Watch provides default callbacks for any that you fail to specify. Other than negatively impacting performance, they perform the standard action that you'd expect, so the variable behaves "normally."

Here are two callbacks for a scalar. The fetch (read) callback does nothing other than illustrate the fact that it returns the value to assign the variable. The store (write) callback uppercases the variable.

```
my $fetch_scalar = sub {
    my($self) = @ARG;
    $self->Fetch;
};
my $store_scalar = sub {
    my($self, $new_val) = @ARG;
    $self->Store(uc $new_val);
};
```

Here are fetch and store callbacks for either an array or hash. They do essentially the same thing as the scalar callbacks, but provide a little more information.

```
my $fetch = sub {
    my($self, $key) = @ARG;
    my $val = $self->Fetch($key);
    print "In fetch callback, key=$key, val=", $self->Say($val);
    my $args = $self->Args(-fetch);
    print ", args=('", join("', '",  @{$args}), "')" if $args;
    print ".\n";
    $val;
};
my $store = sub {
    my($self, $key, $new_val) = @ARG;
    my $val = $self->Fetch($key);
    $new_val = uc $new_val;
    $self->Store($key, $new_val);
    print "In store callback, key=$key, val=", $self->Say($val),
       ", new_val=", $self->Say($new_val);
    my $args = $self->Args(-store);
    print ", args=('", join("', '",  @{$args}), "')" if $args;
    print ".\n";
    $new_val;
};
```

In all cases, the first parameter is a reference to the Watch object. You can use this to invoke useful class methods.

Methods

`$watch = Tie::Watch->new(-options => values);`
> -variable = a *reference* to a scalar, array or hash variable.
>
> -debug = 1 to activate debug print statements internal to Tie::Watch.
>
> Specify any of the following relevant callback parameters, in the format described above: -fetch -store -destroy -clear -delete -exists -firstkey and/ or -nextkey.

`$args = $watch->Args(-fetch);`
> Returns a reference to a list of arguments for the specified callback, or undef() if none.

`$watch->Delete;`
> Stop watching the variable.

`$watch->Fetch; $watch->Fetch($key);`

> Return a variable's current value. `$key` is required for an array or hash.

`%vinfo = $watch->Info;`

> Returns a hash detailing the internals of the Watch object, with these keys:

```
%vinfo = {
    -variable =>  SCALAR(0x200737f8)
    -fetch    =>  ARRAY(0x200f8558)
    -store    =>  ARRAY(0x200f85a0)
    -destroy  =>  ARRAY(0x200f86cc)
    -debug    =>  '1'
    -value    =>  'HELLO SCALAR'
    -legible  =>  above data formatted as a list of string,
for printing
}
```

> For array and hash Watch objects, the **value** key is replaced with a **ptr** key, which is a reference to the parallel array or hash. Additionally, for hashes, there are key/value pairs to the hash-specific callback options.

`$watch->Say($val);`

> Used mainly for debugging, it returns `$val` in quotes if required, or the string **undefined** for undefined values.

`$watch->Store($new_val); $watch->Store($key, $new_val);`

> Store a variable's new value. `$key` is required for an array or hash.

Efficiency Considerations

If you can live using the class methods provided, please do so. You can meddle with the object hash directly and improved watch performance, at the risk of your code breaking in the future.

Author

Stephen O. Lidie, *lusol@Lehigh.edu*

Copyright

Copyright © 1996–1997 Stephen O. Lidie. All rights reserved.

This program is free software; you can redistribute it and/or modify it under the same terms as Perl itself.

Time::CTime — format times à la POSIX `asctime`

Synopsis

```
use Time::CTime
print ctime(time);
print asctime(timelocal(time));
print strftime(template, localtime(time));
```

strftime conversions

```
%%  PERCENT
%a  day of the week abbr
%A  day of the week
```

```
%b   month abbr
%B   month
%c   ctime format: Sat Nov 19 21:05:57 1994
%d   numeric day of the month
%e   DD
%D   MM/DD/YY
%h   month abbr
%H   hour, 24 hour clock, leading 0's
%I   hour, 12 hour clock, leading 0's
%j   day of the year
%k   hour
%l   hour, 12 hour clock
%m   month number, starting with 1
%M   minute, leading 0's
%n   NEWLINE
%o   ornate day of month--"1st", "2nd", "25th", etc.
%p   AM or PM
%r   time format: 09:05:57 PM
%R   time format: 21:05
%S   seconds, leading 0's
%t   TAB
%T   time format: 21:05:57
%U   week number, Sunday as first day of week
%w   day of the week, numerically, Sunday == 0
%W   week number, Monday as first day of week
%x   date format: 11/19/94
%X   time format: 21:05:57
%y   year (2 digits)
%Y   year (4 digits)
%Z   timezone in ASCII. e.g., PST
```

Description

This module provides routines, corresponding to the `libc` routines, to format dates. `&strftime()` supports a pretty good set of coversions—more than most C libraries.

strftime supports a pretty good set of conversions.

The POSIX module has very similar functionality. You should consider using it instead of CTime if you do not have allergic reactions to system libraries.

Author

Written by David Muir Sharnoff, *muir@idiom.com*

The starting point for this package was a posting by Paul Foley (*paul@ascent.com*).

Time::DaysInMonth—simply report the number of days in a month

Synopsis

```
use Time::DaysInMonth;
$days = days_in($year, $month_1_to_12);
$leapyear = is_leap($year);
```

Description

DaysInMonth is simply a package to report the number of days in a month. That's all it does. Really!

Author

David Muir Sharnoff, *muir@idiom.com*

Time::HiRes—Perl extension for `ualarm`, `usleep`, and `gettimeofday`

Synopsis

```
use Time::HiRes qw( usleep ualarm gettimeofday tv_interval );
usleep ($microseconds);
ualarm ($microseconds);
ualarm ($microseconds, $interval_microseconds);
$t0 = [gettimeofday];
($seconds, $microseconds) = gettimeofday;
$elapsed = tv_interval ( $t0, [$seconds, $microseconds]);
$elapsed = tv_interval ( $t0, [gettimeofday]);
$elapsed = tv_interval ( $t0 );
use Time::HiRes qw ( time alarm sleep );
$now_fractions = time;
sleep ($floating_seconds);
alarm ($floating_seconds);
alarm ($floating_seconds, $floating_interval);
```

Description

The `Time::HiRes` package implements a Perl interface to the `usleep`, `ualarm`, and `gettimeofday` system calls. See the following "Examples" section and the test scripts for usage; see your system documentation for the description of the underlying `gettimeofday`, `usleep`, and `ualarm` calls.

If your system lacks `gettimeofday()`, you don't get `gettimeofday()` or the one-arg form of `tv_interval()`. If you don't have `usleep()` or `select()`, you don't get `usleep()` or `sleep()`. If you don't have `ualarm()`, you don't get `ualarm()` or `alarm()`. If you try to import an unimplemented function in the `use` statement, it will fail at compile time.

Functions

`gettimeofday`

> Returns a two-element array with the seconds and microseconds since the epoch.

`usleep ( $useconds )`

> Issues a `usleep` for the number of microseconds specified. See also Time::HiRes::sleep.

`ualarm ( $useconds [, $interval_useconds ] )`

> Issues a `ualarm` call; *$interval_useconds* is optional and will be 0 if unspecified, resulting in alarm-like behaviour.

tv_interval (*$ref_to_gettimeofday* [, *$ref_to_later_gettimeofday*])
> Returns the floating seconds between the two times, which should have been
> returned by Time::HiRes::gettimeofday. If the second is omitted, then the current
> time is used.

time
> Returns the floating seconds since the epoch. This function can be imported,
> resulting in a nice drop-in replacement for the time provided with Perl; see the
> "Examples" below.

sleep (*$floating_seconds*)
> Converts *$floating_seconds* to microseconds and issues a usleep for the
> result. This function can be imported, resulting in a nice drop-in replacement for
> the sleep provided with perl, see the "Examples" below.

alarm (*$floating_seconds* [, *$interval_floating_seconds*])
> Converts *$floating_seconds* and *$interval_floating_seconds* and issues a
> ualarm for the results. *$interval_floating_seconds* is optional and will be 0
> if unspecified, resulting in alarm-like behavior. This function can be imported,
> resulting in a nice drop-in replacement for the alarm provided with Perl; see the
> "Examples" below.

Examples

```
use Time::HiRes qw(usleep ualarm gettimeofday tv_interval);
$microseconds = 750_000;
usleep $microseconds;
# signal alarm in 2.5s & every .1s thereafter
ualarm 2_500_000, 100_000;
# get seconds and microseconds since the epoch
($s, $usec) = gettimeofday;
# measure elapsed time
# (could also do by subtracting 2 gettimeofday return values)
$t0 = [gettimeofday];
# do bunch of stuff here
$t1 = [gettimeofday];
# do more stuff here
$t0_t1 = tv_interval $t0, $t1;

$elapsed = tv_interval ($t0, [gettimeofday]);
$elapsed = tv_interval ($t0); # equivalent code
#
# replacements for time, alarm and sleep that know about floating
# seconds
#
use Time::HiRes;
$now_fractions = Time::HiRes::time;
Time::HiRes::sleep (2.5);
Time::HiRes::alarm (10.6666666);

use Time::HiRes qw ( time alarm sleep );
$now_fractions = time;
sleep (2.5);
alarm (10.6666666);
```

Authors

D. Wegscheid, *wegscd@whirlpool.com*; R. Schertler, *roderick@argon.org*; J. Hietaniemi *jhi@iki.fi*

Copyright

Time::JulianDay—Julian calendar manipulations

Synopsis

```
use Time::JulianDay

$jd = julian_day($year, $month_1_to_12, $day)
$jd = local_julian_day($seconds_since_1970);
$jd = gm_julian_day($seconds_since_1970);
($year, $month_1_to_12, $day) = inverse_julian_day($jd)
$dow = day_of_week($jd)

print (Sun,Mon,Tue,Wed,Thu,Fri,Sat)[$dow];

$seconds_since_jan_1_1970 = jd_secondslocal($jd, $hour, $min, $sec)
$seconds_since_jan_1_1970 = jd_secondsgm($jd, $hour, $min, $sec)
$seconds_since_jan_1_1970 = jd_timelocal($sec,$min,$hours,$mday,$month_
0_to_11,$year)
$seconds_since_jan_1_1970 = jd_timegm($sec,$min,$hours,$mday,$month_0_
to_11,$year)
```

Description

JulianDay is a package that manipulates dates as the number of days since some time a long time ago. It's easy to add and subtract time using Julian dates.

The `day_of_week` returned by `day_of_week()` is 0 for Sunday, 6 for Saturday, and everything else is in between.

Author

Written by David Muir Sharnoff (*muir@idiom.com*), with help from previous work by Kurt Jaeger (a.k.a. PI) (*zrzr0111@helpdesk.rus.uni-stuttgart.de*). Based on postings from Ian Miller (*ian_m@cix.compulink.co.uk*); Gary Puckering (*garyp%cognos.uucp@uunet.uu.net*) based on "Collected Algorithms of the ACM"; and the unknown-to-me author of Time::Local.

Time::ParseDate—relative and absolute date parsing

Synopsis

```
use Time::ParseDate;
$seconds_since_jan1_1970 = parsedate("12/11/94 2pm", NO_RELATIVE => 1)
$seconds_since_jan1_1970 = parsedate("12/11/94 2pm", %options)
```

Description

Options

Date parsing can use the following options:

FUZZY

It's okay not to parse the entire date string.

NOW

The "current" time for relative times (defaults to `time()`)

ZONE

The local time zone (defaults to `$ENV{TZ}`).

WHOLE

The whole input string must be parsed.

GMT

The input time is assumed to be GMT, not local time.

UK

Prefer UK-style dates (dd/mm over mm/dd).

DATE_REQUIRED

Do not use default date.

TIME_REQUIRED

Do not use default time.

NO_RELATIVE

The input time is not relative to NOW.

TIMEFIRST

Try parsing the time before the date [not the default].

PREFER_PAST

When the year or day of week is ambiguous, assume it is past.

PREFER_FUTURE

When the year or day of week is ambiguous, assume it is in the future.

Date Formats Recognized

Absolute date formats:

```
Dow, dd Mon yy
Dow, dd Mon yyyy
Dow, dd Mon
dd Mon yy
dd Mon yyyy
Month day{st,nd,rd,th}, year
Month day{st,nd,rd,th}
Mon dd yyyy
yyyy/mm/dd
yyyy/mm
mm/dd/yy
mm/dd/yyyy
mm/yy
yy/mm       (only if year > 12, or > 31 if UK)
yy/mm/dd    (only if year > 12 and day < 32, or year > 31 if UK)
dd/mm/yy    (only if UK, or an invalid mm/dd/yy or yy/mm/dd)
```

```
dd/mm/yyyy (only if UK, or an invalid mm/dd/yyyy)
dd/mm      (only if UK, or an invalid mm/dd)
```

Relative date formats:

```
count "days"
count "weeks"
count "months"
count "years"
Dow "after next"
Dow          (requires PREFER_PAST or PREFER_FUTURE)
"next" Dow
"tomorrow"
"today"
"yesterday"
"last" dow
"last week"
"now"
"now" "+" count units
"now" "-" count units
"+" count units
"-" count units
```

Absolute time formats:

```
hh:mm:ss
hh:mm
hh:mm[AP]M
hh[AP]M
hhmmss[[AP]M]
"noon"
"midnight"
```

Relative time formats:

```
count "minuts"
count "seconds"
count "hours"
"+" count units
"+" count
"-" count units
"-" count
```

Time zone formats:

```
[+-]dddd
GMT[+-]d+
[+-]dddd (TZN)
TZN
```

Special formats:

```
[ d]d/Mon/yyyy:hh:mm:ss [[+-]dddd]
yy/mm/dd.hh:mm
```

This module recognizes the above date and time formats. Usually a date and a time are specified. There are numerous options for controlling what is recognized and what is not.

The return code is always the time in seconds since January 1, 1970, or zero if Parse-Date was unable to parse the time.

If a time zone is specified, it must be after the time. Year specifications can be tacked onto the end of absolute times.

Examples

```
$seconds = parsedate("Mon Jan  2 04:24:27 1995");
$seconds = parsedate("Tue Apr 4 00:22:12 PDT 1995");
$seconds = parsedate("04.04.95 00:22", ZONE => PDT);
$seconds = parsedate("122212 950404", ZONE => PDT, TIMEFIRST => 1);
$seconds = parsedate("+3 secs", NOW => 796978800);
$seconds = parsedate("2 months", NOW => 796720932);
$seconds = parsedate("last Tuesday");
```

Author

David Muir Sharnoff, *muir@idiom.com*

Patch for UK-style dates: Sam Yates, *syates@maths.adelaide.edu.au*

Time::Period—deals with time periods

Synopsis

```
use Time::Period;
$result = inPeriod($time, $period);
```

Description

The `inPeriod` function determines if a given time falls within a given period. `inPeriod` returns 1 if the time does fall within the given period, 0 if not, and –1 if inPeriod detects a malformed time or period.

The time is specified as per the `time()` function, which is assumed to be the number of non-leap seconds since January 1, 1970.

The period is specified as a string, which adheres to the format:

```
sub-period[, sub-period...]
```

where a sub-period is of the form:

```
scale {range [range ...]} [scale {range [range ...]}]
```

Scale must be one of nine different scales (or their equivalent codes):

Scale	Scale Code	Valid Range Values
year	yr	n, where n is an integer 0<=n<=99 or n>=1970
month	mo	1–12, or jan,feb,mar,apr,may,jun,jul,
		aug,sep,oct,nov,dec
week	wk	1–6
yday	yd	1–365
mday	md	1–31

Scale	Scale Code	Valid Range Values
wday	wd	1–7, or su,mo,tu,we,th,fr,sa
hour	hr	0–23, or 12am, 1am–11am, 12noon, 12pm, 1pm–11pm
minute	min	0–59
second	sec	0–59

The same scale type may be specified multiple times. Additional scales simply extend the range defined by previous scales of the same type.

The range for a given scale must be a valid value in the form of:

```
v
```

or

```
v-v
```

For the range specification v-v, if the second value is larger than the first value, the range wraps around unless the scale specification is year.

Year does not wrap, because the year is never really reset; it just increments. Ignoring that fact has lead to the dreaded year 2000 nightmare. When the year rolls over from 99 to 00, it has really rolled over a century, not gone back a century. inPeriod supports the dangerous two-digit year notation because it is so rampant; however, inPeriod converts the two-digit notation to four digits by prepending the first two digits from the current year. In the case of 99–1972, the 99 is translated to whatever the current century is (probably 20th), and then the range 99-1972 is treated as 1972-1999. If it were the 21st century, then the range would be 1972–2099.

Anyway, if v-v is 9-2 and the scale is month, September, October, November, December, January, and February are the months that the range specifies. If v-v is 2-9, then the valid months are February, March, April, May, Jun, July, August, and September. 9-2 is the same as Sep-Feb.

v isn't a point in time. In the context of the hour scale, 9 specifies the time period from 9:00:00 am to 9:59:59 am. This is what most people would call 9-10. In other words, v is discrete in its time scale. 9 changes to 10 when 9:59:59 changes to 10:00:00, but it is 9 from 9:00:00 to 9:59:59. Just before 9:00:00, v was 8.

Note that whitespace can be anywhere, and case is not important. Note also that scales must be specified either in long form (year, month, week, etc.) or in code form (yr, mo, wk, etc.). Scale forms may be mixed in a period statement.

Furthermore, when using letters to specify ranges, only the first two for weekdays or the first three for months are significant. January is a valid specification for jan, and Sunday is a valid specification for su. Sun is also valid for su.

Period Examples

To specify a time period from Monday through Friday, 9am to 5pm, use a period like:

```
wd {Mon-Fri} hr {9am-4pm}
```

To specify a time period from Monday through Friday, 9am to 5pm on Monday, Wednesday, and Friday, and 9am to 3pm on Tuesday and Thursday, use a period like:

```
wd {Mon Wed Fri} hr {9am-4pm}, wd {Tue Thu} hr {9am-2pm}
```

To specify a time period that extends Mon–Fri 9am–5pm, but alternates weeks in a month, use a period such as:

```
wk {1 3 5} wd {Mon Wed Fri} hr {9am-4pm}
```

Or, how about a period that specifies winter?

```
mo {Nov-Feb}
```

This is equivalent to the previous example:

```
mo {Jan-Feb Nov-Dec}
```

As is:

```
mo {jan feb nov dec}
```

And this is too:

```
mo {Jan Feb}, mo {Nov Dec}
```

Wait! So is this:

```
mo {Jan Feb} mo {Nov Dec}
```

To specify a period that describes every half-hour, use something like:

```
minute { 0-29 }
```

To specify the morning, use:

```
hour { 12am-11am }
```

Remember, 11am is not 11:00:00am, but rather 11:00:00am–11:59:59am.

Hmmmm, every 5 seconds could be a fun period. . . .

```
sec {0-4 10-14 20-24 30-34 40-44 50-54}
```

To specify every first half-hour on alternating week days, and the second half-hour the rest of the week, use the period:

```
wd {1 3 5 7} min {0-29}, wd {2 4 6} min {30-59}
```

Version

1.12

Author

Patrick Ryan, *pgryan@geocities.com*

Copyright

Copyright © 1997 Patrick Ryan. All rights reserved. This Perl module uses the conditions given by Perl. This module may only be distributed and or modified under the conditions given by Perl.

Source

This distribution can be found at:

http://www.geocities.com/SiliconValley/Lakes/8456/

and other places, but probably CPAN, which can be found at:

> *http://www.perl.com/CPAN/modules/by-module/Time/*

If that doesn't work, give:

> *http://www.perl.com/perl/CPAN*

a shot.

Authenticity Verification

A signature for *Period.pm* came with this distribution. It is called *Period.pm.sig*. The module can be verified with the public PGP key called "Patrick Ryan <pryan@sleepy>". That public PGP key is available through:

> *http://www.geocities.com/SiliconValley/Lakes/8456/*

Time::Timezone—miscellaneous time zone manipulation routines

Synopsis

```
use Time::Timezone;
print tz2zone();
print tz2zone($ENV{'TZ'});
print tz2zone($ENV{'TZ'}, time());
print tz2zone($ENV{'TZ'}, undef, $isdst);
$offset = tz_local_offset();
$offset = tz_offset($TZ);
```

Description

This is a collection of miscellaneous time zone manipulation routines:

tz2zone()
> Parses the TZ environment variable and returns a time zone string suitable for inclusion in the date manpage-like output. It optionally takes a time zone string, a time, and an is-dst flag.

tz_local_offset()
> Determines the offset from GMT time in seconds. It only does the calculation once.

tz_offset()
> Determines the offset from GMT in seconds of a specified timezone.

tz_name()
> Determines the name of the timezone based on its offset.

Authors

Graham Barr, *gbarr@pobox.com*; David Muir Sharnoff, *muir@idiom.com*; Paul Foley, *paul@ascent.com*

Time::Zone—miscellaneous time zone manipulation routines

Synopsis

```
use Time::Zone;
print tz2zone();
```

```
print tz2zone($ENV{'TZ'});
print tz2zone($ENV{'TZ'}, time());
print tz2zone($ENV{'TZ'}, undef, $isdst);
$offset = tz_local_offset();
$offset = tz_offset($TZ);
```

Description

This is a collection of miscellaneous time zone manipulation routines.

tz2zone()

Parses the TZ environment variable and returns a time zone string suitable for inclusion in **date**-like output. It optionally takes a time zone string, a time, and an **is-dst** flag.

tz_local_offset()

Determines the offset from GMT time in seconds. It only does the calculation once.

tz_offset()

Determines the offset from GMT in seconds of a specified time zone.

tz_name()

Determines the name of the time zone based on its offset.

Authors

Graham Barr, *gbarr@pobox.com*; David Muir Sharnoff, *muir@idiom.com*; Paul Foley, *paul@ascent.com*

7

Database Interfaces

This section describes tools to work with databases and aid in database programming; SQL and Sybase utilities are included.

CDB_File—Perl extension for access to cdb databases

Synopsis

```
use CDB_File;
tie %h, 'CDB_File', 'file.cdb' or die "tie failed: $!\n";
$t = new CDB_File ('t.cdb', 't.tmp') or die ...;
$t->insert('key', 'value');
$t->finish;
CDB_File::create %t, $file, "$file.$$";
```

or

```
use CDB_File 'create';
create %t, $file, "$file.$$";
```

Description

CDB_File is a module which provides a Perl interface to Dan Berstein's cdb package (cdb is a fast, reliable, lightweight package for creating and reading constant databases).

After the tie shown above, accesses to %h will refer to the cdb file *file.cdb*, as described in tie.

A cdb file is created in three steps. First call new CDB_File (*$final*, *$tmp*), where *$final* is the name of the database to be created, and *$tmp* is the name of a temporary file which can be automatically renamed to *$final*. Secondly, call the insert method once for each *(key, value)* pair. Finally, call the finish method to complete the creation and renaming of the cdb file.

A simpler interface to cdb file creation is provided by CDB_File::create %t, *$final*, *$tmp*. This creates a cdb file named *$final* containing the contents of %t. As before, *$tmp* must name a temporary file which can be atomically renamed to *$final*. CDB_File::create may be imported.

Examples

These are all complete programs.

Convert a Berkeley DB (B-tree) database to cdb format.

```
use CDB_File;
use DB_File;
tie %h, DB_File, $ARGV[0], O_RDONLY, undef, $DB_BTREE or
        die "$0: can't tie to $ARGV[0]: $!\n";
CDB_File::create %h, $ARGV[1], "$ARGV[1].$$" or
        die "$0: can't create cdb: $!\n";
```

Convert a flat file to cdb format. In this example, the flat file consists of one key per line, separated by a colon from the value. Blank lines and lines beginning with # are skipped.

```
use CDB_File;
$cdb = new CDB_File("data.cdb", "data.$$") or
        die "$0: new CDB_File failed: $!\n";
while (<>) {
        next if /^$/ or /^#/;
        chop;
        ($k, $v) = split /:/, $_, 2;
        if (defined $v) {
                $cdb->insert($k, $v);
        } else {
                warn "bogus line: $_\n";
        }
}
$cdb->finish or die "$0: CDB_File finish failed: $!\n";
```

Perl version of cdbdump.

```
tie %data, 'CDB_File', $ARGV[0] or
        die "$0: can't tie to $ARGV[0]: $!\n";
while (($k, $v) = each %data) {
        print '+', length $k, ',', length $v, ":$k->$v\n";
}
print "\n";
```

Although a cdb file is constant, you can simulate updating it in Perl. This is an expensive operation, as you have to create a new database, and copy into it everything that's unchanged from the old database. (As compensation, the update does not affect database readers. The old database is available for them, till the moment the new one is finished.)

```
use CDB_File;
$file = 'data.cdb';
$new = new CDB_File($file, "$file.$$") or
        die "$0: new CDB_File failed: $!\n";
# Add the new values; remember which keys we've seen.
while (<>) {
        chop;
        ($k, $v) = split;
        $new->insert($k, $v);
        $seen{$k} = 1;
}
```

```
# Add any old values that haven't been replaced.
tie %old, 'CDB_File', $file or die "$0: can't tie to $file: $!\n";
while (($k, $v) = each %old) {
        $new->insert($k, $v) unless $seek{$k};
}
$new->finish or die "$0: CDB_File finish failed: $!\n";
```

Repeated Keys

Most users can ignore this section.

A cdb file can contain repeated keys. If the insert method is called more than once with the same key during the creation of a cdb file, that key will be repeated.

Here's an example.

```
$cdb = new CDB_File ("$file.cdb", "$file.$$") or die ...;
$cdb->insert('cat', 'gato');
$cdb->insert('cat', 'chat');
$cdb->finish;
```

Normally, any attempt to access a key retrieves the first value stored under that key. This code snippet always prints gato.

```
$catref = tie %catalogue, CDB_File, "$file.cdb" or die ...;
print "$catalogue{cat}";
```

However, all the usual ways of iterating over a hash—keys, values, and each—do the Right Thing, even in the presence of repeated keys. This code snippet prints cat cat gato chat.

```
print join(' ', keys %catalogue, values %catalogue);
```

Internally, CDB_File stores extra information to keep track of where it is while iterating over a file. But this extra information is not attached to multiple keys returned by keys: if you use them to retrieve values, they will always retrieve the first value stored under that key.

This means that this code probably doesn't do what you want; it prints cat:gato cat:gato.

```
foreach $key (keys %catalogue) {
        print "$key:$catalogue{$key} ";
}
```

The correct version uses each, and prints cat:gato cat:chat.

```
while (($key, $val) = each %catalogue) {
        print "$key:$val ";
}
```

In general, there is no way to retrieve all the values associated with a key, other than to loop over the entire database (i.e. there is no equivalent to DB_File's get_dup method). However, the multi_get method retrieves the values associated with the first occurrence of a key, and all consecutive identical keys. If you ensure that all occurrences of each key are adjacent in the database (perhaps by sorting them during database creation), then multi_get can be used to retrieve all the values associated with a key. This code prints gato chat.

```
print $catref->multiget('cat');
```

Return Values

The routines tie, new, and finish return false if the attempted operation failed; $!
contains the reason for failure.

Diagnostics

The following fatal errors may occur. (See eval if you want to trap them.)

Modification of a CDB_File attempted
> You attempted to modify a hash tied to a CDB_File.

CDB database too large
> You attempted to create a cdb file larger than 4 gigabytes.

Bad CDB_File format
> You tried to use CDB_File to access something that isn't a cdb file.

[Write to | Read of | Seek in] CDB_File failed: <error string>
> The reported operation failed; the operating system's error string is shown. These
> errors can occur only if there is a serious problem—for example, if you have run
> out of disk space.

Use CDB_File::FIRSTKEY before CDB_File::NEXTKEY
> If you are using the NEXTKEY method directly (I can't think of a reason why
> you'd want to do this), you need to call FIRSTKEY first.

Bugs

It isn't lightweight after you've plumbed Perl into it.

The Perl interface to cdb imposes the restriction that data must fit into memory.

Author

Tim Goodwin, *tim@uunet.pipex.com*

See Also

cdb(3)

DBD::Informix—access to Informix databases

Synopsis

```
use DBD::Informix;
```

Description

This document describes DBD::Informix version 0.25 and later.

It has a biased view on how to use DBI and DBD::Informix. Because there is no better
documentation of how to use DBI, this covers both DBI and DBD::Informix. The extant
documentation on DBI suggests that things should be done differently, but gives no solid
examples of how it should be done differently or why it should be done differently.

Be aware that on occasion, it gets complex because of differences between different
versions of Informix software. The key factor is the version of ESQL/C used when building
DBD::Informix. Basically, there are two groups of versions to worry about, the 5.0x family
of versions (5.00.UC1 through 5.08.UC1 at the moment), and the 6.0x and later family of

versions (6.00.UE1 through 7.21.UC1 at the moment). All version families acquire extra versions on occasion.

Note that DBD::Informix does not work with 4.1x or earlier versions of ESQL/C because it uses SQL descriptors and these are not available prior to version 5.00.

Use of DBD::Informix

Loading DBD::Informix

To use the DBD::Informix software, you need to load the DBI software.

```
use DBI;
```

Under normal circumstances, you should then connect to your database using the notation in the section "Connecting to a Database," which calls **DBI->connect()**. Note that the DBD::Informix test code does not operate under normal circumstances, and therefore uses the non-preferred techniques in the section "Driver Attributes and Methods".

Driver Attributes and Methods

If you have a burning desire to do so, you can explicitly install the Informix driver independently of connecting to any database using:

```
$drh = DBI->install_driver('Informix');
```

This gives you a reference to the driver, aka the driver handle. If the load fails, your program stops immediately (unless, perhaps, you **eval** the statement).

Once you have the driver handle, you can interrogate the driver for some basic information:

```
print "Driver Information\n";
# Type is always 'dr'.
print "    Type:                 $drh->{Type}\n";
# Name is always 'Informix'.
print "    Name:                 $drh->{Name}\n";
# Version is the version of DBD::Informix (eg 0.51).
print "    Version:              $drh->{Version}\n";
# The Attribution identifies the culprits who provided you
# with this software.
print "    Attribution:          $drh->{Attribution}\n";
# The ProductName is the version of ESQL/C; it corresponds to
# the first line of the output from "esql -V".
print "    Product:              $drh->{ix_ProductName}\n";
# The ProductVersion is an integer version number such as 721
# for ESQL/C version 7.21.UC1.
print "    Product Version:      $drh->{ix_ProductVersion}\n";
# The MultipleConnections indicates whether the driver
# supports multiple connections (1) or not (0).
print "    Multiple Connections: $drh->{ix_MultipleConnections}\n";
# -- Not implemented in DBD::Informix yet --
# ActiveConnections identifies the number of open connections.
print "    Active Connections:   $drh->{ix_ActiveConnections}\n";
# CurrentConnection identifies the current connection.
print "    Current Connections:  $drh->{ix_CurrentConnection}\n";
```

Once you have the driver loaded, you can connect to a database, or you can sever all connections to databases with disconnect_all.

```
$drh->disconnect_all;
```

There is also an unofficial function which can be called using:

```
@dbnames = $drh->func('_ListDBs');
```

You can test whether this worked with:

```
if (defined @dbnames) { ...process array... }
else                  { ...process error... }
```

Connecting to a Database

To connect to a database, you can use the connect function, which yields a valid reference or database handle if it is successful. If the driver itself cannot be loaded (by the DBI->install_driver() method mentioned above), DBI aborts the script (and DBD::Informix can do nothing about it because it wasn't loaded successfully).

```
$dbh = DBI->connect($database, $username, $password, 'Informix');
```

Note that if you omit the fourth argument ('Informix'), then DBI will load the driver specified by $ENV{DBI_DRIVER}. If you omit the fourth argument, you can also omit the $password and $username arguments if desired. If you specify the fourth argument, you can leave the $password and $username arguments empty and they will be ignored.

```
$dbh = DBI->connect($database, $username, $password);
$dbh = DBI->connect($database, $username);
$dbh = DBI->connect($database);
```

The 5.0x versions ignore the username and password data, and the statement is equivalent to EXEC SQL DATABASE :database;. The 6.0x versions only use the username and password if both are supplied, but it is then equivalent to:

```
EXEC SQL CONNECT TO :database AS :connection
     USER :username USING :password
     WITH CONCURRENT TRANSACTIONS
```

The connection is given a name by DBD::Informix.

For Informix, the database name is any valid format for the DATABASE or CONNECT statements. Examples include:

```
dbase              # 'Local' database
//machine1/dbase   # Database on remote machine
dbase@server1      # Database on (remote) server
                   # (as defined in sqlhosts)
@server1           # Connection to (remote) server but no database
/some/where/dbase  # Connect to local SE database
```

The database name is not supplied implicitly by DBD::Informix, but the DBI driver will supply the value in $ENV{DBI_DBNAME} if the environment variable is set and no database name is supplied in the connect call. If DBD::Informix sees an empty string, then it makes no connection to any database with ESQL/C 5.0x, and it makes a default connection with ESQL/C 6.00 and later. There is an additional string, .DEFAULT., which can be specified explicitly as the database name and which will be interpreted as a request for a default connection. Note that this is not a valid Informix database name, so there can be no confusion.

Once you have a database handle, you can interrogate it for some basic information about the database, etc.

```
print "Database Information\n";
# Type is always 'db'
print "    Type:                    $dbh->{Type}\n";
# Name is the name of the database specified at connect
print "    Database Name:           $dbh->{Name}\n";
# AutoCommit is 1 (true) if the database commits each statement.
print "    AutoCommit:              $dbh->{AutoCommit}\n";
# ix_InformixOnLine is 1 (true) if the handle is connected to an
# Informix-OnLine server.
print "    Informix-OnLine:         $dbh->{ix_InformixOnLine}\n";
# ix_LoggedDatabase is 1 (true) if the database has
# transactions.
print "    Logged Database:         $dbh->{ix_LoggedDatabase}\n";
# ix_ModeAnsiDatabase is 1 (true) if the database is MODE ANSI.
print "    Mode ANSI Database:      $dbh->{ix_ModeAnsiDatabase}\n";
# ix_AutoErrorReport is 1 (true) if errors are reported as they
# are detected.
print "    AutoErrorReport:         $dbh->{ix_AutoErrorReport}\n";
# ix_InTransaction is 1 (true) if the database is in a transaction
print "    Transaction Active:      $dbh->{ix_InTransaction}\n";
# ix_ConnectionName is the name of the ESQL/C connection.
# Mainly applicable with Informix-ESQL/C 6.00 and later.
print "    Connection Name:         $dbh->{ix_ConnectionName}\n";
```

If $dbh->{ix_AutoErrorReport} is true, then DBD::Informix will report each error automatically on STDERR when it is detected. The error is also available via the package variables $DBI::errstr and $DBI::err. Note that $DBI::errstr includes the SQL error number and the ISAM error number if there is one, and ends with a new line. The message may or may not extend over several lines, and is generally formatted so that it will display neatly within 80 columns.

If $dbh->{ix_AutoErrorReport} is false, then DBD::Informix does not report any errors when it detects them; it is up to the user to note that errors have occurred and to report them.

If you connect using the DBI->connect() method, or if you have forgotten the driver, you can discover it again using:

```
$drh = $dbh->{Driver};
```

This allows you to access the driver methods and attributes described previously.

Disconnecting from a Database

You can also disconnect from the database:

```
$dbh->disconnect;
```

This will rollback any uncommitted work. Note that this does not destroy the database handle. You need to do an explicit undef $dbh to destroy the handle. Any statements prepared using this handle are finished (see below) and cannot be used again. All space associated with the statements is released.

If you are using an Informix driver for which $drh->{ProductVersion} >= 600, then you can have multiple concurrent connections. This means that multiple calls to $drh->connect will give you independent connections to one or more databases.

If you are using an Informix driver for which $drh->{ProductVersion} < 600, then you cannot have multiple concurrent connections. If you make multiple calls to $drh ->connect, you will achieve the same effect as executing several database statements in a row. This will generally switch databases successfully, but may invalidate any statements previously prepared. It may fail if the current database is not local, or if there is an active transaction, etc.

Simple Statements

Given a database connection, you can execute a variety of simple statements using a variety of different calls:

```
$dbh->commit;
$dbh->rollback;
```

These two operations commit or rollback the current transaction. If the database is unlogged, they do nothing. If the database is not MODE ANSI and AutoCommit is set to 0 then a new transaction is automatically started. If the database is not MODE ANSI and AutoCommit is set to 1 (the default), then no explicit transaction is started.

You can execute most preparable parameterless statements using:

```
$dbh->do($stmt);
```

The statement must not be either SELECT (other than SELECT...INTO TEMP) or EXECUTE PROCEDURE where the procedure returns data. This will use the ESQL/C EXECUTE IMMEDIATE statement.

You can execute an arbitrary statement with parameters using:

```
$dbh->do($stmt, @parameters);
$dbh->do($stmt, $param1, $param2);
```

Again, the statement must not be a SELECT or EXECUTE PROCEDURE which returns data. The values in @parameters (or the separate values) are bound to the question marks in the statement string. However, this cannot use EXECUTE IMMEDIATE because it does not accept parameters.

```
$sth = $dbh->prepare($stmt);
$sth->execute(@parameters);
```

Unlike previous releases, which used some code from the DBI package, DBD::Informix v0.26, now handles the do operation exclusively with its own code.

You can embed an arbitrary string inside a statement with any quote marks correctly handled by invoking:

```
$dbh->quote($string);
```

This method is provided by the DBI package implementation and is inherited by the DBD::Informix package. The string is enclosed in single quotes, and any embedded single quotes are doubled up, which conforms to the SQL-92 standard.

Creating Statements

You can also prepare a statement for multiple uses, and you can do this for SELECT and EXECUTE PROCEDURE statements which return data (cursory statements) as well as non-cursory statements which return no data. You create a statement handle (another reference) using:

```
$sth = $dbh->prepare($stmt);
```

If the statement is a SELECT which returns data (not SELECT...INTO TEMP) or an EXECUTE PROCEDURE for a procedure which returns values, then a cursor is declared for the prepared statement.

According to the DBI specification, the prepare call accepts an optional attributes parameter which is a reference to a hash. At the moment, no parameters are recognized. It would be reasonable to add, for example, {ix_CursorWithHold => 1} to specify that the cursor should be declared WITH HOLD. Similarly, you could add {ix_BlobLocation => 'InFile'} to support per-statement blob location, and {ix_ScrollCursor => 1} to support scroll cursors.

Note: in versions of DBD::Informix prior to 0.25, preparing a statement also executed non-cursory statements and opened the cursor for cursory statements. This no longer occurs.

More typically, you need to do error checking, and this is achieved by using:

```
die "Failed to prepare '$stmt'\n"
    unless ($sth = $dbh->prepare($stmt));
```

Once the statement is prepared, you can execute it: $sth->execute;

For a non-cursory statement, this simply executes the statement. For a cursory statement, it opens the cursor. You can also specify the parameters for a statement using:

```
$sth->execute(@parameters);
```

The first parameter will be supplied as the value for the first placeholder question mark in the statement, the second parameter for the second placeholder, etc.

For cursory statements, you can discover what the returned column names, types, nullability, etc are. You do this with:

```
@name = @{$sth->{NAME}};        # Column names
@null = @{$sth->{NULLABLE}};     # True => accepts nulls
@type = @{$sth->{TYPE}};         # ODBC Data Type numbers
@prec = @{$sth->{PRECISION}};    # ODBC PRECISION numbers (or undef)
@scal = @{$sth->{SCALE}};        # ODBC SCALE numbers (or undef)
# Native (Informix) type equivalents
@tnam = @{$sth->{ix_NativeTypeName}}; # Type name
@tnum = @{$sth->{ix_ColType}};   # Type number from
                                 #   SysColumns.ColType
@tlen = @{$sth->{ix_ColLength}}; # Type length from
                                 #   SysColumns.ColLength
```

If the statement is a cursory statement, you can retrieve the values in either of two ways:

```
$ref = $sth->fetch;
@row = @{$ref};
@row = @{$sth->fetch};  # Shorthand for above...
@row = $sth->fetchrow;
```

As usual, you have to worry about whether this worked or not. You would normally, therefore, use:

```
while ($ref = $sth->fetch)
{
    # We know we got some data here
    ...
}
# Investigate whether an error occurred or the SELECT
# simply had nothing more to return.
if ($sth->{sqlcode} < 0)
{
    # Process error...
}
```

The returned data includes blobs mapped into strings. Note that byte blobs might contain ASCII NUL '\0' characters. Perl knows how long the strings are and does preserve NUL in the middle of a byte blob. However, you may need to be careful deciding how to handle this string.

There is provision to specify how you want blobs handled. You can set the attribute:

```
$sth->{BlobLocation} = 'InMemory';      # Default
$sth->{BlobLocation} = 'InFile';        # In a named file
$sth->{BlobLocation} = 'DummyValue';    # Return dummy values
$sth->{BlobLocation} = 'NullValue';     # Return undefined
```

The InFile mode returns the name of a file in the fetched array, and that file can be accessed by Perl using normal file access methods. The DummyValue mode returns <<TEXT VALUE>> for text blobs or <<BYTE VALUE>> for byte (binary) blobs. The NullValue mode returns undefined (meaning that Perl's "defined" operator would return false) values. Note that these two options do not necessarily prevent the Server from returning the data to the application, but the user does not get to see the data—this depends on the internal implementation of the ESQL/C FETCH operation in conjunction with SQL descriptors.

You can also set the BlobLocation attribute on the database, overriding it at the statement level.

When you have fetched as many rows as required, you close the cursor using `$sth->finish;`

This simply closes the cursor; it does not free the cursor or the statement. That is done when you destroy (**undef**) the statement handle:

```
undef $sth;
```

You can also implicitly rebind a statement handle to a new statement by simply using the same variable again. This does not cause any memory leaks.

Cursors for Update

With DBD::Informix v0.51 and later, you can use the attribute `$sth->{CursorName}` to retrieve the name of a cursor. If the statement for `$sth` is actually a SELECT, and the cursor is in a MODE ANSI database or is declared with the FOR UPDATE [OF col,... tag, then you can use the cursor name in a DELETE...WHERE CURRENT OF or UPDATE...WHERE CURRENT OF statement.

```
$st1 = $dbh->prepare("SELECT * FROM SomeTable FOR UPDATE");
$wc = "WHERE CURRENT OF $st1->{CursorName}";
$st2 = $dbh->prepare("UPDATE SomeTable SET SomeColumn = ? $wc");
$st3 = $dbh->prepare("DELETE FROM SomeTable $wc");
```

```
$st1->execute;
$row = $st1->fetch;
$st2->execute("New Value");
$row = $st1->fetch;
$st3->execute();
```

Accessing the Sqlca Record

You can access the SQLCA record via either a database handle or a statement handle.

```
$sqlcode = $sth->{ix_sqlcode};
$sqlerrm = $sth->{ix_sqlerrm};
$sqlerrp = $sth->{ix_sqlerrp};
@sqlerrd = $sth->{ix_sqlerrd};
@sqlwarn = $sth->{ix_sqlwarn};
```

Note that the warning information is treated as an array (as in Informix-4GL) rather than as a bunch of separate fields (as in Informix-ESQL/C). Inspect the code in the print_sqlca() function in *InformixTest.pm* for more ideas on the use of these. You cannot set the sqlca record.

Transaction Management

The Interactions of AutoCommit with Informix Databases

There are three types of Informix databases to consider: MODE ANSI, Logged, and UnLogged. Although MODE ANSI databases also have a transaction log, the category of Logged databases specifically excludes MODE ANSI databases. In OnLine, this refers to databases created WITH LOG or WITH BUFFERED LOG; in SE, to databases created WITH LOG IN */some/file/name.*

There are two AutoCommit modes to consider: On, Off.

There are two possible transaction states: In-TX (In transaction), No-TX (Outside transaction).

There are at least 13 types of statements (in four groups and nine sub-groups) to consider:

```
$drh->connect('xyz');                       # Group 1A
$dbh->do('DATABASE xyz');                   # Group 1B
$dbh->do('CREATE DATABASE xyz');            # Group 1B
$dbh->do('ROLLFORWARD DATABASE xyz');       # Group 1B
$dbh->do('START DATABASE xyz');             # Group 1B
$dbh->disconnect();                         # Group 2A
$dbh->do('CLOSE DATABASE');                 # Group 2B
$dbh->commit();                             # Group 3A
$dbh->rollback();                           # Group 3A
$dbh->do('BEGIN WORK');                     # Group 3B
$dbh->do('ROLLBACK WORK');                  # Group 3C
$dbh->do('COMMIT WORK');                    # Group 3C
$dbh->prepare('SELECT ...');                # Group 4A
$dbh->prepare('UPDATE ...');                # Group 4B
```

The Group 1 statements establish the default AutoCommit mode for a database handle. Group 1A is the primary means of connecting to a database; the Group 1B statements can change the default AutoCommit mode by virtue of changing the current database.

For a MODE ANSI database, the default AutoCommit mode is Off. For a Logged database, the default AutoCommit mode is On. For an UnLogged database, the default AutoCommit mode is On and it cannot be changed. Any attempt to change Auto-Commit mode to Off with an UnLogged database generates a non-fatal warning.

The Group 2 statements sever the connection to a database. The Group 2A statement renders the database handle unusable; no further operations are possible except undef or re-assigning with a new connection. The Group 2B statement means that no operations other than those in Group 1B or DROP DATABASE are permitted. The value of AutoCommit is irrelevant after the database is closed.

The Group 3 and 4 statements interact in many complicated ways. Although UPDATE is cited in Group 4B, it represents any statement which is not a SELECT statement. Note that SELECT ... INTO TEMP is a Group 4B statement because it returns no data to the program. An EXECUTE PROCEDURE statement is in Group 4A if it returns data, and in Group 4B if it does not, and you cannot tell which of the two groups applies until after the statement is prepared.

MODE ANSI Databases

By default, a MODE ANSI database operates with AutoCommit Off. When the connection is established, a transaction is started implicitly, and the program will be inside a transaction (In-TX) at all times. Whenever either of the group 3A functions is used, a new transaction is automatically (but implicitly) started. The DBD::Informix code does not do an explicit BEGIN WORK because the user is entitled to write their own BEGIN WORK immediately after COMMIT WORK or ROLLBACK WORK (and hence $dbh->commit or $dbh->rollback), and if DBD::Informix did this, the user would get an unwarranted error. Before disconnecting, the code does ROLLBACK WORK to ensure that the disconnect can occur cleanly.

If the user elects to switch to AutoCommit On, things get trickier. All cursors need to be declared WITH HOLD so that Group 4B statements being committed do not close the active cursors. Whenever a Group 4B statement is executed, the statement needs to be committed. With OnLine (and theoretically with SE, I think), if the statement fails there is no need to do a rollback—the statement failing did the rollback anyway. And the commit will automatically start a new transaction. As before, the code can do ROLLBACK WORK before disconnecting, though it should not actually be necessary.

Logged Databases

Unlike MODE ANSI databases, Logged databases can be in either one of two transaction states—In-TX and No-TX.

AutoCommit is set to On when the connection is established, and the transaction state is No-TX. No further action is required by DBD::Informix in this state. Neither $dbh->commit nor $dbh->rollback should be used in this state—there is no transaction for them to work on. If they are called, the effect will be a no-op; all previous operations were already committed or rolled back, so they will succeed. Note that cursors established in this state are not declared WITH HOLD. If the user executes $dbh->do('BEGIN WORK') or equivalent, then the AutoCommit functionality is suspended and the transaction state is In-TX until the transaction is terminated. If a Group 3A function is executed, a new transaction is not started explicitly and the transaction state is once more No-TX, and the user can execute BEGIN WORK as required. If the state at $dbh->disconnect is In-TX, then DBD::Informix does a rollback before attempting to disconnect. If the user attempts to close the database (or open a new one) while in the In-TX state, an error will be generated by Informix.

If the user sets AutoCommit off explicitly, DBD::Informix does an explicit BEGIN WORK to start a transaction and the transaction state is In-TX (and will stay like that until AutoCommit is set to On). Cursors declared while AutoCommit is off do not need to be declared WITH HOLD either, so cursors in Logged databases are not WITH HOLD regardless of AutoCommit. However, it might be a good option to allow $dbh->{CursorsWithHold} to indicate that they are to be declared WITH HOLD. When the user executes a Group 3A function, a new transaction is started explicitly (meaning that the user cannot successfully execute BEGIN WORK) and the transaction state is In-TX.

UnLogged Databases

The transaction state is No-TX and AutoCommit is On, and this cannot be changed. Any attempt to set AutoCommit to Off generates a non-fatal warning but the program will continue; setting it to On generates neither a warning nor an error. Both $dbh->commit and $dbh->rollback succeed but do nothing. Executing any Group 3B or 3C statement will generate an error.

Attribute Name Changes

Note that most (theoretically all) of the Informix-specific attributes have been renamed so that they start ix_ (eg: $dbh->{ix_AutoErrorReport}), and the old names that do not have this systematic prefix are now officially deprecated. An additional attribute, $dbh->{ix_Deprecated} was invented which could be set to 0 to suppress the warning reports in earlier (0.51..0.53) releases when a deprecated attribute was used. The deprecated form {Deprecated} is also supported.

In this release (0.55), the deprecated warnings will alert you to the fact that the old-style attributes did not achieve anything, and there will be no mechanism to switch the warnings off. In the next release (0.56), using the old-style attribute names will generate an error. In the release after that (0.57), using the old-style attribute names will do nothing silently. The exact time scale for these releases is not clear (but will probably be completed in Q3 of 1997 (give or take a year or two), so if you don't upgrade for a few releases, you could run into problems unexpectedly.

Note that some names may retain the form with no prefix if they are accepted by the larger DBD/DBD community. Two of the prime candidates for not having to change are ProductName and ProductVersion.

Mapping Between ESQL/C and DBD::Informix

A crude form of the mapping between DBD::Informix functions and ESQL/C equivalents follows—there are a number of ways in which it isn't quite precise (e.g., the influence of AutoCommit), but it is accurate enough for most purposes.

```
DBI->connect            => DATABASE in 5.0x
$dbh->disconnect        => CLOSE DATABASE in 5.0x
DBI->connect            => CONNECT in 6.0x and later
$dbh->disconnect        => DISCONNECT in 6.0x and later
$dbh->commit            => COMMIT WORK (+BEGIN WORK)
$dbh->rollback          => ROLLBACK WORK (+BEGIN WORK)
$dbh->do                => EXECUTE IMMEDIATE
$dbh->prepare           => PREPARE, DESCRIBE (DECLARE)
```

```
$sth->execute              => EXECUTE or OPEN
$sth->fetch                => FETCH
$sth->fetchrow             => FETCH
$sth->finish               => CLOSE
undef $sth                 => FREE cursor, FREE statement, etc
```

Known Restrictions

Blobs can be located only in memory (reliably).

Some driver attributes (notably CurrentConnection and ActiveConnections) cannot be queried.

The new DBI spec (version 1.64) from Tim Bunce has not been assimilated into the 0.52 version of DBD::Informix.

Author

At various times:

- Tim Bunce, *Tim.Bunce@ig.co.uk*
- Alligator Descartes, *descartes@hermetica.com*
- Jonathan Leffler, *johnl@informix.com*

See Also

perl(1), perldoc for DBI

DBD::InformixTest—test harness for DBD::Informix

Synopsis

```
use DBD::InformixTest;
```

Description

This document describes DBD::InformixTest for DBD::Informix version 0.25 and later. This is pure Perl code which exploits DBI and DBD::Informix to make it easier to write tests. Most notably, it provides a simple mechanism to connect to the user's chosen test database and a uniform set of reporting mechanisms.

Loading DBD::InformixTest

To use the DBD::InformixTest software, you need to load the DBI software and then install the Informix driver:

```
use DBD::InformixTest;
```

Connecting to Test Database

This gives you a reference to the database connection handle, aka the database handle. If the load fails, your program stops immediately. The functionality available from this handle is documented in the *DBD::Informix* manpage. This function does not report success when it succeeds because the test scripts for blobs, for example, need to know whether they are working with an online system before reporting how many tests will be run.

```
$dbh = &connect_to_test_database;
```

This code exploits four environment variables:

DBD_INFORMIX_DATABASE
DBD_INFORMIX_SERVER
DBD_INFORMIX_USERNAME
DBD_INFORMIX_PASSWORD

The database variable can be simply the name of the database, or it can be *database@server*, or it can be one of the SE notations such as */opt/dbase* or *//hostname/dbase*. If the database name does not contain either slashes or at-signs, then the value in the server variable, which defaults to $INFORMIXSERVER (which must be set for 6.00 and later Informix database systems) is appended to the database name after an at-sign. If INFORMIXSERVER is not set, then you had better be on a 5.0x system, as otherwise the connection will fail. With 6.00 and above, you can optionally specify a username and password in the environment. This is horribly insecure—do not use it for production work. The test scripts do not print the password.

Using stmt_test

Once you have a database connection, you can execute simple statements (those which do not return any data) using &stmt_test():

```
&stmt_test($dbh, $stmt, $flag, $tag);
```

The first argument is the database handle. The second is a string containing the statement to be executed. The third is optional and is a boolean. If it is 0, then the statement must execute without causing an error or the test will terminate. If it is set to 1, then the statement may fail and the error will be reported but the test will continue. The fourth argument is an optional string which will be used as a tag before the statement when it is printed. If omitted, it defaults to Test.

Using stmt_retest

The &stmt_retest() function takes three arguments, which have the same meaning as the first three arguments of &stmt_test():

```
&stmt_retest($dbh, $stmt, $flag);
```

It calls:

```
&stmt_test($dbh, $stmt, 0, "Retest");
```

Using print_sqlca

The &print_sqlca() function takes a single argument which can be either a statement handle or a database handle and prints out the current values of the SQLCA record.

```
&print_sqlca($dbh);
&print_sqlca($sth);
```

Using all_ok

The &all_ok() function can be used at the end of a test script to report that everything was OK. It exits with status 0.

```
&all_ok();
```

Using stmt_ok

This routine adds ok N to the end of a line. The N increments automatically each time &stmt_ok() or &stmt_fail() is called. If called with a non-false argument, it prints the contents of DBI::errstr as a warning message too. This routine is used internally by stmt_test() but is also available for your use.

```
&stmt_ok(0);
```

Using stmt_fail

This routine adds not ok N to the end of a line, then reports the error message in DBI::errstr, and then dies. The N is incremented automatically, as with &stmt_ok(). This routine is used internally by stmt_test() but is also available for your use.

```
&stmt_fail();
```

Using stmt_err

This routines prints a caption (defaulting to Error Message) and the contents of DBI::errstr, ensuring that each line is prefixed by #. This routine is used internally by the InformixTest module, but is also available for your use.

```
&stmt_err('Warning Message');
```

Using stmt_note

This routine writes a string (without any new line unless you include it). This routine is used internally by stmt_test() but is also available for your use.

```
&stmt_note("Some string or other");
```

Using select_some_data

This routine takes three arguments:

```
&select_some_data($dbh, $nrows, $stmt);
```

The first argument is the database handle. The second is the number of rows that should be returned. The third is a string containing the SELECT statement to be executed. It prints all the data returned with a # preceding the first field and two colons separating the fields. It reports OK if the select succeeds and the correct number of rows are returned; it fails otherwise.

Using select_zero_data

This routine takes a database handle and a SELECT statement and invokes &select_some_data with 0 rows expected.

```
&select_zero_data($dbh, $stmt);
```

Note

All these routines can also be used without parentheses or the &, so that the following is also valid:

```
select_zero_data $dbh, $stmt;
```

Author

Jonathan Leffler, *johnl@informix.com*

See Also

perl(1), DBD::Informix, DBI(1)

DBD::Ingres—Ingres access interface for Perl5

Synopsis

```
$dbh = DBI->connect($dbname, $user, $options, 'Ingres')
$sth = $dbh->prepare($statement)
$sth->execute
@row = $sth->fetchrow
$sth->finish
$dbh->commit
$dbh->rollback
$dbh->disconnect
and many more
```

Description

DBD::Ingres is an extension to Perl that allows access to Ingres databases. It is built on top of the standard DBI extension an implements the methods that DBI requires.

This document describes the differences between the "generic" DBD and DBD::Ingres.

Not Implemented

Binding

Parameter binding is not implented in this version of DBD::Ingres. It is planned for a future release—but it does not have high priority.

As there is no binding, there is no need for reexecution of statements—not that anything in the code prevents it (to my knowledge).

`$h->state`

SQL_STATE is not implemented yet. It is planned for the (not so) near future.

OpenIngres new features

The new features of OpenIngres are not (yet) supported in DBD::Ingres.

This includes BLOBS, decimal datatypes, and spatial datatypes.

Support will be added when the need arises—if you need it, you add it.

Extensions/Changes

`$dbh->do`

This is implemented as a call to EXECUTE IMMEDIATE. (The generic way is through **prepare, bind, execute**). This will probably change when binds are added.

`$sth->{Statement}`

Contains the text of the SQL statement. Used mainly for debugging.

`$sth->{TYPE}`

Returns an array of the "Perl" type of the **return** fields of a SELECT statement.

The types are represented as:

'i': integer

All integer types, i.e., `int1`, `int2`, and `int4`.

'f': float

The types `float`, `float8`, and **money**.

's': string

All other supported types, i.e., **char**, **varchar**, **text**, **date**, etc.

`$sth->SqlLen`

Returns an array containing the lengths of the fields in Ingres; e.g., an `int2` will return 2, a `varchar(7)` 7, and so on.

Note that `money` and `date` will have `length` returned as 0.

`$sth->SqlType`

Returns an array containing the Ingres types of the fields. The types are given as documented in the Ingres SQL Reference Manual.

Notes

I wonder if I have forgotten something? There is no authoritative DBI documentation (other than the code); it is difficult to document the differences from a non-existent document.

Authors

DBI/DBD was developed by Tim Bunce, *Tim.Bunce@ig.co.uk*, who also developed the DBD::Oracle that is the closest we have to a generic DBD implementation.

Henrik Tougaard, *ht@datani.dk*, developed the DBD::Ingres extension.

See Also

The DBI documentation.

DBD::Pg—PostgreSQL database driver for the DBI module

Synopsis

```
use DBI;
$dbh = DBI->connect("dbi:Pg:$dbname", $user, $passwd);
# See the DBI module documentation for full details
```

Description

DBD::Pg is a Perl module which works with the DBI module to provide access to PostgreSQL databases.

Connecting to PostgreSQL

To connect to a database you can say:

```
$dbh = DBI->connect('dbi:Pg:DB', 'username', 'password');
```

The first parameter specifies the driver and the database. The second and third parameter specify the username and password. This returns a database handle which can be used for subsequent database interactions.

Simple Statements

Given a database connection, you can execute an arbitrary statement using:

```
$dbh->do($stmt);
```

The statement must not be a SELECT statement (except SELECT...INTO TABLE).

Preparing and Executing Statements

You can prepare a statement for multiple uses, and you can do this for SELECT statements which return data as well as for statements which return no data. You create a statement handle using:

```
$sth = $dbh->prepare($stmt);
```

Once the statement is prepared, you can execute it:

```
$numrows = $sth->execute;
```

For statements which return data, $numrows is the number of selected rows. You can retrieve the values in the following way:

```
while ($ary_ref = $sth->fetch) {
}
```

Another possibility is to bind the fields of a SELECT statement to Perl variables. Whenever a row is fetched from the database the corresponding Perl variables will be automatically updated:

```
$sth->bind_columns(undef, @list_of_refs_to_vars_to_bind);
while ($sth->fetch) {
}
```

When you have fetched as many rows as required, you close the statement handle using:

```
$sth->finish;
```

This frees the statement, but it does not free the related data structures. This is done when you destroy (undef) the statement handle:

```
undef $sth;
```

Disconnecting from a Database

You can disconnect from the database:

```
$dbh->disconnect;
```

Note that this does not destroy the database handle. You need to do an explicit undef $dbh to destroy the handle.

Dynamic Attributes

The following attributes are supported:

```
$DBI::err      # error status
$DBI::errstr   # error message
$DBI::rows     # row count
```

Statement Handle Attributes

For statement handles of a SELECT statement you can discover what the returned column names, types, sizes are:

```
@name = @{$sth->{'NAME'}};    # Column names
@type = @{$sth->{'TYPE'}};    # Data types
@size = @{$sth->{'SIZE'}};    # Numeric size
```

There is also support for two PostgreSQL-specific attributes:

```
$oid_status = $sth->{'pg_oid_status'};  # oid of last insert
$cmd_status = $sth->{'pg_cmd_status'};  # type of last command
```

Transactions

PostgreSQL supports simple transactions. They cannot be named and they cannot be nested. You start a transaction with:

```
$dbh->do('begin');
```

The transaction can be aborted or finished with:

```
$dbh->do('abort');
$dbh->do('end');
```

Note that the following functions can also be used:

```
$dbh->rollback;
$dbh->commit;
```

Blobs

Blobs are not fully supported. The only way is to use the two registered built-in functions `lo_import()` and `lo_export()`. See the *large_objects* manpage for further information.

Known Restrictions

- PostgreSQL does not has the concept of preparing a statement. Here the **prepare** method just stores the statement.

- Currently PostgreSQL does not return the number of affected rows for non-SELECT statements.

- Transactions cannot be named or nested.

- Although PostgreSQL has a cursor concept, it has not been used in the current implementation. Cursors in PostgreSQL can only be used inside a transaction block. Because transactions in PostgreSQL cannot be nested, this would have implied the restriction not to use any nested SELECT statements. Hence, the **execute** method fetches all data at once into data structures located in the front-end application. This has to be considered when selecting large amounts of data!

- $DBI::state is not supported.

- $sth->bind_param() is not supported.

- Some statement handle attributes are not supported.

Acknowledgments

See also *DBI/Acknowledgments*.

Authors

DBI and DBD-Oracle by Tim Bunce, *Tim.Bunce@ig.co.uk*

DBD-Pg by Edmund Mergl, *E.Mergl@bawue.de*

Major parts of this package have been copied from DBD-Oracle.

Copyright

The DBD::Pg module is free software; you can redistribute it and/or modify it under the same terms as Perl itself.

See Also

DBI

DBD::Solid::Const — constants for DBD::Solid Perl extension

Synopsis

```
use DBD::Solid::Const qw(:sql_types);
if ($sth->{TYPE}->[5] == SQL_LONGVARCHAR) {
    do_something_very_different;
}
```

Description

This module import some of the constants used by DBD::Solid into your namespace. This is useful for querying some of the values returned by the DBD::Solid interface.

Author

T.Wenrich, *wenrich@ping.at*

See Also

perl(1), DBD::Solid(perldoc), DBI, Exporter(perldoc)

DB_File — Perl5 access to Berkeley DB

Synopsis

```
use DB_File ;

[$X =] tie %hash,  'DB_File', [$filename, $flags, $mode, $DB_HASH] ;
[$X =] tie %hash,  'DB_File', $filename, $flags, $mode, $DB_BTREE ;
[$X =] tie @array, 'DB_File', $filename, $flags, $mode, $DB_RECNO ;
$status = $X->del($key [, $flags]) ;
$status = $X->put($key, $value [, $flags]) ;
$status = $X->get($key, $value [, $flags]) ;
$status = $X->seq($key, $value, $flags) ;
$status = $X->sync([$flags]) ;
$status = $X->fd ;
# BTREE only
$count = $X->get_dup($key) ;
@list  = $X->get_dup($key) ;
%list  = $X->get_dup($key, 1) ;
# RECNO only
$a = $X->length;
$a = $X->pop ;
$X->push(list);
$a = $X->shift;
$X->unshift(list);
untie %hash ;
untie @array ;
```

Description

DB_File is a module which allows Perl programs to make use of the facilities provided by Berkeley DB. If you intend to use this module you should really have a copy of the *Berkeley DB* manual pages at hand. The interface defined here mirrors the Berkeley DB interface closely.

Please note that this module will only work with version 1.x of Berkeley DB. Once Berkeley DB version 2 is released, DB_File will be upgraded to work with it.

Berkeley DB is a C library which provides a consistent interface to a number of database formats. DB_File provides an interface to all three of the database types currently supported by Berkeley DB.

The file types are:

DB_HASH

> This database type allows arbitrary key/value pairs to be stored in data files. This is equivalent to the functionality provided by other hashing packages like DBM, NDBM, ODBM, GDBM, and SDBM. Remember, though, the files created using DB_HASH are not compatible with any of the other packages mentioned.

> A default hashing algorithm, which will be adequate for most applications, is built into Berkeley DB. If you do need to use your own hashing algorithm it is possible to write your own in Perl and have DB_File use it instead.

DB_BTREE

> The btree format allows arbitrary key/value pairs to be stored in a sorted, balanced binary tree.

> As with the DB_HASH format, it is possible to provide a user-defined Perl routine to perform the comparison of keys. By default, though, the keys are stored in lexical order.

DB_RECNO

> DB_RECNO allows both fixed-length and variable-length flat text files to be manipulated using the same key/value pair interface as in DB_HASH and DB_BTREE. In this case the key will consist of a record (line) number.

Interface to Berkeley DB

DB_File allows access to Berkeley DB files using the `tie()` mechanism in Perl 5 (for full details, see `tie`). This facility allows DB_File to access Berkeley DB files using either an associative array (for DB_HASH and DB_BTREE file types) or an ordinary array (for the DB_RECNO file type).

In addition to the `tie()` interface, it is also possible to access most of the functions provided in the Berkeley DB API directly. See "The API Interface."

Opening a Berkeley DB Database File

Berkeley DB uses the function `dbopen()` to open or create a database. Here is the C prototype for `dbopen()`:

```
DB*
dbopen (const char * file, int flags, int mode,
        DBTYPE type, const void * openinfo)
```

The parameter **type** is an enumeration which specifies which of the three interface methods (DB_HASH, DB_BTREE or DB_RECNO) is to be used. Depending on which of these is actually chosen, the final parameter, **openinfo** points to a data structure which allows tailoring of the specific interface method.

This interface is handled slightly differently in DB_File. Here is an equivalent call using DB_File:

```
tie %array, 'DB_File', $filename, $flags, $mode, $DB_HASH ;
```

The `filename`, `flags` and `mode` parameters are the direct equivalent of their `dbopen()` counterparts. The final parameter $DB_HASH performs the function of both the `type` and `openinfo` parameters in `dbopen()`.

In the example above $DB_HASH is actually a pre-defined reference to a hash object. DB_File has three of these pre-defined references. Apart from $DB_HASH, there is also $DB_BTREE and $DB_RECNO.

The keys allowed in each of these pre-defined references is limited to the names used in the equivalent C structure. So, for example, the $DB_HASH reference will only allow keys called `bsize`, `cachesize`, `ffactor`, `hash`, `lorder` and `nelem`.

To change one of these elements, just assign to it like this:

```
$DB_HASH->{'cachesize'} = 10000 ;
```

The three predefined variables $DB_HASH, $DB_BTREE, and $DB_RECNO are usually adequate for most applications. If you do need to create extra instances of these objects, constructors are available for each file type.

Here are examples of the constructors and the valid options available for DB_HASH, DB_BTREE, and DB_RECNO respectively.

```
$a = new DB_File::HASHINFO ;
$a->{'bsize'} ;
$a->{'cachesize'} ;
$a->{'ffactor'};
$a->{'hash'} ;
$a->{'lorder'} ;
$a->{'nelem'} ;
$b = new DB_File::BTREEINFO ;
$b->{'flags'} ;
$b->{'cachesize'} ;
$b->{'maxkeypage'} ;
$b->{'minkeypage'} ;
$b->{'psize'} ;
$b->{'compare'} ;
$b->{'prefix'} ;
$b->{'lorder'} ;
$c = new DB_File::RECNOINFO ;
$c->{'bval'} ;
$c->{'cachesize'} ;
$c->{'psize'} ;
$c->{'flags'} ;
$c->{'lorder'} ;
$c->{'reclen'} ;
$c->{'bfname'} ;
```

The values stored in the hashes above are mostly the direct equivalent of their C counterpart. Like their C counterparts, all are set to default values, which means you don't have to set *all* of the values when you only want to change one. Here is an example:

```
$a = new DB_File::HASHINFO ;
$a->{'cachesize'} =  12345 ;
tie %y, 'DB_File', "filename", $flags, 0777, $a ;
```

A few of the options need extra discussion here. When used, the C equivalent of the keys hash, compare and prefix store pointers to C functions. In DB_File these keys are used to store references to Perl subs. Below are templates for each of the subs:

```perl
sub hash
{
    my ($data) = @_ ;
    ...
    # return the hash value for $data
    return $hash ;
}
sub compare
{
    my ($key, $key2) = @_ ;
    ...
    # return  0 if $key1 eq $key2
    #        -1 if $key1 lt $key2
    #         1 if $key1 gt $key2
    return (-1 , 0 or 1) ;
}
sub prefix
{
    my ($key, $key2) = @_ ;
    ...
    # return number of bytes of $key2 which are
    # necessary to determine that it is greater than $key1
    return $bytes ;
}
```

See "Changing the BTREE Sort Order" below for an example of using the compare template.

If you are using the DB_RECNO interface and you intend making use of bval, you should check out "The 'bval' Option."

Default Parameters

It is possible to omit some or all of the final four parameters in the call to tie and let them take default values. As DB_HASH is the most common file format used, the call:

```perl
tie %A, "DB_File", "filename" ;
```

is equivalent to:

```perl
tie %A, "DB_File", "filename", O_CREAT|O_RDWR, 0666, $DB_HASH ;
```

It is also possible to omit the filename parameter as well, so the call:

```perl
tie %A, "DB_File" ;
```

is equivalent to:

```perl
tie %A, "DB_File", undef, O_CREAT|O_RDWR, 0666, $DB_HASH ;
```

See "In Memory Databases" below for a discussion on the use of undef in place of a filename.

In Memory Databases

Berkeley DB allows the creation of in-memory databases by using NULL (that is, a (char *)0 in C) in place of the filename. DB_File uses **undef** instead of NULL to provide this functionality.

DB_HASH

The DB_HASH file format is probably the most commonly used of the three file formats that DB_File supports. It is also very straightforward to use.

A simple example

This example shows how to create a database, add key/value pairs to the database, delete keys/value pairs and finally how to enumerate the contents of the database.

```
use strict ;
use DB_File ;
use vars qw( %h $k $v ) ;
tie %h, "DB_File", "fruit", O_RDWR|O_CREAT, 0640, $DB_HASH
    or die "Cannot open file 'fruit': $!\n";
# Add a few key/value pairs to the file
$h{"apple"} = "red" ;
$h{"orange"} = "orange" ;
$h{"banana"} = "yellow" ;
$h{"tomato"} = "red" ;
# Check for existence of a key
print "Banana Exists\n\n" if $h{"banana"} ;
# Delete a key/value pair.
delete $h{"apple"} ;
# print the contents of the file
while (($k, $v) = each %h)
    { print "$k -> $v\n" }
untie %h ;
```

here is the output:

```
Banana Exists

orange -> orange
tomato -> red
banana -> yellow
```

Note that the like ordinary associative arrays, the order of the keys retrieved is apparently random.

DB_BTREE

The DB_BTREE format is useful when you want to store data in a given order. By default, the keys will be stored in lexical order, but as you will see from the example shown in the next section, it is very easy to define your own sorting function.

Changing the BTREE Sort Order

This script shows how to override the default sorting algorithm that BTREE uses. Instead of using the normal lexical ordering, a case-insensitive **compare** function will be used.

```
use strict ;
use DB_File ;
my %h ;
sub Compare
{
    my ($key1, $key2) = @_ ;
    "\L$key1" cmp "\L$key2" ;
}
# specify the Perl sub that will do the comparison
$DB_BTREE->{'compare'} = \&Compare ;
tie %h, "DB_File", "tree", O_RDWR|O_CREAT, 0640, $DB_BTREE
    or die "Cannot open file 'tree': $!\n" ;
# Add a key/value pair to the file
$h{'Wall'} = 'Larry' ;
$h{'Smith'} = 'John' ;
$h{'mouse'} = 'mickey' ;
$h{'duck'}  = 'donald' ;
# Delete
delete $h{"duck"} ;
# Cycle through the keys printing them in order.
# Note it is not necessary to sort the keys as
# the btree will have kept them in order automatically.
foreach (keys %h)
    { print "$_\n" }
untie %h ;
```

Here is the output from the code above.

```
mouse
Smith
Wall
```

There are a few point to bear in mind if you want to change the ordering in a BTREE database:

1. The new **compare** function must be specified when you create the database.

2. You cannot change the ordering once the database has been created. Thus you must use the same **compare** function every time you access the database.

Handling Duplicate Keys

The BTREE file type optionally allows a single key to be associated with an arbitrary number of values. This option is enabled by setting the flags element of $DB_BTREE to R_DUP when creating the database.

There are some difficulties in using the tied hash interface if you want to manipulate a BTREE database with duplicate keys. Consider this code:

```
use strict ;
use DB_File ;
use vars qw($filename %h ) ;
$filename = "tree" ;
unlink $filename ;

# Enable duplicate records
$DB_BTREE->{'flags'} = R_DUP ;
```

```
tie %h, "DB_File", $filename, O_RDWR|O_CREAT, 0640, $DB_BTREE
    or die "Cannot open $filename: $!\n";

# Add some key/value pairs to the file
$h{'Wall'} = 'Larry' ;
$h{'Wall'} = 'Brick' ; # Note the duplicate key
$h{'Wall'} = 'Brick' ; # Note the duplicate key and value
$h{'Smith'} = 'John' ;
$h{'mouse'} = 'mickey' ;
# iterate through the associative array
# and print each key/value pair.
foreach (keys %h)
    { print "$_  -> $h{$_}\n" }
untie %h ;
```

Here is the output:

```
Smith   -> John
Wall    -> Larry
Wall    -> Larry
Wall    -> Larry
mouse   -> mickey
```

As you can see, three records have been successfully created with key Wall—the only thing is, when they are retrieved from the database they *seem* to have the same value, namely Larry. The problem is caused by the way that the associative array interface works. Basically, when the associative array interface is used to fetch the value associated with a given key, it will always retrieve only the first value.

Although it may not be immediately obvious from the code above, the associative array interface can be used to write values with duplicate keys, but it cannot be used to read them back from the database.

The way to get around this problem is to use the Berkeley DB API method called **seq**. This method allows sequential access to key/value pairs. See "The API Interface" for details of both the **seq** method and the API in general.

Here is the script above rewritten using the **seq** API method:

```
use strict ;
use DB_File ;

use vars qw($filename $x %h $status $key $value) ;
$filename = "tree" ;
unlink $filename ;

# Enable duplicate records
$DB_BTREE->{'flags'} = R_DUP ;

$x = tie %h, "DB_File", $filename, O_RDWR|O_CREAT, 0640, $DB_
BTREE
    or die "Cannot open $filename: $!\n";

# Add some key/value pairs to the file
$h{'Wall'} = 'Larry' ;
$h{'Wall'} = 'Brick' ; # Note the duplicate key
```

```
$h{'Wall'} = 'Brick' ; # Note the duplicate key and value
$h{'Smith'} = 'John' ;
$h{'mouse'} = 'mickey' ;

# iterate through the btree using seq
# and print each key/value pair.
$key = $value = 0 ;
for ($status = $x->seq($key, $value, R_FIRST) ;
     $status == 0 ;
     $status = $x->seq($key, $value, R_NEXT) )
   { print "$key -> $value\n" }

undef $x ;
untie %h ;
```

that prints:

```
Smith    -> John
Wall     -> Brick
Wall     -> Brick
Wall     -> Larry
mouse    -> mickey
```

This time we have got all the key/value pairs, including the multiple values associated with the key `Wall`.

The get_dup() Method

DB_File comes with a utility method, called **get_dup**, to assist in reading duplicate values from BTREE databases. The method can take the following forms:

```
$count = $x->get_dup($key) ;
@list  = $x->get_dup($key) ;
%list  = $x->get_dup($key, 1) ;
```

In a scalar context the method returns the number of values associated with the key, $key.

In list context, it returns all the values which match $key. Note that the values will be returned in an apparently random order.

In list context, if the second parameter is present and evaluates TRUE, the method returns an associative array. The keys of the associative array correspond to the values that matched in the BTREE, and the values of the array are a count of the number of times that particular value occurred in the BTREE.

So assuming the database created above, we can use **get_dup** like this:

```
my $cnt  = $x->get_dup("Wall") ;
print "Wall occurred $cnt times\n" ;
my %hash = $x->get_dup("Wall", 1) ;
print "Larry is there\n" if $hash{'Larry'} ;
print "There are $hash{'Brick'} Brick Walls\n" ;
my @list = $x->get_dup("Wall") ;
print "Wall =>     [@list]\n" ;
@list = $x->get_dup("Smith") ;
print "Smith =>    [@list]\n" ;

@list = $x->get_dup("Dog") ;
print "Dog =>      [@list]\n" ;
```

and it will print:

```
Wall occurred 3 times
Larry is there
There are 2 Brick Walls
Wall =>      [Brick Brick Larry]
Smith =>     [John]
Dog =>       []
```

Matching Partial Keys

The BTREE interface has a feature that allows partial keys to be matched. This functionality is *only* available when the **seq** method is used along with the R_CURSOR flag.

```
$x->seq($key, $value, R_CURSOR) ;
```

Here is the relevant quote from the *dbopen* manpage where it defines the use of the R_CURSOR flag with seq:

> Note, for the DB_BTREE access method, the returned key is not necessarily an exact match for the specified key. The returned key is the smallest key greater than or equal to the specified key, permitting partial key matches and range searches.

In the example script below, the **match** sub uses this feature to find and print the first matching key/value pair given a partial key.

```
use strict ;
use DB_File ;
use Fcntl ;
use vars qw($filename $x %h $st $key $value) ;
sub match
{
    my $key = shift ;
my $value = 0;
    my $orig_key = $key ;
    $x->seq($key, $value, R_CURSOR) ;
    print "$orig_key\t-> $key\t-> $value\n" ;
}
$filename = "tree" ;
unlink $filename ;
$x = tie %h, "DB_File", $filename, O_RDWR|O_CREAT, 0640, $DB_
BTREE
    or die "Cannot open $filename: $!\n";

# Add some key/value pairs to the file
$h{'mouse'} = 'mickey' ;
$h{'Wall'} = 'Larry' ;
$h{'Walls'} = 'Brick' ;
$h{'Smith'} = 'John' ;

$key = $value = 0 ;
print "IN ORDER\n" ;
for ($st = $x->seq($key, $value, R_FIRST) ;
     $st == 0 ;
     $st = $x->seq($key, $value, R_NEXT) )

    { print "$key -> $value\n" }
```

```
print "\nPARTIAL MATCH\n" ;
match "Wa" ;
match "A" ;
match "a" ;
undef $x ;
untie %h ;
```

Here is the output:

```
IN ORDER
Smith -> John
Wall  -> Larry
Walls -> Brick
mouse -> mickey
PARTIAL MATCH
Wa -> Wall  -> Larry
A  -> Smith -> John
a  -> mouse -> mickey
```

DB_RECNO

DB_RECNO provides an interface to flat text files. Both variable and fixed length records are supported.

In order to make RECNO more compatible with Perl, the array offset for all RECNO arrays begins at 0 rather than 1 as in Berkeley DB.

As with normal Perl arrays, a RECNO array can be accessed using negative indexes. The index –1 refers to the last element of the array, –2 the second last, and so on. Attempting to access an element before the start of the array will raise a fatal run-time error.

The bval Option

The operation of the **bval** option warrants some discussion. Here is the definition of bval from the *Berkeley DB 1.85 recno* manpage:

> The delimiting byte to be used to mark the end of a record for variable-length records, and the pad character for fixed-length records. If no value is specified, newlines ("\n") are used to mark the end of variable-length records and fixed-length records are padded with spaces.

The second sentence is wrong. In actual fact, **bval** will only default to \n when the **openinfo** parameter in **dbopen** is NULL. If a non-NULL **openinfo** parameter is used at all, the value that happens to be in **bval** will be used. That means you always have to specify **bval** when making use of any of the options in the open-info parameter. This documentation error will be fixed in the next release of Berkeley DB.

That clarifies the situation in regard to Berkeley DB itself. What about DB_File? Well, the behavior defined in the quote above is quite useful, so DB_File conforms to it.

That means that you can specify other options (e.g. **cachesize**) and still have **bval** default to \n for variable-length records, and space for fixed-length records.

A Simple Example

Here is a simple example that uses RECNO.

```
use strict ;
use DB_File ;
my @h ;
tie @h, "DB_File", "text", O_RDWR|O_CREAT, 0640, $DB_RECNO
    or die "Cannot open file 'text': $!\n" ;
# Add a few key/value pairs to the file
$h[0] = "orange" ;
$h[1] = "blue" ;
$h[2] = "yellow" ;
# Check for existence of a key
print "Element 1 Exists with value $h[1]\n" if $h[1] ;
# use a negative index
print "The last element is $h[-1]\n" ;
print "The 2nd last element is $h[-2]\n" ;
untie @h ;
```

Here is the output from the script:

```
Element 1 Exists with value blue
The last element is yellow
The 2nd last element is blue
```

Extra Methods

As you can see from the example above, the tied array interface is quite limited. To make the interface more useful, a number of methods are supplied with DB_File to simulate the standard array operations that are not currently implemented in Perl's tied array interface. All these methods are accessed via the object returned from the tie call.

Here are the methods:

$X-push(*list*) ;
: Pushes the elements of *list* to the end of the array.

$value = $X-pop ;
: Removes and returns the last element of the array.

$X-shift
: Removes and returns the first element of the array.

$X-unshift(*list*) ;
: Pushes the elements of *list* to the start of the array.

$X-length
: Returns the number of elements in the array.

Another Example

Here is a more complete example that makes use of some of the methods described above. It also makes use of the API interface directly (see "The API Interface").

```
use strict ;
use vars qw(@h $H $file $i) ;
use DB_File ;
use Fcntl ;
```

```
$file = "text" ;
unlink $file ;
$H = tie @h, "DB_File", $file, O_RDWR|O_CREAT, 0640, $DB_RECNO
    or die "Cannot open file $file: $!\n" ;

# first create a text file to play with
$h[0] = "zero" ;
$h[1] = "one" ;
$h[2] = "two" ;
$h[3] = "three" ;
$h[4] = "four" ;

# Print the records in order.
#
# The length method is needed here because evaluating a tied
# array in a scalar context does not return the number of
# elements in the array.
print "\nORIGINAL\n" ;
foreach $i (0 .. $H->length - 1) {
    print "$i: $h[$i]\n" ;
}
# use the push & pop methods
$a = $H->pop ;
$H->push("last") ;
print "\nThe last record was [$a]\n" ;
# and the shift & unshift methods
$a = $H->shift ;
$H->unshift("first") ;
print "The first record was [$a]\n" ;
# Use the API to add a new record after record 2.
$i = 2 ;
$H->put($i, "Newbie", R_IAFTER) ;
# and a new record before record 1.
$i = 1 ;
$H->put($i, "New One", R_IBEFORE) ;
# delete record 3
$H->del(3) ;
# now print the records in reverse order
print "\nREVERSE\n" ;
for ($i = $H->length - 1 ; $i >= 0 ; -- $i)
    { print "$i: $h[$i]\n" }
# same again, but use the API functions instead
print "\nREVERSE again\n" ;
my ($s, $k, $v)  = (0, 0, 0) ;
for ($s = $H->seq($k, $v, R_LAST) ;
        $s == 0 ;
        $s = $H->seq($k, $v, R_PREV))
    { print "$k: $v\n" }
undef $H ;
untie @h ;
```

and this is what it outputs:

```
ORIGINAL
0: zero
```

```
1: one
2: two
3: three
4: four
The last record was [four]
The first record was [zero]
REVERSE
5: last
4: three
3: Newbie
2: one
1: New One
0: first
REVERSE again
5: last
4: three
3: Newbie
2: one
1: New One
0: first
```

Notes

1. Rather than iterating through the array, @h, like this:

   ```
   foreach $i (@h)
   ```

   it is necessary to use either this:

   ```
   foreach $i (0 .. $H->length - 1)
   ```

   or this:

   ```
   for ($a = $H->get($k, $v, R_FIRST) ;
        $a == 0 ;
        $a = $H->get($k, $v, R_NEXT) )
   ```

2. Notice that both times the put method was used the record index was specified using a variable, $i, rather than the literal value itself. This is because
   put will return the record number of the inserted line via that parameter.

The API Interface

As well as accessing Berkeley DB using a tied hash or array, it is also possible to make
direct use of most of the API functions defined in the Berkeley DB documentation.

To do this you need to store a copy of the object returned from the tie.

```
$db = tie %hash, "DB_File", "filename" ;
```

Once you have done that, you can access the Berkeley DB API functions as DB_File
methods directly like this:

```
$db->put($key, $value, R_NOOVERWRITE) ;
```

Important: If you have saved a copy of the object returned from tie, the underlying database file will *not* be closed until both the tied variable is untied and all copies of the saved
object are destroyed.

```
use DB_File ;
$db = tie %hash, "DB_File", "filename"
    or die "Cannot tie filename: $!" ;
```

```
...
undef $db ;
untie %hash ;
```

See "The untie( ) Gotcha" for more details.

All the functions defined in the *dbopen* manpage are available except for close() and dbopen() itself. The DB_File method interface to the supported functions have been implemented to mirror the way Berkeley DB works whenever possible. In particular note that:

- The methods return a status value. All return 0 on success. All return −1 to signify an error and set $! to the exact error code. The return code 1 generally (but not always) means that the key specified did not exist in the database.

- Other return codes are defined. See below and in the Berkeley DB documentation for details. The Berkeley DB documentation should be used as the definitive source.

- Whenever a Berkeley DB function returns data via one of its parameters, the equivalent DB_File method does exactly the same.

- If you are careful, it is possible to mix API calls with the tied hash/array interface in the same piece of code. Although only a few of the methods used to implement the tied interface currently make use of the cursor, you should always assume that the cursor has been changed any time the tied hash/array interface is used. As an example, this code will probably not do what you expect:

```
$X = tie %x, 'DB_File', $filename, O_RDWR|O_CREAT, 0777, $DB_BTREE
    or die "Cannot tie $filename: $!" ;
# Get the first key/value pair and set  the cursor
$X->seq($key, $value, R_FIRST) ;
# this line will modify the cursor
$count = scalar keys %x ;
# Get the second key/value pair.
# oops, it didn't, it got the last key/value pair!
$X->seq($key, $value, R_NEXT) ;
```

The code above can be rearranged to get around the problem, like this:

```
$X = tie %x, 'DB_File', $filename, O_RDWR|O_CREAT, 0777, $DB_BTREE
    or die "Cannot tie $filename: $!" ;
# this line will modify the cursor
$count = scalar keys %x ;
# Get the first key/value pair and set  the cursor
$X->seq($key, $value, R_FIRST) ;
# Get the second key/value pair.
# worked this time.
$X->seq($key, $value, R_NEXT) ;
```

All the constants defined in the *dbopen* manpage for use in the flags parameters in the methods defined below are also available. Refer to the Berkeley DB documentation for the precise meaning of the **flags** values.

Below is a list of the methods available.

$status = $X-get(*$key*, *$value* [, *$flags*]) ;

Given a key (*$key*) this method reads the value associated with it from the database. The value read from the database is returned in the *$value* parameter. If the key does not exist the method returns 1.

No flags are currently defined for this method.

`$status = $X-put($key, $value [, $flags]) ;`
> Stores the key/value pair in the database.
>
> If you use either the R_IAFTER or R_IBEFORE flags, the *$key* parameter will have the record number of the inserted key/value pair set.
>
> Valid flags are R_CURSOR, R_IAFTER, R_IBEFORE, R_NOOVERWRITE, and R_SETCURSOR.

`$status = $X-del($key [, $flags]) ;`
> Removes all key/value pairs with key *$key* from the database.
>
> A return code of 1 means that the requested key was not in the database.
>
> R_CURSOR is the only valid flag at present.

`$status = $X-fd ;`
> Returns the file descriptor for the underlying database.
>
> See "Locking Databases" for an example of how to make use of the **fd** method to lock your database.

`$status = $X-seq($key, $value, $flags) ;`
> This interface allows sequential retrieval from the database. See the *dbopen* manpage for full details.
>
> Both the *$key* and *$value* parameters will be set to the key/value pair read from the database.
>
> The *$flags* parameter is mandatory. The valid flag values are R_CURSOR, R_FIRST, R_LAST, R_NEXT, and R_PREV.

`$status = $X-sync([$flags]) ;`
> Flushes any cached buffers to disk.
>
> R_RECNOSYNC is the only valid flag at present.

Hints and Tips

Locking Databases

Concurrent access of a read-write database by several parties requires them all to use some kind of locking. Here's an example of Tom's that uses the **fd** method to get the file descriptor, and then a careful **open()** to give something Perl will **flock()** for you. Run this repeatedly in the background to watch the locks granted in proper order.

```
use DB_File;
use strict;
sub LOCK_SH { 1 }
sub LOCK_EX { 2 }
sub LOCK_NB { 4 }
sub LOCK_UN { 8 }
my($oldval, $fd, $db, %db, $value, $key);
$key = shift || 'default';
$value = shift || 'magic';
$value .= " $$";
$db = tie(%db, 'DB_File', '/tmp/foo.db', O_CREAT|O_RDWR, 0644)
        || die "dbcreat /tmp/foo.db $!";
$fd = $db->fd;
print "$$: db fd is $fd\n";
open(DB_FH, "+<&=$fd") || die "dup $!";
```

```
unless (flock (DB_FH, LOCK_SH | LOCK_NB)) {
    print "$$: CONTENTION; can't read during write update!
            Waiting for read lock ($!) ....";
    unless (flock (DB_FH, LOCK_SH)) { die "flock: $!" }
}
print "$$: Read lock granted\n";
$oldval = $db{$key};
print "$$: Old value was $oldval\n";
flock(DB_FH, LOCK_UN);
unless (flock (DB_FH, LOCK_EX | LOCK_NB)) {
    print "$$: CONTENTION; must have exclusive lock!
            Waiting for write lock ($!) ....";
    unless (flock (DB_FH, LOCK_EX)) { die "flock: $!" }
}
print "$$: Write lock granted\n";
$db{$key} = $value;
$db->sync;   # to flush
sleep 10;
flock(DB_FH, LOCK_UN);
undef $db;
untie %db;
close(DB_FH);
print "$$: Updated db to $key=$value\n";
```

Sharing Databases with C Applications

There is no technical reason why a Berkeley DB database cannot be shared by both a
Perl and a C application.

The vast majority of problems that are reported in this area boil down to the fact that
C strings are NULL terminated, while Perl strings are not.

Here is a real example. Netscape 2.0 keeps a record of the locations you visit along
with the time you last visited them in a DB_HASH database. This is usually stored in
the file *~/.netscape/history.db*. The key field in the database is the location string and
the value field is the time the location was last visited stored as a 4-byte binary value.

If you haven't already guessed, the location string is stored with a terminating NULL.
This means you need to be careful when accessing the database.

Here is a snippet of code that is loosely based on Tom Christiansen's *ggh* script (available from your nearest CPAN archive in *authors/id/TOMC/scripts/nshist.gz*).

```
use strict ;
use DB_File ;
use Fcntl ;
use vars qw( $dotdir $HISTORY %hist_db $href $binary_time $date ) ;
$dotdir = $ENV{HOME} || $ENV{LOGNAME};
$HISTORY = "$dotdir/.netscape/history.db";
tie %hist_db, 'DB_File', $HISTORY
    or die "Cannot open $HISTORY: $!\n" ;;
# Dump the complete database
while ( ($href, $binary_time) = each %hist_db ) {
    # remove the terminating NULL
    $href =~ s/\x00$// ;
    # convert the binary time into a user friendly string
    $date = localtime unpack("V", $binary_time);
```

```
        print "$date $href\n" ;
    }
    # check for the existence of a specific key
    # remember to add the NULL
    if ( $binary_time = $hist_db{"http://mox.perl.com/\x00"} ) {
        $date = localtime unpack("V", $binary_time) ;
        print "Last visited mox.perl.com on $date\n" ;
    }
    else {
        print "Never visited mox.perl.com\n"
    }
    untie %hist_db ;
```

The untie() Gotcha

If you make use of the Berkeley DB API, it is *very* strongly recommended that you read this section.

Even if you don't currently make use of the API interface, it is still worth reading it.

Here is an example that illustrates the problem from a DB_File perspective:

```
    use DB_File ;
    use Fcntl ;
    my %x ;
    my $X ;
    $X = tie %x, 'DB_File', 'tst.fil' , O_RDWR|O_TRUNC
        or die "Cannot tie first time: $!" ;
    $x{123} = 456 ;
    untie %x ;
    tie %x, 'DB_File', 'tst.fil' , O_RDWR|O_CREAT
        or die "Cannot tie second time: $!" ;
    untie %x ;
```

When run, the script will produce this error message:

```
    Cannot tie second time: Invalid argument at bad.file line 14.
```

Although the error message above refers to the second tie() statement in the script, the source of the problem is really with the untie() statement that precedes it.

Having read the *perltie* manpage you will probably have already guessed that the error is caused by the extra copy of the tied object stored in $X. If you haven't, then the problem boils down to the fact that the DB_File destructor, DESTROY, will not be called until *all* references to the tied object are destroyed. Both the tied variable, %x, and $X above hold a reference to the object. The call to untie() will destroy the first, but $X still holds a valid reference, so the destructor will not get called and the database file *tst.fil* will remain open. The fact that Berkeley DB then reports the attempt to open a database that is already open via the catch-all "Invalid argument" doesn't help.

If you run the script with the -w flag the error message becomes:

```
    untie attempted while 1 inner references still exist
    at bad.file line 12.
    Cannot tie second time: Invalid argument at bad.file line 14.
```

which pinpoints the real problem. Finally the script can now be modified to fix the original problem by destroying the API object before the untie:

```
...
$x{123} = 456 ;
undef $X ;
untie %x ;
$X = tie %x, 'DB_File', 'tst.fil' , O_RDWR|O_CREAT
...
```

Common Questions

Why Is There Perl Source in My Database?

If you look at the contents of a database file created by DB_File, there can sometimes be part of a Perl script included in it.

This happens because Berkeley DB uses dynamic memory to allocate buffers which will subsequently be written to the database file. Being dynamic, the memory could have been used for anything before DB malloced it. As Berkeley DB doesn't clear the memory once it has been allocated, the unused portions will contain random junk. In the case where a Perl script gets written to the database, the random junk will correspond to an area of dynamic memory that happened to be used during the compilation of the script.

Unless you don't like the possibility that part of your Perl scripts will be embedded in a database file, this is nothing to worry about.

How Do I Store Complex Data Structures with DB_File?

Although DB_File cannot do this directly, there is a module that can layer transparently over DB_File to accomplish this feat.

Check out the MLDBM module, available on CPAN in the directory *modules/by-module/MLDBM.*

What Does "Invalid Argument" Mean?

You will get this error message when one of the parameters in the `tie` call is wrong. Unfortunately there are quite a few parameters to get wrong, so it can be difficult to figure out which one it is.

Here are a couple of possibilities:

1. Attempting to reopen a database without closing it.
2. Using the O_WRONLY flag.

What Does "Bareword 'DB_File' not allowed" Mean?

You will encounter this particular error message when you have the **strict subs** pragma (or the full strict pragma) in your script. Consider this script:

```
use strict ;
use DB_File ;
use vars qw(%x) ;
tie %x, DB_File, "filename" ;
```

Running it produces the error in question:

```
Bareword "DB_File" not allowed while "strict subs" in use
```

To get around the error, place the word **DB_File** in either single or double quotes, like this:

```
tie %x, "DB_File", "filename" ;
```

Although it might seem like a real pain, it is really worth the effort of having a use
strict in all your scripts.

Bugs

Some older versions of Berkeley DB had problems with fixed length records using the
RECNO file format. The newest version at the time of writing was 1.85; this seems to have
fixed the problems with RECNO.

I am sure there are bugs in the code. If you do find any, or can suggest any enhancements,
I would welcome your comments.

Availability

DB_File comes with the standard Perl source distribution. Look in the directory *ext/DB_File.*

This version of DB_File will only work with version 1.x of Berkeley DB. It is *not* yet
compatible with version 2.

Version 1 of Berkeley DB is available at your nearest CPAN archive in *src/misc/
db.1.85.tar.gz*, or via the host *ftp.cs.berkeley.edu* in */ucb/4bsd/db.tar.gz*. Alternatively,
check out the Berkeley DB home page at *http://www.bostic.com/db*. It is *not* under the GPL.

If you are running IRIX, then get Berkeley DB from *http://reality.sgi.com/ariel*. It has the
patches necessary to compile properly on IRIX 5.3.

As of January 1997, version 1.86 of Berkeley DB is available from the Berkeley DB home
page. Although this release does fix a number of bugs that were present in 1.85, you
should be aware of the following information (taken from the Berkeley DB home page)
before you consider using it:

DB version 1.86 includes a new implementation of the hash access method that
fixes a variety of hashing problems found in DB version 1.85. We are making it
available as an interim solution until DB 2.0 is available.

Please note: the underlying file format for the hash access method changed
between version 1.85 and version 1.86, so you will have to dump and reload all
of your databases to convert from version 1.85 to version 1.86. If you do not absolutely require the fixes from version 1.86, we strongly urge you to wait until DB
2.0 is released before upgrading from 1.85.

Author

The DB_File interface was written by Paul Marquess, *pmarquess@bfsec.bt.co.uk*. Questions
about the DB system itself may be addressed to, *db@sleepycat.com*.

See Also

the perl(1) manpage, the dbopen(3) manpage, the hash(3) manpage, the recno(3)
manpage, the btree(3) manpage

DBI — database independent interface for Perl

Author's Note

This is a draft only.

Synopsis

```
use DBI;

@databases = DBI->data_sources($driver);
$dbh = DBI->connect($database, $username, $auth);
$dbh = DBI->connect($database, $username, $auth, $driver);
$dbh = DBI->connect($database, $username, $auth, $driver, \%attr);

$rc  = $dbh->disconnect;

$rv  = $dbh->do($statement);
$rv  = $dbh->do($statement, \%attr);

$sth = $dbh->prepare($statement);
$sth = $dbh->prepare($statement, \%attr);

$rv = $sth->execute;

$ary_ref  = $sth->fetch;
@row_ary  = $sth->fetchrow;
$hash_ref = $sth->fetchhash;

$tbl_ary_ref  = $sth->fetch_all;

$rc = $sth->finish;

$rv = $sth->rows;

$sql = $dbh->quote($string);

$rc  = $h->err;
$str = $h->errstr;
$rv  = $h->state;
```

Description

The Perl DBI is a database access Application Programming Interface (API) for the Perl language. The DBI defines a set of functions, variables and conventions that provide a consistent database interface independent of the actual database being used.

It is important to remember that the DBI is just an interface, a thin layer of "glue" between an application and one or more database drivers. The drivers do the real work. The DBI provides a standard interface and framework for the drivers to operate within.

This document is a *work in progress*. Although it is incomplete, it should be useful in getting started with the DBI.

Note

This documentation is a new draft. Revision 1.1, 08/21/1997.

It is expected to evolve and expand quite quickly (relative to previous drafts :-)) so it is important to check that you have the latest copy.

Architecture of a DBI Application

```
                         |<- Scope of DBI ->|
                          .-.    .--------------.    .-------------.
   .-------.              | |---| XYZ Driver   |---| XYZ Engine  |
   | Perl  |              |S|   '--------------'    '-------------'
   | script|    |A|       |w|   .--------------.    .-------------.
   | using |--|P|--|i|---|Oracle Driver |---|Oracle Engine|
   | DBI   |    |I|       |t|   '--------------'    '-------------'
   | API   |              |c|...
   |methods|              |h|... Other drivers
   '-------'              | |...
                          '_'
```

The API is the Application Perl-script (or Programming) Interface. The call interface and variables provided by DBI to Perl scripts. The API is implemented by the DBI Perl extension.

The switch is the code that "dispatches" the DBI method calls to the appropriate driver for actual execution. The switch is also responsible for the dynamic loading of drivers, error checking/handling and other general duties.

The drivers implement support for a given type of engine (database). Drivers contain implementations of the DBI methods written using the private interface functions of the corresponding engine. Only authors of sophisticated/multi-database applications or generic library functions need be concerned with drivers.

Notation and Conventions

DBI	static 'top-level' class name
$dbh	Database handle object
$sth	Statement handle object
$drh	Driver handle object (rarely seen or used in applications)
$h	Any of the $??h handle types above
$rc	General Return Code (boolean: true=ok, false=error)
$rv	General Return Value (typically an integer)
@ary	List of values returned from the database, typically a row of data
$rows	Number of rows processed by a function (if available, otherwise -1)
$fh	A filehandle
undef	NULL values are represented by undefined values in Perl

Note that Perl will automatically destroy database and statement objects if all references to them are deleted.

Handle object attributes are shown as:

```
    $h->{attribute_name}    (type)
```

where *type* indicates the type of the value of the attribute (if it's not a simple scalar):

```
    \$   reference to a scalar: $h->{attr}       or  $a = ${$h->{attr}}
    \@   reference to a list:   $h->{attr}->[0]  or  @a = @{$h->{attr}}
    \%   reference to a hash:   $h->{attr}->{a}  or  %a = %{$h->{attr}}
```

General Interface Rules and Caveats

The DBI does not have a concept of a current session. Every session has a handle object (e.g., a $dbh) returned from the connect method and that handle object is used to invoke database-related methods.

Most data is returned to the Perl script as Perl strings (NULL values are returned as undef). This allows arbitrary precision numeric data to be handled without loss of accuracy. Be aware that Perl may not preserve the same accuracy when the string is used as a number.

Dates and times are returned as character strings in the native format of the corresponding engine. Time zone effects are engine/driver dependent.

Perl supports binary data in Perl strings and the DBI will pass binary data to and from the driver without change. It is up to the driver implementors to decide how they wish to handle such binary data.

Multiple SQL statements may not be combined in a single statement handle, e.g., a single $sth.

Non-sequential record reads are not supported in this version of the DBI. For example, records can only be fetched in the order that the database returned them, and once fetched, they are forgotten.

Positioned updates and deletes are not directly supported by the DBI. See the description of the CursorName attribute for an alternative.

Individual driver implementors are free to provide any private functions and/or handle attributes that they feel are useful. Private functions can be invoked using the DBI call method. Private attributes are accessed just like standard attributes.

Character sets: Most databases that understand character sets have a default global charset and text stored in the database that is, or should be, stored in that charset. (If it's not, that's the fault of either the database or the application that inserted the data.) When text is fetched it should be (automatically) converted to the charset of the client (presumably based on the locale). If a driver needs to set a flag to get that behavior, it should do so. It should not require the application to do that.

Naming Conventions

The DBI package and all packages below it (DBI::*) are are reserved for use by the DBI. Package names begining with DBD:: are reserved for use by DBI database drivers. All environment variables used by the DBperl Switch or Adaptors begin with DBI_.

The letter case used for attribute names is significant and plays an important part in the portability of DBI scripts. The case of the attribute name is used to signify who defined the meaning of that name and its values.

Case of name	Has a meaning defined by
UPPER_CASE	Standards; e.g., X/Open, SQL92 etc (portable)
MixedCase	DBI API (portable); underscores are not used
lower_case	Driver- or engine-specific (non-portable)

It is of the utmost importance that driver developers use only lowercase attribute names when defining private attributes.

Data Query Methods

The DBI allows an application to 'prepare' a statement for later execution. A prepared statement is identified by a statement handle object, e.g., `$sth`.

Typical method call sequence for a SELECT statement:

```
connect,
  prepare,
    execute, fetch, fetch, ... finish,
    execute, fetch, fetch, ... finish,
    execute, fetch, fetch, ... finish.
```

Typical method call sequence for a non-SELECT statement:

```
connect,
  prepare,
    execute,
    execute,
    execute.
```

The DBI Class

DBI Class Methods

connect

Establishes a database connection (session) to the requested database.

```
$dbh = DBI->connect($database, $username, $password);
$dbh = DBI->connect($database, $username, $password,
                    $driver);
$dbh = DBI->connect($database, $username, $password,
                    $driver, \%attr);
```

Returns a database handle object. `DBI->connect` installs the requested driver if it has not yet been installed. It then returns the result of `$drh->connect`. It is important to note that driver installation always returns a valid driver handle or it dies with an error message that includes the string `install_driver` and the underlying problem. So, `DBI->connect` will die on a driver installation failure and will only return undef on a connect failure, for which `$DBI::errstr` will hold the error.

The `$database`, `$username`, and `$password` arguments are passed to the driver for processing. The DBI does not define ANY interpretation for the contents of these fields. As a convenience, if the `$database` field is undefined or empty, the switch will substitute the value of the environment variable DBI_DBNAME if any.

If `$driver` is not specified, the environment variable DBI_DRIVER is used. If that variable is not set and the switch has more than one driver loaded, the connect fails and `undef` is returned.

The driver is free to interpret the `database`, `username` and `password` fields in any way and supply whatever defaults are appropriate for the engine being accessed.

Portable applications should not assume that a single driver will be able to support multiple simultaneous sessions and also should check the value of $dbh->{AutoCommit}.

Where possible, each session ($dbh) is independent from the transactions in other sessions. This is useful where you need to hold cursors open across transactions, e.g., use one session for your long-lifespan cursors (typically read-only) and another for your short update transactions.

available_drivers

Returns a list of all available drivers by searching for DBD::* modules through the directories in @INC. By default a warning will be given if some drivers are hidden by others of the same name in earlier directories. Passing a true value for $quiet will inhibit the warning.

```
@ary = DBI->available_drivers;
@ary = DBI->available_drivers($quiet);
```

data_sources

Returns a list of all data sources (databases) available via the named driver. The driver will be loaded if not already. If $driver is empty or undef then the value of the DBI_DRIVER environment variable will be used.

```
@ary = DBI->data_sources($driver);
```

Note that many drivers have no way of knowing what data sources might be available for it and thus, typically, return an empty list.

DBI Utility Functions

neat

Returns a string containing a neat (and tidy) representation of the supplied value. Strings will be quoted, and undefined (NULL) values will be shown as undef. Unprintable characters will be replaced by dot (.) and the string will be truncated and terminated with ... if longer than $maxlen (0 or undef defaults to 400 characters).

```
$str = DBI::neat($value, $maxlen);
```

neat_list

Calls DBI::neat on each element of the list and returns a string containing the results joined with $field_sep. $field_sep defaults to ",".

```
$str = DBI::neat_list(\@listref, $maxlen, $field_sep);
```

dump_results

Fetches all the rows from $sth, calls DBI::neat_list for each row and prints the results to $fh (defaults to STDOUT) separated by $lsep (default "\n"). $fsep defaults to ", " and $maxlen defaults to 35. This function is designed as a handy utility for prototyping and testing queries.

```
$rows = DBI::dump_results($sth, \@listref, $maxlen, $lsep,
                          $fsep, $fh);
```

DBI Dynamic Attributes

These attributes are always associated with the last handle used.

Where an attribute is equivalent to a method call, then refer to the method call for all related documentation.

`$DBI::err`
> Equivalent to `$h->err`.

`$DBI::errstr`
> Equivalent to `$h->errstr`.

`$DBI::state`
> Equivalent to `$h->state`.

`$DBI::rows`
> Equivalent to `$h->rows`.

Methods Common to All Handles

`err`
> Returns the native database engine error code from the last driver function called.
>
> $rv = $dbh->err;

`errstr`
> Returns the native database engine error message from the last driver function called.
>
> $str = $dbh->errstr;

`state`
> Returns an error code in the standard SQLSTATE five-character format. Note that the specific success code 00000 is translated to 0 (false). If the driver does not support SQLSTATE then state will return S1000 (General Error) for all errors.
>
> $rv = $dbh->state;

Attributes Common to All Handles

These attributes are common to all types of DBI handle.

Some attributes are inherited by *child* handles. That is, the value of an inherited attribute in a newly created statement handle is the same as the value in the parent database handle. Changes to attributes in the new statement handle do not affect the parent database handle and changes to the database handle do not affect *existing* statement handles, only future ones.

`Warn (inherited)`
> Enables useful warnings for certain bad practices. Enabled by default. Some emulation layers, especially those for Perl4 interfaces, disable warnings.
>
> $h->{Warn}

`CompatMode (inherited)`
> Used by emulation layers (such as Oraperl) to enable compatible behavior in the underlying driver (e.g., DBD::Oracle) for this handle. Not normally set by application code.
>
> $h->{CompatMode}

`InactiveDestroy`
> This attribute can be used to disable the effect of destroying a handle (which would normally close a prepared statement or disconnect from the database, etc). It is specifically designed for use in UNIX applications that "fork" child processes. Either the parent or the child process, but not both, should set InactiveDestroy on all their handles.
>
> $h->{InactiveDestroy}

RaiseError (inherited)

This attribute can be used to force errors to raise exceptions rather than simply return error codes in the normal way. It defaults to **off**. When set **on**, any method which results in an error occuring ($DBI::err being set true) will cause the DBI to effectively **die** ($DBI::errstr).

```
$h->{RaiseError}
```

Note that the contents of $@ are currently just $DBI::errstr, but that may change and should not be relied upon.

ChopBlanks (inherited)

This attribute can be used to control the trimming of trailing space characters from fixed width char fields. No other field types are affected.

```
$h->{ChopBlanks}
```

The default is false (it is possible that this may change). Applications that need specific behavior should set the attribute as needed. Emulation interfaces should set the attribute to match the behavior of the interface they are emulating.

Drivers are not required to support this attribute, but any driver that does not must arrange to return undef as the attribute value.

DBI Database Handle Objects

Database Handle Methods

prepare

Prepares a single statement for execution by the database engine and returns a reference to a statement handle object that can be used to get attributes of the statement and invoke the **$sth->execute** method.

```
$sth = $dbh->prepare($statement);
$sth = $dbh->prepare($statement, \%attr);
```

Drivers for engines that don't have the concept of preparing a statement will typically just store the statement in the returned handle and process it when **$sth->execute** is called. Such drivers are likely to be unable to give much useful information about the statement, such as **$sth->{NUM_OF_FIELDS}**, until after **$sth->execute** has been called. **Prepare** *never* executes the statement, even if it is not a SELECT statement.

do

Prepares and executes a statement. This method is typically most useful for non-SELECT statements which either cannot be prepared in advance (due to a limitation in the driver) or which do not need to be executed repeatedly.

```
$rc  = $dbh->do($statement);
$rc  = $dbh->do($statement, \%attr);
```

commit

Commits (makes permanent) the most recent series of database changes if the database supports transactions.

```
$rc  = $dbh->commit;
```

rollback

Rolls back (undoes) the most recent series of uncommited database changes if the database supports transactions.

```
$rc  = $dbh->rollback;
```

disconnect

Disconnects the database from the database handle. Typically used only before exiting the program. The handle is of little use after disconnecting.

```
$rc = $dbh->disconnect;
```

The transaction behavior of disconnect is undefined. Applications should explicitly call commit or rollback before calling disconnect.

The database is automatically disconnected (by the DESTROY method) if still connected when there are no longer any references to the handle. The DESTROY method for each driver should explicitly call rollback to undo any uncommited changes. This is *vital* behavior to ensure that incomplete transactions don't get commited simply because Perl calls DESTROY on every object before exiting.

ping

Attempts to determine, in the most efficient way, whether the database server is still running and the connection to it is still working. The default implementation currently always returns true without actually doing anything. Individual drivers should implement this function in the most suitable manner for their database engine.

```
$rc = $dbh->ping;
```

quote

Quotes a string for use in an SQL statement by escaping any special characters (such as quotation marks) contained within the string and adding the required type of outer quotation marks.

```
$sql = $dbh->quote($string);
```

For Oracle, the following example of quote would return 'Don''t', and for Ingres it would return 'Don'+X'27+'t' (including the outer quotation marks).

```
$sql = sprintf "select foo from bar where baz = %s",
               $dbh->quote("Don't\n");
```

An undefined $string value will be returned as NULL (without quotation marks).

Database Handle Attributes

AutoCommit

If true, then database changes cannot be rolled back (undone). If false, then database changes occur within a 'transaction' that must either be committed or rolled back using the commit or rollback methods.

```
$sth->{AutoCommit}      ($)
```

Drivers for databases that support transactions should always default to Auto-Commit mode.

Some drivers only support AutoCommit mode and thus after an application sets AutoCommit it should check that it now has the desired value. All portable applications must explicitly set and check for the desired Auto-Commit mode.

DBI Statement Handle Objects

Statement Handle Methods

execute

Performs whatever processing is necessary to execute the prepared statement. An undef is returned if an error occurs.

```
$rc  = $sth->execute;
```

For a non-SELECT statement, **execute** returns the number of rows affected (if available). Zero rows is returned as "0E0" which Perl will treat as 0 but will regard as **true**.

For SELECT statements, **execute** simply starts the query within the engine. Use one of the fetch methods to retreive the data. Note that the execute method does *not* return the number of rows that will be returned by the query (because for most engines it can't tell in advance).

fetch

Fetches the next row of data and returns a reference to an array holding the field values. If there are no more rows, **fetch** returns **undef**. NULL values are returned as **undef**.

```
$ary_ref = $sth->fetch;
```

fetchrow

An alternative to **fetch**. Fetches the next row of data and returns it as an array holding the field values. If there are no more rows, **fetchrow** returns an empty list. NULL values are returned as **undef**.

```
@ary = $sth->fetchrow;
```

fetchhash

An alternative to **fetchrow**. Fetches the next row of data and returns it as a reference to a hash containing field name and field value pairs. NULL values are returned as **undef**. If there are no more rows, **fetchhash** returns **undef**.

```
$hash_ref = $sth->fetchhash;
```

The keys of the hash are the same names returned by $sth->{NAME}. If more than one field has the same name, only one will be returned. For this reason, **fetchhash** should not be used to fetch data from such queries.

Because of the extra work **fetchhash** and Perl have to perform, **fetchhash** is not as efficient as **fetch** or **fetchrow** and not recommended where performance is very important.

fetch_all

The **fetch_all** method can be used to fetch all the data to be returned from a prepared statement. It returns a reference to an array which contains one array reference per row (as returned by **fetch**).

```
$tbl_ary_ref = $sth->fetch_all;
```

If there are no rows to return, **fetch_all** returns a reference to an empty array.

finish

Indicates that no more data will be fetched from this statement before it is either prepared again via **prepare** or destroyed. It is helpful to call this method where appropriate in order to allow the server to free up any internal resources (such as read locks) currently being held. It does not affect the transaction status of the session in any way.

```
$rc = $sth->finish;
```

rows

Returns the number of rows affected by the last database-altering command, or -1 if not known or available.

```
$rv = $sth->rows;
```

Generally you can rely on a row count only after a do() or non-select execute(). Some drivers offer a row count only after executing some specific operations (e.g., update and delete).

It is generally not possible to know how many rows will be returned from an arbitrary SELECT statement except by fetching and counting them. Also note that some drivers, such as DBD::Oracle, implement read-ahead row caches for SELECT statements, which means that the row count may be incorrect while there are still more records to fetch.

bind_col

Binds a column (field) of a SELECT statement to a Perl variable. Whenever a row is fetched from the database, the corresponding Perl variable is automatically updated. There is no need to fetch and assign the values manually. See bind_columns below for an example. Note that column numbers count up from 1.

```
$rv = $sth->bind_col($column_number, \$var_to_bind);
$rv = $sth->bind_col($column_number, \$var_to_bind, \%attr);
```

The binding is performed at a very low level using Perl aliasing, so there is no extra copying taking place. So long as the driver uses the correct internal DBI call to get the array the fetch function returns, it will automatically support column binding.

bind_columns

Calls bind_col for each column of the SELECT statement. bind_columns will croak if the number of references does not match the number of fields.

```
$rv = $sth->bind_columns(\%attr, @refs_to_vars_to_bind);
```

For example:

```
$sth->prepare(q{ select region,
                 sales from sales_by_region }) or die ...;
my($region, $sales);
# Bind perl variables to columns.
# Note use of perl's handy \(...) syntax.
$rv = $sth->bind_columns(undef, \($region, $sales));
# Column binding is the most eficient way to fetch data
while($sth->fetch) {
    print "$region: $sales\n";
}
```

Statement Handle Attributes

NUM_OF_FIELDS

Number of fields (columns) the prepared statement will return. Non-SELECT statements will have NUM_OF_FIELDS == 0.

```
        $sth->{NUM_OF_FIELDS}   ($)
```

NUM_OF_PARAMS

The number of parameters (placeholders) in the prepared statement.

```
        $sth->{NUM_OF_PARAMS}   ($)
```

NAME

Returns a *reference* to an array of field names for each column.

```
        $sth->{NAME}                (\@)
```

For example:

```
        print "First column name: $sth->{NAME}->[0]\n";
```

NULLABLE

Returns a *reference* to an array indicating the possibility of each column returning a null.

```
        $sth->{NULLABLE}            (\@)
```

For example:

```
        print "First column may return NULL\n"
            if $sth->{NULLABLE}->[0];
```

CursorName

Returns the name of the cursor associated with the statement handle if available. If not available or the database driver does not support the **where current of ...** SQL syntax then it returns **undef**.

```
        $sth->{CursorName}      ($)
```

Simple Example

```
my $dbh = DBI->connect($database, $user, $password, 'Oracle')
    or die "Can't connect to $database: $DBI::errstr";
my $sth = $dbh->prepare( q{
        SELECT name, phone
        FROM mytelbook
}) or die "Can't prepare statement: $DBI::errstr";
my $rc = $sth->execute
    or die "Can't execute statement: $DBI::errstr";
print "Query will return $sth->{NUM_FIELDS} fields.\n\n";
print "$sth->{NAME}->[0]: $sth->{NAME}->[1]\n";
while (($name, $phone) = $sth->fetchrow()) {
    print "$name: $phone\n";
}
# check for problems which may have terminated the fetch early
warn $DBI::errstr if $DBI::err;
$sth->finish;
```

Debugging

Detailed debugging can be enabled for a specific handle (and any future children of that handle) by executing:

```
$h->debug($level);
```

Where **$level** is at least 2 (recommended). Disable with **$level==0;**

You can also enable debugging by setting the PERL_DBI_DEBUG environment variable to the same values. On UNIX-like systems using a Bourne-like shell, you can do this easily for a single command:

```
PERL_DBI_DEBUG=2 perl your_test_script.pl
```

The debugging output is detailed and typically very useful.

Warnings

The DBI is *alpha* software. It is alpha *only* because the interface (API) is not finalized. The alpha status does not reflect code quality or stability.

Frequently Asked Questions

Why doesn't my CGI script work right?

Read the information in the references below. Please do *not* post CGI-related questions to the dbi-users mailing list (or to me).

> *http://www.perl.com/perl/faq/idiots-guide.html*
> *http://www3.pair.com/webthing/docs/cgi/faqs/cgifaq.shtml*
> *http://www.perl.com/perl/faq/perl-cgi-faq.html*
> *http://www-genome.wi.mit.edu/WWW/faqs/www-security-faq.html*
> *http://www.boutell.com/faq/*
> *http://www.perl.com/perl/faq/*

General problems and good ideas:

- Use the CGI::ErrorWrap module.
- Remember that many environment variables won't be set for CGI scripts.

How can I maintain a WWW connection to a database?

For information on the Apache httpd server and the mod_perl module, see *http://www.osf.org/~dougm/apache/*.

A driver build fails because it can't find DBIXS.h.

The installed location of the *DBIXS.h* file changed with 0.77 (it was being installed into the 'wrong' directory but that's where driver developers came to expect it to be). The first thing to do is check to see if you have the latest version of your driver. Driver authors will be releasing new versions that use the new location. If you have the latest, ask for a new release. You can edit the *Makefile.PL* file yourself. Change the part that reads `-I.../DBI` so it reads `-I.../auto/DBI` (where ... is a string of non-space characters).

Has the DBI and DBD::Foo been ported to NT / Win32?

The latest version of the DBI and, at least, the DBD::Oracle module will build—without changes—on NT/Win32 *if* your are using the standard Perl 5.004 and *not* the ActiveWare port.

Jeffrey Urlwin, *jurlwin@access.digex.net*, (or *jurlwin@hq.caci.com*) is helping me with the port. (Actually, he's doing it and I'm integrating the changes.)

What about ODBC?

See the statement and following notes in the DBI README file.

Acknowledgments

I would like to acknowledge the valuable contributions of the many people I have worked with on the DBI project, especially in the early years (1992-1994): Kevin Stock, Buzz Moschetti, Kurt Andersen, Ted Lemon, William Hails, Garth Kennedy, Michael Peppler, Neil S. Briscoe, David J. Hughes, Jeff Stander, Forrest D Whitcher, Larry Wall, Jeff Fried, Roy Johnson, Paul Hudson, Georg Rehfeld, Steve Sizemore, Ron Pool, Jon Meek, Tom Christiansen, Steve Baumgarten, Randal Schwartz, and a whole lot more.

Authors

DBI by Tim Bunce. This pod text by Tim Bunce, J. Douglas Dunlop and others. Perl by Larry Wall and the Perl5 Porters.

Copyright

The DBI module is copyright © 1995, 1996, 1997 Tim Bunce, England. The DBI module is free software; you can redistribute it and/or modify it under the same terms as Perl itself.

This document is copyright © 1997 by Tim Bunce. All rights reserved. Permission to distribute this document, in full or part, via email, Usenet or ftp/http archives or printed copy is granted providing that no charges are involved, reasonable attempt is made to use the most current version, and all credits and copyright notices are retained. Requests for other distribution rights, including incorporation in commercial products, such as books, magazine articles, or CD-ROMs should be made to *Tim.Bunce@ig.co.uk* (please *don't* use this mail address for other DBI-related mail—use the *dbi-users* mailing list).

The DBI is free software. IT COMES WITHOUT WARRANTY OF ANY KIND.

Commercial support agreements for Perl and the DBI, DBD::Oracle, and Oraperl, modules can be arranged via The Perl Clinic. See *http://www.perl.co.uk/tpc* for more details.

See Also

Database Documentation
SQL Language Reference Manual

Books and Journals
Programming Perl, 2nd ed. by Larry Wall, Tom Christiansen, and Randal Schwartz

Learning Perl, 2nd ed., by Randal Schwartz and Tom Christiansen

Dr Dobb's Journal, November 1996

The Perl Journal, April 1997

Manual Pages
the perl(1) manpage, the perlmod(1) manpage, the perlbook(1) manpage

Mailing List
The dbi-users mailing list is the primary means of communication among uses of the DBI and its related modules. Subscribe and unsubscribe via:

> *http://www.fugue.com/dbi*

Mailing list archives are held at:

> *http://www.rosat.mpe-garching.mpg.de/mailing-lists/PerlDB-Interest/*
> *http://www.coe.missouri.edu/~faq/lists/dbi.html*

Assorted Related WWW Links

The DBI home page (not maintained by me):

> *http://www.hermetica.com/technologia/DBI*

Other related links:

> *http://www-ccs.cs.umass.edu/db.html*
> *http://www.odmg.org/odmg93/updates_dbarry.html*
> *http://www.jcc.com/sql_stnd.html*
> *ftp://alpha.gnu.ai.mit.edu/gnu/gnusql-0.7b3.tar.gz*

Known Driver Modules

Oracle—DBD::Oracle
> Tim Bunce, *dbi-users@fugue.com*

Ingres—DBD::Ingres
mSQL—DBD::mSQL
DB2—DBD::DB2
Empress—DBD::Empress
Informix—DBD::Informix
> Jonathan Leffler, *dbi-users@fugue.com*

Solid—DBD::Solid
> Tomis Wenrich, *wenrich@site58.ping.at* or *dbi-users@fugue.com*

Postgres—DBD::Pg
> Edmund Mergl, *mergl@nadia.s.bawue.de* or *dbi-users@fugue.com*

Other Related Works and Perl Modules

Apache::DBI by E.Mergl@bawue.de
> To be used with the Apache daemon together with an embedded Perl interpreter like mod_perl. Establishes a database connection which remains open for the lifetime of the http daemon. This way the CGI connect and disconnect for every database access becomes superfluous.

JDBC Server by Stuart 'Zen' Bishop, zen@bf.rmit.edu.au
> The server is written in Perl. The client classes that talk to it are of course in Java. Thus, a Java applet or application will be able to comunicate via the JDBC API with any database that has a DBI driver installed. The URL used is in the form *jdbc:dbi://host.domain.etc:999/Driver/DBName*. It seems to be very similar to some commercial products, such as jdbcKona.

Remote Proxy DBD support
> Under construction by Carl Declerck (*carl@miskatonic.inbe.net*) and Terry Greenlaw (*z50816@mip.mar.lmco.com*).
>
> Carl is developing a generic proxy object module which could form the basis of a DBD::Proxy driver in the future. Terry is doing something similar.

DBI::W32ODBC—an experimental DBI emulation layer for Win32::ODBC

Synopsis

```
use DBI::W32ODBC;
# apart from the line above everything is just the same as with
# the real DBI when using a basic driver with few features.
```

```
$dbh = DBI->connect(...);
$rc  = $dbh->do($statement);
$sth = $dbh->prepare($statement);
$rc = $sth->execute;
@row_ary = $sth->fetchrow;
$row_ref = $sth->fetch;
$rc = $sth->finish;
$rv = $sth->rows;
$rc = $dbh->disconnect;
$sql = $dbh->quote($string);
$rv  = $h->err;
$str = $h->errstr;
```

Description

This is a very experimental pure Perl DBI emulation layer for Win32::ODBC.

It was developed for use with an Access database, and the quote() method is very likely to need reworking.

If you can improve this code I'd be interested in hearing about it. If you are having trouble using it, please respect the fact that it's very experimental.

Author

Tim Bunce

MLDBM—store multi-level hash structure in single-level tied hash

Synopsis

```
use MLDBM;                    # this gets the default, SDBM
#use MLDBM qw(DB_File);

$dbm = tie %o, MLDBM [..other DBM args..] or die $!;
```

Description

This module, intended primarily for use with DBM packages, can serve as a transparent interface to any TIEHASH package that must be used to store arbitrary Perl data, including nested references.

It works by converting the values in the hash that are references, to their string representation in Perl syntax. When using a DBM database, it is this string that gets stored.

It requires the Data::Dumper package, available at any CPAN site.

See the "Bugs" section for important limitations.

Configuration Variables or Methods

$MLDBM::UseDB or $OBJ->UseDB([DBNAME])

You may want to set $MLDBM::UseDB to default to something other than SDBM_File, in case you have a more efficient DBM, or if you want to use this with some other TIEHASH implementation. Alternatively, you can specify the name of the package at use time. Nested module names can be specified as Foo::Bar.

$MLDBM::Key or $OBJ->Key([KEYSTRING])

> Defaults to the magic string used to recognize MLDBM data. It is a six-character wide, unique string. This is best left alone, unless you know what you're doing.

$MLDBM::DumpMeth or $OBJ->DumpMeth([METHNAME])

> This controls which of the two dumping methods available from Data::Dumper are used. By default, this is set to Dumpxs, the faster of the two methods, but only if MLDBM detects that Dumpxs is supported on your platform. Otherwise, defaults to the slower Dump method.

Example

```
use MLDBM;                            # this gets SDBM
#use MLDBM qw(DB_File);
use Fcntl;                            # to get 'em constants

$dbm = tie %o, MLDBM, 'testmldbm', O_CREAT|O_RDWR, 0640 or die $!;

$c = [\ 'c'];
$b = {};
$a = [1, $b, $c];
$b->{a} = $a;
$b->{b} = $a->[1];
$b->{c} = $a->[2];
@o{qw(a b c)} = ($a, $b, $c);


#
# to see what was stored
#
use Data::Dumper;
print Data::Dumper->Dump([@o{qw(a b c)}], [qw(a b c)]);
#
# to modify data in a substructure
#
$tmp = $o{a};
$tmp[0] = 'foo';
$o{a} = $tmp;


#
# can access the underlying DBM methods transparently
#
# print $dbm->fd, "\n";              # DB_File method
```

Bugs

- Adding or altering substructures to a hash value is not entirely transparent in current Perl. If you want to store a reference or modify an existing reference value in the DBM, it must first be retrieved and stored in a temporary variable for further modifications. In particular, something like this will *not* work properly:

```
$mldb{key}{subkey}[3] = 'stuff';   # won't work
```

  Instead, that must be written as:

```
$tmp = $mldb{key};                 # retrieve value
$tmp->{subkey}[3] = 'stuff';
$mldb{key} = $tmp;                 # store value
```

This limitation exists because the Perl TIEHASH interface currently has no support for multidimensional ties.

- MLDBM was first released along with the Data::Dumper package as an example. If you got serious with that and have a DBM file from that version, you can do something like this to convert the old records to the new format:

```
use MLDBM (DB_File);          # be sure it's the new MLDBM
use Fcntl;
tie %o, MLDBM, 'oldmldbm.file', O_RDWR, 0640 or die $!;
for $k (keys %o) {
    my $v = $o{$k};
    if ($v =~ /^\$CrYpTiCkEy/o) {
        $v = eval $v;
        if ($@) { warn "Error: $@\twhile evaluating $v\n"; }
        else    { $o{$k} = $v; }
    }
}
```

Author

Gurusamy Sarathy, *gsar@umich.edu*

Copyright © 1995 Gurusamy Sarathy. All rights reserved. This program is free software; you can redistribute it and/or modify it under the same terms as Perl itself.

See Also

perl(1), perltie(1), perlfunc(1)

Msql::RDBMS—Relational database management system for Msql

Synopsis

```
use Msql::RDBMS;
$rdbms = new Msql::RDBMS;
$rdbms->show;
```

Description

This is a fully catalog-driven database management system for Perl 5 and mini-SQL. You should use it in conjunction with the *sqldef.pl* script, found in the *utility/* subdirectory of the installation; this script will generate data definition language for your tables.

Generating Data Definition Language

You must pass the name of a schema definition file to *sqldef.pl* (an example, *schema.def*, is included in the *examples/* subdirectory of the distribution). Example usage:

```
sqldef.pl schema.def
```

The above example will send the data definition language to STDOUT. To send it to mini-SQL (this will wipe out all of the data in the specified database):

```
sqldef.pl schema.def | msql database-name
```

The *schema.def* file contains a little bit of documentation on how the data is organized within the file, and how you can set up your own tables.

Usage

You can call up the entire relational database management system from your browser with a URL like this:

> *http://bozos.on.the.bus/sample.cgi?db=demo*

Where *sample.cgi* is a Perl script containing the three lines of code shown in the Synopsis.

Debugging

You can get some debugging information, which consists of a CGI::dump, and an SQL statement, if relevant, by including `debug=1` in the URL.

To Do

- Generate forms for interactive data definition.
- Enforce referential integrity (cascade/block deletes).
- Add support for many-to-many relationships.*
- Enforce uniqueness for label columns.*
- Add fancy display options that support automagic hyperlinking of URLs and email addresses.*

An asterisk (*) denotes features present in the original PHP/FI version.

Author

Brian Jepson, *bjepson@conan.ids.net*

Copyright

Copyright © Brian Jepson. This program is free software; you may distribute this under the same terms as Perl itself.

See Also

CGI::CGI, CGI::Carp, Msql, File::Counterfile

Oraperl—Perl access to Oracle databases for old Oraperl scripts

Synopsis
```
$lda = &ora_login($system_id, $name, $password)
$csr = &ora_open($lda, $stmt [, $cache])
&ora_bind($csr, $var, ...)
&ora_fetch($csr [, $trunc])
&ora_close($csr)
&ora_logoff($lda)
&ora_do($lda, $stmt)
&ora_titles($csr)
&ora_lengths($csr)
&ora_types($csr)
```

```
&ora_commit($lda)
&ora_rollback($lda)
&ora_autocommit($lda, $on_off)
&ora_version()
$ora_cache
$ora_long
$ora_trunc
$ora_errno
$ora_errstr
$ora_verno
$ora_debug
```

Description

Oraperl is an extension to Perl which allows access to Oracle databases.

The functions that make up this extension are described in the following sections. All functions return a `false` or undefined (in the Perl sense) value to indicate failure. You do not need to understand the references to OCI in these descriptions. They are here to help those who wish to extend the routines or to port them to new machines.

The text in this document is largely unchanged from the original Perl4 Oraperl manual written by Kevin Stock, *kstock@auspex.fr*. Any comments specific to the DBD::Oracle Oraperl emulation are prefixed by DBD:.

Principal Functions

The main functions for database access are &ora_login(), &ora_open(), &ora_bind(), &ora_fetch(), &ora_close(), &ora_do(), and &ora_logoff().

ora_login

> In order to access information held within an Oracle database, a program must first log in to it by calling the &ora_login() function. This function is called with three parameters: the system ID (see below) of the Oracle database to be used, and the Oracle username and password. The value returned is a login identifier (actually an Oracle Login Data Area) referred to below as $lda.

> ```
> $lda = &ora_login($system_id, $username, $password)
> ```

> Multiple logins may be active simultaneously. This allows a simple mechanism for correlating or transferring data between databases.

> Most Oracle programs (for example, SQL*Plus or SQL*Forms) examine the environment variable ORACLE_SID or TWO_TASK to determine which database to connect to. In an environment that uses several different databases, it is easy to make a mistake and attempt to run a program on the wrong one. Also, it is cumbersome to create a program that works with more than one database simultaneously. Therefore, Oraperl requires the system ID to be passed as a parameter. However, if the system ID parameter is an empty string, Oracle will use the existing value of ORACLE_SID or TWO_TASK in the usual manner.

> Example:

> ```
> $lda = &ora_login('personnel', 'scott', 'tiger') ||
>         die $ora_errstr;
> ```

> This function is equivalent to the OCI olon and orlon functions.

DBD: note that a name is assumed to be a TNS alias if it does not appear as the name of a SID in */etc/oratab* or */var/opt/oracle/oratab*. See the code in *Oracle.pm* for the full logic of database name handling.

DBD: Since the returned $lda is a Perl5 reference the database login identifier is now automatically released if $lda is overwritten or goes out of scope.

ora_open

To specify an SQL statement to be executed, the program must call the &ora_open() function. This function takes at least two parameters: a login identifier (obtained from &ora_login()) and the SQL statement to be executed. An optional third parameter specifies the size of the row cache to be used for a SELECT statement. The value returned from &ora_open() is a statement identifier (actually an Oracle Cursor) referred to below as $csr.

```
$csr = &ora_open($lda, $statement [, $cache])
```

If the row cache size is not specified, a default size is used. As distributed, the default is five rows, but this may have been changed at your installation (see the &ora_version() function and $ora_cache variable below).

Examples:

```
$csr = &ora_open($lda, 'select ename, sal from emp order by
                ename', 10);
$csr = &ora_open($lda, 'insert into dept values(:1, :2, :3)');
```

This function is equivalent to the OCI **oopen** and **oparse** functions. For statements that do not contain substitution variables (see the section "Substitution Variables" below), it also uses of the oexec function. For SELECT statements, it also makes use of the odescr and odefin functions to allocate memory for the values to be returned from the database.

ora_bind

If an SQL statement contains substitution variables (see the section Substitution Variables below), &ora_bind() is used to assign actual values to them. This function takes a statement identifier (obtained from &ora_open()) as its first parameter, followed by as many parameters as are required by the statement.

```
&ora_bind($csr, $var, ...)
```

Example:

```
&ora_bind($csr, 50, 'management', 'Paris');
```

This function is equivalent to the OCI **obndrn** and **oexec** statements.

The OCI obndrn function does not allow empty strings to be bound. As distributed, $ora_bind therefore replaces empty strings with a single space. However, a compilation option allows this substitution to be suppressed, causing &ora_bind() to fail. The output from the &ora_version() function specifies which is the case at your installation.

ora_fetch

The &ora_fetch() function is used in conjunction with a SQL SELECT statement to retrieve information from a database. This function takes one mandatory parameter, a statement identifier (obtained from &ora_open()).

```
$nfields = &ora_fetch($csr)
@data = &ora_fetch($csr [, $trunc])
```

Used in a scalar context, the function returns the number of fields returned by the query but no data is actually fetched. This may be useful in a program which allows a user to enter a statement interactively.

Example:

```
$nfields = &ora_fetch($csr);
```

Used in an array context, the value returned is an array containing the data, one element per field.

An optional second parameter may be supplied to indicate whether the truncation of a LONG or LONG RAW field is to be permitted (non-zero) or considered an error (zero). If this parameter is not specified, the value of the global variable $ora_trunc is used instead. Truncation of other datatypes is always considered a error.

DBD: The optional second parameter to ora_fetch is not supported. A DBI usage error will be generated if a second parameter is supplied. Use the global variable $ora_trunc instead. Also note that the experimental DBI readblob method can be used to retrieve a long:

```
$csr->readblob($field, $offset, $len [, \$dest, $destoffset]);
```

If truncation occurs, $ora_errno will be set to 1406. &ora_fetch() will complete successfully if truncation is permitted, otherwise it will fail.

&ora_fetch() will fail at the end of the data or if an error occurs. It is possible to distinguish between these cases by testing the value of the variable $ora_errno. This will be zero for end of data, non-zero if an error has occurred.

Example:

```
while (($deptno, $dname, $loc) = &ora_fetch($csr))
{
  warn "Truncated!!!" if $ora_errno == 1406;
  # do something with the data
}
warn $ora_errstr if $ora_errno;
```

This function is equivalent to the OCI ofetch function.

ora_close

If an SQL statement is no longer required (for example, all the data selected has been processed, or no more rows are to be inserted) then the statement identifier should be released. This is done by calling the &ora_close() function with the statement identifier as its only parameter.

```
&ora_close($csr)
```

This function is equivalent to the OCI oclose function.

DBD: Since $csr is a Perl5 reference the statement/cursor is now automatically closed if $csr is overwritten or goes out of scope.

ora_do

Not all SQL statements return data or contain substitution variables. In these cases the &ora_do() function may be used as an alternative to &ora_open() and &ora_close(). This function takes two parameters: a login identifier and the statement to be executed.

```
&ora_do($lda, $statement)
```

Example:

```
&ora_do($lda, 'drop table employee');
```

This function is roughly equivalent to:

```
&ora_close( &ora_open($lda, $statement) )
```

DBD: Oraperl v2 used to return the string 'OK' to indicate success with a zero numeric value. The Oraperl emulation now uses the string '0E0' to achieve the same effect since it does not cause any -w warnings when used in a numeric context.

ora_logoff

When the program no longer needs to access a given database, the login identifier should be released using the &ora_logoff() function.

```
&ora_logoff($lda)
```

This function is equivalent to the OCI ologoff function.

DBD: Since $lda is a Perl5 reference, the database login identifier is now automatically released if $lda is overwritten or goes out of scope.

Ancillary Functions

Additional functions available are: &ora_titles(), &ora_lengths(), &ora_types(), &ora_autocommit(), &ora_commit(), &ora_rollback(), and &ora_version().

The first three are of most use within a program which allows statements to be entered interactively. See, for example, the sample program SQL which is supplied with Oraperl and may have been installed at your site.

ora_titles

A program may determine the field titles of an executed query by calling &ora_titles(). This function takes a single parameter: a statement identifier (obtained from &ora_open()) indicating the query for which the titles are required. The titles are returned as an array of strings, one for each column.

```
@titles = &ora_titles($csr)
```

Titles are truncated to the length of the field, as reported by the &ora_lengths() function.

DBD: Oraperl v2.2 actually changed the behavior such that the titles were not truncated unless an optional second parameter was true. This was not reflected in the Oraperl manual. The Oraperl emulation adopts the non-truncating behavior and doesn't support the truncate parameter.

ora_lengths

A program may determine the length of each of the fields returned by a query by calling the &ora_lengths() function. This function takes a single parameter, a statement identifier (obtained from &ora_open()) indicating the query for which the lengths are required. The lengths are returned as an array of integers, one for each column.

```
@lengths = &ora_lengths($csr)
```

ora_types

A program may determine the type of each of the fields returned by a query by calling the &ora_types() function. This function takes a single parameter, a statement identifier (obtained from &ora_open()) indicating the query for which the lengths are required. The types are returned as an array of integers, one for each field.

```
@types = &ora_types($csr)
```

These types are defined in your OCI documentation. The correct interpretation for Oracle v6 is given in the file *oraperl.ph*.

ora_autocommit

Autocommit mode (in which each transaction is committed immediately, without waiting for an explicit commit) may be enabled or disabled using &ora_auto-commit(). This function takes two parameters, a login identifier (obtained from &ora_login()) and a true/false value indicating whether autocommit is to be enabled (non-zero) or disabled (zero). By default, autocommit is off.

```
&ora_autocommit($lda, $on_or_off)
```

Note that autocommit can only be set per login, not per statement. If you need to control autocommit by statement (for example, to allow deletions to be rolled back, but insertions to be committed immediately) you should make multiple calls to &ora_login() and use a separate login identifier for each statement.

ora_commit, ora_rollback

Modifications to a database may be committed or rolled back using the &ora_commit() and &ora_rollback() functions. These functions take a single parameter, a login identifier obtained from &ora_login().

```
&ora_commit($lda)
&ora_rollback($lda)
```

Transactions which have been committed (either explicitly by a call to &ora_commit() or implicitly through the use of &ora_autocommit()) cannot be subsequently rolled back.

Note that commit and rollback can only be used per login, not per statement. If you need to commit or rollback by statement, you should make multiple calls to &ora_login() and use a separate login identifier for each statement.

ora_version

The &ora_version() function prints the version number and copyright information concerning Oraperl. It also prints the values of various compilation time options. It does not return any value, and should not normally be used in a program.

```
&ora_version()
```

Example:

```
perl -MOraperl -e 'ora_version()'
This is Oraperl, version 2, patch level 0.
Debugging is available, including the -D flag.
Default fetch row cache size is 5.
Empty bind values are replaced by a space.
Perl is copyright by Larry Wall; type oraperl -v for details.
Additions for oraperl: Copyright 1991, 1992, Kevin Stock.
Oraperl may be distributed under the same conditions as Perl.
```

This function is the equivalent of Perl's –v flag.

DBD: The Oraperl emulation printout is similar but not identical.

Variables

Six special variables are provided: $ora_cache, $ora_long, $ora_trunc, $ora_errno, $ora_errstr and $ora_verno.

Customization Variables

These variables are used to dictate the behavior of Oraperl under certain conditions.

$ora_cache

The $ora_cache variable determines the default cache size used by the &ora_open() function for SELECT statements if an explicit cache size is not given.

It is initialized to the default value reported by &ora_version() but may be set within a program to apply to all subsequent calls to &ora_open(). Cursors which are already open are not affected. As distributed, the default value is 5, but may have been altered at your installation.

As a special case, assigning 0 to $ora_cache resets it to the default value. Attempting to set $ora_cache to a negative value results in a warning.

$ora_long

Normally, Oraperl interrogates the database to determine the length of each field and allocates buffer space accordingly. This is not possible for fields of type LONG or LONGRAW. To allocate space according to the maximum possible length (65535 bytes) would obviously be extremely wasteful of memory.

Therefore, when &ora_open() determines that a field is a LONG type, it allocates the amount of space indicated by the $ora_long variable. This is initially set to 80 (for compatibility with Oracle products) but may be set within a program to whatever size is required.

$ora_trunc

Since Oraperl cannot determine exactly the maximum length of a LONG field, it is possible that the length indicated by $ora_long is not sufficient to store the data fetched. In such a case, the optional second parameter to &ora_fetch() indicates whether the truncation should be allowed or should provoke an error.

If this second parameter is not specified, the value of $ora_trunc is used as a default. This applies only to LONG and LONGRAW data types. Truncation of a field of any other type is always considered an error (principally because it indicates a bug in Oraperl).

Status Variables

These variables report information about error conditions or about Oraperl itself. They may only be read; a fatal error occurs if a program attempts to change them.

$ora_errno

$ora_errno contains the Oracle error code provoked by the last function call.

There are two cases of particular interest concerning &ora_fetch(). If a LONG or LONGRAW field is truncated (and truncation is allowed), &ora_fetch() will complete successfully but $ora_errno will be set to 1406 to indicate the truncation. When &ora_fetch() fails, $ora_errno will be set to 0 if this was due to the end of data, or an error code if it was due to an actual error.

$ora_errstr

The $ora_errstr variable contains the Oracle error message corresponding to the current value of $ora_errno.

$ora_verno

The $ora_verno variable contains the version number of Oraperl in the form v.ppp where v is the major version number and ppp is the patchlevel. For example, in Oraperl version 3, patch level 142, $ora_verno would contain the value 3.142 (more or less, allowing for floating point error).

Substitution Variables

Oraperl allows an SQL statement to contain substitution variables. These consist of a colon followed by a number. For example, a program which added records to a telephone list might use the following call to &ora_open():

```
$csr = &ora_open($csr, "insert into telno values(:1, :2)");
```

The two names :1 and :2 are called substitution variables. The function &ora_bind() is used to assign values to these variables. For example, the following statements would add two new people to the list:

```
&ora_bind($csr, "Annette", "472-8836");
&ora_bind($csr, "Brian", "937-1823");
```

Note that the substitution variables must be assigned consecutively beginning from 1 for each SQL statement, as &ora_bind() assigns its parameters in this order. Named substitution variables (for example, :NAME, :TELNO) are not permitted.

DBD: Substitution variables are now bound as type 1 (VARCHAR2) and not type 5 (STRING) by default. This can alter the behavior of SQL code which compares a char field with a substitution variable. See the String Comparison section in the Datatypes chapter of the Oracle OCI manual for more details.

You can work around this by using DBD::Oracle's ability to specify the Oracle type to be used on a per field basis:

```
$char_attrib = { ora_type => 5 }; # 5 = STRING (ala oraperl2.4)
$csr = ora_open($dbh, "select foo from bar where
                       x=:1 and y=:2");
$csr->bind_param(1, $value_x, $char_attrib);
$csr->bind_param(2, $value_y, $char_attrib);
ora_bind($csr);   # bind with no parameters since
                  # we've done bind_param()'s
```

Debugging

DBD: The Oraperl $ora_debug variable is not supported. However, detailed debugging can be enabled at any time by executing:

```
$h->debug(2);
```

where $h is either a $lda or a $csr. If debugging is enabled on an $lda, it is automatically passed on to any cursors returned by &ora_open().

Example

```
format STDOUT_TOP =
Name Phone
==== =====
.
format STDOUT =
@<<<<<<<<< @>>>>>>>>>
$name, $phone
.

die "You should use oraperl, not perl\n" unless defined &ora_login;
$ora_debug = shift if $ARGV[0] =~ /^\-#/;
$lda = &ora_login('t', 'kstock', 'kstock')
        || die $ora_errstr;
$csr = &ora_open($lda, 'select * from telno order by name')
        || die $ora_errstr;
$nfields = &ora_fetch($csr);
print "Query will return $nfields fields\n\n";
while (($name, $phone) = &ora_fetch($csr)) { write; }
warn $ora_errstr if $ora_errno;
die "fetch error: $ora_errstr" if $ora_errno;
do ora_close($csr) || die "can't close cursor";
do ora_logoff($lda) || die "can't log off Oracle";
```

Notes

In keeping with the philosophy of Perl, there is no predefined limit to the number of simultaneous logins or SQL statements that may be active, nor to the number of data fields that may be returned by a query. The only limits are those imposed by the amount of memory available, or by Oracle.

Warning

The Oraperl emulation software shares no code with the original Oraperl. It is built on top of the new Perl5 DBI and DBD::Oracle modules. These modules are still evolving. (One of the goals of the Oraperl emulation software is to allow useful work to be done with the DBI and DBD::Oracle modules while insulating users from the ongoing changes in their interfaces.)

It is quite possible, indeed probable, that some differences in behavior will exist. These are probably confined to error handling.

All differences in behavior which are not documented here should be reported to *Tim.Bunce@ig.co.uk* and cc'd to *dbi-users@fugue.com*.

Authors

Perl by Larry Wall, *larry@wall.org*.

ORACLE by Oracle Corporation, California.

Original Oraperl 2.4 code and documentation by Kevin Stock, *kstock@auspex.fr*.

DBI and Oraperl emulation using DBD::Oracle by Tim Bunce, *Tim.Bunce@ig.co.uk*.

See Also

Oracle Documentation

SQL Language Reference Manual. Programmer's guide to the Oracle Call Interfaces.

Books

Programming Perl by Larry Wall, Tom Christiansen, and Randal Schwartz. *Learning Perl* by Randal Schwartz and Tom Christiansen.

Manual Pages

perl(1)

Postgres—Perl interface to the Postgres95 SQL database engine

Synopsis

```
use Postgres;
$conn = db_connect($database,$host,$port)
    or die "could not connect -- $Postgres::error";
The parameters $host and $port are optional (or may be undef).
This will use the default Postgres95 values for them.
print "Connected Database: ", $conn->db();
print "Connected Host: ", $conn->host();
print "Connection Options: ", $conn->options();
print "Connected Port: ", $conn->port();
print "Connected tty: ", $conn->tty();
print "Connection Error Message: ", $conn->errorMessage();
```

This method is identical to PQreset(conn):

```
$conn->reset();
```

This method executes an SQL statement or query:

```
$query = $conn->execute($sql_statement)
    or die "Error -- $Postgres::error";
```

Retrieve the values from a SELECT query:

```
@array = $query->fetchrow();
```

Get information from the results of the last query:

```
$val = $query->cmdStatus();
$val = $query->oidStatus();
```

Calling the following functions on a result handle that is not from a SELECT is undefined:

```
$val = $query->ntuples();
$val = $query->nfields();
$val = $query->fname($column_index);
$val = $query->fnumber($column_name);
$val = $query->ftype($column_index);
$val = $query->fsize($column_index);
```

These functions are provided for completeness but are not intended to be used. The fetchrow() method will return **undef** for a field that is null.

```
$val = $query->getvalue($tuple_index,$column_index);
$val = $query->getlength($tuple_index,$column_index);
$val = $query->getisnull($tuple_index,$column_index);
```

The putline() and getline() functions are called as follows:

```
$query->putline($string);
$value = $query->getline();
$query->endcopy();
```

Description

This package is designed to be as close as possible to its C API counterpart, but to be more like Perl in how you interact with the API. The C Programmer Guide that comes with Postgres describes most things you need.

The following functions are currently not implemented: PQtrace(), PQendtrace(), and the asynchronous notification. I do not believe that binary cursors will work, either.

Once you db_connect() to a database, you can issue commands to the execute() method. If either of them returns an error from the underlying API, the value returned will be undef and the variable $Postgres::error will contain the error message from the database. The $port parameter to db_connect() is optional and will use the default port if not specified. All environment variables used by the PQsetdb() function are honored.

The method fetchrow() returns an array of the values from the next row fetched from the server. It returns an empty list when there is no more data available. Fields that have a NULL value return undef as their value in the array. Calling fetchrow() or the other tuple-related functions on a statement handle that is *not* from a SELECT statement has undefined behavior, and may well crash your program. Other functions work identically to their similarly named C API functions.

No finish or clear Statements

Whenever the scalar that holds the statement or connection handle loses its value, the underlying data structures will be freed and appropriate connections closed. This can be accomplished by performing one of these actions:

- undef the handle
- use the handle for another purpose
- let the handle run out of scope
- exit the program

Error Messages

A global variable $Postgres::error always holds the last error message. It is never reset except on the next error. The only time it holds a valid message is after execute() or db_connect() returns undef.

Prerequisites

You need to have the Postgres95 database server installed and configured on your system to use this module.

Be sure to set the proper directory locations in the *Makefile.PL* file for your installation.

Author

Vivek Khera, *vivek@khera.org*. Many ideas were taken from the MsqlPerl module.

Sprite——Perl 5.0 module to manipulate text delimited databases

Synopsis

```
use Sprite;
$rdb = new Sprite ();
$rdb->set_delimiter ("Read", "::");
$rdb->set_delimiter ("Write", "::");
$rdb->set_os ("UNIX");
$rdb->sql (<<Query);
    .
    .
    .

Query
$rdb->close ();
$rdb->close ($database);
```

Description

Here is a simple database where the fields are delimited by commas:

```
Player,Years,Points,Rebounds,Assists,Championships
...
Larry Joe Bird,12,28,10,7,3
Michael Jordan,10,33,6,5,3
Earvin Magic Johnson,12,22,7,12,5
...
```

Note: The first line must contain the field names (case-sensitive).

Supported SQL Commands

Here are a list of the SQL commands that are supported by Sprite:

select
> Retrieves records that match specified criteria:
>
> ```
> select col1 [,col2] from database
>     where (cond1 OPERATOR value1)
>     [and|or cond2 OPERATOR value2 ...]
> ```
> The * operator can be used to select all columns.
>
> The *database* is simply the file that contains the data. If the file is not in the current directory, the path must be specified.
>
> Sprite does *not* support multiple tables (commonly known as "joins").
>
> Valid column names can be used where [cond1..n] and [value1..n] are expected, such as:
>
> ```
> select Player, Points from my_db
>     where (Rebounds > Assists)
> ```

The following SQL operators can be used: =, <, >, <=, >=, <> as well as Perl's special operators: =~ and !~. The =~ and !~ operators are used to specify regular expressions, such as:

```
select * from my_db
    where (Name =~ /Bird$/i)
```

Selects records where the Name column ends with "Bird" (case-insensitive). For more information, look at a manual on **regexps**.

update

Updates records that match specified criteria.

```
update database set (cond1 OPERATOR value1)[,
                     (cond2 OPERATOR value2)...]
    where (cond1 OPERATOR value1)
    [and|or cond2 OPERATOR value2 ...]
```

Support for the feature of accepting multiple conditions was added as of version 3.1.

Example:

```
update my_db
    set Championships = (Championships + 1)
    where (Player = 'Larry Joe Bird')
update my_db
    set Championships = (Championships + 1), Years = (12)
    where (Player = 'Larry Joe Bird')
```

delete

Removes records that match specified criteria:

```
delete from database
    where (cond1 OPERATOR value1)
    [and|or cond2 OPERATOR value2 ...]
```

Example:

```
delete from my_db
    where (Player =~ /Johnson$/i) or
          (Years > 12)
```

alter

Simplified version of SQL-92 counterpart.

Removes the specified column from the database. The other standard SQL functions for **alter table** are not supported:

```
alter table database
    drop column column-name
```

Example:

```
alter table my_db
    drop column Championships
```

insert

Inserts a record into the database:

```
insert into database
    (col1, col2, ... coln)
values
    (val1, val2, ... valn)
```

Example:
```
insert into my_db
    (Player, Years, Points, Championships)
values
    ('Kareem Abdul-Jabbar', 21, 27, 5)
```
Note: You do not have to specify all of the fields in the database! Sprite also does not require you to specify the fields in the same order as that of the database.

You should make it a habit to quote strings.

Methods

Here are the four methods that are available:

set_delimiter

> The set_delimiter function sets the read and write delimiter for the SQL command. The delimiter is not limited to one character; you can have a string and even a regexp (for reading only).
>
> *Return Value*
> > None

set_os

> The set_os function can be used to notify Sprite as to the operating system that you're using. Valid arguments are: UNIX, VMS, MSDOS, NT, and MacOS. UNIX is the default.
>
> *Return Value*
> > The previous OS value

sql

> The sql function is used to pass a SQL command to this module. All of the SQL commands described above are supported. The select SQL command returns an array containing the data, where the first element is the status. All of the other other SQL commands simply return a status.
>
> *Return Value*
> > 1: Success; 0: Error

close

> The close function closes the file and destroys the database object. You can pass a filename to the function, in which case Sprite will save the database to that file.
>
> *Return Value*
> > None

Examples

Here are two simple examples that illustrate some of the functions of this module:

Example 1
```
#!/usr/local/bin/perl5
use Sprite;
$rdb = new Sprite ();
# Sets the read delimiter to a comma (,) character. The delimiter
# is not limited to one character; you can have a string, or even
# a regexp.
$rdb->set_delimiter ("Read", ",");
# Retrieves all records that match the criteria.
```

```
@data = $rdb->sql (<<End_of_Query);
    select * from /shishir/nba
        where (Points > 25)
End_of_Query
# Close the database and destroy the database object (i.e $rdb).
# Since we did not pass a argument to this function, the data
# is not updated in any manner.
$rdb->close ();
# The first element of the array indicates the status.
$status = shift (@data);
$no_records = scalar (@data);
if (!$status) {
    die "Sprite database error. Check your query!", "\n";
} elsif (!$no_records) {
    print "There are no records that match your criteria!", "\n";
    exit (0);
} else {
    print "Here are the records that match your criteria: ", "\n";
    # The database returns a record where each field is
    # separated by the "\0" character.
    foreach $record (@data) {
        $record =~ s/\0/,/g;
        print $record, "\n";
    }
}
```

Example 2

```
#!/usr/local/bin/perl5
use Sprite;
$rdb = new Sprite ();
$rdb->set_delimiter ("Read", ",");
# Deletes all records that match the specified criteria. If the
# query contains an error, Sprite returns a status of 1.
$rdb->sql (<<Delete_Query)
            || die "Database Error. Check your query", "\n";
    delete from /shishir/nba
        where (Rebounds <= 5)
Delete_Query
# Access the database again! This time, select all the records that
# match the specified criteria. The database is updated internally
# after the previous delete statement.
# Notice the fact that the full path to the database does not
# need to specified after the first SQL command. This
# works correctly as of version 3.1.
@data = $rdb->sql (<<End_of_Query);
    select Player from nba
        where (Points > 25)
End_of_Query
# Sets the write delimiter to the (:) character, and outputs the
# updated information to the file: "nba.new". If you do not pass
# an argument to the close function after you update the database,
# the modified information will not be saved.
$rdb->set_delimiter ("Write", ":");
$rdb->close ("nba.new");
```

```
    # The first element of the array indicates the status.
    $status = shift (@data);
    $no_records = scalar (@data);
    if (!$status) {
        die "Sprite database error. Check your query!", "\n";
    } elsif (!$no_records) {
        print "There are no records that match your criteria!", "\n";
        exit (0);
    } else {
        print "Here are the records that match your criteria: ", "\n";
        # The database returns a record where each field is
        # separated by the "\0" character.
        foreach $record (@data) {
            $record =~ s/\0/,/g;
            print $record, "\n";
        }
    }
```

Advantages

Here are the advantages of Sprite over mSQL by David Hughes available on the Net:

- It allows for column names to be specified in the **update** command.
- Perl's Regular Expressions allows for powerful pattern matching.
- The database is stored as text. (Very important! Information can be added/modified/ removed with a text editor.)
- It can add/delete columns quickly and easily.

Disadvantages

Here are the disadvantages of Sprite compared to mSQL:

In performance speed, Sprite comes nowhere close to mSQL. Sprite was designed to be used to manipulate very small databases (~1000–2000 records).

It does not have the ability to "join" multiple tables (databases) during a search operation. This will be added soon!

Restrictions

- If a value for a field contains the comma (,) character or the field delimiter, then you need to quote the value. Here is an example:

    ```
    insert into $database
    (One, Two)
    values
    ('$some_value', $two)
    ```

    The information in the variable **$some_value** *might* contain the delimiter, so it is quoted—you can use either the single quote (') or the double quote (").

- All single quotes and double quotes within a value must be escaped. Looking back at the previous example, if you think the variable **$some_value** contains quotes, do the following:

    ```
    $some_value =~ s/([A If a field's value contains a new line
    character, you need to convert the new line to some other
    character (or string):
    $some_value =~ s/\n/<BR>/g;
    ```

- If you want to search a field by using a regular expression:

```
select * from $database
    where (Player =~ /Bird/i)
```

- the only delimiter you are allowed is the standard one (i.e /../). You *cannot* use any other delimeter:

```
select * from $database
    where (Player =~ m|Bird|i)
```

- Field names can only be made up of the following characters:

```
"A-Z", "a-z", and "_"
```

In other words,

```
[A-Za-z_]
```

- If your update value contains parentheses, you need to escape them:

```
$rdb->sql (<<End_of_Query);
update my_db
    set Phone = ('\\(111\\) 222 3333')
    where (Name = /Gundavaram\$/i)
End_of_Query
```

Notice how the "$" (matches end of line) is escaped as well!

See Also

RDB (available at the Metronet Perl archive)

Acknowledgements

I would like to thank the following people for finding bugs and offering suggestions:

Dave Moore (*dmoore@videoactv.com*), Shane Hutchins (*hutchins@ctron.com*), Josh Hochman (*josh@bcdinc.com*), Barry Harrison (*barryh@topnet.net*), Lisa Farley (*lfarley@segue.com*), Loyd Gore (*lgore@ascd.org*), Tanju Cataltepe (*tanju@netlabs.net*).

Copyright

Sybase::BCP—simple front end to the Sybase BCP API

Synopsis

```
use Sybase::BCP;
$bcp = new Sybase::BCP ...;
```

```
$bcp->config(...);
$bcp->run;
```

Description

The Sybase::BCP module serves as a simplified front end for Sybase's Bulk Copy library. It is sub-classed from the Sybase::DBlib module, so all the features of the Sybase::DBlib module are available in addition to the specific Sybase::BCP methods.

So how does it work?

Let's say we want to copy the contents of a filename *foo.bcp* into the table *mydb.dbo.bar*. The fields in the file are separated by a '|'.

```
#!/usr/local/bin/perl
use Sybase::BCP;
$bcp = new Sybase::BCP $user, $passwd;
$bcp->config(INPUT => 'foo.bcp',
             OUTPUT => 'mydb.dbo.bar',
             SEPARATOR => '|');
$bcp->run;
```

That's it!

Of course, there are several things you can do to cater for non-standard input files (see "Configuration Parameters," below).

Features

- Automatic conversions from non-standard date formats.
- Automatic retries of failed batches.

  If there are errors in the input file, or if there are duplicate rows that are rejected, the invalid rows are stored in an error log file, and the batch is retried, so that only the failed rows are not uploaded.

- Handles column reordering and/or skipping of unneeded data.
- Row- or column-based callbacks.
- Allows vetoing of rows, or arbitrary processing of data on input.

Methods

$bcp = new Sybase::BCP [*$user*[, *$password* [, *$server* [, *$appname*]]]]

Allocate a new BCP handle. Opens a new connection to Sybase via the Sybase::DBlib module, and enables BCP IN on this handle.

$bcp->config([*parameters*])

Sets up the Bulk Copy operation. See "Configuration Parameters" below for details.

$bcp->describe(*$colid*, {*parameters*})

Adds a specific configuration element for column $colid. Columns are numbered starting at 1, as is standard in the Sybase APIs.

$bcp->run

Perform the BCP operation, returns the actual number of rows sent to the server.

Configuration Parameters

The general form for configuration is to pass (**parameter** => **value**) pairs via the config() or describe() methods. Some parameters take slightly more complex arguments (see REORDER).

Parameters for config()

DIRECTION

The direction in which the bulkcopy operation is done. Can be IN or OUT. Default: IN (Note: OUT is not implemented yet.)

INPUT

Where BCP should take its input from. It's a filename for `bcp IN`, and a table name for `bcp OUT`.

For `bcp IN INPUT` can also be a reference to a perl subroutine that returns the array to be inserted via `bcp_sendrow()`.

OUTPUT

Where BCP should place it's output. It's a table name for `bcp IN`, and a file-name for `bcp OUT`.

ERRORS

The file where invalid rows should be recorded. Default: *bcp.err.*

SEPARATOR

The pattern that separates fields in the input file, or that should be used to separate fields in the output file. Default: TAB.

FIELDS

Number of fields in the input file for `bcp IN` operations. Default: Number of fields found in the first line. This parameter is ignored for `bcp OUT`.

BATCH_SIZE

Number of rows to be batched together before committing to the server for `bcp IN` operations. Defaults to 100. If there is a risk that retries could be required due to failed batches (e.g. duplicate rows/keys errors) then you should not use a large batch size: one failed row in a batch requires the entire batch to be resent.

NULL

A pattern to be used to detect NULL values in the input file. Defaults to a zero-length string.

DATE

The default format for DATE fields in the input file. The parameter should be a symbolic value representing the format. Currently, the following values are recognized: CTIME (the Unix ctime(3) format), or the numbers 0–12, 100–112, corresponding to the conversion formats defined in Table 2–4 of the *SQL Server Reference Manual.*

BCP detects `datetime` targets by looking up the target table structure in the Sybase system tables.

REORDER

The ordering of the fields in the input file does not correspond to the order of columns in the table, or there are columns that you wish to skip. The REORDER parameter takes a hash that describes the reordering operation:

```
$bcp->config(...
            REORDER => { 1 => 2,
                         3 => 1,
                         2 => 'foobar',
                         12 => 4},
        ...);
```

In this example, field 1 of the input file goes in column 2 of the table, field 3 goes in column 1, field 2 goes in the column named *foobar*, and field 12 goes in column 4. Fields 4–11 and anything beyond 12 are skipped. As you can see you can use the column *name* instead of its position. The default is to not do any reordering.

CALLBACK

The callback subroutine is called for each row (after any reordering), and allows the user to do global processing on the row, or to veto its processing. Example:

```perl
$bcp->config(...
                CALLBACK => \&row_cb,
                ...);
sub row_cb {
    my $row_ref = shift;
    # Skip rows where the first field starts with FOO:
    return undef if $$row_ref[0] =~ /^FOO/;
    1;
}
```

CONDITION

A where clause to be used in bcp OUT operations. Not implemented.

Parameters for describe()

CALLBACK

Specifies a callback for this column. The field value is passed as the first parameter, and the callback should return the value that it wants BCP to use.

Example:

```perl
$dbh->describe(2, {CALLBACK, \&col_cb});
sub col_cb {
    my $data = shift;
    # Convert to lower case...
    $data =~ tr/A-Z/a-z/;
}
```

SKIP

If this is defined then this field is skipped. This is useful if only one or two fields need to be skipped and you don't want to define a big REORDER hash to handle the skipping.

Examples:

```perl
#!/usr/local/bin/perl

use Sybase::BCP;
require 'sybutil.pl';
$bcp = new Sybase::BCP sa, undef, TROLL;
$bcp->config(INPUT => '../../Sybperl/xab',
                OUTPUT => 'excalibur.dbo.t3',
                BATCH_SIZE => 200,
                FIELDS => 4,
                REORDER => {1 => 'account',
                            3 => 'date',
                            2 => 'seq_no',
                           11 => 'broker'},
```

```
                        SEPARATOR => '|');
        $bcp->run;
```

Bugs

The current implementation seems to run about 2.5 to 3 times slower than plain **bcp**.

Author

Michael Peppler, *mpeppler@bix.com.* Send mail directly to the Sybperl mailing list (rather than to me directly) at *sybperl-l@trln.lib.unc.edu* if you have any questions.

Sybase::Login—database login widget

Description

Login is a widget that presents a dialog box to the user so that the user may enter his or her login name and password, as well as select the appropriate database and server.

One uses Login by creating a new login widget, adding at least one database via the **addDatabase** method, configuring via the **configure** method, and then getting a valid login via the **getVerification** method.

```
#!/usr/local/bin/perl -w
use Tk;
use Sybase::DBlib;
use Sybase::Login;
use strict;
my($main) = MainWindow->new;
my($Login) = $main->Login;
$Login->addDatabase('DB',      'SYBSRV1','SYB11');
$Login->addDatabase('DBBACK',  'SYBSRV1','SYB11');
$Login->configure(-User => $ENV{'USER'},
                  -ULabel => 'User Name:',
                  -Title => 'Please Login');
my($msg) = $main->Message(-text => 'Ready to go')->pack;
$main->Button(-text => 'kick me!',
              -command => sub {
                  my($pwd, $usr, $db, $srv, $mDB);
                  if ($Login->getVerification(-Force => 1)) {
                      $pwd = $Login->cget(-Password);
                      $usr = $Login->cget(-User);
                      $db = $Login->cget(-Database);
                      $srv = $Login->cget(-Server);
                      print "Results good:\n\tUser:\t\t$usr\n";
                      print "\tPassword:\t$pwd\n\tDatabase:\t$db\n";
                      print "\tServer:\t\t$srv\n";
                      print "Verifying Login...\n";
                      $mDB = Sybase::DBlib->dblogin("$usr","$pwd", "$srv");
                      $mDB->dbuse($db);
                      $mDB->dbclose;
                      print "Login worked!!!\n";
                  } else {
                      print "Login cancelled at User request.\n";
                  }
```

```
          })->pack;
$main->Button(-text => 'exit',
              -command => sub {$main->destroy;})->pack;
MainLoop;
print "And I'm on my way home!\n";
exit;
```

The user is presented with a dialog box. The focus is on the username entry if no user name has been configured; otherwise, it is on the password entry. If multiple databases have been configured, the user may select the appropriate database from the menu button. If multiple servers have been configured for the selected database, the user may select the appropriate server from the menu button.

When the user has finished entering information, she may press the OK button to attempt to login, or the Cancel button to abort the process. If the user presses the OK button, and the login succeeds, control returns to the caller. If the login fails, an error dialog box is displayed, and the user may press Retry, or may press Cancel, in which case control returns to the caller exactly as if the user had pressed Cancel at the main login screen.

When control returns to the caller, the return value will be 1 if the login was successful, or 0 if not.

A caller may define a message or error handler either before or after calling any of the methods of this object. `getCurrentVerification` will restore the handlers extant when invoked.

Methods

`getCurrentVerification;`
> Returns 1 if the current configuration will result in a valid login, 0 otherwise. No GUI is ever displayed.

`getVerification(-Force = ?);`
> If the current configuration is NOT valid, activate the login frame. This will return 1 with a valid configuration, or 0 if the user hit cancel. If the **-Force** parameter is passed as t, y, or 1, the login frame will be activated even if the current configuration is valid.

`addDatabase(Database, Server List);`
> Adds a database/server set. The first parameter is the name of the database, the second is a list of associated servers. See the code above for examples.
>
> Note that the first server in the list is the default server for that database. Further note that adding a database a second time simply alters the servers.

`clearDatabase([Database[, Database,...]]);`
> Clears the given database entries, or all databases if if none are specified.
>
> Any of the following configuration items may be set via the **configure** method, or retrieved via the **cget** method.

Author

Brent B. Powers, Merrill Lynch (B2Pi), *powers@ml.com*

Copyright

Copyright © Brent B. Powers. This code may be distributed under the same conditions as Perl itself.

Sybase::Sybperl—Sybase extensions to Perl

Synopsis

```
use Sybase::DBlib;
use Sybase::CTlib;
use Sybase::Sybperl;
```

Description

Sybperl implements three Sybase extension modules to Perl (version 5.002 or higher). Sybase::DBlib adds a subset of the Sybase DB-Library API. Sybase::CTlib adds a subset of the Sybase CT-Library (aka the Client Library) API. Sybase::Sybperl is a backwards compatibility module (implemented on top of Sybase::DBlib) to enable scripts written for Sybperl 1.0xx to run with Perl 5. Using both the Sybase::Sybperl and Sybase::DBlib modules explicitly in a single script is not garanteed to work correctly.

The general usage format for both Sybase::DBlib and Sybase::CTlib is this:

```
use Sybase::DBlib;
# Allocate a new connection, usually refered to as a database handle
$dbh = new Sybase::DBlib username, password;
# Set an attribute for this dbh:
$dbh->{UseDateTime} = TRUE;
# Call a method with this dbh:
$dbh->dbcmd(sql code);
```

The DBPROCESS or CS_CONNECTION that is opened with the call to **new()** is automatically closed when the $dbh goes out of scope:

```
sub run_a_query {
    my $dbh = new Sybase::CTlib $user, $passwd;
    my @dat = $dbh->ct_sql("select * from sysusers");
    return @dat;
}
# The $dbh is automatically closed when we exit the subroutine.
```

Attributes

The Sybase::DBlib and Sybase::CTlib modules make a use of attributes that are either package-global or associated with a specific $dbh. These attributes control certain behavior aspects, and are also used to store status information.

Package-global attributes can be set using the %Att hash table in either modules. The %Att variable is not exported, so it must be fully qualified:

```
$Sybase::DBlib::Att{UseDateTime} = TRUE;
```

Note: setting an attribute via the %Att variable does *not* change the status of currently allocated database handles.

In this version, the available attributes for a $dbh are set when the $dbh is created. You can't add arbitrary attributes during the life of the $dbh. This has been done to implement a stricter behavior and to catch attribute errors.

It *is* possible to add your own attributes to a $dbh at creation time. The Sybase::BCP module adds two attributes to the normal Sybase::DBlib attribute set by passing an additional attribute variable to the Sybase::DBlib new() call:

```
$d = new Sybase::DBlib $user,$passwd,$server,
                $appname, {Global => {}, Cols => {}};
```

DateTime, Money and Numeric Data Behavior

As of version 2.04, the Sybase DATETIME and MONEY datatypes can be kept in their native formats in both the Sybase::DBlib and Sybase::CTlib modules. In addition, NUMERIC or DECIMAL values can also be kept in their native formats when using the Sybase::CTlib module. This behavior is normally turned off by default, because there is a performance penalty associated with it. It is turned on by using package or database handle specific attributes.

Please see "Special Handling of DATETIME, MONEY, and NUMERIC/DECIMAL Values" below for details.

Compatibility with Sybase Open Client Documentation

In general, I have tried to make the calls in this package behave the same way as their C language equivalents. In certain cases the parameters are different, and certain calls (dblogin() for example) don't do the same thing in C as in Perl. This has been done to make the life of the Perl programmer easier.

You should, if possible, have the Sybase Open Client documentation available when writing Sybperl programs.

Sybase::DBlib

A generic Perl script using Sybase::DBlib would look like this:

```
use Sybase::DBlib;
$dbh = new Sybase::DBlib 'sa', $pwd, $server, 'test_app';
$dbh->dbcmd("select * from sysprocesses\n");
$dbh->dbsqlexec;
$dbh->dbresults;
while(@data = $dbh->dbnextrow)
{
.... do something with @data ....
}
```

The API calls that have been implemented use the same calling sequence as their C equivalents, with a couple of exceptions, detailed below.

Please see also "Common Sybase::DBlib and Sybase::CTlib routines" below.

List of API Calls

Following is a list of all the API calls for the DBlib module.

Standard Routines

$dbh = new Sybase::DBlib [$user [, $server [, $appname [, {additional attributes}]]]]

$dbh = Sybase::DBlib->dblogin([$user [, $pwd [, $server [, $appname, [{additional attributes}]]]]])

Initiates a connection to a Sybase dataserver, using the supplied user, password, server and application name information. Uses the default values (see DBSETLUSER(), DBSETLPWD(), etc. in the Sybase DB-library documentation) if the parameters are omitted.

Both forms of the call are identical.

This call can be used multiple times if connecting to multiple servers with different username/password combinations is required, for example.

The additional attributes parameter allows you to define application specific attributes that you wish to associate with the $dbh.

$dbh = Sybase::DBlib->dbopen([$server [, $appname, [{attributes}]]])

Opens an additional connection, using the current LOGINREC information.

$status = $dbh->dbuse($database)

Executes use database $database for the connection $dbh.

$status = $dbh->dbcmd($sql_cmd)

Appends the string $sql_cmd to the current command buffer of this connection.

$status = $dbh->dbsqlexec

Sends the content of the current command buffer to the dataserver for execution. See the DB-library documentation for a discussion of return values.

$status = $dbh->dbresults

Retrieves result information from the dataserver after having executed dbsqlexec().

$status = $dbh->dbcancel

Cancels the current command batch.

$status = $dbh->dbcanquery

Cancels the current query within the currently executing command batch.

$dbh->dbfreebuf

Frees the command buffer (required only in special cases—if you don't know what this is you probably don't need it :-)).

$dbh->dbclose

Forces the closing of a connection. Note that connections are automatically closed when the $dbh goes out of scope.

$dbh->DBDEAD

Returns TRUE if the DBPROCESS has been marked *DEAD* by *DBlibrary*.

$status = $dbh->DBCURCMD

Returns the number of the currently executing command in the command batch. The first command is number 1.

$status = $dbh->DBMORECMDS

Returns TRUE if there are additional commands to be executed in the current command batch.

$status = $dbh->DBCMDROW

Returns SUCCEED if the current command can return rows.

$status = $dbh->DBROWS

Returns SUCCEED if the current command did return rows.

$status = $dbh->DBCOUNT

Returns the number of rows that the current command affected.

$row_num = $dbh->DBCURROW

Returns the number (counting from 1) of the currently retrieved row in the current result set.

$status = $dbh->dbhasretstat

> Did the last executed stored procedure return a status value? **dbhasretstats** must only be called after **dbresults** returns NO_MORE_RESULTS, i.e., after all the select, insert, and update operations of the stored procedure have been processed.

$status = $dbh->dbretstatus

> Retrieves the return status of a stored procedure. As with **dbhasretstat**, call this function after all the result sets of the stored procedure have been processed.

$status = $dbh->dbnumcols

> Returns the number of columns in the current result set.

$status = $dbh->dbcoltype(*$colid*)

> Returns the column type of column *$colid* in the current result set.

$status = $dbh->dbcollen(*$colid*)

> Returns the length (in bytes) of column *$colid* in the current result set.

$string = $dbh->dbcolname(*$colid*)

> Returns the name of column *$colid* in the current result set.

@dat = $dbh->dbnextrow([*$doAssoc*])

> Retrieves one row. **dbnextrow()** returns an array of scalars, one for each column value. If *$doAssoc* is non-zero, then **dbnextrow()** returns a hash (a.k.a. associative array) with column name/value pairs. This relieves the programmer from having to call **dbbind()** or **dbdata()**. The return value of the C version of **dbnextrow()** can be accessed via the Perl DBPROCESS attribute field, as in:

```
@arr = $dbh->dbnextrow;              # read results
if($dbh->{DBstatus} != REG_ROW) {
  take some appropriate action...
}
```

> When the results row is a COMPUTE row, the `ComputeID` field of the DBPROCESS is set:

```
@arr = $dbh->dbnextrow;              # read results
if($dbh->{ComputeID} != 0) { # it's a 'compute by' row
  take some appropriate action...
}
```

> **dbnextrow()** can also return a hash keyed on the column name:

```
$dbh->dbcmd("select Name=name, Id = id from test_table");
$dbh->dbsqlexec; $dbh->dbresults;
while(%arr = $dbh->dbnextrow(1)) {
    print "$arr{Name} : $arr{Id}\n";
}
```

@dat = $dbh->dbretdata[*$doAssoc*])

> Retrieves the value of the parameters marked as OUTPUT in a stored procedure. If *$doAssoc* is non-zero, then retrieve the data as an associative array with parameter name/value pairs.

$string = $dbh->dbstrcpy

> Retrieves the contents of the command buffer.

```
$ret = $dbh->dbsetopt($opt [, $c_val [, $i_val]])
```
Sets option *$opt* with optional character parameter *$c_val* and optional integer parameter *$i_val*. *$opt* is one of the option values defined in the Sybase DBlibrary manual (e.g., DBSHOWPLAN, DBTEXTSIZE). For example, to set SHOWPLAN on, you would use:

```
$dbh->dbsetopt(DBSHOWPLAN);
```
See also dbclropt() and dbisopt() below.

```
$ret = $dbh->dbclropt($opt [, $c_val])
```
Clears the option *$opt*, previously set using dbsetopt().

```
$ret = $dbh->dbisopt($opt [, $c_val])
```
Returns TRUE if the option *$opt* is set.

```
$string = $dbh->dbsafestr($string [,$quote_char])
```
Converts *$string* to a "safer" version by inserting single or double quotes where appropriate, so that it can be passed to the dataserver without syntax errors.

The second argument to dbsafestr() (normally DBSINGLE, DBDOUBLE, or DBBOTH) has been replaced with a literal ' or " (meaning DBSINGLE or DBDOUBLE, respectively). Omitting this argument means DBBOTH.

```
$status = $dbh->dbwritetext($colname, $dbh_2, $colnum, $text [,
$log])
```
Inserts, or updates, data in a TEXT or IMAGE column. The usage is a bit different from that of the C version; the calling sequence is different, and logging is off by default.

$dbh_2 and *$colnum* are the DBPROCESS and column number of a currently active query. Example:

```
$dbh_2->dbcmd('select the_text,
              t_index from text_table where t_index = 5');
$dbh_2->dbsqlexec; $dbh_2->dbresults;
@data = $dbh_2->dbnextrow;
$d->dbwritetext ("text_table.the_text", $dbh_2, 1,
    "This is text which was added with Sybperl", TRUE);
```

```
$packet_size = $dbh->dbgetpacket
```
Returns the TDS packet size currently in use for this *$dbh*.

BCP Routines

See also the Sybase::BCP module.

```
BCP_SETL($state)
```
This is an exported routine (i.e., it can be called without a *$dbh* handle) which sets the BCP IN flag to TRUE/FALSE.

It is necessary to call BCP_SETL(TRUE) before opening the connection with which one wants to run a BCP IN operation.

```
$state = bcp_getl
```
Retrieves the current BCP flag status.

```
$status = $dbh->bcp_init($table, $hfile, $errfile, $direction)
```
Initializes the BCP library. *$direction* can be DB_OUT or DB_IN.

`$status = $dbh->bcp_meminit(`*`$numcols`*`)`

This is a utility function that does not exist in the normal BCP API. Its use is to initialize some internal variables before starting a BCP operation from program variables into a table. This call avoids setting up translation information for each of the columns of the table being updated, obviating the use of the `bcp_colfmt` call.

See information on Examples, below.

`$status = $dbh->bcp_sendrow(`*`LIST`*`)`
`$status = $dbh->bcp_sendrow(`*`ARRAY_REF`*`)`

Sends the data in *LIST* to the server. The *LIST* is assumed to contain one element for each column being updated. To send a NULL value, set the appropriate element to the Perl undef value.

In the second form you pass an array reference instead of passing the *LIST*, which makes processing a little bit faster on wide tables.

`$rows = $dbh->bcp_batch`

Commits rows to the database. You usually use it like this:

```
while(<IN>) {
    chop;
    @data = split(/\|/);
    $d->bcp_sendrow(\@data);    # Pass the array reference
    # Commit data every 100 rows.
    if((++$count % 100) == 0) {
            $d->bcp_batch;
    }
}
```

`$status = $dbh->bcp_done`
`$status = $dbh->bcp_control(`*`$field`*`, `*`$value`*`)`
`$status = $dbh->bcp_columns(`*`$colcount`*`)`
`$status = $dbh->bcp_colfmt(`*`$host_col`*`, `*`$host_type`*`, `*`$host_`*`
`prefixlen`*`, `*`$host_collen`*`, `*`$host_term`*`, `*`$host_termlen`*`, `*`$table_`*`
`col`* `[, `*`$precision`*`, `*`$scale`*`])`

If you have DBlibrary for System 10 or higher, then you can pass the additional *$precision* and *$scale* parameters, and have Sybperl call `bcp_colfmt_ps()` instead of `bcp_colfmt()`.

`$status = $dbh->bcp_collen(`*`$varlen`*`, `*`$table_column`*`)`
`$status = $dbh->bcp_exec`
`$status = $dbh->bcp_readfmt(`*`$filename`*`)`
`$status = $dbh->bcp_writefmt(`*`$filename`*`)`

Please see the DB-library documentation for these calls.

DBMONEY Routines

Note: In this version it is possible to avoid calling the routines below and still get DBMONEY calculations done with the correct precision. See the Sybase::DBlib::Money discussion below.

```
($status, $sum) = $dbh->dbmny4add($m1, $m2)
$status = $dbh->dbmny4cmp($m1, $m2)
($status, $quotient) = $dbh->dbmny4divide($m1, $m2)
($status, $dest) = $dbh->dbmny4minus($source)
($status, $product) = $dbh->dbmny4mul($m1, $m2)
($status, $difference) = $dbh->dbmny4sub($m1, $m2)
($status, $ret) = $dbh->dbmny4zero
($status, $sum) = $dbh->dbmnyadd($m1, $m2)
$status = $dbh->dbmnycmp($m1, $m2)
($status, $ret) = $dbh->dbmnydec($m1)
($status, $quotient) = $dbh->dbmnydivide($m1, $m2)
($status, $ret, $remainder) = $dbh->dbmnydown($m1, $divisor)
($status, $ret) = $dbh->dbmnyinc($m1)
($status, $ret, $remain) = $dbh->dbmnyinit($m1, $trim)
($status, $ret) = $dbh->dbmnymaxneg
($status, $ret) = $dbh->dbmnymaxpos
($status, $dest) = $dbh->dbmnyminus($source)
($status, $product) = $dbh->dbmnymul($m1, $m2)
($status, $m1, $digits, $remain) = $dbh->dbmnyndigit($m1)
($status, $ret) = $dbh->dbmnyscale($m1, $multiplier, $addend)
($status, $difference) = $dbh->dbmnysub($m1, $m2)
($status, $ret) = $dbh->dbmnyzero
```

All of these routines correspond to their DB-library counterpart, with the following exception: the routines which in the C version take pointers to arguments (in order to return values) return these values in an array instead:

```
status = dbmnyadd(dbproc, m1, m2, &result) becomes
($status, $result) = $dbproc->dbmnyadd($m1, $m2)
```

RPC Routines

Note: Check out eg/rpc-example.pl for an example on how to use these calls.

$dbh->dbrpcinit($rpcname, $option)

Initialize an RPC call to the remote procedure *$rpcname*. See the DB-library manual for valid values for *$option*.

$dbh->dbrpcparam($parname, $status, $type, $maxlen, $datalen, $value)

Add a parameter to an RPC call initiated with dbrpcinit(). Please see the *DB-library* manpage for details and values for the parameters.

Note: All floating-point types (MONEY, FLOAT, REAL, DECIMAL, etc.) are converted to FLOAT before being sent to the RPC.

$dbh->dbrpcsend

Execute an RPC initiated with dbrpcinit().

Note: This call executes both dbrpcsend() and dbsqlok(). You can call $dbh->dbresults direcly after calling $dbh->dbrpcsend.

dbrpwset($srvname, $pwd)

Set the password for connecting to a remote server.

dbrpwclr

Clear all remote server passwords.

Two-Phase Commit Routines

```
$dbh = Sybase::DBlib->open_commit($user, $pwd, $server, $appname)
$id = $dbh->start_xact($app_name, $xact_name, $site_count)
$status = $dbh->stat_xact($id)
$status = $dbh->scan_xact($id)
$status = $dbh->commit_xact($id)
$status = $dbh->abort_xact($id)
$dbh->close_commit
$string = Sybase::DBlib::build_xact_string($xact_name, $service_
    name, $id)
$status = $dbh->remove_xact($id, $site_count)
```

> Please see the Sybase documentation for these routines.

> Note: These routines have not been thoroughly tested!

Exported Routines

```
$old_handler = dberrhandle($err_handle)
$old_handler = dbmsghandle($msg_handle)
```

> Registers an error (or message) handler for DB-library to use. Handler exam-
> ples can be found in *sybutil.pl* in the Sybperl distribution. Returns a reference
> to the previously defined handler (or undef if none were defined). Passing
> undef as the argument clears the handler.

```
dbsetifile($filename)
```

> Sets the name of the 'interfaces' file. This file is normally found by DB-library
> in the directory pointed to by the $SYBASE environment variable.

```
dbrecftos($filename)
```

> Starts recording all SQL sent to the server in file *$filename*.

```
dbversion
```

> Returns a string identifying the version of DB-library that this copy of Sybperl
> was built with.

```
DBSETLCHARSET($charset)
DBSETLNATLANG($language)
DBSETLPACKET($packet_size)
$time = DBGETTIME
$time = dbsettime($seconds)
$time = dbsetlogintime($seconds)
```

> These utility routines are probably very seldom used. See the DB-library
> manual for an explanation of their use.

```
dbexit
```

> Tell DB-library that we're done. Once this call has been made, no further
> activity requiring DB-library can be performed in the current program.

Utility Routines

These routines are not part of the DB-library API, but have been added because
they can make our life as programers easier, and exploit certain strenghts of Perl.

$ret|@ret = $dbh->sql($cmd [, \&rowcallback [, $flag]])

Runs the sql command and returns the result as a reference to an array of the rows. In a LIST context, return the array itself (instead of a reference to the array). Each row is a reference to an array of scalars.

If you provide a second parameter it is taken as a procedure to call for each row. The callback is called with the values of the row as parameters.

If you provide a third parameter, this is used in the call to dbnextrow() to retrieve associative arrays rather than 'normal' arrays for each row, and store them in the returned array. To pass the third parameter without passing the &rowcallback value you should pass the special value undef as second parameter:

```
@rows = $dbh->sql("select * from sysusers", undef, TRUE);
foreach $row_ref (@rows) {
    if($$row_ref{'uid'} == 10) {
        ....
    }
}
```

See also *eg/sql.pl* for an example.

Contributed by Gisle Aas.

Note: This routine loads all the data into memory. It should not be run with a query that returns a large number of rows. To avoid the risk of overflowing memory, you can limit the number of rows that the query returns by setting the MaxRows field of the $dbh attribute field:

```
$dbh->{'MaxRows'} = 100;
```

This value is *not* set by default.

Constants: Most of the #defines from *sybdb.h* can be accessed as Sybase::DBlib::NAME (e.g., Sybase::DBlib::STDEXIT) Additional constants are:

$Sybase::DBlib::Version

The Sybperl version. Can be interpreted as a string or as a number.

DBLIBVS

The version of DB-library that Sybperl was built against.

Attributes

The behavior of certain aspects of the Sybase::CTlib module can be controlled via global or connection specific attributes. The global attributes are stored in the %Sybase::DBlib::Att variable, and the connection-specific attributes are stored in the $dbh. To set a global attribute, you would code:

$Sybase::CTlib::Att{'AttributeName'} = value;

and to set a connection-specific attribute you would code:

$dbh->{"AttributeName'} = value;

Warning

Global attribute setting changes do not affect existing connections, and changing an attribute inside a ct_fetch() does *not* change the behavior of the data retrieval during that ct_fetch() loop.

The following attributes are currently defined:

dbNullIsUndef

> If set, NULL results are returned as the Perl undef value, otherwise as the string NULL. Default: set.

dbKeepNumeric

> If set, numeric results are not converted to strings before returning the data to Perl. Default: set.

dbBin0x

> If set, BINARY results are preceded by '0x' in the result. Default: unset.

useDateTime

> Turns the special handling of DATETIME values on. Default: unset. See the section on special datatype handling below.

useMoney

> Turns the special handling of MONEY values on. Default: unset. See the section on special datatype handling below.

Status Variables

These status variables are set by Sybase::DBlib internal routines, and can be accessed using the `$dbh->{'variable'}` syntax.

DBstatus

> The return status of the last call to **dbnextrow**.

ComputeID

> The compute ID of the current returned row. Is 0 if no COMPUTE BY clause is currently being processed.

Examples

BCP from program variables

> See also Sybase::BCP for a simplified bulk copy API.

```
&BCP_SETL(TRUE);
$dbh = new Sybase::DBlib $User, $Password;
$dbh->bcp_init("test.dbo.t2", '', '', DB_IN);
$dbh->bcp_meminit(3);    # we wish to copy three columns into
                         # the 't2' table
while(<>)
{
    chop;
    @dat = split(' ', $_);
    $dbh->bcp_sendrow(@dat);
}
$ret = $dbh->bcp_done;
Using the sql() routine
$dbh = new Sybase::DBlib;
$ret = $dbh->sql("select * from sysprocesses");
foreach (@$ret)    # Loop through each row
{
    @row = @$_;
    # do something with the data row...
}
$ret = $dbh->sql("select * from sysusers",
                 sub { print "@_"; });
# This will select all the info from sysusers, and print it
```

Getting SHOWPLAN and STATISTICS information within a script

You can get SHOWPLAN and STATISTICS information when you run a Sybperl script. To do so, you must first turn on the respective options, using dbsetopt(), and then you need a special message handler that will filter the SHOWPLAN and/ or STATISTICS messages sent from the server.

The following message handler differentiates the SHOWPLAN or STATICSTICS messages from other messages:

```perl
# Message number 3612-3615 are statistics time / statistics io
# message. Showplan messages are numbered 6201-6225.
# (I hope I haven't forgotten any...)
@sh_msgs = (3612 .. 3615, 6201 .. 6225);
@showplan_msg{@sh_msgs} = (1) x scalar(@sh_msgs);
sub showplan_handler {
    my ($db, $message, $state, $severity, $text,
        $server, $procedure, $line) = @_;

    # Don't display 'informational' messages:
    if ($severity > 10) {
        print STDERR ("Sybase message ", $message, ",
            Severity ", $severity, ", state ", $state);
        print STDERR ("\nServer '", $server, "'")
            if defined ($server);
        print STDERR ("\nProcedure '", $procedure, "'")
            if defined ($procedure);
        print STDERR ("\nLine ", $line) if defined ($line);
        print STDERR ("\n    ", $text, "\n\n");
    }
    elsif($showplan_msg{$message}) {
    # This is a HOWPLAN or STATISTICS message, so print it out:
        print STDERR ($text, "\n");
    }
    elsif ($message == 0) {
        print STDERR ($text, "\n");
    }

    0;
}
```

This could then be used like this:

```perl
use Sybase::DBlib;
dbmsghandle(\&showplan_handler);
$dbh = new Sybase::DBlib 'mpeppler', $password, 'TROLL';
$dbh->dbsetopt(DBSHOWPLAN);
$dbh->dbsetopt(DBSTAT, "IO");
$dbh->dbsetopt(DBSTAT, "TIME");
$dbh->dbcmd("select * from xrate where date = '951001'");
$dbh->dbsqlexec;
while($dbh->dbresults != NO_MORE_RESULTS) {
    while(@dat = $dbh->dbnextrow) {
        print "@dat\n";
    }
}
```

Et voila!

Bugs

The 2PC calls have not been well tested.

Sybase::Sybperl

The Sybase::Sybperl package is designed for backwards compatibility with Sybperl 1.0xx (for Perl 4.x). Its main purpose is to allow Sybperl 1.0xx scripts to work unchanged with Perl 5 & Sybperl 2. Using this API for new scripts is not recommended, unless portability with older versions of Sybperl is essential.

The *sybperl 1.0xx* manpage is included in this package in *pod/sybperl-1.0xx.man.*

Sybase::Sybperl is layered on top of the Sybase::DBlib package, and could therefore suffer a small performance penalty.

Sybase::CTlib

The CT-library module has been written in collaboration with Sybase. It is still in Beta.

Description

```
$dbh = new Sybase::CTlib $user [, $passwd [, $server [, $appname [,
    {attributes}]
$dbh = Sybase::CTlib->ct_connect($user [, $passwd [, $server
    [,$appname, [{attributes}]]]]])
```

Establishes a connection to the database engine. Initializes and allocates resources for the connection, and registers the username, password, target server and application name.

Additional attributes can be set by passing a hash reference.

```
$status = $dbh->ct_execute($sql)
```

Sends the SQL commands *$sql* to the server. Multiple commands are allowed. However, you must call **ct_results()** until it returns CS_END_RESULTS or CS_FAIL, or call **ct_cancel()** before submitting a new set of SQL commands to the server.

Return values

CS_SUCCEED, CS_FAIL, or CS_CANCELED (the operation was canceled).

Note: **ct_execute()** is equivalent to calling **ct_command()** followed by **ct_send()**.

```
$status = $dbh->ct_command(type, buffer, len, option)
```

Appends a command to the current SQL command buffer. Please check the **Open-Client** documentation for exact usage.

Note: You should only need to call **ct_command()**/**ct_send()** directly if you want to do RPCs or cursor operations. For straight queries you should use **ct_execute()** or **ct_sql()** instead.

```
$status = $dbh->ct_send
```

Sends the current command buffer to the server for execution.

Note: You only need to call **ct_send()** directly if you've used **ct_command()** to set up your SQL query. ·

```
$status = $dbh->ct_results($res_type)
```

This routine returns a results type to indicate the status of returned data. "Command Done:" result type is returned if one result set has been processed.

"Row result" token is returned if regular rows are returned. This output is stored in *$res_type*.

The commonly used values for *$res_type* are CS_ROW_RESULT, CS_CMD_ DONE, CS_CMD_SUCCEED, CS_COMPUTE_RESULT, CS_CMD_FAIL. The full list of values is on page 3–203 OpenClient reference manual.

See also the description of `ct_fetchable()` below.

The $status value takes the following values: CS_SUCCEED, CS_END_RESULTS, CS_FAIL, CS_CANCELED.

@names = $dbh->ct_col_names

Retrieves the column names of the current query. If the current query is not a SELECT statement, then an empty array is returned.

@types = $dbh->ct_col_types([*$doAssoc*])

Retrieves the column types of the currently executing query. If *$doAssoc* is non–0, then a hash (aka associative array) is returned with column names/column type pairs.

@data = $dbh->ct_describe([*$doAssoc*])

Retrieves the description of each of the output columns of the current result set. Each element of the returned array is a reference to a hash that describes the column. The following fields are set: NAME, TYPE, MAXLENGTH, SCALE, PRECI- SION, STATUS.

You could use it like this:

```
$dbh->ct_execute("select name, uid from sysusers");
while(($rc = $dbh->ct_results($restype)) == CS_SUCCEED) {
    next unless $dbh->ct_fetchable($restype);
    @desc = $dbh->ct_describe;
    print "$desc[0]->{NAME}\n";        # prints 'name'
    print "$desc[0]->{MAXLENGTH}\n";   # prints 30
    ....
}
```

The STATUS field is a bitmask which can be tested for the following values: CS_ CANBENULL, CS_HIDDEN, CS_IDENTITY, CS_KEY, CS_VERSION_KEY, CS_ TIMESTAMP, and CS_UPDATEABLE. See Table 3-46 of the *Open Client Client- Library/C Reference Manual* for a description of each of these values.

@data = $dbh->ct_fetch([*$doAssoc*])

Retrieves one row of data. If *$doAssoc* is non–0, a hash is returned with column name/value pairs.

An empty array is returned if there is no data to fetch.

$dbh->ct_cancel(*$type*)

Issues an attention signal to the server about the current transaction. If *$type* == CS_CANCEL_ALL, then cancels the current command immediately. If *$type* == CS_CANCEL_ATTN, then discard all results when next time the application reads from the server.

$old_cb = ct_callback(*$type*, *$cb_func*)

Installs a callback routine. Valid callback types are CS_CLIENTMSG_CB and CS_ SERVERMSG_CB. Returns a reference to the previously installed callback of the specified type, or **undef** if no callback of that type exists. Passing undef as $cb_func unsets the callback for that type.

$res_info = $dbh->ct_res_info(*$info_type*)

Retrieves information on the current result set. The type of information returned depends on *$info_type*. Currently supported values are: CS_NUM_COMPUTES, CS_NUMDATA, CS_NUMORDERCOLS, CS_ROW_COUNT.

($status, $param) = $dbh->ct_option(*$action*, *$option*, *$param*, *$type*)

This routine will set, retrieves or clear the values of server query-processing options. Valid values for the arguments are:

$action

> CS_SET, CS_GET, CS_CLEAR

$option

> see p 3–170 of the OpenClient reference manual.

$param

> > When setting an option, *$param* can be a integer or a string. When retrieving an option, *$param* is set and returned. When clearing an option, *$param* is ignored.

$type

> > CS_INT_TYPE if *$param* is of integer type, CS_CHAR_TYPE if *$param* is a string.

$ret = $dbh->ct_cursor(*$type*, *$name*, *$text*, *$option*)

Initiates a cursor command. Usage is similar to the CTlibrary ct_cursor() call, except that when in C you would pass NULL as the value for *$name* or *$text* you pass the special Perl value **undef** instead.

See *eg/ct_cursor.pl* for an example.

$ret = $dbh->ct_param(\%*datafmt*)

Defines a command parameter. The %*datafmt* hash is used to pass the appropriate parameters to the call. The following fields are defined: name (parameter name), datatype, status, indicator, and value). These fields correspond to the equivalent fields in the CS_DATAFMT structure, which is used in the CTlibrary ct_param call, and includes the two additional parameters **value** and **indicator**.

The hash should be used like this:

```
    %param = (name => '@acc', datatype => CS_CHAR_TYPE,
              status => CS_INPUTVALUE, value => 'CIS 98941',
              indicator => CS_UNUSED);
    $dbh->ct_param(\%param);
```

Note that **ct_param()** converts all parameter types to CS_CHAR_TYPE, CS_FLOAT_TYPE, CS_DATETIME_TYPE, CS_MONEY_TYPE, or CS_INT_TYPE.

See *eg/ct_param.pl* for an example.

$dbh2 = $dbh->ct_cmd_alloc

Allocates a new CS_COMMAND structure. The new $dbh2 shares the CS_CONNECTION with the original $dbh, so this is really only useful for interleaving cursor operations (see **ct_cursor()** above, and the section on cursors in Chapter 2 of the *Open Client Client-Library/C Reference Manual*.

The attributes values are copied from $dbh to $dbh2.

$rc = $dbh->ct_cmd_realloc

> Drops the current *CS_COMMAND* structure, and reallocates a new one. Returns CS_SUCCEED on successful completion.

$ret = ct_config($action, $property, $value)

> Calls ct_config() to change some basic parameter, like the interfaces file location. Valid values for the arguments are:

> *$action*
>> CS_SET or CS_GET.

> *$property*
>> Settable via ct_config() (see your *OpenClient* manpage on ct_config() for a complete list).

> *$value*
>> The input value if *$action* is CS_GET, and the output value if *$action* is CS_GET.

> *$ret*
>> The return status of the ct_config() call.

> Example:
> ```
> $ret = ct_config(CS_SET, CS_IFILE, "/home/mpeppler/foo");
> print "$ret\n";
> $ret = ct_config(CS_GET, CS_IFILE, $out);
> print "$ret - $out\n";   #prints 1 - /home/mpeppler/foo
> ```

$ret|@ret = $dbh->ct_sql($cmd [, \&rowcallback [, $doAssoc]])

> Runs the sql command and returns the result as a reference to an array of the rows. Each row is a reference to an array of scalars. In a LIST context, ct_sql returns an array of references to each row.

> If the *$doAssoc* parameter is CS_TRUE, then each row is a reference to an associative array (keyed on the column names) rather than a normal array (see ct_fetch(), above).

> If you provide a second parameter it is taken as a procedure to call for each row. The callback is called with the values of the row as parameters.

> This routine is very useful to send SQL commands to the server that do not return rows, such as:

> ```
> $dbh->ct_sql("use BugTrack");
> ```

> Examples can be found in *eg/ct_sql.pl*.

> Note: This routine loads all the data into memory. Memory consumption can therefore become quite important for a query that returns a large number of rows, unless the MaxRows attribute has been set.

> Two additional attributes are set after calling ct_sql(): ROW_COUNT holds the number of rows affected by the command, and RC holds the return code of the last call to ct_execute().

$ret = $dbh->ct_fetchable($restype)

> Returns TRUE if the current result set has fetchable rows. Use like this:

> ```
> $dbh->ct_execute("select * from sysprocesses");
> while($dbh->ct_results($restype) == CS_SUCCEED) {
>     next if(!$dbh->ct_fetchable($restype));
> ```

```
        while(@dat = $dbh->ct_fetch) {
            print "@dat\n";
        }
    }
```

Examples

```
#!/usr/local/bin/perl
use Sybase::CTlib;
ct_callback(CS_CLIENTMSG_CB, \&msg_cb);
ct_callback(CS_SERVERMSG_CB, "srv_cb");
$uid = 'mpeppler'; $pwd = 'my-secret-password'; $srv = 'TROLL';
$X = Sybase::CTlib->ct_connect($uid, $pwd, $srv);
$X->ct_execute("select * from sysusers");
while(($rc = $X->ct_results($restype)) == CS_SUCCEED) {
    next if($restype == CS_CMD_DONE || $restype == CS_CMD_FAIL ||
            $restype == CS_CMD_SUCCEED);
    if(@names = $X->ct_col_names()) {
        print "@names\n";
    }
    if(@types = $X->ct_col_types()) {
        print "@types\n";
    }
    while(@dat = $X->ct_fetch) {
        print "@dat\n";
    }
}
print "End of Results Sets\n" if($rc == CS_END_RESULTS);
print "Error!\n" if($rc == CS_FAIL);
sub msg_cb {
    my($layer, $origin, $severity, $number, $msg, $osmsg) = @_;
    printf STDERR "\nOpen Client Message: (In msg_cb)\n";
    printf STDERR "Message number: LAYER = (%ld) ORIGIN = (%ld) ",
            $layer, $origin;
    printf STDERR "SEVERITY = (%ld) NUMBER = (%ld)\n",
            $severity, $number;
    printf STDERR "Message String: %s\n", $msg;
    if (defined($osmsg)) {
        printf STDERR "Operating System Error: %s\n", $osmsg;
    }
    CS_SUCCEED;
}
sub srv_cb {
    my($cmd, $number, $severity, $state, $line, $server,
            $proc, $msg) = @_;
    printf STDERR "\nServer message: (In srv_cb)\n";
    printf STDERR "Message number: %ld, Severity %ld, ",
            $number, $severity;
    printf STDERR "State %ld, Line %ld\n", $state, $line;
    if (defined($server)) {
        printf STDERR "Server '%s'\n", $server;
    }
    if (defined($proc)) {
        printf STDERR " Procedure '%s'\n", $proc;
    }
```

```
        printf STDERR "Message String: %s\n", $msg;   CS_SUCCEED;
    }
```

Attributes

The behavior of certain aspects of the Sybase::CTlib module can be controlled via global or connection-specific attributes. The global attributes are stored in the %Sybase::CTlib::Att variable, and the connection-specific attributes are stored in the $dbh. To set a global attribute, you would code:

```
    $Sybase::CTlib::Att{'AttributeName'} = value;
```

and to set a connection specific attribute you would code:

```
    $dbh->{"AttributeName'} = value;
```

Warning

Global attribute setting changes do not affect existing connections, and changing an attribute inside a ct_fetch() does *not* change the behavior of the data retrieval during that ct_fetch() loop.

The following attributes are currently defined:

UseDateTime
> If TRUE, then keep DATETIME data retrieved via ct_fetch() in native format instead of converting the data to a character string. Default: FALSE.

UseMoney
> If TRUE, keep MONEY data retrieved via ct_fetch() in native format instead of converting the data to double-precision floating point. Default: FALSE.

UseNumeric
> If TRUE, keep NUMERIC or DECIMAL data retrieved via ct_fetch() in native format, instead of converting to double-precision floating point. Default: FALSE.

MaxRows
> If non–0, limit the number of data rows that can be retrieved via ct_sql(). Default: 0.

Common Sybase::DBlib and Sybase::CTlib routines

$module_name::debug($bitmask)
> Turns the debugging trace on or off. The $module_name should be one of Sybase::DBlib or Sybase::CTlib. The value of $bitmask determines which features are going to be traced. The following trace bits are currently recognized:

TRACE_CREATE
> Traces all CTlib and/or DBlib object creations.

TRACE_DESTROY
> Traces all calls to DESTROY.

TRACE_SQL
> Traces all SQL language commands (i.e., calls to dbcmd(), ct_execute() or ct_command()).

TRACE_RESULTS
> Traces calls to dbresults()/ct_results().

TRACE_FETCH

>Traces calls to **dbnextrow()**/**ct_fetch()**, and traces the values that are pushed on the stack.

TRACE_CUSROR

>Traces calls to **ct_cursor()** (not available in Sybase::DBlib).

TRACE_PARAMS

>Traces calls to **ct_param()** (not implemented in Sybase::DBlib).

TRACE_OVERLOAD

>Traces all overloaded operations involving DateTime, Money or Numeric datatypes.

Two special trace flags are TRACE_NONE, which turns off debug tracing, and TRACE_ ALL which (you guessed it!) turns everything on.

The traces are pretty obscure, but they can be useful when trying to find out what is *really* going on inside the program.

For the TRACE_* flags to be available in your scripts, you must load the Sybase::??lib module with the following syntax:

```
use Sybase::CTlib qw(:DEFAULT /TRACE/);
```

This tells the autoloading mechanism to import all the default symbols, plus all the trace symbols.

Special Handling of DATETIME, MONEY, and NUMERIC/DECIMAL Values

Note: This feature is turned off by default for performance reasons. You can turn it on per datatype and **dbh**, or via the module attribute hash (%Sybase::DBlib::Att and %Sybase::CTlib::Att).

The Sybase::CTlib and Sybase::DBlib modules include special features to handle DATETIME, MONEY, and NUMERIC/DECIMAL (CTlib only) values in their native formats correctly. What this means is that when you retrieve a date using **ct_fetch()** or **dbnextrow()** it is not converted to a string, but kept in the internal format used by the Sybase libraries. You can then manipulate this date as you see fit, and in particular crack the date into its components.

The same is true for MONEY (and for CTlib NUMERIC values), which otherwise are converted to floating point values, and hence are subject to loss of precision in certain situations. Here they are stored as MONEY values, and by using operator overloading we can give you intuitive access to the **cs_calc()**/**dbmnyxxx()** routines.

This feature has been implemented by creating new classes in both Sybase::DBlib and Sybase::CTlib. These are: Sybase::DBlib::DateTime, Sybase::DBlib::Money, Sybase::CTlib::DateTime, Sybase::CTlib::Money, and Sybase::CTlib::Numeric (hereafter referred to as **DateTime**, **Money** and **Numeric**). All the examples below use the CTlib module. The syntax is identical for the DBlib module, except that the **Numeric** class does not exist.

To create data items of these types, you call:

```
$dbh = new Sybase::CTlib user, password;
...  # code deleted
# Create a new DateTime object, and initialize to Jan 1, 1995:
$date = $dbh->newdate('Jan 1 1995');
# Create a new Money object
```

```
$mny = $dbh->newmoney;          # Default value is 0
# Create a new Numeric object
$num = $dbh->newnumeric(11.111);
```

The DateTime class defines the following methods:

$date->str

Converts to string (calls cs_convert()/dbconvert()).

@arr = $date->crack

'Cracks' the date into its components.

$date->cmp($date2)

Compares $date with $date2.

$date2 = $date->calc($days, $msecs)

Adds or subtracts $days and $msecs from $date, and returns the new date.

($days, $msecs) = $date->diff($date2)

Computes the difference, in $days and $msecs between $date and $date2.

$val = $date->info($datepart)

Calls cs_dt_info to return the string representation for a $datepart. Valid dateparts are CS_MONTH, CS_SHORTMONTH and CS_DAYNAME.

Note: Not implemented in DBlib.

$time = $date->mktime
$time = $date->timelocal
$time = $date->timegm

Converts a Sybase DateTime value to a UNIX time_t value. The mktime and timelocal methods assume the date is stored in local time; timegm assumes GMT. The mktime method uses the POSIX module (note that unavailability of the POSIX module is not a fatal error.)

Both the str and the cmp methods will be called transparently when they are needed, so that:

```
print "$date"
```

will print the date string correctly, and:

```
$date1 cmp $date2
```

will do a comparison of the two dates, not the two strings.

crack executes cs_dt_crack()/dbdatecrack() on the date value, and returns the following list:

```
($year, $month, $month_day, $year_day, $week_day, $hour,
         $minute, $second, $millisecond, $time_zone) = $date->crack;
```

Compare this with the value returned by the standard Perl function localtime():

```
($sec,$min,$hour,$mday,$mon,$year,$wday,$yday,$isdst) =
                                              localtime(time);
```

In addition, the values returned for the week_day can change depending on the location that has been set.

Please see the discussion on cs_dt_crack() or dbdatecrack() in the *Open Client / Open Server Common Libraries Reference Manual*, Chapter 2.

The `Money` and `Numeric` classes define these methods:

`$mny->str`

> Converts to string (calls `cs_convert()`/`dbconvert()`).

`$mny->num`

> Converts to a floating-point number (calls `cs_convert()`/`dbconvert()`).

`$mny->cmp(`*`$mny2`*`)`

> Compares two `Money` or `Numeric` values.

`$mny->set(`*`$number`*`)`

> Sets the value of `$mny` to *`$number`*.

`$mny->calc(`*`$mny2, $op`*`)`

> Performs the calculation specified by *`$op`* on `$mny` and *`$mny2`*. `$op` is one of '+',
> '-', '*' or '/'.

As with the `DateTime` class, the `str` and `cmp` methods will be called automatically for
you when required. In addition, you can perform normal arithmetic on `Money` or
`Numeric` datatypes without calling the `calc` method explicitly.

Warning

> You must call the `set` method to assign a value to a `Money`/`Numeric` data item. If
> you use
>
> $mny = 4.05
>
> then `$mny` will lose its special `Money` or `Numeric` behavior and become a normal
> Perl data item.

When a new `Numeric` data item is created, the SCALE and PRECISION values are
determined by the initialization. If the data item is created as part of a SELECT statement, then the SCALE and PRECISION values will be those of the retrieved item. If the
item is created via the `newnumeric` method (either explicitly or implicitly) the SCALE
and PRECISION are deduced from the initializing value. For example, `$num = $dbh->`
`newnumeric(11.111)` will produce an item with a SCALE of 3 and a PRECISION of 5.
This is totally transparent to the user.

Acknowledgments

Larry Wall—for Perl

Tim Bunce and Andreas König—for all the work on MakeMaker

Jeffrey Wong for the Sybase::DBlib DBMONEY routines

Dave Bowen and Amy Lin for help with Sybase::CTlib

Author

Michael Peppler, *mpeppler@itf.ch*

Numerous folks have contributed ideas and bug fixes for which they have my undying
thanks.

The Sybperl mailing list (*sybperl-l@trln.lib.unc.edu*) is the best place to ask questions.

TABLEOp—table-level operations

Synopsis

```
use TABLEop;
$titles = new TABLEop ( $dbh, "titles" );
$titles->insert ( \%data );
$titles->update ( \%data, \%where );
$titles->delete ( \%where );
@all_rows = $titles->select (" where title_id < 10 ");
%one_row = $titles->select ( " where title_id = 4 ");
```

Description

These routines allow you to treat your data as hashes. They generate `insert`, `delete`, and `update` statments and actually run them against the server. It does the work of generating SQL for you. It puts the necessary quotes if the datatype is `char`, `datetime`, etc. Additionally you could also do SELECT and get all rows as an array of hash-references or get just one row as a single hash-reference.

Specification of table follows the usual Sybase conventions, i.e., if you did not specify an absolute name, it looks as if the user has a table by the same name. The module remembers the full pathname of the table and uses it for all operations. This avoids the risk of inadvertant changes to your application's database context.

Creating a handle

```
use TABLEop;
$titles = new TABLEop ( $dbh, "titles" );
```

Inserting

```
%data = ('title_id' => 50,
         'title' => 'Perl Book',
         'price' => 50.24,
         'pub_date' => 'Jan 1 1900' );
$titles->insert ( \%data );
```

Deleting

```
%where = ( 'title_id' => 50 );
$titles->delete ( \%where );
```

Updating

```
%data = ('title' => 'Perl New Book',
         'price' => 150.24,
         'pub_date' => 'Jan 1 2100' );
%where = ('title_id' = 50 );
$titles->update ( \%data, \%where );
```

Selecting

The SELECT behaves defferently depending on whether you are expecting one row or many rows. If you want an array, you get an array of hash-references, or you get just a single hash-reference.

```
@all_rows = $titles->select ("where title_id < 50");
```

or

```
@all_rows = $titles->select (""); #Select all the rows !
foreach $row ( @all_rows) {
    printf "title is %s\n", $row->{'title'};
}
```

or:

```
$arow = $title->select ( "where title_id = 30");
printf "The title is %s.\n", $arow->{'title'};
```

Features wanted, unwanted

Currently does not handle NULL in update/delete/insert. This will cause an error. All error handling is left to the caller. It would be nice to automatically generate single row updates by figuring out unique key columns.

Author

Manish I Shah, *mshah@bfm.com*

Velocis::SQL—Perl interface to the Raima Velocis SQL database engine

Synopsis

```
use Velocis::SQL;
$conn = db_connect($database,$user,$password)
   or die "could not connect -- ($Velocis::errorstate)
$Velocis::errorstr";
$query = $conn->execute($sql_statement)
   or die "Error -- ($Velocis::errorstate) $Velocis::errorstr";
@array = $query->fetchrow();
$val = $query->numrows();
$val = $query->numcolumns();
$val = $query->columntype($column_index);
$val = $query->columnname($column_index);
$val = $query->columnlength($column_index);
```

Description

This package is designed as close as possible to its C API counterpart. The C Programmer Guide that comes with Velocis describes most things you need.

Once you **db_connect()** to a database, you can issue commands to the **execute()** method. If either of them returns an error from the underlying API, the value returned will be **undef** and the variable $Velocis::errorstr will contain the error message from the database, and the variable $Velocis::errorstate will contain the Velocis error state.

The function **fetchrow()** returns an array of the values from the next row fetched from the server. It returns an empty list when there is no more data available. Calling **fetchrow()** on a statement handle which is *not* from a SELECT statement has undefined behavior. Other functions work identically to their similarly named C API functions.

To import all the SQL-type definitions for use with **columntype()**, use:

```
use Velocis::SQL qw(:DEFAULT :SQLTYPES);
```

No Disconnect or Free Statements

Whenever the scalar that holds the statement or connection handle loses its value, the underlying data structures will be freed and appropriate connections closed. This can be accomplished by performing one of the following actions.

- **undef** the handle
- Use the handle for another purpose
- Let the handle run out of scope
- Exit the program

Error Messages

A global variable $Velocis::errorstr always holds the last error message. It is never reset except on the next error. The only time it holds a valid message is after **execute()** or **db_connect()** returns **undef**. If **fetchrow()** encountered an error from the database, it will set the error string to indicate the error and return an empty array; however, it will not clear the error string upon successful return, so you must first set it to the empty string if you wish to check it later (when **fetchrow()** returns an empty array).

Prerequisites

You need to have the Velocis database server installed and configured on your system to use this module.

Be sure to set the proper DEFINES in the *Makefile.PL* file for your architecture.

Author

Vivek Khera, *vivek@khera.org*. Many ideas were taken from the MsqlPerl module.

Xbase—Perl module to read Xbase DBF files and FoxPro IDX indexes

Abstract

This is a Perl module to access Xbase files with simple IDX indexes. At the moment only read access to the files is provided by this package. Writing is more complex with IDX updates and is currently under development. Since the read functionality is useful in and of itself, this version is being released.

Installation

To install this package, change to the directory where this file is present and type.

```
perl Makefile.PL
make
make install
```

This will copy *Xbase.pm* to the Perl library directory (provided you have the permission to do so). To use the module in your programs you will use the line:

```
use Xbase;
```

If you cannot install it in the system directory, put it wherever you like and tell Perl where to find it by using the following in the beginning of your script:

```
BEGIN {
    unshift(@INC,'/usr/underprivileged/me/lib');
}
use Xbase;
```

Description

The various methods that are supported by this module are given below. There is a very distinct Xbase-like flavor to most of the commands.

Methods

Creating a new Xbase object

This will create an object $database that will be used to interact with the various methods the module provides.

```
$database = new Xbase;
```

Opening a database

Associates the DBF file and optionally the IDX file with the object. It opens the files and, if an associated MEMO file is present, automatically opens it. Only Foxpro Memo files are currently supported. It assumes the same filename as the DBF with a FPT extension.

```
$database->open_dbf($dbf_name, $idx_name);
```

Database type

Returns a string telling you if the Xbase file opened is DBF3, DBF4, or FOX.

```
print $database->dbf_type;
```

Last update date

Returns a date string telling you when the database was last updated.

```
print $database->last_update;
```

Last record number

Returns the record number of the last record in the database file.

```
$end=$database->lastrec;
```

Database status information

This prints out on to STDOUT a display of the status/structure of the database. It is similar to the Xbase command DISPLAY STATUS. Since it prints field names and structure it is commonly used to see if the module is reading the database as intended and finding out the field names.

```
$database->dbf_stat;
```

Index file status information

Prints on to STDOUT the status information of an open IDX file.

```
$database->idx_stat;
```

Go to top

Moves the record pointer to the top of the database. This is the physical top of database if no index is present; otherwise, it is the first record according to index order.

```
$database->go_top;
```

Go to bottom

Moves the record pointer to the bottom of the database. This is the physical bottom of database if no index is present; otherwise, it is the last record according to index order.

```
$database->go_bottom;
```

Go to next

Equivalent to the Xbase command SKIP 1, which moves the record pointer to the next record.

```
$database->go_next;
```

Go to previous

Equivalent to the Xbase command SKIP −1, which moves the record pointer to the previous record.

```
$database->go_prev;
```

Seek

This command positions the record pointer on the first matching record that has the key value specified. The database should be opened with an associated index. Seek without an available index will print an error message and abort. The return value indicates whether the key value was found or not.

```
$stat=$database->seek($keyvalue);
```

Record number

Returns the record number that the record pointer is currently at.

```
$current_rec=$database->recno;
```

Beginning of file

Tells you whether you are at the beginning of the file. Like in Xbase, it is not true when you are at record number 1 but rather it is set when you try to $database->go_prev when you are at the top of the file.

```
if ($database->bof) {
    print "At the very top of the file \n";
}
```

End of file

Tells you whether you are at the end of the file. Like in Xbase, it is not true when you are at the last record but rather it is set when you try to $database->go_ next from the last record.

```
if ($database->eof) {
    print "At the very end of the file \n";
}
```

Read individual field values

Returns as a string the contents of a field name specified from the current record. Using the pseudo field name _DELETED will tell you if the current record is marked for deletion.

```
print $database->get_field("NAME");
```

Read field values into array

Returns as an array all the fields from the current record. The fields are in the same order as in the database.

```
@fields = $database->get_record;
```

Close database

This closes the database files, index files and memo files that are associated with the $database object with $database->open_dbf

```
$database->close_dbf;
```

Acknowledgments

Thanks are due to Chung Huynh (*chuynh@nero.finearts.uvic.ca*), Jim Esposito (*jgespo@exis.net*), Dick Sutton (*suttond@federal.unisys.com*), Andrew Vasquez (*praka@ophelia.fullcoll.edu*), Leonard Samuelson (*lcs@synergy.smartpages.com*) and Gilbert Ramirez Jr. (*gram@merece.uthscsa.edu*).

Author

Pratap Pereira, *pereira@ee.eng.ohio-state.edu*

Copyright

I request that if you use this module at a Web site, make a link to:

   http://eewww.eng.ohio-state.edu/~pereira/software/xbase/

This is just so that others might find it, and is not required.

More Titles from O'Reilly

Perl

Perl Resource Kit—UNIX Edition

By Larry Wall, Clay Irving, Nate Patwardhan, Ellen Siever & Brian Jepson
1st Edition November 1997 (est.)
1700 pages (est.)
ISBN 1-56592-370-7

The *Perl Resource Kit* is the most comprehesive collection of documentation and commercially enhanced software tools yet published for Perl programmers. The UNIX edition, the first in a series, is the definitive Perl distribution for webmasters, programmers, and system administrators.

Software tools on the Kit's CD include:

* A Java/Perl back-end to the Perl compiler, written by Larry Wall, creator of Perl

* Snapshot of the freeware Perl archives on CPAN, with an Install program and a web-aware interface for identifying more recent online CPAN tools

This new Java/Perl tool allows programmers to write Java classes with Perl implementations (innards), and run the code through a compiler back-end to produce Java byte-code. Using this new tool, programmers can exploit Java's wide availability on the browser (as well as on the server), while using Perl for the things that it does better than Java (such as string processing).

The Kit also includes four tutorial and reference books that contain systematic documentation for the most important Perl extension modules, as well as documentation for the commercially enhanced and supported tools on the CD. The books in the Kit are not available elsewhere or separatelyand include:

* *Perl Module Programmer's Guide*, by Clay Irving and Nate Patwardhan.

* *Perl Module Reference Manual* (two volumes), compiled and edited by Ellen Siever and David Futato.

* *Perl Utilities*, by Brian Jepson.

The *Perl Resource Kit* is the first comprehensive tutorialand reference documentation for hundreds of essential third-party Perl extension modules used for creating CGI applications and more. It features commercially enhanced Perl utilities specially developed for the Kit by Perl's creator, Larry Wall. And, it is all brought to you by the premier publisher of Perl and UNIX books and documentation, O'Reilly & Associates.

Programming Perl, 2nd Edition

By Larry Wall, Tom Christiansen & Randal L. Schwartz
2nd Edition September 1996
670 pages, ISBN 1-56592-149-6

Programming Perl, second edition, is the authoritative guide to Perl version 5, the scripting utility that has established itself as the programming tool of choice for the World Wide Web, UNIX system administration, and a vast range of other applications. Version 5 of Perl includes object-oriented programming facilities. The book is coauthored by Larry Wall, the creator of Perl.

Perl is a language for easily manipulating text, files, and processes. It provides a more concise and readable way to do many jobs that were formerly accomplished (with difficulty) by programming with C or one of the shells. Perl is likely to be available wherever you choose to work.And if it isn't, you can get it and install it easily and free of charge.

This heavily revised second edition of *Programming Perl* contains a full explanation of the features in Perl version 5.003. Contents include:

* An introduction to Perl

* Explanations of the language and its syntax

* Perl functions

* Perl library modules

* The use of references in Perl

* How to use Perl's object-oriented features

* Invocation options for Perl itself, and also for the utilities that come with Perl

Perl 5 Desktop Reference

By Johan Vromans
1st Edition February 1996
46 pages, ISBN 1-56592-187-9

This is the standard quick-reference guide for the Perl programming language. It provides a complete overview of the language, from variables to input and output, from flow control to regular expressions, from functions to document formats—all packed into a convenient, carry-around booklet. Updated to cover Perl version 5.003.

Perl

Learning Perl, 2nd Edition

By Randal L. Schwartz & Tom Christiansen,
Foreword by Larry Wall
2nd Edition July 1997
302 pages, ISBN 1-56592-284-0

In this update of a bestseller, two leading
Perl trainers teach you to use the most
universal scripting language in the age of
the World Wide Web. With a foreword by
Larry Wall, the creator of Perl, this
smooth, carefully paced book is the "official" guide for both formal (classroom) and informal learning. It is now current for
Perl version 5.004.

Learning Perl is a hands-on tutorial designed to get you writing
useful Perl scripts as quickly as possible. Exercises (with complete solutions) accompany each chapter. A lengthy, new chapter
in this edition introduces you to CGI programming, while touching also on the use of library modules, references, and Perl's
object-oriented constructs.

Perl is a language for easily manipulating text, files, and processes. It comes standard on most UNIX platforms and is available
free of charge on all other important operating systems. Perl
technical support is informally available—often within minutes—from a pool of experts who monitor a USENET newsgroup
(comp.lang.perl.misc) with tens
of thousands of readers.

Contents include:

- A quick tutorial stroll through Perl basics
- Systematic, topic-by-topic coverage of Perl's broad capabilities
- Lots of brief code examples
- Programming exercises for each topic, with fully worked-out answers
- How to execute system commands from your Perl program
- How to manage DBM databases using Perl
- An introduction to CGI programming for the Web

Advanced Perl Programming

By Sriram Srinivasan
1st Edition August 1997
434 pages, ISBN 1-56592-220-4

This book covers complex techniques for
managing production-ready Perl programs
and explains methods for manipulating
data and objects that may have looked like
magic before. It gives you necessary background for dealing with networks, data-
bases, and GUIs, and includes a discussion of internals to help
you program more efficiently and embed Perl within C or C within Perl.

Learning Perl on Win32 Systems

By Randal L. Schwartz, Erik Olson &
Tom Christiansen
1st Edition August 1997
306 pages, ISBN 1-56592-324-3

In this carefully paced course, leading
Perl trainers and a Windows NT practitioner teach you to program in the language that promises to emerge as the
scripting language of choice on NT. Based
on the "llama" book, this book features tips for PC users and
new, NT-specific examples, along with a foreword by Larry Wall,
the creator of Perl, and Dick Hardt, the creator of Perl for
Win32.

Mastering Regular Expressions

By Jeffrey E. F. Friedl
1st Edition January 1997
368 pages, ISBN 1-56592-257-3

Regular expressions, a powerful tool for
manipulating text and data, are found in
scripting languages, editors, programming
environments, and specialized tools. In
this book, author Jeffrey Friedl leads you
through the steps of crafting a regular
expression that gets the job done. He examines a variety of tools
and uses them in an extensive array of examples, with a major
focus on Perl.

Java Programming

Java in a Nutshell, DELUXE EDITION

By David Flanagan, et al.
1st Edition June 1997
628 pages, includes CD-ROM and book,
ISBN 1-56592-304-9

Java in a Nutshell, Deluxe Edition, brings together on CD-ROM five volumes for Java developers and programmers, linking related info across books. *Exploring Java, 2nd Edition*, covers Java basics. *Java Language Reference, 2nd Edition, Java Fundamental Classes Reference*, and *Java AWT Reference* provide a definitive set of documentation on the Java language and the Java 1.1 core API. *Java in a Nutshell, 2nd Edition*, our bestselling quick reference, is included both on the CD-ROM and in a companion desktop edition. This deluxe library is an indispensable resource for anyone doing serious programming with Java 1.1.

Exploring Java, Second Edition

By Pat Niemeyer & Josh Peck
2nd Edition September 1997 (est.)
628 pages (est.)
ISBN 1-56592-271-9

Whether you're just migrating to Java or working steadily in the forefront of Java development, this book, fully revised for Java 1.1, gives a clear, systematic overview of the language. It covers the essentials of hot topics like Beans and RMI, as well as writing applets and other applications, such as networking programs, content and protocol handlers, and security managers.

Java Language Reference, Second Edition

By Mark Grand
2nd Edition July 1997
492 pages, ISBN 1-56592-326-X

This book helps you understand the subtle nuances of Java—from the definition of data types to the syntax of expressions and control structures—so you can ensure your programs run exactly as expected. The second edition covers the new language features that have been added in Java 1.1, such as inner classes, class literals, and instance initializers.

Java Fundamental Classes Reference

By Mark Grand &
Jonathan Knudsen
1st Edition May 1997
1114 pages, ISBN 1-56592-241-7

The *Java Fundamental Classes Reference* provides complete reference documentation on the core Java 1.1 classes that comprise the *java.lang, java.io, java.net, java.util, java.text, java.math, java.lang.reflect*, and *java.util.zip* packages. Part of O'Reilly's Java documentation series, this edition describes Version 1.1 of the Java Development Kit. It includes easy-to-use reference material and provides lots of sample code to help you learn by example.

Java AWT Reference

By John Zukowski
1st Edition April 1997
1074 pages, ISBN 1-56592-240-9

The *Java AWT Reference* provides complete reference documentation on the Abstract Window Toolkit (AWT), a large collection of classes for building graphical user interfaces in Java. Part of O'Reilly's Java documentation series, this edition describes both Version 1.0.2 and Version 1.1 of the Java Development Kit, includes easy-to-use reference material on every AWT class, and provides lots of sample code.

Java in a Nutshell, Second Edition

By David Flanagan
2nd Edition May 1997
628 pages, ISBN 1-56592-262-X

The bestselling Java book just got better. Newly updated, it now describes all the classes in the Java 1.1 API, with the exception of the still-evolving Enterprise APIs. And it still has all the great features that have made this the Java book most often recommended on the Internet: practical, real-world examples and compact reference information. It's the only quick reference you'll need.

O'REILLY™

TO ORDER: **800-998-9938** • **order@oreilly.com** • **http://www.oreilly.com/**

OUR PRODUCTS ARE AVAILABLE AT A BOOKSTORE OR SOFTWARE STORE NEAR YOU.

FOR INFORMATION: **800-998-9938** • **707-829-0515** • **info@oreilly.com**

Java Programming *continued*

Java Distributed Computing

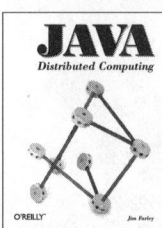

By Jim Farley
1st Edition November 1997 (est.)
350 pages (est.), ISBN 1-56592-206-9

Java Distributed Computing offers a general introduction to distributed computing, meaning programs that run on two or more systems. It focuses primarily on how to structure and write distributed applications and, therefore, discusses issues like designing protocols, security, working with databases, and dealing with low bandwidth situations.

Java Examples in a Nutshell

By David Flanagan
1st Edition September 1997 (est.)
400 pages (est.), ISBN 1-56592-371-5

Java Examples in a Nutshell is chock full of practical, real-world Java programming examples. The author of the bestselling *Java in a Nutshell* has created an entire book of example programs that you can learn from and modify for your own use. If you learn best "by example," this companion volume to *Java in a Nutshell* is the book for you.

Netscape IFC in a Nutshell

By Dean Petrich with David Flanagan
1st Edition August 1997
370 pages, ISBN 1-56592-343-X

This desktop quick reference and programmer's guide is all the documentation programmers need to start creating highly customizable graphical user interfaces with the Internet Foundation Classes (IFC), Version 1.1. The IFC is a Java class library freely available from Netscape. It is also bundled with Communicator, making it the preferred development environment for the Navigator 4.0 web browser. Master the IFC now for a head start on the forthcoming Java Foundation Classes (JFC).

Developing Java Beans

By Robert Englander
1st Edition June 1997
316 pages, ISBN 1-56592-289-1

Developing Java Beans is a complete introduction to Java's component architecture. It describes how to write Beans, which are software components that can be used in visual programming environments. This book discusses event adapters, serialization, introspection, property editors, and customizers, and shows how to use Beans within ActiveX controls.

Java Virtual Machine

By Jon Meyer & Troy Downing
1st Edition March 1997
452 pages, includes diskette
ISBN 1-56592-194-1

This book is a comprehensive programming guide for the Java Virtual Machine (JVM). It gives readers a strong overview and reference of the JVM so that they may create their own implementations of the JVM or write their own compilers that create Java object code. A Java assembler is provided with the book, so the examples can all be compiled and executed.

Database Programming with JDBC and Java

By George Reese
1st Edition June 1997
240 pages, ISBN 1-56592-270-0

Database Programming with JDBC and Java describes the standard Java interfaces that make portable, object-oriented access to relational databases possible and offers a robust model for writing applications that are easy to maintain. It introduces the JDBC and RMI packages and includes a set of patterns that separate the functions of the Java application and facilitate the growth and maintenance of your application.

Java Network Programming

By Elliotte Rusty Harold
1st Edition February 1997
442 pages, ISBN 1-56592-227-1

The network is the soul of Java. Most of what is new and exciting about Java centers around the potential for new kinds of dynamic, networked applications. *Java Network Programming* teaches you to work with Sockets, write network clients and servers, and gives you an advanced look at the new areas like multicasting, using the server API, and RMI. Covers Java 1.1.

Java Threads

By Scott Oaks and Henry Wong
1st Edition January 1997
268 pages, ISBN 1-56592-216-6

With this book, you'll learn how to take full advantage of Java's thread facilities: where to use threads to increase efficiency, how to use them effectively, and how to avoid common mistakes like deadlock and race conditions. Covers Java 1.1.

O'REILLY™

TO ORDER: **800-998-9938** • **order@oreilly.com** • **http://www.oreilly.com/**
OUR PRODUCTS ARE AVAILABLE AT A BOOKSTORE OR SOFTWARE STORE NEAR YOU.
FOR INFORMATION: **800-998-9938** • **707-829-0515** • **info@oreilly.com**

How to stay in touch with O'Reilly

1. Visit Our Award-Winning Web Site

http://www.oreilly.com/

★ "Top 100 Sites on the Web" —*PC Magazine*
★ "Top 5% Web sites" —*Point Communications*
★ "3-Star site" —*The McKinley Group*

Our web site contains a library of comprehensive product information (including book excerpts and tables of contents), downloadable software, background articles, interviews with technology leaders, links to relevant sites, book cover art, and more. File us in your Bookmarks or Hotlist!

2. Join Our Email Mailing Lists

New Product Releases

To receive automatic email with brief descriptions of all new O'Reilly products as they are released, send email to: **listproc@online.oreilly.com**
Put the following information in the first line of your message (*not* in the Subject field):
subscribe oreilly-news "Your Name" of "Your Organization" (for example: subscribe oreilly-news Kris Webber of Fine Enterprises)

O'Reilly Events

If you'd also like us to send information about trade show events, special promotions, and other O'Reilly events, send email to: **listproc@online.oreilly.com**
Put the following information in the first line of your message (*not* in the Subject field):
subscribe oreilly-events "Your Name" of "Your Organization"

3. Get Examples from Our Books via FTP

There are two ways to access an archive of example files from our books:

Regular FTP

- ftp to:
  ftp.oreilly.com
  (login: anonymous
  password: your email address)
- Point your web browser to:
  ftp://ftp.oreilly.com/

FTPMAIL

- Send an email message to:
  ftpmail@online.oreilly.com
  (Write "help" in the message body)

4. Visit Our Gopher Site

- Connect your gopher to:
  gopher.oreilly.com

- Point your web browser to:
  gopher://gopher.oreilly.com/

- Telnet to:
  gopher.oreilly.com
  login: gopher

5. Contact Us via Email

order@oreilly.com
To place a book or software order online. Good for North American and international customers.

subscriptions@oreilly.com
To place an order for any of our newsletters or periodicals.

books@oreilly.com
General questions about any of our books.

software@oreilly.com
For general questions and product information about our software. Check out O'Reilly Software Online at **http://software.oreilly.com/** for software and technical support information. Registered O'Reilly software users send your questions to: **website-support@oreilly.com**

cs@oreilly.com
For answers to problems regarding your order or our products.

booktech@oreilly.com
For book content technical questions or corrections.

proposals@oreilly.com
To submit new book or software proposals to our editors and product managers.

international@oreilly.com
For information about our international distributors or translation queries. For a list of our distributors outside of North America check out:
http://www.oreilly.com/www/order/country.html

O'Reilly & Associates, Inc.
101 Morris Street, Sebastopol, CA 95472 USA
TEL 707-829-0515 or 800-998-9938
     (6am to 5pm PST)
FAX 707-829-0104

Titles from O'Reilly

Please note that upcoming titles are displayed in italic.

WEBPROGRAMMING

Apache: The Definitive Guide
Building Your Own Web
 Conferences
Building Your Own Website
CGI Programming for the World
 Wide Web
Designing for the Web
HTML: The Definitive Guide,
 2nd Ed.
JavaScript: The Definitive Guide,
 2nd Ed.
Learning Perl
Programming Perl, 2nd Ed.
Mastering Regular Expressions
WebMaster in a Nutshell
Web Security & Commerce
Web Client Programming with
 Perl
World Wide Web Journal

USING THE INTERNET

Smileys
The Future Does Not Compute
The Whole Internet User's Guide
 & Catalog
The Whole Internet for Win 95
Using Email Effectively
Bandits on the Information
 Superhighway

JAVA SERIES

Exploring Java
Java AWT Reference
Java Fundamental Classes
 Reference
Java in a Nutshell
Java Language Reference, 2nd
 Edition
Java Network Programming
Java Threads
Java Virtual Machine

SOFTWARE

WebSite™ 1.1
WebSite Professional™
Building Your Own Web
 Conferences
WebBoard™
PolyForm™
Statisphere™

SONGLINE GUIDES

NetActivism   NetResearch
Net Law   NetSuccess
NetLearning   NetTravel
Net Lessons

SYSTEM ADMINISTRATION

Building Internet Firewalls
Computer Crime: A
 Crimefighter's Handbook
Computer Security Basics
DNS and BIND, 2nd Ed.
Essential System Administration,
 2nd Ed.
Getting Connected: The Internet
 at 56K and Up
Linux Network Administrator's
 Guide
Managing Internet Information
 Services
Managing NFS and NIS
Networking Personal Computers
 with TCP/IP
Practical UNIX & Internet
 Security, 2nd Ed.
PGP: Pretty Good Privacy
sendmail, 2nd Ed.
sendmail Desktop Reference
System Performance Tuning
TCP/IP Network Administration
termcap & terminfo
Using & Managing UUCP
Volume 8: X Window System
 Administrator's Guide
Web Security & Commerce

UNIX

Exploring Expect
Learning VBScript
Learning GNU Emacs, 2nd Ed.
Learning the bash Shell
Learning the Korn Shell
Learning the UNIX Operating
 System
Learning the vi Editor
Linux in a Nutshell
Making TeX Work
Linux Multimedia Guide
Running Linux, 2nd Ed.
SCO UNIX in a Nutshell
sed & awk, 2nd Edition
Tcl/Tk Tools
UNIX in a Nutshell: System V
 Edition
UNIX Power Tools
Using csh & tsch
When You Can't Find Your UNIX
 System Administrator
Writing GNU Emacs Extensions

WEB REVIEW STUDIO SERIES

Gif Animation Studio
Shockwave Studio

WINDOWS

Dictionary of PC Hardware and
 Data Communications Terms
Inside the Windows 95 Registry
Inside the Windows 95 File
 System
Windows Annoyances
Windows NT File System
 Internals
Windows NT in a Nutshell

PROGRAMMING

Advanced Oracle PL/SQL
 Programming
Applying RCS and SCCS
C++: The Core Language
Checking C Programs with lint
DCE Security Programming
Distributing Applications Across
 DCE & Windows NT
Encyclopedia of Graphics File
 Formats, 2nd Ed.
Guide to Writing DCE
 Applications
lex & yacc
Managing Projects with make
Mastering Oracle Power Objects
Oracle Design: The Definitive
 Guide
Oracle Performance Tuning, 2nd
 Ed.
Oracle PL/SQL Programming
Porting UNIX Software
POSIX Programmer's Guide
POSIX.4: Programming for the
 Real World
Power Programming with RPC
Practical C Programming
Practical C++ Programming
Programming Python
Programming with curses
Programming with GNU Software
Pthreads Programming
Software Portability with imake,
 2nd Ed.
Understanding DCE
Understanding Japanese
 Information Processing
UNIX Systems Programming for
 SVR4

BERKELEY 4.4 SOFTWARE DISTRIBUTION

4.4BSD System Manager's
 Manual
4.4BSD User's Reference Manual
4.4BSD User's Supplementary
 Documents
4.4BSD Programmer's Reference
 Manual
4.4BSD Programmer's
 Supplementary Documents
X Programming
Vol. 0: X Protocol Reference
 Manual
Vol. 1: Xlib Programming Manual
Vol. 2: Xlib Reference Manual
Vol. 3M: X Window System User's
 Guide, Motif Edition
Vol. 4M: X Toolkit Intrinsics
 Programming Manual, Motif
 Edition
Vol. 5: X Toolkit Intrinsics
 Reference Manual
Vol. 6A: Motif Programming
 Manual
Vol. 6B: Motif Reference Manual
Vol. 6C: Motif Tools
Vol. 8 : X Window System
 Administrator's Guide
Programmer's Supplement for
 Release 6
X User Tools
The X Window System in a
 Nutshell

CAREER & BUSINESS

Building a Successful Software
 Business
The Computer User's Survival
 Guide
Love Your Job!
Electronic Publishing on CD-
 ROM

TRAVEL

Travelers' Tales: Brazil
Travelers' Tales: Food
Travelers' Tales: France
Travelers' Tales: Gutsy Women
Travelers' Tales: India
Travelers' Tales: Mexico
Travelers' Tales: Paris
Travelers' Tales: San Francisco
Travelers' Tales: Spain
Travelers' Tales: Thailand
Travelers' Tales: A Woman's
 World

Perl Module Reference

Perl Module Reference
Volume 2

Ellen Siever and David Futato

O'REILLY™

Cambridge · Köln · Paris · Sebastopol · Tokyo

Perl Module Reference, Volume 2
compiled and edited by Ellen Siever and David Futato

Compilation Copyright © 1997 O'Reilly & Associates, Inc. All rights reserved.
Printed in the United States of America.
Copyright for individual modules and associated documentation appears in the text.

Published by O'Reilly & Associates, Inc., 101 Morris Street, Sebastopol, CA 95472.

Editor: Susan B. Peck

Production Editors: Nancy Wolfe Kotary and Nicole Gipson Arigo

Printing History:

      November 1997:   First Edition.

Table of Contents

Preface

The modules available on CPAN (Comprehensive Perl Archive Network) are an invaluable resource for the Perl programmer. The functionality covered by modules on CPAN range from the seemingly trivial to the absolutely essential, from tiny modules that simplify a tedious task to extensive packages that push the envelope of Perl's capabilities.

The documentation for these modules is embedded into the code itself, using a markup language called *pod*, for Plain Old Documentation. pod makes it easy for module developers to document their module as they go along, and update the documentation as needed.

While the pod infrastructure makes the documentation for a single module easy to access, this book (and its companion volume) mark the first time that the pod for the majority of the CPAN modules has been published in print. Although we do not cover every module on CPAN, we tried to include the ones that we determined to be most stable or most essential. If one of your favorite modules is missing from these volumes, however, it's not necessarily because we didn't think they were "good enough"; we were also restricted by what was available at the time of compilation, and whether the author(s) gave us permission to include their modules in the book.

Please note that while we made every effort to include only modules that are stable and that work as advertised, we were not able to test them ourselves and neither we nor O'Reilly & Associates can accept any responsibility for them.

About the Perl Resource Kit

Until now, Perl has been something that was accessible only to an "in crowd"— much as the Internet itself was a few years ago. Perl is widely available on the

Net, but it hasn't had any kind of standard packaged distribution. This has limited its availability both to new users and to many corporate users who must have a supported distribution before they can adopt a product. The Perl Resource Kit addresses this need, while providing valuable resources, technical knowledge, and software tools to those member of the in-crowd who already use Perl on a regular basis.

The Perl Resource Kit, UNIX Edition, is a definitive Perl distribution, complete with essential documentation, for all Perl users. It contains a collection of Perl software and over 1500 pages of documentation, including the first printed documentation for more than 600 widely used Perl modules. The Kit is for programmers, webmasters, system administrators, and others who use—or want to use—Perl.

The modules documented in the Perl Resource Kit were created by members of the Perl freeware community. O'Reilly actively supports the Perl freeware community and has since the publication of our first Perl book, *Programming Perl*. With the Perl Resource Kit and our Perl books, Perl conferences, and other efforts, we seek to extend the visibility of Perl and help ensure the healthy growth of Perl and its community.

The Perl Resource Kit contains:

- *Programming with Perl Modules*, an introduction to programming with some of the most important Perl modules

- *Perl Module Reference* (two volumes), a comprehensive reference for significant Perl modules

- *Perl Utilities Guide*, documentation for Perl software tools contained in the Kit

- Perl Resource Kit Software (on CD-ROM). This includes a Java/Perl tool (JPL) written by Larry Wall, which allows programmers to write Java classes with Perl implementations; a snapshot of the freeware Perl tools on CPAN (Comprehensive Perl Archives Network), with an install program, a search tool, and a web-aware interface for identifying more recent online CPAN tools; and many bits of example code and sample programs.

- The Autumn 1997 issue of *The Perl Journal*, a quarterly magazine devoted to the Perl language

Conventions Used in This Book

This section lists the conventions we used. We've applied them as consistently as possible, but given the number of authors, who of course used their own conventions, we have not always been successful.

Italic

> is used for URLs, filenames, and email addresses, as well as for emphasis.

`Constant width`

> is used for functions, methods, and other fragments of Perl code in regular text, as well as for blocks of code examples.

`Constant width italic`

> is used for arguments of functions and methods, to be replaced with a user-supplied value (or expression).

Horizontal rules separate each module's documentation from the next.

Contacting Technical Support

If you've thoroughly investigated other sources for help (see Chapter 1 of the *Perl Utilities Guide* for suggestions) and still need assistance, technical support is available for the Perl Resource Kit. Before contacting technical support, make sure you have registered your copy of the Resource Kit online at *http://perl.oreilly.com/register.html*. Registering your copy helps us provide better service and keep you up-to-date on what is happening with Perl at O'Reilly.

Support for the Perl Resource Kit comes in three flavors:

- Once you register your Resource Kit, you have up to 30 days of free initial installation support on Solaris 2.5.* and higher and Linux 2.0.* and higher for the software included on the CD-ROM. This support is available by phone at (707) 829-0515 from 7:00 a.m. to 5:00 p.m. (Pacific Time, U.S.A.), Monday through Friday.

- After the 30 days or for software problems beyond installation, technical support is available for a fee through the Perl Clinic, which you can reach in several ways:
  - on the Web at *http://www.perlclinic.com/*
  - by email at *info@perlclinic.com*
  - by phone in the United States and Canada at (604) 606-4611
  - by phone in Europe and elsewhere at 44 (0) 1483 424424.

- For help and information on the books included in the Resource Kit, technical support is available by email at *perltech@oreilly.com*. Please use this email address to ask questions about and/or report errors in the books.

Acknowledgments

First and foremost, we want to thank all the module authors and maintainers who graciously gave us permission to include their documentation in this book and without whom there would be no Perl Module Reference. We wish we could list them all, but there are too many. In most cases, they are credited in the documentation for their modules.

Thanks also to the many people here at O'Reilly, without whom this book would never have gotten done. Thanks to our editor, Susan Peck, for her advice and support; to Linda Mui, for additional editorial support; to Gina Blaber, who oversaw everything, managed the process of getting the permissions, and provided chocolates; to the rest of the Resource Kit team for support, encouragement, and the answers to many questions; and to Laura Schmier and Trina Jackson for managing the task of organizing and maintaining lists of modules, authors, and permissions.

Thanks to our production editors, Nancy Wolfe Kotary and Nicole Gipson Arigo, who did an incredible job of pulling everything together on an unbelievably short schedule and also did quality control. Thanks to Sheryl Avruch for production management and quality control, Robert Romano for the figures, Ted Meister for the cover design, Nancy Priest and Edie Freedman for the interior design, Mike Sierra for FrameMaker support, and Madeleine Newell for production assistance. Kristin Barendsen and Lunaea Hougland proofread, and Elissa Haney and Kathleen Faughnan helped with FrameMaker formatting.

Ellen would like to thank Stephen and Michael for their support and patience while she spent most of her time glued to the computer, and David for being so easy to work with.

David would like to thank his partner Ron for his patience, his friends Scott and Hilary for their understanding, and his parents for their support. And thanks also to his co-conspirator, Ellen, for working with his insane hours.

8

User Interfaces

In this section we list a variety of user interface tools, from curses to Tcl and X11. Terminal utilities are also listed here.

Curses—terminal screen handling and optimization

Synopsis

```
use Curses;
initscr;
...
endwin;
```

Description

Curses is the interface between Perl and your system's curses(3) library. For descriptions on the usage of a given function, variable, or constant, consult your system's documentation, as such information invariably varies (:-) between different curses(3) libraries and operating systems. This document describes the interface itself, and assumes that you already know how your system's curses(3) library works.

Unified Functions

Many curses(3) functions have variants starting with the prefixes w-, mv-, and/or wmv-. These variants differ only in the explicit addition of a window, or by the addition of two coordinates that are used to move the cursor first. For example, addch() has three variants: waddch(), mvaddch(), and mvwaddch(). The variants aren't very interesting; in fact, we could roll all of the variants into the original function by allowing a variable number of arguments and analyzing the argument list for which variant the user wanted to call.

Unfortunately, curses(3) predates varargs(3), so in C we were stuck with all the variants. However, Curses is a Perl interface, so we are free to "unify" these variants into one function. The section "Supported Functions" later in this module lists all curses (3) functions supported by Curses, indicating whether each is *unified*. If so, it takes a varying number of arguments as follows:

```
function( [win], [y, x], args );
```

win is an optional window argument, defaulting to **stdscr** if not specified.

y, x is an optional coordinate pair used to move the cursor, defaulting to no move if not specified.

args are the function's required arguments. These are the arguments you would specify if you were just calling the base function and not any of the variants.

This makes the variants obsolete, since their functionality has been merged into a single function, so Curses does not define them by default. You can still get them if you want, by setting the variable **$Curses::OldCurses** to a non-zero value before using the Curses package. See "Perl 4.X cursperl compatibility" for an example of this.

Objects

Objects are supported. Example:

```
$win = new Curses;
$win->addstr(10, 10, 'foo');
$win->refresh;
...
```

Any function that has been marked as unified (see "Supported Functions" below and "Unified Functions" above) can be called as a method for a Curses object.

Do not use **initscr()** if using objects, as the first call to get a **new** Curses does it for you.

Compatibility

Perl 4.X cursperl compatibility

Curses has been written to take advantage of the new features of Perl. I felt it better to provide an improved Curses programming environment rather than to be 100% compatible. However, many old **cursperl** applications will probably still work by starting the script with:

```
BEGIN { $Curses::OldCurses = 1; }
use Curses;
```

Any old application that still does not work should print an understandable error message explaining the problem.

Some functions and variables are not supported by Curses, even with the **BEGIN** line. They are listed under "curses(3) items not supported by Curses."

The variables **$stdscr** and **$curscr** are also available as the functions **stdscr** and **curscr**. This is because of a Perl bug. See the "Bugs" section for details.

Incompatibilities with previous versions of Curses

In previous versions of this software, some Perl functions took a different set of parameters than their C counterparts. This is no longer true. You should now use getstr($str) and getyx($y, $x) instead of $str = getstr() and ($y, $x) = getyx().

Incompatibilities with other Perl programs

There were various interaction problems between Curses and *menu.pl* v3.0 and v3.1. Please upgrade to the latest version, which was v3.3 as of 3/16/96.

Diagnostics

Curses function '%s' called with too %s arguments at ...
> You have called a Curses function with a wrong number of arguments.

argument %d to Curses function '%s' is not a Curses window at ...
argument is not a Curses window at ...
> The window argument you gave to the function wasn't really a window.
>
> This probably means that you didn't give the right arguments to a unified function. See the section "Unified Functions" for more information.

Curses function '%s' is not defined by your vendor at ...
> You have a Curses function in your code that your system's curses(3) library doesn't define.

Curses constant '%s' is not defined by your vendor at ...
> You have a Curses constant in your code that your system's curses(3) library doesn't define.

Curses does not support the curses function '%s', used at ...
> You have a curses(3) function in your code that the Curses module doesn't support.

Curses does not support the curses variable '%s', used at ...
> You have a curses(3) variable in your code that the Curses module doesn't support.

Curses does not support the curses constant '%s', used at ...
> You have a bareword in your code that Curses is trying to interpret as a constant, but Curses doesn't know anything about it.

Curses::Vars::FETCH called with bad index at ...
Curses::Vars::STORE called with bad index at ...
> You've been playing with the tie interface to the Curses variables. Don't do that. :-)

Anything else
> Check out the perldiag manpage to see if the error is in there.

Synopsis of Perl Curses Support

Supported Functions

Supported	Unified?	Supported via $OldCurses[a]
addch	Yes	waddch mvaddch mvwaddch
addchnstr	Yes	waddchnstr mvaddchnstr mvwaddchnstr
addchstr	Yes	waddchstr mvaddchstr mvwaddchstr
addnstr	Yes	waddnstr mvaddnstr mvwaddnstr
addstr	Yes	waddstr mvaddstr mvwaddstr
attroff	Yes	wattroff
attron	Yes	wattron
attrset	Yes	wattrset
baudrate	No	

Supported	Unified?	Supported via $OldCurses[a]
beep	No	
bkgd	Yes	wbkgd
bkgdset	Yes	wbkgdset
border	Yes	wborder
box	Yes	
can_change_color	No	
cbreak	No	
clear	Yes	wclear
clearok	Yes	
clrtobot	Yes	wclrtobot
clrtoeol	Yes	wclrtoeol
color_content	No	
COLOR_PAIR	No	
copywin	No	
delch	Yes	wdelch mvdelch mvwdelch
deleteln	Yes	wdeleteln
delwin	Yes	
derwin	Yes	
doupdate	No	
echo	No	
echochar	Yes	wechochar
endwin	No	
erase	Yes	werase
erasechar	No	
flash	No	
flushinp	No	
flusok	Yes	
getattrs	Yes	
getbegyx	Yes	
getbkgd	Yes	
getcap	No	
getch	Yes	wgetch mvgetch mvwgetch
getmaxyx	Yes	
getnstr	Yes	wgetnstr mvgetnstr mvwgetnstr
getparyx	Yes	
getstr	Yes	wgetstr mvgetstr mvwgetstr
gettmode	No	

Supported	Unified?	Supported via $OldCurses[a]
getyx	Yes	
halfdelay	No	
has_colors	No	
has_ic	No	
has_il	No	
hline	Yes	whline
idcok	Yes	
idlok	Yes	
immedok	Yes	
inch	Yes	winch mvinch mvwinch
inchnstr	Yes	winchnstr mvinchnstr mvwinchnstr
inchstr	Yes	winchstr mvinchstr mvwinchstr
init_color	No	
init_pair	No	
initscr	No	
innstr	Yes	winnstr mvinnstr mvwinnstr
insch	Yes	winsch mvinsch mvwinsch
insdelln	Yes	winsdelln
insertln	Yes	winsertln
insnstr	Yes	winsnstr mvinsnstr mvwinsnstr
insstr	Yes	winsstr mvinsstr mvwinsstr
instr	Yes	winstr mvinstr mvwinstr
intrflush	Yes	
is_linetouched	Yes	
is_wintouched	Yes	
isendwin	No	
keyname	No	
keypad	Yes	
killchar	No	
leaveok	Yes	
longname	No	
meta	Yes	
move	Yes	wmove
mvcur	No	
mvwin	Yes	
newpad	No	
newwin	No	

Supported	Unified?	Supported via $OldCurses[a]
nl	No	
nocbreak	No	
nodelay	Yes	
noecho	No	
nonl	No	
noqiflush	No	
noraw	No	
notimeout	Yes	
noutrefresh	Yes	wnoutrefresh
overlay	No	
overwrite	No	
pair_content	No	
PAIR_NUMBER	No	
pechochar	No	
pnoutrefresh	No	
prefresh	No	
qiflush	No	
raw	No	
refresh	Yes	wrefresh
resetty	No	
savetty	No	
scrl	Yes	wscrl
scroll	Yes	
scrollok	Yes	
setscrreg	Yes	wsetscrreg
setterm	No	
slk_clear	No	
slk_init	No	
slk_label	No	
slk_noutrefresh	No	
slk_refresh	No	
slk_restore	No	
slk_set	No	
slk_touch	No	
standend	Yes	wstandend
standout	Yes	wstandout
start_color	No	
subpad	No	

Supported	Unified?	Supported via $OldCurses[a]
subwin	Yes	
syncok	Yes	
timeout	Yes	wtimeout
touchline	Yes	
touchln	Yes	wtouchln
touchoverlap	No	
touchwin	Yes	
typeahead	No	
unctrl	No	
ungetch	No	
vline	Yes	wvline

[a] To use any functions in this column, the variable $Curses::OldCurses *must* be set to a non-zero value before using the Curses package. See "Perl 4.X cursperl Compatibility" for an example of this.

Supported Variables

LINES	COLS	stdscr[a]	curscr[a]

[a] stdscr and curscr are also available via the Perl functions stdscr and curscr. See "Perl 4.X cursperl Compatibility" for more information.

Supported Constants

OK	ERR		
ACS_BLOCK	ACS_BOARD	ACS_BTEE	ACS_BULLET
ACS_CKBOARD	ACS_DARROW	ACS_DEGREE	ACS_DIAMOND
ACS_HLINE	ACS_LANTERN	ACS_LARROW	ACS_LLCORNER
ACS_LRCORNER	ACS_LTEE	ACS_PLMINUS	ACS_PLUS
ACS_RARROW	ACS_RTEE	ACS_S1	ACS_S9
ACS_TTEE	ACS_UARROW	ACS_ULCORNER	ACS_URCORNER
ACS_VLINE			
A_ALTCHARSET	A_ATTRIBUTES	A_BLINK	A_BOLD
A_CHARTEXT	A_COLOR	A_DIM	A_INVIS
A_NORMAL	A_PROTECT	A_REVERSE	A_STANDOUT
A_UNDERLINE			
COLOR_BLACK	COLOR_BLUE	COLOR_CYAN	COLOR_GREEN
COLOR_MAGENTA	COLOR_RED	COLOR_WHITE	COLOR_YELLOW
KEY_A1	KEY_A3	KEY_B2	KEY_BACKSPACE
KEY_BEG	KEY_BREAK	KEY_BTAB	KEY_C1
KEY_C3	KEY_CANCEL	KEY_CATAB	KEY_CLEAR

KEY_CLOSE	KEY_COMMAND	KEY_COPY	KEY_CREATE
KEY_CTAB	KEY_DC	KEY_DL	KEY_DOWN
KEY_EIC	KEY_END	KEY_ENTER	KEY_EOL
KEY_EOS	KEY_EXIT	KEY_F0	KEY_FIND
KEY_HELP	KEY_HOME	KEY_IC	KEY_IL
KEY_LEFT	KEY_LL	KEY_MARK	KEY_MAX
KEY_MESSAGE	KEY_MIN	KEY_MOVE	KEY_NEXT
KEY_NPAGE	KEY_OPEN	KEY_OPTIONS	KEY_PPAGE
KEY_PREVIOUS	KEY_PRINT	KEY_REDO	KEY_REFERENCE
KEY_REFRESH	KEY_REPLACE	KEY_RESET	KEY_RESTART
KEY_RESUME	KEY_RIGHT	KEY_SAVE	KEY_SBEG
KEY_SCANCEL	KEY_SCOMMAND	KEY_SCOPY	KEY_SCREATE
KEY_SDC	KEY_SDL	KEY_SELECT	KEY_SEND
KEY_SEOL	KEY_SEXIT	KEY_SF	KEY_SFIND
KEY_SHELP	KEY_SHOME	KEY_SIC	KEY_SLEFT
KEY_SMESSAGE	KEY_SMOVE	KEY_SNEXT	KEY_SOPTIONS
KEY_SPREVIOUS	KEY_SPRINT	KEY_SR	KEY_SREDO
KEY_SREPLACE	KEY_SRESET	KEY_SRIGHT	KEY_SRSUME
KEY_SSAVE	KEY_SSUSPEND	KEY_STAB	KEY_SUNDO
KEY_SUSPEND	KEY_UNDO	KEY_UP	

curses(3) items not supported by Curses

Functions

    tstp printw wprintw mvprintw mvwprintw scanw wscanw mvscanw mvws-
    canw _putchar fullname

Variables

    ttytype Def_term My_term

Bugs

If you use the variables $stdscr and $curscr instead of their functional counterparts (stdscr and curscr), you might run into a bug in Perl where the "magic" isn't called early enough. This is manifested by the Curses package telling you $stdscr isn't a window. One workaround is to put a line like $stdscr = $stdscr near the front of your program.

There are probably many more.

Author

William Setzer, *William_Setzer@ncsu.edu*

Sx—front-end to Athena and Xlib for Perl GUI progamming

Description

Using the Sx package is pretty simple. At the minimum, you:

```
use Sx;
```

To actually have X windows pop open and such, you need to do the following:

1. To get everything started, you should call `OpenDisplay()`. If `OpenDisplay()` returns a non-zero value, it's ok to go on. `OpenDisplay()` creates what will eventually be your first window.

2. After calling `OpenDisplay()`, you can go on to create all sorts of widgets with the `MakeXXX()` calls. You can lay them out with calls to `SetWidgetPos()`.

3. When you are done creating the user interface, call `ShowDisplay()`. This causes the window and components you've created to be displayed on the workstation screen.

   Until you call `ShowDisplay()`, the user cannot see your window, and drawing into drawing areas has *no* effect.

4. If you need to, you can call any of the color allocation functions such as `GetStandardColors()`, etc.

5. Finally, once the window is displayed and you've done all the initializations you wish, you must call `MainLoop()`. After you call `MainLoop()`, events get processed as they come in and your callback functions are called as necessary.

   After calling `MainLoop()`, the correct way for your program to exit is to have one of your callback routines call `exit()` when appropriate (like after the user clicks on a quit button).

That's all you need to do. Even though that may look like a lot to do, it's really pretty simple in practice. For example, here is a "hello world" program with **libsx**:

```
use Sx;
OpenDisplay(@ARGV);
MakeLabel("Hello World!");
ShowDisplay;
MainLoop;
```

Granted it's one more line than a standard `printf()`–type of "hello world" program, but it's not all that bad.

"Hello world" programs are nice, but you don't tend to write very many of them. Real applications need to be able to do much more. Even these "real" programs aren't all that bad in **libsx**.

Here is a simple program that opens a window with a quit button and a drawing area that you can use to draw whatever graphics you want:

```
use Sx;
sub quit { exit }
sub draw_stuff {
  my($widget, $width, $height, $data) = @_;
  ClearDrawArea;
  DrawLine(0,0, $width, $height);   # just draw a diagonal line
}
$res = OpenDisplay("My Window",@ARGV);
```

```
exit unless($res);
$w[0] = MakeButton("Quit", \&quit, Nullsx);
$w[1] = MakeDrawArea(300,300, \&draw_stuff, Nullsx);
SetWidgetPos($w[1], PLACE_UNDER, $w[0], NO_CARE, Nullsx);
ShowDisplay;
GetStandardColors;
MainLoop;   # off we go!
```

The code above is the basic skeleton for an Sx program, even a complicated one. First you open the display with OpenDisplay(). Then you build your interface by creating a bunch of widgets with the MakeXXX() calls. Next, you lay out the display by specifying the relative positions of the widgets to each other. Then you get any fonts or colors you may need, and finally, you just enter the main loop.

In Sx, your callback functions are where all the real work happens. The program above has two callback functions, quit() and draw_stuff(). They are tied to events that happen in the interface. When the user clicks on the quit button, your quit() function is called. When the drawing area gets resized or needs to be redrawn, your draw_stuff() function gets called.

Usually the process of creating the interface gets split out into a separate function that is easy to modify (instead of cluttering up main). However, the basic outline is the same as above. The only real difference with more complicated interfaces is that they usually have many more calls to the MakeXXX() functions, and they tend to make use of the extra void pointer argument in the callback routines.

General Notes

Specifying callbacks

A callback for Sx is a code reference. As such, you can use whatever syntax you prefer to specify it:

```
MakeButton('Quit',\&MyExit,$data);  # Direct Hard reference
MakeButton('Quit','MyExit',$data);  # Direct Soft reference
$callback = \&MyExit; MakeButton('Quit',$callback,$data);
                              # Hard reference in a variable
$callback = 'MyExit'; MakeButton('Quit',$callback,$data);
                              # Soft reference in a variable
MakeButton('Quit',sub { &MyExit }, $data);     # Anon sub
```

The $data parameter

Most widgets (all those with a callback function associated) take a $data parameter. This value is passed to the callback along with other values, depending on the widget. This parameter can be any kind of scalar value, i.e., you can use it to pass a reference to other variables or anonymous constructs. If you don't need it, just use undef.

X resources

OpenDisplay can be called with a list of arguments. The first argument should be the name of the application. The remaining arguments are parsed, and any X-like commands are taken in account. OpenDisplay returns the list of all arguments that couldn't be recognized as standard X command-line arguments.

All non-list widgets (i.e., anything but MakeScrollList and MakeThreeList) can take a last, optional, name argument. You can use this in conjunction with the application name passed to `OpenDisplay` to make your widget sensitive to resource management through **xrdb**. By default, if you don't specify a name, widgets are created with their type as a name (all widgets resulting from **Make-Button** calls are called "button" and so on).

Labels

A label widget is a widget that displays some text or a bitmap, but cannot be clicked on or interacted with by the user. Generally, a label is for informational purposes, such as providing the current filename.

MakeLabel(*txt*)

> This function creates a label that contains the text in the string pointed to by *txt*. The text is simply displayed, with no fancy borders or special highlighting. If the text contains newline characters, they are interpreted properly.

> If the argument *txt* is NULL, then no label is set for the widget. This is convenient if you plan to put a bitmap on this widget with the `SetWidgetBitmap()` function.

> This widget is useful for displaying a piece of textual information such as a filename or user name.

> If this routine fails, FALSE is returned.

Buttons

A button widget is a button that a user can click on with the left mouse button to indicate an action. When a button is pressed, it is drawn in reverse video and some action takes place.

A button is connected to your code by a callback function that is called when the user clicks on the button widget with the left mouse button.

MakeButton(*label, callback, data*)

> This function creates a small rectangular button that the user can click on. The character string pointed at by *label* is printed inside the button. If the string has newline characters in it, they are interpreted properly (i.e., you get a multiline label). The next two arguments are a callback function and an arbitrary Perl value that is passed to the function.

> If you plan to attach a bitmap to this widget, you can specify **Nullsx** for the label text (see the documentation for `SetWidgetBitmap()`).

> When the button is pressed, the callback is called. This function has two arguments: the widget that the user clicked on (which you can ignore if you do not need it) and the data, specified in the call to `MakeButton()`.

Make3Button(*label, call1, call2, call3, data*)

> This is just a convenience function to avoid some translation table munging. This function creates a button, but you can specify a different callback (or **undef** if unwanted) for button 1, 2, or 3.

Toggles

A toggle widget is similar to a button widget, except that it maintains state. That is, when a user clicks a toggle widget, it remains highlighted until it is clicked again. This is similar to an on/off switch.

Toggle widgets can also be used to create a group of "radio buttons." A radio button group is a set of toggle widgets in which at most one of them can be selected at any one time (it is possible for none of them to be selected).

MakeToggle(*txt, state, widget, func, data*)

This function makes a widget that toggles between a highlighted "on" state and an unhighlighted "off" state.

The first argument is the text that will be displayed inside the widget. The *state* argument is a Boolean value indicating the initial state of the toggle button (TRUE = on/highlighted, FALSE = off). The next argument, *widget*, is NULL if this widget is a simple toggle button by itself and not part of a radio group (described below).

If you plan to display a bitmap for the toggle button, you may specify NULL for the *txt* argument (and then call SetWidgetBitmap()).

The *func* argument is a standard callback function. The first argument is the widget, the second argument the data you specified in the MakeToggle call.

Each time the widget changes state, your callback function is called. That is, each time the user clicks the toggle, your function is called.

Radio Groups

It is possible to connect toggle widgets together to form a group of widgets that are mutually exclusive. That is to say, with a radio group, you can have a set of widgets in which at most one of them will be highlighted at any given time. Therefore, if you had three widgets, A, B, and C, only one could be highlighted at any one time, and clicking on another unhighlights the current one and highlights the toggle clicked on. This is useful for selecting one choice of several (such as a size, which is either small, medium, or large, but not two of those at the same time). Keep in mind that it is possible for none of them to be selected.

To build a radio group, you use the *widget* argument of the MakeToggle() function. If you specify another valid toggle widget in the call to MakeToggle(), the new widget becomes connected to the widget you specified. All the widgets you connect together form a radio group. Any single widget can *only* be in one radio group.

Example:

```
$widg1 = MakeToggleWidget("Thing 1", 1, Nullsx, 'func1', Nullsx);
$widg2 = MakeToggleWidget("Thing 2", 0, $widg1, 'func2', Nullsx);
$widg3 = MakeToggleWidget("Thing 3", 0, $widg1, 'func3', Nullsx);
```

Notice how $widg2 and $widg3 specify $widg1 as their **widget** argument. This connects all three into a radio group, in which only one can be set at a time. We initialize $widg1 to be set and the others off. If you specify more than one widget as "on", the results are undefined.

The callback functions are called whenever a widget is highlighted or unhighlighted. The callbacks when the widget is unhighlighted happen before the callbacks when the widget is highlighted.

SetToggleState(*widget, state*)

SetToggleState() explicitly sets the state of a widget.

The *state* argument is either TRUE (sets the toggle to its highlighted state), or FALSE (unhighlights the widget). The callback routine for the widget is only called if there is a change in state.

`GetToggleState(`*`widget`*`)`

> This function returns the current state of the toggle widget. The return values are either TRUE (the widget is selected) or FALSE (the widget is not highlighted).

Scroll List

A scroll list is a scrollable list of items organized in a vertical fashion. The user can scroll through the list of items using the mouse and select individual items from the available choices.

`MakeScrollList(`*`width`*`, `*`height`*`, `*`callback`*`, `*`data`*`, `*`list`*`)`

> This function creates a scrollable list of items from which a user can select individual items. The list contains text strings. The area allocated for displaying the list is *width* and *height* pixels large. If the entire list does not fit into this space, scrollbars appear that let the user easily scroll through the list.
>
> The callback function, should expect to be called with a *widget* argument, the string of text the user clicked on, the string's index in your table, and whatever user data you gave at widget-creation time
>
> The list of strings passed to `MakeScrollList()` must not be `free()`'d or otherwise deallocated for the entire lifetime of the widget (or until the list of strings is changed with `ChangeScrollList()`).

`GetCurrentListItem(`*`widget`*`)`

> This function returns the index of the currently selected item in the specified list *widget*. The index value returned is an index into the table displayed by the list (specified when the widget was created or with `ChangeScrollList()`).
>
> If no item is selected in the list widget, this routine returns –1.

`ChangeScrollList(`*`widget`*`, `*`new_list`*`)`

> This function changes the list of strings displayed by the list *widget*. The new list of items is taken from the argument *new_list*. After this function is called, the old list can be `free()`'d. Of course, you cannot free *new_list* until the application is done or you change the list again.

`SetCurrentListItem(`*`widget`*`, `*`index`*`)`

> This function causes the item with the specified *index* to be highlighted in the list *widget*. You must make sure that *index* is a valid index into the currently displayed list; the results are undefined otherwise.
>
> After calling this function, the item with this index is highlighted in the list widget.

`Make3List(`*`width`*`, `*`height`*`, `*`callback`*`, `*`data`*`, `*`array`*`)`

> This function does the same job as the standard MakeList call, but the callback function is called on any button_down event and has a new fourth argument, which is the event mask (see *X11/X.h* for values).

Menus

Menus provide standard drop-down menus that let the user select from a variety of choices. The Athena widgets do not support cascaded menus, so a menu is a single list of items. A menu contains menu items that are tied to callback functions in the application. Menu items must be text and cannot be bitmaps.

MakeMenu(*name***)**

> This function creates a menu button that contains the text pointed to by the character string *name*. When the button is clicked, a menu pops up. The menu contains items created with MakeMenuItem().

> You need to save the return value of this function and pass it to *MakeMenu-Item()* so that menu items can be attached to a menu.

> If this function fails, it returns NULL.

MakeMenuItem(*menu, name, func, arg***)**

> This function adds a menu item to *menu*. The menu item contains the text pointed to by the string *name*. Whenever the user selects this menu item, the callback function, *func*, is called. The final argument is an arbitrary value that is passed to the callback function.

> The first argument must be a widget returned by MakeMenu() (the results are undefined if it is not).

> If MakeMenuItem() fails for any reason, NULL is returned.

> Whenever the user selects this menu item, the callback is called.

> Setting widget attributes with SetFgColor(), SetBgColor(), etc., work normally except that only one background color may be specified, which takes effect for the entire menu. You can set different fonts for each menu item.

> Note: You do not need to call SetWidgetPos() for menu items. Successive menu items are placed below previous menu items.

SetMenuItemChecked(*widget, state***)**

> This function sets the "checked" state of a menu item. If a menu item is in the checked state, a bitmap of a check mark appears to the left of the menu item text.

> The first argument, *widget*, is a menu item widget created with MakeMenu-Item(). The second argument, *state*, is a Boolean value of either TRUE (1) or FALSE (0), indicating whether or not the check mark should be drawn. If the state argument is TRUE, the check mark is drawn. If the *state* argument is FALSE, the check mark is removed.

GetMenuItemChecked(*widget***)**

> This function returns a Boolean result indicating whether the menu item referred to by the specified widget is checked or not.

> If the menu item referred to by *widget* is checked, a value of TRUE (1) is returned. If the menu item does not currently have a check mark next to it, a value of FALSE (0) is returned.

Scrollbars

A scrollbar is a widget that allows a user to control some numeric quantity interactively by using the mouse to scroll a slider, similar to the volume slider on some radios. The slider is called the "thumb" or "thumb area" in X terminology.

MakeHorizScrollbar(*length, scroll_func, data***)**
MakeVertScrollbar(*height, scroll_func, data***)**

> These two routines create scrollbars. Scrollbars allow the user to interactively control some numeric quantity with the mouse.

When the user presses the left mouse button, the value represented by the scrollbar increases. Pressing the middle mouse button interactively adjusts the value. Clicking the right mouse button decreases the value represented by the scrollbar.

The arguments for creating a scrollbar are its length or height in pixels, a callback function to call when the scrollbar changes value, and an extra void pointer argument that is passed to the callback function.

If these routines fail, they return NULL.

To set the values a scrollbar represents, you must use `SetScrollbar()`. These two routines only make a scrollbar; they do not set it to return useful values. (See the documentation for `SetScrollbar()` for more information.)

Your callback routine is called every time the scrollbar changes. Since the calculations are done in floating point, the value may not have changed enough to be interesting, but your routine is still called. You should take care to see that the value changed enough to be interesting to your applications (i.e., it is wasteful for a text editor to repaint the window when the new value is 0.003 different from the old value).

A scrollbar callback routine should look like:

```
sub scroll_func {
    my($widget, $new_val, $data) = @_;
}
```

The first argument is the scrollbar widget that the user is manipulating. The second argument is a floating-point value that represents the new value of the scrollbar. The third argument is the argument that was passed to `Make{Horiz,Vert}Scrollbar()`.

`SetScrollbar(`*widget, where, max, size_shown*`)`

This function lets you set the values that a scrollbar represents. The first argument is a scrollbar widget. The next three arguments are floating-point numbers that specify the parameters of the scrollbar.

Before discussing the details of the three float arguments, let us get some terms straight. When we refer to the "container" of a scrollbar, we mean the entire box that makes up the scrollbar. The "thumb"' of a scrollbar is the gray area that the user can grab to manipulate. We refer to the size or length of the thumb area (the amount of grey) as the "size shown." The total amount represented by the scrollbar is called "max."

The arguments mean the following:

where

This floating-point number specifies where in the container the top of the thumb area should start. If you have a maximum value of 100, and **where** is 50, the beginning of the thumb will be in the middle of the container.

max

The maximum value that the scrollbar can have. You will receive numbers in the range 0 to **max** (inclusive). Obviously, **max** should be a positive number and is a float.

size_shown

> This float value controls the size of the grey area that the user can grab. This represents how much of whatever you are representing is visible. For example, a text editor that shows 24 lines of text would set *size_shown* to 24 (out of whatever *max* is). If you want the scrollbar to represent a percentage of something, such that when it is 100%, the grey area is also 100% of the box, then you should set the *size_shown* be equal to *max*. If this is confusing, there are examples below.

Now, some examples to clarify things (in the following, assume that the argument, w, represents a scrollbar widget created with the `MakeHorizScrollbar()` or `MakeVertScrollbar()` routines).

For the first example, let's assume you want a scrollbar to let you set a color value that can range between 0 and 255, with an initial value of 67. Set the scrollbar as follows:

```
SetScrollbar($w, 67.0, 255.0, 1.0);
```

The first value, 67.0, is where we want the beginning of the thumb area to appear. The next value, 255, is the maximum value the scrollbar can attain. The third value, 1, is the size of the thumb area (the amount represented by the thumb relative to the maximum size). This scrollbar will now return values in the range of 0 to 255 (inclusive). The thumb area is small, representing one value of the 255 possible divisions. The position of the thumb area in the container represents its value.

For the next example, suppose we wish to make a scrollbar represent some percentage of a value. That is, the size of the thumb area should be proportional to the value of the scrollbar relative to its maximum (so when the value is at its maximum, the thumb area is 100% of the scrollbar).

In this case, we want the size of the thumb area to represent the amount of the variable (note the difference from the above example). Let us suppose we want a scrollbar that can represent a percentage, 0 to 100, with an initial value of 50:

```
SetScrollbar($w, 50.0, 100.0, 100.0);
```

The first value, 50, is where the thumb area begins (in the middle of the container). The next number is 100 and represents the maximum value of the scrollbar. The next number, again 100, is the size shown. Making this value the same as the *max* value (in this case 100) causes the thumb area to vary according to the value the scrollbar represents.

As a final example, let us take a text editor that is displaying a file. In this case, let us assume the text file is 259 lines long, the window can display 47 lines, and the top line currently displayed is 72. To create the correct scrollbar, we would do the following:

```
SetScrollbar($w, 72.0, 259.0, 47.0);
```

This creates a scrollbar that has a thumb area whose size is 47/259 of the entire container and that is positioned 72/259ths of the way down the container.

String Entry

A string entry widget is a widget that lets a user enter a single line of ASCII text. When the user presses Return in the widget, a callback is made to your application with a pointer to the new text. Support routines also exist to Set and Get the text in the widget.

If you want multiple lines of text, see the text edit widget documentation.

MakeStringEntry(*txt, size, func, data*)

This function makes a string input widget. A string input widget is a widget that lets a user enter or edit a single line string value such as a filename.

The first argument is any default text you would like in the string entry widget. You can specify "" if you don't want anything to appear.

The next argument is the width in pixels of the string entry area. Be careful in specifying the width, since the default font used by the widget may not be wide enough to contain the text you want. It is best if you call **GetWidgetFont()** and then call **TextWidth()** on a string of reasonable length and use the value returned by **TextWidth()** to be the width of the widget. If you're lazy, a value of 150–200 is usually pretty good.

The next argument is a callback function that is called whenever the user presses Return in the string entry widget. The first argument to the callback is the widget where the user pressed Return. For the most part, you can ignore this (unless you want to change the text). The second argument is the string of text the user entered. The final argument is the user data you passed to **MakeStringEntry()**.

SetStringEntry(*widget, new_text*)

This function allows you to change the string of text displayed in a string entry widget.

The first argument is the widget in which you would like to change the string (this widget should be a string entry widget). The second argument is a pointer to the new text you would like displayed in the string entry area.

GetStringEntry(*widget*)

This function lets you retrieve the text a user entered in a string widget. The widget argument should be a string entry widget.

The return value of this function is the string that is the contents of the string entry widget.

If there is a problem, the function returns NULL.

Text Edit

A text edit widget is an area used to display and optionally edit multiple lines of text. You can specify the text to be displayed as either an in-memory string or as a filename. The text edit area manages its scrollbars and internal affairs; you need not do anything (in fact there are no callbacks for the text edit widget).

MakeTextWidget(*txt, is_file, editable, width, height*)

This function lets you create a text edit widget that displays some text and optionally lets the user edit and manipulate it. The first argument, *txt*, is a string (empty string is ok). The second argument, *is_file*, is a Boolean value indicating if the first argument should be interpreted as a filename or not. The next argument, *editable*, is a Boolean value indicating whether or not the user is allowed to edit the text. The final two arguments specify the width and height of the drawing area box. If the area is too small to display the text, scrollbars appear.

The *txt* argument can either contain the entire string that you would like the user to edit, or it can contain the name of a file to be loaded into the text edit widget. If the second argument, *is_file*, is TRUE (1), then the first argument gets interpreted as a filename. If *is_file* is FALSE (0), then the first argument contains the actual text to be displayed.

The argument *editable* is a Boolean value indicating whether or not to allow editing of the text in the widget. If you just want to display some text (such as a help file), set the *editable* argument to FALSE (0) and the user is not allowed to modify the text.

SetTextWidgetText(*widget, text, is_file*)

This argument lets you modify the text displayed in a text edit widget. The first argument identifies the text edit widget to change. The second argument is a string that either contains the actual text to display or the name of a file to read in. If the *is_file* argument is TRUE (1), then the string pointed to by the argument *text* is interpreted as a filename. If *is_file* is FALSE, the string pointed to by *text* is directly displayed in the text edit widget.

If you want to update the displayed text again, you should call **SetTextWidget-Text()** again.

Bugs: The function name is way too long.

GetTextWidgetText(*widget*)

This function lets you retrieve the text contained in a text edit widget. The only argument should be a text edit widget created with **MakeTextWidget()**.

The return from this function is a string that contains the current text in the widget. If there is an error, a NULL is returned.

Bugs: The function name is way too long.

Forms

MakeForm(*parent, where1, from1, where2, from2*)

This function lets you create a new form widget in which to put child widgets. A form widget is a container that holds other widgets. Normally there is no need to call this function, but if you want to have separate "groups" of widgets in your display and you can't lay them out that way with **SetWidgetPos()**, then using multiple form widgets may be the right thing. In addition, a nifty little box gets drawn around the form widget (and all the children) and this can be a nice visual cue in your interface indicating what groups of widgets belong together. A form widget creates a box that surrounds all the widgets contained inside of it (but the form widget itself is inactive and can't be clicked on by the user).

If you use multiple form widgets in your display, the basic logic of how you create the display is a little different. You can think of form widgets as miniature windows inside a larger window.

Once you create a form widget, any other widgets you create with calls like **Make-Button()** and **MakeLabel()** become children of this form widget. Before you create another form widget, you must lay out all the children of the current form widget with calls to **SetWidgetPos()**. After you lay out all the children of the current widget, then you can create another form widget and repeat the process (or call **SetForm()**).

Form widgets are laid out in a manner similar to regular widgets, except that usually their placement is relative to other form widgets. When you create a new form widget (after the first one), you specify where it should be placed relative to other form widgets that you created. The first form widget is always placed in the top left corner of the window.

The *parent* argument to MakeForm() specifies at what level the new form should be created. If you specify TOP_LEVEL_FORM (which is the usual thing to do) the new form is created at the top level of the window. If you pass another form widget for *parent*, then this new form widget is a child of the other form widget. This lets you create hierarchical "boxes" in your display.

The arguments *where1*, *from1*, *where2*, *from2* are the same as in SetWidgetPos(). That is, you specify either NO_CARE, PLACE_UNDER, or PLACE_RIGHT for *where1* and *where2*, and the *from1/from2* arguments are the widgets you would like to place something to the right of or under (or they are NULL if you specified NO_CARE). See SetWidgetPos() for more documentation.

Now for an example.

Let's say we want a display something like this figure:

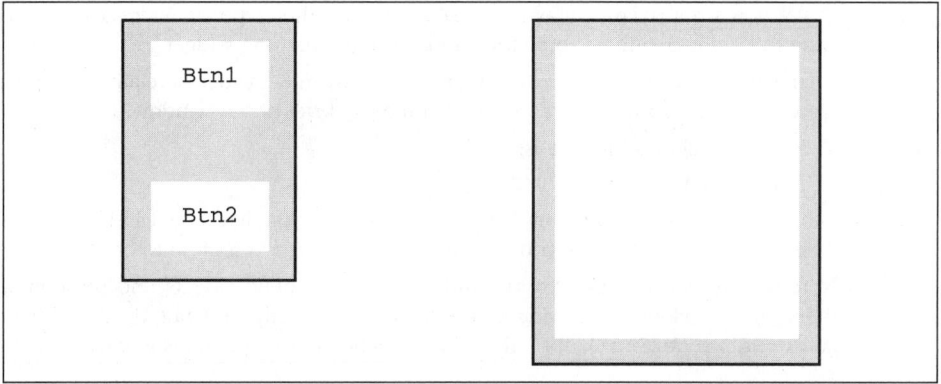

We have two rectangles (forms) that contain other widgets. Inside the leftmost form are two buttons. The form on the right has a single drawing area. Skipping some of the unnecessary details, we could accomplish the above display with the following code:

```
$form1 = MakeForm(TOP_LEVEL_FORM, NO_CARE, Nullsx, NO_CARE,
                  Nullsx);
$w[0]  = MakeButton("Btn1", Nullsx, Nullsx);
$w[1]  = MakeButton("Btn2", Nullsx, Nullsx);
SetWidgetPos($w[1], PLACE_UNDER, $w[0], NO_CARE, Nullsx);
$form2 = MakeForm(TOP_LEVEL_FORM, PLACE_RIGHT, $form1, NO_CARE,
                  Nullsx);
$w[2]  = MakeDrawArea(200, 200, Nullsx, Nullsx);
```

As you can see, we create the first form and specify that we don't care where it goes (the first form widget is always placed in the top left corner of the window). Then we create some widgets to place inside of our new form. Next, and this is important, we lay out all the widgets inside the first form. In this case, we only need to make one call to SetWidgetPos(). Then we create the next form and specify that we want to place it to the right of form1. Finally we create a drawing area widget, which is placed inside of form2.

If you want to create hierarchies of form widgets, you specify the form widget that should be the parent as the first argument to MakeForm(). This can get quite complicated, so you should make sure you know what you're doing if you want to create big hierarchies.

Note: It is important that you lay out all your widgets before you create a new form (unless you're creating a child form).

SetForm(*widget*)

The SetForm() function allows you to change what is considered the current form. Normally, you only use this function to set the current form to TOP_LEVEL_FORM. You can cause your program to crash if you are not careful about what you set as the current form.

The main purpose of this function is to let you create displays that have both form widgets and other "normal" widgets at the same level. You might want to do this if you want a large drawing area (or some other type of widget) but don't want to bother creating a form widget just to hold that one widget.

After calling this function, you can position any new widgets relative to other widgets (usually form widgets) created at the top level of the window.

The normal calling sequence is:

```
SetForm(TOP_LEVEL_FORM)
```

although you can specify any other form widget you like. Be careful, as it is possible to confuse the X layout routines and cause your program to crash.

Note: Before you call SetForm() and start creating new widgets and positioning them, any previous form widgets should be completely laid out (i.e., you have called SetWidgetPos() for all child widgets of any previously created form widgets).

Windows

Here are descriptions of the main high-level startup and window-creation functions.

OpenDisplay(args)

Sx uses this function to initiate everything. You should call this function before you call any of the other functions. A correctly written application will call Open-Display(), passing its command-line arguments and count. The return value from this function is the new list of arguments (or zero if an error occurred). The X libraries accept various standard command-line options, such as -display or -font, and if your application passes the command-line arguments to OpenDis-play(), they are handled properly. Any X options are removed from the return array; therefore it is best if you do your command-line processing *after* calling.

You only need to call this function once to initialize the first window your program uses. Any other windows you need should be created with MakeWindow().

This function returns FALSE (0) if something went wrong (like being unable to open the display, etc). If everything went ok, it returns the new list of arguments as its result.

`ShowDisplay()`

This function displays the currently active window (user interface) you've created with the `MakeXXX()` calls. After this call completes, the interface is visible on the display.

Until you call this function, your interface is not visible, and drawing into a draw area has no effect.

Usually one calls `ShowDisplay()`, allocates some colors, and then immediately calls `MainLoop()`.

`MainLoop()`

After calling this function, your program yields control to the user interface, and is entirely driven by what the user does and the callbacks associated with the various widgets. For a single window application, the general flow of events is:

```
OpenDisplay(@ARGV);        # initialize the first window
MakeXXX(....);             # create widgets
ShowDisplay;               # put the window on the screen
                           # optionally allocate colors
MainLoop;                  # start the main loop going
```

When you call this function after calling `ShowDisplay()` for your first window (created by `OpenDisplay()`), the `MainLoop()` function never returns. Your application should have some callback function that will `exit()` the program (such as a quit button or menu option).

You should not call `MainLoop()` for NONEXCLUSIVE mode windows created with `MakeWindow()`. Such windows have their callbacks handled by the `Main-Loop()` function that is already executing (i.e., the one you called for your original window).

If the window is an EXCLUSIVE mode window, then `MainLoop()` keeps executing until `CloseWindow()` is called on the EXCLUSIVE mode window. That is, `MainLoop()` blocks until the EXCLUSIVE mode window is closed, and then it returns.

If you create a non-exclusive mode window, the general order of events is:

```
MakeWindow(NONEXCLUSIVE_WINDOW, ....);
MakeXXX(...);
ShowDisplay;
```

This creates a window, puts interface objects into it, and then puts that window on the screen. No other actions need to be taken, and when the callback that created this new window returns, all processing takes place normally, including the processing of the new window and its callbacks.

For a window of EXCLUSIVE_WINDOW mode (like a popup), the general order of execution is:

```
MakeWindow(EXCLUSIVE_WINDOW, ....);
MakeXXX(...);
ShowDisplay;
MainLoop;      # blocks until CloseWindow() is called
# do something with whatever values the popup got for us
```

When `MainLoop()` returns for an EXCLUSIVE_WINDOW, the window has been closed.

`SyncDisplay(void)`

This function synchronizes the display with all drawing requests you have made. Normally, it is not necessary to call this function, but if you make many repeated function calls to draw graphics, they will be updated in a chunky fashion because X buffers drawing requests and sends a bunch of them at once.

After this function completes, all drawing requests you have made are visible on the screen.

Note: Normally you do not need to call this function because X ensures that everything you request gets drawn, but sometimes it is necessary to ensure the synchronization of the display.

`MakeWindow(window_name, display_name, exclusive)`

Note: Do not call this function to open your first window. Your application's first window is opened for you by `OpenDisplay()`. If your application only needs one window, do *not* call this function.

This function opens a new window, possibly on a different display (workstation). The new window has the name specified by the argument *window_name* and is opened on the display named by *display_name* (a string usually in the form of *machine_name*:`0.0`). The final argument indicates whether the window should be an exclusive window or not (described below).

After this function returns, the current window is the one you just created, and you can begin adding widgets to it with the `MakeXXX()` calls. After you have created and added any widgets you want, you should call `ShowDisplay()`, and if the window is an EXCLUSIVE_MODE window, then you should call `MainLoop()` (which blocks until the window is closed). If you opened the window with the NONEXCLUSIVE_WINDOW option, you should *not* call `MainLoop()`.

If you pass SAME_DISPLAY, for the display name, the window opens on the same display as the original window that was opened by `OpenDisplay()`.

The argument *exclusive* indicates what type of window to open. A normal window is a NONEXCLUSIVE_WINDOW. That is, it does not block the user from interacting with your existing window. An EXCLUSIVE_WINDOW is a popup window that blocks input to your main window until the popup is closed with `CloseWindow()`.

The EXCLUSIVE_WINDOW mode is useful for requestors that need an answer, and the user should not be able to do other things in the application. Of course, some user-interface folks don't think modal windows like this are good, but tough cookies for them because sometimes it's necessary.

`SetCurrentWindow(widget)`

This function sets the currently active window for other function calls, such as `CloseWindow()`. If you have multiple windows open on several displays, you must call this function to switch the currently active one when you wish to manipulate the various windows.

The argument must be a valid value returned by `MakeWindow()`. If you would like to set the current window to be the original window opened by `OpenDisplay()`, you can pass the `#define`, ORIGINAL_WINDOW.

When you change windows, the current drawing area is also changed to be the last current drawing area in the new window (if there is a drawing area in the new window).

CloseWindow()

This function closes the currently active window and removes it from the display.

After calling this function, you should not refer to any of the widgets contained in the window, as they are invalid (as is the window handle).

Predefined Pop-ups

Pop-up windows are simple dialog boxes that get a simple yes/no or string answer from the user. When these windows pop up, they block input to the previously active window.

GetYesNo(*question*)

This function allows you to prompt the user for the answer to a simple yes or no type of question. It simply pops up a dialog box with the text contained in the string *question*, an okay button, and a cancel button.

If the user clicks Okay, this function returns TRUE. If the user clicks Cancel, the function returns FALSE. The text in the *question* string can have embedded newlines (\n characters) to break things up or to add space.

See also: GetString()

GetString(*msg, default*)

This function allows you to prompt the user for an input string. The first argument, *msg*, is a pointer to a string that will be displayed in the dialog box. The next argument, *default*, is the default string to place in the text string box (it can be NULL or "").

When you call this function, it pops up a small dialog box on the screen, and the user can enter the line of text. When the user clicks OK, the function returns a pointer to the string of text the user entered.

If the user clicks Cancel, you get a NULL return value.

See also: GetYesNo()

Draw Areas

A drawing area is a rectangular area that supports drawing into, receiving input from (mouse clicks, mouse motion, and keypresses), and redisplaying as requested by X. You can draw any sort of graphics into a drawing area as well as perform various types of interaction with mouse and keyboard input.

MakeDrawArea(*width, height, callback, data*)

The function MakeDrawArea() creates a drawing area that you can later use to draw graphics into and receive mouse and keyboard input from. The drawing area has the *width* and *height* you specify. The *callback* function is called whenever the drawing area should be redisplayed (because it was obscured or resized). The argument *data* is any kind of Sxperl object you want, and it is passed directly to the resize callback (and the other callbacks as well).

The redisplay callback is where you should put all of your drawing code. It is called for you when the application opens the window for the first time (by calling MainLoop()). The redisplay callback function should look like:

```
sub redisplay {
    my($widget, $width, $height, $data) = @_;
}
```

The first argument is the drawing-area widget that needs to be redrawn. The second and third arguments are the new width and height of the drawing area (which may have been resized). The final argument is the data passed to `MakeDrawArea()`.

If you are interested in receiving other types of input, see `SetButtonDownCB()`, `SetButtonUpCB()`, `SetKeypressCB()`, and `SetMouseMotionCB()`. These functions let you set callbacks for the other types of input.

Each drawing area you create has its own state (foreground and background colors, drawing mode, and line width). Only one drawing area can be active at any given time. When an event happens for a drawing area, that drawing area becomes the active drawing area. You can make other drawing areas active with `SetDrawArea()`.

If something goes wrong in creating the *DrawArea*, a FALSE value is returned.

`SetButtonDownCB(`*w, callback*`)`

This function sets up a callback that is called every time the user presses a mouse button in the specified drawing area widget *w*.

The callback function should look like:

```
sub  callback {
    my($widget, $which_button, $x, $y, $data) = @_;
}
```

Then, whenever the user presses a mouse button in the drawing area, your callback is called. The first argument is the drawing-area widget where the event happened. The next argument is an integer specifying which button was pressed. It is a small positive integer. A value of one is the left mouse button, two is the middle mouse button and three is the right mouse button. Technically, values of four and five are also possible, though I've never seen a mouse with five buttons. The *x* and *y* arguments are the position of the mouse when the user pressed the mouse button. The final argument is the data argument given to `MakeDrawArea()`.

You can specify a `null` string for the function to turn off receiving button-down events.

`SetButtonUpCB(`*widget, button_up*`)`

This function sets up a callback that is called every time the user releases a mouse button in the specified drawing area widget *w*.

It exhibits the same behavior as `SetButtonDownCB()`.

`SetKeypressCB(`*widget, callback*`)`

This function lets you set a callback so that you will receive keyboard input in the drawing area.

The callback function should look like:

```
sub  callback {
    my($widget, $input, $up_or_down, $data) = @_;
}
```

Then, whenever the user presses keys in the drawing area, your callback function is called. The first argument is the drawing-area widget where the event happened. The next argument is a string that contains what was typed by the user. The *up_or_down* argument indicates whether the key was pressed or released (0 indicates a press, 1 indicates a key release). The final argument is the argument given to `MakeDrawArea()`.

It is useful to know that the string returned to your program is not necessarily a single ASCII character. You will get the usual ASCII characters, including control characters (such as ^C or ^H). But the workstation's function keys will also be returned in a string such as `F11` or `F23`. You will also get other longer strings, such as `Control_L`, `Alt_R`, or `Shift_L`. It is important to understand that even if you just press the shift key to get a capital letter, you will first receive the string `Shift_L` or `Shift_R`, then you will receive the capital letter (say, `H`). You should probably ignore the `Shift_L` or `Shift_R` messages (but who knows, you may find some use for them).

The argument *up_or_down* tells you whether the given key was pressed or released. If the key was pressed down, *up_or_down* is zero (0); if the key was released, *up_or_down* contains 1. This is useful for doing things like shift-clicking with the mouse or handling control-key combinations in an editor or other program.

The arrow keys return strings such as `Left`, `Up`, `Right`, or `Down`. Other keys on the keyboard may return strings such as `Home`, `Prior`, `Next`, `Undo`, `Help`, etc. Of course not all keyboards generate all of the strings (because they aren't set up to).

You can specify a NULL for the function to turn off receiving keypress events.

`SetMouseMotionCB(`*widget, callback*`)`

This function sets a callback so that whenever the mouse moves in your drawing area, the specified function is called. It is important to keep in mind that the function you specify is called *every* time the mouse moves in the drawing area, even if it is just passing through.

The callback function should look like:

```
sub  callback {
    my($widget, $x, $y, $data) = @_;
}
```

The first argument is (as usual) the widget in which the mouse was moved. The next two arguments are the current *x* and *y* values of the mouse. The final argument is the argument passed into `MakeDrawArea()`.

You should be very frugal with what happens in this function so as not to cause the application to lag behind the user too much. Calling functions like `sleep()` are definitely out of the question.

You can specify a `NULL` for the function to turn off receiving mouse motion events.

Drawing

This contains documentation about the routines that let you draw in a drawing area.

The documentation for these functions is quite brief because they are not all that complicated (how much can one really say about `DrawLine()`).

Keep in mind that for all the drawing functions, the top-left corner of a drawing area is considered to be 0,0.

Also, all primitives are drawn in the current foreground color (set either by
`SetColor()` or `SetFgColor()`. Text is drawn with the current foreground color and
the background color. Line, arc, and box primitives are drawn with the current line
width (as set by `SetLineWidth()`), and all primitives are drawn in the current draw
mode (set by `SetDrawMode()`).

`SetDrawArea(w)`

This sets the current drawing area to be that named by the widget *w*. If *w* is not a
drawing-area widget, nothing happens.

You need to call this function when you want to switch between multiple
drawing areas.

If you only have one drawing area, you do not need to worry about this function
at all.

Any callbacks for a drawing area already have the current drawing area set to be
the one where the event happened (so it is not necessary to call this function in a
callback for a drawing area).

`SetColor(color)`

This sets the foreground color to draw with in the current drawing area (each
drawing area has its own foreground color). The argument `color` should be a
valid color obtained with one of the color functions (such as `GetNamedColor()`
or `GetRGBColor()`, etc.).

To some extent this function duplicates the `SetFgColor()` function, but exists
because it is faster than `SetFgColor()`.

`SetLineWidth(width)`

This function sets the width of lines drawn in the current drawing area. Each
drawing area has its own line width.

A width of zero is valid and tells the X server to draw lines as fast as it possibly
can, possibly being a little inaccurate. Larger numbers, of course, draw wider lines.

`SetDrawMode(mode)`

This function sets the drawing mode for the current drawing area. A drawing
mode is one of:

```
GXcopy, GXxor, GXinvert, GXor, GXclear,
GXand, GXandReverse, GXnoop, GXnor, GXequiv,
GXinvert, GXorReverse, GXcopyInverted,
GXorInverted, GXnand, and GXset
```

Most of these are stupid/useless modes defined by X (so ignore them).

The primary mode is GXcopy (the default mode). This causes all primitives to
draw in the foreground color, overwriting any pixels already drawn.

Libsx also defines a special mode: SANE_XOR. The SANE_XOR mode actually
draws primitives in a true XOR mode so that you can draw things like rubber-
band boxes that the user stretches with the mouse. You must use SANE_XOR if
you want true XOR'ed primitives; GXxor will definitely *not* work as you expect.

When you are done using SANE_XOR, you normally call `SetDrawMode()` with an
argument of GXcopy to restore normal drawing.

`GetDrawAreaSize(`*width, height*`)`

This is a convenience function that returns the size of the current drawing area. The window dimensions are returned in the two variables.

`ClearDisplay()`

This function completely clears the current drawing area and sets it to the current background color (which may not be white).

Generally, when your redisplay callback is called, this is the first thing you want to do.

`DrawPixel(`*x1, y1*`)`

This function draws a point in the current foreground color at the location *x1, y1* in your current drawing area. The top left corner of the drawing area is considered 0,0.

`GetPixel(`*x1, y1*`)`

This function retrieves the pixel value at the location *x1, y1* in the current drawing area. The top left corner of the drawing area is considered 0,0.

A pixel value between 0 and 255 (inclusive) is returned to you. This value should be treated as an index into a colormap. To find out what actual color is displayed at that location, you need to look up the color in the colormap (which you should be maintaining, as there is no way to get it after you've set it).

Note: This function is *not* very high performance. It has to call `GetImage()` to do the bulk of the work. This is unfortunate, but unavoidable, because X does not provide an easy way to read individual pixels.

`DrawLine(`*x1, y1, x2, y2*`)`

This function draws a line from *x1,y1* to *x2,y2* in the current foreground color in the current drawing area. The top left corner of the drawing area is considered 0,0.

`DrawPolyline(@points)`

This function accepts an array of points and draws them as a connected polyline on the display. The line is drawn in the current foreground color in the current drawing area. The top left corner of the drawing area is considered 0,0.

The `points` argument is a list of consecutive x,y pairs.

`DrawFilledPolygon (@points)`

This function takes an array of points and draws them as a filled polygon on the display. The polygon is filled with the current foreground color and is drawn in the current drawing area. The top left corner of the drawing area is considered 0,0.

`DrawBox(`*x, y, width, height*`)`

This function draws a rectangular box starting at *x,y* with a *width* and *height* as specified. If you make the call:

```
DrawBox(50,50,75,75)
```

you get a box that starts at position 50,50 and goes for 75 pixels in the x and y directions (i.e., the other extreme of the box would be at 125,125). The box is drawn in the current foreground color in the current drawing area. The top left corner of the drawing area is considered 0,0.

If the width and height are negative, the box is still drawn properly.

DrawFilledBox(*x*, *y*, *width*, *height*)

This function draws a filled rectangular box starting at *x,y* with a *width* and *height* as specified. If you make the call:

```
DrawFilledBox(50,50,75,75)
```

you get a filled box that starts at position 50,50 and goes for 75 pixels in the x and y directions (i.e., the other extreme of the box would be at 125,125). The box is filled with the current foreground color in the current drawing area. The top left corner of the drawing area is considered 0,0.

If the width and height are negative, the box is still drawn properly.

DrawText(*string*, *x*, *y*)

This function prints the text string *string* starting at *x,y*. The text is drawn in the current foreground color. The background of the text is filled with the current background color of the drawing area widget. The top left of the drawing area is 0,0. The x,y position you specify is the bottom left corner of where the text is drawn.

DrawArc(*x*, *y*, *width*, *height*, *angle1*, *angle2*)

This function draws an arc/ellipse from the location x,y that is bounded by the box defined by *x*, *y*, *width*, and *height*. That is, the arc/ellipse is always contained in the box defined by the x,y position and the *width* and *height* arguments. The *x,y* arguments are not the center of the arc/circle.

The arc begins at *angle1* degrees and continues for *angle2* degrees around the circle. The arc is drawn in the current foreground color in the current drawing area. The top left corner of the drawing area is considered 0,0.

If you want a circle, specify *angle1* as 0 and *angle2* as 360.

If *width* and *height* are negative, the arc is still drawn properly.

DrawFilledArc(*x*, *y*, *width*, *height*, *angle1*, *angle2*)

This function draws a filled arc/ellipse from the location x,y that is bounded by the box defined by *x*, *y*, *width*, and *height*. That is, the arc/ellipse is always contained in the box defined by the x,y position and the *width* and *height* arguments. The x,y arguments are not the center of the arc/circle.

The arc begins at *angle1* degrees and continues for *angle2* degrees around the circle. The arc is filled with the current foreground color in the current drawing area. The top left corner of the drawing area is considered 0,0.

If you want a circle, specify *angle1* as 0, and *angle2* as 360.

If *width* and *height* are negative, the arc is still drawn properly.

DrawImage(*data*, *x*, *y*, *width*, *height*)

This function draws a bitmap image that has a width and height as specified by the arguments. The image is drawn at location *x,y* in the current drawing area. The **data** argument should contain at least *width*height* bytes of data.

Each byte of the data is interpreted as a color value to draw the corresponding pixel with.

Normally, you would use this function when you have taken over the colormap with **GetAllColors()** (so you can be guaranteed that certain colors are in a given range). If you have not taken over the colormap, you need to make sure that the bytes in the image data contain valid values that you've allocated with the color allocation functions (GetNamedColor(), GetRGBColor(), or GetPrivateColor()).

The top left corner of the drawing area is considered 0,0.

GetImage(*x, y, width, height, result*)

This function retrieves a bitmap image from your drawing area that has a width and height as specified by the arguments. The image is taken from the starting location *x,y* in the current drawing area.

The *result* variable is filled with the eight-bit pixel values of the current drawing area. Note that the pixel values are not the actual color values. If you want the actual color values, you need to know what the current colormap is (which you know if you've set the colormap) and then use the pixel values to index the colormap.

The memory pointed to by data is packed with *width*height* bytes, with no extra padding or filling. That is, the first *width* bytes correspond to line 0, the next *width* bytes correspond to line 1 of the image, etc.

It is important to keep in mind that if you plan to save the pixel data in an image file, you need to also keep track of the colormap so that you can save that as well. By themselves, the pixel values don't correspond to any particular color.

A serious drawback of this function arises from the way X operates. If the drawing area from which you are "getting" the image is obscured by another window, that part of the bitmap will be empty. The only way around this is to make sure that your window is in front of all the others before you call GetImage(). This is a serious limitation, but it's the way X operates.

The top left corner of the drawing area is considered 0,0. If you specify starting *x,y* and **width** and **height** dimensions that are larger than your drawing area, you get a *BadMatch* error and X terminates your program (so be careful).

ScrollDrawArea(*dx, dy, x1, y1, x2, y2*)

This function scrolls the box defined by (*x1,y1*) (*x2,y2*) by the amounts *dx* and *dy* in the x and y directions respectively. This means that the box whose upper left corner is (*x1,y1*) and whose lower right corner is (*x2,y2*) is scrolled by *dx* and *dy* pixels in x and y.

A positive value for *dx* causes the drawing area to scroll its contents to the left. That is, whatever is at the left edge gets pushed off and the *dx* columns of pixels on the righthand side are cleared to the background color. A negative value has the opposite effect.

A positive value for *dy* corresponds to scrolling upwards. That is, whatever is at the top of the drawing area is pushed up by *dy* pixels and the bottom *dy* rows of pixels are cleared to the background color. A negative value has the opposite effect.

This function is useful for scrolling the drawing area to draw new information (such as a text editor might do to scroll text up or down).

The new area exposed by the scroll is filled with the current background color of the drawing area.

Color Stuff

This describes the routines for managing colors in your window, for example, if you want to change the foreground color or need to get specific colors. To get specific colors, you use the functions discussed in this section. It is important to remember that you cannot call any of these functions until you have called ShowDisplay().

Colors are represented by integers. When you get a color, you are returned an integer that you can use in calls to SetFgColor(), SetBgColor(), and SetColor(). You should attach no meaning to the numbers, and just because green is 17 does not mean that 18 is a lighter or darker shade of green.

There are three ways to manipulate colors with Sxperl. The first way handles most of the common cases and is done with GetNamedColor() or GetRGBColor().

The next method, GetPrivateColor(), allows your application to modify the actual display color represented by a color number (something you cannot do with the other methods).

The final method gives you complete control in specifying the entire colormap. That is, you can determine exactly what integers map to what colors so you can obtain smooth gradients (so that, for example, black is color 0, and white is 255). These routines work best on eight-bit displays, but also work on 24-bit displays.

Note: You cannot call any color function until you have called ShowDisplay().

The way colors work for drawing is like this. There are usually 256 available colors on a workstation. This is called an eight-bit display because $2^8 = 256$. These colors are stored in a table (array) of 256 entries. If you allocate a color, and it is in entry 37, then to draw with the color that is stored there, you must use 37 as an argument to the SetColor() function. When you ask for a color, it may be taken from anywhere in the array of 256 entries, and there is *no* guarantee that if you allocate a green color that the next color in the table will be a lighter or darker green. Even if you allocate many colors using GetNamedColor() or GetRGBColor(), you have *no* assurance about where those colors are in the array (chances are they won't be contiguous). If you need to have a contiguous set of numbers, you must use GetAllColors(), and then SetColorMap() or SetMyColorMap() to set up a custom colormap with a known set of values. When you get a private color, your application can specify what values that color index should have. This is useful when you want to interactively modify a color.

It is important to remember that "getting a color" really means getting an index into the color table where the actual color is stored.

GetStandardColors()

> This function sets six functions returning the standard colors RED, GREEN, BLUE, YELLOW, BLACK, and WHITE. The values returned can be used in calls to SetColor(), SetFgColor(), SetBgColor(), etc.

> Do not call RED, GREEN, BLUE, YELLOW, BLACK, or WHITE before calling GetStandardColors(). The results are undefined if you do this.

> Note: You can only call GetStandardColors() after calling the ShowDisplay() function.

GetNamedColor(*name*)

This function allocates an entry in the color table for the color given by the ASCII string **name**. You can view the list of available color names with the **showrgb** command in a shell (some nice ones are peachpuff, burlywood3, aquamarine, and paleturquoise3). Color names can have spaces in them. The return value of the function is an integer that you can use in calls to **SetColor()** (or any of the other **SetXXColor()** calls). If an error occurs trying to allocate the color (very possible if you allocate a lot of colors), –1 is returned.

GetRGBColor(*red, green, blue*)

This function tries to allocate the color given by the red, green, blue triple (r,g,b). The arguments **red, green,** and **blue** should be between 0 and 255. Overflow is not checked for. The return value is an integer value usable in the **SetColor()** calls or –1 if an error occurs.

GetPrivateColor()

This function allocates a private color cell for use by the application. A private color cell is one for which you can change the color it represents. For example, if you would like to let the user interactively manipulate some color, you need to allocate a private color cell.

The integer returned by this function is a reference to a color cell whose values you can set with **SetPrivateColor()**. The initial contents of the private color cell are undefined, and you should probably call **SetPrivateColor()** immediately to set it to some known value.

If an error occurs, –1 is returned.

When you are done with a private color cell, you should free it with **FreePrivateColor()**.

SetPrivateColor(*which, r, g, b*)

This function sets the color cell referred to by **which** to have the *r,g,b* values specified. The *r,g,b* values are given in the range 0–255 (inclusive). Once this function is called, anything drawn in the display with the color **which** has the new color determined by the *r,g,b* arguments.

FreePrivateColor(*which*)

This function returns the color associated with the private color cell **which** to the system. You should have allocated the color referred to by **which** with **GetPrivateColor()**.

GetAllColors()

This function is rather drastic and should be used with caution. It immediately grabs an entire 256-entry colormap for private use. This has the unfortunate effect of (temporarily) wiping out the colors in all the other windows on the display. However, this is necessary if you wish to get a smooth colormap to use in displaying a smooth-shaded or continuous-tone picture. Once **GetAllColors()** has been called, the entire colormap is free for manipulation by your program. The colormap remains allocated until you call **FreeAllColors()**, at which time everything goes back to normal.

If an error occurs (quite possible), this routine returns FALSE. If everything goes ok, and the colormap is successfully allocated, TRUE is returned.

If you can avoid using this function, try to. It is disconcerting for users to have the colormap get wacked out and have most of their windows disappear (the windows don't really disappear of course, you just can't see them, usually). However, it is sometimes necessary to do this, as there is no other way to get a smoothly continuous color map.

Usually, you will want to call `SetColorMap()` or `SetMyColorMap()` right after this function.

Note: On a 24-bit machine (like the SGI Indigo Elan I tested this with), only the current drawing area gets the colormap; other widgets and windows are not affected.

FreeAllColors()

This function frees a private colormap that was allocated with `GetAllColors()`. It has the beneficial effect of immediately restoring the rest of the colors on the screen and in other windows to those that existed prior to the call to `GetAllColors()`. This function is useful if you wish to let users restore their original colors temporarily (although this happens automatically when the mouse moves outside the window).

SetColorMap(*num*)

This function creates several predefined color maps that are very smoothly continuous. It saves you the hassle of writing them yourself (even though they are mostly easy). The *num* argument you pass in should be one of the following variables:

```
GREY_SCALE_1    0
GREY_SCALE_2    1
RAINBOW_1       2
RAINBOW_2       3
```

The colormap GREY_SCALE_2 is a complete smooth color ramp from pure black (color 0) to pure white (color 255). The other grey-scale, GREY_SCALE_1 is a nearly pure ramp from black (color 0) to white (color 252), but it has a few additional colors thrown in near the end of the colormap. The two RAINBOW_? colormaps have different types of smoothly changing rainbows of color. These are really only useful for drawing pretty patterns or doing false coloring.

Note: You should call `GetAllColors()` before you call this routine. It is not necessary, but if you don't, and `GetAllColors()` fails, you will never know about it, and your application may not work very well.

SetMyColorMap(*red1, green1, blue1, ..., redN, greenN, blueN*)

Occasionally, it is necessary to have absolute control over your colormap, and this function lets you do that. It lets you completely specify each and every color that will be in the colormap. The values for *redi, greeni,* or *bluei* range from 0 to 255. You need not specify a full list of 256 triplets; you can in fact specify only a few.

Note: You should call `GetAllColors()` before you call this routine. It is not necessary, but if you don't and `GetAllColors()` fails, you will never know about it, and your application may not work very well.

Fonts

Fonts are different type styles that can be used in various widgets. You load a font by name and get a handle in return. The handle you get allows you to set the font in the various widgets and font information calls.

`GetFont(`*`fontname`*`)`

> This function loads the font named by *fontname* and returns a handle to the font, or FALSE if there is an error. The handle returned by this function is an XFont object and should be treated as an opaque data type.

> After you've loaded a font, you can then set that font in any widget that displays text. You can also use the handle in calls to `TextWidget()` and `FontHeight()`.

> When you are done with a font, you should free it with `FreeFont()`.

`SetWidgetFont(`*`widget, font`*`)`

> This function sets the font used by the widget *widget* to be the font referred to by the argument *font*. The argument `font` should have been obtained with `GetFont()`.

`GetWidgetFont(`*`widget`*`)`

> This function returns a handle to the font currently used by the widget *widget*. If an error occurs or there is no default font for the widget, FALSE is returned.

> You should *not* call `FreeFont()` on any value returned by this function unless you are sure that you allocated the font with `GetFont()`.

`FreeFont(`*`font`*`)`

> This function frees the resources associated with the font. You should call this function when your application is done using a particular font.

> Of course, you should make sure that no widget still uses the identified font.

`FontHeight(`*`font`*`)`

> This function returns an integer value that is the height in pixels of the specified font. The height is defined to be the ascent of the characters (from the baseline to the top of a capital letter) plus the descent of the characters (the distance from the baseline to bottom of a descender character like "g" or "p").

`TextWidth(`*`font, txt`*`)`

> This function returns the width in pixels used by the string pointed to by *txt* in the specified *font*. The entire string is used to determine the width.

Miscellaneous

The following function allows you to specify how the display should be laid out. It lets you logically position the components you created with the `MakeXXX()` functions. You use this function to lay out the arrangement of your buttons, labels, and drawing area(s).

`SetWidgetPos(`*`widget, where1, from1, where2, from2`*`)`

> This function lets you position a widget in your window. The idea is that you specify logical placement of the widget (i.e., place it to the right of this widget and under that widget). Many layouts are possible, and you can even specify that you don't care where a specific widget is placed.

> There are three types of placement. You can place a widget to the right of another widget with PLACE_RIGHT. If the argument *where1* is PLACE_RIGHT, then the specified widget is placed to the right of the widget *from1*. If *where1* is

equal to PLACE_UNDER, the widget is placed under the widget *from1*. The same holds true for the argument *where2* and widget *from2*. Having two arguments is necessary to be able to unambiguously specify where you want components placed in the display. If you don't care where a widget is placed, you can use NO_ CARE for the *where* argument and a Nullsx value for the *from* argument.

Generally, the first widget created need not be specified; it will always be in the top left corner. Other widgets can then be placed relative to that widget. For example, if you created four widgets ($w[0..4]) and wanted to arrange them in a column, you would do the following :

```
SetWidgetPos($w[1], PLACE_UNDER, $w[0], NO_CARE, Nullsx);
SetWidgetPos($w[2], PLACE_UNDER, $w[1], NO_CARE, Nullsx);
SetWidgetPos($w[3], PLACE_UNDER, $w[2], NO_CARE, Nullsx);
```

Notice how the third argument changes; we are placing the next widget underneath the previous widget. The "zeroth" widget ($w[0]) doesn't have to be placed because it is always in the top left corner (this can not be changed).

If you wanted to arrange things in a row, use PLACE_RIGHT instead of PLACE_ UNDER.

As a more complicated example, suppose you want to create two rows of widgets and a drawing area. You would do the following:

```
# first three across the top
SetWidgetPos($w[1], PLACE_RIGHT, $w[0], NO_CARE, Nullsx);
SetWidgetPos($w[2], PLACE_RIGHT, $w[1], NO_CARE, Nullsx);
SetWidgetPos($w[3], PLACE_RIGHT, $w[2], NO_CARE, Nullsx);
# next three underneath the top row
SetWidgetPos($w[4], PLACE_UNDER, $w[0], NO_CARE, Nullsx);
SetWidgetPos($w[5], PLACE_UNDER, $w[0], PLACE_RIGHT, $w[4]);
SetWidgetPos($w[6], PLACE_UNDER, $w[0], PLACE_RIGHT, $w[5]);
# put the drawing area under the second row
SetWidgetPos($w[7], PLACE_UNDER, $w[4], NO_CARE, Nullsx);
```

It is useful to think of the window as a kind of grid in which you can put various pieces. Just draw a picture of what you want and then use SetWidgetPos() to indicate to the system what is next to or underneath what.

Also, not all imaginable layouts are possible with SetWidgetPos(). For example, you cannot specify specific pixel offsets for a widget, or that it be centered in the display, or right-justified. This limitation is for the sake of simplicity. Generally, this should not be a problem (if it is, you are probably getting beyond the scope of what libsx was intended to provide, i.e., you're becoming an X hacker).

You can simulate more complicated layouts by cheating and creating label widgets whose label is just spaces and then placing other widgets to the left or underneath the label. This works, but is kind of hackish. See also SetWid-getInt() for another way to cheat.

SetFgColor(*widget, color*)

This function sets the foreground color of a widget. If the widget is a drawing area, all future primitives are drawn with the specified color. If the widget is some other type of widget, it sets the foreground color of the widget (such as its text) to be the specified color.

The argument *color* should be an integer that was returned from the colormap functions (GetNamedColor(), GetRGBColor(), GetPrivateColor(), or GetStandardColors()).

SetBgColor(*widget, color*)

This function sets the background color of a widget. If the specified widget is a drawing area, the next call to ClearDisplay() clears the drawing area to the specified background color.

The argument *color* should be an integer that was returned from the colormap functions (GetNamedColor(), GetRGBColor(), GetPrivateColor(), or GetStandardColors()).

SetBorderColor(*widget, color*)

This argument sets the border color that is drawn around a widget. The same effect happens for all of the different widgets—the border is redrawn with the new color. This can be very useful for giving a nice visual offset to an important or dangerous button. Of course, you should avoid garish combinations of colors that are hard to look at.

GetFgColor(*widget*)

This routine is a convenience function that returns the current foreground color of any kind of widget. This is mainly useful for drawing widgets to make sure that you draw things in the proper foreground color. This can arise as a problem if you assume that black is going to be the default foreground color (which it normally is). However, the user can change this default by using the -fg color option on the command line. This is an X command-line option and cannot be overriden by your program. A real application would use this function to check the value and use it to draw in the user's preferred foreground color. Other programs can just ignore the problem and still work ok as long as the user doesn't change the program's colors.

This function returns the integer value of the foreground color that you can use in later calls to SetFgColor() or SetColor(). It returns −1 if you passed an invalid widget to it.

GetBgColor(*widget*)

This routine is a convenience function that returns the current background color of any kind of widget. This is mainly useful for drawing widgets to make sure that you draw things in the proper background color. This can be a problem if you assume that white is going to be the default background color (which it normally is). However, the user can change this default by using the -bg color option on the command line. This is an X command-line option, and cannot be overriden by your program. A real application would use this function to check the value and use it to draw in the user's preferred background color. Other programs can just ignore the problem and still work ok as long as the user doesn't change the program's colors.

The other problem that crops up if you ignore the background color is that if you go to erase something by just drawing in white and white doesn't happen to be the actual background color, your program will look funny.

This function returns the integer value of the background color that you can use in later calls to SetBgColor() or SetColor(). It returns −1 if you passed an invalid widget to it.

AddTimeOut(*interval, func, data*)

If you would like to animate a display or do some periodic processing (such as an autosave feature for an editor), you can use timeouts.

A timeout is a callback function that gets called when the specified amount of time has expired (or, more precisely, when at *least* that much time has passed; UNIX ain't no real-time system).

The argument *interval* is an unsigned long and is specified in milliseconds. That is, a timeout of 1 second would be an argument of 1000.

The callback should look like:

```
sub  func {
    my($data) = @_;
}
```

The function is only called once; if you would like the function to be called repeatedly (to update an animation, for example), the last thing the function should do is to call AddTimeOut() again.

The value returned by AddTimeOut() can be used with RemoveTimeOut() to cancel that timeout.

RemoveTimeOut(*id*)

Cancels a timeout callback that was previously registered with AddTimeOut().

Argument id is an identifier returned by AddTimeOut().

SetWidgetState(*widget, state*)

This function lets you enable or disable particular widgets in an interface. If, for example, choosing one item from a menu should disable various other widgets, you can call this function.

The *widget* argument is the widget in question. The *state* argument is a Boolean, which indicates whether the widget should be active or not. A value of TRUE indicates that the widget should accept input, and a value of FALSE indicates that the widget should not accept input (it becomes greyed out).

When you disable a widget, the user can no longer interact with that widget in *any* way (it is greyed out and ignores all input).

GetWidgetState(*widget*)

This function returns a Boolean value indicating whether or not the specified widget is currently active.

If the widget is active and accepting input, the return is TRUE; if the widget is inactive, the return value is FALSE.

Beep()

This function is really complicated: it beeps the workstation speaker.

SetWidgetBitmap(*widget, data, width, height*)

This function lets you attach a bitmap, instead of the default text, to a widget. This function only works correctly on Button, Toggle, and Label widgets. Using it on another type of widget yields undefined results.

The widget displays the bitmap data given by the argument *data*, whose width and height are given as the last two arguments.

The bitmap data is only one bitplane deep and is usually produced by an X program called bitmap. The output of the bitmap program is a file you can almost always directly **require** in your source code. The contents of the file is an array of characters and two **#defines** that give the width and height of the bitmap.

Thus, making a widget with a bitmap is a three-step process. First, you edit a bitmap using the **bitmap** program, then you need to edit the resulting file to convert it to Perl syntax, and finally you do the following:

```
require  'bmap.ph';
$w = MakeButton(Nullsx, 'func', $a_value);
SetWidgetBitmap($w, $bmap_bits,$bmap_width,$bmap_height);
```

Bits that are a one in the bitmap are drawn in the widget's current foreground color, and zero bits are drawn in the current background color.

Addition to the Original libsx

All the following functions and widgets were added to **libsx**:

DestroyWidget(*widget*)
> This function call destroys a given widget and all its descendants. Care should be taken not to reuse the widget after that.

SetWidgetInt(*widget, resource, value*)
> Sets the named resource with an integer value for a given widget.

SetWidgetDat(*widget, resource, value*)
> Sets the named resource with a string value for a given widget.

GetWidgetInt(*widget, resource*)
> Gets the integer value of the named resource.

GetWidgetDat(*widget, resource*)
> Gets the string value of the named resource.

The following functions are intended for Text widgets:

AppendText(*widget, text*)
> Appends the given text to the end of widget, which should be a text entry widget.

InsertText(*widget, text*)
> Inserts the given text in a text entry widget at the current caret position.

ReplaceText(*widget, text, left, right*)
> Replaces the text in the widget between position *left* and *right* with the *text*.

GetSelection(*widget, buf*)
> Returns (in *buf*) the selected string from the given text widget.

GetTextSelectionPos(*widget,* left, right)
> Returns (in left and right) the start and the end of the selected area.

SetTextSelection(*widget, left, right*)
> Sets the start (*left*) and the end (*right*) of the selected area.

UnsetTextSelection(*widget, left, right*)
> Unsets the selection.

Miscellaneous functions:

WarpPointer(*widget, x, y*)
> Moves the pointer to the (*x, y*) coordinates relative to the given widget.

AddReadCallback(*fd*, *func*, *data*)

> Adds an input callback that gets called if some data are readable for a given file descriptor *fd.*

AddWriteCallback(*fd*, *func*, *data*)

> Like AddReadCallback(), but checks for data writable.

RemoveReadWriteCallback(*id*)

> Cancels an AddReadCallback() or AddWriteCallback() request; *id* is the value as returned by AddReadCallback() or AddWriteCallback().

AddTranslation(*widget*, *translation_table*)

> Add (override) a translation table for the specified widget. Each translation should associate an event to a Perl action. This action takes the widget as its first argument, then the event as packed data, followed by the rest of the specified arguments. Be warned that the arguments are passed as strings. So if you want to pass Perl variables, you should quote them and use eval in the callback.

> For example:

```
sub pargs {
   my($w,$ev,@a) = @_;
   print "args are [@_]\n";
   SetLabel($w,join('-',@a));
}
sub quit { exit }
@ARGV = OpenDisplay('test',@ARGV);
$w1 = MakeButton('quit',\&quit,undef);
AddTranslation($w1,
               '<Btn1Up>' => 'pargs(button1,up)',
               '<Btn1Down>' => 'pargs(button1,down)',
               '<Btn2Up>' => 'pargs(button2,up)',
               '<Btn2Down>' => 'pargs(button2,down)',
               '<Btn3Up>' => 'pargs(button3,up)',
               '<Btn3Down>' => 'pargs(button3,down)',
               '<Motion>' => 'pargs(motion)');
ShowDisplay;
MainLoop;
```

Author

Original by Dominic Giampaolo, *dbg@sgi.com*

Rewritten for Sx by Frederic Chauveau, *fmc@pasteur.fr*

Term::ANSIColor—color screen output using ANSI escape sequences

Synopsis

```
use Term::ANSIColor;
print color 'bold blue';
print "This text is bold blue.\n";
print color 'reset';
print "This text is normal.\n";
print colored ("Yellow on magenta.\n", 'yellow on_magenta');
print "This text is normal.\n";
```

```
use Term::ANSIColor qw(:constants);
print BOLD, BLUE, "This text is in bold blue.\n", RESET;
use Term::ANSIColor qw(:constants);
$Term::ANSIColor::AUTORESET = 1;
print BOLD BLUE "This text is in bold blue.\n";
print "This text is normal.\n";
```

Description

This module has two interfaces, one through `color()` and `colored()` and the other through constants.

`color()` takes any number of strings as arguments and considers them to be space-separated lists of attributes. It then forms and returns the escape sequence to set those attributes. It doesn't print it out, just returns it, so you'll have to print it yourself if you want to (this is so that you can save it as a string, pass it to something else, send it to a file handle, or do anything else with it that you might care to).

The recognized attributes (all of which should be fairly intuitive) are `clear`, `reset`, `bold`, `underline`, `underscore`, `blink`, `reverse`, `concealed`, `black`, `red`, `green`, `yellow`, `blue`, `magenta`, `on_black`, `on_red`, `on_green`, `on_yellow`, `on_blue`, `on_magenta`, `on_cyan`, and `on_white`. Case is not significant. Underline and underscore are equivalent, as are clear and reset, so use whichever is the most intuitive to you. The color alone sets the foreground color, and `on_color` sets the background color.

Note that attributes, once set, last until they are unset (by sending the attribute `reset`). Be careful to do this, or your attribute will persist after your script is done running, and people get very annoyed at having their prompt and typing changed to weird colors.

As an aid, `colored()` takes a scalar as the first argument and any number of attribute strings as the second argument. It returns the scalar wrapped in escape codes, so that the attributes will be set as requested before the string and reset to normal after the string. Normally, `colored()` just puts attribute codes at the beginning and end of the string, but if you set `$Term::ANSIColor::EACHLINE` to some string, that string is considered the line delimiter and the attribute is set at the beginning of each line of the passed string and reset at the end of each line. This is often desirable if the output is being sent to a program like a pager that can be confused by attributes that span lines. Normally, you'll want to set `$Term::ANSIColor::EACHLINE` to \n to use this feature.

Alternately, if you import `:constants`, you can use the constants CLEAR, RESET, BOLD, UNDERLINE, UNDERSCORE, BLINK, REVERSE, CONCEALED, BLACK, RED, GREEN, YELLOW, BLUE, MAGENTA, ON_BLACK, ON_RED, ON_GREEN, ON_YELLOW, ON_BLUE, ON_MAGENTA, ON_CYAN, and ON_WHITE directly. These are the same as `color('attribute')` and can be used if you prefer typing:

```
print BOLD BLUE ON_WHITE "Text\n", RESET;
```

to:

```
print colored ("Text\n", 'bold blue on_white');
```

When using the constants, if you don't want to have to remember to add the ", RESET" at the end of each print line, you can set `$Term::ANSIColor::AUTORESET` to a true value. Then the display mode is automatically reset if there is no comma after the constant. In other words, with that variable set:

```
print BOLD BLUE "Text\n";
```

resets the display mode afterwards, whereas:

```
print BOLD, BLUE, "Text\n";
```

does not.

The subroutine interface has the advantage over the constants interface in that only two subroutines are exported into your namespace, versus 22 in the constants interface. On the flip side, the constants interface has the advantage of better compile-time error checking, since misspelled names of colors or attributes in calls to `color()` and `colored()` aren't caught until runtime, whereas misspelled names of constants are caught at compile time. So, pollute your namespace with almost two dozen subroutines that you may not even use that often, or risk a silly bug by mistyping an attribute. Your choice, TMTOWTDI after all.

Diagnostics

Invalid attribute name %s
> You passed an invalid attribute name to either `color()` or `colored()`.

Identifier %s used only once: possible typo
> You probably mistyped a constant color name such as:
>
> ```
> print FOOBAR "This text is color FOOBAR\n";
> ```
>
> It's probably better to always use commas after constant names in order to force the next error.

No comma allowed after filehandle
> You probably mistyped a constant color name such as:
>
> ```
> print FOOBAR, "This text is color FOOBAR\n";
> ```
>
> Generating this fatal compile error is one of the main advantages of using the constants interface, since you'll immediately know if you mistype a color name.

Bareword %s not allowed while "strict subs" in use
> You probably mistyped a constant color name such as:
>
> ```
> $Foobar = FOOBAR . "This line should be blue\n";
> ```
>
> or:
>
> ```
> @Foobar = FOOBAR, "This line should be blue\n";
> ```
>
> This only shows up under **use strict** (another good reason to run under **use strict**).

Restrictions

It would be nice if one could leave off the commas around the constants entirely and just say:

```
print BOLD BLUE ON_WHITE "Text\n" RESET;
```

but the syntax of Perl doesn't allow this. You need a comma after the string. (Of course, you may consider it a bug that commas between all the constants aren't required, in which case you may feel free to insert commas unless you're using `$Term::ANSIColor::AUTORESET`.)

For easier debugging, you may prefer to always use the commas when not setting `$Term::ANSIColor::AUTORESET` so that you'll get a fatal compile error rather than a warning.

Authors

Original idea (using constants) by Zenin (*zenin@best.com*), reimplemented using subs by Russ Allbery (*rra@cs.stanford.edu*), and then combined with the original idea by Russ with input from Zenin.

Term::Gnuplot—low-level graphics using gnuplot drawing routines

Synopsis

```
use Term::Gnuplot ':ALL';
change_term('dumb') or die "Cannot set terminal.\n";
init();
graphics();
$xmax = xmax();
$ymax = ymax();
linetype(-2);
move(0,0);
vector($xmax-1,0);
vector($xmax-1,$ymax-1);
vector(0,$ymax-1);
vector(0,0);
justify_text(LEFT);
put_text(h_char()*5, $ymax - v_char()*3,"Terminal Test, Perl");
$x = $xmax/4;
$y = $ymax/4;
$xl = h_tic()*5;
$yl = v_tic()*5;
linetype(2);
arrow($x,$y,$x+$xl,$y,1);
arrow($x,$y,$x+$xl/2,$y+$yl,1);
arrow($x,$y,$x,$y+$yl,1);
arrow($x,$y,$x-$xl/2,$y+$yl,0);
arrow($x,$y,$x-$xl,$y,1);
arrow($x,$y,$x-$xl,$y-$yl,1);
arrow($x,$y,$x,$y-$yl,1);
arrow($x,$y,$x+$xl,$y-$yl,1);
text();
Term::Gnuplot::reset();
```

Description

Exports

None by default

Exportable

```
change_term test_term init_terminal
LEFT CENTER RIGHT
name description xmax ymax v_char h_char v_tic h_tic
init scale graphics linetype move vector point text_angle
justify_text put_text arrow text
```

Export tags

:ALL for all stuff, :SETUP for the first row above, :JUSTIFY for the second, :FIELDS for the third, :METHODS for the rest

Semantics

Below I include the contents of the file *term/README* from the gnuplot distribution. It explains the meaning of the above methods. Everything is supported under Perl except the options method. The description below includes underscores, which are deleted in the Perl interface.

The only functions that are not included are change_term($newname), test_term() and init_terminal(), which should be self-explanatory. Currently, it is impossible to find names of supported terminals; this would require a patch to gnuplot.

"Documentation for gnuplot Terminal Driver Writers," by Russell Lang

Information on each terminal device driver is contained in *term.c* and the *term/*.trm* files. Each driver is contained in a *.trm* file and is #included into *term.c*. Each driver has a set of initializers in *term.c* for term_tbl[], an array of struct termentry.

Here is the definition of the struct termentry from *plot.h*:

```
struct termentry {
    char *name;
    char *description;
    unsigned int xmax,ymax,v_char,h_char,v_tic,h_tic;
    FUNC_PTR options,init,reset,text,scale,graphics,move,
            vector,linetype, put_text,text_angle,
            justify_text,point,arrow;
};
```

Here's a brief description of each variable:

The char *name is a pointer to a string containing the name of the terminal. This name is used by the set terminal and show terminal commands. The name must be unique and must not be confused with an abbreviation of another name. For example, if the name postscript exists, it is not possible to have another name postscript2. Keep the name under 15 characters.

The char *description is a pointer to a string containing a description of the terminal, which is displayed in response to the set terminal command. Keep the description under 60 characters.

xmax is the maximum number of points in the x direction. The range of points used by gnuplot is 0 to xmax-1.

ymax is the maximum number of points in the y direction. The range of points used by gnuplot is 0 to ymax-1.

v_char is the height of characters, in the same units as xmax and ymax. The border for labeling at the top and bottom of the plot is calculated using v_char. v_char is used as the vertical line spacing for characters.

h_char is the width of characters, in the same units as xmax and ymax. The border for labeling at the left and right of the plot is calculated using h_char. If the _justify_ text function returns FALSE, h_char is used to justify text right or center. If characters are not fixed width, then the _justify_text function must correctly justify the text.

v_tic is the vertical size of tics along the x axis, in the same units as ymax.

h_tic is the horizontal size of tics along the y axis, in the same units as xmax.

Here's a brief description of what each *term.c* function does:

_options()

> Called when terminal type is selected. This procedure should parse options on the command line. A list of the currently selected options should be stored in term_options[] in a form suitable for use with the **set term** command. term_options[] is used by the **save** command. Use options_null() if no options are available.

_init()

> Called once, when the device is first selected. This procedure should set up things that only need to be set once, like handshaking and character sets, etc.

_reset()

> Called when gnuplot is exited, the output device changes or the terminal type changes. This procedure should reset the device, possibly flushing a buffer somewhere or generating a form feed.

_scale(*xs,ys*)

> Called just before _graphics(). This takes the x and y scaling factors as information. If the terminal would like to do its own scaling, it returns TRUE. Otherwise, it can ignore the information and return FALSE; do_plot will do the scaling for you. null_scale is provided to do just this, so most drivers can ignore this function entirely. The LaTeX driver is currently the only one providing its own scaling.

_graphics()

> Called just before a plot is going to be displayed. This procedure should set the device into graphics mode. Devices that can't be used as terminals (like plotters) will probably always be in graphics mode and therefore won't need this.

_text()

> Called immediately after a plot is displayed. This procedure should set the device back into text mode if it is also a terminal, so that commands can be seen as they're typed. Again, this will probably do nothing if the device can't be used as a terminal.

_move(*x, y*)

> Called at the start of a line. The cursor should move to the (x, y) position without drawing.

_vector(*x, y*)

> Called when a line is to be drawn. This should display a line from the last (*x, y*) position given by _move() or _vector() to this new (*x, y*) position.

_linetype(*lt*)

> Called to set the line type before text is displayed or line(s) plotted. This procedure should select a pen color or line style if the device has these capabilities:
>
> - lt is an integer from –2 to 0 or greater
> - An *lt* of –2 is used for the border of the plot
> - An *lt* of –1 is used for the x and axes
> - *lt* 0 and upwards are used for plots 0 and upwards

If _linetype() is called with *lt* greater than the available line types, it should map it to one of the available line types. Most drivers provide nine different line-types (*lt* of 0 to 8).

_put_text(*x,y,str*)

Called to display text at the (*x,y*) position, while in graphics mode. The text should be vertically (with respect to the text) justified about (*x,y*). The text is rotated according to _text_angle and then horizontally (with respect to the text) justified according to _justify_text.

_text_angle(*ang*)

Called to rotate the text angle when placing the y label. If *ang* = 0, then text is horizontal. If *ang* = 1, then text goes vertically upwards. Returns TRUE if text can be rotated, FALSE otherwise.

_justify_text(*mode*)

Called to justify text left, right, or center.

If *mode* = LEFT, then the text placed by _put_text is flush left against (x,y).

If *mode* = CENTRE, then the center of the text is at (x,y).

If *mode* = RIGHT, then text is placed flush right against (x,y).

Returns TRUE if text can be justified. Returns FALSE otherwise and then _put_text assumes text is flush left; in that case, justification of text is performed by calculating the text width using strlen(text) * h_char.

_point(*x,y,point*)

Called to place a point at position (*x,y*). *point* is −1 or an integer from 0 upwards. Six point types (numbered 0 to 5) are normally provided. Point type −1 is a dot. If point is greater than the available point types, then it should be mapped back to one of the available points. Two _point() functions called do_point() and line_and_point() are provided in *term.c* and should be suitable for most drivers. do_point() draws the points in the current line type. If your driver uses dotted line types (generally because it is monochrome), you should use line_and_point(), which changes to line type 0 before drawing the point. Line type 0 should be solid.

_arrow(*sx,sy,ex,ey,head*)

Called to draw an arrow from (*sx,sy*) to (*ex,ey*). A head is drawn on the arrow if *head* = TRUE. An _arrow() function called do_arrow() is provided in term.c that draws arrows using the _move() and _vector() functions. Drivers should use do_arrow unless it causes problems.

The following illustrates the order in which calls to these routines are made:

```
_init()
 _scale(xs,ys)
 _graphics()
  _linetype(lt)
  _move(x,y)
  _vector(x,y)
   _point(x,y,point)
 _text_angle(angle)
 _justify(mode)
 _put_text(x,y,text)
 _arrow(sx,sy,ex,ey)
```

```
        _text()
        _graphics()
              .
              .
              .
        _text()
     _reset()
```

Term::Query—intelligent user prompt/response driver

Synopsis

```
use Term::Query
qw( query query_table query_table_set_defaults query_table_process );
$result = query $prompt, $flags, [ $optional_args ];
$ok = query_table \@array;
query_table_set_defaults \@array;
$ok = query_table_process \@array, \&flagsub, \&querysub;
```

Description

Subroutines

query

The query subroutine fulfills the need for a generalized question-response subroutine, with programmatic defaulting, validation, condition, and error checking.

Given $prompt and $flags, and possibly additional arguments depending upon the characters in $flags, query issues a prompt to STDOUT and solicits input from STDIN. The input is validated against a set of test criteria as configured by the characters in $flags; if any of the tests fail, an error message is noted, and the query is retried.

When STDIN is not a tty (not interactive), prompts are not issued, and errors cause a return rather than attempting to obtain more input.

query_table

The query_table subroutine performs multiple queries by invoking query and setting associated variables with the results of each query. Prompts, flags, and other arguments for each query are given in an array, called a *query table*, which is passed to the query_table subroutine by reference.

query_table_set_defaults

The query_table_set_defaults subroutine causes any variables named in the given query table array to be assigned their corresponding default values, if any. This is a non-interactive subroutine.

query_table_process

A general interface to processing a query table is available with the query_table_process subroutine. It accepts a query table array and two subroutine references, &flagsub and &querysub. The &flagsub subroutine is invoked on each flag character in the $flags argument of the query table (see following information). The &querysub subroutine is invoked for each query in the query table.

The query_table and query_table_set_defaults subroutines both use query_table_process to perform their functions.

Query Table

The format of the query table array passed to query_table, query_table_set_defaults, and query_table_process subroutines is:

```
@array = ( $prompt1, $flags1, [ $arglist1, ... ],
           $prompt2, $flags2, [ $arglist2, ... ],
           ...
           $promptN, $flagsN, [ $arglistN, ... ] );
```

In English, there are three items per query: a prompt string, a flags string, and an array of arguments. Note that the syntax used above uses [...] to denote a Perl 5 anonymous array, not an optional set of arguments. Of course, if there are no arguments for a particular query, the corresponding anonymous array can be the null string or zero.

The query table design is such that a query table can be created with a set of variables, their defaults, value constraints, and help strings, and it can be used to both initialize the variables' values and to interactively set their new values. The query_table_set_defaults subroutine performs the former, while query_table does the latter.

Flag Characters

With typical usage, given $prompt and $flags, query prints $prompt and then waits for input from the user. The handling of the response depends upon the flag characters given in the $flags string.

The flag characters indicate the type of input, how to process it, acceptable values, etc. Some flags simply indicate the type or processing of the input, and do not require additional arguments. Other flags require that subsequent arguments to the query subroutine be given. The arguments must be given in the same order as their corresponding flag characters.

The ordering of the flags in the $flags argument is important—it determines the ordering of the tests. For example, if both the a and m flags are given as am, then this indicates that an *after* subroutine call should be performed first, followed by a regular expression *match* test.

All tests are applied in the order given in $flags until a particular test fails. When a test fails, an error message is generated and the input is retried, except in the case of the I flag.

Flag Characters Without Arguments

i	The input must be an integer.
n	The input must be a number, real or integer.
Y	The input is a **yes** or **no**, with a default answer of **yes**.
N	The input is a **yes** or **no**, with a default answer of **no**.
r	Some input is required; an empty response is refused. This option is only meaningful when there is no default input (see the d flag character below).

s   Strip and squeeze the input. Leading and trailing blanks are eliminated,
         and embedded whitespace is "squeezed" to a single blank character.
         This flag is implied by the k and K flags.

H   Do not treat input of ? as a request for help. This disables automatic
         help, unless implemented with the `after` (a flag) subroutine.

Flag Characters with Arguments

The following flag characters indicate the presence of an argument to query. The arguments must occur in the same order as their corresponding flag characters. For
example, if both the V and h flags are given as Vh, then the first argument must be the
variable name, and the next the help string, in that order.

a `\&after`
   The next argument is the *after* subroutine, to be invoked after the input has
   been solicited. This feature provides for an "open-ended" input validation,
   completely at the control of the user of the Query module. The `after` subroutine
   is invoked in this manner:

   ```
   &$after( \$input );
   ```

   If the *after* sub returns an `undef`, then query processing stops with an immediate `undef` return value.

   If the *after* sub returns a null or zero value, then the input is rejected and resolic-
   ited. No error messages are displayed except the "Please try again" message.

   Since the *after* sub has the reference to the `$input` variable, it is free to change
   the value of input, indirectly; i.e.:

   ```
   $$input = $some_new_value;
   ```

b `\&before`
   The next argument is the *before* subroutine, to be invoked before any input is
   attempted. If the *before* subroutine returns a non-null, non-zero value, the
   current query is attempted. If a null or zero value is returned, the current query is
   abandoned, with a null return.

   This feature, used in a *query table*, allows for selective queries to be programmed
   by using *before* subs on the optional queries. For example, using the following
   anonymous sub as the b flag argument:

   ```
   sub { $> == 0; }
   ```

   causes the corresponding query to be issued only for the `root` user.

   The ordering of the b flag in the `$flags` argument is unimportant, since, by definition, this test is always performed before attempting any input.

d `$default`
   The next argument is the *default* input. This string is used instead of an empty
   response from the user. The default value can be a scalar value, a reference to a
   scalar value, or a reference to a subroutine, which is invoked for its result only if
   a default value is needed (no input is given).

h `$help_string`
   The next argument is the *help_string*, which is printed in response to an input
   of ?. In order to enter a ? as actual text, it must be prefixed with a backslash: `\?`.

k *\@array*

The next argument is a reference to an array of allowable keywords. The input is matched against the array elements in a case-insensitive manner, with unambiguous abbreviations allowed. This flag implies the **s** flag.

The matching can be made case-sensitive by setting the following variable prior to the invocation of **query**:

```
$Query::Case_sensitive = 1;
```

By default, this variable is null.

K *\@array*

The next argument is a reference to an array of disallowed keywords. In this case, for the input to be unacceptable, it must match exactly, case-insensitive, one of the array elements. This flag implies the **s** flag.

The **k** option is useful for soliciting new, unique keywords for a growing list, such as adding new fields to a database.

The matching can be made case-sensitive by setting the **$Query::Case_sensitive** variable (see above).

l *$maxlen*

The next argument specifies the maximum length of the input.

m *$regular_expression*

The next argument specifies a regular expression pattern against which the input is matched.

I *$reference*

The next argument is the input: either a simple scalar value, or a *reference* to a value, such as a **SCALAR** variable reference (e.g., **\$somevar**), or a **CODE** reference (e.g., **sub {..}**). In any case, the resulting value is used as input instead of reading from STDIN.

If the input returned by the reference does not match other constraints, no additional attempt is made to get input. An error message is noted, and an **undef** return is taken.

This option is handy for applications that have already acquired the input, and wish to use the validation features of **query**.

It is also useful to embed in a query table a query definition that does not actually perform a query, but instead does a variable assignment dynamically, using the **I** reference value.

J *$reference*

The next argument is the input *reference*. This is like the **I** flag, except that if the input fails any of the constraints, additional input is solicited. In other words, the **J** flag sets a *one-time* only input reference. Think of it as *jumping* into the query loop with an initial input.

V *variable_name_or_ref*

The next argument is the name of the variable or reference that is to receive the validated input as its value. This option, and its corresponding variable name, are normally present on all entries used with **query_table** in order to retain the values resulting from each query.

The value can either be a string representing the variable name or a reference to a variable, e.g., \\$some_var.

Details

The query processing proceeds like this:

- If the b flag was given, the *before* subroutine is invoked as a "pre-input" test. If the subroutine returns a 0 or **undef**, the query is abandoned. Otherwise, processing continues.

- If the I or J flags were given, then input is obtained, without prompting, from the associated reference. If the reference type is **CODE**, then it is invoked and the resulting return value is used as the input. Otherwise, the reference is evaluated in a scalar context and used as the input. The J flag test is only done once, on the first entry into the input loop.

- In the absence of either the I or J flags, **query** issues the given prompt and obtains input from STDIN. If an EOF occurs, an **undef** value results.

- If the s, k, or K flags were given, the input is trimmed of leading and trailing blanks and all whitespace is "squeezed" to a single blank.

- If the input is an empty response, and there is a *default* input (d flag), the default input is used instead.

- Unless the H flag is given, if the input is the character ? with nothing else, then some helpful information is printed. If the user has supplied a *help_string*, it is printed, otherwise the message:

      You are being asked "$prompt"

  is displayed. Also, some information about the expected response, according to any given flag characters, is displayed. Finally, the user is returned to the prompt and given another opportunity to enter a response.

- If input is *required* (as indicated by the r flag), and if the input is empty, an error message is produced, and the query is repeated.

- If the query was flagged Y or N, the input is matched against the pattern:

      /^(y(es?)?|no?)$/i

  If the match fails, an error message is printed and the query is repeated. When the match succeeds, the input is replaced with either the complete word **yes** or **no**.

- If an integer response is required (i is flagged), a check is made for integer input. If the input is not an integer, an error is printed, and the query is repeated. A successful integer input is returned.

- If a numeric response is required (n flagged), a check is made for proper numeric input (in either integer or real format). Errors produce a warning and another query.

- If the query was given a *keyword* table (flagged with k), the input is matched against the allowable keyword list. If an exact match is found, the keyword is returned as the input. Failing an exact match, an abbreviation search is performed against the keywords. If a single match is found, it is returned as the input. If no match is found, an error message is produced, and the user is returned to the query to try again. Otherwise, the input was ambiguous, an error is noted showing the matches, and the user is queried again.

The matching is case-insensitive or not, according to the value of the variable `$Query::Case_sensitive`, which is null by default. The variable may be set by the user to change the matching from case-insensitive to case-sensitive.

- If the query was given an unacceptable-keyword list (flagged with K), the input is compared against the unacceptable keywords. If it matches any keywords exactly, an error is noted, and the query is performed again.

  The matching is case-insensitive by default. Set the variable `$Query::Case_sensitive` to a non-null, non-zero value to make the keyword matching case-sensitive.

- If the query was m-flagged with a Perl regular expression pattern, then the input is matched against the pattern. Failures are noted with an error message, and the query is retried.

- If the query was l-flagged with a maximum input length, the length of the input is checked against the maximum. A length violation is noted with an error message, and the user is queried again.

- If the query has a variable defined with the V flag, the variable is assigned the input string. This is always done last, after and only if all tests are successful.

  If the variable is a string name and not qualified with a package name (i.e., `$foo::variable`), then the variable is qualified at the level outside of the *Query.pm* module.

- Finally, having passed whatever conditions were flagged, the input is returned to the user.

Example

The following are typical usage examples:

- To perform a simple yes or no query, with no as the default answer:

  ```
  $ans = &query("Do you wish to quit? (yn)",'N');
  ```

- An equivalent alternative is:

  ```
  query "Do you wish to quit? (yn)", 'NV', \$ans;
  ```

- To perform the same query, with some helpful information supplied:

  ```
  $ans = &query("Do you wish to quit? (yn)",'Nh',<<'EOF');
  You are being asked if you wish to quit.  If you answer "yes",
  then all changes will be lost.  An answer of "no" will allow
  you to return to continue making changes.
  EOF
  ```

- To solicit an integer input:

  ```
  $mode = &query("Please enter the file
  mode:",'idh','644',<<'EOF');
  Please enter the 3 digit numeric file mode; if you are unsure
  of how the file mode is used, please see the manpage for
  "chmod".
  EOF
  ```

- To solicit one of several keywords:

  ```
  @keys = split(' ','SGI DEC IBM Sun HP Apple');
  $vendor = &query('Please enter a vendor:','rkd',\@keys,'SGI');
  ```

- To solicit a new, unique keyword to be used as a database field name, with a regexp pattern to check it against:

```
@fields = split(' ','Index Vendor Title'); # existing fields
$newfield = &query('New field name:','rKm',\@fields,'^\w+$');
```

Environment

COLUMNS

This variable is used to control the width of output when listing the keyword arrays. If not defined, 80 is used by default.

Dependencies

Carp.pm

Used to produce usage error messages

PrintArray.pm

Used to produce displays of the keyword arrays

Files

None

Diagnostics

Input is required

Issued when an empty response is given, and there is no default input.

Please answer with 'yes' or 'no', or enter '?' for help

Issued for Y- or N-flagged queries, and the input is not recognizable.

Please enter an integer number

Printed when non-integer input is given for i-flagged queries.

Please enter a number, real or integer

Printed when non-numeric input is given for n-flagged queries.

The input '$input' is ambiguous; it matches the following:

Issued in response to k-flagged queries with input that matches more than one of the allowed keywords.

The input '$input' fails to match any of the allowed keywords:

Printed when input to a k-flagged query does not match any of the keywords.

The input '%s' matches a disallowed keyword '%s'

Printed when the input matches one of the unacceptable keywords given on a K-flagged query.

'%s' fails to match '%s'

Results from input failing to match the regular expression given on an m-flagged query.

Input is %d characters too long; cannot exceed %d characters

The length of the input exceeded the maximum length given with the l-flag argument.

Please try again, or enter '?' for help

query: The k flag needs an array reference

The next argument in the argument list to **query** wasn't an array reference.

query: The K flag needs an array reference

The next argument in the argument list to **query** wasn't an array reference.

Author

Copyright © 1995 Alan K. Stebbens, *aks@hub.ucsb.edu*

This program is free software; you can redistribute it and/or modify it under the terms of the GNU General Public License as published by the Free Software Foundation; either version 2 of the License, or (at your option) any later version.

This program is distributed in the hope that it will be useful, but WITHOUT ANY WARRANTY; without even the implied warranty of MERCHANTABILITY or FITNESS FOR A PARTICULAR PURPOSE. See the GNU General Public License for more details.

You should have received a copy of the GNU General Public License along with this program; if not, write to the Free Software Foundation, Inc., 675 Mass Ave, Cambridge, MA 02139, USA.

Term::ReadKey—a Perl module for simple terminal control

Description

Term::ReadKey is a compiled Perl module dedicated to providing simple control over terminal driver modes (cbreak, raw, cooked, etc.), support for non-blocking reads if the architecture allows, and some generalized handy functions for working with terminals. One of the main goals is to have the functions as portable as possible, so you can just plug in use `Term::ReadKey` on any architecture and have a good likelihood of it working.

Functions

ReadMode *MODE* [, *Filehandle*]

   Takes an integer argument, which can currently be one of the following values:

```
0    Restore original settings.
1    Change to cooked mode.
2    Change to cooked mode with echo off.
       (Good for passwords)
3    Change to cbreak mode.
4    Change to raw mode.
5    Change to ultra-raw mode.
       (LF to CR/LF translation turned off)
```

   Or you may use the synonyms:

```
restore
normal
noecho
cbreak
raw
ultra-raw
```

   These functions are automatically applied to the STDIN handle if no other handle is supplied. Modes 0 and 5 have some special properties worth mentioning: not only does mode 0 restore original settings, but it causes the next `ReadMode` call to save a new set of default settings. Mode 5 is similar to mode 4, except no CR/LF translation is performed, and if possible, parity is disabled (only if it's not being used by the terminal, however).

If you are executing another program that may be changing the terminal mode, you either want to say:

```
ReadMode 1;
system('someprogram');
ReadMode 1;
```

which resets the settings after the program has run, or:

```
$somemode=1;
ReadMode 0;
system('someprogram');
ReadMode 1;
```

which records any changes the program may have made before it resets the mode.

ReadKey *MODE* [, *Filehandle*]

Takes an integer argument, which currently can be one of the following values:

```
 0   Perform a normal read using getc
-1   Perform a non-blocked read
>0   Perform a timed read
```

(If the filehandle is not supplied, it defaults to STDIN.) If there is nothing waiting in the buffer during a non-blocked read, then undef is returned. Note that if the OS does not provide any known mechanism for non-blocking reads, then a ReadKey -1 can die with a fatal error. This hopefully is not common.

If *MODE* is greater then zero, then ReadKey uses it as a timeout value in seconds (fractional seconds are allowed) and doesn't return undef until that time has expired. (Note, again, that some OSs may not support this timeout behavior.) If *MODE* is less then zero, then this is treated as a timeout of zero and thus returns immediately if no character is waiting. A *MODE* of zero, however, acts like a normal getc.

ReadLine *MODE* [, *Filehandle*]

Takes an integer argument, which currently can be one of the following values:

```
 0   Perform a normal read using scalar(<FileHandle>)
-1   Perform a non-blocked read
>0   Perform a timed read
```

If there is nothing waiting in the buffer during a non-blocked read, then undef is returned. Note that if the OS does not provide any known mechanism for non-blocking reads, then a ReadLine 1 can die with a fatal error. This hopefully is not common. Note that a non-blocking test is only performed for the first character in the line, not the entire line. This call probably does *not* do what you assume, especially with ReadModes greater then 1. For example, pressing Space and then Backspace appears to leave you where you started, but any timeouts are now suspended.

GetTerminalSize [*Filehandle*]

Returns either an empty array if this operation is unsupported or a four-element array containing the width of the terminal in characters, the height of the terminal in characters, the width in pixels, and the height in pixels.

SetTerminalSize *WIDTH, HEIGHT, XPIX, YPIX* [, *Filehandle*]

Returns −1 on failure, 0 otherwise. Note that this terminal size is only for *informative* value, and changing the size via this mechanism does *not* change the size of the screen. For example, XTerm uses a call like this when it resizes the screen. If any of the new measurements vary from the old, the OS will probably send a SIGWINCH signal to anything reading that tty or pty.

GetSpeeds [*Filehandle*]

Returns either an empty array if the operation is unsupported, or a two-value array containing the terminal in and out speeds, in *decimal*. For example, an in speed of 9600 baud and an out speed of 4800 baud are returned as (9600,4800). Note that currently the in and out speeds are always identical in some OSs.

GetControlChars [*Filehandle*]

Returns an array containing key/value pairs suitable for a hash. The pairs consist of a key, the name of the control character/signal, and the value of that character, as a single character.

Each key is an entry from the following list:

```
DISCARD
DSUSPEND
EOF
EOL
EOL2
ERASE
ERASEWORD
INTERRUPT
KILL
MIN
QUIT
QUOTENEXT
REPRINT
START
STATUS
STOP
SUSPEND
SWITCH
TIME
```

Thus, the following always returns the current interrupt character, regardless of platform:

```
%keys = GetControlChars;
$int = $keys{INTERRUPT};
```

SetControlChars [*Filehandle*]

Takes an array containing key/value pairs, such as a hash produces. The pairs should consist of a key that is the name of a legal control character/signal and a value that is either a single character or a number in the range 0-255. SetControl-Chars will die with a runtime error if an invalid character name is passed or there is an error changing the settings. The list of valid names is easily available via:

```
%cchars = GetControlChars();
@cnames = keys %cchars;
```

Term::ReadLine::Gnu—Perl extension for the GNU Readline/History Library

Synopsis

```
use Term::ReadLine;
$term = new Term::ReadLine 'ProgramName';
```

```
while ( defined ($_ = $term->readline('prompt>')) ) {
...
}
```

Description

Overview

This is an implementation of Term::ReadLine using the GNU Readline/History Library.

For basic functions an object-oriented interface is provided. These functions are described in the following sections on methods.

This package also has an interface with almost all the variables and functions that are documented in the GNU Readline/History Library Manual. These variables and functions are documented briefly in the section "Custom Completion: Variables and Functions." For more detail of the GNU Readline/History Library, see the "GNU Readline Library Manual" and "GNU History Library Manual."

Minimal Set of Methods Defined by Readline.pm

ReadLine
> Returns the actual package that executes the commands. If you have installed this package, a possible value is Term::ReadLine::Gnu.

new(*NAME*, [*IN*[, *OUT*]])
> Returns the handle for subsequent calls to following functions. The argument is the name of the application, which can optionally be followed by two arguments for IN and OUT file handles. These arguments should be globs.

readline(*PROMPT*[, *PREPUT*])
> Gets an input line, with actual GNU Readline support. A trailing newline is removed. Returns undef on EOF. *PREPUT* is an optional argument meaning the initial input value.
>
> The optional argument *PREPUT* is allowed only if the value preput is present in Features.

addhistory(*LINE1*, *LINE2*, ...)
> Adds the lines to the history of input, from which it can be used if the actual readline is present.

IN, OUT
> Returns the file handles for input and output, or undef if readline input and output cannot be used for Perl.

MinLine([*MAX*])
> If the argument *MAX* is specified, it is an advice on minimal size of the line to be included into history. undef means do not include anything into history. Returns the old value.

findConsole
> Returns an array with two strings that give the most appropriate names for files for input and output using the conventions <$in and $out>.

Attribs
> Returns a reference to a hash that describes the internal configuration (variables) of the package. The names of the keys in this hash conform to standard conventions, with the leading rl_ stripped.

See "Variables" for the supported variables.

Features

Returns a reference to a hash with the keys being features present in the current implementation. Several optional features are used in the minimal interface: `appname` should be present if the first argument to `new` is recognized, and `minline` should be present if the `MinLine` method is not a dummy. `autohistory` should be present if lines are put into history automatically (maybe subject to `MinLine`), and `addHistory` if the `AddHistory` method is not a dummy. `preput` means that the second argument to the `readline` method is processed. `getHistory` and `setHistory` denote that the corresponding methods are present. `tkRunning` denotes that a Tk application may run while ReadLine is getting input (this is an undocumented feature).

Additional Supported Methods

All these GNU Readline/History Library functions are callable via the method interface and have names that conform to standard conventions with the leading `rl_` stripped.

Almost the methods have lower-level functions in the `Term::ReadLine::Gnu::XS` package. To use them, the fully qualified name is required. Using the method interface is preferred.

Readline Convenience Functions

Naming Function

add_defun(*NAME*, *FUNC* [,*KEY*=-1])

Add *NAME* to the Perl function *FUNC*. If the optional argument *KEY* is specified, bind it to the *FUNC*. Returns a reference to `FunctionPtr`.

Example:

```
# name name 'reverse-line' to a function reverse_line(),
# and bind it to "\C-t"
$term->add_defun('reverse-line', \&reverse_line, "\ct");
```

Selecting a Keymap

make_bare_keymap
:   Keymap   rl_make_bare_keymap()

copy_keymap(*MAP*)
:   Keymap   rl_copy_keymap(Keymap|str map)

make_keymap
:   Keymap   rl_make_keymap()

discard_keymap(*MAP*)
:   Keymap   rl_discard_keymap(Keymap|str map)

get_keymap
:   Keymap   rl_get_keymap()

set_keymap(*MAP*)
:   Keymap   rl_set_keymap(Keymap|str map)

get_keymap_by_name(*NAME*)
:   Keymap   rl_get_keymap_by_name(str name)

get_keymap_name(*MAP*)
:   str   rl_get_keymap_name(Keymap map)

Binding Keys

bind_key(*KEY*, *FUNCTION* [,*MAP*])

Bind *KEY* to the *FUNCTION*. *FUNCTION* is the name added by the **add_defun** method. If the optional argument *MAP* is specified, it binds in *MAP*. Returns non-zero in case of error.

```
int    rl_bind_key(int key, FunctionPtr|str function,
                   Keymap|str map = rl_get_keymap())
```

unbind_key(*KEY* [,*MAP*])

Bind *KEY* to the null function. Returns non-zero in case of error.

```
int    rl_unbind_key(int key, Keymap|str
                     map = rl_get_keymap())
```

generic_bind(*TYPE*, *KEYSEQ*, *DATA*, [,*MAP*])

```
int    rl_generic_bind(int type, str keyseq,
                       FunctionPtr|Keymap|str data,
                       Keymap|str map = rl_get_keymap())
```

parse_and_bind(*LINE*)

Parse *LINE* as if it had been read from the *~/.inputrc* file and perform any key bindings and variable assignments found. For more detail see the "GNU Readline Library Manual."

```
void   rl_parse_and_bind(str line)
```

read_init_file([*FILENAME*])

```
int    rl_read_init_file(str filename = '~/.inputrc')
```

Associating Function Names and Bindings

call_function(*FUNCTION*, [*COUNT* [,*KEY*]])

```
int    rl_call_function(FunctionPtr|str function,
                        count = 1, key = -1)
```

named_function(*NAME*)

```
FunctionPtr rl_named_function(str name)
```

get_function_name(*FUNCTION*)

```
str    rl_get_function_name(FunctionPtr function)
```

function_of_keyseq(*KEYMAP* [,*MAP*])

```
(FunctionPtr|Keymap|str data, int type)
    rl_function_of_keyseq(str keyseq,
                          Keymap|str map = rl_get_keymap())
```

invoking_keyseqs(*FUNCTION* [,*MAP*])

```
(@str)  rl_invoking_keyseqs(FunctionPtr|str function,
                            Keymap|str map =
                            rl_get_keymap())
```

function_dumper([*READABLE*])

```
void   rl_function_dumper(int readable = 0)
```

list_funmap_names

```
void   rl_list_funmap_names()
```

Allowing Undoing

begin_undo_group

```
int    rl_begin_undo_group()
```

end_undo_group
        int   rl_end_undo_group()

add_undo(*WHAT*, *START*, *END*, *TEXT*)
        int   rl_add_undo(int what, int start, int end, str text)

free_undo_list
        void   free_undo_list()

do_undo
        int   rl_do_undo()

modifying([*START* [,*END*]])
        int   rl_modifying(int start = 0, int end = rl_end)

Redisplay

redisplay
        void   rl_redisplay()

forced_update_display
        int   rl_forced_update_display()

on_new_line
        int   rl_on_new_line()

reset_line_state
        int   rl_reset_line_state()

message(*FMT*[, ...])
        int   rl_message(str fmt, ...)

clear_message
        int   rl_clear_message()

Modifying Text

insert_text(*TEXT*)
        int   rl_insert_text(str text)

delete_text([*START* [,*END*]])
        int   rl_delete_text(start = 0, end = rl_end)

copy_text([*START* [,*END*]])
        str   rl_copy_text(start = 0, end = rl_end)

kill_text([*START* [,*END*]])
        int   rl_kill_text(start = 0, end = rl_end)

Utility Functions

read_key
        int   rl_read_key()

getc(*FILE*)
        int   rl_getc(FILE *)

stuff_char(C)
        int   rl_stuff_char(int c)

initialize
        int   rl_initialize()

reset_terminal([*TERMINAL_NAME*])
        int   rl_reset_terminal(str terminal_name = getenv($TERM))

ding
        int   ding()

Alternate Interface

> callback_handler_install(*PROMPT*, *LHANDLER*)
>> void   rl_callback_handler_install(str prompt,
>>   pfunc lhandler)

> callback_read_char
>> void   rl_callback_read_char()

> callback_handler_remove
>> void   rl_callback_handler_remove()

Completion Functions

complete_internal([*WHAT_TO_DO*])
> int   rl_complete_internal(int what_to_do = TAB)

completion_matches(*TEXT* [,*FUNC*])
> (@str) completion_matches(str text,
>   pfunc func = filename_completion_function)

filename_completion_function(*TEXT*, *STATE*)
> str   filename_completion_function(str text, int state)

username_completion_function(*TEXT*, *STATE*)
> str   username_completion_function(str text, int state)

listname_completion_function(*TEXT*, *STATE*)
> str   list_completion_function(str text, int state)

History Functions

Initializing history and state management

> using_history
>> void   using_history()

History list management

> add_history(*STRING*)
>> void   add_history(str string)

> StifleHistory(*MAX*)
>> Stifles the history list, remembering only the last **MAX** entries. If **MAX** is **undef**, remembers all entries.
>>
>>> int   stifle_history(int max|undef)

> SetHistory(*LINE1* [, *LINE2*, ...])
>> Sets the history of input, from where it can be used if the actual **readline** is present.

> remove_history(*WHICH*)
>> str   remove_history(int which)

> replace_history_entry(*WHICH*, *LINE*)
>> str   replace_history_entry(int which, str line)

> clear_history
>> void   clear_history()

> history_is_stifled
>> int   history_is_stifled()

Information about the history list

> where_history
>> int   where_history()

> current_history
>> str   current_history()

> history_get(*OFFSET*)
>> str   history_get(offset)

> history_total_bytes
>> int   history_total_bytes()

> GetHistory
>> Returns the history of input as a list, if the actual **readline** is present.

Moving around the history list

> history_set_pos(*POS*)
>> int   history_set_pos(int pos)

> previous_history
>> str   previous_history()

> next_history
>> str   next_history()

Searching the history list

> history_search(*STRING* [,*DIRECTION* [,*POS*]])
>> int   history_search(str string,
>>   int direction = -1, int pos = where_history())

> history_search_prefix(*STRING* [,*DIRECTION*])
>> int   history_search_prefix(str string, int direction = -1)

Managing the history file

> ReadHistory([*FILENAME* [,*FROM* [,*TO*]]])
>> Adds the contents of *FILENAME* to the history list, a line at a time. If *FILE-NAME* is false, then reads from *~/.history*. Starts reading at line *FROM* and ends at *TO*. If *FROM* is omitted or zero, starts at the beginning. If *TO* is omitted or less than *FROM*, then reads until the end of the file. Returns true if successful, or false if not.
>>
>>> int   read_history_range(str filename = '~/.history',
>>>   int from = 0, int to = -1)

> WriteHistory([*FILENAME*])
>> Writes the current history to *FILENAME*, overwriting *FILENAME* if necessary. If *FILENAME* is false, then writes the history list to *~/.history*. Returns true if successful, or false if not.
>>
>>> int   write_history(str filename = '~/.history')

> append_history(*NELEMENTS* [,*FILENAME*])
>> int   append_history(int nelements,
>>   str filename = '~/.history')

> history_truncate_file([*FILENAME* [,*NLINES*]])
>> int   history_truncate_file(str filename = '~/.history',
>>   int nlines = 0)

History expansion

history_expand(*LINE*)
>   (int result, str expansion) history_expand(str line)

Internal variable access

>   These functions are only for internal use. You should use **Attribs** method to
>   access GNU Readline/History Library variables.

fetch_var(*NAME*)
>   any   rl_fetch_var(str name)

store_var(*NAME*, *VAL*)
>   any   rl_store_var(str name, any val)

Variables

The following GNU Readline/History Library variables can be accessed from a Perl
program. See the "GNU Readline Library Manual" and "GNU History Library Manual"
for the details of each variable. You can access them with the **Attribs** methods. The
names of the keys in this hash conform to standard conventions, with the leading rl_
stripped.

Examples:

```
$attribs = $term->Attribs;
$v = $attribs->{library_version};    # rl_library_version
$v = $attribs->{history_base};       # history_base
$v = Term::ReadLine::GNU::XS::rl_fetch_var('rl_library_version');
```

Readline Variables

```
str rl_line_buffer
int rl_point
int rl_end
int rl_mark
int rl_done
int rl_pending_input
str rl_prompt (read only)
str rl_library_version (read only)
str rl_terminal_name
str rl_readline_name
filehandle rl_instream
filehandle rl_outstream
pfunc rl_startup_hook
pfunc rl_event_hook
pfunc rl_getc_function
pfunc rl_redisplay_function
Keymap rl_executing_keymap (read only)
Keymap rl_binding_keymap (read only)
```

Completion Variables

```
pfunc rl_completion_entry_function
pfunc rl_attempted_completion_function
rl_filename_quoting_function (not implemented)
rl_filename_dequoting_function (not implemented)
rl_char_is_quoted_p (not implemented)
int rl_completion_query_items
str rl_basic_word_break_characters
```

```
str rl_basic_quote_characters
str rl_completer_word_break_characters
str rl_completer_quote_characters
str rl_filename_quote_characters
str rl_special_prefixes
int rl_completion_append_character
int rl_ignore_completion_duplicates
int rl_filename_completion_desired
int rl_filename_quoting_desired
int rl_inhibit_completion
rl_ignore_some_completion_function (not implemented)
rl_directory_completion_hook (not implemented)
```

History Variables

```
int history_base
int history_length
int max_input_history (not implemented)
char history_expansion_char
char history_subst_char
char history_comment_char
str history_no_expand_chars
str history_search_delimiter_chars
int history_quotes_inhibit_expansion
```

Function References

```
rl_getc
rl_callback_read_char
filename_completion_function
username_completion_function
list_completion_function
```

Term::ReadLine::Gnu-Specific Variables

```
do_expand          # if true history expansion is enabled
completion_word    # for list_completion_function
```

Custom Completion: Variables and Functions

In this section, variables and functions for custom completion are described, with examples.

Most of the descriptions in this section are cited from the "GNU Readline Library" manual.

rl_completion_entry_function

This variable refers to a generator function for completion_matches().

A generator function is called repeatedly from completion_matches(), returning a string each time. The arguments to the generator function are TEXT and STATE. TEXT is the partial word to be completed. STATE is zero the first time the function is called, allowing the generator to perform any necessary initialization, and a positive non-zero integer for each subsequent call. When the generator function returns undef, this signals completion_matches() that there are no more possibilities left.

If the value is undef, built-in filename_completion_function is used.

A sample generator function, `list_completion_function`, is defined in *Gnu.pm*. You can use it as follows;

```
use Term::ReadLine;
...
my $term = new Term::ReadLine 'sample';
my $attribs = $term->Attribs;
...
$attribs->{rl_completion_entry_function} =
    $attribs->{'list_completion_function'};
...
$attribs->{completion_word} =
    [qw(reference to a list of words which you want to use for
completion)];
$term->readline("custom completion>");
```

See also `completion_matches`.

rl_attempted_completion_function

A reference to an alternative function to create matches.

The function is called with **TEXT**, **LINE_BUFFER**, **START**, and **END**. **LINE_BUFFER** is a current input buffer string. **START** and **END** are indices in **LINE_BUFFER** saying what the boundaries of **TEXT** are.

If this function exists and returns a null list or **undef**, or if this variable is set to **undef**, then an internal function, rl_complete(), calls the value of $rl_completion_entry_function to generate matches. Otherwise, the array of strings returned is used.

The default value of this variable is **undef**. You can use it as follows:

```
use Term::ReadLine;
...
my $term = new Term::ReadLine 'sample';
my $attribs = $term->Attribs;
...
sub sample_completion {
    my ($text, $line, $start, $end) = @_;
    # If first word then username completion,
    # else filename completion
    if (substr($line, 0, $start) =~ /^\s*$/) {
        return $term->completion_matches($text,
                $attribs->{'username_completion_function'});
    } else {
        return ();
    }
}
...
$attribs->{attempted_completion_function} =
                                    \&sample_completion;
completion_matches(TEXT, ENTRY_FUNC)
```

This returns an array of strings that is a list of completions for **TEXT**. If there are no completions, it returns **undef**. The first entry in the returned array is the substitution for **TEXT**. The remaining entries are the possible completions.

ENTRY_FUNC is a generator function that takes two arguments and returns a string. The first argument is TEXT. The second is a state argument; it is zero on the first call and non-zero on subsequent calls. ENTRY_FUNC returns undef to the caller when there are no more matches.

If the value of ENTRY_FUNC is undef, the built-in `filename_completion_func-tion` is used.

`completion_matches` is a Perl wrapper function for the internal `completion_matches()` function. See also $rl_completion_entry_function.

list_completion_function(TEXT, STATE)

A sample generator function defined by Term::ReadLine::Gnu.pm. The example code at rl_completion_entry_function shows how to use this function.

Files

~/.inputrc

Readline init file. You can use this file if you want to use a different set of key bindings. When a program that uses the Readline library starts up, the init file is read, and the key bindings are set.

Conditional key binding is also available. The program name that is specified by the first argument of the new method is used as the application construct.

For example, when your program calls the new method like this:

```
...
$term = new Term::ReadLine 'PerlSh';
...
```

your *~/.inputrc* can define key bindings only for it as follows:

```
...
$if PerlSh
Meta-Rubout: backward-kill-word
"\C-x\C-r": re-read-init-file
"\e[11~": "Function Key 1"
$endif
...
```

Exports

None

To Do

Test routines for the following variable and functions are required:

```
rl_read_key()
rl_stuff_char()
rl_callback_handler_install()
rl_callback_read_char()
rl_callback_handler_remove()
rl_complete_internal()
history_search()
history_search_prefix()
```

Bugs

rl_add_defun() can define up to 16 functions.

rl_message() does not work. See display_readline_version() in *t/readline.t*.

Author

Hiroo Hayashi, *hayashi@pdcd.ilab.toshiba.co.jp*

See Also

GNU Readline Library Manual, GNU History Library Manual

Term::ReadLine, Term::ReadLine::Perl (Term-ReadLine-xx.tar.gz)

Term::Screen—a simple all-Perl Term::Cap-based screen-positioning module

Synopsis

```
require Term::Screen;
$scr = new Term::Screen;
unless ($scr) { die " Something's wrong \n"; }
$scr->clrscr();
$scr->at(5,3);
$scr->puts("this is some stuff");
$scr->at(10,10)->bold()->puts("hi!")->normal();
    # you can concatenate many calls (not getch)
$c = $scr->getch();     # doesn't need Enter key
...
if ($scr->key_pressed()) { print "ha you hit a key!"; }
```

Description

Term::Screen is a very simple screen-positioning module that should work wherever Term::Cap does. It is set up for UNIX using stty's, but these dependences are isolated by evals in the **new** constructor. Thus, you may create a child module implementing Screen with MS-DOS, ioctl, or other means to get raw and unblocked input. This is not a replacement for Curses—it has no memory. This was written so that it could be easily changed to fit nasty systems and to be available first thing.

The input functions **getch**, **key_pressed**, **echo**, and **noecho** are implemented so as to work under a fairly standard UNIX system. They use **stty** to set raw and no-echo modes and turn on auto-flush. All of these are **eval**ed so that this class can be inherited for new definitions easily.

Term::Screen was designed to be **required**, then used with object syntax as shown above. One quirk (which the author was used to so he didn't care) is that for function-key translation, no delay is set. So for many terminals, to get an **esc** character you have to hit another character after it, generally another **esc**.

You may access the screen size and the actual compiled termcap entries in $scr->{ROWS}, COLS, and TERM, respectively, and $scr->{IN} is the input buffer, but you should never update these items directly—use the provided object methods.

Public Interface

Term::Screen has a very minimal set of fixed-character terminal position and character-reading commands:

new()

    Initializes the screen. Does not clear the screen, but does home the cursor.

`resize(r, c)`

Tells the screen the new number of rows and columns, physically. You can omit the `r` and `c` and get new checked vals from stty or termcap. Term::Screen does not handle resize signals internally, but you can do it by checking and updating the screen size using this function.

What follows are capabilities that are assumed to be in termcap. They apply to all the terminals I've used.

`at(row, col)`

Moves the cursor to (`row, col`), where (0, 0) is the upper left corner. If the location is illegal, it does whatever cm in termcap does, since that is what it uses.

`normal()`

Turns off any highlighting (bold, reverse).

`bold()`

The md value from termcap; usually turns on bold. Defaults to whatever is available.

`reverse()`

The mr value from termcap; often turns on reverse text. Defaults to whatever is available.

`clrscr()`

Clears the screen and homes the cursor.

`clreol()`

Clears to the end of the line; the cursor doesn't move.

`clreos()`

Clears to the end of the screen—right and down; the cursor doesn't move.

`il()`

Inserts a blank line before the line the cursor is on, moving lower lines down.

`dl()`

Deletes the line the cursor is on, moving lower lines up.

The following are useful, but not always there; use the **exists** methods to find out.

`exists_ic()`

Insert-character option is available.

`exists_dc()`

Delete-char option exists and is available.

`ic()`

Inserts character at current position and moves the rest to the right.

`dc()`

Deletes character at current position, moving the rest to the left.

The following are the I/O functions. They provide standard useful, single-character reading values. getch returns either a single character or the name of a function key when a key is pressed. The only exception is that if you hit a character that is the start of a function-key sequence, getch keeps waiting for the next char, to see if it is a function key. Generally this is the escape key, which is why you need to hit ESC twice. To get a straight character, just use the regular **gets** Perl function. You need to echo it yourself if you want.

puts(*str*)

Prints $str and returns the screen object. Used to do things like:

```
$scr->at(10,0)->puts("Hi!")->at(0,0);
```

You can just use print if you want.

getch()

Returns a character in raw mode. Function keys are returned as their capability names, e.g., the up key returns ku. See the get_fn_keys function to find many of the names. This waits for the next character if it's in a possible function-key string, so you probably need to type esc esc to get out of getch, since esc is usually the leading character for function keys. You can use Perl's getc to go "underneath" getch if you want. See the table in Screen::get_fn_keys() for more information.

def_key(*name, input_string*)

Lets you define your own function-key sequence. 'name' is what is returned by getch. *input_string* is what the fn key sends, literally. This overrides any previous definitions of the input. A whole bunch of defaults are defined for xterms, rxvt's, etc., in the get_fn_keys function.

key_pressed([*sec*])

Returns true if there is a character waiting. You can pass as an option the time in seconds to wait.

flush_input()

Clears the input buffer and removes any incoming characters.

stuff_input(*str*)

Lets you stuff characters into the input buffer to be read like keystrokes. This only applies to the getch method buffer; the underlying getc stuff is not touched.

echo()

Tells getch to echo the input to the screen (the default).

noecho()

Tells getch *not* to echo the input to the screen.

Author

Mark Kaehny, *kaehny@execpc.com*

See Also

Term::Cap, termcap, curses, stty, select

Term::Size—Perl extension for retrieving terminal size

Synopsis

```
use Term::Size;
($columns, $rows) = Term::Size::chars *STDOUT{IO};
($x, $y) = Term::Size::pixels;
```

Description

Term::Size is a Perl module that provides a straightforward way to retrieve the terminal size.

Both functions take an optional filehandle argument, which defaults to `*STDIN{IO}`. They both return a list of two values, which are the current width and height, respectively, of the terminal associated with the specified filehandle.

Term::Size::chars returns the size in units of characters, whereas Term::Size::pixels uses units of pixels.

In a scalar context, both functions return the first element of the list, that is, the terminal width.

The functions may be imported.

If you need to pass a filehandle to either of the Term::Size functions, beware that the `*STDOUT{IO}` syntax is only supported in Perl 5.004 and later. If you have an earlier version of Perl, or are interested in backwards compatibility, use `*STDOUT` instead.

Examples

Refuse to run in a too narrow window:

```
use Term::Size;
die "Need 80 column screen" if Term::Size::chars *STDOUT{IO} < 80;
```

Track window size changes:

```
use Term::Size 'chars';
my $changed = 1;
while (1) {
        local $SIG{'WINCH'} = sub { $changed = 1 };
        if ($changed) {
                ($cols, $rows) = chars;
                # Redraw, or whatever.
                $changed = 0;
        }
}
```

Return Values

Both functions return **undef** if there is an error.

If the terminal size information is not available, the functions normally return (0,0), but this depends on your system. On character-only terminals, **pixels** normally returns (0,0).

Bugs

It only works on UNIX systems.

Author

Tim Goodwin, *tim@uunet.pipex.com*

Tk::Cloth — An object-oriented Tk canvas

Synopsis

```
use Tk::Cloth;

$cloth = $parent->Cloth;
```

```
$cloth->pack(-fill => 'both', -expand => 1);

$rect = $cloth->Rectangle(
    -coords => [ 0,0,100,100],
    -fill => 'red'
);

$tag = $cloth->tag;
$tag->Line(
    -coords => [10,10,100,100],
    -foreground => 'black'
);
$tag->Line(
    -coords => [50,50,100,100],
    -foreground => 'black'
);
$tag->move(30,30);

$tag->bind("<1>", [ &button1 ]);
```

Description

Tk::Cloth provides an object-oriented approach to a canvas and canvas items.

Author

Graham Barr, *gbarr@pobox.com*

Copyright

Copyright © 1997 Graham Barr. All rights reserved. This program is free software; you can redistribute it and/or modify it under the same terms as Perl itself.

Tk::Dial—an alternative to the scale widget

Synopsis

```
use Tk::Dial;
$dial = $top->Dial(-margin => 20,
                   -radius => 48,
                   -min => 0,
                   -max => 100,
                   -value => 0,
                   -format => '%d');
```

The values shown above are the default values.

margin
> Blank space to leave around dial

radius
> Radius of dial

min, max
> Range of possible values

value
> Current value

format
> `printf`-style format for displaying format

Description

A dial looks like a speedometer: a 3/4 circle with a needle indicating the current value. Below the graphical dial is an entry that displays the current value and that can be used to enter a value by hand.

The needle is moved by pressing button 1 in the canvas and dragging. The needle follows the mouse, even if the mouse leaves the canvas, which allows for high precision. Alternatively, the user can enter a value in the entry space and press Return to set the value; the needle is set accordingly.

To Do

Configure, tick marks, step size

Authors

Roy Johnson, *rjohnson@shell.com*

Based on a similar widget in XV, a program by John Bradley, *bradley@cis.upenn.edu*.

History

August 1995: Released for critique by pTk mailing list.

Tk::FileDialog —highly configurable File Dialog widget for Perl/Tk

Synopsis

Usage Description

To use FileDialog, simply create your FileDialog objects during initialization (or at least before a Show). When you wish to display the FileDialog, invoke the Show method on the FileDialog object; The method returns either a filename, a pathname, or undef. undef is returned only if the user pressed the Cancel button.

Example Code

The following code creates a FileDialog and calls it. Note that `perl5.002gamma` is required.

```
#!/usr/local/bin/perl -w

use Tk;
use Tk::FileDialog;
use strict;

my($main) = MainWindow->new;
my($Horiz) = 1;
my($fname);
```

```
    my($LoadDialog) = $main->FileDialog(-Title =>'This is my title',
                                        -Create => 0);
    print "Using FileDialog Version ",$LoadDialog->Version,"\n";
    $LoadDialog->configure(-FPat => '*pl',
                           -ShowAll => 'NO');

    $main->Entry(-textvariable => \$fname)
          ->pack(-expand => 1,
                 -fill => 'x');

    $main->Button(-text => 'Kick me!',
                 -command => sub {
                     $fname = $LoadDialog->Show(-Horiz => $Horiz);
                     if (!defined($fname)) {
                         $fname = "Fine,Cancel, but no Chdir
                                  anymore!!!";
                         $LoadDialog->configure(-Chdir =>'NO');
                     }
                 })
          ->pack(-expand => 1,
                 -fill => 'x');

    $main->Checkbutton(-text => 'Horizontal',
                      -variable => \$Horiz)
          ->pack(-expand => 1,
                 -fill => 'x');

    $main->Button(-text => 'Exit',
                 -command => sub {
                     $main->destroy;
                 })
          ->pack(-expand => 1,
                 -fill => 'x');

    MainLoop;
    print "Exit Stage right!\n";
    exit;
```

Description

The widget is composed of a number of subwidgets—namely, a listbox for files and (optionally) directories, an entry for filename, an (optional) entry for pathname, an entry for a filter pattern, a ShowAll checkbox (for enabling display of .* files and directories), and three buttons: OK, Rescan, and Cancel. Note that the labels for all subwidgets (including the text for the buttons and Checkbox) are configurable for foreign language support. The listboxes respond to characters typed over them by scrolling to the first line that starts with the given character (or next, etc., if this character is not present).

Methods

The following non-standard methods may be used with a FileDialog object:

Show

Displays the file dialog box for the user to operate. Additional configuration items may be passed in at Show-time. In other words, this code snippet:

```
$fd->Show(-Title => 'Ooooh, Preeeeeety!');
```

is the same as this code snippet:

```
$fd->configure(-Title => 'Ooooh, Preeeeeety!');
$fd->Show;
```

Version

Returns the current version of FileDialog

Configuration

Any of the following configuration items may be set via the configure (or Show) method, or retrieved via the cget method:

Flags

Flags may be configured with either 1, true, or yes for 1, or 0, false, or no for 0. Any portion of true, yes, false, or no may be used, and case does not matter.

-Chdir

Enables the user to change directories. The default is 1. If disabled, the directory listbox is not shown.

-Create

Enables the user to specify a file that does not exist. If not enabled, and the user specifies a non-existent file, a dialog box is shown informing the user of the error (this dialog box is configurable via the EDlg* switches: see following information).

The default is 1.

-ShowAll

Determines whether hidden files (.*) are displayed in the File and Directory listboxes. The default is 0. The ShowAll checkbox reflects the setting of this switch.

-DisableShowAll

Disables the ability of the user to change the status of the ShowAll flag. The default is 0 (the user is by default allowed to change the status).

-Grab

Enables the File dialog to do an application Grab when displayed. The default is 1.

-Horiz

True sets the File listbox to be to the right of the Directory listbox. If 0, the File listbox is below the Directory listbox. The default is 1.

-SelDir

If True, enables selection of a directory rather than a file and disables the actions of the File listbox. The default is 0.

Special

-FPat

Sets the default file-selection pattern. The default is *. Only files matching this pattern are displayed in the File listbox.

-Geometry

Sets the geometry of the File dialog. Setting the size is a dangerous thing to do. If not configured, or if set to "", the File dialog is centered.

-SelHook

SelHook is configured with a reference to a routine that is to be called when a file is chosen. The file is called with a single parameter of the full path and filename of the file chosen. If the Create flag is disabled (and the user is not allowed to specify new files), the file has to be known to exist at the time that SelHook is called. Note that SelHook is also called with directories if the SelDir flag is enabled, and that the FileDialog box is still displayed. The File-Dialog box should *not* be destroyed from within the SelHook routine, although it may generally be configured.

SelHook routines return 0 to reject the selection and allow the user to reselect, and any other value to accept the selection. If a SelHook routine returns non-zero, the FileDialog is immediately withdrawn, and the file is returned to the caller.

There may be only one SelHook routine active at any time. Configuring the SelHook routine replaces any existing SelHook routine. Configuring the SelHook routine with 0 removes the SelHook routine. The default SelHook routine is **undef**.

Strings

The following two switches may be used to set default variables and to get final values after the **Show** method has returned (but has not been explicitly destroyed by the caller)

-File

The file selected, or the default file. The default is ' '.

-Path

The path of the selected file, or the initial path. The default is $ENV{'HOME'}.

Labels and Captions

For support of internationalization, the text on any of the subwidgets may be changed.

-Title

The title of the dialog box. The default is "Select File:".

-DirLBCaption

The caption above the Directory listbox. The default is "Directories".

-FileLBCaption

The caption above the File listbox. The default is "Files".

-FileEntryLabel

The label to the left of the File Entry. The default is "Filename:".

-PathEntryLabel

The label to the left of the Path Entry. The default is "Pathname:".

-FltEntryLabel

The label to the left of the Filter entry. The default is "Filter:".

-ShowAllLabel

The text of Show All Checkbutton. The default is "Show All".

Button Text

For support of internationalization, the text on the three buttons may be changed.

-OKButtonLabel

The text for the OK button. The default is "OK".

-RescanButtonLabel

The text for the Rescan button. The default is "Rescan".

-CancelButtonLabel

The text for the Cancel button. The default is "Cancel".

Error Dialog Switches

If the Create switch is set to 0, and the user specifies a file that does not exist, a dialog box is displayed informing the user of the error. These switches allow some configuration of that dialog box.

-EDlgTitle

The title of the Error Dialog Box. The default is "File does not exist!".

-EDlgText

The message in the Error Dialog Box. The variables $path, $file, and $filename (the full path and filename of the selected file) are available. The default is *"You must specify an existing file.\n(\ $filename not found)."*

Author

Brent B. Powers, Merrill Lynch (B2Pi), *powers@ml.com*

Copyright

This code may be distributed under the same conditions as Perl itself.

Tk::Pane—a window paner

Synopsis

```
use Tk::Pane;

$pane = $mw->Scrolled(Pane, Name => 'fred',
    -scrollbars => 'soe',
    -sticky => 'we',
    -gridded => 'y'
);
$pane->Frame;
$pane->pack;
```

Description

Tk::Pane provides creates a widget that allows you to view only part of a subwidget.

Author

Graham Barr, *gbarr@pobox.com*

Copyright

Copyright © 1997 Graham Barr. All rights reserved. This program is free software; you can redistribute it and/or modify it under the same terms as Perl itself.

Tk::TFrame——a titled frame widget

Synopsis

```
use Tk::TFrame;

$frame = $parent->TFrame(
    -label => [ -text => 'Title' ]
    -borderwidth => 2,
    -relief => 'groove'
);
$frame->pack;
```

Description

Tk::TFrame provides a frame, but with a title that overlaps the border by half of its height.

Author

Graham Barr, *gbarr@pobox.com*

Copyright

Copyright © 1997 Graham Barr. All rights reserved. This program is free software; you can redistribute it and/or modify it under the same terms as Perl itself.

Tk::WaitBox——an object-oriented Wait dialog for Perl/Tk, of the "please wait" variety

Synopsis

Usage Description

Basic Usage

To use, create your WaitDialog objects during initialization, or at least before a Show. When you wish to display the WaitDialog object, invoke the Show method on the WaitDialog object; when you wish to cease displaying the WaitDialog object, invoke the unShow method on the object.

Configuration

Configuration may be done at creation or via the **configure** method.

Example Code

```
#!/usr/local/bin/perl -w
use Tk;
use Tk::WaitBox;
use strict;
my($root) = MainWindow->new;
my($utxt) = "Initializing...";
```

```
my($wd) = $root->WaitBox(
        -bitmap =>'questhead', # Default would be 'hourglass'
        -txt2 => 'tick-tick-tick', #default would be 'Please Wait'
        -title => 'Takes forever to get service around here',
        -cancelroutine => sub {
            print "\nI'm canceling....\n";
            $wd->unShow;
            $utxt = undef;
        });
$wd->configure(-txt1 => "Hurry up and Wait, my Drill Sergeant told
me");
$wd->configure(-foreground => 'blue',-background => 'white');
### Do something quite boring with the user frame
my($u) = $wd->{SubWidget}(uframe);
$u->pack(-expand => 1, -fill => 'both');
$u->Label(-textvariable => \$utxt)->pack(-expand => 1, -fill =>
'both');
## It would definitely be better to do this with a canvas... this
is dumb
my($base) = $u->Frame(-background =>'gray',
                      -relief => 'sunken',
                      -borderwidth => 2,
                      -height => 20)
        ->pack(-side => 'left', -anchor => 'w',-expand => 1,
               -fill => 'both');
my($bar) = $base->Frame(-borderwidth => 2,
                        -relief => 'raised', -height => 20,
                        -width => 0, -background => 'blue')
        ->pack(-fill => 'y', -side => 'left');
$wd->configure(-canceltext => 'Halt, Cease, Desist'); # default is
'Cancel'
$wd->Show;
for (1..15) {
    sleep(1);
    $bar->configure(-width => int($_/15*$base->Width));
    $utxt = 100*$_/15 . "% Complete";
    $root->update;
    last if !defined($utxt);
}
$wd->unShow;
```

Description

A WaitBox consists of a number of subwidgets:

Subwidgets

bitmap

> A bitmap (configurable via the **-bitmap** command; the default is an hourglass) on the left side of the WaitBox

label

> A label (configurable via the **-txt1** command), with text in the upper portion of the right-hand frame

secondary label
>Another label (configurable via the **-txt2** command; the default is "Please Wait"), with text in the lower portion of the right hand-frame

userframe
>A frame displayed, if required, between the label and the secondary label. For details, see the example code and the "Advertised Widget" section.

cancel button
>If a cancel routine (configured via the **-cancelroutine** command) is defined, a frame is packed below the labels and bitmap, with a single button. The text of the button is "Cancel" (configurable via the **-canceltext** command), and the button calls the supplied subroutine when pressed.

Advertised Subwidgets

uframe
>**uframe** is a frame created between the two messages. It may be used for anything the user has in mind, including exciting cycle-wasting displays of sand dropping through an hour glass, Zippy riding either a Gnu or a bronc, etc.

>Assuming that the WaitBox is referenced by $w, the **uframe** may be addressed as $w->subwidget{'uframe'}. Having gotten the address, you can do anything (I think) you would like with it.

Author

Brent B. Powers (B2Pi), Merrill Lynch, *powers@ml.com*

This code may be distributed under the same conditions as Perl itself.

X11::Auth—Perl module to read X11 authority files

Synopsis
```
require X11::Auth;
$a = new X11::Auth;
($auth_type, $auth_data) = $a->get_by_host($host, $disp_num);
```

Description

This module is an approximate Perl replacement for the libXau C library and the xauth(1) program. It reads and interprets the files (usually *~/.Xauthority*) that hold authorization data used in connecting to X servers. Since it was written mainly for the use of X11::Protocol, its functionality is currently restricted to reading, not writing, of these files.

Methods

new
>Opens an authority file and creates an object to handle it. The filename is taken from the XAUTHORITY environment variable, if present, or *.Xauthority* in the user's home directory, or it may be overridden by an argument. **open** may be used as a synonym.

```
$auth = X11::Auth->new;
$auth = X11::Auth->open($filename);
```

get_one

> Reads one entry from the file. Returns a null list at end-of-file. *$family* is usually Internet or Local, and $display_num can be any string.

```
($family, $host_addr, $display_num, $auth_name, $auth_data)
    = $auth->get_one;
```

get_all

> Reads all of the entries in the file. Each member of the array returned is an array ref similar to the list returned by get_one().

```
@auth_data = $auth->get_all;
```

get_by_host

> Get authentication data for a connection of type *$family* to display *$display_num* on *$host*. If *$family* is Internet, the host is translated into an appropriate address by gethostbyname().

```
($auth_name, $auth_data)
    = $auth->get_by_host($host, $family, $display_num);
```

Compatibility

The following table shows the (rough) correspondence between libXau calls and X11::Auth methods

```
libXau                          X11::Auth
------                          ---------
XauFileName                     $ENV{XAUTHORITY}
                                || "$ENV{HOME}/.Xauthority"
fopen(XauFileName(), "rb")      $auth = new X11::Auth
XauReadAuth                     $auth->get_one
XauWriteAuth
XauGetAuthByAddr                $auth->get_by_host
XauGetBestAuthByAddr
XauLockAuth
XauUnlockAuth
XauDisposeAuth
```

Author

Stephen McCamant, *alias@mcs.com*

See Also

perl(1), X11::Protocol, Xau(3), xauth(1), lib/Xau/README in the X11 source distribution

---

X11::Fvwm — Perl extension for the Fvwm2 X11 Window Manager

Synopsis

```
use X11::Fvwm;
$handle = new X11::Fvwm;
$handle->initModule;
$handle->addHandler(M_CONFIGURE_WINDOW, \&configure_a_window);
$handle->addHandler(M_CONFIG_INFO, \&some_other_sub);
$handle->eventLoop;
$handle->endModule;
```

Description

The X11::Fvwm package is designed to provide access via Perl 5 to the module API of Fvwm 2. This code is based upon Fvwm 2.0.45 beta.

The most common track to interfacing with Fvwm is to create an object of the X11::Fvwm class and use it to create or destroy event handlers and to catch and route such events from Fvwm. Event handlers can be tied to specific event types or given masks that include multiple events, for which the handler is passed the data for any of the events it accepts.

Exported constants

The following constants are exported automatically by X11::Fvwm. Most of these are defined either in the *modules.tex* file that is part of the *docs/* directory in the Fvwm distribution, or within the code itself (particularly the files *fvwm.h* and *module.h* in the actual source directory):

C_ALL	C_FRAME	C_ICON
C_L1	C_L2	C_L3
C_L4	C_L5	C_LALL
C_NO_CONTEXT	C_R1	C_R2
C_R3	C_R4	C_R5
C_RALL	C_ROOT	C_SIDEBAR
C_TITLE	C_WINDOW	F_ALL_COMMON_FLAGS
F_BORDER	F_CirculateSkip	F_CirculateSkipIcon
F_ClickToFocus	F_DoesWmTakeFocus	F_DoesWm-DeleteWindow
F_HintOverride	F_ICON_MOVED	F_ICON_OURS
F_ICON_UNMAPPED	F_ICONIFIED	F_Lenience
F_MAP_PENDING	F_MAPPED	F_MAXIMIZED
F_MWMButtons	F_MWMBorders	F_NOICON_TITLE
F_ONTOP	F_PIXMAP_OURS	F_RAISED
F_SHAPED_ICON	F_SHOW_ON_MAP	F_STARTICONIC
F_STICKY	F_SUPPRESSICON	F_SloppyFocus
F_StickyIcon	F_TITLE	F_TRANSIENT
F_VISIBLE	F_WINDOWLISTSKIP	HEADER_SIZE
MAX_BODY_SIZE	MAX_MASK	MAX_PACKET_SIZE
M_ADD_WINDOW	M_CONFIGURE_WINDOW	M_CONFIG_INFO
M_DEFAULTICON	M_DEICONIFY	M_DESTROY_WINDOW
M_DEWINDOWSHADE	M_END_CONFIG_INFO	M_END_WINDOWLIST
M_ERROR	M_FOCUS_CHANGE	M_ICONIFY
M_ICON_FILE	M_ICON_LOCATION	M_ICON_NAME
M_LOWER_WINDOW	M_MAP	M_MINI_ICON
M_NEW_DESK	M_NEW_PAGE	M_RAISE_WINDOW

M_RES_CLASS	M_RES_NAME	M_STRING
M_WINDOWSHADE	M_WINDOW_NAME	P_LAZY_HANDLERS
P_PACKET_PASSALL	P_STRIP_NEWLINES	START_FLAG

See the following section "Constants and Flags" for short definitions.

Methods

Object manipulation is provided via these methods. $self is assumed to be an object of this class, and all methods aside from new are assumed to be prefixed as $self-> method.

new

> Creates and returns an object of the X11::Fvwm class. The return value is the blessed reference. Any combination of INIT, CONFIG, MASK, NAME, OPTIONS, and DEBUG may be passed in with corresponding values to specify certain parameters at creation time. Each of these is treated as a key/value pair, so even options such as INIT, which are only meaningful if set to "1", still must have that value.

> ```
> $self = new X11::Fvwm %params
> ```

> If INIT is specified and evaluates to true, initModule is run.

> If CONFIG is specified and evaluates to true, getConfigInfo is run, but no values are returned from it. It is run only to warm up the internal cache.

> If MASK is specified, the value passed in is sent to Fvwm as the packet mask this application requires.

> If NAME is specified, it is stored as the internal name for the application, which is used primarily for selecting configuration options intended for the running application.

> If OPTIONS is specified, it is stored as the Perl options for the object. Otherwise, the options default to P_STRIP_NEWLINES.

> If DEBUG is specified and evaluates to true, debugging is enabled for this object.

mask

> Gets or sets the current mask for this object. If called with no argument, then the current value of the mask is returned. Otherwise, the single argument is sent to Fvwm as a new mask request.

> ```
> $old_mask = $self->mask($new_mask)
> ```

name

> Gets or sets the name by which the running object expects to be identified. This defaults to the last element of $0, the script name, but they do not have to be identical. Do understand that Fvwm will attempt some communications based on the name by which it knows the running module. name() has no bearing on this. This is the value used for pattern-matching if the getConfigInfo method is called with the *trimname option.

> ```
> $name = $self->name($new_name)
> ```

options

> Gets or sets the Perl-level options that this object uses. These are the P_* constants. See also the setOptions method, described below.

> ```
> $opts = $self->options($new_options)
> ```

initModule

Initializes this object with respect to the **Fvwm** communication streams. Takes the **Fvwm**-related items out of the arguments list and leaves any remaining arguments in an instance variable called **argv**. The read and write pipes are recorded for use by the communication methods, and the configuration file, window ID, and context are stored on instance variables as well (see "Instance Variables").

initModule takes one optional argument, a packet mask to send after the communications pipes are set up. If passed, it overrides any value that may have been specified in the call to **new**. If not specified, then the value from **new** is used, and if there was no specific mask given to **new**, then no mask is sent, meaning that the object will get every packet sent out by Fvwm.

```
$self->initModule($mask)
```

sendInfo

Sends to Fvwm a data packet with a possible window specification. The contents of $data sents, encoded as Fvwm specifies. $win_id may be 0, in which case Fvwm handles the transaction itself, unless the transaction is in fact window-specific, in which case Fvwm prompts the user to select a target window.

```
$self->sendInfo($win_id, $data)
```

readPacket

Reads a data packet from *Fvwm* via the input handle the module received at start-up. Returns the triple ($len, $packet, $type) and also stores this on the instance variable lastPacket. This call blocks until there is data available on the pipe to be read.

```
$self->readPacket()
```

processPacket

Breaks down the contents of $packet based on $type. Dispatches all packet handlers that accept packets of type $type, passing as arguments $type followed by the contents of the packet itself. If $len is undef, then the triple stored in lastPacket is used. If $len is equal to −1, then this method immediately returns a value of 0.

```
$self->processPacket($len, $packet, $type)
```

If the $stop flag passed when a handler was created (see **addHandler**) was true, then a false (zero) return value from the handler causes processPacket to return 0. Setting the option P_LAZY_HANDLERS causes all handlers created to set their **stop** value to 0.

The execution of handlers is done in a two-stage loop. The first loops incrementally through all the masks for which known handlers exist and the second goes through in the order in which the handlers were added for a given mask. If two handlers are created for the packet **M_ERROR** and one for the combination of **M_ERROR** and **M_STRING**, then the two for **M_ERROR** alone are evaluated first, in the order in which they were created. Afterwards, the one handler is executed. This is because the value of **M_ERROR** and **M_STRING** combined are greater than **M_ERROR** alone.

In general, if multiple handlers are going to be assigned to a given packet type, they should be as independent of each other as possible, and reliance on execution order should be avoided.

addHandler

Adds a new handler routine to the internal table, set to be called for any packets whose type is included in $mask. The mask argument may contain more than one of the known packet types (see information on Packet Types later in this module), or may be the special string EXIT. All handlers of type EXIT are called by eventLoop at termination (or they may be explicitly called within signal catchers and the like with invokeHandler). Others are called when a packet of the flagged type arrives.

```
$new_id = $self->addHandler($mask, $reference)
```

The return value from **addHandler** is an identifier into the internal table kept and tracked by the X11::Fvwm object. This identifier is used in the case where a handler should be deleted. The return value itself should not be directly used, as its format is internal and does not give any indication of execution priority.

The second argument to **addHandler** is a reference to a subroutine (or closure). This is the code (or callback, if you prefer) that is executed with the packet contents as arguments. Every handler gets arguments of the form:

```
($self, $type, $id, $frameid, $ptr, [, @args])
```

where $type is the packet type itself (or EXIT), $id is the X Windows window ID of the application main window, $frameid is the X window ID of the frame created by Fvwm to house the window decorations, and $ptr is an index into the internal database that Fvwm maintains for all managed windows. $self is the reference to the X11::Fvwm object that invoked the **addHandler** method, allowing the routine access to the instance variables. If the packet, by definition, has additional arguments, these follow after the initial four, in the order described by the module API documentation packaged with Fvwm. All packets, however, contain at least these three initial values (the $type argument is provided by processPacket for the sake of handlers written to manage multiple packet types).

The $ptr argument is guaranteed to be unique for all windows currently being managed. It can prove useful as an index itself (see the PerlTkWL sample application, which uses this value in such a way).

The **addHandler** method does not allow or support symbolic references to subroutines.

deleteHandler

Deletes the specified handler from the internal table. $id must be a value returned from an earlier call to **addHandler**.

```
$self->deleteHandler($id)
```

invokeHandler

Forces the execution of all handlers that would trigger on a packet of type $type. @args is passed to each called routine immediately following $type itself, as is the behavior of **processPacket**.

```
$self->invokeHandler($type, @args)
```

setOptions

A more extensive way to set and clear Perl object options. All flags set in the value $set are added (via logical OR) to the current options. All flags in $clear are removed from the current options. If $preserve is passed, it is expected to be a scalar reference, and the current option settings are stored in it before alteration. Either of `$set` or `$clear` can be undef, in which case they have no effect. The return value is the new option set.

This differs from the **options** method described earlier, which only fetches or assigns the options; it does not allow for the detail provided here.

```
$new_opts = $self->setOptions($set, $clear, $preserve)
```

getConfigInfo

Fetches information from the running Fvwm process through the configuration interface. Configuration lines are those lines in the configuration file that start with a leading * character. The first time this method is called, the module fetches all configuration information, discarding the leading asterisk from the names. Specific values may be requested or the entire contents fetched. A module has access to all configuration data, not just the lines that match the name of the program. The return value is a hash table whose keys are the name part of the configuration lines (sans asterisk) and whose values are the contents of the lines.

```
%hash = $self->getConfigInfo(@keys)
```

In addition to the configuration lines, Fvwm also sends the following parameters: IconPath, PixmapPath, ColorLimit and ClickTime. These are also retrievable by those names.

The values in the optional arguments @keys can be a specific name to look up (or names), or any of the following special directives:

-refresh

Forces `getConfigInfo` to reread the data from Fvwm.

-all

Causes the method to return the full configuration table, not just those names that contain the module name as a substring of the configuration item name (this value is taken from the NAME instance variable).

-trimname

Instructs the method to excise the module name (the value of the NAME instance variable) from any keys in the final return set that contain the name as a substring. As an example, a module named TkWinList can get back names such as Foreground rather than TkWinListForeground. Keys not containing the substring are not affected.

If any specific keys are requested in @args, then the returned hash table only contains those keys that were in fact present in the internal table. -trimname can still be used to remove the module name from the keys.

If an option is intended to be lengthy and possibly span lines, multiple occurrences of that configuration name can appear in the configuration file. In cases where the same name appears more than once, the value returned for that key is an array reference rather than a scalar. The contents of the referred array are all the values from the series of lines.

Again, the PerlTkWL sample application utilizes these features and may be referenced for further information.

Note: Alpha versions of this module used the asterisk (*) to specify directives to **getConfigInfo**. That has been deprecated with the first beta release (0.3), and will be removed entirely in the first official release.

eventLoop

An endless loop is entered in which **readPacket** and **processPacket** are called. When **processPacket** indicates a completion (by an exit code of zero), any EXIT handlers are called and the module exits.

```
$self->eventLoop($top)
```

endModule

Sends a final packet to Fvwm indicating that the module is exiting, then closes the input and output pipes.

```
$self->endModule
```

Instance Variables

In addition to the methods above, there are also several instance variables available to the programmer. Not all of the instance variables are intended to be accessed or altered by the programmer, but the ones in the following listing are meant to be public:

MASK

This is the current mask registered with Fvwm. Setting this does not automatically set a new mask. Use the **mask()** method above for that.

NAME

This is the current application name, for the purpose of associating module configuration options. Set it with **name()** described above.

OPTIONS

The current Perl-level module options. Can be tested against the P_* constants. Can be set with the either the **setOptions** method or the **options** method, both described above.

DEBUG

A flag used to note when debugging information is requested. Can be used in handler routines to supplement debugging or set and unset as desired for selective debugging.

fvwmWinId

The X window ID for the window from whose context the module was launched, if applicable. If the module was not launched from the context of a specific window, this value is zero.

fvwmContext

The actual context of the launch, if applicable. Can be compared against the C_* constants. Also set to zero if the module was not launched in the context of a specific window.

fvwmRcfile

The configuration file that *Fvwm* reads at its own start-up. In earlier API models, the module was responsible for reading this file directly to obtain configuration information. That is no longer necessary, but having the path to the file handy may still be useful to some applications.

packetTypes

This is a reference to the internal hash table of unpack formats used in the processing of packet data. Most likely, a module developer will not need this, as the handlers are invoked with the data already unpacked and sent as subroutine arguments. However, some cases arise (such as the initialization in the PerlTkWL sample application) when it is necessary to talk to and understand the results from Fvwm directly. Modify this at your own peril.

lastPacket

A list-reference containing the data from the most recent packet read, as a triple *($len, $packet, $type)*. Is undefined until the first packet has been read.

Constants and Flags

The lines of communication between Fvwm and the module are maintained via the well-defined flags and constants from the header files in the source. The following values are exported by default into the namespace of the application or package using X11::Fvwm. They are taken directly from the header files, so should be portable across platforms:

Packet Types

Most of the packets have the same first three parameters as explained in the definition of the addHandler method. For this section, assume that $id, $frameid, and $ptr have the same meaning as defined there. Much of this text is based on the file *modules.tex* in the Fvwm distribution.

M_ADD_WINDOW

This packet is essentially identical to M_CONFIGURE_WINDOW below, differing only in that M_ADD_WINDOW is sent once, when the window is created, and the M_CONFIGURE_WINDOW packet is sent when the viewport on the current desktop changes, or when the size or location of the window is changed. They contain 24 values. The first three identify the window and the next twelve identify the location and size, as described in the list below. The flags field is a bitwise OR of the flags defined below in Flags:

Arg #	Usage
0	$id
1	$frameid
2	$ptr
3	X location of the window frame
4	Y location of the window frame
5	Width of the window frame (pixels)
6	Height of the window frame (pixels)
7	Desktop number
8	Windows flags field
9	Window title height (pixels)
10	Window border width (pixels)
11	Window base width (pixels)
12	Window base height (pixels)
13	Window resize width increment(pixels)
14	Window resize height increment (pixels)
15	Window minimum width (pixels)

Arg #	Usage
16	Window minimum height (pixels)
17	Window maximum width increment(pixels)
18	Window maximum height increment (pixels)
19	Icon label window ID, or 0
20	Icon pixmap window ID, or 0
21	Window gravity
22	Pixel value of the text color
23	Pixel value of the window border color

M_CONFIGURE_WINDOW

Same structure and contents as M_ADD_WINDOW.

M_CONFIG_INFO

Fvwm records all configuration commands it encounters that begin with the character *. When the built-in command Send_ConfigInfo is invoked by a module, this entire list is transmitted to the module in packets (one line per packet) of this type. The packet consists of three zeros, followed by a variable length character string. In addition, the PixmapPath, IconPath, ColorLimit and ClickTime parameters are sent to the module.

M_DEFAULTICON

This packet identifies the default icon for the session. The first three arguments are all zero, and the fourth is a text string containing the name of the icon to use.

M_DEICONIFY

This packet contains the standard three arguments. It is sent whenever the indicated window is de-iconified.

M_DESTROY_WINDOW

The three default arguments identify a window that was just destroyed and is no longer on the display.

M_DEWINDOWSHADE

The three default arguments identify a window that was just unshaded (applicable only if window-shading was enabled in the configuration).

M_END_CONFIG_INFO

After Fvwm sends all of its M_CONFIG_INFO packets to a module, it sends a packet of this type to indicate the end of the configuration information. This packet contains no values.

M_END_WINDOWLIST

This packet is sent to mark the end of transmission in response to a Send_WindowList request. A module that requests Send_WindowList and then processes all packets received between the request and the M_END_WINDOWLIST will have a snapshot of the status of the desktop.

M_ERROR

When Fvwm has an error message to report, it is echoed to the modules in a packet of this type. This packet has three values, all zero, followed by a variable-length string that contains the error message. It does not have the standard first three values.

M_FOCUS_CHANGE

This packet signifies that the window manager focus has changed. The first three parameters are the common three. There are also a fourth and fifth parameter, the pixel value of the window's text focus color and the window's border focus color, respectively. If the window that now has the focus is not a window recognized by Fvwm, then only the first of these five values, the X window ID, is set. The rest are zeros.

M_ICONIFY

This packet contains seven values. The first three are the usual identifiers, and the next four describe the location and size of the icon window, as described below. Note that M_ICONIFY packets are sent whenever a window is first iconified, or when the icon window is changed via the XA_WM_HINTS in a property notify event. An M_ICON_LOCATION packet is sent when the icon is moved. If a window that has transients is iconified, then an M_ICONIFY packet is sent for each transient window, with the X, Y, width, and height fields set to 0. This packet is sent even if the transients were already iconified. Note that no icons are actually generated for the transients in this case.

Arg #	Usage
0	$id
1	$frameid
2	$ptr
3	X location of the icon frame
4	Y location of the icon frame
5	Width of the icon frame (pixels)
6	Height of the icon frame (pixels)

M_ICON_FILE

This packet has the three standard arguments identifying the window, then a text string with the name of the file used as the icon image. This packet is sent only to identify the icon used by the module itself.

M_ICON_LOCATION

Similar to the M_ICONIFY packet described earlier, this packet has the same arguments in the same order. It is sent whenever the associated icon is moved.

M_ICON_NAME

This packet is like the M_RES_CLASS and M_RES_NAME packets. It contains the usual three window identifiers, followed by a variable-length character string that is the icon name.

M_LOWER_WINDOW

The three default arguments identify a window that was just moved to the bottom of the stacking order.

M_MAP

Contains the standard three values. The packets are sent when a window is mapped, if it is not being de-iconified. This is useful to determine when a window is finally mapped, after being added.

M_MINI_ICON

Not yet documented.

M_NEW_DESK

This packet type does not have the usual three leading arguments. The body of this packet consists of a single long integer, whose value is the number of the currently active desktop. This packet is transmitted whenever the desktop number is changed.

M_NEW_PAGE

These packets also differ from the standard in not having the usual first three arguments. Instead, they contain five integers. The first two are the X and Y coordinates of the upper left corner of the current viewport on the virtual desktop. The third value is the number of the current desktop. The fourth and fifth values are the maximum allowed values of the coordinates of the upper-lefthand corner of the viewport.

M_RAISE_WINDOW

The three default arguments identify a window that was just moved to the top of the stacking order.

M_RES_CLASS

This packet contains the usual three window identifiers, followed by a variable-length character string. The RES_CLASS and RES_NAME fields are fields in the XClass structure for the window. The RES_CLASS and RES_NAME packets are sent on window creation and in response to a Send_WindowList request from a module.

M_RES_NAME

This packet is identical to M_RES_CLASS, identifying instead the resource name for the window.

M_STRING

Similar to the other text packets such as M_ICON_NAME or M_RES_CLASS, this packet contains zeros for the first three arguments, and a variable-length text string as its fourth. This is sent to all modules whose name matches the name pattern from a SendToModule command.

M_WINDOWSHADE

The three default arguments identify a window that was just shaded (applicable only if window-shading was enabled in the configuration).

M_WINDOW_NAME

This packet is like the M_ICON_NAME, M_RES_CLASS, and M_RES_NAME packets. It contains the usual three window identifiers, followed by a variable-length character string that is the window name.

Packet Values

These values are used in disassembling a raw packet into data that is then passed to a handler. In general, a developer does not need these, as the bulk of the work that they are used for occurs in `readPacket`. They are here for completeness and in case an application does have a need.

START_FLAG

This is the value that should be in the first word of the packet. It is set to `0xffffffff` (if the word size is 32 bits). If this is not the first word in the packet, the packet cannot be considered usable.

HEADER_SIZE

The size, in words, of the header. This is used to separate the words that comprise the header from the packet body.

MAX_BODY_SIZE

Maximum size of a packet body, in words.

MAX_MASK

A mask that matches all M_* packet-type values, useful as an operator to a logical AND.

MAX_PACKET_SIZE

Maximum packet size (in words), including both header and body.

Context Specifiers

When a module is launched, one of the parameters passed on the command line is the context in which the module was started. This is stored on the X11::Fvwm object instance in the variable `fvwmContext`. These flags can be used in tests against this value to determine where the running module was launched from.

C_ALL

A mask that matches all C_* flags. Useful as a logical AND operand.

C_NO_CONTEXT

The module has no launch context. These are modules that are launched from the configuration file as Fvwm starts up.

C_ROOT

The module was launched from the root window (via PopUp menu or hot-key).

C_SIDEBAR

Launch was from the sidebar decorating an application.

C_TITLE

Launch occurred from the titlebar itself (but not any of the buttons).

C_WINDOW

The module was launched from within the window of a running application.

C_FRAME

Launch was from the frame of a managed window.

C_ICON

Launch was from the icon of a managed application.

C_L1

The first (leftmost) button on the left of the titlebar.

C_L2

Second left-side button (to the right of C_L1).

C_L3

Third left-side button (to the right of C_L2).

C_L4
Fourth left-side button (to the right of C_L3).

C_L5
Fifth left-side button (to the right of C_L4).

C_LALL
A mask that matches any of the C_L[12345] context flags.

C_R1
The first (rightmost) button on the right of the titlebar.

C_R2
Second right-side button (to the left of C_R1).

C_R3
Third right-side button (to the left of C_R2).

C_R4
Fourth right-side button (to the left of C_R3).

C_R5
Fifth right-side button (to the left of C_R4).

C_RALL
A mask that matches any of the C_R[12345] context flags.

Flags

These are the flags, from the file *fvwm.h*, that are packed into the FLAGS value of M_ADD_WINDOW and M_CONFIGURE_WINDOW packets. Unlike the other constants and flags used by the X11::Fvwm module, these have slightly different names than their native Fvwm counterparts. This is because the values in *fvwm.h* have no distinct prefix, such as C_ or M_. To reduce the risk of name conflict, all of these flags were given a prefix of F_.

F_ALL_COMMON_FLAGS
A mask covering the more commonly used style flags: F_STARTICONIC, F_ONTOP, F_STICKY, F_WINDOWLISTSKIP, F_SUPPRESSICON, F_NOICON_TITLE, F_Lenience, F_StickyIcon, F_CirculateSkipIcon, F_CirculateSkip, F_ClickToFocus, F_SloppyFocus, F_SHOW_ON_MAP.

F_BORDER
This window has a border drawn with it.

F_CirculateSkip
This window has the CirculateSkip style property set.

F_CirculateSkipIcon
This window has the CirculateSkipIcon style property set.

F_ClickToFocus
Whether the window focus style is ClickToFocus.

F_DoesWmTakeFocus
Whether the _XA_WM_TAKE_FOCUS property is set on the window.

F_DoesWmDeleteWindow
Whether the _XA_WM_DELETE_WINDOW property is set on the window.

F_HintOverride
Not documented yet.

F_ICON_MOVED
> Not documented yet.

F_ICON_OURS
> The icon window was provided by Fvwm and should be freed by Fvwm.

F_ICON_UNMAPPED
> Not documented yet.

F_ICONIFIED
> This window is currently iconified.

F_Lenience
> Not documented yet.

F_MAP_PENDING
> This application still awaits mapping.

F_MAPPED
> This window (application) is mapped on the display.

F_MAXIMIZED
> This window is currently maximized.

F_MWMButtons
> This window has its style set to include MWM-ish buttons.

F_MWMBorders
> This window has its style set to include MWM-ish borders.

F_NOICON_TITLE
> This window does not have a title with its icon.

F_ONTOP
> This window is set with the StaysOnTop style setting, meaning that it will always be raised over any windows that obscure it even partially (except other StaysOnTop windows).

F_PIXMAP_OURS
> The pixmap used for the icon was loaded and provided by Fvwm and should be freed by Fvwm when no longer needed.

F_RAISED
> If it is a sticky window, this indicates whether or not it needs to be raised.

F_SHAPED_ICON
> The icon for this window is a shaped icon.

F_SHOW_ON_MAP
> When this window is mapped, the desktop should switch to the appropriate quadrant and desk.

F_STARTICONIC
> This window was instructed to start in an iconic state.

F_STICKY
> This window is considered sticky.

F_SUPPRESSICON
> This application should not be displayed when iconic.

F_SloppyFocus
> This window responds to a focus style of SloppyFocus.

F_StickyIcon
:   The icon for this window is considered sticky.

F_TITLE
:   This window is assigned a title bar.

F_TRANSIENT
:   This window is a transient window.

F_VISIBLE
:   This window is considered fully visible (the only things obscuring it should be windows that are set to StaysOnTop).

F_WINDOWLISTSKIP
:   This window should be skipped over in generated lists of windows.

Perl Values

These are values that relate to the Perl objects directly. They are not defined anywhere in *Fvwm*, but exist as a convenience to the module programmer.

P_LAZY_HANDLERS
:   If this option is set, then any new handlers created are set automatically to ignore return codes when evaluated in the loop that processPacket executes. Since the idea is to use return values to detect errors, setting this is of dubious usefulness. But it can have its application (though some would say that explicitly setting the handlers in this fashion is clearer).

P_PACKET_PASSALL
:   This option tells **processPacket** not to strip out any extra arguments from packets such as M_STRING that may have extra data after the variable-length string. It is not set by default.

P_STRIP_NEWLINES
:   If this option is set, then those packets that pass text data (such as M_ICON_NAME or M_STRING) have any trailing newlines stripped (but not internal ones). This option is set by default.

P_ALL_OPTIONS
:   A combination of all P_* values, useful as a mask for a logical AND.

Examples

Examples are provided in the scripts directory of the distribution. These are:

PerlWinList
:   A simple window-listing program that demonstrates simple module/Fvwm communication, without a lot of features to clutter up the source code. Outputs to */dev/console*.

Bugs

Would not surprise me in the least.

Caveats

In keeping with the UNIX philosophy, X11::Fvwm does not keep you from doing stupid things, as that would also keep you from doing clever things. What this means is that there are several areas with which you can hang your module or even royally confuse your running *Fvwm* process. This is due to flexibility, not bugs.

The ColorLimit parameter that is fetched by `getConfigInfo` is only accessible if you have applied the color-limiting patch to *Fvwm* 2.0.45. The fate of that patch (and others) in future releases of *Fvwm* remains to be seen.

The contents of the M_WINDOWSHADE and M_DEWINDOWSHADE packets is based on a patch submitted by the author. Without this patch, these packets only return one integer value, the X window ID of the window in question. Access to the frame ID or the database ID is dependent on this patch.

Author

Randy J. Ray, *randy@byz.org*

Additional Credits

Considerable text used in defining the packet types was taken from or based heavily upon the *modules.tex* file written by Robert J. Nation, which is distributed with *Fvwm*.

See Also

Fvwm manpage, X11::Fvwm::Tk

X11::Fvwm::Defaults—X11::Fvwm default packet handlers for some packet types

Synopsis

```
use X11::Fvwm;
use X11::Fvwm::Defaults 'FvwmError';
$handle = new X11::Fvwm;
$handle->initModule;
$handle->addHandler(M_ERROR, \&FvwmError);
...
$handle->eventLoop;
$handle->endModule;
```

Description

The X11::Fvwm package is designed to provide access via Perl 5 to the module API of Fvwm 2. This code is based upon Fvwm 2.0.45 beta.

The X11::Fvwm::Defaults package is intended to offer some simple handlers for those packets that lend themselves to such, in an effort to encourage code-reuse and to simplify development.

Routines

There are currently two routines available for import. Neither are exported by default, so you must explicitly request those routines if desired when you use the Defaults package. Both of these are for the M_ERROR packet:

FvwmError

This packet sends the text of the error sent by Fvwm to STDERR using the Carp package from the Perl core, specifically the routine **carp.** This routine by default includes some stack-trace information in the generated output, which may aid in tracking down the problem in question. You may also wish to look at the special signal-class __WARN__, documented in the `perlfunc` manpage.

This does not suppress the error message that Fvwm itself displays to STDERR, which is the same source to which your application writes (unless you use $SIG{_ _WARN__} to completely redirect the messages).

`TkFvwmError`

This handler creates a dialog box using the Tk widgets to notify you that an error has been reported by Fvwm. The dialog has three buttons, labelled Exit, Stack Trace, and Dismiss. Selecting the Dismiss button closes the dialog and allows your application to continue (the TkFvwmError routine grabs the pointer until the dialog is closed). Choosing the Exit button causes the handler to return a zero (0) exit code to the `processPacket` method, which in turn triggers the exit handlers and terminates the running module. If the Stack Trace button is pressed, then a current trace of the stack is produced, showing the sequence of calls that led up to the error. After exiting that window, the application continues as if the Dismiss button had been pressed.

As with the non-Tk routine above, Fvwm still produces its own error message that this routine has no power to suppress.

Examples

The PerlTkWL sample script uses the TkFvwmError default to handle any instances of Fvwm errors. To force this behavior, bind a mouse button to invoke a non-existent module, then click that button in an active PerlTkWL.

Bugs

None known.

Caveats

Currently, only the M_ERROR packet type has any defaults to offer. Other types don't appear to lend themselves well to default handlers.

I don't really like the way stack traces are displayed in the TkFvwmError routine, but it will have to do for now.

Author

Randy J. Ray, *randy@byz.org*

See Also

Fvwm manpage , X11::Fvwm, Tk

X11::Fvwm::Tk—X11::Fvwm with the Tk widget library attached

Synopsis

```
use Tk;
use X11::Fvwm::Tk;
$top = new MainWindow;
$handle = new X11::Fvwm::Tk $top;
$handle->initModule;
```

```
$handle->addHandler(M_CONFIGURE_WINDOW, \&configure_Toplevel);
$handle->addHandler(M_CONFIG_INFO, \&some_other_sub);
$handle->eventLoop;
$handle->endModule;
```

Description

The X11::Fvwm package is designed to provide access via Perl 5 to the module API of Fvwm 2. This code is based upon Fvwm 2.0.45 beta.

The X11::Fvwm::Tk package is a subclass of X11::Fvwm that overloads the methods **new** and **eventLoop** to manage Tk objects as well.

This manual page details only those differences. For details on the API itself, see X11::Fvwm.

Methods

Only those methods that are not available in X11::Fvwm or are overloaded are covered here:

new

> Create and return an object of the X11::Fvwm::Tk class. The return value is the blessed reference. This **new** method is identical to the parent **class** method, with the exception that a Tk toplevel of some sort (MainWindow, TopLevel, Frame, etc.) must be passed before the hash of options. The options themselves are as specified in X11::Fvwm.

```
$self = new X11::Fvwm::Tk $top, %params
```

eventLoop

> From outward appearances, this method operates just as the parent **eventLoop** does. It is worth mentioning, however, that this version enters into the Tk Main-Loop subroutine, ostensibly not to return.

```
$self->eventLoop
```

toplevel

> Returns the Tk toplevel that this object was created with. Unlike other instance variable-related methods, the toplevel cannot be changed, so this method ignores any arguments passed to it.

```
$self->toplevel
```

Instance Variables

The following are instance variables not present in the parent class:

topLevel

> The Tk object that was passed as the toplevel this object will use, should it need to call any Tk widget methods (such as dialog creation). It is recommended that you use the **access** method **toplevel** instead of reading this directly.

Examples

Examples are provided in the scripts directory of the distribution. These are:

PerlTkWL

> A much more robust WinList clone, it looks and acts very much like the Fvwm-WinList module that comes with Fvwm. It differs in some subtle ways, however. This one handles more packet types, as well as demonstrating the interaction between X11::Fvwm and the Tk extension. Requires Tk 400.200 or better.

`TkPerlConsole`

A combination of the FvwmConsole and FvwmDebug modules from the extras directory of the Fvwm distribution. Allows the user to send commands to Fvwm, and if debugging is enabled, also shows traffic from Fvwm in a format slightly cleaned up for ease of reading.

Bugs

Would not surprise me in the least.

Caveats

In keeping with the UNIX philosophy, X11::Fvwm does not keep you from doing stupid things, as that would also keep you from doing clever things. What this means is that there are several areas with which you can hang your module or even royally confuse your running Fvwm process. This is due to flexibility, not bugs.

Author

Randy J. Ray, *randy@byz.org*

Additional Thanks to

Nick Ing-Simmons (*Nick.Ing-Simmons@tiuk.ti.com)* for the incredible Tk Perl extension.

See Also

Fvwm manpage, X11::Fvwm, Tk

X11::Fvwm::Xforms—X11::Fvwm with the Xforms widget library attached

Synopsis

```
use X11::Xforms;
use X11::Fvwm::Xforms;
fl_initialize("Xforms example");
$top = fl_bgn_form(...);
...
fl_end_form();
fl_show_form($top, ...);
$handle = new X11::Fvwm::Xforms $top;
$handle->initModule;
$handle->addHandler(M_CONFIGURE_WINDOW, \&configure_Toplevel);
$handle->addHandler(M_CONFIG_INFO, \&some_other_sub);
$handle->eventLoop;
$handle->endModule;
```

Description

The X11::Fvwm package is designed to provide access via Perl 5 to the module API of Fvwm 2. This code is based upon Fvwm 2.0.45 beta.

The X11::Fvwm::Xforms package is a sub-class of X11::Fvwm that overloads the methods **new** and **eventLoop** to manage Xforms GUI objects as well.

This manual page details only those differences. For details on the API itself, see X11::Fvwm.

Methods

Only those methods that are not available in X11::Fvwm or are overloaded are covered here:

new

> Create and return an object of the X11::Fvwm::Xforms class. The return value is the blessed reference. This **new** method is identical to the parent **class** method, with the exception that a Xforms form object must be passed before the hash of options. The options themselves are as specified in X11::Fvwm. As Xforms does not necessarily require an object instance for most calls, this value can be passed as either an empty string or **undef** if it will not be needed in packet handlers. It is provided as a means of giving access to the topmost form to subroutines.

> ```
> $self = new X11::Fvwm::Xforms $top, %params
> ```

eventLoop

> From outward appearances, this method operates just as the parent **eventLoop** does. It is worth mentioning, however, that this version enters into the Xforms **fl_ do_forms** subroutine, ostensibly not to return. Any arguments passed to **event-Loop** are passed along unmodified to **fl_do_forms**.

> ```
> $self->eventLoop(@optional_args)
> ```

topform

> Returns the Xforms form object that this object was created with. Unlike other instance variable-related methods, the form cannot be changed, so this method ignores any arguments passed to it.

> ```
> $self->topform
> ```

Instance Variables

The following are instance variables not present in the parent class:

topForm

> The Xforms object that was passed as the toplevel this object will use, should it need to call any Xforms routines (such as dialog creation). It is recommended that you use the **access** method topform instead of reading this directly.

Examples

Examples are provided in the scripts directory of the distribution. No Xforms-related examples are available yet.

Bugs

Would not surprise me in the least.

Caveats

In keeping with the UNIX philosophy, X11::Fvwm does not keep you from doing stupid things, as that would also keep you from doing clever things. What this means is that there are several areas with which you can hang your module or even royally confuse your running Fvwm process. This is due to flexibility, not bugs.

The X11::Xforms module itself is still in early development stages, and as such may be somewhat noisy if −w is used.

Author

Randy J. Ray, *randy@byz.org*

Additional Thanks to

Martin Bartlett, *martin@nitram.demon.co.uk*, who developed the X11::Xforms Perl extension

See Also

Fvwm manpage, X11::Fvwm, X11::Xforms

X11::Keysyms—Perl module for names of X11 keysyms

Synopsis

```
use X11::Keysyms '%Keysyms', qw(MISCELLANY XKB_KEYS LATIN1);
%Keysyms_name = reverse %Keysyms;
$ks = $Keysyms{'BackSpace'};
$name = $Keysysms_name{$ks};
```

Description

This module exports a hash mapping the names of X11 keysyms, such as A or Linefeed or Hangul_J_YeorinHieuh onto the numbers that represent them. The first argument to use is the name of the variable the hash should be exported into, and the rest are names of subsets of the keysysms to export: one or more of:

```
'MISCELLANY', 'XKB_KEYS', '3270', 'LATIN1', 'LATIN2',
'LATIN3', 'LATIN4', 'KATAKANA', 'ARABIC', 'CYRILLIC',
'GREEK', 'TECHNICAL', 'SPECIAL', 'PUBLISHING', 'APL',
'HEBREW', 'THAI', 'KOREAN'.
```

If this list is omitted, the list:

```
'MISCELLANY', 'XKB_KEYS', 'LATIN1', 'LATIN2', 'LATIN3',
'LATIN4', 'GREEK'
```

is used.

Author

This module was generated semi-automatically by Stephen McCamant (*alias@mcs.com*), from the header file *X11/keysymdef.h*, distributed by the X Consortium.

See Also

perl(1), X11::Protocol, X Window System Protocol (X Version 11)

X11::Protocol—Perl module for the X Window System Protocol, version 11

Synopsis

```
use X11::Protocol;
$x = X11::Protocol->new();
$win = $x->new_rsrc;
$x->CreateWindow($win, $x->root, 'InputOutput',
                 $x->root_depth, 'CopyFromParent',
                 ($x_coord, $y_coord), $width,
                 $height, $border_w);
...
```

Description

X11::Protocol is a client-side interface to the X11 Protocol (see X(1) for information about X11), allowing Perl programs to display windows and graphics on X11 servers.

A full description of the protocol is beyond the scope of this document; for complete information, see the *X Window System Protocol, X Version 11*, available as Postscript or *roff source from *ftp://ftp.x.org*, or *Volume 0: X Protocol Reference Manual* of O'Reilly & Associates' series of books about X (ISBN 1-56592-083-X, *http://www.oreilly.com*), which contains most of the same information.

Disclaimer

"The protocol contains many management mechanisms that are not intended for normal applications. Not all mechanisms are needed to build a particular user interface. It is important to keep in mind that the protocol is intended to provide mechanism, not policy."—Robert W. Scheifler

Basic Methods

new

> Open a connection to a server.

```
$x = X11::Protocol->new();
$x = X11::Protocol->new($display_name);
$x = X11::Protocol->new($connection);
$x = X11::Protocol->new($display_name,
                         [$auth_type, $auth_data]);
$x = X11::Protocol->new($connection, [$auth_type, $auth_data]);
```

> *$display_name* should be an X display name, of the form host:display_num.screen_num; if no arguments are supplied, the contents of the DISPLAY environment variable are used. Alternatively, a pre-opened connection, of one of the X11::Protocol::Connection classes (X11::Protocol::Connection, X11::Protocol::Connection::FileHandle, X11::Protocol::Connection::Socket, X11::Protocol::Connection::UNIXFH, X11::Protocol::Connection::INETFH, X11::Protocol::Connection::UNIXSocket, X11::Protocol::Connection::INETSocket) can be given. The authorization data is obtained using X11::Auth or the second argument. If the display is specified by *$display_name*, rather than by *$connection*, a choose_screen() is then also performed, defaulting to screen 0 if the .screen_num of the display name is not present. Returns the new protocol object.

new_rsrc

Returns a new resource identifier. A unique resource ID is required for every object that the server creates on behalf of the client: windows, fonts, cursors, etc. (IDs are chosen by the client instead of the server for efficiency—the client doesn't have to wait for the server to acknowledge the creation before starting to use the object).

```
$x->new_rsrc;
```

handle_input

Get one chunk of information from the server and do something with it. If it's an error, handle it using the protocol object's handler (error_handler—the default is kill the program with an explanatory message). If it's an event, pass it to the chosen event handler, or put it in a queue if the handler is queue. If it's a reply to a request, save using the object's replies hash for further processing.

```
$x->handle_input;
```

atom_name

Returns the string corresponding to the atom $atom. This is similar to the GetAtomName request, but caches the result for efficiency.

```
$name = $x->atom_name($atom);
```

atom

The inverse operation; returns the (numeric) atom corresponding to $name. This is similar to the InternAtom request, but caches the result.

```
$atom = $x->atom($name);
```

choose_screen

Indicates that you prefer to use a particular screen of the display.

```
$x->choose_screen($screen_num);
```

Per-screen information, such as root, width_in_pixels, and white_pixel are made available as:

```
$x->{'root'}
```

instead of:

```
$x->{'screens'}[$screen_num]{'root'}
```

Symbolic Constants

Generally, symbolic constants used by the protocol, like CopyFromParent or PieSlice are passed to methods as strings, and converted into numbers by the module. Their names are the same as those in the protocol specification, including capitalization, but with hyphens (–) changed to underscores (_) to look more Perl-ish. If you want to do the conversion yourself for some reason, the following methods are available:

num

Given a string representing a constant and a string specifying what type of constant it is, returns the corresponding number. $type should be a name like VisualClass or GCLineStyle. If the name is not recognized, it is returned intact.

```
$num = $x->num($type, $str)
```

interp

The inverse operation; given a number and string specifying its type, returns a string representing the constant.

```
$name = $x->interp($type, $num)
```

You can disable `interp()` and the module's internal interpretation of numbers by setting `$x->{'do_interp'}` to zero. Of course, this isn't very useful, unless you have your own definitions for all the constants.

Here is a list of available constant types:

```
AccessMode, AllowEventsMode, AutoRepeatMode, BackingStore,
BitGravity, Bool, ChangePropertyMode, CirculateDirection,
CirculatePlace, Class, ClipRectangleOrdering, CloseDownMode,
ColormapNotifyState, CoordinateMode, CrossingNotifyDetail,
CrossingNotifyMode, DeviceEvent, DrawDirection, Error,
EventMask, Events, FocusDetail, FocusMode, GCArcMode,
GCCapStyle, GCFillRule, GCFillStyle, GCFunction, GCJoinStyle,
GCLineStyle, GCSubwindowMode, GrabStatus, HostChangeMode,
HostFamily, ImageFormat, InputFocusRevertTo, KeyMask, LedMode,
MapState, MappingChangeStatus, MappingNotifyRequest,
PointerEvent, PolyShape, PropertyNotifyState, Request,
ScreenSaver, ScreenSaverAction, Significance, SizeClass,
StackMode, SyncMode, VisibilityState, VisualClass, WinGravity
```

Server Information

At connection time, the server sends a large amount of information about itself to the client. This information is stored in the protocol object for future reference. It can be read directly, like:

```
$x->{'release_number'}
```

or, for object-oriented True Believers, using a method:

```
$x->release_number
```

The method **method** also has a one-argument form for setting variables, but it isn't really useful for some of the more complex structures.

Here is an example of what the object's information might look like:

```
'connection' => X11::Connection::UNIXSocket(0x814526fd),
'byte_order' => 'l',
'protocol_major_version' => 11,
'protocol_minor_version' => 0,
'authorization_protocol_name' => 'MIT-MAGIC-COOKIE-1',
'release_number' => 3110,
'resource_id_base' => 0x1c000002,
'motion_buffer_size' => 0,
'maximum_request_length' => 65535, # units of 4 bytes
'image_byte_order' => 'LeastSiginificant',
'bitmap_bit_order' => 'LeastSiginificant',
'bitmap_scanline_unit' => 32,
'bitmap_scanline_pad' => 32,
'min_keycode' => 8,
'max_keycode' => 134,
'vendor' => 'The XFree86 Project, Inc',
'pixmap_formats' => {1 => {'bits_per_pixel' => 1,
                           'scanline_pad' => 32},
                     8 => {'bits_per_pixel' => 8,
                           'scanline_pad' => 32}},
'screens' => [{'root' => 43, 'width_in_pixels' => 800,
               'height_in_pixels' => 600,
```

```
                    'width_in_millimeters' => 271,
                    'height_in_millmerters' => 203,
                    'root_depth' => 8,
                    'root_visual' => 34,
                    'default_colormap' => 33,
                    'white_pixel' => 0, 'black_pixel' => 1,
                    'min_installed_maps' => 1,
                    'max_installed_maps' => 1,
                    'backing_stores' => 'Always',
                    'save_unders' => 1,
                    'current_input_masks' => 0x58003d,
                    'allowed_depths' =>
                        [{'depth' => 1, 'visuals' => []},
                         {'depth' => 8, 'visuals' => [
                             {'visual_id' => 34, 'blue_mask' => 0,
                              'green_mask' => 0, 'red_mask' => 0,
                              'class' => 'PseudoColor',
                              'bits_per_rgb_value' => 6,
                              'colormap_entries' => 256},
                             {'visual_id' => 35, 'blue_mask' => 0xc0,
                              'green_mask' => 0x38, 'red_mask' => 0x7,
                              'class' => 'DirectColor',
                              'bits_per_rgb_value' => 6,
                              'colormap_entries' => 8}, ...]}]],
        'visuals' => {34 => {'depth' => 8, 'class' => 'PseudoColor',
                             'red_mask' => 0, 'green_mask' => 0,
                             'blue_mask'=> 0, 'bits_per_rgb_value' => 6,
                             'colormap_entries' => 256},
                      35 => {'depth' => 8, 'class' => 'DirectColor',
                             'red_mask' => 0x7, 'green_mask' => 0x38,
                             'blue_mask'=> 0xc0, 'bits_per_rgb_value' => 6,
                             'colormap_entries' => 8}, ...}
        'error_handler' => &\X11::Protocol::default_error_handler,
        'event_handler' => sub {},
        'do_interp' => 1
```

Requests

request

Sends a protocol request to the server and gets the reply.

```
    $x->request('CreateWindow', ...);
    $x->req('CreateWindow', ...);
    $x->CreateWindow(...);
```

For names of and information about individual requests, see below and/or the protocol reference manual.

add_reply

Adds a stub for an expected reply to the object's **replies** hash. When a reply numbered *$sequence_num* comes, it is stored in *$var.*

```
    $x->add_reply($sequence_num, \$var);
```

delete_reply

Deletes the entry in **replies** for the specified reply. (This should be done after the reply is received).

```
    $x->delete_reply($sequence_num);
```

send

> Sends a request, but does not wait for a reply. You must handle the reply, if any, yourself, using `add_reply()`, `handle_input()`, `delete_reply()`, and `unpack_reply()`, generally in that order.
>
> ```
> $x->send('CreateWindow', ...);
> ```

unpack_reply

> Interprets the raw reply data *$data*, according to the reply format for the named request. Returns data in the same format as `request(`*$request_name*`, ...)`.
>
> ```
> $x->unpack_reply('GetWindowAttributes', $data);
> ```

This section includes only a short calling summary for each request; for full descriptions, see the protocol standard. Argument order is usually the same as listed in the spec, but you generally don't have to pass lengths of strings or arrays, since Perl keeps track. Symbolic constants are generally passed as strings. Most replies are returned as lists, but when there are many values, a hash is used. Lists usually come last; when there is more than one, each is passed by reference. In lists of multipart structures, each element is a list reference. Parentheses are inserted in argument lists for clarity, but are optional. Requests are listed in order by major opcode, so related requests are usually close together. Replies follow the =>.

```
$x->CreateWindow($wid, $parent, $class, $depth, $visual, ($x, $y),
                 $width, $height, $border_width,
                 'attribute' => $value, ...)
$x->ChangeWindowAttributes($window, 'attribute' => $value, ...)
$x->GetWindowAttributes($window)
=>
('backing_store' => $backing_store, ...)
```

This is an example of a return value that is meant to be assigned to a hash.

```
$x->DestroyWindow($win)
$x->DestroySubwindows($win)
$x->ChangeSaveSet($window, $mode)
$x->ReparentWindow($win, $parent, ($x, $y))
$x->MapWindow($win)
$x->MapSubwindows($win)
$x->UnmapWindow($win)
$x->UnmapSubwindows($win)
$x->ConfigureWindow($win, 'attribute' => $value, ...)
$x->CirculateWindow($win, $direction)
```

Note that this request actually circulates the subwindows of **$win**, not the window itself.

```
$x->GetGeometry($drawable)
=>
('root' => $root, ...)
$x->QueryTree($win)
=>
($root, $parent, @kids)
$x->InternAtom($name, $only_if_exists)
=>
$atom
$x->GetAtomName($atom)
=>
```

```
$name
$x->ChangeProperty($window, $property, $type, $format, $mode,
$data)
$x->DeleteProperty($win, $atom)
$x->GetProperty($window, $property, $type, $offset, $length,
$delete)
=>
($value, $type, $format, $bytes_after)
```

Notice that the value comes first, so you can easily ignore the rest.

```
$x->ListProperties($window)
=>
(@atoms)
$x->SetSelectionOwner($selection, $owner, $time)
$x->GetSelectionOwner($selection)
=>
$owner
$x->ConvertSelection($selection, $target, $property, $requestor,
$time)
$x->SendEvent($destination, $propagate, $event_mask, $event)
```

The $event argument should be the result of a **pack_event**() (see "Events").

```
$x->GrabPointer($grab_window, $owner_events, $event_mask,
                $pointer_mode, $keyboard_mode, $confine_to,
                $cursor, $time)
=>
$status
$x->UngrabPointer($time)
$x->GrabButton($modifiers, $button, $grab_window, $owner_events,
               $event_mask, $pointer_mode, $keyboard_mode,
               $confine_to, $cursor)
$x->UngrabButton($modifiers, $button, $grab_window)
$x->ChangeActivePointerGrab($event_mask, $cursor, $time)
$x->GrabKeyboard($grab_window, $owner_events, $pointer_mode,
                 $keyboard_mode, $time)
=>
$status
$x->UngrabKeyboard($time)
$x->GrabKey($key, $modifiers, $grab_window, $owner_events,
            $pointer_mode, $keyboard_mode)
$x->UngrabKey($key, $modifiers, $grab_window)
$x->AllowEvents($mode, $time)
$x->GrabServer
$x->UngrabServer
$x->QueryPointer($window)
=>
('root' => $root, ...)
$x->GetMotionEvents($start, $stop, $window)
=>
([$time, ($x, $y)], [$time, ($x, $y)], ...)
$x->TranslateCoordinates($src_window, $dst_window, $src_x, $src_y)
=>
($same_screen, $child, $dst_x, $dst_y)
$x->WarpPointer($src_window, $dst_window, $src_x, $src_y, $src_
```

```
                        width,
                        $src_height, $dst_x, $dst_y)
    $x->SetInputFocus($focus, $revert_to, $time)
    $x->GetInputFocus
    =>
    ($focus, $revert_to)
    $x->QueryKeymap
    =>
    $keys
```

$keys is a bit vector, so you should use vec() to read it.

```
    $x->OpenFont($fid, $name)
    $x->CloseFont($font)
    $x->QueryFont($font)
    =>
    ('min_char_or_byte2' => $min_char_or_byte2,
    ...,
    'min_bounds' =>
     [$left_side_bearing, $right_side_bearing, $character_width,
      $ascent,
      $descent, $attributes],
    ...,
     'char_infos' =>
     [[$left_side_bearing, $right_side_bearing, $character_width,
       $ascent,
       $descent, $attributes],
     ...],
     'properties' => {$prop => $value, ...}
     )
    $x->QueryTextExtents($font, $string)
    =>
    ('draw_direction' => $draw_direction, ...)
    $x->ListFonts($pattern, $max_names)
    =>
    @names
    $x->ListFontsWithInfo($pattern, $max_names)
    =>
    ({'name' => $name, ...}, {'name' => $name, ...}, ...)
```

The information in each hash is the same as the information returned by QueryFont, but without per-character size information. This request is special in that it is the only request that can have more than one reply. This means you should probably only use request() with it, not send(), as the reply counting is complicated. Luckily, you never need this request anyway, as its function is completely duplicated by other requests.

```
    $x->SetFontPath(@strings)
    $x->GetFontPath
    =>
    @strings
    $x->CreatePixmap($pixmap, $drawable, $depth, $width, $height)
    $x->FreePixmap($pixmap)
    $x->CreateGC($cid, $drawable, 'attribute' => $value, ...)
    $x->ChangeGC($gc, 'attribute' => $value, ...)
    $x->CopyGC($src, $dest, 'attribute', 'attribute', ...)
```

```
$x->SetDashes($gc, $dash_offset, (@dashes))
$x->SetClipRectangles($gc, ($clip_x_origin, $clip_y_origin),
                      $ordering, [$x, $y, $width, $height], ...)
$x->ClearArea($window, ($x, $y), $width, $height, $exposures)
$x->CopyArea($src_drawable, $dst_drawable, $gc, ($src_x, $src_y),
             $width, $height, ($dst_x, $dst_y))
$x->CopyPlane($src_drawable, $dst_drawable, $gc, ($src_x, $src_y),
              $width, $height, ($dst_x, $dst_y), $bit_plane)
$x->PolyPoint($drawable, $gc, $coordinate_mode,
              ($x, $y), ($x, $y), ...)
$x->PolyLine($drawable, $gc, $coordinate_mode,
             ($x, $y), ($x, $y), ...)
$x->PolySegment($drawable, $gc, ($x, $y) => ($x, $y),
                ($x, $y) => ($x, $y), ...)
$x->PolyRectangle($drawable, $gc,
                  [($x, $y), $width, $height], ...)
$x->PolyArc($drawable, $gc,
            [($x, $y), $width, $height, $angle1, $angle2], ...)
$x->FillPoly($drawable, $gc, $shape, $coordinate_mode,
             ($x, $y), ...)
$x->PolyFillRectangle($drawable, $gc,
                      [($x, $y), $width, $height], ...)
$x->PolyFillArc($drawable, $gc,
                [($x, $y), $width, $height, $angle1, $angle2], ...)
$x->PutImage($drawable, $gc, $depth, $width, $height,
             ($dst_x, $dst_y), $left_pad, $format, $data)
```

Currently, the module has no code to handle the various bitmap formats that the server might specify. Therefore, this request does not work portably without a lot of work.

```
$x->GetImage($drawable, ($x, $y), $width, $height, $plane_mask,
             $format)
$x->PolyText8($drawable, $gc, ($x, $y),
              ($font OR [$delta, $string]), ...)
$x->PolyText16($drawable, $gc, ($x, $y),
               ($font OR [$delta, $string]), ...)
$x->ImageText8($drawable, $gc, ($x, $y), $string)
$x->ImageText16($drawable, $gc, ($x, $y), $string)
$x->CreateColormap($mid, $visual, $window, $alloc)
$x->FreeColormap($cmap)
$x->CopyColormapAndFree($mid, $src_cmap)
$x->InstallColormap($cmap)
$x->UninstallColormap($cmap)
$x->ListInstalledColormaps($window)
=>
@cmaps
$x->AllocColor($cmap, ($red, $green, $blue))
=>
($pixel, ($red, $green, $blue))
$x->AllocNamedColor($cmap, $name)
=>
($pixel, ($exact_red, $exact_green, $exact_blue),
 ($visual_red, $visual_green, $visual_blue))
$x->AllocColorCells($cmap, $colors, $planes, $contiguous)
```

```
                    =>
                    ([@pixels], [@masks])
                    $x->AllocColorPlanes($cmap, $colors, ($reds, $greens, $blues),
                                         $contiguous)
                    =>
                    (($red_mask, $green_mask, $blue_mask), @pixels)
                    $x->FreeColors($cmap, $plane_mask, @pixels)
                    $x->StoreColors($cmap, [$pixel, $red, $green, $blue, $do_mask],
                    ...)
```

The 1, 2, and 4 bits in **$mask** are **do-red**, **do-green**, and **do-blue**. **$mask** can be omitted, defaulting to 7, the usual case—change the whole color.

```
                    $x->StoreNamedColor($cmap, $pixel, $name, $do_mask)
```

$do_mask has the same interpretation as above, but is mandatory.

```
                    $x->QueryColors($cmap, @pixels)
                    =>
                    ([$red, $green, $blue], ...)
                    $x->LookupColor($cmap, $name)
                    =>
                    (($exact_red, $exact_green, $exact_blue),
                     ($visual_red, $visual_green, $visual_blue))
                    $x->CreateCursor($cid, $source, $mask,
                                     ($fore_red, $fore_green, $fore_blue),
                                     ($back_red, $back_green, $back_blue),
                                     ($x, $y))
                    $x->CreateGlyphCursor($cid, $source_font, $mask_font,
                                          $source_char, $mask_char,
                                          ($fore_red, $fore_green, $fore_blue),
                                          ($back_red, $back_green, $back_blue))

                    $x->FreeCursor($cursor)
                    $x->RecolorCursor($cursor, ($fore_red, $fore_green, $fore_blue),
                                      ($back_red, $back_green, $back_blue))
                    $x->QueryBestSize($class, $drawable, $width, $height)
                    =>
                    ($width, $height)
                    $x->QueryExtension($name)
                    =>
                    ($major_opcode, $first_event, $first_error)
```

If the extension is not present, an empty list is returned.

```
                    $x->ListExtensions
                    =>
                    (@names)
                    $x->ChangeModifierMapping($first_keycode, $keysysms_per_keycode,
                                              @keysyms)
                    $x->GetKeyboardMapping($first_keycode, $count)
                    =>
                    ($keysysms_per_keycode, [$keysym, ...], [$keysym, ...], ...)
                    $x->ChangeKeyboardControl('attribute' => $value, ...)
                    $x->GetKeyboardControl
                    =>
                    ('global_auto_repeat' => $global_auto_repeat, ...)
```

```
$x->Bell($percent)
$x->ChangePointerControl($do_acceleration, $do_threshold,
                        $acceleration_numerator,
                        $acceleration_denominator, $threshold)
$x->GetPointerControl
=>
($accerleration_numerator, $acceleration_denominator, $threshold)
$x->SetScreenSaver($timeout, $interval, $prefer_blanking,
                   $allow_exposures)
$x->GetScreenSaver
=>
($timeout, $interval, $prefer_blanking, $allow_exposures)
$x->ChangeHosts($mode, $host_family, $host_address)
$x->ListHosts
=>
($mode, [$family, $host], ...)
$x->SetAccessControl($mode)
$x->SetCloseDownMode($mode)
$x->KillClient($resource)
$x->RotateProperties($win, $delta, @props)
$x->ForceScreenSaver($mode)
$x->SetPointerMapping(@map)
=>
$status
$x->GetPointerMapping
=>
@map
$x->SetModifierMapping(@keycodes)
=>
$status
$x->GetModiferMapping
=>
@keycodes
$x->NoOperation($length)
```

$length specifies the length of the entire useless request, in four-byte units and is optional.

Events

To receive events, first set the **event_mask** attribute on a window to indicate what types of events you desire (see *pack_event_mask*). Then, set the protocol object's **event_handler** to a subroutine reference that will handle the events. Alternatively, set **event_handler** to queue, and retrieve events using **dequeue_event**(). In both cases, events are returned as a hash. For instance, a typical MotionNotify event might look like this:

```
%event = ('name' => 'MotionNotify', 'sequence_number' => 12,
          'state' => 0, 'event' => 58720256, 'root' => 43,
          'child' => None, 'same_screen' => 1, 'time' => 966080746,
          'detail' => 'Normal', 'event_x' => 10, 'event_y' => 3,
          'code' => 6, 'root_x' => 319, 'root_y' => 235);
```

pack_event_mask

Makes an event mask (suitable as the **event_mask** of a window) from a list of strings specifying event types.

```
$mask = $x->pack_event_mask('ButtonPress', 'KeyPress',
'Exposure');
```

unpack_event_mask

The inverse operation; converts an event mask obtained from the server into a list
of names of event categories.

```
@event_types = $x->unpack_event_mask($mask);
```

dequeue_event

If there is an event waiting in the queue, returns it.

```
%event = $x->dequeue_event;
```

next_event

Like Xlib's **XNextEvent()**, this function:

```
%event = $x->next_event;
```

is equivalent to:

```
$x->handle_input until %event = dequeue_event;
```

pack_event

Given an event in hash form, packs it into a string. This is only useful as an argument to **SendEvent()**.

```
$data = $x->pack_event(%event);
```

unpack_event

The inverse operation; given the raw data for an event (32 bytes), unpacks it into
hash form. Normally, this is done automatically.

```
%event = $x->unpack_event($data);
```

Extensions

Protocol extensions add new requests, event types, and error types to the protocol.
Support for them is compartmentalized in modules in the X11::Protocol::Ext:: hierarchy. For an example, see X11::Protocol::Ext:SHAPE. You can tell if the module has
loaded an extension by looking at:

```
$x->{'ext'}{$extension_name}
```

If the extension has been initialized, this value is an array reference, [**$major_request_
number**, **$first_event_number**, **$first_error_number**, $obj], where *$obj* is
an object containing information private to the extension.

init_extension

Initializes an extension: queries the server to find the extension's request number,
then loads the corresponding module. Returns 0 if the server does not support the
named extension or if no module to interface with it exists.

```
$x->init_extension($name);
```

init_extensions

Initializes protocol extensions. This does a ListExtensions request, then calls **init_
extension()** for each extension that the server supports.

```
$x->init_extensions;
```

Writing Extensions

Internally, the X11::Protocol module is table-driven. All an extension has to do is to add new entries to the protocol object's tables. An extension module should use X11::Protocol, and should define an new() method:

```
X11::Protocol::Ext::NAME
    ->new($x, $request_num, $event_num, $error_num)
```

where $x is the protocol object and *$request_num*, *$event_num*, and *$error_num* are the values returned by QueryExtension().

The new() method should add new types of constant like:

```
$x->{'ext_const'}{'ConstantType'} = ['Constant', 'Constant', ...]
```

and set up the corresponding name-to-number translation hashes like:

```
$x->{'ext_const_num'}{'ConstType'} =
    {make_num_hash($x->{'ext_const'}{'ConstType'})}
```

Even names go in:

```
$x->{'ext_const'}{'Events'}[$event_number]
```

while specifications for event contents go in:

```
$x->{'ext_event'}[$event_number]
```

each element of which is either [\&unpack_sub, \&pack_sub] or [$pack_format, $field, $field, ...], where each $field is name, [name, const_type], or [name, [special_name_for_zero, special_name_for_one]], where special_name_for_one is optional.

Finally:

```
$x->{'ext_request'}{$major_request_number}
```

should be an array of arrays, with each array either [$name, \&packit] or [$name, \&packit, \&unpackit], and:

```
$x->{'ext_request_num'}{$request_name}
```

should be initialized with [$minor_num, $major_num] for each request the extension defines. For code examples that do all of this, look at X11::Protocol::Ext::SHAPE.

X11::Protocol exports several functions that might be useful in extensions (note that these are *not* methods):

padding
> Given an integer, computes the number needed to round it up to a multiple of 4. For instance, padding(5) is 3.
>
> ```
> $p = padding $x;
> ```

pad
> Given a string, returns the number of extra bytes needed to make a multiple of 4. Equivalent to padding(length($str)).
>
> ```
> $p = pad $str;
> ```

padded
> Returns a format string, suitable for pack(), for a string padded to a multiple of 4 bytes. For instance, pack(padded('Hello'), 'Hello') gives Hello\0\0\0.
>
> ```
> $data = pack(padded($str), $str);
> ```

`hexi`

> Formats a number in hexadecimal and adds **0x** to the front.
>
> $str = hexi $n;

`make_num_hash`

> Given a reference to a list of strings, returns a hash mapping the strings onto numbers representing their position in the list, as used by `$x->{'ext_const_num'}`.
>
>   %hash = make_num_hash(['A', 'B', 'C']);

Bugs

This module is too big (~2500 lines), too slow (10 second to load on a slow machine), too inefficient (request args are copied several times), and takes up too much memory (3000K for basicwin).

If you have more than 65,535 replies outstanding at once, sequence numbers can collide.

The protocol is too complex.

Author

Stephen McCamant, *alias@mcs.com*

See Also

perl(1), X(1), X11::Keysyms, X11::Protocol::Ext::SHAPE, X11::Protocol::Ext::BIG_REQUESTS, X11::Auth, X Window System Protocol (X Version 11), Inter-Client Communications Conventions Manual, X Logical Font Description Conventions

---

X11::Protocol::Connection—Perl module abstract base class for X11 client-to-server connections

Synopsis

```
# In connection object module
package X11::Protocol::Connection::CarrierPigeon;
use X11::Protocol::Connection;
@ISA = ('X11::Protocol::Connection');
sub open { ... }
sub give { ... }
sub get { ... }
sub fh { ... }
...
# In program
$connection = X11::Protocol::Connection::CarrierPigeon
  ->open($host, $display_number);
$x = X11::Protocol->new($connection);
$connection->give($data);
$reply = unpack("I", $connection->get(4));
use IO::Select;
$sel = IO::select->new($connection->fh);
if ($sel->can_read == $connection->fh) ...
```

Description

This module is an abstract base class for the various X11::Protocol::Connection::* modules that provide connections to X servers for the X11::Protocol module. It provides stubs for the following methods:

open
> Opens a connection to the specified display (numbered from 0) on the specified *$host*.
>
> ```
> $conn = X11::Protocol::Connection::Foo->open($host,
>                                              $display_num)
> ```

give
> Sends the given data to the server. Normally, this method is used only by the protocol module itself.
>
> ```
> $conn->give($data)
> ```

get
> Reads $n bytes of data from the server. Normally, this method is used only by the protocol module itself.
>
> ```
> $data = $conn->get($n)
> ```

fh
> Returns an object suitable for use as a filehandle. This is mainly useful for doing select() and other such system calls.
>
> ```
> $filehandle = $conn->fh
> ```

Author

Stephen McCamant, *alias@mcs.com*

See Also

perl(1), X11::Protocol, X11::Protocol::Connection::Socket, X11::Protocol::Connection::File-Handle, X11::Protocol::Connection::INETSocket, X11::Protocol::Connection::UNIXSocket, X11::Protocol::Connection::INETFH, X11::Protocol::Connection::UNIXFH.

X11::Protocol::Connection::FileHandle —Perl module base class for FileHandle-based X11 connections

Synopsis

```
package X11::Protocol::Connection::WeirdFH;
use X11::Protocol::Connection::FileHandle;
@ISA = ('X11::Protocol::Connection::FileHandle')
```

Description

This module defines get(), give(), and fh() methods common to X11::Protocol::Connection types that are based on the FileHandle package. They expect the object they are called with to be a reference to a FileHandle.

Author

Stephen McCamant, *alias@mcs.com*

See Also

perl(1), X11::Protocol, X11::Protocol::Connection::INETFH, X11::Protocol::Connection::UNIXFH, FileHandle

X11::Protocol::Connection::INETFH —Perl module for File-Handle-based TCP/IP X11 connections

Synopsis

```
use X11::Protocol;
use X11::Protocol::Connection::INETFH;
$conn = X11::Protocol::Connection::INETFH
  ->open($host, $display_number);
$x = X11::Protocol->new($conn);
```

Description

This module is used by X11::Protocol to establish a connection and communicate with a server over an Internet-type TCP/IP socket connection, using the FileHandle module.

Author

Stephen McCamant, *alias@mcs.com*

See Also

perl(1), X11::Protocol, X11::Protocol::Connection::UNIXFH, X11::Protocol::Connection::File-Handle, FileHandle

X11::Protocol::Connection::INETSocket —Perl module for IO::Socket::INET-based X11 connections

Synopsis

```
use X11::Protocol;
use X11::Protocol::Connection::INETSocket;
$conn = X11::Protocol::Connection::INETSocket
  ->open($host, $display_number);
$x = X11::Protocol->new($conn);
```

Description

This module is used by X11::Protocol to establish a connection and communicate with a server over a TCP/IP connection, using the IO::Socket::INET module.

Author

Stephen McCamant, *alias@mcs.com*

See Also

perl(1), X11::Protocol, X11::Protocol::Connection::Socket, X11::Protocol::Connection::UNIX-Socket, IO::Socket

X11::Protocol::Connection::Socket —Perl module base class for IO::Socket-based X11 connections

Synopsis

```
package X11::Protocol::Connection::WeirdSocket;
use X11::Protocol::Connection::Socket;
@ISA = ('X11::Protocol::Connection::Socket')
```

Description

This module defines get(), give(), and fh() methods common to X11::Protocol::Connection types that are based on IO::Socket. They expect the object they are called with to be a reference to an IO::Socket.

Author

Stephen McCamant, *alias@mcs.com*

See Also

perl(1),   X11::Protocol,   X11::Protocol::Connection::INETSocket,   X11::Protocol::Connection::UNIXSocket, IO::Socket.

X11::Protocol::Connection::UNIXFH —Perl module for File-Handle-based UNIX-domain X11 connections

Synopsis

```
use X11::Protocol;
use X11::Protocol::Connection::UNIXFH;
$conn = X11::Protocol::Connection::UNIXFH
  ->open($host, $display_number);
$x = X11::Protocol->new($conn);
```

Description

This module is used by X11::Protocol to establish a connection and communicate with a server over a local UNIX-domain socket connection, using the FileHandle module. The host argument is ignored.

Author

Stephen McCamant, *alias@mcs.com*

See Also

perl(1), X11::Protocol, X11::Protocol::Connection::INETFH, X11::Protocol::Connection::FileHandle, FileHandle

X11::Protocol::Connection::UNIXSocket   —Perl module for
IO::Socket::UNIX-based X11 connections

Synopsis
```
use X11::Protocol;
use X11::Protocol::Connection::UNIXSocket;
$conn = X11::Protocol::Connection::UNIXSocket
  ->open($host, $display_number);
$x = X11::Protocol->new($conn);
```

Description
This module is used by X11::Protocol to establish a connection and communicate with a server over a local UNIX-domain socket connection, using the IO::Socket::UNIX module. The host argument is ignored.

Author
Stephen McCamant, *alias@mcs.com*

See Also
perl(1),   X11::Protocol,   X11::Protocol::Connection::INETSocket,   X11::Protocol::Connection::Socket, IO::Socket

---

X11::Protocol::Ext::BIG_REQUESTS   —Perl module for the X11
protocol Big Requests extension

Synopsis
```
use X11::Protocol;
$x = X11::Protocol->new($ENV{'DISPLAY'});
$x->init_extension('BIG_REQUESTS') or die;
```

Description
This module is used by the X11::Protocol module to participate in the Big Requests extension to the X protocol. Once initialized, it transparently allows requests of more than 262140 (65535 * 4) bytes. The new maximum request length is available as:

```
$x->maximum_request_length.
```

Author
Stephen McCamant, *alias@mcs.com*

See Also
perl(1), X11::Protocol, Big Requests Extension (X Consortium Standard)

X11::Protocol::Ext::SHAPE—Perl module for the X11 Protocol Nonrectangular Window Shape Extension

Synopsis

```
use X11::Protocol;
$x = X11::Protocol->new($ENV{'DISPLAY'});
$x->init_extension('SHAPE') or die;
```

Description

This module is used by the X11::Protocol module to participate in the shaped-window extension to the X protocol, allowing windows to be of any shape, not just rectangles.

Symbolic Constants

This extension adds the constant types **ShapeKind** and **ShapeOp**, with values as defined in the standard.

Events

This extension adds the event type **ShapeNotify**, with values as specified in the standard. This event is selected using the **ShapeSelectInput()** request.

Requests

This extension adds several requests, called as shown below:

```
$x->ShapeQueryVersion
=>
($major, $minor)
$x->ShapeRectangles($dest, $destKind, $op, $xOff, $yOff,
                    $ordering, @rectangles)
$x->ShapeMask($dest, $destKind, $op, $xOff, $yOff, $source)
$x->ShapeCombine($dest, $destKind, $op, $xOff, $yOff, $source,
                 $sourceKind)
$x->ShapeOffset($dest, $destKind, $xOff, $yOff)
$x->ShapeQueryExtents($dest)
=>
($boundingShaped, $clipShaped,
 ($xBoundingShape, $yBoundingShape,
  $widthBoundingShape, $heightBoundingShape)
 ($xClipShape, $yClipShape, $widthClipShape, $heightClipShape))
$x->ShapeSelectInput($window, $enable)
$x->ShapeInputSelected($window)
=>
$enable
$x->ShapeGetRectangles($window, $kind)
=>
($ordering, [$x, $y, $width, $height], ...)
```

Author

Stephen McCamant, *alias@mcs.com*

See Also

perl(1), X11::Protocol, Nonrectangular Window Shape Extension (X Consortium Standard)

9

Interfaces to Other Languages

This section documents interfaces to, and emulations of, other programming languages. For brevity, only C and Tcl are documented. Check your nearest CPAN mirror for utilities to be used with other languages.

C::Scan — scan C language files for easily recognized constructs

Synopsis

```
$c = new C::Scan 'filename' => $filename, 'filename_filter' => $filter,
                 'add_cppflags' => $addflags;
$c->set('includeDirs' => [$Config::Config{shrpdir}]);

my $fdec = $c->get('parsed_fdecls');
```

Description

This description is very incomplete.

This module uses the Data::Flow interface, thus one uses it in the following fashion:

```
$c = new C::Scan(attr1 => $value1, attr2 => $value2);
$c->set( attr3 => $value3 );
$value4 = $c->get('attr4');
```

Attributes are dependent on some other attributes. The only *required* attribute is **filename**, which denotes which file to parse.

All other attributes are either optional or are calculated based on the values of the required and other optional attributes.

Output Attributes

includes
> Reference to a list of included files.

defines_args

Reference to a hash of macros with arguments. The values are references to an array of length 2; the first element is a reference to the list of arguments and the second one is the expansion. Newlines are not unescaped, thus:

```
#define C(x,y)  E\
              F
```

finishes with ("C" => [["x", "y"], "E\nF"]).

defines_no_args

Reference to a hash of macros without arguments. Newlines are not escaped, thus:

```
#define A B
```

finishes with ("A" => "B").

fdecls

Reference to a list of function declarations.

inlines

Reference to a list of function definitions.

parsed_fdecls

Reference to a list of parsed function declarations.

A parsed declaration is a reference to a list of (rt, nm, args, ft, mod), where rt is the return type of a function, nm is the name, args is the list of arguments, ft is the full text of the declaration, and mod is the modifier (which is always undef).

Each entry in the list args is of the same form (ty, nm, args, ft, mod), where ty is the type of an argument, nm is the name (generated, if it's missing in the declaration), args is undef, and mod is the string of array modifiers.

typedef_hash

Reference to a hash that contains known typedefs as keys.

typedef_texts

Reference to a list that contains known expansions of typedefs.

typedefs_maybe

Reference to a list of typedefed names. (Synchronized with typedef_texts).

vdecls

Reference to a list of extern variable declarations.

Tcl—Tcl extension module for Perl

Synopsis

```
use Tcl;
$interp = new Tcl;
$interp->Eval('puts "Hello world"');
```

Description

The Tcl extension module gives access to the Tcl library, with functionality and interface similar to the C functions of Tcl. In other words, you can:

• Create Tcl interpreters. The Tcl interpreters so created are Perl objects whose destructors delete the interpreters cleanly when appropriate.

- Execute Tcl code in an interpreter. The code can come from strings, files, or Perl file-handles.

- Bind in new Tcl procedures. The new procedures can be either C code (with addresses presumably obtained using **dl_open** and **dl_find_symbol**) or Perl subroutines (by name, reference, or as anonymous subroutines). The (optional) **deleteProc** **callback** in the latter case is another Perl subroutine that is called when the command is explicitly deleted by name or when the destructor for the interpreter object is explicitly or implicitly called.

- Manipulate the result field of a Tcl interpreter

- Set and get values of variables in a Tcl interpreter

- Tie Perl variables to variables in a Tcl interpreter. The variables can be either scalars or hashes.

Methods in Class Tcl

To create a new Tcl interpreter, use:

```
$i = new Tcl;
```

The following methods and routines can then be used on the Perl object returned (the object argument is omitted in each case).

Init ()

    Invokes Tcl_Init on the interpreter.

Eval (*STRING*)

    Evaluates script *STRING* in the interpreter. If the script returns successfully (TCL_OK), then the Perl return value corresponds to **interp->result**, otherwise a **die** exception is raised with the **$@** variable corresponding to **interp->result**. In each case, *corresponds* means that if the method is called in scalar context, then the string **interp->result** is returned, but if the method is called in list context, then **interp->result** is split as a Tcl list and returned as a Perl list.

GlobalEval (*STRING*)

    Evaluates script *STRING* at global level. Otherwise, the same as **Eval()** above.

EvalFile (*FILENAME*)

    Evaluates the contents of the file with name *FILENAME*. Otherwise, the same as **Eval()** above.

EvalFileHandle (*FILEHANDLE*)

    Evaluates the contents of the Perl filehandle *FILEHANDLE*. Otherwise, the same as **Eval()** above. Useful when using the filehandle DATA to tack on a Tcl script following an __END__ token.

call (*PROC, ARG, ...*)

    Looks up procedure *PROC* in the interpreter and invokes it directly with arguments (*ARG, . . .*), without passing through the Tcl parser. For example, spaces embedded in any *ARG* do not cause it to be split into two Tcl arguments before being passed to *PROC*.

result ()

    Returns the current **interp->result** field. List versus scalar context is handled as in **Eval()** above.

CreateCommand (*CMDNAME, CMDPROC, CLIENTDATA, DELETEPROC*)

Binds a new procedure named *CMDNAME* into the interpreter. The *CLIENTDATA* and *DELETEPROC* arguments are optional. There are two cases:

- *CMDPROC* is the address of a C function (presumably obtained using dl_open and dl_find_symbol. In this case, *CLIENTDATA* and *DELETEPROC* are taken to be raw data of the ClientData and deleteProc fields, presumably obtained in a similar way.

- *CMDPROC* is a Perl subroutine (either a subroutine name, a subroutine reference or an anonymous subroutine). In this case, *CLIENTDATA* can be any Perl scalar (e.g., a reference to some other data) and *DELETEPROC* must also be a Perl subroutine. When *CMDNAME* is invoked in the Tcl interpreter, the arguments passed to the Perl subroutine *CMDPROC* are:

  (*CLIENTDATA, INTERP, LIST*)

  where *INTERP* is a Perl object for the Tcl interpreter that made the call and *LIST* is a Perl list of the arguments *CMDNAME* was called with. As usual in Tcl, the first element of the list is *CMDNAME* itself. When *CMDNAME* is deleted from the interpreter (either explicitly with DeleteCommand or because the destructor for the interpreter object is called), it is passed the single argument *CLIENTDATA*.

DeleteCommand (*CMDNAME*)

Deletes command *CMDNAME* from the interpreter. If the command was created with *DELETEPROC* (see CreateCommand above), then it is invoked at this point. When a Tcl interpreter object is destroyed, either explicitly or implicitly, an implicit DeleteCommand happens on all its currently registered commands.

SetResult (*STRING*)

Sets interp->result to *STRING*.

AppendResult (*LIST*)

Appends each element of *LIST* to interp->result.

AppendElement (*STRING*)

Appends *STRING* to interp->result as an extra Tcl list element.

ResetResult ()

Resets interp->result.

SplitList (*STRING*)

Splits *STRING* as a Tcl list. Returns a Perl list or the empty list if there is an error (i.e., *STRING* is not a properly formed Tcl list). In that case, the error message is left in interp->result.

SetVar (*VARNAME, VALUE, FLAGS*)

The *FLAGS* field is optional. Sets the Tcl variable *VARNAME* in the interpreter to *VALUE*. The *FLAGS* argument is the usual Tcl one and can be a bitwise OR of the constants $Tcl::GLOBAL_ONLY, $Tcl::LEAVE_ERR_MSG, $Tcl::APPEND_VALUE, and $Tcl::LIST_ELEMENT.

SetVar2 (*VARNAME1, VARNAME2, VALUE, FLAGS*)

Sets the element *VARNAME1*(*VARNAME2*) of a Tcl array to *VALUE*. The optional argument *FLAGS* behaves as in SetVar above.

GetVar (*VARNAME*, *FLAGS*)

> Returns the value of the Tcl variable *VARNAME*. The optional argument *FLAGS* behaves as in `SetVar` above.

GetVar2 (*VARNAME1*, *VARNAME2*, *FLAGS*)

> Returns the value of the element *VARNAME1*(*VARNAME2*) of a Tcl array. The optional argument FLAGS behaves as in `SetVar` above.

UnsetVar (*VARNAME*, *FLAGS*)

> Unsets the Tcl variable *VARNAME*. The optional argument *FLAGS* behaves as in `SetVar` above.

UnsetVar2 (*VARNAME1*, *VARNAME2*, *FLAGS*)

> Unsets the element *VARNAME1*(*VARNAME2*) of a Tcl array. The optional argument *FLAGS* behaves as in `SetVar` above.

Linking Perl and Tcl variables

You can `tie` a Perl variable (scalar or hash) into class Tcl::Var so that changes to a Tcl variable automatically "change" the value of the Perl variable. In fact, as usual with Perl tied variables, the current value is just fetched from the Tcl variable when needed, and setting the Perl variable triggers the setting of the Tcl variable.

To tie a Perl scalar `$scalar` to the Tcl variable `tclscalar` in interpreter `$interp` with optional flags `$flags` (see `SetVar` above), use:

```
tie $scalar, Tcl::Var, $interp, "tclscalar", $flags;
```

Omit the `$flags` argument if not wanted.

To tie a Perl hash `%hash` to the Tcl array variable `array` in interpreter `$interp` with optional flags `$flags` (see `SetVar` above), use:

```
tie %hash, Tcl::Var, $interp, "array", $flags;
```

Omit the `$flags` argument if not wanted. Any alteration to Perl variable `$hash{"key"}` affects the Tcl variable `array(key)` and vice versa.

Author

Malcolm Beattie, *mbeattie@sable.ox.ac.uk*

Tcl::Tk — extension module for Perl giving access to Tk via the Tcl extension

Synopsis

```
use Tcl;
use Tcl::Tk qw(:widgets :misc);
$interp = new Tcl::Tk;
label(".l", -text => "Hello world");
tkpack ".l";
MainLoop;
```

Description

The Tcl::Tk submodule of the Tcl module gives access to the Tk library. It does this by creating a Tcl interpreter object (using the Tcl extension) and binding in all of Tk into the interpreter (in the same way that `wish` or other Tcl/Tk applications do).

Access to the Tcl and Tcl::Tk Extensions

To get access to the Tcl and Tcl::Tk extensions, put the commands:

```
use Tcl;
use Tcl::Tk;
```

near the top of your program. You can also import shortcut functions into your namespace from Tcl::Tk if you want to avoid using method calls for everything.

Creating a Tcl Interpreter for Tk

To create a Tcl interpreter initialized for Tk, use:

```
$i = new Tcl::Tk (DISPLAY, NAME, SYNC);
```

All arguments are optional. This creates a Tcl interpreter object $i, and creates a main top-level window. The window is created on display *DISPLAY* (defaulting to the display named in the DISPLAY environment variable) with name *NAME* (defaulting to the name of the Perl program, i.e., the contents of Perl variable $0). If the *SYNC* argument is present and true then an XSynchronize() call is made, ensuring that X events are processed synchronously (and thus slowly). This is there for completeness and is only very occasionally useful for debugging errant X clients (usually at a much lower level than Tk users will want).

Entering the Main Event Loop

The Perl method call:

```
$i->MainLoop;
```

on the Tcl::Tk interpreter object enters the Tk event loop. If you prefer, you can do Tcl::Tk::MainLoop or `Tcl::Tk->MainLoop` instead. You can even do simply MainLoop if you import it from Tcl::Tk in the **use** statement. Note that commands in the Tcl and Tcl::Tk extensions closely follow the C interface names with the leading Tcl_ or Tk_ removed.

Creating Widgets

If desired, widgets can be created and handled entirely by Tcl/Tk code evaluated in the Tcl interpreter object $i (created above). However, there is an additional way of creating widgets in the interpreter, directly from Perl. The names of the widgets (frame, toplevel, label, etc.) can be imported as direct commands from the Tcl::Tk extension. For example, if you have imported the label command, then:

```
$l = label(".l", -text => "Hello world);
```

executes the command:

```
$i->call("label", ".l", "-text", "Hello world);
```

and hence gets Tcl to create a new label widget *.l* in your Tcl/Tk interpreter. You can either import such commands one by one with, for example:

```
use Tcl::Tk qw(label canvas MainLoop winfo);
```

or you can use the predefined Exporter tags :widgets and :misc. The :widgets tag imports all the widget commands, and the :misc tag imports all non-widget commands (see the next section).

Let's return to the creation of the label widget above. Since Tcl/Tk creates a command .l in the interpreter and creating a similarly named subroutine in Perl isn't a good idea, the Tcl::Tk extension provides a slightly more convenient way of manipulating the widget. Instead of returning the name of the new widget as a string, the above label command returns a Perl reference to the widget's name, blessed into an almost empty class. Perl method calls on the object are translated into commands for the Tcl/Tk interpreter in a very simplistic fashion. For example, the Perl command:

```
$l->configure(-background => "green");
```

is translated into the command:

```
$i->call($$l, "configure", "-background", "green");
```

for execution in your Tcl/Tk interpreter. Notice that it simply dereferences the object to find the widget name. There is no automagic conversion that happens: if you use a Tcl command that wants a widget pathname, and you only have an object returned by `label()` (or `button()` or `entry()` or whatever) then you must dereference it yourself.

Non-Widget Tk Commands

For convenience, the non-widget Tk commands (such as **destroy**, **focus**, **wm**, **winfo**, and so on) are also available for export as Perl commands and translate into their Tcl equivalents for execution in your Tk/Tcl interpreter. The names of the Perl commands are the same as their Tcl equivalents except for two: Tcl's **pack** command becomes **tkpack** in Perl, and Tcl's **bind** command becomes **tkbind** in Perl. The arguments you pass to any of these Perl commands are not touched by the Tcl parser. Each Perl argument is passed as a separate argument to the Tcl command.

Author

Malcolm Beattie, *mbeattie@sable.ox.ac.uk*

10

File Names, File Systems, and File Locking

Many tools for working with files and file systems can be found in this section. Included are utilities to find, compare, copy, and lock files. In addition, modules for working with directories and directory structures are in this section.

Cwd— get pathname of current working directory

Synopsis

```
use Cwd;
$dir = cwd();            # get current working directory safest way
$dir = getcwd();         # like getcwd(3) or getwd(3)
$dir = fastcwd();        # faster and more dangerous
use Cwd 'chdir';         # override chdir; keep PWD up to date
chdir "/tmp";
print $ENV{PWD};         # prints "/tmp"
```

Description

cwd() gets the current working directory using the most natural and safest form for the current architecture. For most systems, it is identical to pwd (but without the trailing line terminator).

getcwd() does the same thing by re-implementing getcwd(3) or getwd(3) in Perl.

fastcwd() looks the same as getcwd(), but runs faster. It's also more dangerous, because you might chdir out of a directory that you can't chdir back into.

It is recommended that one of these functions be used in all code to ensure portability, because the pwd program probably only exists on UNIX systems.

If you consistently override your chdir built-in function in all packages of your program, then your PWD environment variable is automatically kept up-to-date. Otherwise, you shouldn't rely on it. (Which means you probably shouldn't rely on it.)

File::BasicFlock—file locking with `flock`

Synopsis

```
use File::BasicFlock;
lock($filename);
lock($filename, 'shared');
lock($filename, undef, 'nonblocking');
lock($filename, 'shared', 'nonblocking');
unlock($filename);
```

Description

Lock files using the `flock()` call. The file to be locked must already exist.

Author

David Muir Sharnoff, *muir@idiom.com*

File::CheckTree—run many tests on a collection of files

Synopsis

```
use File::CheckTree;

$warnings += validate( q{
    /vmunix             -e || die
    /boot               -e || die
    /bin                cd
        csh             -ex
        csh             !-ug
        sh              -ex
        sh              !-ug
    /usr                -d || warn "What happened to $file?"
});
```

Description

The `validate()` routine takes a single multiline string, each line of which contains a filename plus a file test to try on it. (The file test may be given as `cd`, causing subsequent relative filenames to be interpreted relative to that directory.) After the file test, you may put `|| die` to make it a fatal error if the file test fails. The default is:

```
|| warn
```

You can reverse the sense of the test by prepending `!`. If you specify `cd` and then list some relative filenames, you may want to indent them slightly for readability. If you supply your own `die` or `warn` message, you can use `$file` to interpolate the filename.

File tests may be grouped: `-rwx` tests for all of `-r`, `-w`, and `-x`. Only the first failed test of the group produces a warning.

`validate()` returns the number of warnings issued, presuming it didn't `die`.

File::Compare — compare files or filehandles

Synopsis

```
use File::Compare;
if (compare("file1","file2") == 0) {
    print "They're equal\n";
}
```

Description

The File::Compare::compare function compares the contents of two sources, each of which can be a file or a filehandle. It is exported from File::Compare by default.

File::Compare::cmp is a synonym for File::Compare::compare. It is exported from File::Compare only by request.

Return

File::Compare::compare returns 0 if the files are equal, 1 if the files are unequal, or -1 if an error was encountered.

Author

Nick Ing-Simmons, *Nick.Ing-Simmons@tiuk.ti.com*

Original documentation by Chip Salzenberg

File::Copy — copy files or filehandles

Synopsis

```
use File::Copy;
copy("file1","file2");
copy("Copy.pm",\*STDOUT);'
use POSIX;
use File::Copy cp;
$n=FileHandle->new("/dev/null","r");
cp($n,"x");'
```

Description

The Copy module provides two functions, copy and copydir.

copy

The copy function takes two parameters: a file to copy from and a file to copy to. Either argument may be a string, a FileHandle reference, or a FileHandle glob. If the first argument is a filehandle of some sort, copy reads from the file; if it is a file *name*, copy opens the file for reading. Likewise, the file named in the second argument is written to (and created if need be). If the first argument is the name of a directory, this function simply calls copydir.

An optional third parameter can be used to specify the buffer size used for copying. This is the number of bytes from the first file, that will be held in memory at any given time, before being written to the second file. The default buffer size depends upon the file, but will generally be the whole file (up to 2Mb), or 1k for filehandles that do not reference files (e.g., sockets).

You may use the syntax `use File::Copy "cp"` to get at the `"cp"` alias for this function. The syntax is *exactly* the same.

Returns 1 on success, 0 on failure. `$!` will be set if an error was encountered.

`copydir`

> `copydir` takes two directory names. If the second directory does not exist, it is created. If it does exist, a directory is created in it to copy to. `copydir` copies every file and directory from the source directory (first parameter) to the destination directory (second parameter). The structure of the source directory is preserved, and warnings are issued if a particular file or directory cannot be accessed or created.
>
> `copydir` returns true on success and false on failure, though failure to copy a single file or directory from the source tree may still result in success. The return value simply indicates whether or not *anything* was done.

Author

Aaron Sherman, *ajs@ajs.com*

See Also

File::Tools

File::CounterFile — persistent counter class

Synopsis

```
use File::CounterFile;
$c = new File::CounterFile "COUNTER", "aa00";
$id = $c->inc;
open(F, ">F$id");
```

Description

This module implements a persistent counter class. Each counter is represented by a separate file in the filesystem. File locking is applied, so multiple processes that might try to access the same counters at the same time do so without risk of counter destruction.

You give the filename as the first parameter to the object constructor (new). The file is created if it does not exist.

If the filename does not start with "/" or ".", then it is interpreted as a file relative to $File::CounterFile::DEFAULT_DIR. The default value for this variable is initialized from the environment variable TMPDIR, or */usr/tmp* if no environment variable is defined. You may want to assign a different value to this variable before creating counters.

If you pass a second parameter to the constructor, that parameter sets the initial value for a new counter. The parameter only takes effect when the file is created (i.e., it does not exist before the call).

When you call the `inc()` method, you increment the counter value by one. When you call `dec()`, the counter value is decremented. In both cases, the new value is returned. The `dec()` method only works for numerical counters (digits only).

You can peek at the value of the counter (without incrementing it) by using the `value()` method.

The counter can be locked and unlocked with the **lock()** and **unlock()** methods. Incrementing and value retrieval is faster when the counter is locked, because we do not have to update the counter file all the time. You can query whether the counter is locked by using the **locked()** method.

There is also an operator-overloading interface to the File::CounterFile object. This means that you might use the **++** operator for incrementing the counter, the **--** operator for decrementing it, and you can interpolate counters directly into strings.

Installation
Copy this file to the *File* subdirectory of your Perl 5 library directory (often */usr/local/lib/perl5*).

Bugs
It uses **flock(2)** to lock the counter file. This does not work on all systems. Perhaps we should use the File::Lock module?

Author
Gisle Aas, *aas@sn.no*

Copyright
Copyright © 1995–1996 Gisle Aas. All rights reserved.

This library is free software; you can redistribute it and/or modify it under the same terms as Perl itself.

File::Df—Perl df

Synopsis
```
use File::Df;
($fs_type, $fs_desc, $used, $avail, $fused, $favail) = df ($dir);
```

Description
This routine displays information on a filesystem such as its type, the amount of disk space occupied, the total disk space, and the number of inodes. It tries **syscall(SYS_statfs)** and **syscall(SYS_statvfs)** in several ways. If all fails, it **croaks**.

Options
$fs_type
Type of the filesystem [number]

$fs_desc
Description of this **fs** [string]

$used
Size used (in Kb) [number]

$avail
Size available (in Kb) [number]

$ffree
Free inodes [number]

`$fused`
> Inodes used [number]

Installation

See the INSTALL file.

Notes

Tested with Perl 5.003 under these systems:

- Solaris 2.[4/5]
- SunOS 4.1.[2/3/4]
- HP-UX 9.05, 10.[1/20] (see below)
- OSF1 3.2, 4.0
- Linux 2.0.*

Note for HP-UX users: if you get this message:

```
Undefined subroutine &main::SYS_statfs called at File/Df.pm line
XXX
```

and if you are using an HP9000s700, then edit the *syscall.ph* file (in the Perl *lib* tree) and copy the line containing `SYS_statfs {196;}` outside the `if (defined &__ hp9000s800)` block (around line 356).

Author

Fabien Tassin, *tassin@eerie.fr*

Copyright

This module is copyright 1996, 1997 by Fabien Tassin.

File::Find—traverse a file tree

Synopsis

```
use File::Find;
find(&wanted, 'dir1', 'dir2'...);
sub wanted { ... }

use File::Find;
finddepth(&wanted, 'dir1', 'dir2'...);  # traverse depth-first
sub wanted { ... }
```

Description

`find()` is similar to the UNIX `find(1)` command in that it traverses the specified directories, performing whatever tests or other actions you request. However, these actions are given in the subroutine `wanted()`, which you must define (but see `find2perl` below).

For example, to print out the names of all executable files, you could define **wanted()** this way:

```
sub wanted {
    print "$File::Find::name\n" if -x;
}
```

$File::Find::dir contains the current directory name, and $_ has the current filename within that directory. $File::Find::name contains "$File::Find::dir/$_". You are chdired to $File::Find::dir when find() is called. You can set $File::Find::prune to true in wanted() in order to prune the tree; that is, find() does not descend into any directory when $File::Find::prune is set.

This library is primarily for use with the find2perl(1) command, which is supplied with the standard Perl distribution and converts a find(1) invocation to an appropriate wanted() subroutine. The command:

```
find2perl / -name .nfs* -mtime +7
                -exec rm -f {} ; -o -fstype nfs -prune
```

produces something like:

```
sub wanted {
    /^.nfs.*$/ &&
    (($dev, $ino, $mode, $nlink, $uid, $gid) = lstat($_)) &&
    int(-M _) > 7 &&
    unlink($_)
    ||
    ($nlink || (($dev, $ino, $mode, $nlink, $uid, $gid) =
                lstat($_))) &&
    $dev < 0 &&
    ($File::Find::prune = 1);
}
```

Set the variable $File::Find::dont_use_nlink if you're using the AFS.

finddepth() is just like find(), except that it does a depth-first search.

Here's another interesting wanted() function. It finds all symbolic links that don't resolve:

```
sub wanted {
    -l and not -e and print "bogus link: $File::Find::name\n";
}
```

File::Flock—file locking with flock

Synopsis

```
use File::Flock;

lock($filename);
lock($filename, 'shared');
lock($filename, undef, 'nonblocking');
lock($filename, 'shared', 'nonblocking');
unlock($filename);
```

Description

Lock files using the `flock()` call. If the file to be locked does not exist, then the file is created. If the file was created, then it is removed when it is unlocked (assuming it's still an empty file).

Bugs

File::Flock does not work on Solaris. It works well on many other operating systems, though.

Author

David Muir Sharnoff, *muir@idiom.com*

File::Lockf—Perl interface to the lockf system call

Synopsis

```
use POSIX;
use File::lockf;
$status = File::lockf::lock(FH, size = 0);
$status = File::lockf::tlock(FH, size = 0);
$status = File::lockf::ulock(FH, size = 0);
$status = File::lockf::test(FH, size = 0);
```

Description

File::Lockf is a wrapper around the `lockf` system call. Perl supports the `flock` system call natively, but that does not acquire network locks. Perl also supports the `fcntl` system call, but that is somewhat ugly to use. There are other locking modules available for Perl, but none of them provide what I wanted—a simple, clean interface to the `lockf` system call, without any bells or whistles getting in the way.

File::Lockf contains four functions, which map to the four `lockf` modes: F_LOCK, F_TLOCK, F_ULOCK, and F_TEST. Each function takes an open filehandle as the first argument and, optionally, a size as the second argument.

The functions return 0 (zero) on success and the system error number from errno on failure. If you use the POSIX module, you can compare the return values symbolically:

```
while (File::lockf::tlock(FH) == EAGAIN) {
    sleep 5;
}
```

Please see your system `lockf` manpage for more details about `lockf` functionality on your system.

Author

Paul Henson, *henson@acm.org*

See Also

perl(1)

File::Path—create or remove a series of directories

Synopsis

```
use File::Path

mkpath([ 'blurfl/quux'], 1, 0711);
rmtree([ 'blurfl/quux'], 1, 1);
```

Description

The `mkpath()` function provides a convenient way to create directories, even if your `mkdir(2)` won't create more than one level of directory at a time. `mkpath()` takes three arguments:

- The name of the path to create, or a reference to a list of paths to create

- A Boolean value, which if true causes `mkpath()` to print the name of each directory as it is created (defaults to false)

- The numeric mode to use when creating the directories (defaults to 0777)

It returns a list of all directories created, including intermediate directories, which are assumed to be delimited by the UNIX path separator, /.

Similarly, the `rmtree()` function provides a convenient way to delete a subtree from the directory structure, much like the UNIX `rm -r` command. `rmtree()` takes three arguments:

- The root of the subtree to delete, or a reference to a list of roots. All of the files and directories below each root, as well as the roots themselves, are deleted.

- A Boolean value, which if true causes `rmtree()` to print a message each time it examines a file, giving the name of the file and indicating whether it's using `rmdir(2)` or `unlink(2)` to remove it, or whether it's skipping it. (This argument defaults to false.)

- A Boolean value, which if true causes `rmtree()` to skip any files to which you do not have delete access (if running under VMS) or write access (if running under another operating system). This will change in the future when a criterion for "delete permission" under operating systems other than VMS is settled. (This argument defaults to false.)

`rmtree()` returns the number of files successfully deleted. Symbolic links are treated as ordinary files.

File::PathConvert—convert file paths

`realpath`
Make a canonicalized absolute pathname

`abs2rel`
Make a relative path from an absolute path

`rel2abs`
Make an absolute path from a relative path

Synopsis

```
use File::PathConvert;
$path = realpath($path);
```

```
$path = abs2rel($path);
$path = abs2rel($path, $base);
$path = rel2abs($path);
$path = rel2abs($path, $base);
```

Description

Functions

realpath

> realpath makes a canonicalized absolute pathname and resolves all symbolic links, extra / characters, and references to /./ and /../ in the path. realpath resolves both absolute and relative paths. It returns the resolved name on success, otherwise it returns undef and sets the variable $resolved to the pathname that caused the problem.
>
> All but the last component of the path must exist.
>
> This implementation is based on 4.4BSD realpath(3).

abs2rel

> abs2rel makes a relative path from an absolute path. By default, the base is the current directory. If you specify a second parameter, it's assumed to be the base.
>
> The returned path may include symbolic links. abs2rel doesn't check whether or not any path exists.

rel2abs

> rel2abs makes an absolute path from a relative path. By default, the base directory is the current directory. If you specify a second parameter, it's assumed to be the base.
>
> The returned path may include symbolic links. abs2rel doesn't check whether or not any path exists.

Examples

realpath

> If '/sys' is a symbolic link to '/usr/src/sys':

```
chdir('/usr');
$path = realpath('../sys/kern');
```

> or in anywhere ...

```
$path = realpath('/sys/kern');
```

> yields

```
$path eq '/usr/src/sys/kern'
```

abs2rel

```
chdir('/usr/local/lib');
$path = abs2rel('/usr/src/sys');
```

> or in anywhere:

```
$path = abs2rel('/usr/src/sys', '/usr/local/lib');
```

> yields:

```
$path eq '../../src/sys'
```

> Similarly,

```
$path1 = abs2rel('/usr/src/sys', '/usr');
$path2 = abs2rel('/usr/src/sys', '/usr/src/sys');
```

yields:

```
$path1 eq 'src/sys'
$path2 eq '.'
```

If the base directory includes symbolic links, **abs2rel** produces the wrong path. For example, if '**/sys**' is a symbolic link to '**/usr/src/sys**',

```
$path = abs2rel('/usr/local/lib', '/sys');
```

yields:

```
$path eq '../usr/local/lib'        # It's wrong!!
```

You should convert the base directory into a real path in advance:

```
$path = abs2rel('/sys/kern', realpath('/sys'));
```

yields:

```
$path eq '../../../sys/kern'       # It's correct but ...
```

That is correct, but a little redundant. If you wish get the simple answer 'kern', do the following:

```
$path = abs2rel(realpath('/sys/kern'), realpath('/sys'));
```

realpath() gets the correct result, but don't forget that **realpath** requires that all but the last component of the path exist.

rel2abs

```
chdir('/usr/local/lib');
$path = rel2abs('../../src/sys');
```

or in anywhere:

```
$path = rel2abs('../../src/sys', '/usr/local/lib');
```

yields:

```
$path eq '/usr/src/sys'
```

Similarly,

```
$path = rel2abs('src/sys', '/usr');
$path = rel2abs('.', '/usr/src/sys');
```

yields:

```
$path eq '/usr/src/sys'
```

Author

Shigio Yamaguchi, *shigio@ca2.so-net.or.jp*

File::Recurse — recurse over files, performing some function

Synopsis

```
use File::Recurse;
use File::Copy;
recurse { print } "/tmp";
recurse {copy($_,"elsewhere") if -f $_} "dir";
recurse(\&func, "/");
```

Description

The File::Recurse module is designed for performing an operation on a tree of directories and files. The basic usage is similar to the *find.pl* library. Once you use the File::Recurse module, you need only call the **recurse** function in order to perform recursive directory operations.

The function takes two parameters: a function reference and a directory. The function referenced by the first parameter should expect to take one parameter, which is the full path to the file currently being operated on. This function is called once for every file and directory under the directory named by the second parameter.

For example:

```
recurse(\&func, "/");
```

starts at the top level of the filesystem and calls **func** for every file and directory found (not including "/").

Perl allows a second form of calling this function that can be useful for situations where you want to do something simple in the function. In such cases, you can define an anonymous function by using braces like this:

```
recurse {print $_[0]} "/";
```

This prints every file and directory in the filesystem. However, as an added convenience, you can access the pathname in the variable $_. So the above could be rewritten as:

```
recurse { print } "/";
```

Context

There is an optional third parameter, which can be any scalar value (including a reference). This value is ignored by **recurse**, but is passed as the second parameter to the user-defined function. This can be useful for building library routines that use **recurse**, so that they do not have to pass state to the function as global variables.

Controlling Recursion

If you want to control how recursion happens, you have several options. First, there are some global variables that affect the overall operation of the **recurse** routine:

$MAX_DEPTH
> This variable controls how far down a tree of directories **recurse** will go before it assumes that something bad has happened. The default is 100.

$FOLLOW_SYMLINKS
> This variable tells **recurse** if it should descend into directories that are symbolic links. The default is 0.

Normally, the return value of the called function is not used, but if it is –1 or –2, a special action is taken.

If the function returns –1 and the current filename refers to a directory, **recurse** does *not* descend into that directory. This can be used to prune searches and focus only on those directories that should be followed.

If the function returns –2, the search is terminated, and **recurse** returns. This can be used to bail out when a problem occurs and you don't want to exit the program, or to end the search for some file once it has been found.

See Also

File::Tools

Author

Aaron Sherman, *ajs@ajs.com*

File::Slurp—single-call read and write file routines; read directories

Synopsis

```
use File::Slurp;

$all_of_it = read_file($filename);
@all_lines = read_file($filename);
write_file($filename, @contents)
overwrite_file($filename, @new_contnts);
append_file($filename, @additional_contents);
@files = read_dir($directory);
```

Description

These are quickie routines that are meant to save a couple of lines of code over and over again. They do not do anything fancy.

read_file()

> Does what you would expect. If you are using its output in array context, then it returns an array of lines. If you are calling it from scalar context, then it returns the entire file in a single string.
>
> It croaks()s if it can't open the file.

write_file()

> Creates or overwrites files.

append_file()

> Appends to a file.

overwrite_file()

> Does an in-place update of an existing file or creates a new file if the file doesn't already exist. Write_file also replaces a file. The difference is that the first thing that write_file() does is truncate the file, whereas the last thing that overwrite_file() does is truncate the file. Overwrite_file() should be used in situations where you have a file that always needs to have some content, even in the middle of an update.

read_dir()

> Returns all of the entries in a directory except ".". and "..". It croaks if it cannot open the directory.

Author

David Muir Sharnoff, *muir@idiom.com*

File::Sync—Perl access to fsync() and sync() function calls

Synopsis

```
use File::Sync qw(fsync sync);
fsync(FILEHANDLE) or die "fsync: $!";
sync();

use IO::File;
$fh = IO::File->new("> /tmp/foo")
    or die "new IO::File: $!";
...
$fh->fsync() or die "fsync: $!";
```

Description

The `fsync()` function takes a Perl filehandle as its only argument and passes its `fileno()` to the C function `fsync()`. It returns **undef** on failure, or true on success. The `fsync_fd()` function is used internally by `fsync()`; it takes a file descriptor as its only argument. The `sync()` function is identical to the C function `sync()`.

This module does not export any methods by default, but `fsync()` is made available as a method of the FileHandle and IO::Handle classes.

Notes

Doing `fsync()` if the stdio buffers aren't flushed (with `$|` or the **autoflush** method) is probably pointless.

Calling `sync()` too often on a multi-user system is slightly antisocial.

See Also

perl(1), fsync(2), sync(2), perlvar(1)

Author

Carey Evans, *c.evans@clear.net.nz*

File::Tools—this module is a wrapper for the various File modules

Synopsis

```
use File::Tools;
copy("x", *STDOUT);
recurse { print } "/etc";
```

Description

Provides the routines that are defined in File::Recurse and File::Copy.

Other modules will be added at a later date, but File::Tools will always encapsulate them.

See Also

File::Copy, File::Recurse

Author

Aaron Sherman, *ajs@ajs.com*

11

String and Language Text Processing, Parsing, and Searching

The modules in this section run the gamut of text processing, from the simple (manipulation modules such as Text::Wrap) to the complex (the SGML parsing of SGMLS). Font and string utilities are also located here.

Font::AFM—interface to Adobe Font Metrics files

Synopsis

```
use Font::AFM;
$h = new Font::AFM "Helvetica";
$copyright = $h->Notice;
$w = $h->Wx->{"aring"};
$w = $h->stringwidth("Gisle", 10);
$h->dump;  # for debugging
```

Description

This module implements the Font::AFM class. Objects of this class are initialized from an AFM-file and allow you to obtain information about the font and the metrics of the various glyphs in the font.

All measurements in AFM files are given in terms of units equal to 1/1000 of the scale factor of the font being used. To compute actual sizes in a document, these amounts should be multiplied by (scale factor of font)/1000.

Methods

new($*fontname*)

> Object constructor. Takes the name of the font as argument. It **croaks** if the font cannot be found.

latin1_wx_table()

> Returns a 256-element array, where each element contains the width of the corresponding character in the ISO-8859-1 character set.

stringwidth(*$string*, [*$fontsize*])

Returns the width of the string passed as argument. The string is assumed to be encoded in the ISO-8859-1 character set. A second argument can be used to scale the width according to the font size.

FontName

The name of the font as presented to the PostScript language `findfont` operator, for instance, Times-Roman.

FullName

Unique, human-readable name for an individual font, for instance, Times Roman.

FamilyName

Human-readable name for a group of fonts that are stylistic variants of a single design. All fonts that are members of such a group should have exactly the same `FamilyName`. Example of a family name is Times.

Weight

Human-readable name for the weight, or boldness attribute of a font. Examples are Roman, Bold, Light.

ItalicAngle

Angle in degrees counterclockwise from the vertical of the dominant vertical strokes of the font.

IsFixedPitch

If the value is `true`, it indicates that the font is a fixed-pitch (monospaced) font.

FontBBox

A string of four numbers giving the lower-left **x**, lower-left **y**, upper-right **x**, and upper-right **y** coordinates of the font bounding box. The font bounding box is the smallest rectangle enclosing the shape that would result if all the characters of the font were placed with their origins coincident and then painted.

UnderlinePosition

Recommended distance from the baseline for positioning underline stokes. This number is the **y** coordinate of the center of the stroke.

UnderlineThickness

Recommended stroke width for underlining.

Version

Version number of the font.

Notice

Trademark or copyright notice, if applicable.

Comment

Comments found in the AFM file.

EncodingScheme

The name of the standard encoding scheme for the font. Most Adobe fonts use AdobeStandardEncoding. Special fonts might state FontSpecific.

CapHeight

Usually, the **y** value of the top of the capital H.

XHeight

Typically, the **y** value of the top of the lowercase x.

Ascender
> Typically, the y value of the top of the lowercase d.

Descender
> Typically, the y value of the bottom of the lowercase p.

Wx
> Returns a hash table that maps from glyph names to the widths of the glyphs.

BBox
> Returns a hash table that maps from glyph names to bounding-box information. The bounding box consist of four numbers: llx, lly, urx, ury.

dump
> Dumps the contents of the Font::AFM object to STDOUT. Might sometimes be useful for debugging.

The AFM specification can be found at: *ftp://ftp.adobe.com/pub/adobe/DeveloperSupport/TechNotes/PSfiles/5004.AFM_Spec.ps*

Environment

METRICS
> Contains the path to search for AFM files. Format is the same as for the PATH environment variable. The default path built into this library is:

```
/usr/lib/afm:/usr/local/lib/afm:/usr/openwin/lib/fonts/afm/:
```

Bugs

Kerning data and composite character data is not yet parsed. Ligature data is not parsed.

Copyright

Copyright © 1995 Gisle Aas. All rights reserved.

This program is free software; you can redistribute it and/or modify it under the same terms as Perl itself.

Font::TFM — read and work with TeX font metric files

Synopsis

```
use Font::TFM;
my $cmr = new Font::TFM "cmr10";
(defined $cmr) or die "Error reading font\n";
print "Designsize: ", $cmr->designsize(), "\n";
print $cmr->width("A"), ", ", $cmr->kern('Wo'), "\n";
```

should print on the output:

```
Designsize: 10
491513.749980927, -54612.9166603088
```

Description

Method Font::TFM::new creates a new TFM object in memory, loading all the necessary information from the *.tfm* file. Second (optional) parameter means scale. You can also use Font::TFM::new_at and as the second parameter put requested size in pt.

The list of comma-separated directories to be searched is in the variable $Font::TFM::TEXFONTSDIR. These directories are searched for a given *.tfm* file (the extension *.tfm* is optional in the call to Font::TFM::new). The variable $Font::TFM::TEXFONTSUSELS can be set to zero to disable using ls-R files. If it is kept equal to 1, once it finds a file with name $Font::TFM::LSFILENAME, it doesn't search through the subdirectories and uses only the information in this file to find the *.tfm* file.

Methods

designsize, fontsize
> Returns the design size and the actual size of the font in pt.

width, height, depth, italic
> Returns the requested dimension for a specified character of the font.

kern, lig, ligpassover
> For a two-letter string, returns the kern between them, the ligature formed, and the number of characters to pass over after the ligature.

expand
> One-string parameter undergoes ligature expansion and then kernings are inserted. Returns array of string, kern, string, ...

word_dimensions
> Returns the width, height, and depth of a word. Does the ligature/kern expansion, so the result is the real space it will take on output.

word_width, word_height, word_depth
> Calls word_dimensions and returns the appropriate element. No caching is done, so it is better to call word_dimensions yourself if you are going to need more than one dimension of one word.

param
> Returns the parameter of the font, indexed from 1.

slant, x_height, em_width, quad
space, space_stretch, space_shrink, extra_space
> Returns the parameter of the font.

name
> Returns the name of the font.

Dimensions are multiplied by ($Font::TFM::MULTIPLY * actual size of the font). The value of $Font::TFM::MULTIPLY defaults to 65536, so the dimensions can be used directly when writing the *.dvi* file.

The variable $Font::TFM::DEBUG may be set to 1 to get the processing messages on the standard error output.

Version

0.04

See Also

TeX::DVI(3), perl(1).

Author

Jan Pazdziora, *adelton@fi.muni.cz*

Copyright

SGMLS—class for post-processing the output from the sgmls and nsgmls parsers

Synopsis

```
use SGMLS;
my $parse = new SGMLS(STDIN);
my $event = $parse->next_event;
while ($event) {
  SWITCH: {
    ($event->type eq 'start_element') && do {
      my $element = $event->data;     # An object of class SGMLS_Element
      [[your code for the beginning of an element]]
      last SWITCH;
    };
    ($event->type eq 'end_element') && do {
      my $element = $event->data;     # An object of class SGMLS_Element
      [[your code for the end of an element]]
      last SWITCH;
    };
    ($event->type eq 'cdata') && do {
      my $cdata = $event->data;       # A string
      [[your code for character data]]
      last SWITCH;
    };
    ($event->type eq 'sdata') && do {
      my $sdata = $event->data;       # A string
      [[your code for system data]]
      last SWITCH;
    };
    ($event->type eq 're') && do {
      [[your code for a record end]]
      last SWITCH;
    };
    ($event->type eq 'pi') && do {
      my $pi = $event->data;          # A string
      [[your code for a processing instruction]]
      last SWITCH;
    };
    ($event->type eq 'entity') && do {
      my $entity = $event->data;      # An object of class SGMLS_Entity
      [[your code for an external entity]]
      last SWITCH;
    };
```

```
    ($event->type eq 'start_subdoc') && do {
      my $entity = $event->data;        # An object of class SGMLS_Entity
      [[your code for the beginning of a subdoc entity]]
      last SWITCH;
    };
    ($event->type eq 'end_subdoc') && do {
      my $entity = $event->data;        # An object of class SGMLS_Entity
      [[your code for the end of a subdoc entity]]
      last SWITCH;
    };
    ($event->type eq 'conforming') && do {
      [[your code for a conforming document]]
      last SWITCH;
    };
    die "Internal error: unknown event type " . $event->type . "\n";
  }
  $event = $parse->next_event;
}
```

Description

The SGMLS package consists of several related classes: see SGMLS, SGMLS_Event, SGMLS_
Element, SGMLS_Attribute, SGMLS_Notation, and SGMLS_Entity. All of these classes are
available when you specify:

```
use SGMLS;
```

Generally, the only object that you create explicitly belongs to the SGMLS class; all of the
others are then created automatically for you over the course of the parse. Much fuller
documentation is available in the *.sgml* files in the DOC/ directory of the SGMLS.pm
distribution.

The SGMLS Class

This class holds a single parse. When you create an instance of it, you specify a file
handle as an argument (if you are reading the output of **sgmls** or **nsgmls** from a
pipe, the file handle is ordinarily STDIN):

```
my $parse = new SGMLS(STDIN);
```

The most important method for this class is **next_event**, which reads and returns the
next major event from the input stream. It is important to note that the SGMLS class
deals with most ESIS events itself: attributes and entity definitions, for example, are
collected and stored automatically and invisibly to the user. The following list contains
all of the methods for the SGMLS class:

Methods

next_event()

    Returns an SGMLS_Event object containing the next major event from the SGML
    parse.

element()

    Returns an SGMLS_Element object containing the current element in the
    document.

file()

    Returns a string containing the name of the current SGML source file (this works
    only if the -1 option was given to **sgmls** or **nsgmls**).

`line()`

> Returns a string containing the current line number from the source file (this works only if the `-l` option was given to **sgmls** or **nsgmls**).

`appinfo()`

> Returns a string containing the APPINFO parameter (if any) from the SGML declaration.

`notation(`*NNAME*`)`

> Returns an SGMLS_Notation object representing the notation named *NNAME*. With newer versions of **nsgmls**, all notations are available; otherwise, only the notations that are actually used are available.

`entity(`*ENAME*`)`

> Returns an SGMLS_Entity object representing the entity named *ENAME*. With newer versions of nsgmls, all entities are available; otherwise, only external data entities and internal entities used as attribute values are available.

`ext()`

> Returns a reference to an associative array for user-defined extensions.

The SGMLS_Event Class

This class holds a single major event, as generated by the **next_event** method in the SGMLS class. It uses the following methods:

`type()`

> Returns a string describing the type of event: **start_element**, **end_element**, **cdata**, **sdata**, **re**, **pi**, **entity**, **start_subdoc**, **end_subdoc**, and **conforming**. See the "Synopsis" for the values associated with each of these.

`data()`

> Returns the data associated with the current event (if any). For **start_element** and **end_element**, returns an SGMLS_ELement object; for **entity**, **start_ subdoc**, and **end_subdoc**, returns an SGMLS_Entity object; for **cdata**, **sdata**, and **pi**, returns a string; and for **re** and **conforming**, returns the empty string. See the "Synopsis," above, for an example of this method's use.

`key()`

> Returns a string key to the event, such as an element or entity name (otherwise, the same as `data()`).

`file()`

> Returns the current file name, as in the SGMLS class.

`line()`

> Returns the current line number, as in the SGMLS class.

`element()`

> Returns the current element, as in the SGMLS class.

`parse()`

> Returns the SGMLS object that generated the event.

`entity(`*ENAME*`)`

> Looks up an entity, as in the SGMLS class.

`notation(`*NNAME*`)`

> Looks up a notation, as in the SGMLS class.

`ext()`
> Returns a reference to an associative array for user-defined extensions.

The SGMLS_Element Class

This class is used for elements and contains all associated information (such as the element's attributes). It recognizes the following methods:

`name()`
> Returns a string containing the name, or Generic Identifier, of the element, in uppercase.

`parent()`
> Returns the SGMLS_Element object for the element's parent (if any).

`parse()`
> Returns the SGMLS object for the current parse.

`attributes()`
> Returns a reference to an associative array of attribute names and SGMLS_ Attribute structures. Attribute names are all in uppercase.

`attribute_names()`
> Returns an array of strings containing the names of all attributes defined for the current element, in uppercase.

`attribute(ANAME)`
> Returns the `SGMLS_Attribute` structure for the attribute *ANAME*.

`set_attribute(ATTRIB)`
> Adds the `SGMLS_Attribute` object *ATTRIB* to the current element, replacing any other attribute structure with the same name.

`in(GI)`
> Returns true (1) if the string *GI* is the name of the current element's parent, or false (0) if it is not.

`within(GI)`
> Returns true (1) if the string *GI* is the name of any of the ancestors of the current element, or false (0) if it is not.

`ext()`
> Returns a reference to an associative array for user-defined extensions.

The SGMLS_Attribute Class

Each instance of an attribute for each SGMLS_Element is an object belonging to this class, which recognizes the following methods:

`name()`
> Returns a string containing the name of the current attribute, all in uppercase.

`type()`
> Returns a string containing the type of the current attribute, all in uppercase. Available types are IMPLIED, CDATA, NOTATION, ENTITY, and TOKEN.

`value()`
> Returns the value of the current attribute, if any. This is an empty string if the type is IMPLIED, a string of some sort if the type is CDATA or TOKEN (if it is TOKEN, you may want to split the string into a series of separate tokens), an `SGMLS_Notation` object if the type is NOTATION, or an `SGMLS_Entity` object if the type is

ENTITY. Note that if the value is CDATA, it does not have escape sequences for 8-bit characters, record ends, or SDATA processed—that is your responsibility.

`is_implied()`

Returns true (1) if the value of the attribute is implied, or false (0) if it is specified in the document.

`set_type(TYPE)`

Changes the type of the attribute to the string *TYPE* (which should be all in upper-case). Available types are IMPLIED, CDATA, NOTATION, ENTITY, and TOKEN.

`set_value(VALUE)`

Changes the value of the attribute to *VALUE*, which may be a string, an `SGMLS_Entity` object, or an `SGMLS_Notation` subject, depending on the attribute's type.

`ext()`

Returns a reference to an associative array available for user-defined extensions.

The SGMLS_Notation Class

All declared notations appear as objects belonging to this class, which recognizes the following methods:

`name()`

Returns a string containing the name of the notation.

`sysid()`

Returns a string containing the system identifier of the notation, if any.

`pubid()`

Returns a string containing the public identifier of the notation, if any.

`ext()`

Returns a reference to an associative array available for user-defined extensions.

The SGMLS_Entity Class

All declared entities appear as objects belonging to this class, which recognizes the following methods:

`name()`

Returns a string containing the name of the entity, in mixed case.

`type()`

Returns a string containing the type of the entity, in uppercase. Available types are CDATA, SDATA, NDATA (external entities only), SUBDOC, PI (newer versions of `nsgmls` only), or TEXT (newer versions of `nsgmls` only).

`value()`

Returns a string containing the value of the entity, if it is internal.

`sysid()`

Returns a string containing the system identifier of the entity (if any), if it is external.

`pubid()`

Returns a string containing the public identifier of the entity (if any), if it is external.

`filenames()`

Returns an array of strings containing any filenames generated from the identifiers, if the entity is external.

`notation()`

    Returns the `SGMLS_Notation` object associated with the entity, if it is external.

`data_attributes()`

    Returns a reference to an associative array of data attribute names (in uppercase) and the associated `SGMLS_Attribute` objects for the current entity.

`data_attribute_names()`

    Returns an array of data attribute names (in uppercase) for the current entity.

`data_attribute(`*ANAME*`)`

    Returns the `SGMLS_Attribute` object for the data attribute named *ANAME* for the current entity.

`set_data_attribute(`*ATTRIB*`)`

    Adds the `SGMLS_Attribute` object *ATTRIB* to the current entity, replacing any other data attribute with the same name.

`ext()`

    Returns a reference to an associative array for user-defined extensions.

Copyright

Copyright © 1994 and 1995 by David Megginson, *dmeggins@aix1.uottawa.ca*. Distributed under the terms of the Gnu General Public License (version 2, 1991)—see the file *COPYING*, which is included in the *SGMLS.pm* distribution.

See Also

SGMLS::Output, SGMLS::Refs

SGMLS::Output — stack-based output procedures

Synopsis

```
use SGMLS::Output;
```

To print a string to the current output destination:

```
output($data);
```

To push a new output level to the filehandle DATA:

```
push_output('handle',DATA);
```

To push a new output level to the file *foo.data* (which is opened and closed automatically):

```
push_output('file','foo.data');
```

To push a new output level to a pipe to the shell command **sort**:

```
push_output('pipe','sort');
```

To push a new output level appending to the file *foo.data*:

```
push_output('append','foo.data');
```

To push a new output level to an empty string:

```
push_output('string');
```

To push a new output level appending to the string "**David is** ":

```
push_output('string',"David is ");
```

To push a new output level to The Great Beyond:

```
push_output('nul');
```

To revert to the previous output level:

```
pop_output();
```

To revert to the previous output level, returning the contents of an output string:

```
$data = pop_output();
```

Description

This library allows redirectable, stack-based output to files, pipes, handles, strings, or `nul`. It is especially useful for packages like SGMLS, since handlers for individual SGML elements can temporarily change and restore the default output destination. It is also particularly useful for capturing the contents of an element (and its subelements) in a string:

```
sgmls('<title>', sub{ push_output('string'); });
sgmls('</title>', sub{ $title = pop_output(); });
```

In between, anything sent to output (such as CDATA) is accumulated in the string returned from `pop_output()`:

```
sgmls('<tei.header>', sub { push_output('nul'); });
sgmls('</tei.header>', sub { pop_output(); });
```

All output is ignored until the header has finished.

Copyright

Copyright © 1994 and 1995 by David Megginson, *dmeggins@aix1.uottawa.ca*. Distributed under the terms of the Gnu General Public License (version 2, 1991)—see the file *COPYING*, which is included in the *SGMLS.pm* distribution.

See Also

SGMLS::Refs

SGMLS::Refs——maintain a database of forward references from one processing pass to another

Synopsis

```
use SGMLS::Refs;
```

To create a new reference-manager object using the file *foo.refs*:

```
my $refs = new SGMLS::Refs("foo.refs");
```

To create a new reference-manager object using the file *foo.refs* and logging changes to the file *foo.log*:

```
my $refs = new SGMLS::Refs("foo.refs","foo.log");
```

To record a reference:

```
$refs->put("document title",$title);
```

To retrieve a reference:

```
$title = $refs->get("document title");
```

To return the number of references changed since the last run:

```
$num = $refs->changed;
```

To print a LaTeX-like warning if any references have changed:

```
$refs->warn;
```

Description

This library can be used together with the SGMLS package to keep track of forward references from one run to another, like the LaTeX *.aux* files. Each reference manager is an object that reads and then rewrites a file of Perl source, with the filename provided by the caller.

Example

```
# Start up the reference manager before the parse.
sgml('start', sub { $refs = new SGMLS::Refs("foo.refs"); });
# Warn about any changed references at the end.
sgml('end', sub { $refs->warn; });
# Look up the title from the last parse, if available.
sgml('<div>', sub {
  my $element = shift;
  my $id = $element->attribute(ID)->value;
  my $title = $refs->get("title:$id") || "[no title available]";
  $current_div_id = $id;
  output "\\section{$title}\n\n";
});
# Save the title for the next parse.
sgml('<head>', sub { push_output('string'); });
sgml('</head>', sub {
  my $title = pop_output();
  my $id = $current_div_id;
  $refs->put("title:$id",$title);
});
```

Copyright

Copyright © 1994 and 1995 by David Megginson, *dmeggins@aix1.uottawa.ca*. Distributed under the terms of the Gnu General Public License (version 2, 1991)—see the file *COPYING*, which is included in the *SGMLS.pm* distribution.

See Also

SGMLS, SGMLS::Output

---

sscanf—emulate the sscanf() of the C stdio library

Synopsis

```
use String::Scanf;      # this will import sscanf() into the
                        # current namespace
@values = sscanf($scanf_format_string, $scalar_to_scan);
# the default scan target is the $_
@values = sscanf($scanf_format_string);
# converting scanf formats to regexps (::format_to_re
```

```
# is never exported to the current namespace)
$regexp_string = String::Scanf::format_to_re($scanf_format_string);
```

Description

Perl sscanf() can be used very much like the C stdio sscanf(); for detailed sscanf() documentation, please refer to your usual documentation resources. The supported formats are: [diuoxefgsc] and the character class [].

All of the format must match. Otherwise, an empty list is returned, and all the values end up empty.

The c format returns an anonymous list (see perlref) containing the numeric values of the characters it matched.

The format_to_re() function may be helpful if one wants to develop his or her own parsing routines.

Features

Embedded underscores are accepted in numbers just as in Perl, even in octal/hexadecimal numbers (Perl does not currently support this). Please note the word *embedded*, not leading or trailing.

If the oh formats are used, the octal/hexadecimal interpretation is forced even without the leading 0 or 0x.

Limitations

Certain features of the C sscanf() are unsupported:

- The formats [npSC]
- In the [efg] formats, the INF and various NaNs

The numeric formats are scanned in as strings; this means that numeric overflows may occur. For example, 1.2345e67890 match the %g format, but in most machines Perl cannot handle such large floating-point numbers and bizarre values may end up in the Perl variable. Similar caveats apply for integer-type numbers. Results of such huge numbers (or very tiny numbers, say, 1.24345e-67890) are implementation-defined, which translates quite often as *garbage*. Note: If you really want big numbers please consider using the Math::BigInt and Math::BigFloat packages, which come standard with Perl 5, or the Math::Pari package, available from CPAN.

For Perl, integers and floating-point numbers are the same thing. Also, the possible hl modifiers for the *integers* mean nothing: they are accepted, but they still do nothing, because Perl does not care about short/long integer differences.

The character-class format is not so rigorously checked for correctness that an illegal character-class definition cannot be sneaked in. For example, [z-a,X] is completely illegal as a character class, but String::Scanf happily accepts it. Beware.

The format_to_re() only does the scanf format to regular expression conversion. It ignores tricky things like the c format (see above) and the %n$ argument reordering. If you want these, you may as well use the full sscanf().

Examples

```
# business as usual
($i, $s, $x) = sscanf('%d %3s %g', ' -5_678     abc 3.14e-99 9');
# 'skip leading whitespace': $x becomes 42 despite the leading
# space
```

```
# 'the illegal character': $y becomes 'ab' despite the '3'
# 'c' format: $z becomes [120 100], the numeric values of 'x'
# and 'd' (assuming ASCII or ISO Latin 1)
($x, $y, $z) = sscanf('%i%3[a-e]%2c', ' 42acxde');
# reordering the arguments: $a becomes 34, $b becomes 12
($a, $b) = sscanf('%2$d %1$d', '12 34');
# converting scanf formats to regexps
$re = String::Scanf::format_to_re('%x');
```

There are more examples in the test set *t/scanf.t*.

Internals

The Perl `sscanf()` turns the C-stdio style `sscanf()` format string into a Perl regexp (see `perlre`), which captures the wanted values into submatches and returns the submatches as a list.

Originally written for debugging, but also useful for educational purposes:

```
String::Scanf::debug(1);       # turn on debugging: shows the regexps
                               # used and the possible reordering list
                               # and the character (%c) conversion
                               # targets
String::Scanf::debug(0);                 # turn off debugging
print String::Scanf::debug(), "\n";      # the current debug status
```

Author

Jarkko Hietaniemi, *Jarkko.Hietaniemi@iki.fi*

String::Approx—match and substitute approximately (a.k.a. fuzzy matching)

Synopsis

```
use String::Approx qw(amatch asubstitute);
```

Description

Approximate is defined here as *k-differences*. One difference is an insertion, a deletion, or a substitution of one character. The *k* in the k-differences is the maximum number of differences.

For example *1-difference* means that a match is found if there is one character too many (insertion), or one character missing (deletion), or one character changed (substitution). Those are exclusive ors: that is, not one of each type of modification but *exactly one.*

The Default Approximateness

The default approximateness is 10% of the length of the approximate pattern or at least 1, where 0-differences is the exact matching, which can be done very effectively using the usual Perl function **index()** or normal regular-expression matching.

amatch

```
use String::Approx qw(amatch);
amatch("PATTERN");
amatch("PATTERN", @LIST);
amatch("PATTERN", [ @MODS ]);
amatch("PATTERN", [ @MODS ], @LIST);
```

The *PATTERN* is a string, not a regular expression. The regular expression metanotation (. ? * + {...,...} ( ) | [ ] ^ $ \w ...) is understood as literal characters, that is, a * means (in regex terms) *, not "match 0 or more times".

The *LIST* is the list of strings to match against the pattern. If no LIST is given, matches against $_.

The *MODS* are the modifiers that tell how approximately to match. See below for more detailed explanation. Note: The syntax really is [*@MODS*], the square brackets [ ] must be in there. See below for examples.

In scalar context, amatch() returns the number of successful matches. In list context, amatch() returns the strings that had matches.

Example:

```
use String::Approx qw(amatch);
open(WORDS, '/usr/dict/words') or die;
while (<WORDS>) {
    print if amatch('perl');
}
```

or the same, ignoring case:

```
use String::Approx qw(amatch);
open(WORDS, '/usr/dict/words') or die;
while (<WORDS>) {
    print if amatch('perl', ['i']);
}
```

asubstitute

```
use String::Approx qw(asubstitute);
asubstitute("PATTERN", "SUBSTITUTION");
asubstitute("PATTERN", "SUBSTITUTION", @LIST);
asubstitute("PATTERN", "SUBSTITUTION", [ @MODS ]);
asubstitute("PATTERN", "SUBSTITUTION", [ @MODS ], @LIST);
```

The *PATTERN* is a string, not a regular expression. The regular expression metanotation (. ? * + {...,...} ( ) | [ ] ^ $ \w ...) is understood as literal characters; that is, a * means (in regex terms) *, not "match 0 or more times".

Also the *SUBSTITUTION* is a string, not a regular expression. Well, mostly. Most of the regular expression metanotation (., ?, *, +, ...) is not understood as literal characters; that is, a * means (in regex terms) *, not "match 0 or more times". The understood notations are

$`

The part before the approximate match

$&

The approximately matched part

$'

The part after the approximate match

The *MODS* are the modifiers that tell how approximately to match. See below for a more detailed explanation. Note: Yes, the syntax is really [@MODS]; the square brackets [ ] must be in there. See below for examples.

The *LIST* is the list of strings to substitute against the pattern. If no LIST is given, substitutes against $_.

In scalar context `asubstitute()` returns the number of successful substitutions. In list context `asubstitute()` returns the strings that had substitutions.

Examples:

```
use String::Approx qw(asubstitute);
open(WORDS, '/usr/dict/words') or die;
while (<WORDS>) {
    print if asubstitute('perl', '($&)');
}
```

or the same ignoring case:

```
use String::Approx qw(asubstitute);
open(WORDS, '/usr/dict/words') or die;
while (<WORDS>) {
    print if asubstitute('perl', '($&)', [ 'i' ]);
}
```

Modifiers

The *MODS* argument both in `amatch()` and `asubstitute()` is a list of strings that control the matching of *PATTERN*. The first two, i and g, are the usual regular expression match/substitute modifiers; the rest are special for approximate matching/substitution.

i

Match/substitute ignoring case, case-insensitively.

g

Substitute globally; that is, find all the approximate matches, not just the first one.

k

The maximum number of differences. For example, 2.

Ik

The maximum number of insertions. For example, I2.

Dk

The maximum number of deletions. For example, D2.

Sk

The maximum number of substitutions. For example, S2.

k%

The maximum relative number of differences. For example, 10%.

Ik%

The maximum relative number of insertions. For example, I5%.

Dk%

The maximum relative number of deletions. For example, D5%.

Sk%

The maximum relative number of substitutions. For example, S5%.

The regular expression modifiers o, m, s, and x are not supported, because their definitions for approximate matching are less than clear.

The relative number of differences is relative to the length of the PATTERN, rounded up; if, for example, the PATTERN is 'bouillabaise' and the MODS is ['20%'] then k becomes 3.

If you want to disable a particular kind of difference, you need to explicitly set it to zero. For example, 'D0' allows no deletions.

In case of conflicting definitions, the later ones silently override, for example:

```
[2, 'I3', 'I1']
```

equals:

```
['I1', 'D2', 'S2']
```

Examples

These examples assume the following template:

```
use String::Approx qw(amatch asubstitute);
open(WORDS, "/usr/dict/words") or die;
while (<WORDS>) {
        # <---
}
```

where the examples replace the # <--- line.

Matching from the $_

Match "perl" with one difference
```
print if amatch('perl');
```

The *one difference* is automatically the result in this case, because first the rule of the *10%* of the length of the pattern ("perl") is used and then the *at least 1* rule.

Match "perl" with case ignored
```
print if amatch('perl', [ 'i' ]);
```

The case is ignored in matching (i).

Match "perl" with one insertion
```
print if amatch('perl', [ '0', 'I1' ]);
```

The *one insertion* is most easily achieved by first disabling any approximateness (0) and then enabling one insertion (I1).

Match "perl" with zero deletions
```
print if amatch('perl', [ 'D0' ]);
```

The *zero deletion* is easily achieved by simply disabling any deletions (D0); the other types of differences, the insertions, and the substitutions, are still enabled.

Substitute "perl" approximately with HTML emboldening
```
print if amatch('perl', '<B>$&</B>', [ 'g' ]);
```

All (g) of the approximately matching parts of the input are surrounded by the HTML emboldening markup.

Matching from a list

The above examples match against the default variable $_. The rest of the examples show how the match from a list works. The template is now:

```
use String::Approx qw(amatch asubstitute);
open(WORDS, "/usr/dict/words") or die;
@words = <words>;
# <---
```

and the examples still go where the # <--- line is.

Match "perl" with one difference from a list

```
@matched = amatch('perl', @words);
```

The @matched contains the elements of the @words that matched approximately.

Substitute "perl" approximately with HTML emphasizing from a list

```
@substituted = asubstitute('perl', '<EM$&</EM', [ 'g' ],
@words);
```

The @substituted contains, *with all (g) the substitutions*, the elements of the @words that matched approximately.

Error Messages

```
amatch: $_ is undefined: what are you matching against?
asubstitute: $_ is undefined: what are you matching against?
```

These happen when you have nothing in $_ and try to amatch() or asubstitute(). Perhaps you are using the Perl option -e, but did you forget the Perl option -n?

```
amatch: too long pattern.
```

This happens when the pattern is too long for matching.

When matching long patterns, String::Approx attempts to partition the match. In other words, it tries to do the matching incrementally in smaller pieces.

If this fails, the above message is shown. Please try using shorter match patterns.

See the section below on "Limitations/Pattern length" for a more detailed explanation of why this happens.

```
asubstitute: too long pattern.
```

This happens when the pattern is too long for substituting.

The partitioning scheme explained above that is used for matching long patterns cannot, sadly enough, be used for substituting.

Please try using shorter substitution patterns.

See the section below on "Limitations/Pattern length" for a more detailed explanation of why this happens.

Limitations

Fixed pattern

The PATTERNs of amatch() and asubstitute() are fixed strings, they are not regular expressions. The SUBSTITUTION of asubstitute() is a bit more flexible than that, but not by much.

Pattern length

The approximate matching algorithm is very aggressive. In mathematical terms, it is $O(exp(n) * x**2)$. This means that when the pattern length and/or the approximateness grows, the matching or substitution take a much longer time and more memory.

For amatch() this can be avoided by *partitioning* the pattern, matching it in shorter subpatterns. This makes matching a bit slower and a bit fuzzier, more approximate. For asubstitute(), this partitioning cannot be done; the absolute maximum for the substitution pattern length is 19, but sometimes (for example, it the approximateness is increased), even shorter patterns are too much. When this happens, you must use patterns that are still shorter.

Speed

Despite the about 20-fold speed increase over String::Approx version 1, **agrep** is still faster. If you do not know what **agrep** is, it is a program like UNIX grep, but it knows, among other things, how to do approximate matching. **agrep** is still about 30 times faster than Perl and String::Approx. Note: All these speeds were measured on one particular system using one particular set of tests; your mileage will vary.

Incompatibilities with String::Approx v1.*

If you have been using regular expression modifiers (i, g), you lose. Sorry about that. The syntax simply is not compatible. I had to choose between having **amatch()** match and **asubstitute()** substitute elsewhere than just in $_ and the old messy way of having an unlimited number of modifiers. The first need won.

There is a backward-compatibility mode, though, if you do not want to change your **amatch()** and **asubstitute()** calls. You *have* to change your **use** line, however:

```
use String::Approx qw(amatch compat1);
```

That is, you must add the **compat1** symbol if you want to be compatible with the String::Approx version 1 call syntax.

Version

Version 2.1.

Author

Jarkko Hietaniemi, *jhi@iki.fi*

Acknowledgments

Nathan Torkington, *gnat@frii.com*

String::BitCount—count number of 1 bits in string

Synopsis

```
use String::BitCount;
```

Description

BitCount *LIST*

Joins the elements of *LIST* into a single string and returns the number of bits in this string.

showBitCount *LIST*

Copies the elements of *LIST* to a new list and converts the new elements to strings of digits showing the number of bits that were set in the original byte. In array context, returns the new list. In scalar context, joins the elements of the new list into a single string and returns the string.

Author

Winfried Koenig, *win@in.rhein-main.de*

See Also

perl(1)

String::Parity—Parity (odd/even/mark/space)-handling functions

Synopsis

```
use String::Parity;
use String::Parity qw(:DEFAULT /show/);
```

Description

setEvenParity *LIST*

Copies the elements of *LIST* to a new list and converts the new elements to strings of bytes with even parity. In array context, returns the new list. In scalar context, joins the elements of the new list into a single string and returns the string.

setOddParity *LIST*

Like setEvenParity function, but converts to strings with odd parity.

setSpaceParity *LIST*

Like setEvenParity function, but converts to strings with space (high-bit cleared) parity.

setMarkParity *LIST*

Like setEvenParity function, but converts to strings with mark (high-bit set) parity.

EvenBytes *LIST*

Returns the number of even parity bytes in the elements of *LIST*.

OddBytes *LIST*

Returns the number of odd parity bytes in the elements of *LIST*.

SpaceBytes *LIST*

Returns the number of space parity bytes in the elements of *LIST*.

MarkBytes *LIST*

Returns the number of mark parity bytes in the elements of *LIST*.

isEvenParity *LIST*

Returns true if the *LIST* contains no byte with odd parity, false otherwise.

isOddParity *LIST*

Returns true if the *LIST* contains no byte with even parity, false otherwise.

isSpaceParity *LIST*

Returns true if the *LIST* contains no byte with mark parity, false otherwise.

isMarkParity *LIST*

Returns true if the *LIST* contains no byte with space parity, false otherwise.

showParity *LIST*

Like setEvenParity function, but converts bytes with even parity to 'e' and other bytes to 'o'. The function showParity must be imported by a specialized import list.

showMarkSpace *LIST*

Like `setEvenParity` function, but converts bytes with space parity to 's' and other bytes to 'm'. The function **showMarkSpace** must be imported by a specialized import list.

Notes

Don't use this module unless you have to communicate with some old device or protocol. Please make your application 8-bit clean and use the internationally standardized ISO-8859-1 character set.

Author

Winfried Koenig, *win@in.rhein-main.de*

See Also

perl(1), Exporter(1)

String::ShellQuote—quote strings for passing through the shell

Synopsis

```
$string = shell_quote @list;
$string = shell_comment_quote $string;
```

Description

This module contains some functions that are useful for quoting strings that are going to pass through the shell or a shell-like object.

shell_quote [*string*]...

shell_quote quotes strings so they can be passed through the shell. Each string is quoted, so that the shell will pass it along as a single argument and without further interpretation. If no strings are given, an empty string is returned.

shell_comment_quote [*string*]

shell_comment_quote quotes the string so that it can safely be included in a shell-style comment (the current algorithm is that a sharp character is placed after any newlines in the string).

This routine might be changed to accept multiple string arguments in the future. I haven't done this yet, because I'm not sure if the strings should be joined with blanks (`$"`) or nothing (`$,`). Cast your vote today! Be sure to justify your answer.

Examples

```
$cmd = 'fuser 2>/dev/null ' . shell_quote @files;
@pids = split ' ', '$cmd';
print CFG "# Configured by: ",
          shell_comment_quote($ENV{LOGNAME}), "\n";
```

Author

Roderick Schertler, *roderick@argon.org*

See Also

perl(1)

Text::English — Porter's stemming algorithm

Synopsis

```
use Text::English;
@stems = Text::English::stem( @words );
```

Description

This routine applies the Porter Stemming Algorithm to its parameters, returning the stemmed words. It is derived from the C program *stemmer.c*, as found in freewais and elsewhere, which contains these notes:

```
Purpose:    Implementation of the Porter stemming algorithm documented
            in: Porter, M.F., "An Algorithm For Suffix Stripping,"
            Program 14 (3), July 1980, pp. 130-137.
Provenance: Written by B. Frakes and C. Cox, 1986.
```

I have re-interpreted areas that use Frakes and Cox's WordSize function. My version may misbehave on short words starting with "y", but I can't think of any examples.

The step numbers correspond to Frakes and Cox and are probably in Porter's article (which I've not seen). Porter's algorithm still has rough spots (e.g., current/currency, -ings words), which I have not attempted to cure, although I have added support for the British -ise suffix.

Notes

This is version 0.1. I welcome feedback, especially improvements to the punctuation-stripping step.

Author

Ian Phillipps, *ian@unipalm.pipex.com*

Copyright

Copyright Public IP Exchange Ltd (PIPEX). Available for use under the same terms as Perl.

Text::GenderFromName — Guess the gender of a "Christian" first name.

Synopsis

```
use Text::GenderFromName;

print gender("Jon");    # prints "m"
```

Text::GenderFromName is available at a CPAN site near you.

Description

This module provides a single function: gender(), which returns one of three values: m for male, f for female, or undef if it doesn't know. For instance, gender("Chris") is undef.

The original code assumed a default of male, and I am happy to contribute to the destruction of the oppressive patriarchy by returning an undef value if no rule triggers. Ha ha! Seriously, it'll be useful to know when gender() has no clue.

For the curious, I ran Text::GenderFromName on *The Perl Journal*'s subscriber list. The result?

```
Male:    68%
Female:  32%
```

Bugs

gender() can never be perfect.

I'm sure that many of these rules could return immediately upon firing. However, it's possible that the original author arranged them in a very deliberate order, with more specific rules at the end overruling earlier rules. Consequently, I can't turn all of these rules into the speedier form return "f" if /.../ without throwing away the meaning of the ordering. If you have the stamina to plod through the rules and determine when the ordering doesn't matter, let me know!

The rules should probably be made case-insensitive, but I bet there's some funky situation in which that'll lose.

Author

Jon Orwant, *The Perl Journal* and MIT Media Lab, *orwant@tpj.com*

This is an adaptation of an 8/91 awk script by Scott Pakin in the December 1991 issue of *Computer Language Monthly.*

Small contributions by Andrew Langmead and John Strickler.

Text::German—German grundform reduction

Synopsis

```
use Text::German;
$stem = Text::German::reduce($word)
```

Description

This is a rather incomplete implementation of work done by Gudrun Putze-Meier, *gudrun.pm@t-online.de.* I have to confess that I never read her original paper. So all credit belongs to her, all bugs are mine. I tried to get some insight from an implementation of two students of mine. They remain anonymous because their work was the worst piece of code I ever saw. My code behaves mostly as their implementation did except it is about 75 times faster.

Author

Ulrich Pfeifer, *pfeifer@ls6.informatik.uni-dortmund.de*

Text::Refer—parse UNIX refer files

Synopsis

Pull in the module:

```
use Text::Refer;
```

Parse a refer stream from a filehandle:

```
while ($ref = input Text::Refer \*FH)  {
    # ...do stuff with $ref...
}
defined($ref) or die "error parsing input";
```

Do the same, but using a parser object for more control:

```
# Create a new parser:
$parser = new Text::Refer::Parser LeadWhite=>'KEEP';
# Parse:
while ($ref = $parser->input(\*FH)) {
# ...do stuff with $ref...
}
defined($ref) or die "error parsing input";
```

Manipulate reference objects, using high-level methods:

```
# Get the title, author, etc.:
$title      = $ref->title;
@authors    = $ref->author;        # list context
$lastAuthor = $ref->author;        # scalar context

# Set the title and authors:
$ref->title("Cyberiad");
$ref->author(["S. Trurl", "C. Klapaucius"]);   # arrayref for >1 value!

# Delete the abstract:
$ref->abstract(undef);
```

Do the same, using low-level methods:

```
# Get the title, author, etc.:
$title      = $ref->get('T');
@authors    = $ref->get('A');      # list context
$lastAuthor = $ref->get('A');      # scalar context

# Set the title and authors:
$ref->set('T', "Cyberiad");
$ref->set('A', "S. Trurl", "C. Klapaucius");

# Delete the abstract:
$ref->set('X');                            # sets to empty array of values
```

Output:

```
print $ref->as_string;
```

Description

This module supersedes the old Text::Bib.

This module provides routines for parsing in the contents of refer-format bibliographic databases: these are simple text files that contain one or more bibliography records. They are usually found lurking on UNIX-like operating systems, with the extension *.bib*.

Each record in a refer file describes a single paper, book, or article. Users of nroff/troff often employ such databases when typesetting papers.

Even if you don't use *roff, this simple, easily parsed parameter-value format is still useful for recording or exchanging bibliographic information. With this module, you can easily post-process refer files: search them, convert them into LaTeX, whatever.

Example

Here's a possible refer file with three entries:

```
%T Cyberiad
%A Stanislaw Lem
%K robot fable
%I Harcourt/Brace/Jovanovich

%T Invisible Cities
%A Italo Calvino
%K city fable philosophy
%X In this surreal series of fables, Marco Polo tells an
   aged Kublai Khan of the many cities he has visited in
   his lifetime.

%T Angels and Visitations
%A Neil Gaiman
%D 1993
```

The lines separating the records must be *completely blank*; that is, they cannot contain anything but a single newline.

See `refer(1)` or `grefer(1)` for more information on refer files.

Syntax

From the GNU manpage, `grefer(1)`:

The bibliographic database is a text file consisting of records separated by one or more blank lines. Within each record fields start with a % at the beginning of a line. Each field has a one character name that immediately follows the %. It is best to use only upper- and lowercase letters for the names of fields. The name of the field should be followed by exactly one space, and then by the contents of the field. Empty fields are ignored. The conventional meaning of each field is as follows:

A

The name of an author. If the name contains a title such as Jr. at the end, it should be separated from the last name by a comma. There can be multiple occurrences of the A field. The order is significant. It is a good idea always to supply an A field or a Q field.

B

For an article that is part of a book, the title of the book.

C

The place (city) of publication.

D

The date of publication. The year should be specified in full. If the month is specified, the name rather than the number of the month should be used, but only the first three letters are required. It is a good idea always to supply a D field; if the date is unknown, a value such as "in press" or "unknown" can be used.

E

For an article that is part of a book, the name of an editor of the book. Where the work has editors and no authors, the names of the editors should be given as A fields and , (ed) or , (eds) should be appended to the last author.

G

U.S. Government ordering number.

I

The publisher (issuer).

J

For an article in a journal, the name of the journal.

K

Keywords to be used for searching.

L

Label

Note: Uniquely identifies the entry. For example, "Able94".

N

Journal issue number.

O

Other information. This is usually printed at the end of the reference.

P

Page number. A range of pages can be specified as m-n.

Q

The name of the author, if the author is not a person. This will only be used if there are no A fields. There can only be one Q field.

Note: Thanks to Mike Zimmerman for clarifying this for me: it means a "corporate" author: when the "author" is listed as an organization such as the U.N., or RAND Corporation, or whatever.

R

Technical report number.

S

Series name.

T

Title. For an article in a book or journal, this should be the title of the article

V

   Volume number of the journal or book.

X

   Annotation. Basically, a brief abstract or description.

For all fields except A and E, if there is more than one occurrence of a particular field in a record, only the last such field is used.

If accent strings are used, they should follow the character to be accented. This means that the AM macro must be used with the -ms macros. Accent strings should not be quoted; use one \ rather than two.

Parsing records from refer files

You will nearly always use the `input()` constructor to create new instances and nearly always as shown in the "Synopsis."

Internally, the records are parsed by a parser object; if you invoke the class method `Text::Refer::input()`, a special default parser is used; this is good enough for most tasks. However, for more complex tasks, feel free to use class Text::Refer::Parser to build (and use) your own fine-tuned parser, and `input()` from that instead.

CLASS Text::Refer

Each instance of this class represents a single record in a refer file.

Construction and input

new

   Class method, constructor. Builds an empty refer record.

input FILEHANDLE

   Class method. Inputs a new refer record from a filehandle. The default parser is used:

```
while ($ref = input Text::Refer \*STDIN) {
    # ...do stuff with $ref...
}
```

   Do *not* use this as an instance method; it does not re-initialize the object you give it.

Getting/setting attributes

attr ATTR, [VALUE]

   Instance method. Gets or sets the attribute by its one-character name, *ATTR*. The *VALUE* is optional and may be given in a number of ways:

   • If the *VALUE* is given as undefined, the attribute is deleted:

```
$ref->attr('X', undef);        # delete the abstract
```

   • If a defined, non-reference scalar *VALUE* is given, it is used to replace the existing values for the attribute with that *single* value:

```
$ref->attr('T', "The Police State Rears Its Ugly Head");
$ref->attr('D', 1997);
```

   • If an arrayref *VALUE* is given, it is used to replace the existing values for the attribute with all elements of that array:

```
$ref->attr('A', ["S. Trurl", "C. Klapaucius"]);
```

We use an arrayref, since an empty array would be impossible to distinguish from the next two cases, where the goal is to "get" instead of "set."

This method returns the current (or new) value of the given attribute, just as `get()` does:

- If invoked in a scalar context, the method returns the *last* value (this is to mimic the behavior of **groff**). Hence, given the above, the code:

      $author = $ref->attr('A');

  sets `$author` to "C. Klapaucius".

- If invoked in an array context, the method returns the list of *all* values, in order. Hence, given the above, the code:

      @authors = $ref->attr('A');

  sets `@authors` to ("S. Trurl", "C. Klapaucius").

Note: this method is used as the basis of all "named" access methods; hence, the following are equivalent in every way:

    $ref->attr(T => $title)   <=> $ref->title($title);
    $ref->attr(A => \@authors) <=> $ref->author(\@authors);
    $ref->attr(D => undef)   <=> $ref->date(undef);
    $auth = $ref->attr('A')   <=> $auth = $ref->author;
    @auths = $ref->attr('A')   <=>   @auths = $ref->author;

author, book, city, ... [*VALUE*]

Instance methods. For every one of the standard fields in a refer record, this module has designated a high-level attribute name:

    A   author   G   govt_no   N   number   S   series
    B   book   I   publisher   O   other_info   T   title
    C   city   J   journal   P   page   V   volume
    D   date   K   keywords   Q   corp_author X   abstract
    E   editor   L   label   R   report_no

Then, for each field F with high-level attribute name *FIELDNAME*, the method **FIELDNAME()** works as follows:

    $ref->attr('F', @args)   <=> $ref->FIELDNAME(@args)

Which means:

    $ref->attr(T => $title)   <=> $ref->title($title);
    $ref->attr(A => \@authors) <=> $ref->author(\@authors);
    $ref->attr(D => undef)   <=> $ref->date(undef);
    $auth = $ref->attr('A')   <=> $auth = $ref->author;
    @auths = $ref->attr('A')   <=>   @auths = $ref->author;

See the documentation of `attr()` for the argument list.

get *ATTR*

Instance method. Gets an attribute by its one-character name. In an array context, it returns all values (empty if none):

    @authors = $ref->get('A');   # returns list of all
                                     # authors

In a scalar context, it returns the *last* value (undefined if none):

    $author = $ref->get('A');   # returns the last author

`set` *ATTR, VALUES...*

> *Instance method.* Sets an attribute by its one-character name.
>
> ```
> $ref->set('A', "S. Trurl", "C. Klapaucius");
> ```
>
> An empty array of *VALUES* deletes the attribute:
>
> ```
> $ref->set('A');       # deletes all authors
> ```
>
> No useful return value is currently defined.

Output

`as_string` [*OPTSHASH*]

> *Instance method.* Returns the refer record as a string, usually for printing:
>
> ```
> print $ref->as_string;
> ```
>
> The options are:
>
> `Quick`
>
> > If true, do it quickly, but unsafely. This does no fixup on the values at all: they are output as-is. That means if you use parser options that destroy any of the formatting whitespace (e.g., `Newline=TOSPACE` with `LeadWhite=KILLALL`), there is a risk that the output object will be an invalid refer record.
>
> The fields are output with `%L` first (if it exists) and then the remaining fields in alphabetical order. The following "safety measures" are normally taken:
>
> - Lines longer than 76 characters are wrapped (if possible, at a non-word character a reasonable length in, but there is a chance that they will simply be "split" if no such character is available).
>
> - Any occurrences of `%` immediately after a newline are preceded by a single space.
>
> These safety measures are slightly time-consuming and are silly if you are merely outputting a refer object that you have read in verbatim (i.e., using the default parser options) from a valid refer file. In these cases, you may want to use the `Quick` option.

CLASS *Text::Refer::Parser*

Instances of this class do the actual parsing.

Parser options

The options you may give to `new()` are as follows:

`ForgiveEOF`

> Normally, the last record in a file must end with a blank line, or else this module suspects it of being incomplete and returns an error. However, if you give this option as true, it allows the last record to be terminated by an EOF.

`GoodFields`

> By default, the parser accepts any (one-character) field name that is a printable ASCII character (no whitespace). Formally, this is:
>
> ```
> [\041-\176]
> ```
>
> However, when compiling parser options, you can supply your own regular expression for validating (one-character) field names. (Note that you must supply the square brackets; they are there to remind you that you should

give a well-formed single-character expression). One standard expression is provided for you:

```
$Text::Refer::GroffFields = '[A-EGI-LN-TVX]';
                                    # legal groff fields
```

Illegal fields that are encountered during parsing result in a syntax error.

Note: You really shouldn't use this unless you absolutely need to. The added regular expression test slows down the parser.

LeadWhite

In many refer files, continuation lines (the second, third, etc., lines of a field) are written with leading whitespace, like this:

```
%T Incontrovertible Proof that Pi Equals Three
    (for Large Values of Three)
%A S. Trurl
%X The author shows how anyone can use various common
household
    objects to obtain successively less-accurate estimations
of
    pi, until finally arriving at a desired integer
approximation,
    which nearly always is three.
```

This leading whitespace serves two purposes: (1) it makes it impossible to mistake a continuation line for a field, since % can no longer be the first character, and (2) it makes the entries easier to read. The **LeadWhite** option controls what is done with this whitespace:

KEEP

Default; the whitespace is untouched.

KILLONE

Exactly one character of leading whitespace is removed.

KILLALL

All leading whitespace is removed.

See the section below "Notes on the parser options" for hints and warnings.

Newline

The **Newline** option controls what is done with the newlines that separate adjacent lines in the same field:

KEEP

Default; the newlines are kept in the field value.

TOSPACE

Convert each newline to a single space.

KILL

The newlines are removed.

See the section below "Notes on the parser options" for hints and warnings.

Default values are used for any options that are left unspecified.

Notes on the parser options

The default values for **Newline** and **LeadWhite** preserve the input text exactly.

The **Newline=TOSPACE** option, when used in conjunction with the **LeadWhite=KILLALL** option, effectively "word-wraps" the text of each field into a single line.

Be careful! If you use the `Newline=KILL` option with either the Lead-
White=KILLONE or the `LeadWhite=KILLALL` option, you could end up
eliminating all whitespace that separates the word at the end of one line from
the word at the beginning of the next line.

Public interface

`new` *PARAMHASH*

> *Class method, constructor.* Create and return a new parser. See above for the
> *parser options* that you may give in the *PARAMHASH.*

`create` *[CLASS]*

> *Instance method.* The class of objects to create. The default is Text::Refer.

`input` *FH*

> *Instance method.* Creates a new object from the next record in a refer stream.
> The actual class of the object is given by the `class()` method.
>
> Returns the object on success, 0 on *expected* end-of-file, and undefined on
> error.
>
> Having two false values makes parsing very simple: just `input()` records
> until the result is false, then check to see if that last result was 0 (end of file)
> or `undef` (failure).

NOTES

Under the hood

Each refer object has instance variables corresponding to the actual field names
(`'T'`, `'A'`, etc.). Each of these is a reference to an array of the actual values.

Notice that for maximum flexibility and consistency (but at the cost of some space
and access-efficiency), the semantics of refer records do not come into play at this
time: since everything resides in an array, you can have as many *%K*, *%D*, etc.,
records as you like and give them entirely different semantics.

For example, the Library Of Boring Stuff That Everyone Reads (LOBSTER) uses
the unused *%Y* as a "year" field. The parser accommodates this case by politely
not choking on LOBSTER *.bibs* (although why you would want to eat a lobster
bib instead of the lobster is beyond me . . .).

Performance

Tolerable. On my 90MHz/32 MB RAM/I586 box running Linux 1.2.13 and
Perl5.002, it parses a typical 500 KB "refer" file (of 1600 records) as follows:

```
 8 seconds of user time for input and no output
10 seconds of user time for input and "quick" output
16 seconds of user time for input and "safe" output
```

So, figure the individual speeds are:

```
input:            200 records ( 60 KB) per second.
"quick" output:   800 records (240 KB) per second.
"safe" output:    200 records ( 60 KB) per second.
```

By contrast, a C program that does the same work is about eight times as fast. But
of course, the C code is eight times as large, and eight times as ugly. :-)

Note to serious bib-file users

I actually do not use refer files for *roffing. I use them as a quick-and-dirty database for WebLib, and that's where this code comes from. If you're a serious user of refer files, and this module doesn't do what you need it to, please contact me: I'll add the functionality in.

Bugs

Some combinations of parser-options are silly.

Author and Copyright

Copyright © 1997 by Eryq, *eryq@enteract.com*, *http://www.enteract.com/~eryq*.

This program is free software; you can redistribute it and/or modify it under the terms of the GNU General Public License as published by the Free Software Foundation; either version 2 of the License, or (at your option) any later version.

This program is distributed in the hope that it will be useful, but WITHOUT ANY WARRANTY; without even the implied warranty of MERCHANTABILITY or FITNESS FOR A PARTICULAR PURPOSE. See the GNU General Public License for more details.

For a copy of the GNU General Public License, write to the Free Software Foundation, Inc., 675 Mass Ave, Cambridge, MA 02139, USA.

Text::Striphigh—Perl extension to strip the high bit off of ISO-8859-1 text

Synopsis

```
use Text::Striphigh 'striphigh'
$SevenBitsText = striphigh($TextContainingEightBitCharacters);
```

Description

The Text::Striphigh module exports a single function: **striphigh**. This function takes one argument, a string possibly containing high ASCII characters in the ISO-8859-1 character set, and transforms this into a string containing only 7-bit ASCII characters, by substituting every high-bit character with a similar-looking standard ASCII character, or with a sequence of standard ASCII characters.

You can find examples in the source or the test script.

Maintenance

If you ever want to change the **striphigh** function yourself, then don't change the one containing the mile-long **tr{}{}** statement that you see at first; change the one behind the __DATA__ that is a lot more readable.

After you've done that, simply run the *Striphigh.pm* file through Perl to generate a new version of the first routine and in fact of the entire file, something like this:

```
perl -w Striphigh.pm > Striphigh.pm.new
mv Striphigh.pm.new Striphigh.pm
```

Bugs

Assumes the input text is ISO-8859-1, without even looking at the LOCALE settings.

Some translations are probably less than optimal.

People will be offended if you run their names through this function and print the result on an envelope using an outdated printing device. However, it's probably better than having that printer print a name with a high ASCII character in it which happens to be the command to set the printer on fire.

Author

Jan-Pieter Cornet, *johnpc@xs4all.nl*

Text::Tabs —expand and unexpand tabs per UNIX expand(1) and unexpand(1)

Synopsis

```
use Text::Tabs;
$tabstop = 4;
@lines_without_tabs = expand(@lines_with_tabs);
@lines_with_tabs = unexpand(@lines_without_tabs);
```

Description

Text::Tabs does about what the UNIX utilities **expand(1)** and **unexpand(1)** do. Given a line with tabs in it, **expand** replaces the tabs with the appropriate number of spaces. Given a line with or without tabs in it, **unexpand** adds tabs when it can save bytes by doing so. Invisible compression with plain ASCII!

Bugs

expand doesn't handle newlines very quickly—do not feed it an entire document in one string. Instead feed it an array of lines.

Author

David Muir Sharnoff, *muir@idiom.com*

Text::Template —expand template text with embedded Perl

Synopsis

```
use Text::Template;
$template = new Text::Template ('type' => FILE, 'source' => 'f.tmpl');
  # or
$template = new Text::Template ('type' => ARRAY,
                                'source' => [ ... ] );
  # or
$template = new Text::Template ('type' => FILEHANDLE,
                                'source' => $fh );
$recipient = 'King';
$text = $template->fill_in();
print $text;
$T::recipient = 'Josh';
$text = $template->fill_in('package' => T);
print $text;
$text = $template->fill_in('broken' => \&callback);
```

```
use Text::Template fill_this_in;
$text = fill_this_in( <<EOM, 'package' => T);
Dear {$recipient},
Pay me at once.
        Love,
          G.V.
EOM
print Text::Template->Version;
```

Description

This is a library for printing form letters! This is a library for playing Mad Libs!

A template is a piece of text that has little Perl programs embedded in it here and there. When you fill in a template, you evaluate the little programs and replace them with their values.

This is a good way to generate many kinds of output, such as error messages and HTML pages. Here is one way I use it: I am a freelance computer consultant; I write World Wide Web applications. Usually I work with an HTML designer who designs the pages for me.

Often these pages change a lot over the life of the project: The client's legal department takes several tries to get the disclaimer just right; the client changes the background GIF a few times; the text moves around, and so forth. These are all changes that are easy to make. Anyone proficient with the editor can go and make them. But if the page is embedded inside a Perl program, I don't want the designer to change it, because you never know what they might muck up. I'd like to put the page in an external file instead.

The trouble with that is that parts of the page really are generated by the program; it needs to fill in certain values in some places, and maybe conditionally include some text somewhere else. The page can't just be a simple static file that the program reads in and prints out.

A template has blanks, and when you print one out, the blanks are filled in automatically, so this is no trouble. And because the blanks are small and easy to recognize, it's easy to tell the page designer to stay away from them.

Here's a sample template:

```
Dear {$title} {$lastname},
It has come to our attention that you are delinquent in your
{$last_paid_month} payment.  Please remit ${$amount} immediately,
or your patellae may be needlessly endangered.
                Love,
                Mark "Vizopteryx" Dominus
```

Pretty simple, isn't it? Items in curly braces ({ }) get filled in; everything else stays the same. Anyone can understand that. You can totally believe that the art director isn't going to screw this up while editing it.

You can put any Perl code you want into the braces, so instead of {$amount}, you might want to use {sprintf("%.2f", $amount)}, to print the amount rounded off to the nearest cent.

This is good for generating form letters, HTML pages, error messages, and probably a lot of other things.

Detailed documentation follows.

Constructor

`new`

This creates a new template object. You specify the source of the template with a set of attribute-value pairs in the arguments.

```
new Text::Template ( attribute => value, ... );
```

At present, there are only two attributes. One is **type**; the other is **source**. **type** can be FILEHANDLE, FILE, or ARRAY. If type is FILE, then the **source** is interpreted as the name of a file that contains the template to fill out. If **type** is FILEHANDLE, then the **source** is interpreted as the name of a filehandle, which, when read, will deliver the template to fill out. A **type** of ARRAY means that the **source** is a reference to an array of strings; the template is the concatenation of these strings.

Neither **type** nor **source** is optional yet.

Here are some examples of how to call **new**:

```
$template = new Text::Template
        ('type' => 'ARRAY',
         'source' => [ "Dear {\$recipient}\n",
                       "Up your {\$nose}.\n",
                       "Love, {\$me}.\n" ]);
$template = new Text::Template
        ('type' => 'FILE',
         'source' => '/home/mjd/src/game/youlose.tmpl');
```

new returns a template object on success, and **undef** on failure. On an error, it puts an error message in the variable `$Text::Template::ERROR`.

Methods

`fill_in`

Fills in a template. Returns the resulting text.

Like **new**, `fill_in` accepts a set of attribute-value pairs. At present, the only attributes are **package** and **broken**.

Here's an example: Suppose that `$template` contains a template object that we created with this template:

```
Dear {$name},
        You owe me ${sprintf("%.2f", $amount)}.
        Pay or I will break your {$part}.
                        Love,
                        Uncle Dominus.
```

Here's how you might fill it in:

```
$name = 'Donald';
$amount = 141.61;
$part = 'hyoid bone';
$text = $template->fill_in();
```

Here's another example:

```
Your Royal Highness,
        Enclosed please find a list of things I have gotten
        for you since 1907:
        { $list = '';
          foreach $item (@things) {
```

```
            $list .= " o \u$item\n";
            }
            $list
      }
            Signed,
            Lord High Chamberlain
```

We want to pass in an array, which will be assigned to the array `@things`. Here's how to do that:

```
@the_things = ('ivory', 'apes', 'peacocks', );
$template->fill_in();
```

This is not very safe. The reason this isn't as safe is that if you have any variables named `$list` or `$item` in scope in your program at the point you called `fill_in`, their values will be clobbered by the act of filling out the template.

The next section shows how to make this safer.

Here are the attributes:

package

The value of the **package** attribute names a package that contains the variables that should be used to fill in the template. If you omit the **package** attribute, `fill_in` uses the package that was active when it was called.

Here's a safer version of the Lord High Chamberlain example from the previous section:

```
@VARS::the_things = ('ivory', 'apes', 'peacocks', );
$template->fill_in('package' => VARS);
```

This call to `fill_in` clobbers `$VARS::list` and `$VARS::item` instead of clobbering `$list` and `$item`. If your program doesn't use anything in the VARS package, you don't have to worry that filling out the template is altering one of your variables.

broken

If you specify a value for the **broken** attribute, it should be a reference to a function that `fill_in` can call if one of the little programs fails to evaluate.

`fill_in` passes an associative array to the **broken** function. The associative array should have at least these two members:

```
text => (The full text of the little program that failed)
error => (The text of the error message ($@) generated by eval)
```

If the **broken** function returns a text string, `fill_in` inserts it into the template in place of the broken program, just as though the broken program had evaluated successfully and yielded that same string. If the **broken** function returns **undef**, `fill_in` stops filling in the template, and immediately returns undef itself.

If you don't specify a **broken** function, you get a default one that inserts something like this:

```
Warning
This part of the template:
        1/0
Returned the following errors:
        Illegal division by zero at (eval 7) line 2.
```

fill_this_in

Maybe it's not worth your trouble to put the template into a file; maybe it's a small file, and you want to leave it inline in the code. Maybe you don't want to have to worry about managing template objects. In that case, use `fill_this_in`. You give it the entire template as a string argument, follow that with variable substitutions just as in `fill_in`, and it gives you back the filled-in text.

```
An example:
$Q::name = 'Donald';
$Q::amount = 141.61;
$Q::part = 'hyoid bone';
$text = fill_this_in Text::Template ( <<EOM, 'package' => Q);
Dear {\$name},
You owe me {sprintf('%.2f', \$amount)}.
Pay or I will break your {\$part}.
        Love,
        Grand Vizopteryx of Irkutsk.
EOM
```

Version

Returns the current version of the Text::Template package.

```
Version Text::Template ();
```

Template Format

Here's the deal with templates: anything in braces is a little program, which is evaluated and replaced with its Perl value. A backslashed character has no special meaning, so to include a literal { in your template, use \{, and to include a literal \, use \\.

A little program starts at an open brace and ends at the matching close brace. This means that your little programs can include braces, and you don't need to worry about it. See the example below for an example of braces inside a little program.

If an expression at the beginning of the template has side-effects, the side-effects carry over to subsequent expressions. For example:

```
{$x = @things; ''} The Lord High Chamberlain has gotten {$x}
things for me this year.
{ $diff = $x - 17;
  $more = 'more'
  if ($diff == 0) {
    $diff = 'no';
  } elsif ($diff < 0) {
    $more = 'fewer';
  }
}
That is {$diff} {$more} than he gave me last year.
```

Notice that after we set `$x` in the first little program, its value carries over to the second little program, and that we can set `$diff` and `$more` in one place and use their values again later.

All variables are evaluated in the package you specify as an argument to `fill_in`. This means that if your templates don't do anything egregiously stupid, you don't have to worry that evaluation of the little programs will creep out into the rest of your program and wreck something. On the other hand, there's really no way to protect against a template that says:

```
{ $Important::Secret::Security::Enable = 0;
  # Disable security checks in this program
}
```

or even:

```
{ system("rm -rf /") }
```

so *don't* go filling in templates unless you're sure you know what's in them. This package may eventually use Perl's **Safe** extension to fill in templates in a safe compartment.

Author

Mark-Jason Dominus, Plover Systems, *mjd@pobox.com*

Support

This software is version 0.1 beta. It probably has bugs. It is inadequately tested. Suggestions and bug reports are always welcome.

Bugs and Caveats

This package is in beta testing and should not be used in critical applications.

This package should fill in templates in a **Safe** compartment.

The callback function that **fill_in** calls when a template contains an error should be able to return an error message to the rest of the program.

My variables in **fill_in** are still susceptible to being clobbered by template evaluation. Perhaps it is safer to make them **local** variables.

Maybe there should be a utility method for emptying out a package?

Maybe there should be a utility function for doing **#include**. It would be easy. (John Cavanaugh, *sdd@hp.com*)

Maybe there should be a control item for doing **#if**. Perl's **if** is sufficient, but a little cumbersome to handle the quoting.

Text::TeX—Perl module for parsing of TeX.

Synopsis

```
use Text::TeX;
sub report {
  my($eaten,$txt) = (shift,shift);
  print "Comment: '", $eaten->[1], "'\n" if defined $eaten->[1];
  print "@{$txt->{waitfors}} ", ref $eaten, ": '", $eaten->[0], "'";
  if (defined $eaten->[3]) {
    my @arr = @{ $eaten->[3] };
    foreach (@arr) {
      print " ", $_->print;
    }
  }
  print "\n";
}
my $file = new Text::TeX::OpenFile 'test.tex',
  'defaultact' => \&report;
$file->process;
```

Description

A new TeX parser is created by:

```
$file = new Text::TeX::OpenFile $filename, attr1 => $val1, ...;
```

$filename may be undef; in that case, the text to parse may be specified in the attribute string.

Recognized attributes are:

string
> Contains the text to parse before parsing *$filename*.

defaultact
> Denotes a procedure to submit output tokens to.

tokens
> Gives a hash of descriptors for input token. A sane default is provided.

A call to the method process launches the parser.

Tokenizer

When the parser is running, it processes the input stream by splitting it into input tokens using some heuristics similar to the actual rules of the TeX tokenizer. However, since it does not use the exact rules, the resulting tokens may be wrong if some advanced TeX commands are used; for example, if the character classes are changed.

This should not be of any concern if the stream in question is a "user" file, but it is important for "packages."

Digester

The processed input tokens are handed to the digester, which handles them according to the provided tokens attribute.

Tokens Attribute

This is a hash reference that describes how the input tokens should be handled. A key to this hash is a literal like ^ or \fraction. A value should be another hash reference, with the following keys recognized:

class
> Into which class to bless the token. Several predefined classes are provided. The default is Text::TeX::Token.

Type
> What kind of special processing to do with the input after the class methods are called. Recognized Types are:

report_args
> > When a token of this Type is encountered, it is converted into a Text::Tex::BegArgsToken. Then the arguments are processed as usual, and an output token of type Text::Tex::ArgToken is inserted between them. Finally, after all the arguments have been processed, an output token Text::Tex::EndArgsToken is inserted.
>
> > The first element of these simulated output tokens is an array reference with the first element being the initial output token that generated this sequence.

The second element of the internal array is the number of arguments required by the input token. The Text::Tex::ArgToken token has a third element, which is the ordinal of the argument that ends immediately before this token.

If requested, a token Text::Tex::LookAhead may be returned instead of Text::Tex::EndArgsToken. The additional elements of `$token->[0]` are the reference to the corresponding `lookahead` attribute, the relevant key (text of following token), and the corresponding value.

In such a case, the input token that was looked-ahead would generate an output token of type Text::Tex::BegArgsTokenLookedAhead (if it usually generates Text::Tex::BegArgsToken).

`local`

Means that this macro introduces a local change, which should be undone at the end of the enclosing block. At the end of the block, an output event Text::TeX::EndLocal is delivered, with `$token->[0]` being the output token for the local event starting.

Useful for font switching.

Some additional keys may be recognized by the code for the particular `class`.

`count`

Number of arguments to the macro.

`waitfor`

Gives the matching token for a starting delimiter token.

`eatargs`

Number of tokens to swallow literally and put into the relevant slot of the output token. The surrounding braces are stripped.

`selfmatch`

Used with `eatargs==1`. Denotes that the matching token is also `eatargs==1`, and the swallowed tokens should coincide (like with \begin{blah} ... \end{blah}).

`lookahead`

A hash with keys that are texts of tokens which need to be treated specially after the end of arguments for the current token. If the corresponding text follows the token indeed, a token Text::Tex::LookAhead is returned instead of Text::Tex::EndArgsToken.

Symbol Font Table

The hash `%Text::TeX::xfont` contains the translation table from TeX tokens into the corresponding font elements. The values are array references of the form [`fontname`, `char`]. Currently the only font supported is `symbol`.

Author

Ilya Zakharevich, *ilya@math.ohio-state.edu*

See Also

perl(1)

Text::Vpp—Perl extension for a versatile text preprocessor

Synopsis

```
use Text::Vpp ;
$fin = Text::Vpp-> new('input_file_name') ;
$fin->setVar('one_variable_name' => 'value_one',
                     'another_variable_name' => 'value_two') ;
$res = $fin -> substitute ;
print "Result is : \n\n",join("\n",@$res) ,"\n";
```

Description

This class enables preprocessing of a file somewhat like **cpp**.

First, you create a Vpp object that passes the name of the file to process and then you call **setvar()** to set the variables you need.

Finally, you call **substitute** on the Vpp object.

Non-Description

Note that it's not designed to replace the well-known **cpp**. Note also that if you think of using it to preprocess a Perl script, you're likely to shoot yourself in the foot. Perl has a lot of built-in mechanism so that a preprocessor is not necessary.

Input File Syntax

Comments

All lines beginning with **#** are skipped. (This may be changed with **setCommentChar()**.)

in-line eval

Lines beginning with **@EVAL** (@ being pompously named the action char) are evaluated as small Perl scripts.

When **setActionChar()** is called with **#** as a parameter, Vpp doesn't skip lines beginning with **#**. In this case, there's no comment possible.

Multiline input

Lines ending with \ are concatenated with the following line.

Variables substitution

You can specify in your text variables beginning with $ (as in perl). These variables can be set either by the **setVar()** method or by the **eval** capability of Vpp (see below).

Setting variables

Lines beginning with @ are **eval**ed using variables defined by **setVar()**. You can only use scalar variables. That way you can also define variables in your text that can be used later.

Conditional statements

Text::Vpp understands **@IF**, **@ELSIF**, **@ENDIF**, and so on. **@INCLUDES** and **@IF** can be nested.

@IF and **@ELSIF** are followed by a string that is **eval**ed using the variable you defined (either with **setVar()** or in the text).

Inclusion

Text::Vpp understands **@INCLUDE**

Constructor

new(*file_name*, *optional_var_hash_ref*, *optional_action_char*)

Creates the file object. The second parameter can be a hash containing all variables needed for the substitute method.

Methods

substitute([*output_file*])

Performs the substitute, inclusion, and so on, and writes the result in *output_file*. Returns 1 on completion, 0 in case of an error.

If *output_file* is not specified, this function stores the substitution result in an internal variable. The result can be retrieved with getText().

getText()

Returns an array ref containing the result.

getError()

Returns an array ref containing the errors.

setVar(*key1* => *value1*, *key2* => *value2* ,...) or setVar(*hash_ref*)

Declares variables for the substitute. Note that calling this function clobbers previously stored values.

setActionChar(*char*)

Enables the user to use another char as action char. (The default is @.)

Example: setActionChar('#') enables Vpp to understand #include, #ifdef, etc.

setCommentChar(*char*)

Enables the user to use another char as comment char. (The default is #.)

Author

Dominique Dumont, *Dominique_Dumont@grenoble.hp.com*

Copyright

Copyright © 1996 Dominique Dumont. All rights reserved. This program is free software; you can redistribute it and/or modify it under the same terms as Perl itself.

Version

Version 0.1

See Also

perl(1),Text::Template(3)

Text::Wrap — line-wrapping to form simple paragraphs

Synopsis

```
use Text::Wrap
print wrap($initial_tab, $subsequent_tab, @text);
use Text::Wrap qw(wrap $columns);
$columns = 132;
```

Description

`Text::Wrap::wrap()` is a very simple paragraph formatter. It formats a single paragraph at a time by breaking lines at word boundaries. Indentation is controlled for the first line (`$initial_tab`) and all subsequent lines (`$subsequent_tab`) independently. `$Text::Wrap::columns` should be set to the full width of your output device.

Example

```
print wrap("\t","","This is a bit of text that forms
        a normal book-style paragraph");
```

Bugs

It's not clear what the correct behavior should be when **wrap()** is presented with a word that is longer than a line. The previous behavior was to die. Now the word is split at line-length.

Author

David Muir Sharnoff, *muir@idiom.com* (with help from Tim Pierce and others)

TeX::DVI—write out DVI (DeVice Independent) file

Synopsis

```
use TeX::DVI;
use Font::TFM;
my $dvi = new TeX::DVI "texput.dvi";
my $font = new_at Font::TFM "cmr10", 12;
$dvi->preamble();
$dvi->begin_page();
$dvi->push();
my $fn = $dvi->font_def($font);
$dvi->font($fn);
$dvi->word("difficulty");
$dvi->hskip($font->space());
$dvi->word("AVA");
$dvi->black_box($font->em_width(), $font->x_height());
$dvi->pop();
$dvi->end_page();
$dvi->postamble();
```

Description

Method `TeX::DVI::new()` creates a new DVI object in memory and opens the output DVI file. After that, elements can be written into the file using appropriate methods.

These are the methods available on the Font::TFM object.

Methods

`preamble, postamble, begin_page, end_page, push, pop`
    Writes out appropriate command of the *.dvi* file.

font_def

> The parameter is a reference to a Font::TFM object. Information from this object is printed out. The method returns the internal number of the font in this *.dvi* file.

font

> Writes out the `font_sel` command; the parameter is the number returned by `font_def`.

hskip, vskip

> Skips.

black_box

> Creates a black box, can be used for hrules and vrules.

special

> Writes out the special command; one parameter is written as the command.

word

> Writes out the word given as the first parameter. The currently selected font is used to gather information about ligatures and kernings.

Bugs

The error-handling is rather weak—the module currently assumes you know why you call the method you call.

Version

0.04

See Also

Font::TFM, perl(1).

Copyright

Copyright © 1996, 1997 Jan Pazdziora (*adelton@fi.muni.cz*), Faculty of Informatics, Masaryk University, Brno

12

Option, Argument, Parameter, and Configuration File Processing

This section covers tools for handling run-time options and configuration file-specific directives.

ConfigReader—read directives from a configuration file

Description

The ConfigReader library is a set of classes that reads directives from a configuration file. The library is completely object-oriented, and it is envisioned that parsers for new styles of configuration files can be easily added.

ConfigReader::Spec encapsulates a specification for configuration directives. You can specify which directives can be in the configuration file, aliases for each directive, whether the directive is required or has a default value, and how to parse the directive value.

Here's an example of how one directive might be specified:

```
required $spec 'HomePage', 'new URI::URL';
```

This defines a required directive called HomePage. To parse the value from the configuration file, the URI::URL::new() method is called with the string value as its argument.

If the directive name is a simple string, it is used both to refer to the directive in the Perl program and as the name in the configuration file. You can also specify an alias by using an array ref. For example, suppose you wanted to use "index" as the name of the directive in the configuration file, but to avoid confusion with Perl's index() function, you wanted to refer to the directive inside the program as the "file_index". This will do the trick:

```
['file_index', 'index']
```

You can specify any number of aliases for the directive:

```
['file_index', 'index', 'file_index', 'contents', ...]
```

The parsing function or method is called to translate the value string from the configuration file into the value used by the program. It can be specified in several different ways:

- Code ref
- Static method
- Object method
- Undefined

You can also specify a default value to be used if a directive is not specified in the configuration file.

- String value
- Code ref
- Undefined

ConfigReader::Values stores a set of directive values that have been read from a configuration file. It stores a reference to an associated Spec as a member variable. Separating the specification from the values makes it possible to use a single specification for multiple sets of values.

ConfigReader::DirectiveStyle implements a reader for a common style of configuration file. It is a subclass of ConfigReader::Values. Directive names are followed by their value, one per line:

```
HomePage    http://www.w3.org/
Services    /etc/services
```

ConfigReader::DirectiveStyle—read a configuration file of directives and values

Configuration File Synopsis

```
# comments start with a #, and blank lines are ignored

Input      /etc/data_source      # the value follows the directive name
HomePage   http://www.w3.org/

# values can be quoted
Comment    "here is a value with trailing spaces    "
```

Code Synopsis

```
my $c = new ConfigReader::DirectiveStyle;

directive $c 'Input', undef, '~/input';  # specify default value,
                                          #   but no parsing needed
required  $c 'HomePage', 'new URI::URL'; # create URI::URL object
ignore    $c 'Comment';                  # Ignore this directive.

$c->load('my.config');
open(IN, $c->value("Input"));

$c->define_accessors();                  # creates Input() and HomePage()
retrieve(HomePage());
```

Description

This class reads a common style of configuration files, where directive names are followed by values. For each directive, you can specify whether it has a default value or is required, and a function or method to use to parse the value. Errors and warnings are caught while parsing, and the location where the offending value came from (either from the configuration file, or your Perl source for default values) is reported.

DirectiveStyle is a subclass of ConfigReader::Values. The methods to define the directives in the configuration file are documented there.

Comments are introduced by the # character and continue until the end of line. As in Perl, the backslash character (\) may be used in the directive value for the various standard sequences:

\t	Tab
\n	Newline
\r	Return
\f	Form feed
\v	Vertical tab (whatever that is)
\b	Backspace
\a	Alarm (bell)
\e	Escape
\033	Octal char
\x1b	Hex char

The value may also be quoted, which lets you include leading or trailing spaces. The quotes are stripped off before the value is returned.

DirectiveStyle itself only reads the configuration file. Most of the hard work of defining the directives and parsing the values is done in its superclass, ConfigReader::Values. You should be able to easily modify or subclass DirectiveStyle to read a different style of configuration file.

Public Methods

new([*$spec*])

> This static method creates and returns a new DirectiveStyle object. For information about the optional *$spec* argument, see `DirectiveStyle::new()`.

load(*$file*, [*$untaint*])

> Before calling `load()`, you'll want to define the directives using the methods described in ConfigReader::Values.

> Reads a configuration from *$file*. The default values for any directives not present in the file are assigned.

> Normally, configuration values are tainted like any data read from a file. If the configuration file comes from a trusted source, you can untaint all the values by setting the optional *$untaint* argument to a true value (such as `UNTAINT`).

Subclassable Methods

You can stop reading here if you just want to use DirectiveStyle. The following methods could be overridden in a subclass to provide additional or alternate functionality.

`parse_line($line, $whence, $untaint)`

Parses *$line*. *$whence* is a string describing the source of the line. Returns a two-element array of the directive and the value string, or the empty array () if the line is blank or only contains a comment.

`parse_value_string($str, $whence)`

Interprets quotes, backslashes, and comments in the value part. (Note that after the value string is returned, it still gets passed to the directive's parsing function or method if one is defined).

ConfigReader::Spec—store a specification about configuration directives

Description

The ConfigReader::Spec class stores a specification about configuration directives: their names, whether they are required or if they have default values, and what parsing function or method to use.

ConfigReader::Values—store a set of configuration values

Description

This class stores a set of configuration values that have been read from a configuration file. Methods are provided to define directives, assign and retrieve values, and to create accessor subroutines.

As this class is usually subclassed to implement a reader for a specific style of configuration file, the user-oriented methods are described first. Methods used to help implement a subclass are described later.

User Methods

`directive($directive, [$parser, [$default, [$whence]]])`

Defines a directive named `$directive` for the configuration file. You may optionally specify a parsing function or method for the directive and a default value.

If *$directive* is a simple string, it is used as both the name of the directive inside the program and in the configuration file. You can use an array ref of the form:

```
['program-name', 'name1', 'name2', 'name3' ...]
```

to use **program-name** inside the program, but to recognize any of **name1**, **name2**, or **name3** as the name of the directive in the configuration file.

A directive is set to **undef** if you don't specify a default value and no value is set in the configuration file.

Any errors or warnings that occur while parsing the default value are normally reported as orginating in the caller's module. You can change the reported location by specifying *$whence*.

`required($directive, [$parser, [$whence]])`

Defines a directive that must be specified in the configuration file.

`ignore($directive, [$whence])`

Defines a directive that is accepted, but ignored, in the configuration file.

`directives()`

Returns an array of the configuration directive names.

`value($directive, [$whence])`

Returns the value of the configuration directive `$directive`.

`define_accessors([$package, [@names]])`

Creates subroutines in the caller's package to access configuration values. For example, if one of the configuration directives is named **Input_File**, you can do:

```
$config->define_accessors();
...
open(IN, Input_File());
```

The names of the created subroutines are returned in an array. If you'd like to export the accessor subroutines, you can say:

```
push @EXPORT, $config->define_accessors();
```

You can specify the package in which to create the subroutines with the optional *$package* argument. You may also specify which configuration directives to create accessor subroutines for. By default, subroutines are created for all the directives.

Implementation Methods

The following methods will probably be called by a subclass implementing a reader for a particular style of configuration files.

`new( [$spec] )`

The static method **new()** creates and returns a new ConfigReader::Values object.

Unless the optional *$spec* argument is present, a new ConfigReader::Spec object is created to store the configuration specification. The **directive()**, **required()**, **ignore()**, **value()**, and **directive()** methods described above are passed through to the spec object.

By setting *$spec*, you can use a different class (perhaps a subclass) to store the specification.

You can also set *$spec* if you want to use one specification for multiple sets of values. Files like */etc/termcap* describe a configuration for multiple objects (terminals, in this case), but use the same directives to describe each object.

`values()`

Returns the hash ref that actually stores the configuration directive values. The key of the hash ref is the directive name.

`spec()`

Returns the internal spec object used to store the configuration specification.

```
assign($directive, $value_string, $whence)
```
> Normally called while reading the configuration file, assigns a value to the directive named *$directive*. The *$value_string* is parsed by the directive's parsing function or method, if any. *$whence* should describe the line in the configuration file that contains the value string.

```
assign_defaults($whence)
```
> After the configuration file is read, the **assign_defaults()** method is called to assign the default values for directives that were not specified in the configuration file. *$whence* should describe the name of the configuration file.

Getopt::EvaP—evaluate Perl command-line parameters

Synopsis
```
use vars qw(@PDT @MM %OPT);
use Getopt::EvaP;
EvaP \@PDT, \@MM, \%OPT;
```

Description

@PDT is the Parameter Description Table, which is a reference to a list of strings describing the command-line parameters, aliases, types, and default values. **@MM** is the Message Module, which is also a reference to a list of strings describing the command and its parameters. **%OPT** is an optional hash reference that says where Evaluate Parameters should place its results. If specified, the historical behavior of modifying the calling routine's namespace by storing option values in **%Options**, **%options**, and **$opt*** is disabled.

Introduction

The function Evaluate Parameters parses a Perl command line in a simple and consistent manner, performs type checking of parameter values, and provides the user with first-level help. Evaluate Parameters is also embeddable in your application; refer to the **evap_pac(2)** manpage for complete details. Evaluate Parameters handles command lines in the following format:

```
command [-parameters] [file_list]
```

where **parameters** and **file_list** are optional. A typical example is the C compiler:

```
cc -O -o chunk chunk.c
```

In this case, there are two parameters and a **file_list** consisting of a single filename for the **cc** command.

Parameter Description Table (PDT) Syntax

Here is the PDT syntax. Optional constructs are enclosed in [], and the | character separates possible values in a list.

```
PDT [program_name, alias]
   [parameter_name[, alias]: type [ = [default_variable,]
                                    default_value]]
   PDTEND [optional_file_list | required_file_list | no_file_list]
```

So the simplest possible PDT would be:

```
PDT
PDTEND
```

This PDT simply defines a -help switch for the command, but it is rather useless.

A typical PDT would look more like this:

```
PDT frog
   number, n: integer = 1
PDTEND no_file_list
```

This PDT, for command **frog**, defines a single parameter, **number** (or **n**), of type **integer**, with a default value of 1. The PDTEND **no_file_list** indicator indicates that no trailing **file_list** can appear on the command line. Of course, the -help switch is defined automatically.

The **default_variable** is an environment variable—see "Usage Notes" for complete details.

Usage Notes

Usage is similar to getopt/getopts/newgetopt: define a Parameter Description Table declaring a list of command-line parameters, their aliases, types, and default values. The command-line parameter -help (alias -h) is automatically included by Evaluate Parameters. After the evaluation, the values of the command-line parameters are stored in variable names of the form $opt_parameter, except for lists, which are returned as @opt_parameter, where parameter is the full spelling of the command-line parameter. Note that values are also returned in the hashes %options and %Options, with lists being passed as a reference to a list.

Of course, you can specify where you want Evaluate Parameters to return its results, in which case this historical feature of writing into your namespace is disabled.

An optional PDT line can be included that tells Evaluate Parameters whether or not trailing filenames can appear on the command line after all the parameters. It can read no_file_list, optional_file_list, or required_file_list and, if not specified, it defaults to optional. Although placement is not important, this line is by convention the last line of the PDT declaration.

Additionally a Message Module is declared that describes the command and provides examples. Following the main help text an optional series of help text messages can be specified for individual command-line parameters. In the following sample program all the parameters have this additional text that describes that parameter's type. The leading character is a dot in column one, followed by the full spelling of the command-line parameter. Use -full_help rather than -help to see this supplemental information. This sample program illustrates the various types and how to use EvaP(). The key type is a special type that enumerates valid values for the command-line parameter. The Boolean type may be specified as TRUE/FALSE, YES/NO, ON/OFF, or 1/0. Parameters of type **file** have ~ and $HOME expanded, and the default values **stdin** and **stdout** converted to - and >-, respectively. Of special note is the default value $required: when it is specified, Evaluate Parameters ensures that a value is given for that command-line parameter.

All types except **switch** may be "list of", like the tty parameter in the example below. A list parameter can be specified multiple times on the command line. Note: In general, you should *always* quote components of your lists, even if they're not type **string**, since Evaluate Parameters uses **eval** to parse them. Doing this prevents **eval** from evaluating expressions that it shouldn't, such as filename shortcuts like $HOME, and backticked items like `hostname`. Although the resulting PDT looks cluttered, Evaluate Parameters knows what to do and eliminates superfluous quotes appropriately.

Finally, you can specify a default value via an environment variable. If a command-line parameter is not specified, and there is a corresponding environment variable defined, then Evaluate Parameters uses the value of the environment variable. Examine the command parameter for the syntax. With this feature, users can easily customize command parameters to their liking. Although the name of the environment variable can be whatever you choose, the following scheme is suggested for consistency and to avoid conflicts in names:

- Use all uppercase characters.
- Begin the variable name with D_, to suggest a default variable.
- Continue with the name of the command or its alias followed by an underscore.
- Complete the variable name with the name of the parameter or its alias.

So, for example, D_DISCI_DO would name a default variable for the display_option (do) parameter of the display_command_information (disci) command. Works for MS-DOS and UNIX.

Example:

```
#!/usr/local/bin/perl

use Getopt::EvaP;
@PDT = split /\n/, <<'end-of-PDT';
PDT sample
   verbose, v: switch
   command, c: string = D_SAMPLE_COMMAND, "ps -el"
   scale_factor, sf: real = 1.2340896e-1
   millisecond_update_interval, mui: integer = $required
   ignore_output_file_column_one, iofco: boolean = TRUE
   output, o: file = stdout
   queue, q: key plotter, postscript, text, printer,
      keyend = printer
   destination, d: application = 'hostname'
   tty, t: list of name = ("/dev/console", "/dev/tty0", "/dev/tty1")
PDTEND optional_file_list
end-of-PDT
@MM = split /\n/, <<'end-of-MM';
sample
        A sample program demonstrating typical Evaluate Parameters
        usage.
        Examples:
          sample
          sample -usage_help
          sample -help
          sample -full_help
          sample -mui 1234
.verbose
        A switch type parameter emulates a typical standalone
        switch. If the switch is specified Evaluate Parameters
        returns a '1'.
.command
        A string type parameter is just a list of characters,
        which must be quoted if it contains whitespace.
```

> NOTE: for this parameter you can also create and
> initialize the environment variable D_SAMPLE_COMMAND to
> override the standard default value for this command
> line parameter. All types except switch may have a
> default environment variable for easy user customization.

.scale_factor

> A real type parameter must be a real number that may
> contain a leading sign, a decimal point and an exponent.

.millisecond_update_interval

> An integer type parameter must consist of all digits
> with an optional leading sign. NOTE: this parameter's
> default value is $required, meaning that
> Evaluate Parameters ensures that this parameter is
> specified and given a valid value. All types except
> switch may have a default value of $required.

.ignore_output_file_column_one

> A boolean type parameter may be TRUE/YES/ON/1 or
> FALSE/NO/OFF/0, either upper or lower case. If TRUE,
> Evaluate Parameters returns a value of '1', else '0'.

.output

> A file type parameter expects a filename. For Unix
> $HOME and ~ are expanded. For EvaP/Perl stdin and
> stdout are converted to '-' and '>-' so they can be
> used in a Perl *open()* function.

.queue

> A key type parameter enumerates valid values. Only the
> specified keywords can be entered on the command line.

.destination

> An application type parameter is not type-checked in
> any - the treatment of this type of parameter is
> application specific. NOTE: this parameter' default
> value is enclosed in grave accents (or "backticks").
> Evaluate Parameters executes the command and uses its
> standard output as the default value for the parameter.

.tty

> A name type parameter is similar to a string except
> that embedded white-space is not allowed. NOTE: this
> parameter is also a LIST, meaning that it can be
> specified multiple times and that each value is pushed
> onto a Perl LIST variable. In general you should quote
> all list elements. All types except switch may be
> 'list of'.

```
end-of-MM
EvaP \@PDT, \@MM;                # evaluate parameters
print "\nProgram name:\n  $Options{'help'}\n\n";
if (defined $Options{'verbose'}) {print "\nverbose =
                                   $Options{'verbose'}\n";}
print "command = \"$Options{'command'}\"\n";
print "scale_factor  = $Options{'scale_factor'}\n";
print "millisecond_update_interval =
      $Options{'millisecond_update_interval'}\n";
print "ignore_output_file_column_one =
      $Options{'ignore_output_file_column_one'}\n";
print "output = $Options{'output'}\n";
```

```
print "queue = $Options{'queue'}\n";
print "destination = $Options{'destination'}\n";
print "'list of' tty = \"", join('", "',
                                  @{$Options{'tty'}}), "\"\n";
print "\nFile names:\n  ", join ' ', @ARGV, "\n" if @ARGV;
```

Using the PDT as a guide, Evaluate Parameters parses a user's command line, returning the results of the evaluation to global variables of the form $opt_*parameter*, @opt_*parameter*, %Options{'*parameter*'}, or %options{'*parameter*'}, where parameter is the full spelling of the command-line parameter.

Of course, you can specify where you want Evaluate Parameters to return its results, in which case this historical feature of writing into your namespace is disabled.

Every command using Evaluate Parameters automatically has a -help switch that displays parameter help; no special code is required in your application.

Customization of EvaP's Help Output

There are several Help Hook strings that can be altered to customize EvaP's help output. Currently, there is only one general area that can be customized: usage and error text dealing with the trailing file_list. For instance, if a command requires one or more trailing filenames after all the command-line switches, the default -help text is:

```
file(s) required by this command
```

Some commands do not want trailing "filenames", but rather some other type of information. An example is display_command_information, where a single Program_Name is expected. The following code snippet shows how to do this:

```
$Getopt::EvaP::evap_Help_Hooks{'P_HHURFL'} = " Program_Name\n";
$Getopt::EvaP::evap_Help_Hooks{'P_HHBRFL'} =
        "\nA Program_Name is required by this command.\n\n";
$Getopt::EvaP::evap_Help_Hooks{'P_HHERFL'} =
        "A trailing Program_Name is required by this command.\n";
EvaP \@PDT, \@MM;
```

As you can see, the hash %evap_Help_Hooks is indexed by a simple ordinal. The ordinals are shown below and are mostly self-explanatory. In case you don't have access to the source for Evaluate Parameters, here are the default values of the Help Hook strings:

```
$Getopt::EvaP:evap_Help_Hooks{'P_HHURFL'} = " file(s)\n";
$Getopt::EvaP:evap_Help_Hooks{'P_HHUOFL'} = " [file(s)]\n";
$Getopt::EvaP:evap_Help_Hooks{'P_HHUNFL'} = "\n";
$Getopt::EvaP:evap_Help_Hooks{'P_HHBRFL'} =
        "\nfile(s) required by this command\n\n";
$Getopt::EvaP:evap_Help_Hooks{'P_HHBOFL'} =
        "\n[file(s)] optionally required by this command\n\n";
$Getopt::EvaP:evap_Help_Hooks{'P_HHBNFL'} = "\n";
$Getopt::EvaP:evap_Help_Hooks{'P_HHERFL'} =
        "Trailing file name(s) required.\n";
$Getopt::EvaP:evap_Help_Hooks{'P_HHENFL'} =
        "Trailing file name(s) not permitted.\n";
```

The Help Hooks naming convention is rather simple:

```
P_HHtf
  where:
    P_HH  implies an Evaluate Parameters Help Hook
  t     type:
            U=Usage Help
            B=Brief and Full Help
            E=error message
  f     file_list:
            RFL=required_file_list
            OFL=optional_file_list
            NFL=no_file_list
```

Note to `genPerlTk` and `genTclTk` users: using these Help Hooks may cause the `genTk` programs to generate an unusable Tk script. This happens because the `genTk` programs look for the strings required by this command or optionally required by this command in order to generate the `file_list` `Entry` widget—if these string are missing, the widget is not created. An easy solution is to ensure that your Help Hook text contains said string, just like the code snippet above; otherwise you must manually add the required Tk code yourself.

Human Interface Guidelines

To make Evaluate Parameters successful, you, the application developer, must follow certain conventions when choosing parameter names and aliases.

Parameter names consist of one or more words, separated by underscores, and they describe the parameter (for example, `verbose` and `spool_directory`).

You can abbreviate parameters: use the first letter of each word in the parameter name. Do not use underscores. For example, you can abbreviate `command` as `c` and `delay_period` as `dp`.

There are exceptions to this standard:

- `password` is abbreviated `pw`.
- The words `minimum` and `maximum` are abbreviated `min` and `max`. So the abbreviation for the parameter `maximum_byte_count` is `maxbc`.
- There are no abbreviations for the parameters `usage_help` and `full_help`; I do not want to prevent `uh` and `fh` from being used as valid command-line parameters.

MANPAGER, PAGER, and D_EVAP_DO_PAGE

The environment variable MANPAGER (or PAGER) is used to control the display of help information generated by Evaluate Parameters. If defined and non-null, the value of the environment variable is taken as the name of the program to pipe the help output through. If no paging program is defined, then the program `more` is used.

The Boolean environment variable D_EVAP_DO_PAGE can be set to FALSE/NO/OFF/0, case-insensitive, to disable this automatic paging feature (or you can set your paging program to `cat`).

Return Values

EvaP() behaves differently depending upon whether it's called to parse an application's command line, or as an embedded command-line parser (for instance, when using evap_pac()).

	Application Command Line	Embedded Command Line
error	exit(1)	return(0)
success	return(1)	return(1)
help	exit(0)	return(-1)

See Also

evap(2), evap.c(2), EvaP.pm(2), evap.tcl(2), evap_pac(2), addmm, add_message_modules(1), disci, display_command_information(1), genmp, generate_man_page(1), genpdt, generate_pdt(1), genPerlTk, generate_PerlTk_program(1), genTclTk, generate_TclTk_program(1). They are all available from the directory *ftp.Lehigh.EDU:/pub/evap/evap-2.x.*

Author

Stephen O. Lidie, *lusol@Lehigh.EDU*

Copyright

Copyright © 1993–1997 Stephen O. Lidie. All rights reserved.

This program is free software; you can redistribute it and/or modify it under the same terms as Perl itself.

Getopt::Long—extended processing of command-line options

Synopsis

```
use Getopt::Long;
$result = GetOptions (...option-descriptions...);
```

Description

The Getopt::Long module implements an extended **getopt** function called **GetOptions()**. This function adheres to the POSIX syntax for command-line options, with GNU extensions. In general, this means that options have long names instead of single letters and are introduced with a double dash (--). Support for bundling of command-line options, as was the case with the more traditional single-letter approach, is provided, but not enabled, by default. For example, the UNIX **ps** command can be given the command-line "option":

```
-vax
```

which means the combination of **-v**, **-a** and **-x**. With the new syntax, **--vax** would be a single option, probably indicating a computer architecture.

Command-line options can be used to set values. These values can be specified in one of two ways:

```
--size 24
--size=24
```

`GetOptions` is called with a list of option-descriptions, each of which consists of two elements: the option specifier and the option linkage. The option specifier defines the name of the option and, optionally, the value it can take. The option linkage is usually a reference to a variable that is set when the option is used. For example, the following call to GetOptions:

```
GetOptions("size=i" => \$offset);
```

accepts a command-line option `size`, which must have an integer value. A command line with `--size 24` causes the variable `$offset` to get the value 24.

Alternatively, the first argument to `GetOptions` may be a reference to a hash describing the linkage for the options. The following call is equivalent to the example above:

```
%optctl = ("size" => \$offset);
GetOptions(\%optctl, "size=i");
```

Linkage may be specified using either of the above methods or both. Linkage specified in the argument list takes precedence over the linkage specified in the hash.

The command-line options are taken from array `@ARGV`. Upon completion of `GetOptions`, `@ARGV` contains the rest (i.e., the non-options) of the command line.

Each option specifier designates the name of the option, optionally followed by an argument specifier. Values for argument specifiers are:

<none>
> Option does not take an argument. The option variable is set to 1.

!
> Option does not take an argument and may be negated, i.e., prefixed by "no". For example, "foo!" allows `--foo` (with value 1) and `--nofoo` (with value 0). The option variable is set to 1, or 0 if negated.

=s
> Option takes a mandatory string argument. This string is assigned to the option variable. Note that even if the string argument starts with - or --, it is not considered an option on itself.

:s
> Option takes an optional string argument. This string is assigned to the option variable. If omitted, it is assigned `""` (an empty string). If the string argument starts with - or --, it is considered an option on itself.

=i
> Option takes a mandatory integer argument. This value is assigned to the option variable. Note that the value may start with - to indicate a negative value.

:i
> Option takes an optional integer argument. This value is assigned to the option variable. If omitted, the value 0 is assigned. Note that the value may start with - to indicate a negative value.

=f
> Option takes a mandatory real-number argument. This value is assigned to the option variable. Note that the value may start with - to indicate a negative value.

:f
> Option takes an optional real-number argument. This value is assigned to the option variable. If omitted, the value 0 is assigned.

A lone dash (–) is considered an option; the corresponding option name is the empty string.

A double dash by itself (––) signals the end of the options list.

Linkage Specification

The linkage specifier is optional. If no linkage is explicitly specified, but a ref HASH is passed, GetOptions places the value in the hash. For example:

```
%optctl = ();
GetOptions (\%optctl, "size=i");
```

performs the equivalent of the assignment:

```
$optctl{"size"} = 24;
```

For array options, a reference to an array is used, e.g.:

```
%optctl = ();
GetOptions (\%optctl, "sizes=i@");
```

with the command line –sizes 24 –sizes 48 performs the equivalent of the assignment:

```
$optctl{"sizes"} = [24, 48];
```

For hash options (an option whose argument looks like name=value), a reference to a hash is used, e.g.:

```
%optctl = ();
GetOptions (\%optctl, "define=s%");
```

with the command line ––define foo=hello ––define bar=world performs the equivalent of the assignment:

```
$optctl{"define"} = {foo=>'hello', bar=>'world')
```

If no linkage is explicitly specified and no ref HASH is passed, GetOptions puts the value in a global variable named after the option, prefixed by opt_. To yield a usable Perl variable, characters that are not part of the syntax for variables are translated to underscores. For example, ––fpp-struct-return sets the variable $opt_fpp_struct_return. Note that this variable resides in the namespace of the calling program, not necessarily main. For example:

```
GetOptions ("size=i", "sizes=i@");
```

with the command line –size 10 –sizes 24 –sizes 48 performs the equivalent of the assignments:

```
$opt_size = 10;
@opt_sizes = (24, 48);
```

A lone dash (–) is considered an option; the corresponding Perl identifier is $opt_ .

The linkage specifier can be a reference to a scalar, a reference to an array, a reference to a hash, or a reference to a subroutine.

If a ref SCALAR is supplied, the new value is stored in the referenced variable. If the option occurs more than once, the previous value is overwritten.

If a ref ARRAY is supplied, the new value is appended (pushed) to the referenced array.

If a ref HASH is supplied, the option value should look like `key` or `key=value` (if the `=value` is omitted then a value of 1 is implied). In this case, the element of the referenced hash with the key `key` is assigned `value`.

If a ref CODE is supplied, the referenced subroutine is called with two arguments: the option name and the option value. The option name is always the true name, not an abbreviation or alias.

Aliases and Abbreviations

The option name may actually be a list of option names, separated by `|`, e.g., `foo|bar|blech=s`. In this example, `foo` is the true name of this option. If no linkage is specified, options `foo`, `bar` and `blech` all set `$opt_foo`.

Option names may be abbreviated to uniqueness, depending on the configuration option `auto_abbrev`.

Non-Option Callback Routine

A special option specifier, `<>`, can be used to designate a subroutine to handle non-option arguments. `GetOptions` immediately calls this subroutine for every non-option it encounters in the options list. This subroutine gets the name of the non-option passed. This feature requires the configuration option `permute`; see the section "Configuration Options."

See also the examples.

Option Starters

On the command line, options can start with `-` (traditional), `--` (POSIX), and `+` (GNU, now being phased out). The latter is not allowed if the environment variable POSIXLY_CORRECT has been defined.

Options that start with `--` may have an argument appended, separated with an `=`, e.g., `--foo=bar`.

Return Value

A return status of 0 (false) indicates that the function detected one or more errors.

Compatibility

`Getopt::Long::GetOptions()` is the successor of *newgetopt.pl*, which came with Perl4. It is fully upward-compatible. In fact, the Perl5 version of *newgetopt.pl* is just a wrapper around the module.

If an `@` sign is appended to the argument specifier, the option is treated as an array. Value(s) are not set, but are pushed into the array `@opt_name`. If explicit linkage is supplied, this must be a reference to an ARRAY.

If a `%` sign is appended to the argument specifier, the option is treated as a hash. Value(s) of the form `name=value` are set by setting the element of the hash `%opt_name` with the key `name` to `value` (if the `=value` portion is omitted, it defaults to 1). If explicit linkage is supplied, this must be a reference to a HASH.

If the configuration option `getopt_compat` is set (see the section "Configuration Options"), options that start with `+` or `-` may also include their arguments, e.g., `+foo=bar`. This is for compatibility with older implementations of the GNU `getopt` routine.

If the first argument to GetOptions is a string consisting of only non-alphanumeric characters, it is taken to specify the option starter characters. Everything starting with one of these characters is considered an option. Using a starter argument is strongly deprecated.

For convenience, option specifiers may have a leading - or --, so it is possible to write:

```
GetOptions qw(-foo=s --bar=i --ar=s);
```

Examples

If the option specifier is one:i (i.e., it takes an optional integer argument), then the following situations are handled:

```
-one -two          -> $opt_one = '', -two is next option
-one -2            -> $opt_one = -2
```

Also, assume specifiers foo=s and bar:s:

```
-bar -xxx          -> $opt_bar = '', '-xxx' is next option
-foo -bar          -> $opt_foo = '-bar'
-foo --            -> $opt_foo = '--'
```

In GNU or POSIX format, option names and values can be combined:

```
+foo=blech         -> $opt_foo = 'blech'
--bar=             -> $opt_bar = ''
--bar=--           -> $opt_bar = '--'
```

Example of using variable references:

```
$ret = GetOptions ('foo=s', \$foo, 'bar=i', 'ar=s', \@ar);
```

With the command-line options -foo blech -bar 24 -ar xx -ar yy, this results in:

```
$foo = 'blech'
$opt_bar = 24
@ar = ('xx','yy')
```

Example of using the <> option specifier:

```
@ARGV = qw(-foo 1 bar -foo 2 blech);
GetOptions("foo=i", \$myfoo, "<>", \&mysub);
```

Results:

```
mysub("bar")  will be called (with $myfoo being 1)
mysub("blech")  will be called (with $myfoo being 2)
```

Compare this with:

```
@ARGV = qw(-foo 1 bar -foo 2 blech);
GetOptions("foo=i", \$myfoo);
```

This leaves the non-options in @ARGV:

```
$myfoo -> 2
@ARGV -> qw(bar blech)
```

Configuration Options

GetOptions can be configured by calling subroutine Getopt::Long::config. This subroutine takes a list of quoted strings, each specifying a configuration option to be set, e.g., ignore_case. Options can be reset by prefixing with no_, e.g., no_ignore_ case. Case does not matter. Multiple calls to config are possible.

Previous versions of Getopt::Long used variables for the purpose of configuring. Although manipulating these variables still works, you are strongly encouraged to use the new `config` routine. Besides, it is much easier.

The following options are available:

`default`

Causes all configuration options to be reset to their default values.

`auto_abbrev`

Allows option names to be abbreviated to uniqueness. The default is set unless the environment variable POSIXLY_CORRECT has been set, in which case `auto_abbrev` is reset.

`getopt_compat`

Allows + to start options. The default is set unless the environment variable POSIXLY_CORRECT has been set, in which case `getopt_compat` is reset.

`require_order`

Determines whether non-options are allowed to be mixed with options. The default is set unless the environment variable POSIXLY_CORRECT has been set, in which case `require_order` is reset.

See also `permute`, which is the opposite of `require_order`.

`permute`

Determines whether non-options are allowed to be mixed with options. The default is set unless the environment variable POSIXLY_CORRECT has been set, in which case `permute` is reset. Note that `permute` is the opposite of `require_order`.

If `permute` is set, this means that:

```
-foo arg1 -bar arg2 arg3
```

is equivalent to:

```
-foo -bar arg1 arg2 arg3
```

If a non-option call-back routine is specified, @ARGV is always empty upon successful return of GetOptions, since all options have been processed, unless `--` is used:

```
-foo arg1 -bar arg2 -- arg3
```

calls the call-back routine for **arg1** and **arg2** and terminates, leaving **arg2** in @ARGV.

If `require_order` is set, options processing terminates when the first non-option is encountered.

```
-foo arg1 -bar arg2 arg3
```

is equivalent to:

```
-foo -- arg1 -bar arg2 arg3
```

`bundling (default: reset)`

Setting this variable to a non-zero value allows single-character options to be bundled. To distinguish bundles from long option names, long options must be introduced with `--` and single-character options (and bundles) must be introduced with `-`. For example:

```
ps -vax --vax
```

is equivalent to:

```
ps -v -a -x --vax
```

provided that **vax**, **v**, **a**, and **x** have been defined to be valid options.

Bundled options can also include a value in the bundle; this value has to be the last part of the bundle, e.g.:

```
scale -h24 -w80
```

is equivalent to:

```
scale -h 24 -w 80
```

Note: Resetting `bundling` also resets `bundling_override`.

`bundling_override` (default: reset)

If `bundling_override` is set, bundling is enabled as with `bundling` but now long option names override option bundles. In the above example, `-vax` is interpreted as the option **vax**, not the bundle **v**, **a**, **x**.

Note: Resetting `bundling_override` also resets `bundling`.

Note: Using option bundling can easily lead to unexpected results, especially when mixing long options and bundles. *Caveat emptor.*

`ignore_case` (default: set)

If set, case is ignored when matching options.

Note: Resetting `ignore_case` also resets `ignore_case_always`.

`ignore_case_always` (default: reset)

When bundling is in effect, case is ignored on single-character options also.

Note: Resetting `ignore_case_always` also resets `ignore_case`.

`pass_through` (default: reset)

Unknown options are passed through in `@ARGV` instead of being flagged as errors. This makes it possible to write wrapper scripts that process only part of the user-supplied options and pass the remaining options to some other program.

This can be very confusing, especially when `permute` is also set.

`debug` (default: reset)

Enables copious debugging output.

Other Useful Variables

`$Getopt::Long::VERSION`

Returns the version number of this Getopt::Long implementation in the format `major.minor`. This can be used to have Exporter check the version, e.g.:

```
use Getopt::Long 3.00;
```

You can inspect `$Getopt::Long::major_version` and `$Getopt::Long::minor_version` for the individual components.

`$Getopt::Long::error`

Internal error flag. May be incremented from a call-back routine to cause options parsing to fail.

Getopt::Mixed—getopt processing with both long and short options

Synopsis

```
use Getopt::Mixed;
Getopt::Mixed::getOptions(...option-descriptions...);
...examine $opt_* variables...
```

or:

```
use Getopt::Mixed "nextOption";
Getopt::Mixed::init(...option-descriptions...);
while (($option, $value) = nextOption()) {
    ...process option...
}
Getopt::Mixed::cleanup();
```

Description

This package is my response to the standard modules Getopt::Std and Getopt::Long. Std doesn't support long options, and Long doesn't support short options. I wanted both, since long options are easier to remember and short options are faster to type.

This package is intended to be the "Getopt-to-end-all-Getops". It combines (I hope) flexibility and simplicity. It supports both short options (introduced by -) and long options (introduced by --). Short options that do not take an argument can be grouped together. A short option that does take an argument must be the last option in its group, because everything following the option is considered to be its argument.

There are two methods for using Getopt::Mixed: the simple method and the flexible method. Both methods use the same format for option descriptions.

Option Descriptions

The option-description arguments required by `init` and `getOptions` are strings composed of individual option descriptions. Several option descriptions can appear in the same string if they are separated by whitespace.

Each description consists of the option name and an optional trailing argument specifier. Option names may consist of any characters but whitespace, =, :, and >.

Values for argument specifiers are:

`<none>`
Option does not take an argument.

`=s :s`
Option takes a mandatory (=) or optional (:) string argument.

`=i :i`
Option takes a mandatory (=) or optional (:) integer argument.

`=f :f`
Option takes a mandatory (=) or optional (:) real number argument.

`>new`
Option is a synonym for option new.

The > specifier is not really an argument specifier. It defines an option as being a synonym for another option. For example, `a=i  apples>a` would define -a as an option that requires an integer argument and --apples as a synonym for -a. Only one level of synonyms is supported, and the root option must be listed first. For example, `apples>a a=i` and `a=i apples>a oranges>apples` are illegal; use `a=i apples>a oranges>a` if that's what you want.

For example, in the option description `a b=i c:s apple baker>b charlie:s`, `-a` and `--apple` do not take arguments, `-b` takes a mandatory integer argument, `--baker` is a synonym for `-b -c`, and `--charlie` takes an optional string argument.

If the first argument to `init` or `getOptions` consists entirely of non-alphanumeric characters with no whitespace, it represents the characters that can begin options.

User Interface

From the user's perspective, short options are introduced by a dash (-) and long options are introduced by a double dash (--). Short options may be combined (`-a -b` can be written `-ab`), but an option that takes an argument must be the last one in its group, because anything following it is considered part of the argument. A double dash by itself marks the end of the options; all arguments following it are treated as normal arguments, not options. A single dash by itself is treated as a normal argument, *not* an option.

Long options may be abbreviated. The option `--all-the-time` can be abbreviated `--all`, `--a--tim`, or even `--a`. Note that `--time` does not work; the abbreviation must start at the beginning of the option name. If an abbreviation is ambiguous, an error message is printed.

In the following examples, `-i` and `--int` take integer arguments, `-f` and `--float` take floating-point arguments, and `-s` and `--string` take string arguments. No other options take an argument.

```
-i24            -f24.5                  -sHello
-i=24 --int=-27 -f=24.5 --float=0.27 -s=Hello --string=Hello
```

If an argument is required, it can also be separated from the option by whitespace:

```
-i 24 --int -27 -f 24.5 --float 0.27 -s Hello --string Hello
```

Note that if the option is followed by =, whatever follows the = *is* the argument, even if it's the null string. In the example:

```
-i= 24 -f= 24.5 -s= Hello
```

`-i` and `-f` cause an error, because the null string is not a number, but `-s` is perfectly legal; its argument is the null string, not "Hello".

Remember that optional arguments *cannot* be separated from the option by whitespace.

The Simple Method

The simple method is:

```
use Getopt::Mixed;
Getopt::Mixed::getOptions(...option-descriptions...);
```

You then examine the `$opt_*` variables to find out what options were specified and the `@ARGV` array to see what arguments are left.

If `-a` is an option that doesn't take an argument, then `$opt_a` is set to 1 if the option is present, or left undefined if the option is not present.

If **-b** is an option that takes an argument, then **$opt_b** is set to the value of the argument if the option is present, or left undefined if the option is not present. If the argument is optional but not supplied, **$opt_b** is set to the null string.

Note that even if you specify that an option *requires* a string argument, you can still get the null string (if the user specifically enters it). If the option requires a numeric argument, you will never get the null string (because it isn't a number).

When converting the option name to a Perl identifier, any non-word characters in the name are converted to underscores (_).

If the same option occurs more than once, only the last occurrence is recorded. If that's not acceptable, you have to use the flexible method instead.

The Flexible Method

The flexible method is:

```
use Getopt::Mixed "nextOption";
Getopt::Mixed::init(...option-descriptions...);
while (($option, $value, $pretty) = nextOption()) {
    ...process option...
}
Getopt::Mixed::cleanup();
```

This lets you process arguments one at a time. You can then handle repeated options any way you want to. It also lets you see option names with non-alphanumeric characters without any translation. This is also the only method that lets you find out what order the options and other arguments were in.

First, you call Getopt::Mixed::init with the option descriptions. Then you keep calling **nextOption** until it returns an empty list. Finally, you call Getopt::Mixed::cleanup when you're done. The remaining (non-option) arguments will be found in **@ARGV**.

Each call to **nextOption** returns a list of the next option, its value, and the option as the user typed it. The value is undefined if the option does not take an argument. The option is stripped of its starter (e.g., you get **a** and **foo**, not **-a** or **--foo**). If you want to print an error message, use the third element, which does include the option starter.

Other Functions

Getopt::Mixed provides one other function you can use. **abortMsg** prints its arguments on STDERR, plus your program's name and a newline. It then exits with status 1. For example, if *foo.pl* calls **abortMsg** like this:

```
Getopt::Mixed::abortMsg("Error");
```

The output is:

```
foo.pl: Error
```

Customization

There are several customization variables you can set. All of these variables should be set *after* calling Getopt::Mixed::init and *before* calling **nextOption**.

If you set any of these variables, you *must* check the version number first. The easiest way to do that is like this:

```
use Getopt::Mixed 1.006;
```

If you are using the simple method, and you want to set these variables, you need to call init before calling getOptions, like this:

```
use Getopt::Mixed 1.006;
Getopt::Mixed::init(...option-descriptions...);
...set configuration variables...
Getopt::Mixed::getOptions();    # IMPORTANT: no parameters
```

$order

$order can be set to $REQUIRE_ORDER, $PERMUTE, or $RETURN_IN_ORDER. The default is $REQUIRE_ORDER if the environment variable POSIXLY_CORRECT has been set, $PERMUTE otherwise.

$REQUIRE_ORDER means that no options can follow the first argument that isn't an option.

$PERMUTE means that all options are treated as if they preceded all other arguments.

$RETURN_IN_ORDER means that all arguments maintain their ordering. When nextOption is called, and the next argument is not an option, it returns the null string as the option and the argument as the value. nextOption never returns the null list until all the arguments have been processed.

$ignoreCase

Ignore case when matching options. Default is 1 unless the option descriptions contain an uppercase letter.

$optionStart

A string of characters that can start options. Default is -.

$badOption

A reference to a function that is called when an unrecognized option is encountered. The function receives three arguments. $_[0] is the position in @ARGV where the option was. $_[1] is the option as the user typed it (including the option start character). $_[2] is either undef or a string describing the reason the option was not recognized. (Currently, the only possible value is ambiguous, for a long option with several possible matches.) The option has already been removed from @ARGV. To put it back, you can say:

```
splice(@ARGV,$_[0],0,$_[1]);
```

The function can do anything you want to @ARGV. It should return whatever you want nextOption to return.

The default is a function that prints an error message and exits the program.

$checkArg

A reference to a function that is called to make sure the argument type is correct. The function receives four arguments. $_[0] is the position in @ARGV where the option came from. $_[1] is the text following the option, or undefined if there was no text following the option. $_[2] is the name of the option as the user typed it (including the option start character), suitable for error messages. $_[3] is the argument type specifier.

The function can do anything you want to @ARGV. It should return the value for this option.

The default is a function that prints an error message and exits the program if the argument is not the right type for the option. You can also adjust the behavior of the default function by changing `$intRegexp` or `$floatRegexp`.

`$intRegexp`

A regular expression that matches an integer. Default is `^[-+]?\d+$`, which matches a string of digits preceded by an optional sign. Unlike other configuration variables, this cannot be changed after `nextOption` is called, because the pattern is compiled only once.

`$floatRegexp`

A regular expression that matches a floating-point number. Default is `^[-+]?(\d*\.?\d+|\d+\.)$`, which matches the following formats: 123, 123., 123.45, and .123 (plus an optional sign). It does not match exponential notation. Unlike other configuration variables, this cannot be changed after `nextOption` is called, because the pattern is compiled only once.

`$typeChars`

A string of the characters that are legal argument types. The default is `sif`, for string, integer, and floating-point arguments. The string should consist only of letters. Uppercase letters are discouraged, since this hampers the case-folding of options. If you change this, you should set `$checkType` to a function that checks arguments of your new type. Unlike other configuration variables, this must be set *before* calling `init()` and cannot be changed afterwards.

`$checkType`

If you add new types to `$typeChars`, you should set this to a function that checks arguments of the new types.

Bugs

* This document should be expanded.

* A long option must be at least two characters long. Sorry.

* The Getopt::Long ! argument specifier is not supported, but you can have the options `--foo` and `--nofoo` and then do something like:

  ```
  $opt_foo = 0 if $opt_nofoo;
  ```

* The @ argument specifier of Getopt::Long is not supported. If you want your values pushed into an array, you have to use `nextOption` and do it yourself.

Author

Christopher J. Madsen, *ac608@yfn.ysu.edu*

Thanks are also due to Andreas Koenig for helping Getopt::Mixed conform to the standards for Perl modules and for answering a bunch of questions. Any remaining deficiencies are my fault.

License

Getopt::Mixed is distributed under the terms of the GNU General Public License as published by the Free Software Foundation; either version 2, or (at your option) any later version.

This means it is distributed in the hope that it will be useful, but *without any warranty*, without even the implied warranty of *merchantability* or *fitness for a particular purpose*. See the GNU General Public License for more details.

Since Perl scripts are only compiled at runtime, and simply calling Getopt::Mixed does *not* bring your program under the GPL, the only real restriction is that you can't use Getopt::Mixed in a binary-only distribution produced with dump (unless you also provide source code).

Getopt::Regex — handle command-line options flexibly using regular expressions

Synopsis

```
use Getopt::Regex;
GetOptions(\@ARGV,[$regex,$ref,$takesarg],...);
```

\@ARGV

Reference to array of command-line arguments

$regex

Regular expression for identifying the option

$ref

Reference to a variable to be set or a function that is passed the argument if it exists

$takesarg

If 1, subsequent command-line argument is taken as its argument

Description

This package provides a flexible, yet simple, method for handling command-line options. It does not stamp over the caller's namespace or, currently, enforce any particular standard for the options—users can do this if they want. By using anonymous closures, sophisticated option specifications can be constructed.

The function GetOptions, exported from the package, takes a reference to the argument list, followed by a set of option specifications that are references to arrays containing at least a regular expression to match for the option and a reference to a variable to be set or a function to be called. A third optional argument for each option, if set to 1, pulls off the following command-line argument as an argument for that option.

The simplest use is to set a Boolean variable if an argument is set:

```
GetOptions(\@ARGV,['-[v|V]',\$bool,0]);
```

If one of the options –v or –V is present, $bool is set to 1, otherwise it is left unchanged.

A subsequent command-line argument may be used as an option argument as follows:

```
GetOptions(\@ARGV,['-f',\$fname,1]);
```

will set $fname to fname if –f fname is specified on the command line.

Processed arguments are removed from the argument list. Only the first occurrence of an argument is processed, if a variable is being set, as in the above examples.

More complex argument specifications are possible, using anonymous functions as arguments. If the option takes an argument, the argument is passed to the function. Parts of the regular expression may also be used in the anonymous closure being executed. e.g.:

```
GetOptions(\@ARGV,
  ['-D(.+)=(.+)',sub { diagnostic $1,$2; }   ,0],
  ['-D(.+)',    sub { diagnostic $1; $_[0]; },1]);
```

The first option specification matchs options in the format -DDIAGNOSTIC=VALUE; the second matches occurrences of the format -DDIAGNOSTIC VALUE. As this shows, the regex matching variables can be used in handling the options.

When `GetOptions` is called with a function reference, the function is called for all matching occurrences of the regular expression, and the processed options are removed from the argument list.

Here is another useful example:

```
GetOptions(\@ARGV,['-(no-)*optimization',0,sub
       { $optimization=!$1; }]);
```

This identifies the option statements –optimization and –no-optimization, setting $optimization true or false appropriately.

The option -- ends the search for matching options—additional arguments are not checked.

Note

Requires at least Perl 5.000, or Perl 5.001m if anonymous closures are used.

Bugs

Please let me know.

To Do

Possibly integrate default behavior of other option functions in this package.

Author

John A.R. Williams, *J.A.R.Williams@aston.ac.uk*

Getopt::Std—process single-character switches with switch clustering

Synopsis

```
use Getopt::Std;
getopt('oDI');      # -o, -D & -I take arg.  Sets opt_* as a side effect.
getopt('oDI', \%opts);   # -o, -D & -I take arg.  Values in %opts
getopts('oif:');  # -o & -i are boolean flags, -f takes an argument
                  # Sets opt_* as a side effect.
getopts('oif:', \%opts);  # options as above.  Values in %opts
```

Description

The `getopt()` functions process single-character switches with switch clustering. Pass one argument, which is a string containing all switches that take an argument. For each switch, $opt_x (where x is the switch name) is set to the value of the argument, or 1 if no argument. Switches that take an argument don't care whether there is a space between the switch and the argument.

For those of you who don't like additional variables being created, `getopt()` and `getopts()` also accept a hash reference as an optional second argument. Hash keys are **x** (where **x** is the switch name) with key values the value of the argument, or 1 if no argument is specified.

Getopt::Tabular—table-driven argument parsing for Perl5

Synopsis

```
use Getopt::Tabular;
```

or:

```
use Getopt::Tabular qw/GetOptions
                       SetHelp SetHelpOption
                       SetError GetError/;

...
&Getopt::Tabular::SetHelp (long_help, usage_string);
@opt_table = (
                [section_description, "section"],
                [option, type, num_values, option_data, help_string],
                ...
             );
&GetOptions (\@opt_table, \@ARGV [, \@newARGV]) || exit 1;
```

Description

Getopt::Tabular is a Perl5 module for table-driven argument parsing, vaguely inspired by John Ousterhout's Tk_ParseArgv. All you really need to do to use the package is set up a table describing all your command-line options, and call &GetOptions with three arguments: a reference to your option table, a reference to @ARGV (or something like it), and an optional third array reference (say, to @newARGV). &GetOptions processes all arguments in @ARGV, and copies any leftover arguments (i.e., those that are not options or arguments to some option) to the @newARGV array. (If the @newARGV argument is not supplied, GetOptions replaces @ARGV with the stripped-down argument list.) If there are any invalid options, GetOptions prints an error message and returns 0.

Before I tell you why Getopt::Tabular is a wonderful thing, let me explain some of the terminology that will keep popping up here.

Terminology

argument

> Any single word appearing on the command line, i.e., one element of the @ARGV array.

option

> An argument that starts with a certain sequence of characters; the default is -. (If you like GNU-style options, you can change this to --.) In most Getopt::Tabular–based applications, options can come anywhere on the command line, and their order is unimportant (unless one option overrides a previous option). Also, Getopt::Tabular allows any non-ambiguous abbreviation of options.

option argument (or value)

An argument that immediately follows certain types of options. For instance, if –foo is a scalar-valued integer option, and –foo 3 appears on the command line, then 3 is the argument to –foo.

option type

Controls how GetOptions deals with an option and the arguments that follow it. (Actually, for most option types, the type interacts with the num_values field, which determines whether the option is scalar- or vector-valued. This will be fully explained in due course.)

Features

Now for the advertising, i.e., why Getopt::Tabular is a good thing:

- Command-line arguments are carefully type-checked, both by pattern and number; e.g., if an option requires two integers, GetOptions makes sure that exactly two integers follow it!

- The valid command-line arguments are specified in a data structure separate from the call to GetOptions; this makes it easier to have very long lists of options and to parse options from multiple sources (e.g., the command line, an environment variable, and a configuration file).

- Getopt::Tabular can intelligently generate help text based on your option descriptions.

- The type system is extensible, and if you can define your desired argument type using a single Perl regular expression, then it's particularly easy to extend.

- To make your program look smarter, options can be abbreviated and can appear in any order.

In general, I have found that Getopt::Tabular tends to encourage programs with long lists of sophisticated options, leading to great flexibility, intelligent operation, and the potential for insanely long command lines.

Basic Operation

The basic operation of Getopt::Tabular is driven by an *option table*, which is just a list of *option descriptions* (otherwise known as option-table entries, or just entries). Each option description tells GetOptions everything it needs to know when it encounters a particular option on the command line. For instance:

```
["-foo", "integer", 2, \@Foo, "set the foo values"]
```

means that whenever –foo is seen on the command line, GetOptions is to make sure that the next two arguments are integers, and copy them into the caller's @Foo array. (Well, really into the @Foo array where the option table is defined. This is almost always the same as GetOptions' caller, though.)

Typically, you'll group a bunch of option descriptions together like this:

```
@options =
    (["-range", "integer", 2, \@Range,
      "set the range of allowed values"],
     ["-file", "string", 1, \$File,
       "set the output file"],
     ["-clobber", "boolean", 0, \$Clobber,
       "clobber existing files"],
     ...
    );
```

and then call GetOptions like this:

```
&GetOptions (\@options, \@ARGV) || exit 1;
```

This replaces @ARGV with a new array containing all the arguments left over after the options and their arguments have been removed. You can also call GetOptions with three arguments, like this:

```
&GetOptions (\@options, \@ARGV, \@newARGV) || exit 1;
```

In this case, @ARGV is left alone, and @newARGV gets the leftover arguments.

In case of error, GetOptions prints enough information for the user to figure out what's going wrong. If you supply one, it will even print out a brief usage message in case of error. Thus, it's enough to just **exit 1** when GetOptions indicates an error by returning 0.

Detailed descriptions of the contents of an option-table entry are given next, followed by the complete rundown of available types, full details on error handling, and how help text is generated.

Option Table Entries

The fields in the option table control how arguments are parsed, so it's important to understand each one. First, the format of entries in the table is fairly rigid, even though this isn't really necessary with Perl. It's done that way to make the Getopt::Tabular code a little easier; the drawback is that some entries will have unused values (e.g., the num_values field is never used for Boolean options, but you still have to put something there as a placeholder). The fields are as follows:

option

> This is the option name, e.g., -verbose or -some_value. For most option types, this is simply an option prefix followed by text; for Boolean options, however, it can be a little more complicated. (The exact rules are discussed under "Option Types.") And yes, even though you tell Getopt::Tabular the valid option prefixes, you still have to put one onto the option names in the table.

type

> The option type decides what action is taken when this option is seen on the command line, and (if applicable) what sort of values are accepted for this option. There are three broad classes of types: those that imply copying data from the command line into some variable in the caller's space; those that imply copying constant data into the caller's space without taking any more arguments from the command line; and those that imply some other action to be taken. The available option types are covered in greater detail below (see "Option Types"), but briefly: string, integer, and float all imply copying values from the command line to a variable; constant, boolean, copy, arrayconst, and hash-const all imply copying some pre-defined data into a variable; call and eval allow the execution of some arbitrary subroutine or chunk of code; and help options cause GetOptions to print out all available help text and return 0.

num_values

> For string, integer, and float options, this determines whether the option is a scalar (num_values = 1) or a vector (num_values > 1) option. (Note that whether the option is scalar- or vector-valued has an important influence on what you must supply in the option_data field.) For constant, copy, arrayconst,

and `hashconst` option types, `num_values` is a bit of a misnomer: it actually contains the value (or a reference to it, if array or hash) to be copied when the option is encountered. For `call` options, `num_values` can be used to supply extra arguments to the called subroutine. In any case, though, you can think of `num_values` as an input value. For `boolean` and `eval` options, `num_values` is ignored and should be `undef` or 0.

option_data

> For `string`, `integer`, `float`, `boolean`, `constant`, `copy`, `arrayconst`, and `hashconst` types, this must be a reference to the variable into which you want `GetOptions` to copy the appropriate thing. The "appropriate thing" is either the argument(s) following the option, the constant supplied as `num_values`, or 1 or 0 (for Boolean options).

> For `boolean`, `constant`, `copy`, and scalar-valued `string`, `integer`, and `float` options, this must be a scalar reference. For vector-valued `string`, `integer`, and `float` options (`num_values` > 1), and for `arrayconst` options, this must be an array reference. For `hashconst` options, this must be a hash reference.

> Finally, `option_data` is also used as an input value for `call` and `eval` options. For `call`, it should be a subroutine reference, and for `eval` options, it should be a string containing valid Perl code to evaluate when the option is seen. The subroutine called by a `call` option should take at least two arguments: a string, which is the actual option that triggered the call (because the same subroutine could be tied to many options), and an array reference, which contains all command-line arguments after that option. (Further arguments can be supplied in the `num_values` field.) The subroutine may freely modify this array, and those modifications affect the behavior of `GetOptions` afterwards.

> The chunk of code passed to an `eval` option is evaluated in the package from which `GetOptions` is called, and does not have access to any internal Getopt::Tabular data.

help_string *(optional)*

> A brief description of the option. Don't worry about formatting this in any way; when `GetOptions` has to print out your help, it does so quite nicely without any intervention. If the help string is not defined, then that option is not included in the option help text. (However, you could supply an empty string—which is defined—to make `GetOptions` just print out the option name but nothing else.)

arg_desc *(optional)*

> An even more brief description of the values that you expect to follow your option. This is mainly used to supply placeholders in the help string and is specified separately so that `GetOptions` can act fairly intelligently when formatting a help message. See "Help Text" for more information.

Option Types

The option-type field is the single most important field in the table, as the type for an option `-foo` determines (along with `num_values`) what action `GetOptions` takes when it sees `-foo` on the command line: how many following arguments become `-foo`'s arguments, what regular expression those arguments must conform to, or whether some other action should be taken.

For conciseness, I've omitted the `help_string` and `argdesc` entries in all of the example entries shown here. In reality, you should religiously supply help text in order to make your programs easier to use and easier to maintain.

As mentioned above, there are three main classes of argument types:

argument-driven options

These are options that imply taking one or more option arguments from the command line after the option itself is taken. The arguments are then copied into some variable supplied (by reference) in the option-table entry.

constant-valued options

These are options that have a constant value associated with them; when the option is seen on the command line, that constant is copied to some variable in the caller's space. (Both the constant and the value are supplied in the option-table entry.) Constants can be scalars, arrays, or hashes.

other options

These imply some other action to be taken, usually supplied as a string to `eval` or a subroutine to call.

Argument-driven option types

`string`, `integer`, `float`

These are the option types that imply "option arguments", i.e., arguments after the option that are consumed when that option is encountered on the command line and are copied into the caller's space via some reference. For instance, if you have an option table entry like:

```
["-foo", "string", 1, \$Foo]
```

then, when `GetOptions` sees `-foo` on the command line, it copies one argument immediately following it into the scalar variable `$Foo` in your program. If `num_values` is some *n* greater than one, then the `option_data` field must be an array reference, and *n* arguments are copied from the command line into that array. (The array is clobbered, not appended to, each time `-foo` is encountered.) In this case, `-foo` is referred to as a *vector-valued* option, as it must be followed by a fixed number of arguments. (Eventually, I plan to add *list-valued* options, which take a variable number of arguments.) For example an option table like:

```
["-foo", "string", 3, \@Foo]
```

results in the `@Foo` array being set to the three strings immediately following any `-foo` option on the command line.

The only difference between string, integer, and float options is how picky `GetOptions` is about the value(s) it will accept. For string options, anything is okay; for integer options, the values must look like integers (i.e., they must match /[+-]?\d+/); for float options, the values must look like C floating-point numbers (trust me, you don't want to see the regexp for this). Note that since string options accept anything, they might accidentally slurp up arguments that are meant to be further options if the user forgets to put the correct string. For instance, if `-foo` and `-bar` are both scalar-valued string options, and the arguments `-foo -bar` are seen on the command line, then `-bar` becomes the argument to `-foo` and is never processed as an option itself. (This could be construed as either a bug or a feature. If you feel really strongly that it's a bug, then complain, and I'll consider doing something about it.)

If not enough arguments are found that match the required regular expression, `GetOptions` prints a clear and useful error message to standard error, followed by the usage summary (if you supplied one), and returns 0. The error messages look something like "-foo option must be followed by an integer", or "-foo option must be followed by 3 strings", so it really is enough for your program to `exit 1` without printing any further message.

user-defined patterns

Since the three option types described above are defined by nothing more than a regular expression, it's easy to define your own option types. For instance, let's say you want an option to accept only strings of uppercase letters. You could then call &Getopt::Tabular::AddPatternType as follows:

```
&Getopt::Tabular::AddPatternType
   ("upperstring", "[A-Z]+", "uppercase string")
```

Note that the third parameter is optional and is only supplied to make error messages clearer. For instance, if you now have a scalar-valued option `-zap` of type `upperstring`:

```
["-zap", "upperstring", 1, \$Zap]
```

and if the user gets it wrong and puts an argument that doesn't consist of all uppercase letters after `-zap`, then `GetOptions` complains that "-zap option must be followed by an uppercase string." If you haven't supplied the third argument to `&AddType`, then the error message is the slightly less helpful "-zap option must be followed by an upperstring". Also, you might have to worry about how `GetOptions` pluralizes your description: in this case, it simply adds an "s", which works fine much of the time, but not always. Alternatively, you can supply a two-element list containing the singular and plural forms:

```
&Getopt::Tabular::AddPatternType
   ("upperstring", "[A-Z]+",
      ["string of uppercase letters",
       "strings of uppercase letters"])
```

So, if `-zap` expects three `upperstrings` and the user goofs, then the error message is (in the first example) "-zap option must be followed by 3 uppercase strings" or "-zap option must be followed by three strings of uppercase letters" (in the second example).

Of course, if you don't intend to have vector-valued options of your new type, pluralization hardly matters. Also, while it might seem that this is a nice stab in the direction of multilingual support, the error messages are still hardcoded to English in other places. Maybe in the next version...

Constant-valued option types

boolean

For `boolean` options, `option_data` must be a scalar reference; `num_values` is ignored (you can just set it to `undef` or 0). Booleans are slightly weird in that every `boolean` option implies *two* possible arguments, called the positive and negative alternatives, that are accepted on the command line. The positive alternative (which is what you specify as the option name) results in a true value, while the negative alternative results in false. Most of the time, you can let `GetOptions` pick the negative alternative for you: it just inserts "no" after the option prefix, so `-clobber` becomes `-noclobber`. (More precisely, `GetOptions` tests all option prefixes until one of them matches at the beginning of the option name. It then inserts "no" between this prefix and the rest of the string. So, if you want to support both GNU-style options (like `--clobber`) and one-hyphen options (`-c`), be sure to give `--` *first* when setting the option patterns with `&SetOptionPatterns`. Otherwise, the negative alternative to `--clobber` will be `-no-clobber`, which might not be what you wanted.) Sometimes, though, you want to explicitly specify the negative alternative. This is done by putting both alternatives in the option name, separated by a vertical bar, e.g., `-verbose|-quiet`.

For example, the above two examples might be specified as:

```
["-clobber", "boolean", undef, \$Clobber],
["-verbose|-quiet", "boolean", undef, \$Verbose],...);
```

If `-clobber` is seen on the command line, `$Clobber` is set to 1; if `-noclobber` is seen, then `$Clobber` is set to 0. Likewise, `-verbose` results in `$Verbose` being set to 1, and `-quiet` sets `$Verbose` to 0.

const

For `const` options, put a scalar value (*not* reference) in `num_values`, and a scalar reference in `option_data`. For example:

```
["-foo", "const", "hello there", \$Foo]
```

On encountering `-foo`, `GetOptions` will copy "hello there" to `$Foo`.

arrayconst

For `arrayconst` options, put an array reference (input) (*not* an array value) in `num_values`, and another array reference (output) in `option_data`. For example:

```
["-foo", "arrayconst", [3, 6, 2], \@Foo]
```

On encountering `-foo`, `GetOptions` copies the array (3,6,2) into `@Foo`.

hashconst

For `hashconst` options, put a hash reference (input) (*not* a hash value) in `num_values`, and another hash reference (output) in `option_data`. For example:

```
["-foo", "hashconst", { "Perl"   => "Larry Wall",
                        "C"      => "Dennis Ritchie",
                        "Pascal" => "Niklaus Wirth" },
    \%Inventors]
```

On encountering `-foo`, `GetOptions` copies into `%Inventors` a hash relating various programming languages to the culprits primarily responsible for their invention.

copy

`copy` options act just like `const` options, except when `num_values` is undefined. In that case, the option name itself is copied to the scalar referenced by `option_data`, rather than the `undef` value that would be copied under these circumstances with a `const` option. This is useful when one program accepts options that it simply passes to a subprogram; for instance, if `prog1` calls `prog2`, and `prog2` might be run with the `-foo` option, then `prog1`'s argument table might have this option:

```
["-foo", "copy", undef, \$Foo,
  "run prog2 with the -foo option"]
```

and later on, you would run `prog2` like this:

```
system ("prog2 $Foo ...");
```

That way, if -foo is never seen on prog1's command line, $Foo is untouched and expands to the empty string when building the command line for prog2.

If num_values is anything other than undef, then copy options behave just like constant options.

Other Option Types

call

For call options, option_data must be a reference to a subroutine. The subroutine is called with at least two arguments: a string containing the option that triggered the call (because the same subroutine might be activated by many options), a reference to an array containing all remaining command-line arguments after the option, and other arguments specified using the NUM_VALUES field. (To be used for this purpose, num_values must be an array reference; otherwise, it is ignored.) For example, you might define a subroutine:

```
sub process_foo
{
    my ($opt, $args, $dest) = @_;
    $$dest = shift @$args;
}
```

with a corresponding option table entry:

```
["-foo", "call", [\$Foo], \&process_foo]
```

Then -foo acts like a scalar-valued string option that copies into $Foo. (Well, *almost* . . . read on.)

A subtle point that might be missed from the above code: the value returned by &process_foo *does* matter: if it is false, then GetOptions returns 0 to its caller, indicating failure. To make sure that the user gets a useful error message, you should supply one by calling SetError; doing so prevents GetOptions from printing out a rather mysterious (to the end user, at least) message along the lines of "subroutine call failed". The above example has two subtle problems: first, if the argument following -foo is an empty string, then process_foo will return the empty string—a false value—thus causing GetOptions to fail confusingly. Second, if there no arguments after -foo, then process_foo will return undef—again, a false value, causing GetOptions to fail.

To solve these problems, we have to define the requirements for the -foo option a little more rigorously. Let's say that any string (including the empty string) is valid, but that there must be something there. Then process_foo is written as follows:

```
sub process_foo
{
    my ($opt, $args, $dest) = @_;
    $$dest = shift @$args;
    (defined $$dest) && return 1;
    &Getopt::Tabular::SetError
      ("bad_foo", "$opt option must be followed by a string");
    return 0;
}
```

The `SetError` routine actually takes two arguments: an error class and an error message. This is explained fully in the "Error Handling" section, below. And, if you find yourself writing a lot of routines like this, `SetError` is optionally exported from `Getopt::Tabular`, so you can of course import it into your main package like this:

```
use Getopt::Tabular qw/GetOptions SetError/;
```

eval

An `eval` option specifies a chunk of Perl code to be executed (`eval`'d) when the option is encountered on the command line. The code is supplied (as a string) in the `option_data` field; again, `num_values` is ignored. For example:

```
["-foo", "eval", undef,
 'print "-foo seen on command line\n"']
```

causes `GetOptions` to print out (via an `eval`) the string `-foo seen on the command line\n` when `-foo` is seen. No other action is taken, apart from any you include in the `eval` string. The code is evaluated in the package from which `GetOptions` was called, so you can access variables and subroutines in your program easily. If any error occurs in the `eval`, `GetOptions` complains loudly and returns 0.

Note that the supplied code is always evaluated in a `no strict` environment—that's because Getopt::Tabular is itself `use strict`-compliant, and I didn't want to force strictness on every quick hack that uses the module. (Especially since `eval` options seem to be used mostly in quick hacks.) (Anyone who knows how to fetch the strictness state for another package or scope is welcome to send me hints!) However, the -w state is untouched.

section

`section` options are used to help format the help text. See "Help Text" later in this module for more details.

Error Handling

Generally, handling errors in the argument list is pretty transparent: `GetOptions` (or one of its minions) generates an error message and assigns an error class, `GetOptions` prints the message to the standard error, and it returns 0. You can access the error class and error message using the `GetError` routine:

```
($err_class, $err_msg) = &Getopt::Tabular::GetError ();
```

(Like `SetError`, `GetError` can also be exported from Getopt::Tabular.) The error message is pretty simple—it is an explanation for the end user of what went wrong, which is why `GetOptions` just prints it out and forgets about it. The error class contains further information that might be useful for your program; the current values are:

bad_option

Set when something that looks like an option is found on the command line, but it's either unknown or an ambiguous abbreviation.

bad_value

Set when an option is followed by an invalid argument (i.e., one that doesn't match the regexp for that type), or the wrong number of arguments.

bad_call

> Set when a subroutine called via a `call` option or the code evaluated for an `eval` option returns a false value. The subroutine or `eval`'d code can override this by calling `SetError` itself.

bad_eval

> Set when the code evaluated for an `eval` option has an error in it.

help

> Set when the user requests help.

Note that most of these are errors on the end user's part, such as bad or missing arguments. There are also errors that can be caused by you, the programmer, such as bad or missing values in the option table; these generally result in `GetOptions` croaking so that your program dies immediately with enough information that you can figure out where the mistake is. `bad_eval` is a borderline case; there are conceivably cases where the end user's input can result in bogus code to evaluate, so I grouped this one in the "user errors" class. Finally, asking for help isn't really an error, but the assumption is that you probably shouldn't continue normal processing after printing out the help—so `GetOptions` returns 0 in this case. You can always fetch the error class with `GetError` if you want to treat real errors differently from help requests.

Help Text

One of Getopt::Tabular's niftier features is the ability to generate and format a pile of useful help text from the snippets of help you include in your option table. The best way to illustrate this is with some brief examples. First, it's helpful to know how the user can trigger a help display. This is quite simple: by default, `GetOptions` always has a `-help` option, the presence of which on the command line triggers a help display. (Actually, the help option is really your preferred option prefix plus "help". So, if you like to make GNU-style options take precedence as follows:

```
&Getopt::Tabular::SetOptionPatterns qw|(--)([\w-]+) (-)(\w+)|;
```

then the help option is `--help`. There is only one help option available, and you can set it by calling `&SetHelpOption` (another optional export).

Note that in addition to printing the option help embedded in the option table, `GetOptions` has the ability to print out two other messages: descriptive text (usually a short paragraph giving a rough overview of what your program does, possibly referring the user to the fine manual page), and usage text. These are both supplied by calling `&SetHelp`, e.g.:

```
$Help = <<HELP;
This is the foo program.  It reads one file (specified by -infile),
operates on it some unspecified way (possibly modified by
-threshold), and does absolutely nothing with the results.
(The utility of the -clobber option has yet to be established.)
HELP
$Usage = <<USAGE;
usage: foo [options]
       foo -help to list options
USAGE
&Getopt::Tabular::SetHelp ($Help, $Usage)
```

Note that either of the long help or usage strings may be empty, in which case `GetOptions` simply doesn't print them. If both are supplied, the long help message is printed first, followed by the option help summary, followed by the usage. `GetOp-`

tions inserts enough blank lines to make the output look just fine on its own, so you shouldn't pad either the long help or usage message with blanks. (It looks best if each ends with a newline, though, so setting the help strings with here-documents—as in this example—is the recommended approach.)

As an example of the help display generated by a typical option table, let's take a look at the following:

```
@argtbl = (["-verbose|-quiet", "boolean", 0, \$Verbose,
           "Be noisy [default; opposite is -quiet]"],
          ["-clobber", "boolean", 0, \$Clobber,
           "Overwrite existing files [default: -noclobber]"],
          ["-infile", "string", 1, \$InFile,
           "specify the input file from which to read a large " .
           "and sundry variety of data, to which many " .
           "interesting operations will be applied", "<f>"],
          ["-threshold", "float", 2, \@Threshold
           "only consider values between <v1> and <v2>"
           "<v1> <v2>"]);
```

Assuming you haven't supplied long help or usage strings, when **GetOptions** encounters the help option, it immediately stops parsing arguments and prints out the following option summary:

```
Summary of options:
  -verbose    Be noisy [default; opposite is -quiet]
  -clobber    Overwrite existing files [default:
              -noclobber]
  -infile <f> specify the input file from which to read a
              large and sundry variety of data, to which
              many interesting operations will be applied
  -threshold <v1> <v2>
              only consider values between <v1> and <v2>
```

There are a number of interesting things to note here. First, there are three option table fields that affect the generation of help text: **option**, **help_string**, and **argdesc**. Note how the **argdesc** strings are simply option placeholders, usually used to:

• Indicate how many values are expected to follow an option

• (Possibly) imply what form they take (although that's not really shown here)

• Explain the exact meaning of the values in the help text

argdesc is just a string like the help string; you can put whatever you like in it. What I've shown above is my personal preference (which may well change over time).

Also, I've included hints in the help string about the default values of various options. Ideally, this would be handled by Getopt::Tabular, but it isn't (yet).

The formatting is done as follows: enough room is made on the right-hand side for the longest option name, initially omitting the argument placeholders. Then, if an option has placeholders, and there is room for them between the option and the help string, everything (option, placeholders, help string) is printed together. An example of this is the **-infile** option: here, **-infile <f>** is just small enough to fit in the 12-character column (10 characters because that is the length of the longest option, and two blanks), so the help text is placed right after it on the same line. However, the

-threshold option becomes too long when its argument placeholders are appended to it, so the help text is pushed onto the next line.

In any event, the help string supplied by the caller starts at the same column and is filled to make a nice help paragraph. GetOptions fills to the width of the terminal (or 80 columns if it fails to find the terminal width).

Finally, you can have pseudo-entries of type *section*, which are important for making long option lists readable (and one consequence of using Getopt::Tabular is programs with ridiculously long option lists—not altogether a bad thing, I suppose). For example, this table fragment:

```
@argtbl = (...,
           ["-foo", "integer", 1, \$Foo,
            "set the foo value", "f"],
           ["-enterfoomode", "call", 0, \&enter_foo_mode,
            "enter foo mode"],
           ["Non-foo related options", "section"],
           ["-bar", "string", 2, \@Bar,
            "set the bar strings (which have nothing whatsoever " .
            "to do with foo", "<bar1> <bar2>"],
           ...);
```

results in the following chunk of help text:

```
    -foo f         set the foo value
    -enterfoomode  enter foo mode


 -- Non-foo related options --------------------------------
    -bar b1 b2     set the bar strings (which have nothing
                   whatsoever to do with foo
```

(This example also illustrates a slightly different style of argument placeholder. Take your pick, or invent your own.)

Author

Greg Ward, *greg@bic.mni.mcgill.ca*

Started in July 1995 as ParseArgs.pm, with John Ousterhout's Tk_ParseArgv.c as a loose inspiration. Many, many features added over the ensuing months; documentation written in a mad frenzy April 16–18, 1996. Renamed to Getopt::Tabular, revamped, reorganized, and documentation expanded November 8–11, 1996.

Copyright © 1995–96 Greg Ward. All rights reserved. This program is free software; you can redistribute it and/or modify it under the same terms as Perl itself.

Bugs

The documentation is bigger than the code, and I still haven't covered option patterns or extending the type system (apart from pattern types). Yow!

No support for list-valued options, although you can roll your own with call options. (See the demo program included with the distribution for an example.)

Error messages are hard-coded to English.

IniConf—a module for reading .ini-style configuration files

Description

IniConf provides a way to have readable configuration files outside your Perl script. The configuration can be safely reloaded upon receipt of a signal.

Usage

Get a new IniConf object with the **new** method:

```
$cfg = IniConf->new( -file => "/path/configfile.ini" );
$cfg = new IniConf -file => "/path/configfile.ini";
```

Optional named parameters may be specified after the configuration file name. See **new** in the following "Methods" section.

.ini files consist of a number of sections, each preceded with the section name in square brackets. Parameters are specified in each section as **name=value**. Any spaces around the equals sign are ignored, and the value extends to the end of the line:

```
[section]
Parameter=Value
```

Both the hash mark (#) and the semicolon (;) are comment characters. Lines that begin with either of these characters are ignored. Any amount of whitespace may precede the comment character.

Multiline or multivalued fields may also be defined a la UNIX "here document" syntax:

```
Parameter=<<EOT
value/line 1
value/line 2
EOT
```

You may use any string you want in place of EOT. Note that what follows the << and what appears at the end of the text *must* match exactly, including any trailing whitespace.

See the following "Methods" section for settable options.

Values from the config file are fetched with the **val** method:

```
$value = $cfg->val('Section', 'Parameter');
```

If you want a multiline value field returned as an array, just specify an array as the receiver:

```
@values = $cfg->val('Section', 'Parameter');
```

Methods

new (-file=>*$filename*, [-option=>*value* ...])

Returns a new configuration object (or **undef** if the configuration file has an error). One IniConf object is required per configuration file. The following named parameters are available:

default *section*

Specifies a section used for default values. For example, if you look up the **permissions** parameter in the **users** section, but there is no **users** section, IniConf looks in your default section for a **permissions** value before returning **undef**.

reloadsig signame

> You may specify a signal (such as SIGHUP) that causes the configuration file to be read. This is useful for static daemons where a full restart in order to realize a configuration change would be undesirable. Note that your application must be tolerant of the signal you choose. If a signal handler is already in place before the IniConf object is created, it is called after the configuration file is reread. The signal handler is not re-enabled until after the configuration file has been reread and the previous signal handler returns.

reloadwarn 0|1

> Set -reloadwarn => 1 to enable a warning message (output to STDERR) whenever the config file is reloaded. The reload message is of the form:

```
PID <PID> reloading config file <file> at YYYY.MM.DD HH:MM:SS
```

> See your system documentation for information on valid signals.

nocase 0|1

> Set -nocase => 1 to handle the config file in a case-insensitive manner (case in values is preserved, however). By default, config files are case-sensitive (i.e., a section named Test is not the same as a section named test). Note that there is added overhead for turning off case-sensitivity.

val (*$section*, *$parameter*)

Returns the value of the specified parameter in section *$section*.

setval (*$section*, *$parameter*, *$value*, [*$value2*, ...])

> Sets the value of parameter *$section* in section *$section* to *$value* (or to a set of values). See below for methods to write the new configuration back out to a file.

> You may not set a parameter that didn't exist in the original configuration file. setval returns undef if this is attempted. Otherwise, it returns 1.

ReadConfig

> Forces the config file to be re-read. Also see the -reloadsig option to the new method for a way to connect this method to a signal (such as SIGHUP).

Sections

> Returns an array containing section names in the configuration file. If the nocase option was turned on when the config object was created, the section names are returned in lowercase.

Parameters (*$sectionname*)

Returns an array containing the parameters in the specified section.

GroupMembers (*$group*)

> Returns an array containing the members of the specified *$group*. Groups are specified in the config file as new sections of the form:

```
[GroupName MemberName]
```

> This is useful for building up lists. Note that parameters within a "member" section are referenced normally (i.e., the section name is still "Groupname Membername", including the space).

WriteConfig (*$filename*)

> Writes out a new copy of the configuration file. A temporary file (ending in *.new*) is written out and then renamed to the specified filename. Also see "Bugs" below.

RewriteConfig
> Same as WriteConfig, but specifies that the original configuration file should be rewritten.

Diagnostics

@IniConf::errors
> Contains a list of errors encountered while parsing the configuration file. If the **new** method returns **undef**, check the value of this list to find out what's wrong. This value is reset each time a config file is read.

Bugs

- IniConf won't know if you change the signal handler that it's using for config reloads.

- The signal-handling stuff is almost guaranteed not to work on non-UNIX systems.

- The output from [Re]WriteConfig/OutputConfig might not be as pretty as it be. Comments are tied to whatever was immediately below them.

- No locking is done by [Re]WriteConfig. When writing servers, take care that only the parent ever calls this and consider making your own backup.

- The Windows *.ini* specification (if there is one) probably isn't followed exactly. First and foremost, IniConf is for making easy-to-maintain (and read) configuration files.

Version

Version 0.9 (beta)

Author

Scott Hutton, *shutton@indiana.edu*

Copyright

Copyright © 1996 Scott Hutton. All rights reserved. This program is free software; you can redistribute it and/or modify it under the same terms as Perl itself.

Resources—handling application defaults in Perl

Synopsis

```
use Resources;
$res = new Resources;
$res = new Resources "resfile";
```

Description

Resources are a way to specify information of interest to program or packages.

Applications use resource files to specify and document the values of quantities or attributes of interest.

Resources can be loaded from, or saved to, resource files. Methods are provided to search, modify, and create resources.

Packages use resources to hardwire into their code the default values for their attributes, along with documentation for the attributes themselves.

Packages inherit resources when subclassed, and the resource names are updated dynamically to reflect a class hierarchy.

Methods are provided for interactive resource inspection and editing.

Resource Inheritance

Package attributes are inherited from base and member classes, their names are dynamically updated to reflect the inheritance, and values specified in derived/container classes override those inherited from base/member classes.

More precisely, there a few rules governing the inheritance of resource names and values, and they are explained by way of examples.

As far as resource names, the rules are:

Base class
> If Vehicle has a "speed" property, then it can use a resource named `vehicle.speed` to specify its default value.

Derived class
> If Car *is a* Vehicle, then Car has a `car.speed` resource automagically defined by inheritance from the base class.

Container class
> If Car *has a* member object called Tire, and Tire has a `tire.pressure` resource, then Car inherits a `car.tire.pressure` resource from the member class.

Application class
> All resources of Car objects used by a program named `race` have the prefix `race.` prepended to their names, e.g., `race.car.speed`, `race.car.tire.pressure`, etc.

With regard to assigning values to resources, the rules are:

Specification in a file
> Resources specified in a resource file always override hardcoded resources (with the exception of "hidden" resources, see below).

Inheritance
> Resources defined in a derived class (like Car) override those specified in a base class. Likewise, resources defined in a container class override those specified in the members.

> In the above example, a default value for `car.speed` in Car overrides the value of `vehicle.speed` in any Car object; otherwise, `car.speed` assumes the value of `vehicle.speed`. Same for `car.tire.pressure`.

Resource Files

A resource specification in a (text) resource file is a line of the form:

```
sequence: value
```

There may be any amount of whitespace between the name and the colon, and between the colon and the value.

`sequence` can have four forms:

*   word
*   word.sequence

- word*sequence

- *sequence

A word does not contain whitespace, colons (:), dots (.) or asterisks (*), nor does it start with an underscore (_).

The asterisks in a resource name act as wildcards, matching any sequence of characters.

For cases 3 and 4, the word must be or match the current application class, otherwise the resource specification is silently ignored (this means that an application loads only its own resources and those whose application class is a wildcard from a file).

No distinction is made between uppercase and lowercase letters.

`value` can be:

- An unadorned word or a quoted sequence of whitespace-separated words. Both single (`' '`) and double quotes (`" "`) are allowed, and they must be paired.

- Any *constant* scalar constructor in Perl, including anonymous references to constant arrays or hashes.

- The special words `yes`, `true`, `no`, and `false` (case-insensitive) are treated as Boolean resources and converted to 1 and 0, unless they are quoted.

Examples of valid resource specifications:

```
car*brand : Ferrari            # A word
car.price : 200K               # Another word
car.name : '312 BB'            # A quoted sentence
car*runs*alot : yes            # A Boolean, converted to 1
car*noise*lotsa : 'yes'        # yes, taken verbatim
car.size : [1, [2, 3]]         # An anon array
car.lett : {"P"=>1, "Q"=>[2, 3]} # An anon hash
```

Examples of illegal resource names:

```
car pedal     # Whitespace in the name
.carpedal     # Leading dot in name
car._pedal    # Leading underscore in _dog
carpedal*     # Trailing asterisk
carpedal.     # Trailing dot
```

A resource file may contain comments; anything from a hash (#) character to the end of a line is ignored, unless the hash character appears inside a quoted-value string.

Resource specifications may be split across successive lines, by terminating the split lines with a backslash, as in `cpp(1)`.

The Resources Hash

A non-`my` hash named `%Resources` can be used to specify the default values for the attributes of a package in its source code, along with documentation for the attributes themselves. The documentation itself is "dynamic" (as opposed to the static, pod-like variety) in that it follows a class hierarchy and is suitable for interactive display and editing.

The `%Resources` hash is just a hash of:

```
$Name => [$Value, $Doc]
```

Each hash key $Name is a resource name in the above sequence form. Each hash value is a reference to an anon array [$Value, $Doc], with $Doc being an optional resource documentation.

The resource $Name *cannot* contain wildcard (*) or colon (:) characters, and it cannot start or end with a dot (.). Also, it must *not* be prefixed with the package name (which is automatically prepended by the **merge** method; see below). Names starting with an underscore (_) character are special in that they define "hidden" resources, which may not be specified in resource files or dynamically viewed or edited; they are handy for specifying global parameters when you do not want to use global application-wide variables, and/or you want to take advantage of the inheritance mechanism.

The resource $Value can be any *constant* scalar Perl constructor, including references to arrays and/or hashes of constants (or references thereof). Boolean values must be specified as 1 or 0.

The resource documentation is a just string of any length; it is appropriately broken into lines for visualization purposes. It can also be missing, in which case an inherited documentation is used (if any exists, see the **merge** method below).

The content of a resource hash is registered in a global Resource object using the **merge** method.

Here is an example of defaults specification for a package:

```
package Car;
@ISA = qw( Vehicle );
use vars qw( %Resources );
%Resources = (
    brand    => ["FIAT", "The carmaker"],
    noise    => ["Asthmatic", "Auditory feeling"],
    sucks    => [1, "Is it any good?"],
    nuts     => [ { on => 2, off => [3, 5] }, "Spares"],
    '_ghost' => [0, "Hidden. Mr. Invisible"]
    'tire.flat' => [0],
);
```

The last line overrides a default in member class Tire. The corresponding documentation string is supposedly in the source of that class. The last two hash keys are quoted because of the non-alphanumeric characters in them.

Objects and Resources

The recommended way to use resources with Perl objects is to pass a Resource object to the **new** method of a package. The method itself merges the passed resources with the package defaults, and the passed resource overrides the defaults where needed.

Resource inheritance via subclassing is then easily achieved via the **merge** method, as shown in the previous section onf examples.

Methods in Class Resources
Creation and initialization

new Resources (*$resfile*);

Creates a new resource database, initialized with the defaults for class Resources (see below for a list of them).

If a nonempty filename is specified in `$resfile`, it initializes the object with the content of the so-named resource file. For safe (non-overwriting) loading, see the `load` method below.

If the special filename _RES_NODEFAULTS is specified, the object is created completely empty, with not even the **Resources** class defaults in it.

Returns the new object, or **undef** in case of error.

load(*$resfile*, *$nonew*);

Loads resources from a file named *$resfile* into a resource database.

The *$nonew* argument controls whether loading of resources that have not yet been defined is allowed. If *$nonew* is true, safe loading is performed; attempting to load non-wildcarded resource names that do not match those already present in the database causes an error. This can be useful if you want to make sure that only predefined resources (for which you presumably have hardwired defaults) are loaded. It can be a safety net against typos in a resource file.

Use is made of Safe::reval to parse values specified through Perl constructors (only constants, anonymous hashes and anonymous arrays are allowed).

Returns 1 if ok, 0 if error.

merge(*$class*, *@memberclasses*);

Merges the %Resources hash of the package defining *$class* with those of its *@memberclasses*, writing the result in the resource database.

The merging reflects the resource inheritance explained above: the %Resources of all base classes and member classes of *$class* are inherited along the way. Eventually, all these resources have their names prefixed with the name of the package in which *$class* is defined (lowercased and stripped of all foo::bar:: prefixes), and with the application class as well.

In the above example, the defaults of a Car object are renamed, after merging. as:

```
car.brand, car.noise, ...,
car.tire.flat
```

and for a Civic object, where Civic is a (i.e. **ISA**) Car, they are translated instead as:

```
civic.brand, civic.noise, ...,
civic.tire.flat
```

Finally, the application name ($0, a.k.a. $PROGRAM_NAME in English) is prepended to all resource names, so, if the above Civic package is used by a Perl script named *ilove.pl*, the final names after merging are:

```
ilove.civic.brand, ilove.civic.noise, ...,
ilove.civic.tire.flat
```

The new names are the ones to use when accessing these resources by name.

The resource values are inherited according to the rules previously indicated, with resource files having priority over hardcoded defaults and derived or container classes over base or member classes.

Returns 1 if for success, otherwise 0.

Looking up resources

The values and documentation strings stored in a Resource object can be accessed by specifying their names in three basic ways:

directly ("byname" methods)

As in `my.nice.cozy.couch.`

by a pattern ("bypattern" methods)

As in `m??nice.*` .

hierarchically ("byclass" methods)

If class Nice *is a* Cozy, then asking for "couch" in package Cozy gets you the value/doc of `my.couch.` If, instead, Nice *has a* Cozy member, then the method gets you `my.nice.cozy.couch.` This behavior is essential for the proper initialization of subclassed and member packages, as explained in detail below.

It is also possible to retrieve the entire contents of a resource database (`names` and `each` methods)

Note that all the resource lookup methods return named (non-wildcarded) resources only. Wildcarded resources (i.e., those specified in resource files and whose names contain one or more asterisks (`*`)) are best thought of as placeholders, to be used when the value of an actual named resource is set.

For example, a line in a resource file like:

```
*background : yellow
```

fixes to yellow the color of all resources whose name ends with "background". However, your actual packages will never worry about that, unless they really need a background. In that case, they either have a "background" resource in their defaults hash, or they subclass a package that has one.

`valbyname($name);`

Retrieves the value of a named resource from a Resource database. The $name argument is a string containing a resource name with no wildcards.

Returns the undefined value if no such resource is defined.

`docbyname($name);`

Retrieves the documentation string of a named resource from a Resource database. The $name argument is a string containing a resource name with no wildcards.

Returns the undefined value if no such resource is defined.

`bypattern($pattern);`

Retrieves the full names, values, and documentation strings of all the named (non-wildcarded) resources whose name matches the given $pattern. The pattern itself is string containing a Perl regular expression, *not* enclosed in slashes.

Returns a new Resource object containing only the matching resources, or the undefined value if no matches are found.

`valbypattern($pattern);`

Retrieves the full names and values of all named (non-wildcarded) resources whose name matches the given pattern.

Returns a new Resource object containing only names and values of the matching resources (i.e., with undefined documentation strings), or the undefined value if no matches are found.

docbypattern(*$pattern*);

Retrieves the full names and documentation strings of all named (non-wildcarded) resources whose name matches the given pattern.

Returns a new Resource object containing only names and documentation of the matching resources (i.e. with undefined resource values), or the undefined value if no matches are found.

byclass(*$object*, *$suffix*);

To properly initialize the attributes of a package via resources, we need a way to know whether the package defaults (contained in its %Resources hash) have been overridden by a derived or container class. For example, to set a field like $dog->{Weight} in a Dog object, we must know if this $dog is being subclassed by Poodle or Bulldog, or if it is a member of Family, since all these other classes might override whatever "weight" default is defined in the %Resources hash of *Dog.pm*.

This information must of course be gathered at runtime: if you tried to name explicitly a resource like family.dog.weight inside *Dog.pm* all the OOP crowd would start booing at you. Your object would no longer be reusable, being explicitly tied to a particular container class. After all, we do use objects mainly because we want to easily reuse code.

Enter the "by class" resource-lookup methods: byclass, valbyclass, and docbyclass.

Given an *$object* and a resource *$suffix* (i.e., a resource name stripped of all container and derived class prefixes), the byclass method returns a three-element list containing the name/value/documentation of that resource in *$object*. The returned name is fully qualified with all derived/container classes, up to the application class.

For example, in a program called bark, the statements:

```
$dog = new Dog ($res); # $res is a Resources database
($name,$value,$doc) = $res->byclass($dog, "weight");
```

set $name, $value, and $doc equal to those of the bark.poodle.weight resource if this Dog is subclassed by Poodle, and to those of bark.family.dog.weight, if it is a member of Family instead.

The passed name suffix must not contain wildcards or dots.

Be careful not to confuse the "byclass" with the "byname" and "bypattern" retrieval methods: they are used for two radically different goals. See the previous section on Examples for more information.

Returns the empty list if no resources are found for the given suffix, or if the suffix is incorrect.

namebyclass(*$obj*, *$suffix*);

Like the byclass method above, but returns just the resource name (i.e., the suffix with all the subclasses prepended).

valbyclass(*$obj*, *$suffix*);

Like the byclass method above, but returns just the resource value.

docbyclass(*$suffix*);
> Like the byclass method above, but returns just the resource documentation.

each;
> Returns the next name/[value,doc] pair of the named (non-wildcarded) resources in a resource database, exactly as the each Perl routine.

names;
> Returns a list of the names of all named (non-wildcarded) resources in a resource database, or undef if the database is empty.

Assigning and Removing Resources

put(*$name*, *$value*, *$doc*);
> Writes the value and documentation of a resource in the database. It is possible to specify an empty documentation string, but name and value must be defined.

> Wildcards (* characters) are allowed in the *$name*, but the *$doc* is ignored in this case (documentation is intended for single resources, not for sets of them).

> The value is written unchanged unless the resource database already contains a wildcarded resource whose name includes *$name* (foo*bar includes foo.bar, foo.baz.bar, etc.). In that case, the value of the wildcarded resource overrides the passed *$value*.

> Returns 1 if ok, 0 if error.

removebyname(*$name*);
> Removes the named (non-wildcarded) resources from the database.

> Returns 1 if okay, 0 if the resource is not found in the database.

removebypattern(*$pattern*);
> Removes from the database all resources (both named *and* wildcarded) whose name matches *$pattern*. An exactly matching name must be specified for wildcarded resources (foo*bar to remove foo*bar).

> Returns the number of removed resources.

Viewing and Editing Resources

view;
> Outputs the current content of a Resource object by piping to a pager program.

> The environment variable $ENV{RESPAGER}, the resources.pager resource, and the environment variable $ENV{PAGER} are looked up, in that order, to find the pager program. Defaults to */bin/more*.

> The output format is the same as a resource file, with the resource names alphabetically ordered, and the resource documentation strings written as comments.

> Returns 1 if okay, 0 if error.

edit(*$nonew*);
> Provides dynamic resource editing of a Resource object via an external editor program. Only resource names and values can be edited (anyway, what would be the point of editing a resource comment on the fly?).

The environment variables `$ENV{RESEDITOR}` and the `resources.editor` resource are looked up, in that order, to find the editor program. Defaults to */bin/vi* .

The editor buffer is initialized in the same format as a resource file, with the resource names alphabetically ordered and the resource documentation strings written as comments. The temporary file specified by the `resources.tmpfil` resource is used to initialize the editor, or */tmp/resedit<pid>* if that resource is undefined.

When the editor has been exited (after the buffer has been saved) the method attempts to reload the edited resources. If an error is found, the initial object is left unchanged, a warning with the first offending line in the file is printed, and the method returns with `undef`. Controlled resource loading is obtained by specifying a true value for the *$nonew* argument (see `load`).

If the loading is successful, a new (edited) resource object is returned, which can be assigned to the old one for replacement.

After a successful edit, the value of the resource `resources.updates` (which is always defined as 0 whenever a new resource is created) is increased by one. This is meant to notify program and/or the packages of the resource change, so they can proceed accordingly if they wish.

Miscellaneous methods

`write($filename);`

>   Outputs all resources of a resource database into a resource file (over-writing it).

>   The resource documentation strings are normally written as comments, so the file itself is immediately available for resource loading. However, if the Boolean resource `resources.writepod` is true, then the (non-wildcarded) resources are output in pod format for your documentation pleasure.

>   As usual in Perl, the filename can also be of the form *|command*, in which case the output is piped into *command.*

>   For resources whose value is a reference to an anonymous array or hash, it produces the appropriate constant Perl constructor by reverse parsing. The parser itself is available as a separate method named _ `parse` (see package source for documentation).

>   Returns 1 if okay, 0 if error.

Resources of Resources

As you may have guessed at this point, the default configuration of this package itself is defined by resources. The resource class is, of course, `resources` (meaning that all the names have a leading `resources.`).

To prevent chaos, however, these resources cannot be subclassed. This should not be a problem in normal applications, since the Resource package itself is not meant to be subclassed, but to help building a hierarchy of classes instead.

The currently recognized resources and their default values are:

`resources.appclass : "$PROGRAM_NAME"`

>   The application name of this Resource object

resources.editor : /bin/vi
>   Resource editor

resources.mergeclass : true
>   Boolean. If true, merge with class inheritance.

resources.pager : /bin/more
>   Resource pager

resources.separator : ':'
>   Pattern separating names from values in resource files

resources.tmpfil : ''
>   Temporary editor file

resources.updates : 0
>   Number of resource updates

resources.verbosity : 1
>   If true, print warnings

resources.viewcols : 78
>   Width of view/edit window

resources.writepod : false
>   Boolean. True if the write method should output in pod format.

Examples

Here is an example of resource inheritance. HotDog is a subclass of Food and has a member Wiener, which happens to be a Food as well.

The subclass has defaults for two resources defined by the base classes (edible and wiener.mustard), and their values override the base-class defaults.

Remember that after merging all resources, names are prefixed with the current class name.

```
use Resources;
package Food;
%Resources = (
  edible => [1, "Can it be eaten."],
  tasty  => ["sort_of",  "D'ya like it?"],
);

sub new {
   my ($type, $res) = @_;
   $res || $res =  new Resources || (return undef);
   $res->merge($type) || die ("can't merge defaults");

   my $food= bless({}, type);
   $food->{Edible} = $res->valbyclass("edible");
   $food->{Tasty}  = $res->valbyclass("tasty");
   # Use valbyclass so a subclass like HotDog can change this
   # by its defaults.
}

# A Food method to say if it can be eaten.
sub eatok {
```

```
        my $food=shift;
        return $food->{Edible};
    }
package Wiener;
@ISA = qw( Food );
%Resources = (
        tasty => ["very"], # this overrides a base class default
        mustard => ["plenty", "How much yellow stuff?"],
);
# Nothing else: all methods are inherited from the base class.
package HotDog;
@ISA = qw( Food );
%Resources = (
        edible     => [0],
        tasty      => ["yuck!"],
        'wiener.mustard' => ["none"], # To override member class
                                      # default.
);
sub new {
    my ($type, $res) = @_;

    $res || $res =  new Resources || (return undef);
    $res->merge($type) || die ("can't merge defaults");

    my $hd = bless(new Food ($res), $type);
    $hd->{Wien} = new Wiener ($res);
    return $hd;
}
# All tastes of hotdog
sub tastes {
    my $hd = shift;
    return ($hd->{Tasty}, $hd->{Wien}->{Tasty});
}

package main;
# Whatever
#
$res = new Resources("AppDefltFile") || die;
$snack = new HotDog($res);
$gnam = $snack->eat();  # hotdog.edible overridees food.edible,
                        # so here $gnam equals 0
@slurp = $snack->tastes()    # @slurp equals ("yuck!", "very")
                             # the resources were overridden
                             # by a subclass of HotDog , or
                             # differently specified in
                             # "AppDefltFile"
```

See Also

Safe(3)

Bugs

The underlying idea is to use a centralized resource database for the whole application. This ensures uniformity of behavior across kin objects, but allows special characterizations only at the cost of subclassing.

Author

Francesco Callari (*franco@cim.mcgill.ca*), Artificial Perception Laboratory, Center for Intelligent Machines, McGill University.

On the Web, go to *http://www.cim.mcgill.ca/~franco/Home.html*.

Copyright

Copyright © 1996 Francesco Callari, McGill University

Permission to use, copy, modify, and distribute this software and its documentation for any purpose without fee is hereby granted without fee, provided that the above copyright notice appear in all copies and that both that copyright notice and this permission notice appear in supporting documentation, and that the name of McGill not be used in advertising or publicity pertaining to distribution of the software without specific, written prior permission. McGill makes no representations about the suitability of this software for any purpose. It is provided "as is" without express or implied warranty.

MCGILL DISCLAIMS ALL WARRANTIES WITH REGARD TO THIS SOFTWARE, INCLUDING ALL IMPLIED WARRANTIES OF MERCHANTABILITY AND FITNESS. IN NO EVENT SHALL MCGILL BE LIABLE FOR ANY SPECIAL, INDIRECT OR CONSEQUENTIAL DAMAGES OR ANY DAMAGES WHATSOEVER RESULTING FROM LOSS OF USE, DATA OR PROFITS, WHETHER IN AN ACTION OF CONTRACT, NEGLIGENCE OR OTHER TORTIOUS ACTION, ARISING OUT OF OR IN CONNECTION WITH THE USE OR PERFORMANCE OF THIS SOFTWARE.

13

Internationalization and Locale

In this section, modules to aid in internationalization are documented.

I18N::Collate—compare 8-bit scalar data according to the current locale

Synopsis

```
use I18N::Collate;

setlocale(LC_COLLATE, $locale);          # uses POSIX::setlocale
$s1 = new I18N::Collate "scalar_data_1";
$s2 = new I18N::Collate "scalar_data_2";
```

Description

This module provides you with objects that can be collated (ordered) according to your national character set, provided that Perl's POSIX module and the POSIX setlocale(3) and **strxfrm**(3) functions are available on your system. $locale in the setlocale() invocation shown above must be an argument acceptable to setlocale(3) on your system. See the setlocale(3) manpage for further information. Available locales depend upon your operating system.

Here is an example of collation within the standard C locale:

```
use I18N::Collate;

setlocale(LC_COLLATE, 'C');
$s1 = new I18N::Collate "Hello";
$s2 = new I18N::Collate "Goodbye";
# following line prints "Hello comes before Goodbye"
print "$$s1 comes before $$s2" if $s2 le $s1;
```

The objects returned by the **new()** method are references. You can get at their values by dereferencing them—for example, $$s1 and $$s2. However, Perl's built-in comparison operators are overloaded by I18N::Collate, so that they operate on the objects returned by **new()** without the necessity of dereference. The print line above dereferences $s1 and

$s2 to access their values directly, but does not dereference the variables passed to the le operator. The comparison operators you can use in this way are the following:

```
<    <=   >    >=   ==   !=   <=>
lt   le   gt   ge   eq   ne   cmp
```

I18N::Collate uses POSIX::setlocale() and POSIX::strxfrm() to perform the collation. Unlike strxfrm(), however, I18N::Collate handles embedded NULL characters gracefully.

To determine which locales are available with your operating system, check whether the command:

```
locale -a
```

lists them. You can also check the locale(5) or nlsinfo manpages, or look at the file-names within one of these directories (or their subdirectories): */usr/lib/nls, /usr/share/lib/locale*, or */etc/locale*. Not all locales that your vendor supports are necessarily installed. Please consult your operating system's documentation and possibly your local system administrator.

Locale::Country—ISO two-letter codes for country identification (ISO 3166)

Synopsis

```
use Locale::Country;

$country = code2country('jp');        # $country gets 'Japan'
$code    = country2code('Norway');    # $code gets 'no'

@codes   = all_country_codes();
@names   = all_country_names();
```

Description

The Locale::Country module provides access to the ISO two-letter codes for identifying countries, as defined in ISO 3166. You can either access the codes via the *conversion routines* (described below), or with the two functions that return lists of all country codes or all country names.

Conversion Routines

There are two conversion routines: **code2country()** and **country2code()**.

code2country()
> This function takes a two-letter country code and returns a string that contains the name of the country. If the code is not a valid country code, as defined by ISO 3166, then undef is returned:
> ```
> $country = code2country('fi');
> ```

country2code()
> This function takes a country name and returns the corresponding two-letter country code, if one exists. If the argument cannot be identified as a country name, then undef is returned:
> ```
> $code = country2code('Norway');
> ```

The case of the country name is not important. See the section "Known Bugs and Limitations" below.

Query Routines

There are two functions that can be used to obtain a list of all codes or all country names:

`all_country_codes()`

> Returns a list of all two-letter country codes. The codes are guaranteed to be all lowercase, in no particular order.

`all_country_names()`

> Returns a list of all country names for which there is a corresponding two-letter country code. The names are capitalized and returned in no particular order.

Example

The following example illustrates use of the **code2country()** function. The user is prompted for a country code and is then told the corresponding country name:

```
$| = 1;   # turn off buffering

print "Enter country code: ";
chop($code = <STDIN>);
$country = code2country($code);
if (defined $country)
{
    print "$code = $country\n";
}
else
{
    print "'$code' is not a valid country code!\n";
}
```

Domain Names

Most top-level domain names are based on these codes, but there are certain names that don't map to a code. If you are using this module to identify the country from the hostname, your best bet is to preprocess the country code.

For example, edu, com, gov, and friends map to us; uk maps to gb. Any others?

Known Bugs and Limitations

* When using country2code(), the country name currently must appear exactly as it does in the source of the module. For example:

  ```
  country2code('United States')
  ```

  returns us, as expected. But the following all return undef:

  ```
  country2code('United States of America')
  country2code('U.S.A.')
  country2code('Great Britain')
  ```

  If there's a need for it, a future version could have variants for country names.

* In the current implementation, all data is read in when the module is loaded and then held in memory. A lazy implementation would be more memory-friendly.

Author

Neil Bowers, *neilb@cre.canon.co.uk*

Copyright

Copyright © 1997 Canon Research Centre Europe (CRE)

This module is free software; you can redistribute it and/or modify it under the same terms as Perl itself.

See Also

Locale::Language
> The ISO two-letter codes for the identification of language (ISO 639).

ISO 3166
> The ISO standard that defines these codes.

ftp://info.ripe.net/iso3166-countrycodes
> An online file with the two-letter codes, three-letter codes, and country code numbers. Maintained by the RIPE Network Coordination Centre.

Locale::Language—ISO two-letter codes for language identification (ISO 639)

Synopsis

```
use Locale::Language;

$lang = code2language('en');        # $lang gets 'English'
$code = language2code('French');    # $code gets 'fr'

@codes   = all_language_codes();
@names   = all_language_names();
```

Description

The Locale::Language module provides access to the ISO two-letter codes for identifying languages, as defined in ISO 639. You can either access the codes via the *conversion routines* (described below), or with the two functions that return lists of all language codes or all language names.

Conversion Routines

There are two conversion routines: code2language() and language2code().

code2language()
> This function takes a two-letter language code and returns a string that contains the name of the language. If the code is not a valid language code, as defined by ISO 639, then undef is returned.

```
$lang = code2language($code);
```

language2code()

This function takes a language name and returns the corresponding two-letter language code, if one exists. If the argument cannot be identified as a language name, then **undef** is returned.

```
$code = language2code('French');
```

The case of the language name is not important. See the section "Known Bugs and Limitations" below.

Query Routines

There are two functions that can be used to obtain a list of all language codes or all language names:

all_language_codes()

Returns a list of all two-letter language codes. The codes are guaranteed to be all lowercase and in no particular order.

all_language_names()

Returns a list of all language names for which there is a corresponding two-letter language code. The names are capitalized and are not returned in any particular order.

Example

The following example illustrates the use of the **code2language()** function. The user is prompted for a language code and is then told the corresponding language name:

```
$| = 1;     # turn off buffering

print "Enter language code: ";
chop($code = <STDIN>);
$lang = code2language($code);
if (defined $lang)
{
    print "$code = $lang\n";
}
else
{
    print "'$code' is not a valid language code!\n";
}
```

Known Bugs and Limitations

In the current implementation, all data is read in when the module is loaded and then held in memory. A lazy implementation would be more memory friendly.

Author

Neil Bowers, *neilb@cre.canon.co.uk*

Copyright

Copyright © 1997 Canon Research Centre Europe (CRE)

This module is free software; you can redistribute it and/or modify it under the same terms as Perl itself.

See Also

Locale::Country

The ISO two-letter codes for the identification of country (ISO 3166).

ISO 639:1988 (E/F)

The code for the representation of names of languages.

14

Authentication, Security, andEncryption

This section documents encryption algorithms and security. Note that PGP is not included here; for PGP modules please check the nearest CPAN mirror. To locate the CPAN mirror nearest you, go to *http://www.perl.com/CPAN* (note the absence of the trailing slash).

DES—Perl interface to DES block cipher

Synopsis

```
use Crypt::DES;
```

Description

This Perl extension is an implementation of the DES block-cipher algorithm. The module implements the Crypt::BlockCipher interface, which has the following methods.

Methods

blocksize
> Returns the size (in bytes) of the block cipher.

keysize
> Returns the size (in bytes) of the key.

new
> Creates a new DES BlockCipher object, using *$key*, where *$key* is a key of **keysize()** bytes.
>
>  ```
>  my $cipher = new DES $key;
>  ```

encrypt
> This function encrypts *$plaintext* and returns $ciphertext where *$plaintext* and $ciphertext should be **blocksize()** bytes.
>
>  ```
>  my $cipher = new DES $key;
>  my $ciphertext = $cipher->encrypt($plaintext);
>  ```

decrypt

This function decrypts *$ciphertext* and returns the *$plaintext* where *$plaintext* and *$ciphertext* should be `blocksize()` bytes.

```
my $cipher = new DES $key;
my $plaintext = $cipher->decrypt($ciphertext);
```

Example

```
my $key = pack("H16", "0123456789ABCDEF");
my $cipher = new DES $key;
my $ciphertext = $cipher->encrypt("plaintex");   # NB - 8 bytes
print unpack("H16", $ciphertext), "\n";
```

See Also

Crypt::IDEA

Author

Bruce Schneier, *Applied Cryptography*, 1995, Second Edition, John Wiley & Sons, Inc.

Copyright

The implementation of the DES algorithm was developed by, and is copyright of, Eric Young, *eay@mincom.oz.au*. Other parts of this Perl extension are copyright of Systemics Ltd. (*http://www.systemics.com/*).

MD5 — Perl interface to the RSA Data Security Inc. MD5 Message-Digest Algorithm

Synopsis

```
use MD5;

$context = new MD5;
$context->reset();

$context->add(LIST);
$context->addfile(HANDLE);

$digest = $context->digest();
$string = $context->hexdigest();
$digest = MD5->hash(SCALAR);
$string = MD5->hexhash(SCALAR);
```

Description

The MD5 module allows you to use the RSA Data Security Inc. MD5 Message Digest algorithm from within Perl programs.

A new MD5 context object is created with the **new** operation. Multiple simultaneous digest contexts can be maintained, if desired. The context is updated with the **add** operation which adds the strings contained in the LIST parameter. Note, however, that add('foo', 'bar'), add('foo') followed by add('bar'), and add('foobar') should all give the same result.

The final message digest value is returned by the **digest** operation as a 16-byte binary string. This operation delivers the result of **add** operations since the last **new** or **reset** operation. Note that the **digest** operation is effectively a destructive, read-once operation.

Once `digest` has been performed, the context must be `reset` before being used to calculate another digest value.

Several convenience functions are also provided. The `addfile` operation takes an open filehandle and reads it to end-of-file in 1024-byte blocks, adding the contents to the context. The filehandle can either be specified by name or passed as a type-glob reference, as shown in the examples below. The `hexdigest` operation calls `digest` and returns the result as a printable string of hexadecimal digits. This is exactly the same operation as that performed by the `unpack` operation in the examples below.

The `hash` operation can act as either a static member function (i.e., you invoke it on the MD5 class as in the synopsis above) or as a normal virtual function. In both cases, it performs the complete MD5 cycle (`reset`, `add`, `digest`) on the supplied scalar value. This is convenient for handling small quantities of data. When invoked on the class, a temporary context is created. When invoked through an already-created context object, that context is used. The latter form is slightly more efficient. The `hexhash` operation is analogous to `hexdigest`.

Examples

```
use MD5;

$md5 = new MD5;
$md5->add('foo', 'bar');
$md5->add('baz');
$digest = $md5->digest();

print("Digest is " . unpack("H*", $digest) . "\n");
```

The above example prints out the message:

```
Digest is 6df23dc03f9b54cc38a0fc1483df6e21
```

provided that the implementation is working correctly.

Remembering the Perl motto ("There's more than one way to do it"), the following should all give the same result:

```
use MD5;
$md5 = new MD5;
die "Can't open /etc/passwd ($!)\n" unless open(P, "/etc/passwd");
seek(P, 0, 0);
$md5->reset;
$md5->addfile(P);
$d = $md5->hexdigest;
print "addfile (handle name) = $d\n";
seek(P, 0, 0);
$md5->reset;
$md5->addfile(\*P);
$d = $md5->hexdigest;
print "addfile (type-glob reference) = $d\n";
seek(P, 0, 0);
$md5->reset;
while (<P>)
{
    $md5->add($_);
}
$d = $md5->hexdigest;
```

```
print "Line at a time = $d\n";
seek(P, 0, 0);
$md5->reset;
$md5->add(<P>);
$d = $md5->hexdigest;
print "All lines at once = $d\n";
seek(P, 0, 0);
$md5->reset;
while (read(P, $data, (rand % 128) + 1))
{
    $md5->add($data);
}
$d = $md5->hexdigest;
print "Random chunks = $d\n";
seek(P, 0, 0);
$md5->reset;
undef $/;
$data = <P>;
$d = $md5->hexhash($data);
print "Single string = $d\n";
close(P);
```

Author

Neil Winton, *winton_neil@jpmorgan.com*

Copyright

The MD5 extension may be redistributed under the same terms as Perl. The MD5 algorithm is defined in RFC 1321. The basic C code implementing the algorithm is derived from that in the RFC and is covered by the following copyright:

This copyright does not prohibit distribution of any version of Perl containing this extension under the terms of the GNU or Artistic licenses.

See Also

perl(1)

SHA—Perl interface to the NIST Secure Hash Algorithm

Synopsis

```
use SHA;

$context = new SHA;
$context->reset();

$context->add(LIST);
$context->addfile(HANDLE);

$digest = $context->digest();
$string = $context->hexdigest();
$digest = $context->hash($string);
$string = $context->hexhash($string);
```

Description

The SHA module allows you to use the NIST SHA message digest algorithm from within Perl programs.

A new SHA context object is created with the **new** operation. Multiple simultaneous digest contexts can be maintained, if desired. The context is updated with the **add** operation, which adds the strings contained in the LIST parameter. Adding two strings separately is equivalent to adding their concatenation: add('foo', 'bar') produces the same effect as add('foo'), add('bar'), which in turn produces the same effect as add('foobar').

The final message-digest value is returned by the **digest** operation as a 16-byte binary string. This operation delivers the result of operations since the last **new** or **reset** operation. Once the operation has been performed, the context must be **reset** before being used to calculate another digest value.

Several convenience functions are also provided. The **addfile** operation takes an open filehandle and reads it until end-of-file in 8192-byte blocks, adding the contents to the context. The **hexdigest** operation calls **digest** and returns the result as a printable string of hexdecimal digits in eight-digit groups. The **hash** operation performs the complete series of steps: reset, add, and digest on the supplied scalar value and returns the result as a 16-byte binary string. The **hexhash** operation does the same thing, but returns the result in the format of the **hexdigest** operation.

Example and Validation

```
use SHA 1.1;
$sha = new SHA;
print "EXPECT:   0164b8a9 14cd2a5e 74c4f7ff 082c4d97 f1edf880\n";
$sha->reset();
$sha->add("abc");
print "RESULT 1: " . $sha->hexdigest() . "\n";
$sha->reset();
$sha->add("a", "bc");
print "RESULT 2: " . $sha->hexdigest() . "\n";
$sha->reset();
$sha->add("ab", "c");
print "RESULT 3: " . $sha->hexdigest() . "\n";
$sha->reset();
```

```
$sha->add("a", "b", "c");
print "RESULT 4: " . $sha->hexdigest() . "\n";
$sha->reset();
$sha->add("ab");
$sha->add("c");
print "RESULT 5: " . $sha->hexdigest() . "\n";
$sha->reset();
$sha->add("a");
$sha->add("bc");
print "RESULT 6: " . $sha->hexdigest() . "\n";
$sha->reset();
$sha->add("a");
$sha->add("b");
$sha->add("c");
print "RESULT 7: " . $sha->hexdigest() . "\n";
print "RESULT 8: " . $sha->hexhash("abc") . "\n";
$sha->reset();
$sha->add("ab", "c");
print "result a: " . unpack("H*", ($sha->digest())) . "\n";
print "result b: " . unpack("H*", ($sha->hash("abc"))) . "\n";
```

The above example will produce the output:

```
EXPECT:    0164b8a9 14cd2a5e 74c4f7ff 082c4d97 f1edf880
RESULT 1:  0164b8a9 14cd2a5e 74c4f7ff 082c4d97 f1edf880
RESULT 2:  0164b8a9 14cd2a5e 74c4f7ff 082c4d97 f1edf880
RESULT 3:  0164b8a9 14cd2a5e 74c4f7ff 082c4d97 f1edf880
RESULT 4:  0164b8a9 14cd2a5e 74c4f7ff 082c4d97 f1edf880
RESULT 5:  0164b8a9 14cd2a5e 74c4f7ff 082c4d97 f1edf880
RESULT 6:  0164b8a9 14cd2a5e 74c4f7ff 082c4d97 f1edf880
RESULT 7:  0164b8a9 14cd2a5e 74c4f7ff 082c4d97 f1edf880
RESULT 8:  0164b8a9 14cd2a5e 74c4f7ff 082c4d97 f1edf880
result a:  0164b8a914cd2a5e74c4f7ff082c4d97f1edf880
result b:  0164b8a914cd2a5e74c4f7ff082c4d97f1edf880
```

provided that the implementation is working correctly.

Author

The SHA interface was written by Uwe Hollerbach (*ub@alumni.caltech.edu*) shamelessly stealing from the MD5 interface written by Neil Winton (*winton_neil@jpmorgan.com*).

Copyright

The SHA extension may be redistributed under the same terms as Perl. The SHA code is in the public domain. It was heavily modified by Uwe Hollerbach following the implementation by Peter Gutmann.

15

World Wide Web, HTML, HTTP, CGI, and MIME

The bulk of Perl5 modules are concentrated in this section. Included are Apache server interfaces and HTTP protocol utilities, as well as tools for URL encoding, HTML manipulation, MIME mailing, Web searches, and of course CGI programming. Note that the fundamental networking modules are not contained in this chapter, but rather in Chapter 5, *Networking, Devices, and InterProcess Communication.*

Apache::AccessLimitNum—limit user access by number of requests

Synopsis

```
#server config or .htaccess
#use any authentication module
AuthName SomeRealm
Auth[DBM]UserFile /path/to/password/file

PerlAccessHandler Apache::AccessLimitNum
PerlSetVar        AccessLimitNum  100
PerlSetVar        AccessLimitFile /path/to/limit/file
<Limit GET>
require valid-user #or some such
</Limit>
```

Description

Decides if an authenticated user has exceeded an access limit for the requested realm, if so, forbids access.

AccessLimitFile is a **dbm** file consisting of **username = number** value pairs. This file must be writable by the **httpd** server process.

Author

Doug MacEachern, *dougm@osf.org*

See Also

Apache(3)

Apache::AuthenDBI—authentication via Perl's DBI

Synopsis

```
# Configuration in httpd.conf or srm.conf
PerlModule Apache::AuthenDBI
# Authentication in .htaccess
AuthName DBI
AuthType Basic
#authenticate via DBI
PerlAuthenHandler Apache::AuthenDBI
PerlSetVar AuthDBIDB      dbname
PerlSetVar AuthDBIUser    username
PerlSetVar AuthDBIAuth    auth
PerlSetVar AuthDBIDriver driver
#DBI->connect(DB, User, Auth, Driver)
PerlSetVar AuthDBIUserTable table
PerlSetVar AuthDBINameField user
PerlSetVar AuthDBIPasswordField password
#SELECT PasswordField from UserTable WHERE NameField='$user_sent'
<Limit GET POST>
require valid-user
</Limit>
```

The `AuthType` is limited to Basic. The `require` directive is limited to "valid-user" and "user xxx" (no group support).

Description

This module allows the Apache server to authenticate against a database. It should be used together with Apache::DBI to gain the benefit of a persistent database connection. Remember that the authentication accesses the database once for every request! Make sure that in *httpd.conf* or *srm.conf* the module Apache::DBI comes first:

```
PerlModule Apache::DBI
PerlModule Apache::AuthenDBI
```

The authentication module makes use of persistent connections only if the appropriate module Apache::DBI is already loaded.

The database access uses Perl's DBI. For supported DBI drivers see *http://www.hermetica.com/technologia/DBI/*.

Authors

mod_perl by Doug MacEachern, *dougm@osf.org*
DBI by Tim Bunce, *Tim.Bunce@ig.co.uk*
Apache::AuthenDBI by Edmund Mergl, *E.Mergl@bawue.de*

See Also

Apache(3), DBI(3)

Apache::AuthzAge — authorize based on age

Synopsis

```
#access control directives
#use standard authentication modules
AuthName SomeRealm
Auth[DBM]UserFile /path/to/password/file

PerlAuthzHandler Apache::AuthzAge
PerlSetVar       UserAgeFile  /path/to/dbm_file
#user must be at least 21
<Limit GET>
require age 21
</Limit>
```

Description

Decide if an authenticated user is authorized to complete a request based on age.

UserAgeFile is a **dbm** file consisting of **username** = **age** value pairs.

Author

Doug MacEachern, *dougm@osf.org*

See Also

Apache(3)

Apache::Constants — constants defined in httpd.h

Synopsis

```
use Apache::Constants;
use Apache::Constants ':common'; #OK,DECLINED,etc.
```

Description

Server constants used by Apache modules are defined in *httpd.h*. This module gives Perl access to those constants.

Authors

Gisle Aas, *aas@sn.no*; Doug MacEachern, *dougm@osf.org*

Apache::DCELogin — obtain a DCE Login context

Synopsis

```
#access.conf or some such
AuthType Basic
AuthName "DCE-Perl Login"
PerlAuthenHandler Apache::DCELogin
PerlLogHandler    Apache::DCELogin::purge
```

Description

Apache::DCELogin obtains a DCE login context with the username and password obtained via the Basic authentication challenge.

Author

Doug MacEachern, *dougm@osf.org*

See Also

mod_perl(3), Apache(3), DCE::Login(3)

Apache::DumpHeaders—watch HTTP transaction via headers

Synopsis

```
#httpd.conf or some such
perlLogHandler Apache::DumpHeaders
PerlSetVar     DumpHeadersFile -
```

Description

This module is used to watch an HTTP transaction, looking at client and servers headers. DumpHeadersFile may be a filename or "–" for STDOUT. With Apache::ProxyPassThur configured, you are able to watch your browser talk to any server besides the one with this module living inside.

Author

Doug MacEachern, *dougm@osf.org*

See Also

mod_perl(3), Apache(3), Apache::ProxyPassThru(3)

Apache::Include—utilities for mod_perl/mod_include integration

Synopsis

```
<!--#perl sub="Apache::Include" arg="/perl/ssi.pl" -->
```

Description

The Apache::Include module provides a handler, making it simple to include Apache::Registry scripts with the mod_include Perl directive.

Apache::Registry scripts can also be used in mod_include parsed documents using "virtual include"; however, Apache::Include is faster.

Author

Doug MacEachern, *dougm@osf.org*

See Also

perl(1), mod_perl(3), mod_include

Apache::MsqlProxy—translate URIs into mSQL database queries

Synopsis

```
#httpd.conf or srm.conf
PerlTransHandler Apache::MsqlProxy::translate
PerlHandler      Apache::MsqlProxy::handler
PerlModule       Apache::MsqlProxy
```

Description

This module is meant as an example to show how one can use Apache and **mod_perl** to handle HTTP proxy requests, or simply translating a URL.

It may not be very useful other than as an example, but feel free to change that.

Configure your browser's HTTP proxy to point at the host running Apache configured with this module:

```
http://hostname.domain/
```

When connecting to the server via normal HTTP (not proxy), URLs are not translated.

URLs are translated as follows:

```
http://hostname/database_name/table_name
```

Connect to **hostname** via TCP, select database **database_name**, query table **table_name** with:

```
SELECT * from table_name
http://hostname/database_name/table_name?login_name=dougm
```

Same as above, only with query:

```
SELECT login_name from table where login_name=dougm
http://hostname/database_name/table_name/*?login_name=dougm
```

Same as above with query:

```
SELECT * from table where login_name=dougm
```

Of course:

```
http:///database_name/table_name
```

A null hostname connects via UNIX socket:

```
http://hostname:9876/database_name/table_name
```

Connect via TCP to hostname and port 9876.

Author

Doug MacEachern, *dougm@osf.org*

See Also

Apache(3), Msql(3)

Apache::Options—OPT_* defines from httpd_core.h

Synopsis

```
use Apache::Options;
```

Description

The Apache::Options module will export the following bitmask constants:

```
OPT_NONE
OPT_INDEXES
OPT_INCLUDES
OPT_SYMLINKS
OPT_EXECCGI
OPT_UNSET
OPT_INCNOEXEC
OPT_SYM_OWNER
OPT_MULTI
OPT_ALL
```

These constants can be used to check the return value from `Apache->request->allow_options()` method.

This module is simply a stub which imports from Apache::Constants, just as if you had said `use Apache::Constants ':options';`

See Also

Apache, Apache::Constants

Apache::ProxyPassThru — skeleton for vanilla proxy

Synopsis

```
#httpd.conf or some such
PerlTransHandler  Apache::ProxyPassThru::translate
PerlHandler       Apache::ProxyPassThru
```

Description

This module uses `libwww-perl` as its web client, feeding the response back into the Apache API `request_rec` structure. `PerlHandler` will only be invoked if the request is a proxy request, otherwise, your normal server configuration will handle the request.

Author

Doug MacEachern, *dougm@osf.org*

See Also

mod_perl(3), Apache(3), LWP::UserAgent(3)

Apache::Session — maintain client-httpd instance session

Synopsis

```
#httpd.conf or some such
PerlFixupHandler Apache::Session
#where to store session config files (default is /tmp/httpd_sessions)
PerlSetVar       SessionBaseDir
```

Description

This module starts a session based on **httpd** for a specific client. By using HTTP cookies, the server redirects the client to its session on a dynamically allocated port.

Author

Doug MacEachern, *dougm@osf.org*

See Also

mod_perl(3), Apache(3), File::CounterFile(3)

Apache::SSI—implement Server Side Includes in Perl

Synopsis

Wherever you choose:

```
<Files *.phtml> SetHandler perl-script PerlHandler Apache::SSI </Files>
```

You may wish to subclass Apache::SSI for your own extensions:

```
package MySSI;
use Apache::SSI ();
@ISA = qw(Apache::SSI);
#embedded syntax:
#<!--#something cmd=doit -->
sub something {
    my($self, $attr) = @_;
    my $cmd = $attr->{cmd};
    ...
    return $a_string;
}
```

Description

Apache::SSI implements the functionality of **mod_include** for handling server-parsed html documents. Each "command" or element is handled by an Apache::SSI method of the same name. **attribute=value** pairs are parsed and passed to the method in an anonymous hash.

This module supports the same directives as **mod_include**, see its documentation for commands and syntax.

In addition, Apache::SSI supports the following methods.

Method
perlsub

This directive calls a Perl subroutine:

```
Hello user from <!--#perlsub sub=remote_host -->
```

Caveats

This module is not complete; it does not provide the full functionality of **mod_include**.

There is no support for **xssi** directives.

Author

Doug MacEachern, *dougm@osf.org*

See Also

For much more power, see the *HTML::Embperl* and *Apache::ePerl* modules.

mod_include, mod_perl(3), HTML::TreeBuilder(3), Apache(3), HTML::Embperl(3), Apache::ePerl(3)

CGI—simple Common Gateway Interface class

Synopsis

```
use CGI;
# the rest is too complicated for a synopsis; keep reading
```

Abstract

This Perl library uses Perl5 objects to make it easy to create Web fill-out forms and parse their contents. This package defines CGI objects, entities that contain the values of the current query string and other state variables. Using a CGI object's methods, you can examine keywords and parameters passed to your script, and create forms whose initial values are taken from the current query (thereby preserving state information).

The current version of *CGI.pm* is available at:

    http://www.genome.wi.mit.edu/ftp/pub/software/WWW/cgi_docs.html

    ftp://ftp-genome.wi.mit.edu/pub/software/WWW/

Installation

To install this package, just change to the directory in which this file is found and type the following:

```
perl Makefile.PL
make
make install
```

This will copy *CGI.pm* to your Perl library directory for use by all Perl scripts. You probably must be root to do this. Now you can load the CGI routines in your Perl scripts with the line:

```
use CGI;
```

If you don't have sufficient privileges to install *CGI.pm* in the Perl library directory, you can put *CGI.pm* into some convenient spot, such as your home directory, or in cgi-bin itself and prefix all Perl scripts that call it with something along the lines of the following preamble:

```
use lib '/home/davis/lib';
use CGI;
```

If you are using a version of Perl earlier than 5.002 (such as NT Perl), use this instead:

```
BEGIN {
        unshift(@INC,'/home/davis/lib');
}
use CGI;
```

The CGI distribution also comes with a cute module called CGI::Carp. It redefines the **die()**, **warn()**, **confess()**, and **croak()** error routines so that they write nicely formatted error messages into the server's error log (or to the output stream of your choice). This avoids long hours of groping through the error and access logs, trying to figure out which CGI script is generating error messages. If you choose, you can even have fatal error messages echoed to the browser to avoid the annoying and uninformative "Server Error" message.

Description

Creating a New Query Object

This will parse the input (from both POST and GET methods) and store it into a Perl5 object called $query.

```
$query = new CGI;
```

Creating a New Query Object from an Input File

If you provide a file handle to the **new()** method, it will read parameters from the file (or STDIN, or whatever). The file can be in any of the forms describing below under debugging (i.e., a series of newline delimited TAG=VALUE pairs will work). Conveniently, this type of file is created by the **save()** method (see below). Multiple records can be saved and restored.

```
$query = new CGI(INPUTFILE);
```

Perl purists will be pleased to know that this syntax accepts references to file handles, or even references to file handle globs, which is the "official" way to pass a file handle:

```
$query = new CGI(\*STDIN);
```

You can also initialize the query object from an associative array reference:

```
$query = new CGI( {'dinosaur'=>'barney',
                   'song'=>'I love you',
                   'friends'=>[qw/Jessica George Nancy/]}
                );
```

or from a properly formatted, URL-escaped query string:

```
$query = new CGI('dinosaur=barney&color=purple');
```

To create an empty query, initialize it from an empty string or hash:

```
$empty_query = new CGI("");
    -or-
$empty_query = new CGI({});
```

Fetching a List of Keywords from the Query

If the script was invoked as the result of an <ISINDEX> search, the parsed keywords can be obtained as an array using the **keywords()** method.

```
@keywords = $query->keywords
```

Fetching the Names of All the Parameters Passed to Your Script

If the script was invoked with a parameter list (for example, invoked with **name1=value1&name2=value2&name3=value3**), the **param()** method will return the parameter names as a list. If the script was invoked as an <ISINDEX> script, there will be a single parameter named **keywords**.

```
@names = $query->param
```

Note

As of version 1.5, the array of parameter names returned will be in the same order as they were submitted by the browser. Usually this order is the same as the order in which the parameters are defined in the form. However, this isn't part of the spec, and so isn't guaranteed.

Fetching the Value(s) of a Single Named Parameter

Pass the `param()` method a single argument to fetch the value of the named parameter. If the parameter is multivalued (e.g., from multiple selections in a scrolling list), you can ask to receive an array. Otherwise the method will return a single value.

```
@values = $query->param('foo');
          -or-
$value = $query->param('foo');
```

Setting the Value(s) of a Named Parameter

This sets the value for the named parameter foo to an array of values. This is one way to change the value of a field *after* the script has been invoked once before. (Another way is with the `-override` parameter accepted by all methods that generate form elements.)

```
$query->param('foo','an','array','of','values');
```

`param()` also recognizes a named parameter style of calling described in more detail later:

```
$query->param(-name=>'foo',-values=>['an','array','of','values']);
                          -or-
$query->param(-name=>'foo',-value=>'the value');
```

Appending Additional Values to a Named Parameter

This adds a value or list of values to the named parameter. The values are appended to the end of the parameter if it already exists. Otherwise the parameter is created. Note that this method only recognizes the named argument calling syntax.

```
$query->append(-name=>;'foo',-values=>['yet','more','values']);
```

Importing All Parameters into a Namespace

This creates a series of variables in the R namespace. For example, `$R::foo`, `@R::foo`. For keyword lists, a variable `@R::keywords` will appear. If no namespace is given, this method will assume Q.

```
$query->import_names('R');
```

Warning

Don't import anything into main; this is a major security risk!

In older versions, this method was called `import()`. As of version 2.20, this name has been removed completely to avoid conflict with the built-in Perl module `import` operator.

Deleting a Parameter Completely

This completely clears a parameter. It sometimes useful for resetting parameters that you don't want passed down between script invocations.

```
$query->delete('foo');
```

Deleting All Parameters

This clears the CGI object completely. It might be useful to ensure that all the defaults are taken when you create a fill-out form.

```
$query->delete_all();
```

Saving the State of the Form to a File

This will write the current state of the form to the provided file handle. You can read it back in by providing a file handle to the **new()** method. Note that the file handle can be a file, a pipe, or whatever!

```
$query->save(FILEHANDLE)
```

The format of the saved file is:

```
NAME1=VALUE1
NAME1=VALUE1'
NAME2=VALUE2
NAME3=VALUE3
=
```

Both name and value are URL escaped. Multi-valued CGI parameters are represented as repeated names. A session record is delimited by a single = symbol. You can write out multiple records and read them back in with several calls to **new()**. You can do this across several sessions by opening the file in append mode, allowing you to create primitive guest books, or to keep a history of users' queries. Here's a short example of creating multiple session records:

```
use CGI;
open (OUT,">>test.out") || die;
$records = 5;
foreach (0..$records) {
    my $q = new CGI;
    $q->param(-name=>'counter',-value=>$_);
    $q->save(OUT);
}
close OUT;
# reopen for reading
open (IN,"test.out") || die;
while (!eof(IN)) {
    my $q = new CGI(IN);
    print $q->param('counter'),"\n";
}
```

The file format used for save/restore is identical to that used by the Whitehead Genome Center's data exchange format Boulderio, and can be manipulated and even databased using Boulderio utilities. See *http://www.genome.wi.mit.edu/genome_software/other/boulder.html* for further details.

Creating a Self-Referencing URL That Preserves State Information

self_url() will return a URL, that, when selected, will reinvoke this script with all its state information intact.

```
$myself = $query->self_url;
print "<A HREF=$myself>I'm talking to myself.</A>";
```

This is most useful when you want to jump around within the document using internal anchors but you don't want to disrupt the current contents of the form(s). Something like this will do the trick.

```
$myself = $query->self_url;
print "<A HREF=$myself#table1>See table 1</A>";
print "<A HREF=$myself#table2>See table 2</A>";
print "<A HREF=$myself#yourself>See for yourself</A>";
```

If you don't want to get the whole query string, call the method **url()** to return just the URL for the script:

```
$myself = $query->url;
print "<A HREF=$myself>No query string in this baby!</A>\n";
```

You can also retrieve the unprocessed query string with **query_string()**:

```
$the_string = $query->query_string;
```

Ensuring Compatibility with cgi-lib.pl

To make it easier to port existing programs that use *cgi-lib.pl* the compatibility routine ReadParse is provided. Porting is simple:

Old version

```
require "cgi-lib.pl"; &ReadParse;
print "The value of the antique is $in{antique}.\n";
```

New version

```
use CGI; CGI::ReadParse
print "The value of the antique is $in{antique}.\n";
```

CGI.pm's **ReadParse()** routine creates a tied variable named **%in**, which can be accessed to obtain the query variables. Like **ReadParse**, you can also provide your own variable. Infrequently used features of **ReadParse**, such as the creation of **@in** and **$in** variables, are not supported.

Once you use **ReadParse**, you can retrieve the query object itself this way:

```
$q = $in{CGI};
print $q->textfield(-name=>'wow',
                    -value=>'does this really work?');
```

This allows you to start using the more interesting features of *CGI.pm* without rewriting your old scripts from scratch.

Calling CGI Functions That Take Multiple Arguments

In versions of *CGI.pm* prior to 2.0, it could get difficult to remember the proper order of arguments in CGI function calls that accepted five or six different arguments. As of 2.0, there's a better way to pass arguments to the various CGI functions. In this style, you pass a series of **name=>argument** pairs, like this:

```
$field = $query->radio_group(-name=>'OS',
                             -values=>[Unix,Windows,Macintosh],
                             -default=>'Unix');
```

The advantages of this style are that you don't have to remember the exact order of the arguments, and if you leave out a parameter, in most cases it will default to some reasonable value. If you provide a parameter that the method doesn't recognize, it will usually do something useful with it, such as incorporating it into the HTML form tag.

For example if Netscape decides next week to add a new JUSTIFICATION parameter to the text field tags, you can start using the feature without waiting for a new version of *CGI.pm*:

```
$field = $query->textfield(-name=>'State',
                           -default=>'gaseous',
                           -justification=>'RIGHT');
```

This will result in an HTML tag that looks like this:

```
<INPUT TYPE="textfield" NAME="State" VALUE="gaseous"
       JUSTIFICATION="RIGHT">
```

Parameter names are case insensitive: you can use **-name**, or **-Name** or **-NAME**. You don't have to use the hyphen if you don't want to. After creating a CGI object, call the **use_named_parameters**() method with a nonzero value. This will tell *CGI.pm* that you intend to use named parameters exclusively:

```
$query = new CGI;
$query->use_named_parameters(1);
$field = $query->radio_group('name'=>'OS',
                             'values'=>
['Unix','Windows','Macintosh'],
                               'default'=>'Unix');
```

Actually, *CGI.pm* only looks for a hyphen in the first parameter. So you can leave it off subsequent parameters if you like. Something to be wary of is the potential that a string constant like **values** will collide with a keyword (and in fact it does!). While Perl usually figures out when you're referring to a function and when you're referring to a string, you probably should put quotation marks around all string constants just to play it safe.

Creating the HTTP Header

header() returns the Content-type: header. You can provide your own MIME type if you choose, otherwise it defaults to **text/html**. An optional second parameter specifies the status code and a human-readable message.

```
print $query->header;
     -or-
print $query->header('image/gif');
     -or-
print $query->header('text/html','204 No response');
     -or-
print $query->header(-type=>'image/gif',
                     -nph=>1,
                     -status=>'402 Payment required',
                     -expires=>'+3d',
                     -cookie=>$cookie,
                     -Cost=>'$2.00');
```

For example, you can specify 204, "No response," to create a script that tells the browser to do nothing at all. If you want to add additional fields to the header, just tack them on to the end:

```
print $query->header('text/html','200 OK','Content-Length: 3002');
```

The last example shows the named argument style for passing arguments to the CGI methods using named parameters. Recognized parameters are **-type**, **-status**,

-expires, and -cookie. Any other parameters will be stripped of their initial hyphens and turned into header fields, allowing you to specify any HTTP header you desire.

Most browsers will not cache the output from CGI scripts. Every time the browser reloads the page, the script is invoked anew. You can change this behavior with the -expires parameter. When you specify an absolute or relative expiration interval with this parameter, some browsers and proxy servers will cache the script's output until the indicated expiration date. The following forms are all valid for the -expires field:

+30s	30 seconds from now
+10m	Ten minutes from now
+1h	One hour from now
−1d	Yesterday (i.e., ASAP!)
now	Immediately
+3M	In three months
+10y	In ten years time
Thursday, 25-Apr-96 00:40:33 GMT	At the indicated time and date

(CGI::expires() is the static function call used internally that turns relative time intervals into HTTP dates. You can call it directly if you wish.)

The -cookie parameter generates a header that tells the browser to provide a "magic cookie" during all subsequent transactions with your script. Netscape cookies have a special format that includes interesting attributes such as expiration time. Use the cookie() method to create and retrieve session cookies.

The -nph parameter, if set to a true value, will issue the correct headers to work with a NPH (no-parse-header) script. This is important to use with certain servers, such as Microsoft Internet Explorer, which expect all their scripts to be NPH.

Generating a Redirection Instruction

Redirects the browser elsewhere. If you use redirection like this, you should not print out a header as well. As of version 2.0, we produce both the unofficial Location: header and the official URI: header. This should satisfy most servers and browsers.

```
print $query->redirect('http://somewhere.else/in/movie/land');
```

One hint I can offer is that relative links may not work correctly when you generate a redirection to another document on your site. This is due to a well-intentioned optimization that some servers use. The solution to this is to use the full URL (including the http: part) of the document you are redirecting to.

You can use named parameters:

```
print $query->redirect(-uri=>'http://somewhere.else/in/movie/land',
                       -nph=>1);
```

The -nph parameter, if set to a true value, will issue the correct headers to work with a NPH (no-parse-header) script. This is important to use with certain servers, such as Microsoft Internet Explorer, which expect all their scripts to be NPH.

Creating the HTML Header

This will return a canned HTML header and the opening <BODY> tag. All parameters are optional. In the named parameter form, recognized parameters are -title, -author, -base, -xbase, and -target (see below for the explanation). Any additional parameters you provide, such as the Netscape unofficial BGCOLOR attribute, are added to the <BODY> tag.

```
print $query->start_html(-title=>'Secrets of the Pyramids',
                         -author=>'fred@capricorn.org',
                         -base=>'true',
                         -target=>'_blank',
                         -meta=>{'keywords'=>'pharaoh secret mummy',
                            'copyright'=>'copyright 1996 King Tut'},
                         -style=>{'src'=>'/styles/style1.css'},
                         -BGCOLOR=>'blue');
-or-
print $query->start_html('Secrets of the Pyramids',
                         'fred@capricorn.org','true',
                         'BGCOLOR="blue"');
```

The argument -xbase allows you to provide an HREF for the <BASE> tag different from the current location, as in:

```
-xbase=>"http://home.mcom.com/"
```

All relative links will be interpreted relative to this tag.

The argument -target allows you to provide a default target frame for all the links and fill-out forms on the page. See the Netscape documentation on frames for details of how to manipulate this.

```
-target=>"answer_window"
```

All relative links will be interpreted relative to this tag. You add arbitrary meta information to the header with the -meta argument. This argument expects a reference to an associative array containing name/value pairs of meta information. These will be turned into a series of header <META> tags that look something like this:

```
<META NAME="keywords" CONTENT="pharaoh secret mummy">
<META NAME="description" CONTENT="copyright 1996 King Tut">
```

There is no support for the HTTP-EQUIV type of <META> tag. This is because you can modify the HTTP header directly with the **header()** method. For example, if you want to send the Refresh: header, do it in the **header()** method:

```
print $q->header(-Refresh=>'10; URL=http://www.capricorn.com');
```

The -style tag is used to incorporate cascading stylesheets into your code. See the section on Cascading Stylesheets for more information.

You can place other arbitrary HTML elements to the <HEAD> section with the -head tag. For example, to place the rarely-used <LINK> element in the head section, use:

```
print $q->header(-head=>link({-rel=>'next',
                     -href=>'http://www.capricorn.com/s2.html'}));
```

To incorporate multiple HTML elements into the <HEAD> section, just pass an array reference:

```
print $q->header(-head=>[ link({-rel=>'next',
                     -href=>'http://www.capricorn.com/s2.html'}),
```

```
              link({-rel=>'previous',
                  -href=>'http://www.capricorn.com/s1.html'})
                  ]
       );
```

JavaScripting

The -script, -noScript, -onLoad and -onUnload parameters are used to add Netscape JavaScript calls to your pages. -script should point to a block of text containing JavaScript function definitions. This block will be placed within a <SCRIPT> block inside the HTML (not HTTP) header. The block is placed in the header in order to give your page a fighting chance of having all its JavaScript functions in place even if the user presses the stop button before the page has loaded completely. *CGI.pm* attempts to format the script in such a way that Java-Script-naive browsers will not choke on the code: unfortunately there are some browsers, such as Chimera for UNIX, that get confused by it nevertheless.

The -onLoad and -onUnload parameters point to fragments of JavaScript code to execute when the page is respectively opened and closed by the browser. Usually these parameters are calls to functions defined in the -script field:

```
$query = new CGI;
print $query->header;
$JSCRIPT=<<END;
// Ask a silly question
function riddle_me_this() {
    var r = prompt("What walks on four legs in the morning, " +
                   "two legs in the afternoon, " +
                   "and three legs in the evening?");
    response(r);
}
// Get a silly answer
function response(answer) {
    if (answer == "man")
        alert("Right you are!");
    else
        alert("Wrong!  Guess again.");
}
END
print $query->start_html(-title=>'The Riddle of the Sphinx',
                         -script=>$JSCRIPT);
```

Use the -noScript parameter to pass some HTML text that will be displayed on browsers that do not have JavaScript (or browsers where JavaScript is turned off).

Netscape 3.0 recognizes several attributes of the <SCRIPT> tag, including LANGUAGE and SRC. The latter is particularly interesting, as it allows you to keep the JavaScript code in a file or CGI script rather than cluttering up each page with the source. To use these attributes pass a HASH reference in the -script parameter containing one or more of -language, -src, or -code:

```
print $q->start_html(-title=>'The Riddle of the Sphinx',
                     -script=>{-language=>'JAVASCRIPT',
                               -src=>'/javascript/sphinx.js'}
                    );
```

```
print $q->(-title=>'The Riddle of the Sphinx',
          -script=>{-language=>'PERLSCRIPT'},
                   -code=>'print "hello world!\n;"'
        );
```

See *http://home.netscape.com/eng/mozilla/2.0/handbook/javascript/* for more information about JavaScript.

The old-style positional parameters are as follows:

1   The title

2   The author's email address (will create a `<LINK REV="MADE">` tag if present)

3   A **true** flag if you want to include a `<BASE>` tag in the header. This helps resolve relative addresses to absolute ones when the document is moved, but makes the document hierarchy non-portable. Use with care!

4, 5, 6 . . .

Any other parameters you want to include in the `<BODY>` tag. This is a good place to put Netscape extensions, such as colors and wallpaper patterns.

Ending the HTML Document

This ends an HTML document by printing the `</BODY></HTML>` tags.

```
print $query->end_html
```

Creating Forms

The various form-creating methods all return strings to the caller, containing the tag or tags that will create the requested form element. You are responsible for actually printing out these strings. It's set up this way so that you can place formatting tags around the form elements.

The default values that you specify for the forms are only used the *first* time the script is invoked (when there is no query string). On subsequent invocations of the script (when there is a query string), the former values are used even if they are blank.

If you want to change the value of a field from its previous value, you have two choices:

- Call the **param()** method to set it.

- Use the **-override** (alias **-force**) parameter (a new feature in version 2.15). This forces the default value to be used, regardless of the previous value:

```
print $query->textfield(-name=>'field_name',
                        -default=>'starting value',
                        -override=>1,
                        -size=>50,
                        -maxlength=>80);
```

By default, the text and labels of form elements are escaped according to HTML rules. This means that you can safely use <CLICK ME> as the label for a button. However, it also interferes with your ability to incorporate special HTML character sequences, such as Á, into your fields. If you wish to turn off automatic escaping, call the **autoEscape()** method with a false value immediately after creating the CGI object:

```
$query = new CGI;
$query->autoEscape(undef);
```

Creating an ISINDEX tag

Prints out an `<ISINDEX>` tag. Not very exciting. The parameter `-action` specifies the URL of the script to process the query. The default is to process the query with the current script.

```
print $query->isindex(-action=>$action);
      -or-
print $query->isindex($action);
```

Starting and ending a form

`startform()` will return a `<FORM>` tag with the optional method, action and form encoding that you specify. The defaults are `method:` `POST`, action: *this_ script*, encoding: `application/x-www-form-urlencoded`.

`endform()` returns the closing `</FORM>` tag.

```
print $query->startform(-method=>$method,
                        -action=>$action,
                        -encoding=>$encoding);
  <... various form stuff ...>
print $query->endform;
    -or-
print $query->startform($method,$action,$encoding);
  <... various form stuff ...>
print $query->endform;
```

`startform()`'s encoding method tells the browser how to package the various fields of the form before sending the form to the server. Two values are possible:

`application/x-www-form-urlencoded`

> This is the older type of encoding used by all browsers prior to Netscape 2.0. It is compatible with many CGI scripts and is suitable for short fields containing text data. For your convenience, *CGI.pm* stores the name of this encoding type in $CGI::URL_ENCODED.

`multipart/form-data`

> This is the newer type of encoding introduced by Netscape 2.0. It is suitable for forms that contain very large fields or that are intended for transferring binary data. Most importantly, it enables the "file upload" feature of Netscape 2.0 forms. For your convenience, *CGI.pm* stores the name of this encoding type in $CGI::MULTIPART.

> Forms that use this type of encoding are not easily interpreted by CGI scripts unless they use *CGI.pm* or another library designed to handle them.

For compatibility, the `startform()` method uses the older form of encoding by default. If you want to use the newer form of encoding by default, you can call `start_multipart_form()` instead of `startform()`.

JavaScripting

The `-name` and `-onSubmit` parameters are provided for use with JavaScript. The `-name` parameter gives the form a name so that it can be identified and manipulated by JavaScript functions. `-onSubmit` should point to a JavaScript function that will be executed just before the form is submitted to your server. You can use this opportunity to check the contents of the form for consistency and completeness. If you find something wrong, you can put up an alert box or maybe fix things up yourself. You can abort the submission by returning false from this function.

Usually the bulk of JavaScript functions are defined in a <SCRIPT> block in the HTML header and -onSubmit points to one of these function call. See start_html() for details.

Creating a text field

textfield() will return a text input field.

```
print $query->textfield(-name=>'field_name',
                        -default=>'starting value',
                        -size=>50,
                        -maxlength=>80);
    -or-
print $query->textfield('field_name','starting value',50,80);
```

Parameters:

name

A required parameter giving the name for the field

default

An optional parameter giving the default starting value for the field contents

size

An optional parameter giving the size of the field in characters

maxlength

An optional parameter giving the maximum number of characters the field will accept

As with all these methods, the field will be initialized with its previous contents from earlier invocations of the script. When the form is processed, the value of the text field can be retrieved with:

```
$value = $query->param('foo');
```

If you want to reset it from its initial value after the script has been called once, you can do so like this:

```
$query->param('foo',"I'm taking over this value!");
```

A new feature (as of version 2.15): If you don't want the field to take on its previous value, you can force its current value by using the -override (alias -force) parameter:

```
print $query->textfield(-name=>'field_name',
                        -default=>'starting value',
                        -override=>1,
                        -size=>50,
                        -maxlength=>80);
```

JavaScripting

You can also provide -onChange, -onFocus, -onBlur, and -onSelect parameters to register JavaScript event handlers. The onChange handler will be called whenever the user changes the contents of the text field. You can do text validation if you like. onFocus and onBlur are called respectively when the insertion point moves into and out of the text field. `onSelect` is called when the user changes the portion of the text that is selected.

Creating a big text field

`textarea()` is just like `textfield`, but it allows you to specify rows and columns for a multiline text entry box. You can provide a starting value for the field, which can be long and contain multiple lines.

```
print $query->textarea(-name=>'foo',
                       -default=>'starting value',
                       -rows=>10,
                       -columns=>50);
    -or
print $query->textarea('foo','starting value',10,50);
```

JavaScripting

The -onChange, -onFocus, -onBlur and -onSelect parameters are recognized. See `textfield()`.

Creating a password field

`password_field()` is identical to `textfield()`, except that its contents will be starred-out on the web page.

```
print $query->password_field(-name=>'secret',
                             -value=>'starting value',
                             -size=>50,
                             -maxlength=>80);
    -or-
print $query->password_field('secret','starting value',50,80);
```

JavaScripting

The -onChange, -onFocus, -onBlur, and -onSelect parameters are recognized. See `textfield()`.

Creating a file upload field

`filefield()` will return a file upload field for Netscape 2.0 browsers. In order to take full advantage of this *you must use the new multipart encoding scheme* for the form. You can do this either by calling `startform()` with an encoding type of $CGI::MULTIPART, or by calling the new method `start_multipart_form()` instead of vanilla `startform()`.

```
print $query->filefield(-name=>'uploaded_file',
                        -default=>'starting value',
                        -size=>50,
                        -maxlength=>80);
    -or-
print $query->filefield('uploaded_file',
                        'starting value',50,80);
```

Parameters:

name

A required parameter giving the name for the field

default

An optional parameter giving the default starting value for the field contents size

> An optional parameter giving the size of the field in characters

maxlength

> An optional parameter giving the maximum number of characters the field will accept

When the form is processed, you can retrieve the entered filename by calling param().

```
$filename = $query->param('uploaded_file');
```

In Netscape Gold, the filename that gets returned is the full local filename on the *remote user*'s machine. If the remote user is on a UNIX machine, the filename will follow UNIX conventions:

```
/path/to/the/file
```

On MS-DOS/Windows and OS/2 machines, the filename will follow DOS conventions:

```
C:\PATH\TO\THE\FILE.MSW
```

On a Macintosh machine, the filename will follow Mac conventions:

```
HD 40:Desktop Folder:Sort Through:Reminders
```

The filename returned is also a file handle. You can read the contents of the file using standard Perl file reading calls:

```
# Read a text file and print it out
while (<$filename>) {
    print;
}
# Copy a binary file to somewhere safe
open (OUTFILE,">>/usr/local/web/users/feedback");
while ($bytesread=read($filename,$buffer,1024)) {
    print OUTFILE $buffer;
}
```

When a file is uploaded the browser usually sends along some information along with it in the format of headers. The information usually includes the MIME content type. Future browsers may send other information as well (such as modification date and size). To retrieve this information, call uploadInfo(). It returns a reference to an associative array containing all the document headers.

```
$filename = $query->param('uploaded_file');
$type = $query->uploadInfo($filename)->{'Content-Type'};
unless ($type eq 'text/html') {
    die "HTML FILES ONLY!";
}
```

If you are using a machine that recognizes text and binary data modes, be sure to understand when and how to use them (see the Camel book). Otherwise you may find that binary files are corrupted during file uploads.

JavaScripting

> The -onChange, -onFocus, -onBlur, and -onSelect parameters are recognized. See textfield() for details.

Creating a popup menu

`popup_menu()` creates a menu.

```
print $query->popup_menu('menu_name',
                         ['eenie','meenie','minie'],
                         'meenie');
   -or-
%labels = ('eenie'=>'your first choice',
           'meenie'=>'your second choice',
           'minie'=>'your third choice');
print $query->popup_menu('menu_name',
                         ['eenie','meenie','minie'],
                         'meenie',\%labels);
     -or (named parameter style)-
print $query->popup_menu(-name=>'menu_name',
                         -values=>['eenie','meenie','minie'],
                         -default=>'meenie',
                         -labels=>\%labels);
```

Parameters:

name

The required first argument is the menu's name

values

The required second argument is an array *reference* containing the list of menu items in the menu. You can pass the method an anonymous array, as shown in the example, or a reference to a named array, such as \@foo.

default

The optional third parameter is the name of the default menu choice. If not specified, the first item will be the default. The values of the previous choice will be maintained across queries.

labels

The optional fourth parameter is provided for people who want to use different values for the user-visible label inside the popup menu and the value returned to your script. It's a pointer to an associative array relating menu values to user-visible labels. If you leave this parameter blank, the menu values will be displayed by default. (You can also leave a label undefined if you want to).

When the form is processed, the selected value of the popup menu can be retrieved using:

```
$popup_menu_value = $query->param('menu_name');
```

JavaScripting

`popup_menu()` recognizes the following event handlers: -onChange, -onFocus, and -onBlur. See the `textfield()` section for details on when these handlers are called.

Creating a scrolling list

`scrolling_list()` creates a scrolling list.

```
print $query->scrolling_list('list_name',
                             ['eenie','meenie','minie','moe'],
                             ['eenie','moe'],5,'true');
```

```
      -or-
  print $query->scrolling_list('list_name',
                              ['eenie','meenie','minie','moe'],
                              ['eenie','moe'],5,'true',
                              \%labels);
      -or-
  print $query->scrolling_list(-name=>'list_name',
                              -values=>['eenie','meenie','minie','moe'],
                              -default=>['eenie','moe'],
                              -size=>5,
                              -multiple=>'true',
                              -labels=>\%labels);
```

Parameters:

name
values

>   The first and second arguments are the list name and values. As in the popup menu, the second argument should be an array reference.

default

>   The optional third argument can be either a reference to a list containing the values to be selected by default, or can be a single value to select. If this argument is missing or undefined, then nothing is selected when the list first appears. In the named parameter version, you can use the synonym -defaults for this parameter.

size

>   The optional fourth argument is the size of the list.

multiple

>   The optional fifth argument can be set to true to allow multiple simultaneous selections. Otherwise only one selection will be allowed at a time.

labels

>   The optional sixth argument is a pointer to an associative array containing long user-visible labels for the list items. If not provided, the values will be displayed.

When this form is processed, all selected list items will be returned as a list under the parameter name list_name. The values of the selected items can be retrieved with:

```
  @selected = $query->param('list_name');
```

JavaScripting

>   scrolling_list() recognizes the following event handlers: -onChange, -onFocus, and -onBlur. See textfield() for the description of when these handlers are called.

Creating a group of related checkboxes

checkbox_group() creates a list of checkboxes that are related by the same name.

```
  print $query->checkbox_group(-name=>'group_name',
                              -values=>['eenie','meenie','minie','moe'],
                              -default=>['eenie','moe'],
                              -linebreak=>'true',
                              -labels=>\%labels);
```

```
print $query->checkbox_group('group_name',
                         ['eenie','meenie','minie','moe'],
                         ['eenie','moe'],'true',\%labels);
HTML3-COMPATIBLE BROWSERS ONLY:
print $query->checkbox_group(-name=>'group_name',
                  -values=>['eenie','meenie','minie','moe'],
                  -rows=2,-columns=>2);
```

Parameters:

name
values

> The first and second arguments are the checkbox name and values, respectively. As in the popup menu, the second argument should be an array reference. These values are used for the user-readable labels printed next to the checkboxes as well as for the values passed to your script in the query string.

default

> The optional third argument can be either a reference to a list containing the values to be checked by default, or a single value to checked. If this argument is missing or undefined, then nothing is selected when the list first appears.

linebreak

> The optional fourth argument (-linebreak) can be set to true to place line breaks between the checkboxes so that they appear as a vertical list. Otherwise, they will be strung together on a horizontal line.

labels

> The optional fifth argument is a pointer to an associative array relating the checkbox values to the user-visible labels that will be printed next to them. If not provided, the values will be used as the default.

rows
columns

> HTML3-compatible browsers (such as the latest release of Netscape Navigator or Internet Explorer) can take advantage of the optional parameters -rows, and -columns. These parameters cause checkbox_group() to return an HTML3 compatible table containing the checkbox group formatted with the specified number of rows and columns. You can provide just the -columns parameter if you wish; checkbox_group will calculate the correct number of rows for you.

To include row and column headings in the returned table, you can use the -rowheader and -colheader parameters. Both of these accept a pointer to an array of headings to use. The headings are just decorative. They don't reorganize the interpretation of the checkboxes—they're still a single named unit.

When the form is processed, all checked boxes will be returned as a list under the parameter name **group_name**. The values of the "on" checkboxes can be retrieved with:

```
@turned_on = $query->param('group_name');
```

The value returned by checkbox_group() is actually an array of button elements. You can capture them and use them within tables, lists, or in other creative ways:

```
@h = $query->checkbox_group(-name=>'group_name',
                            -values=>\@values);
&use_in_creative_way(@h);
```

JavaScripting

checkbox_group() recognizes the -onClick parameter. This specifies a JavaScript code fragment or function call to be executed every time the user clicks on any of the buttons in the group. You can retrieve the identity of the particular button clicked on using the **this** variable.

Creating a standalone checkbox

checkbox() is used to create an isolated checkbox that isn't logically related to any others.

```
print $query->checkbox(-name=>'checkbox_name',
                       -checked=>'checked',
                       -value=>'ON',
                       -label=>'CLICK ME');
    -or-
print $query->checkbox('checkbox_name','checked',
                       'ON','CLICK ME');
```

Parameters:

name

The first parameter is the required name for the checkbox. It will also be used for the user-readable label printed next to the checkbox.

checked

The optional second parameter specifies that the checkbox is turned on by default. Synonyms are **-selected** and **-on**.

value

The optional third parameter specifies the value of the checkbox when it is checked. If not provided, the word "on" is assumed.

label

The optional fourth parameter is the user-readable label to be attached to the checkbox. If not provided, the checkbox name is used.

The value of the checkbox can be retrieved using:

```
$turned_on = $query->param('checkbox_name');
```

JavaScripting

checkbox() recognizes the -onClick parameter. See checkbox_group() for further details.

Creating a radio button group

radio_group() creates a set of logically related radio buttons (turning one member of the group on turns the others off):

```
print $query->radio_group(-name=>'group_name',
                          -values=>['eenie','meenie','minie'],
```

```
                         -default=>'meenie',
                         -linebreak=>'true',
                         -labels=>\%labels);
        -or-
   print $query->radio_group('group_name',['eenie','meenie',
                                           'minie'],
                         'meenie','true',\%labels);
   HTML3-COMPATIBLE BROWSERS ONLY:
   print $query->radio_group(-name=>'group_name',
                         -values=>['eenie','meenie',
                                   'minie','moe'],
                         -rows=2,-columns=>2);
```

Parameters:

name

The first argument is the name of the group and is required.

values

The second argument is the list of values for the radio buttons. The values and the labels that appear on the page are identical. Pass an array *reference* in the second argument, either using an anonymous array, as shown, or by referencing a named array as in \@foo.

default

The optional third parameter is the name of the default button to turn on. If not specified, the first item will be the default. You can provide a nonexistent button name, such as "-" to start up with no buttons selected.

linebreak

The optional fourth parameter can be set to 'true' to put line breaks between the buttons, creating a vertical list.

labels

The optional fifth parameter is a pointer to an associative array relating the radio button values to user-visible labels to be used in the display. If not provided, the values themselves are displayed.

rows
columns

HTML3-compatible browsers (such as the latest versions of Netscape Navigator and Internet Explorer) can take advantage of the optional parameters -rows, and -columns. These parameters cause radio_group() to return an HTML3 compatible table containing the radio group formatted with the specified number of rows and columns. You can provide just the -columns parameter if you wish; radio_group will calculate the correct number of rows for you.

To include row and column headings in the returned table, you can use the -rowheader and -colheader parameters. Both of these accept a pointer to an array of headings to use. The headings are just decorative. They don't reorganize the interpretation of the radio buttons—they're still a single named unit.

When the form is processed, the selected radio button can be retrieved using:

```
$which_radio_button = $query->param('group_name');
```

The value returned by `radio_group()` is actually an array of button elements. You can capture them and use them within tables, lists, or in other creative ways:

```
@h = $query->radio_group(-name=>'group_name',
                         -values=>\@values);
&use_in_creative_way(@h);
```

Creating a submit button

`submit()` will create the query submission button. Every form should have one of these.

```
print $query->submit(-name=>'button_name',
                     -value=>'value');
    -or-
print $query->submit('button_name','value');
```

Parameters:

name

> This first argument is optional. You can give the button a name if you have several submission buttons in your form and you want to distinguish between them. The name will also be used as the user-visible label. Be aware that a few older browsers don't deal with this correctly and *never* send back a value from a button.

value

> The second argument is also optional. This gives the button a value that will be passed to your script in the query string.

You can figure out which button was pressed by using different values for each one:

```
$which_one = $query->param('button_name');
```

JavaScripting

> `radio_group()` recognizes the `-onClick` parameter. See `checkbox_group()` for further details.

Creating a reset button

`reset()` creates the "reset" button. Note that it restores the form to its value from the last time the script was called, *not* necessarily to the defaults.

```
print $query->reset
```

Creating a default button

`defaults()` creates a button that, when invoked, will cause the form to be completely reset to its defaults, wiping out all the changes the user ever made.

```
print $query->defaults('button_label');
```

Creating a hidden field

`hidden()` produces a text field that can't be seen by the user. It is useful for passing state variable information from one invocation of the script to the next.

```
print $query->hidden(-name=>'hidden_name',
                     -default=>['value1','value2'...]);
        -or-
print $query->hidden('hidden_name','value1','value2'...);
```

Parameters:

`name`
> The first argument is required and specifies the name of this field (–name).

`default`
> The second argument is also required and specifies its value (–default). In the named parameter style of calling, you can provide a single value here or a reference to a whole list

Fetch the value of a hidden field this way:

```
$hidden_value = $query->param('hidden_name');
```

Note that just like all the other form elements, the value of a hidden field is "sticky." If you want to replace a hidden field with some other values after the script has been called once you'll have to do it manually:

```
$query->param('hidden_name','new','values','here');
```

Creating a clickable image button

`image_button()` produces a clickable image. When it's clicked on the position of the click is returned to your script as button_name.x and button_name.y, where button_name is the name you've assigned to it.

```
print $query->image_button(-name=>'button_name',
                           -src=>'/source/URL',
                           -align=>'MIDDLE');
    -or-
print $query->image_button('button_name',
                           '/source/URL','MIDDLE');
```

Parameters:

`name`
> The first argument is required and specifies the name of this field.

`src`
> The second argument is also required and specifies the URL of the image.

`align`
> The third argument is optional and specifies an alignment type of TOP, BOTTOM, or MIDDLE.

Fetch the value of the button this way:

```
$x = $query->param('button_name.x');
$y = $query->param('button_name.y');
```

JavaScripting

> `image_button()` recognizes the -onClick parameter. See checkbox_group() for further details.

Creating a JavaScript Action Button

`button()` produces a button that is compatible with Netscape 2.0's JavaScript. When it's pressed the fragment of JavaScript code pointed to by the -onClick parameter will be executed. On non-JavaScript browsers this form element will probably not even display.

```
print $query->button(-name=>'button_name',
                     -value=>'user visible label',
                     -onClick=>"do_something()");
  -or-
print $query->button('button_name',"do_something()");
```

Cookies

Most browsers support a so-called "cookie" designed to help maintain state within a browser session. *CGI.pm* has several methods that support cookies.

A cookie is a **name=value** pair much like the named parameters in a CGI query string. CGI scripts create one or more cookies and send them to the browser in the HTTP header. The browser maintains a list of cookies that belong to a particular Web server, and returns them to the CGI script during subsequent interactions.

In addition to the required **name=value** pair, each cookie has several optional attributes:

- A time/date string (in a special GMT format) that indicates when a cookie expires. The cookie will be saved and returned to your script until this expiration date is reached if the user exits Netscape and restarts it. If an expiration date isn't specified, the cookie will remain active until the user quits Netscape.

- A partial or complete domain name for which the cookie is valid. The browser will return the cookie to any host that matches the partial domain name. For example, if you specify a domain name of *.capricorn.com*, then Netscape will return the cookie to web servers running on any of the machines *www.capricorn.com*, *www2.capricorn.com*, *feckless.capricorn.com*, etc. Domain names must contain at least two periods to prevent attempts to match on top level domains like *.edu*. If no domain is specified, then the browser will only return the cookie to servers on the host the cookie originated from.

- An optional cookie path attribute. If you provide a cookie path attribute, the browser will check it against your script's URL before returning the cookie. For example, if you specify the path */cgi-bin*, then the cookie will be returned to each of the scripts */cgi-bin/tally.pl*, */cgi-bin/order.pl*, and */cgi-bin/customer_service/complain.pl*, but not to the script */cgi-private/site_admin.pl*. By default, path is set to "/", which causes the cookie to be sent to any CGI script on your site.

- If the "secure" attribute is set, the cookie will only be sent to your script if the CGI request is occurring on a secure channel, such as SSL.

The interface to cookies is the **cookie()** method:

```
$cookie = $query->cookie(-name=>'sessionID', -value=>'xyzzy',
                         -expires=>'+1h',
                         -path=>'/cgi-bin/database',
                         -domain=>'.capricorn.org', -secure=>1);
print $query->header(-cookie=>$cookie);
```

cookie() creates a new cookie. Its parameters include:

name

The name of the cookie (required). This can be any string at all. Although Netscape limits its cookie names to non-whitespace alphanumeric characters, *CGI.pm* removes this restriction by escaping and unescaping cookies behind the scenes.

value

The value of the cookie. This can be any scalar value, array reference, or even associative array reference. For example, you can store an entire associative array into a cookie this way:

```
$cookie=$query->cookie(-name=>'family information',
                       -value=>\%childrens_ages);
```

path

The optional partial path for which this cookie will be valid, as described above.

domain

The optional partial domain for which this cookie will be valid, as described above.

expires

The optional expiration date for this cookie. The format is as described in the section on the header() method:

```
"+1h"   one hour from now
```

secure

If set to true, this cookie will only be used within a secure SSL session.

The cookie created by cookie() must be incorporated into the HTTP header within the string returned by the header() method:

```
print $query->header(-cookie=>$my_cookie);
```

To create multiple cookies, give header() an array reference:

```
$cookie1 = $query->cookie(-name=>'riddle_name',
                          -value=>"The Sphynx's Question");
$cookie2 = $query->cookie(-name=>'answers',
                          -value=>\%answers);
print $query->header(-cookie=>[$cookie1,$cookie2]);
```

To retrieve a cookie, request it by name by calling cookie() method without the -value parameter:

```
use CGI;
$query = new CGI;
%answers = $query->cookie(-name=>'answers');
# $query->cookie('answers') will work too!
```

The cookie and CGI namespaces are separate. If you have a parameter named **answers** and a cookie named **answers**, the values retrieved by **param()** and **cookie()** are independent of each other. However, it's simple to turn a CGI parameter into a cookie, and vice versa:

```
# turn a CGI parameter into a cookie
$c=$q->cookie(-name=>'answers',-value=>[$q->param('answers')]);
# vice-versa
$q->param(-name=>'answers',-value=>[$q->cookie('answers')]);
```

See the *cookie.cgi* example script for some ideas on how to use cookies effectively.

Note

There appear to be some restrictions on cookies, including limits on the length of cookies. If you need to store a lot of information, it's probably better to create a unique session ID, store it in a cookie, and use the session ID to locate an external file/database saved on the server's side of the connection.

Working with Frames

It's possible for *CGI.pm* scripts to write into several browser panels and windows using either Netscape Navigator's or Internet Explorer's frame mechanism. There are three techniques for defining new frames programmatically:

- After writing out the HTTP header, instead of creating a standard HTML document using the **start_html()** call, create a **<FRAMESET>** document that defines the frames on the page. Specify your script(s) (with appropriate parameters) as the SRC for each of the frames.

  There is no specific support for creating **<FRAMESET>** sections in *CGI.pm*, but the HTML is very simple to write. See the frame documentation in Netscape's home pages for details, *http://home.netscape.com/assist/net_sites/frames.html*.

- You may provide a **-target** parameter to the **header()** method:

  ```
  print $q->header(-target=>'ResultsWindow');
  ```

  This will tell Netscape to load the output of your script into the frame named **ResultsWindow**. If a frame of that name doesn't already exist, Netscape will pop up a new window and load your script's document into that. There are a number of magic names that you can use for targets. See the frame documents on Netscape's home pages for details.

- You can specify the frame to load in the FORM tag itself. With *CGI.pm* it looks like this:

  ```
  print $q->startform(-target=>'ResultsWindow');
  ```

When your script is reinvoked by the form, its output will be loaded into the frame named ResultsWindow. If one doesn't already exist a new window will be created.

The script *frameset.cgi* in the examples directory shows one way to create pages in which the fill-out form and the response live in side-by-side frames.

Limited Support for Cascading Stylesheets

CGI.pm has limited support for HTML3's cascading style sheets (CSS). To incorporate a stylesheet into your document, pass the **start_html()** method a **-style** parameter. The value of this parameter may be a scalar, in which case it is incorporated directly into a **<STYLE>** section, or it may be a hash reference. In the latter case you should provide the hash with one or more of **-src** or **-code**. **-src** points to a URL where an externally defined stylesheet can be found. **-code** points to a scalar value to be incorporated into a **<STYLE>** section. Style definitions in **-code** override similarly named ones in **-src**, hence the name "cascading."

To refer to a style within the body of your document, add the **-class** parameter to any HTML element:

```
print h1({-class=>'Fancy'},'Welcome to the Party');
```

Or define styles on the fly with the **-style** parameter:

```
print h1({-style=>'Color: red;'},'Welcome to Hell');
```

You may also use the new **span()** element to apply a style to a section of text:

```
print span({-style=>'Color: red;'},
           h1('Welcome to Hell'),
```

```
            "Where did that handbasket get to?"
            );
```

Note that you must import the :html3 definitions to have the **span()** method available. Here's a quick and dirty example of using CSS definitions. See the CSS specification at *http://www.w3.org/pub/WWW/TR/Wd-css-1.html* for more information.

```
use CGI qw/:standard :html3/;
#here's a stylesheet incorporated directly into the page
$newStyle=<<END;
<!--
P.Tip {
    margin-right: 50pt;
    margin-left: 50pt;
    color: red;
}
P.Alert {
    font-size: 30pt;
    font-family: sans-serif;
    color: red;
}
-->
END
print header();
print start_html( -title=>'CGI with Style',
                  -style=>{-src=>
'http://www.capricorn.com/style/st1.css',
                          -code=>$newStyle}
                );
print h1('CGI with Style'),
    p({-class=>'Tip'},
      "Better read the cascading style sheet spec" +
      "before playing with this!"),
    span({-style=>'color: magenta'},
        "Look Mom, no hands!",
        p(),
        "Whooo wee!"
        );
print end_html;
```

Debugging

If you are running the script from the command line or in the Perl debugger, you can pass the script a list of keywords or **parameter=value** pairs on the command line or from standard input (you don't have to worry about tricking your script into reading from environment variables). You can pass keywords in any of these ways:

```
your_script.pl keyword1 keyword2 keyword3
your_script.pl keyword1+keyword2+keyword3
your_script.pl name1=value1 name2=value2
your_script.pl name1=value1&name2=value2
```

or even as newline-delimited parameters on standard input.

When debugging, you can use quotes and backslashes to escape characters in the familiar shell manner, letting you place spaces and other funny characters in your **parameter=value** pairs:

```
your_script.pl "name1='I am a long value'" "name2=two\ words"
```

Dumping out all the name/value pairs

The dump() method produces a string consisting of all the query's name/value pairs formatted nicely as a nested list. This is useful for debugging purposes:

```
print $query->dump
```

Produces something that looks like:

```
<UL>
<LI>name1
    <UL>
    <LI>value1
    <LI>value2
    </UL>
<LI>name2
    <UL>
    <LI>value1
    </UL>
</UL>
```

You can pass a value of true to dump() in order to get it to print the results out as plain text, suitable for incorporating into a <PRE> section.

As a shortcut, as of version 1.56 you can interpolate the entire CGI object into a string and it will be replaced with the a nice HTML dump shown above:

```
$query=new CGI;
print "<H2>Current Values</H2> $query\n";
```

Fetching Environment Variables

Some of the more useful environment variables can be fetched through this interface. The methods are as follows:

accept()

> Return a list of MIME types that the remote browser accepts. If you give this method a single argument corresponding to a MIME type, as in $query->accept('text/html'), it will return a floating point value corresponding to the browser's preference for this type from 0.0 (don't want) to 1.0. Glob types (e.g., text/*) in the browser's accept list are handled correctly.

raw_cookie()

> Returns the HTTP_COOKIE variable, an HTTP extension implemented by Netscape browsers version 1.1 and higher. Cookies have a special format, and this method call just returns the raw form (cookie dough?). See cookie() for ways of setting and retrieving cooked cookies.

user_agent()

> Returns the HTTP_USER_AGENT variable. If you give this method a single argument, it will attempt to pattern match on it, allowing you to do something like:
>
> ```
> $query->user_agent(netscape);
> ```

path_info()

> Returns additional path information from the script URL. e.g., fetching */cgi-bin/your_script/additional/stuff* will result in $query->path_info() returning additional/stuff.

Note

The Microsoft Internet Information Server is broken with respect to additional path information. If you use the Perl DLL library, the IIS server will attempt to execute the additional path information as a Perl script. If you use the ordinary file associations mapping, the path information will be present in the environment, but incorrect. The best thing to do is to avoid using additional path information in CGI scripts destined for use with IIS.

`path_translated()`

As per `path_info()` but returns the additional path information translated into a physical path, e.g., */usr/local/etc/httpd/htdocs/additional/stuff.*

The Microsoft IIS is broken with respect to the translated path as well.

`remote_host()`

Returns either the remote host name or IP address, if the former is unavailable.

`script_name()`

Returns the script name as a partial URL, for self-referring scripts.

`referer()`

Returns the URL of the page the browser was viewing prior to fetching your script. Not available for all browsers.

`auth_type()`

Returns the authorization/verification method in use for this script, if any.

`server_name()`

Returns the name of the server, usually the machine's host name.

`virtual_host()`

When using virtual hosts, returns the name of the host that the browser attempted to contact

`server_software()`

Returns the server software and version number.

`remote_user()`

Returns the authorization/verification name used for user verification, if this script is protected.

`user_name()`

Attempt to obtain the remote user's name, using a variety of different techniques.

`request_method()`

Returns the method used to access your script, usually one of POST, GET, or HEAD.

Creating HTML Elements

In addition to its shortcuts for creating form elements, *CGI.pm* defines general HTML shortcut methods as well. HTML shortcuts are named after a single HTML element and return a fragment of HTML text that you can then print or manipulate as you like.

This example shows how to use the HTML methods:

```
$q = new CGI;
print $q->blockquote(
                    "Many years ago on the island of",
                    $q->a({href=>"http://crete.org/"},"Crete"),
                    "there lived a minotaur named",
```

```
                          $q->strong("Fred."),
                      ),
    $q->hr;
```

This results in the following HTML code (extra newlines have been added for readability):

```
<blockquote>
Many years ago on the island of
<a HREF="http://crete.org/">Crete</a> there lived
a minotaur named <strong>Fred.</strong>
</blockquote>
<hr>
```

If you find the syntax for calling the HTML shortcuts awkward, you can import them into your namespace and dispense with the object syntax completely (see the next section for more details):

```
use CGI shortcuts;       # IMPORT HTML SHORTCUTS
print blockquote(
                "Many years ago on the island of",
                a({href=>"http://crete.org/"},"Crete"),
                "there lived a minotaur named",
                strong("Fred."),
            ),
    hr;
```

Providing arguments to HTML shortcuts

The HTML methods will accept zero, one, or multiple arguments. If you provide no arguments, you get a single tag:

```
print hr;
#  gives "<hr>"
```

If you provide one or more string arguments, they are concatenated together with spaces and placed between opening and closing tags:

```
print h1("Chapter","1");
# gives "<h1>Chapter 1</h1>"
```

If the first argument is an associative array reference, then the keys and values of the associative array become the HTML tag's attributes:

```
print a({href=>'fred.html',target=>'_new'},
        "Open a new frame");
# gives <a href="fred.html",target="_new">Open a new frame</a>
```

You are free to use *CGI.pm*-style dashes in front of the attribute names if you prefer:

```
print img {-src=>'fred.gif',-align=>'LEFT'};
# gives <img ALIGN="LEFT" SRC="fred.gif">
```

Generating new HTML tags

Since no mere mortal can keep up with Netscape and Microsoft as they battle it out for control of HTML, the code that generates HTML tags is general and extensible. You can create new HTML tags freely just by referring to them on the import line:

```
use CGI shortcuts,winkin,blinkin,nod;
```

Now, in addition to the standard CGI shortcuts, you've created HTML tags named `winkin`, `blinkin`, and `nod`. You can use them like this:

```
print blinkin {color=>'blue',rate=>'fast'},"Yahoo!";
# <blinkin COLOR="blue" RATE="fast">Yahoo!</blinkin>
```

Importing CGI Method Calls into Your Namespace

As a convenience, you can import most of the CGI method calls directly into your namespace. The syntax for doing this is:

```
use CGI <list of methods>;
```

The listed methods will be imported into the current package; you can call them directly without creating a CGI object first. This example shows how to import the `param()` and `header()` methods, and then use them directly:

```
use CGI param,header;
print header('text/plain');
$zipcode = param('zipcode');
```

You can import groups of methods by referring to a number of special names:

`cgi`

Import all CGI-handling methods, such as `param()`, `path_info()`, and the like.

`form`

Import all fill-out form generating methods, such as `textfield()`.

`html2`

Import all methods that generate HTML 2.0 standard elements.

`html3`

Import all methods that generate HTML 3.0 proposed elements (such as <TABLE>, <SUPER> and <SUB>).

`netscape`

Import all methods that generate Netscape-specific HTML extensions.

`shortcuts`

Import all HTML-generating shortcuts (i.e., `'html2'` + `'html3'` + `'netscape'`).

`standard`

Import "standard" features (`html2` + `form` + `cgi`).

`all`

Import all the available methods. For the full list, see the *CGI.pm* code, where the variable `%TAGS` is defined.

Note that in the interests of execution speed *CGI.pm* does *not* use the standard *Exporter* syntax for specifying load symbols. This may change in the future.

If you import any of the state-maintaining CGI or form-generating methods, a default CGI object will be created and initialized automatically the first time you use any of the methods that require one to be present. This includes `param()`, `textfield()`, `submit()`, and the like. (If you need direct access to the CGI object, you can find it in the global variable $CGI::Q). By importing *CGI.pm* methods, you can create visually elegant scripts:

```
use CGI standard,html2;
print
    header,
```

```
            start_html('Simple Script'),
            h1('Simple Script'),
            start_form,
            "What's your name? ",textfield('name'),p,
            "What's the combination?",
            checkbox_group(-name=>'words',
                            -values=>['eenie','meenie','minie','moe'],
                            -defaults=>['eenie','moe']),p,
            "What's your favorite color?",
            popup_menu(-name=>'color',
                        -values=>['red','green','blue','chartreuse']),p,
            submit,
            end_form,
            hr,"\n";
    if (param) {
        print
            "Your name is ",em(param('name')),p,
            "The keywords are: ",em(join(", ",param('words'))),p,
            "Your favorite color is ",em(param('color')),".\n";
    }
    print end_html;
```

Using NPH Scripts

NPH, or no-parsed-header, scripts bypass the server completely by sending the complete HTTP header directly to the browser. This has slight performance benefits, but is of most use for taking advantage of HTTP extensions that are not directly supported by your server, such as server push and PICS headers.

Servers use a variety of conventions for designating CGI scripts as NPH. Many UNIX servers look at the beginning of the script's name for the prefix **nph-**. The Macintosh WebSTAR server and Microsoft's Internet Information Server, in contrast, try to decide whether a program is an NPH script by examining the first line of script output.

CGI.pm supports NPH scripts with a special NPH mode. When in this mode, *CGI.pm* will output the necessary extra header information when the **header()** and **redirect()** methods are called.

The Microsoft Internet Information Server requires NPH mode. As of version 2.30, *CGI.pm* will automatically detect when the script is running under IIS and put itself into this mode. You do not need to do this manually, although it won't hurt anything if you do.

There are a number of ways to put *CGI.pm* into NPH mode:

In the use statement
    Simply add **:nph** to the list of symbols to be imported into your script:

```
        use CGI qw(:standard :nph)
```

By calling the nph() method
    Call **nph()** with a non-zero parameter at any point after using *CGI.pm* in your program:

```
        CGI->nph(1)
```

By using –nph parameters in the header() and redirect() statements:

```
        print $q->header(-nph=>1);
```

Example

```perl
#!/usr/local/bin/perl

use CGI;

$query = new CGI;
print $query->header;
print $query->start_html("Example CGI.pm Form");
print "<H1> Example CGI.pm Form</H1>\n";
&print_prompt($query);
&do_work($query);
&print_tail;
print $query->end_html;

sub print_prompt {
my($query) = @_;

print $query->startform;
print "<EM>What's your name?</EM><BR>";
print $query->textfield('name');
print $query->checkbox('Not my real name');

print "<P><EM>Where can you find English Sparrows?</EM><BR>";
print $query->checkbox_group(
                         -name=>'Sparrow locations',
                         -values=>[England,France,Spain,Asia,Hoboken],
                             -linebreak=>'yes',
                             -defaults=>[England,Asia]);

print "<P><EM>How far can they fly?</EM><BR>",
      $query->radio_group(
                     -name=>'how far',
                     -values=>['10 ft','1 mile','10 miles','real far'],
                     -default=>'1 mile');

print "<P><EM>What's your favorite color?</EM>";
print $query->popup_menu(-name=>'Color',
                         -values=>['black','brown','red','yellow'],
                         -default=>'red');

print $query->hidden('Reference','Monty Python and the Holy Grail');

print "<P><EM>What have you got there?</EM><BR>";
print $query->scrolling_list(
                          -name=>'possessions',
                          -values=>['A Coconut','A Grail','An Icon',
                                    'A Sword','A Ticket'],
                          -size=>5,
                          -multiple=>'true');

print "<P><EM>Any parting comments?</EM><BR>";
print $query->textarea(-name=>'Comments',
```

```
                             -rows=>10,
                             -columns=>50);

    print "<P>",$query->reset;
    print $query->submit('Action','Shout');
    print $query->submit('Action','Scream');
    print $query->endform;
    print "<HR>\n";
}

sub do_work {
    my($query) = @_;
    my(@values,$key);
    print "<H2>Here are the current settings in this form</H2>";
    foreach $key ($query->param) {
        print "<STRONG>$key</STRONG> -> ";
        @values = $query->param($key);
        print join(", ",@values),"<BR>\n";
    }
}

sub print_tail {
    print <<END;
    <HR>
    <ADDRESS>Lincoln D. Stein</ADDRESS><BR>
    <A HREF="/">Home Page</A>
    END
}
```

Bugs

This module has grown large and monolithic. Furthermore it's doing many things, such as handling URLs, parsing CGI input, writing HTML, etc., that are also done in the LWP modules. It should be discarded in favor of the CGI::* modules, but somehow I continue to work on it.

Note that the code is truly contorted in order to avoid spurious warnings when programs are run with the -w switch.

Acknowledgments

Thanks very much to:

Matt Heffron, *heffron@falstaff.css.beckman.com*
James Taylor, *james.taylor@srs.gov*
Scott Anguish, *sanguish@digifix.com*
Mike Jewell, *mlj3u@virginia.edu*
Timothy Shimmin, *tes@kbs.citri.edu.au*
Joergen Haegg, *jh@axis.se*
Laurent Delfosse, *delfosse@csgrad1.cs.wvu.edu*
Richard Resnick, *applepi1@aol.com*
Craig Bishop, *csb@barwonwater.vic.gov.au*
Tony Curtis, *tc@vcpc.univie.ac.at*
Tim Bunce, *Tim.Bunce@ig.co.uk*
Tom Christiansen, *tchrist@convex.com*

Andreas Koenig, *k@franz.ww.TU-Berlin.DE*
Tim MacKenzie, *Tim.MacKenzie@fulcrum.com.au*
Kevin B. Hendricks, *kbhend@dogwood.tyler.wm.edu*
Stephen Dahmen, *joyfire@inxpress.net*
Ed Jordan, *ed@fidalgo.net*
David Alan Pisoni, *david@cnation.com*
and many, many more,

for suggestions and bug fixes.

Author

Lincoln D. Stein, *lstein@genome.wi.mit.edu*

Copyright

Copyright 1995, 1996, Lincoln D. Stein. All rights reserved. It may be used and modified freely, but I do request that this copyright notice remain attached to the file. You may modify this module as you wish, but if you redistribute a modified version, please attach a note listing the modifications you have made.

See Also

CGI::Carp, URI::URL, CGI::Request, CGI::MiniSvr, CGI::Base, CGI::Form, CGI::Apache, CGI::Switch, CGI::Push, CGI::Fast

---

CGI Lite —Perl 5.0 module to process and decode WWW form information

Synopsis

```
use CGI_Lite;
$cgi = new CGI_Lite;
$cgi->set_platform ($platform);
    where $platform (case insensitive) can be one of:
    Unix, Windows, Windows95, DOS, NT, PC, Mac or Macintosh
$cgi->set_file_type ("handle" or "file");
$size = $cgi->set_buffer_size ($some_size);
$status = $cgi->set_directory ('/some/dir');
$cgi->set_directory ('/some/dir') || die "Directory doesn't exist.\n";
$form = $form->parse_form_data;
%form = $cgi->parse_form_data;
$cookies = $form->parse_cookies;
%cookies = $cgi->parse_cookies;
$cgi->print_form_data;
$cgi->print_cookie_data;
$new_string  = $cgi->wrap_textarea ($string, $length);
@all_options = $cgi->get_multiple_values ($options);
$cgi->create_variables (\%form);
$cgi->create_variables ($form);
```

Description

You can use this module to decode form information or cookies in a very simple manner; you need not concern yourself with the actual details behind the decoding process.

This module can handle the traditional GET and POST URL encoded data, as well the new multipart form data (i.e., file upload).

Methods

Here are the methods you can use to process your forms:

parse_form_data

> This will handle all types of requests: GET, HEAD, and POST (for both encoding methods). For multipart/form-data, uploaded files are stored in the user selected directory (see **set_directory**). The files are named in the following format:
>
> > timestamp__filename
>
> where the filename is specified in the "Content-disposition" header. Note that the browser URL encodes the name of the file. This module makes no effort to decode the information for security reasons.
>
> *Return Value*
>
> > Returns either a hash or a reference to the hash, which contains all of the key/value pairs. For fields that contain file information, the value contains either the path to the file, or the file handle (see the **set_file_type** method).

parse_cookies

> Parses any cookies passed by the browser. This method works in much the same manner as **parse_form_data**.

set_platform

> This method will set the end of line characters for uploaded text files so that they display properly on the specified platform (the platform your HTTP server is running on).
>
> You can specify either:

Unix	EOL: \012	= \n
Windows, Windows95, DOS, NT, PC	EOL: \015\012	= \r\n
Mac or Macintosh	EOL: \015	= \r

> "Unix" is the default.

set_directory

> Used to set the directory where the uploaded files will be stored (only applies to the multipart/form-data encoding scheme).
>
> This function should be called *before* you call **parse_form_data**, or else the directory defaults to /tmp. If the application cannot write to the directory for whatever reason, an error status is returned.
>
> *Return Value*
>
> > 0   Failure
> > 1   Success

set_file_type

> The *names* of uploaded files are returned by default, when you call the **parse_form_data** method. But, if pass the string "handle" to this method, the *handles* to the files are returned. However, the name of the handle corresponds to the filename.
>
> This function should be called *before* you call **parse_form_data**, or else it will not work.

`set_buffer_size`

This method allows you to set the buffer size when dealing with multipart form data. However, the *actual* buffer size that the algorithm uses *will* be 2–3 times that of the value you specify. This ensures that boundary strings are not "split" between multiple reads. So take this into consideration when setting a buffer size.

You cannot set a buffer size below 256 bytes and above the total amount of multi-part form data. The default value is 1024 bytes.

Return Value

The buffer size.

`print_form_data`

Displays all of the key/value pairs. If a key contains multiple values, all the values are displayed.

`print_cookie_data`

Displays all the cookie key/value pairs. If a key contains multiple values, all the values are displayed.

`wrap_textarea`

You can use this function to "wrap" a long string into one that is separated by a combination of carriage return and newline (see `set_platform`) at fixed lengths. The two arguments that you need to pass to this method are the string and the length at which you want the line separator added.

Return Value

The modified string.

`get_multiple_values`

One of the major changes to this module as of v1.7 is that multiple values for a single key are returned as an reference to an array, and *not* as a string delimited by the null character (\0). You can use this function to return the actual array.

There was no way I could make this backward compatible. I apologize!

Return Value

Array consisting of the multiple values.

`create_variables`

Sometimes, it is convenient to have scalar variables that represent the various keys in a hash. You can use this method to do just that. Say you have a hash like the following:

```
%form = ('name'   => 'shishir gundavaram',
         'sport'  => 'track and field',
         'events' => '100m');
```

If you call this method in the following manner:

```
$cgi->create_variables (\%hash);
```

it will create three scalar variables: `$name`, `$sport`, and `$events`. Convenient, huh?

Acknowledgments

I'd like to thank the following for finding bugs and offering suggestions:

Eric D. Friedman, *friedman@uci.edu*

Thomas Winzig, *tsw@pvo.com*

Len Charest, *len@cogent.net*
Achim Bohnet, *ach@rosat.mpe-garching.mpg.de*
John E. Townsend, *John.E.Townsend@BST.BLS.com*
Andrew McRae, *mcrae@internet.com*
and many others!

Author

Shishir Gundavaram

Copyright

See Also

You should look at the various other CGI modules, and use the one that best suits you. For more information, you can subscribe to the CGI Module Development List at:

> *CGI-perl@webstorm.com*

Contact: Marc Hedlund *(hedlund@best.com)* for more information. This list is *not* for general CGI support. It only deals with CGI module development.

The CGI modules and *CGI.pm* are maintained by Lincoln Stein *(lstein@genome.wi.mit.edu)* and can be found on his web site:

> *http://www-genome.wi.mit.edu/WWW/tools/scripting*

CGI::BasePlus — HTTP CGI base class with handling of multipart forms

Description

This module implements a CGI::BasePlus object that is identical in behavior to CGI::Base except that it provides special handling for postings of MIME type multipart/form-data (which may get very long). In the case of these types of postings, parts that are described as being from a file upload are copied into a temporary file in */usr/tmp*, a file handle is opened on the temporary files, and the name of the file handle is returned to the caller in the $CGI::Base:QUERY_STRING variable.

Please see CGI::Base for more information.

See Also

URI::URL, CGI::Request, CGI::MiniSvr, CGI::Base

CGI::Fast — CGI interface for fast CGI

Synopsis

```
use CGI::Fast qw(:standard);
$COUNTER = 0;
```

```
while (new CGI::Fast) {
    print header;
    print start_html("Fast CGI Rocks");
    print
        h1("Fast CGI Rocks"),
        "Invocation number ",b($COUNTER++),
        " PID ",b($$),".",
        hr;
    print end_html;
}
```

Description

CGI::Fast is a subclass of the CGI object created by *CGI.pm*. It is specialized to work well with the Open Market FastCGI standard, which greatly speeds up CGI scripts by turning them into persistently running server processes. Scripts that perform time-consuming initialization processes, such as loading large modules or opening persistent database connections, will see large performance improvements.

Other Pieces of the Puzzle

In order to use CGI::Fast you'll need a FastCGI-enabled web server. Open Market's server is FastCGI-savvy. There are also freely redistributable FastCGI modules for NCSA httpd 1.5 and Apache. FastCGI-enabling modules for Microsoft Internet Information Server and Netscape Communications Server have been announced.

In addition, you'll need a version of the Perl interpreter that has been linked with the FastCGI I/O library. Precompiled binaries are available for several platforms, including DEC Alpha, HP-UX and SPARC/Solaris, or you can rebuild Perl from source with patches provided in the FastCGI developer's kit. The FastCGI Perl interpreter can be used in place of your normal Perl without ill consequences.

You can find FastCGI modules for Apache and NCSA httpd, precompiled Perl interpreters, and the FastCGI developer's kit all at the following URL:

http://www.fastcgi.com/

Writing FastCGI Perl Scripts

FastCGI scripts are persistent: one or more copies of the script are started up when the server initializes, and stay around until the server exits or they die a natural death. After performing whatever one-time initialization it needs, the script enters a loop waiting for incoming connections, processing the request, and waiting some more.

A typical FastCGI script will look like this:

```
#!/usr/local/bin/perl    # must be a FastCGI version of perl!
use CGI::Fast;
&do_some_initialization();
while ($q = new CGI::Fast) {
    &process_request($q);
}
```

Each time there's a new request, CGI::Fast returns a CGI object to your loop. The rest of the time your script waits in the call to new(). When the server requests that your script be terminated, new() will return undef. You can of course exit earlier if you choose. A new version of the script will be respawned to take its place (this may be necessary in order to avoid Perl memory leaks in long-running scripts).

CGI.pm's default CGI object mode also works. Just modify the loop this way:

```
while (new CGI::Fast) {
    &process_request;
}
```

Calls to `header()`, `start_form()`, etc., will all operate on the current request.

Installing FastCGI Scripts

See the FastCGI developer's kit documentation for full details. On the Apache server, the following line must be added to *srm.conf*:

```
AddType application/x-httpd-fcgi .fcgi
```

FastCGI scripts must end in the extension *.fcgi*. For each script you install, you must add something like the following to *srm.conf*:

```
AppClass /usr/etc/httpd/fcgi-bin/file_upload.fcgi -processes 2
```

This instructs Apache to launch two copies of *file_upload.fcgi* at startup time.

Using FastCGI Scripts as Normal CGI Scripts

Any script that works correctly as a FastCGI script will also work correctly when installed as a vanilla CGI script. However, it will not see any performance benefit.

Author

Lincoln D. Stein, *lstein@genome.wi.mit.edu*

Copyright

Copyright © 1996, Lincoln D. Stein. All rights reserved. It may be used and modified freely, but I do request that this copyright notice remain attached to the file. You may modify this module as you wish, but if you redistribute a modified version, please attach a note listing the modifications you have made.

See Also

CGI::Carp, CGI

CGI::Form—build smart HTML forms on top of the CGI::* modules

Abstract

This Perl library uses Perl5 objects to make it easy to create web fill-out forms and parse their contents. This package defines CGI objects, entities that contain the values of the current query string and other state variables. Using a CGI object's methods, you can examine keywords and parameters passed to your script, and create forms whose initial values are taken from the current query (thereby preserving state information).

Installation

To use this package, install it in your Perl library path (usually */usr/local/lib/perl5/*) and add the following to your Perl CGI script:

```
Use CGI::Form;
```

Description

Creating a New Form Object and Processing Parameters

This will parse the input (from both POST and GET methods) and store it into a Perl5 object called $query. This method is inherited from CGI::Request. See its manpage for details.

```
$query = new CGI::Form;
```

Similarly, CGI::Form uses CGI::Request to get and set named query parameters, e.g.:

```
@values = $query->param('foo');
          -and-
$query->param('foo','an','array','of','values');
```

or whatever!

Calling CGI::Form Functions That Take Multiple Arguments

In versions of *Form.pm* prior to 2.8, it could get difficult to remember the proper order of arguments in CGI function calls that accepted five or six different arguments. As of 2.8, there's a better way to pass arguments to the various CGI functions. In this style, you pass a series of **name=>argument** pairs, like this:

```
$field = $query->radio_group(-name=>'OS',
                             -values=>[Unix,Windows,Macintosh],
                             -default=>'Unix');
```

The advantages of this style are that you don't have to remember the exact order of the arguments, and if you leave out a parameter, in most cases it will default to some reasonable value. If you provide a parameter that the method doesn't recognize, it will usually do something useful with it, such as incorporating it into the HTML form tag. For example if Netscape decides next week to add a new JUSTIFICATION parameter to the text field tags, you can start using the feature without waiting for a new version of *CGI.pm*:

```
$field = $query->textfield(-name=>'State',
                           -default=>'gaseous',
                           -justification=>'RIGHT');
```

This will result in an HTML tag that looks like this:

```
<INPUT TYPE="textfield" NAME="State" VALUE="gaseous"
       JUSTIFICATION="RIGHT">
```

Parameter names are case insensitive: you can use **-name**, or **-Name**, or **-NAME**. You don't have to use the hyphen if you don't want to. After creating a CGI object, call the **use_named_parameters()** method with a nonzero value. This will tell *CGI.pm* that you intend to use named parameters exclusively:

```
$query = new CGI;
$query->use_named_parameters(1);
$field = $query->radio_group('name'=>'OS',
                             'values'=>['Unix','Windows','Macintosh'],
                             'default'=>'Unix');
```

Actually, *CGI.pm* only looks for a hyphen in the first parameter. So you can leave it off subsequent parameters if you like. Something to be wary of is the potential that a string constant like **values** will collide with a keyword (and in fact it does!). While Perl usually figures out when you're referring to a function and when you're referring to a string, you probably should put quotation marks around all string constants just to play it safe.

Creating a Self-Referencing URL that Preserves State Information

`self_url()` will return a URL, that, when selected, will reinvoke this script with all its state information intact.

```
$myself = $query->self_url
print "<A HREF=$myself>I'm talking to myself.</A
```

This is most useful when you want to jump around within the document using internal anchors, but you don't want to disrupt the current contents of the form(s). Something like this will do the trick:

```
$myself = $query->self_url
print "<A HREF=$myself#table1>See table 1</A
print "<A HREF=$myself#table2>See table 2</A
print "<A HREF=$myself#yourself>See for yourself</A
```

This method is actually defined in CGI::Base, but is passed through here for compatibility with *CGI.pm*

Creating the HTTP Header

`header()` returns the Content-type: header. you can provide your own MIME type if you choose, otherwise it defaults to `text/html`.

```
print $query->header;
      -or-
print $query->header('image/gif');
```

This method is provided for compatibility with *CGI.pm* only. It is much better to use the `SendHeaders()` method of CGI::Base.

Note that this is a temporary method that will be replaced by the CGI::Response module as soon as it is released.

Generating a Redirection Instruction

Redirect the browser elsewhere. If you use redirection like this, you should *not* print out a header as well.

```
print $query->redirect('http://somewhere.else/in/movie/land');
```

This method is provided for compatibility with *CGI.pm* only. New scripts should use CGI::Base's `redirect()` method instead.

Creating the HTML Header

This will return a canned HTML header and the opening <BODY> tag. All parameters are optional. In the named parameter form, recognized parameters are -title, -author, and -base (see below for the explanation). Any additional parameters you provide, such as the Netscape unofficial BGCOLOR attribute, are added to the <BODY> tag.

```
print $query->start_html(-title=>'Secrets of the Pyramids',
                         -author=>'fred@capricorn.org',
                         -base=>'true',
                         -BGCOLOR=>"#00A0A0");
```

```
-or-
print $query->start_html('Secrets of the Pyramids',
                         'fred@capricorn.org','true',
                         'BGCOLOR="#00A0A0"');
```

Positional parameters are as follows:

1   The title

2   The author's email address (will create a `<LINK REV="MADE">` tag if present

3   A `'true'` flag if you want to include a `<BASE>` tag in the header. This helps resolve relative addresses to absolute ones when the document is moved, but makes the document hierarchy non-portable. Use with care!

4, 5, 6 . . .

Any other parameters you want to include in the `<BODY>` tag. This is a good place to put Netscape extensions, such as colors and wallpaper patterns.

Ending the HTML document

This ends an HTML document by printing the `</BODY></HTML>` tags.

```
print $query->end_html
```

Creating Forms

The various form-creating methods all return strings to the caller, containing the tag or tags that will create the requested form element. You are responsible for actually printing out these strings. It's set up this way so that you can place formatting tags around the form elements.

The default values that you specify for the forms are only used the *first* time the script is invoked. If there are already values present in the query string, they are used, even if blank. If you want to change the value of a field from its previous value, call the `param()` method to set it.

By default, the text and labels of form elements are escaped according to HTML rules. This means that you can safely use `<CLICK ME>` as the label for a button. However, it also interferes with your ability to incorporate special HTML character sequences, such as `&Aacute;`, into your fields. If you wish to turn off automatic escaping, call the `autoEscape()` method with a false value immediately after creating the CGI object:

```
$query = new CGI::Form;
$query->autoEscape(undef);
```

Creating an ISINDEX tag

```
print $query->isindex($action);
```
Prints out an `<ISINDEX>` tag. Not very exciting. The optional parameter specifies an `ACTION="<URL>"` attribute.

Starting and ending a form

`startform()` will return a `<FORM>` tag with the optional method, action and form encoding that you specify.

```
print $query->startform($method,$action,$encoding);
   <... various form stuff ...>
print $query->endform;
```

The default values are:

```
method: POST
action: this script encoding:
application/x-www-form-urlencoded
```

The encoding method tells the browser how to package the various fields of the form before sending the form to the server. Two values are possible:

application/x-www-form-urlencoded

This is the older type of encoding used by all browsers prior to Netscape 2.0. It is compatible with many CGI scripts and is suitable for short fields containing text data.

multipart/form-data

This is the newer type of encoding introduced by Netscape 2.0. It is suitable for forms that contain very large fields or that are intended for transferring binary data. Most importantly, it enables the "file upload" feature of Netscape 2.0 forms.

Forms that use this type of encoding are not easily interpreted by CGI scripts unless they use *CGI.pm* or another library designed to handle them.

For your convenience, *Form.pm* defines two subroutines that contain the values of the two alternative encodings:

```
use CGI::Form(URL_ENCODED,MULTIPART);
```

For compatibility, the **startform()** method uses the older form of encoding by default. If you want to use the newer form of encoding by default, you can call **start_multipart_form()** instead of **startform()**. **endform()** returns a **</FORM>** tag.

Creating a text field

textfield() will return a text input field.

```
print $query->textfield(-name=>'field_name',
                        -default=>'starting value',
                        -size=>50,
                        -maxlength=>80);
```

or:

```
print $query->textfield('field_name','starting value',50,80);
```

Parameters:

1. The first parameter is the required name for the field (**-name**).

2. The optional second parameter is the default starting value for the field contents (**-default**).

3. The optional third parameter is the size of the field in characters (**-size**).

4. The optional fourth parameter is the maximum number of characters the field will accept (**-maxlength**).

As with all these methods, the field will be initialized with its previous contents from earlier invocations of the script. When the form is processed, the value of the text field can be retrieved with:

```
$value = $query->param('foo');
```

If you want to reset it from its initial value after the script has been called once, you can do so like this:

```
$query->param('foo',"I'm taking over this value!");
```

Creating a big text field

`textarea()` is just like textfield, but it allows you to specify rows and columns for a multiline text entry box. You can provide a starting value for the field, which can be long and contain multiple lines.

```
print $query->textarea(-name=>'foo',
                       -default=>'starting value',
                       -rows=>10,
                       -columns=>50);
```

or:

```
print $query->textarea('foo','starting value',10,50);
```

Creating a password field

`password_field()` is identical to `textfield()`, except that its contents will be starred out on the web page.

```
print $query->password_field(-name=>'secret',
                             -value=>'starting value',
                             -size=>50,
                             -maxlength=>80);
```

or:

```
print $query->password_field('secret','starting value',50,80);
```

Creating a file upload field

`filefield()` will return a file upload field for Netscape 2.0 browsers. In order to take full advantage of this *you must use the new multipart encoding scheme* for the form. You can do this either by calling `startform()` with an encoding type of $CGI::MULTIPART, or by calling the new method `start_multipart_form()` instead of vanilla `startform()`.

```
print $query->filefield(-name=>'uploaded_file',
                        -default=>'starting value',
                        -size=>50,
                        -maxlength=>80);
```

or:

```
print $query->filefield('uploaded_file','starting
value',50,80);
```

Parameters:

1. The first parameter is the required name for the field (**-name**).

2. The optional second parameter is the starting value for the field contents to be used as the default file name (**-default**).

   The beta2 version of Netscape 2.0 currently doesn't pay any attention to this field, and so the starting value will always be blank. Worse, the field loses its "sticky" behavior and forgets its previous contents. The starting value field is called for in the HTML specification, however, and possibly later versions of Netscape will honor it.

3. The optional third parameter is the size of the field in characters (**-size**).

4. The optional fourth parameter is the maximum number of characters the field will accept (**-maxlength**).

When the form is processed, you can retrieve the entered filename by calling **param()**.

```
$filename = $query->param('uploaded_file');
```

In Netscape Beta 1, the filename that gets returned is the full local filename on the *remote user*'s machine. If the remote user is on a UNIX machine, the filename will follow UNIX conventions:

```
/path/to/the/file
```

On an MS-DOS/Windows machine, the filename will follow DOS conventions:

```
C:\PATH\TO\THE\FILE.MSW
```

On a Macintosh machine, the filename will follow Mac conventions:

```
HD 40:Desktop Folder:Sort Through:Reminders
```

In Netscape Beta 2, only the last part of the file path (the filename itself) is returned. I don't know what the release behavior will be.

The filename returned is also a file handle. You can read the contents of the file using standard Perl file reading calls:

```
# Read a text file and print it out
while (<$filename>) {
   print;
}
# Copy a binary file to somewhere safe
open (OUTFILE,">>/usr/local/web/users/feedback");
while ($bytesread=read($filename,$buffer,1024)) {
   print OUTFILE $buffer;
}
```

Creating a popup menu

popup_menu() creates a menu:

```
print $query->popup_menu('menu_name',
                         ['eenie','meenie','minie'],
                         'meenie');
```

or:

```
%labels = ('eenie'=>'your first choice',
           'meenie'=>'your second choice',
           'minie'=>'your third choice');
print $query->popup_menu('menu_name',
                         ['eenie','meenie','minie'],
                         'meenie',\%labels);
```

or (named parameter style):

```
print $query->popup_menu(-name=>'menu_name',
                         -values=>['eenie','meenie','minie'],
                         -default=>'meenie',
                         -labels=>\%labels);
```

Parameters:

1. The required first argument is the menu's name (-name).

2. The required second argument (-values) is an array *reference* containing the list of menu items in the menu. You can pass the method an anonymous array, as shown in the example, or a reference to a named array, such as \@foo.

3. The optional third parameter (-default) is the name of the default menu choice. If not specified, the first item will be the default. The values of the previous choice will be maintained across queries.

4. The optional fourth parameter (-labels) is provided for people who want to use different values for the user-visible label inside the popup menu and the value returned to your script. It's a pointer to an associative array relating menu values to user-visible labels. If you leave this parameter blank, the menu values will be displayed by default. (You can also leave a label undefined if you want to.)

When the form is processed, the selected value of the popup menu can be retrieved using:

```
$popup_menu_value = $query->param('menu_name');
```

Creating a scrolling list

scrolling_list() creates a scrolling list.

```
print $query->scrolling_list('list_name',
                             ['eenie','meenie','minie','moe'],
                             ['eenie','moe'],5,'true');
```

or:

```
print $query->scrolling_list('list_name',
                             ['eenie','meenie','minie','moe'],
                             ['eenie','moe'],5,'true',
                             \%labels);
```

or:

```
print $query->scrolling_list(-name=>'list_name',
                             -values=>['eenie','meenie','minie','moe'],
                             -default=>['eenie','moe'],
                             -size=>5,
                             -multiple=>'true',
                             -labels=>\%labels);
```

Parameters:

1. The first and second arguments are the list name (-name) and values (-values). As in the popup menu, the second argument should be an array reference.

2. The optional third argument (-default) can be either a reference to a list containing the values to be selected by default, or can be a single value to select. If this argument is missing or undefined, then nothing is selected when the list first appears. In the named parameter version, you can use the synonym -defaults for this parameter.

3. The optional fourth argument is the size of the list (-size).

4. The optional fifth argument can be set to true to allow multiple simultaneous selections (-multiple). Otherwise only one selection will be allowed at a time.

5. The optional sixth argument is a pointer to an associative array containing long user-visible labels for the list items (-labels). If not provided, the values will be displayed.

When this form is processed, all selected list items will be returned as a list under the parameter name list_name. The values of the selected items can be retrieved with:

```
@selected = $query->param('list_name');
```

Creating a group of related checkboxes

checkbox_group() creates a list of checkboxes that are related by the same name.

```
print $query->checkbox_group(-name=>'group_name',
                   -values=>['eenie','meenie','minie','moe'],
                   -default=>['eenie','moe'],
                   -linebreak=>'true',
                   -labels=>\%labels);
print $query->checkbox_group('group_name',
                      ['eenie','meenie','minie','moe'],
                      ['eenie','moe'],'true',\%labels);
```

HTML3-compatible browsers only:

```
print $query->checkbox_group(-name=>'group_name',
                   -values=>['eenie','meenie','minie','moe'],
                   -rows=2,-columns=>2);
```

Parameters:

1. The first and second arguments are the checkbox name and values, respectively (-name and -values). As in the popup menu, the second argument should be an array reference. These values are used for the user-readable labels printed next to the checkboxes as well as for the values passed to your script in the query string.

2. The optional third argument (-default) can be either a reference to a list containing the values to be checked by default, or can be a single value to checked. If this argument is missing or undefined, then nothing is selected when the list first appears.

3. The optional fourth argument (-linebreak) can be set to true to place line breaks between the checkboxes so that they appear as a vertical list. Otherwise, they will be strung together on a horizontal line.

4. The optional fifth argument is a pointer to an associative array relating the checkbox values to the user-visible labels that will be printed next to them (-labels). If not provided, the values will be used as the default.

HTML3-compatible browsers (such as Netscape) can take advantage of the optional parameters -rows, and -columns. These parameters cause checkbox_group() to return an HTML3-compatible table containing the checkbox group formatted with the specified number of rows and columns. You can provide just the -columns parameter if you wish; checkbox_group will calculate the correct number of rows for you.

To include row and column headings in the returned table, you can use the `-rowheader` and `-colheader` parameters. Both of these accept a pointer to an array of headings to use. The headings are just decorative. They don't reorganize the interpretation of the checkboxes—they're still a single named unit.

When the form is processed, all checked boxes will be returned as a list under the parameter name **group_name**. The values of the "on" checkboxes can be retrieved with:

```
@turned_on = $query->param('group_name');
```

Creating a standalone checkbox

`checkbox()` is used to create an isolated checkbox that isn't logically related to any others.

```
print $query->checkbox(-name=>'checkbox_name',
                       -checked=>'checked',
                       -value=>'ON',
                       -label=>'CLICK ME');
```
or
```
print $query->checkbox('checkbox_name','checked'
                       'ON','CLICK ME');
```

Parameters:

1. The first parameter is the required name for the checkbox (**-name**). It will also be used for the user-readable label printed next to the checkbox.

2. The optional second parameter (**-checked**) specifies that the checkbox is turned on by default. Synonyms are **-selected** and **-on**.

3. The optional third parameter (**-value**) specifies the value of the checkbox when it is checked. If not provided, the word "on" is assumed.

4. The optional fourth parameter (**-label**) is the user-readable label to be attached to the checkbox. If not provided, the checkbox name is used.

The value of the checkbox can be retrieved using:

```
$turned_on = $query->param('checkbox_name');
```

Creating a radio button group

`radio_group()` creates a set of logically related radio buttons (turning one member of the group on turns the others off):

```
print $query->radio_group(-name=>'group_name',
                          -values=>['eenie','meenie','minie'],
                          -default=>'meenie',
                          -linebreak=>'true',
                          -labels=>\%labels);
```
or:
```
print $query->radio_group('group_name',
                          ['eenie','meenie','minie'],
                          'meenie','true',\%labels);
```

HTML3-compatible browsers only:

```
print $query->checkbox_group(-name=>'group_name',
                             -values=>['eenie','meenie','minie','moe'],
                             -rows=2,-columns=>2);
```

Parameters:

1. The first argument is the name of the group and is required (**-name**).

2. The second argument (**-values**) is the list of values for the radio buttons. The values and the labels that appear on the page are identical. Pass an array *reference* in the second argument, either using an anonymous array, as shown, or by referencing a named array as in \@foo.

3. The optional third parameter (**-default**) is the name of the default button to turn on. If not specified, the first item will be the default. You can provide a nonexistent button name, such as "-" to start up with no buttons selected.

4. The optional fourth parameter (**-linebreak**) can be set to **true** to put line breaks between the buttons, creating a vertical list.

5. The optional fifth parameter (**-labels**) is a pointer to an associative array relating the radio button values to user-visible labels to be used in the display. If not provided, the values themselves are displayed.

6. HTML3-compatible browsers (such as Netscape) can take advantage of the optional parameters **-rows**, and **-columns**. These parameters cause **radio_group()** to return an HTML3-compatible table containing the radio group formatted with the specified number of rows and columns. You can provide just the **-columns** parameter if you wish; **radio_group** will calculate the correct number of rows for you.

To include row and column headings in the returned table, you can use the **-rowheader** and **-colheader** parameters. Both of these accept a pointer to an array of headings to use. The headings are just decorative. They don't reorganize the interpretation of the radio buttons—they're still a single named unit.

When the form is processed, the selected radio button can be retrieved using:

```
$which_radio_button = $query->param('group_name');
```

Creating a submit button

submit() will create the query submission button. Every form should have one of these.

```
print $query->submit(-name=>'button_name',
                     -value=>'value');
```

or:

```
print $query->submit('button_name','value');
```

Parameters:

1. The first argument (**-name**) is optional. You can give the button a name if you have several submission buttons in your form and you want to distinguish between them. The name will also be used as the user-visible label. Be aware that a few older browsers don't deal with this correctly and *never* send back a value from a button.

2. The second argument (**-value**) is also optional. This gives the button a value that will be passed to your script in the query string.

You can figure out which button was pressed by using different values for each one:

```
$which_one = $query->param('button_name');
```

Creating a reset button

reset() creates the "reset" button. Note that it restores the form to its value from the last time the script was called, *not* necessarily to the defaults.

```
print $query->reset
```

Creating a default button

defaults() creates a button that, when invoked, will cause the form to be completely reset to its defaults, wiping out all the changes the user ever made.

```
print $query->defaults('button_label')
```

Creating a hidden field

hidden() produces a text field that can't be seen by the user. It is useful for passing state variable information from one invocation of the script to the next.

```
print $query->hidden(-name=>'hidden_name',
                      -default=>['value1','value2'...]);
```

or:

```
print $query->hidden('hidden_name','value1','value2'...);
```

Parameters:

1. The first argument is required and specifies the name of this field (-name).

2. The second argument is also required and specifies its value (-default). In the named parameter style of calling, you can provide a single value here or a reference to a whole list

Fetch the value of a hidden field this way:

```
$hidden_value = $query->param('hidden_name');
```

Note that just like all the other form elements, the value of a hidden field is "sticky." If you want to replace a hidden field with some other values after the script has been called once you'll have to do it manually:

```
$query->param('hidden_name','new','values','here');
```

Creating a clickable image button

image_button() produces a clickable image. When it's clicked on the position of the click is returned to your script as button_name.x and button_name.y, where button_name is the name you've assigned to it:

```
print $query->image_button(-name=>'button_name',
                           -src=>'/source/URL',
                           -align=>'MIDDLE');
```

or:

```
print $query->image_button('button_
name','/source/URL','MIDDLE');
```

Parameters:

1. The first argument (-name) is required and specifies the name of this field.

2. The second argument (-src) is also required and specifies the URL.

3. The third option (-align, optional) is an alignment type, and may be TOP, BOTTOM, or MIDDLE.

Fetch the value of the button this way:

```
$x = $query->param('button_name.x');
$y = $query->param('button_name.y');
```

Debugging

If you are running the script from the command line or in the Perl debugger, you can pass the script a list of keywords or **parameter=value** pairs on the command line or from standard input (you don't have to worry about tricking your script into reading from environment variables). You can pass keywords like this:

```
your_script.pl keyword1 keyword2 keyword3
```

or this:

```
your_script.pl keyword1+keyword2+keyword3
```

or this:

```
your_script.pl name1=value1 name2=value2
```

or this:

```
your_script.pl name1=value1&name2=value2
```

or even as newline-delimited parameters on standard input.

When debugging, you can use quotes and backslashes to escape characters in the familiar shell manner, letting you place spaces and other funny characters in your **parameter=value** pairs:

```
your_script.pl name1='I am a long value' name2=two\ words
```

Dumping Out All the Name/Value Pairs

The **dump()** method produces a string consisting of all the query's name/value pairs formatted nicely as a nested list. This is useful for debugging purposes:

```
print $query->dump
```

produces something that looks like:

```
<UL>
<LI>name1
    <UL>
    <LI>value1
    <LI>value2
    </UL>
<LI>name2
    <UL>
    <LI>value1
    </UL>
</UL>
```

You can pass a value of **true** to **dump()** in order to get it to print the results out as plain text, suitable for incorporating into a <PRE> section.

Fetching Environment Variables

All the environment variables, such as REMOTE_HOST and HTTP_REFERER, are available through the CGI::Base object. You can get at these variables using with the **cgi()** method (inherited from CGI::Request):

```
$query->cgi->var('REMOTE_HOST');
```

A Complete Example of a Simple Form-Based Script

```perl
#!/usr/local/bin/perl

use CGI::Form;

$query = new CGI::Form;
print $query->header;
print $query->start_html("Example CGI.pm Form");
print "<H1> Example CGI.pm Form</H1>\n";
&print_prompt($query);
&do_work($query);
&print_tail;
print $query->end_html;

sub print_prompt {
    my($query) = @_;

    print $query->startform;
    print "<EM>What's your name?</EM><BR>";
    print $query->textfield('name');
    print $query->checkbox('Not my real name');

    print "<P><EM>Where can you find English Sparrows?</EM><BR>";
    print $query->checkbox_group('Sparrow locations',
                                 [England,France,Spain,Asia,Hoboken],
                                 [England,Asia]);

    print "<P><EM>How far can they fly?</EM><BR>",
          $query->radio_group('how far',
                    ['10 ft','1 mile','10 miles','real far'],
                    '1 mile');

    print "<P><EM>What's your favorite color?</EM>   ";
    print $query->popup_menu('Color',
                             ['black','brown','red','yellow'],'red');

    print $query->hidden('Reference',
                         'Monty Python and the Holy Grail');

    print "<P><EM>What have you got there?</EM>   ";
    print $query->scrolling_list('possessions',
                                 ['A Coconut','A Grail','An Icon',
                                  'A Sword','A Ticket'],
                                 undef,10,'true');

    print "<P><EM>Any parting comments?</EM><BR>";
    print $query->textarea('Comments',undef,10,50);
```

```
        print "<P>",$query->reset;
        print $query->submit('Action','Shout');
        print $query->submit('Action','Scream');
        print $query->endform;
        print "<HR>\n";
    }

sub do_work {
    my($query) = @_;
    my(@values,$key);
    print "<H2>Here are the current settings in this form</H2>";
    foreach $key ($query->param) {
        print "<STRONG>$key</STRONG> -> ";
        @values = $query->param($key);
        print join(", ",@values),"<BR>\n";
    }
}

sub print_tail {
    print <<END;
    <HR>
    <ADDRESS>Lincoln D. Stein</ADDRESS><BR>
    <A HREF="/">Home Page</A>
    END
}
```

Bugs

This module doesn't do as much as *CGI.pm*, and it takes longer to load. Such is the price of flexibility.

Author

Lincoln D. Stein, *lstein@genome.wi.mit.edu*

Copyright

This code is copyright © 1995 by Lincoln Stein and the Whitehead Institute for Biomedical Research. It may be used and modified freely. I request, but do not require, that this credit appear in the code.

See Also

URI::URL, CGI::Request, CGI::MiniSvr, CGI::Base, CGI

CGI::Imagemap—imagemap behavior for CGI programs

Synopsis

```
use CGI::Imagemap;

$map = new CGI::Imagemap;
$map->setmap(@map);
$action = $map->action($x,$y);
```

or:

```
use CGI::Imagemap 'action_map';

$action = action_map($x,$y,@map);
```

Description

CGI::Imagemap allows CGI programmers to place **type=image** form fields on their HTML fill-out forms, with either client-side or server-side maps emulated.

The imagemap file follows that of the NCSA imagemap program. Each point is an **x,y** tuple. Each line in the map consists of one of the following formats. Comment lines start with **#**.

```
circle action center edgepoint
rect action upperleft lowerright
point action point
poly action point1 point2 ... pointN
default action
```

Using **point** and **default** in the same map makes no sense. If **point** is used, the action for the closest one is selected.

To use CGI::Imagemap, define an image submit map on your form with something like:

```
<input type=image name=mv_todo
    SRC="image_url">
```

You can pass a "client-side" imagemap like this:

```
<input type="hidden" name="todo.map"
            value="rect action1 0,0 25,20">
<input type="hidden" name="todo.map"
            value="rect action2 26,0 50,20">
<input type="hidden" name="todo.map"
            value="rect action3 51,0 75,20">
<input type="hidden" name="todo.map"
            value="default action0">
```

If the **@map**-passed parameter contains a NUL (\0) in the first array position, the map is assumed to be null-separated and **@map** is built by splitting it. This allows a null-separated *todo.map* with multiple values (parsed by a *cgi-lib.pl* or the like) to be referenced.

All of the following examples assume the above definitions in your form.

Static Methods

CGI::Imagemap allows the export of two routines, **action_map** and **map_untaint**. If you choose to use CGI::Imagemap statically, call the module with:

```
use CGI::Imagemap qw(action_map map_untaint);
```

action_map(x,y,map)

> We are assuming the map definition above, with the **type=image** variable named **todo**, and the map in *todo.map*. You can pass the map in one of two ways. The first is compatible with the *CGI.pm* (or CGI::*) modules, and passes the map as an array:

```
$query = new CGI;
my $x = $query->param('todo.x');
my $y = $query->param('todo.y');
```

```
my $map = $query->param('todo.map');
$action = action_map($x, $y, $map);
```

If you are using the old *cgi-lib.pl* library, which places multiple instances of the same form variable in a scalar, separated by null (\0) characters, you can do this:

```
ReadParse(*FORM);
my $x = $FORM{'todo.x'};
my $y = $FORM{'todo.y'};
my $map = $FORM{'todo.map'};
$action = action_map($x, $y, $map);
```

map_untaint(*$untaint*)

> If you are running with taint checking, as is suggested for CGI programs, you can use **map_untaint(1)** to set map untainting on a global basis. (If using class methods, each has its own instance of untainting).
>
> It ensures all characters in the action fit pattern of [-\w.+@]+, meaning alphanumerics, underscores, dashes (-), periods, and the @ sign. It also checks the methods (**rect**, **poly**, **point**, **default**, **circle**) and ensures that points/tuples are only integers. Once that is done, it untaints the passed form variables.

```
map_untaint(1);     # Turns on untainting
map_untaint('yes'); # Same as above
map_untaint(0);     # Disable untainting
map_untaint('no');  # Same as above

$status = map_untaint(); # Get status
```

> Default is no untainting.

Class Methods

The class methods for CGI::Imagemap are much the same as above, with the exception that multiple imagemaps are then maintained by the module, with full independence. The following method definitions assume the CGI::Form module is being used, like this:

```
use CGI::Form;
use CGI::Imagemap;
$query = new CGI::Form;
$map   = new CGI::Imagemap;
```

setmap(*@map*)

> This sets the map for the instance.

```
$map = new CGI::Imagemap;
$map->setmap($query->param('todo.map'));
```

addmap(*@map*)

> This adds a new map action specification *to the current map*.

```
$map->addmap('point action5 3,9'));
```

action(*x,y*)

> This finds the action, based on the active map and the values of x and y:

```
$x = $query->param('todo.x');
$y = $query->param('todo.y');
$action = $map->action($x, $y);
```

untaint()
>   Sets, unsets, or returns the taint status for the instance.

```
    $map->untaint(1);          # Turns on untainting
    $map->untaint('yes');      # Same as above
    $map->untaint(1);          # Disables untainting
    $map->untaint('yes');      # Same as above
    $status = $map->untaint(); # Get status
```

version()
>   Returns the version number of the module.

Example

A couple of self-contained examples are included in the CGI::Imagemap package. They are:

testmap
>   Uses the CGI::Form module.

testmap.old
>   Uses the old *cgi-lib.pl*

Bugs

The untainting stuff is not totally independent—threading might not work very well. This can be fixed if it is important—in the CGI world, I doubt it.

Author

Mike Heins, Internet Robotics, *mikeh@iac.net*

Acknowledgments

This work is heavily kited from the Perl imagemap program originally written by V. Khera (*khera@kciLink.com*).

CGI::MiniSvr—adds to CGI::Base the ability for a CGI script to become a mini-HTTP server

Synopsis

```
    use CGI::MiniSvr;

    $cgi = new CGI::MiniSvr;
    $cgi = new CGI::MiniSvr $port_or_path;
    $cgi = new CGI::MiniSvr $port_or_path, $timeout_mins;

    $cgi->port;          # return MiniSvr port number with leading colon
    $cgi->spawn;         # fork/detach from httpd

    $cgi->get;           # get input

    $cgi->pass_thru($host, $port);
    $cgi->redirect($url);

    $cgi->done;          # end 'page' and close connection (high-level)
    $cgi->close;         # just close connection (low-level)
```
See also the CGI::Base methods.

Description

This file implements the CGI::MiniSvr object. This object represents an alternative *interface* between the application and an HTTP daemon.

In a typical CGI scenario the *interface* is just a collection of environment variables passed to a process which then generated some output and exits. The CGI::Base class implements this standard interface.

The CGI::MiniSvr class inherits from CGI::Base and extends it to implement a "mini HTTP daemon" which can be spawned (forked) from a CGI script in order to maintain state information for a client "session."

This is very useful. It neatly sidesteps many of the painful issues involved in writing real-world multiscreen applications using the standard CGI interface (namely saving and restoring state between screens).

Another use for the MiniSvr is to allow CGI scripts to produce output pages with dynamically generated in-line graphics (for example). To do this the script would spawn a MiniSvr and refer to its port number in the URLs for the embedded images. The MiniSvr would then sit on the port, with a relatively short timeout, ready to serve the requests for those images. Once all the images have been served the MiniSvr would simply exit.

Like the CGI::Base module the CGI::MiniSvr module does not do any significant data parsing. Higher level query processing (forms, etc.) is performed by the CGI::Request module.

Note that the implementation of these modules means that you should invoke **new CGI::Base;** before **new CGI::MiniSvr;**. This is the natural order anyway and so should not be a problem.

Warning

This module is *not* a good solution to many problems! It is only a good solution to some. It should only be used by those who understand why it is *not* a good solution to many problems!

For those who don't see the pitfalls of the mini-server approach, consider just this one example: what happens to your machine if new "sessions" start, on average, faster than abandoned ones time out?

Security and short-lifespan URLs are some of the other problems.

If in doubt, don't use it! If you do, then don't blame me for any of the problems you may (will) experience. *You have been warned!*

Direct Access Usage

In this mode the MiniSvr creates an Internet domain socket and returns to the client a page with URLs which contain the MiniSvr's own port number.

```
$q = GetRequest();          # get initial request
$cgi = new CGI::MiniSvr;    # going to switch to CGI::MiniSvr later
$port = $cgi->port; # get port number (as ':NNNN') for use in URL's
$me = "http://$SERVER_NAME$port$SCRIPT_NAME"; # build my url
print "Hello... <A HREF="$me?INSIDE"> Step Inside ...</A>\r\n";
$cgi->done(1);              # flush out page, include debugging
$cgi->spawn and exit 0;     # fork, original cgi process exits
CGI::Request::Interface($cgi); # default to new interface
```

```
while($q = GetQuery() or $cgi->exit){ # await request/timeout
   ...
}
```

Indirect Access Usage

In this mode the MiniSvr creates a UNIX domain socket and returns to the client a page with a hidden field containing the path to the socket.

```
$q = GetRequest(); # get initial request
$path = $q->param('_minisvr_socket_path');
if ($path) {
    # just pass request on to our mini server
    $q->cgi->pass_thru('', $path) or (...handle timeout...)
    $q->cgi->done;
} else {
    # launch new mini server
    $path = "/tmp/cgi.$$";
    $cgi = new CGI::MiniSvr $path; # unix domain socket
    # code here mostly same as 'DIRECT ACCESS' above except that
    # the returned page has an embedded field _minisvr_socket_path
    # set to $path
    ...
}
```

Subclassing the MiniSvr

In some cases you may wish to have more control over the behavior of the mini-server, such as handling some requests at a low level without disturbing the application. Subclassing the server is generally a good approach. Use something like this:

```
# Define a specialised subclass of the MiniSvr for this application
{
    package CGI::MiniSvr::FOO;
    use CGI::MiniSvr;
    @ISA = qw(CGI::MiniSvr);
    # Default behaviour for everything except GET requests for
    # .(gif|html|jpg) Note that we must take great care not to:
    # a) try to pass_thru to ourselves (it would hang), or
    # b) pass_thru to the server a request which it will try
    # to satisfy by starting another instance of this same script!
    sub method_GET {
        my $self = shift;
        if ($self->{SCRIPT_NAME} =~ m/\.(gif|jpg|html)$/){
            $self->pass_thru('', $self->{ORIG_SERVER_PORT});
            $self->done;
            return 'NEXT';
        }
        1;
    }
    # ... other overriding methods can be defined here ...
}
```

Once defined you can use your new customized mini-server by changing:

```
$cgi = new CGI::MiniSvr;
```

into:

```
$cgi = new CGI::MiniSvr::FOO;
```

With the example code above any requests for GIF, JPG, or HTML will be forwarded to the server which originally invoked this script. The application no longer has to deal with them. Note: this is just an example usage for the mechanism; you would typically generate pages in which any embedded images had URLs which refer explicitly to the main httpd.

With a slight change in the code above you can arrange for the handling of the pass-thru to occur in a subprocess. This frees the main process to handle other requests. Since the MiniSvr typically only exists for one process, forking off a subprocess to handle a request is only useful for browsers such as Netscape, which make multiple parallel requests for inline images.

```
if ($self->{SCRIPT_NAME} =~ m/\.(gif|html|jpg)$/){
    if ($self->fork == 0) {
        $self->pass_thru('', $self->{ORIG_SERVER_PORT});
        $self->exit;
    }
    $self->done;
    return 'NEXT';
}
```

Note that forking can be expensive. It might not be worth doing for small images.

Features

Object-oriented and sub-classable.

Transparent low-level peer validation (no application involvement but extensible through subclassing).

Transparent low-level pass-thru/redirecting of URLs the application is not interested in (no application involvement but extensible through subclassing).

Effective timeout mechanism with default and per-call settings.

Good emulation of standard CGI interface (for code portability).

Support

Please use *comp.infosystems.www.** and *comp.lang.perl.misc* for support. Do not contact me directly; I'm sorry, but I just don't have the time.

Author

Tim Bunce

Acknowledgments

This module includes ideas from Pratap Pereira (*pereira@ee.eng.ohio-state.edu*), Jack Shirazi (*js@biu.icnet.uk*), and others.

Copyright

This code is copyright © Tim Bunce 1995. All rights reserved. This program is free software; you can redistribute it and/or modify it under the same terms as Perl itself.

IN NO EVENT SHALL THE AUTHORS BE LIABLE TO ANY PARTY FOR DIRECT, INDI-
RECT, SPECIAL, INCIDENTAL, OR CONSEQUENTIAL DAMAGES ARISING OUT OF THE
USE OF THIS SOFTWARE AND ITS DOCUMENTATION (INCLUDING, BUT NOT LIMITED
TO, LOST PROFITS) EVEN IF THE AUTHORS HAVE BEEN ADVISED OF THE POSSIBILITY
OF SUCH DAMAGE.

See Also

CGI::Base, CGI::Request, URI::URL

CGI::Push—simple interface to server push

Synopsis

```
use CGI::Push qw(:standard);
do_push(-next_page=>\&next_page,
        -last_page=>\&last_page,
        -delay=>0.5);
sub next_page {
    my($q,$counter) = @_;
    return undef if $counter >= 10;
    return start_html('Test'),
           h1('Visible'),"\n",
           "This page has been called ", strong($counter)," times",
           end_html();
}
sub last_page {
    my($q,$counter) = @_;
    return start_html('Done'),
           h1('Finished'),
           strong($counter),' iterations.',
           end_html;
}
```

Description

CGI::Push is a subclass of the CGI object created by *CGI.pm*. It is specialized for server
push operations, which allow you to create animated pages whose content changes at
regular intervals.

You provide CGI::Push with a pointer to a subroutine that will draw one page. Every time
your subroutine is called, it generates a new page. The contents of the page will be transmitted to the browser in such a way that it will replace what was there beforehand. The
technique will work with HTML pages as well as with graphics files, allowing you to create
animated GIFs.

Using CGI::Push

CGI::Push adds one new method to the standard CGI suite, do_push(). When you
call this method, you pass it a reference to a subroutine that is responsible for drawing
each new page, an interval delay, and an optional subroutine for drawing the last
page. Other optional parameters include most of those recognized by the CGI
header() method.

You may call **do_push()** in the object-oriented manner or not, as you prefer:

```
use CGI::Push;
$q = new CGI::Push;
$q->do_push(-next_page=>\&draw_a_page);
```

or:

```
use CGI::Push qw(:standard);
do_push(-next_page=>\&draw_a_page);
```

Parameters are as follows:

-next_page

> This required parameter points to a reference to a subroutine responsible for drawing each new page.

```
do_push(-next_page=>\&my_draw_routine);
```

> The subroutine should expect two parameters consisting of the CGI object and a counter indicating the number of times the subroutine has been called. It should return the contents of the page as an *array* of one or more items to print. It can return a false value (or an empty array) in order to abort the redrawing loop and print out the final page (if any):

```
sub my_draw_routine {
    my($q,$counter) = @_;
    return undef if $counter > 100;
    return start_html('testing'),
           h1('testing'),
           "This page called $counter times";
}
```

-last_page

> This optional parameter points to a reference to the subroutine responsible for drawing the last page of the series. It is called after the **-next_page** routine returns a false value. The subroutine itself should have exactly the same calling conventions as the **-next_page** routine.

-type

> This optional parameter indicates the content type of each page. It defaults to **text/html**. Currently, server push of heterogeneous document types is not supported.

-delay

> This indicates the delay, in seconds, between frames. Smaller delays refresh the page faster. Fractional values are allowed.
>
> If not specified, **-delay** will default to 1 second.

-cookie, -target, -expires

> These have the same meaning as the like-named parameters in **CGI::header()**.

Installing CGI::Push Scripts

Server push scripts *must* be installed as no-parsed-header (NPH) scripts in order to work correctly. On UNIX systems, this is most often accomplished by prefixing the script's name with **nph-**. Recognition of NPH scripts happens automatically with WebSTAR and Microsoft IIS. Users of other servers should see their documentation for help.

Caveats

This is a new module. It hasn't been extensively tested.

Author

Lincoln D. Stein, *lstein@genome.wi.mit.edu*

Copyright

Copyright © 1996 Lincoln Stein. This program may be used and modified freely, but I do request that this copyright notice remain attached to the file. You may modify this module as you wish, but if you redistribute a modified version, please attach a note listing the modifications you have made.

See Also

CGI::Carp, CGI

CGI::Out—buffer output when building CGI programs

Synopsis

```
use CGI;
use CGI::Out;
$query = new CGI;
savequery $query;                   # to reconstruct input
$CGI::Out::mailto = 'fred';         # override default of $<
out $query->header();
out $query->start_html(
        -title=>'A test',
        -author=>'muir@idiom.com');
croak "We're outta here!";
confess "It was my fault: $!";
carp "It was your fault!";
warn "I'm confused";
die  "I'm dying.\n";
use CGI::Out qw(carpout);
carpout(\*LOG);
```

Description

This is a helper routine for building CGI programs. It buffers stdout until you've completed building your output. If you should get an error before you are finished, then it will display a nice error message (in HTML), log the error, and send email about the problem.

It wraps all of the functions provided by CGI::Carp and Carp. Do not "use" them directly, instead just use CGI::Out.

Instead of `print`, use `out`.

Bugs

No support for `formats` is provided by CGI::Out.

Author

David Muir Sharnoff, *muir@idiom.com*

See Also

Carp, CGI::Carp, CGI, CGI::Wrap

CGI::Response — respond to CGI requests

Synopsis

Simple Interface:

```
use CGI::Response qw(:Simple);
print ContentType;
print "<html><head>\n"; # .....
```

Full Interface:

```
use CGI::Response;
$response = new CGI::Response;
$response->content_type;
print $response->as_string;
print "<html><head>\n"; # .....
```

Description

CGI::Response is a Perl5 module for constructing responses to Common Gateway Interface (CGI) requests. It is designed to be lightweight and efficient for the most common tasks, and also to provide access to all HTTP response features for more advanced CGI applications.

There are two ways to use CGI::Response. For basic applications, the Simple Interface provides a number of plain functions that cover the most commonly used CGI response headers. More advanced applications may employ the Full Interface object methods to access any HTTP header, or to add experimental or non-standard headers. Both interfaces try to generate reasonable defaults whenever possible.

For efficiency, just the Simple Interface functions are compiled on start-up. Full Interface methods are compiled only when they are called. This helps to make CGI::Response usable in a variety of applications. See "SelfLoader" for more information.

Simple Interface

The Simple Interface methods are *not* exported by default. In order to use them, you must import them explicitly. You can import all of the methods at once by saying:

```
use CGI::Response qw(:Simple);
```

Or, you can import just one function by listing it by name, as in:

```
use CGI::Response qw(ContentType);
```

Only one Simple Interface function should be called in a response, since all of these functions terminate the response header (that is, send the blank line denoting the end of the header) immediately upon execution. If you need to use a combination of headers not provided by the Simple Interface, use the Full Interface instead.

All of the Simple Interface functions force a flush on the currently selected output channel (that is, they set $| = 1$). This is done to prevent a common problem in CGI scripts, where a `system()` or `exec()` call causes output before the response header, and generates a server error. If you do not want $| = 1$, you should either set it back to 0 after using the Simple Interface, or you should employ the Full Interface, which does not have this side effect.

For reference, below is a list of the headers sent by each function, and the default header values, if any. Arguments are listed in the order they should appear. Square brackets ([ ]) indicate optional arguments; angled brackets (<>) indicate required arguments.

Function	Argument(s)	Header(s)	Default(s)
&ContentType	[content-type]	Content-Type	text/html
&Redirect	<Location/URI> [permanent?] Content-Type Status	Location URI text/html 302 Moved Temporarily	[none] [none]
&NoCache	[content-type] Pragma Expires	Content-Type no-cache [now]	text/html
&NoContent	Status	204 No Content	

Each of these functions is documented more completely below, and examples for each are provided.

Functions

&ContentType

> This is the most commonly used function. It identifies the Internet Media Type of the entity that follows. If you call it without an argument, it will send `text/html` as the content-type.
>
> ```
> use CGI::Response qw(:Simple);
> print &ContentType;   # defaults to text/html
> ```
>
> Otherwise, you can specify some other content-type:
>
> ```
> use CGI::Response qw(:Simple);
> print &ContentType('image/gif');
> ```
>
> This function should be called as early as possible to prevent server errors (see the note on $| above).

&Redirect

> A redirect causes the user-agent to make a follow-up request for some other resource. Some user-agents will be better than others at complying with a redirect, so this function tries to be as explicit as possible.
>
> You are required to give one argument, specifying the URL which the user-agent should request. A second argument is accepted as a Boolean value—if any second argument is present, the browser will be told that the requested resource has moved permanently to a new URL (that is, future requests for the document should be to the new URL, not to the one which was first requested).

```
use CGI::Response qw(:Simple);
print &Redirect('http://www.company.com/', 'permanent');
# this resource has moved permanently, status 301
```

If no second argument is given, the redirect will be specified as temporary.

```
use CGI::Response qw(:Simple);
print &Redirect('http://www.company.com/');
# this resource has moved temporarily, status 302
```

A brief HTML page is output after the header so that users whose user-agents fail to recognize the redirect will get an informative message with a link to the redirect. Use the Full Interface to supply some other page or none at all.

&NoCache

This function tries to inform user-agents and proxy servers that the included resource should not be cached. It does so by sending both an **Expires** header, set for immediate expiration, and a **Pragma: no-cache** header, which older user-agents and servers might not recognize.

Preventing caching is important to CGI applications which produce output based on some factor of the request (such as which user-agent made the request). For instance, a shopping-basket application would not want to allow caching of an order information page, which may contain user-specific information.

It must be noted, however, that caches prevent excess network load and cache-friendly applications are always preferable to use of the **&NoCache** function. This function should only be used when there is no other alternative.

&NoCache takes one optional argument, the content-type of the entity to follow. Therefore, its call is nearly identical to the **&ContentType** function, and the two functions may be interchanged easily. As with **&ContentType**, if you call **&NoCache** without an argument, it will send **text/html** as the content-type.

```
use CGI::Response qw(:Simple);
print &NoCache;   # defaults to text/html
```

Otherwise, you can specify some other content-type:

```
use CGI::Response qw(:Simple);
print &NoCache('image/gif');
```

As noted earlier, this function should be called as early as possible to prevent server errors (see the note on $| above).

&NoContent

&NoContent allows a script to accept input without changing the current page in the user-agent's view. This may be useful for a successful form input that requires no response, or for an imagemap click that does not have a defined link.

A No Content response does not reset form fields after submission. HTTP/1.1 will include a "205 Reset Document" status for this purpose, and a future version of this module will provide a **&Reset** function to support this status.

This function sends only one header, "Status: 204 No Content," and it takes no arguments.

```
use CGI::Response qw(:Simple);
print &NoContent;
```

Full Interface

The Full Interface is still under development and is not currently documented.

Note

Please note that future versions are not guaranteed to be backwards-compatible with this version. The interface will be frozen at version 0.1 (first beta release).

Author

Marc Hedlund, *hedlund@best.com*

Copyright

Copyright 1995, All rights reserved

See Also

CGI::Base(3pm), CGI::BasePlus(3pm), CGI::Request(3pm), CGI::Lite(3pm), CGI(3pm), CGI::Form(3pm), LWP(3pm), SelfLoader(3pm)

CGI::Switch—try more than one constructor and return the first object available

Synopsis

```
use CGISwitch;
```

or:

```
use CGI::Switch This, That, CGI::XA, Foo, Bar, CGI;
my $q = new CGI::Switch;
```

Description

Per default the `new()` method tries to call `new()` in the three packages Apache::CGI, CGI::XA, and CGI. It returns the first CGI object it succeeds with.

The import method allows you to set up the default order of the modules to be tested.

See Also

perl(1), Apache(3), CGI(3), CGI::XA(3)

Author

Andreas Koenig, *a.koenig@mind.de*

CGI::Wrap—buffer output when building CGI programs

Synopsis

```
use CGI;
use CGI::Croak;
use CGI::Wrap;
```

```
$query = new CGI;
savequery $query;                # to reconstruct input
$CGI::Out::mailto = 'fred';      # override default of $<
run \&myfunc, @myargs            # a function
run sub { code }                 # an inline function
run 'code'                       # something to eval
sub myfunc {
        out $query->header();
        out $query->start_html(
                -title=>'A test',
                -author=>'muir@idiom.com');
}
```

Description

This is a helper routine for building CGI programs. It buffers stdout until you've completed building your output. If you should get an error before you are finished, then it will display a nice error message (in HTML), log the error, and send email about the problem.

To use it, you must condense your program down to a single function call and then use CGI::Wrap::run to call it.

Instead of print, use out.

Bugs

No support for formats is provided by CGI::Wrap.

Author

David Muir Sharnoff, *muir@idiom.com*

See Also

Carp, CGI::Carp, CGI::Out, CGI

---

encode, decode—encode characters in a string using HTML entities, or expand HTML entities in a string

Synopsis

```
use HTML::Entities;
$a = "V&aring;re norske tegn b&oslash;r &#230res";
decode_entities($a);
encode_entities($a, "\200-\377");
```

Description

The decode_entities() routine replaces valid HTML entities found in the string with the corresponding ISO-8859/1 character.

The encode_entities() routine replaces the characters specified by the second argument with their entity representation. The default set of characters to expand are control chars, high-bit chars and the <, &, >, and " characters.

Both routines modify the string passed in as the first argument and return it.

If you prefer not to import these routines into your namespace you can call them as:

```
use HTML::Entities ();
$encoded = HTML::Entities::encode($a);
$decoded = HTML::Entities::decode($a);
```

The module can also export the `%char2entity` and the `%entity2char` hashes which contain the mapping from all characters to the corresponding entities.

Author

Gisle Aas, *aas@sn.no*

Copyright

Copyright 1995, 1996 Gisle Aas. All rights reserved.

This library is free software; you can redistribute it and/or modify it under the same terms as Perl itself.

---

encode_base64, decode_base64—encode/decode string using base64 encoding

Synopsis

```
use MIME::Base64;
$encoded = encode_base64('Aladdin:open sesame');
$decoded = decode_base64($encoded);
```

Description

This module provides functions to encode and decode strings into the Base64 encoding specified in RFC 2045: *MIME (Multipurpose Internet Mail Extensions)*. The Base64 encoding is designed to represent arbitrary sequences of octets in a form that need not be humanly readable. A 65-character subset (`[A-Za-z0-9+/=]`) of US-ASCII is used, enabling 6 bits to be represented per printable character.

Functions

encode_base64($str, [$eol])

Encode data by calling the **encode_base64()** function. The first argument is the string to encode. The second argument is the line-ending sequence to use (it is optional and defaults to \n). The returned encoded string is broken into lines of no more than 76 characters each, and it ends with $eol unless it is empty. Pass an empty string as the second argument if you do not want the encoded string broken into lines.

decode_base64($str)

Decode a base64 string by calling the **decode_base64()** function. This function takes a single argument that is the string to decode and returns the decoded data. Any character not one of the legal base64 characters is ignored. The **decode_base64()** function might croak if the sequence to decode ends prematurely.

If you prefer not to import these routines into your namespace, you can call them as:

```
use MIME::Base64 ();
$encoded = MIME::Base64::encode($decoded);
$decoded = MIME::Base64::decode($encoded);
```

Author

Gisle Aas, *aas@sn.no*

Copyright

Copyright © 1995–1997 Gisle Aas.

This library is free software; you can redistribute it and/or modify it under the same terms as Perl itself.

Distantly based on LWP::Base64 written by Martijn Koster (*m.koster@nexor.co.uk*) and Joerg Reichelt (*j.reichelt@nexor.co.uk*) and on code posted to *comp.lang.perl* (*3pd2lp$6gf@wsinti07.win.tue.nl*) by Hans Mulder (*hansm@wsinti07.win.tue.nl*).

The XS implementation uses code from metamail. Copyright © 1991 Bell Communications Research, Inc. (Bellcore)

HTML::AsSubs—functions that construct a HTML syntax tree

Synopsis

```
use HTML::AsSubs;
$h = body(
        h1("This is the heading"),
        p("This is the first paragraph which contains a ",
          a({href=>'link.html'}, "link"),
          " and an ",
          img({src=>'img.gif', alt=>'image'}),
          "."
         ),
       );
print $h->as_HTML;
```

Description

This module exports functions that can be used to construct various HTML elements. The functions are named after the tags of the corresponding HTML element and are all written in lowercase. If the first argument is a hash then it will be used to initialize the attributes of this element. The remaining arguments are regarded as content.

Acknowledgment

This module was inspired by the following message:

```
Date: Tue, 4 Oct 1994 16:11:30 +0100
Subject: Wow! I have a large lightbulb above my head!
Take a moment to consider these lines:
%OVERLOAD=( '""' => sub { join("", @{$_[0]}) } );
sub html { my($type)=shift; bless ["<$type>", @_, "</$type>"]; }
:-)  I *love* Perl 5!  Thankyou Larry and Ilya.
Regards,
Tim Bunce.
p.s. If you didn't get it, think about recursive data types:
html(html())
```

p.p.s. I'll turn this into a much more practical example in a day or
two.
p.p.p.s. It's a pity that overloads are not inherited. Is this a bug?

Bugs

The exported `link()` function overrides the built-in `link()` function. The exported `tr()`
function must be called using `&tr(...)` syntax because it clashes with the built-in
`tr/../../ ` operator.

See Also

HTML::Element

HTML::Element—class for objects that represent HTML elements

Synopsis

```
require HTML::Element;
$a = new HTML::Element 'a', href => 'http://www.oslonett.no/';
$a->push_content("Oslonett AS");
$tag = $a->tag;
$tag = $a->starttag;
$tag = $a->endtag;
$ref = $a->attr('href');
$links = $a->extract_links();
print $a->as_HTML;
```

Description

Objects of the HTML::Element class can be used to represent elements of HTML. These
objects have attributes and content. The content is an array of text segments and other
HTML::Element objects. Thus a tree of HTML::Element objects as nodes can represent the
syntax tree for a HTML document.

Methods

`$h = HTML::Element->new(tag, attrname => value,...)`
> The object constructor. Takes a tag name as argument. Optionally, allows you to
> specify initial attributes at object creation time.

`$h->tag()`
> Returns (optionally sets) the tag name for the element. The tag is always
> converted to lower case.

`$h->starttag()`
> Returns the complete start tag for the element. Including leading <, trailing >, and
> attributes.

`$h->endtag()`
> Returns the complete end tag. Includes leading </ and the trailing >.

`$h->parent([$newparent])`
> Returns (optionally sets) the parent for this element.

`$h->implicit([`*`$bool`*`])`

Returns (optionally sets) the implicit attribute. This attribute is used to indicate that the element was not originally present in the source, but was inserted in order to conform to HTML structure.

`$h->is_inside(`*`tag`*`,...)`

Returns true if this tag is contained inside one of the specified tags.

`$h->pos()`

Returns (and optionally sets) the current position. The position is a reference to a HTML::Element object that is part of the tree that has the current object as root. This restriction is not enforced when setting `pos()`, but unpredictable things will happen if this is not true.

`$h->attr(`*`attr`*`, [`*`$value`*`])`

Returns (and optionally sets) the value of some attribute.

`$h->content()`

Returns the content of this element. The content is represented as a reference to an array of text segments and references to other HTML::Element objects.

`$h->is_empty()`

Returns true if there is no content.

`$h->insert_element(`*`$element`*`, `*`$implicit`*`)`

Inserts a new element at current position and updates `pos()` to point to the inserted element. Returns `$element`.

`$h->push_content(`*`$element_or_text`*`,...)`

Adds to the content of the element. The content should be a text segment (scalar) or a reference to a HTML::Element object.

`$h->delete_content()`

Clears the content.

`$h->delete()`

Frees memory associated with the element and all children. This is needed because Perl's reference counting does not work since we use circular references.

`$h->traverse(\&`*`callback`*`, [`*`$ignoretext`*`])`

Traverse the element and all of its children. For each node visited, the callback routine is called with the node, a startflag and the depth as arguments. If the *$ignoretext* parameter is true, then the callback will not be called for text content. The flag is 1 when we enter a node and 0 when we leave the node.

If the returned value from the callback is false then we will not traverse the children.

`$h->extract_links([`*`@wantedTypes`*`])`

Returns links found by traversing the element and all of its children. The return value is a reference to an array. Each element of the array is an array with two values; the link value and a reference to the corresponding element.

You might specify that you just want to extract some types of links. For instance if you only want to extract `<A HREF="...">` and `<IMG SRC="...">` links you might code it like this:

```
for (@{ $e->extract_links(qw(a img)) }) {
    ($link, $linkelem) = @$_;
    ...
}
```

`$h->dump()`
> Prints the element and all its children to STDOUT. Mainly useful for debugging. The structure of the document is shown by indentation (no end tags).

`$h->as_HTML()`
> Returns a string (the HTML document) that represents the element and its children.

Bugs

If you want to free the memory associated with a tree built of HTML::Element nodes then you will have to delete it explicitly. The reason for this is that Perl currently has no proper garbage collector, but depends on reference counts in the objects. This scheme fails because the parse tree contains circular references (parents have references to their children and children have a reference to their parent).

Author

Gisle Aas, *aas@sn.no*

Copyright

Copyright 1995, 1996 Gisle Aas. All rights reserved.

This library is free software; you can redistribute it and/or modify it under the same terms as Perl itself.

See Also

HTML::AsSubs

HTML::FormatPS—format HTML as PostScript

Synopsis

```
require HTML::FormatPS;
$html = parse_htmlfile("test.html");
$formatter = new HTML::FormatPS
                FontFamily => 'Helvetica',
                PaperSize  => 'Letter';
print $formatter->format($html);
```

Description

The HTML::FormatPS is a formatter that outputs PostScript code. Formatting of HTML tables and forms is not implemented.

You might specify the following parameters when constructing the formatter:

PaperSize
> What kind of paper should we format for. The value can be one of these: A3, A4, A5, B4, B5, Letter, Legal, Executive, Tabloid, Statement, Folio, 10x14, Quarto.
>
> The default is A4.

PaperWidth
> The width of the paper in points. Setting PaperSize also defines this value.

PaperHeight

> The height of the paper in points. Setting PaperSize also defines this value.

LeftMargin

> The left margin in points.

RightMargin

> The right margin in points.

HorizontalMargin

> Both left and right margin at the same time. The default value is 4 cm.

TopMargin

> The top margin in points.

BottomMargin

> The bottom margin in points.

VerticalMargin

> Both top and bottom margin at the same time. The default value is 2 cm.

PageNo

> The parameter determines if we should put page numbers on the pages. The default is yes, so you have to set this value to 0 in order to suppress page numbers.

FontFamily

> The parameter specifies which family of fonts to use for the formatting. Legal values are Courier, Helvetica, and Time. The default is Times.

FontScale

> All fontsizes might be scaled by this factor.

Leading

> How much space between lines. This is a factor of the fontsize used for that line. Default is 0.1.

Author

Gisle Aas, *aas@sn.no*

Copyright

Copyright © 1995 Gisle Aas. All rights reserved.

This library is free software; you can redistribute it and/or modify it under the same terms as Perl itself.

See Also

HTML::Formatter

HTML::Formatter—base class for HTML formatters

Synopsis

```
package HTML::FormatXX;
require HTML::Formatter;
@ISA=qw(HTML::Formatter);
```

Description

HTML formatters are able to format a HTML syntax tree into various printable formats. Different formatters produce output for different output media. Common for all formatters are that they will return the formatted output when the `format()` method is called. `format()` takes a HTML::Element as parameter.

Author

Gisle Aas, *aas@sn.no*

Copyright

Copyright © 1995 Gisle Aas. All rights reserved.

This library is free software; you can redistribute it and/or modify it under the same terms as Perl itself.

See Also

HTML::FormatText, HTML::FormatPS, HTML::Element

HTML::FormatText—format HTML as text

Synopsis

```
require HTML::FormatText;
$html = parse_htmlfile("test.html");
$formatter = new HTML::FormatText;
print $formatter->format($html);
```

Description

The HTML::FormatText is a formatter that outputs plain latin1 text. All character attributes (bold/italic/underline) are ignored. Formatting of HTML tables and forms is not implemented.

Author

Gisle Aas, *aas@sn.no*

Copyright

Copyright © 1995 Gisle Aas. All rights reserved.

This library is free software; you can redistribute it and/or modify it under the same terms as Perl itself.

See Also

HTML::Formatter

HTML::HeadParser—parse <HEAD> section of an HTML document

Synopsis

```
require HTML::HeadParser;
$p = HTML::HeadParser->new;
```

```
$p->parse($text) and  print "not finished";
$p->header('Title')           # to access <title>....</title>
$p->header('Content-Base')    # to access <base href="http://...">
$p->header('Foo')             # to access <meta http-equiv="Foo"
                              # content="...">
```

Description

The HTML::HeadParser is a specialized (and lightweight) HTML::Parser that will only parse the `<HEAD>...</HEAD>` section of a HTML document. The `parse()` and `parse_file()` methods will return a FALSE value as soon as a `<BODY>` element is found, and should not be called again after this.

The HTML::HeadParser constructor takes a HTTP::Headers object reference as argument. The parser will update this header object as the various head elements are recognized.

The following header fields are initialized from elements found in the `<HEAD>` section of a HTML document:

Content-Base
> The *Content-Base* header is initialized from the `<BASE HREF="...">` element.

Title
> The *Title* header is initialized from the `<TITLE>...</TITLE>` element.

Isindex
> The *Isindex* header will be added if there is a `<ISINDEX>` element in the `<HEAD>`. The header value is initialized from the *prompt* attribute if it is present.

X-Meta-Foo
> All `<META>` elements will initialize headers with the prefix `X-Meta-`. If the element contains a `http-equiv` attribute, then it will be honored as the header name.

Examples

```
$h = HTTP::Headers->new;
$p = HTML::HeadParser->new($h);
$p->parse(<<EOT);
<title>Stupid example</title>
<base href="http://www.sn.no/libwww-perl/">
Normal text starts here.
EOT
undef $p;
print $h->title;   # should print "Stupid example"
```

Author

Gisle Aas, *aas@sn.no*

Copyright

Copyright © 1996 Gisle Aas. All rights reserved.

This library is free software; you can redistribute it and/or modify it under the same terms as Perl itself.

See Also

HTML::Parser, HTTP::Headers

HTML::LinkExtor—extract links from an HTML document

Synopsis
```
require HTML::LinkExtor;
$p = HTML::LinkExtor->new(\&cb, "http://www.sn.no/");
sub cb {
    my($tag, %links);
    print "$tag @{[%links]}\n";
}
$p->parse_file("index.html");
```

Description

The HTML::LinkExtor (link extractor) is an HTML parser that takes a callback routine as parameter. This routine is then called as the various link attributes are recognized.

The HTML::LinkExtor is a subclass of HTML::Parser. This means that the document should be given to the parser by calling the $p->parse() or $p->parse_file() methods.

Methods

$p = HTML::LinkExtor->new([$callback[, $base]])

The constructor takes two optional argument. The first is a reference to a callback routine. It will be called as links are found. If a callback is not provided, then links are just accumulated internally and can be retrieved by calling the $p->links() method. The *$base* is an optional base URL used to absolutize all URLs found.

The callback is called with the lowercase tag name as first argument, and then all link attributes as separate key/value pairs. All non-link attributes are removed.

$p->links

Returns a list of all links found in the document. The returned values will be anonymous arrays with the following elements:

```
[$tag, $attr => $url1, $attr2 => $url2,...]
```

The $p->links method will also truncate the internal link list. This means that if the method is called twice without any parsing in between then the second call will return an empty list.

Also note that $p->links will always be empty if a callback routine was provided when the HTML::LinkExtor was created.

Example

This is an example showing how you can extract links as a document is received using LWP:

```
use LWP::UserAgent;
use HTML::LinkExtor;
use URI::URL;
$url = "http://www.sn.no/";  # for instance
$ua = new LWP::UserAgent;
# Set up a callback that collect image links
my @imgs = ();
sub callback {
    my($tag, %attr) = @_;
```

```
        return if $tag ne 'img';  # we only look closer at <img ...>
        push(@imgs, values %attr);
    }
    # Make the parser.  Unfortunately, we don't know the base yet (it might
    # be diffent from $url)
    $p = HTML::LinkExtor->new(\&callback);
    # Request document and parse it as it arrives
    $res = $ua->request(HTTP::Request->new(GET => $url),
                        sub {$p->parse($_[0])});
    # Expand all image URLs to absolute ones
    my $base = $res->base;
    @imgs = map { $_ = url($_, $base)->abs; } @imgs;
    # Print them out
    print join("\n", @imgs), "\n";
```

Author

Gisle Aas, *aas@sn.no*

See Also

HTML::Parser

HTML::Parser—HTML parser class

Synopsis

```
    require HTML::Parser;
    $p = HTML::Parser->new;  # should really a be subclass
    $p->parse($chunk1);
    $p->parse($chunk2);
    #...
    $p->parse(undef)          # signal EOF
    # Parse directly from file
    $p->parse_file("foo.html");
    # or
    open(F, "foo.html") || die;
    $p->parse_file(\*F);
```

Description

The HTML::Parser will tokenize an HTML document when the $p->**parse**() method is called. The document to parse can be supplied in arbitrary chunks. Call $p->**parse**(**undef**) at the end of the document to flush any remaining text. The return value from **parse**() is a reference to the parser object.

The $p->**parse_file**() method can be called to parse text from a file. The argument can be a filename or an already opened file handle. The return value from **parse_file**() is a reference to the parser object.

In order to make the parser do anything interesting you must make a subclass where you override one or more of the following methods as appropriate.

Methods

`$self->declaration($decl)`

> This method is called when a *markup declaration* has been recognized. For typical HTML documents, the only declaration you are likely to find is `<!DOCTYPE ...>`. The initial `<!` and ending `>` is not part of the string passed as argument. Comments are removed and entities have *not* been expanded yet.

`$self->start($tag, $attr)`

> This method is called when a complete start tag has been recognized. The first argument is the tag name (in lowercase) and the second argument is a reference to a hash that contain all attributes found within the start tag. The attribute keys are converted to lowercase. Entities found in the attribute values are already expanded.

`$self->end($tag)`

> This method is called when a end tag has been recognized. The argument is the lowercase tag name.

`$self->text($text)`

> This method is called as plain text in the document is recognized. The text is passed on unmodified and might contain multiple lines. Note that for efficiency reasons, entities in the text are *not* expanded. You should call **HTML::Entities::decode**(`$text`) before you process the text any further.

`$self->comment($comment)`

> This method is called as comments are recognized. The leading and trailing "`--`" sequences have been stripped off the comment text.

> The default implementation of these methods does nothing, i.e., the tokens are just ignored.

There is really nothing in the basic parser that is HTML-specific, so it is likely that the parser can parse many kinds of SGML documents, but SGML has many obscure features (not implemented by this module) that prevent us from renaming this module as SGML::Parser.

Author

Gisle Aas, *aas@sn.no*

Copyright

Copyright © 1996 Gisle Aas. All rights reserved.

This library is free software; you can redistribute it and/or modify it under the same terms as Perl itself.

See Also

HTML::TreeBuilder, HTML::HeadParser, HTML::Entities

HTML::Stream——HTML output stream class and some markup utilities

Description

The HTML::Stream module provides you with an object-oriented (and subclassable) way of outputting HTML. Basically, you open up an "HTML stream" on an existing file handle, and then do all of your output to the HTML stream. You can intermix HTML-stream-output and ordinary-print-output, if you like.

Here's small sample of some of the non-OO ways you can use this module:

```
use HTML::Stream qw(:funcs);

print html_tag('A', HREF=>$link);
print html_escape("<<Hello & welcome!>>");
```

And some of the OO ways as well:

```
use HTML::Stream;
$HTML = new HTML::Stream \*STDOUT;

# The vanilla interface...
$HTML->tag('A', HREF=>"$href");
$HTML->tag('IMG', SRC=>"logo.gif", ALT=>"LOGO");
$HTML->text($copyright);
$HTML->tag('_A');

# The chocolate interface...
$HTML -> A(HREF=>"$href");
$HTML -> IMG(SRC=>"logo.gif", ALT=>"LOGO");
$HTML -> t($caption);
$HTML -> _A;

# The chocolate interface, with whipped cream...
$HTML -> A(HREF=>"$href")
      -> IMG(SRC=>"logo.gif", ALT=>"LOGO")
      -> t($caption)
      -> _A;
# The strawberry interface...
output $HTML [A, HREF=>"$href"],
             [IMG, SRC=>"logo.gif", ALT=>"LOGO"],
             $caption,
             [_A];
```

There's even a small built-in subclass, HTML::Stream::Latin1, which can handle Latin-1 input right out of the box. But all in good time . . .

Introduction (The Neopolitan Dessert)

Function interface

Let's start out with the simple stuff. This module provides a collection of non-OO utility functions for escaping HTML text and producing HTML tags, like this:

```
use HTML::Stream qw(:funcs);    # imports functions from @EXPORT_OK

print html_tag(A, HREF=>$url);
print '&copy; 1996 by', html_escape($myname), '!';
print html_tag('/A');
```

By the way, that last line could be rewritten as:

```
print html_tag(_A);
```

And if you need to get a parameter in your tag that doesn't have an associated value, supply the *undefined* value (*not* the empty string!):

```
print html_tag(TD, NOWRAP=>undef, ALIGN=>'LEFT');

    <TD NOWRAP ALIGN=LEFT>

print html_tag(IMG, SRC=>'logo.gif', ALT=>'');

    <IMG SRC="logo.gif" ALT="">
```

There are also some routines for reversing the process, like:

```
$text = "This <i>isn't</i> &quot;fun&quot;...";
print html_unmarkup($text);

    This isn't &quot;fun&quot;...

print html_unescape($text);

    This isn't "fun"...
```

Yeah, yeah, yeah, I hear you cry. *We've seen this stuff before.* But wait! There's more...

Object-Oriented Interface, Vanilla

Using the function interface can be tedious, so we also provide an "HTML output stream" class. Messages to an instance of that class generally tell that stream to output some HTML. Here's the above example, rewritten using HTML streams:

```
use HTML::Stream;
$HTML = new HTML::Stream \*STDOUT;

$HTML->tag(A, HREF=>$url);
$HTML->ent('copy');
$HTML->text(" 1996 by $myname!");
$HTML->tag(_A);
```

As you've probably guessed:

text()
: Outputs some text, which will be HTML-escaped.

tag()
: Outputs an ordinary tag, like <A>, possibly with parameters. The parameters will all be HTML-escaped automatically.

ent()
: Outputs an HTML entity, like the © or <. You mostly don't need to use it; you can often just put the Latin-1 representation of the character in the text().

You might prefer to use t() and e() instead of text() and ent(); they're absolutely identical, and easier to type:

```
$HTML -> tag(A, HREF=>$url);
$HTML -> e('copy');
$HTML -> t(" 1996 by $myname!");
$HTML -> tag(_A);
```

Now, it wouldn't be nice to give you those `text()` and `ent()` shortcuts without giving you one for `tag()`, would it? Of course not...

Object-Oriented Interface, Chocolate

The known HTML tags are even given their own tag-methods, compiled on demand. The above code could be written even more compactly as:

```
$HTML -> A(HREF=>$url);
$HTML -> e('copy');
$HTML -> t(" 1996 by $myname!");
$HTML -> _A;
```

As you've probably guessed:

```
A(HREF=>$url)    ==    tag(A, HREF=>$url)    ==    <A HREF="/the/url">
_A               ==    tag(_A)               ==    </A>
```

All of the autoloaded "tag-methods" use the tagname in *all-uppercase*. An _ prefix on any tag-method means that an end-tag is desired. The _ was chosen for several reasons:

- It's short and easy to type.

- It doesn't produce much visual clutter to look at.

- **_TAG** looks a little like /**TAG** because of the straight line.

Note: I know it looks like a private method. You get used to it. Really.

I should stress that this module will only auto-create tag methods for *known* HTML tags. So you're protected from typos like this (which will cause a fatal exception at runtime):

```
$HTML -> IMGG(SRC=>$src);
```

(You're not yet protected from illegal tag parameters, but it's a start, ain't it?)

If you need to make a tag known (sorry, but this is currently a *global* operation, and not stream-specific), do this:

```
accept_tag HTML::Stream 'MARQUEE';       # for you MSIE fans...
```

Note: there is no corresponding "reject_tag". I thought and thought about it, and could not convince myself that such a method would do anything more useful than cause other people's modules to suddenly stop working because some bozo function decided to reject the **FONT** tag.

Object-Oriented Interface, with Whipped Cream

In the grand tradition of C++, output method chaining is supported in both the Vanilla Interface and the Chocolate Interface. So you can (and probably should) write the above code as:

```
$HTML -> A(HREF=>$url)
      -> e('copy') -> t(" 1996 by $myname!")
      -> _A;
```

Object-Oriented Interface, Strawberry

I was jealous of the compact syntax of HTML::AsSubs, but I didn't want to worry about clogging the namespace with a lot of functions like `p()`, `a()`, etc. (especially when markup-functions like `tr()` conflict with existing Perl functions). So I came up with this:

```
output $HTML [A, HREF=>$url], "Here's my $caption", [_A];
```

Conceptually, array refs are sent to `html_tag()`, and strings to `html_escape()`.

Advanced Topics

Auto-Formatting and Inserting Newlines

Auto-formatting is the name I give to the Chocolate Interface feature whereby newlines (and maybe, in the future, other things) are inserted before or after the tags you output in order to make your HTML more readable. So, by default, this:

```
$HTML -> HTML
      -> HEAD
      -> TITLE -> t("Hello!") -> _TITLE
      -> _HEAD
      -> BODY(BGCOLOR=>'#808080');
```

Actually produces this:

```
<HTML><HTML>
<HEAD>
<TITLE>Hello!</TITLE>
</HEAD>
<BODY BGCOLOR="#808080">
```

To turn off autoformatting altogether on a given HTML::Stream object, use the **auto_format()** method:

```
$HTML->auto_format(0);          # stop autoformatting!
```

To change whether a newline is automatically output before/after the begin/end form of a tag *at a global level*, use **set_tag()**:

```
# 15 means "\n<B>\n \n</B>\n"
HTML::Stream->set_tag('B', Newlines=>15);
# 7 means   "\n<I>\n \n</I>  "
HTML::Stream->set_tag('I', Newlines=>7);
```

To change whether a newline is automatically output before/after the begin/end form of a tag *for a given stream*, give the stream its own private "tag info" table, and then use **set_tag()**:

```
$HTML->private_tags;
$HTML->set_tag('B', Newlines=>0);     # won't affect anyone else!
```

To output newlines explicitly, just use the special **nl** method in the Chocolate Interface:

```
$HTML->nl;     # one newline
$HTML->nl(6);  # six newlines
```

I am sometimes asked, "Why don't you put more newlines in automatically?" Well, mostly because:

- Sometimes you'll be outputting stuff inside a PRE environment.
- Sometimes you really do want to jam things (like images, or table cell delimiters and the things they contain) right up against each other.

So I've stuck to outputting newlines in places where it's most likely to be harmless.

Entities

As shown above, you can use the `ent()` (or `e()`) method to output an entity:

```
$HTML->t('Copyright ')->e('copy')->t(' 1996 by Me!');
```

But this can be a pain, particularly for generating output with non-ASCII characters:

```
$HTML -> t('Copyright ')
      -> e('copy')
      -> t(' 1996 by Fran') -> e('ccedil') -> t('ois, Inc.!');
```

Granted, Europeans can always type the 8-bit characters directly in their Perl code, and just have this:

```
$HTML -> t("Copyright \251 1996 by Fran\347ois, Inc.!");
```

But folks without 8-bit text editors can find this kind of output cumbersome to generate. Which brings me to...

Auto-Escaping: Changing the Way Text Is Escaped

Auto-escaping is the name I give to the act of taking an "unsafe" string (one with ">", "&", etc.), and magically outputting "safe" HTML.

The default "auto-escape" behavior of an HTML stream can be a drag if you've got a lot character entities that you want to output, or if you're using the Latin-1 character set, or some other input encoding. Fortunately, you can use the `auto_escape()` method to change the way a particular HTML::Stream works at any time.

First, here's a couple of special invocations:

```
# Default; escapes [<>"&] and 8-bit chars.
$HTML->auto_escape('ALL');
# Like ALL, but uses Latin-1 entities instead of decimal
# equivalents.
$HTML->auto_escape('LATIN_1');
# Like ALL, but leaves "&" alone.
$HTML->auto_escape('NON_ENT');
```

You can also install your own auto-escape function (note that you might very well want to install it for just a little bit only, and then de-install it):

```
sub my_auto_escape {
    my $text = shift;
    HTML::Entities::encode($text);      # start with default
    $text =~ s/\(c\)/&copy;/ig;         # (C) becomes copyright
    $text =~ s/\\,(c)/\&$1cedil;/ig;    # \,c becomes a cedilla
    $text;
}


# Start using my auto-escape:
my $old_esc = $HTML->auto_escape(\&my_auto_escape);

# Output some stuff:
$HTML-> IMG(SRC=>'logo.gif', ALT=>'Fran\,cois, Inc');
output $HTML 'Copyright (C) 1996 by Fran\,cois, Inc.!';

# Stop using my auto-escape:
$HTML->auto_escape($old_esc);
```

If you find yourself in a situation where you're doing this a lot, a better way is to create a *subclass* of HTML::Stream which installs your custom function when constructed. For an example, see the HTML::Stream::Latin1 subclass in this module.

Outputting HTML to Things Besides File Handles

As of Revision 1.21, you no longer need to supply `new()` with a file handle: any object that responds to a `print()` method will do. Of course, this includes blessed FileHandles, and IO::Handles.

If you supply a GLOB reference (like `\*STDOUT`) or a string (like `"Module::FH"`), HTML::Stream will automatically create an invisible object for talking to that file handle (I don't dare bless it into a FileHandle, since the underlying descriptor would get closed when the HTML::Stream is destroyed, and you might not want that).

You say you want to print to a string? For kicks and giggles, try this:

```
package StringHandle;
sub new {
    my $self = '';
    bless \$self, shift;
}
sub print {
    my $self = shift;
    $$self .= join('', @_);
}


package main;
use HTML::Stream;

my $SH = new StringHandle;
my $HTML = new HTML::Stream $SH;
$HTML -> H1 -> t("Hello & <<welcome>>!") -> _H1;
print "PRINTED STRING: ", $$SH, "\n";
```

Subclassing

This is where you can make your application-specific HTML-generating code *much* easier to look at. Consider this:

```
package MY::HTML;
@ISA = qw(HTML::Stream);

sub Aside {
    $_[0] -> FONT(SIZE=>-1) -> I;
}
sub _Aside {
    $_[0] -> _I -> _FONT;
}
```

Now you can do this:

```
my $HTML = new MY::HTML \*STDOUT;

$HTML -> Aside
      -> t("Don't drink the milk, it's spoiled... pass it on...")
      -> _Aside;
```

If you're defining these markup-like, chocolate-interface-style functions, I recommend using mixed case with a leading capital. You probably shouldn't use all-uppercase, since that's what this module uses for real HTML tags.

Public Interface

Functions

html_escape *TEXT*

Given a *TEXT* string, turn the text into valid HTML by escaping "unsafe" characters. Currently, the "unsafe" characters are 8-bit characters plus:

    <   >   =   &

Note: Provided for convenience and backwards-compatibility only. You may want to use the more-powerful HTML::Entities::encode function instead.

html_tag *TAG* [, *PARAM*=>*VALUE*, ...]

Return the text for a given *TAG*, possibly with parameters. As an efficiency hack, only the values are HTML-escaped currently: it is assumed that the tag and parameters will already be safe.

For convenience and readability, you can say _A instead of /A for the first tag, if you're into barewords.

html_unescape *TEXT*

Remove angle-tag markup, and convert the standard ampersand-escapes (lt, gt, amp, quot, and #ddd) into ASCII characters.

Note: provided for convenience and backwards-compatibility only. You may want to use the more-powerful HTML::Entities::decode function instead: unlike this function, it can collapse entities like copy and ccedil into their Latin-1 byte values.

html_unmarkup *TEXT*

Remove angle-tag markup from *TEXT*, but do not convert ampersand-escapes. Cheesy, but theoretically useful if you want to, say, incorporate externally provided HTML into a page you're generating, and are worried that the HTML might contain undesirable markup.

Vanilla

new [*PRINTABLE*]

Class method. Create a new HTML output stream.

The *PRINTABLE* may be a FileHandle, a glob reference, or any object that responds to a print() message. If no *PRINTABLE* is given, does a select() and uses that.

auto_escape [*NAME*|*SUBREF*]

Instance method. Set the auto-escape function for this HTML stream.

If the argument is a subroutine reference *SUBREF*, then that subroutine will be used. Declare such subroutines like this:

```
sub my_escape {
    my $text = shift;      # it's passed in the first argument
    ...
    $text;
}
```

If a textual NAME is given, then one of the appropriate built-in functions is used. Possible values are:

ALL

> Default for HTML::Stream objects. This escapes angle brackets, ampersands, double-quotes, and 8-bit characters. 8-bit characters are escaped using decimal entity codes (like #123).

LATIN_1

> Like "ALL", but uses Latin-1 entity names (like ccedil) instead of decimal entity codes to escape characters. This makes the HTML more readable but it is currently not advised, as "older" browsers (like Netscape 2.0) do not recognize many of the ISO-8859-1 entity names (like deg).
>
> *Warning*: If you specify this option, you'll find that it attempts to "require" HTML::Entities at run time. That's because I didn't want to force you to have that module just to use the rest of HTML::Stream. To pick up problems at compile time, you are advised to say:
>
> ```
> use HTML::Stream;
> use HTML::Entities;
> ```
>
> in your source code.

NON_ENT

> Like "ALL", except that ampersands (&) are *not* escaped. This allows you to use &-entities in your text strings, while having everything else safely escaped:
>
> ```
> output $HTML "If A is an acute angle, then A > 90&deg;";
> ```
>
> Returns the previously installed function, in the manner of select(). No arguments just returns the currently installed function.

auto_format *ONOFF*

> *Instance method.* Set the auto-formatting characteristics for this HTML stream. Currently, all you can do is supply a single defined Boolean argument, which turns auto-formatting ON (1) or OFF (0). The self object is returned.
>
> Please use no other values; they are reserved for future use.

comment *COMMENT*

> Instance method. Output an HTML comment. As of 1.29, a newline is automatically appended.

ent *ENTITY*

> *Instance method.* Output an HTML entity. For example, here's how you'd output a non-breaking space:
>
> ```
> $html->ent('nbsp');
> ```
>
> You may abbreviate this method name as e:
>
> ```
> $html->e('nbsp');
> ```
>
> *Warning*: This function assumes that the entity argument is legal.

io

> *Instance method.* Return the underlying output handle for this HTML stream. All you can depend upon is that it is some kind of object which responds to a print() message:
>
> ```
> $HTML->io->print("This is not auto-escaped or nuthin!");
> ```

nl [*COUNT*]

> *Instance method.* Output *COUNT* newlines. If undefined, *COUNT* defaults to 1.

tag *TAGNAME* [, *PARAM=>VALUE*, ...]

> *Instance method.* Output a tag. Returns the self object, to allow method chaining. You can say _A instead of /A, if you're into barewords.

text *TEXT*, ..., *TEXT*

> *Instance method.* Output some text. Returns the self object, to allow method chaining. You may abbreviate this method name as t:

```
$html->t('Hi there, ', $yournamehere, '!');
```

Strawberry

output *ITEM*, ..., *ITEM*

> *Instance method.* Go through the items. If an item is an array ref, treat it like the array argument to html_tag() and output the result. If an item is a text string, escape the text and output the result. Like this:

```
output $HTML [A, HREF=>$url], "Here's my $caption!", [_A];
```

Chocolate

accept_tag *TAG*

> *Class method.* Declares that the tag is to be accepted as valid HTML (if it isn't already). For example, this:

```
# Assure methods MARQUEE and _MARQUEE are compiled on demand:
HTML::Stream->accept_tag('MARQUEE');
```

> gives the Chocolate Interface permission to create (via AUTOLOAD) definitions for the MARQUEE and _MARQUEE methods, so you can then say:

```
$HTML -> MARQUEE -> t("Hi!") -> _MARQUEE;
```

> If you want to set the default attribute of the tag as well, you can do so via the set_tag() method instead; it will effectively do an accept_tag() as well.

```
# Make sure methods MARQUEE and _MARQUEE are compiled on demand,
#   *and*, set the characteristics of that tag.
HTML::Stream->set_tag('MARQUEE', Newlines=>9);
```

private_tags

> *Instance method.* Normally, HTML streams use a reference to a global table of tag information to determine how to do such things as auto-formatting, and modifications made to that table by set_tag will affect everyone.

> However, if you want an HTML stream to have a private copy of that table to munge with, just send it this message after creating it. Like this:

```
my $HTML = new HTML::Stream \*STDOUT;
$HTML->private_tags;
```

> Then, you can say stuff like:

```
$HTML->set_tag('PRE',   Newlines=>0);
$HTML->set_tag('BLINK', Newlines=>9);
```

> And it won't affect anyone else's *auto-formatting* (although they will possibly be able to use the BLINK tag method without a fatal exception).

> Returns the self object.

set_tag *TAG,* [*TAGINFO...*]

> *Class/instance method.* Accept the given *TAG* in the Chocolate Interface, and (if *TAGINFO* is given) alter its characteristics when being output.
>
> - If invoked as a class method, this alters the "master tag table", and allows a new tag to be supported via an autoloaded method:
>
>   ```
>   HTML::Stream->set_tag('MARQUEE', Newlines=>9);
>   ```
>
>   Once you do this, *all* HTML streams you open from then on will allow that tag to be output in the chocolate interface.
>
> - If invoked as an instance method, this alters the "tag table" referenced by that HTML stream, usually for the purpose of affecting things like the auto-formatting on that HTML stream.
>
> *Warning:* By default, an HTML stream just references the "master tag table" (this makes **new()** more efficient), so *by default, the instance method will behave exactly like the class method.*
>
> ```
> my $HTML = new HTML::Stream \*STDOUT;
> $HTML->set_tag('BLINK', Newlines=>0);   # changes it for others!
> ```
>
> If you want to diddle with *one* stream's auto-formatting *only,* you'll need to give that stream its own *private* tag table. Like this:
>
> ```
> my $HTML = new HTML::Stream \*STDOUT;
> $HTML->private_tags;
> $HTML->set_tag('BLINK', Newlines=>0);   # doesn't affect
>                                         # other streams
> ```
>
> *Note:* This will still force an default entry for BLINK in the *master* tag table: otherwise, we'd never know that it was legal to AUTOLOAD a BLINK method. However, it will only alter the *characteristics* of the BLINK tag (like auto-formatting) in the *object's* tag table.
>
> The *TAGINFO,* if given, is a set of **key=>value** pairs with the following possible keys:
>
> **Newlines**
>
> > Assumed to be a number which encodes how newlines are to be output before/after a tag. The value is the logical OR (or sum) of a set of flags:
> >
> > | | | | | | |
> > |---|---|---|---|---|---|
> > | 0x01 | newline before <TAG> | .<TAG>. | | .</TAG>. | |
> > | 0x02 | newline after <TAG> | \| | \| | \| | \| |
> > | 0x04 | newline before </TAG> | 1 | 2 | 4 | 8 |
> > | 0x08 | newline after </TAG> | | | | |
> >
> > Hence, to output BLINK environments which are preceded/followed by newlines:
> >
> > ```
> > set_tag HTML::Stream 'BLINK', Newlines=>9;
> > ```
>
> Returns the self object on success.

tags

> *Class/instance method.* Returns an unsorted list of all tags in the class/instance tag table (see **set_tag** for class/instance method differences).

Subclasses

HTML::Stream::Latin1

A small public package for outputting Latin-1 markup. Its default auto-escape function is `LATIN_1`, which tries to output the mnemonic entity markup (e.g., `&ccedil;`) for ISO-8859-1 characters.

So using HTML::Stream::Latin1 like this:

```
use HTML::Stream;

$HTML = new HTML::Stream::Latin1 \*STDOUT;
output $HTML "\253A right angle is 90\260, \277No?\273\n";
```

Prints this:

```
&laquo;A right angle is 90&deg;, &iquest;No?&raquo;
```

Instead of what HTML::Stream would print, which is this:

```
&#171;A right angle is 90&#176;, &#191;No?&#187;
```

Warning: A lot of Latin-1 HTML markup is not recognized by older browsers (e.g., Netscape 2.0). Consider using HTML::Stream; it will output the decimal entities which currently seem to be more "portable".

Note: Using this class "requires" that you have HTML::Entities.

Performance

Slower than I'd like. Both the `output()` method and the various "tag" methods seem to run about five times slower than the old just-hardcode-the-darn stuff approach. That is, in general, this:

```
### Approach #1...
tag  $HTML 'A', HREF=>"$href";
tag  $HTML 'IMG', SRC=>"logo.gif", ALT=>"LOGO";
text $HTML $caption;
tag  $HTML '_A';
text $HTML $a_lot_of_text;
```

And this:

```
### Approach #2...
output $HTML [A, HREF=>"$href"],
             [IMG, SRC=>"logo.gif", ALT=>"LOGO"],
             $caption,
             [_A];
output $HTML $a_lot_of_text;
```

And this:

```
### Approach #3...
$HTML -> A(HREF=>"$href")
      -> IMG(SRC=>"logo.gif", ALT=>"LOGO")
      -> t($caption)
      -> _A
      -> t($a_lot_of_text);
```

Each run about 5x slower than this:

```
### Approach #4...
    print '<A HREF="', html_escape($href), '">',
```

```
            '<IMG SRC="logo.gif" ALT="LOGO">',
            html_escape($caption),
            '</A>';
    print html_escape($a_lot_of_text);
```

Of course, I'd much rather use any of first three *(especially #3)* if I had to get something done right in a hurry. Or did you not notice the typo in approach #4?[*]

(BTW, thanks to Benchmark:: for allowing me to . . . er . . . benchmark stuff.)

Acknowledgments

Warmest thanks to:

John Buckman
> For suggesting that I write an "html2perlstream", and inspiring me to look at supporting Latin-1.

Tony Cebzanov
> For suggesting that I write an "html2perlstream".

John D Groenveld
> For bug reports, patches, and suggestions.

B. K. Oxley (binkley)
> For suggesting the support of "writing to strings" which became the "printable" interface.

Author

Eryq, *eryq@rhine.gsfc.nasa.gov*

HTTP::Daemon—a simple HTTP server class

Synopsis

```
    use HTTP::Daemon;
    use HTTP::Status;
    $d = new HTTP::Daemon;
    print "Please contact me at: <URL:", $d->url, ">\n";
    while ($c = $d->accept) {
        $r = $c->get_request;
        if ($r) {
            if ($r->method eq 'GET' and $r->url->path eq "/xyzzy") {
                # this is *not* recommened practice
                $c->send_file_response("/etc/passwd");
            } else {
                $c->send_error(RC_FORBIDDEN);
            }
        }
        $c = undef;  # close connection
    }
```

---

[*] The typo is the missing closing double quotation mark in the first line. It should read:
```
    print '<A HREF="', html_escape($href), '">',
```

Description

Instances of the HTTP::Daemon class are HTTP/1.1 servers that listens on a socket for incoming requests. The HTTP::Daemon is a subclass of IO::Socket::INET, so you can do socket operations directly on it.

The `accept()` method will return when a connection from a client is available. The returned value will be a reference to a object of the HTTP::Daemon::ClientConn class which is another IO::Socket::INET subclass. Calling the `get_request()` method on this object will read data from the client and return an HTTP::Request object reference.

This HTTP daemon does not `fork(2)` for you. Your application, i.e., the user of the HTTP::Daemon is responsible for forking if that is desirable. Also note that the user is responsible for generating responses that conforms to the HTTP/1.1 protocol. The HTTP::Daemon::ClientConn provide some methods that make this easier.

Methods

The following is a list of methods that are new (or enhanced) relative to the IO::Socket::INET base class.

$d = new HTTP::Daemon
> The object constructor takes the same parameters as the IO::Socket::INET constructor. It can also be called without specifying any parameters. The daemon will then set up a listen queue of five connections and allocate some random port number. A server that want to bind to some specific address on the standard HTTP port will be constructed like this:
>
> ```
>     $d = new HTTP::Daemon
>         LocalAddr => 'www.someplace.com',
>         LocalPort => 80;
> ```

$c = $d->accept
> Same as IO::Socket::accept but will return an HTTP::Daemon::ClientConn reference. It will return **undef** if you have specified a timeout and no connection is made within that time.

$d->url
> Returns a URL string that can be used to access the server root.

$d->product_tokens
> Returns the name that this server will use to identify itself. This is the string that is sent with the **Server** response header.

The HTTP::Daemon::ClientConn is also a IO::Socket::INET subclass. Instances of this class are returned by the `accept()` method of the HTTP::Daemon. The following additional methods are provided:

$c->get_request
> Will read data from the client and turn it into a HTTP::Request object which is then returned. Will return undef if reading of the request failed. If it fails, then the HTTP::Daemon::ClientConn object ($c) should be discarded.
>
> The $c->get_request method support HTTP/1.1 content bodies, including *chunked* transfer encoding with footer and *multipart/** types.

$c->antique_client
> Returns TRUE if the client speaks the HTTP/0.9 protocol, i.e., no status code or headers should be returned.

$c->send_status_line([$code, [$mess, [$proto]]])
> Sends the status line back to the client.

$c->send_basic_header([$code, [$mess, [$proto]]])
> Sends the status line and the **Date:** and **Server:** headers back to the client.

$c->send_response([$res])
> Takes a HTTP::Response object as parameter and send it back to the client as the response.

$c->send_redirect($loc, [$code, [$entity_body]])
> Sends a redirect response back to the client. The location (*$loc*) can be an absolute or a relative URL. The *$code* must be one the redirect status codes, and it defaults to "301 Moved Permanently."

$c->send_error([$code, [$error_message]])
> Send an error response back to the client. If the *$code* is missing, a "Bad Request" error is reported. The *$error_message* is a string that is incorporated in the body of the HTML entity body.

$c->send_file_response($filename)
> Send back a response with the specified *$filename* as content. If the file happen to be a directory we will generate a HTML index for it.

$c->send_file($fd);
> Copies the file back to the client. The file can be a string (which will be interpreted as a filename) or a reference to a glob.

$c->daemon
> Return a reference to the corresponding HTTP::Daemon object.

Author

Gisle Aas, *aas@sn.no*

Copyright

Copyright © 1996, Gisle Aas

This library is free software; you can redistribute it and/or modify it under the same terms as Perl itself.

See Also

IO::Socket, Apache

HTTP::Headers — class encapsulating HTTP message headers

Synopsis

```
require HTTP::Headers;
$request = new HTTP::Headers;
```

Description

The HTTP::Headers class encapsulates HTTP-style message headers. The headers consist of attribute-value pairs, which may be repeated, and which are printed in a particular order.

Instances of this class are usually created as member variables of the HTTP::Request and HTTP::Response classes, internal to the library.

Methods

$h = new HTTP::Headers

Constructs a new HTTP::Headers object. You might pass some initial attribute-value pairs as parameters to the constructor, e.g.:

```
$h = new HTTP::Headers
    Date        => 'Thu, 03 Feb 1994 00:00:00 GMT',
    Content_Type => 'text/html; version=3.2',
    Content_Base => 'http://www.sn.no/';
```

$h->header(*$field* [=> *$val*],...)

Get or set the value of a header. The header field name is not case sensitive. To make the life easier for Perl users who wants to avoid quoting before the => operator, you can use "_" as a synonym for "-" in header names.

The value argument may be a scalar or a reference to a list of scalars. If the value argument is not defined, then the header is not modified.

The **header**() method accepts multiple (*$field* => *$value*) pairs.

The list of previous values for the last *$field* is returned. Only the first header value is returned in scalar context.

```
$header->header(MIME_Version => '1.0',
                User_Agent   => 'My-Web-Client/0.01');
$header->header(Accept => "text/html, text/plain, image/*");
$header->header(Accept => [qw(text/html text/plain image/*)]);
@accepts = $header->header('Accept');
```

$h->scan(\\&*doit*)

Apply a subroutine to each header in turn. The callback routine is called with two parameters; the name of the field and a single value. If the header has more than one value, then the routine is called once for each value. The field name passed to the callback routine has case as suggested by HTTP Spec, and the headers will be visited in the recommended "Good Practice" order.

$h->as_string([*$endl*])

Return the header fields as a formatted MIME header. Since it internally uses the **scan**() method to build the string, the result will use case as suggested by HTTP Spec, and it will follow recommended "Good Practice" of ordering the header fields. Long header values are not folded.

The optional parameter specifies the line ending sequence to use. The default is \n. Embedded \n characters in the header will be substituted with this line ending sequence.

$h->push_header(*$field*, *$val*)

Add a new field value of the specified header. The header field name is not case sensitive. The field need not already have a value. Previous values for the same field are retained. The argument may be a scalar or a reference to a list of scalars.

```
$header->push_header(Accept => 'image/jpeg');
```

$h->remove_header(*$field*,...)

This function removes the headers with the specified names.

$h->clone

Returns a copy of this HTTP::Headers object.

Convenience Methods

The most frequently used headers can also be accessed through the following convenience methods. These methods can both be used to read and to set the value of a header. The header value is set if you pass an argument to the method. The old header value is always returned.

Methods that deal with dates and times always convert their value to system time (seconds since January 1, 1970) and they also expect this kind of value when the header value is set.

$h->date

This header represents the date and time at which the message was originated.

```
$h->date(time);  # set current date
```

$h->expires

This header gives the date and time after which the entity should be considered stale.

$h->if_modified_since

This header is used to make a request conditional. If the requested resource has not been modified since the time specified in this field, then the server will return a "304 Not Modified" response instead of the document itself.

$h->last_modified

This header indicates the date and time at which the resource was last modified.

```
# check if document is more than 1 hour old
if ($h->last_modified < time - 60*60) {
    . . .
}
```

$h->content_type

The Content-Type header field indicates the media type of the message content.

```
$h->content_type('text/html');
```

The value returned will be converted to lowercase, and potential parameters will be chopped off and returned as a separate value if in an array context. This makes it safe to do the following:

```
if ($h->content_type eq 'text/html') {
    # we enter this place even if the real header value
    # happens to be 'TEXT/HTML; version=3.0'
    . . .
}
```

$h->content_encoding

The Content-Encoding header field is used as a modifier to the media type. When present, its value indicates what additional encoding mechanism has been applied to the resource.

$h->content_length

A decimal number indicating the size in bytes of the message content.

`$h->title`

>The title of the document. In libwww-perl this header will be initialized automatically from the `<TITLE>...</TITLE>` element of HTML documents. *This header is no longer part of the HTTP standard.*

`$h->user_agent`

>This header field is used in request messages and contains information about the user agent originating the request:

>>   `$h->user_agent('Mozilla/1.2');`

`$h->server`

>The server header field contains information about the software being used by the originating server program handling the request.

`$h->from`

>This header should contain an Internet email address for the human user who controls the requesting user agent. The address should be machine-usable, as defined by RFC 822:

>>   `$h->from('Gisle Aas <aas@sn.no>');`

`$h->referer`

>Used to specify the address (URI) of the document from which the requested resource address was obtained.

`$h->www_authenticate`

>This header must be included as part of a "401 Unauthorized" response. The field value consist of a challenge that indicates the authentication scheme and parameters applicable to the requested URI.

`$h->authorization`

>A user agent that wishes to authenticate itself with a server, may do so by including this header.

`$h->authorization_basic`

>This method is used to get or set an authorization header that use the "Basic Authentication Scheme." In array context it will return two values; the username and the password. In scalar context it will return `uname:password` as a single string value.

>When used to set the header value, it expects two arguments:

>>   `$h->authorization_basic($uname, $password);`

HTTP::Message—class encapsulating HTTP messages

Synopsis

```
package HTTP::Request;   # or HTTP::Response
require HTTP::Message;
@ISA=qw(HTTP::Message);
```

Description

A HTTP::Message object contains some headers and a content (body). The class is abstract, i.e., it is only used as a base class for HTTP::Request and HTTP::Response and should never instantiated as itself.

Methods

$mess = new HTTP::Message;

This is the object constructor. It should only be called internally by this library. External code should construct HTTP::Request or HTTP::Response objects.

$mess->clone()

Returns a copy of the object.

$mess->protocol([*$proto*])

Sets the HTTP protocol used for the message. $proto is a string like "HTTP/1.0" or "HTTP/1.1".

$mess->content([*$content*])

The content() method sets the content if an argument is given. If no argument is given the content is not touched. In either case the previous content is returned.

$mess->add_content(*$data*)

The add_content() methods appends more data to the end of the previous content.

$mess->content_ref

The content_ref() method will return a reference to content string. It can be more efficient to access the content this way if the content is huge, and it can be used for direct manipulation of the content, for instance:

```
${$res->content_ref} =~ s/\bfoo\b/bar/g;
```

Header Methods

$mess->headers_as_string([*$endl*])

Call the HTTP::Headers->as_string() method for the headers in the message.

All unknown HTTP::Message methods are delegated to the HTTP::Headers object that is part of every message. This allows convenient access to these methods. Refer to HTTP::Headers for details of these methods:

```
$mess->header($field => $val);
$mess->scan(&doit);
$mess->push_header($field => $val);
$mess->remove_header($field);
$mess->date;
$mess->expires;
$mess->if_modified_since;
$mess->last_modified;
$mess->content_type;
$mess->content_encoding;
$mess->content_length;
$mess->title;
$mess->user_agent;
$mess->server;
$mess->from;
$mess->referer;
$mess->www_authenticate;
$mess->authorization;
$mess->authorization_basic;
```

HTTP::Request—class encapsulating HTTP requests

Synopsis

```
require HTTP::Request;
$request = new HTTP::Request 'GET', 'http://www.oslonett.no/';
```

Description

HTTP::Request is a class encapsulating HTTP-style requests, consisting of a request line, a MIME header, and optional content. Note that the LWP library also uses this HTTP-style request for non-HTTP protocols.

Instances of this class are usually passed to the **request()** method of an LWP::UserAgent object:

```
$ua = new LWP::UserAgent;
$request = new HTTP::Request 'http://www.oslonett.no/';
$response = $ua->request($request);
```

Methods

HTTP::Request is a subclass of HTTP::Message and therefore inherits its methods. The inherited methods are **header()**, **push_header()**, **remove_header()**, **headers_as_ string()**, and **content()**. See HTTP::Message for details.

$r = new HTTP::Request *$method*, *$url*, *[$header, [$content]]*
> Constructs a new HTTP::Request object describing a request on the object *$url* using method *$method*. The *$url* argument can be either a string, or a reference to a URI::URL object. The *$header* argument should be a reference to a HTTP::Headers object.

> ```
> $request = new HTTP::Request 'GET', 'http://www.oslonett.no/';
> ```

$r->method([$val])
$r->url([$val])
> These methods provide public access to the member variables containing respectively the method of the request and the URL object of the request.

> If an argument is given the member variable is given that as its new value. If no argument is given the value is not touched. In either case the previous value is returned.

> The **url()** method accept both a reference to a URI::URL object and a string as its argument. If a string is given, then it should be parseable as an absolute URL.

$r->as_string()
> Method returning a textual representation of the request. Mainly useful for debugging purposes. It takes no arguments.

HTTP::Request::Common—construct common HTTP::Request objects

Synopsis

```
use HTTP::Request::Common;
$ua = LWP::UserAgent->new;
$ua->request(GET 'http://www.sn.no/');
$ua->request(POST 'http://somewhere/foo', [foo => bar, bar => foo]);
```

Description

This module provides functions that return newly created HTTP::Request objects. These functions are usually more convenient than the standard HTTP::Request constructor for these common requests.

Functions

GET $url, [Header => Value,...]

The GET() function returns a HTTP::Request object initialized with the GET method and the specified URL. Without additional arguments it is exactly equivalent to the following call:

```
HTTP::Request->new(GET => $url)
```

but is less cluttered. It also reads better when used together with the LWP::User-Agent->request() method:

```
my $ua = new LWP::UserAgent;
my $res = $ua->request(GET 'http://www.sn.no')
if ($res->is_success) { ...
```

You can also initialize the header values in the request by specifying some key/value pairs as optional arguments. For instance:

```
$ua->request(GET 'http://www.sn.no',
             If_Match => 'foo',
             From     => 'gisle@aas.no',
         );
```

A header key called "Content" is special and when seen the value will initialize the content part of the request instead of setting a header.

HEAD $url, [Header => Value,...]

Like GET() but the method in the request is HEAD.

PUT $url, [Header => Value,...]

Like GET() but the method in the request is PUT.

POST $url, [$form_ref], [Header => Value,...]

This works mostly like GET() with POST as method, but this function also takes a second optional array reference parameter ($form_ref). This argument can be used to pass key/value pairs for the form content. By default we will initialize a request using the application/x-www-form-urlencoded content type. This means that you can emulate a HTML <FORM> POSTing like this:

```
POST 'http://www.perl.org/survey.cgi',
    [ name   => 'Gisle',
      email  => 'gisle@aas.no',
      gender => 'm',
      born   => '1964',
      trust  => '3%',
    ];
```

This will create a HTTP::Request object that looks like this:

```
POST http://www.perl.org/survey.cgi
Content-Length: 61
Content-Type: application/x-www-form-urlencoded
name=Gisle&email=gisle%40aas.no&gender=m&born=1964&trust=3%25
```

The POST method also supports the `multipart/form-data` content used for *Form-based File Upload* as specified in RFC 1867. You trigger this content format by specifying a content type of `'form-data'`. If one of the values in the *$form_ref* is an array reference, then it is treated as a file part specification with the following values:

```
[ $file, $filename, Header => Value... ]
```

The first value in the array (*$file*) is the name of a file to open. This file will be read and its contents placed in the request. The routine will croak if the file can't be opened. Use an undef as *$file* value if you want to specify the content directly. The *$filename* is the filename to report in the request. If this value is undefined, then the basename of the *$file* will be used. You can specify an empty string as *$filename* if you don't want any filename in the request.

Sending my ~/.profile to the survey used as example above can be achieved by this:

```
POST 'http://www.perl.org/survey.cgi',
    Content_Type => 'form-data',
    Content      => [ name  => 'Gisle Aas',
                      email => 'gisle@aas.no',
                      gender => 'm',
                      born  => '1964',
                      init  => ["$ENV{HOME}/.profile"],
                    ]
```

This will create a HTTP::Request object that almost looks like this (the boundary and the content of your ~/.profile is likely to be different):

```
POST http://www.perl.org/survey.cgi
Content-Length: 388
Content-Type: multipart/form-data; boundary="6G+f"
--6G+f
Content-Disposition: form-data; name="name"

Gisle Aas
--6G+f
Content-Disposition: form-data; name="email"

gisle@aas.no
--6G+f
Content-Disposition: form-data; name="gender"

m
--6G+f
Content-Disposition: form-data; name="born"

1964
--6G+f
Content-Disposition: form-data; name="init";
filename=".profile"
Content-Type: text/plain

PATH=/local/perl/bin:$PATH
export PATH
--6G+f--
```

Author

Gisle Aas, *aas@sn.no*

Copyright

Copyright © 1997, Gisle Aas

This library is free software; you can redistribute it and/or modify it under the same terms as Perl itself.

See Also

HTTP::Request, LWP::UserAgent

HTTP::Response—class encapsulating HTTP responses

Synopsis

```
require HTTP::Response;
```

Description

The HTTP::Response class encapsulate HTTP-style responses. A response consist of a response line, some headers, and a (potential empty) content. Note that the LWP library will use HTTP-style responses also for non-HTTP protocol schemes.

Instances of this class are usually created and returned by the **request()** method of an LWP::UserAgent object:

```
...
$response = $ua->request($request)
if ($response->is_success) {
    print $response->content;
} else {
    print $response->error_as_HTML;
}
```

Methods

HTTP::Response is a subclass of HTTP::Message and therefore inherits its methods. The inherited methods are **header()**, **push_header()**, **remove_header()**, **headers_ as_string()**, and **content()**. The header convenience methods are also available. See HTTP::Message for details.

$r = new HTTP::Response (*$rc*, [*$msg*, [*$header*, [*$content*]]])
> Constructs a new HTTP::Response object describing a response with response code $rc and optional message *$msg*.

$r->code([*$code*])
$r->message([*$message*])
$r->request([*$request*])
$r->previous([*$previousResponse*])
> These methods provide public access to the member variables. The first two contain, respectively, the response code and the message of the response.

The *request* attribute is a reference to the request that gave this response. It does not have to be the same request as passed to the `$ua->request()` method, because there might have been redirects and authorization retries in between.

The previous attribute is used to link together chains of responses. You get chains of responses if the first response is redirect or unauthorized.

`$r->base`

Returns the base URL for this response. The return value will be a reference to a URI::URL object.

The base URL is obtained from one the following sources (in priority order):

1. Embedded in the document content, for instance `<BASE HREF="...">` in HTML documents.

2. A "Content-Base:" or a "Content-Location:" header in the response.

   For backwards compatibility with older HTTP implementations we will also look for the "Base:" header.

3. The URL used to request this response. This might not be the original URL that was passed to `$ua->request()` method, because we might have received some redirect responses first.

When the LWP protocol modules produce the HTTP::Response object, then any base URL embedded in the document (step 1) will already have initialized the "Content-Base:" header. This means that this method only performs the last two steps (the content is not always available, either).

`$r->as_string()`

Method returning a textual representation of the request. Mainly useful for debugging purposes. It takes no arguments.

`$r->is_info`
`$r->is_success`
`$r->is_redirect`
`$r->is_error`

These methods indicate if the response was informational, successful, a redirection, or an error.

`$r->error_as_HTML()`

Return a string containing a complete HTML document indicating what error occurred. This method should only be called when `$r->is_error` is TRUE.

`$r->current_age`

This function will calculate the "current age" of the response as specified by *<draft-ietf-http-v11-spec-07>* section 13.2.3. The age of a response is the time since it was sent by the origin server. The returned value is a number representing the age in seconds.

`$r->freshness_lifetime`

This function will calculate the "freshness lifetime" of the response as specified by *<draft-ietf-http-v11-spec-07>* section 13.2.4. The freshness lifetime is the length of time between the generation of a response and its expiration time. The returned value is a number representing the freshness lifetime in seconds.

If the response does not contain an "Expires" or a "Cache-Control" header, then this function will apply some simple heuristic based on "Last-Modified" to determine a suitable lifetime.

`$r->is_fresh`

Returns TRUE if the response is fresh, based on the values of `freshness_lifetime()` and `current_age()`. If the response is not longer fresh, then it has to be refetched or revalidated by the origin server.

`$r->fresh_until`

Returns the time when this entity is no longer fresh.

HTTP::Status—HTTP status code processing

Synopsis

```
use HTTP::Status;
if ($rc != RC_OK) {
    print status_message($rc), "\n";
}
if (is_success($rc)) { ... }
if (is_error($rc)) { ... }
if (is_redirect($rc)) { ... }
```

Description

HTTP::Status is a library of routines for defining and classification of HTTP status codes for *libwww-perl*. Status codes are used to encode the overall outcome of a HTTP response message. Codes correspond to those defined in RFC 2068.

Constants

The following constant functions can be used as mnemonic status code names:

RC_CONTINUE	(100)
RC_SWITCHING_PROTOCOLS	(101)
RC_OK	(200)
RC_CREATED	(201)
RC_ACCEPTED	(202)
RC_NON_AUTHORITATIVE_INFORMATION	(203)
RC_NO_CONTENT	(204)
RC_RESET_CONTENT	(205)
RC_PARTIAL_CONTENT	(206)
RC_MULTIPLE_CHOICES	(300)
RC_MOVED_PERMANENTLY	(301)
RC_MOVED_TEMPORARILY	(302)
RC_SEE_OTHER	(303)
RC_NOT_MODIFIED	(304)
RC_USE_PROXY	(305)
RC_BAD_REQUEST	(400)
RC_UNAUTHORIZED	(401)
RC_PAYMENT_REQUIRED	(402)
RC_FORBIDDEN	(403)

```
RC_NOT_FOUND                          (404)
RC_METHOD_NOT_ALLOWED                 (405)
RC_NOT_ACCEPTABLE                     (406)
RC_PROXY_AUTHENTICATION_REQUIRED      (407)
RC_REQUEST_TIMEOUT                    (408)
RC_CONFLICT                           (409)
RC_GONE                               (410)
RC_LENGTH_REQUIRED                    (411)
RC_PRECONDITION_FAILED                (412)
RC_REQUEST_ENTITY_TOO_LARGE           (413)
RC_REQUEST_URI_TOO_LARGE              (414)
RC_UNSUPPORTED_MEDIA_TYPE             (415)
RC_INTERNAL_SERVER_ERROR              (500)
RC_NOT_IMPLEMENTED                    (501)
RC_BAD_GATEWAY                        (502)
RC_SERVICE_UNAVAILABLE                (503)
RC_GATEWAY_TIMEOUT                    (504)
RC_HTTP_VERSION_NOT_SUPPORTED         (505)
```

Functions

The following additional functions are provided. Most of them are exported by default.

status_message(*$code*)

> The status_message() function translates status codes to human readable strings. The string is the same as found in the constant names above.

is_info(*$code*)

> Returns TRUE if $code is an *Informational* status code.

is_success(*$code*)

> Returns TRUE if $code is a *Successful* status code.

is_redirect(*$code*)

> Returns TRUE if $code is a *Redirection* status code.

is_error(*$code*)

> Returns TRUE if *$code* is an *Error* status code. The function returns TRUE for both a client error or a server error status codes.

is_client_error(*$code*)

> Returns TRUE if *$code* is an *Client Error* status code. This function is *not* exported by default.

is_server_error(*$code*)

> Returns TRUE if *$code* is an *Server Error* status code. This function is *not* exported by default.

HTTPD::Authen—HTTP server authentication class

Synopsis

```
use HTTPD::Authen ();
```

Description

This module provides methods for authenticating a user. It uses HTTPD::UserAdmin to lookup passwords in a database. Subclasses provide methods specific to the authentication mechanism.

Currently, under HTTP/1.0 the only supported authentication mechanism is Basic Authentication. NCSA Mosaic and NCSA HTTPD understand the proposed Message Digest Authentication, which should make it into the HTTP spec someday. This module supports both.

Methods

`new ()`

> Since HTTPD::Authen uses HTTPD::UserAdmin for database lookups it needs many of the same attributes. Or, if the first argument passed to the `new()` object constructor is a reference to an HTTPD::UserAdmin, the attributes are inherited.
>
> The following attributes are recognized from HTTPD::UserAdmin:
>
> > `DBType, DB, Server, Path, DBMF, Encrypt`
>
> And, if you wish to query an SQL server:
>
> > `Host, User, Auth, Driver, UserTable, NameField, PasswordField`
>
> The same defaults are assumed for these attributes, as in HTTPD::UserAdmin. See HTTPD::UserAdmin for details.
>
> > `$authen = new HTTPD::Authen (DB => "www-users");`

`basic()`

> Shortcut to return an HTTPD::Authen::Basic object.
>
> > `$basic = $authen->basic;`

`digest()`

> Shortcut to return an HTTPD::Authen::Digest object.
>
> > `$digest = $authen->digest;`

`type($authorization_header_value)`

> This method will guess the authorization scheme based on the "Authorization" header value, and return an object bless into that scheme's class.
>
> By using this method, it is simple to authenticate a user without even knowing what scheme is being used:
>
> ```
> $authtype = HTTPD::Authen->type($authinfo);
> @info = $authtype->parse($authinfo)
> if( $authtype->check(@info) ) {
>     #response 200 OK, etc.
> }
> ```

Subclasses

The following sections detail the subclasses of HTTPD::Authen.

HTTPD::Authen::Basic methods

`new([$hashref])`

> *$hashref* should be an HTTPD::Authen object, it must be present when looking up users. Optionally, you can pass the attribute USER with the value of an HTTPD::UserAdmin object.

Normally, this method isn't called directly, but rather by the HTTPD::Authen-> basic method.

`parse ($authorization_header_value)`

This method expects the value of the HTTP "Authorization" header of type Basic. This should look something like:

```
'Basic ZG91Z206anN0NG11'
```

This string will be parsed and decoded, returning the username and password. Note that the MIME::Base64 module is required for decoding.

```
($username,$password) =
         HTTPD::Authen::Basic->parse($authinfo)

#or, assuming $authen is an HTTPD::Authen object
($username,$password) = $authen->basic->parse($authinfo)
#or check the info at the same time
$OK = $authen->check($authen->basic->parse($authinfo))
```

`check($username, $password)`

This method expects a username and *clear text* password as arguments. Returns true if the username was found, and passwords match, otherwise returns false.

```
if($authen->check("JoeUser", "his_clear_text_password")) {
    print "Well, the passwords match at least\n";
}
else {
    print "Password mismatch! Intruder alert!\n";
}
```

HTTPD::Authen::Digest methods

Note: The MD5 module is required to use these methods.

`new([$hashref])`

$hashref should be an HTTPD::Authen object. Normally, this method is not called directly, but rather by the HTTPD::Authen->digest method.

`parse ($authorization_header_value)`

This method expects the value of the HTTP "Authorization" header of type Basic. This should look something like:

```
Digest username="JoeUser", realm="SomePlace",
nonce="826407380", uri="/test/blah.html",
response="0306f29f88690fb9203451556c376ae9",
opaque="5e09061a062a271c8fcc686c5be90c2a"
```

This method returns a hashref containing all *name = value* pairs from the header.

```
$mda = HTTPD::Authen::Digest->parse($authinfo);
#or, assuming $authen is an HTTPD::Authen object
$mda = $authen->digest->parse($authinfo)
#or check the info at the same time
$OK = $authen->check($authen->digest->parse($authinfo))
```

`check ($hashref[, $request [, $seconds [, $client_ip ]]])`

This method expects a hashref of *name = value* pairs normally found in the "Authorization" header. With this argument alone, the method will return true without checking "nonce" or the opaque string if the client response checksum matches ours.

If *$request* is present, it must be a hashref or an HTTP::Request method. From here, we fetch the request `uri` and `request` method. Otherwise, we default to the value of `uri` present in `$hashref`, and GET for the method.

If *$seconds* is present, the value of "nonce" will be checked, returning `false` if it is stale.

If *$client_ip* is present, the value of the `opaque` string will be checked, returning `false` if the string is not valid.

This implementation is based on the Digest Access Authentication Internet draft *http://hopf.math.nwu.edu/digestauth/draft.rfc* and NCSA's implementation *http://hoohoo.ncsa.uiuc.edu/docs/howto/md5_auth.html*.

Author

Doug MacEachern, *dougm@osf.org*

Copyright

Copyright © 1996, Doug MacEachern, OSF Research Institute

This library is free software; you can redistribute it and/or modify it under the same terms as Perl itself.

See Also

HTTPD::UserAdmin, MD5, HTTP::Request, MIME::Base64

HTTPD::GroupAdmin—management of HTTP server group databases

Synopsis

```
use HTTPD::GroupAdmin ();
```

Description

This software is meant to provide a generic interface that hides the inconsistencies across HTTP server implementations of user and group databases.

Methods

new ()

Here's where we find out what's different about your server.

Some examples:

```
@DBM = (DBType => 'DBM',
        DB     => '.htgroup',
        Server => 'apache');
$group = new HTTPD::GroupAdmin @DBM;
```

This creates an object who's database is a DBM file named *.htgroup*, in a format that the Apache server understands.

```
@Text = (DBType => 'Text',
         DB     => '.htgroup',
         Server => 'ncsa');
$group = new HTTPD::GroupAdmin @Text;
```

This creates an object whose database is a plain text file named *.htgroup* in a format that the NCSA server understands.

Note: Support is not yet available for SQL servers.

Full list of constructor attributes:

Name
> Group name

DBType
> The type of database, one of DBM, Text, or SQL (default is DBM)

DB
> The database name (default is *.htpasswd* for DBM and Text databases)

Server
> HTTP server name (default is the generic class, which works with NCSA, Apache and possibly others).
>
> Note: Run perl t/support.t matrix to see what support is currently available.

Path
> Relative DB files are resolved to this value (default is ".").

Locking
> Boolean, Lock Text, and DBM files (default is true).

Debug
> Boolean, turn on debug mode.

Specific to DBM files:

DBMF
> The DBM file implementation to use (default is NDBM).

Flags
> The read, write, and create flags. There are four modes—rwc: the default, open for reading, writing, and creating; rw: open for reading and writing; r: open for reading only; w: open for writing only.

Mode
> The file creation mode (defaults to 0644).

From here on out, things should look the same for everyone.

add($username[, $groupname])
> Add user $username to group $groupname, or whatever the Name attribute is set to.
>
> Fails if $username exists in the database.

```
if($group->add('dougm', 'www-group')) {
    print "Welcome!\n";
}
```

delete($username[, $groupname])
> Delete user $username from group $groupname, or whatever the Name attribute is set to.

```
if($group->delete('dougm')) {
    print "He's gone from the group\n";
}
```

`exists(`*`$groupname,`* *`[$username]`*`)`

True if *$groupname* is found in the database.

```
if($group->exists('web-heads')) {
    die "oh no!";
}
if($group->exists($groupname, $username) {
    #$username is a member of $groupname
}
```

`list([`*`$groupname]`*`)`

Returns a list of group names, or users in a group if *$groupname* is given.

```
@groups = $group->list;
@users = $group->list('web-heads');
```

`user()`

Shortcut for creating an HTTPD::UserAdmin object. All applicable attributes are inherited, but can be overridden.

```
$user = $group->user();
```

(See HTTPD::UserAdmin)

`convert(`*`@Attributes`*`)`

Convert a database.

```
#not yet
```

`remove(`*`$groupname`*`)`

Remove group *$groupname* from the database.

`name(`*`$groupname`*`)`

Change the value of **Name** attribute.

```
$group->name('bew-ediw-dlrow');
```

`debug(`*`$boolean`*`)`

Turn debugging on or off.

`lock([`*`$timeout]`*`)`
`unlock()`

These methods give you control of the locking mechanism.

```
$group = new HTTPD::GroupAdmin (Locking => 0); # turn off
                                                # auto-locking
$group->lock; #lock the object's database
$group->add($username,$passwd); #write while database is locked
$group->unlock; release the lock
```

`db(`*`$dbname`*`);`

Select a different database.

```
$olddb = $group->db($newdb);
print "Now we're reading and writing '$newdb',
    done with '$olddb'n\";
```

`flags([`*`$flags]`*`)`

Get or set read, write, create flags.

`commit`

Commit changes to disk (for Text files).

Author

Doug MacEachern, *dougm@osf.org*

Copyright

Copyright © 1996, 1997 Doug MacEachern.

This library is free software; you can redistribute it and/or modify it under the same terms as Perl itself.

See Also

HTTPD::UserAdmin(3)

HTTPD::UserAdmin—management of HTTP server user databases

Synopsis

```
use HTTPD::UserAdmin ();
```

Description

This software is meant to provide a generic interface that hides the inconsistencies across HTTP server implementations of user and group databases.

Methods

new ()

Here's where we find out what's different about your server.

Some examples:

```
@DBM = (DBType => 'DBM',
        DB     => '.htpasswd',
        Server => 'apache');
$user = new HTTPD::UserAdmin @DBM;
```

This creates an object whose database is a DBM file named *.htpasswd*, in a format that the Apache server understands.

```
@Text = (DBType => 'Text',
         DB     => '.htpasswd',
         Server => 'ncsa');
$user = new HTTPD::UserAdmin @Text;
```

This creates an object whose database is a plain text file named *.htpasswd*, in a format that the NCSA server understands.

```
@SQL = (DBType =>    "SQL",
        Host =>      "",            # server hostname
        DB =>        "www",         # database name
        User =>      "",            # database login name
        Auth =>      "",            # database login password
        Driver =>    "mSQL",        # driver for DBI
        Server =>    "apache",      # HTTP server type, not
                                    # required
        UserTable => "www-users",   # table with field names
                                    # below
        NameField => "user",        # field for the name
```

```
                      PasswordField => "password", #field for the password
                      );
       $user = new HTTPD::UserAdmin @SQL;
```

This creates an object whose mSQL database is named *www*, with a schema that the Apache server (extension) understands.

Full list of constructor attributes (note that these are case-insensitive):

DBType
: The type of database, one of DBM, Text, or SQL (default is DBM).

DB
: The database name (default is *.htpasswd* for DBM and Text databases).

Server
: HTTP server name (default is the generic class, that works with NCSA, Apache and possibly others).

: Note: Run perl t/support.t matrix to see what support is currently available.

Encrypt
: One of crypt or MD5 (default is crypt).

Locking
: Boolean, Lock Text, and DBM files (default is true).

Path
: Relative DB files are resolved to this value (default is ".").

Debug
: Boolean, turn on debug mode.

Flags
: The read, write, and create flags. There are four modes—rwc: the default, open for reading, writing, and creating; rw: open for reading and writing; r: open for reading only; w: open for writing only.

Specific to DBM files:

DBMF
: The DBM file implementation to use (default is 'NDBM').

Mode
: The file creation mode (default is '0644').

Specific to DBI:

We talk to an SQL server via Tim Bunce's DBI switch; for more information, see *http://www.hermetica.com/technologia/DBI/* .

Host
: Server hostname.

User
: Database login name.

Auth
: Database login password.

Driver
: Driver for DBI (default is mSQL).

UserTable
: Table with field names below.

NameField
>   Field for the name (default is **user**).

PasswordField
>   Field for the password (default is **password**).

From here on out, things should look the same for everyone.

add(*$username, $password*[, *$noenc, @fields*])
>   Add a user.
>
>   If *$noenc* is true, the password is not encrypted, useful for copying/converting, or if you just prefer to store passwords in plain text.
>
>   Fails if *$username* exists in the database.
>
>    ```
>    if($user->add('dougm', 'secret')) {
>        print "You have the power!\n";
>    }
>    ```
>
>   You may need to pass additional fields, such as the user's real name. This depends on your server, of course.
>
>    ```
>    $user->add('JoeUser', 'try2guess', '', 'Joseph A. User');
>    ```

delete(*$username*)
>   Delete a user.
>
>    ```
>    if($user->delete('dougm')) {
>        print "He's gone\n";
>    }
>    ```

exists(*$username*)
>   True if *$username* is found in the database.
>
>    ```
>    if($user->exists('dougm')) {
>        die "oh no!";
>    }
>    ```

password()
>   Returns the encrypted password for a user.
>
>    ```
>    $passwd = $user->password("dougm");
>    ```
>
>   Useful for copying users to another database.

list()
>   Returns a list of usernames in the current database.
>
>    ```
>    @users = $user->list
>    ```

update(*$username, $password*)
>   Update *$username* with a new *$password*.
>
>    ```
>    if($user->update('dougm', 'idunno')) {
>        print "Updated\n";
>    }
>    ```

group()
>   Shortcut for creating an HTTPD::GroupAdmin object. All applicable attributes are inherited, but can be overridden.
>
>    ```
>    $group = $user->group(NAME => 'www-group');
>    ```
>
>   (See HTTPD::GroupAdmin.)

convert(@*Attributes*)

> Convert a database.

```
$dbmuser = $user->convert(@Apache);
```

lock([[$*timeout*]])

unlock()

> These methods give you control of the locking mechanism.

```
$user = new HTTPD::UserAdmin (Locking => 0); # turn off auto-
                                             # locking
$user->lock; #lock the object's database
$user->add($username,$passwd); #write while file is locked
$user->unlock; release the lock
```

db($*dbname*);

> Select a different database.

```
$olddb = $user->db($newdb);
print "Now we're reading and writing '$newdb', done with
'$olddb'n\";
```

flags([$*flags*])

> Get or set read, write, create flags.

commit

> Commit changes to disk (for Text files).

Message Digest User Databases

Currently, you can store user info in a format for servers who support Message Digest Authentication. Here's an example:

```
$user = new HTTPD::UserAdmin (DB => '.htdigest', Encrypt => 'MD5');

($username,$realm,$password) = ('JoeUser', 'SomePlace', '14me');
#The checksum contains more info that just a password
$user->add($username, "$username:$realm:$password");
$user->update($username, "$username:$realm:newone");
$info = $user->password($username);
($realm, $checksum) = split(":", $info);
$user->delete($username);
```

See *http://booboo.ncsa.uiuc.edu/docs/howto/md5_auth.html* for NCSA's implementation.

So, it's a little more work, but don't worry, a nicer interface is on the way.

Author

Doug MacEachern, *dougm@osf.org*

Copyright

Copyright © 1996, Doug MacEachern

This library is free software; you can redistribute it and/or modify it under the same terms as Perl itself.

See Also

HTTPD::GroupAdmin(3), HTTPD::Authen(3)

LWP—library for WWW access in Perl

Synopsis

```
use LWP;
print "This is libwww-perl-$LWP::VERSION\n";
```

Description

libwww-perl is a collection of Perl modules which provides a simple and consistent programming interface (API) to the World Wide Web. The main focus of the library is to provide classes and functions that allow you to write WWW clients, thus *libwww-perl* is said to be a WWW client library. The library also contain modules that are of more general use.

The main architecture of the library is object oriented. The user agent, requests sent and responses received from the WWW server are all represented by objects. This makes a simple and powerful interface to these services. The interface should be easy to extend and customize for your needs.

The main features of the library are:

- Contains various reusable components (modules) that can be used separately or together.

- Provides an object-oriented model of HTTP-style communication. Within this framework we currently support access to http, gopher, ftp, news, file, and mailto resources.

- Allows use through the full object-oriented interface or a very simple procedural interface.

- Supports the basic and digest authorization schemes.

- Gives transparent redirect handling.

- Supports access through proxy servers.

- Provides URL handling (both absolute and relative URLs are supported).

- Provides a parser for *robots.txt* files and a framework for constructing robots.

- Gives an experimental HTML parser and formatters (for PostScript and plain text).

- Cooperates with Tk. A simple Tk-based GUI browser called *tkweb* is distributed with the Tk extension for Perl.

- Implements of the HTTP content negotiation algorithm that can be used both in protocol modules and in server scripts (like CGI scripts).

- Provides a simple command-line client application called `lwp-request`.

HTTP-Style Communication

The *libwww-perl* library is based on HTTP-style communication. This section tries to describe what that means.

Let us start with this quote from the HTTP specification document, found online at *http://www.w3.org/pub/WWW/Protocols/*:

> The HTTP protocol is based on a request/response paradigm. A client establishes a connection with a server and sends a request to the server in the form of a request method, URI, and protocol version, followed by a MIME-like message containing request modifiers, client information, and possible body content. The

server responds with a status line, including the message's protocol version and a success or error code, followed by a MIME-like message containing server information, entity meta-information, and possible body content.

What this means to *libwww-perl* is that communication always take place through these steps. First, a *request* object is created and configured. This object is then passed to a server and we get a *response* object in return that we can examine. A request is always independent of any previous requests, i.e., the service is stateless. The same simple model is used for any kind of service we want to access.

For example, if we want to fetch a document from a remote file server, then we send it a request that contains a name for that document and the response will contain the document itself. If we access a search engine, then the content of the request will contain the query parameters and the response will contain the query result. If we want to send a mail message to somebody then we send a request object which contains our message to the mail server, and the response object will contain an acknowledgment that tells us that the message has been accepted and will be forwarded to the recipient(s).

It is as simple as that!

The Request Object

The request object has the class name HTTP::Request in *libwww-perl*. The fact that the class name uses HTTP:: as a name prefix only implies that we use the HTTP model of communication. It does not limit the kind of services we can try to pass this *request* to. For instance, we will send HTTP::Requests both to ftp and gopher servers, as well as to the local filesystem.

The main attributes of the request objects are:

- The method is a short string that tells what kind of request this is. The most used methods are GET, PUT, POST and HEAD.

- The url is a string denoting the protocol, server and the name of the "document" we want to access. The url might also encode various other parameters.

- The headers contain additional information about the request and can also used to describe the content. The headers is a set of keyword/value pairs.

- The content is an arbitrary amount of data.

The Response Object

The request object has the class name HTTP::Response in *libwww-perl*. The main attributes of objects of this class are:

- The code is a numerical value that encode the overall outcome of the request.

- The message is a short (human-readable) string that corresponds to the code.

- The headers contain additional information about the response and they also describe the content.

- The content is an arbitrary amount of data.

Since we don't want to handle all possible *code* values directly in our programs, the *libwww-perl* response object have methods that can be used to query what kind of response this is. The most commonly used response classification methods are:

`is_success()`

The request was successfully received, understood or accepted.

`is_error()`

> The request failed. The server or the resource might not be available, access to the resource might be denied or other things might have failed for some reason.

The User Agent

Let us assume that we have created a *request* object. What do we actually do with it in order to receive a *response?*

The answer is that you pass it on to a *user agent* object and this object will take care of all the things that need to be done (low-level communication and error handling). The user agent will give you back a *response* object. The user agent represents your application on the network and it provides you with an interface that can accept *requests* and will return *responses*.

You should think about the user agent as an interface layer between your application code and the network. Through this interface you are able to access the various servers on the network.

The *libwww-perl* class name for the user agent is LWP::UserAgent. Every *libwww-perl* application that wants to communicate should create at least one object of this kind. The main method provided by this object is `request()`. This method takes an HTTP::Request object as argument and will (eventually) return a HTTP::Response object.

The user agent has many other attributes that let you configure how it will interact with the network and with your application code.

- The timeout attribute specifies how much time we give remote servers in creating responses before the library disconnect and creates an internal timeout response.

- The agent attribute specifies the name that your application should use when it presents itself on the network.

- The from attribute can be set to the e-mail address of the person responsible for running the application. If this is set, then the address will be sent to the servers with every request.

- The use_alarm attribute specifies if it is OK for the user agent to use the alarm(2) system to implement timeouts.

- The use_eval attribute specifies if the agent should raise an exception (`die` in Perl) if an error condition occurs.

- The parse_head attribute specifies whether we should initialize response headers from the <HEAD> section of HTML documents.

- The proxy and no_proxy attributes specify if and when communication should go through a proxy server. See *http://www.w3.org/pub/WWW/Proxies/.*

- The credentials attribute provides a way to set up usernames and passwords that is needed to access certain services.

Many applications would want even more control over how they interact with the network and they get this by specializing the LWP::UserAgent by subclassing. The library provides a specialization called LWP::RobotUA that is used by robot applications.

Example

This example shows how the user agent, a request, and a response are represented in actual Perl code:

```
# Create a user agent object
use LWP::UserAgent;
$ua = new LWP::UserAgent;
$ua->agent("AgentName/0.1 " . $ua->agent);
# Create a request
my $req = new HTTP::Request POST => 'http://www.perl.com/cgi-
bin/BugGlimpse';
$req->content_type('application/x-www-form-urlencoded');
$req->content('match=www&errors=0');
# Pass request to the user agent and get a response back
my $res = $ua->request($req);
# Check the outcome of the response
if ($res->is_success) {
    print $res->content;
} else {
    print "Bad luck this time\n";
}
```

The attribute specifies is created once when the application starts up. New request objects are normally created for each request sent.

Network Support

This section goes through the various protocol schemes and describes the HTTP-style methods that are supported and the headers that might have any effect.

For all requests, a "User-Agent" header is added and initialized from the $ua->agent value before the request is handed to the network layer. In the same way, a "From" header is initialized from the $ua->from value.

For all responses, the library will add a header called "Client-Date". This header will encode the time when the response was received by your application. This format and semantics of the header is just like the server-created "Date" header.

HTTP Requests

HTTP requests are really just handed off to an HTTP server and it will decide what happens. Few servers implement methods beside the usual GET, HEAD, POST, and PUT, but CGI scripts can really implement any method they like.

If the server is not available then the library will generate an internal error response.

The library automatically adds a "Host" and a "Content-Length" header to the HTTP request before it is sent over the network.

For GET request you might want to add the "If-Modified-Since" header to make the request conditional.

For POST request you should add the "Content-Type" header. When you try to emulate HTML <FORM> handling you should usually let the value of the "Content-Type" header be application/x-www-form-urlencoded. See the lwpcook manpage for examples of this.

The *libwww-perl* HTTP implementation currently supports the HTTP/1.0 protocol. HTTP/0.9 servers are also handled correctly.

The library allows you to access proxy server through HTTP. This means that you can set up the library to forward all types of requests through the HTTP protocol module. See LWP::UserAgent for documentation of this.

FTP Requests

The library currently supports GET, HEAD, and PUT requests. GET will retrieve a file or a directory listing from an FTP server. PUT will store a file on a FTP server.

You can specify an FTP account for servers that want this in addition to username and password. This is specified by passing an "Account" header in the request.

Username/password can be specified using basic authorization or be encoded in the URL. Bad logins return an UNAUTHORIZED response with "WWW-Authenticate: Basic" and can be treated as basic authorization for HTTP.

The library supports ftp ASCII transfer mode by specifying `type=a` parameter in the URL.

Directory listings are by default returned unprocessed (as returned from the FTP server) with the content media type reported to be `text/ftp-dir-listing`. The File::Listing module provides functionality for parsing of these directory listings.

The FTP module is also able to convert directory listings to HTML and this can be requested via the standard HTTP content negotiation mechanisms (add an "Accept: text/html" header in the request if you want this).

For normal file retrievals, the "Content-Type" is guessed based on the filename suffix. See LWP::MediaTypes.

The "If-Modified-Since" header is not honored yet.

Example

```
$req = HTTP::Request->new(GET =>
'ftp://me:passwd@ftp.some.where.com/');
$req->header(Accept => "text/html, */*;q=0.1");
```

News Requests

Access to the Usenet News system is implemented through the NNTP protocol. The name of the news server is obtained from the NNTP_SERVER environment variable and defaults to "news". It is not possible to specify the hostname of the NNTP server in the *news:* URLs.

The library support GET and HEAD to retrieve news articles through the NNTP protocol. You can also post articles to newsgroups by using (surprise!) the POST method.

GET on newsgroups is not implemented yet.

Example

```
$req = HTTP::Request->new(GET => 'news:abc1234@a.sn.no');
$req = HTTP::Request->new(POST => 'news:comp.lang.perl.test');
$req->header(Subject => 'This is a test',
             From    => 'me@some.where.org');
$req->content(<<EOT);
```

```
This is the content of the message that we are sending to
the world.
EOT
```

Gopher Requests

The library supports the GET and HEAD methods for gopher requests. All request header values are ignored. HEAD cheats and will return a response without even talking to the server.

Gopher menus are always converted to HTML.

The response "Content-Type" is generated from the document type encoded (as the first letter) in the request URL path itself.

Example

```
$req = HTTP::Request->new('GET', 'gopher://gopher.sn.no/');
```

File Requests

The library supports GET and HEAD methods for file requests. The "If-Modified-Since" header is supported. All other headers are ignored. The *host* component of the file URL must be empty or set to "localhost". Any other *host* value will be treated as an error. Directories are always converted to an HTML document. For normal files, the "Content-Type" and "Content-Encoding" in the response are guessed based on the file suffix.

Example

```
$req = HTTP::Request->new(GET => 'file:/etc/passwd');
```

Mailto Requests

You can send (or "POST") mail messages using the library. All headers specified for the request are passed on to the mail system. The "To" header is initialized from the mail address in the URL.

Example

```
$req = HTTP::Request->new(POST => 'mailto:libwww-perl-
request@ics.uci.edu');
$req->header("Subject", "subscribe");
$req->content("Please subscribe me to the libwww-perl mailing
list!\n");
```

Overview of Classes and Packages

This table should give you a quick overview of the classes provided by the library. Indentation shows class inheritance.

LWP::MemberMixin	Access to member variables of Perl5 classes
LWP::UserAgent	WWW user agent class
LWP::RobotUA	When developing a robot applications
LWP::Protocol	Interface to various protocol schemes
LWP::Protocol::http	http:// access
LWP::Protocol::file	file:// access
LWP::Protocol::ftp	ftp:// access
...	

LWP::Socket	Socket creation and IO
HTTP::Headers	MIME/RFC 822 style header (used by HTTP::Message)
HTTP::Message	HTTP-style message
HTTP::Request	HTTP request
HTTP::Response	HTTP response
HTTP::Daemon	An HTTP server class
URI::URL	Uniform Resource Locators
WWW::RobotRules	Parse *robots.txt* files
WWW::RobotRules::AnyDBM_File	Persistent RobotRules
HTML::Parser	Parse HTML documents
HTML::TreeBuilder	Build an HTML syntax tree
HTML::HeadParser	Parse the `<HEAD>` section of an HTML document
HTML::LinkExtor	Extract links from an HTML document
HTML::Element	Building block for the HTML::TreeBuilder
HTML::Formatter	Convert HTML syntax trees to readable formats
HTML::FormatText	Output is plain text
HTML::FormatPS	Output is PostScript

The following modules provide various functions and definitions.

LWP	This file (library version number and documentation)
LWP::MediaTypes	MIME types configuration (`text/html`, etc.)
LWP::Debug	Debug logging module
LWP::Simple	Simplified procedural interface for common functions
HTTP::Status	HTTP status code (200 OK, etc)
HTTP::Date	Date-parsing module for HTTP date formats
HTTP::Negotiate	HTTP content negotiation calculation
HTML::Entities	Expand or unexpand entities in HTML text
File::Listing	Parse directory listings

HTTP use the Base64 encoding at some places. The QuotedPrint module is just included to make the MIME:: collection more complete.

MIME::Base64	Base64 encoding/decoding routines
MIME::QuotedPrint	Quoted Printable encoding/decoding routines

The following modules do not have much to do with the World Wide Web, but are included just because I did not bother to make separate distributions for them. Regard them as a bonus, provided free for your pleasure.

Font::AFM	Parse Adobe Font Metric files
File::CounterFile	Persistent counter class

More Documentation

All modules contain detailed information on the interfaces they provide. The `lwpcook` manpage is the *libwww-perl* cookbook that contains examples of typical usage of the library. You might want to take a look at how the scripts `lwp-request`, `lwp-rget`, and `lwp-mirror` are implemented.

Bugs

The library cannot handle multiple simultaneous requests yet. The HTML:: modules are still experimental. Also, check out what's left in the TODO file.

Acknowledgments

This package owes a lot in motivation, design, and code to the *libwww-perl* library for Perl 4, maintained by Roy Fielding (*fielding@ics.uci.edu*).

That package used work from Alberto Accomazzi, James Casey, Brooks Cutter, Martijn Koster, Oscar Nierstrasz, Mel Melchner, Gertjan van Oosten, Jared Rhine, Jack Shirazi, Gene Spafford, Marc VanHeyningen, Steven E. Brenner, Marion Hakanson, Waldemar Kebsch, Tony Sanders, and Larry Wall; see the *libwww-perl-0.40* library for details.

The primary architects for this Perl5 library are Martijn Koster and Gisle Aas, with lots of help from Graham Barr, Tim Bunce, Andreas Koenig, Jared Rhine, and Jack Shirazi.

Copyright

Copyright © 1995–1997, Gisle Aas

Copyright © 1995, Martijn Koster

This library is free software; you can redistribute it and/or modify it under the same terms as Perl itself.

LWP::Debug— debug routines for the libwww-perl library

Synopsis

```
use LWP::Debug qw(+ -conns);
# Used internally in the library
LWP::Debug::trace('send()');
LWP::Debug::debug('url ok');
LWP::Debug::conns("read $n bytes: $data");
```

Description

LWP::Debug provides tracing facilities. The `trace()`, `debug()`, and `conns()` functions are called within the library and they log information at increasing levels of detail. Which level of detail is actually printed is controlled with the `level()` function.

Functions

`level(...)`

> The `level()` function controls the level of detail being logged. Passing + or – indicates full and no logging respectively. Individual levels can be switched on and off by passing the name of the level with a + or – prepended. The levels are:

```
trace    : trace function calls
debug    : print debug messages
conns    : show all data transferred over the connections
```

The LWP::Debug module provide a special `import()` method that allows you to pass the `level()` arguments with initial use statement. If a **use** argument starts with + or – then it is passed to the level function, else the name is exported as usual. The following two statements are thus equivalent (if you ignore the fact that the second pollutes your namespace):

```
use LWP::Debug qw(+);
use LWP::Debug qw(level); level('+');
```

trace(*$msg*)

The **trace()** function is used for tracing function calls. The package and calling subroutine name is printed along with the passed argument. This should be called at the start of every major function.

debug(*$msg*)

The **debug()** function is used for high-granularity reporting of state in functions.

conns(*$msg*)

The **conns()** function is used to show data being transferred over the connections. This may generate considerable output.

LWP::IO — low-level I/O capability

Synopsis

```
use LWP::IO ();
```

Description

LWP::IO::read(*$fd*, *$data*, *$size*, *$offset*, *$timeout*)
LWP::IO::write(*$fd*, *$data*, *$timeout*)

These routines provide low-level I/O with timeout capability for the LWP library. These routines will only be installed if they are not already defined. This fact can be used by programs that need to override these functions. Just provide replacement functions before you require LWP. See also LWP::TkIO.

LWP::MemberMixin — member access mixin class

Synopsis

```
package Foo;
require LWP::MemberMixin;
@ISA=qw(LWP::MemberMixin);
```

Description

A mixin class to get methods that provide easy access to member variables in the %$self.

Method

_elem(*$elem* [, *$val*])

> Internal method to get/set the value of member variable *$elem*. If *$val* is defined it is used as the new value for the member variable. If it is undefined, the current value is not touched. In both cases, the previous value of the member variable is returned.

Bugs

Ideally, there should be better Perl language support for this.

LWP::Protocol—base class for LWP protocols

Synopsis

```
package LWP::Protocol::foo;
require LWP::Protocol;
@ISA=qw(LWP::Protocol);
```

Description

This class is used as the base class for all protocol implementations supported by the LWP library.

When creating an instance of this class using **LWP::Protocol::create(*$url*)**, you get an initialized subclass appropriate for that access method. In other words, the LWP::Protocol::create() function calls the constructor for one of its subclasses.

All derived LWP::Protocol classes need to override the **request()** method which is used to service a request. The overridden method can make use of the **collect()** function to collect together chunks of data as it is received.

Methods and Functions

$prot = new HTTP::Protocol;

> The LWP::Protocol constructor is inherited by subclasses. As this is a virtual base class this method should *not* be called directly.

$prot = LWP::Protocol::create(*$url*)

> Create an object of the class implementing the protocol to handle the given scheme. This is a function, not a method. It is more an object factory than a constructor. This is the function user agents should use to access protocols.

$class = LWP::Protocol::implementor(*$scheme*, [*$class*])

> Get and/or set implementor class for a scheme. Returns '' if the specified scheme is not supported.

$prot->request(...)

> Dispatches a request over the protocol, and returns a response object. This method needs to be overridden in subclasses. Referer to LWP::UserAgent for description of the arguments.

```
$response = $protocol->request($request, $proxy, undef);
$response = $protocol->request($request, $proxy, '/tmp/sss');
$response = $protocol->request($request, $proxy, \&callback,
                        1024);
```

$prot->timeout(*$seconds*)

> Get and set the timeout value in seconds.

$prot->use_alarm(*$yesno*)

> Indicates if the library is allowed to use the core **alarm()** function to implement timeouts.

$prot->parse_head(*$yesno*)

> Should we initialize response headers from the <HEAD> section of HTML documents.

$prot->collect(*$arg, $response, $collector*)

> Called to collect the content of a request, and process it appropriately into a scalar, file, or by calling a callback. If *$arg* is undefined, then the content is stored within the *$response*. If *$arg* is a simple scalar, then *$arg* is interpreted as a file name and the content is written to this file. If *$arg* is a reference to a routine, then content is passed to this routine.
>
> The *$collector* is a routine that will be called and that is responsible for returning pieces (as ref to scalar) of the content to process. The *$collector* signals EOF by returning a reference to an empty sting.
>
> The return value from **collect()** is the *$response* object reference.
>
> *Note:* We will only use the callback or file argument if **$response->is_success()**. This avoids sending content data for redirects and authentication responses to the callback which would be confusing.

$prot->collect_once(*$arg, $response, $content*)

> Can be called when the whole response content is available as *$content*. This will invoke **collect()** with a collector callback that returns a reference to *$content* the first time and an empty string the next.

See Also

Inspect the *LWP/Protocol/file.pm* and *LWP/Protocol/http.pm* files for examples of usage.

LWP::RobotUA — a class for Web robots

Synopsis

```
require LWP::RobotUA;
$ua = new LWP::RobotUA 'my-robot/0.1', 'me@foo.com';
$ua->delay(10);  # be very nice, go slowly
...
# just use it just like a normal LWP::UserAgent
$res = $ua->request($req);
```

Description

This class implements a user agent that is suitable for robot applications. Robots should be nice to the servers they visit. They should consult the *robots.txt* file to ensure that they are welcomed and they should not send too frequent requests.

But before you consider writing a robot, take a look on the Web at the URL *http://info.webcrawler.com/mak/projects/robots/robots.html.*

When you use an LWP::RobotUA as your user agent, then you do not really have to think about these things yourself. Just send requests as you do when you are using a normal LWP::UserAgent and this special agent will make sure you are nice.

Methods

The LWP::RobotUA is a subclass of LWP::UserAgent and implements the same methods. The `use_alarm()` method also decides whether we will wait if a request is tried too early (if true), or will return an error response (if false).

In addition these methods are provided:

$ua = LWP::RobotUA->new(*$agent_name, $from*, [*$rules*])

> Your robot's name and the mail address of the human responsible for the robot (i.e., you) is required by the constructor.
>
> Optionally it allows you to specify the WWW::RobotRules object to use.

$ua->delay([*$minutes*])

> Set the minimum delay between requests to the same server. The default is 1 minute.

$ua->rules([*$rules*])

> Set/get which WWW::RobotRules object to use.

$ua->no_visits(*$netloc*)

> Returns the number of documents fetched from this server host.

$ua->host_wait(*$netloc*)

> Returns the number of seconds you must wait before you can make a new request to this host.

$ua->as_string

> Returns a text that describe the state of the UA. Mainly useful for debugging.

Author

Gisle Aas, *aas@sn.no*

See Also

LWP::UserAgent, WWW::RobotRules

LWP::Socket—TCP/IP socket interface

Synopsis

```
$socket = new LWP::Socket;
$socket->connect('localhost', 7); # echo
$quote = 'I dunno, I dream in Perl sometimes...';
$socket->write("$quote\n");
$socket->read_until("\n", \$buffer);
$socket->read(\$buffer);
$socket = undef;  # close
```

Description

This class implements TCP/IP sockets. It groups socket generation, TCP address manipulation and buffered reading. Errors are handled by dying (throws exceptions).

This class should really not be required, something like this should be part of the standard Perl5 library.

Running this module standalone executes a self-test which requires `localhost` to serve `chargen` and `echo` protocols.

Methods

`$sock = new LWP::Socket()`

Constructs a new socket object.

`$sock->connect($host, $port)`

Connects the socket to given host and port.

`$sock->shutdown()`

Shuts down the connection.

`$sock->bind($host, $port)`

Binds a name to the socket.

`$sock->listen($queuesize)`

Sets up listen queue for socket.

`$sock->accept($timeout)`

Accepts a new connection. Returns a new LWP::Socket object if successful. Timeout not implemented yet.

`$sock->getsockname()`

Returns a two-element array ($host, $port).

`$sock->read_until($delim, $data_ref, $size, $timeout)`

Reads data from the socket, up to a delimiter specified by a regular expression. If `$delim` is undefined all data is read. If `$size` is defined, data will be read internally in chunks of `$size` bytes. This does not mean that we will return the data when size bytes are read.

Note that `$delim` is discarded from the data returned.

`$sock->read($bufref, [$size, $timeout])`

Reads data off the socket. Not more than `$size` bytes. Might return less if the data is available. Dies on timeout.

`$sock->pushback($data)`

Puts data back into the socket. Data will be returned next time you `read()`. Can be used if you find out that you have read too much.

`$sock->write($data, [$timeout])`

Write data to socket. The `$data` argument might be a scalar or code.

If data is a reference to a subroutine, then we will call this routine to obtain the data to be written. The routine will be called until it returns `undef` or empty data. Data might be returned from the callback as a scalar or as a reference to a scalar.

Write returns the number of bytes written to the socket.

`_getaddress($host, $port)`

Given a host and a port, this routine returns the address (`sockaddr_in`) suitable as the `name` argument for `connect()` or `bind()`. Might return several addresses in array context if the hostname is bound to several IP addresses.

Self-Test

This self test is only executed when this file is run standalone. It tests its functions against some standard TCP services implemented by inetd. If you do not have them around the tests will fail.

LWP::TkIO—Tk I/O routines for the LWP library

Synopsis

```
use Tk;
require LWP::TkIO;
require LWP::UserAgent;
```

Description

This module provides replacement functions for the LWP::IO functions. Require this module if you use Tk and want non-exclusive IO behavior from LWP. This does not allow LWP to run simultaneous requests though.

See Also

LWP::IO.

LWP::UserAgent—a WWW UserAgent class

Synopsis

```
require LWP::UserAgent;
$ua = new LWP::UserAgent;
$request = new HTTP::Request('GET', 'file://localhost/etc/motd');
$response = $ua->request($request); # or
$response = $ua->request($request, '/tmp/sss'); # or
$response = $ua->request($request, \&callback, 4096);
sub callback { my($data, $response, $protocol) = @_; .... }
```

Description

The LWP::UserAgent is a class implementing a simple World-Wide Web user agent in Perl. It brings together the HTTP::Request, HTTP::Response and the LWP::Protocol classes that form the rest of the core of *libwww-perl* library. For simple uses this class can be used directly to dispatch WWW requests; alternatively it can be subclassed for application-specific behavior.

In normal usage the application creates a UserAgent object, and then configures it with values for timeouts proxies, name, etc. The next step is to create an instance of HTTP::Request for the request that needs to be performed. This request is then passed to the UserAgent request() method, which dispatches it using the relevant protocol, and returns a HTTP::Response object.

The basic approach of the library is to use HTTP-style communication for all protocol schemes, i.e., you will receive an HTTP::Response object also for gopher or ftp requests. In order to achieve even more similarities with HTTP-style communications, gopher menus and file directories will be converted to HTML documents.

The `request()` method can process the content of the response in one of three ways: in core, into a file, or into repeated calls of a subroutine. You choose which one by the kind of value passed as the second argument to `request()`.

The in-core variant simply returns the content in a scalar attribute called `content()` of the response object, and is suitable for small HTML replies that might need further parsing. This variant is used if the second argument is missing (or is `undef`).

The filename variant requires a scalar containing a filename as the second argument to `request()`, and is suitable for large WWW objects which need to be written directly to the file, without requiring large amounts of memory. In this case the response object returned from `request()` will have empty `content()`. If the request fails, then the `content()` might not be empty, and the file will be untouched.

The subroutine variant requires a reference to callback routine as the second argument to `request()` and it can also take an optional chunk size as third argument. This variant can be used to construct "pipe-lined" processing, where processing of received chunks can begin before the complete data has arrived. The callback function is called with three arguments: the data received this time, a reference to the response object and a reference to the protocol object. The response object returned from `request()` will have empty `content()`. If the request fails, then the callback routine will not have been called, and the `response->content()` might not be empty.

The request can be aborted by calling `die()` within the callback routine. The die message will be available as the "X-Died" special response header field.

The library also accepts that you put a subroutine reference as content in the request object. This subroutine should return the content (possibly in pieces) when called. It should return an empty string when there is no more content.

The user of this module can fine-tune timeouts and error handling by calling the `use_alarm()` and `use_eval()` methods.

By default the library uses `alarm()` to implement timeouts, dying if the timeout occurs. If this is not the preferred behavior or it interferes with other parts of the application one can disable the use alarms. When alarms are disabled, timeouts can still occur, for example when reading data, but other cases like name lookups, etc., will not be timed out by the library itself.

The library catches errors (such as internal errors and timeouts) and presents them as HTTP error responses. Alternatively one can switch off this behavior, and let the application handle die.

Methods

`$ua = new LWP::UserAgent;`

   Constructor for the UserAgent. Returns a reference to a LWP::UserAgent object.

`$ua->simple_request($request, [$arg [, $size]])`

   This method dispatches a single WWW request on behalf of a user, and returns the response received. The *$request* should be a reference to a HTTP::Request object with values defined for at least the `method()` and `url()` attributes.

   If *$arg* is a scalar it is taken as a filename where the content of the response is stored.

If *$arg* is a reference to a subroutine, then this routine is called as chunks of the content is received. An optional *$size* argument is taken as a hint for an appropriate chunk size.

If *$arg* is omitted, then the content is stored in the response object itself.

$ua->request(*$request, $arg* [, *$size*])

Process a request, including redirects and security. This method may actually send several different simple requests.

The arguments are the same as for **simple_request()**.

$ua->redirect_ok

This method is called by **request()** before it tries to do any redirects. It should return a true value if the redirect is allowed to be performed. Subclasses might want to override this.

The default implementation will return **false** for POST request and **true** for all others.

$ua->credentials(*$netloc, $realm, $uname, $pass*)

Set the username and password to be used for a realm. It is often more useful to specialize the **get_basic_credentials()** method instead.

$ua->get_basic_credentials(*$realm, $uri*)

This is called by **request()** to retrieve credentials for a realm protected by Basic Authentication or Digest Authentication.

Should return username and password in a list. Return **undef** to abort the authentication resolution attempts.

This implementation simply checks a set of pre-stored member variables. Subclasses can override this method to ask the user for a username/password. An example of this can be found in the **lwp-request** program distributed with this library.

$ua->agent([*$product_id*])

Get/set the product token that is used to identify the user agent on the network. The agent value is sent as the "User-Agent" header in the requests. The default agent name is "libwww-perl/#.##", where "#.##" is substituted with the version number of this library.

The user agent string should be one or more simple product identifiers with an optional version number separated by the "/" character. Examples are:

```
$ua->agent('Checkbot/0.4 ' . $ua->agent);
$ua->agent('Mozilla/5.0');
```

$ua->from([*$email_address*])

Get/set the Internet email address for the human user who controls the requesting user agent. The address should be machine-usable, as defined in RFC 822. The from value is send as the "From" header in the requests. There is no default. Example:

```
$ua->from('aas@sn.no');
```

$ua->timeout([*$secs*])

Get/set the timeout value in seconds. The default **timeout()** value is 180 seconds.

`$ua->use_alarm([`*`$boolean`*`])`

    Get/set a value indicating whether to use `alarm()` when implementing timeouts. The default is `true`, i.e., to use alarm. Disable this on systems that do not implement alarm, or if this interferes with other uses of alarm in your application.

`$ua->use_eval([`*`$boolean`*`])`

    Get/set a value indicating whether to handle internal errors internally by trapping with eval. The default is `true`, i.e., the `$ua->request()` will never die.

`$ua->parse_head([`*`$boolean`*`])`

    Get/set a value indicating whether we should initialize response headers from the `<HEAD>` section of HTML documents. The default is `true`. Do not turn this off, unless you know what you are doing.

`$ua->max_size([`*`$bytes`*`])`

    Get/set the size limit for response content. The default is undef, which means that there is no limit. If the returned response content is only partial, because the size limit was exceeded, then a "X-Content-Range" header will be added to the response.

`$ua->clone;`

    Returns a copy of the LWP::UserAgent object.

`$ua->is_protocol_supported(`*`$scheme`*`)`

    You can use this method to query if the library currently supports the specified `$scheme`. The `$scheme` might be a string (like `http` or `ftp`) or it might be a URI::URL object reference.

`$ua->mirror(`*`$url`*`, `*`$file`*`)`

    Get and store a document identified by a URL, using If-Modified-Since, and checking of the Content-Length. Returns a reference to the response object.

`$ua->proxy(...)`

    Set/retrieve proxy URL for a scheme:

```
$ua->proxy(['http', 'ftp'], 'http://proxy.sn.no:8001/');
$ua->proxy('gopher', 'http://proxy.sn.no:8001/');
```

    The first form specifies that the URL is to be used for proxying of access methods listed in the list in the first method argument, i.e., `http` and `ftp`.

    The second form shows a shorthand form for specifying proxy URL for a single access scheme.

`$ua->env_proxy()`

    Load proxy settings from `*_proxy` environment variables. You might specify proxies like this (`sh-syntax`):

```
gopher_proxy=http://proxy.my.place/
wais_proxy=http://proxy.my.place/
no_proxy="my.place"
export gopher_proxy wais_proxy no_proxy
```

    Csh or tcsh users should use the `setenv` command to define these environment variables.

`$ua->no_proxy(`*`$domain`*`,...)`

    Do not proxy requests to the given domains. Calling `no_proxy` without any domains clears the list of domains:

```
$ua->no_proxy('localhost', 'no', ...);
```

See Also

See *LWP* for a complete overview of *libwww-perl5*. See the **request** manpage and the **mirror** manpage for examples of usage.

MIME-tools—modules for parsing (and creating) MIME entities

Synopsis

Here's some pretty basic code for parsing a MIME message, and outputting its decoded components to a given directory:

```
use MIME::Parser;

# Create parser, and set the output directory:
my $parser = new MIME::Parser;
$parser->output_dir("$ENV{HOME}/mimemail");

# Parse input:
$entity = $parser->read(\*STDIN) or die "couldn't parse MIME stream";

# Take a look at the top-level entity (and any parts it has):
$entity->dump_skeleton;
```

Here's some code which composes and sends a MIME message containing three parts: a text file, an attached GIF, and some more text:

```
use MIME::Entity;
# Create the top-level, and set up the mail headers:
$top = build MIME::Entity Type    =>"multipart/mixed",
                          -From    => "me\@myhost.com",
                          -To      => "you\@yourhost.com",
                          -Subject => "Hello, nurse!";

# Attachment #1: a simple text document:
attach $top  Path=>"./testin/short.txt";

# Attachment #2: a GIF file:
attach $top  Path      => "./docs/mime-sm.gif",
             Type      => "image/gif",
             Encoding  => "base64";

# Attachment #3: some literal text:
attach $top  Data=>$message;

# Send it:
open MAIL, "| /usr/lib/sendmail -t -i" or die "open: $!";
$top->print(\*MAIL);
close MAIL;
```

Description

MIME-tools is a collection of Perl5 MIME:: modules for parsing, decoding, *and generating* single- or multipart (even nested multipart) MIME messages. (Yes, kids, that means you can send messages with attached GIF files).

Parsing, in a Nutshell

You usually start by creating an instance of MIME::Parser (a subclass of the abstract MIME::ParserBase), and setting up certain parsing parameters: what directory to save extracted files to, how to name the files, etc.

You then give that instance a readable file handle on which waits a MIME message. If all goes well, you will get back a MIME::Entity object (a subclass of Mail::Internet), which consists of:

- A MIME::Head (a subclass of Mail::Header) which holds the MIME header data.

- A MIME::Body, which is a object that knows where the body data is. You ask this object to "open" itself for reading, and it will hand you back an "I/O handle" for reading the data: this is a FileHandle-like object, and could be of any class, so long as it conforms to a subset of the IO::Handle interface.

If the original message was a multipart document, the MIME::Entity object will have a non-empty list of "parts", each of which is in turn a MIME::Entity (which might also be a multipart entity, etc.).

Internally, the parser (in MIME::ParserBase) asks for instances of MIME::Decoder whenever it needs to decode an encoded file. MIME::Decoder has a mapping from supported encodings (e.g., 'base64') to classes whose instances can decode them. You can add to this mapping to try out new/experiment encodings. You can also use MIME::Decoder by itself.

Composing, in a Nutshell

On a small scale, the MIME::Decoder can be used to *encode* as well. All the standard encodings are supported:

7bit
> Use this for plain ASCII documents (and multiparts)

8bit
> Use this for small 8-bit character documents

binary
> No encoding

quoted-printable
> Use this for text files with 8-bit characters and long lines

base64
> Use this for binary files

When encoding a text document as a 7-bit mail message, the software will not puke on 8-bit characters; instead, the 8-bit characters are escaped for you into reasonable ASCII sequences, by the MIME::Latin1 module. This feature is for folks who really hate sending out a document as quoted-printable just because it happens to have a couple of French or German names.

I've considered making it so that the content-type and encoding can be automatically inferred from the file's path, but that seems to be asking for trouble, or at least, for Mail::Cap.

Other Stuff

If you want to tweak the way this toolkit works (for example, to turn on debugging), use the routines in the MIME::ToolUtils module.

Contents

Module	DSLI	Description	Info
MIME::			
::Body	adpO	Abstract message holder (file, scalar, etc.)	ERYQ
::Decoder	bdpO	OO interface for decoding MIME messages	ERYQ
::Entity	bdpO	An extracted and decoded MIME entity	ERYQ
::Field::*	bdpO	Mail::Field subclasses for parsing fields	ERYQ
::Head	bdpO	A parsed MIME header (Mail::Header subclass)	ERYQ
::IO	adpO	Simple I/O handles for file handles/scalars	ERYQ
::Latin1	adpO	Encoding 8-bit Latin-1 as 7-bit ASCII	ERYQ
::Parser	bdpO	Parses streams to create MIME entities	ERYQ
::ParserBase	bdpO	For building your own MIME parser	ERYQ
::ToolUtils	adpO	For tweaking the MIME-tools library	ERYQ

Programs in this toolkit

mimedump
> Dump out a summary of the contents of a MIME message

mimeexplode
> Parse/decode a MIME message into its component files

mimesend
> Send a message with attachments from the command line

Manifest

MIME/.pm*
> The MIME-tools classes

Makefile.PL
> The input to MakeMaker

COPYING
> Terms and conditions for copying/using the software

README
> This file

docs/
> HTMLized documentation

etc/
> Convenient copies of other modules you may need

examples
> Sample executables

t/*.t
> The `make test` scripts

testin/
> Files you can use for testing (as in `make test`)

testout/
> The output of `make test`

Requirements

You'll need Perl5.002 or better.

You'll need to obtain and install the following kits from the CPAN:

MIME::(QuotedPrint, Base64)
> These perform the low-level MIME decoding. Get these from Gisle Aas's author directory. They are also reported to be in the LWP distribution.

MailTools (1.06 or higher)
> This is Graham Barr's revamped set of Mail:: modules. Many of them are now superclasses of the MIME:: modules, and perform the core functionality of manipulating headers and fields.

For your convenience, possibly old copies of the MIME:: modules are provided in the *etc/* directory of the distribution, but they are *not* installed for you during the installation procedure.

Installation

Pretty simple:

1. `gunzip` and de-`tar` the distribution, and `cd` to the top level.
2. Type `perl Makefile.PL`
3. Type `make` (this step is optional)
4. Type `make test` (this step is optional)
5. Type `make install`

Other interesting targets in the Makefile are:

```
make config     # to check if the Makefile is up-to-date
make clean      # delete local temp files (Makefile gets renamed)
make realclean  # delete derived files (including ./blib)
```

If you're installing this as a replacement for MIME-parser 1.x or earlier, *please* read the following Compatibility notes.

Notes

Compatibility

If you're installing this as a replacement for the MIME-parser 1.x release, and you really don't want to break existing code, you should do this at any point before the parsing code is invoked:

```
use MIME::ToolUtils;

config MIME::ToolUtils EMULATE_VERSION => 1.0;
```

Try not to get too attached to this, though. Instead, plan on upgrading your code ASAP to the 2.0 style.

Design Issues

Why assume that MIME objects are email objects?

I quote from Achim Bohnet, who gave feedback on v.1.9 (I think he's using the word "header" where I would use "field"; e.g., to refer to "Subject:", "Content-type:", etc.):

> There is also IMHO no requirement [for] MIME::Heads to look like [email] headers; so to speak, the MIME::Head [simply stores] the attributes of a complex object, e.g.:

```
new MIME::Head type => "text/plain",
             charset => ...,
           disposition => ..., ... ;
```

I agree in principle, but (alas and dammit) RFC 1521 says otherwise. RFC 1521 [MIME] headers are a syntactic subset of RFC 822 [email] headers. Perhaps a better name for these modules would be RFC 1521:: instead of MIME::, but we're a little beyond that stage now. (Note: RFC 1521 has recently been obsoleted by RFCs 2045-2049, so it's just as well we didn't go that route. . . .)

However, in my mind's eye, I see a mythical abstract class which does what Achim suggests... so you could say:

```
my $attrs = new MIME::Attrs type => "text/plain",
                     charset => ...,
                   disposition => ..., ... ;
```

We could even make it a superclass or companion class of MIME::Head, such that MIME::Head would allow itself to be initialized from a MIME::Attrs object.

In the meanwhile, look at the `build()` and `attach()` methods of MIME::Entity: they follow the spirit of this mythical class.

To subclass or not to subclass?

When I originally wrote these modules for the CPAN, I agonized for a long time about whether or not they really should subclass from Mail::Internet (then at version 1.17). There were pluses:

- Software reuse
- Inheritance of the mail-sending utilities

And, unfortunately, minuses:

- The Mail::Internet 1.17 model of messages as being short enough to fit into in-core arrays is excellent for most email applications; however, it seemed ill-suited for generic MIME applications, where MIME streams could be mega-bytes long.
- The implementation of Mail::Internet 1.17 was excellent for certain kinds of header manipulation, but the implementation of `get()` was less efficient than I would have liked for MIME applications.
- In my heart of hearts, I honestly felt that the head should be encapsulated as a first-class object, and in Mail::Internet 1.17 it was not.

So I chose to make MIME::Head and MIME::Entity their own standalone modules. Since that time, I worked with Graham Barr (author of most of the MailTools package, and a darn nice guy to "work" with over email), and he has graciously evolved the MailTools modules into a direction that addressed a lot of these issues.

When MailTools hit its 1.06 release, it was finally time to finish what I had started, and release MIME-tools 2.0. We now are almost at the stage of a fully integrated Mail/MIME environment.

Questionable Practices

Fuzzing of CRLF and newline on input

RFC 1521 dictates that MIME streams have lines terminated by CRLF (\r\n). However, it is extremely likely that folks will want to parse MIME streams where each line ends in the local newline character \n instead.

An attempt has been made to allow the parser to handle both CRLF and newline-terminated input.

See MIME::ParserBase for details.

Fuzzing of CRLF and newline when decoding

The 7bit and 8bit decoders will decode both a \n and a \r\n end-of-line sequence into a \n.

The binary decoder (default if no encoding specified) still outputs stuff verbatim... so a MIME message with CRLFs and no explicit encoding will be output as a text file that, on many systems, will have an annoying ^M at the end of each line... *but this is as it should be.*

See MIME::ParserBase for details.

Fuzzing of CRLF and newline when encoding/composing

All encoders currently output the end-of-line sequence as a \n, with the assumption that the local mail agent will perform the conversion from newline to CRLF when sending the mail.

However, there probably should be an option to output CRLF as per RFC 1521. I'm currently working on a good mechanism for this.

See MIME::ParserBase for details.

Inability to handle multipart boundaries with embedded newlines

First, let's get something straight: this is an evil, *evil* practice. If your mailer creates multipart boundary strings that contain newlines, give it two weeks notice and find another one. If your mail robot receives MIME mail like this, regard it as syntactically incorrect, which it is.

See MIME::ParserBase for details.

Support

Please email me directly with questions/problems (see following "Author" information).

If you want to be placed on an email distribution list (not a mailing list) for MIME-tools, and receive bug reports, patches, and updates as to when new MIME-tools releases are planned, just email me and say so. If your project is using MIME-tools, it might not be a bad idea to find out about those bugs *before* they become problems.

Author

Eryq, *eryq@rhine.gsfc.nasa.gov*

Acknowledgments

This kit would not have been possible but for the direct contributions of the following:

Gisle Aas
> The MIME encoding/decoding modules

Laurent Amon
> Bug reports and suggestions

Graham Barr
> The new MailTools

Achim Bohnet
> Numerous good suggestions, including the I/O model

Kent Boortz
> Initial code for RFC-1522-decoding of MIME headers

Andreas Koenig
> Numerous good ideas, tons of beta testing, and help with CPAN-friendly packaging

Igor Starovoitov
> Bug reports and suggestions

Jason L Tibbitts III
> Bug reports and suggestions

Not to mention the Accidental Beta Test Team, whose bug reports (and comments) have been invaluable in improving the whole:

> Phil Abercrombie
> Kurt Freytag
> Jake Morrison
> Rolf Nelson
> Joel Noble
> Tim Pierce
> Andrew Pimlott
> Dragomir R. Radev
> Nickolay Saukh
> Russell Sutherland
> Larry Virden
> Zyx

Please forgive me if I've accidentally left you out. Better yet, email me, and I'll put you in.

Copyright

Copyright © 1996 by Eryq. All rights reserved. This program is free software; you can redistribute it and/or modify it under the same terms as Perl itself.

See the *COPYING* file in the distribution for details.

See Also

Users of this toolkit may wish to read the documentation of Mail::Header and Mail::Internet.

The MIME format is documented in RFCs 1521-1522, and more recently in RFCs 2045-2049.

The MIME header format is an outgrowth of the mail header format documented in RFC 822.

MIME::Body—the body of a MIME message

Synopsis

```
# Create new body:
$body = new MIME::Body::File "/path/to/file";

# Write data to the body:
$IO = $body->open("w")        || die "open body: $!";
$IO->print($message);
$IO->close                    || die "close I/O handle: $!";

# Read data from the body:
$IO = $body->open("r")        || die "open body: $!";
while (defined($_ = $IO->getline)) {
    # do stuff
}
$IO->close                    || die "close I/O handle: $!";
```

For example, this subclass stores the data in a disk file, which is only opened when needed:

```
$body = new MIME::Body::File "/path/to/file";
```

While *this* subclass stores the data in an in-core scalar:

```
$body = new MIME::Body::Scalar \$scalar;
```

In any case, once a MIME::Body has been created, you use the same mechanisms for reading from or writing to it, no matter what the subclass is.

Description

MIME messages can be very long (e.g., tar files, MPEGs, etc.) or very short (short textual notes, as in ordinary mail). Long messages are best stored in files, while short ones are perhaps best stored in core.

This class is an attempt to define a common interface for objects which contain message data, regardless of how the data is physically stored. Figure 15-1 gives an overview.

It works this way:

- An "entity" has a "head" and a "body". Entities are MIME message parts.

- A "body" knows where the data is. You can ask to "open" this data source for *reading* or *writing*, and you will get back an "I/O handle".

- An "I/O handle" knows how to read/write the data. It is an object that is basically like an IO::Handle or a FileHandle... it can be any class, so long as it supports a small, standard set of methods for reading from or writing to the underlying data source.

The lifespan of a "body" usually looks like this:

- Body object is created by a MIME::Parser during parsing. It's at this point that the actual MIME::Body subclass is chosen, and **new**() is invoked. (For example: if the body data is going to a file, then it is at this point that the class MIME::Body::File, and the filename, is chosen).

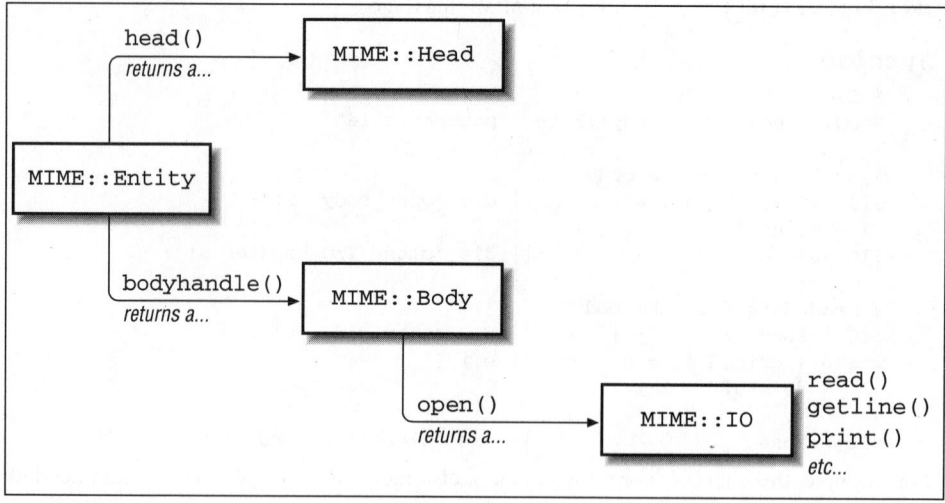

Figure 15-1. Message data in a MIME message

- Data is written (usually by the MIME parser) like this:
  - Body is opened for writing, via open(w). This will trash any previous contents, and return an "I/O handle" opened for writing.
  - Data is written to the I/O handle, via print().
  - I/O handle is closed, via close().
- Data is read (usually by the user application) like this:
  - Body is opened for reading by a user application, via open(r). This will return an "I/O handle" opened for reading.
  - Data is read from the I/O handle, via read(), getline(), or getlines().
  - I/O handle is closed, via close().
- Body object is destructed.

You can write your own subclasses, as long as they follow the interface described below. Implementers of subclasses should assume that steps 2 and 3 may be repeated any number of times, and in different orders (e.g., 1-2-2-3-2-3-3-3-3-2-4).

Users should be aware that unless they know for certain what they have, they should not assume that the body has an underlying file handle.

Defining Your Own Subclasses

So you're not happy with files and scalars? No problem: just define your own MIME::Body subclass, and make a subclass of MIME::Parser or MIME::ParserBase which returns an instance of your body class whenever appropriate in the new_body_for(head) method.

Writing a "body" class

Your "body" class must inherit from MIME::Body (or some subclass of it), and it must either provide or inherit the following methods:

init *ARGS*...

> *Instance method.* This is called automatically by `new()`, with the arguments given to `new()`. The arguments are optional, and entirely up to your class.

open *MODE*

> *Instance method.* This should do whatever is necessary to open the body for either writing (if *MODE* is "w") or reading (if mode is "r"). Return an "I/O handle" on success, false on error.

binmode [*ONOFF*]

> *Instance method.* With argument, flags whether or not `open()` should return an I/O handle which has `binmode()` activated. With no argument, just returns the current value. The inherited action should be fine.

path

> *Instance method.* Oh, the joys of encapsulation. If you're storing the body data in a new disk file, you'll want to give applications the ability to get at that file, if only for cleanup (see `MIME::Entity::purge()` for an example). This method should return the path to the file, or `undef` if there is none (e.g., if the data is in core). The default inherited method just returns `undef`.

Writing/using an "I/O handle" class

Your "body" class's `open()` method must return an "I/O handle" object, which can be any object that supports a small set of standard methods for reading/writing data.

See the documentation on the MIME::IO class for details on what is expected of an I/O handle. *Note that the IO::Handle class already conforms to this interface.*

Notes on Design Issues

One reason I didn't just use FileHandle or IO::Handle objects for message bodies was that I wanted a "body" object to be a form of completely encapsulated program-persistent storage; that is, I wanted users to be able to write code like this:

```
# Get body handle from this MIME message, and read its data:
$body = $entity->bodyhandle;
$IO = $body->open("r");
while (defined($_ = $IO->getline)) {
    print STDOUT $_;
}
$IO->close;
```

without requiring that they know anything more about how the $body object is actually storing its data (disk file, scalar variable, array variable, or whatever).

Storing the body of each MIME message in a persistently open IO::Handle was a possibility, but it seemed like a bad idea, considering that a single multipart MIME message could easily suck up all the available file descriptors on some OSes. This risk increases if the user application is processing more than one MIME entity at a time.

Subclasses

Basically, we have the following classes:

MIME::Body::File

A body class that stores the data in a disk file. The I/O handle is a wrapped file handle. Invoke the constructor as:

```
$body = new MIME::Body::File "/path/to/file";
```

In this case, the `path()` method would return the given path.

You can even use this class to pipe the data through shell commands on input and/or output. For example, here's an easy way to store the data in compressed format without having to explicitly do the compression yourself:

```
$body = new MIME::Body::File "/tmp/somefile.gz";
$body->writer("| gzip > /tmp/somefile.gz");
$body->reader("zcat /tmp/somefile.gz |");
...
$IO = $body->open("w")    || die "open failed: $!";
$IO->print("I'll automatically be stored compressed!\n");
$IO->close               || die "close failed: $!";
```

Notice the semantics of the "path" in this case: it names the file that is created to hold the data, even though that file can't be used directly.

Notes

All of the usual caveats related to shell commands apply! To make sure you won't accidentally do something you'll regret, use taint-checking (`perl -T`) in your application.

I would have had MIME::Body::File return a FileHandle, except that there are some methods that FileHandle does not support in 5.002, and it was too soon to require IO::Handle.

MIME::Body::Scalar

A body class that stores the data in-core, in a simple scalar. Invoke the constructor as:

```
$body = new MIME::Body::Scalar \$scalar;
```

A single scalar argument sets the body to that value, exactly as though you'd opened for the body for writing, written the value, and closed the body again:

```
$body = new MIME::Body::Scalar "Line 1\nLine 2\nLine 3";
```

A single array reference sets the body to the result of joining all the elements of that array together:

```
$body = new MIME::Body::Scalar ["Line 1\n",
                                "Line 2\n",
                                "Line 3"];
```

Uses MIME::IO::Scalar as the I/O handle.

Body class	Stores body data in	When open()ed, returns	Someday soon will return
MIME::Body::File	disk file	MIME::IO::Handle	IO::Handle
MIME::Body::Scalar	scalar	MIME::IO::Scalar	IO::????

Author

Eryq, *eryq@rhine.gsfc.nasa.gov*

Copyright

Copyright © 1996 by Eryq

Thanks to Achim Bohnet for suggesting that MIME::Parser not be restricted to the use of FileHandles.

MIME::Decoder—an object for decoding the body part of a MIME stream

Synopsis

Decoding a data stream

Here's a simple filter program to read quoted-printable data from STDIN (until EOF) and write the decoded data to STDOUT:

```
use MIME::Decoder;

$decoder = new MIME::Decoder 'quoted-printable' or
           die "unsupported";
$decoder->decode(\*STDIN, \*STDOUT);
```

Encoding a data stream

Here's a simple filter program to read binary data from STDIN (until EOF) and write base64-encoded data to STDOUT:

```
use MIME::Decoder;

$decoder = new MIME::Decoder 'base64' or die "unsupported";
$decoder->encode(\*STDIN, \*STDOUT);
```

Installing your own decoders

You can write and install your own decoders so that MIME::Decoder knows about them:

```
use MyBase64Decoder;

install MyBase64Decoder 'base64';
```

Testing for supported encoding

You can also test if an encoding is supported:

```
if (MIME::Decoder->supported('x-uuencode')) {
    # we can uuencode!
}
```

Description

This abstract class and its private concrete subclasses (see below) provide an object-oriented front end to the following actions:

- Decoding a MIME-encoded stream
- Encoding a raw data stream into a MIME-encoded stream.

The constructor for MIME::Decoder takes the name of an encoding (**base64**, **7bit**, etc.) and returns an instance of a *subclass* of MIME::Decoder whose **decode()** method will perform the appropriate decoding action, and whose **encode()** method will perform the appropriate encoding action.

Public Interface

Standard interface

If all you are doing is *using* this class, here's all you'll need:

new *ENCODING*

> *Class method.* Create and return a new decoder object that can handle the given *ENCODING.*
>
> ```
> my $decoder = new MIME::Decoder "7bit";
> ```
>
> Returns the undefined value if no known decoders are appropriate.

decode *INSTREAM, OUTSTREAM*

> *Instance method.* Decode the document waiting in the input handle *INSTREAM,* writing the decoded information to the output handle *OUTSTREAM.*
>
> Read the section in this document on I/O handles for more information about the arguments. Note that you can still supply old-style unblessed file handles for *INSTREAM* and *OUTSTREAM.*

encode *INSTREAM, OUTSTREAM*

> *Instance method.* Encode the document waiting in the input file handle *INSTREAM,* writing the encoded information to the output stream *OUTSTREAM.*
>
> Read the section in this document on I/O handles for more information about the arguments. Note that you can still supply old-style unblessed file handles for *INSTREAM* and *OUTSTREAM.*

encoding

> *Instance method.* Return the encoding that this object was created to handle, coerced to all lowercase (e.g., **base64**).

supported [*ENCODING*]

> *Class method.* With one argument (an *ENCODING* name), returns true if that encoding is currently handled and false otherwise. The *ENCODING* is automatically coerced to lowercase:
>
> ```
> if (MIME::Decoder->supported('7BIT')) {
>     # yes, we can handle it...
> }
> else {
>     # drop back six and punt...
> }
> ```
>
> With no arguments, returns all the available decoders as a hash reference, where the key is the encoding name (all lowercase, like **7bit**), and the associated value is true (it happens to be the name of the class that handles the decoding, but you probably shouldn't rely on that). Hence:
>
> ```
> my $supported = MIME::Decoder->supported;
> if ($supported->{7bit}) {
>     # yes, we can handle it...
> }
> elsif ($supported->{8bit}) {
>     # yes, we can handle it...
> }
> ```

You may safely modify this hash; that does *not* change the way the module performs its lookups. Only `install` can do that.

Thanks to Achim Bohnet for suggesting this method.

Subclass interface

If you are writing (or installing) a new decoder subclass, there are some other methods you'll need to know about:

decode_it *INSTREAM, OUTSTREAM*

> *Abstract instance method.* The backend of the `decode` method. It takes an input handle opened for reading (*INSTREAM*) and an output handle opened for writing (*OUTSTREAM*).
>
> If you are writing your own decoder subclass, you must override this method in your class. Your method should read from the input handle via `getline()` or `read()`, decode this input, and print the decoded data to the output handle via `print()`. You may do this however you see fit, so long as the end result is the same.
>
> Note that unblessed references and globrefs are automatically turned into I/O handles for you by `decode()`, so you don't need to worry about it.
>
> Your method must return either `undef` (to indicate failure), or 1 (to indicate success).

encode_it *INSTREAM, OUTSTREAM*

> *Abstract instance method.* The backend of the `encode` method. It takes an input handle opened for reading (*INSTREAM*) and an output handle opened for writing (*OUTSTREAM*).
>
> If you are writing your own decoder subclass, you must override this method in your class. Your method should read from the input handle via `getline()` or `read()`, encode this input, and print the encoded data to the output handle via `print()`. You may do this however you see fit, so long as the end result is the same.
>
> Note that unblessed references and globrefs are automatically turned into I/O handles for you by `encode()`, so you don't need to worry about it.
>
> Your method must return either `undef` (to indicate failure), or 1 (to indicate success).

init *ARGS...*

> *Instance method.* Do any necessary initialization of the new instance, taking whatever arguments were given to `new()`. Should return the self object on success or `undef` on failure.

install *ENCODING*

> *Class method.* Install this class so that it handles *ENCODING*. You should not override this method.

Built-In Decoder Subclasses

You don't need to `use` any other Perl modules; the following are included as part of MIME::Decoder:

MIME::Decoder::Base64

> The built-in decoder for the `base64` encoding.

The name was chosen to jibe with the pre-existing MIME::Base64 utility package, which this class actually uses to translate each line.

When decoding, the input is read one line at a time. The input accumulates in an internal buffer, which is decoded in multiple-of-4-sized chunks (plus a possible "leftover" input chunk, of course).

When encoding, the input is read 45 bytes at a time; this ensures that the output lines are not too long. We chose 45 since it is a multiple of 3 and produces lines under 76 characters, as RFC 1521 specifies.

Thanks to Phil Abercrombie for locating one idiotic bug in this module, which led me to discover another.

MIME::Decoder::Binary

The built-in decoder for a binary encoding (in other words, no encoding).

The binary decoder is a special case, since it's ill-advised to read the input line-by-line: after all, an uncompressed image file might conceivably have long stretches of bytes without a \n among them, and we don't want to risk blowing out our core. So we read and write fixed-size chunks.

Both the encoder and decoder do a simple pass-through of the data from input to output.

MIME::Decoder::QuotedPrint

The built-in decoder for quoted-printable encoding.

The name was chosen to jibe with the pre-existing MIME::QuotedPrint utility package, which this class actually uses to translate each line.

The decoder does a line-by-line translation from input to output.

The encoder does a line-by-line translation, breaking lines so that they fall under the standard 76-character limit for this encoding.

Note: Just like MIME::QuotedPrint, we currently use the native \n for line breaks, not CRLF. This may need to change in future versions.

MIME::Decoder::Xbit

The built-in decoder for both 7bit and 8bit encodings, which guarantee short lines (a maximum of 1000 characters per line) of US-ASCII data compatible with RFC 821.

The decoder does a line-by-line pass-through from input to output, leaving the data unchanged *except* that an end-of-line sequence of CRLF is converted to a newline (\n).

The encoder does a line-by-line pass-through from input to output, splitting long lines if necessary. If created as a 7-bit encoder, it maps any 8-bit characters to zero or more 7-bit characters. Note that this is a potentially *lossy* encoding if you hand it anything but 7-bit input. Therefore, don't use it on binary files (GIFs) and the like; use it only when it "doesn't matter" if extra newlines are inserted and 8-bit characters are squished.

Don't use this class. Really. Use a more appropriate encoding, like quoted-printable.

There are several possible ways to use this class to encode arbitrary 8-bit text as 7-bit text.

APPROX

Approximate the appearance of the Latin-1 character via Internet conventions; e.g., \c,, \n~, etc. This is the default behavior of this class. It pulls in the MIME::Latin1 module to do the translation. *This will be useless to you if your 8-bit characters are not Latin-1 text.*

STRIP

Strip out any 8-bit characters. Nice if you're *really* sure that any such characters in your input are mistakes to be deleted, but it transforms non-English documents into an abbreviated mess. But then, you should be using quoted-printable for those.

QP

Encode them as though we were doing a quoted-printable encoding; e.g., =A0. This won't help the mail-viewing software, but some humans may get the gist, and at least the original data might be recoverable.

To affect the default scheme, use the class method:

```
MIME::Decoder::Xbit->map_8_to_7_by('STRIP');
```
To affect just one decoder object:

```
$decoder->map_8_to_7_by('STRIP');
```

Notes

Input/output handles

As of MIME-tools 2.0, this class has to play nice with the new MIME::Body class, which means that input and output routines cannot just assume that they are dealing with file handles.

Therefore, all that MIME::Decoder and its subclasses require (and, thus, all that they can assume) is that *INSTREAM*s and *OUTSTREAM*s are objects which respond to the messages defined in MIME::IO (basically, a subset of those defined by IO::Handle).

For backwards compatibility, if you supply a scalar file handle name (like STDOUT) or an unblessed glob reference (like *STDOUT) where an *INSTREAM* or *OUTSTREAM* is expected, this package automatically wraps it in an object that fits the I/O handle criteria.

Thanks to Achim Bohnet for suggesting this more generic I/O model.

Writing a decoder

If you're experimenting with your own encodings, you'll probably want to write a decoder. Here are the basics:

- Create a module, like MyDecoder::, for your decoder. Declare it to be a subclass of MIME::Decoder.

- Create the following instance methods in your class, as described above:
  ```
  decode_it
  encode_it
  init
  ```

- In your application program, activate your decoder for one or more encodings like this:

```
require MyDecoder;
install MyDecoder "7bit";    # use MyDecoder to decode "7bit"
install MyDecoder "x-foo";   # also, use MyDecoder to decode
                             #  "x-foo"
```

To illustrate, here's a custom decoder class for the **quoted-printable** encoding:

```
package MyQPDecoder;
@ISA = qw(MIME::Decoder);
use MIME::Decoder;
use MIME::QuotedPrint;

# decode_it - the private decoding method
sub decode_it {
    my ($self, $in, $out) = @_;

    while (defined($_ = $in->getline())) {
        my $decoded = decode_qp($_);
        $out->print($decoded);
    }
    1;
}

# encode_it - the private encoding method
sub encode_it {
    my ($self, $in, $out) = @_;

    my ($buf, $nread) = ('', 0);
    while ($in->read($buf, 60)) {
        my $encoded = encode_qp($buf);
        $out->print($encoded);
    }
    1;
}
```

That's it.

The task was pretty simple because the **quoted-printable** encoding can easily be converted line-by-line, as can even **7bit** and **8bit** (since all these encodings guarantee short lines, with a maximum of 1000 characters). The good news is that it is very likely that it will be similarly easy to write a MIME::Decoder for any future standard encodings.

The binary decoder, however, really required block reads and writes; see MIME::Decoder::Binary for details.

Author

Eryq, *eryq@rhine.gsfc.nasa.gov*

Copyright

Copyright © 1996 by Eryq

MIME::Field::ContDisp—a "Content-disposition" field

Synopsis

```
use Mail::Field;
use MIME::Head;

# Create an instance from some text:
$field = Mail::Field->new('Content-disposition', $text);

# Inline or attachment?
$type = $field->type;

# Recommended filename?
$filename = $field->filename;
```

Description

A subclass of Mail::Field.

Don't use this class directly... its name may change in the future! Instead, ask Mail::Field for new instances based on the field name!

MIME::Field::ConTraEnc—a "Content-transfer-encoding" field

Synopsis

```
use Mail::Field;
use MIME::Head;

# Create an instance from some text:
$field = Mail::Field->new('Content-transfer-encoding', '7bit');

# Get the encoding.
#     Possible values: 'binary', '7bit', '8bit', 'quoted-printable',
#     'base64' and '' (unspecified).  Note that there can't be a
#     single default for this, since it depends on the content type!
$encoding = $field->encoding;
```

Description

A subclass of Mail::Field.

Don't use this class directly... its name may change in the future! Instead, ask Mail::Field for new instances based on the field name!

MIME::Field::ContType—a "Content-type" field

Synopsis

```
use Mail::Field;
use MIME::Head;

# Create an instance from some text:
```

```
$field = Mail::Field->new('Content-type',
                          'text/HTML; charset="US-ASCII"');

# Get the MIME type, like 'text/plain' or 'x-foobar'.
# Returns 'text/plain' as default, as per RFC-1521:
my ($type, $subtype) = split('/', $field->type);
# Get generic information:
print $field->name;

# Get information related to "message" type:
if ($type eq 'message') {
    print $field->id;
    print $field->number;
    print $field->total;
}

# Get information related to "multipart" type:
if ($type eq 'multipart') {
    print $field->boundary;              # the basic value, fixed up
    print $field->multipart_boundary;    # empty if not a multipart message!
}

# Get information related to "text" type:
if ($type eq 'text') {
    print $field->charset;       # returns 'us-ascii' as default
}
```

Description

A subclass of Mail::Field.

Don't use this class directly... its name may change in the future! Instead, ask Mail::Field for new instances based on the field name!

Public Interface

boundary

> Return the boundary field. The boundary is returned exactly as given in the Content-type: field; that is, the leading double-hyphen (--) is *not* prepended.
>
> Well, *almost* exactly—take this excerpt from RFC 1521:
>
> > If a boundary appears to end with whitespace, the whitespace must be presumed to have been added by a gateway, and must be deleted.
>
> We oblige and remove any trailing spaces.
>
> Returns the empty string if there is no boundary, or if the boundary is illegal (e.g., if it is empty after all trailing whitespace has been removed).

multipart_boundary

> Like boundary(), except that this will also return the empty string if the message is not a multipart message. In other words, there's an automatic sanity check.

type

> Try real hard to determine the content type (e.g., text/plain, image/gif, x-weird-type, which is returned in all-lowercase.

A happy thing: the following code will work just as you would want, even if there's no subtype (as in **x-weird-type**)... in such a case, the $subtype would simply be the empty string:

```
($type, $subtype) = split('/', $head->mime_type);
```

If the content-type information is missing, it defaults to **text/plain**, as per RFC 1521:

> Default RFC 822 messages are typed by this protocol as plain text in the US-ASCII character set, which can be explicitly specified as "Content-type: text/plain; charset=us-ascii". If no Content-Type is specified, this default is assumed.

If *just* the subtype is missing (a syntax error unless the type begins with **x-**, but we'll tolerate it, since some brain-dead mailers actually do this), then it simply is not reported; e.g., **Content-type: TEXT** is returned simply as **text**.

If the content type is present but can't be parsed at all (yow!), the empty string is returned.

Notes

Since nearly all (if not all) parameters must have non-empty values to be considered valid, we just return the empty string to signify missing fields. If you need to get the *real* underlying value, use the inherited **param()** method (which returns **undef** if the parameter is missing).

MIME::Field::ParamVal—subclass of Mail::Field, for structured MIME fields

Description

This is an abstract superclass of most MIME fields. It handles fields with a general syntax like this:

```
Content-Type: Message/Partial;
    number=2; total=3;
    id="oc=jpbe0M2Yt4s@thumper.bellcore.com"
```

Comments are supported *between* items, like this:

```
Content-Type: Message/Partial; (a comment)
    number=2  (another comment) ; (yet another comment) total=3;
    id="oc=jpbe0M2Yt4s@thumper.bellcore.com"
```

Public Interface

set [\%*paramhash* | key=>val,...,key=>val]

Set this field. The ***paramhash*** should contain parameter names in *all lowercase*, with the special "_" parameter name signifying the "default" (unnamed) parameter for the field:

```
# Set up to be...
#
#   Content-type: Message/Partial; number=2; total=3;
#                 id="ocj=pbe0M2"
#
```

```
          $conttype->set('_'        => 'Message/Partial',
                         'number'  => 2,
                         'total'   => 3,
                         'id'      => "ocj=pbe0M2");
```

Note that a single argument is taken to be a *reference* to a **paramhash**, while multiple args are taken to be the elements of the **paramhash** themselves.

Supplying undef for a hashref, or an empty set of values, effectively clears the object.

The self object is returned.

parse_params *STRING*

Class/instance utility method. Extract parameter info from a structured field, and return it as a hash reference. For example, here is a field with parameters:

```
Content-Type: Message/Partial;
    number=2; total=3;
    id="oc=jpbe0M2Yt4s@thumper.bellcore.com"
```

Here is how you'd extract them:

```
$params = $class->parse_params('content-type');
if ($$params{'_'} eq 'message/partial') {
    $number = $$params{'number'};
    $total  = $$params{'total'};
    $id     = $$params{'id'};
}
```

Like field names, parameter names are coerced to lowercase. The special "_" parameter means the default parameter for the field.

NOTE: This has been provided as a public method to support backwards compatibility, but you probably shouldn't use it.

parse *STRING*

Parse the string into the instance. Any previous information is wiped.

The self object is returned.

param *PARAMNAME*, [*VALUE*]

Return the given parameter, or undef if it isn't there. With an argument, set the parameter to that *VALUE*. The *PARAMNAME* is case-insensitive. A "_" refers to the "default" parameter.

stringify

Convert the field to a string, and return it.

tag

Return the tag for this field. Abstract!

MIME::Latin1 — translate ISO-8859-1 into 7-bit approximations

Synopsis

```
use MIME::Latin1 qw(latin1_to_ascii);

$dirty = "Fran\347ois";
print latin1_to_ascii($dirty);      # prints out "Fran\c,ois"
```

Description

This is a small package used by the **7bit** encoder/decoder for handling the case where a user wants to 7bit-encode a document that contains 8-bit (presumably Latin-1) characters. It provides a mapping whereby every 8 bit character is mapped to a unique sequence of two 7-bit characters that approximates the appearance or pronunciation of the Latin-1 character. For example:

This	Maps To
ç (a c with a cedilla)	c,
Ç (a C with a cedilla)	C,
Æ (an "AE" ligature)	AE
æ (an "ae" ligature)	ae
¥ (yen sign)	Y-

I call each of these 7-bit 2-character encodings *mnemonic encodings*, since they (hopefully) are visually reminiscent of the 8-bit characters they are meant to represent.

Functions

latin1_to_ascii STRING, [OPTS]

> Map the Latin-1 characters in the string to sequences of the form:
>
>   \xy
>
> Where **xy** is a two-character sequence that visually approximates the Latin-1 character. For example:
>
>   ç => \c,
>   ñ => \n~
>   Æ => \AE
>   ø => \o/
>
> The sequences are taken almost exactly from the Sun character composition sequences for generating these characters. The translation may be further tweaked by the (optional) OPTS string:

READABLE

> *Currently the default.* Only 8-bit characters are affected, and their output is of the form \xy:
>
>   \<<Fran\c,ois M\u"ller\>>   c:\usr\games

NOSLASH

> Exactly like READABLE, except the leading \ is not inserted, making the output more compact:
>
>   <<Franc,ois Mu"ller>>   c:\usr\games

ENCODE

> Not only is the leading \ output, but any other occurrences of \ are escaped as well by turning them into \\. Unlike the other options, this produces output which may easily be parsed and turned back into the original 8-bit characters, so in a way it is its own full-fledged encoding... and given that \ is a rare-enough character, not much uglier that the normal output:
>
>   \<<Fran\c,ois M\u"ller\>>   c:\\usr\\games
>
> You may use **ascii_to_latin1** to decode this.

Note that as of 3.12, the options string must, if defined, be one of the above options. Composite options like "ENCODE|NOSLASH" will no longer be supported (most will be self-contradictory anyway).

`ascii_to_latin1` STRING

Map the Latin-1 escapes in the string (sequences of the form \xy) back into actual 8-bit characters.

```
# Assume $enc holds the actual text...
# \<<Fran\c,ois \\ M\u"ller\>>
print ascii_to_latin1($enc);
```

Unrecognized sequences are turned into '?' characters.

Note that you must have specified the "ENCODE" option when encoding in order to decode!

Notes

Hex Encoding

Characters in the octal range \200-\237 (hexadecimal \x80-\x9F) currently do not have mnemonic Latin-1 equivalents, and therefore are represented by the hex sequences "80" through "9F", where the second hex digit is upcased. That is:

```
80 81 82 83 84 85 86 87 88 89 8A 8B 8C 8D 8E 8F
90 91 92 93 94 95 96 97 98 99 9A 9B 9C 9D 9E 9F
```

To allow this scheme to work properly for *all* 8-bit-on characters, the general rule is: *the first hex digit is DOWNcased, and the second hex digit is UPcased.* Hence, these are all decodable sequences:

```
a0 a1 a2 a3 a4 a5 a6 a7 a8 a9 aA aB aC aD aE aF
```

This "downcase-upcase" style is so we don't conflict with mnemonically encoded ligatures like "ae" and "AE", the latter of which could reasonably have been represented as "Ae".

Note that we must never have a mnemonic encoding that could be mistaken for a hex sequence from "80" to "fF", since the ambiguity would make it impossible to decode. (However, "12", "34", "Ff", etc. are perfectly fine.)

Thanks to Rolf Nelson for reporting the "gap" in the encoding.

Other Restrictions

The first character of a 2-character encoding can not be a \. This is because \\ represents an encoded \; to allow \\x would introduce an ambiguity for the decoder.

Going Backwards

Since the mappings may fluctuate over time as I get more input, anyone writing a translator would be well-advised to use `ascii_to_latin1()` to perform the reverse mapping. I will strive for backwards-compatibility in that code.

Got a problem?

If you have better suggestions for some of the character representations, please contact me.

Author

Eryq, *eryq@rhine.gsfc.nasa.gov*

Copyright

Copyright © 1996 by Eryq

MIME::Lite—low-calorie MIME generator

Synopsis

```
use MIME::Lite;
```

Create a single-part message:

```
# Create a new single-part message, to send a GIF file:
$msg = new MIME::Lite
        From     =>'me@myhost.com',
        To       =>'you@yourhost.com',
        Cc       =>'some@other.com, some@more.com',
        Subject  =>'Helloooo00, nurse!',
        Type     =>'image/gif',
        Encoding =>'base64',
        Path     =>'hellonurse.gif';
```

Create a multipart message (i.e., one with attachments):

```
# Create a new multipart message:
$msg = new MIME::Lite
        From     =>'me@myhost.com',
        To       =>'you@yourhost.com',
        Cc       =>'some@other.com, some@more.com',
        Subject  =>'A message with 2 parts...',
        Type     =>'multipart/mixed';

# Add parts (each "attach" has same arguments as "new"):
attach $msg
        Type     =>'TEXT',
        Data     =>"Here's the GIF file you wanted";
attach $msg
        Type     =>'image/gif',
        Path     =>'aaa000123.gif',
        Filename =>'logo.gif';
```

Output a message:

```
# As a string...
$str = $msg->as_string;

# To a file handle (say, a "sendmail" stream)...
$msg->print(\*SENDMAIL);
```

Description

In the never-ending quest for great taste with fewer calories, we proudly present: MIME::Lite.

MIME::Lite is intended as a simple, standalone module for generating (not parsing!) MIME messages. Specifically, it allows you to output a simple, decent single- or multi-part message with text or binary attachments. It does not require that you have the Mail:: or MIME:: modules installed.

Warning

This is alpha code. I have not yet fully tested it, and I can't guarantee that the interface won't change in the next few releases in a non-backwards-compatible manner. It is being provided to the community for suggestions and in the hopes that it will be useful.

You can specify each message part as either the literal data itself (in a scalar or array), or as a string which can be given to `open()` to get a readable file handle (e.g., `<filename>` or `somecommand|`).

You don't need to worry about encoding your message data; this module does that for you. It handles the five standard MIME encodings.

If you need more sophisticated behavior, please get the MIME-tools package instead. I am more likely to add stuff to that toolkit than this one.

Construction Methods

`new [`*PARAMHASH*`]`

> *Class method, constructor.* Create a new message object. If any arguments are given, they are passed into `build()`; otherwise, just the empty object is created.

`attach [`*OBJECT*`|`*PARAMHASH*`]`

> *Instance method.* Add a new part to this message, and return the new part. You can attach a MIME::Lite *OBJECT*, or have it create one by specifying a *PARAMHASH* that is automatically given to `new()`.

> One of the possibly-quite-useful hacks thrown into this is the "attach-to-singlepart" hack: if you attempt to attach a part (let's call it "part 1") to a message that *isn't* a multipart message (the "self" object in this case), the following happens:

> - A new part (call it "part 0") is made.
> - The MIME attributes and data (but *not* the other headers) are cut from the "self" message, and pasted into "part 0".
> - The "self" is turned into a "multipart/mixed" message.
> - The new "part 0" is added to the "self", and *then* "part 1" is added.

> One of the nice side-effects is that you can create a text message, and then add zero or more attachments to it, much in the same way that a user agent like Netscape allows you to do.

`build [`*PARAMHASH*`]`

> *Class/instance method, initializer.* Create (or initialize) a MIME message object. *PARAMHASH* can contain the following keys:

(fieldname)

Any field you want placed in the message header, taken from the standard list of header fields (you don't need to worry about case):

Bcc	Encrypted	Organization	Return-Path
Cc	From	Received	Sender
Comments	Keywords	References	Subject
Content-*	Message-ID	Reply-To	To
Date	MIME-Version	Resent-*	X-*

To give experienced users some veto power, these fields are set *after* the ones I set... so be careful: *don't set any MIME fields* (like `Content-type`) unless you know what you're doing!

To specify a fieldname that's *not* in the above list, even one that's identical to an option below, just add a trailing :, e.g., `My-field:`. That *always* signals a mail field (and it sort of looks like one too).

Data

Alternative to "Path". The actual message data. This may be a scalar or a ref to an array of strings; if the latter, the message consists of a simple concatenation of all the strings in the array.

Disposition

Optional. The content disposition, `inline` or `attachment`. The default is `inline`.

Encoding

Optional. The content transfer encoding that should be used to encode your data. The default is `binary`, which means "no encoding": this is generally not suitable for sending anything but ASCII text files with short lines, so consider using one of the following values instead:

Use encoding:	If your message contains:
7bit	Only 7-bit text, all lines <1000 characters
8bit	8-bit text, all lines <1000 characters
quoted-printable	8-bit text or long lines (more reliable than "8bit")
base64	Largely binary data: a GIF, a tar file, etc.

Be sure to pick an appropriate encoding. In the case of 7bit/8bit, long lines are automatically chopped to legal length; in the case of 7bit, all 8-bit characters are automatically converted to ugly QP-like =XX sequences. There's a section called "A MIME Primer" in this document with more info.

Filename

Optional. The name of the attachment. You can use this to supply a filename if the one in the Path is inadequate, or if you're using the Data argument.

Length

Optional. Set the content length explicitly. Normally, this header is automatically computed, but only under certain circumstances (see "Limitations").

Path

Alternative to "Data". Path to a file containing the data. Actually, it can be any `open()`able expression. If it looks like a path, the last element is automatically treated as the filename. Ignored if "Data" is present. See "ReadNow" also.

ReadNow

Optional, for use with "Path". If true, open the path and slurp the contents into core now. This is useful if the Path points to a command, and you don't want to run the command over and over if you're outputting the message several times. A fatal exception is raised if the open fails.

Top

Optional. If defined, indicates whether or not this is a "top-level" MIME message. The parts of a multipart message are not top-level. The default is true.

Type

Optional. The MIME content type, or one of these special values (case-sensitive):

"TEXT" means "text/plain"
"BINARY" means "application/octet-stream"

The default is `TEXT`.

Construction Method Examples

A picture being worth 1000 words (which is of course 2000 bytes, so it's probably more of an "icon" than a "picture", but I digress), here are some examples:

```
$msg = build MIME::Lite
        From    => 'yelling@inter.com',
        To      => 'stocking@fish.net',
        Subject => "Hi there!",
        Type    => 'TEXT',
        Encoding => '7bit',
        Data    => "Just a quick note to say hi!";

$msg = build MIME::Lite
        From    => 'dorothy@emerald-city.oz',
        To      => 'gesundheit@edu.edu.edu',
        Subject => "A gif for U"
        Type    => 'image/gif',
        Path    => "/home/httpd/logo.gif";

$msg = build MIME::Lite
        From    => 'laughing@all.of.us',
        To      => 'scarlett@fiddle.dee.de',
        Subject => "A gzipp'ed tar file",
        Type    => 'x-gzip',
        Path    => "gzip < /usr/inc/somefile.tar |",
        ReadNow => 1,
        Filename => "somefile.tgz";
```

To show you what's really going on, that last example could also have been written:

```
$msg = new MIME::Lite;

$msg->build(Type     => 'x-gzip',
            Path     => "gzip < /usr/inc/somefile.tar |",
            ReadNow  => 1,
            Filename => "somefile.tgz");

$msg->add(From    => "laughing@all.of.us");
$msg->add(To      => "scarlett@fiddle.dee.de");
$msg->add(Subject => "A gzipp'ed tar file");
```

Setting/Getting Headers and Attributes

add *TAG, VALUE*

Add field TAG with the given VALUE to the end of the header. The TAG is converted to all-lowercase, and the VALUE is made "safe" (returns are given a trailing space).

Beware: Any MIME fields you "add" will override any MIME attributes I have when it comes time to output those fields. Normally, you will use this method to add *non-MIME* fields:

```
$msg->add("Subject" => "Hi there!");
```

Giving *VALUE* as an arrayref causes all the values in the array to be added:

```
$msg->add("Received" => ["here", "there", "everywhere"]);
```

Note that add() is probably going to be more efficient than replace(), so you're better off using it for most applications. The name comes from Mail::Header.

attr *ATTR, [VALUE]*

Set MIME attribute *ATTR* to the string *VALUE. ATTR* is converted to all-lowercase. This method is normally used to set/get MIME attributes:

```
$msg->attr("content-type"         => "text/html");
$msg->attr("content-type.charset" => "US-ASCII");
$msg->attr("content-type.name"    => "homepage.html");
```

This causes the final output to look something like this:

```
Content-type: text/html; charset=US-ASCII; name="homepage.html"
```

Note that the special empty subfield tag indicates the anonymous first subfield.

Giving *VALUE* as undefined causes the contents of the named subfield to be deleted.

Supplying no *VALUE* argument just returns the attribute's value:

```
$type = $msg->attr("content-type");       # returns
"text/html"
$name = $msg->attr("content-type.name");  # returns
"homepage.html"
```

delete *TAG*

Delete field *TAG* with the given *VALUE* to the end of the header. The TAG is converted to all-lowercase.

```
$msg->delete("Subject");
```

Note that the name comes from Mail::Header.

fields

Return the full header for the object, as a ref to an array of [*TAG, VALUE*] pairs.

Any fields that the user has explicitly set override the corresponding MIME fields that we would generate. So *don't* say:

```
$msg->set("Content-type" => "text/html; charset=US-ASCII");
```

unless you *mean it*!

I called this "fields" because the **header()** method of Mail::Header returns something different, but similar enough to be confusing.

filename [*FILENAME*]

Set the filename that this data will be reported as. This actually sets both "standard" attributes.

With no argument, returns the filename as dictated by the content-disposition.

get_length

Recompute the content length for the message *if the process is trivial*, setting the "content-length" attribute as a side-effect:

```
$msg->get_length;
```

Returns the length, or undefined if not set.

Note that the content length can be difficult to compute, since it involves assembling the entire encoded body and taking the length of it (which, in the case of multipart messages, means freezing all the subparts, etc.).

This method only sets the content length to a defined value if the message is singlepart with **binary** encoding, *and* the body is available either in-core or as a simple file. Otherwise, the content length is set to the undefined value.

Since content-length is not a standard MIME field anyway (that's right, kids: it's not in the MIME RFCs, it's an HTTP thing), this seems pretty fair.

replace *TAG, VALUE*

Delete all occurrences of fields named *TAG*, and add a new field with the given *VALUE*. *TAG* is converted to all-lowercase.

Beware: Any MIME fields you "replace" will override any MIME attributes I have when it comes time to output those fields. Normally, you will use this method to set *non-MIME* fields:

```
$msg->replace("Subject" => "Hi there!");
```

Giving *VALUE* as undefined simply causes the contents of the named field to be deleted. Giving *VALUE* as an arrayref causes all the values in the array to be added.

Note that the name comes from Mail::Header.

Setting/Getting Message Data

binmode [*OVERRIDE*]

With no argument, returns whether or not it thinks that the data (as given by the "Path" argument of **build()**) should be read using **binmode()** (for example, when **read_now()** is invoked).

The default behavior is that any content type other than **text/*** or **message/*** is binmode'd; this should in general work fine.

With a defined argument, this method sets an explicit "override" value. An undefined argument unsets the override. The new current value is returned.

data [*DATA*]
> Get/set the literal *DATA* of the message. The *DATA* may be either a scalar, or a reference to an array of scalars (which are simply joined).

> ### Warning

> Setting the data causes the "content-length" attribute to be recomputed (possibly to nothing).

path [*PATH*]
> Get/set the *PATH* to the message data.

> ### Warning

> Setting the path recomputes any existing "content-length" field, and re-sets the "filename" (to the last element of the path if it looks like a simple path, and to nothing if not).

read_now [*PATH*]
> Force the path to be read into core immediately. With optional argument, sets the path() first; otherwise, the current path (such as that given during a build()) will be used.

> Note that the in-core data is always used if available.

> Be aware that everything is slurped into a giant scalar: you may not want to use this if sending tar files! The benefit of *not* reading in the data is that very large files can be handled by this module if left on disk until the message is output via print() or print_body().

sign *PARAMHASH*
> Sign the message. This forces the message to be read into core, after which the signature is appended to it.

> Data
>> As in build(): the literal signature data. Can be either a scalar or a ref to an array of scalars.

> Path
>> As in build(): the path to the file.

> If no arguments are given, the default is: Path => "$ENV{HOME}/.signature".

> The content-length is recomputed.

Output Methods

print [*OUTHANDLE*]
> *Instance method.* Print the message to the given output handle, or to the currently selected file handle if none was given.

> All *OUTHANDLE* has to be is a file handle (possibly a glob ref) or any object that responds to a print() message.

print_body [*OUTHANDLE*]
> *Instance method.* Print the body of the message to the given output handle, or to the currently selected file handle if none was given.

> All *OUTHANDLE* has to be is a file handle (possibly a glob ref), or any object that responds to a print() message.

Fatal exception is raised if unable to open any of the input files, or if a part contains no data, or if an unsupported encoding is encountered.

`print_header [`*OUTHANDLE*`]`

Instance method. Print the header of the message to the given output handle or to the currently selected file handle if none was given.

All *OUTHANDLE* has to be is a file handle (possibly a glob ref) or any object that responds to a `print()` message.

`as_string`

Instance method. Return the entire message as a string, with a header and an encoded body.

`body_as_string`

Instance method. Return the encoded body as a string.

Note that this actually prepares the body by "printing" to a scalar. Proof that you can hand the `print*()` methods any blessed object that responds to a `print()` message.

`header_as_string`

Instance method. Return the header as a string.

Sending Methods

`send`

Instance method. Sends the message.

Right now, this is done by piping it into the sendmail command as given by `send-mail()`. It probably works only on UNIX systems.

Returns false if sendmail *seems* to have failed, true otherwise. Fatal exception is raised if the open fails.

`sendmail COMMAND...`

Class method. Set up the sendmail command used by `send()`. You may supply it as either a single string or an array of path-to-command-plus-arguments:

```
sendmail MIME::Lite "/usr/lib/sendmail", "-t", "-oi", "-oem";
```

What you see above is the default.

Miscellaneous Methods

`quiet ONOFF`

Class method. Suppress/unsuppress all warnings coming from this module:

```
quiet MIME::Lite 1;        # I know what I'm doing
```

I recommend that you include that comment as well. And while you type it, say it out loud: if it doesn't feel right, then maybe you should reconsider the whole line. `;-)`

Examples

Create a multipart message exactly as above, but using the "attach to singlepart" hack:

```
# Create a new multipart message:
$msg = new MIME::Lite
            From    =>'me@myhost.com',
            To      =>'you@yourhost.com',
            Cc      =>'some@other.com, some@more.com',
```

```
            Subject =>'A message with 2 parts...',
            Type    =>'TEXT',
            Data    =>"Here's the GIF file you wanted";

# Attach a part:
attach $msg
            Type     =>'image/gif',
            Path     =>'aaa000123.gif',
            Filename =>'logo.gif';
```

Output a message to a file handle:

```
# Write it to a file handle:
$msg->print(\*STDOUT);

# Write just the header:
$msg->print_header(\*STDOUT);

# Write just the encoded body:
$msg->print_body(\*STDOUT);
```

Get a message as a string:

```
# Get entire message as a string:
$str = $msg->as_string;

# Get just the header:
$str = $msg->header_as_string;

# Get just the encoded body:
$str = $msg->body_as_string;
```

Send a message (UNIX systems only!):

```
# Send it!
$msg->send;
```

Notes

Limitations

This is "lite," after all . . .

- There's no parsing. Get MIME-tools if you need to parse MIME messages.

- MIME::Lite messages are currently *not* interchangeable with either Mail::Internet or MIME::Entity objects. This is a completely separate module.

- A content-length field is only inserted if the encoding is binary, the message is singlepart, and all the document data is available at build() time by virtue of residing in a simple path, or in-core. Since content-length is not a standard MIME field anyway, this seems pretty fair.

- MIME::Lite alone cannot help you lose weight. You must supplement your use of MIME::Lite with a healthy diet and exercise.

Cheap and Easy Mailing

I thought putting in a sendmail invocation wasn't too bad an idea, since a lot of Perlers are on UNIX systems. The default arguments to sendmail (which you can change) are:

-t   Scan message for To:, Cc:, Bcc:, etc.

-oi Do *not* treat a single "." on a line as a message terminator. As in, "-oi vey, it truncated my message . . . why?!"

-oem
    On error, mail back the message (I assume to the appropriate address, given in the header). When mail returns, circle is complete.

Under the Hood

This class treats a MIME header in the most abstract sense, as being a collection of high-level attributes. The actual RFC 822-style header fields are not constructed until it's time to actually print the darn thing.

Warnings

The MIME attributes are stored and manipulated separately from the message header fields; when it comes time to print the header out, *any explicitly given header fields override the ones that would be created from the MIME attributes.* That means that this:

```
### DANGER ### DANGER ### DANGER ### DANGER ### DANGER ###
$msg->add("Content-type", "text/html; charset=US-ASCII");
```

sets the exact `Content-type` field in the header I write, *regardless of what the actual MIME attributes are.*

This feature is for experienced users only, as an escape hatch in case the code that normally formats MIME header fields isn't doing what you need. And, like any escape hatch, it's got an alarm on it: MIME::Lite warns you if you attempt to `set()` or `replace()` any MIME header field. Use `attr()` instead.

A MIME Primer

Content Types

The "Type" parameter of `build()` is a *content type*. This is the actual type of the data you are sending. Generally, this is a string of the form `majortype/minortype`.

Here are the major MIME types. A more-comprehensive listing may be found in RFC 2046.

application
    Data which does not fit in any of the other categories, particularly data to be processed by some type of application program. `application/octet-stream`, `application/gzip`, `application/postscript`, etc.

audio
    Audio data. `audio/basic`, etc.

image
    Graphics data. `image/gif`, `image/jpeg`, etc.

message
    A message, usually another mail or MIME message. `message/rfc822`, etc.

multipart

> A message containing other messages. multipart/mixed, multipart/alterna-tive, etc.

text

> Textual data, meant for humans to read. text/plain, text/html, etc.

video

> Video or video+audio data. video/mpeg, etc.

Content Transfer Encodings

The "Encoding" parameter of build(). This is how the message body is packaged up for safe transit.

Here are the five major MIME encodings. A more comprehensive listing may be found in RFC 2045.

7bit

> Basically, no *real* encoding is done. However, this label guarantees that no 8-bit characters are present and that lines do not exceed 1000 characters in length.

8bit

> Basically, no *real* encoding is done. The message might contain 8-bit characters, but this encoding guarantees that lines do not exceed 1000 characters in length.

binary

> No encoding is done at all. Message might contain 8-bit characters and lines might be longer than 1000 characters.
>
> The most liberal encoding type, and the least likely to get through mail gateways. Use sparingly or (better yet) not at all.

base64

> Like uuencode, but very well-defined. This is how you should send essentially binary information (tar files, GIFs, JPEGs, etc.).

quoted-printable

> Useful for encoding messages that are textual in nature, yet that contain non-ASCII characters (e.g., characters from the Latin-1, Latin-2, or any other 8-bit alphabet).

Author

Eryq, *eryq@enteract.com*
(who really should be wrapping holiday presents instead, 11 December 1996)
 http://enteract.com/~eryq/

Copyright

MIME::ParserBase—abstract class for parsing MIME mail

Synopsis

This is an *abstract* class; however, here's how one of its *concrete subclasses* is used:

```
use MIME::Parser;

# Create a new parser object:
my $parser = new MIME::Parser;

# Parse an input stream:
$entity = $parser->read(\*STDIN) or die "couldn't parse MIME stream";

# Congratulations: you now have a (possibly multipart) MIME entity!
$entity->dump_skeleton;           # for debugging
```

There are also some convenience methods:

```
# Parse an in-core MIME message:
$entity = $parser->parse_data($message)
      || die "couldn't parse MIME message";

# Parse already-split input (as "deliver" would give it to you):
$entity = $parser->parse_two("msg.head", "msg.body")
      || die "couldn't parse MIME files";
```

In case a parse fails, it's nice to know who sent it to us. So...

```
# Parse an input stream:
$entity = $parser->read(\*STDIN);
if (!$entity) {            # oops!
    my $decapitated = $parser->last_head;     # last top-level head
}
```

You can also alter the behavior of the parser:

```
# Parse contained "message/rfc822" objects as nested MIME streams:
$parser->parse_nested_messages('REPLACE');

# Automatically attempt to RFC-1522-decode the MIME headers:
$parser->decode_headers(1);
```

Description

This is the class that contains all the knowledge for *parsing* MIME streams. It's an abstract class, containing no methods governing the *output* of the parsed entities: such methods belong in the concrete subclasses.

You can inherit from this class to create your own subclasses that parse MIME streams into MIME::Entity objects. One such subclass, MIME::Parser, is already provided in this kit.

Public Interface

Construction, and setting options

new *ARGS...*

> *Class method.* Create a new parser object. Passes any subsequent arguments onto the init() method.

Once you create a parser object, you can then set up various parameters before doing the actual parsing. Here's an example using one of our concrete subclasses:

```
my $parser = new MIME::Parser;
$parser->output_dir("/tmp");
$parser->output_prefix("msg1");
my $entity = $parser->read(\*STDIN);
```

decode_headers *ONOFF*

Instance method. If set true, then the parser will attempt to decode the MIME headers as per RFC 1522 the moment it sees them. This will probably be of most use to those of you who expect some international mail, especially mail from individuals with 8-bit characters in their names.

If set false, no attempt at decoding will be done.

With no argument, just returns the current setting.

Warning: Some folks already have code which assumes that no decoding is done, and since this is pretty new and radical stuff, I have initially made "off" the default setting for backwards compatibility in 2.05. However, I will possibly change this in future releases, so please: if you want a particular setting, declare it when you create your parser object.

interface *ROLE,* [*VALUE*]

Instance method. During parsing, the parser normally creates instances of certain classes, like MIME::Entity. However, you may want to create a parser subclass that uses your own experimental head, entity, etc., classes (for example, your "head" class may provide some additional MIME-field-oriented methods).

If so, then this is the method that your subclass should invoke during init. Use it like this:

```
package MyParser;
@ISA = qw(MIME::Parser);
...
sub init {
    my $self = shift;
    $self->SUPER::init(@_);                 # do my parent's init
    $self->interface(ENTITY_CLASS => 'MIME::MyEntity');
    $self->interface(HEAD_CLASS   => 'MIME::MyHead');
    $self;                                  # return
}
```

With no *VALUE*, returns the *VALUE* currently associated with that *ROLE*.

last_head

Instance method. Return the top-level MIME header of the last stream we attempted to parse. This is useful for replying to people who sent us bad MIME messages.

```
# Parse an input stream:
$entity = $parser->read(\*STDIN);
if (!$entity) {                                   # oops!
    my $decapitated = $parser->last_head; # last top-level head
}
```

parse_nested_messages *OPTION*

Instance method. Some MIME messages will contain a part of type **message/rfc822**: literally, the text of an embedded mail/news/whatever message. The normal behavior is to save such a message just as if it were a `text/plain` document, without attempting to decode it. However, you can change this: before parsing, invoke this method with the OPTION you want:

If OPTION is false, the normal behavior will be used.

If OPTION is true, the body of the `message/rfc822` part is decoded (after all, it might be encoded!) into a temporary file handle, which is then rewound and parsed by this parser, creating an entity object. What happens then is determined by the OPTION:

NEST *or* 1

> The contained message becomes a "part" of the `message/rfc822` entity, as though the `message/rfc822` were a special kind of `multipart` entity. However, the `message/rfc822` header (and the content-type) *is retained*.
>
> *Warning*: Since it is not legal MIME for anything but `multipart` to have a "part", the `message/rfc822` message *will appear to have no content* if you simply `print()` it out. You will have to have to get at the reparsed body manually, by the `MIME::Entity::parts()` method.
>
> IMHO, this option is probably only useful if you're *processing* messages, but *not* saving or re-sending them. In such cases, it is best to *not* use "parse nested" at all.

REPLACE

> The contained message replaces the `message/rfc822` entity, as though the `message/rfc822` "envelope" never existed.
>
> *Warning*: Notice that, with this option, all the header information in the `message/rfc822` header is lost. This might seriously bother you if you're dealing with a top-level message, and you've just lost the sender's address and the subject line.

Thanks to Andreas Koenig for suggesting this method.

Parsing messages

parse_data *DATA*

> *Instance method.* Parse a MIME message that's already in-core. You may supply the *DATA* in any of a number of ways:
>
> - A scalar which holds the message.
> - A ref to a scalar which holds the message. This is an efficiency hack.
> - A ref to an array of scalars. The array elements are simply joined to produce a scalar; no newlines are inserted!

Returns a MIME::Entity, which may be a single entity, or an arbitrarily nested multi-part entity. Returns `undef` on failure.

Note: Where the parsed body parts are stored (e.g., in-core vs. on-disk) is not determined by this class, but by the subclass you use to do the actual parsing (e.g., MIME::Parser). For efficiency, if you know you'll be parsing a small amount of data, it is probably best to tell the parser to store the parsed parts in core. For example, here's a short test program, using MIME::Parser:

```
use MIME::Parser;

my $msg = <<EOF;
```

```
Content-type: text/html
Content-transfer-encoding: 7bit
<H1>Hello, world!</H1>;
EOF
$parser = new MIME::Parser;
$parser->output_to_core('ALL');
$entity = $parser->parse_data($msg);
$entity->print(\*STDOUT);
```

parse_two *HEADFILE, BODYFILE*

> *Instance method.* Convenience front-end onto **read**(), intended for programs running under mail-handlers like **deliver**, which splits the incoming mail message into a header file and a body file.

> Simply give this method the paths to the respective files. These must be pathnames: Perl "open-able" expressions won't work, since the pathnames are shell-quoted for safety.

> *Warning:* It is assumed that, once the files are **cated** together, there will be a blank line separating the head part and the body part.

> Returns the parsed entity, or **undef** on error.

read *INSTREAM*

> *Instance method.* Takes a MIME-stream and splits it into its component entities, each of which is decoded and placed in a separate file in the splitter's **output_dir**().

> The *INSTREAM* can be given as a readable FileHandle, a globref'd file handle (like *STDIN), or as *any* blessed object conforming to the MIME::IO (or IO::) interface.

> Returns a MIME::Entity, which may be a single entity, or an arbitrarily-nested multi-part entity. Returns **undef** on failure.

Writing Subclasses

All you have to do to write a subclass is to provide or override the following methods:

init *ARGS...*

> *Instance method, private.* Initialize the new parser object, with any args passed to **new**().

> You don't *need* to override this in your subclass. If you override it, however, make sure you call the inherited method to init your parents!

```
package MyParser;
@ISA = qw(MIME::Parser);
...
sub init {
    my $self = shift;
    $self->SUPER::init(@_);          # do my parent's init

    # ...my init stuff goes here...

    $self;                           # return
}
```

> Should return the self object on success, and **undef** on failure.

new_body_for *HEAD*

> *Abstract instance method.* Based on the *HEAD* of a part we are parsing, return a new body object (any desirable subclass of MIME::Body) for receiving that part's data (both will be put into the "entity" object for that part).
>
> If you want the parser to do something other than write its parts out to files, you should override this method in a subclass. For an example, see MIME::Parser.
>
> Note: the reason that we don't use the "interface" mechanism for this is that your choice of (1) which body class to use, and (2) how its new() method is invoked, may be very much based on the information in the header.
>
> You are of course free to override any other methods as you see fit, like new.

Notes

This is an abstract class. If you actually want to parse a MIME stream, use one of the children of this class, like the backwards-compatible MIME::Parser.

Under the Hood

RFC 1521 gives us the following BNF grammar for the body of a multipart MIME message:

```
multipart-body   := preamble 1*encapsulation close-delimiter
epilogue
encapsulation    := delimiter body-part CRLF
delimiter        := "--" boundary CRLF
                            ; taken from Content-Type field.
                            ; There must be no space between "--"
                            ; and boundary.
close-delimiter  := "--" boundary "--" CRLF
                            ; Again, no space by "--"
preamble         := discard-text
                            ; to be ignored upon receipt.
epilogue         := discard-text
                            ; to be ignored upon receipt.
discard-text     := *(*text CRLF)
body-part        := <"message" as defined in RFC 822, with all
                     header fields optional, and with the specified
                     delimiter not occurring anywhere in the message
                     body, either on a line by itself or as a
                     substring anywhere. Note that the semantics of
                     a part differ from the semantics of a message,
                     as described in the text.>
```

From this we glean the following algorithm for parsing a MIME stream:

```
PROCEDURE parse
INPUT
    A FILEHANDLE for the stream.
    An optional end-of-stream OUTER_BOUND
      (for nested multipart message).

RETURNS
    The (possibly-multipart) ENTITY that was parsed.
    A STATE indicating how we left things: "END" or "ERROR".
```

```
BEGIN
     LET OUTER_DELIM = "--OUTER_BOUND".
     LET OUTER_CLOSE = "--OUTER_BOUND--".

     LET ENTITY = a new MIME entity object.
     LET STATE  = "OK".

     Parse the (possibly empty) header, up to and including the
     blank line that terminates it.   Store it in the ENTITY.

     IF the MIME type is "multipart":
         LET INNER_BOUND = get multipart "boundary" from header.
         LET INNER_DELIM = "--INNER_BOUND".
         LET INNER_CLOSE = "--INNER_BOUND--".

         Parse preamble:
             REPEAT:
                 Read (and discard) next line
             UNTIL (line is INNER_DELIM) OR we hit EOF (error).

         Parse parts:
             REPEAT:
                 LET (PART, STATE) = parse(FILEHANDLE, INNER_BOUND).
                 Add PART to ENTITY.
             UNTIL (STATE != "DELIM").

         Parse epilogue:
             REPEAT (to parse epilogue):
                 Read (and discard) next line
             UNTIL (line is OUTER_DELIM or OUTER_CLOSE) OR we hit EOF
             LET STATE = "EOF", "DELIM", or "CLOSE" accordingly.

     ELSE (if the MIME type is not "multipart"):
         Open output destination (e.g., a file)

         DO:
             Read, decode, and output data from FILEHANDLE
         UNTIL (line is OUTER_DELIM or OUTER_CLOSE) OR we hit EOF.
         LET STATE = "EOF", "DELIM", or "CLOSE" accordingly.

     ENDIF

     RETURN (ENTITY, STATE).
END
```

For reasons discussed in MIME::Entity, we can't just discard the "discard text": some mailers actually put data in the preamble.

Questionable Practices

Multipart messages are always read line-by-line

Multipart document parts are read line-by-line, so that the encapsulation boundaries may easily be detected. However, bad MIME composition agents (for example, naive CGI scripts) might return multipart documents where the parts are, say, unencoded bitmap files... and, consequently, where such "lines" might be very long indeed.

A better solution for this case would be to set up some form of state machine for input processing. This will be left for future versions.

Multipart parts read into temp files before decoding

In my original implementation, the MIME::Decoder classes had to be aware of encapsulation boundaries in multipart MIME documents. While this decode-while-parsing approach obviated the need for temporary files, it resulted in inflexible and complex decoder implementations.

The revised implementation uses a temporary file (á la `tmpfile()`) during parsing to hold the *encoded* portion of the current MIME document or part. This file is deleted automatically after the current part is decoded and the data is written to the "body stream" object; you'll never see it, and should never need to worry about it.

Some folks have asked for the ability to bypass this temp-file mechanism, I suppose because they assume it would slow down their application. I considered accommodating this wish, but the temp-file approach solves a lot of thorny problems in parsing, and it also protects against hidden bugs in user applications (what if you've directed the encoded part into a scalar, and someone unexpectedly sends you a 6 MB tar file?). Finally, I'm just not convinced that the temp-file use adds significant overhead.

Fuzzing of CRLF and newline on input

RFC 1521 dictates that MIME streams have lines terminated by CRLF (\r\n). However, it is extremely likely that folks will want to parse MIME streams where each line ends in the local newline character \n instead.

An attempt has been made to allow the parser to handle both CRLF and newline-terminated input.

Fuzzing of CRLF and newline on output

The 7bit and 8bit decoders will decode both a \n and a \r\n end-of-line sequence into a \n.

The `binary` decoder (default if no encoding specified) still outputs stuff verbatim... so a MIME message with CRLFs and no explicit encoding will be output as a text file that, on many systems, will have an annoying ^M at the end of each line... *but this is as it should be.*

Inability to handle multipart boundaries that contain newlines

First, let's get something straight: *this is an evil, EVIL practice,* and is incompatible with RFC-1521... hence, it's not valid MIME.

If your mailer creates multipart boundary strings that contain newlines *when they appear in the message body,* give it two weeks notice and find another one. If your mail robot receives MIME mail like this, regard it as syntactically incorrect MIME, which it is.

Why do I say that? Well, in RFC 1521, the syntax of a boundary is given quite clearly:

```
boundary := 0*69<bchars> bcharsnospace

bchars := bcharsnospace / " "

bcharsnospace :=    DIGIT / ALPHA / "'" / "(" / ")" / "+" /"_"
                 / "," / "-" / "." / "/" / ":" / "=" / "?"
```

All of which means that a valid boundary string cannot have newlines in it, and any newlines in such a string in the message header are expected to be solely the result of folding the string (i.e., inserting to-be-removed newlines for readability and line-shortening only).

Yet, there is at least one brain-damaged user agent out there that composes mail like this:

```
MIME-Version: 1.0
Content-type: multipart/mixed; boundary="----ABC-
 123----"
Subject: Hi... I'm a dork!

This is a multipart MIME message (yeah, right...)

----ABC-
 123----

Hi there!
```

We have *got* to discourage practices like this (and the recent file upload idiocy where binary files that are part of a multipart MIME message aren't base64-encoded) if we want MIME to stay relatively simple, and MIME parsers to be relatively robust.

Thanks to Andreas Koenig for bringing a bad user agent to my attention.

Warnings

New, untested `binmode()` calls were added in module version 1.11 . . . if `binmode()` is *not* a NOOP on your system, please pay careful attention to your output, and report *any* anomalies. *It is possible that "make test" will fail on such systems,* since some of the tests involve checking the sizes of the output files. That doesn't necessarily indicate a problem.

If anyone wants to test out this package's handling of both binary and textual email on a system where `binmode()` is not a NOOP, I would be most grateful. If stuff breaks, send me the pieces (including the original email that broke it, and at the very least a description of how the output was screwed up).

Author

Eryq, *eryq@rhine.gsfc.nasa.gov*

Copyright

Copyright © 1996 by Eryq.

MIME::ToolUtils — MIME-tools kit configuration and utilities

Description

A catch-all place for miscellaneous global information related to the configuration of the MIME-tools kit.

Since most of the MIME-tools modules "use" it by name, this module is really not subclassable.

Public Interface

`config [VARIABLE, [VALUE]]`

> *Class method.* Set/get a configuration variable:
>
> ```
> # Get current debugging flag:
> $current = config MIME::ToolUtils 'DEBUGGING';
>
>
> # Invert it:
> config MIME::ToolUtils DEBUGGING => !$current;
> ```
>
> *Note:* As you can see, I like the "arrow" syntax when setting values.
>
> The complete list of configuration variables is listed below. They are all-upper-case, possibly with underscores. To get a list of all valid config variables in your program, and output their current values, you can say:
>
> ```
> foreach $var (sort (config MIME::ToolUtils)) {
>     print "MIME config $var = ", (config MIME::ToolUtils $var),
>         "\n";
> }
> ```
>
> Note that some of these variables may have nice printed representations, while others may not.
>
> Rationale: I wanted access to the configuration to be done via some kind of controllable public interface, in case "setting a config variable" involved making a subroutine call. This approach is an attempt to do so while preventing an explosion of lots of little methods, many of which will do nothing more than set an entry in the internal %CONFIG hash. I suppose a tied hash would have been slicker.

Configuration Variables

You may set/get all of these via the `config` method.

AUTO_SYNC_HEADERS

> When printing out a MIME entity, you may find it desirable to always output a Content-Length header (even though this is a non-standard MIME header). If you set this configuration option true (the default is false), the toolkit will attempt to precompute the Content-Length of all singleparts in your message, and set the headers appropriately. Otherwise, it will leave the headers alone.
>
> You should be aware that auto-synching the headers can slow down the printing of messages.

DEBUGGING

> Value should be a Boolean: true to turn debugging on, false to turn it off.

EMULATE_TMPFILE

> Determines how to patch a Perl 5.002 bug in `FileHandle::new_tmpfile`, and get a FileHandle object which really *will* be destroyed when it goes out of scope. Possible values are:

> **OPENDUP**
>
> > Always emulate `FileHandle->new_tmpfile`, using an `fd`-opened duplicate file handle. Pretty ugly (two additional file handles sharing the same descriptor are briefly open at one point, though both are closed before the

new tmpfile object is returned): however, it's probably quite portable since it (a) doesn't require POSIX, and (b) doesn't make assumptions as to the underlying implementation of FileHandle objects.

UNLINK

Always emulate `FileHandle->new_tmpfile`, using `tmpnam()` plus `unlink()`. Probably only works on UNIX-like systems, but is very straightforward. Depends on `POSIX::tmpnam()` and on the `autodelete-on-unlink` behavior.

NO

No emulation: always just use `FileHandle->new_tmpfile` to get tmpfile handles.

(a subroutine reference)

Use the given subroutine, with no arguments, to return a `tmpfile`.

If any of the named emulation options ends with ! (e.g., "UNLINK!"), then the package will *always* emulate that way. Otherwise, it will try to make a reasonable guess as to whether emulation is necessary, based on your version of Perl.

The default setting (if you never invoke this method) is OPENDUP.

EMULATE_VERSION

Emulate the behavior of a previous version of the MIME-tools kit (a.k.a. the MIME-parser kit in its version 1.x incarnations). This will *not* turn off warnings about deprecated usage (that would impede progress), but it *will* patch things like the `get()` method of MIME::Head:

```
config MIME::ToolUtils EMULATE_VERSION => 1.0;
```

The value should be '1' or '1.0'. To reliably turn off emulation, set it to **undef**.

VERSION

Read-only. The version of the *toolkit*.

```
config MIME::ToolUtils VERSION => 1.0;
```

Please notice that as of 3.x, this *happens* to be the same as the `$MIME::ToolUtils::VERSION`; however, this was not always the case, and someday may not be the case again.

Author

Eryq, *eryq@rhine.gsfc.nasa.gov*

Copyright

Copyright © 1996 by Eryq

Netscape::Cache—object class for accessing Netscape cache files

Synopsis

The object-oriented interface:

```
use Netscape::Cache;
$cache = new Netscape::Cache;
```

```
   while (defined($url = $cache->next_url)) {
      print $url, "\n";
   }
   while (defined($o = $cache->next_object)) {
      print
         $o->{'URL'}, "\n",
         $o->{'CACHEFILE'}, "\n",
         $o->{'LAST_MODIFIED'}, "\n",
         $o->{'MIME_TYPE'}, "\n";
   }
```

The TIEHASH interface:

```
   use Netscape::Cache;
   tie %cache, 'Netscape::Cache';
   foreach (sort keys %cache) {
      print $cache{$_}->{URL}, "\n";
   }
```

Description

The Netscape::Cache module implements an object class for accessing the filenames and URLs of the cache files used by the Netscape Web browser. You can access the cached URLs offline via Netscape if you set Options ▶ Network Preferences ▶ Verify Document to **Never**.

Constructor

The following creates a new instance of the Netscape::Cache object class. The `-cachedir` argument is optional. By default, the cache directory setting is retrieved from *~/.netscape/preferences*.

```
   $cache = new Netscape::Cache(-cachedir =>
   "$ENV{HOME}/.netscape/cache");
```

If the Netscape cache index file does not exist, a warning message will be generated, and the constructor will return **undef**.

Methods

The Netscape::Cache class implements the following methods:

next_url
> This method returns the next URL from the cache index. Unlike Netscape::History, this method returns a string and not an URI::URL-like object.
>
> This method is faster than **next_object**, since it does only evaluate the URL of the cached file.
>
> ```
>    $url = $history->next_url;
> ```

next_object
> This method returns the next URL from the cache index as a Netscape::Cache::Object object. See below for accessing the components (cache filename, content length, mime type, and more) of this object.
>
> ```
>    $cache->next_object;
> ```

get_object
> This method returns the Netscape::Cache::Object object for a given URL. If the URL does not live in the cache index, then the returned value will be undefined.
>
> ```
>    $cache->get_object;
> ```

delete_object

Deletes URL from cache index and the related file from the cache.

Warning

Do not use delete_object while in a next_object loop! It is better to collect all objects for delete in a list and do the deletion after the loop, otherwise you can get strange behavior (e.g., malloc panics).

rewind

This method is used to move the internal pointer of the cache index to the first URL in the cache index. You don't need to bother with this if you have just created the object, but it doesn't harm anything if you do.

```
$cache->rewind();
```

Netscape::Cache::Object

next_object and get_object return an object of the class Netscape::Cache::Object. This object is simply a hash, from which members have to be accessed directly (no methods).

An example:

```
$o = $cache->next_object;
print $o->{'URL'}, "\n";
```

URL

The URL of the cached object

CACHEFILE

The filename of the cached URL in the cache directory. To construct the full path use ($cache is a Netscape::Cache object and $o a Netscape::Cache::Object object):

```
$cache->{'CACHEDIR'} . "/" . $o->{'CACHEFILE'}
```

CACHEFILE_SIZE

The size of the cache file.

CONTENT_LENGTH

The length of the cache file as specified in the HTTP response header. In general, SIZE and CONTENT_LENGTH are equal. If you interrupt a transfer of a file, only the first part of the file is written to the cache, resulting in a smaller CONTENT_ LENGTH than SIZE.

LAST_MODIFIED

The date of last modification of the URL as UNIX time (seconds since epoch). Use:

```
scalar localtime $o->{'LAST_MODIFIED'}
```

to get a human-readable date.

LAST_VISITED

The date of last visit.

EXPIRE_DATE

If defined, the date of expiry for the URL.

MIME_TYPE

The MIME type of the URL (e.g., text/html or image/jpeg).

ENCODING

The encoding of the URL (e.g,. x-gzip for gzipped data).

CHARSET
>   The charset of the URL (e.g., iso-8859-1).

Notes

You can also use the undocumented pseudo-URLs about:cache, about:memory-cache and about:global-history to access your cache, memory cache, and history.

There is also an interface for using tied hashes.

Environment

The Netscape::Cache module examines the following environment variable:

HOME
>   Home directory of the user, used to find Netscape's preferences (*$HOME/.netscape*). Otherwise, if not set, retrieve the home directory from the *passwd* file.

Example

This program loops through all cache objects and prints a HTML-ified list. The list is sorted by URL, but you can sort it by last visit date or size, too.

```
use Netscape::Cache;
$cache = new Netscape::Cache;
while ($o = $cache->next_object) {
    push(@url, $o);
}
# sort by name
@url = sort {$a->{'URL'} cmp $b->{'URL'}} @url;
# sort by visit time
#@url = sort {$b->{'LAST_VISITED'} <=> $a->{'LAST_VISITED'}} @url;
# sort by mime type
#@url = sort {$a->{'MIME_TYPE'} cmp $b->{'MIME_TYPE'}} @url;
# sort by size
#@url = sort {$b->{'CACHEFILE_SIZE'} <=> $a->{'CACHEFILE_SIZE'}} @url;
print "<ul>\n";
foreach (@url) {
    print
        "<li><a href=\"file:",
        $cache->{'CACHEDIR'}, "/", $_->{'CACHEFILE'}, "\">",
        $_->{'URL'}, "</a> ",
        scalar localtime $_->{'LAST_VISITED'}, "<br>",
        "type: ", $_->{'MIME_TYPE'},
        ",size: ", $_->{'CACHEFILE_SIZE'}, "\n";
}
print "</ul>\n";
```

Bugs

There are still some unknown fields (_XXX_FLAG_{1,2,3}).

You can't use delete_object while looping with next_object. See the question "What happens if I add or remove keys from a hash while iterating over it?" in *perlfaq4*.

keys() or each() on the tied hash are slower than the object oriented equivalents next_object or next_url.

See Also

Netscape::History

Author

Slaven Rezic, *eserte@cs.tu-berlin.de*

Thanks to: Fernando Santagata, *lac0658@iperbole.bologna.it*

Copyright

Copyright © 1997 Slaven Rezic. All rights reserved. This module is free software; you can redistribute it and/or modify it under the same terms as Perl itself.

Netscape::History—object class for accessing Netscape history database

Synopsis

```
use Netscape::History;

$history = new Netscape::History();
while (defined($url = $history->next_url() ))
{
}
```

Description

The Netscape::History module implements an object class for accessing the history database maintained by the Netscape web browser. The history database keeps a list of all URLs you have visited, and is used by Netscape to change the color of URLs which you have previously visited, for example.

Constructor

```
$history = new Netscape::History();
```

This creates a new instance of the Netscape::History object class. You can optionally pass the path to the history database as an argument to the constructor, as in:

```
$history = new Netscape::History('/home/bob/.netscape/history.db');
```

If you do not specify the file, then the constructor will use:

```
$HOME/.netscape/history.db
```

If the Netscape history database does not exist, a warning message will be generated, and the constructor will return **undef**.

Methods

The Netscape::History class implements the following methods:

next_url

Get the next URL from your history database.

```
$url = $history->next_url();
```

This method returns the next URL from your history database. If you want to process all URLs in the database, you should call the **rewind** method before looping over all URLs.

The URL returned is an instance of the Netscape::HistoryURL class, which works just like an instance of URI::URL, but provides an extra method **visit_time()**. This returns the time of your last visit to that URL.

delete_url

Remove a URL from the history database.

```
$history->delete_url($url);
```

This method is used to remove a URL from your history database. The URL passed can be a simple text string with the URL, or an instance of Netscape::HistoryURL, URI::URL, or any other class which can be rendered into a string.

rewind

Reset internal URL pointer to first URL in history.

```
$history->rewind();
```

This method is used to move the history database's internal pointer to the first URL in your history database. You don't need to bother with this if you have just created the object, but it doesn't harm anything if you do.

close

Close the history database.

```
$history->close();
```

This closes the history database. The destructor will do this automatically for you, so most of time you don't actually have to bother calling this method explicitly. Good programming style says you should though :-)

Example

The following example illustrates use of this module, and the **visit_time()** method of the URLs returned. The program will list all URLs visited, along with visit time. The Date::Format module is used to format the visit time.

```
#!/usr/bin/perl -w

use Netscape::History;
use Date::Format;
use strict;

my $history;
my $url;

$history = new Netscape::History;
while (defined($url = $history->next_url() ))
{
    print "$url : ", ctime($url->visit_time());
}
$history->close();
```

Author

Neil Bowers, *neilb@cre.canon.co.uk*, and Richard Taylor, *rit@cre.canon.co.uk*

Copyright

See Also

Netscape::HistoryURL

When you call the **next_url** method, you are returned instances of this class.

URI::URL

The underlying class for Netscape::HistoryURL, which provides the mechanisms for manipulating URLs.

Date::Format

Functions for formatting time and date in strings.

Netscape::HistoryURL—subclass of URI::URL which provides visit time

Synopsis

```
use Netscape::HistoryURL;

$url = new Netscape::HistoryURL('http://foobar.com/', $time);
```

Description

The Netscape::HistoryURL module subclasses URI::URL to provide a URL class with a method for accessing visit time.

Constructor

```
$object = new Netscape::HistoryURL( URL, TIME );
```

This creates a new instance of the Netscape::HistoryURL object class. This supports all the methods supported by the URI::URL class. Please see the documentation for that module.

The first argument passed is a string which contains a valid URL. The second argument is the time of visit, in seconds since the last epoch.

Method

The Netscape::HistoryURL class implements the following methods:

visit_time

Return the time of last visit to this URL.

```
$time = $url->visit_time();
```

This method returns the time you last visited the URL, in seconds since the last epoch. This can then be used with any of the standard routines for formatting as a string. The following example uses **ctime()**, from the Date::Format module:

```
print "Time of last visit for $url : ",
        ctime($url->visit_time);
```

In addition, all the methods of the URI::URL class are supported. See the documentation for that module.

Author

Neil Bowers, *neilb@cre.canon.co.uk*

Copyright

Copyright © 1997 Canon Research Centre Europe. All rights reserved. This module is free software; you can redistribute it and/or modify it under the same terms as Perl itself.

See Also

Netscape::History
  An object class for accessing the Netscape history database

URI::URL
  Base-class, which provides heaps of functionality

time2str, str2time—date conversion routines

Synopsis

```
use HTTP::Date;
$stringGMT = time2str(time);   # Format as GMT ASCII time
$time = str2time($stringGMT);  # convert ASCII date to machine time
```

Description

This module provides two functions that deal with the HTTP date format.

Functions

time2str([*$time*])

  The `time2str()` function converts a machine time (seconds since epoch) to a string. If the function is called without an argument, it will use the current time.

  The string returned is in the format defined by the HTTP/1.0 specification. This is a fixed length subset of the format defined by RFC 1123, represented in Universal Time (GMT). An example of this format is:

```
Thu, 03 Feb 1994 17:09:00 GMT
```

str2time(*$str* [, *$zone*])

  The `str2time()` function converts a string to machine time. It returns **undef** if the format is unrecognized, or the year is not between 1970 and 2038. The function is able to parse the following formats:

"Wed, 09 Feb 1994 22:23:32 GMT"	HTTP format
"Thu Feb 3 17:03:55 GMT 1994"	`ctime(3)` format
"Thu Feb 3 00:00:00 1994"	ANSI C `asctime()` format
"Tuesday, 08-Feb-94 14:15:29 GMT"	Old RFC850 HTTP format
"Tuesday, 08-Feb-1994 14:15:29 GMT"	Broken RFC850 HTTP format
"03/Feb/1994:17:03:55 -0700"	Common logfile format
"09 Feb 1994 22:23:32 GMT"	HTTP format (no weekday)
"08-Feb-94 14:15:29 GMT"	RFC850 format (no weekday)
"08-Feb-1994 14:15:29 GMT"	Broken RFC850 format (no weekday)
"1994-02-03 14:15:29 -0100"	ISO 8601 format
"1994-02-03 14:15:29"	Zone is optional

"1994-02-03"	Only date
"1994-02-03T14:15:29"	Use T as separator
"19940203T141529Z"	ISO 8601 compact format
"19940203"	Only date
"08-Feb-94"	Old RFC850 HTTP format (no weekday, no time)
"08-Feb-1994"	Broken RFC850 HTTP format (no weekday, no time)
"09 Feb 1994"	Proposed new HTTP format (no weekday, no time)
"03/Feb/1994"	Common logfile format (no time, no offset)
"Feb 3 1994"	UNIX `ls -l` format
"Feb 3 17:03"	UNIX `ls -l` format
"11-15-96 03:52PM"	Windows `dir` format

The parser ignores leading and trailing whitespace. It also allows the seconds to be missing and the month to be numerical in most formats.

The `str2time()` function takes an optional second argument that specifies the default time zone to use when converting the date. This zone specification should be numerical (like "-0800" or "+0100") or "GMT". This parameter is ignored if the zone is specified in the date string itself. It this parameter is missing, and the date string format does not contain any zone specification then the local time zone is assumed.

If the year is missing, then we assume that the date is the first matching date *before* current time.

Bugs

Non-numerical time zones (like MET, PST) are all treated like GMT. Do not use them. HTTP does not use them.

The `str2time()` function has been told how to parse far too many formats. This makes the module name misleading. To be sure it is really misleading you can also import the `time2iso()` and `time2isoz()` functions. They work like `time2str()` but produce ISO-8601 formatted strings (YYYY-MM-DD hh:mm:ss).

Author

Gisle Aas, *aas@sn.no*

Copyright

Copyright © 1995–1997, Gisle Aas

This library is free software; you can redistribute it and/or modify it under the same terms as Perl itself.

URI::URL—Uniform Resource Locators (absolute and relative)

Synopsis

```
use URI::URL;
# Constructors
$url1 = new URI::URL 'http://www.perl.com/%7Euser/gisle.gif';
$url2 = new URI::URL 'gisle.gif', 'http://www.com/%7Euser';
$url3 = url 'http://www.sn.no/'; # handy constructor
$url4 = $url2->abs;           # get absolute url using base
$url5 = $url2->abs('http:/other/path');
$url6 = newlocal URI::URL 'test';
# Stringify URL
$str1 = $url->as_string;  # complete escaped URL string
$str2 = $url->full_path;  # escaped path+params+query
$str3 = "$url";           # use operator overloading
# Retrieving Generic-RL components:
$scheme   = $url->scheme;
$netloc   = $url->netloc; # see user,password,host,port below
$path     = $url->path;
$params   = $url->params;
$query    = $url->query;
$frag     = $url->frag;
# Accessing elements in their escaped form
$path     = $url->epath;
$params   = $url->eparams;
$query    = $url->equery;
# Retrieving Network location (netloc) components:
$user     = $url->user;
$password = $url->password;
$host     = $url->host;
$port     = $url->port;   # returns default if not defined
# Retrieve escaped path components as an array
@path     = $url->path_components;
# HTTP query-string access methods
@keywords = $url->keywords;
@form     = $url->query_form;
# All methods above can set the field values, e.g:
$url->scheme('http');
$url->host('www.w3.org');
$url->port($url->default_port);
$url->base($url5);                        # use string or object
$url->keywords(qw(dog bones));
# File methods
$url = new URI::URL "file:/foo/bar";
open(F, $url->local_path) or die;
# Compare URLs
if ($url->eq("http://www.sn.no")) or die;
```

Description

This module implements the URI::URL class representing Uniform Resource Locators (URL). URLs provide a compact string representation for resources available via the Internet. Both absolute (RFC 1738) and relative (RFC 1808) URLs are supported.

URI::URL objects are created by calling `new()`, which takes as argument a string representation of the URL or an existing URL object reference to be cloned. Specific individual elements can then be accessed via the `scheme()`, `user()`, `password()`, `host()`, `port()`, `path()`, `params()`, `query()`, and `frag()` methods. In addition escaped versions of the path, params and query can be accessed with the `epath()`, `eparams()`, and `equery()` methods. Note that some URL schemes will support all these methods.

The object constructor `new()` must be able to determine the scheme for the URL. If a scheme is not specified in the URL itself, it will use the scheme specified by the base URL. If no base URL scheme is defined then `new()` will croak if `URI::URL::strict(1)` has been invoked, otherwise `http` is silently assumed. Once the scheme has been determined `new()` then uses the `implementor()` function to determine which class implements that scheme. If no implementor class is defined for the scheme then `new()` will croak if URI::URL::strict(1) has been invoked, otherwise the internal generic URL class is assumed.

Internally defined schemes are implemented by the URI::URL::*scheme_name* module. The `URI::URL::implementor()` function can be used to explicitly set the class used to implement a scheme if you want to override this.

How and When to Escape

This is an edited extract from a URI specification:

> The printability requirement has been met by specifying a safe set of characters, and a general escaping scheme for encoding "unsafe" characters. This "safe" set is suitable, for example, for use in electronic mail. This is the canonical form of a URI.

There is a conflict between the need to be able to represent many characters including spaces within a URI directly, and the need to be able to use a URI in environments which have limited character sets or in which certain characters are prone to corruption. This conflict has been resolved by use of an hexadecimal escaping method which may be applied to any characters forbidden in a given context. When URLs are moved between contexts, the set of characters escaped may be enlarged or reduced unambiguously. The canonical form for URIs has all white spaces encoded.

Notes

A URL string *must*, by definition, consist of escaped components. Complete URLs are always escaped.

The components of a URL string must be *individually* escaped. Each component of a URL may have a separate requirements regarding what must be escaped, and those requirements are also dependent on the URL scheme.

Never escape an already escaped component string.

This implementation expects an escaped URL string to be passed to `new()` and will return a fully escaped URL string from `as_string()` and `full_path()`.

Individual components can be manipulated in unescaped or escaped form. The following methods return/accept unescaped strings:

scheme	path
user	params
password	query

```
host                    frag
port
```

The following methods return/accept partially escaped strings:

```
netloc                  eparams
epath                   equery
```

Partially escaped means that only reserved characters (i.e. :, @, /, ;, ?, =, & in addition to %, ., and #) needs to be escaped when they are to be treated as normal characters. *Fully escaped* means that all unsafe characters are escaped. Unsafe characters are all control characters (%00-%1F and %7F), all 8-bit characters (%80-%FF) as well as {, }, |, \, ^, [,], ', ", <, and >. Note that the character ~ is *not* considered unsafe by this library as it is common practice to use it to reference personal home pages, but it is still unsafe according to RFC 1738.

Adding New URL Schemes

New URL schemes or alternative implementations for existing schemes can be added to your own code. To create a new scheme class use code like:

```
package MYURL::foo;
@ISA = (URI::URL::implementor());   # inherit from generic scheme
```

The URI::URL::implementor() function call with no parameters returns the name of the class which implements the generic URL scheme behavior (typically URI::URL::_generic). All hierarchical schemes should be derived from this class.

Your class can then define overriding methods (e.g., new(), _parse() as required).

To register your new class as the implementor for a specific scheme, use code like:

```
URI::URL::implementor('x-foo', 'MYURL::foo');
```

Any new URL created for scheme x-foo will be implemented by your MYURL::foo class. Existing URLs will not be affected.

Functions

new URI::URL $url_string [, $base_url]

> This is the object constructor. It will create a new URI::URL object, initialized from the URL string. To trap bad or unknown URL schemes use:
>
> ```
> $obj = eval { new URI::URL "snews:comp.lang.perl.misc" };
> ```
>
> or set URI::URL::strict(0) if you do not care about bad or unknown schemes.

newlocal URI::URL $path;

> Returns an URL object that denotes a path within the local filesystem. Paths not starting with / are interpreted relative to the current working directory. This constructor always return an absolute "file" URL.

url($url_string, [, $base_url])

> Alternative constructor function. The url() function is exported by the URI::URL module and is easier both to type and read than calling URI::URL->new directly. Useful for constructs like this:
>
> ```
> $h = url($str)->host;
> ```
>
> This function is just a wrapper for URI::URL->new.

`URI::URL::strict(`*`$bool`*`)`

If strict is true then we croak on errors. The function returns the previous value.

`URI::URL::implementor([`*`$scheme,`* `[`*`$class`*`]])`

Use this function to get or set implementor class for a scheme. Returns '' if specified scheme is not supported. Returns generic URL class if no scheme specified.

Methods

This section describes the methods available for an URI::URL object. Note that some URL schemes will disallow some of these methods and will croak if they are used. Some URL schemes add additional methods that are described in the sections to follow.

Attribute access methods marked with * can take an optional argument to set the value of the attribute, and they always return the old value.

`$url->abs([`*`$base,`* `[`*`$allow_scheme_in_relative_urls`*`]])`

The `abs()` method attempts to return a new absolute URI::URL object for a given URL. In order to convert a relative URL into an absolute one, a *base* URL is required. You can associate a default base with a URL either by passing a *base* to the `new()` constructor when a URI::URL is created or using the `base()` method on the object later. Alternatively you can specify a one-off base as a parameter to the `abs()` method.

Some older parsers used to allow the scheme name to be present in the relative URL if it was the same as the base URL scheme. RFC 1808 says that this should be avoided, but you can enable this old behavior by passing a **true** value as the second argument to the `abs()` method. The difference is demonstrated by the following examples:

```
url("http:foo")->abs("http://host/a/b")     ==>   "http:foo"
url("http:foo")->abs("http://host/a/b", 1)  ==>
"http:/host/a/foo"
```

The `rel()` method will do the opposite transformation.

`$url->as_string`

Returns a string representing the URL in its canonical form. All unsafe characters will be escaped. This method is overloaded as the Perl "stringify" operator, which means that URLs can be used as strings in many contexts.

`$url->base (*)`

Get/set the base URL associated with the current URI::URL object. The base URL matters when you call the `abs()` method.

`$url->clone`

Returns a copy of the current URI::URL object.

`$url->crack`

Return a nine element array with the following content:

```
0: $url->scheme (*)
1: $url->user
2: $url->password
3: $url->host
4: $url->port
5: $url->epath
6: $url->eparams
7: $url->equery
8: $url->frag
```

All elements except scheme will be undefined if the corresponding URL part is not available.

Note: The scheme (first element) returned by crack will always be defined. This is different from what the $url->scheme returns, since it will return undef for relative URLs.

$url->default_port

Returns the default port number for the URL scheme that the URI::URL belongs to.

$url->eparams (*)

Get/set the URL parameters in escaped form.

$url->epath (*)

Get/set the URL path in escaped form.

$url->eq($other_url)

Compare two URLs to decide if they match or not. The rules for how comparison is made varies for different parts of the URLs; scheme and netloc comparison is case-insensitive, and escaped chars match their %XX encoding unless they are "reserved" or "unsafe".

$url->equery (*)

Get/set the URL query string in escaped form.

$url->full_path

Returns the string /path;params?query. This is the string that is passed to a remote server in order to access the document.

$url->frag (*)

Get/set the fragment (unescaped).

$url->host (*)

Get/set the host (unescaped).

$url->netloc (*)

Get/set the network location in escaped form. Setting the network location will affect user, password, host, and port.

$url->params (*)

Get/set the URL parameters (unescaped)

$url->password (*)

Get/set the password (unescaped)

$url->path (*)

Get/set the path (unescaped). This method will croak if any of the path components in the return value contain the / character. You should use the epath() method to be safe.

$url->path_components (*)

Get/set the path using a list of unescaped path components. The return value will lose the distinction between "." and %2E. When setting a value, a "." is converted to be a literal "." and is therefore encoded as %2E.

$url->port (*)

Get/set the network port (unescaped).

$url->rel([$base])

Return a relative URL if possible. This is the opposite of what the abs() method does. For instance:

```
url("http://www.math.uio.no/doc/mail/top.html",
    "http://www.math.uio.no/doc/linux/")->rel
```

will return a relative URL with path set to *../mail/top.html* and with the same base as the original URL.

If the original URL already is relative or the scheme or `netloc` does not match the base, then a copy of the original URL is returned.

$url->print_on(*FILEHANDLE);

Prints a verbose presentation of the contents of the URL object to the specified file handle (default STDOUT). Mainly useful for debugging.

$url->scheme (*)

Get/set the scheme for the URL.

$url->query (*)

Get/set the query string (unescaped). This method will croak if the string returned contains both + and %2B or = together with %3D or %26. You should use the `equery()` method to be safe.

$url->user (*)

Get/set the URL username (unescaped).

HTTP Methods

For `http` URLs you may also access the query string using the `keywords()` and the `query_form()` methods. Both will croak if the query is not of the correct format. The encodings look like this:

```
word1+word2+word3..        # keywords
key1=val1&key2=val2...     # query_form
```

Note: These functions does not return the old value when they are used to set a value of the query string.

$url->keywords (*)

The `keywords()` method returns a list of unescaped strings. The method can also be used to set the query string by passing in the keywords as individual arguments to the method.

$url->query_form (*)

The `query_form()` method return a list of unescaped key/value pairs. If you assign the return value to a hash you might loose some values if the key is repeated (which it is allowed to do).

This method can also be used to set the query string of the URL like this:

```
$url->query_form(foo => 'bar', foo => 'baz', equal => '=');
```

If the value part of a key/value pair is a reference to an array, then it will be converted to separate key/value pairs for each value. This means that these two calls are equal:

```
$url->query_form(foo => 'bar', foo => 'baz');
$url->query_form(foo => ['bar', 'baz']);
```

File Methods

The `file` URLs implement the `local_path()` method that returns a path suitable for access to files within the current filesystem. These methods cannot be used to set the path of the URL.

`$url->local_path`
> This method is really just an alias for one of the methods below depending on what system you run on.

`$url->unix_path`
> Returns a path suitable for use on a UNIX system. This method will croak if any of the path segments contains a "/" or a NULL character.

`$url->dos_path`
> Returns a path suitable for use on a MS-DOS or MS Windows system.

`$url->mac_path`
> Returns a path suitable for use on a Macintosh system.

`$url->vms_path`
> Returns a path suitable for use on a VMS system. (VMS is a trademark of Digital.)

Gopher Methods

The methods access the parts that are specific for the gopher URLs. These methods access different parts of the `$url->path`.

```
$url->gtype (*)
$url->selector (*)
$url->search (*)
$url->string (*)
```

News Methods

```
$url->group (*)
$url->article (*)
```

WAIS Methods

The methods access the parts that are specific for the WAIS URLs. These methods access different parts of the `$url->path`.

```
$url->database (*)
$url->wtype (*)
$url->wpath (*)
```

Mailto Methods

```
$url->address (*)
```

The mail address can also be accessed with the `netloc()` method.

What a URL Is Not

URL objects do not, and should not, know how to **get** or **put** the resources they specify locations for, anymore than a postal address **knows** anything about the postal system. The actual access/transfer should be achieved by some form of transport agent class (see LWP::UserAgent). The agent class can use the URL class, but should not be a subclass of it.

Compatibility

This is a listing incompatibilities with URI::URL version 3.x:

`unsafe()`, `escape()`, and `unescape()`
> These methods are not supported anymore.

`full_path()` and `as_string()`

These methods no longer take a second argument which specify the set of characters to consider as unsafe.

+ in the query-string

The + character in the query part of the URL was earlier considered to be an encoding of a space. This was just a bad influence from Mosaic. The space character is now encoded as %20.

`path()` and `query()`

These methods will croak if they lose information. Use `epath()` or `equery()` instead. The `path()` method will (for instance) lose information if any path segment contain an (encoded) / character.

The `path()` method now considers a leading / to be part of the path. If the path is empty it will default to /. You can get the old behavior by setting $URI::URL::COMPAT_VER_3 to TRUE before accessing the `path()` method.

`netloc()`

The string passed to `netloc` is now assumed to be escaped. The string returned will also be (partially) escaped.

subclassing

The path, params, and query are now stored internally in unescaped form. This might affect subclasses of the URL scheme classes.

Acknowledgments

This module is (distantly) based on the *wwwurl.pl* code in the *libwww-perl* distribution developed by Roy Fielding (*fielding@ics.uci.edu*), as part of the Arcadia project at the University of California, Irvine, with contributions from Brooks Cutter.

Authors

Gisle Aas (*aas@sn.no*), Tim Bunce (*Tim.Bunce@ig.co.uk*), Roy Fielding (*fielding@ics.uci.edu*), and Martijn Koster (*m.koster@webcrawler.com*) (in English alphabetical order) have collaborated on the complete rewrite for Perl5, with input from other people on the libwww-perl mailing list.

If you have any suggestions, bug reports, fixes, or enhancements, send them to the libwww-perl mailing list at *libwww-perl@ics.uci.edu*.

Copyright

Copyright © 1995–1996 Gisle Aas. Copyright © 1995 Martijn Koster.

This program is free software; you can redistribute it and/or modify it under the same terms as Perl itself.

---

uri_escape, uri_unescape—escape/unescape unsafe characters

Synopsis

```
use URI::Escape;
$safe = uri_escape("10% is enough\n");
$verysafe = uri_escape("foo", "\0-\377");
$str  = uri_unescape($safe);
```

Description

This module provide functions to escape and unescape URI strings. Some characters are regarded as "unsafe" and must be escaped in accordance with RFC 1738. Escaped characters are represented by a triplet consisting of the character "%" followed by two hexadecimal digits.

The `uri_escape()` function takes an optional second argument that overrides the set of characters that are to be escaped. The set is specified as a string that can be used in a regular expression character class (between [ ]). For example:

```
\x00-\x1f\x7f-\xff        # all control and hi-bit characters
a-z                       # all lower case characters
^A-Za-z                   # everything not a letter
```

The default set of characters to be escaped is:

```
\x00-\x20"#%;<>?{}|\\\\^~'\[\]\x7F-\xFF
```

The module can also export the `%escapes` hash which contains the mapping from all characters to the corresponding escape code.

See Also

URI::URL

WWW::Robot—configurable Web traversal engine (for Web robots and agents)

Synopsis

```
use WWW::Robot;

$robot = new WWW::Robot('NAME'      => 'MyRobot',
                        'VERSION'   => '1.000',
                        'EMAIL'     => 'fred@foobar.com');

# ... configure the robot's operation ...

$robot->run('http://www.foobar.com/');
```

Description

This module implements a configurable Web traversal engine, for a *robot* or other Web agent. Given an initial Web page (URL), the robot will get the contents of that page, and extract all links on the page, adding them to a list of URLs to visit.

Features of the robot module include:

* Follows the *Robot Exclusion Protocol.*
* Supports the META element proposed extensions to the Protocol.
* Implements many of the *Guidelines for Robot Writers.*
* Configurable.
* Builds on standard Perl5 modules for WWW, HTTP, HTML, etc.

A particular application (robot instance) has to configure the engine using *hooks*, which are Perl functions invoked by the robot engine at specific points in the control loop.

The robot engine obeys the Robot Exclusion Protocol, as well as a proposed addition. See "See Also" for references to documents describing the Robot Exclusion Protocol and Web robots.

Questions

This section contains a number of questions. I'm interested in hearing what people think, and what you've done faced with similar questions.

- What style of API is preferable for setting attributes? For example, using something like the following:

  ```
  $robot->verbose(1);
  $traversal = $robot->traversal();
  ```

  i.e., a method for setting and getting each attribute, depending on whether you passed an argument?

- Should the robot module support a standard logging mechanism? For example, a LOG-FILE attribute, which is set to either a filename, or a file handle reference. This would need a useful file format.

- Should the AGENT be an attribute, so you can set this to whatever UserAgent object you want to use? Then if the attribute is not set by the first time the `run()` method is invoked, we'd fall back on the default.

- Should TMPDIR and WORKFILE be attributes? I don't see any big reason why they should, but someone else's application might benefit.

- Should the module also support an ERRLOG attribute, with all warnings and error messages sent there?

- At the moment the robot will print warnings and error messages to stderr, as well as returning error status. Should this behavior be configurable—that is, include the ability to turn off warnings?

  The basic architecture of the robot is as follows:

  ```
  Hook: restore-state
  Get Next URL
      Hook: invoke-on-all-url
      Hook: follow-url-test
      Hook: invoke-on-follow-url
      Get contents of URL
      Hook: invoke-on-contents
      Skip if not HTML
      Foreach link on page:
          Hook: invoke-on-link
          Add link to robot's queue
  Continue?
  Hook: continue-test
  Hook: save-state
  Hook: generate-report
  ```

  Each of the hook procedures and functions is described below. A robot must provide a `follow-url-test` hook, and at least one of the following:

- `invoke-on-all-url`
- `invoke-on-followed-url`

- invoke-on-contents
- invoke-on-link

Constructor

Create a new robot engine instance. If the constructor fails for any reason, a warning message will be printed, and undef will be returned.

```
$robot = new WWW::Robot( <attribute-value-pairs> );
```

Having created a new robot, it should be configured using the methods described below. Certain attributes of the Robot can be set during creation; they can be (re)set after creation, using the setAttribute() method.

The attributes of the robot are described in the following "Robot Attributes" section.

Methods

run

Invokes the robot, initially traversing the root URLs provided in LIST, and any which have been provided with the addUrl() method before invoking run(). If you have not correctly configured the robot, the method will return undef.

```
$robot->run( LIST );
```

The initial set of URLs can either be passed as arguments to the run() method, or with the addUrl() method before you invoke run(). Each URL can be specified either as a string, or as a URI::URL object.

Before invoking this method, you should have provided at least some of the hook functions. See the example given in the following "Examples" section.

By default the run() method will iterate until there are no more URLs in the queue. You can override this behavior by providing a continue-test hook function, which checks for the termination conditions. This particular hook function, and use of hook functions in general, are described below.

setAttribute

Change the value of one or more robot attributes.

```
$robot->setAttribute( ... attribute-value-pairs ... );
```

Attributes are identified using a string, and take scalar values. For example, to specify the name of your robot, you set the NAME attribute:

```
$robot->setAttribute('NAME' => 'WebStud');
```

The supported attributes for the Robot module are listed in the following "Robot Attributes" section.

getAttribute

Queries a robot for the value of an attribute.

```
$value = $robot->getAttribute('attribute-name');
```

For example, to query the version number of your robot, you would get the VERSION attribute:

```
$version = $robot->getAttribute('VERSION');
```

The supported attributes for the Robot module are listed in the following "Robot Attributes" section.

addUrl

Used to add one or more URLs to the queue for the robot. Each URL can be passed as a simple string, or as a URI::URL object.

```
$robot->addUrl( $url1, ..., $urlN );
```

Returns true (non-zero) if all URLs were successfully added, false (zero) if at least one of the URLs could not be added.

addHook

Register a *hook* function which should be invoked by the robot at a specific point in the control flow. There are a number of *hook points* in the robot, which are identified by a string. For a list of hook points, see the following "Supported Hooks" section.

```
$robot->addHook($hook_name, \&hook_function);

sub hook_function { ... }
```

If you provide more than one function for a particular hook, then the hook functions will be invoked in the order they were added—that is, the first hook function called will be the first hook function you added.

proxy, no_proxy, env_proxy

These are convenience functions are setting proxy information on the User agent being used to make the requests.

```
$robot->proxy(protocol, proxy);
```

Used to specify a proxy for the given scheme. The protocol argument can be a reference to a list of protocols.

```
$robot->no_proxy(domain1, ... domainN);
```

Specifies that proxies should not be used for the specified domains or hosts.

```
$robot->env_proxy();
```

Load proxy settings from protocol_proxy environment variables: ftp_proxy, http_proxy, no_proxy, etc.

Robot Attributes

This section lists the attributes used to configure a robot object. Attributes are set using the setAttribute() method, and queried using the getAttribute() method.

Some of the attributes *must* be set before you start the robot (with the run() method). These are marked as *mandatory* in the following list.

NAME (mandatory)

The name of the robot. This should be a sequence of alphanumeric characters, and is used to identify your robot. This is used to set the User-Agent field of HTTP requests, and so will appear in server logs.

VERSION (mandatory)

The version number of your robot. This should be a floating point number, in the format N.NNN.

EMAIL (mandatory)

A valid email address which can be used to contact the robot's owner, for example by someone who wishes to complain about the behavior of your robot.

VERBOSE

> A Boolean flag which specifies whether the robot should display verbose status information as it runs.
>
> Default: 0 (`false`)

TRAVERSAL

> Specifies what traversal style should be adopted by the robot. Valid values are `depth` and `breadth`.
>
> Default: depth

REQUEST_DELAY

> Specifies whether the delay (in minutes) between successive GETs from the same server.
>
> Default: 1

IGNORE_TEXT

> Specifies whether the HTML structure passed to the *invoke-on-contents* hook function should include the textual content of the page, or just the HTML elements.
>
> Default: 1 (`true`)

Supported Hooks

This section lists the hooks which are supported by the WWW::Robot module. The first two arguments passed to a hook function are always the robot object followed by the name of the hook being invoked—that is, the start of a hook function should look something like:

```
sub my_hook_function
{
    my $robot = shift;
    my $hook  = shift;
    # ... other, hook-specific, arguments
```

Wherever a hook function is passed a $url argument, this will be a URI::URL object, with the URL fully specified. That is, even if the URL was seen in a relative link, it will be passed as an absolute URL.

restore-state

> This hook is invoked just before entering the main iterative loop of the robot. The intention is that the hook will be used to restore state, if such an operation is required.
>
> ```
> sub hook { my($robot, $hook_name) = @_; }
> ```
>
> This can be helpful if the robot is running in an incremental mode, where state is saved between each run of the robot.

invoke-on-all-url

> This hook is invoked on all URLs seen by the robot, regardless of whether the URL is actually traversed. In addition to the standard $robot and $hook arguments, the third argument is $url, which is the URL being traversed by the robot.
>
> ```
> sub hook { my($robot, $hook_name, $url) = @_; }
> ```
>
> For a given URL, the hook function will be invoked at most once, regardless of how many times the URL is seen by the robot. If you are interested in seeing the URL every time, you can use the `invoke-on-link` hook.

follow-url-test

> This hook is invoked to determine whether the robot should traverse the given URL. If the hook function returns 0 (zero), then the robot will do nothing further with the URL. If the hook function returns non-zero, then the robot will get the contents of the URL, invoke further hooks, and extract links if the contents are HTML.
>
> ```
> sub hook { my($robot, $hook_name, $url) = @_; return $boolean;}
> ```

invoke-on-followed-url

> This hook is invoked on URLs which are about to be traversed by the robot, i.e., URLs which have passed the follow-url-test hook.
>
> ```
> sub hook { my($robot, $hook_name, $url) = @_; }
> ```

invoke-on-get-error

> This hook is invoked if the robot ever fails to get the contents of a URL. The *$response* argument is an object of type HTTP::Response.
>
> ```
> sub hook { my($robot, $hook_name, $url, $response) = @_; }
> ```

invoke-on-contents

> This hook function is invoked for all URLs for which the contents are successfully retrieved.
>
> ```
> sub hook { my($robot, $hook, $url, $response, $structure,
>               $filename) = @_; }
> ```
>
> The *$url* argument is a URI::URL object for the URL currently being processed by the robot engine.
>
> The *$response* argument is an HTTP::Response object, the result of the GET request on the URL.
>
> The *$structure* argument is an HTML::Element object which is the root of a tree structure constructed from the contents of the URL. You can set the IGNORE_TEXT attribute to specify whether the structure passed includes the textual content of the page, or just the HTML elements.
>
> The *$filename* argument is the path to a local temporary file which contains a local copy of the URL contents. You cannot assume that the file will exist after control has returned from your hook function.

invoke-on-link

> This hook function is invoked for all links seen as the robot traverses. When the robot is parsing a page (*$from_url*) for links, for every link seen the invoke-on-link hook is invoked with the URL of the source page, and the destination URL. The destination URL is in canonical form.
>
> ```
> sub hook { my($robot, $hook_name, $from_url, $to_url) = @_; }
> ```

continue-test

> This hook is invoked at the end of the robot's main iterative loop. If the hook function returns non-zero, then the robot will continue execution with the next URL. If the hook function returns zero, then the robot will terminate the main loop, and close down after invoking the following two hooks.
>
> ```
> sub hook { my($robot) = @_; }
> ```
>
> If no continue-test hook function is provided, then the robot will always loop.

save-state

This hook is used to save any state information required by the robot application.

```
sub hook { my($robot) = @_; }
```

generate-report

This hook is used to generate a report for the run of the robot, if such is desired.

```
sub hook { my($robot) = @_; }
```

modified-since

If you provide this hook function, it will be invoked for each URL before the robot actually requests it. The function can return a time to use with the If-Modified-Since HTTP header. This can be used by a robot to only process those pages which have changed since the last visit.

Your hook function should be declared as follows:

```
sub modifed_since_hook
{
    my $robot = shift;        # instance of Robot module
    my $hook  = shift;        # name of hook invoked
    my $url   = shift;        # URI::URL for the url in
                              # question

    # ... calculate time ...
    return $time;
}
```

If your function returns anything other than **undef**, then an "If-Modified-Since:" field will be added to the request header.

invoke-after-get

This hook function is invoked immediately after the robot makes each GET request. This means your hook function will see every type of response, not just successful GETs. The hook function is passed two arguments: the *$url* we tried to GET, and the *$response* which resulted.

If you provided the **modified-since** manpage hook, then provide an **invoke-after-get** function, and look for error code 304 (or RC_NOT_MODIFIED if you are using HTTP::Status, which you should be :-):

```
sub after_get_hook
{
    my($robot, $hook, $url, $response) = @_;

    if ($response->code == RC_NOT_MODIFIED)
    {
    }
}
```

Examples

This section illustrates use of the robot module, with code snippets from several sample robot applications. The code here is not intended to show the right way to code a web robot, but just illustrates the API for using the robot.

Validating Robot

This is a simple robot which you could use to validate your Web site. The robot uses `weblint` to check the contents of URLs of type text/html:

```perl
#!/usr/bin/perl
require 5.002;
use WWW::Robot;

$rootDocument = $ARGV[0];

$robot = new WWW::Robot('NAME'    => 'Validator',
                        'VERSION' => 1.000,
                        'EMAIL'   => 'fred@foobar.com');

$robot->addHook('follow-url-test', \&follow_test);
$robot->addHook('invoke-on-contents', \&validate_contents);

$robot->run($rootDocument);

#--------------------------------------------------------
sub follow_test {
    my($robot, $hook, $url) = @_;

    return 0 unless $url->scheme eq 'http';
    return 0 if $url =~ /\.(gif|jpg|png|xbm|au|wav|mpg)$/;

    #---- we're only interested in pages on our site ----
    return $url =~ /^$rootDocument/;
}

#--------------------------------------------------------
sub validate_contents {
    my($robot, $hook, $url, $response, $filename) = @_;

    return unless $response->content_type eq 'text/html';

    print STDERR "\n$url\n";

    #---- run weblint on local copy of URL contents -----
    system("weblint -s $filename");
}
```

If you are behind a firewall, then you will have to add something like the following, just before calling the `run()` method:

```perl
$robot->proxy(['ftp', 'http', 'wais', 'gopher'],
              'http://firewall:8080/');
```

Module Dependencies

The *Robot.pm* module builds on a lot of existing Net, WWW and other Perl modules. Some of the modules are part of the core Perl distribution, and the latest versions of all modules are available from the Comprehensive Perl Archive Network (CPAN). The modules used are:

HTTP::Request
   This module is used to construct HTTP requests, when retrieving the contents of a URL, or using the HEAD request to see if a URL exists.

HTML::Parse

This module builds a tree data structure from the contents of an HTML page. This is used to extract the URLs from the links on a page. This is also used to check for page-specific robot exclusion commands, using the META element.

URI::URL

This module implements a class for URL objects, providing resolution of relative URLs, and access to the different components of a URL.

LWP::RobotUA

This is a wrapper around the LWP::UserAgent class. A *UserAgent* is used to connect to servers over the network, and make requests. The RobotUA module provides transparent compliance with the Robot Exclusion Protocol.

HTTP::Status

This has definitions for HTTP response codes, so you can say RC_NOT_MODIFIED instead of 304.

All of these modules are available as part of the libwww-perl5 distribution, which is also available from CPAN.

Author

Neil Bowers, *neilb@cre.canon.co.uk*

SAS Group, Canon Research Centre Europe

Copyright

Copyright © 1997, Canon Research Centre Europe.

This module is free software; you can redistribute it and/or modify it under the same terms as Perl itself.

See Also

The SAS Group Home Page
http://www.cre.canon.co.uk/sas.html

This is the home page of the SAS Group at Canon Research Centre Europe, which is responsible for *Robot.pm*.

Robot Exclusion Protocol
http://info.webcrawler.com/mak/projects/robots/norobots.html

This is a *de facto* standard which defines how a "well-behaved" robot client should interact with web servers and web pages.

Guidelines for Robot Writers
http://info.webcrawler.com/mak/projects/robots/guidelines.html

Guidelines and suggestions for those who are (considering) developing a web robot.

Weblint Home Page
http://www.cre.canon.co.uk/~neilb/weblint/

Weblint is a Perl script which is used to check HTML for syntax errors and stylistic problems, in the same way `lint` is used to check C.

Comprehensive Perl Archive Network (CPAN)
http://www.perl.com/CPAN/

This is a well-organized collection of Perl resources, such as modules, documents, and scripts. CPAN is mirrored at FTP sites around the world.

WWW::RobotRules—parse robots.txt files

Synopsis

```
require WWW::RobotRules;
my $robotsrules = new WWW::RobotRules 'MOMspider/1.0';
use LWP::Simple qw(get);
$url = "http://some.place/robots.txt";
my $robots_txt = get $url;
$robotsrules->parse($url, $robots_txt);
$url = "http://some.other.place/robots.txt";
my $robots_txt = get $url;
$robotsrules->parse($url, $robots_txt);
# Now we are able to check if a URL is valid for those servers that
# we have obtained and parsed "robots.txt" files for.
if($robotsrules->allowed($url)) {
    $c = get $url;
    ...
}
```

Description

This module parses a *robots.txt* file as specified in "A Standard for Robot Exclusion," described at *http://info.webcrawler.com/mak/projects/robots/norobots.html*. Webmasters can use the *robots.txt* file to disallow conforming robots access to parts of their WWW server.

The parsed file is kept in the WWW::RobotRules object, and this object provide methods to check if access to a given URL is prohibited. The same WWW::RobotRules object can parse multiple *robots.txt* files.

Methods

`$rules = new WWW::RobotRules 'MOMspider/1.0'`

> This is the constructor for WWW::RobotRules objects. The first argument given to **new()** is the name of the robot.

`$rules->parse($url, $content, $fresh_until)`

> The **parse()** method takes as arguments the URL that was used to retrieve the */robots.txt* file, and the contents of the file.

`$rules->allowed($url)`

> Returns **true** if this robot is allowed to retrieve this URL.

`$rules->agent([$name])`

> Get/set the agent name. Note: Changing the agent name will clear the *robots.txt* rules and expire times out of the cache.

robots.txt

The format and semantics of the */robots.txt* file are as follows (this is an edited abstract of *http://info.webcrawler.com/mak/projects/robots/norobots.html*):

The file consists of one or more records separated by one or more blank lines. Each record contains lines of the form:

> `field-name: value`

The field name is case-insensitive. Text after the # character on a line is ignored during parsing. This is used for comments. The following *field-names* can be used:

User-Agent

> The value of this field is the name of the robot the record is describing access policy for. If more than one *User-Agent* field is present the record describes an identical access policy for more than one robot. At least one field needs to be present per record. If the value is *, the record describes the default access policy for any robot that has not matched any of the other records.

Disallow

> The value of this field specifies a partial URL that is not to be visited. This can be a full path, or a partial path; any URL that starts with this value will not be retrieved.

Examples

The following example *robots.txt* file specifies that no robots should visit any URL starting with *cyberworld/map/* or *tmp/*:

```
# robots.txt for http://www.site.com/
User-agent: *
Disallow: /cyberworld/map/ # This is an infinite virtual URL space
Disallow: /tmp/ # these will soon disappear
```

This example *robots.txt* file specifies that no robots should visit any URL starting with *cyberworld/map/*, except the robot called "cybermapper":

```
# robots.txt for http://www.site.com/
User-agent: *
Disallow: /cyberworld/map/ # This is an infinite virtual URL space
# Cybermapper knows where to go.
User-agent: cybermapper
Disallow:
```

This example indicates that no robots should visit this site further:

```
# go away
User-agent: *
Disallow: /
```

See Also

LWP::RobotUA, WWW::RobotRules::AnyDBM_File

WWW::RobotRules::AnyDBM_File— persistent RobotRules

Synopsis

```
require WWW::RobotRules::AnyDBM_File;
require LWP::RobotUA;
# Create a robot useragent that uses a diskcaching RobotRules
my $rules = new WWW::RobotRules::AnyDBM_File 'my-robot/1.0',
'cachefile';
my $ua = new WWW::RobotUA 'my-robot/1.0', 'me@foo.com', $rules;
# Then just use $ua as usual
$res = $ua->request($req);
```

Description

This is a subclass of WWW::RobotRules that uses the **AnyDBM_File** package to implement persistent diskcaching of *robots.txt* and host visit information.

The constructor (the **new()** method) takes an extra argument specifying the name of the DBM file to use. If the DBM file already exists, then you can specify **undef** as agent name as the name can be obtained from the DBM database.

See Also

WWW::RobotRules, LWP::RobotUA

Authors

Hakan Ardo, *hakan@munin.ub2.lu.se*; Gisle Aas, *aas@sn.no*

WWW::Search—virtual base class for WWW searches

Description

This class is the parent for all access method supported by the WWW::Search library. This library implements a Perl API to web-based search engines.

Current search engines supported include AltaVista (both web and news), Dejanews, Excite (web only), HotBot (web only), Infoseek (email, web, and news) and Lycos.

Search results are limited and there is a pause between each request for results to avoid overloading either the client or the server.

Sample program

Using the library should be straightforward: Here's a sample program:

```
my($search) = new WWW::Search('AltaVista');
$search->native_query(WWW::Search::escape_query($query));
my($result);
while ($result = $search->next_result()) {
    print $result->url, "\n";
};
```

Results are objects of WWW::SearchResult (see "WWW::SearchResult").

Methods and Functions

new

To create a new WWW::Search, call $search = new WWW::Search('Search-EngineName'); where **SearchEngineName** is replaced with a particular search engine. For example:

```
$search = new WWW::Search('AltaVista');
```

If no search engine is specified a default will be chosen for you.

The next step is usually:

```
$search->native_query('search-engine-specific+query+string');
```

native_query

Specify a query (and optional options) to the current search object. The query and options must be escaped; call **WWW::Search::escape_query** to escape a plain query. The actual search is not actually begun until `results` or `next_result` is called.

Example:

```
$search->native_query('search-engine-specific+query+string',
                { option1 => 'able', option2 => 'baker' } );
```

The hash of options following the query string is optional. Both the query string and the hash of options are interpreted in search-engine-specific manner.

Details about how the search string and option hash are interpreted in the search-engine-specific manual pages (WWW::Search::SearchEngineName).

After `native_query`, the next step is usually:

```
@results = $search->results();
```

or:

```
while ($result = $search->next_result()) {
    # do_something;
};
```

`results`

Return all the results of a query as a reference to array of SearchResult objects.

Example:

```
@results = $search->results();
foreach $result (@results) { print $result->url(), "\n"; };
```

On error, `results()` will return `undef` and set `response()` to the HTTP response code.

`next_result`

Return each result of a query as a SearchResult object.

Example:

```
while ($result = $search->next_result()) {
    print $result->url(), "\n";
}
```

On error, `results()` will return `undef` and set `response()` to the HTTP response code.

`response`

Return the HTTP response code for the last query (see "HTTP::Response"). If the query returns `undef`, errors could be reported like this:

```
my($response) = $search->response();
if ($response->is_success) {
    print "no search results\n";
} else {
    print "error: " . $response->as_string() . "\n";
};
```

Note: Even if the back-end does not involve the Web, it should return HTTP::Response-style codes.

`seek_result($offset)`

Set which result `next_result` should return (like `lseek` in UNIX). Results are zero-indexed.

The only guaranteed valid offset is 0, which will replay the results from the beginning. In particular, seeking past the end of the current cached results probably won't do what you might think it should.

Results are cached, so this doesn't re-issue the query or cause I/O (unless you go off the end of the results). To redo the query, create a new search object.

Example: `$search->seek_result(0);`

maximum_to_retrieve

The maximum number of hits to return (approximately). Queries resulting in more than this many hits will return the first hits, up to this limit.

Defaults to 500.

Example: `$max = $search->maximum_to_retrieve(100);`

escape_query

Escape a query. Before queries are made special characters must be escaped so that a proper URL can be formed.

This is like escaping a URL but all non-alphanumeric characters are escaped and spaces are converted to +es.

Example:

```
$escaped = Search::escape_query('+lsam +replication');
```

This returns `%221sam+replication%22`.

See also **unescape_query**.

unescape_query

Unescape a query. See **escape_query** for details.

Example:

```
$unescaped = Search::unescape_query('%221sam+replication%22');
```

This returns `+lsam +replication`.

See also **escape_query**.

http_proxy

Set up an HTTP proxy (perhaps for connections from behind a firewall.)

This routine should be called before the first retrieval is attempted.

Example:

```
$search->http_proxy("http://gateway:8080");
```

setup_search *(PRIVATE)*

This internal routine does generic Search setup. It calls **native_setup_search** to do back-end specific setup.

user_agent(*$NON_ROBOT*) *(PRIVATE)*

This internal routine creates a user-agent for derived classes that query the web. If $NON_ROBOT, a normal user-agent (rather than a robot-style user-agent) is used.

Back-ends should use robot-style user-agents wherever possible. Also, back-ends should call **user_agent_delay** every page retrieval to avoid swamping search-engines.

user_agent_delay *(PRIVATE)*

Derived classes should call this between requests to remote servers to avoid overloading them with many, fast back-to-back requests.

`retrieve_some` *(PRIVATE)*

> An internal routine to interface with `native_retrieve_some`. Checks for overflow.

Implementing New Back-Ends

WWW::Search supports back-ends to separate search engines. Each back-end is implemented as a subclass of WWW::Search. WWW::Search::AltaVista provides a good sample back-end.

A back-end usually has two routines, `native_retrieve_some` and `native_setup_search`.

`native_retrieve_some` is the core of a back-end. It will be called periodically to fetch URLs. Each call it should fetch a page with about 10 or so hits and add them the cache. It should return the number of hits found or `undef` when there are no more hits.

Internally, `native_retrieve_some` typically will parse the HTML, extract the links and descriptions, then find the "next" button and save the URL. See the code for the AltaVista implementation for an example.

`native_setup_search` is invoked before the search. It is passed a single argument: the escaped, native version of the query.

The front- and back-ends share a single object (a hash) The back-end can change any hash element beginning with underscore, `{response}` (an HTTP::Response code) and `{cache}` (the array of WWW::SearchResult objects caching all results).

If you implement a new back-end, please let the authors know.

Author

John Heidemann, *johnh@isi.edu*

Back-ends and applications for WWW::Search have been done by John Heidemann, Wm. L. Scheding, Cesare Feroldi de Rosa, and Glen Pringle.

Copyright

Copyright © 1996 University of Southern California. All rights reserved.

Redistribution and use in source and binary forms are permitted provided that the above copyright notice and this paragraph are duplicated in all such forms and that any documentation, advertising materials, and other materials related to such distribution and use acknowledge that the software was developed by the University of Southern California, Information Sciences Institute. The name of the University may not be used to endorse or promote products derived from this software without specific prior written permission.

THIS SOFTWARE IS PROVIDED "AS IS" AND WITHOUT ANY EXPRESS OR IMPLIED WARRANTIES, INCLUDING, WITHOUT LIMITATION, THE IMPLIED WARRANTIES OF MERCHANTABILITY AND FITNESS FOR A PARTICULAR PURPOSE.

See Also

For more details see LWP.

For specific search engines, see"WWW::Search::TheEngineName (replacing The Engine-Name with a particular search engine).

For details about the results of a search, see WWW::SearchResult.

WWW::Search::AltaVista—class for searching AltaVista

Description

This class is an AltaVista specialization of WWW::Search. It handles making and interpreting AltaVista searches (*http://www.altavista.digital.com/*).

This class exports no public interface; all interaction should be done through WWW::Search objects.

Options

The default is for simple web queries. Specialized back ends for simple and advanced web and news searches are available (refer to one of the following modules: "WWW::Search::AltaVista::Web," "WWW::Search::AltaVista::AdvancedWeb," "WWW::Search:: AltaVista::News," "WWW::Search::AltaVista::AdvancedNews"). These back-ends set different combinations following options.

pg=aq
> Do advanced queries. (It defaults to simple queries.)

what=news
> Search Usenet instead of the Web. (It defaults to search the Web.)

See Also

To make new back-ends, see WWW::Search, or the specialized AltaVista searches described in options.

How Does It Work?

`native_setup_search` is called before we do anything. It initializes our private variables (which all begin with underscores) and sets up a URL to the first results page in `{_next_url}`.

`native_retrieve_some` is called (from WWW::Search::retrieve_some) whenever more hits are needed. It calls the LWP library to fetch the page specified by `{_next_url}`. It parses this page, appending any search hits it finds to `{cache}`. If it finds a "next" button in the text, it sets `{_next_url}` to point to the page for the next set of results, otherwise it sets it to `undef` to indicate we're done.

Author

John Heidemann, *johnh@isi.edu*

Copyright

WWW::Search::AltaVista::AdvancedNews —class for
advanced AltaVista news searching

Description

This class implements the advanced AltaVista news search (specializing AltaVista and WWW::Search). It handles making and interpreting AltaVista web searches (*http://www.altavista.digital.com/*).

Details of AltaVista can be found at WWW::Search::AltaVista.

This class exports no public interface; all interaction should be done through WWW::Search objects.

Author

John Heidemann, *johnh@isi.edu*

Copyright

WWW::Search::AltaVista::AdvancedWeb —class for
advanced Alta Vista Web searching

Description

This class implements the advanced mode of AltaVista web search (specializing AltaVista and WWW::Search). It handles making and interpreting AltaVista searches (*http://www.altavista.digital.com/*).

Details of AltaVista can be found at WWW::Search::AltaVista.

This class exports no public interface; all interaction should be done through WWW::Search objects.

Author

John Heidemann, *johnh@isi.edu*

Copyright

tation, advertising materials, and other materials related to such distribution and use acknowledge that the software was developed by the University of Southern California, Information Sciences Institute. The name of the University may not be used to endorse or promote products derived from this software without specific prior written permission.

WWW::Search::AltaVista::News — class for AltaVista news searching

Description

This class implements the AltaVista news search (specializing in AltaVista and WWW::Search). It handles making and interpreting AltaVista news searches (*http://www.altavista.digital.com/*).

Details about AltaVista can be found at "WWW::Search::AltaVista."

This class exports no public interface; all interaction should be done through WWW::Search objects.

Author

John Heidemann, *johnh@isi.edu*

Copyright

WWW::Search::AltaVista::Web — class for Alta Vista Web searching

Description

This class implements the AltaVista Web search (specializing AltaVista and WWW::Search). It handles making and interpreting AltaVista web searches *(http://www.altavista.digital.com/)*.

Details of AltaVista can be found at "WWW::Search::AltaVista."

This class exports no public interface; all interaction should be done through WWW::Search objects.

Author

John Heidemann, *johnh@isi.edu*

Copyright

WWW::Search::Dejanews—Perl class for searching Dejanews

Description

This class is a WWW::Search back-end for the Dejanews search engine for Usenet news.

This class exports no public interface; all interaction should be done through WWW::Search objects.

Options

`defaultOp`
> AND or OR (defaults to OR).

`groups`
> For example, *comp.foo.bar*. Defaults to all groups.

Author

Cesare Feroldi de Rosa, *C.Feroldi@IT.net* (derived from *AltaVista.pm*)

Copyright

This back-end was contributed to USC/ISI by Cesare Feroldi de Rosa.

See Also

To make new back-ends, see WWW::Search.

WWW::Search::Excite — class for searching Excite

Description

This class is an Excite specialization of WWW::Search. It handles making and interpreting Excite searches (*http://www.excite.com/*).

This class exports no public interface; all interaction should be done through WWW::Search objects.

How Does It Work?

`native_setup_search` is called before we do anything. It initializes our private variables (which all begin with underscores) and sets up a URL to the first results page in {_next_url}.

`native_retrieve_some` is called (from WWW::Search::retrieve_some) whenever more hits are needed. It calls the LWP library to fetch the page specified by {_next_url}. It parses this page, appending any search hits it finds to {`cache`}. If it finds a "next" button in the text, it sets {_next_url} to point to the page for the next set of results, otherwise it sets it to `undef` to indicate we're done.

Bugs

This module should support options and a back-end specific for news.

Author

Glen Pringle, *pringle@cs.monash.edu.au*, based upon WWW::Search::Lycos.

Copyright

This back-end was contributed to USC/ISI by GLen Pringle.

Copyright © 1996 University of Southern California. All rights reserved.

Redistribution and use in source and binary forms are permitted provided that the above copyright notice and this paragraph are duplicated in all such forms and that any documentation, advertising materials, and other materials related to such distribution and use acknowledge that the software was developed by the University of Southern California, Information Sciences Institute. The name of the University may not be used to endorse or promote products derived from this software without specific prior written permission.

THIS SOFTWARE IS PROVIDED "AS IS" AND WITHOUT ANY EXPRESS OR IMPLIED WARRANTIES, INCLUDING, WITHOUT LIMITATION, THE IMPLIED WARRANTIES OF MERCHANTABILITY AND FITNESS FOR A PARTICULAR PURPOSE.

See Also

To make new back-ends, see WWW::Search.

WWW::Search::HotBot — class for searching HotBot

Description

This class is an HotBot specialization of WWW::Search. It handles making and interpreting HotBot searches (*http://www.hotbot.com/*).

This class exports no public interface; all interaction should be done through WWW::Search objects.

How Does It Work?

`native_setup_search` is called before we do anything. It initializes our private variables (which all begin with underscores) and sets up a URL to the first results page in {_next_url}.

`native_retrieve_some` is called (from WWW::Search::retrieve_some) whenever more hits are needed. It calls the LWP library to fetch the page specified by {_next_url}. It parses this page, appending any search hits it finds to {cache}. If it finds a "next" button in the text, it sets {_next_url} to point to the page for the next set of results, otherwise it sets it to `undef` to indicate we're done.

Bugs

This module should support options.

Author

Wm. L. Scheding, based on WWW::Search::AltaVista

Copyright

See Also

To make new back-ends, see WWW::Search.

WWW::Search::Infoseek — class for searching Infoseek

Description

This class is an Infoseek specialization of WWW::Search. It handles making and interpreting AltaVista searches (*http://www.infoseek.com/*).

This is an abstract class: you cannot instance a variable of this type.

Descendant classes must override the `native_retrieve_some` method.

This class exports no public interface; all interaction should be done through WWW::Search objects.

Option
```
operator
```
> Values are AND or OR (defaults to OR).

> If you want to use the native + and – operators directly, use the OR operator.

Author

Cesare Feroldi de Rosa, *C.Feroldi@IT.net* (derived from *AltaVista.pm*)

Copyright

Copyright © 1996 University of Southern California. All rights reserved.

Redistribution and use in source and binary forms are permitted provided that the above copyright notice and this paragraph are duplicated in all such forms and that any documentation, advertising materials, and other materials related to such distribution and use acknowledge that the software was developed by the University of Southern California, Information Sciences Institute. The name of the University may not be used to endorse or promote products derived from this software without specific prior written permission.

THIS SOFTWARE IS PROVIDED "AS IS" AND WITHOUT ANY EXPRESS OR IMPLIED WARRANTIES, INCLUDING, WITHOUT LIMITATION, THE IMPLIED WARRANTIES OF MERCHANTABILITY AND FITNESS FOR A PARTICULAR PURPOSE.

See Also

To make new back-ends, see WWW::Search.

WWW::Search::Infoseek::Email—class for searching for email at Infoseek

Description

Back-end for Infoseek search engine.

This class exports no public interface; all interaction should be done through WWW::Search objects.

Option
```
operator
```
> Values are AND or OR (defaults to OR).

> If you want to use the native + and – operators directly, use the OR operator.

Author

Cesare Feroldi de Rosa, *C.Feroldi@IT.net* (derived from *AltaVista.pm*)

Copyright

Copyright © 1996 University of Southern California. All rights reserved.

Redistribution and use in source and binary forms are permitted provided that the above copyright notice and this paragraph are duplicated in all such forms and that any documentation, advertising materials, and other materials related to such distribution and use acknowledge that the software was developed by the University of Southern California, Information Sciences Institute. The name of the University may not be used to endorse or promote products derived from this software without specific prior written permission.

THIS SOFTWARE IS PROVIDED "AS IS" AND WITHOUT ANY EXPRESS OR IMPLIED WARRANTIES, INCLUDING, WITHOUT LIMITATION, THE IMPLIED WARRANTIES OF MERCHANTABILITY AND FITNESS FOR A PARTICULAR PURPOSE.

See Also

To make new back-ends, see WWW::Search.

WWW::Search::Infoseek::News—class for searching for news at Infoseek

Description

Back end for Infoseek search engine (Usenet news).

This class exports no public interface; all interaction should be done through WWW::Search objects.

Options

operator

Example: `operator=>'AND'`; valid values AND or OR (defaults to OR).

If you want to use the native + and – operators directly, use the OR operator.

groups

Example: `groups=>'comp.foo.bar'`; defaults to all groups.

Author

Cesare Feroldi de Rosa, *C.Feroldi@IT.net* (derived from *AltaVista.pm*)

Copyright

Copyright © 1996 University of Southern California. All rights reserved.

Redistribution and use in source and binary forms are permitted provided that the above copyright notice and this paragraph are duplicated in all such forms and that any documentation, advertising materials, and other materials related to such distribution and use acknowledge that the software was developed by the University of Southern California, Information Sciences Institute. The name of the University may not be used to endorse or promote products derived from this software without specific prior written permission.

THIS SOFTWARE IS PROVIDED "AS IS" AND WITHOUT ANY EXPRESS OR IMPLIED WARRANTIES, INCLUDING, WITHOUT LIMITATION, THE IMPLIED WARRANTIES OF MERCHANTABILITY AND FITNESS FOR A PARTICULAR PURPOSE.

See Also

To make new back-ends, see WWW::Search.

WWW::Search::Lycos—class for searching Lycos

Description

This class is an Lycos specialization of WWW::Search. It handles making and interpreting Lycos searches (*http://www.lycos.com/*).

This class exports no public interface; all interaction should be done through WWW::Search objects.

How Does It Work?

`native_setup_search` is called before we do anything. It initializes our private variables (which all begin with underscores) and sets up a URL to the first results page in {_next_url}.

`native_retrieve_some` is called (from WWW::Search::retrieve_some) whenever more hits are needed. It calls the LWP library to fetch the page specified by {_next_url}. It parses this page, appending any search hits it finds to {cache}. If it finds a "next" button in the text, it sets {_next_url} to point to the page for the next set of results, otherwise it sets it to `undef` to indicate we're done.

Bugs

This module should support options.

Author

Wm. L. Scheding; based upon WWW::Search::AltaVista

Copyright

Copyright © 1996 University of Southern California. All rights reserved.

Redistribution and use in source and binary forms are permitted provided that the above copyright notice and this paragraph are duplicated in all such forms and that any documentation, advertising materials, and other materials related to such distribution and use acknowledge that the software was developed by the University of Southern California, Information Sciences Institute. The name of the University may not be used to endorse or promote products derived from this software without specific prior written permission.

THIS SOFTWARE IS PROVIDED "AS IS" AND WITHOUT ANY EXPRESS OR IMPLIED WARRANTIES, INCLUDING, WITHOUT LIMITATION, THE IMPLIED WARRANTIES OF MERCHANTABILITY AND FITNESS FOR A PARTICULAR PURPOSE.

See Also

To make new back-ends, see WWW::Search.

WWW::Search::Yahoo —class for searching Yahoo

Description

This class is an Yahoo specialization of WWW::Search. It handles making and interpreting Yahoo searches (*http://www.yahoo.com/*).

This class exports no public interface; all interaction should be done through WWW::Search objects.

Warning

This class has not been fully debugged yet. Use at your own risk.

How Does It Work?

native_setup_search is called before we do anything. It initializes our private variables (which all begin with underscores) and sets up a URL to the first results page in {_next_ url}.

native_retrieve_some is called (from WWW::Search::retrieve_some) whenever more hits are needed. It calls the LWP library to fetch the page specified by {_next_url}. It parses this page, appending any search hits it finds to {cache}. If it finds a "next" button in the text, it sets {_next_url} to point to the page for the next set of results, otherwise it sets it to undef to indicate we're done.

Bugs

WWW::Search::Yahoo does not currently work reliably and is not being actively maintained. If you wish to hack on it, please go ahead.

Author

Wm. L. Scheding based upon WWW::Search::AltaVista

Copyright

Copyright © 1996 University of Southern California. All rights reserved.

Redistribution and use in source and binary forms are permitted provided that the above copyright notice and this paragraph are duplicated in all such forms and that any documentation, advertising materials, and other materials related to such distribution and use acknowledge that the software was developed by the University of Southern California, Information Sciences Institute. The name of the University may not be used to endorse or promote products derived from this software without specific prior written permission.

THIS SOFTWARE IS PROVIDED "AS IS" AND WITHOUT ANY EXPRESS OR IMPLIED WARRANTIES, INCLUDING, WITHOUT LIMITATION, THE IMPLIED WARRANTIES OF MERCHANTABILITY AND FITNESS FOR A PARTICULAR PURPOSE.

See Also

To make new back-ends, see WWW::Search.

WWW::SearchResult—class for results returned from WWW::Search

Description

A framework for returning the results of WWW::Search.

Methods and Functions

new

> To create a new WWW::SearchResult, call:

```
$search = new WWW::SearchResult();
```

url

> Return the primary URL. Note that there may be a list of URLs, see also methods urls and add_url. Nothing special is guaranteed about the primary URL other than that it's the first one returned by the back-end.

> Every result is required to have at least one URL.

urls
> Return a reference to an array of URLs. There is also a primary URL (url). See also add_url.

add_url
> Add a URL to the list.

related_urls, add_related_url, related_titles, add_related_title
> Analogous to URLs, these functions provide lists of related URLs and their titles. These point to things the search engine thinks you might want (for example, see Infoseek).

title, description, score, change_date, index_date, size, raw
> Set or get attributes of the result.

> None of these attributes is guaranteed to be provided by a given back-end. If an attribute is not provided its method will return undef.

> Typical contents of these attributes:

title
> The result's title (typically that provided by the "TITLE" HTML command).

description
> A brief description of result. Often the first few sentences of the document.

score
> A back-end specific, numeric "score" of the search result. The exact range of scores is search-engine specific, but if a score is provided, larger scores are required to signify better quality results.

change_date
> When the result was last changed.

index_date
> When the search engine indexed the result.

size
> The size of the result, in bytes.

raw
> The raw HTML for the entire result.

See Also

WWW::Search

16

Server and Daemon Utilities

EventServer is the largest and most thorough of the server utilities, handling all kinds of events.

EventServer—the all-singing, all-dancing server

Synopsis

Functions can be imported and used:

```
use EventServer;

$r1 = register_timed_client($obj1,$time1,$coderef1);
$r2 = register_interval_client($obj2,$time2,$coderef2);
$r3 = register_signal_client($obj3,$signal3,$coderef3);
$r4 = register_io_client($obj4,$mode4,$coderef4_r,
                         $coderef4_w,$coderef4_rw);
$r5 = register_child_termination_client($obj5,$pid5,$coderef5);
$r6 = register_event_client($obj6,$eventName6,$coderef6);

trigger_on_deregistering($r1,$coderef7);
cancel_registration($r3);
$ordered_keys_ref = ordered_keys_ref();

$time = maximum_inactive_server_time();
set_maximum_inactive_server_time($time);
execute_in_array_context_with_timeout($timeout,$timeout_retcode,
                                      $error_retcode,$coderef,@args);

fork_with_child_retaining_clients($r1,$r2,...);

sub something {add_event($eventName)}

start_server();
```

Or the class can be used with methods:

```
require EventServer;
$S = EventServer;

$r1 = $S->registerTimedClient($obj1,$time1,$coderef1);
$r2 = $S->registerIntervalClient($obj2,$time2,$coderef2);
$r3 = $S->registerSignalClient($obj3,$signal3,$coderef3);
$r4 = $S->registerIOClient($obj4,$mode4,$coderef4_r,
                           $coderef4_w,$coderef4_rw);
$r5 = $S->registerChildTerminationClient($obj5,$pid5,$coderef5);
$r6 = $S->registerEventClient($obj6,$eventName6,$coderef6);

$S->triggerOnDeregistering($r1,$coderef7);
$S->cancelRegistration($r3);
$ordered_keys_ref = $S->orderedKeysRef();

$time = $S->maximumInactiveServerTime();
$S->setMaximumInactiveServerTime($time);
$S->executeInArrayContextWithTimeout($timeout,$timeout_retcode,
                                     $error_retcode,$coderef,@args);

$S->forkWithChildRetainingClients($r1,$r2,...);

sub something {$S->addEvent($eventName)}

$S->startServer();
```

Description

This module handles all types of events.

Warning

The ALRM signal is used extensively, as is `alarm()`. You should not call the function `alarm()` as this will corrupt the internal logic of the server. Similarly `sleep()` should not be used either, as this is often implemented in terms of `alarm()`.

Instead use `execute_in_array_context_with_timeout()`, which is better anyway since it allows multiple clients to set alarms simultaneously and allows nested alarms. However, for this reason, registering a client to receive ALRM signals is probably of no use.

Also, if you assign to the %SIG hash, or install signal handlers through POSIX yourself, then you may corrupt the logic of the server. If you need to do this for something other than a signal (e.g. __WARN__), that should be okay, otherwise you should probably create a subclass to install the handlers you want (see "The SIG Hash and Signals" and "Creating Subclasses").

Function and Method Summary

There are 15 public functions/methods:

- 8 dealing with registering clients
- 1 to add user defined events
- 3 dealing with executing code and timeouts

- 1 to fork the process
- 1 to start the server

Functions are:

```
register_interval_client(O/R,INTERVAL,FUNCREF,ARG)
register_timed_client(O/R,TIMEOUT,FUNCREF,ARG)
register_io_client(O/R,MODE,HANDLE,RFUNCREF,WFUNCREF,RWFUNCREF,ARG)
register_signal_client(O/R,SIGNAL,FUNCREF,ARG)
register_child_termination_client(O/R,PID,FUNCREF,ARG)
register_event_client(O/R,EVENT,FUNCREF,ARG)

trigger_on_deregistering(REGISTRY_KEY,FUNCREF)
cancel_registration(REGISTRY_KEY)

add_event(EVENT)

maximum_inactive_server_time()
set_maximum_inactive_server_time(TIME)
execute_in_array_context_with_
timeout(TIMEOUT,TRET,ERET,FUNCREF,ARGS)

fork_with_child_retaining_clients(LIST_OF_REGISTRY_KEYS)

start_server();
```

And defined as methods:

```
$SERVER->registerIntervalClient(O/R,INTERVAL,FUNCREF,ARG)
$SERVER->registerTimedClient(O/R,TIMEOUT,FUNCREF,ARG)
$SERVER->registerIOClient(O/R,MODE,HANDLE,RFUNCREF,WFUNCREF,
                          RWFUNCREF,ARG)
$SERVER->registerSignalClient(O/R,SIGNAL,FUNCREF,ARG)
$SERVER->registerChildTerminationClient(O/R,PID,FUNCREF,ARG)
$SERVER->registerEventClient(O/R,EVENT,FUNCREF,ARG)

$SERVER->triggerOnDeregistering(REGISTRY_KEY,FUNCREF);
$SERVER->cancelRegistration(REGISTRY_KEY);

$SERVER->addEvent(EVENT)

$SERVER->maximumInactiveServerTime()
$SERVER->setMaximumInactiveServerTime(TIME)
$SERVER->
executeInArrayContextWithTimeout(TIMEOUT,TRET,ERET,FUNCREF,ARGS)

$SERVER->forkWithChildRetainingClients(LIST_OF_REGISTRY_KEYS)

$SERVER->startServer();
```

Including the Server in Your Program

The server is included in your program with the line:

```
use EventServer;
```

to import the functions, or:

```
require EventServer;
```

if used as a class.

Starting the Server

The server is started by executing the function or method:

```
start_server();
EventServer->startServer();
```

In either case, if a subclass has been defined correctly, then the server will be started using that subclass.

Registering Clients (General)

Clients are registered with the server using any of the 6 registering methods listed in the next section. They all have various points in common:

- $SERVER is assumed to be EventServer or a subclass.

- All registration methods return a RegistryKey object on success, which holds the registration key, and false on failure. (Note previous versions returned a string—the current version should be fully compatible with previous versions.) The registration key is unique to the registration, depending on all the parameters passed to the registration method—i.e., a single object can be registered multiple times using different parameters or registration methods (multiple *identical* registrations will return the same key, and will result in only one registration). To alter the parameters of an existing registration, pass the registration key to the registration method instead of the object (see *O/R* below). But note that this generates a new RegistryKey object since the registration parameters are now different (the old RegistryKey object is deregistered, and is essentially useless). Reregistering an existing registration so that it is identical to another registration will just deregister the first registration, returning the existing identical RegistryKey object (i.e., as stated above, there will only be one registry entry for identical parameters regardless of how you register them).

- *O/R* is the object being registered or the registration key of an already registered object. The object can be anything (previous versions restricted it to be class names or objects that returned true ref() values). This object is passed to *FUNCREF* (see below) as the first argument.

- *ARG* is anything. It is passed to *FUNCREF* (see below) as the last argument. If nothing is passed, then *ARG* is defaulted to undef().

- At least one *FUNCREF* argument is required. All *FUNCREF* arguments are CODE references to the function which is executed when the client is triggered. Where there is more than one *FUNCREF* to be specified, the one called will depend on the trigger type. When triggered, the *FUNCREF* is called as:

```
&FUNCREF(OBJECT,REGISTRY_KEY,some method specific args,ARG);
```

  where:

  - *OBJECT* is the object registered (the O in O/R above).

  - *REGISTRY_KEY* is the registration key for that registration (the R in O/R above, returned by registration methods).

  - *ARG* is the last argument passed to the registration method (*ARG* above).

  This call to *FUNCREF* takes place within a timeout. The current maximum timeout value can be retrieved using maximum_inactive_server_time(), and can be set using set_maximum_inactive_server_time(). (These access and set the global $EventServer::MAX_INACTIVE_SERVER_TIME.) The default value is 60 seconds. Any fatal errors caused by executing *FUNCREF* are trapped, and cause the client to be deregistered. A timeout will also cause the client to be deregistered.

Note however that a call to `exit()` cannot be trapped and will cause the server process to exit. Similarly, a call to `dump()` also cannot be trapped and will cause the server process to core dump.

Registering Clients (Methods)

register_interval_client *(O/R, INTERVAL, FUNCREF, ARG)*
$SERVER->registerIntervalClient*(O/R, INTERVAL, FUNCREF, ARG)*

> *INTERVAL* is a time (see *Times and Timing*). The client is triggered after every *INTERVAL* seconds. Triggering effects the function call:

&FUNCREF *(OBJECT, REGISTRY_KEY, INTERVAL, ARG)* ;

register_timed_client *(O/R, TIMEOUT, FUNCREF, ARG)*
$SERVER->registerTimedClient*(O/R, TIMEOUT, FUNCREF, ARG)*

> *TIMEOUT* is a time (see "Times and Timing"). The client is triggered after *TIMEOUT* seconds and then deregistered. Triggering effects the function call:

&FUNCREF *(OBJECT, REGISTRY_KEY, TIMEOUT, ARG)* ;

register_io_client*(O/R, MODE, HANDLE, RFUNCREF, WFUNCREF, RWFUNCREF, ARG)*
$SERVER->registerIOClient*(O/R, MODE, HANDLE, RFUNCREF, WFUNCREF,*
> *RWFUNCREF, ARG)*

> *MODE* is r, w, or rw, depending on whether the trigger should be for input pending (read won't block), output possible (write won't block) or both. *HANDLE* is the fully qualified package name of the filehandle which has already been opened, on which I/O is tested. *RFUNCREF*, *WFUNCREF*, and *RWFUNCREF* are three FUNCREFs (see above). If input is pending on *HANDLE*, this triggers the call:

&RFUNCREF *(OBJECT, REGISTRY_KEY, HANDLE, ARG)* ;

> if output is possible on *HANDLE*, this triggers the call:

&WFUNCREF *(OBJECT, REGISTRY_KEY, HANDLE, ARG)* ;

> and if both input and output won't block, then this triggers the call:

&RWFUNCREF *(OBJECT, REGISTRY_KEY, HANDLE, ARG)* ;

> If *MODE* r has been specified, then obviously only *RFUNCREF* can ever get called, and similarly if *MODE* w has been specified, then only *WFUNCREF* can ever get called. However, if *MODE* rw has been specified, then any of the three functions could be called depending on what becomes non-blocking first.

> In all cases of *MODE*, all three FUNCREFs must be CODE references.

> Note, unlike previous versions, if you make multiple registrations for a specific filehandle, then client functions are still only triggered when they are guaranteed to be non-blocking. To paraphrase, if any FUNCREF is called, you are guaranteed to be able to do a `sysread()`, `syswrite()`, or `accept()` (whichever is appropriate).

register_signal_client *(O/R, SIGNAL, FUNCREF, ARG)*
$SERVER->registerSignalClient*(O/R, SIGNAL, FUNCREF, ARG)*

> *SIGNAL* is a valid trappable signal. The signals are obtained from the Config module. (Previous versions specified them explicitly in subroutines). The `allSignals` method returns the list of signals.

The client is triggered after the signal is trapped (and after the signal handler has exited). Triggering effects the function call:

&FUNCREF(*OBJECT, REGISTRY_KEY, SIGNAL, NSIGS, ARG*);

where *NSIGS* is the number of times the signal was received since this function was last called, and *SIGNAL* is the canonical name for the signal (which may be different from what was passed in the case of CHLD/CLD; you can always use either—the correct signal name for the system will be used).

Note that ALRM and CLD (or CHLD or CHILD) are specially handled, and registering for these signals is of little use. For alarms, use execute_in_array_context_with_timeout(), and to find out when a child process has died, register with register_child_termination_client().

Signals which have no clients registered for them will cause the default action to occur (i.e., they will not be trapped).

Signals are not passed to the clients immediately; they are put into the queue and clients are triggered when the signal queue is checked. If you need some action to occur immediately on receipt of the signal, you will need to create a subclass to handle this. (This is because setting up an "immediately signalled" type of client is fraught with difficulties, and is likely to lead to an unstable process—I tried it. And that was even without having signal handlers stacked through recursive calls to it. Mind you, it should be doable with POSIX signals, and is almost, but some bug that I haven't tracked down yet seems to propagate a die past an eval if called from within the handler, so it's not yet implemented for POSIX signals in the server.)

Signal handlers are not installed until the server has been started (see "Starting the Server").

All signal handlers are reset to default if the server loop exits (see "Questions and Answers").

See also "The SIG Hash and Signals."

register_child_termination_client (*O/R, PID, FUNCREF, ARG*)
$SERVER->registerChildTerminationClient(*O/R, PID, FUNCREF, ARG*)

PID is the process *ID* of the child process. When that child dies this triggers the function call:

&FUNCREF(*OBJECT, REGISTRY_KEY, DATA, ARG*);

where data is either the process ID of the terminated child or an array reference with two items in the array—the process ID and the child termination status as given by $?. The choice of which is returned is set by calling always_return_child_termination_status() with a Boolean argument—*true* means return the array reference, *false* means return the PID only. The default is false for backward compatibility.

Note that if forking the server, you should use fork_with_child_retaining_clients() rather than just a fork().

register_event_client (*O/R, EVENT, FUNCREF, ARG*)
$SERVER->registerEventClient(*O/R, EVENT, FUNCREF, ARG*)

EVENT is any string. If any client adds the event *EVENT* into the server's event loop (using add_event(*EVENT*)) then this will trigger the call:

&FUNCREF(*OBJECT, REGISTRY_KEY, EVENT, ARG*);

for this client. This allows clients for user defined events.

add_event (*EVENT*)
$SERVER->addEvent(*EVENT*)

> Simply adds the string *EVENT* to the end of the event queue. Any clients waiting for this event (registered using the **register_event_client()** function) are triggered.

always_return_child_termination_status(*BOOLEAN*)
$SERVER->alwaysReturnChildTerminationStatus(*BOOLEAN*)

> Sets whether the **register_child_termination_client()** call will trigger a callback with just the child's PID as the third argument (*BOOLEAN* **true**), or a reference to an array holding the PID and the termination status (*BOOLEAN* **false**). Note that this affects the call dynamically—the trigger checks as its triggering to see what type of argument it should pass.

> The default is **false** for backward compatibility.

Client Order for Simultaneous Events

If two events occur simultaneously, or an event occurs for which more than one client is registered, more than one client will be triggered in the same server loop. You may want to ensure that for any pair of clients, a specific client is always called before another in this situation.

This can be achieved using the following function:

ordered_keys_ref()
$SERVER->orderedKeysRef()

> This method/function returns a reference to an ARRAY type object. This object holds RegistryKey objects in whatever order you want to specify. In cases where more than one client is to be triggered within a single server loop, the order of the keys within this array determines the ordering of client activation. For example, this:

```
$r1 = register_...;
$r2 = register_...;
push(@{ordered_keys_ref()},$r2,$r1);
```

> will ensure that in such a case, the client registered on key $r2 will always be called before the client registered on key $r1.

> The object returned by **ordered_keys_ref()** is actually an object of class EventServer::OrderedKeys, and there are several methods in this class which may make it easier for you to manipulate the array (though just treating it as an array reference is absolutely fine):

```
$order = ordered_keys_ref();
$order->push_keys(LIST_OF_KEYS);
$order->pop_key();
$order->shift_key();
$order->unshift_keys(LIST_OF_KEYS);
$order->insert_keys_before(INDEX,LIST_OF_KEYS);
$order->delete_key_at(INDEX);
```

Deregistering Clients

There are two methods for deregistering clients. One is to use the fact that FUNCREF calls have fatal **die()** errors trapped—which means that a client can **die()** when it is triggered, and this will cause that client to be deregistered. (Timing out will have the same effect, but is a silly way to do it since all other clients may be blocked until the timeout is finished).

Note that generating an ALRM signal (e.g., with `kill 'ALRM,$$'`) will produce a `die()` since the alarm handler dies. This means that if you produce an ALRM signal, you are effectively timing out the client, and hence deregistering it.

The second method is to use the function/method provided:

```
cancel_registration (REGISTRY_KEY);
$SERVER->cancelRegistration(REGISTRY_KEY);
```
This deregisters the client that was registered on the key *REGISTRY_KEY*.

The server will deregister a client if there are any problems with it. You can find out when a client is deregistered by setting a function to be triggered when the client is deregistered using the function/method:

```
trigger_on_deregistering (REGISTRY_KEY,FUNCREF);
$SERVER->triggerOnDeregistering(REGISTRY_KEY,FUNCREF);
```
This returns `true` (*REGISTRY_KEY*) on success, `false` (`undef`) on failure. On success, the code reference FUNCREF has been added to the client's registration such that when the client is deregistered, this triggers the call:

```
&FUNCREF(OBJECT,REGISTRY_KEY,method specific args,ARG);
```
where the *method specific args* are determined by the type of registration used (as specified in the section "Registering Clients (Methods)"), and the other terms are as previously defined.

Timeouts Within Client Code

Note `alarm()` should not be used. Instead, a function/method has been provided which allows for nested timeouts.

```
execute_in_array_context_with_timeout (TIMEOUT, TRET, ERET,
                                          FUNCREF,ARGS)
$SERVER->executeInArrayContextWithTimeout(TIMEOUT, TRET, ERET,
                                          FUNCREF,ARGS)
```
TIMEOUT is a time (see "Times and Timing"). This sets the timeout for the call (note that times are rounded up to the next integer number of seconds).

TRET is the value/object returned as the first element of the return array if the call is timed out.

ERET is the value/object returned as the first element of the return array if the call produces a fatal error.

FUNCREF is the CODE reference which is called.

ARGS are the arguments which are passed to *FUNCREF* when it is called.

This method calls *FUNCREF* in an array context with arguments *ARGS*, i.e., the call is:

```
@ret = &FUNCREF(ARGS);
```
If you want to make a call in a scalar context, wrap the function and pass the wrapped function reference, e.g.:

```
sub wrapper { (scalar_call(@_)) }
```
and *FUNCREF* = `\&wrapper`.

If the call is not timed out, and does not produce an error, then the array returned by the *FUNCREF* call (@ret) is returned. If a timeout occurred, then the array (*TRET*) is returned, and if an error occurred during the *FUNCREF* call, then the array (*ERET*, $@) is returned.

This method allows timeouts to be nested—i.e., you can call this method within another function which is being timed out by this method.

maximum_inactive_server_time()
$SERVER->maximumInactiveServerTime()

> Returns the current value that this is set to. This determines the maximum time before triggered clients are timed out. Default is 60 (seconds).

set_maximum_inactive_server_time (*TIME*)
$SERVER->setMaximumInactiveServerTime(*TIME*)

> Sets this value to *TIME*. It should be a positive value.

Forking Child Processes

The call fork() works fine, but the resulting child is a copy of the server with all the clients retained. If the fork is to be followed by an **exec**, this is fine. But otherwise, you need to know which clients are still registered, and which ones you don't want.

Instead of worrying about this, I provide a function/method to fork the server retaining only those clients you know you want. All other clients are deregistered in the child.

fork_with_child_retaining_clients (*LIST_OF_REGISTRY_KEYS*)
$SERVER->forkWithChildRetainingClients(*LIST_OF_REGISTRY_KEYS*)

> This function/method works and returns as fork(): On failure, **undef** is returned, on success the process is forked and the child gets 0 returned while the parent gets the process ID of the child returned.

> In addition, only those clients with registry keys specified as arguments when this method is called, have their registration retained in the child. (Note that if you are handling signals in addition to whatever else, you may want to retain those signal handling clients in the child).

> This saves you from needing to think about which clients need to be deregistered in the child—you only need to consider which ones need to be kept.

Times and Timing

Note that all times should be specified in seconds, and can be fractional (e.g., 2.35). However the fractional part may be of no use depending on where it is used.

Currently, timing-out code using **execute_in_array_context_with_timeout**() has values rounded up to the next highest integer, e.g., 2.35 will be used as 3, and 2 will be used as 3 (this latter use is because **alarm**() can be up to one second less). This is because **alarm**() is being used to time out code in this function, and **alarm**() only has a 1-second resolution.

Timing in the Interval and Timer client registration is dependent on the resolution available from a clock timer used from Perl. If the default **time**() is used, then fractional seconds are effectively rounded up to the next integer, since the times can only be ticked down in seconds. Resolutions will specify how many digits after the decimal point are used. The maximum resolution is one microsecond (six digits after the decimal point). Non-significant digits may be rounded up or down.

The server specifies the timing method during initialization. Currently, if `syscall()` and the `gettimeofday()` system call are available, these are used, otherwise `time()` is used.

However, the availability of the `gettimeofday()` call is established with a call to the method `timeClass()` in the OS specific class given by the OS name as obtained from Config, appended to EventServer::.

For example, if this module is run on SunOS, Config says that the OS name (*osname* parameter) is sunos, in which case the call:

```
EventServer::sunos->timeClass()
```

is made. If this call produces a `die()`, that is trapped, and the default time class (using `time()`) is used. If this does not `die`, it is assumed to return a reference to an array, with first element being the time class to use, and the second any initialization.

For example, in the case of SunOS, this returns:

```
['EventServer::Gettimeofday',116];
```

which specifies to use the `Gettimeofday` class, and initializes this class with the syscall number required to make the call to `gettimeofday()`.

Please tell me what is best on any specific platform, I'll try to include support for it. Currently automatically supported are SunOS 4.*, IRIX 5.*, and Linux. You can add specific OS support just be adding the package and `timeClass()` method as shown.

Remember, you can always let it default to the plain Time class—this is usually sufficient.

The SIG Hash and Signals

If you assign to the %SIG hash, or install signal handlers through POSIX yourself, then you may corrupt the logic of the server. If you need to do this for anything other than a signal (e.g., __WARN__), that should be okay, otherwise you should probably create a subclass to install the handlers you want (see "Creating Subclasses").

If you want to trap a signal, do it by registering a signal client. If you want to trap a signal and need to have control during the signal handler, then subclass the Event-Server class and set the handler in the subclass. And note that any handler which dies will deregister any client which sends a signal for that handler. It's usually a bad idea to do too much in a signal handler (see "Possible Problems").

However, if you are definitely not going to register any clients for a particular signal, you can assign your own signal handler for that signal (though not for ALRM and CHLD).

Terminating children have their PIDs removed from the process list before clients receive the CLD signal. For this reason you should not `wait()` for terminating children. If you want to be notified of this, use the `register_child_termination_client()` registration method. For this reason, registering a client to receive CLD signals is probably of no use.

Signals which have no clients registered for them will not be trapped.

See also "Timeouts Within Client Code" and the entries for methods `register_signal_client()` and `register_child_termination_client()`.

Creating Subclasses

The EventServer server is designed with subclassing in mind. There is only so much generality that can be catered to in any class, and specific applications will do much better by subclassing and specializing.

In making a subclass of the server, the following points are of note:

- The server class is specified in the variable:

  ```
  $EventServer::SERVER_CLASS
  ```

  To allow your subclass to handle all methods (including signal handling, initialization and exporting of functions) you need to specify this variable before requiring the EventServer. This is best done as:

  ```
  package MyServer;
  BEGIN {$EventServer::SERVER_CLASS ||= MyServer;}
  @ISA = qw(EventServer);
  require EventServer;
  ```

  Note that the @ISA call *must* be before the **require** since the **require** contains initialization calls that need to do method lookups on **$EventServer::SERVER_CLASS**.

  Making the assignment conditional on the variable being false allows your class to be subclassed as well.

- The initialization is a method called **init()**. Specifying the SERVER_CLASS variable above will ensure that the **init** method is called in the subclass rather than the EventServer class.

  Initialization occurs when EventServer is required.

- The initialization sets several system constants:

  ```
  EINTR EBADF EINVAL EFAULT WNOHANG
  ```

  and will produce a fatal error if they cannot be set.

  These are set when the method **_setConstantsAndTimeClass()** is called from **init()**, which in turn calls **_setConstants()**. The constants are set using the methods **_setEINTR()**, **_setEBADF()**, **_setEINVAL()**, **_setEFAULT()**, and **_setWNOHANG()**.

  So, for example, to specify the values for SunOS 4, you could declare the following method in a subclass:

  ```
  sub _setConstants {
      my($self) = @_;
      $self->_setEINTR(0x4);
      $self->_setEBADF(0x9);
      $self->_setEINVAL(0x16);
      $self->_setEFAULT(0xe);
      $self->_setWNOHANG(0x1);
  }
  ```

- The initialization sets and initializes the variable time class to use. It does this by finding the OS name from **Config** (**$Config{'**osname**'}**) and making the call:

  ```
  EventServer::osname->timeClass()
  ```

  where *osname* is the OS name as found from CONFIG. If this call does not **die()** (any call to **die()** is trapped), then it is assumed to return an array reference to an array consisting of the time class to use as the first element, and values to initialize the time class for subsequent elements.

Typically, this would be EventServer::Gettimeofday as the first element, and the syscall number for the `gettimeofday` call as the second element (e.g., SYS_get-timeofday from *syscall.h* on many systems). However, you could explicitly specify the default EventServer::Time using this method, or a completely different class.

If you roll your own time class, it must have the following methods implemented appropriately:

`initialize(?)`	Whatever
`now()`	Return an object representing the time now
`newFromSeconds(SECONDS)`	Return an object representing SECONDS
`copy()`	Return new object representing the time in `self`
`newFromDiff(OTHER)`	Return an object representing the time difference between `self` and OTHER
`original()`	Return the time in its original format
`isPositive`	Is the time positive? Return Boolean
`smallerTime(OTHER)`	Return object with smaller time, `self` or OTHER
`time()`	Return the time as a number (a float if needed)
`wholeSecondsRoundedDown()`	Return time as an integer, ignoring fractions

The method `timeClass()` gives the class being used to handle times. Available are EventServer::Time using the `time()` function in Perl (resolution 1 second) and EventServer::Gettimeofday which uses the `gettimeofday()` C system call using `syscall`.

• The `init()` sets the list of signals that can be registered for. The list is obtained from the Config module, minus the untrappable KILL and STOP signals.

• The `setSignalHandlers()` method creates the signal handlers if necessary, and installs those that are to be permanently installed. All signals have a signal handler assigned.

Unlike previous versions, in order to eliminate possible reentrancy bugs, the signal handlers do not execute in subclasses. They are functions in their own namespace which do the absolute minimum possible (mostly just incrementing a variable).

To reimplement a signal handler, you need to respecify the `signalHandler-For()` method. This method takes as argument the signal name, and returns the name of the handler. The handlers should increment the global `$Event-Server::Signal::SIGNAME`, e.g., the TERM signal handler should increment the global `$EventServer::Signal::TERM` (This is all they do by default.)

The ALRM handler is implemented slightly differently, and should not be reimplemented unless you know what you're doing.

Handlers are normally only installed when a client registers for that signal. However, ALRM and CHLD are permanently registered. You can specify which handlers are permanently registered by reimplementing the isSpecialSig-nalHandler() method. This returns true for those signals which should have permanently installed handlers. But note that if you reimplement this, you should include ALRM and CHLD (or CLD) among the set of signals which return true.

Note that any handler which is set to **die** on receipt of a signal will deregister any client which sends a that signal.

The server can be started using:

```
start_server();
```

or:

```
EventServer->startServer();
```

or:

```
MyServer->startServer();
```

since startServer() actually starts the server using the class specified in $Event-Server::SERVER_CLASS.

Example Subclasses

The SunOS example is not necessary, and is just here for illustrative purposes (though it can be used).

```
###############################################################
# Subclass for SunOS4. Speeds up initialization and
# ensures the use of gettimeofday(2) system call.
# Also SunOS doesn't need to have handlers reinstalled
# when they are called.
# NOTE that you can use EventServer
# on SunOS or any other OS without this subclass.
#
package EventServer_SunOS4;

BEGIN {
   if ('/bin/uname -sr' =~ /^SunOS\s+4/i) {
      $EventServer::SERVER_CLASS ||=
        EventServer_SunOS4;
   } else {
      warn "Warning: system is not SunOS4--" +
           "using plain EventServer class\n";
   }
}

@ISA = qw(EventServer);
require EventServer;

sub _setConstantsAndTimeClass {
    my($self) = @_;
    $self->_setConstants();
    $self->_setTimeClass(EventServer::Gettimeofday,116);
}
sub _setConstants {
    my($self) = @_;
    $self->_setEINTR(0x4);
```

```
        $self->_setEBADF(0x9);
        $self->_setEINVAL(0x16);
        $self->_setEFAULT(0xe);
        $self->_setWNOHANG(0x1);
    }


    # No need to reset signal handlers within signal handlers for SunOS
    # Though this is redundant, since POSIX handlers will be used.
    sub signalHandlerForSpecialSignal {
        my($self,$signal) = @_;
        $signal =~ tr/A-Z/a-z/;
        'EventServer::Signal::posix_' . $signal;
    }
    sub defaultSignalHandlerFor {
        my($self,$signal) = @_;

        my $handler = $self->_handlerPrefix() . $signal;
        unless ( defined(&{$handler}) ) {
            eval sprintf('sub %s {$%s++;die "\n"} $%s=0;',
                         $handler,$handler,$handler);
        }
        $handler;
    }


    1;
    __END__
```

Possible Problems

Posting from Todd Hoff:

```
    From: tmh@ictv.com (Todd Hoff)
    Newsgroups: comp.lang.perl
    Subject: Re: Perl 5: alarm BSD vs. SysV
    Date: 3 Apr 1995 10:38:35 -0700
    Organization: ICTV, Inc.
    Lines: 24
    Message-ID: <31pbqr$gbm@anxious.ictv.com>

    In article <31omapINN334@calvin.lif.icnet.uk>,
    >Have you guys tried re-setting the signal handler within the
    >handler. Some systems reset the signal handler to default
    >after it is called.
    >
    >sig handler {
    >    $SIG{'ALRM'} = 'handler';
    >    ...
    >}


    Each UNIX vendor has chosen which version of the "old" signal
    semantics to emulate, thus signal work is not very portable and
    bug prone. Setting the handler in the handler breaks miserably
    because an interrupt can occur before the handler is set. What
    sucks is that you are unlikely to see problems unless you have a
    loaded machine or high interrupt rate, both of which I usually
    have :-(
```

```
The only solution is for perl to use POSIX signals which are safe
(but harder to understand). As an aside do not do anything in a
signal handler but set a flag which tells you if you should call a
handler in the main line logic. Reentrancy bugs are intermitent
and nasty.
--
Todd Hoff       | My words are my own.
tmh@ictv.com    | And i have all this extra white space...
```

In addition, Perl has the problem that signals can interrupt a `malloc`—and this seems prone to causing a SIGSEGV.

The problems are decreased in this server because most of the time it will probably be in the select call, in which case signals are likely to hit it mostly during a select call, not a `malloc`. But you should be prepared for your server to **die**, and have some automated procedure to restart it—like a **cron** job. This is a general problem of signals and Perl (and C), not a specific problem of the server.

If you want the general problem illustrated in a simple way, the following is nice and clear, and will give a core dump after a few seconds:

```perl
@a = qw(1, 2, 3, 4);
$sig_happened = 0;

$SIG{'ALRM'} = 'sig_handler';
alarm(1);

while (1)
{
    foreach $z (@a)
    {
        reset_handler() if ($sig_happened);
    }
}

sub reset_handler
{
    print "Reset the handler\n";
    $sig_happened = 0;
    $SIG{'ALRM'} = 'sig_handler';
    alarm(1);
}

sub sig_handler
{
    $sig_happened = 1;
}
__END__
```

Questions and Answers

How do I exit the start_server loop?

When there are no more clients registered with the server, the method **noClients()** is called. If this method returns a false value then the **start_server** loop terminates. If this returns a true value, then the loop continues.

The default action is for the server to print the message:

```
Error: No clients are registered with the server ...
```

to STDERR and then exit.

To change the default behavior, create a subclass which redefines noClients, and use that subclass. For example:

```
package MyServer;
BEGIN {$EventServer::SERVER_CLASS ||= MyServer;}
@ISA = qw(EventServer);
require EventServer;
sub noClients {0} # Just terminate the loop if no clients left.
```

Note that you don't need this to go into a separate module—it can be in your main program as an initialization if this is all you need, e.g. :

```
$EventServer::SERVER_CLASS ||= MyServer;
@MyServer::ISA = qw(EventServer);
require EventServer;
sub MyServer::noClients {0}
```

Example

Note that you can execute this example with `perl5 -x EventServer.pm` assuming you are in the Perl *lib* directory where you installed this module.

The example program below registers all the various types of clients:

- A timer client (expiring after 3 seconds), which is also told that it is being deregistered when it dies.

- An interval client (sending a SIGCONT every 4.3 seconds for 4 times, then deregistering)—on the fourth triggering this client calls a function to test nested timeouts. That should time out after 3 seconds, though an interrupt could terminate it quicker.

- A signal client which also tests reregistering (triggered on receiving the first CONT from the interval client, at which point it reregisters, changing the function that is called to cont_test2 which makes it catch the second SIGCONT from the interval client, and then deregister).

- An event client, which waits for the event CHECK—that event is sent on the third triggering of the interval client. The Event client calls a nested timeout which tests the functionality of nested timeouts. That should time out after 3 seconds, though an interrupt could terminate it quicker.

- An I/O client, which waits for some input on STDIN (requires a RETURN to be triggered) and then deregisters.

- A child termination client (the process forks right at the beginning, and the child sleeps for 10 seconds then terminates).

- A signal client which will take two SIGINTs (usually generated by typing Ctrl-C) and then deregister, which means that the next SIGINT will cause the default signal action to occur (program termination).

Note that the server will terminate when all clients are deregistered, so if you want to see everything you need to run this at least twice—the first time, you can terminate by giving three Ctrl-Cs *before* all the other clients have deregistered (you can keep the I/O client registered by not typing RETURN), and the second time you can let the program terminate by letting all the clients deregister (two Ctrl-Cs and a RETURN get rid of the SIGINT client and the I/O client—all other clients get deregistered within the first 20 seconds).

```perl
#!perl5
BEGIN {print "Initializing, process id is $$\n";}
use EventServer;

# Timer test client (after 3 seconds)
$r = register_timed_client([],3,sub {print STDERR "Timed test\n"})
        || die "Timed test not registered";

# Deregistering Trigger test
trigger_on_deregistering($r,
  sub {print STDERR "Deregistering Trigger test\n"}) ||
        die "Deregistering Trigger test not registered";

# Interval test client (every 4.3 seconds, 4 times)
register_interval_client([],4.3,\&interval_test)
        || die "Interval test not registered";

sub interval_test {
    $C++;print STDERR "Interval test $C\n";
    kill 'CONT',$$;
    if ($C == 3) {
        add_event('CHECK');
    } elsif ($C > 3) {
        $t=time;
        execute_in_array_context_with_timeout(2.5,0,0,\&t4_test);
        print STDERR "Nested timeout returned after ",
                    time-$t," secs\n";
        die;
    }
}

sub t3_test {
    execute_in_array_context_with_timeout(2.5,0,0,
                            sub {select(undef,undef,undef,9)});
}

sub t4_test {
     execute_in_array_context_with_timeout(6.5,0,0,
                            sub {select(undef,undef,undef,9)});
}

sub t1_test {
    print STDERR "Event client test\n";
    $t=time;
    execute_in_array_context_with_timeout(6.5,0,0,\&t3_test);
    print STDERR 'Nested timeout returned after ',time-$t," secs\n";
    die;
}

register_event_client([],'CHECK',\&t1_test) ||
    die "Event test not registered";
```

```
# Signal test client (once after first Interval test)
$r = register_signal_client([],'CONT',\&cont_test)
        || die "Signal test not registered";

# Reregistration test client (once after second Interval test)
sub cont_test {
    print STDERR "Signal test\n";
    register_signal_client($r,'CONT',\&cont_test2)
}
sub cont_test2 {print STDERR "Reregistering test\n";die}

# IO test client (once after user types <RETURN>)
register_io_client([],'r',STDIN,\&io,\&io,\&io) ||
        die "STDIN test not registered";
sub io {$l=<STDIN>;print STDERR "IO test: $l";die}

# Child Termination test client (after 10 seconds)
defined($pid = fork) || die "Couldn't fork";
if($pid==0){
    #Keep the child around for 10 seconds
    $SIG{'INT'} = 'IGNORE';sleep(10);warn "Child Died\n";exit(23);
}
print STDERR "Start child process pid = $pid\n";
always_return_child_termination_status(1);
register_child_termination_client([],$pid,
    sub {print STDERR "Child (pid=$_[2]->[0]) terminated with status ",
                    $_[2]->[1]>>8,"\n"}) ||
        die "Not registered";

# Signal test client (catches 2 ^C, then uses default SIGINT)
register_signal_client([],'INT',
    sub {$A++;print STDERR "INT caught $A\n";$A1 && die})
          || die "Signal test not registered";

print "Starting server now\n";
start_server();

__END__
```

Author

This software was developed by Jack Shirazi (*js@biu.icnet.uk*) in the Biomedical Informatics Unit at the Imperial Cancer Research Fund, and was partly funded by the European Union Computer Executive Committee under EP6708 "APPLAUSE: Application and Assessment of Parallel Programming Using Logic."

Copyright

This program is free software; you can redistribute it and/or modify it under the terms of either:

- the GNU General Public License as published by the Free Software Foundation; either version 1, or (at your option) any later version, or
- the "Artistic License" which comes with Perl.

This program is distributed in the hope that it will be useful, but WITHOUT ANY WARRANTY; without even the implied warranty of MERCHANTABILITY or FITNESS FOR A PARTICULAR PURPOSE. See either the GNU General Public License or the Artistic License for more details.

17

Archiving and Compression

This section contains utilities for file conversion and compression.

AppleII::Disk — block-level access to Apple II disk image files

Synopsis

```
use AppleII::Disk;
my $disk = AppleII::Disk->new('image.dsk');
my $data = $disk->read_block(1);    # Read block 1
$disk->write_block(1, $data);       # And write it back :-)
```

Description

AppleII::Disk provides block-level access to the Apple II disk image files used by most Apple II emulators. (For information about Apple II emulators, try the Apple II Emulator Page at *http://www.ecnet.net/users/mumbv/pages/apple2.shtml*.) For a higher-level interface, use the AppleII::ProDOS module.

AppleII::Disk provides the following methods.

Methods

`$disk = AppleII::Disk->new($filename, [$mode])`

Constructs a new AppleII::Disk object. *$filename* is the name of the image file. The optional *$mode* is a string specifying how to open the image. It can consist of the following characters (case-sensitive):

r   Allow reads (this is actually ignored; you can always read)

w   Allow writes

d   Disk image is in DOS 3.3 order

p   Disk image is in ProDOS order

If you don't specify d or p, then the format is guessed from the filename. *.PO* and *.HDV* files are ProDOS order, and anything else is assumed to be DOS 3.3 order.

If you specify w to allow writes, then the image file is created if it doesn't already exist.

$size = $disk->blocks([*$newsize*])

Gets or sets the size of the disk in blocks. *$newsize* is the new size of the disk in blocks. If *$newsize* is omitted, then the size is not changed. Returns the size of the disk image in blocks.

This refers to the *logical* size of the disk image. Blocks outside the physical size of the disk image read as all zeros. Writing to such a block will expand the image file.

When you create a new image file, you must use **blocks** to set its size before writing to it.

$contents = $disk->read_block(*$block*)

Reads one block from the disk image. $block is the block number to read.

$contents = $disk->read_blocks(*@blocks*)

Reads a sequence of blocks from the disk image. *@blocks* is a reference to an array of block numbers.

$contents = $disk->read_sector(*$track*, *$sector*)

Reads one sector from the disk image. *$track* is the track number, and *$sector* is the DOS 3.3 logical sector number. This is currently implemented only for DOS 3.3 order images.

$disk->write_block(*$block*, *$contents*, [*$pad*])

Writes one block to the disk image. *$block* is the block number to write. $contents is the data to write. The optional *$pad* is a character to pad the block with (out to 512 bytes). If *$pad* is omitted or **null**, then *$contents* must be exactly 512 bytes.

$disk->write_blocks(*@blocks*, *$contents*, [*$pad*])

Writes a sequence of blocks to the disk image. *@blocks* is a reference to an array of block numbers to write. *$contents* is the data to write. It is broken up into 512 byte chunks and written to the blocks. The optional *$pad* is a character to pad the data with (out to a multiple of 512 bytes). If *$pad* is omitted or **null**, then *$contents* must be exactly 512 bytes times the number of blocks.

$disk->write_sector(*$track*, *$sector*, *$contents*, [*$pad*])

Writes one sector to the disk image. *$track* is the track number, and *$sector* is the DOS 3.3 logical sector number. *$contents* is the data to write. The optional *$pad* is a character to pad the sector with (out to 256 bytes). If *$pad* is omitted or null, then *$contents* must be exactly 256 bytes. This is currently implemented only for DOS 3.3 order images.

$padded = AppleII::Disk->pad_block(*$data*, [*$pad*, [*$length*]])

Pads *$data* out to *$length* bytes with *$pad*. Returns the padded string; the original is not altered. Dies if *$data* is longer than *$length*. The default *$pad* is \0, and the default *$length* is 512 bytes.

If *$pad* is the null string (not **undef**), just checks to make sure that *$data* is exactly *$length* bytes and returns the original string. Dies if *$data* is not exactly *$length* bytes.

pad_block can be called either as AppleII::Disk->pad_block or $disk->pad_block.

Author

Christopher J. Madsen, *ac608@yfn.ysu.edu*

Compress::Zlib—interface to zlib compression library

Synopsis
```
use Compress::Zlib ;

($d, $status) = deflateInit( [OPT] ) ;
($out, $status) = $d->deflate($buffer) ;
($out, $status) = $d->flush() ;
$d->dict_adler() ;

($i, $status) = inflateInit( [OPT] ) ;
($out, $status) = $i->inflate($buffer) ;
$i->dict_adler() ;

$dest = compress($source) ;
$dest = uncompress($source) ;

$gz = gzopen($filename or filenamdle, $mode) ;
$status = $gz->gzread($buffer [,$size]) ;
$status = $gz->gzreadline($line) ;
$status = $gz->gzwrite($buffer) ;
$status = $gz->gzflush($flush) ;
$status = $gz->gzclose() ;
$errstring = $gz->gzerror() ;
$gzerrno

$crc = adler32($buffer [,$crc]) ;
$crc = crc32($buffer [,$crc]) ;

ZLIB_VERSION
```

Description

The Compress::Zlib module provides a Perl interface to the **zlib** compression library (see "Authors" for details about where to get **zlib**). Most of the functionality provided by **zlib** is available in Compress::Zlib.

Warning

The interface defined in this document is alpha and is liable to change.

The module can be split into two general areas of functionality, namely in-memory compression/decompression and read/write access to *gzip* files. Each of these areas is discussed separately below.

The interface that Compress::Zlib provides to the in-memory `deflate` and `inflate` functions has been modified to fit into a Perl model.

The main difference is that for both inflation and deflation, the Perl interface *always* consumes the complete input buffer before returning. Also the output buffer returned is automatically grown to fit the amount of output available.

deflate Interface

Here is a definition of the interface available:

```
($d, $status) = deflateInit( [OPT] )
```

This initializes a deflation stream.

It combines the features of the `zlib` functions `deflateInit`, `deflateInit2` and `deflateSetDictionary`.

If successful, it returns the initialized deflation stream, `$d` and `$status` of `Z_OK` in a list context. In scalar context, it returns the deflation stream, `$d`, only.

If not successful, the returned deflation stream (`$d`) is `undef` and `$status` holds the exact `zlib` error code.

The function optionally takes a number of named options specified as `-Name=>value` pairs. This allows individual options to be tailored without having to specify them all in the parameter list.

For backward compatibility, it is also possible to pass the parameters as a reference to a hash containing the `name=>value` pairs.

The function takes one optional parameter, a reference to a hash. The contents of the hash allow the deflation interface to be tailored.

Here is a list of the valid options:

`-Level`

    Defines the compression level. Valid values are 1 through 9, `Z_BEST_SPEED`, `Z_BEST_COMPRESSION`, and `Z_DEFAULT_COMPRESSION`.

    The default is `-Level=>Z_DEFAULT_COMPRESSION`.

`-Method`

    Defines the compression method. The only valid value at present (and the default) is `-Method =>Z_DEFLATED`.

`-WindowBits`

    For a definition of the meaning and valid values for `WindowBits` refer to the `zlib` documentation for `deflateInit2`.

    Defaults to `-WindowBits=>MAX_WBITS`.

`-MemLevel`

    For a definition of the meaning and valid values for `MemLevel` refer to the `zlib` documentation for `deflateInit2`.

    Defaults to `-MemLevel=>MAX_MEM_LEVEL`.

-Strategy

Defines the strategy used to tune the compression. The valid values are Z_DEFAULT_STRATEGY, Z_FILTERED and Z_HUFFMAN_ONLY.

The default is -Strategy=>Z_DEFAULT_STRATEGY.

-Dictionary

When a dictionary is specified Compress::Zlib automatically calls deflateSetDictionary directly after calling deflateInit. The Adler32 value for the dictionary can be obtained by calling the method $d->dict_adler().

The default is no dictionary.

-Bufsize

Sets the initial size for the deflation buffer. If the buffer has to be reallocated to increase the size, it grows in increments of Bufsize.

The default is 4096.

Here is an example of using the deflateInit optional parameter list to override the default buffer size and compression level. All other options take their default values.

```
deflateInit( -Bufsize => 300, -Level => Z_BEST_SPEED  ) ;
```

($out, $status) = $d->deflate($buffer)

Deflates the contents of $buffer. When finished, $buffer is completely processed (assuming there were no errors). If the deflation was successful it returns the deflated output, $out, and a status value, $status, of Z_OK.

On error, $out is undef and $status contains the zlib error code.

In a scalar context, deflate returns $out only.

As with the deflate function in zlib, it is not necessarily the case that any output will be produced by this method. So don't rely on the fact that $out is empty for an error test.

($out, $status) = $d->flush()

Finishes the deflation. Any pending output is returned via $out. $status has a value Z_OK if successful.

In a scalar context, flush returns $out only.

Note that flushing can degrade the compression ratio, so it should only be used to terminate a decompression.

$d->dict_adler()

Returns the adler32 value for the dictionary.

Example

Here is a trivial example of using deflate. It simply reads standard input, deflates it and writes it to standard output.

```
use Compress::Zlib ;
$x = deflateInit()
   or die "Cannot create a deflation stream\n" ;
while (<>)
{
    ($output, $status) = $x->deflate($_) ;

    $status == Z_OK
```

```
            or die "deflation failed\n" ;
        print $output ;
    }
    ($output, $status) = $x->flush() ;
    $status == Z_OK
        or die "deflation failed\n" ;
    print $output ;
```

inflate Interface

Here is a definition of the interface:

```
    ($i, $status) = inflateInit()
```

This initializes an inflation stream.

In a list context, the function returns the inflation stream, $i, and the zlib status code ($status). In a scalar context, it returns the inflation stream only.

If the inflation is successful, $i holds the inflation stream and $status is Z_OK.

If it is not successful, $i is undef and $status holds the zlib error code.

The function optionally takes a number of named options specified as –Name=>value pairs. This allows individual options to be tailored without having to specify them all in the parameter list.

For backward compatibility, it is also possible to pass the parameters as a reference to a hash containing the name=>value pairs.

The function takes one optional parameter, a reference to a hash. The contents of the hash allow the deflation interface to be tailored.

Here is a list of the valid options:

–WindowBits

For a definition of the meaning and valid values for WindowBits, refer to the zlib documentation for inflateInit2.

Defaults to –WindowBits=>MAX_WBITS.

–Bufsize

Sets the initial size for the inflation buffer. If the buffer has to be reallocated to increase the size, it grows in increments of Bufsize.

The default is 4096.

–Dictionary

The default is no dictionary.

Here is an example of using the inflateInit optional parameter to override the default buffer size:

```
    inflateInit( -Bufsize => 300 ) ;
    ($out, $status) = $i->inflate($buffer)
```

Inflates the complete contents of $buffer.

Returns Z_OK if successful and Z_STREAM_END if the end of the compressed data has been reached.

```
    $i->dict_adler()
```

Example

Here is an example of using `inflate`:

```
use Compress::Zlib ;
$x = inflateInit()
    or die "Cannot create a inflation stream\n" ;
$input = '' ;
while (read(STDIN, $input, 4096))
{
    ($output, $status) = $x->inflate($input) ;
    print $output
        if $status == Z_OK or $status == Z_STREAM_END ;
    last if $status != Z_OK ;
}
die "inflation failed\n"
    unless $status == Z_STREAM_END ;
```

compress/uncompress Interface

Two high-level functions are provided by `zlib` to perform in-memory compression. They are `compress` and `uncompress`. Two Perl subroutines are provided which offer similar functionality.

`$dest = compress(`*$source*`) ;`
>Compresses *$source*. If successful, it returns the compressed data. Otherwise, it returns `undef`.

`$dest = uncompress(`*$source*`) ;`
>Uncompresses *$source*. If successful, it returns the uncompressed data. Otherwise, it returns `undef`.

gzip Interface

A number of functions are supplied in `zlib` for reading and writing `gzip` files. This module provides an interface to most of them. In general, the interface provided by this module operates identically to the functions provided by `zlib`. Any differences are explained below.

`$gz = gzopen(`*filename or filehandle, mode*`)`
>This function operates identically to the `zlib` equivalent except that it returns an object that is used to access the other `gzip` methods.

>As with the `zlib` equivalent, the *mode* parameter is used to specify both whether the file is opened for reading or writing and, optionally, a compression level. Refer to the `zlib` documentation for the exact format of the *mode* parameter.

>If a reference to an open filehandle is passed in place of the filename, `gzdopen` is called behind the scenes. The third example at the end of this section, `gzstream`, uses this feature.

`$status = $gz->gzread(`*$buffer* `[, ` *$size*`]) ;`
>Reads *$size* bytes from the compressed file into *$buffer*. If *$size* is not specified, it defaults to 4096. If the scalar *$buffer* is not large enough, it is extended automatically.

`$status = $gz->gzreadline(`*$line*`) ;`
>Reads the next line from the compressed file into *$line*.

>It is legal to intermix calls to `gzread` and `gzreadline`.

At this time `gzreadline` ignores the variable $/ (`$INPUT_RECORD_SEPARATOR` or `$RS` when `English` is in use). The end of a line is denoted by the C character `\n`.

`$status = $gz->gzwrite($buffer)` ;

Writes the contents of *$buffer* to the compressed file.

`$status = $gz->gzflush($flush)` ;

Flushes all pending output into the compressed file. Works identically to the `zlib` function it interfaces to. Note that the use of `gzflush` can degrade compression.

Refer to the `zlib` documentation for the valid values of *$flush*.

`$gz->gzclose`

Closes the compressed file. Any pending data is flushed to the file before it is closed.

`$gz->gzerror`

Returns the `zlib` error message or number for the last operation associated with `$gz`. The return value is the `zlib` error number when used in a numeric context and the `zlib` error message when used in a string context. The `zlib` error number constants, shown below, are available for use:

Z_OK	Z_STREAM_END	Z_ERRNO
Z_STREAM_ERROR	Z_DATA_ERROR	Z_MEM_ERROR
Z_BUF_ERROR		

`$gzerrno`

The `$gzerrno` scalar holds the error code associated with the most recent *gzip* routine. Note that unlike `gzerror()`, the error is *not* associated with a particular file.

As with `gzerror()`, `$gzerrno` returns an error number in numeric context and an error message in string context. Unlike `gzerror()`, though, the error message corresponds to the `zlib` message when the error is associated with `zlib` itself, or to the UNIX error message when it is not (i.e., `zlib` returned Z_ERRORNO).

As there is an overlap between the error numbers used by `zlib` and UNIX, `$gzerrno` should only be used to check for the presence of *an* error in numeric context. Use `gzerror()` to check for specific `zlib` errors. The `gzcat` example below shows how the variable can be used safely.

Examples

Here is an example script that uses the interface. It implements a `gzcat` function:

```
use Compress::Zlib ;
die "Usage: gzcat file...\n"
    unless @ARGV ;
foreach $file (@ARGV) {
    $gz = gzopen($file, "rb")
        or die "Cannot open $file: $gzerrno\n" ;
    print $buffer
        while $gz->gzread($buffer) > 0 ;
    die "Error reading from $file: $gzerrno\n"
        if $gzerrno != Z_STREAM_END ;

    $gz->gzclose() ;
}
```

Below is a script which makes use of **gzreadline**. It implements a very simple **grep**-like script:

```
use Compress::Zlib ;
die "Usage: gzgrep pattern file...\n"
    unless @ARGV >= 2;
$pattern = shift ;
foreach $file (@ARGV) {
    $gz = gzopen($file, "rb")
        or die "Cannot open $file: $gzerrno\n" ;

    while ($gz->gzreadline($_) > 0) {
        print if /$pattern/ ;
    }

    die "Error reading from $file: $gzerrno\n"
        if $gzerrno != Z_STREAM_END ;

    $gz->gzclose() ;
}
```

This script, **gzstream**, does the opposite of the **gzcat** script above. It reads from standard input and writes a **gzip** file to standard output.

```
use Compress::Zlib ;
my $gz = gzopen(\*STDOUT, "wb")
        or die "Cannot open stdout: $gzerrno\n" ;
while (<>) {
    $gz->gzwrite($_)
        or die "error writing: $gzerrno\n" ;
}
$gz->gzclose ;
```

Checksum Functions

Two functions are provided by **zlib** to calculate a checksum. For the Perl interface, the order of the two parameters in both functions has been reversed. This allows both running checksums and one-off calculations to be done.

```
$crc = adler32($buffer [,$crc]) ;
$crc = crc32($buffer [,$crc]) ;
```

Constants

All the **zlib** constants are automatically imported when you make use of Compress::Zlib.

Authors

The Compress::Zlib module was written by Paul Marquess, *pmarquess@bfsec.bt.co.uk*. The latest copy of the module can be found on CPAN in *modules/by-module/Compress/Compress-Zlib-x.x.tar.gz*.

The **zlib** compression library was written by Jean-loup Gailly (*gzip@prep.ai.mit.edu*), and Mark Adler (*madler@alumni.caltech.edu*). It is available at *ftp://ftp.uu.net/pub/archiving/zip/zlib** and *ftp://swrinde.nde.swri.edu/pub/png/src/zlib**. Alternatively, check out the **zlib** home page at *http://quest.jpl.nasa.gov/zlib/*.

Questions about zlib itself should be sent to *zlib@quest.jpl.nasa.gov* or, if this fails, to the addresses given for the authors above.

Convert::UU—Perl module for uuencode and uudecode

Synopsis

```
use Convert::UU qw(uudecode uuencode);
$encoded_string = uuencode($string,[$filename],[$mode]);
($string,$filename,$mode) = uudecode($string);
$string = uudecode($string); # in scalar context
```

Description

uuencode() takes as the first argument a string that is to be uuencoded. Note that it is the string that is encoded, not a filename. Alternatively, a filehandle may be passed that must be opened for reading. It returns the uuencoded string, including begin and end. The second and third arguments are optional and specify filename and mode. If unspecified, they default to *uuencode.uu* and 644.

uudecode() takes a string to be uudecoded as its argument. If the argument is a filehandle, the handle is read instead. If it is a reference to an ARRAY, the elements are treated like lines that form a string. Leading and trailing garbage is ignored. The function returns the uudecoded string for the first begin/end pair. In array context, it returns an array whose first element is the uudecoded string, the second is the filename, and the third is the mode.

Export

Both uudecode and uuencode are in @EXPORT_OK.

Portability

No effort has been made yet to port this module to non-UNIX operating systems. Volunteers are welcome.

Author

Andreas Koenig, *andreas.koenig@mind.de*. With code stolen from Hans Mulder, *hansm@wsinti05.win.tue.nl*, and Randal L. Schwartz, *merlyn@teleport.com*.

See Also

puuencode(1), puudecode(1) for examples of how to use this module

18

Image, Pixmap, and Bitmap Manipulation

In this section we include utilities for working with pre-existing images as well as modules to aid in the creation of new ones. VRML is also in this section, along with various graphing and drawing utilities.

GD — interface to GD graphics library

Description

GD.pm is a port of Thomas Boutell's GD graphics library (see below). GD allows you to create color drawings using a large number of graphics primitives, and emit the drawings as GIF files.

GD defines the following three classes:

GD::Image
   An image class, which holds the image data and accepts graphic primitive method calls

GD::Font
   A font class, which holds static font information and used for text rendering

GD::Polygon
   A simple polygon object, used for storing lists of vertices prior to rendering a polygon into an image

A Simple Example

```
#!/usr/local/bin/perl
use GD;

# create a new image
$im = new GD::Image(100,100);
# allocate some colors
$white = $im->colorAllocate(255,255,255);
$black = $im->colorAllocate(0,0,0);
$red = $im->colorAllocate(255,0,0);
$blue = $im->colorAllocate(0,0,255);
```

```
# make the background transparent and interlaced
$im->transparent($white);
$im->interlaced('true');
# Put a black frame around the picture
$im->rectangle(0,0,99,99,$black);
# Draw a blue oval
$im->arc(50,50,95,75,0,360,$blue);
# And fill it with red
$im->fill(50,50,$red);
# Convert the image to GIF and print it on standard output
print $im->gif;
```

Notes

To create a new, empty image, send a **new()** message to GD::Image, passing it the width and height of the image you want to create. An image object will be returned. Other class methods allow you to initialize an image from a preexisting GIF, GD or XBM file.

Next you will ordinarily add colors to the image's color table. colors are added using a **colorAllocate()** method call. The three parameters in each call are the red, green and blue (RGB) triples for the desired color. The method returns the index of that color in the image's color table. You should store these indexes for later use.

Now you can do some drawing! The various graphics primitives are described below. In this example, we do some text drawing, create an oval, and create and draw a polygon.

Polygons are created with a **new()** message to GD::Polygon. You can add points to the returned polygon one at a time using the **addPt()** method. The polygon can then be passed to an image for rendering.

When you're done drawing, you can convert the image into GIF format by sending it a **gif()** message. It will return a (potentially large) scalar value containing the binary data for the image. Ordinarily you will print it out at this point or write it to a file.

Methods

GD::Image::new(*width,height*)

> *Class method.* To create a new, blank image, send a **new()** message to the GD::Image class. For example:

> > `$myImage = new GD::Image(100,100) || die;`

> This will create an image that is 100 x 100 pixels wide. If you don't specify the dimensions, a default of 64 x 64 will be chosen. If something goes wrong (e.g., insufficient memory), this call will return **undef**.

GD::Image::newFromGif(*filehandle*)

> *Class method.* This will create an image from a GIF file read in through *file-handle*. The filehandle must previously have been opened on a valid GIF file or pipe. If successful, this call will return an initialized image which you can then manipulate as you please. If it fails, which usually happens if the thing at the other end of the filehandle is not a valid GIF file, the call returns **undef**. Notice that the call doesn't automatically close the filehandle for you.

> To get information about the size and color usage of the information, you can call the image query methods described below.

Example usage:

```
open (GIF,"barnswallow.gif") || die;
$myImage = newFromGif GD::Image(GIF) || die;
close GIF;
```

GD::Image::newFromXbm(*filehandle*)

Class method. This works in exactly the same way as **newFromGif**, but reads the contents of an X Bitmap file:

```
open (XBM,"coredump.xbm") || die;
$myImage = newFromXbm GD::Image(XBM) || die;
close XBM;
```

GD::Image::newFromGd(*filehandle*)

Class method. This works in exactly the same way as **newFromGif**, but reads the contents of a GD file. GD is Tom Boutell's disk-based storage format, intended for the rare case when you need to read and write the image to disk quickly. It's not intended for regular use, because, unlike GIF or JPEG, no image compression is performed and these files can become (very) big.

```
open (GDF,"godzilla.gd") || die;
$myImage = newFromGd GD::Image(GDF) || die;
close GDF;
```

GD::Image::gif

Object method. This returns the image data in GIF format. You can then print it, pipe it to a display program, or write it to a file. Example:

```
$gif_data = $myImage->gif;
open (DISPLAY,"| display -") || die;
print DISPLAY $gif_data;
close DISPLAY;
```

GD::Image::gd

Object method. This returns the image data in GD format. You can then print it, pipe it to a display program, or write it to a file. Example:

```
print MYOUTFILE $myImage->gd;
```

Color Control

GD::Image::colorAllocate(*red,green,blue*)

Object method. This allocates a color with *red, green* and *blue* components and returns its index in the color table, if specified. The first color allocated in this way becomes the image's background color. (255,255,255) is white (all pixels on). (0,0,0) is black (all pixels off). (255,0,0) is fully saturated red. (127,127,127) is 50% gray. You can find plenty of examples in */usr/X11/lib/X11/rgb.txt*.

If no colors are allocated, then this function returns −1.

Example:

```
$white = $myImage->colorAllocate(0,0,0); #background color
$black = $myImage->colorAllocate(255,255,255);
$peachpuff = $myImage->colorAllocate(255,218,185);
```

GD::Image::colorDeallocate(*colorIndex*)

Object method. This marks the color at the specified index as being ripe for reallocation. The next time **colorAllocate** is used, this entry will be replaced. You can call this method several times to deallocate multiple colors. There's no function result from this call.

Example:

```
$myImage->colorDeallocate($peachpuff);
$peachy = $myImage->colorAllocate(255,210,185);
```

GD::Image::colorClosest(*red,green,blue*)

Object method. This returns the index of the color closest in the color table to the *red, green,* and *blue* components specified. If no colors have yet been allocated, then this call returns −1.

Example:

```
$apricot = $myImage->colorClosest(255,200,180);
```

GD::Image::colorExact(*red,green,blue*)

Object method. This returns the index of a color that exactly matches the specified *red, green,* and *blue* components. If such a color is not in the color table, this call returns −1.

```
$rosey = $myImage->colorExact(255,100,80);
warn "Everything's coming up roses.\n" if $rosey >= 0;
```

GD::Image::colorsTotal()

Object method. This returns the total number of colors allocated in the object.

```
$maxColors = $myImage->colorsTotal;
```

GD::Image::getPixel(*x,y*)

Object method. This returns the color table index underneath the specified point. It can be combined with **rgb()** to obtain the RGB color underneath the pixel.

Example:

```
$index = $myImage->getPixel(20,100);
($r,$g,$b) = $myImage->rgb($index);
```

GD::Image::rgb(*colorIndex*)

Object method. This returns a list containing the red, green, and blue components of the specified color index.

Example:

```
@RGB = $myImage->rgb($peachy);
```

GD::Image::transparent(*colorIndex*)

Object method. This marks the color at the specified index as being transparent. Portions of the image drawn in this color will be invisible. This is useful for creating paintbrushes of odd shapes, as well as for making GIF backgrounds transparent for displaying on the Web. Only one color can be transparent at any time. To disable transparency, specify −1 for the index.

If you call this method without any parameters, it will return the current index of the transparent color, or −1 if none.

Example:

```
open(GIF,"test.gif");
$im = newFromGif GD::Image(GIF);
$white = $im->colorClosest(255,255,255); # find white
$im->transparent($white);
print $im->gif;
```

Special Colors

GD implements a number of special colors that can be used to achieve special effects. They are constants defined in the GD:: namespace, but automatically exported into your namespace when the GD module is loaded.

`GD::Image::setBrush()` *and* `GD::gdBrushed`

> You can draw lines and shapes using a brush pattern. Brushes are just images that you can create and manipulate in the usual way. When you draw with them, their contents are used for the color and shape of the lines.
>
> To make a brushed line, you must create or load the brush first, then assign it to the image using `setBrush`. You can then draw in that with that brush using the `gdBrushed` special color. It's often useful to set the background of the brush to transparent so that the non-colored parts don't overwrite other parts of your image.
>
> Example:

```
# Create a brush at an angle
$diagonal_brush = new GD::Image(5,5);
$white = $diagonal_brush->allocateColor(255,255,255);
$black = $diagonal_brush->allocateColor(0,0,0);
$diagonal_brush->transparent($white);
$diagonal_brush->line(0,4,4,0,$black); # NE diagonal
# Set the brush
$myImage->setBrush($diagonal_brush);

# Draw a circle using the brush
$myImage->arc(50,50,25,25,0,360,gdBrushed);
```

`GD::Image::setStyle(@colors)` *and* `GD::gdStyled`

> Styled lines consist of an arbitrary series of repeated colors and are useful for generating dotted and dashed lines. To create a styled line, use `setStyle` to specify a repeating series of colors. It accepts an array consisting of one or more color indexes. Then draw using the `gdStyled` special color. Another special color, `gdTransparent` can be used to introduce holes in the line, as the example shows.
>
> Example:

```
# Set a style consisting of 4 pixels of yellow,
# 4 pixels of blue, and a 2 pixel gap
$myImage->setStyle($yellow,$yellow,$yellow,$yellow,
                   $blue,$blue,$blue,$blue,
                   gdTransparent,gdTransparent);
$myImage->arc(50,50,25,25,0,360,gdStyled);
```

> To combine the `gdStyled` and `gdBrushed` behaviors, you can specify `gdStyled-Brushed`. In this case, a pixel from the current brush pattern is rendered wherever the color specified in `setStyle()` is neither `gdTransparent` nor 0.

`gdTiled`

> Draw filled shapes and flood fills using a pattern. The pattern is just another image. The image will be tiled multiple times in order to fill the required space, creating wallpaper effects. You must call `setTile` in order to define the particular tile pattern you'll use for drawing when you specify the `gdTiled` color.

gdStyled

The gdStyled color is used for creating dashed and dotted lines. A styled line can contain any series of colors and is created using the **setStyled** command.

Drawing Commands

GD::Image::setPixel(*x,y,color*)

Object method. This sets the pixel at (*x, y*) to *color*. No value is returned from this method. The coordinate system starts at the upper left at (0,0) and gets larger as you go down and to the right. You can use a real color, or one of the special colors gdBrushed, gdStyled, or gdStyledBrushed can be specified.

Example:

```
# This assumes $peach already allocated
$myImage->setPixel(50,50,$peach);
```

GD::Image::line(*x1,y1,x2,y2,color*)

Object method. This draws a line from (*x1, y1*) to (*x2, y2*) of the specified *color*. You can use a real color, or one of the special colors gdBrushed, gdStyled, and gdStyledBrushed.

Example:

```
# Draw a diagonal line using the currently defind
# paintbrush pattern.
$myImage->line(0,0,150,150,gdBrushed);
```

GD::Image::dashedLine(*x1,y1,x2,y2,color*)

Object method. This draws a dashed line from (*x1, y1*) to (*x2, y2*) in the specified *color*. A more powerful way to generate arbitrary dashed and dotted lines is to use the **setStyle()** method described below and to draw with the special color gdStyled.

Example:

```
$myImage->dashedLine(0,0,150,150,$blue);
```

GD::Image::rectangle(*x1,y1,x2,y2,color*)

Object method. This draws a rectangle with the specified *color*. (*x1, y1*) and (*x2, y2*) are the upper left and lower right corners respectively. Both real color indexes and the special colors gdBrushed, gdStyled and gdStyledBrushed are accepted.

Example:

```
$myImage->rectangle(10,10,100,100,$rose);
```

GD::Image::filledRectangle(*x1,y1,x2,y2,color*)

Object method. This draws a rectangle filed with the specified *color*. You can use a real color, or the special fill color gdTiled to fill the polygon with a pattern.

Example:

```
# read in a fill pattern and set it
open(GIF, "happyface.gif") || die;
$tile = newFromGif GD::Image(GIF);
$myImage->setTile($tile);
# draw the rectangle, filling it with the pattern
$myImage->filledRectangle(10,10,150,200,gdTiled);
```

GD::Image::polygon(*polygon, color*)

> *Object method.* This draws a *polygon* with the specified *color*. The polygon must be created first (see the example). The polygon must have at least three vertices. If the last vertex doesn't close the polygon, the method will close it for you. Both real color indexes and the special colors gdBrushed, gdStyled, and gdStyledBrushed can be specified.
>
> Example:
>
> ```
> $poly = new GD::Polygon;
> $poly->addPt(50,0);
> $poly->addPt(99,99);
> $poly->addPt(0,99);
> $myImage->polygon($poly,$blue);
> ```

GD::Image::filledPolygon(*polygon, color*)

> *Object method.* This draws a *polygon* filled with the specified *color*. You can use a real color, or the special fill color gdTiled to fill the polygon with a pattern.
>
> Example:
>
> ```
> # make a polygon
> $poly = new GD::Polygon;
> $poly->addPt(50,0);
> $poly->addPt(99,99);
> $poly->addPt(0,99);
> # draw the polygon, filling it with a color
> $myImage->filledPolygon($poly,$peachpuff);
> ```

GD::Image::arc(*cx, cy, width, height, start, end, color*)

> *Object method.* This draws arcs and ellipses of the specified *color*. *cx, cy* are the center of the arc, and *width, height* specify the width and height, respectively. The portion of the ellipse covered by the arc are controlled by *start* and *end*, both of which are given in degrees from 0 to 360. Zero is at the top of the ellipse, and angles increase clockwise. To specify a complete ellipse, use 0 and 360 as the starting and ending angles. To draw a circle, use the same value for width and height.
>
> You can specify a normal color or one of the special colors gdBrushed, gdStyled, or gdStyledBrushed.
>
> Example:
>
> ```
> # draw a semicircle centered at 100,100
> $myImage->arc(100,100,50,50,0,180,$blue);
> ```

GD::Image::fill(*x, y, color*)

> *Object method.* This method flood-fills regions with the specified *color*. The color will spread through the image, starting at point (*x, y*), until it is stopped by a pixel of a different color from the starting pixel (this is similar to the "paint-bucket" in many popular drawing toys). You can specify a normal color, or the special color gdTiled, to flood-fill with patterns.
>
> Example:
>
> ```
> # Draw a rectangle, and then make its interior blue
> $myImage->rectangle(10,10,100,100,$black);
> $myImage->fill(50,50,$blue);
> ```

GD::Image::fillToBorder(*x,y,bordercolor,color*)

> *Object method.* Like fill, this method flood-fills regions with the specified *color*, starting at position (*x, y*). However, instead of stopping when it hits a pixel of a different color than the starting pixel, flooding will only stop when it hits the color specified by *bordercolor*. You must specify a normal indexed color for *bordercolor*. However, you are free to use the gdTiled color for the fill.

> Example:

```
# This has the same effect as the previous example
$myImage->rectangle(10,10,100,100,$black);
$myImage->fillToBorder(50,50,$black,$blue);
```

Image Copying Commands

Two methods are provided for copying a rectangular region from one image to another. One method copies a region without resizing it. The other allows you to stretch the region during the copy operation.

With either of these methods it is important to know that the routines will attempt to flesh out the destination image's color table to match the colors that are being copied from the source. If the destination's color table is already full, then the routines will attempt to find the best match, with varying results.

GD::Image::copy(*sourceImage,dstX,dstY,srcX,srcY,width,height*)

> *Object method.* This is the simpler of the two copy operations, copying the specified region from the source image to the destination image (the one performing the method call). *srcX, srcY* specify the upper left corner of a rectangle in the source image, and *width, height* give the width and height of the region to copy. *dstX, dstY* control where in the destination image to stamp the copy. You can use the same image for both the source and the destination, but the source and destination regions must not overlap or strange things will happen.

> Example:

```
$myImage = new GD::Image(100,100);
... various drawing stuff ...
$srcImage = new GD::Image(50,50);
... more drawing stuff ...
# copy a 25x25 pixel region from $srcImage to
# the rectangle starting at (10,10) in $myImage
$myImage->copy($srcImage,10,10,0,0,25,25);
```

GD::Image::copyResized(*sourceImage,dstX,dstY,srcX,srcY,destW,destH,*
> > > > *srcW,srcH*)

> *Object method.* This method is similar to copy() but allows you to choose different sizes for the source and destination rectangles. The source and destination rectangle's are specified independently by (*srcW,srcH*) and (*destW,destH*) respectively. copyResized() will stretch or shrink the image to accommodate the size requirements.

> Example:

```
$myImage = new GD::Image(100,100);
... various drawing stuff ...
$srcImage = new GD::Image(50,50);
... more drawing stuff ...
# copy a 25x25 pixel region from $srcImage to
```

```
# a larger rectangle starting at (10,10) in $myImage
$myImage->copyResized($srcImage,10,10,0,0,50,50,25,25);
```

Character and String Drawing

GD allows you to draw characters and strings, either in normal horizontal orientation or rotated 90 degrees. These routines use a GD::Font object, described in more detail below. There are four built-in fonts, available in global variables gdLargeFont, gdMediumBoldFont, gdSmallFont, and gdTinyFont. Currently there is no way of dynamically creating your own fonts.

GD::Image::string(*font*,*x*,*y*,*string*,*color*)
> *Object method.* This method draws a *string* starting at position (*x*, *y*) in the specified *font* and *color.* Your choices of fonts are gdSmallFont, gdMediumBoldFont, gdTinyFont, and gdLargeFont.

> Example:

```
$myImage->string(gdSmallFont,2,10,"Peachy Keen",$peach);
```

GD::Image::stringUp(*font*,*x*,*y*,*string*,*color*)
> *Object method.* Just like the previous call, but draws the text rotated counterclockwise 90 degrees.

GD::Image::char(*font*,*x*,*y*,*char*,*color*)
GD::Image::charUp(*font*,*x*,*y*,*char*,*color*)
> *Object methods.* These methods draw single characters at position (*x*, *y*) in the specified font and color. They're carryovers from the C interface, where there is a distinction between characters and strings. Perl is insensitive to such subtle distinctions.

Miscellaneous Image Methods

GD::Image::interlaced( )
> *Object method.* This method sets or queries the image's interlaced setting. Interlace produces a cool venetian-blinds effect on certain viewers. Provide a true parameter to set the interlace attribute. Provide undef to disable it. Call the method without parameters to find out the current setting.

GD::Image::getBounds( )
> *Object method.* This method will return a two-member list containing the width and height of the image. You can query, but not change, the size of the image once it's created.

Polygon Methods

A few primitive polygon creation and manipulation methods are provided. They aren't part of the GD library, but I thought they might be handy to have around (they're borrowed from my *qd.pl* Quickdraw library).

GD::Polygon::new
> *Class method.* Create an empty polygon with no vertices.

```
$poly = new GD::Polygon;
```

GD::Polygon::addPt(*x*,*y*)
> *Object method.* Add point (*x*, *y*) to the polygon.

```
$poly->addPt(0,0);
$poly->addPt(0,50);
$poly->addPt(25,25);
$myImage->fillPoly($poly,$blue);
```

`GD::Polygon::getPt(`*index*`)`
> *Object method.* Retrieve the point at the specified vertex.
>
>> `($x,$y) = $poly->getPt(2);`

`GD::Polygon::setPt(`*index,x,y*`)`
> *Object method.* Change the value of an already existing vertex. It is an error to set a vertex that isn't already defined.
>
>> `$poly->setPt(2,100,100);`

`GD::Polygon:deletePt(`*index*`)`
> *Object method.* Delete the specified vertex, returning its value.
>
>> `($x,$y) = $poly->deletePt(1);`

`GD::Polygon::length`
> *Object method.* Return the number of vertices in the polygon.
>
>> `$points = $poly->length;`

`GD::Polygon::vertices`
> *Object method.* Return a list of all the vertices in the polygon object. Each member of the list is a reference to an `(x,y)` array.
>
>> ```
>> @vertices = $poly->vertices;
>> foreach $v (@vertices)
>>     print join(",",@$v),"\n";
>> }
>> ```

`GD::Polygon::bounds`
> *Object method.* Return the smallest rectangle that completely encloses the polygon. The return value is an array containing the `(left,top,right,bottom)` of the rectangle.
>
>> `($left,$top,$right,$bottom) = $poly->bounds;`

`GD::Polygon::offset(`*dx,dy*`)`
> *Object method.* Offset all the vertices of the polygon by the specified horizontal (*dx*) and vertical (*dy*) amounts. Positive numbers move the polygon down and to the right.
>
>> `$poly->offset(10,30);`

`GD::Polygon::map(`*srcL,srcT,srcR,srcB,destL,dstT,dstR,dstB*`)`
> *Object method.* Map the polygon from a source rectangle to an equivalent position in a destination rectangle, moving it and resizing it as necessary. See *polys.pl* for an example of how this works. Both the source and destination rectangles are given in `(left,top,right,bottom)` coordinates. For convenience, you can use the polygon's own bounding box as the source rectangle.
>
>> ```
>> # Make the polygon really tall
>> $poly->map($poly->bounds,0,0,50,200);
>> ```

Font Utilities

GD's support for fonts is minimal. Basically you have access to **gdSmallFont** and **gdLargeFont** for drawing, and not much else. However, for future compatibility, I've made the fonts into Perl objects of type GD::Font that you can query and, perhaps someday manipulate.

`GD::Font::gdSmallFont`
> *Constant.* This is the basic small font, "borrowed" from a well-known public domain 6×12 font.

GD::Font::gdLargeFont
> *Constant.* This is the basic large font, "borrowed" from a well-known public domain 8×16 font.

GD::Font::gdMediumBoldFont
> *Constant.* This is a bold font intermediate in size between the small and large fonts, borrowed from a public domain 7×13 font;

GD::Font::gdTinyFont
> *Constant.* This is a tiny, almost unreadable font, 5×8 pixels wide.

GD::Font::nchars
> *Object method.* This returns the number of characters in the font.

```
print "The large font contains ",gdLargeFont->nchars,"
                              characters\n";
```

GD::Font::offset
> *Object method.* This returns the ASCII value of the first character in the font

GD::Font::width
GD::Font::height
> *Object methods.* These return the width and height of the font.

```
($w,$h) = (gdLargeFont->width,gdLargeFont->height);
```

Obtaining the C-Language Version of gd

libgd, the C-language version of GD, can be obtained at *http://www.boutell.com/gd/gd.html*. Directions for installing and using it can be found at that site. Please do not contact me for help with libgd.

Author

Lincoln D. Stein, *ldstein@genome.wi.mit.edu*

Copyright

The GD.pm interface is Copyright © 1995, Lincoln D. Stein. You are free to use it for any purpose, commercial or noncommercial, provided that if you redistribute the source code, this statement of copyright remains attached. The GD library is covered separately under a 1994 copyright by Quest Protein Database Center, Cold Spring Harbor Labs and Thomas Boutell. For usage information see the GD documentation at:

> *http://www.boutell.com/gd/gd.html*

The latest versions of GD.pm are available at:

> *http://www.genome.wi.mit.edu/ftp/pub/software/WWW/GD.html*
> *ftp://ftp-genome.wi.mit.edu/pub/software/WWW/GD.pm.tar.gz*

GIFgraph— graph plotting module for Perl 5

Description

GIFgraph is a Perl5 module to create and display GIF output for a graph. The following classes for graphs with axes are defined:

`GIFgraph::lines`
> Create a line chart.

`GIFgraph::bars`
> Create a bar chart.

`GIFgraph::points`
> Create a chart, displaying the data as points.

`GIFgraph::linespoints`
> Combination of lines and points.

`GIFgraph::area`
> Create a graph, representing the data as areas under a line.

Additional types:

`GIFgraph::pie`
> Create a pie chart.

Usage

Fill an array of arrays with the **x** values and the values of the data sets. Make sure that every array is the same size.

```
@data = (
    ["1st","2nd","3rd","4th","5th","6th","7th", "8th", "9th"],
    [   1,    2,    5,    6,    3,  1.5,    1,     3,     4]
);
```

Create a new Graph object by calling the **new** operator on the graph type you want to create (**chart** is **bars, lines, points, linespoints** or **pie**):

```
$my_graph = new GIFgraph::chart( );
```

Set the graph options:

```
$my_graph->set( 'x_label'        => 'X Label',
                'y_label'        => 'Y label',
                'title'          => 'A Simple Line Graph',
                'y_max_value'    => 8,
                'y_tick_number'  => 8,
                'y_label_skip'   => 2 );
```

Output the graph:

```
$my_graph->plot_to_gif( "sample01.gif", \@data );
```

Methods

Methods for All Graphs

`new GIFgraph::chart([width,height])`
> Create a new object $graph with optional *width* and *height*. Default width is 400, default height 300. **chart** is either **bars, lines, points, linespoints, area** or **pie**.

`set_text_clr( colorname )`
> Set the color of the text.

`set_title_font( fontname )`
> Set the font that will be used for the title of the chart. Possible choices are defined in GD. If you want to use this function, you'll need to use GD.

`plot( \@data )`

> Plot the chart, and return the GIF data.

`plot_to_gif( "filename", \@data )`

> Plot the chart, and write the GIF data to `filename`.

`ReadFile ( "filename", some array of columns? )`

> Read data from `filename`, which must be a data file formatted for GNUplot. *N.B.* I still have to figure out how to call the function.

`set( key1 => value1, key2 => value2 .... )`

> Set chart options. See the section "Options."

Methods for Pie Charts

`set_label_font( fontname )`
`set_value_font( fontname )`

> Set the font that will be used for the label of the pie or the values on the pie. Possible choices are defined in GD. If you want to use this function, you'll need to use GD.

Methods for Charts With Axes

`set_x_label_font ( fontname )`
`set_y_label_font ( fontname )`
`set_x_axis_font ( fontname )`
`set_y_axis_font ( fontname )`

> Set the font for the x and y axis label, and for the x and y axis value labels. If you want to use this function, you'll need to use GD.

Options

Options for all graphs

`gifx`, `gify`

> The width and height of the GIF file in pixels. Default: 400×300.

`t_margin`, `b_margin`, `l_margin`, `r_margin`

> Top, bottom, left and right margin of the GIF. These margins will be left blank. Default: 0 for all.

`logo`

> Name of the logo file. This should be a GIF file. Default: no logo.

`logo_resize`, `logo_position`

> Factor to resize the logo by, and the position on the canvas of the logo. Possible values for logo_position are LL, LR, UL, and UR. (lower and upper left and right). Default: LR.

`transparent`

> If 1, the produced GIF will have the background color marked as transparent. Default: 1.

`interlaced`

> If 1, the produced GIF will be interlaced. Default: 1.

`bgclr`, `fgclr`, `textclr`, `labelclr`, `axislabelclr`, `accentclr`

> Background, foreground, text, label, axis label, and accent colors.

Options for Graphs with Axes

Options for `bars`, `lines`, `points`, `linespoints`, and `area` charts.

`long_ticks, tick_length`

If `long_ticks` = 1, ticks will be drawn the same length as the axes. Otherwise ticks will be drawn with length `tick_length`. Default: `long_ticks` = 0, `tick_length` = 4.

`y_tick_number`

Number of ticks to print for the y axis. Default: 5.

`x_label_skip, y_label_skip`

Print every `x_label_skip`th number under the tick on the x axis, and every `y_label_skip`th number next to the tick on the y axis. Default: 1 for both.

`x_plot_values, y_plot_values`

If set to 1, the values of the ticks on the x or y axes will be plotted next to the tick. Also see `x_label_skip, y_label_skip`. Default: 1 for both.

`box_axis`

Draw the axes as a box, if 1. Default: 1.

`two_axes`

Use two separate axes for the first and second data set. The first data set will be set against the left axis, the second against the right axis. If this is set to 1, trying to use anything else than 2 datasets will generate an error. Default: 0.

`marker_size`

The size of the markers used in `points` and `linespoints` graphs, in pixels. Default: 4.

`line_width`

The width of the line used in `lines` and `linespoints` graphs, in pixels. Default: 2.

`axis_space`

This space will be left blank between the axes and the text. Default: 4.

`overwrite`

In bar graphs, if this is set to 1, bars will be drawn on top of each other, otherwise next to each other. Default: 0.

Options for Pie Graphs

`3d`

If 1, the pie chart will be drawn with a 3D look. Default: 1.

`pie_height`

The thickness of the pie when *3d* is 1. Default: 0.1 × GIF y size.

`start_angle`

The angle at which the first data slice will be displayed, with 0 degrees being "3 o'clock". Default: 0.

Author

Martien Verbruggen, *mgjv@comdyn.com.au*

Copyright

GIFgraph::Colour—color manipulation routines for use with GIFgraph

Description

The Colour Package provides a few routines to convert some color names to RGB values. Also included are some functions to calculate the hue and luminance of the colors, mainly to be able to sort them.

Functions

Colour::list(*number of colors*)
> Returns a list of *number of colors* color names known to the package.

Colour::sorted_list(*number of colors*)
> Returns a list of *number of colors* color names known to the package, sorted by luminance.

Colour::rgb(*color name*)
> Returns a list of the RGB values of *color name*.

Colour::hue(*R,G,B*)
> Returns the hue of the color with the specified RGB values.

Colour::luminance(*R,G,B*)
> Returns the luminance of the color with the specified RGB values.

Graph::Edge—object class for an edge in a directed graph

Synopsis

```
use Graph::Node;
use Graph::Edge;

$parent = new Graph::Node('LABEL' => 'Parent Node');
$child  = new Graph::Node('LABEL' => 'Child Node');
$edge   = new Graph::Edge('FROM' => $parent,
                          'TO'   => $child);

$parent->save('simple.daVinci', 'daVinci');
```

Description

The Graph::Edge is a class implementing an edge, or arc, in a directed graph. A graph is constructed using Node and Edge objects, with nodes being defined with the Graph::Node class.

An Edge takes four standard attributes: ID, LABEL, FROM, and TO. In addition, you may also define any number of custom attributes. Attributes are manipulated using the **setAttribute**, **getAttribute** methods, which are defined in the base class, Graph::Element.

Constructor

```
$edge = new Graph::Edge( . . . );
```

This creates a new instance of the Graph::Edge object class, used in conjunction with the Graph::Node class to construct directed graphs.

You *must* specify the FROM and TO attributes of an edge when creating it:

```
$edge = new Graph::Edge('FROM'  => $parent,
                        'TO'    => $child,
                        'ID'    => 'identifier'
                        );
```

where the *$parent* and *$child* are Graph::Node objects. The ID attribute is optional, and must be a unique string identifying the edge. If you do not specify the ID attribute, the edge will be assigned a unique identifier automatically.

Author

Neil Bowers, *neilb@cre.canon.co.uk*

Copyright

Copyright © 1997 Canon Research Centre Europe. All rights reserved. This module is free software; you can redistribute it and/or modify it under the same terms as Perl itself.

See Also

Graph::Node
> for a description of the Node class.

Graph::Element
> for a description of the base class, including the attribute methods.

Graph::Element—base class for elements of a directed graph

Synopsis

```
$object->setAttribute('ATTR_NAME', $value);
$value = $object->getAttribute('ATTR_NAME');
```

Description

The Graph::Element module implements the base class for elements of a directed graph. It is subclassed by the Graph::Node and Graph::Edge modules. This module provides a constructor, and attribute setting mechanisms.

If you want to inherit this class, see the following section "Inheriting This Class."

Constructor

```
$edge = new Graph::Element( . . . );
```

This creates a new instance of the Graph::Element object class, which is the base class for Graph::Node and Graph::Edge.

You can set attributes of new object by passing arguments to the constructor.

```
$element = new Graph::Element('ATTR1'  => $value1,
                             'ATTR2'  => $value2
                             );
```

If you do not set the ID attribute at creation time a unique value will be automatically assigned.

Methods

This module provide three methods, described in separate sections below:

setAttribute
> Change an attribute of an object.
>
> ```
> $object->setAttribute('ATTR_A' => $valueA,
>                       'ATTR_B' => $valueB);
> ```
>
> This method is used to set user-defined attributes on an object. These are different from the standard attributes, such as ID and LABEL.

getAttribute
> Query the value of a object's attribute.
>
> ```
> $value = $object->getAttribute('ATTRIBUTE_NAME');
> ```
>
> This method is used to get the value of a single attribute defined on an object. If the attribute name given has not been previously set on the object, **undef** is returned.

addAttributeCallback
> Add an attribute callback to object.
>
> ```
> $object->addAttributeCallback('ATTR_NAME',
>                               \&callback_function);
>
>
> sub callback_function
> {
>     my $self       = shift;
>     my $attr_name  = shift;    # name of attribute which changed
>     my $attr_value = shift;    # new value of attribute
>
>     # do some stuff here
> }
> ```
>
> This is used to add a callback function to an object, associated with a particular attribute. Whenever the attribute is changed, the callback function is invoked, with the attribute name and new value passed as arguments.

Virtual Methods for Accessing Attributes

In addition to the **getAttribute** and **setAttribute** methods, this class also supports virtual methods for accessing attributes.

For example, if you have set an attribute FOOBAR, then you can call method **foobar()** on the object:

```
$object->setAttribute('FOOBAR', $value);
$value = $object->foobar;
```

This capability assumes that all attribute names will be in UPPERCASE; the resulting method names will be all lowercase.

This feature is particularly useful for manipulating the ID, LABEL, FROM, and TO attributes:

```
$node->label('label for my node');
$id = $node->id;
$edge-to($node);
```

Note

This feature won't work if you use an attribute name which is the same as an existing method for your object class, such as **new**, or DESTROY.

Inheriting This Class

If you want to provide attribute methods for your class, you just need the following lines in your module:

```
use Graph::Element;
@ISA = qw(Graph::Element);
```

This will give your objects the `getAttribute()`, `setAttribute()`, and **addAttributeCallback()** methods.

When subclassing Graph::Element you shouldn't need to override the constructor (`new()`), but should be able to get away with overriding the `initialise()` function.

Restrictions

This class assumes that the object instance for your class is a blessed hash (associative array) reference.

Author

Neil Bowers, *neilb@cre.canon.co.uk*

Copyright

Copyright © 1997 Canon Research Centre Europe. All rights reserved. This module is free software; you can redistribute it and/or modify it under the same terms as Perl itself.

See Also

Graph::Node
> For a description of the Node class.

Graph::Edge
> For a description of the Edge class.

Graph::Node—object class for a node in a directed graph

Synopsis

```
use Graph::Node;
use Graph::Edge;
$parent = new Graph::Node('LABEL' => 'Parent Node');
$child  = new Graph::Node('LABEL' => 'Child Node');
$edge   = new Graph::Edge('FROM' => $parent,
                          'TO'   => $child);
$parent->save('simple.daVinci', 'daVinci');
```

Description

The Graph::Node module implements a *node* in a *directed graph*. A graph is constructed using Node and Edge objects; edges are defined with the Graph::Edge class.

Constructor

Create a new Node object. Returns a reference to a Graph::Node object:

```
$node = new Graph::Node('ID'    => 'identifier',
                        'LABEL' => 'text string'
                        );
```

The ID attribute is optional, and must be a unique string identifying the edge. If you do not specify the ID attribute, the edge will be assigned a unique identifier automatically.

The LABEL attribute is also optional, and specifies a text string which should be associated with the node. This should be used when drawing the Node, for example.

Methods

This class implements the following methods:

`setAttribute()`
   Set the value of an attribute on the node

`getAttribute()`
   Get the value of an attribute of the node

`save()`
   Save the graph under the node in a specified file

The save method is described below. The **setAttribute** and **getAttribute** methods are described in the documentation for the base class Graph::Element, where they are defined.

`save ( $filename [, $format] )`
   Save directed graph to a file. The arguments are:

   `$filename`
      The name or full path of the file to save the directed graph into.

   `$format`
      An optional string which specifies the format which the graph should be saved as. At the moment the only format supported is daVinci, which generates the file format used by the daVinci graph visualization system.

The **save()** method is used to save a directed graph into a file. At the moment the graph is saved in the format used by the daVinci graph visualization system (daVinci v2.0).

The filename extension should be *.daVinci*, otherwise daVinci will complain.

Author

Neil Bowers, *neilb@cre.canon.co.uk*

Copyright

Copyright © 1997 Canon Research Centre Europe. All rights reserved. This module is free software; you can redistribute it and/or modify it under the same terms as Perl itself.

See Also

Graph::Node
   For a description of the Node class.

Graph::Element
    For a description of the base class, including the attribute methods.

Image::Magick—Perl extension for calling ImageMagick's *libmagick* routines

Synopsis

```
use Image::Magick;
p = new Image::Magick;
p->Read("imagefile");
p->Set(attribute => value, ...)
($a, ...) = p->Get("attribute", ...)
p->routine(parameter => value, ...)
p->Mogrify("Routine", parameter => value, ...)
p->Write("filename");
```

Description

This Perl extension allows the reading, manipulation, and writing of a large number of image file formats using the magick library from ImageMagick by John Cristy (*cristy@dupont.com*). It was originally developed to be used by CGI scripts for web pages.

A web page has been set up for this extension. See:

> *http://www.wizards.dupont.com/cristy/www/perl.html*

Author

Kyle Shorter, *magick@sympatico.org*

Bugs

Has all the bugs of ImageMagick and much, much more!

See Also

perl(1)

Image::Size—read the dimensions of an image in several popular formats

Synopsis

```
use Image::Size;
# Get the size of globe.gif
($globe_x, $globe_y) = imgsize("globe.gif");
# Assume X=60 and Y=40 for remaining examples
use Image::Size 'html_imgsize';
# Get the size as "HEIGHT=X WIDTH=Y" for HTML generation
$size = html_imgsize("globe.gif");
# $size == "HEIGHT=60 WIDTH=40"
use Image::Size 'attr_imgsize';
# Get the size as a list passable to routines in CGI.pm
@attrs = attr_imgsize("globe.gif");
# @attrs == ('-HEIGHT', 60, '-WIDTH', 40)
use Image::Size;
```

```
# Get the size of an in-memory buffer
($buf_x, $buf_y) = imgsize($buf);
```

Description

The Image::Size library is based upon the **wwwis** script written by Alex Knowles *(alex@ed.ac.uk)*, and is a tool to examine HTML and add HEIGHT and WIDTH parameters to image tags. The sizes are cached internally based on filename, so multiple calls on the same filename (such as images used in bulleted lists, for example) do not result in repeated computations.

Image::Size provides three interfaces for possible import:

imgsize(*stream*)
> Returns a three-item list of the **x** and **y** dimensions (height and width, in that order) and image type of *stream*. Errors are noted by undefined **undef** value for the first two elements, and an error string in the third. The third element can be (and usually is) ignored, but is useful when sizing data whose type is unknown.

html_imgsize(*stream*)
> Returns the height and width (**x** and **y**) of *stream* pre-formatted as a single string "**HEIGHT=X WIDTH=Y**" suitable for addition into generated HTML IMG tags. If the underlying call to **imgsize** fails, **undef** is returned.

attr_imgsize(*stream*)
> Returns the height and width of *stream* as part of a 4-element list useful for routines that use hash tables for the manipulation of named parameters, such as the Tk or CGI libraries. A typical return value looks like (**"-HEIGHT"**, X, **"-WIDTH"**, Y). If the underlying call to **imgsize** fails, **undef** is returned.

By default, only **imgsize()** is imported. Any one or combination of the three may be imported, or all three may be with the tag **:all**.

Input Types

The sort of data passed as *stream* can be one of three forms:

string
> If an ordinary scalar (string) is passed, it is assumed to be a filename (either absolute or relative to the current working directory of the process) and is searched for and opened (if found) as the source of data. Possible error messages (see "Diagnostics" below) may include file-access problems.

scalar reference
> If the passed-in stream is a scalar reference, it is interpreted as pointing to an in-memory buffer containing the image data.
>
> ```
> # Assume that &read_data gets data somewhere (WWW, etc.)
> $img = &read_data;
> ($x, $y, $id) = imgsize(\$img);
> # $x and $y are dimensions, $id is the type of the image
> ```

IO::File object reference
> The third option is to pass in an object of the IO::File class that has already been instantiated on the target image file. The file pointer will necessarily move, but will be restored to its original position before subroutine end.
>
> ```
> # $fh was passed in, is IO::File reference:
> ($x, $y, $id) = imgsize($fh);
> # Same as calling with filename, but more abstract.
> ```

Recognized Formats

Image::Size understands and sizes data in the following formats:

GIF	JPG	XBM
XPM	PPM family (PPM/PGM/PBM)	PNG

When using the `imgsize` interface, there is a third, unused value returned if the programmer wishes to save and examine it. This value is the three-letter identity of the data type. This is useful when operating on open file handles or in-memory data, where the type is as unknown as the size. The two support routines ignore this third return value, so those wishing to use it must use the base `imgsize` routine.

Diagnostics

The base routine, `imgsize`, returns `undef` as the first value in its list when an error has occurred. The third element contains a descriptive error message.

The other two routines simply return `undef` in the case of error.

Caveats

This will reliably work on Perl 5.002 or newer. Perl versions prior to 5.003 do not have the IO::File module by default, which this module requires. You will have to retrieve and install it, or upgrade to 5.003, in which it is included as part of the core.

Caching of size data can only be done on inputs that are filenames. Open filehandles and scalar references cannot be reliably transformed into a unique key for the table of cache data. Buffers could be cached using the MD5 module, and perhaps in the future I will make that an option. I do not, however, wish to lengthen the dependency list by another item at this time.

Authors

Perl module interface by Randy J. Ray *(rjray@uswest.com)*, original image-sizing code by Alex Knowles *(alex@ed.ac.uk)* and Andrew Tong *(werdna@ugcs.caltech.edu)*, used with their joint permission.

Some bug fixes submitted by Bernd Leibing *(bernd.leibing@rz.uni-ulm.de)*. PPM/PGM/PBM sizing code contributed by Carsten Dominik *(dominik@strw.LeidenUniv.nl)*. Tom Metro *(tmetro@vl.com)* re-wrote the JPG and PNG code, and also provided a PNG image for the test suite. Dan Klein *(dvk@lonewolf.com)* contributed a rewrite of the GIF code.

See Also

http://www.tardis.ed.ac.uk/~ark/wwwis/ for a description of **wwwis** and how to obtain it.

PGPLOT—allow subroutines in the PGPLOT graphics library to be called from Perl

Synopsis

```
use PGPLOT;
pgbegin(0,"/xserve",1,1);
pgenv(1,10,1,10,0,0);
pglabel('X','Y','My plot');
pgpoint(7,[2..8],[2..8],17);
```

```
# etc...
pgend;
```

Description

Originally developed in the olden days of Perl4 (when it was known as **pgperl** due to the necessity of making a special Perl executable) PGPLOT is now a dynamically loadable Perl module which interfaces to the FORTRAN graphics library of the same name.

PGPLOT, originally developed as a FORTRAN library, is now available with C bindings (which the Perl module uses), though a FORTRAN compiler is still required to build it.

For every PGPLOT C/FORTRAN function the module provides an equivalent Perl function with the same arguments. Thus the user of the module should refer to the PGPLOT manual to learn all about how to use PGPLOT and for the complete list of available functions. This manual comes with the PGPLOT distribution and is also available at the WWW address:

   http://astro.caltech.edu/~tjp/pgplot/

Also refer to the extensive set of test scripts (*test*.p*) included in the module distribution for examples of usage of all kinds of PGPLOT routines.

How the FORTRAN/C function calls map on to Perl calls is detailed below.

Argument Mapping: Simple Numbers And Arrays

This is more or less as you might expect—use Perl scalars and Perl arrays in place of FORTRAN/C variables and arrays.

Any FORTRAN REAL/INTEGER/CHARACTER scalar variable maps to a Perl scalar (Perl doesn't care about the differences between strings and numbers and ints and floats).

Thus you can say any of the following:

To draw a line to point (42,$x):

```
pgdraw(42,$x);
```

To plot 10 points with data in Perl arrays @x and @y with plot symbol no. 17 (note the Perl arrays are passed by reference):

```
pgpoint(10, \@x, \@y, 17);
```

You can also use the old Perl4 style:

```
pgpoint(10, *x, *y, 17);
```

but this is deprecated in Perl5.

Label the axes:

```
pglabel("X axis", "Data units", $label);
```

Draw *one* point, see how when N=1 **pgpoint**() can take a scalar as well as an array argument:

```
pgpoint(1, $x, $y, 17);
```

Argument Mapping: Images and 2D Arrays

Many of the PGPLOT commands (e.g., **pggray**) take 2D arrays as arguments. Several schemes are provided to allow efficient use from Perl:

- Simply pass a reference to a 2D array, e.g.:

   ```
   # Create 2D array
   $x=[];
   ```

```
      for($i=0; $i<128; $i++) {
         for($j=0; $j<128; $j++) {
            $$x[$i][$j] = sqrt($i*$j);
         }
      }
       pggray( $x, 128, 128, ...);
```

- Pass a reference to a 1D array:

```
      @x=();
      for($i=0; $i<128; $i++) {
         for($j=0; $j<128; $j++) {
            $x[$i][$j] = sqrt($i*$j);
         }
      }
      pggray( \@x, 128, 128, ...);
```

Here @x is a 1D array of 1D arrays. (Confused? See **perldata(1)**). Alternatively, @x could be a flat 1D array with 128×128 elements, 2D routines such as pggray() etc. are programmed to do the right thing as long as the number of elements match.

- If your image data is packed in raw binary form into a character string you can simply pass the raw string. e.g.:

```
      read(IMG, $img, 32768);
      pggray($img, $xsize, $ysize, ...);
```

Here the **read()** function reads the binary data from a file and the **pggray()** function displays it as a grey-scale image.

This saves unpacking the image data in to a potentially very large 2D perl array. However, the types must match. The string must be packed as an **f***, for example, to use **pggray**. This is intended as a shortcut for sophisticated users. Even more sophisticated users will want to download the PDL module, which provides a wealth of functions for manipulating binary data.

Note

As PGPLOT is a Fortran library it expects its images to be stored in row order. Thus a 1D list is interpreted as a sequence of rows end to end. Perl is similar to C in that 2D arrays are arrays of pointers, thus images end up stored in column order.

Thus, using Perl multidimensional arrays, the coordinate ($i,$j) should be stored in $img[$j][$i] for things to work as expected, e.g.:

```
      $img = [];
      for $j (0..$nx-1) for $i (0..$ny-1) {
         $$img[$j][$i] = whatever();
      }}
      pggray($$img, $nx, $ny, ...);
```

Also, PGPLOT displays coordinate (0,0) at the bottom left (this is natural as the subroutine library was written by an astronomer).

Argument Mapping: Function Names

Some PGPLOT functions (e.g., **pgfunx**) take functions as callback arguments. In Perl simply pass a subroutine reference or a name, e.g.:

```
# Anonymous code reference:
pgfunx(sub{ sqrt($_[0]) },  500, 0, 10, 0);
# Pass by ref:
sub foo {
    my $x=shift;
    return sin(4*$x);
}
pgfuny(\&foo, 360, 0, 2*$pi, 0);
# Pass by name:
pgfuny("foo", 360, 0, 2*$pi, 0);
```

Argument Mapping: General Handling of Binary Data

In addition to the implicit rules mentioned above PGPLOT now provides a scheme for explicitly handling binary data in all routines.

If your scalar variable (e.g., x) holds binary data (i.e., "packed") then simply pass PGPLOT a reference to it (e.g., \$x). Thus, one can say:

```
read(MYDATA, $wavelens, $n*4);
read(MYDATA, $spectrum, $n*4);
pgline($n, \$wavelens, \$spectrum);
```

This is very efficient as we can be sure the data never gets copied and will always be interpreted as binary.

Again see the PDL module for sophisticated manipulation of binary data. PDL takes great advantage of these facilities.

Be very careful that binary data is of the right size or your segments might get violated.

VRML — implements VRML nodes independent of specification (1.x or 2.0)

Synopsis

```
use VRML;
$vrml = new VRML;
$vrml->browser('Netscape+Live3D');
$vrml->at('-15 0 20');
$vrml->cube('5 3 1','yellow');
$vrml->back;
$vrml->print;


OR with the same result

use VRML;
VRML
->browser('Netscape+Live3D')
->at('-15 0 20')->cube('5 3 1','yellow')->back
->print;
```

Description

```
$content_type; # for CGI scripts only
content_type is 'x-world/x-vrml' for VRML 1.0
or 'model/vrml' for VRML 2.0
```

Author

Hartmut Palm, *palm@gfz-potsdam.de*

See Also

VRML::VRML1,   VRML::VRML1::Standard,   VRML::VRML2,   VRML::VRML2::Standard,
VRML::Basic

VRML::Basic—implements basic methods

Synopsis

```
use VRML::Basic;
```

Description

The following methods are currently implemented.

new	debug	VRML_init
VRML_head	VRML_add	VRML_trim
VRML_swap	VRML_put	VRML_row
VRML_pos	VRML_comment	VRML_print
VRML_format	as_string	print
print_as_cgi	save (*$filename*)	

Author

Hartmut Palm, *palm@gfz-potsdam.de*

VRML::Color—implements color methods and names

Synopsis

```
use VRML::Color;
```

Description

X11 color names are:

aliceblue	antiquewhite	aqua	aquamarine
azure	beige	bisque	black
blanchedalmond	blue	blueviolet	brown
burlywood	cadetblue	chartreuse	chocolate
coral	cornflowerblue	cornsilk	crimson
cyan	darkblue	darkcyan	darkgoldenrod
darkgray	darkgreen	darkkhaki	darkmagenta
darkolivegreen	darkorange	darkorchid	darkred
darksalmon	darkseagreen	darkslateblue	darkslategray

darkturquoise	darkviolet	deeppink	deepskyblue
dimgray	dodgerblue	firebrick	floralwhite
forestgreen	fuchsia	gainsboro	ghostwhite
gold	goldenrod	gray	green
greenyellow	honeydew	hotpink	indianred
indigo	ivory	khaki	lavender
lavenderblush	lawngreen	lemonchiffon	lightblue
lightcoral	lightcyan	lightgoldenrod-yellow	lightgreen
lightgrey	lightpink	lightsalmon	lightseagreen
lightskyblue	lightslategray	lightsteelblue	lightyellow
lime	limegreen	linen	magenta
maroon	mediumaquamarine	mediumblue	mediumorchid
mediumpurple	mediumseagreen	mediumslateblue	mediumspringgreen
mediumturquoise	mediumvioletred	midnightblue	mintcream
mistyrose	moccasin	navajowhite	navy
oldlace	olive	olivedrab	orange
orangered	orchid	palegoldenrod	palegreen
paleturquoise	palevioletred	papayawhip	peachpuff
peru	pink	plum	powderblue
purple	red	rosybrown	royalblue
saddlebrown	salmon	sandybrown	seagreen
seashell	sienna	silver	skyblue
slateblue	slategray	snow	springgreen
steelblue	tan	teal	thistle
tomato	turquoise	violet	wheat
white	whitesmoke	yellow	yellowgreen

You can also use:

```
red-40 = '0.4 0 0'
yellow%30 = '0.3 0.3 0'
gray%30 = '0.7 0.7 0.7'
```

VRML::VRML1::Standard—implements nodes the VRML 1.x standard

Synopsis

```
use VRML::VRML1::Standard;
```

Description

The following nodes are currently implemented.

```
[Group Nodes] [Geometry Nodes] [Property Nodes]
[Appearance Nodes] [Transform Nodes] [Common Nodes]
```

Group Nodes

These nodes need End !

Group

Group(*$comment*)

Separator

Separator(*$comment*)

Switch

Switch(*$whichChild*, *$comment*)

WWWAnchor

WWWAnchor(*$url*, *$description*, *$target*)

$target works only with *some* browsers.

LOD

LOD(*$range*, *$center*)

$range is a string with comma-separated values.

$center = SFVec3f

Example: LOD('1, 2, 5', '0 0 0')

SpinGroup

SpinGroup(*$rotation*, *$local*)

This is supported only by some browsers.

Geometry Nodes

AsciiText

AsciiText(*$string*, *$width*, *$justification*, *$spacing*)

$justification is a string (LEFT, CENTER, RIGHT).

Cone

Cone(*$radius*, *$height*, *@parts*)

@parts is a list of strings (SIDES, BOTTOM, ALL).

Cube

Cube(*$width*, *$height*, *$depth*)

Cylinder

Cylinder(*$radius*, *$height*, *@parts*)

@parts is a list of strings (SIDES, TOP, BOTTOM, ALL)

IndexedFaceSet

IndexedFaceSet(*$coordIndex_ref*, *$materialIndex_ref*,
             $normalIndex_ref, *$textureCoordIndex_ref*)

$coordIndex_ref is a reference of a list of point index strings like '0 1 3 2',
'2 3 5 4', ...

$materialIndex_ref is a reference of a list of materials.

$normalIndex_ref is a reference of a list of normals.

$textureCoordIndex_ref is a reference of a list of textures.

IndexedLineSet

IndexedLineSet(*$coordIndex_ref*, *$materialIndex_ref*,
             $normalIndex_ref, *$textureCoordIndex_ref*)

$coordIndex_ref is a reference of a list of point index strings like `'0 1 3 2'`, `'2 3 5 4'`, ...

$materialIndex_ref is a reference of a list of materials.

$normalIndex_ref is a reference of a list of normals.

$textureCoordIndex_ref is a reference of a list of textures.

PointSet
> PointSet(*$numPoints*, *$startIndex*)

Sphere
> Sphere(*$radius*)

> *$radius* has to be > 0.

Property Nodes

Coordinate3
> Coordinate3(*@points*)

> *@points* is a list of points with strings like `'1.0 0.0 0.0'`, `'-1 2 0'`.

Fontstyle
> FontStyle(*$size*, *$style*, *$family*)

> Defines the current font style for all subsequent **AsciiText** Nodes.

> *$style* can be NONE, BOLD, ITALIC.

> *$family* can be SERIF, SANS, TYPEWRITER.

Appearance Nodes

Material
> Material(*%materials*)

MaterialBinding
> MaterialBinding(*$value*)

> *$value* can be:

> DEFAULT
>> Use default binding

> OVERALL
>> Whole object has same material

> PER_PART
>> One material for each part of object

> PER_PART_INDEXED
>> One material for each part, indexed

> PER_FACE
>> One material for each face of object

> PER_FACE_INDEXED
>> One material for each face, indexed

> PER_VERTEX
>> One material for each vertex of object

> PER_VERTEX_INDEXED
>> One material for each vertex, indexed

Normal

> Normal(*@vector*)

@vector is a list of vectors with strings like '1.0 0.0 0.0', '-1 2 0'.

NormalBinding

> NormalBinding(*$value*)

$value is the same as MaterialBinding .

Texture2

> Texture2(*$value*)

Transform Nodes

Transform

> Transform(*$translation*, *$rotation*, *$scaleFactor*,
>   *$scaleOrientation*, *$center*)

$translation is a string like 0 1 -2 .

$rotation is a string like 0 0 1 1.57.

$scaleFactor is a string like 1 1 1.

$scaleOrientation is a string like 0 0 1 0.

$center is a string like 0 0 0.

Rotation

> Rotation(*$rotation*)

$rotation is a string like 0 0 1 1.57.

This node is not supported under VRML 2.0. Use Transform.

Scale

> Scale(*$scaleFactor*)

$scaleFactor is a string like 1 1 1.

This node is not supported under VRML 2.0. Use Transform.

Translation

> Translation(*$translation*)

$translation is a string like 0 1 -2.

This node is not supported under VRML 2.0. Use Transform .

Common Nodes

PerspectiveCamera

> PerspectiveCamera(*$position*, *$orientation*, *$heightAngle*,
>   *$focalDistance*, *$nearDistance*, *$farDistance*)

OrthographicCamera

> OrthographicCamera(*$position*, *$orientation*, *$height*,
>   *$focalDistance*, *$nearDistance*, *$farDistance*)

DirectionalLight

> DirectionalLight(*$direction*, *$intensity*,
>   *$ambientIntensity*, *$color*, *$on*)

PointLight

> PointLight(*$location*, *$intensity*, *$color*, *$on*)

```
SpotLight
    SpotLight($location, $direction, $intensity, $color, $on)
DirectedSound
    DirectedSound($name, $description, $location, $direction,
                  $intensity, $maxFrontRange, $maxBackRange,
                  $minFrontRange, $minBackRange, $loop, $pause)
```

Other
```
WWWInline
    WWWInline($name, $bboxSize, $bboxCenter)
Info
    Info($string, $comment)
```
`$comment` is optional.
```
NavigationInfo
    NavigationInfo($headlight, $type)
```
Works only with Live3D and WebFX.
```
USE
    USE($name)
DEF
    DEF($name)
```

Author
Hartmut Palm, *palm@gfz-potsdam.de*

VRML::VRML1 — implements VRML methods with the VRML 1.x standard

Synopsis
```
use VRML::VRML1;
```

Description
The following methods are currently implemented. (Values in "..." must be strings!)

- `begin('comment')`

  ```
  . . .
  ```
  `end('comment')`
- `group_begin('comment')`

  ```
  . . .
  ```
  `group_end`
- `at('type=value ; ...')`

  Parameter; see `transform_begin`.
- `transform_begin('type=value ; ...')`

  Where *type* can be:
  ```
  t = translation
  r = rotation
  ```

```
          c = center
          o = scaleOrientation
          f = scaleFactor
```

- transform_end
- anchor_begin('URL','description','target=parameter')
- anchor_end
- collision_begin
- collision_end
- lod_begin('range','center')
- lod_end
- background('color','imageURL')
- title('string')
- info('string')
- cameras_begin('whichCameraNumber')
- camera('name','positionXYZ','orientationXYZ',heightAngle)//persp. camera
- camera_set('positionXYZ','orientationXYZ',heightAngle)//persp.cameras
- camera_auto_set
- cameras_end
- light('direction','intensity','color','ambientIntensity','on')
- box('width [height [depth]]','appearance')
- cone('radius height','appearance')
- cube('width','appearance')
- cylinder('radius [height]','appearance')
- line('fromXYZ','toXYZ',radius,'appearance','[x][y][z]')
- sphere('radius_x [radius_y radius_z]','appearance')
- text('string','appearance','size style family')
- fixtext('string','appearance','size style family')
- def('name',[code])
- use('name')
- appearance('type=value1,value2 ; ...')

  Where *type* can be:

```
          a = ambientColor
          d = diffuseColor
          e = emissiveColor
          s = specularColor
          sh = shininess
          tr = transparency
          tex = texture filename[,wrapS[,wrapT]]
```

  For color values see:

```
          VRML::Color
```

See Also

VRML, VRML::VRML1::Standard, VRML::Basic

Author

Hartmut Palm, *palm@gfz-potsdam.de*

VRML::VRML2—implements VRML methods with the VRML 2.0 standard

Synopsis

```
use VRML::VRML2;
```

Description

The following methods are currently implemented. (Values in "..." must be strings!)

- `begin(['comment'])`

  `. . .`

  `end(['comment'])`
- `group_begin(['comment'])`

  `. . .`

  `group_end`
- `at('type=value ; ...')`

  Parameter; see `transform_begin`.
- `transform_begin('type=value ; ...')`

  Where *type* can be:
  ```
  t = translation
  r = rotation
  c = center
  o = scaleOrientation
  f = scaleFactor
  ```
- `transform_end`
- `anchor_begin('Url','description','parameter')`
- `anchor_end`
- `collision_begin`
- `collision_end`
- `lod_begin('range','center')`
- `lod_end`
- `background('skycolor','backUrl','groundcolor','bottomURL','topURL','leftUrl','rightUrl','frontUrl')`
- `title('string')`
- `info('string')`
- `cameras_begin('whichCameraNumber')`
- `camera('positionXYZ','orientationXYZ',fieldOfView) // persp. camera`

- `camera_set('positionXYZ','orientationXYZ',fieldOfView)//persp.cameras`
- `camera_auto_set`
- `cameras_end(['comment'])`
- `light('direction','intensity','color','ambientIntensity','on')`
- `box('width [height [depth]]','appearance')`
- `cone('radius height','appearance')`
- `cube('width','appearance')`
- `cylinder('radius [height]','appearance')`
- `line('fromXYZ','toXYZ',radius,'appearance','[x][y][z]')`
- `sphere('radius_x [radius_y radius_z]','appearance')`
- `text('string','appearance','size style family')`
- `fixtext('string','appearance','size style family')`
- `def('name',[code])`
- `use('name')`
- `route('from','to')`
- `appearance('type=value1,value2 ; ...')`

    Where *type* can be:

        a = ambientColor
        d = diffuseColor
        e = emissiveColor
        s = specularColor
        sh = shininess
        tr = transparency
        tex = texture filename[,wrapS[,wrapT]]

    For color values see:

        VRML::Color

See Also

VRML, VRML::VRML2::Standard, VRML::Basic

Author

Hartmut Palm, *palm@gfz-potsdam.de*

19

Mail and Usenet News

These utilities focus on working with Internet mail and Usenet news, and include interfaces with a variety of mailbox folders and mail servers, a *newsrc* file manager, a client for NNTP, and a MIME utility.

Mail::Address—parse mail addresses

Description

Mail::Address extracts and manipulates RFC 822-compliant email addresses. As well as being able to create Mail::Address objects in the normal manner, Mail::Address can extract addresses from the To and Cc lines found in an email message.

Constructors

new(*PHRASE, ADDRESS,* [*COMMENT*])

Create a new object which represent an address with the elements given.

```
Mail::Address->new("Perl5 Porters",
                   "perl5-porters@africa.nicoh.com");
```

In a message these 3 elements would be seen like:

PHRASE <ADDRESS> (*COMMENT*)
ADDRESS (*COMMENT*)

parse(*LINE*)

Parse the given line a return a list of extracted objects. The line would normally be one taken from a To, Cc or Bcc line in a message:

```
Mail::Address->parse($line);
```

Methods

phrase ()

Return the phrase part of the object.

address ()

Return the address part of the object.

`comment ()`
> Return the comment part of the object.

`format ()`
> Return a string representing the address in a suitable form to be placed on a To, Cc, or Bcc line of a message.

`name ()`
> Using the information contained within the object, attempt to identify the person or group's name.

`host ()`
> Return the address excluding the user id and @.

`user ()`
> Return the address excluding the @ and the mail domain.

`path ()`
> Unimplemented, but should return the UUCP path for the message.

`canon ()`
> Unimplemented, but should return the UUCP canon for the message.

Author

Graham Barr, *gbarr@pobox.com*

Copyright

Mail::Alias——manipulate mail alias files of various formats

Synopsis

```
use Mail::Alias;
```

Description

Mail::Alias can read various formats of mail alias. Once an object has been created, it can be used to expand aliases and output them in another format.

Note that this package is unfinished.

Constructor
`new()`

Methods
`read()`
`write()`
`format()`
`exists()`
`expand()`

Author

Graham Barr, *gbarr@pobox.com*

Copyright

Copyright © 1995 Graham Barr. All rights reserved. This program is free software; you can redistribute it and/or modify it under the same terms as Perl itself.

Mail::Cap—parse mailcap files

Description

This module parses mailcap files as specified in RFC 1524—*A User Agent Configuration Mechanism for Multimedia Mail Format Information*. In the description below, *$type* refers to the MIME type as specified in the *Content-Type* header of mail or HTTP messages. Examples of types are:

* image/gif
* text/html
* text/plain; charset=iso-8859-1

Methods

new()

> Create and initialize a new Mail::Cap object. If you give it an argument, it tries to parse the specified file. Without any arguments, it searches for the mailcap file using the standard mailcap path or the MAILCAPS environment variable if it is defined.
>
> ```
> $mcap = new Mail::Cap;
> $mcap = new Mail::Cap "/mydir/mailcap";
> ```

view(*$type, $file*)
compose(*$type, $file*)
edit(*$type, $file*)
print(*$type, $file*)

> These methods invoke a suitable program presenting or manipulating the media object in the specified file. They all return 1 if a command was found, and 0 otherwise. You might test $? for the outcome of the command.

viewCmd(*$type, $file*)
composeCmd(*$type, $file*)
editCmd(*$type, $file*)
printCmd(*$type, $file*)

> These methods return a string that is suitable for feeding to **system**() in order to invoke a suitable program presenting or manipulating the media object in the specified file. They return **undef** if no suitable specification exists.

field(*$type, $file*)

> Returns the specified field for the type. Returns **undef** if no specification exists.

```
description($type)
textualnewlines($type)
x11_bitmap($type)
nametemplate($type)
```
These methods return the corresponding mailcap field for the type. These methods should be more convenient to use than the `field()` method for the same fields.

Author

Gisle Aas, *aas@oslonett.no*

Maintained by Graham Barr, *gbarr@pobox.com*

Copyright

Copyright © 1995 Gisle Aas. All rights reserved.

This library is free software; you can redistribute it and/or modify it under the same terms as Perl itself.

Mail::Field—base class for manipulation of mail header fields

Synopsis
```
use Mail::Field;

$field = Mail::Field->new('Subject', 'some subject text');
print $field->tag,": ",$field->stringify,"\n";
$field = Mail::Field->subject('some subject text');
```

Description

Mail::Field is a base class for packages that create and manipulate fields from email (and MIME) headers. Each different field has its own subclass, defining its own interface.

This document describes the minimum interface that each subclass should provide and also offers guidelines on how the field-specific interface should be defined.

Constructor

Mail::Field and its subclasses define several methods that return new objects. These can all be termed constructors:

new (*TAG* [, *STRING* | *OPTIONS*])

The new constructor creates an object in the class that defines the field specified by the tag argument.

After creation of the object:

- If the tag argument is followed by a single string, then the **parse** method will be called with this string.

- If the tag argument is followed by more than one argument, then the **create** method will be called with these arguments.

extract (*TAG, HEAD* [, *INDEX*])

> This constructor takes as arguments the tag name, a `Mail::Head` object, and optionally an index.

> If the index argument is given, then **extract** retrieves the given tag from the Mail::Head object and creates a new Mail::Field-based object. **undef** is returned if the field does not exist.

> If the index argument is not given, the result depends on the context in which **extract** is called. If called in a scalar context, the result is as if **extract** was called with an index value of zero. If called in an array context, then all tags are retrieved and a list of Mail::Field objects is returned.

combine (*FIELD_LIST*)

> This constructor takes as arguments a list of Mail::Field objects, which should all be of the same subclass, and creates a new object in that same class.

> This constructor is not defined in Mail::Field, as there is no generic way to combine the various field types. Each subclass should define its own combine constructor, if combining is possible/allowed.

Methods

parse
set
tag
stringify

Subclass Package Names

All subclasses should be called Mail::Field::*name*, where *name* is derived from the tag using these rules:

- Consider a tag as being made up of elements separated by "–".

- Convert all characters to lowercase except the first in each element, which should be uppercase.

- Create *name* from these elements by using the first *N* characters from each element.

- Calculate *N* by using the formula :

      int((7 + #elements) / #elements)

- Limit *name* to a maximum of eight characters, using the first eight characters.

For an example, take a look at the definition of the **_header_pkg_name** subroutine in Mail::Field.

Acknowledgments

Eryq (*eryq@rbine.gsfc.nasa.gov*) for all the help in defining this package so that Mail::* and MIME::* can be integrated together.

Author

Graham Barr, *gbarr@pobox.com*

Copyright

This program is free software; you can redistribute it and/or modify it under the same terms as Perl itself.

See Also

MIME::*

Mail::Folder—a folder-independent interface to email folders

Synopsis

```
use Mail::Folder;
```

Description

This base class and companion subclasses provide an object-oriented interface to email folders independent of the underlying folder implementation.

Warning

This code is in alpha release. Expect the interface to change.

The following folder interfaces are provided with this package:

Mail::Folder::Mbox

Ye olde standard mailbox format.

Mail::Folder::Maildir

An interface to maildir (a la *qmail*) folders. This is a very interesting folder format. It is "missing" some of the nicer features that some other folder interfaces have (like the message sequences in MH), but is probably one of the more resilient folder formats around.

Mail::Folder::Emaul

Emaul is a folder interface of my own design (in the loosest sense of the word :-)). It is vaguely similar to MH. I wrote it to flesh out earlier versions of the Mail::Folder package.

Mail::Folder::NNTP

The beginnings of an interface to NNTP. Some of the Mail::Folder methods are not implemented yet, and no regression tests have been written.

Here is a snippet of code that retrieves the third message from a mythical email folder and outputs it to stdout:

```
use Mail::Folder::Emaul;
$folder = new Mail::Folder('emaul', "mythicalfolder");
$message = $folder->get_message(3);
$message->print(\*STDOUT);
$folder->close;
```

Methods

new($foldertype [, %options])
new($foldertype, $folder_name [, %options])

Create a new, empty Mail::Folder object of the specified folder type. If $folder_name is specified, then the open method is automatically called with that argument.

If *$foldertype* is AUTODETECT, then the folder type is deduced by querying each registered folder type for a match.

Options are specified as hash items using key and value pairs.

The following options are currently built-in:

Create

> If set, open creates the folder if it does not already exist.

Content-Length

> If set, the Content-Length header field is automatically created or updated by the append_message and update_message methods.

DotLock

> If set and appropriate for the folder interface, the folder interface uses .lock-style folder locking. Currently, this is only used by the mbox interface—please refer to the documentation for the mbox interface for more information. This mechanism will probably be replaced with something more generalized in the future.

Flock

> If set and appropriate for the folder interface, the folder interface uses flock-style folder locking. Currently, this is only used by the mbox interface—please refer to the documentation for the mbox interface for more information. This mechanism will probably be replaced with something more generalized in the future.

NFSLock

> If set and appropriate for the folder interface, the folder interface takes extra measures necessary to deal with folder-locking across NFS. These measures typically consist of constructing lock files in a special manner that is more immune to the atomicity problems that NFS has when creating a lock file. Use of this option generally requires the ability to use long filenames on the NFS server in question.

NotMUA

> If this option is set, the folder interface still makes updates like deletes and appends, etc., but does not save the message labels or the current message indicator.

> If the option is not set (the default), the folder interface saves the persistent labels and the current message indicator as appropriate for the folder interface.

> The default setting is designed for the types of updates to the state of mail messages that a mail user agent typically makes. Programmatic updates to folders might be better served to turn the option off so that labels like "seen" aren't inadvertently set and saved when they really shouldn't be.

Timeout

> If this option is set, the folder interface uses it to override any default value for Timeout. For folder interfaces that entail network communications, it is used to specify the maximum amount of time, in seconds, to wait for a response from the server. For folder interfaces that entail local file locking, it is used to specify the maximum amount of time, in seconds, to wait for a lock to be acquired. And for the maildir interface, it is, of course, meaningless.

DefaultFolderType

> If the **Create** option is set and AUTODETECT is being used to determine folder type, this option is used to determine what type of folder to create.

open(*$folder_name*)

> Open the given folder and populate internal data structures with information about the messages in the folder. If the **Create** option is set, then the folder is created if it does not already exist.

> The read-only attribute is set if the underlying folder interface determines that the folder is read-only.

> Please note that I have not done any testing for using this module against system folders. I am a strong advocate of using a filter package or mail delivery agent that migrates the incoming email to the home directory of the user. If you try to use **MailFolder** against a system folder, you deserve what you get. Consider yourself warned. I have no intention, at this point in time, of dealing with system folders and the related issues. If you work on it, and get it working in a portable manner, let me know.

> Folder interfaces are expected to perform the following tasks:

> * Call the superclass **new** method.
> * Call **set_readonly** if folder is read-only.
> * Call **remember_message** for each message in the folder.
> * Initialize **current_message**.
> * Initialize any message labels from the persistent storage that the folder has.

close

> Performs any housecleaning to effect a "closing" of the folder. It does not perform an implicit **sync**. Make sure you do a **sync** before the **close** if you want the pending deletes, appends, updates, etc., to be performed on the folder.

> Folder interfaces are expected to perform the following tasks:

> * Do the appropriate cleanup specific to the folder interface.
> * Return the result of calling the superclass **close** method.

sync

> Synchronize the folder with the internal data structures. The folder interface processes deletes, updates, appends, refiles, and dups. It also reads in any new messages that have arrived in the folder since the last time it was either **opened** or **synced**.

> Folder interfaces are expected to perform the following tasks:

> * Call the superclass **sync** method.
> * Lock the folder.
> * Absorb any new messages
> * Perform any pending deletes and updates.
> * Update the folder-persistent storage of the current message.
> * Update the folder-persistent storage of message labels.
> * Unlock the folder.

pack

For folder formats that may have holes in the message number sequence (like MH), this renames the files in the folder so that there are no gaps in the message-number sequence.

Please remember that because this method might renumber the messages in a folder, any code that remembers message numbers outside of the object could get out of sync after a **pack**.

Folder interfaces are expected to perform the following tasks:

- Call the superclass **pack** method.
- Perform the guts of the pack.
- Renumber the **Messages** member of $self.
- Update **current_message** based on the renumbering.

get_message(*$msg_number*)

Retrieve a Mail::Internet reference to the specified *$msg_number*. The base class method returns 0 if a folder has not been opened in the object or if the specified *$msg_number* does not exist.

If present, it removes the **Content-Length** field from the message reference that it returns.

It also caches the header, just as **get_header** does.

Folder interfaces are expected to perform the following tasks:

- Call the superclass **get_message** method.
- Extract the message into a Mail::Internet object.

get_mime_message(*$msg_number* [, *parserobject*] [, *%options*])

Retrieves a MIME::Entity reference for the specified *$msg_number*. Returns **undef** on failure.

It essentially calls **get_message_file** to get a file to parse, creates a MIME::Parser object, configures it a little, and then calls the **read** method of MIME::Parser to create the MIME::Entity object.

If *parserobject* is specified, it is used instead of an internally created parser object. The parser object is expected to be a class instance and a subclass (however far removed) of MIME::ParserBase.

Options are specified as hash items using key and value pairs.

Here is the list of known options. They essentially map into the MIME::Parser methods of the same name. For documentation regarding these options, refer to the documentation for MIME::Parser.

- **output_dir**
- **output_prefix**
- **output_to_core**

get_message_file(*$msg_number*)

Acts like **get_message()** except that a filename is returned instead of a Mail::Internet object reference. This might be useful for dealing with the MIME-tools package.

Please note that get_message_file does *not* perform any "From" escaping or unescaping regardless of the underlying folder architecture. I am working on a mechanism that will resolve any resulting issues with this malfeature.

Folder interfaces are expected to perform the following tasks:

- Call the superclass get_message_file method.
- Extract the message into a temp file (if not already in one) and return the name of the file.

get_header($msg_number)

Retrieves a message header. Returns a reference to a Mail::Header object and caches the result for later use.

Folder interfaces are expected to perform the following tasks:

- Call the superclass get_header method.
- Return the cached entry if it exists.
- Extract the header into a Mail::Internet object.
- Cache it.

get_mime_header($msg_number)

Retrieves the message header for the given message and returns a reference to MIME::Head object. It actually calls get_header, creates a MIME::Head object, then stuffs the contents of the Mail::Header object into the MIME::Head object.

append_message($mref)

Adds a message to a folder. Given a reference to a Mail::Internet object, appends it to the end of the folder. The result is not committed to the original folder until a sync is performed.

The Content-Length field is added to the written file if the Content-Length option is enabled.

This method will, under certain circumstances, alter the message reference that was passed to it. If you are writing a folder interface, make sure you pass a dup of the message reference when calling the SUPER of the method. For examples, see the code for the stock folder interfaces provided with Mail::Folder.

update_message($msg_number, $mref)

Replaces the message identified by *$msg_number* with the contents of the message in reference to a Mail::Internet object *$mref*. The result is not committed to the original folder until a sync is performed.

This method will, under certain circumstances, alter the message reference that was passed to it. If you are writing a folder interface, make sure you pass a dup of the message reference when calling the SUPER of the method. For examples, see the code for the stock folder interfaces provided with Mail::Folder.

Folder interfaces are expected to perform the following tasks:

- Call the superclass update_message method.
- Replace the specified message in the working copy of the folder.

refile($msg_number, $folder_ref)

Moves a message from one folder to another. Note that this method uses delete_message and append_message so the changes show up in the folder objects, but needs a sync performed in order for the change to show up in the actual folders.

dup(*$msg_number*, *$folder_ref*)

> Copies a message to a folder. Works like refile, but does not delete the original message. Note that this method uses append_message so the change shows up in the folder object, but needs a sync performed in order for the change to show up in the actual folder.

delete_message(*@msg_numbers*)

> Mark a list of messages for deletion. The actual delete in the original folder is not performed until a sync is performed. This is merely a convenience wrapper around add_label. It returns 1.

> If any of the items in *@msg_numbers* are array references, delete_message expands the array reference(s) and calls add_label for each of the items in the reference(s).

undelete_message(*@msg_numbers*)

> Unmarks a list of messages marked for deletion. This is merely a convenience wrapper around delete_label. It returns 1.

> If any of the items in *@msg_numbers* are array references, undelete_message expands the array reference(s) and calls delete_label for each of the items in the reference(s).

message_list

> Returns a list of the message numbers in the folder. The list is not guaranteed to be in any specific order.

qty

> Returns the number ("quantity") of messages in the folder.

first_message

> Returns the message number of the first message in the folder.

last_message

> Returns the message number of the last message in the folder.

next_message
next_message(*$msg_number*)

> Returns the message number of the next message in the folder relative to *$msg_number*. If *$msg_number* is not specified, then the message number of the next message relative to the current message is returned. It returns 0 if there is no next message (i.e., at the end of the folder).

prev_message
prev_message(*$msg_number*)

> Returns the message number of the previous message in the folder relative to *$msg_number*. If *$msg_number* is not specified, then the message number of the next message relative to the current message is returned. It returns 0 if there is no previous message (i.e., at the beginning of the folder).

first_labeled_message(*$label*)

> Returns the message number of the first message in the folder that has the label *$label* associated with it. Returns 0 if there are no messages with the given label.

last_labeled_message(*$label*)

> Returns the message number of the last message in the folder that has the label *$label* associated with it. Returns 0 if there are no messages with the given label.

`next_labeled_message($msg_number, $label)`

> Returns the message number of the next message (relative to *$msg_number*) in the folder that has the label *$label* associated with it. It returns 0 if there is no next message with the given label.

`prev_labeled_message($msg_number, $label)`

> Returns the message number of the previous message (relative to *$msg_number*) in the folder that has the label *$label* associated with it. It returns 0 if there is no previous message with the given label.

`current_message`
`current_message($msg_number)`

> When called with no arguments, returns the message number of the current message in the folder. When called with an argument, sets the current message number for the folder to the value of the argument.

> For folder mechanisms that provide persistent storage of the current message, the underlying folder interface updates that storage. For those that do not, changes to `current_message` are in effect while the folder is open.

`sort($func_ref)`

> Returns a sorted list of messages. Conceptually, it works like the regular Perl sort. The *$func_ref* that is passed to `sort` must be a reference to a function. The function is passed two Mail::Header message references, and it must return an integer less than, equal to, or greater than 0, depending on how the list is to be ordered.

`select($func_ref)`

> Returns a list of message numbers that match a set of criteria. The method is passed a reference to a function that is used to determine the match criteria. The function is passed a reference to a Mail::Internet message object containing only a header.

> The list of message numbers returned is not guaranteed to be in any specific order.

`inverse_select($func_ref)`

> Returns a list of message numbers that do not match a set of criteria. The method is passed a reference to a function that is used to determine the match criteria. The function is passed a reference to a Mail::Internet message object containing only a header.

> The list of message numbers returned is not guaranteed to be in any specific order.

`add_label($msg_number, $label)`

> Associates *$label* with *$msg_number*. The label must have a length > 0 and should be a printable string, although there are currently no requirements for this.

> `add_label` returns 0 if *$label* is of zero length, otherwise it returns 1.

> The persistent storage of labels is dependent on the underlying folder interface. Some folder interfaces may not support arbitrary labels. In that case, the labels will not exist when the folder is reopened.

> There are a few standard labels that have implied meaning. Unless stated, those labels are not actually acted on by the module interface; rather, they represent a standard set of labels for MUAs to use.

deleted

This is used by **delete_message** and **sync** to process the deletion of messages. These are not reflected in any persistent storage of message labels.

edited

This tag is added by **update_message** to reflect that the message has been altered. This behavior may go away.

seen

This means that the message has been viewed by the user. The concept of seen is nebulous at best. The **get_message** method sets this label for any message it is asked to retrieve.

filed
replied
forwarded
printed

delete_label(*$msg_number*, *$label*)

Deletes the association of *$label* with *$msg_number*.

Returns 0 if the label *$label* was not associated with *$msg_number*, otherwise returns a 1.

clear_label(*$label*)

Deletes the association of *$label* for all of the messages in the folder.

Returns the number of messages that were associated with the label before they were cleared.

label_exists(*$msg_number*, *$label*)

Returns 1 if the label *$label* is associated with *$msg_number*, otherwise returns 0.

list_labels($msg_number)

Returns a list of the labels that are associated with *$msg_number*.

If **list_labels** is called in a scalar context, it returns the number of labels that are associated with *$msg_number*.

The returned list is not guaranteed to be in any specific order.

list_all_labels

Returns a list of all the labels that are associated with the messages in the folder. The items in the returned list are not guaranteed to be in any particular order.

If **list_all_labels** is called in a scalar context, it returns the number of labels that are associated with the messages.

select_label(*$label*)

Returns a list of message numbers that have the given label *$label* associated with them.

If **select_label** is called in a scalar context, it returns the number of messages that have the given label.

foldername

Returns the name of the folder that the object has open.

message_exists(*$msg_number*)

Returns 1 if the folder object contains a reference for *$msg_number*, otherwise returns 0.

set_readonly

> Sets the readonly attribute for the folder. This causes the sync command to not perform any updates to the actual folder.

is_readonly

> Returns 1 if the readonly attribute for the folder is set, otherwise returns 0.

get_option(*$option*)

> Returns the setting for the given option. Returns undef if the option does not exist. ·

set_option(*$option, $value*)

> Sets *$option* to *$value*.

debug(*$value*)

> Sets the level of debug information for the object. If *$value* is not given, then the current debug level is returned.

debug_print(*$text*)

> Outputs *$text*, along with some other information, to STDERR. The format of the outputted line is as follows:

```
-> $subroutine $self $text
```

Writing a Folder Interface

General Concepts

In general, writing a folder interface consists of writing a set of methods that override some of the native ones in Mail::Folder. Below is a list of the methods that typically need to be overridden. See the code of the folder interfaces provided with the package for specific examples.

Basically, the goal of an interface writer is to map the mechanics of interfacing to the folder format into the methods provided by the base class. If there are any obvious additions to be made, let me know. If it looks like I can fit them in and they make sense in the larger picture, I will add them.

If you set about writing a folder interface and find that something is missing from this documentation, please let me know.

Initialization

The beginning of a new folder interface module should start with something like the following chunk of code:

```
package Mail::Folder::YOUR_FOLDER_TYPE;
@ISA = qw(Mail::Folder);
use Mail::Folder;
Mail::Folder::register_folder_type(
        'Mail::Folder::YOUR_FOLDER_TYPE', 'your_folder_type_name');
```

Envelopes

Please take note that interfolder envelope issues are not completely ironed out yet. Some folder types (maildir via *qmail*) actually store all of the envelope information, some (mbox) only store a portion of it, and others do not store any. Electronic mail has a rich history of various issues related to this issue (anyone out there remember the days when many elm programs were compiled to use the From_ field for replies instead of the fields in the actual header—and then everyone started do non-uucp email?

Depending on the expectations, the scale of the problem is relative. Here is what I have done so far to deal with the problem.

In the stock folder interfaces, the underlying Mail::Internet object is created with the `MailFrom` option set to COERCE. This causes it to rename a `From_` field to a `Mail-From` field. All interface writers should do the same. This prevents the interface writer from needing to deal with it themselves.

For folder interfaces that require part or all of the envelope to be present as part of the stored message, then coercion is sometimes necessary. As an example, the `maildir` folder format uses a `Return-Path` field as the first line in the file to signify the sender portion of the envelope. If that field is not present, then the interfaces tries to synthesize it by way of the `Reply-To`, `From`, and `Sender` fields (in that order). Currently, it croaks if it fails to find any of those fields (this will probably change in the future— feedback please). At some time in the future, I am going to try to provide some generalized routines to perform these processes in a consistent manner across all the interfaces; in the meantime, keep an eye out for issues related to this whole mess.

Every folder interface should take steps to prevent some of the more common problems like being passed in a message with a `From_` field. If all other fields that carry similar information are present, then delete the field. If the interface can benefit from coercing it into another field that would otherwise be missing, go for it. Even if all of the other interfaces do the right thing, a user might hand it a mail message that contains a `From_` field, so one cannot be too careful.

The recipient portion of the envelope is pretty much not dealt with at all. If it presents any major issues, describe them to me, and I will try to work something out.

Methods to Override

The following methods typically need to be overridden in the folder interface:

open	close
sync	pack
get_header	get_message
get_message_file	update_message

Folder Interface Methods

This section describes the methods that are available for use by interface writers. Refer to the stock folder interfaces for examples of their use.

register_folder_type(*$class*, *$type*)
> Registers a folder interface with Mail::Folder.

is_valid_folder_format(*$default*, *$foldername*)
> In a folder interface, this method should return 1 if it thinks the folder is a valid format and return 0 otherwise. The method is used by the Mail::Folder **open** method when AUTODETECT is used as the folder type. The **open** method iterates through the list of known folder interfaces until it finds one that answers yes to the question.

> This method is always overridden by the folder interface.

init
> This is a stub entry called by **new**. The primary purpose is to provide a method for subclasses to override for initialization to be performed at constructor time. It is called after the object members' variables have been initialized and before the optional call to **open**. The **new** method returns **undef** if the init method returns 0. Only interface writers need to worry about this one.

create(*$foldername*)
> In a folder interface, this method should return 1 after it successfully creates a folder with the given name and 0 otherwise.
>
> This method is always overridden by the folder interface. The base class method returns a 0 so that if **create** is not defined in the folder interface, the call to **create** will return failure.

cache_header(*$msg_number*, *$header_ref*)
> Associates *$header_ref* with *$msg_number* in the internal header cache of the object.

invalidate_header(*$msg_number*)
> Clobbers the header cache entry for *$msg_number*.

remember_message(*$msg_number*)
> Adds an entry for *$msg_number* to the internal data structure of the folder object.

forget_message(*$msg_number*)
> Removes the entry for *$msg_number* from the internal data structure of the folder object.

detect_folder_type(*$foldername*)
> Returns the folder type of the given *$foldername*. Returns **undef** if it cannot deduce the folder type.

Caveats

Forking Children

If a script forks while having any folder open, only the parent should make changes to the folder. In addition, when the parent closes the folder, related temporary files will be reaped. This temporary file cleanup does not occur for the child. I am contemplating a more general solution to this problem, but until then *only parents should manipulate mail.*

Folder Locking

Please note that I am not pleased with folder locking as it is currently implemented in Mail::Folder for some of the folder interfaces. It will improve.

Folder locking is problematic in certain circumstances. For those not familiar with some of these issues, I will elaborate.

An interface like *maildir* has no locking issues. This is because the design of the folder format inherently eliminates the need for locking (cheers from the crowd).

An interface like *nntp* has no locking issues, because it merely implements an interface to a network protocol. Locking issues are left as an exercise to the server on the other end of a socket.

Interfaces like *mbox*, on the other hand, are another story.

Taken as a whole, the locking mechanism(s) used for mbox folders are not inherently rock-solid in all circumstances. To further complicate things, there are several variations that have been implemented as attempts to work around the fundamental issues of the design of mbox folder locking.

In the simplest implementation, an mbox folder merely uses a *dotlock* file as a semaphore to prevent simultaneous updates to the folder. All processes are supposed to cooperate and honor the lock file.

In a non-NFS environment, typically the only issue with a dotlock is that the code implementing the lock file needs to be written in such a way as to prevent race conditions by testing for the locking and creating the lockfile. This is usually done with an O_EXCL flag passed to the call to open(2). This allows for an atomic creation of the lock file if and only if the file does not already exist, assuming the operating system implements the O_EXCL feature. Some operating systems' implementations have also resorted to using lockf, fcntl, or flock as way to atomically test and set the folder lock. The major issue for Mail::Folder in this type of environment is to merely detect what flavor(s) is necessary and implement it.

In an NFS environment, the story is somewhat different and a lot more complicated. The O_EXCL is not atomic across NFS, some implementations of flock do not work across NFS, and not all operating systems use flock to lock mbox folders. To further complicate matters, all processes that lock the mbox folder need to do it in such a way that all clients mounting the data can also cooperate in the locking mechanism.

Here are a few of the outstanding folder-locking issues in Mail::Folder for folder interfaces that do not provide a native way to solve locking issues.

- Only DotLock is supported.

  There are snippets of code related to flock, but I have disabled it for a time.

- Not NFS safe.

Author

Kevin Johnson, *kjj@pobox.com*

Copyright

Copyright © 1996–1997 Kevin Johnson.

Mail::Folder::Emaul— an Emaul folder interface for Mail::Folder

Synopsis

```
use Mail::Folder::Emaul;
```

Description

This module provides an interface to the Emaul folder mechanism. It is currently intended to be used as an example of hooking a folder interface into Mail::Folder.

Warning

This code is in alpha release. Expect the interface to change.

The folder structure of Emaul is styled after MH. It uses directories for folders and numerically named files for the individual mail messages. The current message for a particular folder is stored in the file *.current_msg* in the folder directory.

Folder locking is accomplished through the use of a *.lock* file in the folder directory.

If a `Timeout` option is specified when the object is created, that value is used to determine the timeout for attempting to acquire a folder lock. The default is 10 seconds.

Methods

open(*$folder_name*)

Populates the Mail::Folder object with information about the folder.

- Call the superclass `open` method.
- Make sure it is a valid mbox folder.
- Check to see that it is read-only
- Lock the folder if it is not read-only. (This is dubious.)
- For every message file in the *$folder_name* directory, add the `message_number` to the list of messages in the object.
- Load the contents of *$folder_dir/.current_msg* into $self->{Current}.
- Set `current_message`.
- Load message labels.
- Unlock the folder if it is not read-only.

sync

Flushes any pending changes out to the original folder.

- Call the superclass `sync` method.
- Return −1 if the folder is read-only.
- Return −1 if the folder cannot be locked.
- Scan the folder directory for message files that were not present the last time the folder was either `opened` or `synced` and absorb them.
- For every pending delete, unlink that file in the folder directory.
- Clear out the "pending delete" list.
- Update the *.current_msg* file and the *.msg_labels* file if the `NotMUA` option is not set.
- Return the number of new messages found.

pack

Calls the superclass `pack` method.

Returns 0 if the folder is read-only.

Returns 0 if the folder cannot be locked.

Renames the message files in the folder so that there are no gaps in the numbering sequence. It tweaks `current_message` accordingly.

Old deleted message files (ones that start with *,*) are also renamed as necessary.

It abandons the operation and returns 0 if a `rename` fails, otherwise it returns 1.

Please note that `pack` acts on the real folder.

get_message(*$msg_number*)

> Calls the superclass get_message method.
>
> Retrieves the given mail message file into a Mail::Internet object reference and returns the reference.
>
> It coerces the From_ field into a Mail-From field, adds the seen label to the message, removes the Content-Length field if present, and caches the header.
>
> Returns undef on failure.

get_message_file(*$msg_number*)

> Calls the superclass get_message_file method.
>
> Retrieves the given mail message file and returns the name of the file.
>
> Returns undef on failure.

get_header(*$msg_number*)

> Calls the superclass get_header method.
>
> If the particular header has never been retrieved, then get_header loads the header of the given mail message into a member of $self->{Messages}{$msg_number} and returns the object reference.
>
> If the header for the given mail message has already been retrieved in a prior call to get_header, then the cached entry is returned.
>
> The Content-Length field is deleted from the header object it returns.

append_message(*$mref*)

> Calls the superclass append_message method.
>
> Returns 0 if it cannot lock the folder.
>
> Appends the contents of the mail message contained in $mref to the folder.
>
> It also caches the header.
>
> Please note that, contrary to other documentation for Mail::Folder, the Emaul append_message method actually updates the real folder, rather than queueing it up for a subsequent sync. The dup and refile methods are also affected. This will be fixed soon.

update_message(*$msg_number, $mref*)

> Calls the superclass update_message method.
>
> It returns 0 if it cannot lock the folder.
>
> Replaces the message pointed to by *$msg_number* with the contents of the Mail::Internet object reference *$mref*.
>
> Please note that, contrary to other documentation for Mail::Folder, the Emaul update_message method actually updates the real folder, rather than queueing it up for a subsequent sync. This will be fixed soon.

is_valid_folder_format(*$foldername*)

> Returns 0 if the folder is not a directory or looks like a maildir folder. The current logic allows it to handle MH directories, but watch out; you should probably set the NotMUA option so the interface doesn't create its own little folder droppings like *.msg_labels* and such.

create(*$foldername*)

> Returns 0 if the folder already exists.
>
> Creates a new folder named *$foldername* with mode 0700 and then returns 1.

Author

Kevin Johnson, *kjj@pobox.com*

Copyright

Copyright © 1996-1997 Kevin Johnson.

Mail::Folder::Maildir—a maildir folder interface for Mail::Folder

Synopsis

```
use Mail::Folder::Maildir;
```

Description

This module provides an interface to the **maildir** folder mechanism.

Warning

This code is in alpha release. Expect the interface to change.

The **maildir** folder format is the preferred folder mechanism for the *qmail* mail transport agent. It uses directories as folders and files as messages. It also provides separate directories for new and current messages. One of the most distinguishing features of the *maildir* format is that it accomplishes its job without the need for file locking, so it's better equipped to deal with things like NFS mounts and the like.

More information about *qmail* is available from *http://pobox.com/~djb/qmail.html*.

Methods

open(*$folder_name*)

Populates the Mail::Folder object with information about the folder.

- Calls the superclass **open** method.

- Makes sure it is a valid *maildir* folder.

- Detects whether the folder is read-only.

- Cleans the folder **tmp** directory.

- Moves message from the folder **new** directory into the **cur** directory.

- For every message in the folder, adds a new message number to the list of messages in the object and remembers the association between the message number and the message filename.

- Set **current_message** to 1.

close

Deletes the working copy of the folder and calls the superclass **close** method.

sync

Calls the superclass **sync** method and scans for new messages; it absorbs any found. If the folder is not read-only, expunge messages marked for deletion. Updates the **:info** portion of each file in the folder.

Returns the number of new messages found.

pack

> Calls the superclass **pack** method. Reassociates the filenames in the folders with message numbers, deleting holes in the sequence of message numbers.

get_message(*$msg_number*)

> Calls the superclass **get_message** method.

> Retrieves the contents of the file pointed to by *$msg_number* into a Mail::Internet object reference, caches the header, marks the message as **seen**, and returns the reference.

get_message_file(*$msg_number*)

> Calls the superclass **get_message_file** method.

> Retrieves the given mail message file pointed to by *$msg_number* and returns the name of the file.

get_header(*$msg_number*)

> If the particular header has never been retrieved, then **get_header** loads the header of the given mail message into a member of **$self->{Messages}{***$msg_number*} and returns the object reference.

> If the header for the given mail message has already been retrieved in a prior call to **get_header**, then the cached entry is returned.

append_message(*$mref*)

> Calls the superclass **append_message** method.

> Writes a temporary copy of the message in *$mref* to the folder **tmp** directory, then moves that temporary copy into the folder **cur** directory.

> It deletes the **From_** line in the header if one is present.

update_message(*$msg_number*, *$mref*)

> Calls the superclass **update_message** method.

> Writes a temporary copy of the message in *$mref* to the folder **tmp** directory, then moves that temporary copy into the folder **cur** directory, replacing the message pointed to by *$msg_number*.

> It deletes the **From_** line in the header if one is present.

is_valid_folder_format(*$foldername*)

> Returns 1 if the folder is a directory and contains **tmp**, **cur**, and **new** subdirectories; otherwise returns 0.

create(*$foldername*)

> Creates a new folder named *$foldername*. Returns 0 if the folder already exists; otherwise returns 1.

Author

Kevin Johnson, *kjj@pobox.com*

Copyright

Mail::Folder::Mbox— a UNIX mbox interface for Mail::Folder

Synopsis

```
use Mail::Folder::Mbox;
```

Description

This module provides an interface to UNIX mbox folders.

Warning

This code is in alpha release. Expect the interface to change.

The *mbox* folder format is the standard monolithic folder structure prevalent on UNIX. A single folder is contained within a single file. Each message starts with a line matching /^From / and ends with a blank line.

The folder architecture does not provide any persistently stored current message variable, so the current message in this folder interface defaults to 1 and is not retained between opens of a folder.

If the Timeout option is specified when the object is created, that value is used to determine the timeout for attempting to acquire a folder lock. The default is 10 seconds.

If the DotLock option is specified when the object is created, that value is used to determine whether or not to use .lock-style folder locking. The default value is 1.

If the Flock option is specified when the object is created, that value is used to determined whether or not to use flock-style folder locking. By default, the option is not set.

If the NFSLock option is specified when the object is created, that value is used to determine whether or not special measures are taken when doing DotLocking. These special measures consist of constructing the lock file in a manner that is more immune to atomicity problems with NFS when creating a folder lock file. By default, the option is not set. This option requires the ability to use long filenames.

It is currently a fatal error to have both DotLock and Flock disabled.

Note: flock locking is currently disabled until I can sift out the "right way."

Methods

open(*$folder_name*)

Calls the superclass open method.

- Check to see if the folder is a valid mbox folder.
- Mark it as read-only if the folder is not writable.
- Lock the folder.
- Split the folder into individual messages in a temporary working directory.
- Unlock the folder.
- Cache all the headers.
- Update the appropriate labels with information in the Status fields.
- Set current_message to 1.

close

Deletes the internal working copy of the folder and calls the superclass close method.

sync
>   Calls the superclass sync method.
>
>   - Lock the folder.
>   - Extract into the temporary working directory any new messages that have been appended to the folder since the last time the folder was either opened or synced.
>   - Create a new copy of the folder, populate it with the messages in the working copy that are not flagged for deletion, and update the Status fields appropriately.
>   - Move the original folder to a temporary location.
>   - Move the new folder into place.
>   - Delete the old original folder.
>   - Unlock the folder.

pack
>   Calls the superclass pack method.
>
>   Renames the message list so that there are no gaps in the numbering sequence.
>
>   It also tweaks the current_message accordingly.

get_message (*$msg_number*)
>   Calls the superclass get_message method.
>
>   Retrieves the given mail message file into a Mail::Internet object reference, sets the seen label, and returns the reference.
>
>   If the Content-Length option is not set, then get_message unescapes "From " lines in the body of the message.

get_message_file (*$msg_number*)
>   Calls the superclass get_message_file method.
>
>   Retrieves the given mail message file and returns the name of the file.
>
>   Returns undef on failure.
>
>   This method does *not* currently do any "From " unescaping.

get_header(*$msg_number*)
>   If the particular header has never been retrieved, then get_header loads (in a manner similar to get_message) the header of the given mail message into $self->{Messages}{*$msg_number*}{Header} and returns the object reference.
>
>   If the header for the given mail message has already been retrieved in a prior call to get_header, then the cached entry is returned.
>
>   It also calls the superclass get_header method.

append_message(*$mref*)
>   Calls the superclass append_message method.
>
>   Creates a new mail message file, in the temporary working directory, with the contents of the mail message contained in *$mref*. It synthesizes a "From " line if one is not present in $mref.
>
>   If the "Content-Length" option is not set, then get_message escapes "From " lines in the body of the message.

update_message(*$msg_number, $mref*)

Calls the superclass **update_message** method.

Replaces the message pointed to by *$msg_number* with the contents of the Mail::Internet object reference *$mref*.

It synthesizes a "From " line if one is not present in *$mref*.

If the "Content-Length" option is not set, then **get_message** escapes "From " lines in the body of the message.

init

Initializes various items specific to mbox.

- Determines an appropriate temporary directory. If the TMPDIR environment variable is set, it uses that; otherwise it uses */tmp*. The working directory will be a subdirectory in that directory.

- Bumps a sequence number used for unique temporary filenames.

- Initializes $self->{WorkingDir} to the name of a directory that is used to hold the working copies of the messages in the folder.

is_valid_folder_format(*$foldername*)

Returns 1 if the folder is a plain file that starts with the string "**From** ", otherwise it returns 0.

Returns 1 if the folder is a zero-length file and the $Mail::Format::Default-EmptyFileFormat class variable is set to mbox.

Otherwise it returns 0.

create(*$foldername*)

Creates a new folder named *$foldername*. Returns 0 if the folder already exists; otherwise returns 1.

Author

Kevin Johnson, *kjj@pobox.com*

Copyright

Mail::Folder::NNTP—an NNTP folder interface for Mail::Folder

Synopsis

```
use Mail::Folder::Maildir;
```

Description

This module provides an interface to newsgroups accessible via the NNTP protocol.

Warning

This code is in alpha release. Expect the interface to change.

Methods

open(*$foldername*)

Populates the Mail::Folder object with information about the folder.

The given foldername can be in one of two formats. Either news://*news-host/newsgroup* where *newshost* is the NNTP host and *newsgroup* is the newsgroup of interest, or #news:*newsgroup*, in which case the NNTPSERVER environment variable is referenced to determine the news host to connect to.

Please note that an NNTP connection is opened for each open NNTP folder.

If no Timeout option is specified, it defaults to a timeout of 120 seconds.

- Call the superclass open method.
- Make sure *$foldername* is a valid NNTP folder name.
- Connect to the NNTP server referenced in *$foldername*.
- Perform an NNTP group command to determine the quantity and range of articles available.
- Loop through the available article numbers; retrieve and cache the headers.

close

Calls the superclass get_message method and shuts down the connection to the NNTP server.

sync

Currently a no-op; returns 0.

Eventually will expunge articles marked as seen, look for new articles, update the *.newsrc* (or equivalent) file, and return the number of new articles found.

pack

Since the association between article and article number is determined by the server, this method is a no-op.

It returns 1.

get_message(*$msg_number*)

Calls the superclass get_message method.

Retrieves the contents of the news article pointed to by the given *$msg_number* into a Mail::Internet object reference, caches the header, marks the message as seen, and returns the reference.

It returns undef on failure.

get_message_file(*$msg_number*)

Not currently implemented. Returns undef.

get_header(*$msg_number*)

If the particular header has never been retrieved, then get_header retrieves the header for the given news article from the news server, converts it into a Mail::Header object, and returns a reference to the object.

If the header has already been retrieved in a prior call to get_header, then the cached entry is returned.

It returns undef on failure.

append_message(*$mref*)

Not currently implemented. Returns 0.

update_message(*$msg_number*, *$mref*)
> Not currently implemented. Returns 0.

is_valid_folder_format(*$foldername*)
> Returns 1 if *$foldername* either starts with the string *news://* or the string *#news:* and the NNTPSERVER environment variable is set; otherwise returns 0.

create($foldername)
> Not currently implemented. Returns 0.

Author

Kevin Johnson, *kjj@pobox.com*

Copyright

Copyright © 1997 Kevin Johnson. All rights reserved. This program is free software; you can redistribute it and/or modify it under the same terms as Perl itself.

Mail::Header—manipulate mail RFC 822-compliant headers

Synopsis

```
use Mail::Header;

$head = new Mail::Header;
$head = new Mail::Header \*STDIN;
$head = new Mail::Header [<>], Modify => 0;
```

Description

This package provides a class object that can be used for reading, creating, manipulating, and writing RFC 822-compliant headers.

Constructor

new ([*ARG*], [*OPTIONS*])
> *ARG* may be either a file descriptor (a reference to a GLOB) or a reference to an array. If given, the new object is initialized with headers either from the array or read from the file descriptor.
>
> *OPTIONS* is a list of options given in the form of key-value pairs, just like a hash table. Valid options are:

Modify
> If this value is true, then the headers are reformatted; otherwise the format of the header lines remains unchanged.

MailFrom
> This option specifies what to do when a header in the form "From " is encountered. Valid values are IGNORE to ignore and discard the header, ERROR to invoke an error (call die), COERCE to rename the header Mail-From, and KEEP to keep the header.

FoldLength
> This option specifies the default line length to be used when folding header lines.

Methods

modify ([*VALUE*])

If *VALUE* is false then Mail::Header does not do any automatic reformatting of the headers, other than ensuring that the line starts with the tags given.

mail_from (*OPTION*)

OPTION specifies what to do when a "From " line is encountered. Valid values are IGNORE to ignore and discard the header, ERROR to invoke an error (call die), COERCE to rename the header Mail-From, and KEEP to keep the header.

fold ([*LENGTH*])

Fold the header. If *LENGTH* is not given, then Mail::Header uses the following rules to determine what length to fold a line:

* The fold length for the tag that is being processed
* The default fold length for the tag that is being processed
* The default fold length for the object

extract (*ARRAY_REF*)

Extract a header from the given array. extract modifies this array and returns the object that the method was called on.

read (*FD*)

Read a header from the given file descriptor.

empty ()

Empty the Mail::Header object of all lines.

header ([*ARRAY_REF*])

header performs multiple operations. First, it extracts a header from the array, if one is given. It then reformats the header if reformatting is permitted, and finally returns a reference to an array that contains the header in a printable form.

add (*TAG, LINE* [, *INDEX*])

Add a new line to the header. If *TAG* is undef, then the tag is extracted from the beginning of the given line. If *INDEX* is given, the new line is inserted into the header at the given point; otherwise the new line is appended to the end of the header.

replace (*TAG, LINE* [, *INDEX*])

Replace a line in the header. If *TAG* is undef, then the tag is extracted from the beginning of the given line. If *INDEX* is given, the new line replaces the Nth instance of that tag; otherwise the first instance of the tag is replaced. If the tag does not appear in the header, then a new line is appended to the header.

combine (*TAG* [, *WITH*])

Combine all instances of *TAG* into one. The lines are joined together with *WITH*, or a single space if *WITH* is not given. The new item is positioned in the header where the first instance was and all other instances of *TAG* are removed.

get (*TAG* [, *INDEX*])

Get the text from a line. If *INDEX* is given, then the text of the Nth instance is returned. If it is not given, the return value depends on the context in which get was called. In an array context, a list of all text from all instances of *TAG* is returned. In a scalar context, the text for the first instance is returned.

`delete ( `*`TAG`*` [, `*`INDEX`*` ] )`

> Delete a tag from the header. If *INDEX* is given, then the *N*th instance of the tag is removed. If *INDEX* is not given, all instances of the tag are removed.

`count ( `*`TAG`*` )`

> Return the number of times the given tag appears in the header.

`print ( [ `*`FD`*` ] )`

> Print the header to the given file descriptor or to STDOUT if no file descriptor is given.

`fold_length ( [ `*`TAG`*` ], [ `*`LENGTH`*` ] )`

> Set the default fold length for all tags or just one. With no arguments, the default fold length is returned. With two arguments, `fold_length` sets the fold length for the given tag and returns the previous value. If only *LENGTH* is given, it sets the default fold length for the current object.
>
> In the two-argument form, `fold_length` may be called as a static method, setting default fold lengths for tags that are used by *all* Mail::Header objects. See the `fold` method for a description on how Mail::Header uses these values.

`tags ()`

> Return an array of all the tags that exist in the header. Each tag only appears in the list once. The order of the tags is not specified.

`dup ()`

> Create a duplicate of the current object.

`cleanup ()`

> Remove any header line that, other than the tag, only contains whitespace.

`unfold ( [ `*`TAG`*` ] )`

> Unfold all instances of the given tag so that they do not spread across multiple lines. IF *TAG* is not given, then all lines are unfolded.

Author

Graham Barr, *gbarr@pobox.com*

Copyright

Mail::Internet—manipulate Internet format (RFC 822) mail messages

Synopsis

```
use Mail::Internet;
```

Description

This package provides a class object which can be used for reading, creating, manipulating, and writing a message with RFC 822-compliant headers.

Constructor

new ([*ARG*], [*OPTIONS*])

ARG is optional and may be either a file descriptor (reference to a GLOB) or a reference to an array. If given the new object will be initialized with headers either from the array of read from the file descriptor.

OPTIONS is a list of options given in the form of key-value pairs, just like a hash table. Valid options are

Header

The value of this option should be a Mail::Header object. If given then Mail::Internet will not attempt to read a mail header from *ARG*, if it was specified.

Body

The value of this option should be a reference to an array which contains the lines for the body of the message. If given then Mail::Internet will not attempt to read the body from *ARG*, if it was specified.

The Mail::Header options `Modify`, `MailFrom` and `FoldLength` may also be given.

Methods

body ()

Returns the body of the message. This is a reference to an array. Each entry in the array represents a single line in the message.

print_header ([*FILEHANDLE*])
print_body ([*FILEHANDLE*])
print ([*FILEHANDLE*])

Print the header, body or whole message to file descriptor *FILEHANDLE*. $fd should be a reference to a GLOB. If *FILEHANDLE* is not given the output will be sent to STDOUT.

```
$mail->print( \*STDOUT );  # Print message to STDOUT
```

head ()

Returns the Mail::Header object which holds the headers for the current message.

Utility Methods

The following methods are more a utility type than a manipulation type of method.

remove_sig ([*NLINES*])

Attempts to remove a user's signature from the body of a message. It does this by looking for a line equal to "-- " within the last *NLINES* of the message. If found then that line and all lines after it will be removed. If *NLINES* is not given a default value of 10 will be used. This would be of most use in auto-reply scripts.

tidy_body ()

Removes all leading and trailing lines from the body that only contain white spaces.

reply ()

Creates a new object with header initialized for a reply to the current object. And the body will be a copy of the current message indented.

add_signature ([*FILE*])

>Appends a signature to the message. *FILE* is a file which contains the signature, if not given then the file *$ENV{HOME}/.signature* will be checked for.

smtpsend ()

>Sends a Mail::Internet message via SMTP

>The message will be sent to all addresses on the To, Cc and Bcc lines. The SMTP host is found by attempting connections first to hosts specified in $ENV{SMTPHOSTS}, a colon separated list, then `mailhost` and `localhost`.

nntppost ()

>Posts an article via NNTP, require News::NNTPClient.

escape_from ()

>It can cause problems with some applications if a message contains a line starting with "From ", in particular when attempting to split a folder. This method inserts a leading > on any line starting with "From ".

unescape_from ()

>This method will remove the escaping added by `escape_from`.

Author

Graham Barr, *gbarr@pobox.com*

Copyright

Copyright © 1995 Graham Barr. All rights reserved. This program is free software; you can redistribute it and/or modify it under the same terms as Perl itself.

See Also

Mail::Header, Mail::Address

Mail::Mailer—simple interface to electronic mailing mechanisms

Synopsis

```
use Mail::Mailer;
use Mail::Mailer qw(mail);

$mailer = new Mail::Mailer;

$mailer = new Mail::Mailer $type, @args;

$mailer->open(\%headers);

print $mailer $body;

$mailer->close;
```

Description

Sends mail using any of the built-in methods. You can alter the behavior of a method by passing *$command* to the `new` method.

Methods
mail

> Use the UNIX system `mail` program to deliver the mail. *$command* is the path to `mail`.

sendmail

> Use the `sendmail` program to deliver the mail. *$command* is the path to `sendmail`.

test

> Used for debugging; this calls */bin/echo* to display the data. No mail is ever sent. *$command* is ignored.

Mail::Mailer searches for executables in the above order. The default mailer is the first one found. In the case of `mail`, Mail::Mailer searches for `mail`, `mailx`, and `Mail`.

Arguments

`new` can optionally be given a *$command* and *$type*. *$type* is one of `sendmail`, `mail`, etc., given above. The meaning of *$command* depends on *$type*.

`open` is given a reference to a hash. The hash consists of key-value pairs, where the key is the name of the header field (e.g., `To`), and the value is the corresponding contents of the header field. The value can either be a scalar (e.g., *gnat@frii.com*) or a reference to an array of scalars (e.g., *gnat@frii.com, Tim.Bunce@ig.co.uk*).

Authors

Tim Bunce (*Tim.Bunce@ig.co.uk*), with a kick-start from Graham Barr (*gbarr@pobox.com*), and contributions from Gerard Hickey (*hickey@ctron.com*). For support, please contact *comp.lang.perl.misc*. Small fix and documentation by Nathan Torkington (*gnat@frii.com*).

See Also

Mail::Send

Mail::POP3Client—Perl 5 module to talk to a POP3 (RFC 1081) server

Description

This module implements an object-oriented interface to a POP3 server. It is based on RFC 1081.

Usage

Here is a simple example to list the headers in your remote mailbox:

```
#!/usr/local/bin/perl

use Mail::POP3Client;

$pop = new Mail::POP3Client("me", "mypassword", "pop3.do.main");
for ($i = 1; $i <= $pop->Count; $i++) {
    print $pop->Head($i), "\n";
}
```

POP3Client Commands

These commands are intended to make writing a POP3 client easier. They do not necessarily map directly to POP3 commands defined in RFC 1081. Some commands return multiple lines as an array in an array context, but there may be missing places.

new
> Constructs a new POP3 connection. You should give it at least two arguments: username and password. The next two optional arguments are the POP3 host and port number. A final fifth argument is a positive integer that enables debugging on the object (to STDERR).

Head
> Gets the headers of the specified message. Here is a simple biff program:

```
#!/usr/local/bin/perl

use Mail::POP3Client;

$pop = new Mail::POP3Client("me", "mypass", "pop3.do.main");
for ($i = 1; $i <= $pop->Count; $i++) {
    foreach ($pop->Head($i)) {
        /^(From|Subject): / and print $_, "\n";
    }
    print "\n";
}
```

Body
> Gets the body of the specified message.

HeadAndBody
> Gets the head and body of the specified message.

Retrieve
> Does the same as HeadAndBody.

Delete
> Marks the specified message number as DELETED. Becomes effective upon QUIT. Can be reset with a Reset message.

Connect
> Starts the connection to the POP3 server. You can pass in the host and port.

Close
> Closes the connection gracefully. POP3 says this performs any pending deletes on the server.

Alive
> Returns true if the connection is active; otherwise returns false.

Socket
> Returns the file descriptor for the socket.

Size
> Sets/returns the size of the remote mailbox. Set by POPStat.

Count
> Sets/returns the number of remote messages. Set during login.

Message
> Returns the last status message received from the server.

State

Returns the internal state of the connection: DEAD, AUTHORIZATION, or TRANSACTION.

POPStat

Returns the results of a POP3 STAT command. Sets the size of the mailbox.

List

Returns a list containing the size of each message.

Last

Returns the number of the last message retrieved from the server.

Reset

Tells the server to unmark any message marked for deletion.

User

Sets/returns the current username.

Pass

Sets/returns the current username.

Login

Attempts to log in to the server connection.

Host

Sets/returns the current host.

Port

Sets/returns the current port number.

Acknowledgments

Based loosely on News::NNTPClient by Rodger Anderson (*rodger@boi.hp.com*)

Author

Sean Dowd, *ssd@mmts.eds.com*

Copyright

Copyright © 1995, 1996 Electronic Data Systems, Inc. All rights reserved.

This module is free software; you can redistribute it and/or modify it under the same terms as Perl itself.

Mail::Send—simple electronic mail interface

Synopsis

```
require Mail::Send;

$msg = new Mail::Send;

$msg = new Mail::Send Subject=>'example subject', To=>'timbo';

$msg->to('user@host');
$msg->subject('user@host');
$msg->cc('user@host');
```

```
$msg->bcc('someone@else');

$msg->set($header, @values);
$msg->add($header, @values);
$msg->delete($header);

# Launch mailer and set headers. The filehandle returned
# by open() is an instance of the Mail::Mailer class.

$fh = $msg->open;

print $fh "Body of message";

$fh->close;          # complete the message and send it

$fh->cancel;         # not yet implemented
```

Authors

Tim Bunce (*Tim.Bunce@ig.co.uk*), with a kick-start from Graham Barr (*gbarr@pobox.com*) and with contributions from Gerard Hickey (*hickey@ctron.com*).

For support please contact *comp.lang.perl.misc.*

See Also

Mail::Mailer

Mail::Util—mail utility functions

Synopsis

```
use Mail::Util qw( ... );
```

Description

This package provides several mail-related utility functions. Any function required must be explicitly listed on the use line to be exported into the calling package.

Functions

read_mbox(*$file*)

> Read *$file*, a binmail mailbox file, and return a list of references. Each reference is a reference to an array containing one message.

maildomain()

> Attempt to determine the current user's mail domain string via the following methods:
>
> * Look for a *sendmail.cf* file and extract DH parameter.
> * Look for an smail config file and use the first host defined in hostname(s).
> * Try an SMTP connect (if Net::SMTP exists), first to mailhost and then to local-host.
> * Use the value from Net::Domain::domainname (if Net::Domain exists).

```
mailaddress()
```
Return a guess at the current user's mail address. The user can force the return value by setting `$ENV{MAILADDRESS}`.

Author

Graham Barr, *gbarr@pobox.com*

Copyright

News::Newsrc—manage newsrc files

Synopsis

```
use News::Newsrc;

$newsrc    = new News::Newsrc;

$ok        = $newsrc->load;
$ok        = $newsrc->load          ($file);

            $newsrc->save;
            $newsrc->save_as        ($file);

$ok        = $newsrc-> add_group    ($group,                 %options);
$ok        = $newsrc->move_group    ($group,                 %options);
$ok        = $newsrc-> del_group    ($group);

            $newsrc->  subscribe    ($group,                 %options);
            $newsrc->unsubscribe    ($group,                 %options);

            $newsrc->mark           ($group,  $article , %options);
            $newsrc->mark_list      ($group, \@articles, %options);
            $newsrc->mark_range     ($group, $from, $to, %options);

            $newsrc->unmark         ($group,  $article , %options);
            $newsrc->unmark_list    ($group, \@articles, %options);
            $newsrc->unmark_range   ($group, $from, $to, %options);

    ... if $newsrc->exists          ($group);
    ... if $newsrc->subscribed      ($group);
    ... if $newsrc->marked          ($group, $article);

$n         = $newsrc->  num_groups;
@groups    = $newsrc->      groups;
@groups    = $newsrc->  sub_groups;
@groups    = $newsrc->unsub_groups;

@articles = $newsrc->  marked_articles($group,                 %options);
```

```
@articles = $newsrc->unmarked_articles($group, $from, $to, %options);

$articles = $newsrc->get_articles    ($group,              %options);
$ok       = $newsrc->set_articles    ($group, $articles,   %options);
```

Prerequisites

Perl 5.003, Exporter, Set::IntSpan 1.03

Description

News::Newsrc manages *newsrc* files, of the style:

```
alt.foo: 1-21,28,31-34
alt.bar! 3,5,9-2900,2902
```

Methods are provided for:

- Reading and writing *newsrc* files
- Adding and removing newsgroups
- Changing the order of newsgroups
- Subscribing and unsubscribing from newsgroups
- Testing whether groups exist and are subscribed
- Marking and unmarking articles
- Testing whether articles are marked
- Returning lists of newsgroups
- Returning lists of articles

newsrc Files

A *newsrc* file is an ASCII file that lists newsgroups and article numbers. Each line of a *newsrc* file describes a single newsgroup. Each line is divided into three fields: a *group*, a *subscription mark,* and an *article list.*

Lines containing only whitespace are ignored. Whitespace within a line is ignored.

Group

> The *group* is the name of the newsgroup. A group name may not contain colons (:) or exclamation points (!).
>
> Group names must be unique within a *newsrc* file. The group name is required.

Subscription mark

> The *subscription mark* is either a colon (:), for subscribed groups, or an exclamation point (!), for unsubscribed groups. The subscription mark is required.

Article list

> The *article list* is a comma-separated list of positive integers. The integers must be listed in increasing order. Runs of consecutive integers may be abbreviated a-b, where a is the first integer in the run and b is the last. The article list may be empty.

Newsgroup Order

News::Newsrc preserves the order of newsgroups in a *newsrc* file: if a file is loaded and then saved, the newsgroup order will be unchanged.

Methods that add or move newsgroups affect the newsgroup order. By default, these methods put newsgroups at the end of the *newsrc* file. Other locations may be specified by passing an *%options* hash with a `where` key to the method. Recognized locations are:

where => 'first'
    Put the newsgroup first.

where => 'last'
    Put the newsgroup last.

where => 'alpha'
    Put the newsgroup in alphabetical order.

    If the other newsgroups are not sorted alphabetically, put the group at an arbitrary location.

where => [before => $group]
    Put the group immediately before *$group*.

    If *$group* does not exist, put the group last.

where => [after => $group]
    Put the group immediately after *$group*.

    If *$group* does not exist, put the group last.

where => [number => $n]
    Put the group at position *$n* in the group list. Indices are zero-based. Negative indices count backwards from the end of the list.

Methods

$newsrc = $newsrc = new News::Newsrc
    Creates and returns a News::Newsrc object. The object contains no newsgroups.

$ok = $newsrc->load
$ok = $newsrc->load($file)
    Loads the newsgroups in *$file* into $newsrc. If *$file* is omitted, reads *$ENV{HOME}/.newsrc*. Any existing data in $newsrc is discarded. Returns true on success.

    If *$file* can't be opened, load discards existing data from $newsrc and returns null.

    If *$file* contains invalid lines, load will die. When this happens, the state of $newsrc is undefined.

$newsrc->save
    Writes the contents of $newsrc back to the file from which it was loaded. If load has not been called, writes to *$ENV{HOME}/.newsrc*. In either case, if the destination file exists, it is renamed to *file.bak*.

    save will die if there is an error writing the file.

$newsrc->save_as($file)
    Writes the contents of $newsrc to *$file*. If *$file* exists, it is renamed to *$file.bak*. Subsequent calls to save will write to *$file*.

    save_as will die if there is an error writing the file.

$ok = $newsrc->add_group(*$group*, *%options*)

Adds *$group* to the list of newsgroups in $newsrc. *$group* is initially subscribed. The article list for *$group* is initially empty.

By default, *$group* is added to the end of the list of newsgroups. Other locations may be specified in *%options*; see "Newsgroup Order" for details.

By default, add_group does nothing if *$group* already exists. If the replace => 1 option is provided, then add_group will delete *$group* if it exists, and then add it.

add_group returns true if *$group* was added.

$ok = $newsrc->move_group(*$group*, *%options*)

Changes the position of *$group* in $newsrc according to *%options*. See "Newsgroup Order" for details.

If *$group* does not exist, move_group does nothing and returns false. Otherwise, it returns true.

$ok = $newsrc->del_group(*$group*)

If *$group* exists in $newsrc, del_group removes it and returns true. The article list for *$group* is lost.

If *$group* does not exist in $newsrc, del_group does nothing and returns false.

$newsrc->subscribe(*$group*, *%options*)

Subscribes to *$group*.

$group will be created if it does not exist. Its location may be specified in *%options*; see "Newsgroup Order" for details.

$newsrc->unsubscribe(*$group*, *%options*)

Unsubscribes from *$group*.

$group will be created if it does not exist. Its location may be specified in *%options*; see "Newsgroup Order" for details.

$newsrc->mark(*$group*, *$article*, *%options*)

Adds *$article* to the article list for *$group*.

$group will be created if it does not exist. Its location may be specified in *%options*; see "Newsgroup Order" for details.

$newsrc->mark_list(*$group*, \@*articles*, *%options*)

Adds @*articles* to the article list for *$group*.

$group will be created if it does not exist. Its location may be specified in *%options*; see "Newsgroup Order" for details.

$newsrc->mark_range(*$group*, *$from*, *$to*, *%options*)

Adds all the articles from *$from* to *$to*, inclusive, to the article list for *$group*.

$group will be created if it does not exist. Its location may be specified in *%options*; see "Newsgroup Order" for details.

$newsrc->unmark(*$group*, *$article*, *%options*)

Removes *$article* from the article list for *$group*.

$group will be created if it does not exist. Its location may be specified in *%options*; see "Newsgroup Order" for details.

$newsrc->unmark_list(*$group*, \@*articles*, *%options*)

Removes @*articles* from the article list for *$group*.

$group will be created if it does not exist. Its location may be specified in %options; see "Newsgroup Order" for details.

`$newsrc->unmark_range(`*$group*`,` *$from*`,` *$to*`,` %options`)`

Removes all the articles from *$from* to *$to*, inclusive, from the article list for *$group*.

$group will be created if it does not exist. Its location may be specified in %options; see "Newsgroup Order" for details.

`$newsrc->exists(`*$group*`)`

Returns true if *$group* exists in $newsrc.

`$newsrc->subscribed(`*$group*`)`

Returns true if *$group* exists and is subscribed.

`$newsrc->marked(`*$group*`,` *$article*`)`

Returns true if *$group* exists and its article list contains *$article*.

`$n = $newsrc->num_groups`

Returns the number of groups in $newsrc.

`@groups = $newsrc->groups`

Returns the list of groups in $newsrc, in *newsrc* order. In scalar context, returns an array reference.

`@groups = $newsrc->sub_groups`

Returns the list of subscribed groups in $newsrc, in *newsrc* order. In scalar context, returns an array reference.

`@groups = $newsrc->unsub_groups`

Returns the list of unsubscribed groups in $newsrc, in *newsrc* order. In scalar context, returns an array reference.

`@articles = $newsrc->marked_articles(`*$group*`)`

Returns the list of articles in the article list for *$group*. In scalar context, returns an array reference.

$group will be created if it does not exist. Its location may be specified in %options; see "Newsgroup Order" for details.

`@articles = $newsrc->unmarked_articles(`*$group*`,` *$from*`,` *$to*`,` %options`)`

Returns the list of articles from *$from* to *$to*, inclusive, that do **not** appear in the article list for *$group*. In scalar context, returns an array reference.

$group will be created if it does not exist. Its location may be specified in %options; see "Newsgroup Order" for details.

`$articles = $newsrc->get_articles(`*$group*`,` %options`)`

Returns the article list for *$group* as a string, in the format described in "Newsrc files/Article list."

$group will be created if it does not exist. Its location may be specified in %options; see "Newsgroup Order" for details.

If you plan to do any nontrivial processing on the article list, consider converting it to a Set::IntSpan object:

```
$articles = Set::IntSpan->new($newsrc->get_articles('alt.foo'))
```

`$ok = $newsrc->set_articles(`*$group*`,` *$articles*`,` %options`)`

Sets the article list for *$group*. Any existing article list is lost.

$articles is a string, as described in "Newsrc files/Article list."

$group will be created if it does not exist. Its location may be specified in %options; see "Newsgroup Order" for details.

If $articles does not have the format described in "Newsrc files/Article list," set_articles does nothing and returns false. Otherwise, it returns true.

Diagnostics

News::Newsrc::load: Bad newsrc line: $file, line $.: $_

> A line in the *newsrc* file does not have the format described in "Newsrc files."

News::Newsrc::load: Bad article list: %file, line $.: $_

> The article list for a newsgroup does not have the format described in "Newsrc files."

News::Newsrc::save_as: Can't rename $file, $file.bak: $!

News::Newsrc::save_as: Can't open $file: $!

News::Newsrc::save_as: Can't write $file: $!

Error Handling

Don't test for errors that you can't handle.

load returns null if it can't open the *newsrc* file, and dies if the *newsrc* file contains invalid data. This isn't as schizophrenic as it seems.

There are several ways a program could handle an open failure on the *newsrc* file. It could prompt the user to reenter the filename. It could assume that the user doesn't have a *newsrc* file yet. If it doesn't want to handle the error, it could go ahead and die.

On the other hand, it is very difficult for a program to do anything sensible if the *newsrc* file opens successfully and then turns out to contain invalid data. Was there a disk error? Is the file corrupt? Did the user accidentally specify his kill file instead of his *newsrc* file? And what are you going to do about it?

Rather than try to handle an error like this, it's probably better to die and let the user sort things out. By the same rational, save and save_as die on failure.

Programs that must retain control can use eval{...} to protect calls that may die. For example, Perl/Tk runs all callbacks inside an eval{...}. If a callback dies, Perl/Tk regains control and displays $@ in a dialog box. The user can then decide whether to continue or quit from the program.

Author

Steven McDougall, *swmcd@world.std.com*

Copyright

See Also

perl(1), Set::IntSpan

News::NNTPClient—Perl 5 module to talk to NNTP (RFC977) server

Description

This module implements a client interface to NNTP, enabling a Perl 5 application to talk to NNTP servers. It uses the OOP (Object-Oriented Programming) interface introduced with Perl 5.

Usage

To use it in your programs, you can use either:

```
use News::NNTPClient;
```

or:

```
require News::NNTPClient;
```

NNTPClient exports nothing.

A new NNTPClient object must be created with the new method. Once this has been done, all NNTP commands are accessed through this object.

Here are a couple of short examples. The first prints all articles in the test newsgroup:

```
#!/usr/local/bin/perl -w

use News::NNTPClient;

$c = new News::NNTPClient;

($first, $last) = ($c->group("test"));

for (; $first <= $last; $first++) {
    print $c->article($first);
}

__END__
```

This example prints the body of all articles in the test newsgroup newer than one hour:

```
#!/usr/local/bin/perl -w

require News::NNTPClient;

$c = new News::NNTPClient;

foreach ($c->newnews("test", time - 3600)) {
    print $c->body($_);
}

__END__
```

NNTPClient Commands

These commands are used to manipulate the NNTPClient object, and aren't directly related to commands available on any NNTP server.

new

Use this to create a new NNTP connection. It takes three arguments, a hostname, a port, and a debug flag. It calls `initialize`. Use an empty argument to specify defaults.

If port is omitted or blank (""), looks for environment variable NNTPPORT, service nntp, or uses 119.

If host is omitted or empty (""), looks for environment variable NNTPSERVER or uses news.

Examples:

```
$c = new News::NNTPClient;
or
$c = new News::NNTPClient("newsserver.some.where");
or
$c = new News::NNTPClient("experimental", 9999);
or
# Specify debug but use defaults.
$c = new News::NNTPClient("", "", 2);
```

Returns a blessed reference, representing a new NNTP connection.

initialize

Calls `port`, `host`, `connect`, and `response`, in that order. If any of these fail, initialization is aborted.

connect

Connects to current host/port. Not normally needed, as the new method does this for you. Closes any existing connection. Sets the posting status. See the **postok** method.

host

Sets the host that will be used on the next connect. Not normally needed, as the new method does this for you.

Without an argument, returns current host.

Argument can be hostname or dotted quad, for example, `15.2.174.218`.

Returns fully qualified hostname.

port

Sets the port that will be used on the next connect. Not normally needed, as the new method does this for you.

Without an argument, returns current port.

Argument can be port number or name. If it is a name, it must be a valid service.

Returns port number.

debug

Sets the debug level.

Without an argument, returns current debug level.

There are currently three debug levels. Level 0, level 1, and level 2.

At level 0 the messages described for level 1 are not produced. Debug level 0 is a way of turning off messages produced by the default debug level 1. Serious error messages, such as EOF (End Of File) on the filehandle, are still produced.

At level 1, any NNTP command that results in a result code of 400 or greater prints a warning message. This is the default.

At level 2, in addition to level 1 messages, status messages are printed to indicate actions taking place.

Returns old debug value.

ok

Returns Boolean status of most recent command. NNTP return codes less than 400 are considered OK. Not often needed as most commands return false upon failure anyway.

okprint

Returns Boolean status of most recent command. NNTP return codes less than 400 are considered OK. Prints an error message for return codes of 400 or greater unless debug level is set to zero (0).

This method is used internally by most commands, and could be considered to be "for internal use only." You should use the return status of commands directly to determine pass-fail, or if needed the ok method can be used to check status later.

message

Returns the NNTP response message of the most recent command.

Example, as returned by NNTP server version 1.5.11t:

```
$c->slave;
print $c->message;
```

Kinky, kinky. I don't support such perversions.

code

Returns the NNTP response code of the most recent command.

Example:

```
$c->article(1);
print $c->code, "\n";
412
```

postok

Returns the post-ability status that was reported upon connection or after the mode_reader command.

eol

Sets the End-Of-Line termination for text returned from the server.

Returns the old EOL setting.

Default is \n.

To set EOL to nothing, pass it the empty string.

To query the current EOL without setting it, call it with no arguments.

Returns the old EOL termination.

Example:

```
$old_eol = $c->eol();      # Get original.
$c->eol("");               # Set EOL to nothing.
@article = $c->article();  # Fetch an article.
$c->eol($old_eol);         # Restore value.
```

version
> Returns version number.
>
> This document represents @(#) $Revision: 1.1 $.

NNTP Commands

These commands directly correlate to NNTP server commands. They return a false value upon failure, true upon success. The truth value is usually some bit of useful information. For example, the `stat` command returns Message-ID if it is successful.

Some commands return multiple lines. These lines are returned as an array in array context, and as a reference to an array in scalar context. For example, if you do this:

```
@lines = $c->article(14);
```

then *@lines* will contain the article, one line per array element. However, if you do this:

```
$lines = $c->article(14);
```

then *$lines* will contain a *reference* to an array. This feature is for those who don't like passing arrays from routine to routine.

mode_reader
> Some servers require this command to process NNTP client commands. Sets `postok` status. See `postok`.
>
> Returns OK status.

article
> Retrieves an article from the server. This is the main command for fetching articles. Expects a single argument, an article number or Message-ID. If you use an article number, you must be in a newsgroup. See `group`.
>
> Returns the header, a separating blank line, and the body of the article as an array of lines terminated by the current EOL.
>
> In scalar context a reference to the array is returned instead of the array itself.
>
> Examples:
>
> ```
> print $c->article('<art1234@soom.oom>');
> $c->group("test");
> print $c->article(99);
> ```

body
> Expects a single argument, an article number or Message-ID.
>
> Returns the body of an article as an array of lines terminated by the current EOL.
>
> In scalar context a reference to the array is returned instead of the array itself.
>
> See `article`.

head
> Expects a single argument, an article number or Message-ID.
>
> Returns the head of the article as an array of lines terminated by the current EOL.
>
> In scalar context a reference to the array is returned instead of the array itself.
>
> See `article`.

stat
> Expects a single argument, an article number or Message-ID.

The `stat` command is like the `article` command except that it does not return any text. It can be used to set the "current article pointer if passed an article number, or to validate a Message-ID if passed a Message-ID.

Returns Message-ID if successful, otherwise returns `false`.

last

The current article pointer maintained by the server is moved to the previous article in the current newsgroup.

Returns Message-ID if successful, otherwise returns `false`.

next

The current article pointer maintained by the server is moved to the next article in the current newsgroup.

Returns Message-ID if successful, otherwise returns `false`.

group

Expects a single argument, the name of a valid newsgroup.

This command sets the current newsgroup as maintained by the server. It also sets the server-maintained current article pointer to the first article in the group. This enables the use of certain other server commands, such as `article`, `head`, `body`, `stat`, `last`, and `next`. Also sets the current group in the NNTPClient object, which is used by the `newnews` and `xindex` commands.

Returns (`first`, `last`) in list context, or `first-last` in scalar context, where `first` and `last` are the first and last article numbers as reported by the group command. Returns `false` if there is an error.

It is an error to attempt to select a nonexistent newsgroup.

If the estimated article count is needed, it can be extracted from the message. See `message`.

list

Accepts one optional argument that can be used indicate the type of list desired. The list type depends on the server.

With an argument of `active` or with no arguments, this command returns a list of valid newsgroups and associated information. The format is:

```
group last first p
```

where `group` is the newsgroup name, `last` is the article number of the last article, `first` is the article number of the first article, and `p` is a flag indicating if posting is allowed. A `y` flag is an indication that posting is allowed.

Other possible arguments are: `newsgroups`, `distributions`, `subscriptions` for B-News, and `active.times`, `distributions`, `distrib.pats`, `newsgroups`, `overview.fmt` for INN.

Returns an array of lines terminated by the current EOL.

In scalar context a reference to the array is returned instead of the array itself.

newgroups

Expects at least one argument representing the date/time in seconds, or in YYMMDD HHMMSS format. Remaining arguments are used as distributions.

Example: print all new groups in the `comp` and/or `news` hierarchies as of one hour ago:

```
print $c->newgroups(time() - 3600, "comp", "news");
```

Returns list of new newsgroup names as an array of lines terminated by the current EOL.

In scalar context a reference to the array is returned instead of the array itself.

`newnews`

Expects one, two, or more arguments.

If the first argument is a group name, it looks for new news in that group, and the date/time is the second argument. If the first argument represents the date/time in seconds or in YYMMDD HHMMSS format, then the group is the last group set via the `group` command. If no `group` command has been issued then the group is `*`, representing all groups. Remaining arguments are use to restrict search to certain distribution(s).

Returns a list of Message-IDs of articles that have been posted or received since the specified time.

Examples:

```
# Hour old news in newsgroup "test".
$c->newnews("test", time() - 3600);
or
# Hour old in all groups.
$c->newnews(time() - 3600);
or
$c->newnews("*", time() - 3600);
or
# Hour old news in newsgroup "test".
$c->group("test");
$c->newnews(time() - 3600);
```

The group argument can include an asterisk to specify a range of newsgroups. It can also include multiple newsgroups, separated by a comma.

Example:

```
$c->newnews("comp.*.sources,alt.sources", time() - 3600);
```

An exclamation point may be used to negate the selection of certain groups.

Example:

```
$c->newnews("*sources*,!*.d,!*.wanted", time() - 3600);
```

Any additional distribution arguments will be concatenated together and send as a distribution list. The distribution list will limit articles to those that have a "Distribution:" header containing one of the distributions passed.

Example:

```
$c->newnews("*", time() - 3600, "local", "na");
```

Returns Message-IDs of new articles as an array of lines terminated by the current EOL.

In scalar context a reference to the array is returned instead of the array itself.

`help`

Returns any server help information. The format of the information is highly dependent on the server, but usually contains a list of NNTP commands recognized by the server.

Returns an array of lines terminated by the current EOL.

In scalar context a reference to the array is returned instead of the array itself.

post

> Post an article. Expects data to be posted as an array of lines. Most servers expect, at a minimum, Newsgroups and Subject headers. Be sure to separate the header from the body with a blank line.
>
> Example:
>
> ```
> @header = ("Newsgroups: test", "Subject: test");
> @body   = ("This is the body of the article");
> $c->post(@header, "", @body);
> ```
>
> Any \n characters at the end of a line will be trimmed.

ihave

> Transfer an article. Expects an article Message-ID and the article to be sent as an array of lines.
>
> Example:
>
> ```
> # Fetch article from server on $c
> @article = $c->article($artid);
>
> # Send to server on $d
> if ($d->ihave($artid, @article)) {
>     print "Article transfered\n";
> } else {
>     print "Article rejected: ", $d->message, "\n";
> }
> ```

slave

> Doesn't do anything on most servers. Included for completeness.

DESTROY

> This method is called whenever the object created by News::NNTPClient::new is destroyed. It calls quit to close the connection.

quit

> Send the NNTP quit command and close the connection. The connection can be then be re-opened with the connect method. quit will automatically be called when the object is destroyed, so there is no need to explicitly call quit before exiting your program.

Extended NNTP Commands

These commands also directly correlate NNTP server commands, but are not mentioned in RFC 977, and are not part of the standard. However, many servers implement them, so they are included as part of this package for your convenience. If a command is not recognized by a server, the server usually returns code 500, command unrecognized.

authinfo

> Expects two arguments, user and password.

date

> Returns server date in YYYYMMDDhhmmss format.

listgroup

> Expects one argument, a group name. Default is current group.
>
> Returns article numbers as an array of lines terminated by the current EOL.
>
> In scalar context a reference to the array is returned instead of the array itself.

xmotd

Expects one argument of UNIX time in seconds or as a string in the form YYMMDD HHMMSS.

Returns the news servers Message of the Day as an array of lines terminated by the current EOL.

In scalar context a reference to the array is returned instead of the array itself.

For example, the following will always print the message of the day, if there is any:

```
print $c->xmotd(1);
NNTP Server News2
News administrator is Joseph Blough <joeblo@news.foo.com>
```

xgtitle

Expects one argument of a group pattern. Default is current group.

Returns group titles as an array of lines terminated by the current EOL.

In scalar context a reference to the array is returned instead of the array itself.

Example:

```
print $c->xgtitle("bit.listserv.v*");
bit.listserv.valert-l    Virus Alert List. (Moderated)
bit.listserv.vfort-l     VS-Fortran Discussion List.
bit.listserv.vm-util     VM Utilities Discussion List.
bit.listserv.vmesa-l     VM/ESA Mailing List.
bit.listserv.vmslsv-l    VAX/VMS LISTSERV Discussion List.
bit.listserv.vmxa-l      VM/XA Discussion List.
bit.listserv.vnews-l     VNEWS Discussion List.
bit.listserv.vpiej-l     Electronic Publishing Discussion
```

xpath

Expects one argument of an article Message-ID. Returns the path name of the file on the server.

Example:

```
print print $c->xpath(q(<43bq51$7b5@news.dtc.hp.com>))'
hp/test/4469
```

xhdr

Fetches header for a range of articles. First argument is name of header to fetch. If omitted or blank, defaults to Message-ID. Second argument is start of article range. If omitted, defaults to 1. Next argument is end of range.

Returns headers as an array of lines terminated by the current EOL.

In scalar context a reference to the array is returned instead of the array itself.

Examples:

```
# Fetch Message-ID of article 1.
$c->xhdr();
# Fetch Subject of article 1.
$c->xhdr("Subject");
# Fetch Subject of article 3345.
$c->xhdr("Subject", 3345);
# Fetch Subjects of articles 3345-9873
$c->xhdr("Subject", 3345, 9873);
# Fetch Message-ID of articles 3345-9873
$c->xhdr("", 3345,9873);
```

xpat

> Fetches header for a range of articles matching one or more patterns. First argument is name of header to fetch. If omitted or blank, defaults to Subject. Second argument is start of article range. If omitted, defaults to 1. Next argument is end of range. Remaining arguments are patterns to match. Some servers use * for wildcard.
>
> Returns headers as an array of lines terminated by the current EOL.
>
> In scalar context a reference to the array is returned instead of the array itself.
>
> Examples:
>
> ```
> # Fetch Subject header of article 1.
> $c->xpat();
> # Fetch "From" header of article 1.
> $c->xpat("From");
> # Fetch "From" of article 3345.
> $c->xpat("From", 3345);
> # Fetch "From" of articles 3345-9873 matching *foo*
> $c->xpat("From", 3345, 9873, "*foo*");
> # Fetch "Subject" of articles 3345-9873 matching
> # *foo*, *bar*, *and*, *stuff*
> $c->xpat("", 3345,9873, qw(*foo* *bar* *and* *stuff*));
> ```

xover

> Expects an article number or a starting and ending article number representing a range of articles.
>
> Returns overview information for each article as an array of lines terminated by the current EOL.
>
> In scalar context a reference to the array is returned instead of the array itself.
>
> **xover** generally returns items separated by tabs. Here is an example that prints out the **xover** fields from all messages in the **test** newsgroup.
>
> ```
> #!/usr/local/bin/perl
> require News::NNTPClient;
> $c = new News::NNTPClient;
> @fields = qw(numb subj from date mesg refr char line xref);
> foreach $xover ($c->xover($c->group("test"))) {
>     %fields = ();
>     @fields{@fields} = split /\t/, $xover;
>     print map { "$_: $fields{$_}\n" } @fields;
>     print "\n";
> }
> __END__
> ```

xthread

> Expects zero or one argument. Value of argument doesn't matter. If present, dbinit command is sent. If absent, thread command is sent.
>
> Returns binary data as a scalar value.
>
> Format of data returned is unknown at this time.

xindex

> Expects one argument, a group name. If omitted, defaults to the group set by last group command. If there hasn't been a group command, it returns an error.

Returns index information for group as an array of lines terminated by the current EOL.

In scalar context a reference to the array is returned instead of the array itself.

xsearch

Expects a query as an array of lines which are sent to the server, much like post. Returns the result of the search as an array of lines or a reference to same.

Format of query is unknown at this time.

Author

Rodger Anderson, *rodger@boi.hp.com*

Source

The latest version may be retrieved by sending mail to *rodger@boi.hp.com* with the body of the message starting with: send nntpclient.

Copyright

20

Control Flow Utilities

These two utilities provide assistance when working with callback and exception handling.

AtExit—register a subroutine to be invoked at program-exit time

Synopsis

```
use AtExit;

sub cleanup {
    my @args = @_;
    print "cleanup() executing: args = @args\n";
}

$_ = atexit(\&cleanup, "This call was registered first");
print "first call to atexit() returned $_\n";
$_ = atexit("cleanup", "This call was registered second");
print "second call to atexit() returned $_\n";
$_ = atexit("cleanup", "This call should've been unregistered by
rmexit");
rmexit($_)  ||  warn "couldnt' unregister exit-sub $_!";
END {
    print "*** Now performing program-exit processing ***\n";
}
```

Description

The AtExit module provides ANSI C–style exit processing modeled after the `atexit()` function in the standard C library (see the `atexit(3C)` manpage). Various exit processing routines may be registered by calling `atexit()` and passing it the desired subroutine along with any desired arguments. Then, at program-exit time, the subroutines registered with `atexit()` are invoked with their given arguments in the *reverse* order of registration (last one registered is invoked first). Registering the same subroutine more than once will cause that subroutine to be invoked once for each registration.

The `atexit()` function exported by AtExit should be passed a subroutine name or reference, optionally followed by the list of arguments with which to invoke it at program-exit time. Anonymous subroutine references passed to `atexit()` act as "closures" (which are described in the `perlref` manpage). If a subroutine *name* is specified (as opposed to a subroutine reference) then, unless the subroutine name has an explicit package prefix, it is assumed to be the name of a subroutine in the caller's current package. A reference to the specified subroutine is obtained, and, if invocation arguments were specified, it is "wrapped up" in a closure which invokes the subroutine with the specified arguments. The resulting subroutine reference is prepended to the front of the `@AtExit::EXIT_SUBS` list of exit-handling subroutines and the reference is then returned to the caller (just in case you might want to unregister it later using `rmexit()`). If the given subroutine could *not* be registered, then the value zero is returned.

The `rmexit()` function exported by AtExit should be passed one or more subroutine references, each of which was returned by a previous call to `atexit()`. For each argument given, `rmexit()` will look for it in the `@AtExit::EXIT_SUBS` list of exit-handling subroutines and remove the first such match from the list. The value returned will be the number of subroutines that were successfully unregistered.

At program-exit time, the `END{}` block in the AtExit module iterates over the subroutine references in the `@AtExit::EXIT_SUBS` array and invokes each one in turn (each subroutine is removed from the front of the queue immediately before it is invoked). Note that the subroutines in this queue are invoked in first-to-last order (the *reverse* order in which they were registered with `atexit()`).

Invoking atexit() and rmexit() During Program Exit

The variable `$AtExit::IGNORE_WHEN_EXITING` specifies how calls to `atexit()` will be handled if they occur during the time that subroutines registered with `atexit()` are being invoked. By default, this variable is set to a non-zero value, which causes `atexit()` to *ignore* any calls made to it during this time (a value of zero will be returned). This behavior is consistent with that of the standard C library function of the same name. If desired however, the user may enable the registration of subroutines by `atexit()` during this time by setting `$AtExit::IGNORE_WHEN_EXITING` to zero or to the empty string. Just remember that any subroutines registered with `atexit()` during program-exit time will be placed at the *front* of the queue of yet-to-be-invoked exit-processing subroutines.

Regardless of when it is invoked, `rmexit()` will *always* attempt to unregister the given subroutines (even when called during program exit processing). Keep in mind however that if it is invoked during program exit processing then it will *fail* to unregister any exit-processing subroutines that have *already been invoked* by the `END{}` block in the AtExit module (since those subroutine calls have already been removed from the `@AtExit::EXIT_SUBS` list).

The variable `$AtExit::EXITING` may be examined to determine if routines registered using `atexit()` are currently in the process of being invoked. It will be non-zero if they are and zero otherwise.

Notes

The usual Perl way of doing exit processing is through the use of END{} blocks (see "Package Constructors and Destructors"). The AtExit module implements its exit processing with an END{} block that invokes all the subroutines registered by atexit() in the array @AtExit::EXIT_SUBS. If any other END{} block processing is specified in the user's code or in any other packages it uses, then the order in which the exit processing takes place is subject to Perl's rules for the order in which END{} blocks are processed. This may affect when subroutines registered with atexit() are invoked with respect to other exit processing that is to be performed. In particular, if atexit() is invoked from within an END{} block that executes *after* the END{} block in the AtExit module, then the corresponding subroutine that was registered will never be invoked by the AtExit module's exit-processing code.

END{} block processing order

END{} blocks, including those in other packages, get called in the reverse order in which they appear in the code. (atexit() subroutines get called in the reverse order in which they are registered.) If a package gets read via "use", it will act as if the END{} block was defined at that particular part of the "main" code. Packages read via "require" will be executed after the code of "main" has been parsed and will be seen last so will execute first (they get executed in the context of the package in which they exist).

It is important to note that END{} blocks only get called on normal termination (which includes calls to die() or Carp::croak()). They do *not* get called when the program terminates *abnormally* (due to a signal, for example) unless special arrangements have been made by the programmer (e.g., using a signal handler).

See Also

The atexit(3C) manpage describes the atexit() function for the standard C library (the actual UNIX manual section in which it appears may differ from platform to platform—try sections 3C, 3, 2C, and 2). Further information on anonymous subroutines ("closures") may be found in the perlref manpage. For more information on END{} blocks, see "Package Constructors and Destructors." See %SIG{expr} for handling abnormal program termination.

Authors

Andrew Langmead, *aml@world.std.com* (initial draft)

Brad Appleton, *Brad_Appleton-GBDA001@email.mot.com* (final version)

Religion — generate tracebacks, and create and install die() and warn() handlers

Description

This is a second go at a module to simplify installing die() and warn() handlers, and to make such handlers easier to write and control.

For most people, this just means that if you **use Religion;** then you'll get noticably better error reporting from warn() and die(). This is especially useful if you are using eval().

Religion provides four classes, WarnHandler, DieHandler, WarnPreHandler, and DiePreHandler, that when you construct them return closures that can be stored in variables that in turn get invoked by $SIG{__DIE__} and $SIG{__WARN__}. Note that if Religion is in use, you should not modify $SIG{__DIE__} or $SIG{__WARN__}, unless you are careful about invoking chaining to the old handler.

Religion also provides a TraceBack function, which is used by a DieHandler after you die() to give a better handle on the current scope of your situation, and provide information about where you were, which might influence where you want to go next, either returning back to where you were, or going on to the very last.

See below for usage and examples.

Usage

DieHandler SUB

Invoke like this:

```
$Die::Handler = new DieHandler sub {
        #...
    };
```

where #... contains your handler code. Your handler will receive the following arguments:

$message

> The message provided to die(). Note that the default addition of " at FILE line LINE.\n" will have been stripped off if it was present. If you want to add such a message back on, feel free to do so with *$iline* and *$ifile*.

$full_message

> The message with a scope message added on if there was no newline at the end of $message. Currently, this is *not* the original message that die() tacked on, but something along the lines of at line 3 of the eval at line 4 of Foo.pl\n.

$eval

> Non-zero if the die() was invoked inside an eval.

$level
$iline
$ifile
$oline
$ofile
$oscope

> The rest of the arguments are explained in the source for Religion::TraceBack.

Whenever you install a DieHandler, it will automatically store the current value of $Die::Handler so it can chain to it. If you want to install a handler only temporarily, use local().

If your handler returns data using return or by falling off the end, then the items returned will be used to fill back in the argument list, and the next handler in the chain, if any, will be invoked. *Don't fall off the end if you don't want to change the error message.*

If your handler exits using last, then no further handlers will be invoked, and the program will die immediately.

If your handler exits using **next**, then the next handler in the chain will be invoked directly, without giving you a chance to change its arguments as you could if you used **return**.

If your handler invokes **die()**, then **die()** will proceed as if no handlers were installed. If you are inside an **eval**, then it will exit to the scope enclosing the **eval**, otherwise it will exit the program.

WarnHandler SUB

Invoke like this:

```
$Warn::Handler = new WarnHandler sub {
      #...
};
```

For the rest of its explanation, see DieHandler, and substitute **warn()** for **die()**. Note that once the last DieHandler completes (or last is invoked) then execution will return to the code that invoked **warn()**.

DiePreHandler SUB

Invoke like this:

```
$Die::PreHandler = new DiePreHandler sub {
      #...
};
```

This works identically to **$Die::Handler**, except that it forms a separate chain that is invoked *before* the DieHandler chain. Since you can use **last** to abort all the handlers and die immediately, or change the messages or scope details, this can be useful for modifying data that all future handlers will see, or to dispose of some messages from further handling.

This is even more useful in **$Warn::PreHandler**, since you can just throw away warnings that you *know* aren't needed.

WarnPreHandler SUB

Invoke like this:

```
$Warn::PreHandler = new WarnPreHandler sub {
      #...
};
```

This works identically to **$Warn::Handler**, except that it forms a separate chain that is invoked *before* the WarnHandler chain. Since you can use **last** to abort all the handlers and return to the program, or change the messages or scope details, this can be useful for modifying data that all future handlers will see, or to dispose of some messages.

This is very useful, since you can just throw away warnings that you *know* aren't needed.

Examples

A dialog error message

```
$Die::Handler = new DieHandler sub {
    my($msg,$fmsg,$level,$eval) = @_;
    if($eval) {
```

```
                          # if we are in an eval, skip to the next handler
                          next;
                } else {
                          # show a message box describing the error.
                          print "ShowMessageBox $fmsg";

                          # force the program to exit
                          exit 0;
                          next;
                }
        };
```

A handler that changes die() messages back to the original format

```
        local($Die::Handler) = new DieHandler sub {
          my($msg,$fmsg,$level,@trace) = @_;
                $fmsg = $msg . ((substr($msg,-1,1) ne "\n") ?
                                        " at $trace[2] line $trace[1].\n"
                                        : "");
                return ($msg,$fmsg);
        };
```

A warn handler that does nothing

```
        $Warn::Handler = new WarnHandler sub {next;};
```

A warn prehandler that throws away a warning

```
        $Warn::PreHandler = new WarnPreHandler sub {
                my($msg,$fmsg,$level,$eval) = @_;
                if($msg =~ /Use of uninitialized/) {
                        last;
                }
                next;
        };
```

21

File Handle, Directory Handle, and I/O Stream Utilities

This chapter covers tools for working with input/output streams, such as pipes, files, file handles, and sockets.

FileHandle::Multi—print to multiple filehandles with one output call

Synopsis

```
use FileHandle::Multi;
$mult_obj=new FileHandle::Multi;
$mult_obj->open('>-');
$mult_obj->open('>file');
$mult_obj->open(">$file");
$mult_obj->open('>>file2');
$mult_obj->print("This will be printed to several filehandles\n");
$mult_obj->printf("This will be printed to %d filehandles\n",
    scalar @{$mult_obj->{handles}});
$mult_obj->autoflush();
@handle_refs = $mult_obj->members();
$mult_obj->output_field_separator(':');
$mult_obj->output_record_separator('\n');
$mult_obj->format_page_number(2);
$mult_obj->format_lines_per_page(66);
$mult_obj->format_lines_left(10);
$mult_obj->format_name('AN_REPORT');
$mult_obj->format_top_name('AN_REPORT_TOP');
$mult_obj->format_line_break_characters('\n');
$mult_obj->format_formfeed('\l');
$mult_obj->close();
```

Description

This module requires that the user have the FileHandle module installed (it comes with the Perl distribution). Create objects for each of the output filehandles you'll have, then call the `print()` and `printf()` methods to send output to all the filehandles associated with an object.

Examples

Look at the "Synopsis" section. Also, here is a simple implementation of the UNIX tee(1) program (non-append mode):

```
#!/local/bin/perl
use FileHandle::Multi;
$mh=new FileHandle::Multi;
$mh->open('>-');
for (@ARGV) { $mh->open(">$_"); }
while (<STDIN>) { $mh->print($_); }
```

Bugs

I don't think using my()s the way I am in the open() method is all that good. binmode isn't supported (but I don't see anybody using that anyway). In order to use fcntl(), fileno(), or flock() you'll have to access the filehandles yourself by calling members(). There's no write() yet (but I'm working on it!). Also, any limitations to the FileHandle module also apply here. Comments, bugs fixes, and suggestions welcome.

Author

Nem W. Schlecht, *nem@plains.nodak.edu*

IO——load various I/O modules

Synopsis

```
use IO;
```

Description

IO provides a simple mechanism to load all of the I/O modules at one go. Currently this includes:

IO::Handle	IO::Seekable	IO::File
IO::Pipe	IO::Socket	

For more information on any of these modules, please see its respective documentation.

IO::File——supply object methods for filehandles

Synopsis

```
use IO::File;
$fh = new IO::File;
if ($fh->open("< file")) {
    print <$fh>;
    $fh->close;
}
$fh = new IO::File "> file";
if (defined $fh) {
    print $fh "bar\n";
    $fh->close;
}
```

```
$fh = new IO::File "file", "r";
if (defined $fh) {
    print <$fh>;
    undef $fh;          # automatically closes the file
}
$fh = new IO::File "file", O_WRONLY|O_APPEND;
if (defined $fh) {
    print $fh "corge\n";
    $pos = $fh->getpos;
    $fh->setpos($pos);
    undef $fh;              # automatically closes the file
}
autoflush STDOUT 1;
```

Description

IO::File inherits from IO::Handle and IO::Seekable. It extends these classes with methods that are specific to file handles.

Constructor

new ([*ARGS*])

> Creates an IO::File. If it receives any parameters, they are passed to the method open; if the open fails, the object is destroyed. Otherwise, it is returned to the caller.

Methods

open(*FILENAME* [, *MODE* [, *PERMS*]])

> open accepts one, two or three parameters. With one parameter, it is just a front-end for the built-in open function. With two parameters, the first parameter is a filename that may include whitespace or other special characters, and the second parameter is the open mode, optionally followed by a file permission value.

> If IO::File::open receives a Perl mode string (>, +<, etc.) or a POSIX fopen() mode string (w, r+, etc.), it uses the basic Perl open operator.

> If IO::File::open is given a numeric mode, it passes that mode and the optional permissions value to the Perl sysopen operator. For convenience, IO::File::import tries to import the O_XXX constants from the Fcntl module. If dynamic loading is not available, this may fail, but the rest of IO::File will still work.

Author

Derived from *FileHandle.pm* by Graham Barr, *gbarr@pobox.com*.

See Also

perfunc, I/O Operators, IO::Handle IO::Seekable

IO::Handle — supply object methods for I/O handles

Synopsis

```
use IO::Handle;
$fh = new IO::Handle;
if ($fh->fdopen(fileno(STDIN),"r")) {
```

```
    print $fh->getline;
    $fh->close;
}
$fh = new IO::Handle;
if ($fh->fdopen(fileno(STDOUT),"w")) {
    $fh->print("Some text\n");
}
$fh->setvbuf($buffer_var, _IOLBF, 1024);
undef $fh;       # automatically closes the file if it's open
autoflush STDOUT 1;
```

Description

IO::Handle is the base class for all other I/O handle classes. It is not intended that objects of IO::Handle would be created directly, but instead IO::Handle is inherited from by several other classes in the IO hierarchy.

If you are reading this documentation looking for a replacement for the **FileHandle** package, then I suggest you read the documentation for IO::File.

A IO::Handle object is a reference to a symbol (see the **Symbol** package).

Constructors

new ()

> Creates a new IO::Handle object.

new_from_fd (*FD, MODE*)

> Creates an IO::Handle like **new** does. It requires two parameters, which are passed to the method **fdopen**; if the **fdopen** fails, the object is destroyed. Otherwise, it is returned to the caller.

Methods

If the C function setvbuf() is available, then IO::Handle::setvbuf sets the buffering policy for the IO::Handle. The calling sequence for the Perl function is the same as its C counterpart, including the macros _IOFBF, _IOLBF, and _IONBF, except that the buffer parameter specifies a scalar variable to use as a buffer.

Warning

> A variable used as a buffer by IO::Handle::setvbuf must not be modified in any way until the IO::Handle is closed or until IO::Handle::setvbuf is called again, or memory corruption may result!

See the **perlfunc** manpage for complete descriptions of each of the following supported IO::Handle methods, which are just front-ends for the corresponding built-in functions:

close	gets	stat
eof	print	sysread
fileno	printf	syswrite
getc	read	truncate

See the `perlvar` manpage for complete descriptions of each of the following supported IO::Handle methods:

`autoflush`	`format_name`
`input_line_number`	`format_formfeed`
`format_page_number`	`input_record_separator`
`format_line_break_characters`	`format_top_name`
`output_field_separator`	`format_lines_left`
`format_write`	`output_record_separator`

Furthermore, for doing normal I/O you might need these:

`$fh->getline`
> This works like `$fh` described in "I/O Operators" except that it's more readable and can be safely called in an array context while still returning just one line.

`$fh->getlines`
> This works like `$fh` when called in an array context to read all the remaining lines in a file, except that it's more readable. It will also `croak()` if accidentally called in a scalar context.

`$fh->fdopen ( FD, MODE )`
> fdopen is like an ordinary `open` except that its first parameter is not a filename but rather a file handle name, a IO::Handle object, or a file descriptor number.

`$fh->write ( BUF, LEN [, OFFSET ] )`
> `write` is like `write` found in C, that is, it is the opposite of `read`. The wrapper for the Perl `write` function is called `format_write`.

`$fh->opened`
> Returns `true` if the object is currently a valid file descriptor.

Lastly, a special method for working under `-T` and `setuid/gid` scripts:

`$fh->untaint`
> Marks the object as taint-clean, and as such, data read from it will also be considered taint-clean. Note that this is a very trusting action to take, and appropriate consideration for the data source and potential vulnerability should be kept in mind.

Note

An IO::Handle object is a GLOB reference. Some modules that inherit from IO::Handle may want to keep object-related variables in the hash-table part of the GLOB. In an attempt to prevent modules trampling on each other, I propose that any such module should prefix its variables with its own name separated by underscores. For example the IO::Socket module keeps a `timeout` variable in `io_socket_timeout`.

Bugs

Due to backwards compatibility, all filehandles resemble objects of class IO::Handle, or, actually, classes derived from that class. They aren't. Which means you can't derive your own class from IO::Handle and inherit those methods.

Author

Derived from *FileHandle.pm* by Graham Barr, *gbarr@pobox.com*

See Also

perlfunc , I/O Operators, IO::File

IO::Pipe—supply object methods for pipes

Synopsis

```
use IO::Pipe;
$pipe = new IO::Pipe;
if($pid = fork()) { # Parent
    $pipe->reader();
    while(<$pipe> {
        ....
    }
}
elsif(defined $pid) { # Child
    $pipe->writer();
    print $pipe ....
}
or
$pipe = new IO::Pipe;
$pipe->reader(qw(ls -l));
while(<$pipe>) {
    ....
}
```

Description

IO::Pipe provides an interface to creating pipes between processes.

Constructor

new ([*READER, WRITER*])

> Creates an IO::Pipe, which is a reference to a newly created symbol (see the Symbol package). IO::Pipe::new optionally takes two arguments, which should be objects blessed into IO::Handle, or a subclass thereof. These two objects will be used for the system call to **pipe**. If no arguments are given, then method handles is called on the new IO::Pipe object.

> These two handles are held in the array part of the GLOB until either **reader** or **writer** is called.

Methods

reader ([*ARGS*])

> The object is reblessed into a subclass of IO::Handle, and becomes a handle at the reading end of the pipe. If *ARGS* are given, then **fork** is called and *ARGS* are passed to **exec**.

writer ([*ARGS*])

> The object is reblessed into a subclass of IO::Handle, and becomes a handle at the writing end of the pipe. If *ARGS* are given, then **fork** is called and *ARGS* are passed to **exec**.

```
handles ()
```
This method is called during construction by IO::Pipe::new on the newly created IO::Pipe object. It returns an array of two objects blessed into IO::Pipe::End, or a subclass thereof.

Author

Graham Barr, *gbarr@pobox.com*

Copyright

Copyright © 1996 Graham Barr. All rights reserved. This program is free software; you can redistribute it and/or modify it under the same terms as Perl itself.

See Also

IO::Handle

IO::Pty — pseudo-tty object class

Synopsis

```
use IO::Pty;
$pty = new IO::Pty;
$slave  = $pty->slave;
foreach $val (1..10) {
    print $pty "$val\n";
    $_ = <$slave>;
    print "$_";
}
close($slave);
```

Description

IO::Pty provides an interface to allow the creation of a pseudo-tty.

IO::Pty inherits from IO::Handle and so provides all the methods defined by the IO::Handle package.

Constructor

new

The new constructor takes no arguments and returns a new object which represents the master side of the pseudo-tty.

Methods

slave

The slave method will return a new IO::Pty object which represents the slave side of the pseudo-tty.

ttyname

Returns the name of the pseudo-tty. On UNIX machines, this will be the pathname of the device.

Author

Graham Barr, *gbarr@pobox.com*

Based on original Ptty module by Nick Ing-Simmons, *nik@tiuk.ti.com*

Copyright

Most of the C code used in the XS file is covered by the GNU GENERAL PUBLIC LICENSE, See COPYING.

All other code is free software; you can redistribute it and/or modify it under the same terms as Perl itself.

See Also

IO::Handle

IO::Seekable —supply seek-based methods for I/O objects

Synopsis

```
use IO::Seekable;
package IO::Something;
@ISA = qw(IO::Seekable);
```

Description

IO::Seekable does not have a constructor of its own as it is intended to be inherited by other IO::Handle-based objects. It provides methods which allow seeking of the file descriptors.

If the C functions `fgetpos()` and `fsetpos()` are available, then `IO::File::getpos` returns an opaque value that represents the current position of the IO::File, and `IO::File::setpos` uses that value to return to a previously visited position.

See the `perlfunc` manpage for complete descriptions of each of the following supported IO::Seekable methods, which are just front-ends for the corresponding built-in functions:

```
clearerr               seek                    tell
```

Author

Derived from FileHandle.pm by Graham Barr, *gbarr@pobox.com*

See Also

perlfunc, I/O Operators, IO::Handle IO::File

IO::Select —OO interface to the select system call

Synopsis

```
use IO::Select;
$s = IO::Select->new();
$s->add(\*STDIN);
$s->add($some_handle);
@ready = $s->can_read($timeout);
@ready = IO::Select->new(@handles)->read(0);
```

Description

The IO::Select package implements an object-oriented approach to the system **select** function call. It allows the user to see what I/O handles (see IO::Handle) are ready for reading, writing, or have an error condition pending.

Constructor

new ([*HANDLES*])

> The constructor creates a new object and optionally initializes it with a set of handles.

Methods

add (*HANDLES*)

> Adds the list of handles to the IO::Select object. It is these values that will be returned when an event occurs. IO::Select keeps these values in a cache which is indexed by the **fileno** of the handle, so if more than one handle with the same **fileno** is specified then only the last one is cached.

> Each handle can be an IO::Handle object, an integer or an array reference where the first element is a IO::Handle or an integer.

remove (*HANDLES*)

> Remove all the given handles from the object. This method also works by the **fileno** of the handles. So the exact handles that were added need not be passed, just handles that have an equivalent **fileno**.

exists (*HANDLE*)

> Returns a true value (actually the handle itself) if it is present. Returns **undef** otherwise.

handles

> Returns an array of all registered handles.

can_read ([*TIMEOUT*])

> Returns an array of handles that are ready for reading. *TIMEOUT* is the maximum amount of time to wait before returning an empty list. If *TIMEOUT* is not given and any handles are registered then the call will block.

can_write ([*TIMEOUT*])

> Same as **can_read** except checks for handles that can be written to.

has_error ([*TIMEOUT*])

> Same as **can_read** except checks for handles that have an error condition, for example EOF.

count ()

> Returns the number of handles that the object will check for when one of the **can_** methods is called or the object is passed to the **select** static method.

bits()

> Returns the bit string suitable as argument to the core **select()** call.

select (*READ, WRITE, ERROR* [, *TIMEOUT*])

> **select** is a static method, that is, you call it with the package name like **new**. *READ*, *WRITE* and *ERROR* are either **undef** or IO::Select objects. *TIMEOUT* is optional and has the same effect as for the core select call.

The result will be an array of 3 elements, each a reference to an array which will hold the handles that are ready for reading, ready for writing, and have error conditions respectively. Upon error an empty array is returned.

Example

Here is a short example which shows how IO::Select could be used to write a server which communicates with several sockets while also listening for more connections on a listen socket:

```
use IO::Select;
use IO::Socket;
$lsn = new IO::Socket::INET(Listen => 1, LocalPort => 8080);
$sel = new IO::Select( $lsn );

while(@ready = $sel->can_read) {
    foreach $fh (@ready) {
        if($fh == $lsn) {
            # Create a new socket
            $new = $lsn->accept;
            $sel->add($new);
        }
        else {
            # Process socket
            # Maybe we have finished with the socket
            $sel->remove($fh);
            $fh->close;
        }
    }
}
```

Author

Graham Barr, *gbarr@pobox.com*

Copyright

Copyright © 1995 Graham Barr. All rights reserved. This program is free software; you can redistribute it and/or modify it under the same terms as Perl itself.

IO::Socket — object interface to socket communications

Synopsis

```
use IO::Socket;
```

Description

IO::Socket provides an object interface to creating and using sockets. It is built upon the IO::Handle interface and inherits all the methods defined by IO::Handle.

IO::Socket only defines methods for those operations which are common to all types of socket. Operations which are specified to a socket in a particular domain have methods defined in subclasses of IO::Socket.

IO::Socket will export all functions (and constants) defined by Socket.

Constructor

new ([*ARGS*])

> Creates a IO::Socket, which is a reference to a newly created symbol (see the Symbol package). new optionally takes arguments, these arguments are in key-value pairs. new only looks for one key, Domain, which tells new which domain the socket it will be. All other arguments will be passed to the configuration method of the package for that domain. See below.

Methods

See the perlfunc manpage for complete descriptions of each of the following supported IO::Seekable methods, which are just front-ends for the corresponding built-in functions:

socket	socketpair	bind
listen	accept	send
recv	peername (getpeername)	sockname (getsockname)

Some methods take slightly different arguments to those defined in the perlfunc manpage in attempt to make the interface more flexible. These are:

accept ([*PKG*])

> Perform the system call accept on the socket and return a new object. The new object will be created in the same class as the listen socket, unless *PKG* is specified. This object can be used to communicate with the client that was trying to connect. In a scalar context the new socket is returned, or undef upon failure. In an array context a two-element array is returned containing the new socket and the peer address, the list will be empty upon failure.

Additional methods that are provided are:

timeout ([*VAL*])

> Set or get the timeout value associated with this socket. If called without any arguments then the current setting is returned. If called with an argument the current setting is changed and the previous value returned.

sockopt (*OPT* [, *VAL*])

> Unified method to both set and get options in the SOL_SOCKET level. If called with one argument then getsockopt is called, otherwise setsockopt is called.

sockdomain

> Returns the numerical number for the socket domain type. For example, for a AF_INET socket the value of &AF_INET will be returned.

socktype

> Returns the numerical number for the socket type. For example, for a SOCK_STREAM socket the value of &SOCK_STREAM will be returned.

protocol

> Returns the numerical number for the protocol being used on the socket, if known. If the protocol is unknown, as with an AF_UNIX socket, zero is returned.

Subclasses

IO::Socket::INET

IO::Socket::INET provides a constructor to create an AF_INET domain socket and some related methods. The constructor can take the following options:

PeerAddr
>   Remote host address: `<hostname>[:<port>]`

PeerPort
>   Remote port or service: `<service>[(<no>)]` | `<no>`

LocalAddr
>   Local host bind address: `hostname[:port]`

LocalPort
>   Local host bind port: `<service>[(<no>)]` | `<no>`

Proto
>   Protocol name: `"tcp"` | `"udp"` | `...`

Type
>   Socket type: `SOCK_STREAM` | `SOCK_DGRAM` | `...`

Listen
>   Queue size for listen

Reuse
>   Set SO_REUSEADDR before binding

Timeout
>   Timeout value for various operations

If `Listen` is defined then a listen socket is created, unless the socket type, which is derived from the protocol, is SOCK_STREAM, then `connect()` is called.

The `PeerAddr` can be a hostname or an IP-address of the **xx.xx.xx.xx** form. The `PeerPort` can be a number or a symbolic service name. The service name might be followed by a number in parentheses which is used if the service is not known by the system. The `PeerPort` specification can also be embedded in the `PeerAddr` by preceding it with a ":".

Only one of `Type` or `Proto` needs to be specified; one will be assumed from the other. If you specify a symbolic `PeerPort` port, then the constructor will try to derive `Type` and `Proto` from the service name.

Methods

`sockaddr()`
>   Return the address part of the **sockaddr** structure for the socket

`sockport()`
>   Return the port number that the socket is using on the local host

`sockhost()`
>   Return the address part of the **sockaddr** structure for the socket in the text form **xx.xx.xx.xx**

`peeraddr()`
>   Return the address part of the **sockaddr** structure for the socket on the peer host

peerport ()
> Return the port number for the socket on the peer host.

peerhost ()
> Return the address part of the sockaddr structure for the socket on the peer host in the text form **xx.xx.xx.xx**

Examples

```
$sock = IO::Socket::INET->new(PeerAddr => 'www.perl.org',
                              PeerPort => http(80),
                              Proto    => 'tcp');
$sock = IO::Socket::INET->new(PeerAddr => 'localhost:smtp(25)');
$sock = IO::Socket::INET->new(Listen   => 5,
                              LocalAddr => 'localhost',
                              LocalPort => 9000,
                              Proto    => 'tcp');
```

IO::Socket::UNIX

IO::Socket::UNIX provides a constructor to create an AF_UNIX domain socket and some related methods. The constructor can take the following options:

Type
> Type of socket (e.g., SOCK_STREAM or SOCK_DGRAM)

Local
> Path to local `fifo`

Peer
> Path to peer `fifo`

Listen
> Create a listen socket

Methods

hostpath()
> Returns the pathname to the `fifo` at the local end

peerpath()
> Returns the pathname to the `fifo` at the peer end

Author

Graham Barr, *gbarr@pobox.com*

Copyright

See Also

Socket, IO::Handle

Log::Topics—control flow of logging messages

Synopsis

```
use Log::Topics qw(add_topic log_topic topics);
add_topic $topic_name,$filehandle,$overload
add_topic $topic_name,$filename,$overload
log_topic $topic_name,@messages
@topicslist=topics();
```

Description

This package provides services for controlling the output of logging messages from an application. Log messages are identified by named topics, and the messages for each topic can be directed or redirected to file handles or files.

The add_topic() function can be used to associate a named topic with a particular file handle. If a value of 0, then logging of that particular topic is switched off. If the file handle is not connected to a file then it will be created and connected to a file of the same name. add_topic() returns the name of the file handle. The third $overload parameter, if specified and false, will only set the file handle if the specified topic is not already associated with a file handle.

Log messages are written using the log_topic() function which takes the topic name, and if that particular topic is enabled will print its remaining arguments to the associated file handle. It is an error to use a topic name that has not been declared using add_topic() first.

The topics() function returns a list of all the current registered topics.

This package can usefully be used for controlling all the output of a program, not just debugging and logging messages.

If you have the Getopt::Regex package, then the following lines of code allow the user to control the log messages from the command line using either –Lname=FILE or –Lname FILE syntaxes.

```
use Log::Topics qw(add_topic log_topic);
use Getopt::Regex qw(GetOptions);
GetOptions(\@ARGV,
  [K{ add_topic $1,$2; }    ,0],
  ['    sub { add_topic $1; $_[0]; },1]);
```

Bugs

Please let me know of any bugs. Suggestions for improvements gladly received.

Author

John A.R. Williams, *J.A.R.Williams@aston.ac.uk*

Thanks to Tim Bunce (*Tim.Bunce@ig.co.uk*) for helpful suggestions and comments.

22

Microsoft Windows Modules

Chapter 22 on CPAN contains the Microsoft Windows (Win32) modules, which provide functions for interfacing Perl with Windows NT and Windows 95 systems and applications.

We haven't included the full documentation for these modules in this UNIX version of the Perl Resource Kit, but they will be thoroughly documented in the Perl Resource Kit, Windows NT Edition. In the meantime, if you want to use the modules, you can get them through CPAN. For information on CPAN and using CPAN to retrieve the modules, see Chapter 1, *Introduction.*

The following list details the Win32 extensions included with the ActiveState Perl for Win32 distribution (these are also available for the standard distribution via the `libwin32` distribution, available from CPAN). This list was taken from Appendix B of O'Reilly's *Learning Perl on Win32 Systems.*

OLE (Win32::OLE in the `libwin32` distribution)
> Access to OLE automation and OLE variants

Win32::Process
> Access to extended Win32 process creation and management; includes methods to kill, suspend, resume, and set the priorities of processes

Win32::Semaphore
> Provides access to Win32 semaphores and synchronization

Win32::IPC
> Provides synchronization for objects of type Semaphore, Mutex, Process, or ChangeNotify

Win32::Mutex
> Provides access to Win32 mutex objects

Win32::ChangeNotify
> Provides access to Win32 change-notification objects, letting you do things like monitor changes to directory trees

Win32::EventLog
> Provides access to the Windows NT event log

Win32::Registry

Provides access to the Windows NT Registry

Win32::NetAdmin

Lets you manipulate users and groups

Win32::File

Lets you get and set file attributes

Win32::Service

Provides a service control interface: lets you start, pause, resume, and stop services

Win32::NetResource

Lets you work with shares, both as a client and a server

Win32::FileSecurity

Lets you work with file permissions on NTFS

Win32::Error

Provides an interface to the system error codes and messages

The following Win32 extensions are not included in (but are readily available for) the ActiveState distribution, and are included with the `libwin32` distribution.

Win32::Internet

Provides an interface to HTTP and FTP

Win32::ODBC

Provides an interface to ODBC data sources

```
Win32::Shortcut
```

Lets you create Explorer (shell) shortcuts

Win32::Sound

Plays *.wav* files or uses system sounds

Win32::AdminMisc

Provides an extension of Win32::NetAdmin that adds user impersonation, password manipulation, and DNS administration

Win32::Clipboard

Accesses the Windows NT clipboard

Win32::Console

Interfaces to console screen drawing; lets you do colors, boxes, etc.

Win32::Pipe

Provides access to named pipes on Windows NT

In addition to these extensions, a Win32 extension is included with the ActiveState distribution and is available as part of `libwin32`. The Win32 extension provides the following list functions (we've given a brief code snippet to illustrate how you might code each one):

Win32::GetLastError

Returns the last error value generated by a call to a Win32 API function:

```
use Win32;
$err = Win32::GetLastError();
```

Win32::BuildNumber

Returns the build number of Perl for Win32:

```
use Win32:
$build = Win32::BuildNumber(); # $build has 306 (or whatever it is)
```

Win32::LoginName

Returns the username of the owner of the current Perl process:

```
use Win32;
$user = Win32::LoginName();   # $user has eriko (account name of
    current user)
```

Win32::NodeName

Returns the Microsoft Network node name of the current machine:

```
use Win32;
$node = Win32::NodeName(); # $node has machine name
```

Win32::DomainName

Returns the name of the Microsoft Network domain that the owner of the current Perl process is logged into:

```
use Win32;
$domain = Win32::Domain();   # $domain has network domain name (not
    TCP/IP domain name)
```

Win32::FsType

Returns a string naming the filesystem type of the currently active drive:

```
use Win32;
$fs = Win32::FsType();      # $fs contains fs type, like NTFS or FAT
```

Win32::GetCwd

Returns the current active drive and directory; this function does not return a UNC (Universal Naming Convention) path:

```
use Win32;
$cwd = Win32::GetCwd();       # $cwd has current working directory
```

Win32::SetCwd NEW_DIRECTORY

Sets the current active drive and directory; this function does not work with UNC paths:

```
use Win32;
Win32::SetCwd("c:/temp") || die "SetCwd: $!";
```

Win32::GetOSVersion

Returns an array (*$string*, *$major*, *$minor*, *$build*, and *$id*). *$string* is a descriptive string, *$major* is the major version of the operating system, *$minor* is the minor version of the operating system, *$build* is the build number of the OS, and *$id* is a digit that denotes the operating system variety (zero for Win32s, one for Windows 95, and two for Windows NT):

```
use Win32;
($string, $major, $minor, $build, $id) = Win32::GetOSVersion();
@os = qw(Win32s, Win95, WinNT);
print "$os[$id] $major\.$minor $string (Build $build)\n";
```

The output on a Windows NT 4.0 system is:

```
WinNT 4.0 Service Pack 3 (Build 1381)
```

Win32::FormatMessage ERROR_CODE

Converts the supplied Win32 error bitmap (returned by `GetLastError`) to a descriptive string:

```
use Win32;
use Win32::WinError;  # for error constants
$msg = Win32::FormatMessage(ERROR_INTERNAL_ERROR);
# $msg contains the string: There is not enough space on disk
```

Win32::Spawn COMMAND, ARGS, PID

Spawns a new process using the supplied COMMAND, passing in arguments in the string ARGS; the pid of the new process is stored in PID:

```
use Win32;
Win32::Spawn('c:/nt/system32/notepad.exe', undef, $pid); # $pid has
    new pid of notepad
```

Win32::LookupAccountName SYSTEM, ACCOUNT, DOMAIN, SID, SIDTYPE

Looks up ACCOUNT on SYSTEM and returns the domain name, SID, and SID type

Win32::LookupAccountSID SYSTEM, SID, ACCOUNT, DOMAIN, SIDTYPE

Looks up SID (Security ID) on SYSTEM and returns the account name, domain name, and SID type:

```
use Win32;
Win32::LookupAccountSID(undef, $some_sid, $acct, $domain,
$sidtype);
```

Win32::InitiateSystemShutdown MACHINE, MESSAGE, TIMEOUT, FORCECLOSE, REBOOT

Shuts down the specified MACHINE (**undef** means local machine), notifying users with the supplied MESSAGE, within the specified TIMEOUT (in seconds) interval. Forces closing of all documents without prompting the user if FORCECLOSE is **true**, and reboots the machine if REBOOT is **true** (be careful experimenting with this one):

```
use Win32;
Win32::InitiateSystemShutdown(undef, "Bye",  15, undef, 1);
# try to shut down local machine
```

Win32::AbortSystemShutdown MACHINE

Aborts a shutdown on the specified MACHINE:

```
use Win32;
Win32::AbortSystemShutdown(undef);
# stop a shutdown on local machine
```

Win32::GetTickCount

Returns the Win32 tick count, which is the number of milliseconds that have elasped since the system started:

```
use Win32;
$tick = Win32::GetTickCount();
# tick has number of milliseconds since system start
```

Win32::IsWinNT

Returns nonzero if the operating system is Windows NT:

```
use Win32;
$winnt = Win32::IsWinNT();  # true if running on Windows NT
```

Win32::IsWin95

Returns nonzero if the operating system is Windows 95:

```
use Win32;
$win95 = Win32::IsWin95(); # true if running on Windows 95
```

Win32::ExpandEnvironmentStrings STRING

Takes the STRING and builds a return string that has environment-variable strings replaced with their defined values:

```
use Win32;
$path = Win32::ExpandEnvironmentStrings('%PATH%'); # $path
contains expanded PATH
```

Win32::GetShortPathName LONGPATHNAME

Returns the short (8.3) pathname for LONGPATHNAME:

```
use Win32;
$short = Win32::GetShortPathName('words.secret');   # $short now
has 8.3 name (WORDS~1.SEC)
```

Win32::GetNextAvailDrive

Returns a string in the form of q:\ where q is the first available drive letter:

```
use Win32;
$drive = Win32::GetNextAvailDrive();  # $drive has first drive
(e.g,. B:)
```

23

Miscellaneous Modules

Agent—supplies agentspace methods for Perl5

Synopsis

```
use Agent;
```

Description

Agent::new creates agent objects, variables can be stored and retrieved within the agent's agentspace with the Agent::add, Agent::write, and Agent::read methods. When the agent needs to be transported, it can be packed completely via the Agent::sleep method. Once it gets wherever it's going, use Agent::wake to turn it back into an object. To set the importance (priority level) of the agentspace, use the Agent::setpriority method. You can set the level of priority to three different values: Urgent, Normal, and Low. This will eventually define how much precedence the agentspace will have on a remote machine, if lots of other agents are also running. The Agent::addcode method allows you to add some form of code to the agent. It does not matter what language the code is written in, except when a remote machine runs it, the particular remote machine must be able to read and parse that language.

Agent 2.91 should be backwardly compatible with the first release of Agent, even though Agentspace has had data compartments replaced and added.

Methods

Agent::new

Agent::new creates agentspace objects.

```
$my_agent = new Agent;
```

Agent::add

Agent::add allows you to declare new variables inside the agentspace.

```
$my_agent->add ( Name => 'A_Variable',
                 Value => 'Untyped_value' );
```

Agent::write

Agent::write lets you rewrite (modify) existing agentspace variables.

```
$my_agent->write ( Name => 'An_Existing_Variable',
                   Value => 'New_Value' );
```

Agent::read

> Agent::read lets you read variables out of the agentspace.

```
$my_value = $my_agent->read ( Name => 'A Variable' );
```

Agent::addcode

> Agent::addcode lets you add information into the codespace of the agent.

```
$my_agent->addcode ( Code => 'any_code' );
```

Agent::setpriority

> Agent::setpriority allows you to set the execution priority level of the agentspace agent. It has three levels: **Urgent**, **Normal**, and **Low**. All agents start with priority level set at **Normal**.

```
$my_agent->setpriority ( Level => 'Normal' );
```

Agent::sleep

> Agent::sleep returns a packed agentspace variable. The contents of this variable could then be transported in many ways.

```
$my_var = $my_agent->sleep();
```

Agent::wake

> Agent::wake is used to unpack agentspace created with packself.

```
wake $my_agent Agent => $sleeping_agent;
```

Agent::contents

> Agent::contents returns the contents of the various compartments within the agentspace.

```
$my_agent_vars = $my_agent->var_contents();
$my_agent_code = $my_agent->code_contents();
$my_agent_level = $my_agent->getlevel();
```

Author

James Duncan, *jduncan@hawk.igs.net*

Acknowledgments

Thanks go out to Steve Purkis (*spurkis@hawk.igs.net*), and everyone who has submitted oo modules to CPAN.

Bundle::CPAN—a bundle to play with all the other modules on CPAN

Synopsis

```
perl -MCPAN -e 'install Bundle::CPAN'
```

Contents

CPAN

CPAN::WAIT

Description

This bundle includes *CPAN.pm* as the base module and CPAN::WAIT, the first plug-in for CPAN that was developed even before there was an API.

After installing this bundle, it is recommended that you quit the current session and start again in a new process.

Author

Andreas Koenig, *k@franz.ww.TU-Berlin.DE*

Bundle::libnet—a bundle to install all libnet-related modules

Synopsis

```
perl -MCPAN -e 'install Bundle::libnet'
```

Contents

Data::Dumper—For Net::Config

Net::Telnet—For Net::Telnet by Jay Rogers

Net::Cmd—For libnet itself

Description

This bundle includes all the libnet distribution and the Net-Telnet distribution by Jay Rogers, *jay@rgrs.com*, which is a replacement module for the original Net::Telnet module which was in the libnet distribution.

Author

Graham Barr, *gbarr@pobox.com*

Bundle::LWP—a bundle to install all libwww-perl–related modules

Synopsis

```
perl -MCPAN -e 'install Bundle::LWP'
```

Contents

Net::FTP 2.00—If you want *ftp://* (FTP URL) support

IO::Socket 1.13—Used by HTTP::Daemon

MIME::Base64—Used in authentication headers

MD5—Needed for Digest authentication

Description

This bundle defines all prerequired modules for `libwww-perl`.

Author

Gisle Aas, *aas@sn.no*

Bundle::Tk—CPAN Bundle for Tk and its dependencies

Synopsis

```
perl -MCPAN -e 'install Bundle::Tk'
```

Contents

ExtUtils::MakeMaker—Should be in Perl distribution.

Net::NNTP—For proto news reader, also pulls in rest of Net::* which LWP needs.

Mail::Internet—For news again.

LWP—For tkweb.

Tk—Tk itself.

Author

Nick Ing-Simmons

Business::CreditCard—validate/generate credit card checksums/names

Synopsis

```
use Business::CreditCard;

print validate("5276 4400 6542 1319");
print cardtype("5276 4400 6542 1319");
print generate_last_digit("5276 4400 6542 131");
```

Description

These subroutines tell you whether a credit card number is self-consistent—whether the last digit of the number is a valid checksum for the preceding digits.

The validate() subroutine returns 1 if the card number provided passes the checksum test, and 0 otherwise.

The cardtype() subroutine returns a string containing the type of card: "MasterCard", "VISA", and so on. My list is not complete; I welcome additions.

The generate_last_digit() subroutine computes and returns the last digit of the card given the preceding digits. With a 16-digit card, you provide the first 15 digits; the subroutine returns the sixteenth.

This module does *not* tell you whether the number is on an actual card, only whether it might conceivably be on a real card. To verify whether a card is real, whether it's been stolen, or what its balance is, you need a Merchant ID, which gives you access to credit card databases. The *Perl Journal* (*http://tpj.com/tpj/*) has a Merchant ID so that I can accept MasterCard and VISA payments; it comes with the little pushbutton/slide-your-card-through device you've seen in restaurants and stores. That device calculates the checksum for you, so I don't actually use this module.

These subroutines will also work if you provide the arguments as numbers instead of strings, e.g., validate(5276440065421319).

To install this module, change directories to wherever your system keeps Perl modules (e.g., */usr/local/lib/perl5*) and create a *Business* directory if there isn't one already. Then copy this file there. That's it!

Author

Jon Orwant, *orwant@tpj.com*

The Perl Journal and MIT Media Lab

CPAN::FirstTime—utility for CPAN::Config file initialization

Synopsis

```
CPAN::FirstTime::init()
```

Description

The init routine asks a few questions and writes a CPAN::Config file.

CPAN::Nox—wrapper around CPAN.pm without using any XS module

Synopsis

Interactive mode:

```
perl -MCPAN::Nox -e shell;
```

Description

This package has the same functionality as *CPAN.pm*, but tries to prevent the usage of compiled extensions during its own execution. Its primary purpose is a rescue in case you upgraded Perl and broke binary compatibility somehow.

See Also

CPAN(3)

---

get, head, getprint, getstore, mirror—procedural LWP interface

Synopsis

```
perl -MLWP::Simple -e 'getprint "http://www.sn.no"'
use LWP::Simple;
$content = get("http://www.sn.no/")
if (mirror("http://www.sn.no/", "foo") == RC_NOT_MODIFIED) {
    ...
}
if (is_success(getprint("http://www.sn.no/"))) {
    ...
}
```

Description

This interface is intended for those who want a simplified view of the libwww-perl library. This interface should also be suitable for one-liners. If you need more control or access to the header fields in the requests sent and responses received you should use the full OO interface provided by the LWP::UserAgent module.

Functions

This following functions are provided (and exported) by this module:

get(*$url*)

> This function will get the document identified by the given URL. The get() function will return the document if successful or **undef** if it fails. The $url argument can be either a simple string or a reference to a URI::URL object.

> You will not be able to examine the response code or response headers (like "Content-Type") when you are accessing the Web using this function. If you need this you should use the full OO interface.

head(*$url*)

> Get document headers. Returns the following values if successful: $content_type, $document_length, $modified_time, $expires, $server.

> Returns an empty list if it fails.

getprint(*$url*)

> Get and print a document identified by a URL. The document is printed on STDOUT. The error message (formatted as HTML) is printed on STDERR if the request fails. The return value is the HTTP response code.

getstore(*$url, $file*)

> Gets a document identified by a URL and stores it in the file. The return value is the HTTP response code.

mirror(*$url, $file*)

> Get and store a document identified by a URL, using "If-modified-since," and checking of the "Content-Length." Returns the HTTP response code.

Exports

This module also exports the HTTP::Status constants and procedures. These can be used when you check the response code from getprint(), getstore(), and mirror(). The constants are:

RC_CONTINUE	RC_SWITCHING_PROTOCOLS
RC_OK	RC_CREATED
RC_ACCEPTED	RC_REQUEST_TIMEOUT
RC_NO_CONTENT	RC_RESET_CONTENT
RC_PARTIAL_CONTENT	RC_MULTIPLE_CHOICES
RC_MOVED_PERMANENTLY	RC_MOVED_TEMPORARILY
RC_SEE_OTHER	RC_NOT_MODIFIED
RC_USE_PROXY	RC_BAD_REQUEST
RC_UNAUTHORIZED	RC_PAYMENT_REQUIRED
RC_FORBIDDEN	RC_NOT_FOUND

RC_METHOD_NOT_ALLOWED	RC_NOT_ACCEPTABLE
RC_PROXY_AUTHENTICATION_ REQUIRED	RC_NON_AUTHORITATIVE_INFORMA- TION
RC_CONFLICT	RC_GONE
RC_LENGTH_REQUIRED	RC_PRECONDITION_FAILED
RC_REQUEST_ENTITY_TOO_LARGE	RC_REQUEST_URI_TOO_LARGE
RC_UNSUPPORTED_MEDIA_TYPE	RC_INTERNAL_SERVER_ERROR
RC_NOT_IMPLEMENTED	RC_BAD_GATEWAY
RC_SERVICE_UNAVAILABLE	RC_GATEWAY_TIMEOUT
RC_HTTP_VERSION_NOT_SUPPORTED	

The HTTP::Status classification functions are:

is_success(*$rc*)
> Check if response code indicated successful request.

is_error(*$rc*)
> Check if response code indicated that an error occurred.

The module will also export the LWP::UserAgent object as $ua if you ask for it explicitly.

The user agent created by this module will identify itself as LWP::Simple/0.00 and will initialize its proxy defaults from the environment (by calling $ua->env_proxy).

See Also

LWP, LWP::UserAgent, HTTP::Status, the request manpage, the mirror manpage

---

gettext—message-handling functions

Synopsis

```
use gettext;
use POSIX;     # Needed for setlocale()
setlocale(LC_MESSAGES, "");
textdomain("my_program");
print gettext("Welcome to my program"), "\n";
        # (printed in the local language)
```

Description

The gettext module permits access from Perl to the gettext() family of functions for retrieving message strings from databases constructed to internationalize software.

gettext(), dgettext(), and dcgettext() attempt to retrieve a string matching their msgid parameter within the context of the current locale. dcgettext() takes the message's category and the text domain as parameters while dcgettext() defaults to the LC_MESSAGES category and gettext() defaults to LC_MESSAGES and uses the current text domain. If the string is not found in the database, then msgid is returned.

textdomain() sets the current text domain and returns the previously active domain.

bindtextdomain(*domain, dirname*) instructs the retrieval functions to look for the databases belonging to domain *domain* in the directory *dirname*.

Author

Phillip Vandry, *vandry@Mlink.NET*

See Also

gettext(3i), gettext(1), msgfmt(1)

---

guess_media_type,media_suffix— guess/return media type for a file or a URL

Synopsis

```
use LWP::MediaTypes qw(guess_media_type);
$type = guess_media_type("/tmp/foo.gif");
```

Description

This module provides functions for handling of media (also known as MIME) types and encodings. The mapping from file extensions to media types is defined by the *media.types* file. If the *~/.media.types* file exists, it is used as a replacement.

For backwards compatibility we will also look for *~/.mime.types*.

Functions

guess_media_type(*$filename_or_url*, [*$header_to_modify*])

> This function tries to guess media type and encoding for given file. In scalar context it returns only the content-type. In array context it returns an array consisting of content-type followed by any content-encodings applied.

> The **guess_media_type** function also accepts a URI::URL object as argument.

> If the type can not be deduced from looking at the filename only, then **guess_media_type()** will take a look at the actual file using the **-T** Perl operator in order to determine if this is a text file (**text/plain**). If this does not work it will return **application/octet-stream** as the type.

> The optional second argument should be a reference to a HTTP::Headers object (or some HTTP::Message object). When present, this function will set the value of the Content-Type and Content-Encoding for this header.

media_suffix(*$type,...*)

> This function will return all suffixes that can be used to denote the specified media type(s). Wildcard types can be used. In scalar context it will return the first suffix found.

Examples

```
@suffixes = media_suffix('image/*', 'audio/basic');
$suffix = media_suffix('text/html');
```

Krb4—Perl extension for Kerberos 4

Synopsis

```
use Krb4;
```

Description

Krb4 is an object-oriented extension to Perl5 that implements several user-level Kerberos 4 functions. With this module, you can create Kerberized clients and servers written in Perl. It is compatible with both AFS and MIT Kerberos.

Variables and Functions

Note: No methods or variables are exported, so each variable and function should be preceded by `Krb4::`.

error
> Contains the error code of the most recent Kerberos function call.

get_phost(*alias*)
> Returns the instance name of the host **alias**

get_lrealm(*n*)
> Returns the nth realm of the host machine. n is zero by default.

realmofhost(*host*)
> Returns the realm of the machine **host**.

mk_req(*service, instance, realm, checksum*)
> Returns a Krb4::Ticket object for the specified *service*, *instance*, and *realm*. It will return **undef** if there was an error.

rd_req(*ticket, service, instance, fn*)
> Returns a Krb4::AuthDat object, which contains information obtained from the ticket, or **undef** upon failure. Ticket is a variable of the class Krb4::Ticket, which can be obtained from mk_req(). *fn* is a path to the appropriate **srvtab**. /etc/srvtab will be used if *fn* is null.

get_cred(*service, instance, realm*)
> Searched the caller's ticket file for a ticket for the service and instance in the given realm. Returns a Krb4::Creds object, or **undef** upon failure.

get_key_sched(*session*)
> Returns the key schedule for the session key *session*, which can be obtained from rd_req() or get_cred(). The key schedule is a Krb4::KeySchedule object.

Classes and Methods

There are four classes in the Krb4 module: Ticket, AuthDat, Creds, and KeySchedule. They are all simply abstractions of Kerberos 4 structures. You almost never need to worry about creating new objects—the functions which return these objects create them for you (is this the best thing to do?). The one exception is when you need to construct a Ticket object for rd_req(). See below for details.

Ticket
> Contains a ticket for a specified service, instance, and realm.

new(dat)

Returns a new Ticket object containing the data in dat. You must create a new Ticket object on the server side for passing to rd_req().

dat

The data contained in the ticket. Looks like junk to the naked eye.

length

The length of the data contained in dat

AuthDat

Contains the contents of the AUTH_DAT structure returned by rd_req(). See below for the goodies.

pname

Returns the principal's name.

pinst

Returns the principal's instance.

prealm

Returns the principal's realm.

session

The session key. Pass this to get_key_sched() to obtain a key schedule for encryption.

k_flags

Flags from the ticket

checksum

The checksum from the ticket. See mk_req().

life

Life of the ticket

time_sec

The time the ticket was issued. localtime() can convert this to a nicer format.

address

The address in the ticket. Useful for mutual authentication.

reply

Auth reply (not very descriptive, I know...)

Creds

Contains information retrieved from your ticket file.

service

The service name

instance

The instance (duh!)

realm

The realm (duh!)

session

Returns the session key. Pass this to get_key_sched() to obtain a key schedule for encryption.

lifetime

The lifetime of the ticket

kvno
> The key version number

ticket_st
> The ticket itself

issue_date
> The date the ticket was issued

pname
> The name of the principal

pinst
> The instance of the principal

KeySchedule
> You don't need to fool around with this.

Author

Jeff Horwitz, *jhorwitz@umich.edu*

See Also

perl(1)

Logfile — Perl extension for generating reports from logfiles

Synopsis

```
use Logfile::Cern;
$l = new Logfile::Cern  File  => 'cache.log.gz',
                        Group => [Domain,File,Hour];
$l->report(Group => File,   Sort => Records);
$l->report(Group => Domain, Sort => Bytes);
$l->report(Group => Hour, List => [Bytes, Records]);
use Logfile::Wftp;
[...]
```

Description

The Logfile extension will help you generate various reports from different server logfiles. In general there is no restriction as to what information you extract from the logfiles.

Reading the files

The package can be customized by subclassing Logfile.

A subclass should provide a function **next** which reads the next record from the file handle $self->{Fh} and returns an object of type Logfile::Record. In addition a function **norm** may be specified to normalize the various record fields.

Here is a shortened version of the Logfile::Cern class:

```
package Logfile::Cern;
@ISA = qw ( Logfile::Base ) ;
sub next {
    my $self = shift;
    my $fh = $self->{Fh};
```

```
*S = $fh;
my ($line,$host,$user,$pass,$rest,$date,$req,$code,$bytes);
($host,$user,$pass,$rest) = split ' ', $line, 4;
($rest =~ s!\[([^\]]+)\]\s*!!) && ($date = $1);
($rest =~ s!\"([^\"]+)\"\s*!!) && ($req = (split ' ', $1)[1]);
($code, $bytes) = split ' ', $rest;
Logfile::Record->new(Host  => $host,
                     Date  => $date,
                     File  => $req,
                     Bytes => $bytes);
}
```

As stated above, in general you are free to choose the fields you enter in the record.
But:

Date

> Should be a valid date string. For conversion to the seconds elapsed since the
> start of epoch the modules GetDate and Date::DateParse are tried. If both cannot
> be used, a crude build-in module is used.
>
> The record constructor replaces Date by the date in yymmdd form to make it sort-
> able. Also the field Hour is padded in.

Host

> Setting Host will also set field Domain by the verbose name of the country given
> by the domain suffix of the fully qualified domain name (*hostname.domain*).
> foo.bar.PG will be mapped to Papua New. Hostnames containing no dot will be
> assigned to the domain Local. IP numbers will be assigned to the domain Unre-
> solved. Mapping of short to long domain names is done in the Net::Country
> extension which might be useful in other contexts:
>
> ```
> use Net::Country;
> $germany = Net::Country::Name('de');
> ```

Records

> Is always set to 1 in the Record constructor. So this field gives the number of
> successful returns from the next function.

Here is the shortened optional norm method:

```
sub norm { my ($self, $key, $val) = @_;
    if ($key eq File) {
        $val =~ s/\?.*//;                          # remove query
        $val =~ s!%([\da-f][\da-f])!chr(hex($1))!eig;   # decode
    }
    $val;
}
```

The constructor reads in a logfile and builds one or more indices.

```
$l = new Logfile::Cern  File => 'cache.log.gz',
                        Group => [Host,Domain,File,Hour,Date];
```

There is little space but some time overhead in generating additional indexes. If the
File parameter is not given, STDIN is used. The Group parameter may be a field
name or a reference to a list of field names. Only the field names given as constructor
argument can be used for report generation.

Report Generation

The index to use for a report must be given as the `Group` parameter. Output is sorted by the index field unless a `Sort` parameter is given. Also the output can be truncated by a `Top` argument or `Limit`.

The report generator lists the fields `Bytes` and `Records` for a given index. The option `List` may be a single field name or a reference to an array of field names. It specifies which field should be listed in addition to the `Group` field. `List` defaults to `Records`.

```
$l->report(Group => Domain, List => [Bytes, Records])
```

Output is sorted by the `Group` field unless overwritten by a `Sort` option. Default sorting order is increasing for `Date` and `Hour` fields and decreasing for all other fields. The order can be reversed using the `Reverse` option.

This code:

```
$l->report(Group => File, Sort => Records, Top => 10);
```

prints:

```
File                            Records
=======================================
/htbin/SFgate              30 31.58%
/freeWAIS-sf/*             22 23.16%
/SFgate/SFgate              8  8.42%
/SFgate/SFgate-small        7  7.37%
/icons/*                    4  4.21%
/~goevert                   3  3.16%
/journals/SIGMOD            3  3.16%
/SFgate/ciw                 2  2.11%
/search                     1  1.05%
/reports/96/                1  1.05%
```

Here are other examples. Also take a look at the *t/** files.

```
$l->report(Group => Domain, Sort => Bytes);
Domain                     Records
==================================
Germany                  12 12.63%
Unresolved                8  8.42%
Israel                   34 35.79%
Denmark                   4  4.21%
Canada                    3  3.16%
Network                   6  6.32%
US Commercial            14 14.74%
US Educational            8  8.42%
Hong Kong                 2  2.11%
Sweden                    2  2.11%
Non-Profit                1  1.05%
Local                     1  1.05%

$l->report(Group => Hour, List => [Bytes, Records]);
Hour            Bytes           Records
=======================================
07        245093 17.66%        34 35.79%
08        438280 31.59%        19 20.00%
09        156730 11.30%        11 11.58%
```

```
10        255451 18.41%        16 16.84%
11        274521 19.79%        10 10.53%
12         17396  1.25%         5  5.26%
```

Report options

Group => *field*

> Mandatory. *field* must be one of the fields passed to the constructor.

List => *field*
List => [*field*, *field*]

> List the subtotals for *field*s. Defaults to Records.

Sort => *field*

> Sort output by *field*. By default, Date and Hour are sorted in increasing order, whereas all other fields are sorted in decreasing order.

Reverse => 1

> Reverse sorting order.

Top => *number*

> Print only the first *number* subtotals.

Limit => *number*

> Print only the subtotals with Sort field greater than *number* (less than number if sorted in increasing order).

Currently reports are simply printed to STDOUT.

Author

Ulrich Pfeifer, *pfeifer@ls6.informatik.uni-dortmund.de*

See Also

perl(1)

---

lwpcook—libwww-perl cookbook

Description

This document contain some examples that show typical usage of the libwww-perl library. You should consult the documentation for the individual modules for more detail.

All examples should be runnable programs. You can, in most cases, test the code sections by piping the program text directly to Perl.

get

> It is very easy to use this library to just fetch documents from the Net. The LWP::Simple module provides the get() function that returns the document specified by its URL argument:
>
> ```
> use LWP::Simple;
> $doc = get 'http://www.sn.no/libwww-perl/';
> ```
>
> or as a Perl one-liner using the getprint() function:
>
> ```
> perl -MLWP::Simple -e 'getprint "http://www.sn.no/libwww-perl/"'
> ```

or how about fetching the latest Perl by running this:

```
perl -MLWP::Simple -e 'getstore
        "ftp://ftp.sunet.se/pub/lang/perl/CPAN/src/latest.tar.gz",
        "perl.tar.gz"'
```

You will probably first want to find a CPAN site closer to you by running something like the following command:

```
perl -MLWP::Simple -e 'getprint
        "http://www.perl.com/perl/CPAN/CPAN.html"'
```

Enough of this simple stuff! The LWP object-oriented interface gives you more control over the request sent to the server. Using this interface, you have full control over the headers sent and how you want to handle the response returned.

```
use LWP::UserAgent;
$ua = new LWP::UserAgent;
$ua->agent("$0/0.1 " . $ua->agent);
# pretend you are some very new Netscape browser
# $ua->agent("Mozilla/5.0")

$req = new HTTP::Request 'GET' => 'http://www.sn.no/libwww-perl';
$req->header('Accept' => 'text/html');

# send request
$res = $ua->request($req);

# check the outcome
if ($res->is_success) {
    print $res->content;
} else {
    print "Error: " . $res->code . " " . $res->message;
}
```

The lwp-request program (alias GET) that is distributed with the library can also be used to fetch documents from WWW servers.

head

If you just want to check if a document is present (i.e., that the URL is valid) try to run code that looks like this:

```
use LWP::Simple;

if (head($url)) {
    # ok document exists
}
```

The head() function really returns a list of meta-information about the document. The first three values of the list returned are the document type, the size of the document, and the age of the document.

More control over the request or access to all header values returned requires that you use the object-oriented interface described for GET above. Just do: **s/GET/HEAD/g**.

POST

There is no simple interface for posting data to a WWW server. You must use the object-oriented interface for this. The most common POST operation is to access a WWW form application:

```
use LWP::UserAgent;
$ua = new LWP::UserAgent;

my $req = new HTTP::Request 'POST',
                    'http://www.perl.com/cgi-bin/BugGlimpse';
$req->content_type('application/x-www-form-urlencoded');
$req->content('match=www&errors=0');

my $res = $ua->request($req);
print $res->as_string;
```

If your application has the key/value pairs to be posted in an associative array, then we can exploit the URI::URL module to create the content for the POST request message (which handles all the escaping issues):

```
%form = ( search => 'www', errors => 0 );

use URI::URL;
use LWP::UserAgent;
$ua = new LWP::UserAgent;

my $req = new HTTP::Request 'POST',
                    'http://www.perl.com/cgi-bin/BugGlimpse';
$req->content_type('application/x-www-form-urlencoded');

my $curl = url("http:");        # create an empty HTTP URL object
$curl->query_form(%form);
$req->content($curl->equery); # %form content as escaped query
                              # string

print $ua->request($req)->as_string;
```

The lwp-request program (alias POST) that is distributed with the library can also be used for posting data.

Proxies

Some sites use proxies to go through firewall machines or just as a cache in order to improve performance. Proxies can also be used for accessing resources through protocols not supported directly (or supported badly) by the libwww-perl library.

You should initialize your proxy setting before you start sending requests:

```
use LWP::UserAgent;
$ua = new LWP::UserAgent;
$ua->env_proxy; # initialize from environment variables
# or
$ua->proxy(ftp  => 'http://proxy.myorg.com');
$ua->proxy(wais => 'http://proxy.myorg.com');
$ua->no_proxy(qw(no se fi));

my $req = new HTTP::Request 'wais://xxx.com/';
print $ua->request($req)->as_string;
```

The LWP::Simple interface calls env_proxy() for you automatically. Applications that use the $ua->env_proxy() method normally do not use the $ua->proxy() and $ua->no_proxy() methods.

Access to Protected Documents

Documents protected by basic authorization can be easily accessed like this:

```
use LWP::UserAgent;
$ua = new LWP::UserAgent;
$req = new HTTP::Request GET => 'http://www.sn.no/secret/';
$req->authorization_basic('aas', 'mypassword');
print $ua->request($req)->as_string;
```

The other alternative is to provide a subclass of LWP::UserAgent that overrides the get_basic_credentials() method. Study the *lwp-request* program for an example of this.

Mirroring

If you want to mirror documents from a WWW server, then try to run code similar to this at regular intervals:

```
use LWP::Simple;

%mirrors = (
    'http://www.sn.no/'            => 'sn.html',
    'http://www.perl.com/'         => 'perl.html',
    'http://www.sn.no/libwww-perl/' => 'lwp.html',
    'gopher://gopher.sn.no/'       => 'gopher.html',
);

while (($url, $localfile) = each(%mirrors)) {
    mirror($url, $localfile);
}
```

Or as a Perl (almost) one-liner:

```
perl -MLWP::Simple -e 'mirror("http://www.perl.com/",
                             "perl.html")';
```

The document is not transferred unless it has been updated.

Large Documents

If the document you want to fetch is too large to be kept in memory, then you have two alternatives. You can instruct the library to write the document content to a file (the second argument to $ua->request() is a filename):

```
use LWP::UserAgent;
$ua = new LWP::UserAgent;

my $req = new HTTP::Request 'GET',
          'http://www.sn.no/~aas/perl/www/libwww-perl-5.00.tar.gz';
$res = $ua->request($req, "libwww-perl.tar.gz");
if ($res->is_success) {
    print "ok\n";
}
```

Or you can process the document as it arrives (the second $ua->request() argument is a code reference):

```
use LWP::UserAgent;
$ua = new LWP::UserAgent;
$URL = 'ftp://ftp.unit.no/pub/rfc/rfc-index.txt';

my $expected_length;
my $bytes_received = 0;
$ua->request(HTTP::Request->new('GET', $URL),
        sub {
                my($chunk, $res) = @_;
                $bytes_received += length($chunk);
                unless (defined $expected_length) {
                    $expected_length = $res->content_length || 0;
                }
                if ($expected_length) {
                    printf STDERR "%d%% - ",
                            100 * $bytes_received / $expected_length;
                }
                print STDERR "$bytes_received bytes received\n";
                # XXX Should really do something with the chunk itself
                # print $chunk;
            });
```

HTML Formatting

It is easy to convert HTML code to "readable" text:

```
use LWP::Simple;
use HTML::Parse;
print parse_html(get 'http://www.sn.no/libwww-perl/')->format;
```

Parse URLs

To access individual elements of a URL, try this:

```
use URI::URL;
$host = url("http://www.sn.no/")->host;
```

or:

```
use URI::URL;
$u = url("ftp://ftp.sn.no/test/aas;type=i");
print "Protocol scheme is ", $u->scheme, "\n";
print "Host is ", $u->host, " at port ", $u->port, "\n";
```

or even:

```
use URI::URL;
my($host,$port) = (url("ftp://ftp.sn.no/test/aas;
                        type=i")->crack)[3,4];
```

Expand Relative URLs

This code reads URLs and print expanded versions:

```
use URI::URL;
$BASE = "http://www.sn.no/some/place?query";
while (<>) {
    print url($_, $BASE)->abs->as_string, "\n";
}
```

We can expand URLs in an HTML document by using the parser to build a tree that we then traverse:

```
%link_elements =
(
 'a'    => 'href',
 'img'  => 'src',
 'form' => 'action',
 'link' => 'href',
);

use HTML::Parse;
use URI::URL;

$BASE = "http://somewhere/root/";
$h = parse_htmlfile("xxx.html");
$h->traverse(\&expand_urls, 1);

print $h->as_HTML;

sub expand_urls
{
    my($e, $start) = @_;
    return 1 unless $start;
    my $attr = $link_elements{$e->tag};
    return 1 unless defined $attr;
    my $url = $e->attr($attr);
    return 1 unless defined $url;
    $e->attr($attr, url($url, $BASE)->abs->as_string);
}
```

Base URL

If you want to resolve relative links in a page, you have to determine which base URL to use. The HTTP::Response object now has a **base()** method:

```
$BASE = $res->base;
```

---

mod_perl—embed a Perl interpreter in the Apache HTTP server

Description

The Apache/Perl integration project brings together the full power of the Perl programming language and the Apache HTTP server. This is achieved by linking the Perl runtime library into the server and providing an object-oriented Perl interface to the server's C language API. These pieces are seamlessly glued together by the mod_perl server plugin, making it possible to write Apache modules entirely in Perl. In addition, the persistent interpreter embedded in the server avoids the overhead of starting an external interpreter and the penalty of Perl start-up (compile) time.

Without question, the most popular Apache/Perl module is the Apache::Registry module. This module emulates the CGI environment, allowing programmers to write scripts that run under CGI or mod_perl without change. Existing CGI scripts may require some changes, simply because a CGI script has a very short lifetime of one HTTP request, allowing you to get away with "quick and dirty" scripting. Using `mod_perl` and Apache::Registry requires you to be more careful, but it also gives new meaning to the word "quick"! Apache::Registry maintains a cache of compiled scripts, which happens the first time a script is accessed by a child server and again if the file is updated on disk.

Although it may be all you need, a speedy CGI replacement is only a small part of this project. Callback hooks are in place for each stage of a request. Apache-Perl modules may step in during the handler, header parser, uri translate, authentication, authorization, access, type check, fixup and logger stages of a request.

FAQ

Patrick Kane (*modus@enews.com*) maintains the `mod_perl` FAQ available at: *http://chaos.dc.enews.com/mod_perl/*.

Apache/Perl API

See "perldoc Apache" for info on how to use the Perl-Apache API.

See the *lib/* directory for example modules and *apache-modlist.html* for a comprehensive list.

See the *eg/* directory for example scripts.

mod_perl

For using `mod_perl` as a CGI replacement, the recommended configuration is as follows:

```
Alias /perl/  /real/path/to/perl-scripts/
<Location /perl>
SetHandler  perl-script
PerlHandler Apache::Registry
Options ExecCGI
</Location>
```

Now, any file accessed under */perl* will be handled by `mod_perl` and the Apache::Registry module. The file must exist and be executable, in addition, Options ExecCGI must be turned on. See the Apache::Registry module for details.

By default, `mod_perl` does not send any headers by itself, however, you may wish to change this:

```
PerlSendHeader On
```

With the recommended configuration, these options and Perl version 5.003_93 or higher (or 5.003_xx version with `sfio`), scripts running under Apache::Registry will look just like "normal" CGI scripts. See *eg/perlio.pl* as an example.

You may load additional modules via:

```
PerlModule Apache::SSI SomeOther::Module
```

There is a limit of 10 PerlModule's. If you need more to be loaded when the server starts, use one PerlModule to pull in many or use the PerlScript directive described below.

Optionally:

```
PerlScript  /full/path/to/script_to_load_at_startup.pl
```

This script will be loaded when the server starts. See *eg/startup.pl* for an example to start with.

In an `access.conf` `<Directory /foo>` or *.htaccess* you need:

```
PerlHandler sub_routine_name
```

This is the name of the subroutine to call to handle each request. e.g., in the PerlModule Apache::Registry this is Apache::Registry::handler.

If PerlHandler is not a defined subroutine, `mod_perl` assumes it is a package name which defines a subroutine named "handler".

```
PerlHandler    Apache::Registry
```

would load *Registry.pm* (if it is not already) and call its subroutine "handler".

There are several stages of a request where the Apache API allows a module to step in and do something. The Apache documentation will tell you all about those stages and what your modules can do. By default, these hooks are disabled at compile time; see the INSTALL document for information on enabling these hooks. The following configuration directives take one argument, which is the name of the subroutine to call. If the value is not a subroutine name, `mod_perl` assumes it is the name of a package that implements a "handler" subroutine.

```
PerlInitHandler
PerlTransHandler
PerlAuthenHandler
PerlAuthzHandler
PerlAccessHandler
PerlTypeHandler
PerlFixupHandler
PerlLogHandler
PerlHeaderParser (requires apache1.2b5 or higher)
PerlCleanupHandler
```

I/O

Apache's I/O is not stream oriented. So, unless you have Perl version 5.003_93 or higher, by default, you cannot `print()` to STDOUT from your script; use `$r->print()` instead. Nor can you `read()` from STDIN, use `$r->read()` or the `$r->content` methods to read POST data. In post-5.003 versions of Perl, two mechanisms have been introduced which allows redirecting the STDIN and STDOUT streams.

One mechanism takes advantage of the PerlIO abstraction and **sfio** discipline structures, such that STDIN and STDOUT are hooked up to the client by default if you configured perl with `-Dusesfio` (see Perl's INSTALL doc).

Otherwise, `mod_perl` will `tie()` STDOUT and STDIN to the client. In order for this to work, you must have Perl version 5.003_93 or higher.

Environment

Under CGI the Perl hash `%ENV` is magical in that it inherits environment variables from the parent process and will set them should a process spawn a child. However, with **mod_ perl** we're in the parent process that would normally set up the common environment variables before spawning a CGI process. Therefore, `mod_perl` must feed these variables to `%ENV` directly. Normally, this does not happen until the response stage of a request when PerlHandler is called. If you wish to set variables that will be available before then, such as for a PerlAuthenHandler, you may use the PerlSetEnv configuration directive:

```
PerlSetEnv  SomeKey  SomeValue
```

Using CGI.pm and CGI::*

CGI.pm users *must* have version 2.32 of the package or higher; earlier versions will not work under `mod_perl`. If you have Perl version 5.003_93 or higher (or _xx+ version with `sfio`), scripts may `use` CGI. Otherwise, scripts need to use CGI::Switch so I/O goes through Apache-> methods; this will also work with later versions of Perl.

The CGI::* modules (CGI::Request, et al.) can be used untouched if your Perl is configured to use `sfio` and the following directive is present in the directory configuration:

```
PerlSendHeader On
```

If you use the `SendHeaders()` function, be sure to call `$req_obj->cgi->done` when you are done with a request, just as you would under CGI::MiniSrv.

Memory Consumption

No matter what, your `httpd` will be larger than normal to start, simply because you've linked it with Perl's runtime.

Here I'm just running:

```
% /usr/bin/perl -e '1 while 1'
   PID USERNAME PRI NICE   SIZE   RES STATE   TIME   WCPU    CPU COMMAND
 10214 dougm     67    0   668K  212K run    0:04 71.55% 21.13% perl
```

Now with a few random modules:

```
% /usr/bin/perl -MDBI -MDBD::mSQL -MLWP::UserAgent -MFileHandle\
                -MIO -MPOSIX -e '1 while 1'
 10545 dougm     49    0  3732K 3340K run    0:05 54.59% 21.48% perl
```

Here's my `httpd` linked with `libperl.a`, not having served a single request:

```
 10386 dougm      5    0  1032K  324K sleep  0:00  0.12%  0.11% httpd-a
```

You can reduce this if you configure Perl 5.003_xx+ with -Duseshrplib. Here's my `httpd` linked with `libperl.sl`, not having served a single request:

```
 10393 dougm      5    0   476K  368K sleep  0:00  0.12%  0.10% httpd-s
```

Now, once the server starts receiving requests, the embedded interpreter will compile code for each `require` file it has not seen yet, each new Apache::Registry subroutine that's compiled, along with whatever modules it's `using` or `requiring`. Not to mention Auto-Loading. (Modules that you `use` will be compiled when the server starts unless they are inside an `eval` block.) `httpd` will grow just as big as our */usr/bin/perl* would, or a CGI process for that matter, it all depends on your setup.

Newer Perl versions also have other options to reduce runtime memory consumption. See Perl's INSTALL file for details on -DPACK_MALLOC and -DTWO_POT_OPTIMIZE. With these options, my `httpd` shrinks down ~150K.

For me, once everything is compiled, the processes no longer grow, and I can live with the size at that point. For others, this size might be too big, or they might be using a module that leaks or have code of their own that leaks. In any case, using the Apache configuration directive MaxRequestsPerChild is your best bet to keep the size down; but at the same time, you'll be slowing things down when Apache::Registry scripts have to recompile. Tradeoffs.

Switches

Normally when you run Perl from the command line or have the shell invoke it with #!, you may choose to pass Perl switch arguments such as -w or -T. Since the command line is only parsed once, when the server starts, these switches are unavailable to mod_perl scripts. However, most command-line arguments have a Perl special-variable equivalent. For example, the $^W variable corresponds to the -w switch. Consult the **perlvar** manpage for more details. The switch which enables taint checks does not have a special variable, so mod_perl provides the PerlTaintCheck directive to turn on taint checks. In *httpd.conf,* enable it with:

```
PerlTaintCheck On
```

Now any and all code compiled inside httpd will be checked.

Persistent Database Connections

Another popular use of mod_perl is to take advantage of its persistence to maintain open database connections. The basic idea goes like so:

```
#Apache::Registry script
use strict;
use vars qw($dbh);
$dbh ||= SomeDbPackage->connect(...);
```

Since $dbh is a global variable, it will not go out of scope, keeping the connection open for the lifetime of a server process, after establishing it during the script's first request for that process.

It's recommended that you use one of the Apache::* database connection wrappers. Currently for DBI users there is Apache::DBI and for Sybase users Apache::Sybase::DBlib. These modules hide the peculiar code example above. In addition, different scripts may share a connection, minimizing resource consumption. Example:

```
use strict;
my $dbh = Apache::DBI->connect(...);
```

Although $dbh shown here will go out of scope when the script ends, the Apache::DBI module's reference to it does not, so keep the connection open.

Stacked Handlers

With the mod_perl stacked-handlers mechanism, it is possible for more than one Perl*Handler to be defined and run during each stage of a request.

Perl*Handler directives can define any number of subroutines, e.g., in config files.

```
PerlTransHandler OneTrans TwoTrans RedTrans BlueTrans
```

With the method **Apache->push_handlers**, callbacks can be added to the stack by scripts at runtime by mod_perl scripts.

Apache->push_handlers takes the callback hook name as its first argument and a subroutine name or reference as its second. e.g.:

```
Apache->push_handlers("PerlLogHandler", \&first_one);
$r->push_handlers("PerlLogHandler", sub {
    print STDERR "__ANON__ called\n";
    return 0;
});
```

After each request, this stack is cleared out.

All handlers will be called unless a handler returns a status other than OK or DECLINED; this needs to be considered more. Post-Apache-1.2 will have a DONE return code to signal termination of a stage, which we came up with a while back when first discussing the idea of stacked handlers. 2.0 won't come for quite sometime, so `mod_perl` will most likely handle this before then.

Examples

CGI.pm maintains a global object for its plain function interface. Since the object is global, it does not go out of scope, and DESTROY is never called. `CGI->new` can call:

```
Apache->push_handlers("PerlCleanupHandler", \&CGI::_reset_globals);
```

This function will be called during the final stage of a request, refreshing *CGI.pm's* globals before the next request comes in.

Apache::DCELogin establishes a DCE login context which must exist for the lifetime of a request, so the DCE::Login object is stored in a global variable. Without stacked handlers, users must set:

```
PerlCleanupHandler Apache::DCELogin::purge
```

in the configuration files to destroy the context. This is not user-friendly. Now Apache::DCELogin::handler can call:

```
Apache->push_handlers("PerlCleanupHandler", \&purge);
```

Persistent database connection modules such as Apache::DBI could push a PerlCleanupHandler handler that iterates over `%Connected`, refreshing connections or just checking that ones have not gone stale. Remember, by the time we get to PerlCleanupHandler, the client has what it wants and has gone away, so we can spend as much time as we want here without slowing down response time to the client.

PerlTransHandlers may decide, based or URI or other condition, whether or not to handle a request, e.g., Apache::MsqlProxy. Without stacked handlers, users must configure:

```
PerlTransHandler Apache::MsqlProxy::translate
PerlHandler      Apache::MsqlProxy
```

PerlHandler is never actually invoked unless `translate()` sees the request is a proxy request (`$r->proxyreq`); if it is a proxy request, `translate()` set `$r->handler(perl-script)`, only then will PerlHandler handle the request. Now users do not have to specify PerlHandler Apache::MsqlProxy; the `translate()` function can set it with `push_handlers()`.

Includes, footers, headers, etc., piecing together a document, imagine (no need for SSI parsing!):

```
PerlHandler My::Header Some::Body A::Footer
```

This was my first test:

```
#My.pm
package My;
sub header {
    my $r = shift;
    $r->content_type("text/plain");
    $r->send_http_header;
    $r->print("header text\n");
}
```

```
sub body    { shift->print("body text\n")    }
sub footer  { shift->print("footer text\n")  }
1;
__END__
#in config
<Location /foo>
SetHandler "perl-script"
PerlHandler My::header My::body My::footer
</Location>
```

Parsing the output of another PerlHandler? This is a little more tricky, but consider:

```
<Location /foo>
  SetHandler "perl-script"
  PerlHandler OutputParser SomeApp
</Location>
<Location /bar>
  SetHandler "perl-script"
  PerlHandler OutputParser AnotherApp
</Location>
```

Now, OutputParser goes first, but it **unties** *STDOUT and re-**ties** to its own package like so:

```
package OutputParser;
sub handler {
    my $r = shift;
    untie *STDOUT;
    tie *STDOUT => 'OutputParser', $r;
}
sub TIEHANDLE {
    my($class, $r) = @_;
    bless { r => $r}, $class;
}
sub PRINT {
    my $self = shift;
    for (@_) {
        #do whatever you want to $_
        $self->{r}->print($_ . "[insert stuff]");
    }
}
1;
__END__
```

tie of *STDOUT has worked since perl5.003_02 or so, no matter if **sfio** is configured.

To build in this feature, configure with:

```
% perl Makefile.PL PERL_STACKED_HANDLERS=1 [PERL_FOO_HOOK=1,etc]
```

Another method, **Apache->can_stack_handlers**, will return **true** if **mod_perl** was configured with PERL_STACKED_HANDLERS=1, **false** otherwise.

Perl Method Handlers

If a Perl*Handler is prototyped with $$, this handler will be invoked as method:

```
package My;
@ISA = qw(BaseClass);
```

```
sub handler ($$) {
    my($class, $r) = @_;
    ...;
}
package BaseClass;
sub method ($$) {
    my($class, $r) = @_;
    ...;
}
__END__
```

Configuration:

```
PerlHandler My
```

or:

```
PerlHandler My->handler
```

Since the handler is invoked as a method, it may inherit from other classes:

```
PerlHandler My->method
```

In this case, the My class inherits this method from BaseClass.

To build in this feature, configure with:

```
% perl Makefile.PL PERL_METHOD_HANDLERS=1 [PERL_FOO_HOOK=1,etc]
```

Perl Sections

With <Perl></Perl> sections, it is possible to configure your server entirely in Perl.

<Perl> sections can contain *any* and as much Perl code as you wish. These sections are compiled into a special package whose symbol table mod_perl can then walk and grind the names and values of Perl variables/structures through the Apache core config gears. Most of the configuration directives can be represented as $Scalars or @Lists. An @List inside these sections is simply converted into a single-space delimited string for you inside. Here's an example:

```
#httpd.conf
<Perl>
@PerlModule = qw(Mail::Send Devel::Peek);
#run the server as whoever starts it
$User  = getpwuid($>) || $>;
$Group = getgrgid($)) || $);
$ServerAdmin = $User;
</Perl>
```

Block sections such as <Location></Location> are represented in a %Hash, e.g.:

```
$Location{"/~dougm/"} = {
    AuthUserFile => '/tmp/htpasswd',
    AuthType => 'Basic',
    AuthName => 'test',
    DirectoryIndex => [qw(index.html index.htm)],
    Limit => {
        METHODS => 'GET POST',
        require => 'user dougm',
    },
};
```

Other section counterparts include `%VirtualHost`, `%Directory` and `%Files`.

These are somewhat boring examples, but they should give you the basic idea. You can mix in any Perl code your heart desires. See *eg/httpd.conf.pl* and *eg/perl_sections.txt* for some examples.

Currently for `<Perl>` sections to work, the PerlScript configuration directive must be defined; */dev/null* will do just fine.

To configure this feature, build with `perl Makefile.PL PERL_SECTIONS=1`.

mod_perl and mod_include integration

As of Apache 1.2b11, `mod_include` can handle Perl callbacks.

A "`sub`" key value may be anything a Perl*Handler can be: subroutine name, package name (defaults to Package::Handler), `Class->method` call or anonymous sub `{}`.

Example:

```
Child <!--#perl sub="sub {print $$}" --> accessed
<!--#perl sub="sub {print ++$Access::Cnt }" --> times. <br>
<!--#perl sub="Package::handler" arg="one" arg="two" -->
```

The Apache::Include module makes it simple to include Apache::Registry scripts with the `mod_include` Perl directive.

Example:

```
<!--#perl sub="Apache::Include" arg="/perl/ssi.pl" -->
```

You can also use "virtual include" to include Apache::Registry scripts, of course. However, using `#perl` will save the overhead of making Apache go through the motions of creating/destroying a subrequest and making all the necessary access checks to see that the request would be allowed outside of a "virtual include" context.

To enable Perl in `mod_include` parsed files, when building Apache the following must be present in the Configuration file:

```
EXTRA_CFLAGS=-DUSE_PERL_SSI -I. 'perl -MExtUtils::Embed -ccopts'
```

`mod_perl`'s Makefile.PL script can take care of this for you as well:

```
perl Makefile.PL PERL_SSI=1
```

If you're interested in sprinkling Perl code inside your HTML documents, you'll also want to look at the Apache::Embperl, Apache::ePerl and Apache::SSI modules.

Warnings

Your scripts *will not* run from the command line (yet) unless you use CGI::Switch and no direct calls to `Apache->methods`.

Perl's `exit()` built-in function cannot be used in `mod_perl` scripts. Apache::exit should be used instead; however, it is not 100% reliable. Your servers and your code are better off if they are structured such that they do not need to use `exit()`.

If you wish to use a module that is normally linked static with your Perl, it must be listed in `static_ext` in Perl's *Config.pm* to be linked with `httpd` during the `mod_perl` build.

Support

For comments, questions, bug reports, announcements, etc., send mail to *listserv@list-proc.itribe.net* with the string `subscribe modperl` in the body.

Author

Doug MacEachern, *dougm@osf.org*

NetObj—allows you to create a distributed module platform for Perl

Synopsis

```
######  Server creation ######
use NetObj;
use NetObj::Block;

my $server = new NetObj Server;
$server->open();
($peer, $port) = $server->getconnectinfo();
$objectname = $server->getrequest();

$block = new NetObj::Block Object => $objectname;
$module = $block->createblock();
$server->putobj($module);
$server->close();
##### To make a request #####
use NetObj;

my $req = new NetObj Request;
$req->ObjectName($somemodulename);
$req->request(Remote => $remotehostname);
# [ .. you can then use the module like normal .. ]
```

Description

NetObj allows you to distribute modules over a network in real time. Its limitations are that of the B module, so as of this moment, it cannot do XSUBS, and autoloading (I believe) and other funky stuff like that.

More documentation will come as this moves beyond an alpha release, and into something more stable.

Author

James Duncan, *jduncan@hawk.igs.net*

Acknowledgments

Felix Gallo, for providing some initial insight into this sort of thing.

Malcolm Beattie, for the wonderful Perl Compiler (and more specifically the `Bytecode->Asm` part of it).

Penguin::Easy—provides easy access to Penguin module

Synopsis

```
use Penguin::Easy;
my $ep = new Penguin::Easy Title => 'Easy Program',
                           Name => 'James Duncan',
                           Sig => $my_pgp_sig,
                           Code => $my_perl_code;

$results = $ep->run;
print "$results\n";
```

Description

Penguin::Easy is an OO module that provides quick-and-dirty access to the Penguin module for those not wanting to learn the nitty-grittys about it. The Easy module provides transparent access to the Penguin module, even to the extent of deciding whether the Penguin code should be transparently wrapped, or PGP-wrapped (if you include a sig in the call to the new method, it will use PGP).

Notes

While writing this little module, I've decided that "wrapper" is perhaps one of the funniest words I have ever seen. It has completely lost all meaning.

PerlTk::Install—install file for Perl/Tk

Synopsis

Unpack the *tar* file outside the Perl source tree for preference.

To install this (Tk-b9.01) package you need perl5.002beta1 and unofficial patches to f.

The best place to get perl5.002b1f is via the CPAN site nearest you.

```
ftp any-CPAN-site - see www.perl.com for a list:
cd CPAN/authors/id/ANDYD/
binary
get perl5.002b1d.tar.gz
get perl5.002beta1.patch.2b1e.gz
get perl5.002beta1.patch.2b1f.gz
```

When patch.2.b1g shows up it should be safe to apply as well, as there are plans to make it a documentation patch. Latest MakeMaker from CPAN may help too.

See *README.osname* for further hints/warnings.

If you have perl5.002b1f installed in the normal way, you can proceed to build Tk.

It is much simpler to install Perl than to try and use an uninstalled private copy. If you have a private copy you should configure it to install somewhere you have write access to, and install it there, then use that Perl to build Tk.

When you have an up-to-date perl5.002 installed, cd to the directory the distribution unpacks to.

Dynamic Link Version

Then if you have dynamic linking :

```
perl Makefile.PL
make
```

Now built locally—if you have dynamic loading you can now say:

```
perl ./basic_demo
make install
```

You can now run the converted Tk4.0 demos:

```
./demos/widget
```

Static Link Version

For static linking the following is how it is supposed to work (I think, but I don't use static linking normally; this scheme worked as far as this on one trial under SunOS4):

```
perl Makefile.PL
make
make tkperl
```

This builds a Perl with Tk statically linked in the Tk directory, thus:

```
./tkperl ./basic_demo
```

should now work.

It is unclear to me whether **make install** works, and I don't want to try it on my system in case it breaks the dynamic version.

Specifying X11 Libraries

If *Makefile.PL* reports that it cannot find X, or chooses a version you don't like, you can specify a version on the command line:

```
perl Makefile.PL X11=/usr/local/X11R5
```

If X's **include** and **lib** are not under a common parent they can be specified separately:

```
perl Makefile.PL X11INC=/usr/local/share/X11R5/include
                 X11LIB=/usr/local/arch/X11R5/lib
```

Author

Nick Ing-Simmons, *nick@ni-s.u-net.com*

Copyright

Copyright © 1995 Nick Ing-Simmons. All rights reserved. This package is free software; you can redistribute it and/or modify it under the same terms as Perl itself, with the exception of all the files in the pTk sub-directory which have separate terms derived from those of the original Tk4.0 sources. See pTk/license.terms for details of this license.

Regexp—object-oriented interface to Perl's regular expression code

Synopsis

```
use Regexp;
my $re = new Regexp q/Some Pattern/;
```

```
if (match $re "Some String") { ... }
$re->prematch
$re->postmatch
$re->pattern
my @info  = $re->parentheses
my $count = $re->parentheses
```

Author

Nick Ing-Simmons, nick@ni-s.u-net.com

Roman——Perl module for conversion between Roman and Arabic numerals.

Synopsis

```
use Roman;
$arabic = arabic($roman) if isroman($roman);
$roman = Roman($arabic);
$roman = roman($arabic);
```

Description

This package provides some functions which help in the conversion of numeric notation between Roman and Arabic.

Bugs

The domain of valid Roman numerals is limited to less than 4000, since proper Roman digits for the rest are not available in ASCII.

Author

OZAWA Sakuro, *ozawa@prince.pe.u-tokyo.ac.jp*

Copyright

SendmailUtil——utilities for sendmail packages

Synopsis

```
use SyslogScan::SendmailUtil;
open(FH,"/var/log/syslog");
my $transfer;
while ($transfer = SyslogScan::SendmailUtil::getNextMailTranfer(\*FH))
{
    # process the tranfer
}
```

Description

getNextMailTransfer queries a file handle pointing to a syslog for the next line that is a sendmail "To:", "From:", or "Clone:" line, and returns a SyslogScan::SendmailLineFrom, SyslogScan::SendmailLineTo, or SyslogScan::SendmailLineClone object.

canonAddress()

> The canonAddress() routine modifies the address of the Sendmail routines to be all lowercase, removes enclosing brackets, and appends @localhost to local addresses. Modifying this routine changes how SyslogScan canonicalizes.

Author

Rolf Harold Nelson, *rolf@usa.healthnet.org*

Copyright

Copyright © SatelLife, Inc. 1996. All rights reserved.

This code is free software; you can redistribute it and/or modify it under the same terms as Perl itself.

In no event shall SatelLife be liable to any party for direct, indirect, special, incidental, or consequential damages arising out of the use of this software and its documentation (including, but not limited to, lost profits) even if the authors have been advised of the possibility of such damage.

See Also

SyslogScan::SendmailLineFrom, SyslogScan::SendmailLineTo, SyslogScan::SyslogEntry

SyslogScan::ByGroup—organizes a summary of mail statistics into groups of related email users

Synopsis

```
# $summary is a SyslogScan::Summary object
# default is to organize by internet host
my $byGroup = new SyslogScan::ByGroup($summary);
print $byGroup -> dump();
# group by whether users use 'jupiter' or 'satellife' as
# their machine name, and discard users who use neither
my $pointerToGroupingRoutine = sub {
    my $address = shift;
    return 'jupiter' if $address =~ /jupiter.healthnet.org$/;
    return 'satellife' if $address =~ /satellife.healthnet.org$/;
    # ignore all others
    return undef;
}
my $groupByMachine = new SyslogScan::ByGroup($summary,

$pointerToGroupingRoutine);
print $groupByMachine -> dump();
# Extract a SyslogScan::Group object
my $jupiterGroup = $$groupByMachine{jupiter};
```

```
print $jupiterGroup -> dump();
# Extract a SyslogScan::Summary object
my $summaryOfJupiter = $jupiterGroup{byAddress};
print $summaryOfJupiter -> dump();

# Create a summary by group, rather than a summary by address
my $summaryByMachine = $groupByMachine -> createSummary();
```

Description

A SyslogScan::ByGroup object is a hash table of SyslogScan::Group objects, each indexed by the group name as returned by the sorting algorithm fed to **new**.

A SyslogScan::Group is a hash table with two members:

byAddress
>A SyslogScan::Summary of each address that is a member of the group

groupUsage
>A SyslogScan::Usage object containing the total usage of the group.

Author

Rolf Harold Nelson, *rolf@usa.healthnet.org*

Copyright

Copyright © SatelLife, Inc. 1996. All rights reserved.

This code is free software; you can redistribute it and/or modify it under the same terms as Perl itself.

In no event shall SatelLife be liable to any party for direct, indirect, special, incidental, or consequential damages arising out of the use of this software and its documentation (including, but not limited to, lost profits) even if the authors have been advised of the possibility of such damage.

See Also

SyslogScan::Summary, SyslogScan::Usage

SyslogScan::Delivery—encapsulates a logged, successful delivery of mail from a sender to a list of recipients

Synopsis

See SyslogScan::DeliveryIterator.

Description

A Delivery object is an indication that mail was successfully delivered or forwarded from a sender to a list of recipients. You can extract Delivery objects from a syslog file by using SyslogScan::DeliveryIterator.

Variables

`Sender`, `ReceiverList`, `Size`, and `Date` are the most useful:

`Sender`
> Email address of sender, may be **undef** if the sender could not be determined from the syslog.
>
> ```
> my $sender = $$delivery{Sender};
> ```

`ReceiverList`
> Reference to array of email addresses of recipients.
>
> ```
> my $paReceiverList = $$delivery{ReceiverList};
> my @aReceiverList = @$paReceiverList;
> print "The recipient(s) of the message was (were) ",
>     join(' ',@aReceiverList), "\n";
> ```

`Size`
> Size of message, may be **undef** if the size could not be determined from the syslog.
>
> ```
> my $sizeInBytes = $$delivery{Size};
> ```

`Date`
> Date the message was succesfully delivered or forwarded.
>
> ```
> my $date = $$delivery{Date};
> ```

`Id` and `Instance` are more advanced features:

`Id`
> `id` in syslog, useful for cross-referencing.
>
> ```
> my $id = $$delivery{Id};
> ```

`Instance`
> The first delivery of any message has an `Instance` of 1; the next deliveries will have `Instance` > 1, specifically a number equal to the number of people who the message has previously been delivered to, plus 1. This is useful for detecting mass-mailings.
>
> Suppose I send a message to five people, but only three copies are delivered right away; the other two are deferred. The first delivery has instance 1; the next delivery of the same message will have instance 4.
>
> ```
> my $instance = $$delivery{Instance};
> my @aReceiverList = @{$$delivery{ReceiverList}};
> print "This message has so far been delivered to ",
>     $instance + $@aReceiverList - 1, "people so far\n";
> ```

Methods

`new ()`
> Manually create a new delivery object.
>
> ```
> my $delivery = new SyslogScan::Delivery (Date => time(),
>                     Size => 100,
>                     From => 'foo@bar.com',
>                     ReceiverList => [him@baz.edu, her@baz.edu],
>                     Instance => 1,
>                     Id => 'manual' . $id++);
> ```

```
summary()
dump()
```
   Print out contents, either in summary or in verbose mode.

```
        print $delivery -> summary();
        print $delivery -> dump();
```

```
persist()
restore()
```
   Save/restore delivery to/from file.

```
        open(OUT,">save.txt");
        $delivery -> persist(\*OUT);
        close(OUT);
        undef($delivery);

        open(IN,"save.txt");
        $delivery = SyslogScan::Delivery -> restore(\*IN);
```

Author

Rolf Harold Nelson, *rolf@usa.healthnet.org*

Copyright

Copyright © SatelLife, Inc. 1996. All rights reserved.

This code is free software; you can redistribute it and/or modify it under the same terms as Perl itself.

IN NO EVENT SHALL THE AUTHORS BE LIABLE TO ANY PARTY FOR DIRECT, INDIRECT, SPECIAL, INCIDENTAL, OR CONSEQUENTIAL DAMAGES ARISING OUT OF THE USE OF THIS SOFTWARE AND ITS DOCUMENTATION (INCLUDING, BUT NOT LIMITED TO, LOST PROFITS) EVEN IF THE AUTHORS HAVE BEEN ADVISED OF THE POSSIBILITY OF SUCH DAMAGE.

See Also

SyslogScan::DeliveryIterator, SyslogScan::Summary

SyslogScan::DeliveryIterator—scans a syslog file for deliveries, successful transfers of mail to mailboxes or to other machines

Synopsis

```
use SyslogScan::Delivery;
use SyslogScan::DeliveryIterator;

my $iter = new SyslogScan::DeliveryIterator(syslogList =>
                                        ["/var/log/syslog"]);

my $delivery;
while ($delivery = $iter -> next())
{
    print $delivery -> summary();
}
```

Description

A DeliveryIterator goes through your sendmail logging file (which may be */var/log/syslog*, */var/adm/messages*, or something completely different) looking for successful deliveries of mail to local user accounts or successful transfers of mail to remote machines.

Here is an excerpt from a sample syslog:

```
Jun 13 01:50:16 satellife sendmail[29556]: DAA29556:
from=<shookway@fs1.ho.man.ac.uk>, size=954, class=0, pri=30954,
nrcpts=1, msgid=<5B013544E0D@fs1.ho.man.ac.uk>, proto=ESMTP,
relay=curlew.cs.man.ac.uk [130.88.13.7]

Jun 13 01:50:17 satellife sendmail[29558]: DAA29556:
to=<shoko@time.healthnet.org>, delay=00:00:05, mailer=fidogate,
stat=Deferred (Remote host is busy)

...

Jun 13 14:55:50 satellife sendmail[29558]: DAA29556:
to=<shoko@time.healthnet.org>, delay=13:00:05, mailer=fidogate,
stat=Sent
```

The delivery was not registered until 14:55:50. In order to figure out the size and sender, the iterator needs to have gone over the "from" entry associated with message DAA29566; otherwise it returns a delivery with "Sender" and "Size" set to an undefined value (unless you specified defaults when constructing your DeliveryIterator.)

Methods

new

new creates a new iterator.

```
my $iter = new
    SyslogScan::DeliveryIterator(startDate => "06.01.96 18:00:00",
                                 endDate => "06.02.96 06:00:00",
                                 syslogList =>
                                     [/var/log/syslog.090696,
                                      /var/log/syslog.090796],
                                 unknownSender => 'antiquity',
                                 unknownSize => 0,
                                 defaultYear => 1996);
```

All of the above parameters are optional.

startDate and endDate define a span of time; we ignore deliveries that fall before startDate or after endDate. This allows you to generate statistical reports about mail delivered over a given span of time.

syslogList is a list of files to search through for deliveries. The alternative to specifying syslogList is to supply a file handle to a syslog file on each call to the next() method.

unknownSender and unknownSize are what to specify as the sender and the size if we cannot determine from the logs who sent the message and how large the message is.

defaultYear is the year in which the deliveries are assumed to have taken place (this is not specified in the syslog file.) The default is to guess the year that makes the delivery take place close to "now." (For example, if "now" is February 3, 1996, then by default a delivery made on December 14 is assumed to be in 1995, and a delivery made on February 4 is assumed to be in 1996.

The use of **defaultYear** is deprecated; instead, set the default year with SyslogScan::ParseDate::setDefaultYear.

next

Once an iterator has been defined, the **next()** method searches for the next delivery, skipping any deliveries that don't match the time constraints of **startDate** and **endDate.** There are two ways to call **next():**

```
# poll syslogList members
$delivery = $iter -> next;
```

and:

```
# poll filehandle
open(LOG,"/var/log/syslog");
$delivery = $iter -> next(\*LOG);
```

Other Operations

The **appendSyslog** method can add a syslog filename to the list of syslog filenames that were specified at construction time as **syslogList.**

Setting the global variable **$::gbQuiet** to 1 suppresses some of the error messages to STDERR.

Bugs

If two messages have the same message ID through a bad coincidence, a message is produced with sender of **duplicate** and size of 0 rather than using the **unknownSender** and **unknownSize** parameters.

Sender and receiver address are downcased automatically. It would probably be better if this module downcased only the hostname part of the address and not the username.

Some mailings have a **ctladdr** field; DeliveryIterator should probably try to parse this as a backup clue for figuring out the sender.

Author

Rolf Harold Nelson, *rolf@usa.healthnet.org.*

Copyright

Copyright © SatelLife, Inc. 1996. All rights reserved.

This code is free software; you can redistribute it and/or modify it under the same terms as Perl itself.

In no event shall SatelLife be liable to any party for direct, indirect, special, incidental, or consequential damages arising out of the use of this software and its documentation (including, but not limited to, lost profits) even if the authors have been advised of the possibility of such damage.

See Also

SyslogScan::Delivery, SyslogScan::Summary

SyslogScan::SendmailLine—enhances basic SyslogEntry parsing by understanding sendmail to/from message syntax

Description

Suppose I run a new `SyslogEntry` command and read in the following line:

```
Jun 13 01:32:26 satellife sendmail[23498]: WAA18677: to=bar@foo.org,
baz@foo.org, delay=03:50:20, mailer=smtp, relay=relay.ulthar.com
[128.206.5.3], stat=Sent (May, have (embedded, commas))
```

If I have not loaded in SendmailLine, then **new** `SyslogEntry` will return an Unsupported-Entry object looking like this:

```
month => Jun,
day => 13,
time => 01:32:26,
machine => satellife,
executable => sendmail,
tag => 23498,
content => WAA18677: to=bar@foo.org,baz@foo.org, delay=03:50:20, ...
```

On the other hand, if I have a use `SyslogScan::SendmailLine` command before my call to **new** `SyslogEntry`, then I will get a SendmailLine object with all of the above parameters, plus the following additional parameters:

```
messageID => WAA18677
toList => ( bar@foo.org, baz@foo.org )
attrHash => ( to => "bar@foo.org,baz@foo.org",
              delay => "03:50:20",
              mailer => "smtp",
              relay => "relay.ulthar.com [128.206.5.3]",
              stat => "Sent (May, have (embedded, commas))"
            )
```

Also well-supported is the From line:

```
Jun 13 01:34:54 satellife sendmail[26035]: BAA26035:
from=<bar!baz!foo>, size=7000, class=0, pri=37000, nrcpts=1,
msgid=<199606130634.BAA26035@satellife.healthnet.org>, proto=SMTP,
relay=uth.bar.com [155.247.14.2]
```

produces a SendmailLine object with the additional attributes of:

```
messageID => BAA26035
attrHash => ( from => "<bar!baz!foo>",
              size => "7000",
              class => "0",
              pri => "37000",
              nrcpts => "1",
              msgid => "<199606130634.BAA26035@satellife.healthnet.org>",
              proto => "SMTP",
              relay => "uth.bar.com [155.247.14.2]"
            )
```

Other types of lines are legal, but are not currently very thoroughly parsed and therefore return somewhat minimal SendmailLine objects:

```
Jun 13 13:05:35 satellife sendmail[19620]: NAA19606: NAA19620: return
to sender: unknown mailer error 2
```

returns a SendmailLine object with the usual SyslogEntry attributes, plus the single additional attribute of:

```
messageID => NAA19606
```

while lines like the following produce SendmailLine objects with no additional SendmailLine-specific attributes:

```
Jun 13 03:00:05 satellife sendmail[26611]: alias database
/var/yp/nis.healthnet.org/mail.aliases rebuilt by root
```

Note that this is a subclass for SyslogScan::SyslogEntry that handles certain types of logfile lines. See the documentation for SyslogEntry for further details of how SyslogEntry subclassing works.

Also, see the SyslogScan::SendmailLineFrom and SyslogScan::SendmailLineTo modules for examples of returned SendmailLine objects.

Author

Rolf Harold Nelson, *rolf@usa.healthnet.org*

Copyright

Copyright © SatelLife, Inc. 1996. All rights reserved.

This code is free software; you can redistribute it and/or modify it under the same terms as Perl itself.

In no event shall SatelLife be liable to any party for direct, indirect, special, incidental, or consequential damages arising out of the use of this software and its documentation (including, but not limited to, lost profits) even if the authors have been advised of the possibility of such damage.

See Also

SyslogScan::SyslogEntry, SyslogScan::SendmailLineFrom, SyslogScan::SendmailLineTo

---

SyslogScan::SendmailLineFrom—encapsulates a From: line in a syslog file

Description

Here is a sample SendmailLineFrom object.

If new `SyslogScan::SendmailLineEntry` reads in a line like

```
Jun 13 02:34:54 satellife sendmail[26035]: BAA26035:
from=<HELP-NET@BAR.TEMPLE.EDU>, size=7000, class=0, pri=37000,
nrcpts=1, msgid=<199606130634.BAA26035@satellife.healthnet.org>,
proto=SMTP, relay=vm.temple.edu [155.247.14.2]
```

then it returns a SyslogScan::SendmailLineFrom object like this:

```
# generic SyslogScan::SyslogEntry stuff
day => 13,
executable => 'sendmail',
machine => 'satellife',
month => 'Jun',
```

```
    tag => 26035,
    time => '02:34:54',
    content => 'BAA26035: from=<HELP-NET@BAR.TEMPLE.EDU>,
    size=7000, class=0, pri=37000, nrcpts=1,
    msgid=<199606130634.BAA26035@satellife.healthnet.org>,
    proto=SMTP, relay=vm.temple.edu [155.247.14.2]',

    # sendMailLineFrom-specific stuff
    messageID => 'BAA26035',
    attrHash => {
            'class' => 0,
            'from' => 'help-net@bar.temple.edu',
            'msgid' => '<199606130634.BAA26035@satellife.healthnet.org>',
            'nrcpts' => 1,
            'pri' => 37000,
            'proto' => 'SMTP',
            'relay' => 'vm.temple.edu [155.247.14.2]',
            'size' => 7000
            }
```

Author

Rolf Harold Nelson, *rolf@usa.healthnet.org*

Copyright

Copyright © SatelLife, Inc. 1996. All rights reserved.

This code is free software; you can redistribute it and/or modify it under the same terms as Perl itself.

In no event shall SatelLife be liable to any party for direct, indirect, special, incidental, or consequential damages arising out of the use of this software and its documentation (including, but not limited to, lost profits) even if the authors have been advised of the possibility of such damage.

See Also

SyslogScan::SendmailLine

SyslogScan::SendmailLineTo—encapsulates a To: line in a syslog file

Description

Here is a sample SendmailLineTo object.

If new `SyslogScan::SendmailLineEntry` reads in a line like:

```
Jun 13 01:50:48 satellife sendmail[23498]: WAA18677:
to=mbe527@time.nums.nwu.edu,jsm341@anima.nums.nwu.edu, delay=03:52:42,
mailer=smtp, relay=anima.nums.nwu.edu. [165.124.50.10], stat=Sent
(AA097917369 Message accepted for delivery)
```

then it returns a SyslogScan::SendmailLineTo object like this:

```
# generic SyslogScan::SyslogEntry stuff
day => 13,
```

```
        executable => 'sendmail',
        machine => 'satellife',
        messageID => 'WAA18677',
        month => 'Jun',
        tag => 23498,
        content => 'WAA18677: to=mbe527@time.nums.nwu.edu,
        jsm341@anima.nums.nwu.edu, delay=03:52:42, mailer=smtp,
        relay=anima.nums.nwu.edu. [165.124.50.10],
        stat=Sent (AA097917369 Message accepted for delivery)',

        # sendMailLineTo-specific stuff
        messageID => 'WAA18677'
        toList => (mbe527@time.nums.nwu.edu, jsm341@anima.nums.nwu.edu)
        attrHash => (
                'delay' => '03:52:42',
                'mailer' => 'smtp',
                'relay' => 'anima.nums.nwu.edu. [165.124.50.10]',
                'stat' => 'Sent (AA097917369 Message accepted for delivery)',
                'to' => 'mbe527@time.nums.nwu.edu,jsm341@anima.nums.nwu.edu'
                )
```

Author

Rolf Harold Nelson, *rolf@usa.healthnet.org*

Copyright

Copyright © SatelLife, Inc. 1996. All rights reserved.

This code is free software; you can redistribute it and/or modify it under the same terms as Perl itself.

In no event shall SatelLife be liable to any party for direct, indirect, special, incidental, or consequential damages arising out of the use of this software and its documentation (including, but not limited to, lost profits) even if the authors have been advised of the possibility of such damage.

See Also

SyslogScan::SendmailLineTo

SyslogScan::Summary—encapsulates a tally of how many bytes people have sent and received through sendmail

Synopsis

```
        Use SyslogScan::Summary;
        Use SyslogScan::DeliveryIterator;
        my $iter = new SyslogScan::DeliveryIterator(syslogList =>
                                                [/var/log/syslog]);
        my $summary;
        if (defined $DOING_IT_THE_HARD_WAY_FOR_NO_PARTICULAR_REASON)
        {
            # feed a series of SyslogScan::Delivery objects
            $summary = new SyslogScan::Summary();
```

```
    my $delivery;
    while ($delivery = $iter -> next())
    {
        $summary -> registerDelivery($delivery);
        # You would instead use:
        # $summary -> registerDelivery($delivery,'foo\.com\.$')
        # if you only cared to get statistics relating to how
        # much mail users at foo.com sent or received.
    }
}
else
{
    # slurps up all deliveries in the iterator,
    # producing the same effect as the block above
    $summary = new SyslogScan::Summary($iter);
}
print $summary -> dump();
use SyslogScan::Usage;
my $usage = $$summary{'john_doe@foo.com'};
if (defined $usage)
{
    print "Here is the usage of John Doe at foo.com:\n";
    print $usage -> dump();
}
else
{
    print "John Doe has neither sent nor received messages lately.\n";
}
```

Description

A SyslogScan::Summary object "registers" a series of SyslogScan::Delivery objects. All registered deliveries are grouped by sender and receiver email addresses and then added up. Three sums are kept: total bytes received, total bytes sent, and total bytes broadcast.

Methods

new()

> new takes as arguments a (possibly null) list of SyslogScan::DeliveryIterator objects, from which it extracts and registers all queued deliveries.

registerDelivery()

> registerDelivery takes as its first argument a SyslogScan::Delivery object followed by up to two optional patterns. If the first pattern is specified, only those email addresses that match the pattern are tallied. This enables you to create an accounting summary for only those users at your site.

> If the second pattern is also specified, then deliveries are only registered to the person matched by the first pattern if the second pattern matches the address at "the other end of the pipe."

> Pattern matches are case-insensitive. Remember the **(?!regexp)** operation if you want only addresses which do *not* match the pattern to get passed through the filter. For example, if mail to or from support is exempt from billing charges, note that the pattern match:

> /^(?!support)/

> does *not* match **support@foo.com** but *does* match **random_guy@foo.com**.

`registerAllInIterators()`

> Takes as parameters two patterns and a list of iterators, then feeds deliveries in the iterators and the patterns to `registerDelivery()`.
>
> For example:

```
$sum -> registerAllInIterators('foo\.com$','^(?!.*bar\.com$)',
                               @iterList)
```

> bills users at *foo.com* for all mail extracted from *@iterList* that was sent from *foo.com* to somewhere besides *bar.com*, or sent to *foo.com* from somewhere besides *bar.com*.

`dump()`

> `dump` returns a string containing address lines alternating with usage reports. Usage reports are in the form:

```
B#,Bb          S#,Sb          R#,Rb
```

> where:
>
> * B# is the number of messages broadcast
> * Bb is the total number of bytes broadcast
> * S# is the number of messages sent
> * Sb is the total number of bytes sent
> * R# is the number of messages received
> * Rb is the total number of bytes received

`persist()`

> `persist` takes as its single argument an output file handle and persists the state of the summary to the file.

`restore()`

> `restore` takes as its single argument an input file handle that stores the results of a previous `persist()` command and returns a copy of the object in the state in which it was originally persisted.

`addSummary()`

> `addSummary` takes as its single argument a second SyslogScan::Summary object and adds this second summary to the `$self` object.

Example

Suppose I have a function `getTodaySummary()` that gets a summary of the last 24 hours of `sendmail` logging:

```
my $summary = getTodaySummary();
open(SUMMARY1,">summary1.sav");
$summary -> persist(\*SUMMARY1);
close(SUMMARY1);
exit 0;
# wait 24 hours
my $summary = getTodaySummary();
open(SUMMARY2,">summary2.sav");
$summary -> persist(\*SUMMARY2);
close(SUMMARY2);
exit 0;
# some time later, you decide you want a summary of the total
```

```
# for both days.  So, you write this program:
open(INSUM1,"summary1.sav");
my $sum = SyslogScan::Summary -> restore(\*INSUM1);
open(INSUM2,"summary2.sav");
my $sum2 = SyslogScan::Summary -> restore(\*INSUM2);
$sum -> addSummary($sum2);
print "Here is the grand total for both days:\n\n";
print $sum -> dump();
```

Internals

A SyslogScan::Summary object is a hash of SyslogScan::Usage objects, where the key is the email address of the user in question. SyslogScan::Usage has its own manpage, which describes how to extract information without having to use the dump() method.

Author

Rolf Harold Nelson, *rolf@usa.healthnet.org*

Copyright

Copyright © SatelLife, Inc. 1996. All rights reserved.

This code is free software; you can redistribute it and/or modify it under the same terms as Perl itself.

In no event shall SatelLife be liable to any party for direct, indirect, special, incidental, or consequential damages arising out of the use of this software and its documentation (including, but not limited to, lost profits) even if the authors have been advised of the possibility of such damage.

See Also

SyslogScan::Usage, SyslogScan::DeliveryIterator, SyslogScan::Delivery, SyslogScan::ByGroup

---

SyslogScan::SyslogEntry—parses generic lines in syslog files

Synopsis

```
use SyslogScan::SyslogEntry;
open(FH,"/var/log/syslog");
my $entry;
# reads from filehandle $fh and returns an object
# of a subclass of SyslogEntry.
while ($entry = new SyslogScan::SyslogEntry (\*FH))
{
    # process $entry
}
```

Description

All syslog objects share these data structures: month, day, time, machine, executable, tag (optional), and content.

For example, if a syslog line looks like:

```
Jun 13 02:32:27 satellife in.identd[25994]: connect from mail.msu.edu
```

then the line returned by **new SyslogEntry** returns a SyslogEntry-derived object with at least this set of parameters:

```
month => Jun,
day => 13,
time => 02:32:27,
machine => satellife,
executable => in.identd,
tag => 25994,
content => connect from mail.missouri.edu,
unix_time => 834633147,
raw => Jun 13 02:32:27 satellife in.identd[25994]:
        connect from mail.msu.edu
```

Since the executable is *in.identd*, SyslogEntry looks for a class called SyslogScan::In_identd-Line derived from SyslogEntry, and attempts to call that class's **parseContent** method. If no such **In_identdLine** class is in use, then the returned object is of the default SyslogScan::UnsupportedEntry class.

If the **In_identdLine** class throws a **die()** exception, *SyslogEntry.pm* catches the **die()** and returns a SyslogScan::BotchedEntry object containing the exception in **$errorString** and the failed handler in **brokenHandler**.

new SyslogEntry returns the undefined value if at EOF.

Bugs

In retrospect, this model of passing control to subclasses based on the name of the controlling program doesn't work exceptionally elegantly in Perl. I would probably do it more conventionally if I had it to do over again.

Author

Rolf Harold Nelson, *rolf@usa.healthnet.org*

Thanks to Allen S. Rout for his code contributions.

Copyright

Copyright © SatelLife, Inc. 1996. All rights reserved.

This code is free software; you can redistribute it and/or modify it under the same terms as Perl itself.

In no event shall SatelLife be liable to any party for direct, indirect, special, incidental, or consequential damages arising out of the use of this software and its documentation (including, but not limited to, lost profits) even if the authors have been advised of the possibility of such damage.

See Also

SyslogScan::SendmailLine

SyslogScan::Usage—encapsulates the total volumes of mail broadcast, sent, and received through **sendmail** by a single user or group

Synopsis

```
# $summary is a SyslogScan::Summary object

use SyslogScan::Usage;
my $usage = $$summary{'john_doe@foo.com'};
$usage -> dump();

use SyslogScan::Volume;
my $broadcastVolume = $usage -> getBroadcastVolume();
my $sendVolume = $usage -> getSendVolume();
my $receiveVolume = $usage -> getReceiveVolume();

print "John Doe sent $$sendVolume[0] messages with $$sendVolume[1]
bytes\n";
```

Description

Broadcast, Send, and Receive

Volume of messages received has the obvious meaning. Volume of messages sent and volume of messages broadcast require more explanation.

If I send out a message that has three recipients, then for the purposes of the SyslogScan modules, I am *broadcasting* the message once, but I am *sending* it three times.

Usage Methods

new()

    Creates a new, empty Usage object.

addUsage() and deepCopy()

    Note that because we used **deepCopy**, $usage1 is still four messages of 100 bytes.

```
    # $usage1 is 4 messages of 100 bytes Received
    # $usage2 is 1 message of 35 bytes Received

    my $usageTotal = $usage1 -> deepCopy();
    # $usageTotal is 4 messages of 100 bytes Received

    $usageTotal -> addUsage($usage2);
    # $usageTotal is 5 messages of 135 bytes Received
```

registerBroadcast, registerSend, registerReceive

```
    my $usage = new SyslogScan::Usage();
    $usage -> registerSend(512);
    $usage -> registerSend(34);
    $usage -> registerBroadcast(34);
    # $usage is now 2 messages, 546 bytes Sent,
    # and 1 message, 34 bytes Broadcast
```

getBroadcastVolume, getSendVolume, getReceiveVolume

    Returns deep copy of the applicable SyslogScan::Volume objects.

deepCopy
> Returns deep copy of the whole SyslogScan::Usage object.

dump
> Returns a string containing (Message,Bytes) pairs for Broadcast, Send, and Receive volumes.

Volume Methods

new()
> Creates a new Volume object of 0 messages, 0 bytes.

deepCopy()
> Creates a new Volume object with the same number of messages and bytes as the current Volume object.

addVolume(), addSize()
> addVolume() adds the volume of a second Volume object onto the volume of the current Volume object.

> addSize() adds on one message of the given size.

```
use SyslogScan::Volume;
my $volume1 = new SyslogScan::Volume();
$volume1 -> addSize(512);
my $volume2 = $volume1 -> deepCopy();
# $volume2 is 1 message, 512 bytes
$volume2 -> addSize(31);
# $volume2 is 2 messages, 543 bytes
$volume2 -> addVolume($volume1);
# $volume2 is 3 messages, 1055 bytes
$volume2 -> addVolume($volume2);
# $volume2 is 6 messages, 2110 bytes
```

getMessageCount, getByteCount
> Gets the number of messages and the total number of bytes, respectively.

dump()
> Returns the string getMessageCount(),getByteCount().

Volume Internals

A Volume is simply a two-element array of (*$messages*, *$bytes*).

- $$volume[0] is the number of messages.
- $$volume[1] is the number of bytes.

Author

Rolf Harold Nelson, *rolf@usa.healthnet.org*

Copyright

Copyright © SatelLife, Inc. 1996. All rights reserved.

This code is free software; you can redistribute it and/or modify it under the same terms as Perl itself.

In no event shall SatelLife be liable to any party for direct, indirect, special, incidental, or consequential damages arising out of the use of this software and its documentation (including, but not limited to, lost profits) even if the authors have been advised of the possibility of such damage.

See Also

SyslogScan::Summary

SyslogScan::WhereIs::guess—return full path of syslog file where mail messages are logged

Synopsis

```
my $syslogPath =
    new SyslogScan::Whereis::guess("/etc/syslog.conf");
```

Description

Scans a syslog configuration file to try to figure out where *mail.info* messages are sent. Default configuration file is */etc/syslog.conf*.

Returns **undef** if the syslog file cannot be determined.

Bugs

It might have been more elegant to return an array of syslog files; this would, as a bonus, permit multiple syslogs to be returned if mail messages go to more than one place.

Author

Rolf Harold Nelson, *rolf@usa.healthnet.org*

Copyright

Copyright © SatelLife, Inc. 1996. All rights reserved.

This code is free software; you can redistribute it and/or modify it under the same terms as Perl itself.

In no event shall SatelLife be liable to any party for direct, indirect, special, incidental, or consequential damages arising out of the use of this software and its documentation (including, but not limited to, lost profits) even if the authors have been advised of the possibility of such damage.

See Also

SyslogScan::DeliveryIterator

Index

About the Editors

Ellen Siever is a writer at O'Reilly & Associates, where she has also been a production editor and tools specialist. Before that, she was a programmer for many years at various high tech companies in the Boston area, until she decided that she'd rather play with words than bytes. She has degrees from the University of Chicago and MIT, neither of which is in computer science.

David Futato has a Bachelor of Science in Creative Writing from the Massachusetts Institute of Technology, so—with such a unique degree—O'Reilly seemed like the logical choice; David has worked as a production editor at O'Reilly for more than two years. Stepping to the other side of the publishing fence, this is David's first full-fledged writing/editorial assignment. He lives just outside of Boston with his husband Ron, their two cats, Cairo and Minsk, and more CDs and vinyl than any one person should own.

Colophon

The animal featured on the cover of the *Perl Resource Kit, UNIX Edition*, is a camel (one-hump dromedary). Camels are large ruminant mammals, weighing between 1,000 and 1,600 pounds and standing six to seven feet tall at the shoulders. They are well known for their use as draft and saddle animals in the desert regions, especially in Africa and Asia. Camels can go for days without water. If food is scarce, they will eat anything, even their owner's tent. Camels live up to 50 years.

Ted Meister designed this cover and the packaging for the *Perl Resource Kit*. The layouts were produced using Adobe Photoshop 4 and QuarkXpress 3.32, with Adobe ITC Garamond and Helvetica Condensed fonts. The camel image is from the Dover Pictorial Archive.

The interior layout was designed by Nancy Priest and Edie Freedman, and implemented in FrameMaker 5.0 by Mike Sierra. The text and heading fonts are ITC Garamond Light and ITC Garamond Book, by Adobe. The illustrations were created in Macromedia Freehand 7 by Robert Romano.

Whenever possible, our books use RepKover™, a durable and flexible lay-flat binding. If the page count exceeds RepKover's limit, perfect binding is used.

 # More Titles from O'Reilly

Perl

Perl Resource Kit—UNIX Edition

By Larry Wall, Clay Irving, Nate Patwardhan, Ellen Siever & Brian Jepson
1st Edition November 1997 (est.)
1700 pages (est.)
ISBN 1-56592-370-7

The *Perl Resource Kit* is the most comprehensive collection of documentation and commercially enhanced software tools yet published for Perl programmers. The UNIX edition, the first in a series, is the definitive Perl distribution for webmasters, programmers, and system administrators.

Software tools on the Kit's CD include:

- A Java/Perl back-end to the Perl compiler, written by Larry Wall, creator of Perl

- Snapshot of the freeware Perl archives on CPAN, with an Install program and a web-aware interface for identifying more recent online CPAN tools

This new Java/Perl tool allows programmers to write Java classes with Perl implementations (innards), and run the code through a compiler back-end to produce Java byte-code. Using this new tool, programmers can exploit Java's wide availability on the browser (as well as on the server), while using Perl for the things that it does better than Java (such as string processing).

The Kit also includes four tutorial and reference books that contain systematic documentation for the most important Perl extension modules, as well as documentation for the commercially enhanced and supported tools on the CD. The books in the Kit are not available elsewhere or separatelyand include:

- *Perl Module Programmer's Guide*, by Clay Irving and Nate Patwardhan.

- *Perl Module Reference Manual* (two volumes), compiled and edited by Ellen Siever and David Futato.

- *Perl Utilities*, by Brian Jepson.

The *Perl Resource Kit* is the first comprehensive tutorialand reference documentation for hundreds of essential third-party Perl extension modules used for creating CGI applications and more. It features commercially enhanced Perl utilities specially developed for the Kit by Perl's creator, Larry Wall. And, it is all brought to you by the premier publisher of Perl and UNIX books and documentation, O'Reilly & Associates.

Programming Perl, 2nd Edition

By Larry Wall, Tom Christiansen & Randal L. Schwartz
2nd Edition September 1996
670 pages, ISBN 1-56592-149-6

Programming Perl, second edition, is the authoritative guide to Perl version 5, the scripting utility that has established itself as the programming tool of choice for the World Wide Web, UNIX system administration, and a vast range of other applications. Version 5 of Perl includes object-oriented programming facilities. The book is coauthored by Larry Wall, the creator of Perl.

Perl is a language for easily manipulating text, files, and processes. It provides a more concise and readable way to do many jobs that were formerly accomplished (with difficulty) by programming with C or one of the shells. Perl is likely to be available wherever you choose to work.And if it isn't, you can get it and install it easily and free of charge.

This heavily revised second edition of *Programming Perl* contains a full explanation of the features in Perl version 5.003. Contents include:

- An introduction to Perl

- Explanations of the language and its syntax

- Perl functions

- Perl library modules

- The use of references in Perl

- How to use Perl's object-oriented features

- Invocation options for Perl itself, and also for the utilities that come with Perl

Perl 5 Desktop Reference

By Johan Vromans
1st Edition February 1996
46 pages, ISBN 1-56592-187-9

This is the standard quick-reference guide for the Perl programming language. It provides a complete overview of the language, from variables to input and output, from flow control to regular expressions, from functions to document formats—all packed into a convenient, carry-around booklet. Updated to cover Perl version 5.003.

Perl

Learning Perl, 2nd Edition

By Randal L. Schwartz & Tom Christiansen,
Foreword by Larry Wall
2nd Edition July 1997
302 pages, ISBN 1-56592-284-0

In this update of a bestseller, two leading Perl trainers teach you to use the most universal scripting language in the age of the World Wide Web. With a foreword by Larry Wall, the creator of Perl, this smooth, carefully paced book is the "official" guide for both formal (classroom) and informal learning. It is now current for Perl version 5.004.

Learning Perl is a hands-on tutorial designed to get you writing useful Perl scripts as quickly as possible. Exercises (with complete solutions) accompany each chapter. A lengthy, new chapter in this edition introduces you to CGI programming, while touching also on the use of library modules, references, and Perl's object-oriented constructs.

Perl is a language for easily manipulating text, files, and processes. It comes standard on most UNIX platforms and is available free of charge on all other important operating systems. Perl technical support is informally available—often within minutes—from a pool of experts who monitor a USENET newsgroup (*comp.lang.perl.misc*) with tens

of thousands of readers.

Contents include:

- A quick tutorial stroll through Perl basics
- Systematic, topic-by-topic coverage of Perl's broad capabilities
- Lots of brief code examples
- Programming exercises for each topic, with fully worked-out answers
- How to execute system commands from your Perl program
- How to manage DBM databases using Perl
- An introduction to CGI programming for the Web

Advanced Perl Programming

By Sriram Srinivasan
1st Edition August 1997
434 pages, ISBN 1-56592-220-4

This book covers complex techniques for managing production-ready Perl programs and explains methods for manipulating data and objects that may have looked like magic before. It gives you necessary background for dealing with networks, databases, and GUIs, and includes a discussion of internals to help you program more efficiently and embed Perl within C or C within Perl.

Learning Perl on Win32 Systems

By Randal L. Schwartz, Erik Olson &
Tom Christiansen
1st Edition August 1997
306 pages, ISBN 1-56592-324-3

In this carefully paced course, leading Perl trainers and a Windows NT practitioner teach you to program in the language that promises to emerge as the scripting language of choice on NT. Based on the "llama" book, this book features tips for PC users and new, NT-specific examples, along with a foreword by Larry Wall, the creator of Perl, and Dick Hardt, the creator of Perl for Win32.

Mastering Regular Expressions

By Jeffrey E. F. Friedl
1st Edition January 1997
368 pages, ISBN 1-56592-257-3

Regular expressions, a powerful tool for manipulating text and data, are found in scripting languages, editors, programming environments, and specialized tools. In this book, author Jeffrey Friedl leads you through the steps of crafting a regular expression that gets the job done. He examines a variety of tools and uses them in an extensive array of examples, with a major focus on Perl.

Java Programming

Java in a Nutshell, DELUXE EDITION

By David Flanagan, et al.
1st Edition June 1997
628 pages, includes CD-ROM and book,
ISBN 1-56592-304-9

Java in a Nutshell, Deluxe Edition, brings together on CD-ROM five volumes for Java developers and programmers, linking related info across books. *Exploring Java, 2nd Edition*, covers Java basics. *Java Language Reference, 2nd Edition*, *Java Fundamental Classes Reference*, and *Java AWT Reference* provide a definitive set of documentation on the Java language and the Java 1.1 core API. *Java in a Nutshell, 2nd Edition*, our bestselling quick reference, is included both on the CD-ROM and in a companion desktop edition. This deluxe library is an indispensable resource for anyone doing serious programming with Java 1.1.

Exploring Java, Second Edition

By Pat Niemeyer & Josh Peck
2nd Edition September 1997 (est.)
628 pages (est.)
ISBN 1-56592-271-9

Whether you're just migrating to Java or working steadily in the forefront of Java development, this book, fully revised for Java 1.1, gives a clear, systematic overview of the language. It covers the essentials of hot topics like Beans and RMI, as well as writing applets and other applications, such as networking programs, content and protocol handlers, and security managers.

Java Language Reference, Second Edition

By Mark Grand
2nd Edition July 1997
492 pages, ISBN 1-56592-326-X

This book helps you understand the subtle nuances of Java—from the definition of data types to the syntax of expressions and control structures—so you can ensure your programs run exactly as expected. The second edition covers the new language features that have been added in Java 1.1, such as inner classes, class literals, and instance initializers.

Java Fundamental Classes Reference

By Mark Grand &
Jonathan Knudsen
1st Edition May 1997
1114 pages, ISBN 1-56592-241-7

The *Java Fundamental Classes Reference* provides complete reference documentation on the core Java 1.1 classes that comprise the *java.lang, java.io, java.net, java.util, java.text, java.math, java.lang.reflect*, and *java.util.zip* packages. Part of O'Reilly's Java documentation series, this edition describes Version 1.1 of the Java Development Kit. It includes easy-to-use reference material and provides lots of sample code to help you learn by example.

Java AWT Reference

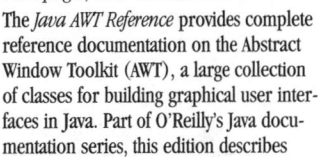

By John Zukowski
1st Edition April 1997
1074 pages, ISBN 1-56592-240-9

The *Java AWT Reference* provides complete reference documentation on the Abstract Window Toolkit (AWT), a large collection of classes for building graphical user interfaces in Java. Part of O'Reilly's Java documentation series, this edition describes both Version 1.0.2 and Version 1.1 of the Java Development Kit, includes easy-to-use reference material on every AWT class, and provides lots of sample code.

Java in a Nutshell, Second Edition

By David Flanagan
2nd Edition May 1997
628 pages, ISBN 1-56592-262-X

The bestselling Java book just got better. Newly updated, it now describes all the classes in the Java 1.1 API, with the exception of the still-evolving Enterprise APIs. And it still has all the great features that have made this the Java book most often recommended on the Internet: practical, real-world examples and compact reference information. It's the only quick reference you'll need.

O'REILLY™

TO ORDER: **800-998-9938** • **order@oreilly.com** • **http://www.oreilly.com/**

OUR PRODUCTS ARE AVAILABLE AT A BOOKSTORE OR SOFTWARE STORE NEAR YOU.

FOR INFORMATION: **800-998-9938** • **707-829-0515** • **info@oreilly.com**

Java Programming *continued*

Java Distributed Computing

By Jim Farley
1st Edition November 1997 (est.)
350 pages (est.), ISBN 1-56592-206-9

Java Distributed Computing offers a general introduction to distributed computing, meaning programs that run on two or more systems. It focuses primarily on how to structure and write distributed applications and, therefore, discusses issues like designing protocols, security, working with databases, and dealing with low bandwidth situations.

Java Examples in a Nutshell

By David Flanagan
1st Edition September 1997 (est.)
400 pages (est.), ISBN 1-56592-371-5

Java Examples in a Nutshell is chock full of practical, real-world Java programming examples. The author of the bestselling *Java in a Nutshell* has created an entire book of example programs that you can learn from and modify for your own use. If you learn best "by example," this companion volume to *Java in a Nutshell* is the book for you.

Netscape IFC in a Nutshell

By Dean Petrich with David Flanagan
1st Edition August 1997
370 pages, ISBN 1-56592-343-X

This desktop quick reference and programmer's guide is all the documentation programmers need to start creating highly customizable graphical user interfaces with the Internet Foundation Classes (IFC), Version 1.1. The IFC is a Java class library freely available from Netscape. It is also bundled with Communicator, making it the preferred development environment for the Navigator 4.0 web browser. Master the IFC now for a head start on the forthcoming Java Foundation Classes (JFC).

Developing Java Beans

By Robert Englander
1st Edition June 1997
316 pages, ISBN 1-56592-289-1

Developing Java Beans is a complete introduction to Java's component architecture. It describes how to write Beans, which are software components that can be used in visual programming environments. This book discusses event adapters, serialization, introspection, property editors, and customizers, and shows how to use Beans within ActiveX controls.

Java Virtual Machine

By Jon Meyer & Troy Downing
1st Edition March 1997
452 pages, includes diskette
ISBN 1-56592-194-1

This book is a comprehensive programming guide for the Java Virtual Machine (JVM). It gives readers a strong overview and reference of the JVM so that they may create their own implementations of the JVM or write their own compilers that create Java object code. A Java assembler is provided with the book, so the examples can all be compiled and executed.

Database Programming with JDBC and Java

By George Reese
1st Edition June 1997
240 pages, ISBN 1-56592-270-0

Database Programming with JDBC and Java describes the standard Java interfaces that make portable, object-oriented access to relational databases possible and offers a robust model for writing applications that are easy to maintain. It introduces the JDBC and RMI packages and includes a set of patterns that separate the functions of the Java application and facilitate the growth and maintenance of your application.

Java Network Programming

By Elliotte Rusty Harold
1st Edition February 1997
442 pages, ISBN 1-56592-227-1

The network is the soul of Java. Most of what is new and exciting about Java centers around the potential for new kinds of dynamic, networked applications. *Java Network Programming* teaches you to work with Sockets, write network clients and servers, and gives you an advanced look at the new areas like multicasting, using the server API, and RMI. Covers Java 1.1.

Java Threads

By Scott Oaks and Henry Wong
1st Edition January 1997
268 pages, ISBN 1-56592-216-6

With this book, you'll learn how to take full advantage of Java's thread facilities: where to use threads to increase efficiency, how to use them effectively, and how to avoid common mistakes like deadlock and race conditions. Covers Java 1.1.

O'REILLY™

TO ORDER: **800-998-9938** • *order@oreilly.com* • *http://www.oreilly.com/*
OUR PRODUCTS ARE AVAILABLE AT A BOOKSTORE OR SOFTWARE STORE NEAR YOU.
FOR INFORMATION: **800-998-9938** • **707-829-0515** • *info@oreilly.com*

Security

Web Security & Commerce

By Simson Garfinkel
with Gene Spafford
1st Edition June 1997
506 pages, ISBN 1-56592-269-7

Web Security & Commerce explains the real risks of the Web and how you can minimize them. Whether you're a casual (but concerned) web surfer or a system administrator responsible for the security of a critical web server, this book will tell you what you need to know. Entertaining as well as illuminating, it looks behind the headlines at the technologies, risks, and benefits of the Web.

Practical UNIX & Internet Security, 2nd Edition

By Simson Garfinkel & Gene Spafford
2nd Edition April 1996
1004 pages, ISBN 1-56592-148-8

This second edition of the classic *Practical UNIX Security* is a complete rewrite of the original book. It's packed with twice the pages and offers even more practical information for UNIX users and administrators. In it you'll find coverage of features of many types of UNIX systems, including SunOS, Solaris, BSDI, AIX, HP-UX, Digital UNIX, Linux, and others. Contents include UNIX and security basics, system administrator tasks, network security, and appendixes containing checklists and helpful summaries.

Building Internet Firewalls

By D. Brent Chapman &
Elizabeth D. Zwicky
1st Edition September 1995
546 pages, ISBN 1-56592-124-0

Building Internet Firewalls is a practical guide to building firewalls on the Internet. If your site is connected to the Internet, or if you're considering getting connected, you need this book. It describes a variety of firewall approaches and architectures and discusses how you can build packet filtering and proxying solutions at your site. It also contains a full discussion of how to configure Internet services (e.g., FTP, SMTP, Telnet) to work with a firewall, as well as a complete list of resources, including the location of many publicly available firewall construction tools.

PGP: Pretty Good Privacy

By Simson Garfinkel
1st Edition January 1995
430 pages, ISBN 1-56592-098-8

PGP is a freely available encryption program that protects the privacy of files and electronic mail. It uses powerful public key cryptography and works on virtually every platform. This book is both a readable technical user's guide and a fascinating behind-the-scenes look at cryptography and privacy. It describes how to use PGP and provides background on cryptography, *PGP*'s history, battles over public key cryptography patents and U.S. government export restrictions, and public debates about privacy and free speech.

Computer Crime

By David Icove, Karl Seger &
William VonStorch
(Consulting Editor Eugene H. Spafford)
1st Edition August 1995
462 pages, ISBN 1-56592-086-4

This book is for anyone who needs to know what today's computer crimes look like, how to prevent them, and how to detect, investigate, and prosecute them if they do occur. It contains basic computer security information as well as guidelines for investigators, law enforcement, and system administrators. It includes computer-related statutes and laws, a resource summary, detailed papers on computer crime, and a sample search warrant.

Computer Security Basics

By Deborah Russell & G.T. Gangemi, Sr.
1st Edition July 1991
464 pages, ISBN 0-937175-71-4

Computer Security Basics provides a broad introduction to the many areas of computer security and a detailed description of current security standards. This handbook uses simple terms to describe complicated concepts like trusted systems, encryption, and mandatory access control, and it contains a thorough, readable introduction to the "Orange Book."

Network Administration

Using and Managing PPP

By Andrew Sun
1st Edition December 1997 (est.)
400 pages (est.), ISBN 1-56592-321-9

Covers all aspects of PPP, including setting up dial-in servers, debugging, and PPP options. Also contains overviews of related areas, like serial communications, DNS setup, and routing.

Managing IP Networks with Cisco Routers

By Scott M. Ballew
1st Edition October 1997 (est.)
250 pages (est.), ISBN 1-56592-320-0

This practical guide to setting up and maintaining a production network covers how to select routing protocols, configure protocols to handle most common situations, evaluate network equipment and vendors, and set up a help desk. Although it focuses on Cisco routers, and gives examples using Cisco's IOS, the principles discussed are common to all IP networks.

sendmail Desktop Reference

By Bryan Costales & Eric Allman
1st Edition March 1997
74 pages, ISBN 1-56592-278-6

This quick-reference guide provides a complete overview of the latest version of sendmail (V8.8), from command-line switches to configuration commands, from options declarations to macro definitions, and from m4 features to debugging switches—all packed into a convenient, carry-around booklet co-authored by the creator of sendmail. Includes extensive cross-references to *sendmail*, second edition.

sendmail, 2nd Edition

By Bryan Costales & Eric Allman
2nd Edition January 1997
1050 pages, ISBN 1-56592-222-0

sendmail, 2nd Edition, covers sendmail Version 8.8 from Berkeley and the standard versions available on most systems. This cross-referenced edition offers an expanded tutorial, solution-oriented examples, and new topics such as the #error delivery agent, sendmail's exit values, MIME headers, and how to set up and use the user database, *mailertable*, and *smrsh*.

DNS and BIND, 2nd Edition

By Paul Albitz & Cricket Liu
2nd Edition December 1996
438 pages, ISBN 1-56592-236-0

This book is a complete guide to the Internet's Domain Name System (DNS) and the Berkeley Internet Name Domain (BIND) software, the UNIX implementation of DNS. This second edition covers Bind 4.8.3, which is included in most vendor implementations today, as well as Bind 4.9.4, the potential future standard.

Getting Connected: The Internet at 56K and Up

By Kevin Dowd
1st Edition June 1996
424 pages, ISBN 1-56592-154-2

A complete guide for businesses, schools, and other organizations who want to connect their computers to the Internet. This book covers everything you need to know to make informed decisions, from helping you figure out which services you really need to providing down-to-earth explanations and configuration instructions for telecommunication options at higher than modem speeds, such as frame relay, ISDN, and leased lines. Once you're online, it shows you how to set up basic Internet services, such as a World Wide Web server. Tackles issues for PC, Macintosh, and UNIX platforms.

Network Administration *continued*

Networking Personal Computers with TCP/IP

By Craig Hunt
1st Edition July 1995
408 pages, ISBN 1-56592-123-2

This book offers practical information as well as detailed instructions for attaching PCs to a TCP/IP network and its UNIX servers. It discusses the challenges you'll face and offers general advice on how to deal with them, provides basic TCP/IP configuration information for some of the popular PC operating systems, covers advanced configuration topics and configuration of specific applications such as email, and includes a chapter on on integrating Netware with TCP/IP.

TCP/IP Network Administration

By Craig Hunt
1st Edition August 1992
502 pages, ISBN 0-937175-82-X

TCP/IP Network Administration is a complete guide to setting up and running a TCP/IP network for practicing system administrators. The book covers setting up your network, configuring important network applications including sendmail, and issues in troubleshooting and security. It covers both BSD and System V TCP/IP implementations.

O'REILLY™

How to stay in touch with O'Reilly

1. Visit Our Award-Winning Web Site

http://www.oreilly.com/

★ "Top 100 Sites on the Web" —*PC Magazine*
★ "Top 5% Web sites" —*Point Communications*
★ "3-Star site" —*The McKinley Group*

Our web site contains a library of comprehensive product information (including book excerpts and tables of contents), downloadable software, background articles, interviews with technology leaders, links to relevant sites, book cover art, and more. File us in your Bookmarks or Hotlist!

2. Join Our Email Mailing Lists

New Product Releases

To receive automatic email with brief descriptions of all new O'Reilly products as they are released, send email to: **listproc@online.oreilly.com**
Put the following information in the first line of your message (*not* in the Subject field):
subscribe oreilly-news "Your Name" of "Your Organization" (for example: subscribe oreilly-news Kris Webber of Fine Enterprises)

O'Reilly Events

If you'd also like us to send information about trade show events, special promotions, and other O'Reilly events, send email to: **listproc@online.oreilly.com**
Put the following information in the first line of your message (*not* in the Subject field):
subscribe oreilly-events "Your Name" of "Your Organization"

3. Get Examples from Our Books via FTP

There are two ways to access an archive of example files from our books:

Regular FTP
- ftp to:
  ftp.oreilly.com
  (login: anonymous
  password: your email address)
- Point your web browser to:
  ftp://ftp.oreilly.com/

FTPMAIL
- Send an email message to:
  ftpmail@online.oreilly.com
  (Write "help" in the message body)

4. Visit Our Gopher Site
- Connect your gopher to:
  gopher.oreilly.com

- Point your web browser to:
  gopher://gopher.oreilly.com/

- Telnet to:
  gopher.oreilly.com
  login: gopher

5. Contact Us via Email

order@oreilly.com
To place a book or software order online. Good for North American and international customers.

subscriptions@oreilly.com
To place an order for any of our newsletters or periodicals.

books@oreilly.com
General questions about any of our books.

software@oreilly.com
For general questions and product information about our software. Check out O'Reilly Software Online at **http://software.oreilly.com/** for software and technical support information. Registered O'Reilly software users send your questions to: **website-support@oreilly.com**

cs@oreilly.com
For answers to problems regarding your order or our products.

booktech@oreilly.com
For book content technical questions or corrections.

proposals@oreilly.com
To submit new book or software proposals to our editors and product managers.

international@oreilly.com
For information about our international distributors or translation queries. For a list of our distributors outside of North America check out:
http://www.oreilly.com/www/order/country.html

O'Reilly & Associates, Inc.
101 Morris Street, Sebastopol, CA 95472 USA
TEL   707-829-0515 or 800-998-9938
       (6am to 5pm PST)
FAX   707-829-0104

Titles from O'Reilly

Please note that upcoming titles are displayed in italic.

WEB PROGRAMMING

Apache: The Definitive Guide
Building Your Own Web Conferences
Building Your Own Website
CGI Programming for the World Wide Web
Designing for the Web
HTML: The Definitive Guide, 2nd Ed.
JavaScript: The Definitive Guide, 2nd Ed.
Learning Perl
Programming Perl, 2nd Ed.
Mastering Regular Expressions
WebMaster in a Nutshell
Web Security & Commerce
Web Client Programming with Perl
World Wide Web Journal

USING THE INTERNET

Smileys
The Future Does Not Compute
The Whole Internet User's Guide & Catalog
The Whole Internet for Win 95
Using Email Effectively
Bandits on the Information Superhighway

JAVA SERIES

Exploring Java
Java AWT Reference
Java Fundamental Classes Reference
Java in a Nutshell
Java Language Reference, 2nd Edition
Java Network Programming
Java Threads
Java Virtual Machine

SOFTWARE

WebSite™ 1.1
WebSite Professional™
Building Your Own Web Conferences
WebBoard™
PolyForm™
Statisphere™

SONGLINE GUIDES

NetActivism   NetResearch
Net Law   NetSuccess
NetLearning   NetTravel
Net Lessons

SYSTEM ADMINISTRATION

Building Internet Firewalls
Computer Crime: A Crimefighter's Handbook
Computer Security Basics
DNS and BIND, 2nd Ed.
Essential System Administration, 2nd Ed.
Getting Connected: The Internet at 56K and Up
Linux Network Administrator's Guide
Managing Internet Information Services
Managing NFS and NIS
Networking Personal Computers with TCP/IP
Practical UNIX & Internet Security, 2nd Ed.
PGP: Pretty Good Privacy
sendmail, 2nd Ed.
sendmail Desktop Reference
System Performance Tuning
TCP/IP Network Administration
termcap & terminfo
Using & Managing UUCP
Volume 8: X Window System Administrator's Guide
Web Security & Commerce

UNIX

Exploring Expect
Learning VBScript
Learning GNU Emacs, 2nd Ed.
Learning the bash Shell
Learning the Korn Shell
Learning the UNIX Operating System
Learning the vi Editor
Linux in a Nutshell
Making TeX Work
Linux Multimedia Guide
Running Linux, 2nd Ed.
SCO UNIX in a Nutshell
sed & awk, 2nd Edition
Tcl/Tk Tools
UNIX in a Nutshell: System V Edition
UNIX Power Tools
Using csh & tsch
When You Can't Find Your UNIX System Administrator
Writing GNU Emacs Extensions

WEB REVIEW STUDIO SERIES

Gif Animation Studio
Shockwave Studio

WINDOWS

Dictionary of PC Hardware and Data Communications Terms
Inside the Windows 95 Registry
Inside the Windows 95 File System
Windows Annoyances
Windows NT File System Internals
Windows NT in a Nutshell

PROGRAMMING

Advanced Oracle PL/SQL Programming
Applying RCS and SCCS
C++: The Core Language
Checking C Programs with lint
DCE Security Programming
Distributing Applications Across DCE & Windows NT
Encyclopedia of Graphics File Formats, 2nd Ed.
Guide to Writing DCE Applications
lex & yacc
Managing Projects with make
Mastering Oracle Power Objects
Oracle Design: The Definitive Guide
Oracle Performance Tuning, 2nd Ed.
Oracle PL/SQL Programming
Porting UNIX Software
POSIX Programmer's Guide
POSIX.4: Programming for the Real World
Power Programming with RPC
Practical C Programming
Practical C++ Programming
Programming Python
Programming with curses
Programming with GNU Software
Pthreads Programming
Software Portability with imake, 2nd Ed.
Understanding DCE
Understanding Japanese Information Processing
UNIX Systems Programming for SVR4

BERKELEY 4.4 SOFTWARE DISTRIBUTION

4.4BSD System Manager's Manual
4.4BSD User's Reference Manual
4.4BSD User's Supplementary Documents
4.4BSD Programmer's Reference Manual
4.4BSD Programmer's Supplementary Documents
X Programming
Vol. 0: X Protocol Reference Manual
Vol. 1: Xlib Programming Manual
Vol. 2: Xlib Reference Manual
Vol. 3M: X Window System User's Guide, Motif Edition
Vol. 4M: X Toolkit Intrinsics Programming Manual, Motif Edition
Vol. 5: X Toolkit Intrinsics Reference Manual
Vol. 6A: Motif Programming Manual
Vol. 6B: Motif Reference Manual
Vol. 6C: Motif Tools
Vol. 8: X Window System Administrator's Guide
Programmer's Supplement for Release 6
X User Tools
The X Window System in a Nutshell

CAREER & BUSINESS

Building a Successful Software Business
The Computer User's Survival Guide
Love Your Job!
Electronic Publishing on CD-ROM

TRAVEL

Travelers' Tales: Brazil
Travelers' Tales: Food
Travelers' Tales: France
Travelers' Tales: Gutsy Women
Travelers' Tales: India
Travelers' Tales: Mexico
Travelers' Tales: Paris
Travelers' Tales: San Francisco
Travelers' Tales: Spain
Travelers' Tales: Thailand
Travelers' Tales: A Woman's World

International Distributors

UK, Europe, Middle East and Northern Africa (except France, Germany, Switzerland, & Austria)

INQUIRIES

International Thomson Publishing
Europe
Berkshire House
168-173 High Holborn
London WC1V 7AA, United Kingdom
Telephone: 44-171-497-1422
Fax: 44-171-497-1426
Email: itpint@itps.co.uk

ORDERS

International Thomson Publishing
Services, Ltd.
Cheriton House, North Way
Andover, Hampshire SP10 5BE,
United Kingdom
Telephone: 44-264-342-832
  (UK orders)
Telephone: 44-264-342-806
  (outside UK)
Fax: 44-264-364418 (UK orders)
Fax: 44-264-342761 (outside UK)
UK & Eire orders: itpuk@itps.co.uk
International orders: itpint@itps.co.uk

France

Editions Eyrolles
61 bd Saint-Germain
75240 Paris Cedex 05
France
Fax: 33-01-44-41-11-44

FRENCH LANGUAGE BOOKS

All countries except Canada
Phone: 33-01-44-41-46-16
Email: geodif@eyrolles.com

ENGLISH LANGUAGE BOOKS

Phone: 33-01-44-41-11-87
Email: distribution@eyrolles.com

Australia

WoodsLane Pty. Ltd.
7/5 Vuko Place, Warriewood NSW 2102
P.O. Box 935, Mona Vale NSW 2103
Australia
Telephone: 61-2-9970-5111
Fax: 61-2-9970-5002
Email: info@woodslane.com.au

Germany, Switzerland, and Austria

INQUIRIES

O'Reilly Verlag
Balthasarstr. 81
D-50670 Köln
Germany
Telephone: 49-221-97-31-60-0
Fax: 49-221-97-31-60-8
Email: anfragen@oreilly.de

ORDERS

International Thomson Publishing
Königswinterer Straße 418
53227 Bonn, Germany
Telephone: 49-228-97024 0
Fax: 49-228-441342
Email: order@oreilly.de

Asia (except Japan & India)

INQUIRIES

International Thomson Publishing Asia
60 Albert Street #15-01
Albert Complex
Singapore 189969
Telephone: 65-336-6411
Fax: 65-336-7411

ORDERS

Telephone: 65-336-6411
Fax: 65-334-1617
thomson@signet.com.sg

New Zealand

WoodsLane New Zealand Ltd.
21 Cooks Street (P.O. Box 575)
Wanganui, New Zealand
Telephone: 64-6-347-6543
Fax: 64-6-345-4840
Email: info@woodslane.com.au

Japan

O'Reilly Japan, Inc.
Kiyoshige Building 2F
12-Banchi, Sanei-cho
Shinjuku-ku
Tokyo 160 Japan
Telephone: 81-3-3356-5227
Fax: 81-3-3356-5261
Email: kenji@oreilly.com

India

Computer Bookshop (India) PVT. LTD.
190 Dr. D.N. Road, Fort
Bombay 400 001
India
Telephone: 91-22-207-0989
Fax: 91-22-262-3551
Email: cbsbom@giasbm01.vsnl.net.in

The Americas

O'Reilly & Associates, Inc.
101 Morris Street
Sebastopol, CA 95472 U.S.A.
Telephone: 707-829-0515
Telephone: 800-998-9938 (U.S. &
Canada)
Fax: 707-829-0104
Email: order@oreilly.com

Southern Africa

International Thomson Publishing
Southern Africa
Building 18, Constantia Park
138 Sixteenth Road
P.O. Box 2459
Halfway House, 1685 South Africa
Telephone: 27-11-805-4819
Fax: 27-11-805-3648

O'REILLY™

TO ORDER: **800-998-9938** • *order@oreilly.com* • *http://www.oreilly.com/*

OUR PRODUCTS ARE AVAILABLE AT A BOOKSTORE OR SOFTWARE STORE NEAR YOU.

FOR INFORMATION: **800-998-9938** • **707-829-0515** • *info@oreilly.com*

O'REILLY & ASSOCIATES, INC. SOFTWARE LICENSE AGREEMENT

O'REILLY & ASSOCIATES, INC. SOFTWARE LICENSE AGREEMENT THIS IS A LEGAL AGREEMENT BETWEEN YOU AND O'REILLY & ASSOCIATES. CAREFULLY READ ALL THE TERMS AND CONDITIONS OF THIS AGREEMENT PRIOR TO INSTALLING THIS SOFTWARE. INSTALLING THIS SOFTWARE INDICATES YOUR ACCEPTANCE OF THESE TERMS AND CONDITIONS. IF YOU DO NOT AGREE TO THESE TERMS AND CONDITIONS, RETURN THE PACKAGE AND ALL COMPONENTS OF THIS PRODUCT TO THE POINT OF PURCHASE FOR REFUND. IF PURCHASED FROM O'REILLY, UPON RETURN OF THE PRODUCT WITHIN 30 DAYS OF PURCHASE, A REFUND WILL BE GIVEN. IF PURCHASED FROM ANOTHER SOURCE, FOLLOW THEIR RETURN POLICY.

1. **License:** This License Agreement ("Agreement") permits you to use one copy of the software in the *oreilly* directory on the CD-ROM ("Software") which is part of the O'Reilly product you have purchased, on any single computer, provided the Software is in use on only one computer at any time. If you have multiple Licenses for the Software, then at any time you may have as many copies of the Software in use as you have Licenses. The Software is "in use" on a computer when it is loaded in temporary memory (i.e., RAM) or installed into the permanent memory (e.g. hard disk, CD-ROM, or other storage device) of that computer. If the anticipated number of users of the Software will exceed the number of applicable Licenses, then you must have a reasonable mechanism or process in place to assure that the number of persons using the Software concurrently does not exceed the number of Licenses. If the Software is permanently installed on the hard disk or other storage device of a computer and one person uses that computer more than 80% of the time it is in use, then that person may also use the Software on a portable or home computer.

2. **Backup and Transfer:** You may make one copy of the Software solely for backup purposes. You may transfer and license the Software to another party if the other party agrees to the terms and conditions of this Agreement and completes an online registration form available at *http://perl.oreilly.com/register.html*. If you transfer the Software, you must also transfer or destroy the Documentation and backup copy.

3. **Copyright:** The Software and the accompanying books, *Perl Utilities Guide*, *Perl Module Reference Volumes 1 and 2*, and *Programming With Perl Modules* ("Documentation"), are owned by O'Reilly & Associates, Inc. The Software and Documentation are protected by United States and international copyright laws and international trade provisions. You may not remove, obscure, or alter any notice of patent, copyright, trademark, trade secret, or other proprietary rights. You must treat the Software like any other copyrighted material (e.g., a book or musical recording) except that you may either (a) make one copy of the software solely for backup or archival purposes, or (b) transfer the Software to a single hard disk provided you keep the original solely for backup or archival purposes. You may not copy the written materials accompanying the Software, except by prior written permission from the owner of such material, as described above. All other copies of the Software and Documentation are in violation of this agreement. This license and your right to use the product terminate automatically if you violate any part of this agreement. In the event of termination, you must immediately destroy all copies of the product or return them to O'Reilly.

4. **Term:** This license is effective until terminated. You may terminate the Agreement by returning or destroying the Software and Documentation and all copies. You agree upon termination to return or destroy within five days all copies of the Software and Documentation and within two (2) weeks after any such termination you must specify in writing to O'Reilly that you have done so through your best efforts and to the best of your knowledge

5. **Limited Warranty (Disclaimer and Limitation of Liability):** O'Reilly warrants the media on which the Licensed Programs are provided to be free from defects in materials and workmanship for 90 days after delivery. Defective media may be returned for replacement without charge during the 90-day warranty period unless the media has been damaged by acts or actions of the Licensee or while under its control. O'Reilly does not warrant any object codes contained in the licensed programs furnished to it by its vendors. In the event the Licensee wishes further information about object codes contained in the license programs that are not created by O'Reilly but which are used by O'Reilly with permission of a vendor, please contact O'Reilly.Due to the complex nature of computer software, O'Reilly does not warrant that the Licensed Programs are completely error free, will operate without interruption, or are compatible with all equipment and software configurations. The Licensee expressly assumes all risk for use of the Licensed Programs. Repair, replacement, or refund (at the option of O'Reilly) is the exclusive remedy, if there is a defect. **In the event this product is discontinued or canceled by O'Reilly, this agreement is null and void.**

O'REILLY MAKES NO OTHER WARRANTIES EXPRESSED OR IMPLIED WITH RESPECT TO THE LICENSED PROGRAMS (INCLUDING ASSOCIATED WRITTEN MATERIALS), THEIR MERCHANTABILITY, OR THEIR FITNESS FOR ANY PARTICULAR PURPOSE. IN NO EVENT WILL O'REILLY BE LIABLE FOR INDIRECT OR CONSEQUENTIAL DAMAGES, INCLUDING, WITHOUT LIMITATIONS, LOSS OF INCOME, USE, OR INFORMATION, NOR SHALL THE LIABILITY OF O'REILLY EXCEED THE AMOUNT PAID FOR THE LICENSED PROGRAMS. THIS LIMITED WARRANTY GIVES YOU SPECIFIC LEGAL RIGHTS. YOU MAY HAVE OTHERS, WHICH VARY FROM STATE TO STATE.

6. **General:** You may not sublicense, assign, or transfer the license, Software, or Documentation except as expressly provided in this Agreement. This Agreement constitutes the entire Agreement between you and O'Reilly and supercedes any prior written or oral Agreement concerning the contents of this package. It shall not be modified except by written agreement dated subsequent to the date of this Agreement and signed by an authorized O'Reilly representative.O'Reilly is not bound by any provision of any purchase order, receipt, acceptance, confirmation, correspondence, or otherwise, unless O'Reilly specifically agrees to the provision in writing. This Agreement is governed by the State of California.

7. **U.S. Government Restricted Rights:** The Software and Documentation are provided with RESTRICTED RIGHTS. Use, duplication, or disclosure by the Government is subject to restrictions as set forth in subparagraph (c)(1)(ii) of the Rights in Technical Data and Computer Software clause at DFARS 252.227-7013 or subparagraphs (c)(1) and (2) of the Commercial Computer Software Restricted Rights at 48 CFR 52.227-19, as applicable. Contractor/manufacturer is O'Reilly & Associates, Inc., 101 Morris Street, Sebastopol, CA 95472

Perl Utilities Guide

Perl Utilities Guide

Brian Jepson

O'REILLY™

Cambridge · Köln · Paris · Sebastopol · Tokyo

Perl Utilities Guide
by Brian Jepson

Published by O'Reilly & Associates, Inc., 101 Morris Street, Sebastopol, CA 95472.

Editor: Susan B. Peck

Production Editor: David Futato

Printing History:

> November 1997:   First Edition.

Table of Contents

Preface

Until now, Perl has been something that was accessible only to an "in crowd"—
much as the Internet itself was a few years ago. Perl is widely available on the
Net, but it hasn't had any kind of standard packaged distribution. This has limited
its availability both to new users and to many corporate users who must have a
supported distribution before they can adopt a product. The Perl Resource Kit
addresses this need, while providing valuable resources, technical knowledge,
and software tools to those members of the in-crowd who already use Perl on a
regular basis.

The Perl Resource Kit, UNIX Edition, is a definitive Perl distribution, complete
with essential documentation, for all Perl users. It contains a collection of Perl software and over 1500 pages of documentation, including the first printed
documentation for more than 600 widely used Perl modules. The Kit is for
programmers, webmasters, system administrators, and others who use—or want
to use—Perl.

The modules documented in the Perl Resource Kit were created by members of
the Perl freeware community. O'Reilly actively supports the Perl freeware community and has since the publication of our first Perl book, *Perl Programming* (in
1991). With the Perl Resource Kit and our Perl books, conferences, and other
efforts, we seek to extend the visibility of Perl and help ensure the healthy growth
of Perl and its community.

The Perl Resource Kit contains:

- *Programming with Perl Modules*, an introduction to programming with some
  of the most important Perl modules.

- *Perl Module Reference* (two volumes), a comprehensive reference for significant Perl modules.

- *Perl Utilities Guide*, documentation for Perl software tools contained in the Kit.

- Perl Resource Kit Software (on CD-ROM), a Java/Perl tool (JPL) written by Larry Wall, which allows programmers to write Java classes with Perl implementations; a snapshot of the freeware Perl tools on CPAN (Comprehensive Perl Archives Network), with an install program, a search tool, and a web-aware interface for identifying more recent online CPAN tools; and many bits of example code and sample programs.

- The Autumn 1997 issue of *The Perl Journal*, a quarterly magazine devoted to the Perl language.

A more thorough description of the contents appears in Chapter 1 of *Perl Utilities Guide,* this book. The remainder of this Preface is devoted to the Utilities Guide.

How to Use this Book

The *Perl Utilities Guide* covers the software included with the Resource Kit and provides instructions, tutorials, and many examples. This overview will help you find what you need quickly.

Chapter 1, *Welcome to the Perl Resource Kit*
> You can use this chapter to obtain a comprehensive overview of the contents of this book and of the Perl Resource Kit. Ideas for using the Kit as well as pointers to other sources of information and available tech support are also included in Chapter 1.

Chapter 2, *Installing the Resource Kit Software*
> This chapter should be one of your first stops. Two forms of installation are covered in this book: installation using the graphical setup tool and manual installation of Perl from source. Also, this chapter explains ways in which you can make the most of the CPAN mirror, with or without the use of the graphical setup tool.

Chapter 3, *Perlez-Vous Java? Using JPL*
> In Chapter 3, you will find a tutorial introduction to installing and using JPL, with numerous useful example programs. JPL is Larry Wall's Java-Perl integration tool, on which the remainder of this book focuses.

Chapter 4, *Going All AWT: Using the Java Abstract Window Toolkit with Perl*
> If you're going to use JPL to develop graphically-rich Perl applications, this is the place to start. This chapter offers tips, tricks, and techniques for working with Java's AWT (Abstract Window Toolkit) to develop graphical user interfaces with JPL.

Chapter 5, *JPL and Applets: Using JPL with RMI*

    If you want a little Perl code in your applets, it can be done. This chapter explains the multi-tier trickery you must employ to do so. The RMI (Remote Method Invocation) API lets your applets invoke methods in objects that reside on your web server.

Chapter 6, *Advanced JPL: SQL Databases and Dynamic Images*

    Java's JDBC API is a call-level SQL interface that enables you to build Java programs that can interact with SQL database engines. GIFgraph is a Perl module that allows you to generate dynamic graphs. This chapter walks through a "case study" in which JPL brings together both JDBC and GIFgraph to generate a graph from data contained in an SQL database.

Appendix A, *JPL Reference*

    Is there something you couldn't find in the other chapters? This appendix offers a topic-oriented way of getting quick reference information on JPL.

Appendix B, *Selected Articles from The Perl Journal*

    An entire copy of *The Perl Journal* for Autumn 1997 is included in the Perl Resource Kit (see the case containing the CD). In addition, we've reprinted a few articles from earlier editions for your reading pleasure and learning. Sit back, relax, and spend a few minutes with some Perl gurus.

Conventions Used in This Book

We use the following typographic conventions.

Italic

    is used for URLs, filenames, and email addresses, as well as for emphasis.

`Constant width`

    is used for functions, methods, and other fragments of Perl code in regular text, as well as for blocks of code examples.

`Constant width italic`

    is used for arguments of functions and methods, to be replaced with a user-supplied value (or expression).

`Constant width bold`

    is used for text to be typed literally by the user.

Contacting Technical Support

If you've thoroughly investigated other sources for help (see Chapter 1 of this book for suggestions) and still need assistance, technical support is available for the Perl Resource Kit. Before contacting technical support, make sure you have registered your copy of the Resource Kit online at *http://perl.oreilly.com/ register.html*. Registering your copy helps us provide better service and keep you up-to-date on what is happening with Perl at O'Reilly.

Support for the Perl Resource Kit comes in three flavors:

- Once you register your Resource Kit, you have up to 30 days of free initial installation support on Solaris 2.5.* and higher and Linux 2.0.* and higher for the software included on the CD-ROM. This support is available by phone at (707) 829-0515 from 7:00 a.m. to 5:00 p.m. (Pacific Time, U.S.A.), Monday through Friday.

- After the 30 days or for software problems beyond installation, technical support is available for a fee through the Perl Clinic, which you can reach in several ways:
  — on the Web at *http://www.perlclinic.com/*
  — by email at *info@perlclinic.com*
  — by phone in the United States and Canada at (604) 606-4611
  — by phone in Europe and elsewhere at 44 (0) 1483 424424

- For help and information on the books included in the Resource Kit, technical support is available by email at *perltech@oreilly.com*. Please use this email address to ask questions about and/or report errors in the books.

Acknowledgments

This book started out as a simple manual, little more than documentation for the utilities bundled with the Perl Resource Kit. What it turned into instead was an amazing journey into the innards of two languages, climaxing in a savage ballet that was performed among the sparks formed where the cutting edges meet between Perl and Java. If you look closely enough, you can see burns and singes where the sparks hit the printed page.

This book has been an exciting endeavor, and could not have been written without the help of many people. Thanks go out to Gina Blaber and Susan Peck, who provided expert guidance and sanity checks during the development of this book. I'd also like to thank Nate Patwardhan for his assistance with the bits of the book that pertained to the Perl Resource Kit Setup Tool, and other "perls" of wisdom. Thanks also to Linda Mui, Ellen Siever, David Futato, the Resource Kit beta testers, and the other random people, household pets, and small furry creatures from Alpha Centauri who provided input and feedback throughout the development of the Resource Kit.

Thanks to David Futato, who shepherded this work through the intricacies of production, and the many others on the O'Reilly production staff who worked hard to bring this book out on schedule: Sheryl Avruch for her wise and balanced management, Robert Romano for his quick turnaround on figures, Seth Maislin, who wrote the index, Ted Meister for his cover design, Mike Sierra for FrameMaker support, and Jane Ellin for quality assurance.

A special thanks goes out to Larry Wall for his "heavy mettle," which enables him to turn out tools (such as Perl and JPL) that are deep, practical, and above all, very interesting. Finally, I'd like to thank Shawn Wallace for the chapter and appendix he contributed to this book. Shawn provided a thorough exploration of the ways in which Java's graphical toolkit could be integrated with Perl, and the book, particularly Chapter 4, is richer for it. Also, the comprehensive nature of Appendix A was the result of his diligent investigation into JPL and JNI.

1

Welcome to the Perl Resource Kit

The Perl Resource Kit, UNIX Edition, aims to be the ultimate companion to Perl—a scripting language written by Larry Wall, assisted by a cast of thousands. Perl brings together the best features of C, the Bourne Shell, and data manipulation utilities such as sed and awk. Its popularity and wide acceptance owes to the fact that you can master the core features quickly, and Perl's smooth learning curve means that you can learn as you go. You will often find that you learn more as your needs increase. As muscles tend to grow with use, so does your Perl knowledge.

Although one of Perl's strongest areas is processing text, it excels in other areas, such as system management, database access, and CGI development. You can also use it for graphical development, and it makes a great tool for quickly prototyping a system.

Perhaps you bought the Perl Resource Kit because you thought it would help you squeeze more power out of a language you already know well. Perhaps you were looking to get deeper insights into some of the hundreds of modules that are available for Perl. Maybe you just bought this because you couldn't bear to leave another Perl-related product stranded on the bookshelves of your favorite bookseller. Whatever your intentions for obtaining this kit were, I'm sure they were noble. To reward such pure motives, the Perl Resource Kit is going to do its best to meet your expectations.

Above all, the culture that surrounds Perl is very good at documenting its accomplishments. The abundance of online documentation is well-written, concise, and often delightfully up-to-date. However, there are a lot of choices available when you are attacking a project with Perl as your weapon. The hundreds of modules that are available can be quite overwhelming. Some modules overlap in very subtle ways, so it is not always easy to pick the right one without turning to sources of wisdom. Further, if you've come up against a programming problem that has not been addressed by one of these modules, what do you do when you need to code the solution yourself?

This is where the Perl Resource Kit comes in handy. The books that comprise it address these issues nicely. *Programming with Perl Modules* provides a tutorial introduction to using the most important Perl modules. This book also includes a chapter titled "Contributing to CPAN," which guides you in creating and deploying your own modules. The two-volume *Perl Module Reference* supplies complete documentation and reference for nearly 600 key Perl modules. This book, the *Perl Utilities Guide*, supplies instructions for installing the software on the CD-ROM and for installing modules both from the CD-ROM and from remote archive sites. Additionally, the *Utilities Guide* offers coverage of JPL, a Java/Perl interface written by Larry Wall. JPL allows you to create hybrid Java and Perl programs, leveraging the power of Perl for tasks such as network connectivity and string processing, while making the most of Java's graphical capabilities. JPL is available nowhere else but the Perl Resource Kit. JPL is included on the Resource Kit's CD-ROM along with other useful tools, information, and samples.

What Comes with the Resource Kit?

The Perl Resource Kit includes a CD-ROM filled with software and reference material. The material on the CD-ROM complements the four books included in the kit. To help you find your way around the Resource Kit, the following roadmap provides brief descriptions of the books and CD-ROM contents.

JPL

JPL is a Java/Perl interface written by Larry Wall exclusively for the Perl Resource Kit. JPL is not necessarily an acronym, but the J stands for Java, and the PL comes from *.pl*, a common file extension used for Perl scripts. JPL allows you to easily embed Perl within Java applications and provides the "glue" between the two languages. Using JPL, you can write embedded Perl methods that manipulate Java objects and primitive data types. Perl methods can accept Java objects and primitive values as arguments, and can also return objects and values to Java methods.

JPL can be used to build graphically rich, network-enabled applications that take advantage of the strengths of both languages. A number of example programs that showcase the wide possibilities available with JPL are developed in the *Perl Utilities Guide*. Many of these examples are included on the CD-ROM for you to use in your own JPL applications. Chapters 3 and 4 of this book cover the basic techniques of using JPL and walk through the examples.

The Graphical Setup Tool

The graphical setup tool lets you easily install the contents of the CD-ROM. It offers options to install a binary version of Perl and/or the source code for Perl, as well as the utilities and examples included with the Resource Kit. The setup tool also includes a facility for managing and installing unbundled Perl modules, which offers the ability to install modules from the CD as well as from remote archive sites. The remote retrieval capability makes it easy to ensure that the modules you have locally are the most current versions available.

CPAN Mirror

The Perl Resource Kit CD-ROM includes a mirror of CPAN (the Comprehensive Perl Archive Network). In the words of the CPAN welcome page, "CPAN aims to be The Perl archive, the only Perl archive you will ever need by definition: the C in CPAN obliges." In addition to the most recent Perl source code (as well as older versions), CPAN includes a vast collection of Perl modules. A module is a freely redistributable chunk of reusable code that can be easily imported into your Perl programs. In general, these modules are extremely easy to use, and often very well-documented. The graphical setup tool lets you search and copy modules from the CPAN mirror on the CD as well as from remote archive sites.

Programming with Perl Modules

Programming with Perl Modules includes an introduction to Perl modules, and tutorials for a number of the most popular and powerful modules. Building-block libraries, such as `getopts`, which allows you to parse command-line options are showcased, as well as high-level modules, such as GD, which offers you the ability to generate GIF images. In addition, *Programming with Perl Modules* includes tutorial coverage of database, network, and web modules, which exposes you to the fundamental building blocks of a web-based business solution. This book is an indispensable handbook for learning how to develop your own applications with Perl modules.

Perl Module Reference (Two Volumes)

The *Perl Module Reference* is a two-volume set that contains documentation for nearly 600 of the most popular Perl modules, organized by the same module categories used on CPAN itself. Not only will this reference enable you to find documentation on a module that you are using, but having the documentation available will help you decide if a given module is the right tool for the job before you install it.

Perl Utilities Guide

This book, the *Perl Utilities Guide*, provides step-by-step instructions on getting the most out of the CD-ROM. The graphical setup tool, which is available for Solaris and Linux users, is explained in detail. Also, this book explains how to build from source and install modules from the CD-ROM for users who cannot or who do not wish to use the graphical setup tool. And that's just Chapter 2!

The rest of the *Utilities Guide* is a comprehensive how-to and reference guide for building applets and applications that make use of JPL. Graphically rich sample programs give you hands-on practice using examples of some of the things that Perl is great for: data manipulation and network programming.

How Can I Use the Resource Kit?

Perl has been called the glue of the Internet. It's used in many places to connect applications to one another and has found one (among many) major niche: generating dynamic content for web sites. Of course, Perl is there for you when you have a multi-megabyte file that needs to be parsed, filed, sorted, indexed, briefed, debriefed, or numbered. So what can this resource kit do for you?

- For any enterprise that has included Perl as part of its development strategy, this kit will be invaluable. The combined development expertise of the Perl Resource Kit authors has been distilled into the reference materials contained in the Kit. Not only are hundreds of the most popular modules identified and documented in the *Perl Module Reference* for your benefit, but a select number of these modules are given tutorial-level coverage in the *Programming with Perl Modules* book. Coupled with the complete mirror of CPAN, this makes for a very practical and indispensable reference.

- Perl has already distinguished itself as the language of choice for Internet and intranet development. Everyone's seen web counters and guestbook scripts written in Perl, but did you know that Perl can be used to develop mission-critical Internet and intranet applications using a browser as a user-interface? The *Programming with Perl Modules* book includes conceptual coverage of the HTML and CGI modules, as well as the DBI. Combining these modules, you can build CGI-based applications that do almost everything that you can do with traditional client-server development tools. Enormously complex applications have been deployed in this fashion. The lesson learned is that Perl/CGI-based systems experience a number of benefits over traditional tools such as Powerbuilder, FoxPro, or Access. For one, there are marvelously few desktop support and configuration issues, since the only desktop component is the browser. Further, rollout of new versions is trivial: it can be as simple as changing a URL to point to the new version of the system. Also, Perl's object-oriented nature and wealth of available modules means that you don't need to reinvent the wheel each time you need a new feature. You can spend more time on user-visible features, and less time on developing interfaces to remote systems or coding up date parsing routines!

- Perhaps you've built a web system using Perl, but you are tired of the limitations of the user interface available in HTML forms. For you, JPL represents an escape route. Through the magic of RMI (Remote Method Invocation), you can build Java applets that run on any desktop, but invoke Perl methods that belong to objects running on your remote server. Now that JavaSoft and the Object Management Group have agreed to guarantee interoperability between RMI and CORBA/IIOP (Common Object Request Broker Architecture/Internet Inter-ORB Protocol), you'll eventually be able to have your applications talk to objects all over the place! Using RMI and JPL is the topic of Chapter 5 of this book.

- Although Perl is commonly thought of as a language for systems programming, web development, or raw text processing, it also makes a great companion to graphically rich languages such as Tk or Java. Using either Perl/Tk or JPL, you can build applications that make use of a sophisticated GUI interface. Both Perl/Tk and JPL are covered in the Resource Kit, and the sky's the limit as far as the sort of applications that can be developed with these tools. Do you need database access, graphing, and network connectivity? Build your front end with Perl/Tk or JPL, and drive the back end with the DBI for SQL access, GIFgraph for charts, and the `libnet` bundle for network connectivity. Oh, did you say it was a financial application that needs to connect to your company's ultra-secret pricing models that are packaged as a C library? Well, then just make use of Perl's XS interface to easily create an extension interface to your libraries!

What You Should Know (And Where to Learn More)

The Perl Resource Kit does not attempt to provide an introduction to Perl programming. Instead, it's a collection of tools that enables you to build on a solid foundation of mid-level Perl experience. If you're still using Perl 4.036 (or a much earlier version), you'll need to upgrade to the latest version to make use of the most current tools, including this Resource Kit. Fortunately, the Resource Kit includes the newest version of Perl. Here we cover some of the basic topics you should know as well as some background on resources for more information.

Basic Concepts and Features of Perl

To make the most efficient use of this Kit, you should have experience with some of the following areas of Perl programming. This information is a distillation of some of the features listed on the `perl` manpage, and is a list of features that are fundamental to understanding what goes into a module:

Data Structures

Perl offers you the ability to create scalar values that are references to variables and subroutines, which makes it possible to create a scalar value that is actually a reference to a scalar variable, hash, array, or even a chunk of code. Since arrays and hashes contain scalar values, each element of a hash or array can be a reference, making it possible to create arrays of arrays, arrays of hashes, arrays of code references, and so on. This feature is a critical part of Perl's object-oriented capabilities. There are a few manpages that are useful for learning more about data structures: `perldata` (*Perl Data Structures*), `perlref` (*Perl References*), `perldsc` (*Perl Data Structures Cookbook*), and `perllol` (*Perl Data Structures: Lists of Lists*). After you have installed Perl, you can view these manpages with the `man` or `perldoc` command, by issuing such commands as `man perldata` or `perldoc perldata` (or the name of the manpage you wish to see).

Perl Modules

Earlier versions of Perl allowed you to extend its functionality by importing library code or by building a new version of the Perl interpreter that was statically linked to a binary extension. The present version of Perl allows modules to be loaded dynamically at run-time. This includes modules written in Perl or binary modules compiled for your operating system. This feature, more than any other, has made it very easy for Perl developers to write reusable code. In addition to the documentation supplied in the *Programming with Perl Modules* book in this Resource Kit, the `perlmod` (*Perl Modules: How They Work*) and `perlmodlib` (*Perl Modules: How To Write and Use*) manpages are quite helpful.

Object-Orientation

Perl modules consist of one or more "packages" contained in a single file. A package offers a namespace that is independent from the default (`main`) namespace and from the namespace of other packages. With some very simple changes to the way you are used to programming, a package can easily be designed as a class. Most modules that are available are designed as classes. There are several good manpages that you can use if you are not familiar with Perl's object-oriented features, the most notable being `perltoot`, the *Perl OO Tutorial*. You may also consult `perlobj` (*Perl Objects*) and `perlbot` (*Perl OO Tricks and Examples*).

CPAN History

CPAN began as an idea offered by Jared Rhine to the *perl-packrats* mailing list on December 6, 1993. This message arrived on the mailing list only four days after the mailing list was created, at a time when the list's membership could have been counted on the fingers of two hands. The packrats had been discussing a strategy for archiving Perl sources in the wake of the accidental deletion of the Coombs archive, which was one of the leading archives of Perl scripts at the time. Jared's proposal suggested that this "comprehensive Perl archive" follow the structure of the CTAN project, "a collection of canonical sites for TeX."

One day after Jared's message was forwarded to the packrats list, Coombs was officially declared to be "no more a Perl archive." That very day, Bill Middleton sent a missive to the caretakers of the CTAN, seeking advice on creating and maintaining such an archive. Although a top-level organization of the CPAN was discussed, the idea slumbered until February 19, 1995, when Jarkko Hietaniemi posted a message, titled "CPAN idea still alive?" to the packrats mailing list. By June 5, after much discussion of how the CPAN should be organized, Jarkko announced a first cut of CPAN, which was located at `ftp.funet.fi`. The organization of the site barely resembled the present state; Perl 4 was still popular, so there was quite a bit of the site devoted to Perl 4 software. The Perl 5 extensions directory, possibly the closest thing to the modules directory of the current CPAN, included all of the extensions lumped into a single directory. It wasn't long before the suggestion was raised that these extensions be given subdirectories that corresponded to their package names.

On August 17, 1995, Andreas Koenig suggested an organization of the modules that led to the current organization of CPAN. The Perl 5 Module list, a master list of all freely available Perl modules, included a code for each author's name. Andreas suggested that the organization of the CPAN follow these author's names; one directory for each author, and all of that author's modules would be stored in the directory. On September 27, 1995, Andreas consolidated suggestions for CPAN's organization. Tim Bunce, then the maintainer of the Perl 5 Module List, suggested that the module categories in the module list be preserved, and this became the *modules/by-category* directory. The *by-module* directory was also adopted, and the *by-author* directory was chosen as the place where files would actually reside. The *by-category* and *by-module* directory contained symbolic links to the files in the *by-author* directory. This is the CPAN as it is known today; a massive (over 200 megabytes), distributed (mirrored by over 50 sites), well-organized archive of Perl materials. CPAN is accessible from the Tom Christiansen's *perl.com* multiplexor, at *http://www.perl.com/CPAN*.

CPAN Organization

The files in CPAN are organized in several ways. You can choose to browse CPAN by the module name, the author's name, or by the module category. Also, search engines are available that let you perform queries on the hundreds of modules available at CPAN. Finally, the Perl 5 Modules List is a widely available document that contains a list of all CPAN modules, as well as information about installing and using the modules. The Perl 5 Modules List is posted regularly to *comp.lang.perl.announce*. The Perl Resource Kit includes a CD-ROM with a complete copy of CPAN—thus, you can browse it or you can use the graphical setup tool (see Chapter 2) to locate and install modules.

You'll probably find browsing by module name and category to be the most useful. Browsing by module name is handy if you have become familiar with the modules that are available. Since related modules are often organized under the same package, if you are looking for something HTML-related, you'll probably browse within the directory set aside for HTML modules. Also, the module categories are organized at a very high level into more than twenty different groups. Browsing by module category can be very handy if you are not familiar with the available modules, or if you simply can't find the module you are looking for when you look in the usual places.

Imagine that you need to develop a script that retrieves email messages from a POP3 server. Of course, you'll write this script in Perl, there's no question about that. But you need to find a module that will help you interact with that POP3 server. Knowing that CPAN is the standard repository of all wisdom and knowledge, you truck on over to CPAN, using the URL:

   http://www.perl.com/CPAN/modules/by-category

When you bring up the directory listing, you find one directory that catches your eye, *19_Mail_and_Usenet_News*. Following that link, you find a directory known as *Mail*. Lo and behold, the *Mail* directory contains a module called POP3Client, which does exactly what you want!

Suppose now, three months later, you need to write a script that manipulates mail folders. Well, you remembered that the *Mail* module directory contained lots of neat stuff, so you head back to CPAN, but this time, you go directly to the *Mail* module directory with:

   http://www.perl.com/CPAN/modules/by-module/Mail

Once you arrive at the *Mail* module directory, you find a package called *Mail-Folder*, which does exactly what you want. Of course, not all stories have such happy endings. Some end with you having to write the module you need, which can be a source of happiness in and of itself. In such cases, you'll find *Programming with Perl Modules* in this resource kit to be indispensable.

What If I Need Help?

If you can't find what you are looking for in the Resource Kit, your first point of outside help should be the Perl Resource Kit online site at *http://perl.oreilly.com/*. At this site you can find information on troubleshooting, technical support, ideas for using Perl, more tools and samples, and links to more information. You will also find a listing of other reference books on Perl and related topics that can help you solve the problem you are facing. The list of O'Reilly books on Perl is growing every month (to say nothing of the list of Java books). Check this site regularly for updated information, news, and help.

There is a wealth of online resources at your disposal, as well. The Perl Language Home page, at *http://www.perl.com/*, includes a comprehensive overview of all things Perl, as well as links to the various Perl FAQs (Frequently Asked Questions) other sites. If you have access to Usenet news, you will find the following newsgroups to be extremely useful sources of information:

comp.lang.perl.misc
    general Perl language issues

comp.lang.perl.modules
    discussions of Perl modules

comp.lang.perl.tk
    issues related to Perl and Tk

However, since your question has probably already been answered, please check the FAQ first, and then an archive of Usenet news such as *http://www.dejanews.com/* or *http://www.altavista.digital.com/*—you will most likely get the fastest answer this way. Failing that, you can try posting your question to one of the appropriate Perl newsgroups.

2

Installing the Resource Kit Software

The Perl Resource Kit CD-ROM includes a wealth of software, including a complete snapshot of CPAN, binary versions of Perl for Linux and Solaris, the source code for Perl, a graphical setup tool, and the Perl Resource Kit utilities. You can use the graphical setup tool to install any or all of these packages, as explained in this chapter. Note that you must be running one of the 2.0 Linux kernels or Solaris 2.5 (or greater) with the X Window System to use the setup tool. If you do not have this setup, follow the manual installation instructions for other platforms located at the end of this chapter.

Starting the Graphical Setup Tool

Before you can start the setup tool, you must mount the CD-ROM on your workstation. To run the setup tool, you should have super-user (*root*) privileges. Use the su command to become the super-user (*root*), if you are not already logged in as *root*.

Before starting the setup tool, review the *README* file contained in the top-level directory. This file includes any late-breaking news as well as general information about the CD-ROM.

The setup tool is located in the *oreilly/* directory on the CD-ROM. That directory includes a script called *setup*, which, when executed, starts the setup tool. After you have mounted the CD-ROM, the following commands will start the setup tool. This example assumes that you have mounted the CD-ROM in */cdrom*:

```
# cd /cdrom/oreilly
# ./setup
```

NOTE   The CD comes with both a maintenance version and a developer
              version of Perl. By default the setup program installs the stable main-
              tenance version; however if you need some special functionality of
              the newer developer version and are willing to put up with the risks
              of using a developer version, you may install it by giving the com-
              mand **setup -devel** instead of **setup**.

The first time you run the setup tool, you will probably encounter the CPAN configuration screen (see Figure 2-1). This screen does not appear if you have a private configuration file (*~/.cpan/CPAN/MyConfig.pm*) for the CPAN module. The purpose of this screen is to allow you to configure the CPAN module, which is used by the setup tool's "Search/Update Existing Modules" feature to locate and install modules from remote sites or the CD-ROM.

The CPAN configuration screen consists of a number of text fields. If you pass your mouse over the label of each field, you will see help balloons that describe each option. In most cases, you should accept the defaults. Each option is described in Table 2-1.

Table 2-1. CPAN Configuration Fields

Option	Explanation
build_cache	This is the size (in megabytes) of the cache directory for extracting and building modules that have been down-loaded from a remote CPAN site or from the CD-ROM.
build_dir	The cache directory for extracting and building modules. It should be a locally accessible directory.
cpan_home	The directory for the CPAN module to keep indexes and other internal information.
ftp	The path to your FTP program, such as */bin/ftp*.
ftp_proxy	The URL of an FTP proxy server. This is used when the CPAN module finds the LWP module installed, which it uses to make FTP and HTTP requests.
getcwd	How to get the current directory.
gzip	Location of the *gzip* utility.
http_proxy	The URL of an HTTP proxy server. This is used when the CPAN module finds the LWP module installed, which it uses to make FTP and HTTP requests.

Table 2-1. CPAN Configuration Fields (continued)

Option	Explanation
inactivity_timeout	Some modules require an interactive configuration session. This option will cause the CPAN module to break an interactive *Makefile.PL* after *n* seconds of inactivity. You may supply a value of zero to never break.
index_expire	The CPAN module keeps a local copy of CPAN index files. This is number of days to wait between refreshing the index files.
inhibit_startup_message	Does not print the startup message if value is 1.
keep_source_where	If you want to keep the source code around after building the module, this is the directory where it is kept.
lynx	The location of the text-based browser *lynx*, if it is installed.
make	Location of your make executable.
make_arg	Arguments that should always be passed to make.
make_install_arg	Same as make_arg for make install.
makepl_arg	Arguments passed to perl Makefile.PL.
ncftp	The location of *ncftp*, an anonymous FTP client, if it is installed.
no_proxy	List of hostnames for which CPAN should not use a proxy server.
pager	Location of your preferred pager, such as *less*.
shell	The location of your favorite shell.
tar	Location of your *tar* program.
unzip	Location of your *unzip* program.
urllist	List of your preferred CPAN site(s). You should include a comma-delimited list of sites, with the URL of the CD-ROM listed last. This causes the CPAN module to query a remote site first for retrieving CPAN index files. CPAN also automatically checks any *file://* URL first when downloading a module, irrespective of the order in which it appears in the list. This way, the CD-ROM is used if it contains the most recent version of a module, but a remote CPAN site is used if *it* has the latest version. (Note that this feature is only used by the setup tool's "Search/Update Existing Modules" option—the "Install Module(s) from CD" option always uses the CD-ROM.) This is also explained in the section at the end of this chapter, "Installing Modules Using the CD-ROM and a Remote CPAN Site." Of course, if you want to only use the CD, you can supply the *file://* URL of the CD-ROM as the only item in the urllist.
wait_list	List of your preferred WAIT site(s).

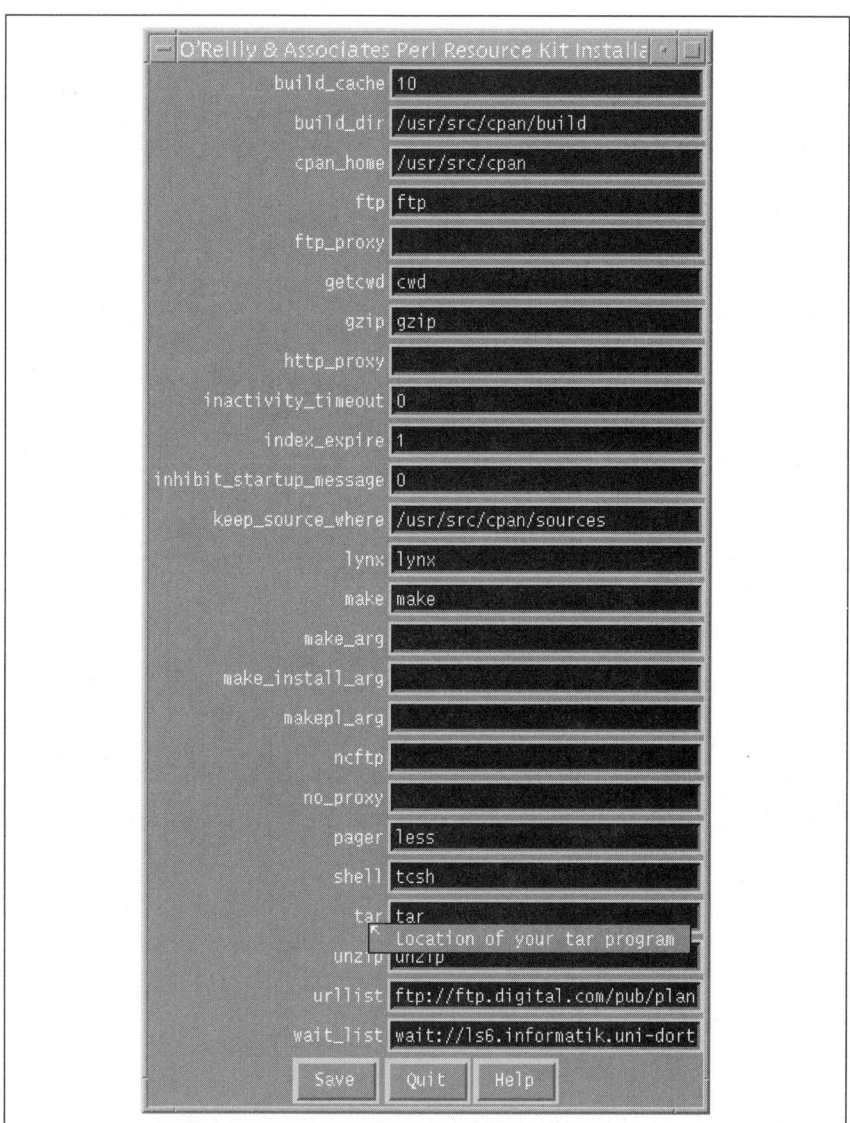

Figure 2-1. Setup tool CPAN configuration screen

After you've finished entering the configuration options you need, click *Save* to save the configuration. You can click *Quit* to exit the setup tool completely without saving the configuration. Clicking *Help* displays the online help. When you save the configuration, it is saved to *~/.cpan/CPAN/MyConfig.pm*. The *Install Perl Modules* screen (see the section titled "Installing, Updating, and Using CPAN Modules") offers an option to *Modify Your CPAN Configuration*, which brings up this screen again.

After you either save or quit the configuration screen, the first screen of the setup tool appears, as shown in Figure 2-2. From this screen, you may choose any of four installation options, each of which is individually explained in the following sections.

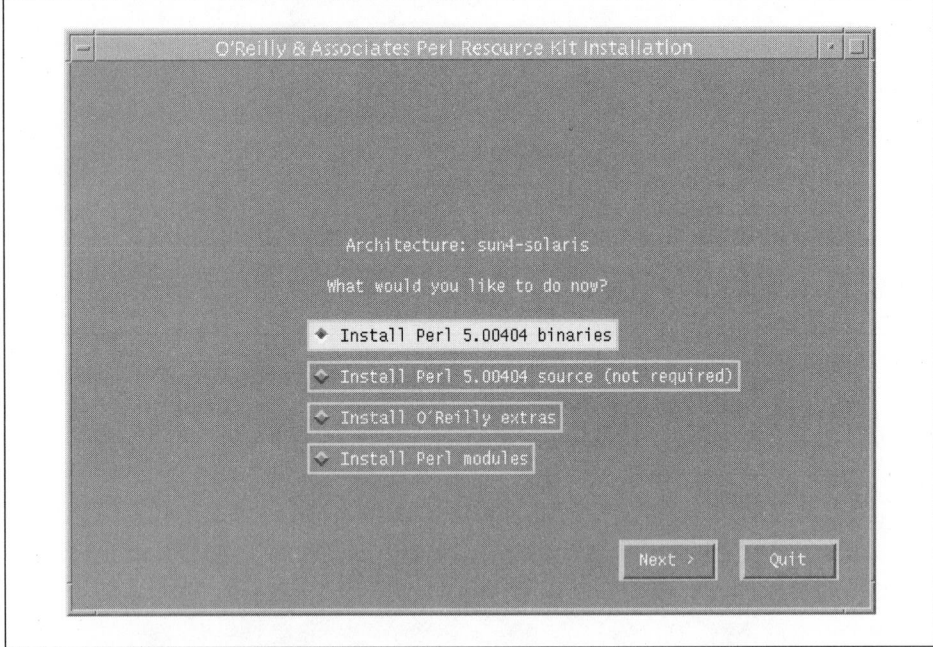

Figure 2-2. Setup tool main screen

Installing a Precompiled Perl Binary

Precompiled Perl binaries are available and supported for SPARC Solaris and Linux running on Intel processors. If a binary is not available for your operating system, you can find instructions for installing and compiling Perl later in this chapter.

Although a binary version of Perl is included for Sparc Solaris and Linux on Intel, you should install from source if you have a compiler other than GNU C (such as Sun's compiler), since the binary version of Perl included on the CD-ROM is configured for GNU C. If you do not have a C compiler installed, you may still install Perl, but there will be many modules and tools that you cannot install, including JPL. See instructions later in this chapter for installing Perl from source. If a binary is available for your operating system, you may choose the *Install Perl 5.004xx binaries* option from the first screen of the setup tool. Click *Next* and you will be prompted to choose an installation directory. Figure 2-3 shows the directory chooser screen.

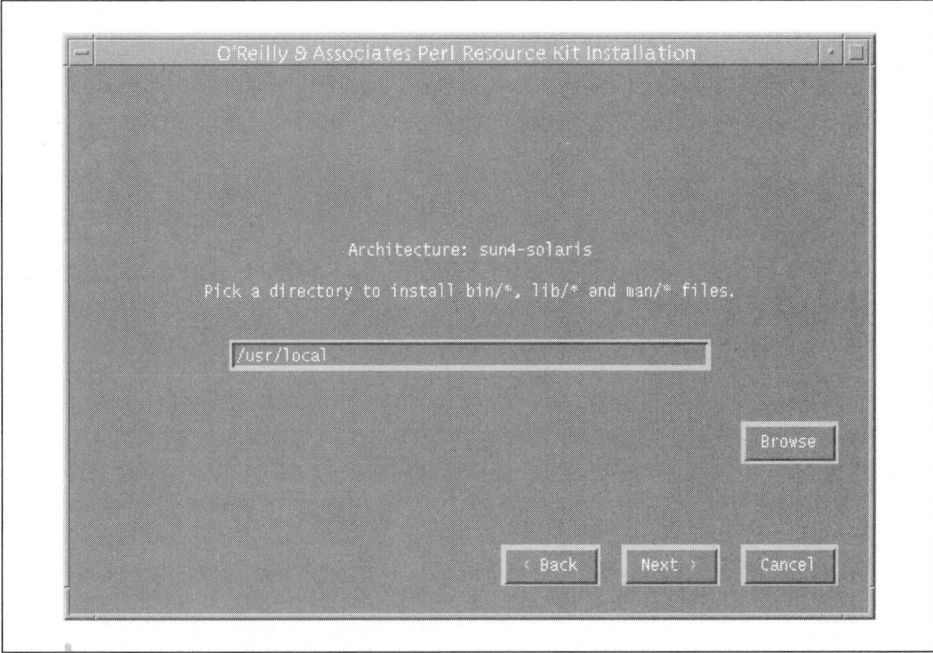

Figure 2-3. Setup tool directory chooser screen

At the end of the installation, if you chose any directory other than */usr*, a dialog box asks if you want to create a symbolic link from */usr/bin/perl* to the installed location of Perl. If you choose to do this, scripts that expect Perl to be in the default location will have no trouble finding it.

Installing the O'Reilly Extras

The Resource Kit also includes an Extras distribution, which includes JPL (a Java-Perl integration kit), sample programs for JPL, and examples from the chapters in this book.

To install the Resource Kit Extras, select *Install O'Reilly Extras* from the installation menu, and click *Next*. You will then be asked to supply an installation directory for the Resource Kit Extras. After you choose the directory, click *Next*. The Resource Kit Extras are installed in the directory of your choice.

The *README* file in the installation directory includes instructions on installing and using the distribution. Chapter 3, *Perlez-Vous Java? Using JPL*, provides detailed instructions on installing and using JPL. Other examples included in the

Extras are discussed in this book. If you wish to use the examples in the book, you must install the Resource Kit Extras. You may also copy them from the *oreilly/ eg/* directory on the CD-ROM to a locally available filesystem.

Installing, Updating, and Using CPAN Modules

The Perl Resource Kit includes a snapshot of CPAN, the Comprehensive Perl Archive Network. CPAN is a distributed collection of Perl modules and is the only place you should ever need to visit for Perl software. The fact that Perl is freely redistributable has encouraged many people to share the fruits of their Perl development in the same fashion as Perl. In fact, most modules on CPAN bear the license, "You may distribute this under the same terms as Perl itself."

Since version 5 of Perl, developers have been able to extend Perl using modules, which are collections of reusable code that can be loaded at run-time. The Perl community has been very zealous about promoting the use of these modules. CPAN includes several useful pieces of documentation to help users find the module they are looking for. The Perl 5 Module List, a widely-disseminated list of the Perl modules, is also helpful in this respect, as it provides an excellent way to locate reusable modules. The module list takes this one step further. In times of plenty, developers are taught how to fish. However, in times of dearth, they are encouraged to grow their own food. The Perl 5 Module List includes a section called "Modules: Creation, Use and Abuse" that explains when it's appropriate to write a new module, how to write the new module, and how to ensure that other developers can learn about and obtain the module. Because of this sort of educational effort, CPAN has grown immensely.

Perl source code may contain documentation that is known as "plain old documentation," or *pod*. Perl source code can be fed into a translator that converts the embedded pod into any of several convenient forms: PostScript, HTML, manpages, or plain text. The ease with which this documentation can be embedded makes it easy to document modules. Since the documentation is embedded in the source code, it's almost trivial for the developer to keep it up-to-date as the module evolves. As part of the Resource Kit, we compiled and edited the pods found on CPAN; you can find this information in the two volumes of the *Perl Module Reference.*

Given the benefits of Perl modules (object-oriented, reusable, well-documented) and the general willingness of members of the Perl community to freely redistribute modules that they have found useful, something like CPAN seems inevitable: a distributed repository of freely redistributable, easy-to-integrate, exceptionally well-documented source code. Chapter 1, *Introduction to Perl*

Modules and CPAN, in *Programming with Perl Modules*, explains how you can use modules in your programs and also provides a more thorough description of modules.

Using the Setup Tool with CPAN

The setup tool main menu (see Figure 2-2) includes an option to *Install Perl Modules*. This option allows you to do one of four tasks:

* Install a CPAN module from the Resource Kit's CD-ROM

* Update a module you have installed with a newer one from CPAN (requires an Internet connection)

* Search and update modules

* Update the CPAN index files on your local system

To complete one of these tasks, select this option and click *Next*. The *Install Perl Modules* screen appears, as shown in Figure 2-4. The following sections explain how to install, update, or search using CPAN modules using the setup tool.

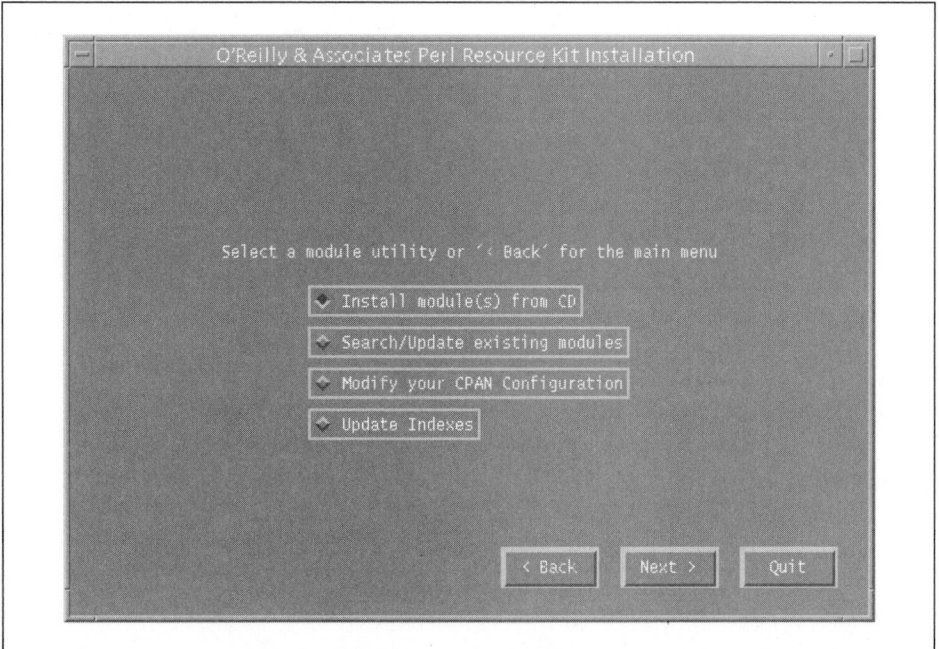

Figure 2-4. The "Install Perl Modules" screen

Install one or more modules

From the *Install Perl Modules* screen, select *Install module(s) from CD* and click *Next*. You are asked to select a directory for the module sources. The default is */usr/local/src/cpan/sources*, which is used as a work area to download, extract, and build module sources. You must either supply a directory or accept the default and click *Next*. At this point, the *Module Selection* screen (Figure 2-5) appears and presents you with an alphabetic list of all modules. Double-click the module that you wish to install. If you wish to install more than one module, select multiple modules by single-clicking on each module, and then clicking *Install Modules*.

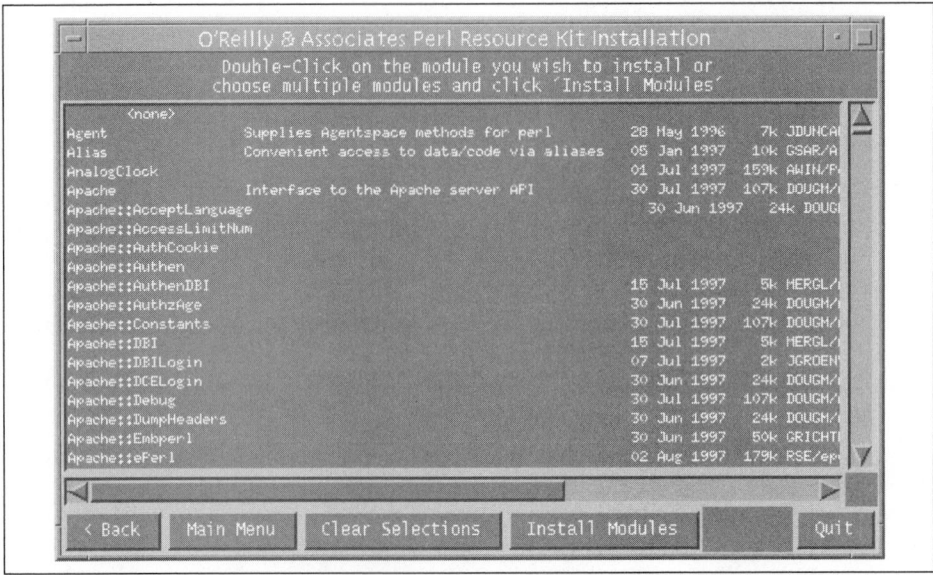

Figure 2-5. The "Module Selection" screen

In some cases, a module may not install correctly. A module may fail to install because there was no *Makefile.PL* file included with the distribution or because the tests for that module failed. If the installation fails, the setup tool directs you to the *README* file for that module. You will often find notes in the *README* file that explain non-standard installation methods or potential areas of trouble for your operating system or configuration.

Search for or update an existing module

The setup tool allows you to view all of the currently installed modules and to update them if you desire. To use this facility, select the *Search/Update Existing Modules* option from the *Install Perl Modules* screen shown in Figure 2-4 and click *Next*. The *Search For a Module* screen appears, which includes a list of all modules. When you click on a module, the version of that module appears in the status bar, as shown in Figure 2-6. The Setup tool also performs an automatic search of CPAN indexes, and displays the version of the latest module.

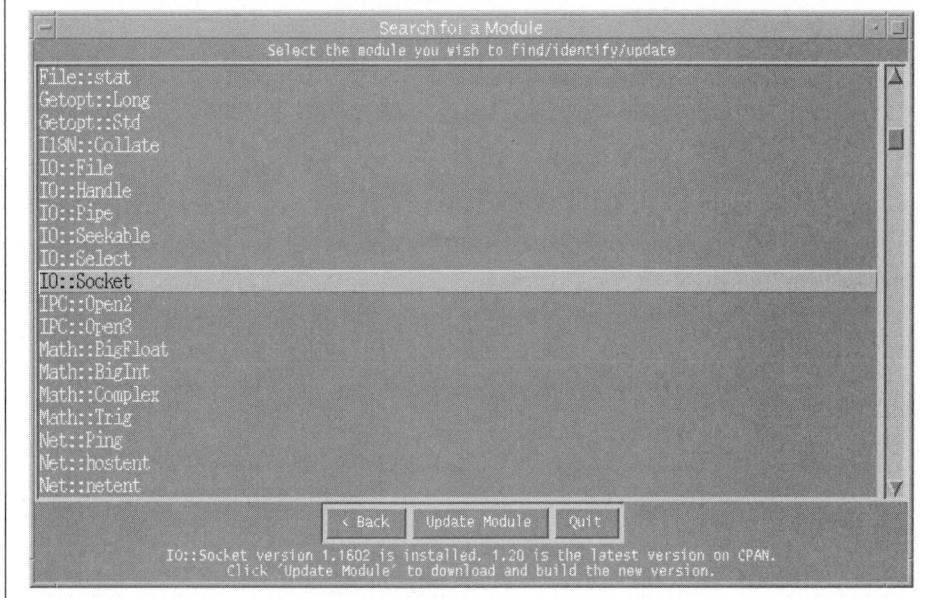

Figure 2-6. The "Search for a Module" screen

If the *Search for a Module* screen indicates that a newer version of the module is available, you can upgrade to the most recent version of the selected module by clicking the *Update Module* button. The setup tool proceeds to download, configure, compile, and install the module from either the CD-ROM or a remote CPAN site, depending upon whether the CD-ROM version is out of date. You can avoid searches of remote CPAN sites by including only the URL of the CD-ROM in the `urllist` configuration parameter, as described in the table shown in the "Starting the Graphical Setup Tool" section earlier in this chapter.

Update module indexes

In order to update your local CPAN index files, click *Update Indexes* on the *Install Perl Modules* screen. The setup tool retrieves the index files from a remote host, if you have specified one in the CPAN configuration, as described in the "Starting the Graphical Setup Tool" section of this chapter.

Installing the Perl Source Code

If the Perl Resource Kit CD-ROM does not contain a precompiled binary for your operating system, or if you wish to build Perl from scratch, you will need to install the Perl source code from the setup tool main menu. To install the source code, you should select the *Install Perl 5.004xx Source* option from the menu and click *Next.* You are prompted to select the directory in which to unpack the source. Follow the instructions included in *"Building Perl from Source"* later in this chapter.

Although a binary version of Perl is included for Sparc Solaris and Linux on Intel, you should install from source if you have a compiler other than GNU C (such as Sun's compiler), since the binary version of Perl included on the CD-ROM is configured for GNU C. If you do not have a C compiler installed, you may still install Perl, but there will be many modules and tools that you cannot install, including JPL.

Installing Software from the CD Manually

If your platform is not supported by the graphical setup tool or if a binary version of Perl is not available for your platform, you can still install software from this CD set without using the graphical setup tool. Before you can install anything else, you will need to have Perl installed. If you already have Perl installed, you can skip directly to the section titled "Installing Modules Using the CD-ROM and a Remote CPAN Site."

Building Perl from Source

If you did not (or were not able to) use the graphical installation tool to install the Perl source, you can install it directly from the CD-ROM. The source code to Perl is included on the CD-ROM in *tar* format, compressed with GNU *zip*. To extract the source, change directory on the local system to the directory of your choice, such as */usr/src*, and issue one of the following commands (either one will create the *perl5.004xx/* directory underneath the current working directory):

For Linux and sites with GNU tar:

```
tar xvfz /cdrom/CPAN/src/latest.tar.gz
```

For systems without GNU tar (you still must have *gzip*):

```
gzip -d -c /cdrom/CPAN/src/latest.tar.gz | tar xvf -
```

You should then change directory to the *perl5.004xx/* directory, and review the *README* and *INSTALL* files. These files will be your guide in case the following instructions do not work for you. Perl has been tested and successfully builds on most Unix systems, as well as on many non-Unix systems. On most Unix systems, the following sequence of commands should build Perl, and are explained in more detail below (note that you must be a root user to install Perl, but for the build process, you do not need to be *root*):

```
# rm -f config.sh
# sh Configure
# make
# make test
# make install
```

Step-by-step: rm -f config.sh

This first step removes any existing configuration file for Perl. When you configure Perl in the next step, the *Configure* script creates a file called *config.sh*. The next time you run the configuration process, it will attempt to use the defaults found in that file, which may override the hints for your operating system. Thus, it's sensible to remove *config.sh* before running *Configure*, especially if you have problems the first time around and this is your second build of Perl.

Step-by-step: sh Configure

This next step runs the *Configure* script, an interactive session in which you are asked many questions. With the exception of one question (see Note), it is best to accept the default answers to these questions, especially the first time you build Perl.

NOTE   During the configuration session, you are asked the following question: "Build a shared *libperl.so*?" The default for this is *no*, but if you are planning to use JPL (the Java/Perl integration tool included with this resource kit), you must answer *yes* here. You must also answer *no* when it asks whether to use the `malloc()` that comes with Perl.

At the end of the configuration process, you will see the following messages:

```
End of configuration questions.

Stripping down executable paths...

Creating config.sh...

If you'd like to make any changes to the config.sh file before I begin
to configure things, do it as a shell escape now (e.g. !vi config.sh).

Press return or use a shell escape to edit config.sh:
```

At this point, you should press Return, after which you will see the following messages:

```
Doing variable substitutions on .SH files...
Extracting Makefile (with variable substitutions)
Extracting cflags (with variable substitutions)
Extracting config.h (with variable substitutions)
Extracting makeaperl (with variable substitutions)
Extracting makedepend (with variable substitutions)
Extracting makedir (with variable substitutions)
Extracting perl.exp
Extracting writemain (with variable substitutions)
Extracting x2p/Makefile (with variable substitutions)
Extracting x2p/cflags (with variable substitutions)

Now you need to generate make dependencies by running "make depend".
You might prefer to run it in background: "make depend > makedepend.out &"
It can take a while, so you might not want to run it right now.

Run make depend now? [y]
```

You should answer *yes* to this question, and wait for the **make depend** process to complete. Then, you may move on the next step, running **make**.

Step-by-step: make

The **make** command processes the *Makefiles* that were generated by the configuration process. Depending on the speed of your machine, this process can take a considerable amount of time. If you chose to build a shared *libperl*, you must set the LD_LIBRARY_PATH environment variable before you run make. The LD_LIBRARY_PATH environment variable is used by the dynamic loader to locate the Perl shared library during certain portions of the make process. Make sure that you are in the same directory in which you ran **sh Configure** and in which you will run **make**, and set LD_LIBRARY_PATH to the current working directory, by issuing the following command in *sh*, *ksh*, or *bash* (note that the quotes shown below are backticks—this will set the LD_LIBRARY_PATH environment variable to the output of the **pwd** command):

```
LD_LIBRARY_PATH=`pwd`
export LD_LIBRARY_PATH
```

The equivalent in *tcsh* or *csh* is shown here:

```
setenv LD_LIBRARY_PATH `pwd`
```

Note that neither of the following are appropriate, since the make process does its work in many subdirectories, and . will always resolve to the current directory:

bash, *sh*, *ksh* (this will not work—use `pwd` as shown earlier):

```
LD_LIBRARY_PATH=.
export LD_LIBRARY_PATH
```

csh, *tcsh* (this will not work—use `` `pwd` `` as shown earlier):

```
setenv LD_LIBRARY_PATH .
```

You may now run the **make** command, and go make a coffee or some soup while you are waiting.

Step-by-step: make test

After the **make** process has run, the next step is to run **make test**, Perl's regression tests. When the tests are complete, you should see the message "All tests successful." If you do not, then you should follow the instructions under "Troubleshooting" later in this chapter.

Step-by-step: make install

This command will install a Perl binary and all of the manpages. When you are done, you can read the online documentation by typing **man perl** or **perldoc perl**. The install step is the only step for which you must be the root user.

Troubleshooting

If the compiled version of Perl fails any of its tests, you may go through the configuration process again, supplying different values for certain questions. There are so many expert-level questions in *Configure*, that it's a good idea to consult sources of higher wisdom, such as the Perl FAQ, mailing list archives, and archives of Usenet postings. The Perl FAQ and mailing list archives are available through *http://www.perl.com/*, and archives of Usenet postings may be found at *http://www.dejanews.com/* or by searching at *http://www.altavista.digital.com/*. The Usenet group *comp.lang.perl.misc* may turn up especially useful information. You may also check *http://perl.oreilly.com/* for setup hints and answers to questions. If all else fails, go back and read the *INSTALL* file that you were supposed to have read earlier, but didn't.

If you believe you have found a genuine problem in building Perl for your platform, you should follow the bug reporting instructions included in the *README* file.

Installing Modules Using the CD-ROM and a Remote CPAN Site

To install modules from the Perl Resource Kit CD-ROM without using the setup tool, use the CPAN module, which is bundled with Perl. The CPAN module offers an interactive shell for installing and updating modules. It includes features for working with remote CPAN sites and can also be configured to use the CD-ROM. In fact, you can use it with both a remote site and the CD-ROM.

To do this, you must include the URL of the CD-ROM's *CPAN* directory in the CPAN `urllist` configuration parameter. The `urllist` configuration parameter is set the first time you run the CPAN shell, and can also be set interactively. Both methods of setting this parameter are discussed below. This URL is a *file://* URL, which points to a path on your local filesystem. This URL should include the full path to the *CPAN* directory on the CD-ROM, such as *file:///cdrom/unixperlre-sourcekit/CPAN* or *file:///cdrom/CPAN*.

Start the CPAN shell with the following command:

```
perl -MCPAN -e shell
```

The first time you run the CPAN tool, you are presented with an interactive configuration session. Part way through the session, you must supply a URL for your favorite CPAN site. This URL sets the `urllist` parameter. This portion of the configuration session is shown below:

```
We need to know the URL of your favorite CPAN site.
Please enter it here:  http://www.perl.com/CPAN

Testing "http://www.perl.com/CPAN" ...

"http://www.perl.com/CPAN" seems to work
```

Next, add the URL of the CD-ROM's *CPAN* directory to the `urllist`. You can do this from within the CPAN shell. *It is critical* that the URL of the CD-ROM appears at the end of the `urllist`, because the **CPAN** module automatically searches any *file://* URLs in the `urllist` first, *except when it is retrieving CPAN indexes* (since CD-ROMs rapidly become out of date and it is essential that the most recent indexes are available). If the *file://* URL appears at the beginning of the `urllist`, the CPAN module will get indexes from there, rather than from the remote CPAN site.

Since the CPAN module automatically tries the next site in the `urllist` in case of a failure, this scheme allows you to get the most out of the CD-ROM. Consider the following scenario: you go to install the module **Foo**, which is currently at version 1.70. However, your CD-ROM contains version 1.68. Since the CPAN indexes come from the remote CPAN site, the CPAN module knows to download version 1.70. It then tries to get that version off the CD-ROM, since all *file://* URLs are tried first. This step, of course, fails, since version 1.70 is not present on the CD-ROM. Next, the CPAN module travels to the next URL in your `urllist`, and tries to get version 1.70, which, of course, succeeds. In the case where the module on the remote CPAN site and the local CD-ROM are the same version, it will use the module on the CD-ROM.

To add the CD-ROM URL to your configuration, start the CPAN shell and use the `o conf urllist push URL` command to push the CD-ROM URL onto the end of the `urllist` and then issue the command o conf commit to write the changes, as shown here:

```
cpan> o conf urllist push file:///cdrom/unixperlresourcekit/CPAN
cpan> o conf commit
commit: wrote /usr/local/lib/perl5/CPAN/Config.pm
```

Keep in mind that if you add any other remote sites to the list, you should move the *file://* URL to the end of the list. You can pop off the last item, add the remote site, and then add the *file://* URL back in, as shown here:

```
cpan> o conf urllist pop
cpan> o conf urllist push ftp://ftp.funet.fi/pub/languages/perl/CPAN
cpan> o conf urllist push file:///cdrom/unixperlresourcekit/CPAN
cpan> o conf commit
commit: wrote /usr/local/lib/perl5/CPAN/Config.pm
```

Of course, a real hacker would just rewrite *Config.pm* using cat.

3

Perlez-Vous Java?
Using JPL

It may be tempting to believe that a massive gulf exists between Perl and Java. While both languages are object-oriented, and bear more than a passing resemblance to C, there seems to be a huge mismatch between the two. For instance, Java is a strongly typed language, unlike Perl. In Perl, you can treat a number as a string, an array as a scalar value, and a hash as an array. This sort of behavior would get you thrown out of Java's high society, to say the least! Further, Java supports method overloading, in that you can have multiple definitions of the same method that are only differentiated by the data types of the method's arguments. Perl's methods will gladly accept any number of arguments, but no overloading is available.

Despite these differences, Perl and Java are willing to cooperate. JPL is Larry Wall's toolkit for creating Java and Perl hybrid applications. It was written from scratch just for the Perl Resource Kit, and it is a preprocessor and run-time module that unites Java and Perl code in the most seamless fashion possible. With JPL, the Perl interpreter can be embedded within Java, and Perl methods can call back into Java, invoking Java methods and accessing Java class and instance fields. In other words, JPL allows you to invoke Java from within Perl, and Perl from within Java. JPL is more than just a link between the two languages; it also provides the syntactic sugar that glues the two languages together in a transparent fashion.

This chapter assumes you have some familiarity with both Perl and Java. To take full advantage of JPL and the material presented in this chapter, you should be familiar with the data types and structures available in both languages, as well as with the mechanisms by which classes are defined and objects are instantiated. The Perl online manual, including the `perldata`, `perlref`, and `perltoot` manpages are good starting points for this sort of information. You may also wish to obtain a copy of *Programming Perl*, by Larry Wall, Randal L. Schwartz, and Tom Christiansen, which provides comprehensive coverage of these and other details of the Perl language.

Installing and Building JPL

The JPL distribution is included on the Resource Kit's CD-ROM in the directory *oreilly/jpl/*. The setup tool has an option to install O'Reilly Extras, including JPL. Selecting the Extras option installs the JPL source code in a directory of your choice. Chapter 2, *Installing the Resource Kit Software*, gives detailed instructions for installing JPL using the setup tool. If you cannot run the setup tool, you may copy the contents of the *oreilly/jpl/* directory to a convenient location. Be sure to preserve the directory structure and permissions when you do that.

NOTE   To use JPL, your Perl *must* have been built as a shared library, and you must be using the system `malloc()`. When you built the version of Perl you plan to use with JPL, make sure that you answered *yes* to the "Build a shared *libperl.so*?" and *no* to the "Do you wish to attempt to use the `malloc` that comes with Perl?" configuration questions. Otherwise, you will need to install and build Perl again, after running the configuration process and answering each question as required. The precompiled versions of Perl from the Perl Resource Kit CD were built as a shared library and use the system `malloc()`, so if you are using one of those distributions, you don't need to worry about these requirements.

To run JPL, you need a fully-functional version of JDK (Java Development Kit) 1.1 or greater. JPL has been tested with Solaris 2.5.1 and Linux 2.0.30, but may work on other operating systems' JDK implementations. The *jpl/* directory includes a subdirectory called *get_jdk*, which contains a script, *get_jdk.pl* that downloads the JDK for your operating system. Make sure you peruse the *README* file in this directory to obtain platform-specific release notes and instructions. Not all platforms are represented in this script, and some versions of the JDK, such as the Irix JDK, require registration and interactive download. For the latest availability of the JDK, including third-party ports such as the Irix JDK, please visit *http://www.javasoft.com/*.

Before you build JPL, make sure that your JDK is in a well-known location, such as */usr/local/java*, */usr/lib/java* or */usr/java*. If your JDK is in none of these locations, set the JAVA_HOME environment variable to the actual location. To build JPL go to the *jpl/* directory and issue the command `install-jpl`. This command begins the compilation and installation of all of the JPL components. This process is self-configuring, except for one interactive step, where it asks you to choose the installation directory for JPL and related components.

After JPL is installed, the **setvars** script is created in the top-level JPL directory you selected when you ran `install-jpl`. You use the **setvars** script to generate environment variable settings for various shells, including *sh*-like shells (*ksh*, *sh*, *bash*), *csh*-like shells (*csh*, *tcsh*) and of course Perl. These environment variables need to be set whenever you are building or executing a JPL application. You can set them each time you start a new shell or you can capture the output and include it in your startup.

To execute **setvars**, you either need to add the location of the top-level JPL directory to your path or to include the full path when invoking **setvars**. You can invoke **setvars** with one of three switches:

```
setvars -sh     # for the sh, bash, or ksh shells
setvars -csh    # for the csh or tcsh shells
setvars -perl   # for Perl
```

You can then capture the output of **setvars** and include the commands in your startup script. To make the variables available in your current shell session, do one of the following:

Bourne Shell:

```
eval `setvars -sh`
or
setvars -sh > .shvars
. .shvars
```

C Shell:

```
eval `setvars -csh`
or
setvars -csh > .cshvars
source .cshvars
```

If you do not include the output of **setvars** in your startup script, you will have to issue one of the commands shown above each time you start a new shell.

Using JPL

Once you have JPL installed and built, the next step is to cover the basics and more of using JPL. To get you started, this section provides a discussion of various concepts and tasks illustrated by examples. You can find the code for the examples used in this section on the Resource Kit's CD-ROM. Follow the general instructions in this section for compiling and running the examples and then work along with the text.

Classes and Objects in JPL

Perl and Java deal with class definitions in a similar fashion. In both languages, collections of classes are organized into packages. In Perl, a definition for a `String` class might reside in the hypothetical Text::String package, while in Java, it would reside in the *java.lang.String* package. Both Perl and Java use the native filesystem to enforce the organization of these packages. In Perl, the String class resides in the source code file *Text/String.pm*, while in Java it resides in the class file *java/lang/String.class*. The actual location of the *Text* or *java* directory depends on the installation, but they must be in a location where the Java or Perl interpreter can find them.

Both languages make use of a special method called a *constructor* to allow the developer to create a new instance of the class. In the case of Perl, all objects are references that have been blessed into being an object. The `bless` operator causes the reference (actually, the item referenced) to know which package it belongs to, allowing it to locate its methods and properties as necessary. A Perl object can be a reference to a scalar variable, array, hash, or subroutine. It is most common to find that the object is a reference to a hash. In practice, the user of the class does not need to be concerned with such details. Within instance methods, the first parameter is the object itself, and the programmer often refers to this with a variable called `$self`. The `$self` variable is automatically created for you in JPL, so you don't need to look for it as you do with regular Perl methods. Not only can you get at Perl methods through this variable, but you can also get at Java methods and fields.

Java hides the details of objects from the developer, which provides a great deal of transparency for working with objects. The Java developer does not have to be concerned with looking for a reference to the object as an argument to instance methods, as you must do with Perl. Like the `$self` reference, Java does support an explicit means of referring to the current object with the `this` identifier. The `this` identifier is automatically available within an instance method. Although Java's approach to class definitions is simple, it can be somewhat restrictive.

Compiling and Running the Examples

The CD-ROM includes examples for this chapter in *oreilly/eg/ch03/*. Each of the examples for this chapter are located in separate subdirectories. The name of the JPL source code file for each example is the same as the directory in which it resides, except for the fact that it has the *.jpl* suffix. For example, the *ArrayExample/* directory has a file called *ArrayExample.jpl*, which contains the array example source code.

To compile each of the examples, you must issue the following commands:

```
perl Makefile.PL
make clean
make
make install
```

The JPL compilation process creates a number of files with the same base file-name as the JPL file. In the case of the array example, these are *ArrayExample.java, ArrayExample.pl, ArrayExample.c, ArrayExample.h, libArrayExample.so,* and *ArrayExample.class*. The name of the shared native library (*libArrayExample.so*) may vary, depending on your operating system's naming convention for shared libraries. Of these files, *ArrayExample.class, libArrayExample.so,* and *ArrayExample.pl* are required to run the application. If you want to experiment with the examples, do not modify any of the intermediate files, as changes are lost when you run **make**. The only file you should edit is the *.jpl* file (*ArrayExample.jpl*) itself.

You can run an example by passing the name of the compiled Java class to the Java interpreter (do not include the *.class* suffix):

```
java ArrayExample
```

With those instructions out of the way, you can work through the following sections using the examples on the CD-ROM.

Defining a Perl Method in a JPL File

JPL's preprocessor needs Perl methods to be defined a little differently than Java methods. For one, they must be declared as a **perl** method and must be enclosed in two sets of curly braces, unlike typical Java methods, which only need one set. Be careful not to use `}}` within your Perl code, since this will confuse the JPL preprocessor. If you must use two curly braces, please insert a space between them.

The *PerlExample/* directory includes the *PerlExample.jpl* file that contains both a Perl and a Java method. Note that the return type (**void**) must be specified for the Perl method, just as in the Java method:

```
/*
 * PerlExample.jpl - a JPL example that compares Java and Perl methods.
 */

public class PerlExample {

    /**
     *
     * A Java method that says hi.
     *
```

```
    */
    void javaExample() {
        System.out.println("    Java says hi!");
    }

    /**
     *
     * A Perl method that says hi.
     *
     */
    perl void plExample() {{
        print "    Perl says hi!\n";
    }}

    /**
     *
     * This method is automatically invoked by the JVM when
     * this compiled class definition is fed to the java
     * interpreter.
     *
     */
    public static void main(String[] argv) {
        PerlExample ex = new PerlExample();

        System.out.println("\n\nNow testing: javaExample()\n");
        ex.javaExample();

        System.out.println("\n\nNow testing: plExample()\n");
        ex.plExample();
    }
}
```

Here is the output of that example:

```
Now testing: javaExample()

    Java says hi!

Now testing: plExample()

    Perl says hi!
```

Working with Primitive Java Data Types and Strings

JPL provides a high degree of transparency for primitive data types and objects of the type *java.lang.String*. Variables having numeric data types such as `int`, `float`, and `double` can be passed to Perl and handled as Perl variables. JPL also freely converts between Java `boolean` and Perl variables, converting `true` to `1` and `false` to `0`, and vice versa. Although `String`s are not primitive data types, JPL converts these to Perl variables automatically as well, so you can use these in your Perl programs with abandon (but see the section "Java Strings and Overloaded Perl Methods," later in this chapter). This simple example, included in the

PrimitiveExample/ subdirectory, sets up some variables and a `String` and passes them to a Perl method. The Perl method displays these values, and also returns a Perl string value, which is converted to a `java.lang.String` object when it is returned to Java:

```
/*
 * PrimitiveExample.jpl - primitive data types and Strings.
 */

public class PrimitiveExample {

    /**
     * An example that prints out primitive data types and a
     * String, and returns a String value.
     */
    perl String primitiveExample(String s, double d, boolean b, byte y) {{

        print qq[    Perl got a string:  "$s"\n];
        print qq[    Perl got a double:   $d\n];
        print qq[    Perl got a boolean:  $b\n];
        print qq[    Perl got a byte:     $y\n];

        return "Thank you!";

    }}

    /**
     * The main() method.
     */
    public static void main(String[] argv) {

        PrimitiveExample ex = new PrimitiveExample();

        // Test out the simple data type and String example.
        //
        System.out.println("\n\nNow testing: primitiveExample()\n");

        String  s = "Hello, World";
        double  d = 1.23456;
        boolean b = true;
        byte    y = -127;

        String result = ex.primitiveExample(s, d, b, y);
        System.out.println("    Result was: " + result);

    }
}
```

Here is the output of this example:

```
Now testing: primitiveExample()

    Perl got a string:  "Hello, World"
    Perl got a double:   1.23456
```

```
Perl got a boolean:  1
Perl got a byte:     -127
Result was: Thank you!
```

Creating Java Objects from Perl

To create a Java object within Perl, you must first issue a **use** statement to import the class definition. This procedure is identical to Perl's own mechanism for importing a class definition before you create an object. In Perl, you must supply the name of the package followed by an optional import list when you issue a **use** statement. In the case of Java classes, your **use** statement will specify the JPL::Class package, and you must supply the fully qualified name of the Java class as the sole value of the import list. Note that the delimiter used in a Java package is a period (full stop), as in **java.awt.Frame**. In Perl, you must specify these packages using Perl's package delimiter, a double colon, as in java::awt::Frame. The following example, which is included in the *ObjectExample/* subdirectory, demonstrates this:

```
/*
 * ObjectExample.jpl - An example that shows how to create a Java object
 * from within a Perl method.
 */

public class ObjectExample {

    /**
     * An example that creates a Java object and tells us
     * something about it.
     */
    perl void objectExample() {{

        # Import the class definition.
        #
        use JPL::Class 'java::awt::Frame';

        # Create a new instance of the Frame.
        #
        my $f = new java::awt::Frame;

        # What does Perl think of this Frame?
        #
        print "   Got a ", ref $f, "\n";

    }}

    /**
     * The main() method.
     */
    public static void main(String[] argv) {
```

```
        ObjectExample ex = new ObjectExample();

        // Invoke the object construction example.
        //
        System.out.println("\n\nNow testing: objectExample()\n");
        ex.objectExample();

    }

}
```

When you execute this program, it will display the following output:

```
Now testing: objectExample()

Got a java::awt::Frame
```

Invoking a Java Method from Perl

To invoke most Java methods other than **new()** (as was demonstrated in the
previous example), you need to look up the method signature. A method signature is a combination of method name, argument types, and return type that is
used by Java to determine which method you actually want to invoke. Java
supports method overloading, so you can have more than one method with the
same name, but each method is differentiated by the number and types of arguments, as well as the return value. Java does not support method overloading
with respect to return values, but it needs to know the type of the return value in
order to find the method.

If you are invoking a method which does not have any arguments or return value,
you do not need to look up the method, and you can invoke it directly. This is
the case with the **new()** method, despite the fact that it returns an object. Internally, the method signature of the constructor specifies that it returns a void data
type. Constructors may take arguments, however, and you can look up a
constructor method if you choose not to use the default **new()**. This situation is
covered below, in the section titled "Inner Classes and Alternate Constructors."

You can use the **getmeth()** function to look up a method. The **getmeth()** function is exported into the namespace of all JPL programs. Its first argument is the
name of the method, followed by an array reference containing a list of types
corresponding to the arguments that the method requires. This array can be a mix
of primitive data types, and fully qualified class definitions such as
java.lang.String. The argument list is followed by an array reference containing a
single value: the type of the return value.

For methods which either take no arguments or are declared **void** (that is, returns
no value), you may include an empty array reference. Here is an example that

looks up the method signature for setSize(int, int). Since this method is declared void, its return type array is empty:

```
my $setSize = getmeth('setSize', ['int','int'], []);
```

In case you're interested, the method signature is setSize__II__V. Keep in mind that the purpose of the getmeth() function is to shield you from complex method signatures. Unless you have a taste for pain, you shouldn't need to concern yourself with them.

Notice that the call to getmeth() doesn't specify a class name. This is because getmeth() is not in the business of returning actual references to a method, rather it merely returns a signature for the method. When you invoke the method for real, Java knows both the method signature and the class, since the object you use to invoke the method belongs to a given class. Using this information, Java can find the correct method. You invoke the method using the same syntax you normally use in Perl, except you supply the string with the method signature instead of the method name:

```
$f->$setSize(100, 100);
```

The *MethodExample/* subdirectory contains a simple example that creates a Frame, sets its size and title, and then prints out the title that it set. There are three method invocations in this example: void setSize(int, int), void SetTitle(java.lang.String), and String getTitle(). Note that the Frame is never displayed on the screen, it's just created and the methods are invoked to set and retrieve its properties. This example also displays the method signature for each method it looks up, something that you may find either informative, frightening, or both:

```
/* .
 *
 * MethodExample.jpl - This example shows how you can invoke Java methods
 * from within Perl.
 *
 */

public class MethodExample {

    /*
     * A Perl method that invokes some Java methods.
     */
    perl void methodExample() {{

        # Create a new instance of a Frame.
        #
        use JPL::Class 'java::awt::Frame';
        my $f = new java::awt::Frame;
```

```
      # Look up the method signature for setSize(int, int).
      #
      my $setSize = getmeth('setSize', ['int','int'], []);
      print "   Method signature for setSize:\n";
      print "       $setSize\n";

      # Look up the method signature for setTitle(String).
      #
      my $setTitle = getmeth('setTitle', ['java.lang.String'], []);
      print "   Method signature for setTitle:\n";
      print "       $setTitle\n";

      # Look up the method signature for String getTitle().
      #
      my $getTitle = getmeth('getTitle', [], ['java.lang.String']);
      print "   Method signature for getTitle:\n";
      print "       $getTitle\n\n";

      # Set the size of the Frame.
      #
      $f->$setSize(100, 100);

      # Set the title of the Frame.
      #
      $f->$setTitle("Sample Title 1");

      # Now, get the title and print it out.
      #
      my $title = $f->$getTitle();
      print "   Title is now: $title\n";

   }}

   /**
    * The main() method.
    */
   public static void main(String[] argv) {

      MethodExample ex = new MethodExample();

      // A Perl method that invokes some Java methods.
      //
      System.out.println("\n\nNow testing: methodExample()\n");
      ex.methodExample();

   }

}
```

Here is the output of this example program:

```
Now testing: methodExample()

   Method signature for setSize:
       setSize__II__V
```

```
Method signature for setTitle:
    setTitle__Ljava_lang_String_2__V
Method signature for getTitle:
    getTitle____Ljava_lang_String_2

Title is now: Sample Title 1
```

Accessing Java Fields from Perl

A Java class definition can include fields (variables or objects) that are accessible from other methods in the class. JPL provides a means to access these from within Perl by creating a method that corresponds to each field. For example, if your Java class definition includes a `String` called `str_field`, you will be able to access it within a Perl method using `$self->str_field()`. If you invoke this method without supplying an argument, the field is returned to you. If you supply an argument to this method, the field is changed; in the case of a variable, it is reassigned, but in the case of an object, the reference to the original is destroyed and a new one created. Note that this does not guarantee that the original object will be immediately destroyed, but it will no longer be available through that identifier.

The following example shows a method, `fieldExample()`, which does different things with three fields that are defined within the Java class definition: the `str_field` is changed from `lumpy gravy` to `Hello!` and the value of an integer field is displayed. Also, two elements are added to the `vec_field`, which is a *java.util.Vector* (a shrinkable and growable array) object.

The *FieldExample* example also includes the `clobberExample()` method, which shows how you can use the field access feature of JPL to overwrite fields that are defined in the Java class. Here is the entire example:

```
/*
 *
 * FieldExample.jpl - An example that demonstrates how to access Java fields
 * from within Perl.
 *
 */

import java.util.Vector;

public class FieldExample {

    // Some fields that we'll access from Perl.
    //
    int    int_field = 1;
    String str_field = "lumpy gravy";
    Vector vec_field = new Vector();
```

```perl
/**
 *
 * This Perl method demonstrates how the Java object's fields can be
 * accessed.
 *
 */
perl void fieldExample() {{

    use JPL::Class 'java::util::Vector';

    # Change the value of the String field by passing a String argument
    # to the method that corresponds to that field.
    #
    print qq[     \$self->str_field is "], $self->str_field, qq[".\n];
    $self->str_field("Hello!");
    print qq[     \$self->str_field was changed to "], $self->str_field,
        qq[".\n];

    # Invoke the int_field() method, which returns the int_field
    # variable, a field belonging to the Java object.
    #
    my $int_field = $self->int_field;

    # Display the value of int_field.
    #
    print "    int_field = $int_field.\n";

    # Do the same for the str_field and vec_field.
    #
    my $str_field = $self->str_field;
    my $vec_field = $self->vec_field;

    # Add the str_field and some other string to the Vector.
    #
    $addElement = getmeth('addElement', ['java.lang.Object'], []);
    $vec_field->$addElement($str_field);
    $vec_field->$addElement("yet another string");

    # Now, let's invoke a method that belongs to the Vector, but invoke
    # it through a call to the vec_field() method that JPL creates for
    # us.
    #
    my $size = getmeth('size', [], ['int']);
    my $vector_size = $self->vec_field->$size();

    print "    The size of the Vector is now: $vector_size.\n";

}}

/**
 *
 * This Perl method demonstrates how the Java object's fields can be
 * clobbered.
 *
```

```
    */
    perl void clobberExample() {{

        # What's the current size of the Vector?
        #
        my $size = getmeth('size', [], ['int']);
        my $vector_size = $self->vec_field->$size();
        print "    Vector's size was $vector_size.\n";

        # Clobber the old Vector with a new one.
        #
        $self->vec_field( new java::util::Vector );

        # It's a different Vector now, and has a size of 0.
        #
        $vector_size = $self->vec_field->$size();
        print "    Vector's size is now $vector_size.\n";

    }}

    /**
     * The main() method.
     */
    public static void main(String[] argv) {

        FieldExample ex = new FieldExample();

        // Call Perl methods that demonstrate means of accessing fields
        // belonging to the Java object.
        //
        System.out.println("\n\nNow Testing: fieldExample()\n");
        ex.fieldExample();

        System.out.println("\n\nNow Testing: clobberExample()\n");
        ex.clobberExample();

    }

}
```

Here is the output of this example:

```
Now Testing: fieldExample()

    $self->str_field is "lumpy gravy".
    $self->str_field was changed to "Hello!".
    int_field = 1.
    The size of the Vector is now: 2.

Now Testing: clobberExample()

    Vector's size was 2.
    Vector's size is now 0.
```

Casting Java Objects Within Perl

There are times you will need a Java object to appear to be an object of another type. For example, you may have a custom component that needs the Java object to behave as though it were an instance of its superclass. Or perhaps you have added an element to a `Vector`. When you retrieve that object with `elementAt()`, you don't get an object of the same type as the one you put in. Instead, you get a *java.lang.Object*. To get back the original object type, you must use Java's casting mechanism. In Java, you accomplish this by prefixing the object's identifier with the name of the class to which you wish to cast it, as in:

```
String s = (java.lang.String) v.elementAt(0);
```

Within Perl methods, you can accomplish the same thing using the two-argument form of `bless()`. The first argument is the object you want to cast and the second is the name of the class you want to cast it to. You will need to import the class with a **use** statement before you **bless** the object, as in:

```
use JPL::Class 'java::util::Random';
bless $obj, "java::util::Random";
```

The following example is in the *CastExample/* subdirectory and includes a Java method and a Perl method demonstrating how casting is performed within their respective languages:

```
/*
 * CastExample.jpl - casting from one class to another.
 */
import java.util.Vector;

public class CastExample {

    /**
     * A Java casting example.
     */
    void javaCastExample() {

        // Create a Vector and add a String to it.
        //
        Vector v = new Vector();
        v.addElement( new String("Hello") );

        // Get the String back.
        //
        String s = (java.lang.String) v.elementAt(0);

        // Print out the String.
        //
        System.out.println("    The Vector said " + s + ".");

    }
```

```perl
/**
 * This example shows the use of bless() to cast from one Java class to
 * another.
 */
perl void castExample() {{

    use JPL::Class 'java::util::Vector';
    use JPL::Class 'java::util::Random';

    # Create a Vector object.
    #
    my $v = new java::util::Vector;

    # Add a random number generator to the empty Vector.
    #
    my $addElement = getmeth('addElement', ['java.lang.Object'], []);
    $v->$addElement(new java::util::Random);

    # Now, how do we deal with the object we just put in the Vector? If
    # we retrieve it, we get a java.lang.Object, not a java.util.Random
    # object.
    #
    my $elementAt = getmeth('elementAt', ['int'], ['java.lang.Object']);
    my $obj = $v->$elementAt(0);
    print "    \$obj is a ", ref $obj, ".\n";

    # Use bless() to turn this Object into a java.util.Random object,
    # so we can call its nextFloat() method.
    #
    bless $obj, "java::util::Random";
    print "    \$obj has been cast to a ", ref $obj, ".\n";

    # Call the object's nextFloat() method, and print out the value of
    # the result.
    #
    my $nextFloat = getmeth('nextFloat', [], ['float']);
    my $random_float = $obj->$nextFloat();
    print "    got random number: $random_float.\n";

}}

/**
 * The main() method.
 */
public static void main(String[] argv) {

    CastExample ex = new CastExample();

    // Invoke the casting demonstration method.
    //
    System.out.println("\n\nNow Testing: castExample()\n");
    ex.castExample();
```

```
        // Invoke the Java casting example.
        //
        System.out.println("\n\nNow Testing: javaCastExample()\n");
        ex.javaCastExample();

    }

}
```

Here is the output that is produced when you run this example:

```
Now Testing: castExample()

    $obj is a java::lang::Object.
    $obj has been cast to a java::util::Random.
    got random number: 0.54251229763031.

Now Testing: javaCastExample()

    The Vector said Hello.
```

Careful with That Ax, Eugene—Object Trouncing 101

When you pass an object to a method, you are merely passing a reference to that object. This allows you to manipulate the object within a method, while being sure that it's the same object that other methods will be working with. However, if you attempt to assign a new object to the identifier, you will only trounce your local reference; when you return from the method, the original is intact, as shown in the following example, from the *TrounceExample/* directory:

```
/**
 * TrounceExample.jpl - shows that you're not always trouncing objects when
 * you think you are.
 */

public class TrounceExample {

    perl void trounceMethod(StringBuffer strbuff) {{

        use JPL::Class "java::lang::StringBuffer";

        # Look up the method signatures for a few of the methods we'll be
        # using.
        #
        my $setLength = getmeth('setLength', ['int'], []);
        my $toString  = getmeth('toString', [], ['java.lang.String']);
        my $append = getmeth('append', ['java.lang.String'],
                            ['java.lang.StringBuffer']);
```

```
    # Set the length of the StringBuffer to 0, and append a new String
    # of text to it.
    #
    $strbuff->$setLength(0);
    $strbuff->$append("This is the new value.");

    # Here, we replace the local reference to the StringBuffer with a
    # new StringBuffer, and append some text to it. However, this does
    # not replace the strbuff object back in the Java method that
    # invoked this method.
    #
    $strbuff = new java::lang::StringBuffer;
    $strbuff->$append("Or is this the new value?");

    # Let's see the current value of the StringBuffer.
    #
    my $str = $strbuff->$toString();
    print "    New value as the Perl method sees it: '$str'.\n";

}}

/**
 * The main() method.
 */
public static void main (String[] argv) {

    TrounceExample ex = new TrounceExample();

    System.out.println("\n\nNow testing: trounceExample()\n");

    // Create a StringBuffer with an initial value.
    //
    StringBuffer strbuff =
        new StringBuffer("This is the original value.");

    // Display the StringBuffer.
    //
    System.out.println("    Original value: '" + strbuff + "'.");

    // Execute the Perl method.
    //
    ex.trounceMethod(strbuff);

    // Display the contents of the StringBuffer at this point.
    //
    System.out.println("    New value as Java sees it: '" +
                        strbuff + "'.");

    }

}
```

As you can see from the output shown below, the Perl method is pretty confident that it knows the value of the `StringBuffer`, but Java has another opinion altogether:

```
Now testing: trounceExample()

    Original value: 'This is the original value.'.
    New value as the Perl method sees it: 'Or is this the new value?'.
    New value as Java sees it: 'This is the new value.'.
```

Inner Classes and Alternate Constructors

Inner classes are a feature of Java that was introduced with version 1.1. Inner classes allow you to define a class within another class, and are used when it does not make sense to define a top-level class for a simple helper class, such as an event handler. While JPL does not supply any direct support for working with inner classes, you can use a wrapper method to return a new instance of an inner class to a Perl method.

In the following example, two inner classes are defined, both of which are event handlers. The first, `buttonWatcher`, is an implementation of the `ActionListener` interface. The second inner class is `closeEventHandler`, which extends the `WindowAdapter` class. The `buttonWatcher` responds to mouse presses on the `Button`, and the `closeEventHandler` responds to any sort of window closing event, such as a click on a Close Window button, or the selection of the Close option from a window menu.

The class definitions are immediately followed by wrappers: `getbuttonWatcher()` and `getcloseEventHandler()`. These wrappers not only create instances of the corresponding inner class, but perform a cast operation on each before returning the object to the caller. This action causes the `buttonWatcher` to be cast to an `ActionListener`, and the `closeEventHandler` to be cast to a `WindowAdapter`. After the Perl method uses the wrapper classes to create these event handlers, it invokes the appropriate method to add each event handler to the `Button` (`addActionListener()`) and the `Frame` (`addWindowListener()`).

This example also demonstrates how you can use an alternate constructor when you instantiate an object. In the case of *java.awt.Frame*, the default constructor, `Frame()`, constructs a `Frame` with a default window title. An alternate constructor is also available so you can invoke the constructor with a `String` argument, which is used as the `Frame`'s window title.

Except for the type of the return value, you can treat a constructor as you would any other method by using the `getmeth()` function. Instead of specifying a

Frame as the return type, however, you should specify **void** (using a **null** list) as the return type, as in:

```
getmeth('new', ['java.lang.String'], []);
```

The method signature for a constructor specifies **void** as the return type, regardless of the type of object being constructed. Figure 3-1 shows this example in action.

Figure 3-1. Results of inner examples

Here is the source code for this example, which you can find in the *InnerExample/* directory:

```
/**
 *
 * InnerExample.jpl - accessing inner classes.
 *
 */
import java.awt.event.*;

public class InnerExample {

    /**
     * An instance of this inner class will be used to respond to action
     * events from the button.
     */
    class buttonWatcher implements ActionListener {
        public void actionPerformed( ActionEvent e) {
            System.out.println("Please do not press this button again.");
        }
    }

    /**
     * This inner class will respond to events generated by the closing of
     * the Frame.
     */
    class closeEventHandler extends WindowAdapter {
        public void windowClosing(WindowEvent e) {
            System.exit(0);
        }
    }

    /**
     * A wrapper method to let the Perl method get an instance of an inner
     * class, in this case a buttonWatcher.
     */
```

```perl
public ActionListener getbuttonWatcher() {
    return (ActionListener) new buttonWatcher();
}

/**
 * A wrapper method to let the Perl method get an instance of
 * closeEventHandler.
 */
public WindowListener getcloseEventHandler() {
    return (WindowListener) new closeEventHandler();
}

/**
 * This method creates a Button and a Frame, and associates them with
 * event handlers that are implemented as inner classes.
 */
perl void awtMethod() {{

    # Import the classes that we'll be using in this method.
    #
    use JPL::Class "java::awt::Frame";
    use JPL::Class "java::awt::FlowLayout";
    use JPL::Class "java::awt::Button";

    # Method lookups for the methods we need to use.
    #
    my $setLayout = getmeth('setLayout', ['java.awt.LayoutManager'], []);
    my $setLabel  = getmeth('setLabel', ['java.lang.String'], []);
    my $setSize   = getmeth('setSize', ['int', 'int'], []);
    my $addActionListener = getmeth('addActionListener',
                                    ['java.awt.event.ActionListener'], []);
    my $add = getmeth('add', ['java.awt.Component'],
                      ['java.awt.Component']);
    my $getbuttonWatcher = getmeth('getbuttonWatcher', [],
                                   ['java.awt.event.ActionListener']);
    my $getcloseEventHandler = getmeth('getcloseEventHandler', [],
                                       ['java.awt.event.WindowListener']);
    my $addWindowListener = getmeth('addWindowListener',
                                    ['java.awt.event.WindowListener'], []);

    # Instantiate a Frame, but use the constructor that takes a window
    # title as an argument.
    #
    my $new_with_title = getmeth('new', ['java.lang.String'], []);
    $f = java::awt::Frame->$new_with_title("AWT Sample");

    # Get a new FlowLayout, and use it as the layout manager for the
    # Frame.
    #
    $fl = new java::awt::FlowLayout;
    $f->$setLayout( $fl );

    # Instantiate a new button and set its label to "Press Me!"
    #
```

```
my $button = new java::awt::Button;
$button->$setLabel("Press Me!");

# Get a new buttonWatcher using the wrapper method
# getbuttonWatcher(), and add it to the button as an
# ActionListener.
#
$al = $self->$getbuttonWatcher();
$button->$addActionListener($al);

# Add the button to the Frame.
#
$f->$add($button);

# Add an event handler to handle the window closing event.
#
my $wl = $self->$getcloseEventHandler();
$f->$addWindowListener( $wl );

# Pick a size for the Frame that lets us see the button and the
# title.
#
$f->$setSize(200, 60);

# Show the Frame.
#
$f->show();

}}

/**
 * The main() method.
 */
public static void main (String[] argv) {

    InnerExample ex = new InnerExample();

    System.out.println("\n\nNow testing: awtExample()\n");

    // Execute the Perl method.
    //
    ex.awtMethod();

}

}
```

Passing and Returning Primitive Arrays

JPL provides facilities that allow you to easily move array data between Perl and Java. While this facility is not implemented as transparently as other features of JPL, it does make it possible to work with arrays. You can pass an array into a

Perl method as an argument, access an array that is an instance or class field, and return arrays from Perl methods.

JPL does not automatically convert Java arrays to Perl arrays. When an array is passed into a Perl method, or when you retrieve an array that is an instance field, the array appears to be a scalar value. To access the elements of a Java array, you need to use the *GetPimitiveTypeArrayElements*() JNI function, substituting the name of the primitive type of the array for *PrimitiveType*, such as Int, Char, Double, etc. This technique is shown below:

```
perl void showArray(int[] int_array) {{

    # Get the values of all the array elements, using the
    # GetIntArrayElements() JNI function.
    #
    my @values = GetIntArrayElements($int_array);
}
```

You may also declare a Perl method as returning an array type. At the end of the method, you must return a reference to an array, as in the following examples:

```
return \@array;
return [1, 2, 3, 4];
```

JPL also supports a transparent means of converting Perl strings to arrays of Java primitive types. To take advantage of this, you need to declare your return type in the Perl method, and simply return the string. It is automatically converted to a Java array of the desired primitive type.

The following example program, which is in the *ArrayExample/* directory, includes four methods. The first method, showArray(), is a Perl method that takes an array of integers as an argument, and displays them. This method also shows the use of the JNI function GetArrayLength(). The second example, showInstanceArray(), is a Perl method that accesses a char[] array defined as an instance field. Note the use of pack() to convert the numeric values into ASCII characters. The third method, getArray() is a Perl method that returns an array of randomly generated double values to Java. Finally, the getBytes() method returns a Perl string as an array of byte values:

```
/*
 * ArrayExample.jpl - a JPL example that demonstrates some array techniques.
 */

public class ArrayExample {

    // An instance array.
    //
    char[] char_array = {'a', 'm', 'z'};
```

```
/**
 * The constructor.
 */
public ArrayExample () {

    // Call a Perl method to display an array of integers.
    //
    System.out.println("\nNow testing: showArray()\n");
    int[] int_array = {1, 2, 3};
    showArray(int_array);

    // Invoke a Perl method to display the char_array.
    //
    System.out.println("\nNow testing: showInstanceArray()\n");
    showInstanceArray();

    // Get an array of doubles from Perl
    //
    System.out.println("\nNow testing: getArray()\n");
    double[] dbl_array = getArray();

    // Display the array.
    //
    for (int i = 0; i < dbl_array.length; i++) {
        System.out.println("    dbl_array[" + i + "] = " + dbl_array[i]);
    }

    // Get an array of bytes from Perl.
    //
    System.out.println("\nNow testing: getBytes()\n");
    byte[] byte_array = getBytes();

    // Create a String from the byte array.
    //
    String byteString = new String(byte_array);

    // Print the String.
    //
    System.out.println("    " + byteString);

}

/**
 * A Perl method that displays an array that was passed to it.
 */
perl void showArray(int[] int_array) {{

    # Get the values of all the array elements, using the
    # GetIntArrayElements() JNI function.
    #
    my @values = GetIntArrayElements($int_array);

    # Loop from the first to the last element the easy way.
    #
```

```perl
    my $i = 0;
    print "    Looping the easy way:\n";
    foreach my $value (@values) {
        print "    int_array[$i]=$value\n";
        $i++;
    }

    # Loop from the first to the last element. This method, while not
    # the easy way, does show the use of GetArrayLength().
    #
    my $length = GetArrayLength($int_array);
    print "\n    Looping the not-so-easy way:\n";
    for (my $i = 0; $i < $length; $i++) {

        # Get the current value of the array element from the @values
        # array created earlier, and print out the value.
        #
        my $value = shift @values;
        print "    int_array[$i]=$value\n";

    }

}}


/**
 * A Perl method that displays an instance array.
 */
perl void showInstanceArray() {{

    # Get the values of all the array elements, using the
    # GetCharArrayElements() JNI function.
    #
    my @values = GetCharArrayElements($self->char_array());

    # Loop from the first to the last element, printing out each element.
    #
    my $length = GetArrayLength($self->char_array());
    for (my $i = 0; $i < $length; $i++) {

        my $value = shift @values;

        # Since the char values are arriving as numbers, we need to do
        # a little conversion to get the characters themselves.
        #
        print "    char_array[$i]=", chr($value), "\n";

    }

}}


/**
 * A Perl method that returns an array of double values.
 */
```

```
perl double[] getArray() {{

    # Generate 10 random numbers and push them onto an array.
    #
    my @retarray;
    for (1..10) {
        push @retarray, rand 255;
    }

    # Return the array.
    #
    return \@retarray;

}}

/**
 * A Perl method that returns a string, which is automatically
 * converted into an array of byte values.
 */
perl byte[] getBytes() {{

    # Return a String
    #
    return "Hello, world\n";

}}

/**
 * The main() method.
 */
public static void main(String[] argv) {
    ArrayExample ex = new ArrayExample();
}
}
```

Here is the output that is generated by running this example:

```
Now testing: showArray()

    Looping the easy way:
    int_array[0]=1
    int_array[1]=2
    int_array[2]=3

    Looping the not-so-easy way:
    int_array[0]=1
    int_array[1]=2
    int_array[2]=3

Now testing: showInstanceArray()

    char_array[0]=a
    char_array[1]=m
    char_array[2]=z
```

```
Now testing: getArray()

        dbl_array[0] = 208.37814331054688
        dbl_array[1] = 192.23831176757812
        dbl_array[2] = 162.1142578125
        dbl_array[3] = 26.933441162109375
        dbl_array[4] = 246.097412109375
        dbl_array[5] = 138.34808349609375
        dbl_array[6] = 138.643798828125
        dbl_array[7] = 14.902496337890625
        dbl_array[8] = 17.6806640625
        dbl_array[9] = 113.16558837890625

Now testing: getBytes()

        Hello, world
```

Developing and Deploying Your Own JPL Applications

With the basics covered and some practice with the preceding examples, you can embark on creating and using your own JPL applications. To give you a hand, we've included a sample JPL application on the CD-ROM. The *Sample/* directory in the top-level JPL directory contains a sample JPL application, as well as a generic JPL *Makefile.PL*. As with the examples shown earlier in this chapter, you must run the *Makefile.PL* through the Perl interpreter with the command **perl Makefile.PL**. This step generates a *Makefile* based on your JPL, Java, and Perl configuration and shields you from having to know all the locations of the various components.

NOTE   Before you generate the *Makefile*, and before you attempt to build
              or run your application, please follow the instructions for using the
              setvars script to prepare your JPL environment given in "Using JPL,"
              earlier in this chapter.

The generic *Makefile.PL* included in the *Sample/* subdirectory assumes that the name of your *.jpl* file is the same as the subdirectory the *Makefile.PL* and *.jpl* file are in. So, if you wish to build a JPL application called **FooBar**, then you should perform the following steps:

1. Prepare your JPL environment with the *setvars* script.

2. Create a subdirectory called *FooBar/*.

3. Copy the *Makefile.PL* from the *Sample* subdirectory into the *FooBar/* subdirectory.

4. Write the *FooBar.jpl* program.

5. Generate your *Makefile* with the command `perl Makefile.PL`.

6. Build your application with the command `make`.

7. Install it with the command `make install`.

8. Finally, run your application with `java FooBar`.

After you have compiled the final version of the application, you only need to perform step 1 and step 8 each time you want to run it.

JPL Known Issues

This section enumerates and explains the few limitations we have encountered with JPL and provides workarounds wherever possible. Because Java is evolving as a language, virtual machine, and API, there are areas that have not yet been perfected, and some that will eventually be perfected. With this in mind, it should not be surprising that trouble areas exist.

JNI I/O Bug

The Solaris version of the JDK relies on a user-level thread package (Green Threads) rather than native Solaris threads. In order for Java to cooperate with this thread package, a number of system calls are overridden by *libjava.so*. As a result, the Java Native Interface (JNI), on which JPL (and other embedded Java solutions) relies, has demonstrated problems with certain Perl modules. Note that JavaSoft is developing a release of the JDK that makes use of native Solaris threads. This should eliminate these problems when it is released.

In particular, database modules that rely on socket-based calls to retrieve data may have problems with JPL. It has been found that the DBD::mSQL, DBD::mySQL, and DBD::Pg DBI drivers are susceptible to this. Other DBI drivers or database APIs may exhibit this problem, as well.

Signal Handlers

Use of a signal handler that intercepts the alarm signal may result in Java's internal alarms not being received properly. As a result, you may receive the message "Alarm Clock," followed by the termination of your program. Whenever possible, you should disable the use of alarm signal handlers, as well as `alarm()`.

If you are using the LWP::UserAgent, you can easily disable the use of the alarm signal handler and `alarm()` for timeouts, as in:

```
use LWP::UserAgent;
$ua=new LWP::UserAgent or die "Could not connect to server!\n";
$ua->use_alarm(0);
```

Java Strings and Overloaded Perl Methods

Some Perl modules, such as HTTP::Request, implement a sort of method over-loading by checking the constructor arguments to determine whether they are simple strings or references. In the case of HTTP::Request, the constructor accepts a URL as one of its arguments. The URL can either be a string containing the URL, or it can be a URI::URL object.

Here's where JPL has problems: if you get the URL from a Java method or instance field, it is considered an object (java::lang::String) rather than a plain old string. However, since JPL overloads the object in such a way that it can be used in places where strings can be used, this is usually completely transparent to the developer. But, if you have some code that uses the `ref` function to determine whether something is a reference, it's going to think your Java string is a reference. Here's the code from the `url()` method in HTTP::Request where this is a problem (the `url()` method is invoked within the HTTP::Request constructor):

```
if (!defined $url) {
    # that's ok
} elsif (ref $url) {
    $url = $url->abs;
} else {
    eval {  $url = URI::URL->new($url); };
    $url = undef if $@;
}
```

If you invoke the constructor using the following bit of code, HTTP::Request will think the string is a URI::URL object:

```
# Get the URL from the textfield.
#
$url = $self->tf->$getText();

# use the LWP::UserAgent module and create a new instance of it.
#
use LWP::UserAgent;
my $ua = new LWP::UserAgent;

# Create the request object.
#
$request = new HTTP::Request('GET', $url);
```

After HTTP::Request determines incorrectly that it is a URI::URL object, it tries to invoke the **abs()** method, which fails, since that method is not defined for *java.lang.String*. However, you can force it to become a Perl string by enclosing $url in quotes:

```
$request = new HTTP::Request('GET', "$url");
```

The following example demonstrates a case where this becomes an issue, but includes the workaround. It displays a **Frame** with a text input field and a **Button**. You may type a URL into the field, and when you press the *Fetch* button, it will download the resource specified in the URL and then display it in the terminal window from which you started the program. This example is included in the *StringRefProblem/* directory, in the file *StringRefProblem.jpl*:

```
/*
 * StringRefProblem.jpl - Strings that you get from Java in JPL aren't really
 * Perl strings - they are references. However, they are overloaded in such a
 * way so as to yield their string value in contexts where the value is
 * needed. Some Perl modules (HTTP::Request, for example) implement
 * overloading by checking certain arguments to see if they are references
 * or not. Since a java::lang::String object will appear to be a reference
 * in the opinion of the 'ref' operator, this causes problems unless you
 * implement the workaround included in this program.
 */
import java.awt.*;
import java.awt.event.*;

public class StringRefProblem {

    Frame f;        // A Frame to show the GUI components.
    TextField tf;   // A text field for the URL.
    Button b;       // A button to perform the fetch action.

    /**
     * The default constructor.
     */
    public StringRefProblem() {

        // Instantiate the new Frame and give it a layout manager.
        //
        f = new Frame();
        f.setLayout(new FlowLayout());

        // Create a text field for the user to supply a URL and add it to
        // the Frame.
        //
        tf = new TextField(64);
        f.add(tf);

        // Add a fetch button, give it an action listener, and add it to
        // the Frame.
        //
```

```
        b = new Button("Fetch");
        b.addActionListener( new buttonAction() );
        f.add(b);

        // Pack and show the Frame.
        //
        f.pack();
        f.show();
    }

/**
 * This actionlistener will invoke the Perl method fetchurl() when
 * someone clicks the button, and will then exit.
 */
class buttonAction implements ActionListener {
    public void actionPerformed ( ActionEvent e ) {
        fetchurl();
        System.exit(0);
    }
}

/**
 * A Perl method to fetch a URL and display the result.
 */
perl void fetchurl() {{

    # Lookup the getText() method.
    #
    my $getText = getmeth('getText', [], ['java.lang.String']);

    # Get the contents of the textfield, which holds the URL.
    #
    use JPL::Class 'java::awt::TextField';
    $url = $self->tf->$getText();

    # use the LWP::UserAgent module and create a new instance of it.
    #
    use LWP::UserAgent;
    my $ua = new LWP::UserAgent;

    # This avoids the alarm() bug with JPL.
    #
    $ua->use_alarm(0);

    # Create a new request object. Note how the $url is enclosed in
    # quotes. This causes it to be evaluated and turned into a Plain
    # Old String Variable before being sent to the Request
    # constructor. Otherwise, when the constructor passes the url to
    # the HTTP::Request->url() method, it thinks the string is a
    # reference, and assumes that it is a URI::URL object. This will
    # cause the program to die on the call to URI::URL->abs(), which
    # is a method not present in java::lang::String.
    #
```

```
            # You can uncomment the next line and then comment out the one that
            # follows if you would like to "taste the pain."
            #
            # $request = new HTTP::Request('GET', $url);
            $request = new HTTP::Request('GET', "$url");

            # Make the request, and display the content.
            #
            $response = $ua->request($request);
            print $response->content();

        }}

        /**
         * The main() method.
         */
        public static void main(String[] argv) {
            StringRefProblem f = new StringRefProblem();
        }
    }
```

Happy JPLing!

The examples in this chapter were designed to address many of the common issues you will encounter as you develop with JPL. It is by no means a complete reference, since this chapter is supplemented by Appendix A, *JPL Reference*. Although this chapter provides enough background information on JPL to aid in your understanding of the chapters that follow, Appendix A is organized as a reference, and may help you as you work through examples in this book. Both this chapter and Appendix A will definitely come in handy when you are building JPL applications of your own!

4

In this chapter:
- *Using and Abusing
  AWT via JPL*
- *Sample Application:
  An Interface to an
  FTP Search Server*
- *What Next?*

Going All AWT:
Using the Java
Abstract Window
Toolkit with Perl

If we were to use a wedding metaphor to describe the nuptials between Perl and Java, then JPL applications that implement the Abstract Window Toolkit (AWT) would be infant stepchildren. The AWT is a collection of Java packages that enables a programmer to describe in broad strokes a Graphical User Interface that is portable across many platforms. With the JPL package you have all the tools you need to embed AWT method calls in your Perl code, or to delegate tasks better handled by Perl from your Java code.

This chapter does not pretend to be an exhaustive reference on the AWT; there are many other, thicker, books that do that and you should probably get one if you intend to do serious AWT programming. However, if you follow the techniques illustrated in this chapter and peruse the sample application at the end of the chapter, you should be able to write Perl code that exploits all of the AWT features that are available from Java.

Using and Abusing AWT via JPL

This section covers the following aspects of AWT:

- Components

- Containers and layouts

- Event handling

The *FtpSearcher* example program at the end of this chapter puts many of these techniques to use, and also provides some examples of working with graphics, color, and fonts. As you work through this chapter, it will help immensely to keep an AWT reference handy. If you have downloaded the JDK documentation and installed it locally, or if you are connected to the Internet as you work through these examples, you can browse the API reference with your favorite web browser. Not only does the java.awt section of the JavaSoft API reference cover the classes and methods used in this chapter, but it includes explanations of some of the more arcane aspects of the AWT, such as the `GridBagLayout` class.

There are several aspects of the AWT that are beyond the scope of this chapter that we will not cover here; however, there is no reason why the syntax and techniques described in this chapter won't apply to the use of these packages also:

Advanced Image Manipulation
> The *java.awt.image* package provides several classes and interfaces for dealing with image processing.

Peer Communication
> The *java.awt.peer* package describes a series of interfaces that are used internally by other AWT classes for communicating with platform-specific peers that do the work of controlling the look and feel of the graphical objects. Note that these classes are hardly ever used explicitly.

Data Transfer
> The *java.awt.datatransfer* package contains a few classes to facilitate the transfer of information between applications.

Running the Examples

The examples in this chapter are included on the CD-ROM in the directory *oreilly/eg/ch04/*. These examples are organized in a manner identical to those of Chapter 3, *Perlez-Vous Java? Using JPL*. Please see the instructions for compiling and running examples in that chapter.

Components: Our Graphical Widget Friends

`Buttons`, `Labels`, text input devices, menus and menu bars, homebrewed doohickies—these are the things that GUIs are made of. They are *components*. The superclass *java.awt.Component* defines many methods that are common to most objects that you will use with AWT, methods that allow access to colors, fonts, sizes, positions, labels and event listeners. There are components, such as the `Canvas`, that are easily extensible into other components. There are checkboxes and lists. Here we describe five of the most common components: `Labels`, `TextFields`, `TextAreas`, `Buttons`, and `Menus`.

Label

A `Label` component displays a single line of static text. Labels are not very useful for anything other than displaying a few words to title adjacent components or as a prompt for some sort of user action. A `Label` can react to events if the events are explicitly sent to the label, but its peer (the underlying platform-specific GUI component) does not send any. Thus, a `Label` cannot respond to a user event, such as a mouse click. If you want a piece of text that will receive events and react to them, you will have to extend the `Canvas` class. An example of this is provided later in this chapter in the `LinkLabel` class that is used by the *FtpSearcher* code to implement hyperlinks.

The following example is included in the *LabelExample/* subdirectory, and creates two labels and sticks them in a window. Note that the example class extends the `Frame` class, which allows us to use this class as the top-level container and display component:

```
/*
 * LabelExample.jpl - An AWT example that shows the use of Labels.
 */

import java.awt.*;

public class LabelExample extends Frame {

    /**
     * A Perl method that adds a Label to this Frame.
     */
    perl void labelExample() {{

        # Import the Label class definition.
        #
        use JPL::Class 'java::awt::Label';

        # Look up the setText() method, which is used to set the Text of
        # certain components such as the Label.
        #
        my $setText = getmeth("setText", ['java.lang.String'], []);

        # Look up the add() method, which adds a Component to the Frame,
        # under the control of its layout manager (see the main() method
        # for the layout manager we're using). The add() method takes a
        # Component as its argument, and returns a reference to that
        # Component, as well. Since the Label is a subclass of Component,
        # it can be passed to this method as an argument.
        #
        my $add =
            getmeth("add", ['java.awt.Component'], ['java.awt.Component']);
```

```
        # Create a new Label, set its text, and add it to this object.
        #
        my $fugLabel = java::awt::Label->new();
        $fugLabel->$setText("The Fugs");
        $self->$add($fugLabel);

        # This time, use the version of the new() constructor that takes
        # a String as an argument - this is the title of the Label.
        #
        my $new = getmeth("new", ['java.lang.String'], []);
        my $edLabel = java::awt::Label->$new("starring Ed Sanders");

        # Add the Label to this object.
        #
        $self->$add($edLabel);

    }}

    /**
     * The main() method.
     */
    public static void main(String[] argv) {

        // Create a new instance of the LabelExample object.
        //
        LabelExample ex = new LabelExample();

        // The GridLayout layout manager arranges components neatly in a
        // grid, as they are added to the LabelExample object (a subclass of
        // Frame).
        //
        ex.setLayout(new GridLayout(0,1,0,0));

        // Call the labelExample() method to add a Label.
        //
        ex.labelExample();

        // pack() and show() the LabelExample object.
        //
        ex.pack();
        ex.show();

    }

}
```

When you run this example, you'll see a window appear with two labels, as shown in Figure 4-1. We haven't introduced any of the event handling features of the AWT, so, to terminate this example, you will need to press CTRL-C in the terminal window from which you ran the example. You will need to do this for each example until we come to the event handling example, which can be closed with a window control.

Figure 4-1. Label example

TextField and TextArea

The AWT provides two components for handling text input: `TextField` and `TextArea`. Both are subclasses of `TextComponent`, which provides several methods for accessing text selections with the components. `TextField` displays a single line of text, and is useful for single field entries in applications, or as a message bar for displaying short textual feedback to the user. `TextArea` displays multiple lines of text, with or without scrollbars. The following example, which is in the *TextExample/* directory, demonstrates both a `TextField` and a `TextArea`. Figure 4-2 shows this example in action. Note that while the `TextField` has stretched to fill half the screen, it still allows only one line of text, unlike the `TextArea`, which accommodates multiple lines of text.

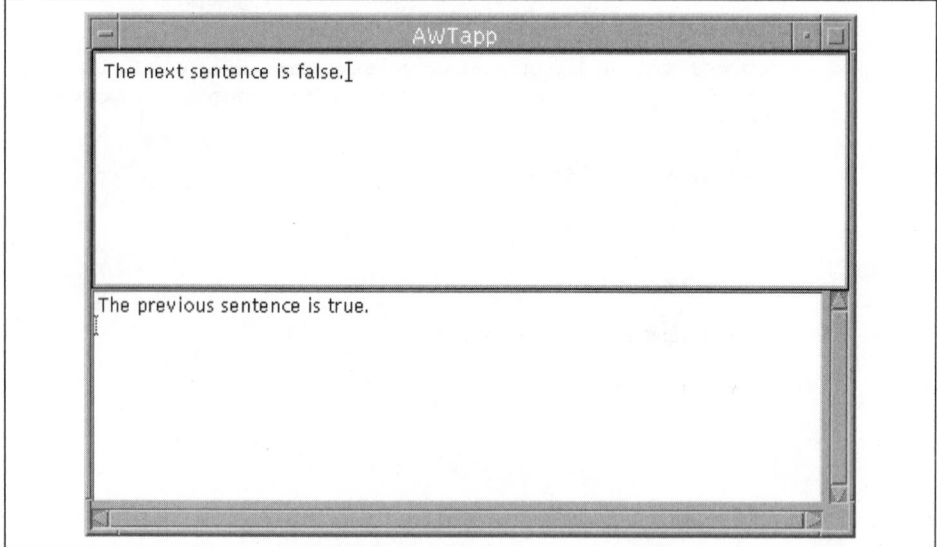

Figure 4-2. TextField and TextArea example

```
/*
 * TextExample.jpl - TextAreas with JPL.
 */

import java.awt.*;
```

```
public class TextExample extends Frame {

    /**
     * Add a couple of TextComponents (TextArea, TextField) to the Frame.
     */
    perl void textExample() {{

        # Import both classes.
        #
        use JPL::Class 'java::awt::TextArea';
        use JPL::Class 'java::awt::TextField';

        # Look up the setText() method, which sets the text of the
        # text component objects.
        #
        my $setText = getmeth("setText", ['java.lang.String'], []);

        # Look up the add method, which lets us add the text components to
        # the Frame.
        #
        my $add = getmeth("add", ['java.awt.Component'],
                          ['java.awt.Component']);

        # Create a new TextField, append some text to it, and add it to
        # the Frame.
        #
        my $tfld = new java::awt::TextField;
        $tfld->$setText("The next sentence is false.\n");
        $self->$add($tfld);

        # Create a new TextArea, append some text to it, and add it to
        # the Frame.
        #
        my $tarea = new java::awt::TextArea;
        $tarea->$setText("The previous sentence is true.\n");
        $self->$add($tarea);

    }}

    /**
     * The main() method.
     */
    public static void main(String[] argv) {

        TextExample ex = new TextExample();

        // Set the layout, invoke the Perl method, and pack() and show()
        // the TextExample.
        //
        ex.setLayout(new GridLayout(0, 1, 0, 0));
        ex.textExample();
        ex.pack();
        ex.show();
```

```
    }


    }
```

Buttons

Buttons are perhaps the most ubiquitous of the AWT primitives. Buttons have a
textual label associated with them that should give some sort of clue about what
will happen if the user clicks the button. An ImageButton subclass that allows an
Image as a label does exist, but it is not included in the standard API. Buttons
may also have an ActionCommand string associated with them by calling the
setActionCommand() method. You would use setActionCommand() if you
wanted a button's event handler to be able to process a string other than the
button's label. For example, if the button were a hyperlink, you would want the
ActionCommand to be the URL to load once the button was clicked.

In the next example, we create 100 pink buttons and add them to a Frame.
Notice that we are only creating and displaying buttons here; none of the buttons
actually *do* anything yet; they won't work until we get to the event handling
section. This example is included in the *ButtonExample/* subdirectory, and the
wall of buttons is shown in Figure 4-3.

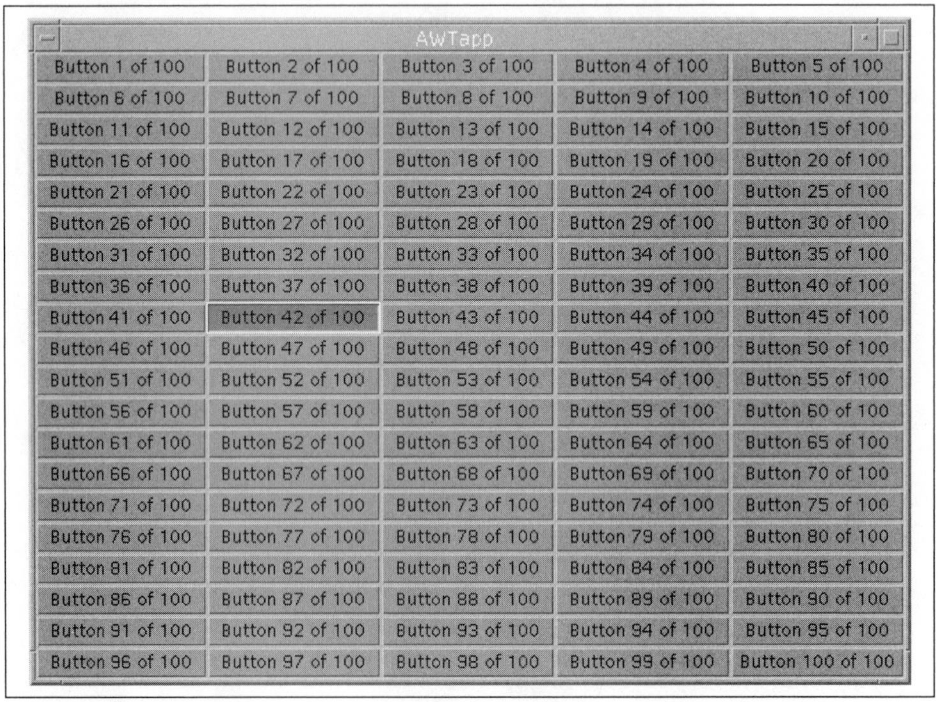

Figure 4-3. Button example

```
/*
 * ButtonExample.jpl - A Button example.
 */

import java.awt.*;

public class ButtonExample extends Frame {

    /**
     * A Perl method that demonstrates the use of Buttons.
     */
    perl void buttonExample() {{

        # Import the Button and Color class definitions.
        #
        use JPL::Class 'java::awt::Button';
        use JPL::Class 'java::awt::Color';

        # Look up the add() method, a new() method that takes a String
        # argument, and the setBackground() method.
        #
        my $add = getmeth("add", ['java.awt.Component'],
                          ['java.awt.Component']);
        my $new = getmeth("new", ['java.lang.String'], []);
        my $setBackground = getmeth("setBackground", ['java.awt.Color'], []);

        # Look up a constructor for a Color. Note that the method signature
        # takes three integers (RGB values) as its arguments.
        #
        my $newColor = getmeth("new", ['int','int','int'], []);

        # This should approximate a pink color.
        #
        my $pinkish = java::awt::Color->$newColor(255, 128, 128);

        # Let's make 100 pink buttons!
        #
        for my $count (1..100) {

            # Create the button.
            #
            my $button = java::awt::Button->$new("Button $count of 100");

            # Set the color of the button and add it to the Frame.
            #
            $button->$setBackground($pinkish);
            $self->$add($button);

        }

    }}

    /**
     * The main() method.
     */
```

```
public static void main(String[] argv) {

    ButtonExample ex = new ButtonExample();

    // Set the layout manager, invoke the Perl method, pack() and
    // show() the Frame.
    //
    ex.setLayout(new GridLayout(0, 5, 0, 0));
    ex.buttonExample();
    ex.pack();
    ex.show();

    }
}
```

Menus

Menus have become a standard part of every GUI system. In the AWT, each `Frame` may contain only one `MenuBar` at a time, but a `MenuBar` can contain as many `Menus` as you can squeeze into it. `Menus` are composite objects that may be disabled, added to, or removed from the `MenuBar` as necessary and can receive and respond to events generated by the user. `Menus` should have `ActionListeners` associated with them to process `ActionEvents`. `ActionListeners` are part of the AWT event handling mechanism, which is covered later in this chapter.

This example, located in the *MenuExample/* subdirectory, creates two simple menus from Perl, one of which is a tear-off menu. Figure 4-4 shows how this example appears when you run it.

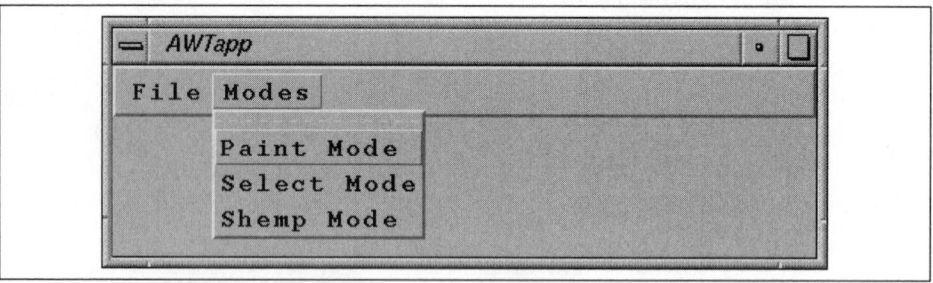

Figure 4-4. Menu example

```
/*
 * MenuExample.jpl - A Menu Example.
 */

import java.awt.*;

public class MenuExample extends Frame {
```

```perl
/**
 * A Perl method that creates a Menu.
 */
perl void menuExample() {{

    # Import the class definitions.
    #
    use JPL::Class 'java::awt::Menu';
    use JPL::Class 'java::awt::MenuBar';

    # A Frame can only have one MenuBar. We must
    # set the Frame's MenuBar with the setMenuBar method
    #
    my $setMenuBar = getmeth("setMenuBar", ['java.awt.MenuBar'], []);

    # Use the Menu constructor that allows us to supply a boolean flag
    # for indicating whether we want a tear-off menu.
    #
    my $new = getmeth("new", ['java.lang.String','boolean'], []);

    # We need a unique name for the Menu and MenuBar add methods
    # because they have different signatures than
    # Container's add method.
    #
    my $addtoMenu    = getmeth("add", ['java.lang.String'], []);
    my $addtoMenuBar = getmeth("add", ['java.awt.Menu'],
                               ['java.awt.Menu']);

    # Create a new menu bar
    #
    my $menuBar = java::awt::MenuBar->new();

    # Let's make two menus, File and Modes.  The second parameter to
    # the constructor is a boolean which indicates whether it is a
    # tear-off menu.
    #
    my $fileMenu = java::awt::Menu->$new("File", 0);
    my $modeMenu = java::awt::Menu->$new("Modes", 1);

    my @fileLabels = ('New', 'Open', 'Save', 'Quit');
    my @modeLabels = ('Paint Mode', 'Select Mode', 'Shemp Mode');

    # Now add the labels to each menu.
    #
    foreach my $label (@fileLabels) {
        $fileMenu->$addtoMenu($label);
    }
    foreach my $label (@modeLabels) {
        $modeMenu->$addtoMenu($label);
    }

    # Add the individual menus to the MenuBar object.
    #
    $menuBar->$addtoMenuBar($fileMenu);
```

```
        $menuBar->$addtoMenuBar($modeMenu);

        # Set the MenuBar object to be this Frame's menu bar.
        #
        $self->$setMenuBar($menuBar);

    }}

    /**
     * The main() method.
     */
    public static void main(String[] argv) {
        MenuExample ex = new MenuExample();
        ex.menuExample();
        ex.pack();
        ex.show();
    }

}
```

Containers

Containers are a special subclass of Component that can hold other Components. We have already seen the Frame container in previous examples. Some other containers are the all-purpose Panel (on which the applet class is based) and the ScrollPane, which helpfully relieves you of all scrollbar maintenance responsibilities. Some Containers come with a default LayoutManager for free: FlowLayout is the default for a Panel and BorderLayout comes with a Frame. A ScrollPane has its own built-in manager that it won't let you change, so don't even try!

This example, which is included in the *ContainerExample/* subdirectory, demonstrates some nested containers—a ScrollPane within a Panel within a Frame, which is shown in Figure 4-5.

```
/*
 * ContainerExample.jpl - A Container example.
 */

import java.awt.*;

public class ContainerExample {

    // This layout manager is for the Frame.
    //
    GridLayout gridLayout = new GridLayout(0, 1, 0, 0);

    /**
     * A Perl method that demonstrates the use of Container classes.
     */
```

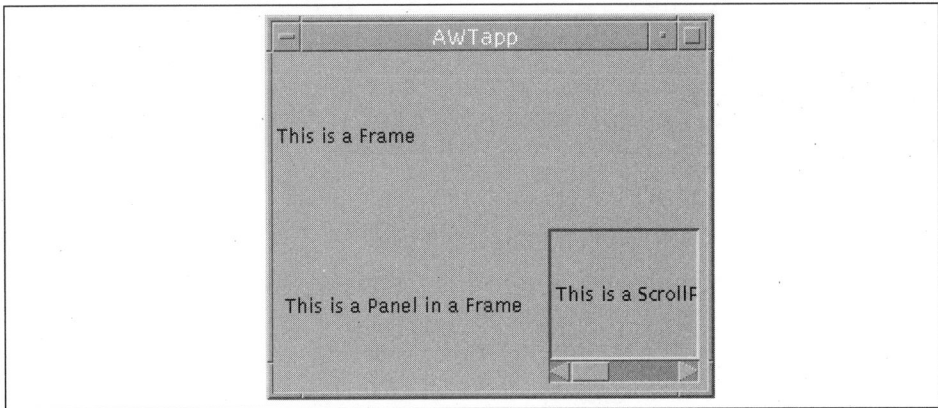

Figure 4-5. Container example

```perl
perl void containerExample() {{

    # Import the classes that we will use in this example. Note that we
    # can pass multiple arguments to JPL::Class.
    #
    use JPL::Class qw(
        java::awt::Frame
        java::awt::Panel
        java::awt::ScrollPane
        java::awt::Label
        java::awt::Color
    );

    # This add() method will work for all three containers because
    # they all have methods with this signature (which they all
    # inherit from Container).
    #
    my $add =
        getmeth("add", ['java.awt.Component'], ['java.awt.Component']);

    # The constructor for a Label.
    #
    my $new = getmeth("new", ['java.lang.String'], []);

    # The setLayout() method for the Frame. This allows us to set a
    # layout manager.
    #
    my $setLayout = getmeth("setLayout", ['java.awt.LayoutManager'], []);

    # Create some Labels.
    #
    my $frameLabel  = java::awt::Label->$new("This is a Frame");
    my $panelLabel =
    java::awt::Label->$new("This is a Panel in a Frame");
```

```perl
    my $scrollLabel =
    java::awt::Label->$new("This is a ScrollPane in a Panel in a Frame");

    # Create a Frame, Panel, and ScrollPane.
    #
    my $frame = new java::awt::Frame;
    my $panel = new java::awt::Panel;
    my $scrollPane = new java::awt::ScrollPane;

    # Frame has a BorderLayout as its default layout manager. We will
    # set it to a GridLayout. Panel has a default layout manager,
    # FlowLayout, and we won't change that. The ScrollPane has *no*
    # layout manager, and none can be assigned, since it can only
    # contain one component, so we won't set that layout manager,
    # either.
    #
    $frame->$setLayout($self->gridLayout);

    # Add the $frameLabel to the Frame, the $panelLabel to the Panel, and
    # the $scrollLabel to the ScrollPane.
    #
    $frame->$add($frameLabel);
    $panel->$add($panelLabel);
    $scrollPane->$add($scrollLabel);

    # Add the ScrollPane to the panel.
    #
    $panel->$add($scrollPane);

    # Add the Panel to the Frame.
    #
    $frame->$add($panel);

    # pack() and show() the Frame.
    #
    $frame->pack();
    $frame->show();

}}

/**
 * The main() method.
 */
public static void main(String[] argv) {
    ContainerExample ex = new ContainerExample();
    ex.containerExample();
}

}
```

Layout Managers

The subclasses of `LayoutManager` (`FlowLayout`, `GridLayout`, `BorderLayout`, and so forth) control the placement and sizing of components within containers for you. A layout manager takes charge when you `add()` a component to a container. Layout managers are an easy, platform-independent tool for making your GUI look nice; they can also be the source of hours of bemusement as you first try to puzzle out the quirks of each one. The `GridBagLayout` is arguably the most useful of the managers that are part of the JDK API, but it is also the most complicated to use and its nuances are well beyond the scope of this humble chapter.

The three managers illustrated in the example below are the `FlowLayout`, `BorderLayout`, and `GridLayout`. This example displays three frames, one with each of the three managers in effect. Note that the `BorderLayout` is handled a little differently—as we add each button to it, we pop off a location from the `@locations` array. Using the `ref` operator, we can determine which of the three layout managers is the `BorderLayout`. This example is shown in Figure 4-6, and the source is included in the *LayoutExample/* subdirectory.

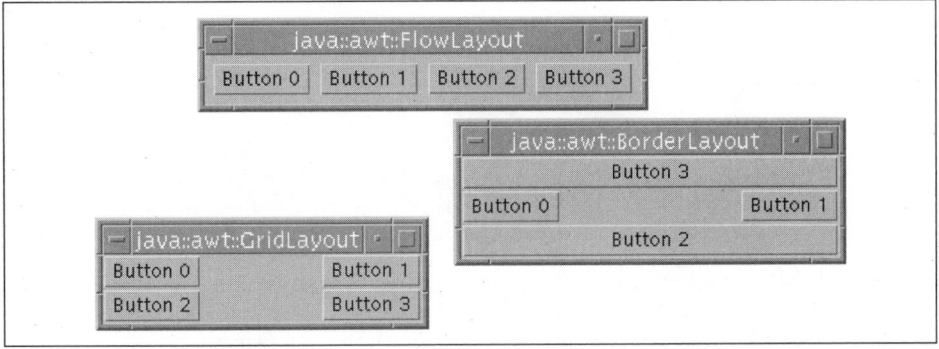

Figure 4-6. Layout example

```
/*
 * LayoutExample.jpl - A Layout Example.
 */

import java.awt.*;

public class LayoutExample extends Frame {

        // Create a FlowLayout layout manager.
        //
        FlowLayout flow = new FlowLayout();
```

```
// For the BorderLayout, keep a big gap between components, so we can
// see the title of the Frame.
//
BorderLayout border = new BorderLayout(60, 0);

// A GridLayout with two columns and a big gap between components.
//
GridLayout grid = new GridLayout(0, 2, 80, 0);

/**
 * A Perl method to demonstrate the layout managers.
 */
perl void layoutExample() {{

    # Import the class definitions that we'll need.
    #
    use JPL::Class 'java::awt::Frame';
    use JPL::Class 'java::awt::Button';

    # Look up method signatures for add(), new(), and setLayout().
    #
    my $add = getmeth("add", ['java.awt.Component'],
                             ['java.awt.Component']);
    my $new = getmeth("new", ['java.lang.String'], []);
    my $setLayout = getmeth("setLayout", ['java.awt.LayoutManager'], []);

    # Here, we're putting each of the four layout managers that were
    # created earlier into an array. We'll loop through this array,
    # create a Frame, set the layout manager, and add some buttons.
    #
    #
    @layout = ($self->flow, $self->border, $self->grid);

    # Locations for the BorderLayout manager.
    #
    @locations = ('North', 'South', 'East', 'West');

    # An add method for use with the BorderLayout manager.
    #
    my $borderadd = getmeth('add',
                            ['java.lang.String', 'java.awt.Component'],
                            ['java.awt.Component']);

    # Create four frames, each with four buttons and a different manager
    #
    foreach my $mgr (@layout) {

        # Create a new Frame. Use the class name of the layout manager
        # as the title.
        #
        my $frame = java::awt::Frame->$new( ref $mgr );
```

```
        # Set the layout manager of the Frame.
        #
        $frame->$setLayout($mgr);

        # Add four buttons.
        #
        for my $cnt (0..3) {

            my $button = java::awt::Button->$new("Button $cnt");

            # If it's a BorderLayout, be sure to specify a location,
            # since it will just keep adding components on top of each
            # other if we don't!
            #
            if (ref $mgr eq 'java::awt::BorderLayout') {
                $frame->$borderadd(pop @locations, $button);
            } else {
                $frame->$add($button);
            }

        }

        # Pack and show the frame.
        #
        $frame->pack();
        $frame->show();
    }

}}

/**
 * The main() method.
 */
public static void main(String[] argv) {
    LayoutExample ex = new LayoutExample();
    ex.layoutExample();
}

}
```

Event Handling

As of the 1.1 release of the JDK, the event-handling mechanism of the AWT has been changed from a case-statement driven single event handler into a delegation model. With this approach comes a new class of event listeners that the programmer can assign to specific components. These event listeners act on events intended for the object to which they listen. ActionListeners keep track of events sent to buttons, input fields, checkboxes, and menus; WindowAdapters watch the application's windows for opening and closing events; MouseListeners and KeyboardListeners wait for input from their respective input devices.

When designing a user interface, it is very important to know what objects are capable of receiving events and which are not. A `Label`, for instance, can react to events, but no events are ever passed to it by its underlying platform-dependent component! If you want to be able to click on some text, you'll have to roll your own component (or expand on the `LinkLabel` class at the end of this chapter). `Canvas` is a good candidate for this sort of all-purpose homemade class because it can receive and react to any event.

One hopes that future revisions of implementations of the `Toolkit` (a collection of peers that do the real work for corresponding AWT components, the platform-dependent troll that lives under the AWT bridge) will address these drawbacks; for now, an up-to-date chart that cross-references the event passing (or lack of it) for each component on several platforms is available at *http://www.oreilly.com/catalog/javaawt/*.

The next example witnesses the creation of two simple event handlers; one to listen for a window closing (at last, we can close the window of an example program!) and one that listens for a button click and performs some arbitrary action upon receiving an `ActionEvent`. For a more involved example of event handling, see the *FtpSearcher* application later in this chapter. Note the use of anonymous classes to create the individual listeners. These anonymous classes follow the call to the constructor, and declare methods of the objects "in place," without the need to create a class definition for each listener. Compare this usage with the *Inner Class* example in the preceding chapter. Figure 4-7 shows the event-handling example.

Figure 4-7. Event Handler example

```
/*
 * EventExample.jpl - An Event Example.
 */

import java.awt.*;
import java.awt.event.*;

public class EventExample extends Frame {

    // Create event listeners using the JDK 1.1 anonymous class
    // feature. The actionPerformed() and windowClosing() methods are
    // defined "in place."
    //
```

```perl
ActionListener buttonListener = new ActionListener() {
    public void actionPerformed(ActionEvent e) {
        System.out.print("Yowza!");
    }
};
WindowAdapter windowListener = new WindowAdapter() {
    public void windowClosing(WindowEvent e) {
        System.exit(0);
    }
};

/**
 * A Perl method that demonstrates event handling.
 */
perl void eventExample() {{

    # Import any classes we'll need.
    #
    use JPL::Class 'java::awt::Frame';
    use JPL::Class 'java::awt::Button';

    # Look up the add() and new() methods.
    #
    my $add = getmeth("add", ['java.awt.Component'],
                      ['java.awt.Component']);
    my $new = getmeth("new", ['java.lang.String'], []);

    # Look up the addActionListener() and addWindowListener() methods.
    #
    my $addActionListener = getmeth("addActionListener",
                                ['java.awt.event.ActionListener'], []);
    my $addWindowListener = getmeth("addWindowListener",
                                ['java.awt.event.WindowListener'], []);

    # Add window listener to this object, which is a subclass of Frame.
    #
    $self->$addWindowListener($self->windowListener);

    # Create a new button and add the action listener to it.
    #
    my $button = java::awt::Button->$new("Say 'Yowza!'");
    $button->$addActionListener($self->buttonListener);

    # Add the button to this object, pack() and show() it.
    #
    $self->$add($button);
    $self->pack();
    $self->show();

}}

/**
 * The main() method.
 */
```

```
public static void main(String[] argv) {
    EventExample ex = new EventExample();
    ex.eventExample();
}
```
}

Sample Application: An Interface to an FTP Search Server

We developed *FtpSearcher* as an example of integrating JPL and the AWT. Combining Perl's data manipulation and network programming strengths with Java's GUI features, this application highlights methods for dealing with complications that arise from the interactions between the languages and shows some slightly involved event-handling techniques. *FtpSearcher* is an uncomplicated, plain interface to an FTP search server, a program that compiles directory listings from FTP sites globally and allows intelligent, direct access to FTP sites through a variety of search methods. Because the FTP search server uses a WWW gateway, many web page–based interfaces are available on the Web. *FtpSearcher* is a dedicated little tool that implements a portion of the features of its web-bound companions.

Running FtpSearcher

Like the other examples, *FtpSearcher* is included with the Chapter 4 examples on the CD-ROM in *oreilly/ch04/*. If you installed the O'Reilly Extras from the CD, this directory is installed on a file system you can read and write to.

Like the other chapter examples, you must first compile the example before running it. Note too, that you must have the LWP bundle installed. FtpSearcher also depends on the CGI module, which is bundled with the latest Perl. *FtpSearcher* relies on recent versions of both LWP (5.14 or greater) and IO::Socket (1.18 or greater). See Chapter 2, *Installing the Resource Kit Software*, for instructions on using the setup tool to install modules.

To build this sample application, go to the *FtpSearcher/* subdirectory, and issue the commands:

```
perl Makefile.PL
make
```

After you complete those commands, you run the application with the command `java FtpSearcher`.

Figure 4-8 shows the FtpSearcher main screen, and Figure 4-9 shows the results window. To submit a query, simply type in a search term and press Return. This will send your query to the remote FTP Search server, and perform an *archie*-like search of many FTP sites. For updates or bug fixes to the *FtpSearcher* application, keep an eye on the Perl Resource Kit web site, at *http://perl.oreilly.com/*.

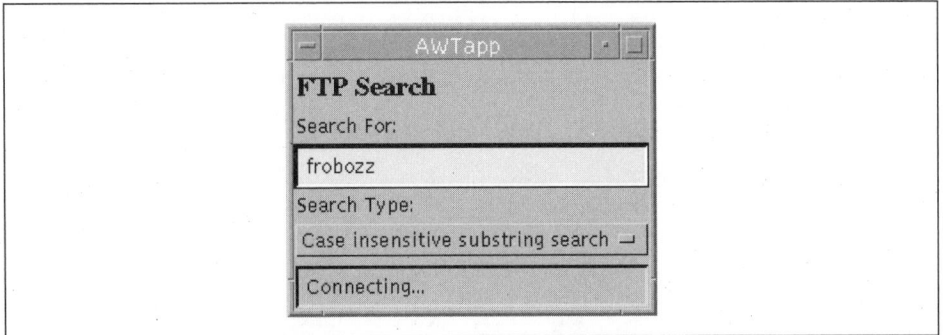

Figure 4-8. FtpSearcher main screen

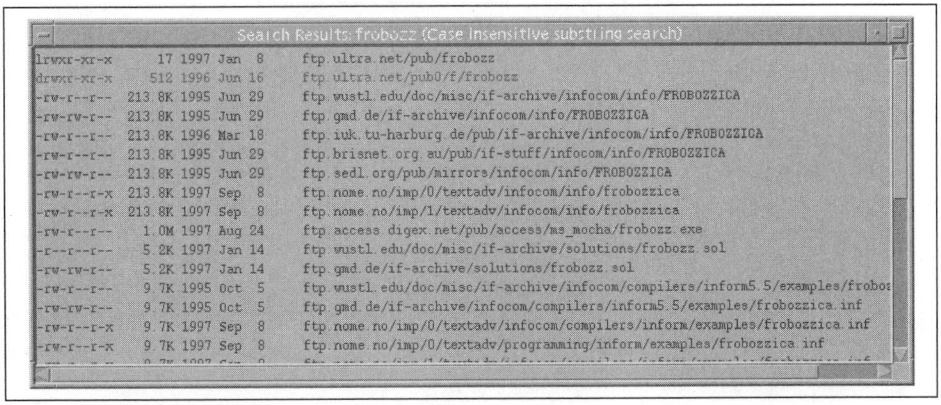

Figure 4-9. FtpSearcher results window

The Interface

Figure 4-10 shows the WWW front-end to FTP Search. The FTP Search server expects CGI requests to appear in a certain format, and if everything goes well, it sends back a nicely formatted response. A request looks something like this:

```
http://ftpsearchhost.somewhere.com/ftpsearch?query=perl+java&doit=Search&
type=Case+insensitive+substring+search&hits=&matches=&hitsprmatch=&limdom=
&limpath=&f1=Mode&f2=Size&f3=Date&f4=Host&f5=Path&f6=-&header=none&sort=none
&trlen=20
```

That request seems a bit cryptic at first, but it's actually fairly easy to understand when you dissect it. When we make a request to the server we are constructing a Uniform Resource Locator (URL) that imparts certain bits of information to the web server, which is then passed on to the FTP Search program. In this case, we

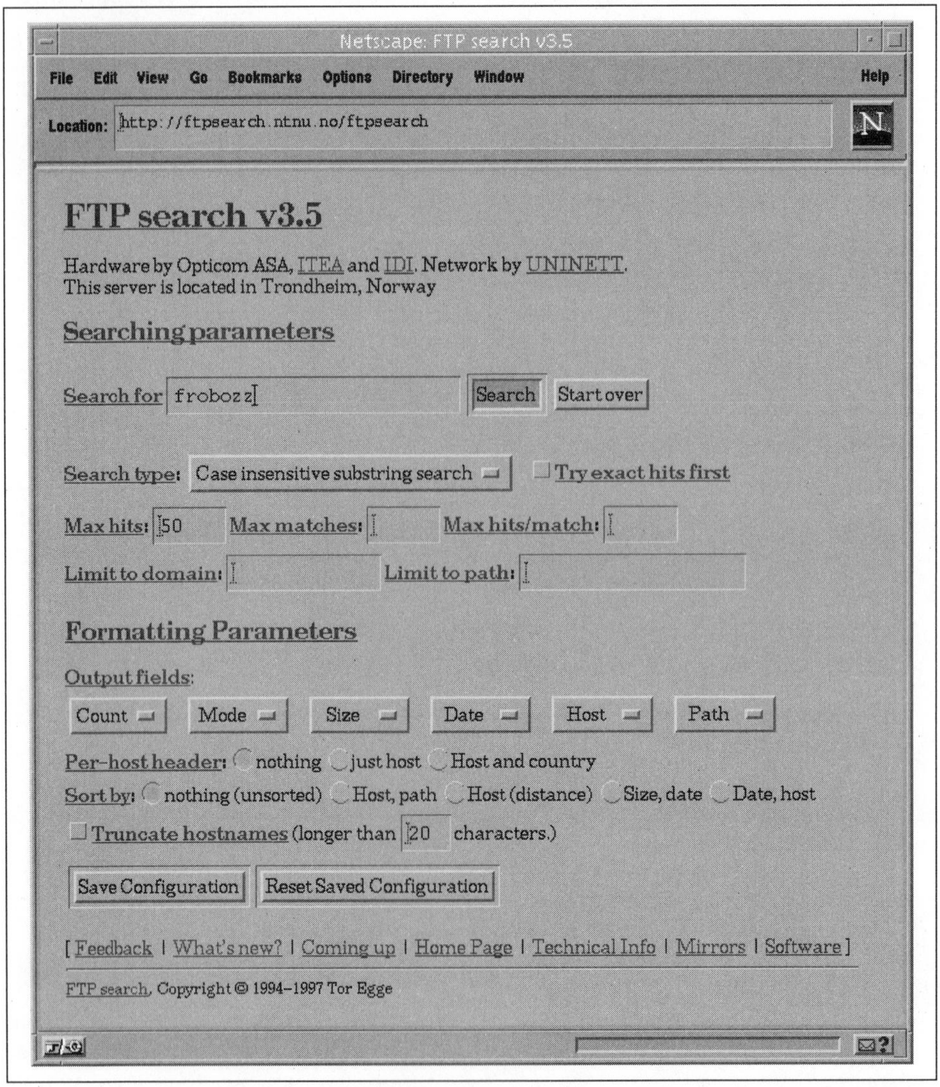

Figure 4-10. WWW front-end to FTP Search

are sending it 17 fields of information (the field names are shown in bold) about what we want to search for and how we want it sent back to us. Note that the field names of this URL are specific to the implementation of the FTP Search program. The interface is documented on the FTP Search technical information web page (*http://ftpsearch.ntnu.no/help/searchparam.html*) and it was easy to reverse engineer the specifics by looking at other peoples' front-ends to FTP Search.

The fields of most interest are `query` and `type`. The `query` field contains the string that we are searching for, and the `type` field indicates one of 12 supported types of searches. Our *FtpSearcher* application only supports six of these, due to the fact that the others return the results in a slightly different format than the first six.

For this application we are only going to let the user specify the values of `query` and `type`, and we hardcode the rest into the URLs that we send to the engine. It would be a fairly trivial task to expand the example into an application that supports the full interface. Such a task is an exercise left to the reader.

After the server receives a request, it sends back a response via a web gateway that will be in the form of an HTML document. Figure 4-11 shows how this output would look in a web browser.

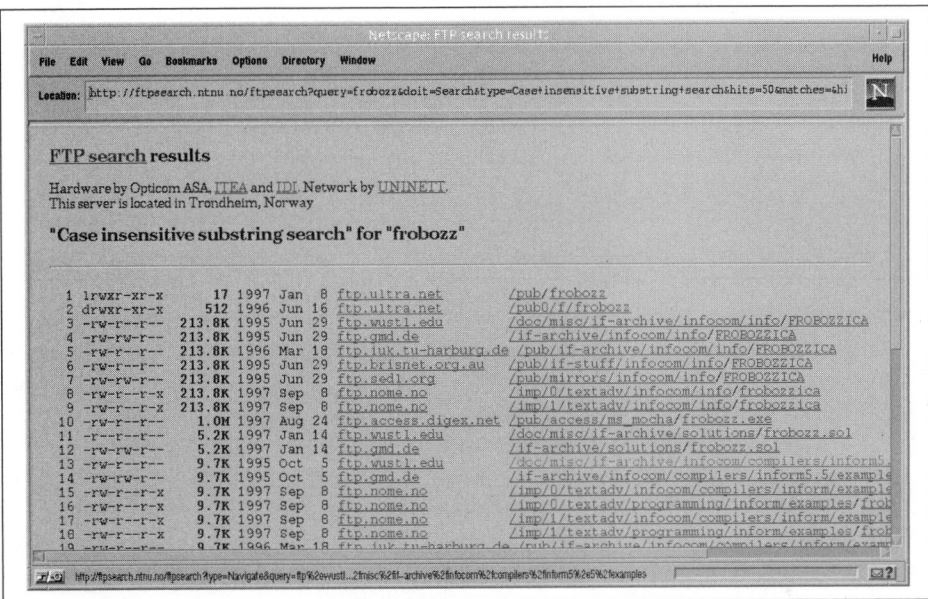

Figure 4-11. HTML response document

The source of that response is shown here:

```
<HTML>
<HEAD>
<TITLE>FTP search results</TITLE>
</HEAD>
<BODY>

<H2><A HREF="/ftpsearch">FTP search</A> results</H2>
```

```
<p>Hardware by Opticom ASA, <A HREF="http://www.itea.ntnu.no/">ITEA</A> and
<A HREF="http://www.idi.ntnu.no/indexe.html">IDI</A>.
Network by <A HREF="http://www.uninett.no/homepage.en.html">UNINETT</A>.
<br>This server is located in Trondheim, Norway
<br>
<h3>&quot;Case insensitive substring search&quot; for &quot;frobozz&quot;</h3>
<hr>
<PRE>
  1 <TT>lrwxr-xr-x</TT> <B>      17</B> 1997 Jan  8
<A HREF="/ftpsearch?type=Navigate&query=ftp%2eultra%2enet%2f">ftp.ultra.net</A>
<A HREF="/ftpsearch?type=Navigate&query=ftp%2eultra%2enet%2fpub">/pub</A>
/<A HREF="ftp://ftp.ultra.net/pub/frobozz">frobozz</A>
  2 <TT>drwxr-xr-x</TT> <B>     512</B> 1996 Jun 16
<A HREF="/ftpsearch?type=Navigate&query=ftp%2eultra%2enet%2f">ftp.ultra.net</A>
<A HREF="/ftpsearch?type=Navigate&query=ftp%2eultra%2enet%2fpub0%2ff%2ffrobozz">
/pub0/f/frobozz</A>

[...]
content removed for brevity
[...]

</PRE>
<HR>34 reported hits
<br>0.120 seconds prospero
<br>0.121 seconds HTTP
<br>0 partial writes.
<br>DONE<hr>
<FONT SIZE=-1><A HREF="http://ftpsearch.ntnu.no">
FTP search</A>, Copyright &#169; 1994-1997 Tor Egge
</FONT>
</BODY></HTML>
```

Our program must be able to parse this HTML document to some extent and isolate all the pertinent information for display. Java does not have built-in classes for handling HTML; in fact, it really doesn't even handle text all that well, which is where Perl comes in.

Several people are working on HTML-friendly Java objects and, of course, Sun has implemented a whole suite of tools for its HotJava web browser. In the interest of simplicity, we are going to extract only the file information and the URLs and labels embedded in the HTML, and then display it using a custom `LinkLabel` class.

For an interesting approach to parsing and displaying HTML from Perl (with a little help from the HTML::Parser module and Perl/Tk) check out the *xword* dictionary client example in Clinton Wong's *Web Client Programming with Perl* (O'Reilly 1997).

The Code

One of the driving design concerns with *FtpSearcher* was to showcase the interaction between the two languages, and minimize the number of times we force JPL to do method lookups and parameter passing. The Java segments of the program deal with initializing and manipulating the graphical interface and the Perl methods do the bulk of the network and parsing work. The work is broken up fairly evenly between Perl and Java methods.

At the top of the program, useful packages are imported, and a number of instance fields are declared and initialized:

```
/**
 * FtpSearcher provides a rudimentary interface to the popular FTP Search
 * program.  ftpsearch is a ftp indexing server that utilizes a WWW
 * gateway to serve responses to queries.
 */

import java.util.*;
import java.awt.*;
import java.awt.event.*;

// The VerticalBagLayout is included in the sun.awt package.
//
import sun.awt.*;

class FtpSearcher extends Panel {

    // This text field accepts the user's search criteria.
    //
    TextField searchField = new TextField();

    // The user can use this choice object to choose one of the available
    // search options.
    //
    Choice searchType = new Choice();

    // This is the status bar.
    //
    TextField msgBar = new TextField();

    // This is the URL of the ftpsearch server we will be using.
    //
    String host = "http://ftpsearch.ntnu.no";
```

The constructor for *FtpSearcher* contains a call to `initGUI()`, which builds the main window. All subsequent search result windows are constructed on the fly by the `handleFtpSearch()` method. Because the `FtpSearcher` class extends the `Panel` class, we must create a `Frame` for the main search window in this method. Because of this approach, *FtpSearcher* is easily embeddable in other Java applications.

```
/**
 * Construct a new FtpSearcher object.
 */
public FtpSearcher() {

    // Initialize the user interface.
    //
    initGUI();

}
```

The `initGUI()` method assembles all the components of the user interface. The `ActionListener` added to the `searchField` object receives an `ActionEvent` when the user presses `Enter` in the `TextField`.

```
/**
 * initGUI() assembles all the components of the user interface. The
 * main window is a Panel managed by a GridBagLayout which controls
 * several textfields and a Choice menu.
 */
public void initGUI() {

    // Gratuitous use of color for the background.
    //
    setBackground(Color.orange);

    // We are hardcoding the size of the Panel here.
    //
    setSize(600, 300);

    // Set the layout manager to be the GridBagLayout object, and set
    // some defaults for the constraints.
    //
    GridBagLayout layout = new GridBagLayout();
    setLayout(layout);

    GridBagConstraints gc = new GridBagConstraints();
    gc.anchor = GridBagConstraints.NORTH;
    gc.fill = GridBagConstraints.BOTH;
    gc.weightx = 1.0;

    // Create a label for the title, set its font, and add it to this
    // Panel under the control of a GridBagLayout manager and the
    // GridBagConstraints.
    //
    Label label1 = new Label("FTP Search");
    label1.setFont( new Font("Serif", Font.BOLD, 18) );
    gc.gridwidth = GridBagConstraints.REMAINDER;
    layout.setConstraints(label1, gc);
    add(label1);

    // This label prompts the user to enter the search terms.
    //
    Label label2 = new Label("Search For:");
```

```
            layout.setConstraints(label2, gc);
            add(label2);

            // The searchField will have its own actionListener that
            // catches an ActionEvent whenever the user presses
            // enter within the searchField. This event tells the
            // listener to call getNewURL(), and pass the value obtained from
            // that to handleFtpSearch().
            //
            searchField.addActionListener(new ActionListener() {

                public void actionPerformed (ActionEvent e) {
                    String search_url = getNewURL();
                    handleFtpSearch(host, search_url);
                }

            });

            // Add the searchfield to the Panel.
            //
            layout.setConstraints(searchField, gc);
            add(searchField);

            // Add a label for the search type.
            //
            Label label3 = new Label("Search Type:");
            layout.setConstraints(label3, gc);
            add(label3);

            // buildChoice is a Perl method that will add options
            // to the searchType Choice object.
            //
            buildChoice();

            // Add the searchType Choice object.
            //
            layout.setConstraints(searchType, gc);
            add(searchType);

            // msgBar is a textField for displaying the status.
            //
            layout.setConstraints(msgBar, gc);
            msgBar.setEditable(false);
            add(msgBar);
        }
```

The **buildChoice()** method is a convenience function that adds options to the **selectionType** choice menu.

```
        /*
         * buildChoice is a native Perl method for adding options to the
         * searchType Choice object. It is a helper method for initGUI().
         */
```

```perl
perl void buildChoice() {{

    # Look up the add() method for java.awt.Choice
    #
    use JPL::Class 'java::awt::Choice';
    my $add = getmeth("add", ['java.lang.String'], []);

    my @choices = (
        "Case insensitive substring search",
        "Case sensitive substring search",
        "Case insensitive glob search",
        "Case sensitive glob search",
        "Regular expression search",
        "Exact search"
        );

    foreach my $choice (@choices) {
        $self->searchType->$add($choice);
    }

}}
```

The **getNewURL()** method constructs the URL for our request based on user input, but only when we are making a brand new request. If we are navigating through the links of a search, the URL is taken from the link it is associated with.

```perl
/**
 * getNewURL will construct a String that will be passed to
 * handleFtpSearch based on user input. This string is a Uniform
 * Resource Locator that will be passed to the ftpsearch server as
 * a request. getNewURL is called whenever the user performs a new
 * search.
 */
perl String getNewURL() {{

    # Import the classes we need.
    #
    use JPL::Class 'java::awt::Choice';
    use JPL::Class 'java::awt::TextField';

    # Look up any methods we need.
    #
    my $getSelectedItem = getmeth("getSelectedItem", [],
                                  ['java.lang.String']);
    my $getText = getmeth("getText", [], ['java.lang.String']);

    # Get the user's query from the searchField object.
    #
    my $searchtxt = $self->searchField->$getText();

    # The CGI::escape module 'escapes' all the spaces and special chars
    #
    use CGI;
    my $querytxt = CGI::escape($searchtxt);
```

```
        # Get the search type, and escape the text of it.
        #
        my $searchTypetxt = $self->searchType->$getSelectedItem();
        my $typetxt = CGI::escape($searchTypetxt);

        # The following are all fields that the ftpsearch server
        # expects.
        #
        my $server = "/ftpsearch";
        my $query  = "?query=$querytxt";
        my $doit   = "&doit=Search";
        my $type   = "&type=$typetxt";
        my $hits   = "&hits=50";

        # The next four optionally control the number of matches and domain
        # and path names of the returned document.  Here they are empty and
        # unimplemented, but they could be supported easily.
        #
        my $matches     = "&matches=";
        my $hitsprmatch = "&hitsprmatch=";
        my $limdom      = "&limdom=";
        my $limpath     = "&limpath=";

        # $fields lists the output fields - this order is important for the
        # parsing routing. $header indicates whether we want a header and
        # $sort indicates how the output should  be sorted. Sometimes path
        # names can be quite long so $trlen tells the server the maximum
        # length of a path name.
        #
        my $fields = "&f1=Mode&f2=Size&f3=Date&f4=Host&f5=Path&f6=-";
        my $header = "&header=none";
        my $sort   = "&sort=none";
        my $trlen  = "&trlen=20";

        # Concatenate the request fields into a URL.
        #
        my $url = "$server$query$doit$type$hits$matches$hitsprmatch" .
                  "$limdom$limpath$fields$header$sort$trlen";

        return $url;

    }}
```

The `newLinkLabel()` method is a convenience function called from the `getSearchResults()` method that eliminates the need for lengthy method lookups in the native method.

```
    /**
     * A helper function to create a new LinkLabel, set up some
     * listeners, and return the LinkLabel to the caller.
     */
    public LinkLabel newLinkLabel(String label, String host, String url) {
```

```
        // Create a new LinkLabel.
        //
        LinkLabel linklabel = new LinkLabel(label, url);

        // We want the flashy colors when you move the mouse over the
        // label, so we'll enable the effects.
        //
        linklabel.enableEffects();

        // Add a LinkListener to the LinkLabel. This is an inner class of
        // this class definition, which will follow links when the user
        // clicks on one.
        //
        linklabel.addMouseListener(new LinkListener(host, url));

        return linklabel;
    }
```

The `handleFtpSearch()` method creates a new window in which to display the search results and calls `getSearchResults()` to make a connection with the server and display the results. This method can be called in one of two ways; from the action event handler of the search `TextField` (when the user clicks **Enter**) or from the `getFtp()` method when the user follows a `LinkLabel` to get more information on the search. In the former case, the `host` parameter is taken from the `host` instance variable and the `url` parameter is formed by the `getNewURL()` method. In the latter case, the `host` and `url` are both passed from the `LinkLabel` that was selected.

```
    /**
     * Create a Frame and fill it with search results.
     */
    public void handleFtpSearch(String host, String url) {

        // Create a new Frame.
        //
        String searchTypetxt = searchType.getSelectedItem();
        Frame resultframe =
            new Frame("Search Results: " + searchField.getText() +
                    " (" + searchTypetxt + ")");

        // Create a new Panel.
        //
        Panel panel = new Panel();

        // Create a new ScrollPane.
        //
        ScrollPane scrollpane = new ScrollPane();
        scrollpane.setSize(800, 300);

        // Add the ScrollPane to the Frame.
        //
        resultframe.add(scrollpane);
        getsearchresults(host, url, panel);
```

```
              // Add the Panel to the ScrollPane.
              //
              scrollpane.add(panel);

              // The Vertical BagLayout is included in the sun.awt package
              // It allows one object per row and sizes each object according to
              // its preferred size
              //
              panel.setLayout(new VerticalBagLayout());

              // Add a WindowListener to the Frame that disposes of it.
              //
              resultframe.addWindowListener(new WindowAdapter() {
                  public void windowClosing(WindowEvent e) {

                      Window w = e.getWindow();
                      w.dispose();

                  }
              });

              // Pack and show the Frame.
              //
              resultframe.pack();
              resultframe.show();

      }
```

The **getSearchResults()** method creates an LWP::UserAgent object that will
handle our interactions with the server. It then removes unnecessary information
from the response (if there is a response) and creates a display in the new **Panel**
passed to it by **handleFtpSearch()**.

```
      /**
       * getSearchResults is a native Perl method that takes a host string,
       * a URL and a Container (in this case a Panel) as parameters and
       * formats output to be displayed in Container. This method connects
       * with the ftpsearch server, retrieves a response, formats it, and
       * adds it to the Container.
       */
      perl void getsearchresults(String host, String url, Panel panel) {{

          # Look up the add() method, and the newLinkLabel() method.
          # (add() is a method of java.awt.Container and newLinkLabel() is
          # a method of ftpSearcher).
          #
          my $add = getmeth("add",
                            ['java.awt.Component'],
                            ['java.awt.Component']);

          my $newLinkLabel = getmeth("newLinkLabel",
                      ['java.lang.String','java.lang.String','java.lang.String'],
                      ['LinkLabel']);
```

```perl
# Get the setText() method to display the status.
#
use JPL::Class 'java::awt::TextField';
$setText = getmeth("setText", ['java.lang.String'], []);

# Create a User Agent to communicate with the server.
#
use LWP::UserAgent;
$ua = new LWP::UserAgent or die "Could not connect to server!\n";
$self->msgBar->$setText("Connecting...");

# The following line is very important!
# UserAgent defaults to using alarm() to implement timeouts. alarm()
# sends a signal which we think Java intercepts. This line disables
# this "feature".
#
$ua->use_alarm(0);

# Use the HTTP package to create $request to give to the UserAgent
#
$request = new HTTP::Request('GET', "$host$url");

# Make the request, and get a response object.
#
$response = $ua->request($request);

# If we actually got a valid response, split it into individual lines
# for later parsing. If not, split the error message that resulted
# from our request. We won't do too much with the error message, but
# we will use most of the links. Note that the response is formatted
# as HTML since we are using a WWW gateway. Formatting and displaying
# the remaining HTML is beyond the scope of this example.
#
my @html;
if ($response->is_success) {

    @html = split(/\n/, $response->content);
    $self->msgBar->$setText("Formatting...");

} else {

    @html = split(/\n/, $response->error_as_HTML);
    $self->msgBar->$setText("Bad response!");

}

# Process and display each line of HTML.
#
foreach my $line (@html) {

    # Extract the links and link labels - match everything before
    # the first <A HREF...
    #
```

```
$line =~ /(.*?)<A/;
my $info = $1;

# Strip trivial (non-nested) HTML.
#
$info =~ s/<[^>]*>//g;
my @path = $line =~ /<A[^>]*>      # Match <A HREF="something">.
                     ([^<]*)       # The text of the link.
                     <\/A>         # The end of the link.
                     (\/*)         # There might be a slash outside of
                                   # the link.
                   /gx;

# Join the @path.
#
my $path = join('', @path);

# This will pull out the last URL in the line.
#
$line =~ /.*<A HREF="([^"]*)/;
my $url = $1;

# Concatenate the info and path to get a label.
#
$label = "$info     $path";

# Skip over any line that doesn't include an info line or a path.
# Also, skip all http urls.
#
if ($info and $path and !($url =~ /^http/)) {

    # Create a new LinkLabel and add it to the Panel.
    #
    $linklabel = $self->$newLinkLabel($label, $host, $url);
    $panel->$add($linklabel);

}

}

# Update the status.
#
$self->msgBar->$setText("Done!");

}}
```

The getFtp() method is called when a LinkLabel MouseListener receives a
mouseClicked event. If the selected link is a link to a file on an FTP server, the
method attempts to download the selected file, using the LWP::UserAgent
module. If the link is a relative URL to another FTP search, it calls
handleSearchResults() with the host and URL of the request.

```perl
/**
 * getFtp is a method called when the user follows a link. If the link is
 * to an ftp site, this method calls up a new UserAgent and tries to get
 * the file. Otherwise, it tries to call handleSearchRequest, since
 * everything other than a link to an ftp site is a request to
 * drill-down deeper into the ftpsearch index.
 */
perl void getftp(String host, String url) {{

    use JPL::Class 'java::awt::TextField';

    # Get the setText method.
    #
    my $setText = getmeth("setText", ['java.lang.String'], []);

    # Does it look like a link to an ftp site?
    #
    if ($url =~ /^ftp:/) {

        # Set the status message.
        #
        $self->msgBar->$setText("Downloading $url");

        # Get a user agent.
        #
        use LWP::UserAgent;
        use HTTP::Request;
        $ua = new LWP::UserAgent or die "Could not connect to server!\n";

        # Don't use signals for timeouts, since Java has problems with
        # signal handlers established in Perl.
        #
        $ua->use_alarm(0);

        # Create a new request with the given URL, and get a response
        # object for it.
        #
        $request  = new HTTP::Request('GET', $url);
        $response = $ua->request($request);

        # If the response is a success, download the file.
        #
        if ($response->is_success) {

            # A successful return, now save it.
            #
            my $file = $response->content;

            # Get the filename from the URL.
            #
            $url =~ /.*\/(.*)/; my $ftpfile = $1;

            $self->msgBar->$setText("Saving to: downloads/$ftpfile");
            print "Saving to: downloads/$ftpfile\n";
```

```
            if (open OUTFILE, ">downloads/$ftpfile") {
                print OUTFILE $file;
                close OUTFILE;
                $self->msgBar->$setText("Got it!");

                if ($ftpfile =~
                        /\.(gif|jpg|jpeg|tiff?|p[bgp]m|bmp|pcx|xpm)$/) {

                    # let's load xv for the heck of it
                    # hardcoded silliness
                    #
                    $self->msgBar->$setText("Trying to open xv...");
                    system("xv downloads/$ftpfile &");

                }

            } else {
                $self->msgBar->$setText("Error saving file: $!");
            }
        } else {
            $self->msgBar->$setText("Error from server!");
        }

    } else {

        # Drill-down into the ftp search index in another window.
        #
        my $handleFtpSearch = getmeth("handleFtpSearch",
                            ['java.lang.String', 'java.lang.String'],
                            []);
        $self->$handleFtpSearch($host, $url);

    }
}}
```

The **LinkListener** class is a **MouseAdaptor** that is added to all **LinkLabels**
when they are created. Because **LinkLabel** is an external class, this **mouseListener** cannot be built into it (and we really shouldn't be doing that anyway, for
the sake of reusable code). The **LinkListener** knows the URL of the **LinkLabel**
it is associated with and calls the **getFtp()** method when a link is clicked.

```
/**
 * The LinkListener class is built to call getFtp when a link is
 * clicked. Because LinkLabel is an external class, we can't build
 * this mouseListener into it (and we really shouldn't, anyway).
 */
class LinkListener extends MouseAdapter {

    String linkurl;
    String linkhost;

    public LinkListener(String host, String url) {
        linkurl  = url;
```

```
            linkhost = host;
        }

        // Follow the link when it's clicked.
        //
        public void mouseClicked(MouseEvent e) {
            getftp(linkhost, linkurl);
        }

    }
```

The `main()` method simply constructs a new `Frame` and a new `FtpSearcher`
object, and adds the `FtpSearcher` object to the `Frame`, demonstrating how easy
it is to embed instances of the `FtpSearcher` class into containers.

```
/**
 * The main() method.
 */
public static void main(String[] argv) {

    // Create the Frame to hold the user interface.
    //
    Frame frame = new Frame();

    // Add a window listener to listen for window closing events
    //
    frame.addWindowListener(new WindowAdapter() {
        public void windowClosing(WindowEvent e) {
            System.exit(0);
        }
    });

    // Add the FtpSearcher object to the Frame.
    //
    frame.add(new FtpSearcher());

    // Pack and show the Frame.
    //
    frame.pack();
    frame.show();

    }

}
```

The `LinkLabel` class is a new class that has been created specifically to imitate
some of the behavior exhibited by hyperlinks on most web browsers. The
`LinkLabel` has several bits of information stored within it: a `Font`, a `Color`, a
URL, and a `Label`. It has two public methods, `enableLinkListener()` and
`paint()`. `EnableLinkListener()` adds a `mouseListener` to the `LinkLabel`
that detects `mouseEnter` and `mouseExit` events and changes the color of the link
to red as the mouse passes over it and leaves links that have been followed a

magenta color. The `paint()` method automatically redraws the `LinkLabel`'s label. The `LinkLabel` extends the `Canvas` class; it fulfills the need for a textual label that can receive and process events.

```
/**
 * LinkLabel is a shiny new class that mimics the behaviour of hyperlinks in
 * web browsers. It "knows" its own font, color, and URL and can change color
 * temporarily when the mouse passes over, or permanently when clicked.
 */
class LinkLabel extends Canvas {

    String linkurl;
    String linklabel;

    Font font = new Font("Monospaced", Font.PLAIN, 12);

    Color color = new Color(10, 20, 240);
    Color savedColor;

    /**
     * Construct a new LinkLabel.
     */
    public LinkLabel(String label, String url) {

        //super();
        linkurl    = url;
        linklabel  = label;

        // Save the current color.
        //
        savedColor = color;

        // Set the size of this label according to the height and descent
        // of its font.
        //
        FontMetrics fm = getFontMetrics(font);
        setSize(fm.stringWidth(linklabel), fm.getHeight() + fm.getDescent());

    }


    // This method enables several listeners that control the LinkLabel's
    // color
    //
    public void enableEffects() {

        addMouseListener(new MouseAdapter() {

            // These "internal" listeners control the color change

            // Set the color to magenta for followed links.
            //
            public void mouseClicked(MouseEvent e) {
```

```
                    color       = Color.magenta;
                    savedColor = Color.magenta;
                    repaint();

                }

                // Make the link red as long as a mouse is over it.
                //
                public void mouseEntered(MouseEvent e) {

                    savedColor = color;
                    color       = Color.red;
                    repaint();

                }

                // Return the color to its original color before we dragged the
                // mouse over it.
                //
                public void mouseExited(MouseEvent e) {

                    color = savedColor;
                    repaint();

                }

            });

    }

    /**
     * Java calls the paint() method whenever the object needs to be
     * redrawn, so this method fully renders the label as needed.
     */
    public void paint(Graphics g) {

        FontMetrics fm = g.getFontMetrics();
        g.setColor(color);
        g.setFont(font);

        // "Draw" the text of the label.
        //
        g.drawString(linklabel, 0, fm.getHeight());

    }

}
```

What Next?

The java.awt package is a flexible and functional means with which to create graphical user interfaces. Much of the promise of JPL lies in the ability to utilize the many resources provided by the AWT for event handling, image manipulation, and graphical component manipulation from within your Perl program.

Even though it is still a fairly young API when compared to other graphical toolkits, AWT is maturing rapidly. Java's AWT also has an edge over other toolkits because it was designed from the bottom up as a platform-independent interface. Even though it still exhibits some platform-specific behavior, it comes very close to full platform independence. The AWT also has the Java marketing juggernaut working for it, which means more installed users, and more functionality as more and more people extend the base classes. The Java community is fairly well organized (though they are by no means as well organized as the Perl activists) and if you search, you will probably find someone else who had the same problem you are having; perhaps you will even find someone who came up with a solution to that problem.

With these techniques and examples under your belt, you can now begin to develop your own applications.

5

JPL and Applets:
Using JPL with RMI

In a perfect world, Java's promise of "compile once, run everywhere" would hold true in every circumstance. However, since JPL uses platform-specific extensions (native code) to embed Perl within Java, it is not possible to distribute a Java applet that has been extended using JPL. Consider the following scenario: a user visits your site using a Macintosh version of the Netscape browser. As with any applet, the applet classes and any supporting classes (including the Perl shared library) that are not already installed in the user's environment must be downloaded over the network. Even if you could get past the security restriction that prevents an applet from downloading native libraries, the shared libraries built on a Unix platform supported by JPL are useless on a different platform, such as the Mac! Therein lies the rub—applications and applets written using pure Java are fully platform independent, but once you introduce a native library, you sacrifice that independence. With every fancy feature comes a price.

The situation is not completely hopeless, however. As of JDK 1.1, Java programs can invoke the methods of objects running on a remote host. This feature is known as RMI, or Remote Method Invocation. To take advantage of RMI, you must develop a class that inherits and implements certain components of the RMI API. This effectively makes it a server; once you start running it, it can respond to remote requests from client programs, including applets and applications.

This chapter starts with a quick introduction to RMI, using a simple example which covers the basics of developing an RMI-enabled applet. With this as a foundation, the remainder of the chapter is devoted to showing how an RMI-enabled applet can be developed that invokes Perl methods within the remote object.

RMI Quick Start

Building an RMI-enabled applet is somewhat more involved than building a typical applet, as you'll see in this section. For starters, you will need to define and instantiate a class that supports RMI, and your applet will need to do a few tricks to interact with remote instances of the class. If you want to use RMI within an applet, the remote object must reside on the same server from which the applet was loaded. This is a fundamental security feature of applets: once an applet has been downloaded and is running within the user's browser, it cannot make a network connection to any host other than the one from which the applet was originally loaded. However, since the remote object is a Java application, it operates under less severe restrictions. Unlike an applet, the remote object can connect to other hosts, use native libraries, and interact with the filesystem of the server on which it is running.

Defining the Remote Class

The remote class must be defined using two classes. The first is actually an *interface*, which declares the methods you want applets to be able to invoke remotely. These methods should have no body, since an interface may only contain abstract classes and it is up to implementations of an interface to actually define the methods. The second class you must define is the implementation of the interface. This *implementation class* must include definitions for the abstract methods declared in the interface. The reason for this unusual arrangement is that applets will actually work with a remote object as an instance of the interface rather than as an instance of the implementation class. In practice, this means that after the applet obtains the class from the `java.rmi.Naming.lookup()` method, it uses Java's casting mechanism to treat it as an instance of the interface class. The `java.rmi.Naming.lookup()` method returns a reference to an instance of a class that is running remotely as though it were an instance of *java.rmi.Remote*, which all remote interfaces extend in their interface declaration.

The examples in this chapter are on the Perl Resource Kit CD-ROM in the directory *oreilly/eg/ch05/*. If you chose to install the O'Reilly Extras using the setup tool, these examples will have been copied to the directory you chose. See Chapter 2, *Installing the Resource Kit Software*, for more details.

To prepare the *Makefile* for the RMI example, in the *RMIIntroApplet/* subdirectory, execute the command `perl Makefile.PL`. This command generates the *Makefile* for these examples and also sets some site-specific constants within the applications (including your hostname and the location of your JDK).

The following listing is from the *RMIIntro.java* program. It defines the interface for a remote object that performs some simple string manipulations. Since it is an interface and not a class, none of the methods may have a body; rather they have a semicolon. It is up to an implementation of this interface to define how the ReverseIt() and ReplaceIt() methods will behave. As stated earlier, the reason is that the RMI API does not allow client applets or applications to work with remote objects as an instance of the remote class; they must treat them as though they were instances of an interface that defines the remote methods. As a result, client applets and applications can only invoke methods declared here in the interface. For example, if you were to add a method called SortIt() to the implementation class, but that method was not declared in the interface listed below, client applets and applications could not invoke the SortIt() method.

```
/*
 * RMIIntro.java
 *
 * Interface for a remote object that can reverse and
 * replace within a String.
 *
 */
import java.rmi.*;

public interface RMIIntro extends Remote {
    public String ReverseIt(String s) throws RemoteException;
    public String ReplaceIt(String s, char oldchar, char newchar)
            throws RemoteException;
}
```

The implementation of this class simply provides a method body for the methods declared in the interface, and defines a main() method. The main() method is executed by default when the name of this class is passed to the Java interpreter, but the main() method is not exposed as a remote method.

The ReverseIt() method traverses the String from the last character to the first, and appends each character along the way into a temporary buffer. This buffer is an instance of StringBuffer, since String objects in Java are immutable. The StringBuffer class, on the other hand, offers an append() method that will add a string to the end of the buffer. After the ReverseIt() method, the ReplaceIt() method appears, which is quite simple—it uses a method that the String object already has, the replace() method, to replace each occurrence of a given character with another character.

The main() method is responsible for setting up the RMI server. As is the case with all Java applications, the main() method is a static method that is automatically invoked by the Java interpreter if the compiled class is named on the command line. In the case of this class, the main() method creates an instance of the RMIIntroImpl class and registers it with the RMI registry, a special process that must be running on the server that the remote object is running on. The RMI registry is a shell script that starts the RMI Naming service, which listens on a TCP/IP port (1099 by default) and allows RMI objects on the local machine to register and deregister themselves. Also, it allows remote clients to look up RMI objects that are running on the host. The "Serving Up the Remote Object" section that appears later in this chapter describes what must be done to start the RMI registry.

The following code shows the implementation class for the **RMIIntro** interface:

```java
/*
 *
 * RMIIntroImpl.java
 *
 * Implementation class for the RMIIntro interface.
 *
 */

import java.rmi.*;
import java.rmi.server.UnicastRemoteObject;

public class RMIIntroImpl extends UnicastRemoteObject implements RMIIntro {

    // This String is the name of the RMI server. It is set
    // by whatever method constructs this class.
    //
    private String name;

    public RMIIntroImpl(String s) throws RemoteException {
        super();  // Call the superclass constructor.
        name = s; // Set the name of this object.
    }

    /**
     *
     * Reverse a String, byte by byte.
     *
     * @param s      the String to reverse.
     * @return       the reversed String.
     */
    public String ReverseIt(String s) throws RemoteException {

        // Create a StringBuffer to hold the reversed value.
        StringBuffer sb = new StringBuffer();

        // Walk over the String backwards.
        //
        for (int i = s.length() - 1; i >= 0; i--) {

                // Append the character at the current index
                // to the StringBuffer.
                //
                sb.append(s.substring(i, i + 1));
        }
```

```java
            // Return a String representation of the
            // StringBuffer.
            //
            return sb.toString();

    }

    /**
     *
     * Single character search and replace.
     *
     * @param s        the String on which to perform the replacement.
     * @param oldchar the character to replace.
     * @param newchar the new character.
     *
     * @return        the modified String.
     *
     */
    public String ReplaceIt(String s, char oldchar, char newchar)
              throws RemoteException {
        return s.replace(oldchar, newchar);
    }

    public static void main(String args[]) {

        // Create and install an RMI security manager.
        //
        System.setSecurityManager(new RMISecurityManager());

        try {
            // Create an instance of the RMIIntroImpl object.
            //
            RMIIntroImpl obj = new RMIIntroImpl("RMIIntroServer");

            // Register this new object with the RMI
            // registry running on this machine.
            //
            Naming.rebind("//yourhost/RMIIntroServer", obj);

            // Tell us something reassuring...
            //
            System.out.println("RMIIntroServer bound in registry");

        } catch (Exception e) {

            System.out.println("RMIIntroImpl err: " + e.getMessage());
            e.printStackTrace();

        }

    }

}
```

The Client Applet

The client applet for this RMI example offers a simple interface to the end user. Figure 5-1 shows the applet running in the Netscape Navigator browser. In the applet, the user is offered a text region at the top of the applet into which he may type any sort of free text. This input region is a `TextArea` object called `input`. Below this region is a read-only output area, a `TextArea` object called `mangled`.

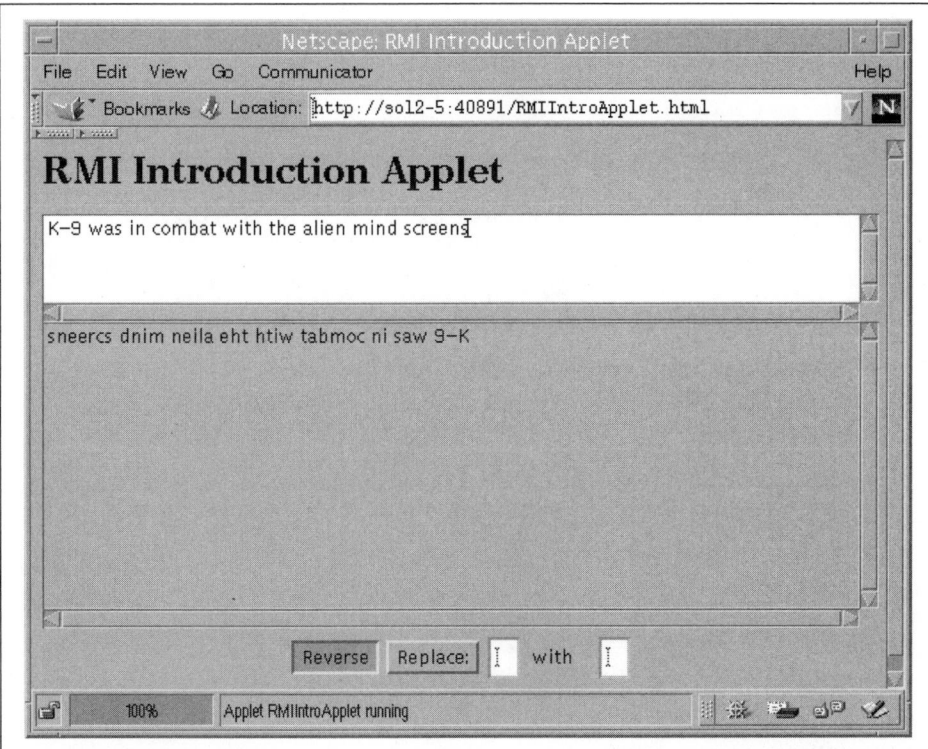

Figure 5-1. RMI client applet

At the bottom of the applet are two buttons. The first button is marked *Reverse*. If the user types some text into the top region and clicks this button, the applet performs an RMI registry lookup on the remote host, finds the remote object, and invokes its `ReverseIt()` method, which returns the same string the user typed, but reversed. After it gets the reversed string, the applet displays the string in the second text region. The second button on the form is marked *Replace* and is followed immediately by two blank text input fields. If the user clicks *Replace*, the applet passes the string from the input region as well as the first character in the search and replace fields and invokes the remote `ReplaceIt()` method, which returns a string that has the search character replaced by the replacement character. It then displays the modified string in the output region. The code for the client applet follows.

```
/**
 *
 * A client applet that invokes methods in the RMIIntro
 * object. It actually manipulates an RMIIntroImpl object,
 * but this applet has no way of knowing that.
 *
 */
import java.awt.*;
import java.awt.event.*;
import java.rmi.*;

public class RMIIntroApplet extends java.applet.Applet {

    TextArea input;      // Input area for the text we'll modify.
    TextArea mangled;    // An output area for the text.

    TextField search;    // The text to search for.
    TextField replace;   // The text to replace the above.

    Button btn_rev;      // A button to reverse the text.
    Button btn_replace;  // A button to search/replace within the text.

    /**
     *
     * The Applet's init() method.
     *
     */
    public void init() {

        // A panel to hold the action buttons and the
        // search/replace text fields.
        //
        Panel button_panel;

        // Set the layout of this Applet to be a
        // BorderLayout.
        //
        setLayout(new BorderLayout());

        // Instantiate two TextArea objects: one for the
        // input and one for the mangled output. Since the
        // mangled output needs to be read-only, its
        // editable property gets set to false.
        //
        input   = new TextArea(4, 65);
        mangled = new TextArea(4, 65);
        mangled.setEditable(false);
```

```
        // Put the input area in the north of the applet and
        // the output area in the center.
        //
        add("North", input);
        add("Center", mangled);

        // Instantiate the panel for the buttons and give it
        // a FlowLayout.
        //
        button_panel = new Panel();
        button_panel.setLayout(new FlowLayout());

        // Add a button labeled Reverse.
        //
        btn_rev   = new Button("Reverse");
        button_panel.add(btn_rev);

        // Add a button labeled Replace.
        //
        btn_replace = new Button("Replace:");
        button_panel.add(btn_replace);

        // Add TextFields for the search and replace texts.
        // They are separated by the word "with", since the
        // button to their left is labeled Replace. Read
        // left to right, the user will see "Replace [blank]
        // with [blank]."
        //
        search = new TextField(1);
        button_panel.add(search);
        button_panel.add(new Label("with"));
        replace = new TextField(1);
        button_panel.add(replace);

        // Add the button panel at the south of the Applet.
        //
        add("South", button_panel);

    }

    /**
     *
     * Unfortunately, Netscape Navigator does not support
     * the newer AWT event handling, although it does
     * support other features from JDK 1.1, including RMI.
     * Since the new AWT event model is not supported, we
     * have to use the old handleEvent() method, and this
     * will generate deprecation errors when compiled with
     * the JDK 1.1 compiler.
     *
     */
    public boolean handleEvent( Event event ) {
```

```
switch(event.id) {

  case Event.ACTION_EVENT:

    // The user clicked the Reverse button.
    //
    if (event.target == btn_rev) {

        RMIIntro obj = null;
        try {

            String remote_name =
                "//" + getCodeBase().getHost() + "/RMIIntroServer";
            obj = (RMIIntro)Naming.lookup(remote_name);

            mangled.setText( obj.ReverseIt( input.getText() ) );

        } catch (Exception e) {

            System.out.println(
                "RMIIntroApplet exception: " + e.getMessage());
            e.printStackTrace();

        }

    }

    // The user clicked the Replace button.
    //
    if (event.target == btn_replace) {

        RMIIntro obj = null;
        try {
            String remote_name =
                "//" + getCodeBase().getHost() + "/RMIIntroServer";
            obj = (RMIIntro)Naming.lookup(remote_name);

            char oldchar = search.getText().toCharArray()[0];
            char newchar = replace.getText().toCharArray()[0];
            mangled.setText( obj.ReplaceIt( input.getText(),
                                            oldchar,
                                            newchar) );

        } catch (ArrayIndexOutOfBoundsException e) {

            String msg = "Please supply a character for both " +
                        "the search and replace input fields.";
            mangled.setText("**ERROR**\n" + msg);

        } catch (Exception e) {

            System.out.println(
                "RMIIntroApplet exception: " + e.getMessage());
            e.printStackTrace();
```

```
                }
              }
            break;

          default:
              return false;
          }
          return true;
       }

    }
```

The HTML File

To view this applet in a browser, it must be loaded from a simple HTML document, which includes a title and an **<applet>** tag. When a client loads this HTML document in a Java-aware browser, the applet is loaded over the network, as well. The HTML necessary is shown below.

```
<html>
<head>
<title>RMI Introduction Applet</title>
</head>

<body>
<h1>RMI Introduction Applet</h1>

<applet codebase="./" code="RMIIntroApplet" width=580 height=320>

</applet>
</body>
</html>
```

Serving Up the Remote Object

Once you have defined the remote object interface and implementation, you should compile the classes and use the **rmic** utility to generate the remote stub and skeleton. The remote stub is the class that is actually loaded by the applet client, and the stub forwards RMI calls to the skeleton, which in turn forwards the method calls to the implementation classes. You compile the classes with the following command:

```
javac RMIIntro.java RMIIntroImpl.java RMIIntroApplet.java
```

You then need to feed the compiled implementation class into the **rmic** utility to generate the stub and skeleton, with this command:

```
rmic RMIIntroImpl
```

This command generates the files **RMIIntroImpl_Skel.class** and **RMIIntroImpl_Stub.class**.

To make all this very simple, you can generate a *Makefile* using the command `perl Makefile.PL`. This command also discovers the location of your JDK and determines your machine's host name (needed by the RMI components). Once you have generated the *Makefile*, use the command `make` to compile the Java files and run `rmic` to generate the stub and skeleton.

Note that the *Makefile* assumes you will be compiling and deploying the RMI server object and applet from the same directory. If not, you will need to specify the deployment directory with the `-d` switch. For example, if you are installing these examples in the directory *~/public_html/RMIIntro*, you would compile and use the `rmic` utility as follows:

```
javac -d ~/public_html/RMIIntro RMIIntro.java RMIIntroImpl.java \
        RMIIntroApplet.java
rmic -d ~/public_html/RMIIntro RMIIntroImpl
```

The example in this chapter is deployed using a simple web server written in Perl, so it should not be necessary for you to use a different deployment directory as you work through this example. The only reason you would need a different deployment directory would be if you wished to use this applet example under a production web server and didn't want the source code to be sitting in the deployment directory.

Running the Demo

To run the demo, you need to install the LWP (libwww) library for Perl since the demo runs a Perl-based web server to serve up the applet from the current directory. You can use the Resource Kit's setup tool to do this, as described in Chapter 2. To start the demo, simply execute it as `perl demo.pl`. Once the demo loads, you should see something similar to the following:

```
RMI Registry PID: 5260
RMI Object Server PID: 5262
RMI Object Status: RMIIntroServer bound in registry

Looks good! Go somewhere warm and do a:

    appletviewer http://sol2-5:34225/RMIIntroApplet.html

(hit CTRL-C to end this demo...)
```

If you have trouble running the demo, or are simply curious as to what goes on inside it, read on. The demo script starts the **rmiregistry** server, which is located in *$JAVA_HOME/bin/rmiregistry*, where $JAVA_HOME is something like */usr/local/java* or */usr/local/jdk1.1.3*. The RMI registry runs in the background, and can be run from the shell with no arguments.

If you want the demo use a TCP/IP port other than the default of 1099, invoke it with a port number as an argument. You will also need to change the assignment of the `remote_name` variable in the *RMIIntroApplet.java* file to use this port number:

```
String remote_name = "//" + getCodeBase().getHost() + ":2001/RMIIntroServer";
```

Also, you will need to change the `Naming.rebind()` method invocation in the *RMIIntroImpl.java.in* file to something like:

```
// Register this new object with the RMI
// registry running on this machine.
//
Naming.rebind("//MYHOSTNAME:2001/RMIIntroServer", obj);
```

The *RMIIntroImpl.java.in* file is processed by *Makefile.PL*, which substitutes the name of your server for MYHOSTNAME. After you make these changes, you should run both `perl Makefile.PL` and `make` again.

Once you have started the RMI registry, you will need to feed the `RMIIntroImpl` class into the Java interpreter. This action implicitly invokes the `main()` method, which constructs an instance of the remote object and registers it with the RMI registry, enabling the applet to connect to the object remotely. To do so, issue the following command, where *$URL* is the URL of the directory containing the Applet and the RMI server application:

```
java -Djava.rmi.server.codebase=$URL RMIIntroImpl
```

To use your own web server, you must configure the directory that contains these examples as a document directory. A mini-web server, which depends upon the LWP bundle, is included in the *demo.pl* script which starts a web server and prints out the URL of the applet after it starts up. The mini-web server uses a different port each time it starts, so the demo script prints the URL when it starts. You can cut and paste the URL into a web browser that understands Java and the RMI API, such as *appletviewer* that comes with the JDK or Netscape Navigator 4.02 or higher. The following listing shows the contents of the *demo.pl* script:

```
#!/usr/local/bin/perl

# HTTP server components from the LWP bundle.
#
use HTTP::Daemon;
use HTTP::Status;

# The configuration constants in Config.demo.pl were set up
# by Makefile.PL
#
eval("require 'Config.demo.pl'")
    or die "Config.demo.pl not found:\n" .
            "Did you remember to run 'perl Makefile.PL'?";
```

```perl
# Location of the rmiregistry script and the java
# interpreter.
#
$RMI_REG   = "$JAVA_HOME/bin/rmiregistry";
$JAVA      = "$JAVA_HOME/bin/java";

# Make sure both of these paths point to executables.
#
unless (-x $RMI_REG) {
    die "Can't find rmiregistry - looked in $RMI_REG";
}
unless (-x $JAVA) {
    die "Can't find java - looked in $JAVA";
}

# Create a new HTTP server and find out what its URL is.
#
$d = new HTTP::Daemon
        LocalAddr => $HOSTNAME;
$URL = $d->url or die "No URL!!!";

# Open a pipe to a new rmiregistry process.
#
$rmipid = open(RMIREGISTRY, "$RMI_REG|")
                or die "Couldn't start the rmiregistry: $!";
print "RMI Registry PID: $rmipid\n";

# Start up the RMI server using a pipe that we can read
# from.
#
$rmisrv = "$JAVA -Djava.rmi.server.codebase=$URL RMIIntroImpl";
$rmisrvpid = open(RMISRV, "$rmisrv|")
                or die "Couldn't start '$rmisrv': $!";

print "RMI Object Server PID: $rmisrvpid\n";
$rmistat = <RMISRV>;
if ($rmistat !~ /bound in registry/) {
    die "Error creating the remote object: $rmistat";
} else {
    print "RMI Object Status: $rmistat\n";
}

# Tell the user the URL to use to view the applet.
#
print <<EOF;
Looks good! Go somewhere warm and do a:

    appletviewer ${URL}RMIIntroApplet.html

(hit CTRL-C to end this demo...)
EOF

# Have the web server wait for connections.
#
```

```
while ($c = $d->accept) {

    # Get a request object from this connection.
    #
    $r = $c->get_request;

    # If the request object is defined, then assume the
    # remote user is looking for a file from us.
    #
    if ($r) {

        # Get the file name from the request, and strip out
        # any leading non-word characters - this will
        # eliminate leading .. and / characters, as well as
        # other stuff we might want to avoid, like ~.
        #
        $file = $r->url->path;
        $file =~ s#^\W+##g;

        # Give them the file they asked for.
        #
        $c->send_file_response($file);
    }

    # Close this connection.
    #
    $c = undef;
}
```

Thoughts to Keep in Mind

Although RMI involves a bit of trickery, it is not so difficult to deploy. It is a simple API that allows you to supply functionality to your applets that would otherwise be unavailable. As will be seen in the next example, this is especially handy to deploy an applet that uses JPL to integrate Perl and Java. Before you look at the JPL applet example, keep in mind the components of an RMI deployment:

The RMI registry

> Allows RMI-enabled objects to register and deregister themselves. It also provides lookup functionality so clients can locate and gain access to remote objects that have been registered.

The RMI-enabled object

> Runs in its own JVM on your server. Each time you run the Java interpreter or run an applet in a web browser, it is running in its own Java Virtual Machine. You can think of RMI as one way to get two Virtual Machines talking to each other.

The web server

> Sends the HTML document and the applet, and nothing more.

The web browser

> Loads an HTML document that contains an applet tag. After it loads the HTML document, it asks the web server to send down the compiled *.class* file that comprises the applet.

The applet

> Runs in a Java Virtual Machine under the web browser and connects to the RMI registry running on the web server to locate and gain access to the remote object.

For further reference, you may want to consult the online Java documentation for the RMI-related classes, and also the "Getting Started with RMI" document, available at:

> *http://www.javasoft.com/products/jdk/1.1/docs/guide/rmi/getstart.doc.html*

Online JDK documentation may be found at:

> *http://www.javasoft.com/products/jdk/1.1/docs/index.html*

and you can download the documentation for local perusal by visiting:

> *http://www.javasoft.com/products/jdk/1.1/index.html#docs*

You should also always check the latest resources at the Perl Resource Kit site:

> *http://perl.oreilly.com/*

Using JPL and RMI

Once you've tackled the RMI part, developing an applet that connects to a JPL-enhanced remote object is extremely simple. Rather than develop an implementation class that lives in a Java file, you need to develop your implementation class as a *.jpl* file and compile it as you would any other JPL application. The *RMIJPL* directory on the CD (or loaded on your system) contains the examples found in this chapter. If you have not yet installed the example, see Chapter 2 for instructions.

Running the JPL-RMI Demo Applet

As it did with the previous RMI example, running `perl Makefile.PL` in the RMIJPL directory sets up the *Makefile* for this example. It also sets up the *Config.demo.pl* file and processes the *RMIDemoImpl.jpl.in* file, producing the *RMIDemoImpl.jpl* file. Once you have generated the *Makefile*, execute the command `make` and run the demo with the command `perl  demo.pl`. You should see output similar to the following:

```
RMI Registry PID: 5668
RMI Object Server PID: 5669
RMI Object Status: RMIDemoServer bound in registry

Looks good! Go somewhere warm and do a:

    appletviewer http://sol2-5:34338/RMIDemoApplet.html

(hit CTRL-C to end this demo...)
```

Figure 5-2 shows the applet in action. Since this applet is Perl-enhanced, it offers a few more features than the Java-only version. For one, there is now a *Sort* button, which will sort everything in the text input field by word. Second, the *Reverse* button reverses the text input by word, rather than by character. Finally, the search and replace functionality is a little bit smarter. Rather than a simple character replacement, the *Replace* button allows you to use the power of Perl's regular expressions!

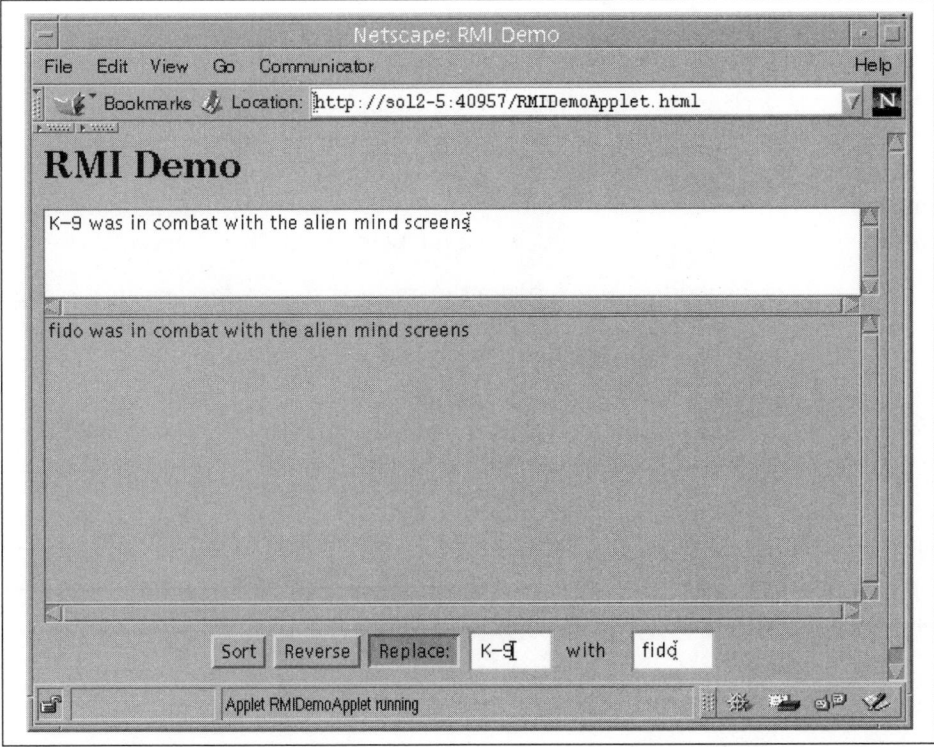

Figure 5-2. RMIJPL applet

The RMIDemo Interface

Like all RMI deployments, you need to have an interface that extends the *java.rmi.Remote* class. The interface contained in the *RMIDemo.java* file does exactly that:

```
/*
 * RMIDemo.java
 *
 * Interface for a remote object that can sort, reverse and
 * replace within a String.
 *
 */
import java.rmi.*;

public interface RMIDemo extends Remote {
    String SortIt(String s) throws RemoteException;
    String ReverseIt(String s) throws RemoteException;
    String ReplaceIt(String s, String left, String right)
        throws RemoteException;
}
```

The RMIDemoImpl Implementation Class

Like the previous example, the implementation class provides a method body for the methods declared in the interface. It also supplies a **main()** method, which is executed when this class is fed to the Java interpreter. The remote classes are simply wrappers to the Perl methods that perform the text processing. The Perl methods can't be exposed as remote methods, since they are actually native methods, so the remote methods delegate the work to the Perl methods.

The **SortIt()** method calls the **plsort()** method to sort the text in the input region by word. It is a brutish sort, since it simply **split()**s the string on any whitespace and then sorts the list that results from the call to the **split()** function. It then joins the sorted list using a single space, which is ultimately returned to the applet. The **ReverseIt()** method is quite similar. It invokes the **plreverse()** method, which does everything that the **plsort()** method does, except it uses the **reverse** operator on the list rather than the **sort** operator.

The **ReplaceIt()** method delegates its work to the **plreplace()** method, which performs a substitution on the input region using Perl's substitution operator. The complete code is shown below:

```
/*
 *
 * RMIDemoImpl.java
 *
 * Implementation class for the RMIDemo interface.
 *
```

```
 */
import java.rmi.*;
import java.rmi.server.UnicastRemoteObject;

public class RMIDemoImpl extends UnicastRemoteObject implements RMIDemo {

    // This String is the name of the RMI server. It is set
    // by whatever method constructs this class.
    //
    private String name;

    public RMIDemoImpl(String s) throws RemoteException {
        super();  // Call the superclass constructor.
        name = s; // Set the name of this object.
    }

    /**
     *
     * Remote method that sorts a String. This is simply a
     * wrapper to the Perl method that does the real work,
     * plsort().
     *
     * @param s     the String to sort.
     * @return      the sorted String.
     *
     */
    public String SortIt(String s) throws RemoteException {
        return plsort(s);
    }

    /**
     *
     * Remote method that reverse the words in a string.
     * This is nothing more than a wrapper to a Perl method
     * that does the grunt work, namely plreverse().
     *
     * @param s     the String to reverse.
     * @return      the reversed String.
     */
    public String ReverseIt(String s) throws RemoteException {
        return plreverse(s);
    }

    /**
     *
     * Remote method that is responsible for performing a
     * search and replace on a string. This method merely
     * acts as a wrapper to a Perl function, plreplace().
     *
     * @param s       the String on which to perform the replacement.
     * @param left    the left-hand side of the s///g; * operation.
     * @param right   the right-hand side of the s///g; * operation.
     *
```

```
 * @return          the modified String.
 */
public String ReplaceIt(String s, String left, String right)
  throws RemoteException {
    return plreplace(s, left, right);
}

/**
 *
 * Sort the words in a string.
 *
 * @param s      the String to sort.
 * @return       the sorted String.
 *
 */
perl String plsort(String s) {{

    # Split the string on one or more whitespace
    # characters, sort the resulting list, and
    # join the result using one space.
    #
    return join(" ", sort split(/\s+/, $s));

}}

/**
 *
 * Reverses the words in a string.
 *
 * @param s      the String to reverse.
 * @return       the reversed String.
 */
perl String plreverse(String s) {{

    # Split the string on one or more whitespace
    # characters, reverse the resulting list, and
    # join the result using one space.
    #
    return join(" ", reverse split(/\s+/, $s));

}}

/**
 *
 * Execute a search and replace operation on a string.
 *
 * @param s         the String on which to perform the replacement.
 * @param left      the left-hand side of the s///g; * operation.
 * @param right     the right-hand side of the s///g; * operation.
 *
 * @return          the modified String.
 */
perl String plreplace(String s, String left, String right) {{
```

```
            # Perform the substitution.
            #
            $s =~ s/$left/$right/g;

            return $s;
    }}

    public static void main(String args[]) {

        // Create and install an RMI security manager.
        //
        System.setSecurityManager(new RMISecurityManager());

        try {
            // Create an instance of the RMIDemoImpl object.
            //
            RMIDemoImpl obj = new RMIDemoImpl("RMIDemoServer");

            // Register this new object with the RMI
            // registry running on this machine.
            //
            Naming.rebind("//sol2-5/RMIDemoServer", obj);

            // Tell us something reassuring...
            //
            System.out.println("RMIDemoServer bound in registry");

        } catch (Exception e) {

            System.out.println("RMIDemoImpl err: " + e.getMessage());
            e.printStackTrace();

        }

    }
}
```

The HTML File

As with any other applet, the RMIDemoApplet needs to be loaded from an HTML file. *RMIDemoApplet.html*, shown below, handles this for our example:

```
<html>
<head>
<title>RMI Demo</title>
</head>

<body>
<h1>RMI Demo</h1>

<applet codebase="./" code="RMIDemoApplet" width=580 height=320>
```

```
</applet>
</body>
</html>
```

The Applet

The applet itself is contained in the file *RMIDemoApplet.java* and is very similar to the applet in the *RMIIntro* example. Like the applet in that example, this applet displays a user interface that consists of two text areas, some buttons, and two text fields. The first text area is a `TextArea` object called `input`, and the second is a read-only `TextArea` object called `mangled`.

In this example, there are three buttons, labeled *Sort, Reverse,* and *Replace*. The `handleEvent()` method checks to see if the user clicked one of these buttons and looks up the remote object, invoking the appropriate remote method. In the case of the *Replace* button, the remote method is handed the values in the search and replace `TextField` objects. In the event handler for each button, the output of the remote method invocation is stored in the `mangled TextArea` object. Readers familiar with improvements in the JDK 1.1 event handling mechanism will notice that the `handleEvent()` method is currently deprecated. Note, too, that Navigator 4.x does not supply a full set of JDK 1.1 features; rather it still uses the old AWT event handling mechanism.

Following is the code for the applet:

```
/**
 *
 * A client applet that invokes methods in the RMIDemo
 * object. It actually manipulates an RMIDemoImpl object,
 * but this applet has no way of knowing that.
 *
 */
import java.awt.*;
import java.awt.event.*;
import java.rmi.*;

public class RMIDemoApplet extends java.applet.Applet {

    TextArea input;        // Input area for the text we'll modify.
    TextArea mangled;      // An output area for the text.

    TextField search;      // The text to search for.
    TextField replace;     // The text to replace the above.

    Button btn_sort;       // A button to sort the text
    Button btn_rev;        // A button to reverse the text.
    Button btn_replace;    // A button to search/replace within the text.
```

```
/**
 *
 * The Applet's init() method.
 *
 */
public void init() {

    // A panel to hold the action buttons and the
    // search/replace text fields.
    //
    Panel button_panel;

    // Set the layout of this Applet to be a
    // BorderLayout.
    //
    setLayout(new BorderLayout());

    // Instantiate two TextArea objects: one for the
    // input and one for the mangled output. Since the
    // mangled output needs to be read-only, its
    // editable property gets set to false.
    //
    input   = new TextArea(4, 65);
    mangled = new TextArea(4, 65);
    mangled.setEditable(false);

    // Put the input area in the north of the applet and
    // the output area in the center.
    //
    add("North", input);
    add("Center", mangled);

    // Instantiate the panel for the buttons and give it
    // a FlowLayout.
    //
    button_panel = new Panel();
    button_panel.setLayout(new FlowLayout());

    // Add a button labeled Sort.
    //
    btn_sort  = new Button("Sort");
    button_panel.add(btn_sort);

    // Add a button labeled Reverse.
    //
    btn_rev   = new Button("Reverse");
    button_panel.add(btn_rev);

    // Add a button labeled Replace.
    //
    btn_replace = new Button("Replace:");
    button_panel.add(btn_replace);
```

```
        // Add TextFields for the search and replace texts.
        //
        search = new TextField(10);
        button_panel.add(search);
        button_panel.add(new Label("with"));
        replace = new TextField(10);
        button_panel.add(replace);

        // Add the button panel at the south of the Applet.
        //
        add("South", button_panel);

    }

    /**
     *
     * Event handler for the applet.
     */
    public boolean handleEvent( Event event ) {

        switch(event.id) {

          case Event.ACTION_EVENT:

            // The user clicked the Sort button.
            //
            if (event.target == btn_sort) {

                RMIDemo obj = null;
                try {

                    // Look up the remote object.
                    //
                    String remote_name =
                        "//" + getCodeBase().getHost() + "/RMIDemoServer";
                    obj = (RMIDemo)Naming.lookup(remote_name);

                    // Invoke the remote object's SortIt()
                    // method and set the text of the
                    // mangled TextArea to the return value.
                    //
                    mangled.setText( obj.SortIt( input.getText() ) );

                } catch (Exception e) {

                    System.out.println(
                        "RMIDemoApplet exception: " + e.getMessage());
                    e.printStackTrace();

                }

            }
```

```
// The user pressed the Reverse button.
//
if (event.target == btn_rev) {

    RMIDemo obj = null;
    try {

        // Look up the remote object.
        //
        String remote_name =
            "//" + getCodeBase().getHost() + "/RMIDemoServer";
        obj = (RMIDemo)Naming.lookup(remote_name);

        // Invoke the remote object's
        // ReverseIt() method, setting the text
        // of the mangled TextArea to the
        // result.
        //
        mangled.setText( obj.ReverseIt( input.getText() ) );

    } catch (Exception e) {

        System.out.println(
            "RMIDemoApplet exception: " + e.getMessage());
        e.printStackTrace();

    }

}

// The user clicked the Replace button.
//
if (event.target == btn_replace) {

    RMIDemo obj = null;
    try {

        // Look up the remote object.
        //
        String remote_name =
            "//" + getCodeBase().getHost() + "/RMIDemoServer";
        obj = (RMIDemo)Naming.lookup(remote_name);

        // Invoke the remote ReplaceIt() method,
        // and set the text of the mangled
        // TextArea to the output.
        //
        mangled.setText( obj.ReplaceIt( input.getText(),
                                        search.getText(),
                                        replace.getText()) );

    } catch (Exception e) {
```

```
                    System.out.println(
                        "RMIDemoApplet exception: " + e.getMessage());
                    e.printStackTrace();


                }
            }
            break;

          default:
            return false;
        }
        return true;
    }

}
```

6

Advanced JPL: SQL Databases and Dynamic Images

If the purpose of a tool such as JPL is to unite two very different languages, then it surpasses expectations if it makes simple tasks simple, difficult tasks possible, and impossible tasks avoidable. This chapter investigates two common, if not somewhat difficult, tasks in application development: the acquisition of data and the generation of graphical output based on that data.

Using JPL, Java's JDBC database access API, the Data::Xtab module, and the GIFGraph module, these tasks become very simple! Although the finished product that unites these pieces is short and sweet, each of the components has a life of its own. Before looking at how these pieces go together, we'll examine each in turn, with the hopes of laying a sufficient foundation upon which you can build your understanding of the final application.

The examples for this chapter are included on the CD-ROM in the directory *oreilly/ eg/ch06/*. Use the setup tool to install them onto a locally available file system. See Chapter 2, *Installing the Resource Kit Software*, for more information on the setup tool.

GIFGraph and Data::Xtab

The example application in this chapter makes use of two user-visible modules: Martien Verbruggen's GIFgraph and Data::Xtab. We say "user-visible" here, because the GIFgraph module uses Lincoln Stein's GD module to render GIF images, but GD is not directly used in any of the code shown in this chapter. The GD module is a Perl interface to Thomas Boutell's gd graphics library. The great thing about GD and GIFgraph is that it is possible to create a GIF image as a string and, since JPL allows you to automagically convert a Perl string into a Java byte array, it is very simple to hand off the image to Java for its own sinister (or benign!) purposes.

NOTE   For the module authors' documentation on these modules, see the
Perl Module Reference in this Resource Kit.

Graphing with GIFgraph

The GIFgraph module requires you to supply a list of labels for the chart's X axis, along with any number of lists that are used for each data series. The X axis is labeled with the labels you supply. Each data series is plotted by value along the Y axis and also along the X axis according to the X axis label that corresponds to that value's position in the data series list. To support this plotting scheme, each data series must have the same number of elements as the list of X-axis labels.

Here is an example data set:

X-Axis Labels:	'JAN'	'FEB'	'MAR'
Y-Axis Series 1:	7	5	3
Y-Axis Series 2:	5	4	7
Y-Axis Series 3:	0	3	5

Figure 6-1 shows how this data looks when plotted using the GIFgraph module. The graph shown in this figure uses both lines and points to plot data. The red line (solid box points) corresponds to the first series, the green (hollow box points) to the second series, and the blue (x marks the point) to the third series. (Yes, we realize you can't see the colors in print, but if you run the example, you'll see them.)

The GIFgraph module, which should be installed along with the GD module using the Perl Resource Kit setup tool, allows you to generate graphs in a variety of styles. For this purpose, several modules are available in the GIFgraph package, including GIFgraph::lines, GIFgraph::bars, GIFgraph::points, GIFgraph::linespoints, GIFgraph::area, and GIFgraph::pie. Depending on how you want the graph to look, you can pick your choice of modules from the GIFgraph package and construct it with the new() method, as in:

```
$my_graph = new GIFgraph::linespoints();
```

Although the graph includes numerous default values, you can use the set() method to control the appearance of the graph. Among the options you may configure are x_label, which is the title for the X axis label values; y_label, the

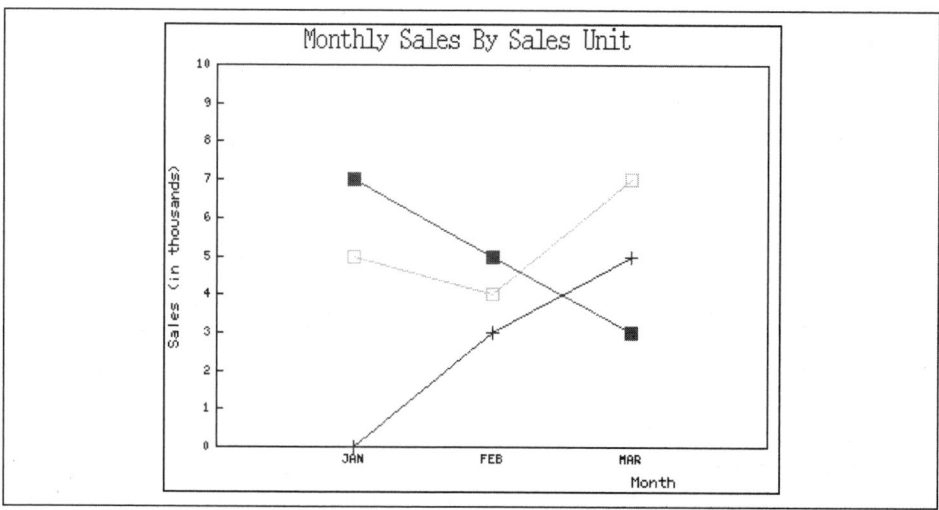

Figure 6-1. Data plotted using the GIFgraph module

title for the Y Axis data points, `title`, which is a title for the graph itself; `y_max_value`, which is the maximum value for the data set; and `y_tick_number`, which is the number of ticks to show along the Y axis. The following code shows these options:

```
$my_graph->set( 'x_label' => 'Month',
                'y_label' => 'Sales (in thousands)',
                'title' => 'Monthly Sales By Sales Unit',
                'y_max_value' => 10,
                'y_tick_number' => 10);
```

There are two methods you can use to produce a graph, `plot_to_gif()` and `plot()`. Both of these methods require you to pass in an array reference to the data array. The data array, in turn, is comprised of references to at least two other arrays: the array of labels for the X axis, and an array for each data set. The `plot_to_gif()` method requires a filename as its first argument, followed by the array reference, as in:

```
my @data = (['JAN', 'FEB', 'MAR'],
            [ 7 ,   5 ,   3],
            [ 5 ,   4 ,   7],
            [ 0 ,   3 ,   5]);
$my_graph->plot_to_gif("simplegraph.gif", \@data );
```

You can use the `plot()` method to retrieve the GIF as a string value, as in:

```
$my_graph->plot(\@data );
```

Following is a simple example, *simplegraph.pl*, which produces the graph shown in Figure 6-1 and saves it to the file *simplegraph.gif.*

```perl
#!/usr/local/bin/perl

use GIFgraph::linespoints;

# Initialize the X-axis labels and each data series. The
# @data array must start with a reference to an array of
# labels, followed by references to the arrays that contain
# the values for each data series.
#
my @data = (['JAN', 'FEB', 'MAR'],
            [ 7 ,    5 ,    3],
            [ 5 ,    4 ,    7],
            [ 0 ,    3 ,    5]);

# Construct a new GIFgraph::linespoints object.
#
$my_graph = new GIFgraph::linespoints();

# Set the X label, Y label, title, maximum value for the
# data series, as well as the number of 'ticks' to display
# along the Y axis.
#
$my_graph->set( 'x_label' => 'Month',
                'y_label' => 'Sales (in thousands)',
                'title' => 'Monthly Sales By Sales Unit',
                'y_max_value' => 10,
                'y_tick_number' => 10);

# Plot the gif to a file.
#
$my_graph->plot_to_gif("simplegraph.gif", \@data );
```

Pivoting the Data with Data::Xtab

As it turns out, when you are working with data in a normalized collection of
tables, you rarely find that the data is "ready to chart." It's unlikely that a
company's sales figures are going to be stored as monthly totals, and it's even
more unlikely that there will be a table that corresponds to each sales group. If
there were, it would be very easy to obtain the three data series lists shown in the
previous data set. In fact, the data is likely to be very raw and probably looked
something like this before the previous data set was generated:

Sales Group	Date of Sale	Dollars
A	JAN-14	$6,874
A	FEB-01	$1,987
A	FEB-18	$3,200
A	MAR-17	$3,459
B	JAN-12	$4,995
B	FEB-02	$3,750

Sales Group	Date of Sale	Dollars
B	MAR-08	$4,192
B	MAR-19	$2,984
C	FEB-27	$2,617
C	MAR-19	$4,697

At first glance, there are a couple of differences between this data set and the one that was used to generate the graph. Not all of these differences are handled by Data::Xtab, so the data must be manipulated somewhat before it is sent to Data::Xtab. One problem that's easy to solve is that the dollar amount isn't in rounded thousands, as it is in the chart data seen in the first example. Also, the dates include the day of the month in them, unlike the data that we used to generate the graph. These problems are easily fixed by first rounding the dollar amounts to the nearest thousand, then by stripping off all but the name of the month from the date. These steps prepare the data to be handed off to Data::Xtab:

Sales Group	Month of Sale	Dollars (in thousands)
A	JAN	7
A	FEB	2
A	FEB	3
A	MAR	3
B	JAN	5
B	FEB	4
B	MAR	4
B	MAR	3
C	FEB	3
C	MAR	5

The function of Data::Xtab is to pivot the data in such a way so that a new table is produced. This new table consists of *n* rows, where *n* is the number of data series in the raw data. In this example, each data series corresponds to a given sales group. Further, each row in this new table has one column for each X axis label, which is the month in this example. Further, Data::Xtab aggregates any data that falls into the same row and column, producing the following new table:

Sales Group	January Sales	February Sales	March Sales
A	7	5	3
B	5	4	7
C	0	3	5

The following example, *simplextab.pl*, uses the Data::Xtab module to perform the same conversion and then uses the GIFgraph module to create the GIF that was shown in Figure 6-1:

```
# !/usr/local/bin/perl

use Data::Xtab;
use GIFgraph::linespoints;

# This is some sample data that is not quite ready to feed
# into the GIFgraph module, but is a very realistic
# depiction of what you might find in a database table!
#
my @data = ( ['A', 'JAN-14', 6874],
             ['A', 'FEB-01', 1987],
             ['A', 'FEB-18', 3200],
             ['A', 'MAR-17', 3459],
             ['B', 'JAN-12', 4995],
             ['B', 'FEB-02', 3750],
             ['B', 'MAR-08', 4192],
             ['B', 'MAR-19', 2984],
             ['C', 'FEB-27', 2617],
             ['C', 'MAR-19', 4697]);

# Massage the data into shape before feeding it to
# Data::Xtab.
#
foreach my $d (@data) {

    # Trim the dash and day number from the date, which is
    # the second (index 1) element in each array.
    #
    $d->[1] =~ s/-..//g;

    # Get the sales amount (the third element in each array)
    # in thousands and round up.
    #
    $d->[2] = int( ($d->[2]/1000) + .5 )

}

# This array is required, since we want the months to appear
# in a certain order, and not sorted by month name, which is
# the default if no such array is passed as an argument to
# the Data::Xtab constructor.
#
my @outputcols = ('JAN', 'FEB', 'MAR');

# Create a new Data::Xtab object with the data that we have.
#
my $xtab = new Data::Xtab(\@data, \@outputcols);
```

```
# Retrieve the pivoted data in a format that is designed to
# play well with GIFgraph.
#
my @graph_data = $xtab->graph_data;

# The output of the Data::Xtab::graph_data() method includes
# a running total data series as the last series in the
# list. I don't want it in my graph, so I'm popping it off.
#
pop @graph_data;

# Create a new GIFGraph::linespoints object.
#
$my_graph = new GIFgraph::linespoints();

# Set up some common graph options.
#
$my_graph->set( 'x_label' => 'Month',
                'y_label' => 'Sales (in thousands)',
                'title' => 'Monthly Sales By Sales Unit',
                'y_max_value' => 10,
                'y_tick_number' => 10);

# Plot the graph, using the data in @graph_data.
#
$my_graph->plot_to_gif("simplextab.gif", \@graph_data );
```

JDBC

JDBC is Java's database access API. JDBC, which most likely stands for Java Data-Base Connectivity, offers a collection of classes that are useful for connecting to a database, issuing updates and queries against the database, and processing the results of queries. It is a very simple API and is mostly concerned with making it possible to create Java programs that interface with SQL data. It does not provide any sort of object-oriented mapping between objects you create in Java and data stored in a relational database. This comes as a surprise and disappointment to many people, who must account for this impedance mismatch as they decompose objects into columns and rows, shoehorning their carefully crafted objects into the relational model. While it is possible to stream certain objects into a database representation, this provides none of the object-oriented benefits at a database level. That is, database engine-level inheritance, polymorphism, and inter-object relationships are not part of JDBC. Such things are the purview of object-relational and object database engines and associated APIs, such as the proposed ODMG binding for Java (*http://www.odmg.org/*).

Although JDBC will not automagically map your objects and their relationships out to the database, it provides more than enough of a database API for you to develop database-enabled Java applications.

JDBC and Database Drivers

In order for JDBC to be of much use to you, you'll need access to some sort of SQL engine. The JDBC classes included with the JDK do not actually provide access to any particular database; rather, these classes comprise a driver manager of sorts. To use JDBC with a particular database engine, you will need to obtain a driver for that database.

Each JDBC driver implements a number of the interfaces in the *java.sql.** package. The *java.sql.DriverManager* class is responsible for determining which JDBC driver you want to use when your Java program makes a call to the `DriverManager.getConnection()` method. One of the arguments that is passed to this method is a JDBC URL, which is very similar to the connection strings used by the Perl DBI. In fact, these JDBC URLs are not true URLs in that they are not an instance of the *java.net.URL* class and are really more like ODBC or DBI connection strings than anything else. The fact that they are called URLs has caused a little bit of confusion among novice users. It's important to think of these JDBC URLs as no more than instructions to the driver manager and to the driver that the driver manager chooses to load.

Anatomy of a JDBC URL

JDBC URLs come in many flavors. They are predictable to the extent that they always start with the string `jdbc`, and this is immediately followed by a string that identifies the JDBC driver. These strings are separated with a colon (`:`) character. Here is an example of the sort of URL that is used by the Mini SQL JDBC driver:

jdbc:msql://localhost:1114/prk_db

In the URL just shown, there are a number of components. The first is the `jdbc` identifier, followed by `msql`, the name of the JDBC driver that uses this sort of URL. After that, a hostname and port number appear, which is not unlike the notation used in typical URLs. They are followed by the string `prk_db` which is the name of the database to open when the driver is instantiated by the driver manager. Each driver is capable of handling a different type of URL. In fact, the driver manager takes advantage of this fact when it determines which driver should handle a given URL. Since you may have more than one JDBC driver installed at a given time, the driver manager instantiates each driver, and asks it if it can handle the URL. The first driver to respond affirmatively is the one that is selected to process the URL. This is why it is vitally important that the URL each driver understands be unique. Since the driver name is usually the second part of the URL, this has not generally been a problem.

Choosing a Driver

Choosing a database driver for JDBC development can be a tricky process. If you've already got a database system in your company, such as Mini SQL, mySQL, Sybase, Oracle or some other product, you should go with whatever JDBC driver is offered by your vendor. Companies such as WebLogic, OpenLink, or Visigenic offer JDBC drivers as an alternative to vendor-supplied JDBC drivers.

Since both a database server and JDBC drivers often cost money, the examples in this chapter are going to make use of a database engine, called tinySQL, that we designed some time ago for the purposes of teaching JDBC. You can't use this engine in an applet, or even over the network, since it's a simple client-side engine that manipulates database files locally. Further, tinySQL implements its join and filtering logic in a brute force, inefficient manner. Nonetheless, we were able to write it in a weekend, and it supports enough SQL that it can be used for demonstration or educational purposes.

If you already have a database server installed and you want to choose your own JDBC driver for the examples in this chapter, then you merely need to change the class name of the driver and the URL that is used in the examples, which we will note at the top of each example program. You will need to determine the appropriate URL to use by consulting the driver vendor's documentation. In practice, the URL that is used for a particular JDBC driver will depend on vendor-specific constraints, as well as site-specific information, such as a hostname, port number, and database name.

Obtaining and Installing tinySQL

The *oreilly/eg/ch06/* directory of the Resource Kit software includes the *tinySQL.tar.gz* file, which contains the complete tinySQL distribution. You can also obtain the most recent tinySQL release from:

> *http://users.ids.net/~bjepson/tinySQL/latest.tar.gz*

Extract this distribution using the *gzip* and *tar* utilities, which creates a top-level *tinySQL/* directory. This directory contains some random files as well as two directories: *classes* and *src*. The *src* directory contains the source code to tinySQL, and the *classes* directory contains the *ORG* directory which supplies precompiled classes that can be used out of the box. To install tinySQL, you can copy the *ORG* directory and all of its subdirectories into a permanent location, and add that location to your **CLASSPATH** environment variable in whatever startup script you use to set your **CLASSPATH** (*.profile, .bash_profile, .cshrc*, etc.). This procedure would look something like:

```
gzip -d -c latest.tar.gz | tar xvf -
cd tinySQL/classes
mkdir /usr/local/classes
mv ORG /usr/local/classes
export CLASSPATH=$CLASSPATH:/usr/local/classes
```

Alternatively, you could copy the *ORG* directory into a directory that is already in your CLASSPATH, such as the *lib/* directory under your Java installation, as in:

```
gzip -d -c latest.tar.gz | tar xvf -
cd tinySQL/classes
cp -r ORG /usr/local/jdk1.1/lib
```

Once you have installed tinySQL, you can test it out using the *tinySQLtest.java* program, which is supplied with the tinySQL distribution. First compile it with **javac tinySQLtest.java** and then try running it with **java tinySQLtest**. If you see the message "I could not find the tinySQL classes. Did you install them as directed in the README file?" you should check to verify that the *ORG* directory is in your CLASSPATH. Otherwise, you should see output similar to the following:

```
Created the test table.
Name                       Id
========================== ===
Brian                      1
Cletus                     2
-1 row(s) affected.
```

Programming with JDBC

Once you have installed a JDBC driver, you can begin developing JDBC-enabled Java applications. Since one of the goals of JDBC is to enable developers to build database-independent applications, JDBC classes are never directly instantiated within your code: the driver manager (*java.sql.DriverManager*) is responsible for locating and instantiating the JDBC driver, after which it hands it back to your application. Despite this fact, you need to engage in some lightweight trickery to load the classes. Typically, you can load a driver in your code with the following invocation:

```
Class.forName(String classname);
```

The **forName()** method is a static method in the *java.lang.Class* package that returns a **Class** object for the class or interface named by the **classname** argument. It usually has the added side effect of executing any static code in the class. We say *usually* because some implementations of Java do not automatically do this, and it has been a topic of heated debate whether or not this feature was even part of the Java specification; so it's often safer to say (generically):

```
Class.forName("DRIVER NAME").newInstance();
```

For example, you can do this with the tinySQL `textFileDriver`, which is located in the package `ORG.as220.tinySQL`, with the following syntax:

```
Class.forName("ORG.as220.tinySQL.textFileDriver").newInstance();
```

The act of loading the class runs a static initializer that is present in all JDBC drivers. This action causes the driver to register itself with the *java.sql.DriverManager* class. The act of registering simply adds the driver to a list of drivers, which is a static **Vector** in the *java.sql.DriverManager* class. This is why you don't need an instance of the **DriverManager** to register a driver—the **Vector** is a class field, as opposed to an instance field.

In the examples that follow, use the `javac` compiler to compile the source code and run it with `java classname`, as in:

```
javac db_connect.java
java db_connect
```

Making a connection

Once you have loaded the JDBC driver class, use the **DriverManager** to get a connection to the class. As mentioned earlier, you will need a URL for this. The tinySQL driver keeps this simple—the URL should simply be *jdbc:tinySQL*. The **DriverManager.getConnection()** method returns a **Connection** object (actually **textFileConnection**) for the JDBC driver. Since JDBC's mission is to protect you from the internals of the driver, the **textFileConnection** object is returned to you as a *java.sql.Connection* object. As a result, the JDK API documentation for the *java.sql.Connection* class tells you everything you need to know about the **textFileConnection** class. The **getConnection()** method requires a URL, user ID, and password as arguments. If your JDBC driver does not require a user ID or password, as is the case with tinySQL, you can leave these blank, as in:

```
Connection con = DriverManager.getConnection("jdbc:tinySQL", "", "");
```

The following example loads the JDBC driver using **Class.forName()**, and then uses the **DriverManager.getConnection()** method to create a new **Connection** object that can be used to send queries to the database. Notice that both the **Class.forName()** and **DriverManager.getConnection()** calls are wrapped in **try...catch** blocks. Normally, **Class.forName()** would only throw a **ClassNotFoundException**, but the **newInstance()** method is included, which can throw an **InstantiationException** or an **IllegalAccessException**. For this reason, the superclass of these three exceptions, **java.lang.Exception**, is caught. However, many of the methods in the JDBC driver manager class and driver interface classes can throw **SQLExceptions**, so that exception is explicitly caught in the **catch()** clause that handles the **DriverManager.getConnection()** call. You can find the following code with the chapter examples, as *db_ connect.java*:

```
/*
 *
 * Connect to a JDBC data source, in this case, tinySQL.
 *
 */

import java.sql.*;

class db_connect {

    public static void main(String argv[]) {

        // Here is the name of the driver to load, and the
        // URL with which to load it. If you are using a
        // different JDBC driver, you will need to follow
        // the driver's documentation, and include the
        // appropriate driver name and URL. If you do
        // that, be sure to recompile this program.
        //
        String driver = "ORG.as220.tinySQL.textFileDriver";
        String url    = "jdbc:tinySQL";

        // Some drivers need a userid and password, but
        // tinySQL doesn't. If you need to change these
        // strings, be sure to recompile this program.
        //
        String userid   = "";
        String password = "";

        try {

            // Register the JDBC driver. Normally, the
            // newInstance() is not needed, but some JVMs
            // have a bug which requires it.
            //
            Class.forName(driver).newInstance();

        } catch (Exception e) {

            System.err.println( "I could not find your JDBC driver.");
            e.printStackTrace();
        }

        // This try{} block will catch any SQLExceptions.
        //
        try {
```

```
              // Make a connection to the database.
              //
              Connection con =
                DriverManager.getConnection(url, userid, password);
              System.out.println("Connected OK!");
              con.close();

          } catch( SQLException e ) {
              System.out.println(e.getMessage());
              e.printStackTrace();
          }
      }

  }
```

Issuing an update

There are two broad types of SQL statements that can be sent to a database engine or server. The first type is considered an update. An update statement changes something in the database, but does not generally return results. Some SQL statements that fall into the category of update are the UPDATE statement (of course) and the DROP TABLE, CREATE TABLE, DELETE, and INSERT statements.

To send an update, you will need a *java.sql.Statement* object. This object can be obtained by invoking the `createStatement()` method of the *java.sql.Connection* object that was created in the previous example. The Statement object offers a method called `executeUpdate(String sqlstatement)`, which causes the database server or engine to execute the SQL statement that is passed as an argument to that method. The following example, *db_update.java*, uses the `executeUpdate()` method to create a table and insert two rows into it.

Notice that the example attempts to drop the table before it issues the CREATE TABLE statement. This is done because the entire process will fail if there is already a table named test_table in your database that has a different structure than the one the INSERT statements expect. Of course, on the off chance that you have a table named test_table that you want to keep around, you should change the name of the table and recompile *db_update.java* before running it. Notice that the DROP TABLE statement sits between a try...catch block that ignores any SQLException. This takes care of the likely case that you don't have the table in your database the first time you run this script. Some JDBC drivers, such as tinySQL, do not have a means of verifying which tables exist in the database, so there is no way to tell in advance if the DROP TABLE statement is needed:

```
  /*
   *
   * Connect to a JDBC data source and issue an update.
   *
   */
```

```java
import java.sql.*;

class db_update {

    public static void main(String argv[]) {

        // See db_connect.java for notes on these variables.
        //
        String driver = "ORG.as220.tinySQL.textFileDriver";
        String url     = "jdbc:tinySQL";
        String userid   = "";
        String password = "";

        try {

            // Register the JDBC driver.
            //
            Class.forName(driver).newInstance();

        } catch (Exception e) {

            System.err.println( "I could not find your JDBC driver.");
            e.printStackTrace();
        }

        try {

            // Make a connection to the database.
            //
            Connection con = DriverManager.getConnection(url, userid,
                                                         password);

            // Get a statement object from the connection.
            //
            Statement stmt = con.createStatement();

            // tinySQL has no way of telling whether a table
            // exists before you try to create it. If you
            // try to create a table that already exists,
            // you'll get an exception. So, we'll ignore any
            // exception raised here when we try to drop the
            // table.
            //
            try {
                stmt.executeUpdate("DROP TABLE test_table");
            } catch (SQLException e) { }


            // Create the table.
            //
            stmt.executeUpdate("CREATE TABLE test_table " +
                        "(weapon CHAR(20), advantage INT)");
            System.out.println("Finished creating the table.");
```

```
                    // Insert two rows of data.
                    //
                    stmt.executeUpdate("INSERT INTO test_table (weapon,advantage) " +
                                       "VALUES ('Beater', 50) ");
                    stmt.executeUpdate("INSERT INTO test_table (weapon,advantage) " +
                                       "VALUES ('Biter',  25) ");

                    System.out.println("Added two rows.");
                    con.close();

                } catch( SQLException e ) {
                    System.out.println(e.getMessage());
                    e.printStackTrace();
                }
            }
        }


        }
```

Making queries

The second broad category of database interactions is a query. A query often takes the form of an SQL **SELECT** statement—when the server is finished processing the statement, it returns a result set, which is made up of a sequence of rows. Stored procedures (compiled programs written in the database server's dialect of SQL) can also return queries. Lightweight engines such as Mini SQL and tinySQL do not offer stored procedures, so your queries will be limited to SQL **SELECT** statements.

To issue a query, you still need to create a *java.sql.Statement* object. However, instead of using the **executeUpdate()** method, you must use the **executeQuery()** method. This returns a *java.sql.ResultSet* object, which offers a number of methods for retrieving data from the result set. Typically, you will need to invoke the **next()** method for each row in the result set. The **next()** method fetches the next row, and returns a boolean **true** value until there are no more rows to fetch. After you have called **next()**, you can use one of the get methods, such as **getString()** or **getInt()** to retrieve a column from the result set. These methods should be passed the column index of the column you wish to retrieve. If you issue the **SELECT** statement **SELECT weapon, advantage FROM test_table**, index one will correspond to the **weapon** column and index two will correspond to the **advantage** column. The **ResultSet** object also accepts method invocations that include the column name, rather than the column index, but if there is no explicit need to do this, you should use the column index, since it is generally faster.

The next example, found in *db_query.java*, uses a **SELECT** statement to retrieve the rows that were inserted in the previous example.

```
/*
 *
 * Connect to a JDBC data source and issue an update.
 *
 */

import java.sql.*;

class db_query {

    public static void main(String argv[]) {

        // See db_connect.java for notes on these variables.
        //
        String driver = "ORG.as220.tinySQL.textFileDriver";
        String url    = "jdbc:tinySQL";
        String userid   = "";
        String password = "";

        try {

            // Register the JDBC driver.
            //
            Class.forName(driver).newInstance();

        } catch (Exception e) {

            System.err.println( "I could not find your JDBC driver.");
            e.printStackTrace();
        }

        try {

            // Make a connection to the database.
            //
            Connection con =
              DriverManager.getConnection(url, userid, password);

            // Get a statement object from the connection.
            //
            Statement stmt = con.createStatement();


            // Execute a query and get a result set.
            //
            ResultSet rs =
              stmt.executeQuery("SELECT weapon, advantage FROM test_table");

            // Print out a header.
            //
            System.out.println(
                "Sword          +to hit");
```

```
            // Loop until the next() method returns false.
            //
            while (rs.next()) {

                // Get the name of the weapon and its
                // advantage.
                //
                String weapon = rs.getString(1);
                int advantage = rs.getInt(2);

                // Print the information.
                //
                System.out.println(weapon + advantage);

            }

            con.close();

        } catch( SQLException e ) {
            System.out.println(e.getMessage());
            e.printStackTrace();
        }
    }

}
```

Putting It All Together: JDBC Meets GIFgraph Meets Data::Xtab

Now that we've been through an exhaustive and possibly exhausting overview of seemingly unconnected technologies, let's walk through a concise example that brings them all together. What good is a graph if its data has to be hard-coded into the graphing program? Using JDBC, we can manage a table that contains our data. The data will be represented in the raw form that was seen earlier in the Data::Xtab example and converted into a form that can be easily graphed.

The following example makes a JDBC connection to a tinySQL database system, creates a table called **data**, and fills it with the sales data shown in the previous examples. It does so by first creating the table, and then using the SQL **INSERT** statement to fill the table with data. It is included on the CD-ROM as *init_db.java*, and can be compiled and executed with the following commands:

```
javac init_db.java
java init_db
```

If you need to use a database engine other than tinySQL, adjust the driver class name, URL, user name, and password, all conveniently included as **String**s at the top of the source file. If you do make this change, recompile the program. The code for the example follows.

```
/*
 * Simple class to initialize a database for the chapter 6
 * JDBCGIF example program.
 */
import java.util.*;
import java.sql.*;

class init_db {

    public static void main(String argv[]) {

        // The name of the driver and JDBC URL. You can
        // customize this for your site.
        //
        String driver   = "ORG.as220.tinySQL.textFileDriver";
        String url       = "jdbc:tinySQL";
        String user      = "";
        String password = "";

        try {

            // Register the driver.
            //
            Class.forName(driver);

        } catch (ClassNotFoundException e) {

            System.err.println( "I could not find your JDBC driver.");
            e.printStackTrace();
        }

        try {

            // Make a connection to the Driver.
            //
            Connection con = DriverManager.getConnection(url, user,
                                                         password);

            // get a Statement object from the Connection
            //
            Statement stmt = con.createStatement();

            // Try to drop the table if it exists.
            // Ignore any exception for DROP TABLE;
            // it will most assuredly throw one if
            // the table does not exist
            //
            try {
                stmt.executeUpdate("DROP TABLE data");
            } catch (Exception e) {
                // do nothing
            }
```

```
                // Create a table
                //
                stmt.executeUpdate("CREATE TABLE data " +
                                "(sales_group CHAR(1), " +
                                " sdate       CHAR(6), " +
                                " sales       INT)");
                System.err.println("Created the data table.");

                // Insert a number of rows
                //
                stmt.executeUpdate("INSERT INTO data (sales_group, sdate, sales)"+
                                " VALUES ('A', 'JAN-14', 6874)");
                stmt.executeUpdate("INSERT INTO data (sales_group, sdate, sales)"+
                                " VALUES ('A', 'FEB-01', 1987)");
                stmt.executeUpdate("INSERT INTO data (sales_group, sdate, sales)"+
                                " VALUES ('A', 'FEB-18', 3200)");
                stmt.executeUpdate("INSERT INTO data (sales_group, sdate, sales)"+
                                " VALUES ('A', 'MAR-17', 3459)");

                stmt.executeUpdate("INSERT INTO data (sales_group, sdate, sales)"+
                                " VALUES ('B', 'JAN-12', 4995)");
                stmt.executeUpdate("INSERT INTO data (sales_group, sdate, sales)"+
                                " VALUES ('B', 'FEB-02', 3750)");
                stmt.executeUpdate("INSERT INTO data (sales_group, sdate, sales)"+
                                " VALUES ('B', 'MAR-08', 4192)");
                stmt.executeUpdate("INSERT INTO data (sales_group, sdate, sales)"+
                                " VALUES ('B', 'MAR-19', 2984)");

                stmt.executeUpdate("INSERT INTO data (sales_group, sdate, sales)"+
                                " VALUES ('C', 'FEB-27', 2617)");
                stmt.executeUpdate("INSERT INTO data (sales_group, sdate, sales)"+
                                " VALUES ('C', 'MAR-19', 4697)");

                System.out.println("Inserted data");

                stmt.close();
                con.close();

        } catch( Exception e ) {
            System.out.println(e.getMessage());
            e.printStackTrace();
        }
    }
}
```

The next step is to run the *JDBCGIF.jpl* program. This program uses JDBC to retrieve information from the data table. It then performs the same manipulations on the data that were performed in the Data::Xtab section of this chapter and generates a GIF with the GIFgraph module. The GIF is then handed back to Java and displayed on the user's desktop in a `Frame`. To run this example, have your working environment set up as directed for JPL in Chapter 3, *Perlez-Vous Java? Using JPL*. To compile and run this example, issue the following commands:

```
perl Makefile.PL
make
java JDBCGIF
```

If you need to change the database driver, you can modify the **driver**, **url**, **user**, and **password** variables to reflect your site's requirements and then run **make** again.

After you run this program, you will see a **Frame** which contains the graph image, as shown in Figure 6-2.

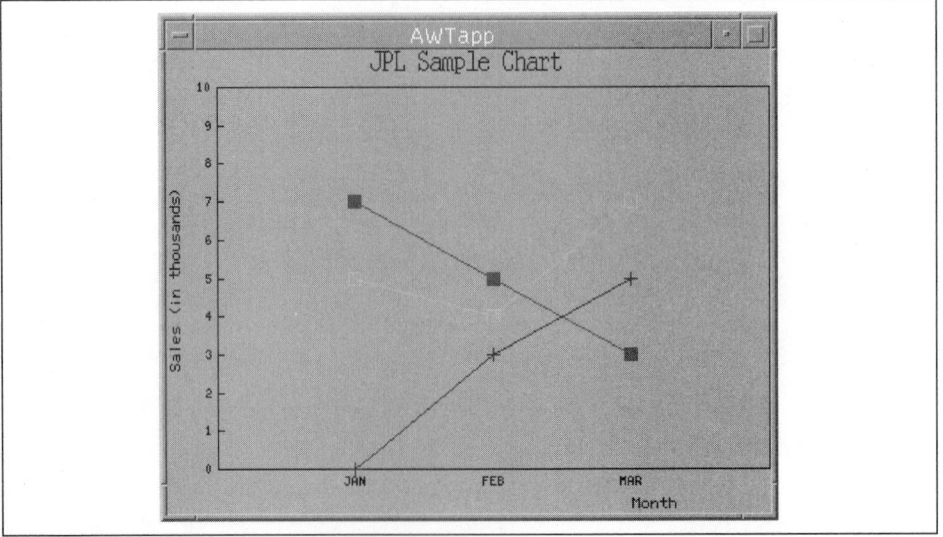

Figure 6-2. Graph output from JDBCGIF.jpl

JDBCGIF.jpl unites the techniques shown in the earlier examples and puts a few twists on things. Derived from the *java.awt.Canvas* class, a JDBCGIF object is suitable for embedding in a container such as a *java.awt.Frame*. This is exactly what happens in the static **main()** method, shown at the bottom of the class definition. First, a **Frame** is constructed, then a JDBCGIF object. The **generateGraph()** method is invoked, and then the JDBCGIF object is added to the **Frame**, which is then **pack()**ed and **show()**n.

The **generateGraph()** method performs a number of important functions. First, it sets up the JDBC connection and issues a query to retrieve the graph data, and then invokes **mkImage()**, passing the **ResultSet** from the query as an argument. The **mkImage()** method returns a **byte** array containing the GIF to the **java.awt.Toolkit.createImage()** method (see the comments in the source code for a detailed description of using a `Toolkit` object). The return type of the `createImage()` method is a *java.awt.Image*, which is stored in the instance field *i*. The *i* instance field is declared as an `Image` at the top of the class.

The `mkImage()` method is very similar to the *simplextab.pl* script shown earlier. The biggest difference is that instead of getting the data from an array, the data is read from the *java.sql.ResultSet* object that was passed into the method. The retrieval of this data uses the same techniques shown in the *db_query.java* example, but these are implemented in Perl, using the `getmeth()` function to obtain a valid method signature for the `getString()`, `getInt()` and `next()` methods, and then invoking them directly through the `ResultSet` object `$rs`. Although the GIF that is returned from this method resides in a Perl string, the fact that the method is declared as returning a `byte` array causes JPL to automagically convert the string to a `byte` array, which not only keeps Java happy, but lets the `createImage()` method get the bytes that it needs to create a *java.awt.Image* object.

The following code is *JDBCGIF.jpl*:

```
/*
 * JDBCGIF - a JPL application that combines Java's
 * graphical capabilities and database API with
 * the Perl GD and GIFgraph modules.
 */
import java.awt.*;
import java.awt.event.*;
import java.awt.image.*;
import java.sql.*;
import java.util.*;

public class JDBCGIF extends Canvas {

    // The java.awt.Image object that will eventually
    // contain our GIF.
    //
    Image i;

    // The class name of the driver to load, and a URL to
    // load it. You can customize this for your site.
    //
    String driver   = "ORG.as220.tinySQL.textFileDriver";
    String url       = "jdbc:tinySQL";
    String user      = "";
    String password = "";

    // This width and height is used for the Canvas as well
    // as the GIFgraph object.
    //
    int width  = 400;
    int height = 300;
```

```
/**
 *
 * Construct a new JDBCGIF object.
 *
 */
public JDBCGIF() {

    // Set the size of this Canvas to the desired width
    // and height.
    //
    this.setSize(width, height);

}

/**
 *
 * generateGraph() drives the graph generation process,
 * as its name implies.
 *
 */
public void generateGraph() {

    try {

        // Load the class for the desired driver.
        //
        Class.forName(driver).newInstance();

        // Make a connection to the database using the
        // JDBC URL.
        //
        Connection con =
          DriverManager.getConnection(url, user, password);

        // Create a Statement object.
        //
        Statement stmt = con.createStatement();

        // Execute an SQL statement to retrieve the
        // sales data.
        //
        String sql = "SELECT sales_group, sdate, sales " +
                     "FROM data";
        ResultSet rs = stmt.executeQuery(sql);

        // The java.awt.Toolkit is a weird sort of
        // class. Its responsibility is to take care of
        // platform-specific operations, and is often
        // doing things behind the scenes when you are
        // using the AWT. The getDefaultToolkit() method
        // is a static method to obtain access to your
        // personal Toolkit. It's best to avoid using
        // the Toolkit object when you can, but it has
```

```
            // this nifty little method called createImage()
            // that I just can't resist using.
            //
            Toolkit kit = Toolkit.getDefaultToolkit();

            // Invoke createImage() to create a GIF image
            // from the byte array that's returned by the
            // mkImage() method.
            //
            i = kit.createImage( mkImage(rs) );

        } catch (Exception e) {

            System.out.println(e.getMessage());
            e.printStackTrace();
            System.exit(0);

        }

    }

    /**
     *
     * This method will draw the image when the Canvas needs
     * to be repainted.
     *
     */
    public void paint(Graphics g) {
        g.drawImage(i, 0, 0, this);
    }

    /**
     *
     * This method will fetch rows from a ResultSet, convert
     * them to a form that is usable by GIFgraph, and return
     * a byte array that contains a GIF image.
     *
     */
    perl byte[] mkImage(ResultSet rs) throws SQLException {{

        use GIFgraph::linespoints;
        use Data::Xtab;

        # Get the method signatures for Java methods that
        # we want to call from Perl.
        #
        my $getString = getmeth("getString", ['int'], ['java.lang.String']);
        my $getInt    = getmeth("getInt",    ['int'], ['int']);
        my $next      = getmeth("next",      [],      ['boolean']);

        # The @data array will hold references to each row
        # of data.
        #
        my @data;
```

```perl
# Process each row in the result set.
#
while( $rs->$next() ) {

    $sales_group = $rs->$getString(1);
    $sdate       = $rs->$getString(2);
    $sales       = $rs->$getInt(3);

    # Add this row to the @data array as a reference
    # to an anonymous array.
    #
    push @data, [$sales_group, $sdate, $sales];

}


# Massage the data into shape before feeding it to
# Data::Xtab.
#
foreach my $d (@data) {

    # Trim the dash and day number from the date, which is
    # the second (index 1) element in each array.
    #
    $d->[1] =~ s/-..//g;

    # Get the sales amount (the third element in each array)
    # in thousands and round up.
    #
    $d->[2] = int( ($d->[2]/1000) + .5 )

}


# Make sure that the first three months of the year
# are included as labels on the graph.
#
my @outputcols = ('JAN', 'FEB', 'MAR');

# Create a new Data::Xtab object.
#
my $xtab = new Data::Xtab(\@data, \@outputcols);

# Retrieve the graph_data and pop off the last data
# series (totals).
#
my @graph_data = $xtab->graph_data;
pop @graph_data;

# Create a new graph made up of lines and points.
#
$my_graph = new GIFgraph::linespoints();

# Set up the graph options.
#
```

```
        $my_graph->set( 'x_label'       => 'Month',
                        'y_label'       => 'Sales (in thousands)',
                        'title'         => 'JPL Sample Chart',
                        'y_max_value'   => 10,
                        'y_tick_number' => 10,
                        'gifx'          => $self->width,
                        'gify'          => $self->height);

        # Plot the GIF to a string and return it. This
        # method is declared as returning a byte array, so
        # the string will be automatically converted into an
        # array.
        #
        $s = $my_graph->plot( \@graph_data );
        return $s;

}}

public static void main(String[] argv) {

    // Create a Frame to hold the JDBCGIF (Canvas)
    // object.
    //
    Frame f = new Frame();

    // Give the Frame a BorderLayout.
    //
    f.setLayout(new BorderLayout());

    // Instantiate a new JDBCGIF object.
    //
    JDBCGIF graph = new JDBCGIF();

    // Generate the graph.
    //
    graph.generateGraph();

    // Add the graph to the frame.
    //
    f.add("Center", graph);

    // Add a Handler object (defined below) to the Frame
    // as a WindowListener.
    //
    f.addWindowListener( new Handler() );

    // Pack and show the Frame.
    //
    f.pack();
    f.show();

}

}
```

```
/**
 *
 * This little class is used as an event handler to allow
 * the user to close the Frame.
 *
 */
class Handler extends WindowAdapter {
    public void windowClosing(WindowEvent e) {
        System.exit(0);
    }
}
```

The strength of JPL lies not only in its ability to develop applications in both Java and Perl, but in its ability to surprise us from time to time as to how easy certain seemingly difficult tasks can be. While Perl and Java both have unique strengths, and certainly some areas of overlap, Java has a certain amount of specialization in the realm of graphical development. In this chapter, we've seen two of Perl's strengths at work: the availability of powerful, flexible modules from the CPAN in the form of GD and GIFgraph, and Perl's ability to rapidly process data of any sort, as evidenced by GIFgraph's ability to rapidly generate graphs from a data set. There are many more possible combinations with JPL, as shown in examples elsewhere in this book. With what you've read in the book and the examples included on the CD-ROM, you should be producing your own Java-Perl applications in no time at all.

JPL Reference

This appendix contains a task-oriented, comprehensive reference to JPL. It revisits many of the features demonstrated in previous chapters, and includes a good deal of information about other methods that are available through JNI, the Java Native Interface that is exposed by the JNI module.

Features and Techniques

This section provides a quick reference to various JPL features and techniques, particularly about methods.

Defining Perl Methods in a JPL File

There are only two syntactic differences between the definition of a Java method and a Perl native method embedded in Java. JPL expects the Perl method to be declared with the keyword **perl** and it expects the body of the method to begin and end with two curly braces, {{...}}. Be careful not to use two curly braces in a row within the Perl code, or you'll confuse the JPL parser. JPL allows other clauses in the method prototype, such as the **throws** exception handling clause. A simple Perl method is shown here:

```
perl void Example() {{
    print "Perl says hi!\n";
}}
```

Comment Styles

JPL may be a Java/Perl hybrid, but there are no hybrid comments, so each language needs to be commented in its own manner. Comment each block as you would normally comment the language that block is in. It is a given that after a while you will find yourself getting syntax errors from using Perl comments in Java and vice versa as the boundaries between the languages begin to blur. Here are samples of each:

```
public void javaCommentExample {
    // Here is a Java comment
    /* And a multi-
       line Java comment */
}

perl void perlCommentExample {{
    # Only the finest Perl comment styles used here
}}
```

The Class and AutoLoader Modules

JPL allows the use of Java and Perl together through the use of the JNI module, which is a Perl module that exposes the Java Native Interface (JNI). The JNI is an API that allows Java code to embed and to be embedded in other languages. Virtually all the JNI interface is available through the JNI module; these JNI functions allow the interaction between languages to happen by giving you the ability to develop Perl methods that create Java objects, invoke methods, catch and throw exceptions. You will not need to call many of the JNI functions directly, because JPL handles a lot of tasks automatically with the JPL::AutoLoader and JPL::Class modules.

The JPL::AutoLoader module automates the following functions:

- Uses Perl's autoloading feature to look up Java methods at run-time.

- Automatically loads the correct JPL::Class package when a Java method returns a Java object of a type that has not yet been loaded.

- Maps **new** into `<init>` internally for you, and does other magic, such as translating method signatures to JNI format.

Note that the JPL preprocessor automatically inserts `use JPL::AutoLoader` in your *.jpl* file so you don't have to. Before you can invoke the constructor for any class not automatically loaded above, you must explicitly import the class with the JPL::Class module. This module maps the same AUTOLOAD function into the given module name. JPL::Class expects its import list to consist of Perl package names, so you must replace the delimiter in the Java package name (.) with the Perl package delimiter (::). If you wish to use the methods of the *java.util.Random* class, for example, you would include the following line in your code:

```
use JPL::Class 'java::util::Random';
```

The methods belonging to the *java.util.Random* class will be autoloaded when you invoke a method from that package, such as when you create a new object with:

```
$foogum = java::util::Random->new();
```

Method Signatures and getmeth()

Because Java methods support overloading, different methods with the same name may be invoked, differentiated from one another only by the number and type of arguments that the method accepts. Each Java method has its own unique signature that is recognized by JNI. This signature is formed by mangling the name of the function with its arguments and return values. When calling Java methods from Perl, JNI requires the method signature to look up the method name, so you will have to supply the mangled name yourselves.

Java method signatures

If you want to see the method signatures for a specific class, use the **-s** option with the **javap** class dissembler to generate the field signatures of the class. You never *have* to do this; this option is only for the curious. For example, the following is the output from **javap** for the class *java.awt.Polygon*:

```
bash-2.00$ javap -s -p java.awt.Polygon

Compiled from Polygon.java
public synchronized class java.awt.Polygon extends java.lang.Object
implements java.awt.Shape , java.io.Serializable
    /* ACC_SUPER bit set */
{
    public int npoints;
        /*   I   */
    public int xpoints[];
        /*   [I   */
    public int ypoints[];
        /*   [I   */
    protected java.awt.Rectangle bounds;
        /*   Ljava/awt/Rectangle;   */
    private static final long serialVersionUID;
        /*   J   */
    public java.awt.Polygon();
        /*   ()V   */
    public java.awt.Polygon(int[],int[],int);
        /*   ([I[II)V   */
    public void translate(int, int);
        /*   (II)V   */
    void calculateBounds(int[], int[], int);
        /*   ([I[II)V   */
    void updateBounds(int, int);
        /*   (II)V   */
```

```
        public void addPoint(int, int);
            /*   (II)V   */
        public java.awt.Rectangle getBounds();
            /*   ()Ljava/awt/Rectangle;   */
        public java.awt.Rectangle getBoundingBox();
            /*   ()Ljava/awt/Rectangle;   */
        public boolean contains(java.awt.Point);
            /*   (Ljava/awt/Point;)Z   */
        public boolean contains(int, int);
            /*   (II)Z   */
        public boolean inside(int, int);
            /*   (II)Z   */
    }
```

The argument and return type signatures follow the method prototype in a comment block in the form (arg-types) ret-type. JNI uses the Java Virtual Machine's encoding of type signatures:

JNI Signature Encoding	Type
V	void
Z	boolean
B	byte
C	char
S	short
I	int
J	long
F	float
D	double
LClassName	A fully qualified Java class
[type	An array of type type

Thus (II)Z indicates that a method is called with two integer arguments and returns a boolean.

The JPL::AutoLoader module expects a slightly different syntax that does not include (or [so that methods can be easily integrated into the Perl caching and module lookup scheme. A Java signature of (I)I would correspond to a JPL signature of __I__I (two underscores before the args and return value). For example, a Java signature for *java.awt.Polygon*'s updateBounds() method is:

```
    (II)V;
```

and its JPL signature is:

```
    updateBounds__II__V
```

Now, what about the signature of a method that passes an object or string? For *java.awt.Polygon*'s `getBoundingBox()` method, which returns an object of class *java.awt.Rectangle*, we would have to provide the following method signature:

```
()Ljava/awt/Rectangle;
```

In JPL, this signature would be:

```
getBoundingBox____Ljava_awt_Rectangle_2
```

Please note that there are four underscores after `getBoundingBox` in the signature just shown. It is not necessary to specify a type when the method's argument list is empty, so there is no type listed after the first two underscores.

The getmeth() function

That's an awful lot to type for every method call. Luckily, we can use the `getmeth()` function to calculate the signature once and assign it to a variable for reuse later in the code. The `getmeth()` function takes three arguments: a string with the name of the method, an anonymous array containing a list of strings with the package and class names or type of the arguments, and another anonymous array with a single string describing the package and class name or type of the return value. Note that the return value array will always have only one element, and that the package names use the standard Java syntax with periods as delimiters.

The signature value returned by `getmeth()` is simply the mangled signature for that method and may be applied to any class that has a method with the same signature. For example, *java.awt.List* and *java.awt.Menu* both have add methods that take a `String` as an argument and return `void`, so the following is perfectly acceptable if `$someList` is a *java.awt.List* and `$someMenu` is a *java.awt.Menu*:

```
$add=getmeth('add', ['java.lang.String'], []);
$someList->$add('List item');
$someMenu->$add('Menu item');
```

You should avoid calling `getmeth()` unnecessarily within loops, because there is a significant overhead to reconstructing the method signature each time. Whenever possible, move your `getmeth()` calls outside the loop. In other words, if you are going to use a method many times within a loop, look it up before you enter the loop, not within the loop. Also, if you are storing the method signatures as package variables, you can short-circuit the assignment in cases where you have already looked up the method signature, as in:

```
$foo ||= getmeth("foo", ['int'], ['double']);
```

Calling Static Methods

To call a static method in the same class, you must prepend JPL:: to the package name of the enclosing class:

```
$foogum=getmeth('foogum',['int'],['boolean']);  # look up Java method foogum
$result=JPL::Sample->$foogum(123);               # result is a 0 or 1
```

To call a static method of a different class, you must prepend the package name of the class:

```
# These lines are from the exception handling example later in the chapter
#
$forName=getmeth("forName",['java.lang.String'],['java.lang.Class']);
$c=java::lang::Class->$forName("java.io.FileNotFoundException");
```

Primitive Java Data Types and Strings

JPL allows easy access to primitive Java data types from within Perl methods. Data of type int, double, short, or float may be passed directly and handled as Perl variables. JPL will also convert a boolean from true or false to 1 to 0. Strings passed from a Java method or instance field are actually considered java::lang::String objects rather than plain old strings. In most cases the string object will behave transparently as a string in Perl, unless you are using code that calls the ref() function to determine whether the variable is a reference. If you are expecting a string in this case, you must convert the String object to a plain old string by enclosing it in quotes. See "Java Strings and Overloaded Perl Methods" in Chapter 3 for a comprehensive discussion of this task.

Casting Java Objects within Perl

Java objects may be cast to another type within Perl by using the two argument form of bless(). The bless() function tells an object that it now belongs to the specified package. You will have to import the target class with the use statement before calling methods on it:

```
use JPL::Class 'java::util::Random';
bless $obj, 'java::util::Random';
```

For examples of circumstances when you may need to cast an object to another type, see "Casting Java Objects within Perl" in Chapter 3.

Accessing Instance Fields

JPL provides a means of accessing variables or objects belonging to a Java class definition via a method of the same name as the field, invoked as a method of

`$self`. These methods are pregenerated by JPL. There are two ways of invoking them:

- Invoking the method without an argument, as in `$self->str_field()`, returns the field to you to do with as you wish, whether the field is a variable or an object.

- Invoking the method with arguments, as in `$self->str_field("Hello!")`, causes the field to be changed; how it is changed depends on whether the field is a variable or an object. If it a variable, the field gets reassigned. If it is an object, the reference to the field is destroyed and a new reference is created.

See "Accessing Java Fields from Perl" in Chapter 3 for a complete discussion.

Dealing with Inner Classes

JPL has no direct means for working with inner classes, which are classes that can be defined within another class. The inner class has access to instance fields and methods of the enclosing class, as well as static fields and methods. Consider the following example, which includes an inner class that prints out the value of an instance field belonging to the enclosing class:

```
public class InnerExample {

    // This String is an instance field of the InnerExample class, but is
    // accessible from the Inner class
    //
    String str_val = "hello, world";

    public InnerExample() {

        // Create an instance of the inner class, and call its printval()
        // method.
        //
        myInnerClass i = new myInnerClass();
        i.printval();

        // Call the Perl method.
        //
        foo();
    }

    /**
     * A Perl method that tries to create an instance of an inner class.
     */
    perl void foo() {{

        use JPL::Class ('InnerExample$myInnerClass');
        my $inner = 'InnerExample$myInnerClass'->new();

    }}
```

```
/**
 * A simple inner class.
 */
class myInnerClass {
    void printval() {

        // Access an instance field of the enclosing class.
        //
        System.err.println(str_val);
    }
}

public static void main(String[] argv) {
    InnerExample f = new InnerExample();
}
}
```

The preceding example, which is included in the *oreilly/apa/InnerExample/* directory, generates the following output (note that we can access the inner class from
within Java, as evidenced by the display of "hello, world"):

```
hello, world
JNI panic: private method or <init> called from outside of the object
InnerExample.<init>(InnerExample.java:18)
at InnerExample.main(InnerExample.java:49)
```

See "Inner Classes and Alternate Constructors" in Chapter 3 for an example that
covers this issue and includes a workaround for the problem. This limitation will
probably be eliminated in the future, as the interface to the JVM's internal
accessor functions that allow the classes to talk to each other becomes better
documented.

Exception Handling

When using Perl methods embedded in Java, the die() and warn() error
handling functions generate a *java.lang.RuntimeException*. You can use the
Throw() and ThrowNew() JNI functions to generate other exceptions, though.
The following example, included in the *ExceptionExample/* subdirectory under
the Appendix A examples directory (*apa/*), shows how a Java method would
handle three Perl methods throwing exceptions three different ways:

- The openFile() method attempts to open a file and uses the JNI Throw()
  function to pass an exception back to Java if it fails. Throw() takes a pre-cre-
  ated exception object as an argument, so we first have to create a new
  instance of the *java.io.FileNotFoundException* class.

- The openFile2() method utilizes the ThrowNew() JNI function, which takes
  a Class object and a string as parameters, creates a new exception object
  and throws the exception. In this example, we get the Class object using the

`forName()` method of class which returns the `Class` object associated with a given string name.

- The `openFile3()` method also uses the `ThrowNew()` JNI function, but gets the class object using the `FindClass()` JNI function. `FindClass()` takes a string and returns the object associated with it. Since it is a JNI function, it expects the sting to be in JNI-style, with slashes as delimiters.

The following code shows various exception handling examples:

```
/**
 * An example of Exception Handling
 *
 */

import java.awt.Frame;

public class ExceptionExample {

    public ExceptionExample() {

        // The following three blocks all catch exceptions thrown by
        // Perl methods. Note that all of these errors are recoverable
        // and the program exits normally.
        //

        try {
            openFile();
        } catch (Exception e) {
            System.err.println("Dag nab it! Couldn't open the file!");
            e.printStackTrace();
        }

        try {
            openFile2();
        } catch (Exception e) {
            System.err.println("Still couldn't open the file!");
            e.printStackTrace();
        }

        try {
            openFile3();
        } catch (Exception e) {
            System.err.println("Can't open it!");
            e.printStackTrace();
        }

    }

    /**
     * These three Perl methods attempt to open a non-existent file, and
     * pass the resulting exception three different ways.
     */
```

```
perl void openFile() {{

    # This is one way to throw an exception using the JNI Throw()
    # function, which requires an Exception object as an argument.
    #
    use JPL::Class 'java::io::FileNotFoundException';
    $new = getmeth("new", ['java.lang.String'], []);

    # Let's create a new exception object to pass to Throw
    #
    my $exception =
        java::io::FileNotFoundException->$new("I can't find it!");

    # Now try to open a non-existent file
    #
    unless (open (INFILE,"SomeFileNameThatProbablyDoesNotExist")) {
        Throw($exception);
        return;
    }

}}

perl void openFile2() {{

    # This is another way to throw an exception using the JNI
    # ThrowNew() function, which expects the Class object and
    # a message string as arguments.
    #
    use JPL::Class 'java::lang::Class';

    # The forName() of Class takes a string and returns the Class
    # corresponding to the string
    #
    $forName = getmeth("forName",
                       ['java.lang.String'],
                       ['java.lang.Class']);
    $c =
      java::lang::Class->$forName("java.io.FileNotFoundException");

    # Now try to open a non-existent file
    #
    unless (open (INFILE, "SomeFileNameThatProbablyDoesNotExist")) {
        ThrowNew($c, "I still can't find it!");
        return;
    }

}}

perl void openFile3() {{

    # There is yet a third way to throw an exception, still using
    # the ThrowNew() function. This time we get the class of the
    # exception using the JNI FindClass() function, which takes a
    # string as an argument and returns a Class object. This is an
```

```
            # uglier way to do Class lookups, since FindClass() expects this
            # string to be mangled JNI-style; i.e., with /'s delimiting the
            # package name instead of ::
            #
            my $s="java/io/FileNotFoundException";
            my $c=FindClass($s);
            unless (open (INFILE,"SomeFileNameThatProbablyDoesNotExist")) {
                ThrowNew($c,"Try another filename!");
                return;
            }
        }}

        public static void main(String[] argv) {
            ExceptionExample ex = new ExceptionExample();
        }
    }
```

The output of this program would look like:

```
Dag nab it! Couldn't open the file!
java.io.FileNotFoundException: I can't find it!
        at Example.<init>(Example.java:23)
        at Example.main(Example.java:130)
Still couldn't open the file!
java.io.FileNotFoundException: I still can't find it!
        at Example.<init>(Example.java:30)
        at Example.main(Example.java:130)
Can't open it!
java.io.FileNotFoundException: Try another filename!
        at Example.<init>(Example.java:37)
        at Example.main(Example.java:130)
```

Arrays

Accessing array elements must be done via JNI array functions. These functions are fully described in the "JPL and the Java Native Interface (JNI)" section later in this appendix.

Accessing arrays of primitive elements

You can use GetTypeArrayElements() to get an array, which returns a Perl array of the same length as the original Java array. You can use normal Perl operations on the resulting array. The array returned by this method is a copy of the array, as opposed to a reference to the original array. If you need to, you can obtain the length of a Java array by calling the JNI function GetArrayLength().

The JNI provides a set of functions to access arrays of every primitive type:

* GetBooleanArrayElements() returns the elements in a Java boolean array
* GetByteArrayElements() returns the elements in a Java byte array

- `GetCharArrayElements()` returns the elements in a `char` array
- `GetShortArrayElements()` returns the elements in a `short` array
- `GetIntArrayElements()` returns the elements in an `int` array
- `GetLongArrayElements()` returns the elements in a `long` array
- `GetFloatArrayElements()` returns the elements in a `float` array
- `GetDoubleArrayElements()` returns the elements in a `double` array

For an example of using these functions to access Java arrays from Perl, see the section "Passing and Returning Primitive Arrays" in Chapter 3. You may also get individual elements or regions of an array using the various `GetTypeArrayRegion()` calls, but it's usually more efficient to process the whole array with one JNI call.

Accessing arrays of objects

JNI provides two separate functions to access the elements of object arrays (there are no JNI functions for accessing all of the elements of an object array):

- `GetObjectArrayElement()` returns the specified object element
- `SetObjectArrayElement()` updates the specified object element

The following example from the *ObjectArrayExample/* subdirectory illustrates how to deal with arrays of objects. The program passes an array to a Perl method which adds two objects (a `Frame` and a `Button`) to the array and then retrieves the objects, adding the `Button` to the `Frame` and displaying it. Figure A-1 shows the `Frame`.

Figure A-1. Frame from ObjectArray example

```
/*
 * ObjectArrayExample.jpl - a JPL example that demonstrates some array
 * techniques for dealing with Objects.
 */

import java.awt.*;
import java.awt.event.*;

public class ObjectArrayExample {

    /**
     * The constructor.
     */
```

```
public ObjectArrayExample () {

    // Create a two-element array of objects.
    //
    Object[] obj_array = new Object[2];

    // Set the second element of the array to be a new, unlabeled
    // Button.
    //
    obj_array[1] = new Button();

    // Call a Perl method with the array, and let it modify that array.
    //
    System.out.println("\nNow testing: getArray()\n");
    showArray(obj_array);

    // Get the Frame out of the array.
    //
    Frame f = (Frame) obj_array[0];

    // Get the button out of the array.
    //
    Button btn = (Button) obj_array[1];

    // Add an action listener to the button.
    //
    btn.addActionListener( new appCloser() );

    // Add the button to the Frame, set its size, and show() it.
    //
    f.add(btn);
    f.setSize(200, 60);
    f.show();

}

class appCloser implements ActionListener {
    public void actionPerformed ( ActionEvent e ) {
        System.exit(0);
    }
}

/**
 * Take an array of objects as an argument, and add a Frame and a
 * Button to the array.
 */
perl void showArray(Object[] obj_array) {{

    # We'll use the same constructor signature for both Frame and
    # Button, so we only need to look it up once.
    #
    my $new = getmeth('new', ['java.lang.String'], []);
```

```
        # Create a new Frame.
        #
        use JPL::Class 'java::awt::Frame';
        $f    = java::awt::Frame->$new("Sample Program");

        # Retrieve the button from the array as an Object.
        #
        $btn = GetObjectArrayElement($obj_array, 1);

        # Bless the Object into being a Button again.
        #
        use JPL::Class 'java::awt::Button';
        bless $btn, 'java::awt::Button';

        # Set the Button's label to 'Close'.
        #
        my $setLabel  = getmeth('setLabel', ['java.lang.String'], []);
        $btn->$setLabel('Close');

        # Add the Frame to the array using the JNI function
        # SetObjectArrayElement.
        #
        SetObjectArrayElement($obj_array, 0, $f);

    }}

    /**
     * The main() method.
     */
    public static void main(String[] argv) {
        ObjectArrayExample ex = new ObjectArrayExample();
    }
}
```

JPL and Applets

Because JPL creates platform-specific code which needs access to the perl shared library at run-time, applications and applets written using JPL are not platform-independent. In addition, security restrictions placed on applets prevent the downloading of native shared libraries. For these reasons, we must take a different tack when creating JPL applets for use by remote web clients.

You can implement a fully functional applet using a feature of JDK 1.1 known as *RMI* (Remote Method Invocation) that allows Java programs to call the methods of objects running on remote servers. You would effectively separate the platform-specific aspects of your code from the pure Java code and create an RMI-enabled client applet that can run anywhere that would connect to your JPL-extended remote object. In this case, the remote JPL object must reside on the same server as the applet because once an applet is running, it cannot establish network connections except to the server from which it originated. For a complete discussion and example, see Chapter 5, *JPL and Applets: Using JPL with RMI*.

Known Problems

For a more complete discussion of JPL caveats, see the section in Chapter 3 called "JPL Known Issues."

JNI I/O Bug

As of this writing, the Solaris version of the JDK was implemented with a user-level thread library that causes the JNI to misbehave with certain Perl modules. This problem should be fixed in the future, as soon as JavaSoft develops a version of the Solaris JDK that relies on the native Solaris threads.

The Alarm() Call

It seems that installing an alarm signal handler within Perl code overrides Java's internal signal handler, resulting in a run-time "Alarm Clock" error that terminates your program. Avoid and/or disable the use of alarm signal handlers if possible.

Java Strings and Overloaded Methods

Some Perl modules utilize a sort of method overloading by allowing either strings or references to be passed as arguments. If you are using a string in Perl that has been retrieved from a Java field, it may seem as if you are using a string when you are actually using a reference to a *java.lang.String* object. This is not normally a problem, as JPL handles the conversion for you automatically. The problem is in sending a *java.lang.String* reference when you think you are sending a simple string to a Perl method that can deal with either a string or reference. In this case, you must force the reference into a string by enclosing it in quotes. See the section in Chapter 3, "Java Strings and Overloaded Perl Methods," for an example.

JPL and the Java Native Interface (JNI)

This section provides information on using JPL with the Java Native Interface.

Using JNI Public Functions

There are a couple of cases that we have already seen in which you may have to use JNI functions explicitly to pass information between the two languages. The two most important cases are for passing exceptions to Java from Perl, and passing arrays for Java to Perl, and vice versa. There are a number of other JNI functions that are available to you (for example, functions for method calling and object creation), but you don't really need those because that functionality is provided for you automatically by JPL.

All the JNI functions (except for superfluous `Release*()` functions) are exported by JPL into your namespace. This means that, whether or not you use them, the names of the JNI functions are taken and should not be used elsewhere in your code. A list of many of these functions is provided below in the *JNI Quick Reference* section.

JNI Public Functions Quick Reference

Refer to the following descriptions and examples for information on various JNI functions and operations.

Exception-handling functions

`Throw(exception_object)`
> Takes a previously created exception object as an argument and causes it to be thrown. Returns 0 on success and –1 on failure.

`ThrowNew(class, msg_string)`
> Creates a new exception object of *class* and associates it with the error message string given in *msg_string*. Returns 0 on success and –1 on failure.

`ExceptionOccurred()`
> `ExceptionOccurred()` returns the exception object that is currently being thrown.

`ExceptionDescribe()`
> `ExceptionDescribe()` is a convenience function used for debugging that will print an exception and a backtrace of the stack, similar to the `printStackTrace()` method of the `Exception` class.

`ExceptionClear()`
> `ExceptionClear()` will clear any exception currently being thrown, or does nothing if there is no exception being thrown.

`FatalError(msg_string)`
> `FatalError()` takes an error message string that it will display on exiting the program. This should not really be used for exception handling purposes; it is to signal fatal JNI errors. Handle a fatal exception the way you would normally, using the system's exit method calls.

Array functions

GetArrayLength(*array*)

> Returns the number of elements in *array*.

NewObjectArray(*len*, *class*, *init*)

> Constructs a new array of length *len* holding objects of *class*. All elements are initially set to *init*.

GetObjectArrayElement(*array*, *index*)

> Returns the element at *index* in *array*.

SetObjectArrayElement(*array*, *index*, *value*);

> Sets the element at *index* in *array* to *value*.

NewBooleanArray(*len*)
NewByteArray(*len*)
NewCharArray(*len*)
NewShortArray(*len*)
NewIntArray(*len*)
NewLongArray(*len*)
NewFloatArray(*len*)
NewDoubleArray(*len*)

> These operations may be used to construct new scalar array objects of the respective type, returning an empty array of length *len*. To set the individual elements of the array, you will have to use the appropriate SetScalarArray-Region() method.

GetBooleanArrayElements(*array*)
GetByteArrayElements(*array*)
GetCharArrayElements(*array*)
GetShortArrayElement(*array*)
GetIntArrayElements(*array*)
GetLongArrayElements(*array*)
GetFloatArrayElements(*array*)
GetDoubleArrayElements(*array*)

> These functions return the elements of *array*. The length of the array may be found using the GetArrayLength() method (or you can just look at the length of the resulting Perl array).

GetBooleanArrayRegion(*array*, *start*, *len*, *buf*)
GetByteArrayRegion(*array*, *start*, *len*, *buf*)
GetCharArrayRegion(*array*, *start*, *len*, *buf*)
GetShortArrayRegion(*array*, *start*, *len*, *buf*)
GetIntArrayRegion(*array*, *start*, *len*, *buf*)

GetLongArrayRegion(*array*, *start*, *len*, *buf*)
GetFloatArrayRegion(*array*, *start*, *len*, *buf*)
GetDoubleArrayRegion(*array*, *start*, *len*, *buf*)

These functions copy a region of a scalar array into an array buffer, where *len* is the number of elements to be copied, *start* is the starting element, *array* is the source array and *buf* is the destination buffer. The following example, included as *oreilly/eg/apa/GetRegionExample/*, demonstrates the use of one of these functions:

```
public class GetRegionExample {

    // Create an array.
    //
    int[] myarray = {1, 1, 2, 3, 5, 8, 13};

    public GetRegionExample() {

        // Call the Perl method.
        //
        foo();
    }

    /**
     * A Perl method that fetches and displays an array region.
     */
    perl void foo() {{

        # create a buffer that can hold three integers
        #
        my $buf = "\0" x 3;

        # Get the array region into the buffer.
        #
        GetIntArrayRegion($self->myarray(), 1, 3, $buf);

        # unpack the buffer.
        #
        my @nums = unpack("l*", $buf);

        # Display the array.
        #
        print "@nums\n";

    }}

    public static void main(String[] argv) {
        GetRegionExample f = new GetRegionExample();
    }
}
```

Notice that the buffer must be unpacked. The following table should guide you in using the correct unpack() template for various Java primitive types. You can obtain more information on pack() and unpack() from the **perlfunc** manpage.

Java Primitive Type	unpack
boolean	C
byte	c
char	S
short	s
int	l
long	q (not supported on all architectures)
float	f
double	d

```
SetBooleanArrayRegion(array, start, len, buf)
SetByteArrayRegion(array, start, len, buf)
SetCharArrayRegion(array, start, len, buf)
SetShortArrayRegion(array, start, len, buf)
SetIntArrayRegion(array, start, len, buf)
SetLongArrayRegion(array, start, len, buf)
SetFloatArrayRegion(array, start, len, buf)
SetDoubleArrayRegion(array, start, len, buf)
```

These functions copy a region of a scalar array from a buffer, where *len* is the number of elements to be copied, *start* is the starting element, *array* is the destination array and *buf* is the source buffer. The following example, included in *oreilly/eg/apa/SetRegionExample/*, demonstrates the use of one of these functions:

```
public class SetRegionExample {

    // Create an empty array.
    //
    int myarray[] = new int[3];

    public SetRegionExample() {

        // Call the Perl method.
        //
        foo();

        // Display the array.
        //
        for (int i = 0; i < myarray.length; i++) {
            System.err.println(myarray[i]);
        }
    }
```

```
/**
 * A Perl method that sets the array elements.
 */
perl void foo() {{

    # create a buffer that can hold three integers
    #
    my $buf = pack("l*", 100, 200, 300);

    # Set the array region using the buffer.
    #
    SetIntArrayRegion($self->myarray(), 0, 3, $buf);

}}

public static void main(String[] argv) {
    SetRegionExample f = new SetRegionExample();
}
}
```

Class and object operations

FindClass(*string*)

This function takes *string* specifying a class name and returns a locally defined class with the specified name. Note that the classname must use JNI-style delimiters (that is, / instead of ::).

GetSuperclass(*class*)

This function takes a Class *class* as an argument and returns its superclass. If class is an *java.lang.Object*, the function returns null.

IsSubclassOf(*class1, class2*)

This function returns a boolean; true if *class1* can be safely cast to *class2*, false otherwise.

IsSameObject(*object1, object2*)

This function returns a boolean; true if *object1* is the same object as *object2*, false otherwise. This is similar in functionality to the Java statement *object1==object2*.

GetObjectClass(*object*)

This function returns the class of the function; it is similar to the Perl ref(*object*) construct.

IsInstanceOf(*object, class*)

This function returns a boolean; true if *object* is an instance of *class*, false otherwise.

How to Find Out More About JNI

The following resources will help you learn more about JNI:

- Sun's JNI tutorial offers a complete (if terse) introduction to programming with the JNI: *http://java.sun.com/docs/books/tutorial/native1.1/implementing/index.html.*

- The Java Native Interface Specification developed by JavaSoft is available at: *http://www.tns.lcs.mit.edu/manuals/java-api-1.1beta2/guide/nativemethod/jni-TOC.doc.html.*

- There is also JNI documentation bundled with the JDK in the directory: *jdk1.1.1/docs/guide/jni/spec/jniTOC.doc.html.*

Debugging JPL Programs

JPL can be set to debug mode by issuing the following command, or equivalent, at the command prompt:

tcsh, csh:

```
setenv JPLDEBUG 1
```

bash, sh, ksh:

```
JPLDEBUG=1
export JPLDEBUG
```

In debug mode, JPL will give you more information on STDERR as the program executes. You will be able to tell what method is executing and can see the method signature lookups as they are performed. Most of your JPL-related errors will likely be the result of improperly defining the arguments to **getmeth()**. Debug mode will help you catch these errors. A reference book—such as *Java in a Nutshell*, by David Flanagan (O'Reilly)—that summarizes the Java method prototypes in one place is indispensable!

Error and Warning Messages

There are a few error and warning messages that you will commonly run across in the course of developing with JPL, as described below.

Errors

Alarm Clock

>   Java has either intercepted a signal from Perl generated by the **alarm()** method or its own alarm handler has been overridden or intercepted.

`ArrayIndexOutOfBoundsException`

Thrown by one of several JNI array access functions if the index parameter passed to it does not specify a valid index in the array.

`ArrayStoreException`

Thrown by `SetObjectArrayElement()` if the class of value is not a subclass of the element class of the array.

`Can't get method id for...`

Generated by JPL::AutoLoader when it could not find a method with the given signature in the appropriate package. Either the method does not exist, the proper package was not imported with an explicit use, or there is a problem with the formation of a `getmeth()` function call.

`Can't locate object method ... via package ...`

The AutoLoader could not find the method, probably because you forgot to explicitly import the package with a `use`.

`Class is not of type jclass at...`

This error is returned by a JNI function that is expecting a class as an argument and got something else. Use the `FindClass()` JNI function to look up the class object based on the string you thought you were supposed to pass.

`JNI panic: private method or <init> called from outside of the object`

This is caused by an attempt to instantiate an Object belonging to an inner class. See the section "Inner Classes and Alternate Constructors" in Chapter 3 for a discussion of a workaround solution.

Warnings

`Can't Allocate Colormap`

This is not a JPL-related warning; it is an error that you may encounter under the X Window System when you try to start Java, and another program has already allocated a lot of system color resources. If you start Java before other programs that are color-greedy, you can avoid this error.

Glossary

AWT (Abstract Window Toolkit)

A set of Java packages that allow the creation of complete graphical user interfaces. The AWT includes the following packages:

- *java.awt*: a group of generic components, containers, graphic and image objects

- *java.awt.image*: more comprehensive classes for manipulating images

- *java.awt.event*: event handling classes and methods

- *java.awt.datatransfer*: classes that simplify the cut and paste between programs

- *java.awt.peer*: classes that handle interactions with platform-specific peer objects

- *java.applet*: classes and methods for creating applets

javac

The `javac` program is the Java source to byte-code compiler.

javap (Java class disassembler)

The `javap` program is the Java class disassembler. It disassembles the classes given to it and produces readable output.

JDK (Java Development Kit)

The JDK is a group of tools for creating Java applications, an API, and a virtual machine for running Java applications.

JNI (Java Native Interface)

A programming interface that allows Java to be embedded in other applications (and vice versa).

JPL

A preprocessor and run-time support kit that allows you to combine Perl and Java.

libPerlInterpreter.so

The native library that allows Java to load the Perl interpreter.

Makefile.PL

A Perl script that generates a *Makefile* and automatically sets up the environment variables for it based on the configuration of your system.

Mangling

Name mangling is used by compilers to differentiate method and function signatures; in the case of Java, a method name is mangled with its arguments and return values to produce a unique name for referring to that method.

RMI (Remote Method Invocation)

A set of Java classes that allow RMI-enabled objects to invoke the methods of objects on remote hosts. A new feature of JDK 1.1.

Embedding Java in Perl

You may have noticed that all of our examples embed Perl in Java rather than Java in Perl. While it is theoretically possible to embed Java in Perl (and in fact, you can try it yourself—just say "`use JNI`" at the front of your Perl script), there is a bug in Sun's current Java implementation that prevents it from being useful, since it dumps core if you try to do any I/O in Java. This capability is expected to improve in the future when Sun switches to a native threads implementation for Java.

B

Selected Articles from The Perl Journal

The Perl Resource Kit contains a complete copy of the Autumn 1997 edition of *The Perl Journal,* the only periodical devoted exclusively to Perl. Under the watchful editorital eye of Jon Orwant, *The Perl Journal* includes articles, news, tips, and resources to help Perl programmers at any level. The articles we've chosen to reprint will give you a flavor of Perl's origin, uses, and technical flexiblity.

The following articles are reprinted courtesy of *The Perl Journal* (*http://tpj.com/*):

- *Wherefore Art, Thou,* by Larry Wall
- *How Perl Saved the Human Genome Project,* by Lincoln Stein
- *Understanding Regular Expressions,* by Jeffrey Friedl
- *CGI Scripts and Cookies,* by Lincoln Stein
- *CGI Programming: The LWP Library,* by Lincoln Stein

We have tried to preserve the author's original formatting as much as possible.

We encourage you to visit *The Perl Journal's* site (*http://tpj.com*) and sign up today to subscribe to this invaluable resource.

Wherefore Art, Thou   by Larry Wall

I don't know whether a picture is really worth a thousand words (most pictures seem to be considerably larger these days), but when I give talks about Perl, I often put up a picture showing where some of the ideas in Perl come from (Figure B-1).

I usually make a joke about Linguistics not really being the opposite of Common Sense, and then proceed to talk a lot about both of them, with some Computer

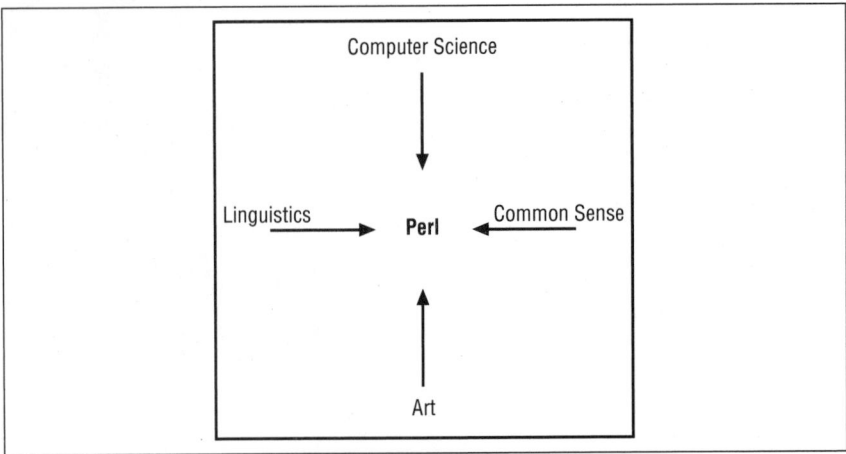

Figure B-1. Where the ideas in Perl come from

Science thrown in for good measure. But last December as I was giving a talk in Stockholm, someone asked me how Perl got its inspiration from Art. I was stumped. I mumbled something semi-irrational (always appropriate when discussing Art) and went on to the rest of my talk.

But the question continued to bother me; or more specifically, it continued to bother my left brain. My right brain continued to be perfectly content with the purported connection. Unfortunately, it's also not at all forthcoming with the verbiage necessary to explain itself. Right brains tend to be like that. So let me see if my left brain can make something of it all.

Art is first of all based on the notion that there exist amoral decisions, that is, choices you can make either way, without feeling like you're being naughty or nice. So let's presume that the Artist has free will of some sort or another, and can therefore behave as your ordinary, everyday Creator.

Now, it's more or less immaterial whether your Artist creates because of a liking for Deluxe Designer Universes or merely because of a liking for caffeine. The simple fact is, we have Artists, and they do Art. We just have to deal with it. We really do. You can make life miserable for the Artist, but the Artist has ways of getting revenge.

(Of course, if you don't make an Artist miserable, they'll make themselves miserable, but that comes into a different story.)

We can further subdivide the Artists into those who enjoy getting their revenge by being MORE than properly miserable, and those who prefer to get their revenge by being LESS than properly miserable. Artists of the first sort will prefer to work in a more formal medium, one that inflicts extra pain on the Artist, such as composing sonnets, dancing ballet, or programming C++. Artists of the second sort tend to be much more fun-loving, free-wheeling and undisciplined, whether the verb in question is composing, dancing, programming, or slinging. (Especially slinging. There's nobody quite so joyful as a B.S. artist. I should know...)

There is, of course, a third category of Artist, the one who oscillates between the two extremes.

Perl was written first of all to let the Artist make amoral decisions. That's why the Perl slogan is "There's More Than One Way To Do It!" Perl doesn't really care whether you use cobalt blue or burnt umber in a particular spot in your painting. It's your choice—you're the Artist. You're responsible for the overall effect. Indeed, your boss will hold *you* responsible for the overall effect, so why should Perl?

But more than that, Perl is intended to be a medium for those who are tired of composing in a formal computer language, and want to write some "free verse" without arbitrary restrictions. Sure, from a motivational point of view, arbitrary restrictions are challenging to work with, but when's the last time you saw a gleeful COBOL programmer?

On the other hand, with Perl 5, we've made strides in making life wonderful for those Artists who oscillate. You can have your cake and eat it too. When you're in a manic mood, you can pour forth unstructured, unreadable (but expressive) code to your heart's content. Later on, when you are in a dour mood, you can put a *-w* and a *use strict* at the top of your script and greatly increase your level of discipline (read "pain"). Next you can prototype your function definitions. While still in your somber state, you can go back and put whitespace in all your regular expressions and comment every last little bit as penance for your past indiscretions. You can restructure all your code into modules and unit test it in a jiffy because the Perl interpreter is so handy to invoke. Then as you swing back into a more carefree frame of mind, you can cheat by tweaking all those carefully encapsulated variables in all those painstakingly restructured modules. Ain't it the life.

Now, Linguistics may not be the opposite of Common Sense, but it's certainly the case that over the last twenty years or so, many Computer Scientists have come out in opposition to the Art of Programming. In trying to make programming predictable, they've mostly succeeded in making it boring. And in so doing, they've lost sight of the idea that programming is a human pursuit. They've designed languages intended more to keep the computer happy than the programmer. Was any SQL programmer ever happy about having to declare a value to be varchar(255)? Oops, now it's a key, and can't be longer than 60. Who comes up with these numbers?

They've also lost sight of the idea known to any Artist, that form and meaning are deeply interdependent. One of the ideas I keep stressing in the design of Perl is that things that ARE different should LOOK different. The reason many people hate programming in Lisp is because everything looks the same. I've said it before, and I'll say it again: Lisp has all the visual appeal of oatmeal with finger-nail clippings mixed in. (Other than that, it's quite a nice language.)

A large part of the design of Perl is driven by the dictates of visual psychology. That's why Perl lets you structure your code with the condition on the left or on the right, depending on which part you want to look important. That's why the large nested structures like *while* loops require an explicit beginning and end, while the small ones like list operators don't. That's why scalars start with $, arrays with @, and hashes with %. That's why filetest operators look like "-M", while numeric tests look like "==", and string tests look like "eq". Perl is very much a What-You-See-Is-What-It-Does language. You can talk about readability all you like, but readability depends first and foremost on recognizability.

Music To My Ears

Like many computer geeks, much of my artistic training has been in music. Of all the arts, it most clearly makes a programmer/interpreter distinction, so perhaps it's natural for a musician to think about how interpeters work. But the interpreters for a computer language are located both in the computer and in the human brain. I don't always know what makes a computer sad (or happy), but I do have a pretty good idea what makes a person mad (or sappy). Er, sorry.

Anyway, when I was young, I was taught that music has progressed through four major periods: Baroque, Classical, Romantic and Modern. (The other so-called fine arts have also gone through these periods, though not necessarily at the same rate.) I always thought it rather curious that we called the current period Modern, since definitionally the idea of modernity seems to be a permanently latched-on state, bound to the cursor of time, so to speak. But that was because the word "modern" still meant something back then. This was, after all, the 1960s. Who could have guessed that Modern period would be followed by the Post-Modern?

If you're willing to concede by now that the design of computer languages is an artistic medium of sorts (and searches), then it's reasonable for us to ask ourselves whether programming languages have been progressing through the same sequence of artistic development. Certainly, people have occasionally claimed that Perl is "baroque," to which my usual retort is, "Thanks, I like Bach too." But this is merest rhetoric (on both sides).

So what do we really mean when we talk about these periods? Let's start at the beginning, which is the Baroque period. Of course, it's not really the beginning. People were producing music long before they ever invented the bucket in which to carry the tune. But before and during the Baroque period, there was tremendous technological progress in both the production and publication of music. Composers and performers could make a name for themselves. Innovators were rewarded, but the forms of expression were heavily influenced both by cultural expectations and by available hardware. People were expected to improvise. What we got was more or less the Cambrian explosion of music.

Similarly, at the dawn of the computer era, there were new opportunities to innovate. The geniuses of that period improvised many forms of assembly language. To them, these languages all looked very different. But nowadays we tend to see all assembly language as the same, just as a lot of Baroque music seems the same to us, because the music tends to follow particular forms and sequences. Baroque music is structured like a weaving on a loom, and it's no accident that punch cards were invented to run looms before they were used to run computers.

It's easy to take a superior attitude toward these innovators, but this is unfair. We owe a great debt to these people. They invented the algorithms we use, even if the music does seem a bit limited at times. (Except for Bach, and Backus, of course.)

The Classical period was a time of standardization. Most of our modern instruments took their current form during this period, and this continued the trend of turning virtuosity into a marketable and portable commodity. Being able to program in FORTRAN was like being able to play the pianoforte. It was a skill you could use on someone else's machinery. Mozart could now go on tour.

The Romantic era was a time of seeing how far the classical forms could be stretched. And considerably stretched they were, in Beethoven and Mahler, as well as PL/1 and COBOL. The word "excessive" has been applied to all of them, as it will always be applied to anyone or anything that attempts to sling the entire universe around by any of its handles. But this is difficult at the best of times.

Finally, the typical overreaction took place, and we arrived in the Modern era, in which subtlety and minimalism were mandated, and antiquated cultural expectations were thrown over and thrown out. Reductionism and deconstructionism were the order of the day, from Bartok to Cage, and from Pascal to C. Music wasn't allowed to be tonal, and computer languages weren't allowed to do fancy I/O. All the gadgetry had to be visible and exposed. Everything had to look difficult, so we got stuck in the Turing Tarpit.

Of course, this is all oversimplified, and every language has aspects of each of these periods in it. And languages specialize in other ways: BASIC is like pop music. Tune into REXX for your easy listening classics. Tcl is fuzzy like jazz—you get to improvise a lot, and you're never quite sure who is interpreting what. Python is like MTV—it rocks, but it gets to be much of a sameness after half an hour or so.

Lisp is like church music down through the ages, adapting to whatever the popular culture is, from organ to electric guitar to synthesizer. That would make Scheme a kind of cult music, sung simply but with great fervor to an acoustic guitar.

C++ is like movie music, of titanic proportions, yet still culturally derivative by and large. Especially large. Sometimes it's hard to sit through the whole movie. And yet, as an intentionally Post-Modern language, it's kinda fun, and gets the job done.

As for Java, using a subset of movie music, it's attempting to be the basis for every good feeling everywhere, the ground of all emotional being. Muzak. It's everywhere you want to be.

Shell programming is a 1950s jukebox—great if it has your song already.

And of course, any language touched by ANSI starts to sound distinctly operatic.

So where does Perl fit in to this glorious mess? Like C++, Perl is a Post-Modern language by design, unashamedly reconstructionist and derivative. Perl is neo-Baroque, neo-Classical, neo-Romantic, and even, in spots, neo-Modern.

What musical genre encompasses so much? Where can you find everything from Wagner to "Shave and a Haircut, Two Bits"? Where can you find multiple levels of abstraction, accessible to newbies and oldsters alike? What kind of music admits everything from harmonica to accordion to pipe organ? What music is object-oriented, in good one-to-one correspondence with the main action? What music is good for programming in the small, but can be expanded to feature length as necessary? What music parodies everything in the world, yet leaves you feeling good about the world? What music is Perl?

Why, cartoon music, of course.

That's all folks!

Larry Wall doesn't mind being blamed for the invention of Perl, to the extent that you can blame any one person for it, which you can't, so there.

How Perl Saved the Human Genome Project

by Lincoln D. Stein

DATE:

Early February, 1996

LOCATION:

Cambridge, England, in the conference room of the largest DNA sequencing center in Europe.

OCCASION:

A high level meeting between the computer scientists of this center and the largest DNA sequencing center in the United States.

THE PROBLEM:

Although the two centers use almost identical laboratory techniques, almost identical databases, and almost identical data analysis tools, they still can't interchange data or meaningfully compare results.

THE SOLUTION:

Perl.

The human genome project was inaugurated at the beginning of the decade as an ambitious international effort to determine the complete DNA sequence of human beings and several experimental animals. The justification for this undertaking is both scientific and medical. By understanding the genetic makeup of an organism in excruciating detail, it is hoped that we will be better able to understand how organisms develop from single eggs into complex multicellular beings, how food is metabolized and transformed into the constituents of the body, how the nervous system assembles itself into a smoothly functioning ensemble. From the medical point of view, the wealth of knowledge that will come from knowing the complete DNA sequence will greatly accelerate the process of finding the causes of (and potential cures for) human diseases.

Six years after its birth, the genome project is ahead of schedule. Detailed maps of the human and all the experimental animals have been completed (mapping out the DNA using a series of landmarks is an obligatory first step before determining the complete DNA sequence). The sequence of the smallest model organism, yeast, is nearly completed, and the sequence of the next smallest, a tiny soil-dwelling worm, isn't far behind. Large scale sequencing efforts for human DNA started at several centers a number of months ago and will be in full swing within the year.

The scale of the human DNA sequencing project is enough to send your average UNIX system administrator running for cover. From the information-handling point of view, DNA is a very long string consisting of the four letters G, A, T and C (the letters are abbreviations for the four chemical units that form the "rungs" of the DNA double helix ladder). The goal of the project is to determine the order of letters in the string. The size of the string is impressive but not particularly mind-boggling: 3×10^9 letters long, or some 3 gigabytes of storage space if you use 1 byte to store each letter with no compression techniques.

Three gigabytes is substantial but certainly manageable by today's standards. Unfortunately, this is only what's required to store the *finished* data. The storage requirements for the experimental data needed to determine this sequence is far more vast. The essential problem is that DNA sequencing technology is currently limited to reading stretches of at most 500 contiguous letters. In order to determine sequences longer than that, the DNA must be sequenced as small overlapping fragments called "reads" and the jigsaw puzzle reassembled by algorithms that look for areas where the sequences match. Because the DNA sequence is nonrandom (similar but not-entirely-identical motifs appear many times throughout the genome), and because DNA sequencing technology is noisy and error-prone, one ends up having to sequence each region of DNA five to ten times in order to reliably assemble the reads into the true sequence. This increases the amount of data to manage by an order of magnitude. On top of this is all the associated information that goes along with laboratory work: who performed the experiment, when it was performed, the section of the genome that was sequenced, the identity and version of the software used to assemble the sequence, any comments someone wants to attach to the experiment, and so forth. In addition, one generally wants to store the raw output from the machine that performs the sequencing. Each 500 letters of sequence generates a data file that's 20-30 kilobytes long!

That's not the whole of it. It's not enough just to determine the sequence of the DNA. Within the sequence are functional areas scattered among long stretches of nonfunctional areas. There are genes, control regions, structural regions, and even a few viruses that got entangled in human DNA long ago and persist as fossilized remnants. Because the genes and control regions are responsible for health and disease, one wants to identify and mark them as the DNA sequence is assembled. This type of annotation generates yet more data.

Altogether, people estimate that some one to ten terabytes of information will need to be stored in order to see the human genome project to its conclusion.

So what's Perl got to do with it? From the beginning, researchers realized that informatics would have to play a large role in the genome project. An informatics core formed an integral part of every genome center that was created. The mission of these cores was two-fold: to provide computer support and databasing services for their affiliated laboratories, and to develop data analysis and management software for use by the genome community as a whole.

It's fair to say that the initial results of the informatics groups efforts were mixed. Things were slightly better on the laboratory management side of the coin. Some groups attempted to build large monolithic systems on top of complex relational databases; they were thwarted time and again by the highly dynamic nature of biological research. By the time a system that could deal with the ins and outs of a complex laboratory protocol had been designed, implemented and debugged, the protocol had been superseded by new technology and the software engineers had to go back to the drawing board.

Most groups, however, learned to build modular, loosely-coupled systems whose parts could be swapped in and out without retooling the whole system. In my group, for example, we discovered that many data analysis tasks involve a sequence of semi-independent steps. Consider the steps that one may want to perform on a bit of DNA that has just been sequenced. First there's a basic quality check on the sequence: is it long enough? Are the number of ambiguous letters below the maximum limit? Then there's the "vector check." For technical reasons, the human DNA must be passed through a bacterium before it can be sequenced (this is the process of "cloning"). Not infrequently, the human DNA gets lost somewhere in the process and the sequence that's read consists entirely of the bacterial vector. The vector check ensures that only human DNA gets into the database. Next there's a check for repetitive sequences. Human DNA is full of repetitive elements that make fitting the sequencing jigsaw puzzle together challenging. The repetitive sequence check tries to match the new sequence against a library of known repetitive elements. A penultimate step is to attempt to match the new sequence against other sequences in a large community database of DNA sequences. Often a match at this point will provide a clue to the function of the new DNA sequence. After performing all these checks, the sequence along with the information that's been gathered about it along the way is loaded into the local laboratory database.

The process of passing a DNA sequence through these independent analytic steps looks kind of like a pipeline, and it didn't take us long to realize that a UNIX pipe could handle the job. We developed a simple Perl-based data exchange format called *boulderio* that allowed loosely coupled programs to add information to a pipe-based I/O stream. *boulderio* is based on tag/value pairs. A Perl module makes it easy for programs to reach into the input stream, pull out only the tags they're interested in, do something with them, and drop new tags into output the stream. Any tags that the program isn't interested in are just passed through to standard output so that other programs in the pipeline can get to them.

Using this type of scheme, the process of analyzing a new DNA sequence looks something like this (this is not exactly the set of scripts that we use, but it's close enough):

```
name_sequence.pl < new.DNA |
quality_check.pl |
vector_check.pl |
find_repeats.pl |
search_big_database.pl |
load_lab_database.pl
```

A file containing the new DNA sequence is processed by a Perl script named *name_sequence.pl*, whose only job is to give the sequence a new unique name and to put it into *boulderio* format. Its output looks like this:

```
NAME=L26P93.2 SEQUENCE=GATTTCAGAGTCCCAGATTTCCCCCAGGGGGTTTCCAGAGAGCCC...
```

The output from *name_sequence.pl* is next passed to the quality checking program, which looks for the SEQUENCE tag, runs the quality checking algorithm, and writes its conclusion to the data stream. The data stream now looks like this:

```
NAME=L26P93.2 SEQUENCE=GATTTCAGAGTCCCAGATTTCCCCCAGGGGGTTTCCAGAGAGCCC...
QUALITY_CHECK=OK
```

Now the data stream enters the vector checker. It pulls the SEQUENCE tag out of the stream and runs the vector checking algorithm. The data stream now looks like this:

```
NAME=L26P93.2
SEQUENCE=GATTTCAGAGTCCCAGATTTCCCCCAGGGGGTTTCCAGAGAGCCC......
QUALITY_CHECK=OK VECTOR_CHECK=OK VECTOR_START=10 VECTOR_LENGTH=300
```

This continues down the pipeline, until at last the *load_lab_database.pl* script collates all the data, makes some final conclusions about whether the sequence is suitable for further use, and enters all the results into the laboratory database.

One of the nice features of the *boulderio* format is that multiple sequence records can be processed sequentially in the same UNIX pipeline. An "=" sign marks the end of one record and the beginning of the next:

```
NAME=L26P93.2 SEQUENCE=GATTTCAGAGTCCCAGATTTCCCCCAGGGGGTTTCCAGAGAGCCC...
=
NAME=L26P93.3 SEQUENCE=CCCCTAGAGAGAGAGAGCCGAGTTCAAAGTCAAAACCCATTCTCTCTC...
=
```

There's also a way to create subrecords within records, allowing for structured data types.

Here's an example of a script that processes *boulderio* format. It uses an object-oriented style, in which records are pulled out of the input stream, modified, and dropped back in:

```
use Boulder::Stream;
$stream = new Boulder::Stream;
while ($record=$stream->read_record('NAME','SEQUENCE')) {
    $name = $record->get('NAME');
    $sequence = $record->get('SEQUENCE');
    ...continue processing...
    $record->add(QUALITY_CHECK=>"OK");
    $stream->write_record($record);
}
```

(If you're interested, more information about the *boulderio* format and the Perl libraries to manipulate it can be found at *http://www.genome.wi.mit.edu/ftp/pub/software/boulderio/*).

The interesting thing is that multiple informatics groups independently converged on solutions that were similar to the *boulderio* idea. For example, several groups involved in the worm sequencing project began using a data exchange format called *.ace*. Although this format was initially designed as the data dump and reload format for the ACE database (a database specialized for biological data), it happens to use a tag/value format that's very similar to *boulderio*. Soon *.ace* files were being processed by Perl script pipelines and loaded into the ACE database at the very last step.

Perl found uses in other aspects of laboratory management. For example, many centers, including my own, use Web based interfaces for displaying the status of projects and allowing researchers to take actions. Perl scripts are the perfect engine for Web CGI scripts. Similarly, Perl scripts run e-mail database query servers, supervise cron jobs, prepare nightly reports summarizing laboratory activity, create instruction files to control robots, and handle almost every other information management task that a busy genome center needs.

So as far as laboratory management went, the informatics cores were reasonably successful. Systems integration, however, was not so rosy.

The problem will be familiar to anyone who has worked in a large, loosely organized software project. Despite best intentions, the project begins to drift. Programmers go off to work on ideas that interest them, modules that need to interface with one another are designed independently, and the same problems get solved several times in different, mutually incompatible ways. When the time comes to put all the parts together, nothing works.

This is what happened in the genome project. Despite the fact that everyone was working on the same problems, no two groups took exactly the same approach.

Programs to solve a given problem were written and rewritten multiple times. While a given piece of software wasn't guaranteed to work better than its counterpart developed elsewhere, you could always count on it to sport its own idiosyncratic user interface and data format. A typical example is the central algorithm that assembles thousands of short DNA reads into an ordered set of overlaps. At last count there were at least six different programs in widespread use, and no two of them use the same data input or output formats.

This lack of interchangeability presents a terrible dilemma for the genome centers. Without interchangeability, an informatics group is locked into using the software that it developed in-house. If another genome center develops a better software tool to attack the same problem, a tremendous effort is required by the first center to adopt that tool.

The long range solution to this problem is to come up with uniform data interchange standards that genome software must adhere to. This would allow common modules to be swapped in and out easily. However, standards require time to agree on, and while the various groups are involved in discussion and negotiation, there is still an urgent need to adapt existing software to the immediate needs of the genome centers.

Here is where Perl again came to the rescue. The Cambridge summit meeting that introduced this article was called in part to deal with the data interchange problem. Despite the fact that the two groups involved were close collaborators and superficially seemed to be using the same tools to solve the same problems, on closer inspection nothing they were doing was exactly the same.

The main software components in a DNA sequencing projects are:

- a *trace editor* to analyze, display and allow biologists to edit the short DNA read chromatograms from sequencing machines.

- a *read assembler*, to find overlaps between the reads and assemble them together into long contiguous sections.

- an *assembly editor*, to view the assemblies and make changes in places where the assembler went wrong.

- a *database* to keep track of it all.

Over the course of a few years, the two groups had developed suites of software that worked well in their hands. Following the familiar genome center model, some of the components were developed in-house while others were imported from outside. Perl was used as the glue to fit these pieces together. Between each pair of interacting modules were one or more Perl scripts responsible for massaging the output of one module into the expected input for another.

When the time came to interchange data, however, the two groups hit a snag. Between them they were now using two trace editors, three assemblers, two assembly editors and (thankfully) one database. If two Perl scripts were required for each pair of components (one for each direction), one would need as many as 62 different scripts to handle all the possible interconversion tasks. Every time the input or ouput format of one of these modules changed, 14 scripts might need to be examined and fixed.

The two groups decided to adopt a common data exchange format known as CAF (an acronym whose exact meaning was forgotten during the course of the meeting). CAF would contain a superset of the data that each of the analysis and editing tools needed. For each module, two Perl scripts would be responsible for converting from CAF into whatever format Module A expects ("CAF2ModuleA") and converting Module A's output back into CAF ("ModuleA2CAF"). This simplified the programming and maintenance task considerably. Now there were only 16 Perl scripts to write; when one module changed, only two scripts would need to be examined.

This episode is not unique. Perl has been the solution of choice for genome centers whenever they need to exchange data, or to retrofit one center's software module to work with another center's system.

So Perl has become the software mainstay for computation within genome centers as well as the glue that binds them together. Although genome informatics groups are constantly tinkering with other high level languages such as Python, Tcl and recently Java, nothing comes close to Perl's popularity. How has Perl achieved this remarkable position?

Several factors are responsible:

1. Perl is remarkably good for slicing, dicing, twisting, wringing, smoothing, summarizing and otherwise mangling text. Although the biological sciences do involve a good deal of numeric analysis now, most of the primary data is still text: clone names, annotations, comments, bibliographic references. Even DNA sequences are textlike. Interconverting incompatible data formats is a matter of text mangling combined with some creative guesswork. Perl's powerful regular expression matching and string manipulation operators simplify this job in a way unequalled by any other modern language.

2. Perl is forgiving. Biological data is often incomplete, fields can be missing, or a field that is expected to be present once occurs several times (because, for example, an experiment was run in duplicate), or the data was entered by hand and doesn't quite fit the expected format. Perl doesn't particularly mind if a value is empty or contains odd characters. Regular expressions can be written to pick up and correct a variety of common errors in data entry. Of

course this flexibility can be also be a curse. I talk more about the problems with Perl below.

3. Perl is component-oriented. Perl encourages people to write their software in small modules, either using Perl library modules or with the classic UNIX tool-oriented approach. External programs can easily be incorporated into a Perl script using a pipe, system call or socket. The dynamic loader introduced with Perl5 allows people to extend the Perl language with C routines or to make entire compiled libraries available for the Perl interpreter. (An effort is currently under way to gather all the world's collected wisdom about biological data into a set of modules called "bioPerl.")

4. Perl programs are easy to write and fast to develop. The interpreter doesn't require you to declare all your function prototypes and data types in advance, new variables spring into existence as needed, calls to undefined functions only cause an error when the function is needed. The debugger works well with Emacs and allows a comfortable interactive style of development.

5. Perl is a good prototyping language. Because Perl is quick and dirty, it often makes sense to prototype new algorithms in Perl before moving them to a fast compiled language. Sometimes it turns out that Perl is fast enough so that of the algorithm doesn't have to be ported; more frequently one can write a small core of the algorithm in C, compile it as a dynamically loaded module or external executable, and leave the rest of the application in Perl. For an example of a complex genome mapping application implemented in this way, see:

http://www.genome.wi.mit.edu/ftp/pub/software/RHMAPPER/

6. Perl is a good language for Web CGI scripting, and is growing in importance as more labs turn to the Web for publishing their data.

My experience in using Perl in a genome center environment has been extremely favorable overall. However I find that Perl has its problems too. Its relaxed programming style leads to many errors that more uptight languages would catch. For example, Perl lets you use a variable before it's been assigned to, a useful feature when that's what you intend but a disaster when you've simply mistyped a variable name. Similarly, it's easy to forget to declare make a variable used in a subroutine local, inadvertently modifying a global variable.

If one uses the -w switch religiously and turns on the use strict vars pragma, then Perl will catch these problems and others. However there are more subtle gotchas in the language that are not so easy to fix. A major one is Perl's lack of type checking. Strings, floats and integers all interchange easily. While this greatly speeds up development, it can cause major headaches. Consider a typical genome center Perl script that's responsible for recording the information of short named subsequences within a larger DNA sequence. When the script was written, the data format was expected to consist of tab-delimited fields: a string followed by two integers representing the name, starting position and length of a DNA subsequence within a larger sequence. An easy way to parse this would to *split()* into an list like this:

```
($name,$start,$length) = split("\t");
```

Later on in this script some arithmetic is performed with the two integer values and the result written to a database or to standard output for further processing.

Then one day the input file format changes without warning. Someone bumps the field count up by one by sticking a comment field between the name and the first integer. Now the unknowing script assigns a string to a variable that's expected to be numeric and silently discards the last field on the line. Rather than crashing or returning an error code, the script merrily performs integer arithmetic on a string, assuming a value of zero for the string (unless it happens to start with a digit). Although the calculation is meaningless, the output may look perfectly good, and the error may not be caught until some point well downstream in the processing.

The final Perl deficiency has been a way to create graphical user interfaces. Although UNIX True Believers know that anything worth doing can be done on the command line, most end-users don't agree. Windows, menus and bouncing icons have become *de rigueur* for programs intended for use by mere mortals.

Until recently, GUI development in Perl was awkward to impossible. However the work of Nick Ing-Simmons and associates on Perl/Tk has made Perl-driven GUIs possible on X-windows systems. My associates and I have written several Perl/Tk-based applications for internal use at the MIT genome center, and it's been a satisfying experience overall. Other genome centers make much more extensive use of Perl/Tk, and in some places its become a mainstay of production.

Unfortunately, I'm sad to confess that a few months ago when I needed to put a graphical front end on a C++ image analysis program I'd written, I turned to the standard Tcl/Tk library rather than to Perl/Tk. I made this choice because I intended the application for widespread distribution. I find Perl/Tk still too unstable for export: new releases of Perl/Tk discover lurking bugs in Perl, and vice-versa. Further, I find that even seasoned system administrators run into glitches when compiling and installing Perl modules, and I worried that users would hit some sort of roadblock while installing either Perl/Tk or the modules needed to support my application, and would give up. In contrast, many systems have the Tcl/Tk libraries preinstalled; if they don't, installation is quick and painless.

In short, when the genome project was foundering in a sea of incompatible data formats, rapidly-changing techniques, and monolithic data analysis programs that were already antiquated on the day of their release, Perl saved the day. Although it's not perfect, Perl fills the needs of the genome centers remarkably well, and is usually the first tool we turn to when we have a problem to solve.

When he's not rushing to meet a deadline, Lincoln sometimes goes out for a coffee.

Understanding Regular Expressions
by Jeffrey Friedl

I'd like to tell you a story about a friend of mine, Fred. Because of the nature of the story, I'll talk a lot about Perl regular expressions and how they really work behind the scenes. To follow the story, I'll assume that you know Perl at least as well as Fred (which is not saying a lot, since he doesn't know it all that well, although he thinks he does).

In the last issue, Tom Christiansen wrote that regular expressions can still be daunting even to the expert. With much due respect for Tom (from whom I've learned a great deal about both Perl and regular expressions), I don't believe that's really fair to say. Regular expressions need not be difficult, and need not be a mystery. Frankly, if you put aside all the theoretical mumbo-jumbo and look from a practical point of view *how* the Perl regular-expression engine works, then you too can think along those lines and *know* how an expression will act in any given situation.

So, I believe that with a bit of explanation and a healthy dose of experience, you'll create an *undaunted* expert. This story covers the whole range, from the Fred level all the way up to the expert level.

Note that the approach I take for explaining regular expressions is perhaps quite different than you or Fred has ever seen before. The story approaches Perl regular expressions "from the back." The manual page and publications tend to provide a raw "these metacharacters do such-and-such" table along with a few examples. Rather than rehashing this old story, I'll present the view from the regular-expression engine's point of view, showing what it actually *does* in attempting a match. Eventually, we will work our way "to the front" to see what relation these workings have to the metacharacters you feed it. It's quite a longer path to get there, but the added understanding will usually make the difference between hoping an expression will work, and Knowing.

This is a long story, and because of the "from the back" approach, you might not always see where I'm heading or the relevance of what I discuss. But, as I said, eventually we will indeed work our way to the front, and things should suddenly become much more clear when you start to compare what I've written with the experience and knowledge you already have.

So, if you feel daunted at all—anything less than utmost confidence around even the most hairy regular·expression—it is my hope you will get something real, tangible, and useful out of this story. Hey, even Fred did!

"Regular Expression" Nomenclature

Before starting with the story, I'd like to comment on a few of the ways "regular expression" is abbreviated. I use "regex." An alternate spelling, "regexp," also seems somewhat popular although I can't quite comprehend why—it is difficult to pronounce and to pluralize. "Regex" just rolls right off the tongue.

The Story of Fred

Fred was a happy programmer. Like with so many projects before, Fred needed to verify some data, but this time the data was pretty simple—just numbers and colons. The (small) catch was that the colons must come in pairs, with no single-tons allowed.

Mmmm... sounds like a regular-expression match is just the hammer for this nail, and that's exactly what Fred used.

Let's see . . . . Fred wants to match the line exactly `/^ ... $/`, allowing a bunch of digits `/[0-9]+/` or pairs of colons `/::/` as many times as happen to be there `/(...)*/`. Putting it all together, Fred gets `/^([0-9]+|::)*$/`.

Well, that was pretty easy, even for Fred. Testing it quickly, he dumps some sample data:

```
::1234::5678901234567890::::1234567890::888
```

into a file *data* and tests via

```
% perl -ne 'die "bad data" unless m/^([0-9]+|::)*$/' data
%
```

Fred realizes that with this test, no news is good news.

Heck, as an aside, Fred even noticed that this task is so simple that he can use the exact same regex to test it with *egrep* or *awk* (two tools, he knows, whose regex flavor is similar to Perl's):

```
% egrep -v '^([0-9]+|::)*$' data
%

% awk '! /^([0-9]+|::)*$/ { print "bad data" }' data
%
```

So anyway, Fred's Perl script is happily using this test to verify the data until one day the program just locks up dead. Debugging, Fred tracks it down to the regex match. The match starts, but never returns a result—it seems that there's some infinite loop during the match.

Fred looks at the particular data that was being checked at the time:

```
::1234::5678901234567890::::1234567890::888:
```

and notices that it is not valid (this is the valid data from above, but with a singleton : tacked onto the end making it invalid).

Dumbfounded, Fred returns to the *egrep* and *awk* tests and finds that they still work, even on this data. Fred even tries the same tests on various other machines, all with the same result—the Perl program locks up when it hits this data. So why does the regex match seem to run forever? Fred thinks it's a bug in Perl.

Reality Check

No Fred, it's not a bug in Perl at all—it's simply doing exactly what you asked it to do. "Well," he replies, "I didn't ask it to lock up. And anyway, the *egrep* and *awk* tests work fine, so it must be a bug in Perl!" The bug, I'm afraid, is Fred's understanding of Perl and regular expressions (or lack thereof).*

The problem is *backtracking*, something the Perl regex engine has to do, but the *egrep* and *awk* engines do not. I'll go into the details a bit later, but the result is that the Perl regex engine needs to perform about 140 billion tests before it can report for sure that the data in question doesn't match m/^([0-9]+|::)*$/. Yes folks, 140 *billion*. Even on Fred's fastest machine, that's likely to take a few hours, thus exhibiting the "lockup" symptom. [*Editor's note: 4 hours on my 175 MHz DEC Alpha.*]

The *awk* and *egrep* regex engines, however, are able to find the answer (match, or in this case, no match) immediately. Fred is confused.

Regular Expression Background

The regular expressions that we know and love started out as a formal algebra in the early 1950s, but believe me, I don't want to get into a discussion of math theory (mostly because I don't know it). What is relevant here is that there are two basic methods to implement a regular expression engine: "NFA engines" and "DFA engines."

---

* Amazingly enough, there is an unrelated bug in versions of Perl 5 before 5.001 which, unfortunately for your author, just happens to result in the test in question appearing to work correctly! From 5.001m that bug has been fixed, allowing these tests to exhibit the "bug" that this article is about. Fred is cool and up to speed with 5.002.

For those that want to impress their mother, nfa and dfa stand for "Nondeterministic Finite Automata" and "Deterministic Finite Automata," but this is the only time in this article you'll see them spelled out. From a theoretical point of view, there's a lot packed into those terms. But who can figure out all that mumbo-jumbo? For practical purposes, just consider "NFA engine" and "DFA engine" as names, like "Moe" or "Shemp."

Perl has always used an NFA engine, as does *vi, sed,* GNU *emacs,* Python, Tcl, *expect,* and most versions of *grep.* On the other hand, most versions of *egrep, awk,* and *lex* are built with DFA engines. The two types are different in important ways, but practically speaking, you don't need to care about one to study the other. So while this article looks at Perl's NFA engine in depth, a few comments about how NFA and DFA engines differ might be useful to whet the appetite of the curious.

DFA vs NFA

When a DFA engine first encounters the regular expression, it spends some time analyzing it, creating an understanding of every type of string it could possibly match. As a particular string is actually checked, the DFA engine always knows the status (no match, partial match, full match) of the text checked so far. Once the text has been scanned to the end, the engine can simply report the final verdict.

An NFA, on the other hand, goes about things quite differently. It is what I call "regex directed," and approaches a match in a way that humans tend to relate to. For example, if something in the regex is optional, it might try the optional match, and come back ("backtrack") and retry by skipping it if the first try didn't work out.

Each of the two types has it's own pluses and minuses, which is why they are both still around. A DFA engine tends to need more time and memory for the initial check of any particular regular expression, but because it is determinate and never needs to backtrack, it will tend to do individual matches much faster. Sometimes much, much faster. But because of how it works internally, a pure DFA can't provide backreferences or the $1, $2, etc. that Perl's NFA so importantly provides. Chapter 3 of Aho, Sethi, and Ullman's *Compilers* (a.k.a. The Dragon Book—1986, 2nd ed., Addison-Wesley) gives an extremely rigorous presentation of the theory behind these engines.

NFA vs NFA, DFA vs DFA

Each program that implements regular expressions has their own special features and special problems. There are "Perl 5.002 regular expressions", "GNU *awk* 2.15 regular expressions", and so on. While there are obvious similarities among them, there is little meaning to talking "regular expressions" out of context of their intended use. This story is about Perl 5.002 regular expressions.

So, what does all this mean?

Fred has a superficial understanding of regular expressions. He knows more or less what the metacharacters do, but doesn't really *understand* how a regex match is attempted, and so is never really sure what will happen with anything nontrivial until he actually tries it. He doesn't really understand the differences among regex flavors, so certainly doesn't know about the backtracking that Perl is forced to do. Fred is often confused when regexes that have /.*/ in them don't work as he expects, and he often wonders why he always seems to be getting the wrong results. When it comes down to it, Fred is never really comfortable around regular expressions. Fred is confused all the time.

Don't Be a Fred

But you don't have to be like Fred. One nice characteristic of an NFA engine is that it is pretty easy to understand. Understanding how it works will take the magic and the wonder out of Perl regular expressions. You'll be in the know. You'll be confident. You won't be a Fred.

Perl Regex Engine Basics

The first thing the regex engine does when it sees a regular expression is to *compile* it. The regex is analyzed, checked for errors, and reduced to an internal form that can be used later to quickly check a particular string for a match. Since the compilation itself is unrelated to an actual match attempt, it needs to be done just once, usually when the whole Perl script is first loaded. The internal form will then be used repeatedly to do the actual matches during the script's execution.

What this article will focus on is how the engine actually applies a regex to a string to see if there is a match. This is definitely a case where what goes on behind the scenes is not out-of-sight-out-of-mind, for as Fred learned, some matches take much longer than others. As it turns out, we can use our (perhaps newfound) knowledge of what goes on behind the scenes to rewrite the regex that Fred used in such a way that it works quickly in every situation. Fred would be very grateful.

A Sample Regex

Let's look at the simple regex /".*"/, ostensibly used to match a double-quoted string. From a superficial point of view, this means: "match a double quote, then any amount of anything (except newlines), and finally another double quote."

With the example text

```
And then "Right," said Fred, "at 12:00" and he was gone.
```

we can easily see that there will certainly be a match, so the question becomes *which text* will actually be matched. Looking at the English description above, there are a variety of ways it could conceptually apply:

```
And then "Right," said Fred, "at 12:00" and he was gone.
```

So which will it be? And more importantly, *why?*

"The longest match wins" and other myths

If you've been using Perl for more than a day or three, you probably already know that /.*/ is "greedy" and will "match as much as it can," so you probably know which of the above is the result you can expect from Perl. Heck, even Fred knows. Fred knows about "greedy," and has heard various other rules such as "the longest match wins" or maybe "the first match wins" or even "the first longest match wins." Fred can't quite keep them all straight, but feels these rules make him a Power User.

The problem is that *none* of these rules apply to Perl. As we will see, some are close, but rather than remember a bunch of rules that aren't even correct, I think it is better to Know What Happens. When it comes to complex situations where the "rules" start to fail, your Knowledge will put you light-years ahead of Fred.

The First Real Rule of Regexes

Matches that start earlier *always* take precedence over matches that start later. Why? Because the regex engine first tries to find a match *starting at the first position in the text*, and only if a match is not found will it then bump along and attempt the match from the next position, and the next, and so on until some individual attempt does yield a match.

Looking at our sample text, we know we can eliminate half of the possibilities because they start later than the three that start at the first quote. We are then left with three possibilities:

```
And then "Right," said Fred, "at 12:00" and he was gone.
```

This doesn't explain one way or the other which of the remaining three will be chosen, as they all start at the same equally-leftmost position. But we know that in attempting this match, the engine will make nine failed attempts on matches starting with the 'A', 'n', 'd', and so on.

There's one particularly interesting effect of this "earlier-starting matches take precedence" rule. Let's look at `/-?[0-9]*\.?[0-9]*/`, which is ostensibly meant to match a floating-point number.* We have an optional minus sign, some digits, perhaps a decimal point, and then perhaps some more digits. Indeed, it will match a wide range of examples such as '1', '3.1415', '-.007', '-1223.3838', '19.', etc. It could even match the '12' from our Fred example.

But will it? Breaking this regex into its component parts, we can view it as

> `/-?/` and then `/[0-9]*/` and then `/\.?/` and then `/[0-9]*/`

The '-' is allowed, but not required. Digits are allowed as well, but also not required. In fact, looking at all the components we realize that *nothing is required* for a match!

Applying it to our Fred example, the engine will first attempt a match starting from the start of the string. Were it to fail, and fail all the other attempts until the start of the '12', it would get a chance to match. But since nothing is required to match, we're *guaranteed* to be successful here with the first try. There is only one plausible match starting at 'And then...', and that's the match of nothingness at the start.

Now, had our text been, say, '4.0, patchlevel 36' there would have been a number of plausible matches right at the start. The nothingness that we know is always allowed with this regex, or perhaps the full '4.0'. Or perhaps just '4.'. All in all, there are five plausible matches. We still don't know anything about *which* it will be, but whichever it is, we know the match will begin at the start of the text:

> Second Cousin of the First Rule: A regex that doesn't require anything for a successful match will *always* succeed with a match beginning at the start of the target.

So, knowing how the Perl regex engine approaches a string overall, let's look at how any one particular attempt behaves. Knowing this will tell us which of the plausible matches will actually be returned, as well as why. This is where things really get interesting.

---

* This regex actually appeared in a book written by a friend of mine (but not a Fred) for a famous publisher. In the unforgettable words of Dave Barry, "I'm not making this up."

A Single Match Attempt

The top half of Figure B-2 shows, from a practical point of view, how the regular expression engine views/`".*"/`. The bottom half shows the metacharacters relating to the top half.

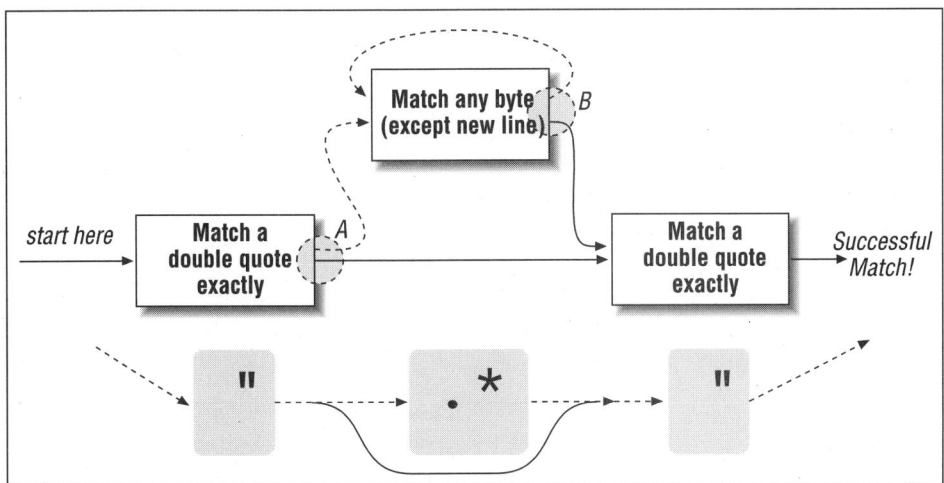

Figure B-2. The regular expression engine

It helps to consider the regex engine as an entity moving from square to square along the solid and dashed connecting lines. If it moves into a square and can make the match noted there, it is then free to move along. If not, it must do something else (that "something else" being backtracking, but I'm getting a bit ahead of myself).

Multiple paths

Sometimes there is more than one path the engine can take at any one point. In the figure, these are marked **A** and **B**. It is useful to note that the solid paths represent the skipping of something that is allowed but not required (i.e. optional). The dashed path from **A** represents an attempt at `/.*/`, while the solid path represents its omission. The omission reflects that `/.*/` can match nothing yet still be successful.

The dashed path from **B** represents the attempt at another `/./` by the `/.*/` construct, while the solid path represents breaking out of the `/.*/` to continue on. This reflects that no matter how much has already been matched by `/.*/`, further matches are still optional.

Perl's NFA regex engine can take only one path at a time, so at these places where there are more than one option, what should it do? This is an extremely important point. It may well be that one path will lead to a match, while others will not. The point is, the NFA regex engine doesn't know which will and will not lead to a match until it actually tries.

Looking at the figure and starting at the marked position in

```
And then "Right," said Fred, "at 12:00" and he was gone.
         ʌ
```

Indeed the first "match a double quote" box is successful. This moves us to ʌRight, in the text, but the engine still has to move to another box. At **A** it has the choice between the solid and dashed arrows. If it happens to choose the solid path over to the second "match a double quote" box, we can see it will fail, since a double quote won't match the 'R' we're currently at. *We* can see it will fail, but the regex engine can't. Remember, it doesn't know until it actually tries.

Which will it choose? What will it do if it chooses wrong? These are the key, fundamental issues of an NFA regex engine. If you understand them, you are 90% of the way to becoming an undaunted expert.

Fortunately, as you'll see soon, these issues are quite easy to understand.

Backtracking

When the regex engine is faced with multiple paths, it chooses one (exactly which it chooses and why is quite important, but discussed a bit later), and marks the others paths as untried. Later during the match, if the regex engine finds it has taken a path that has lead to failure, it can return to the situation where it had been and retry with one of the marked paths. This is known as *backtracking*.

Returning to our example, we found ourselves in the text at ʌRight, and in the regex at **A**. For the purposes of discussion, let's say that the regex chooses the solid path first. In doing so, it will remember that, should the need ever arise, it can retry from that position via the dashed path.

Indeed, the need arises quickly. As mentioned above, the second "match quote" box certainly fails to match the 'R'. Normally, this local failure would mean overall match failure, but because we have a *remembered state*, we know that there are options that were allowed but have not yet been tried. *Backtracking is nothing more than returning to yet-to-be-tried options when the current path fails.*

So, we return to **A** and take the dashed path. This time, the "match any byte" successfully matches the 'R'. Now what to do? At **B** now, we again have a choice. For the purposes of the current discussion, let's say that the dashed path is chosen. In doing so, the engine will remember

```
can take the solid path from B while at R ʌ
```

"Byte" vs. "Character"

Most people don't differentiate between the terms "byte" and "character," although they can be quite different. With normal 7-bit ASCII, for example, there are characters for only the first 128 values that a byte could have. A byte with value of decimal 212 simply has no meaning in normal ASCII, yet is "M" in EBCDIC, "Ô" in the ISO-8859-1 ("Latin-1") encoding, and " ｲ " in the Japanese JIS-Roman encoding.

The difference becomes a very real concern when working with multi-byte encodings such as Unicode, EUC, and Big Five, among others. In the EUC Japanese encoding, for example, two bytes with decimal value 212 together encode the single character " 墺 " (which is an abbreviation for Austria, if you must know).

Text is simply a lump of bytes, and a character encoding tells how to interpret it. Perl regular expressions don't know what encoding the data was *intended* to be taken as—for the most part, it treats everything in a pseudo-ASCIIish way. This is fine when working with straight English text or ASCII, and so in this article, I use "byte" and "character" interchangeably.

You can still use Perl to work with other encodings (I use it often to process text encoded via several different Japanese encodings), but it takes extra work and care. Knowing that / ./ matches a *byte* and not a *character* becomes extremely important, for example. If there is enough interest (as shown by notes to *perl-journal-letters@perl.com*), I'll be more than happy to write on this subject in a future column. Until then, the definitive reference on Asian encodings (which tend to be multibyte) is Ken Lunde's *Understanding Japanese Information Processing* (which is somewhat of a misnomer since it touches on various languages), published by O'Reilly. *[Pub. note: This book is now out of print.]*

So, taking that dashed path we wind up at the same box. This time, the any-byte matched is the 'i'. As before, we have a choice. Let's say that the dashed path is chosen again. In doing so, we're bypassing *another* opportunity to take the solid path, so we add

```
can take the solid path from B while at Ri ʌ
```

to our list of remembered states. In fact, we add a state each time we go through this loop. Assuming we take the dashed path the next time as well, we also add

```
can take the solid path from B while at Rig ʌ
```

during the next loop, leaving us at `Righ`∧ in the text.

Let's say, for the purposes of the discussion, that at this point the regex engine decides to take the solid path. Now we're bypassing a chance to take the dashed path at this juncture, so we add

```
can take the dashed path from B while at Righ∧
```

Unfortunately, the solid path from **B** at this point immediately leads to failure, as the text's 't' can't match the required double-quote. A local failure? No problem! We have plenty of saved states to retry from, and one (or more?!) might eventually lead to a match.

When the regex engine is forced to backtrack, it will always backtrack to the most-recently saved state that is available (the others will be used, in turn, when and if needed).

So we backtrack to:

```
can take the dashed path from B while at Righ∧
```

and take the dashed path. We match the 't' and find ourself at **B** for about the half-dozenth time, and as with each time before, we have two fresh choices.

Okay, so this description is getting a bit long-winded, and I think by now even Fred is getting the picture. And we still haven't gotten to the whole issue of how the engine decides which from among its possible paths to choose at any particular point (remember, all the decisions reported above are for the purposes of discussion and don't necessarily reflect what any known regex engine will actually do in the exact same situation).

So, to make this go a bit quicker, let's assume that from now on the regex engine will always choose the dashed path whenever it reaches **B**. This would result in a lot of looping, with the "any byte" matching each byte of the target text in succession. And, of course, each time we choose the dashed path, the solid is remembered in yet another saved state.

By the time the engine has neared the end of the string, as far as **was gone**∧ we have accumulated quite a few saved states. Listing them in reverse order, we have

```
can take the solid path from B while at  was gon∧
can take the solid path from B while at  was go∧
can take the solid path from B while at  was g∧
...
can take the solid path from B while at  Rig∧
can take the solid path from B while at  Ri∧
can take the solid path from B while at  R∧
```

Anyway, that's the current status, but we still haven't reached an overall match yet. As we've been doing, we take the dashed path, this time adding

```
can take the solid path from B while at  was gone⌄
```

We can match the '.', and so follow with another dashed path, adding

```
can take the solid path from B while at  was gone. ⌄
```

But this time, the "any byte" box can't match because we're at the end of the string. Had it been a "match the end of the text" box, we'd be fine, but it's not, so we have a local failure and need to backtrack. So we go back to this most-recently saved state, but fail there as well (this time because "double quote" can't match the nothingness at the end of the string). Still no worries — we have plenty of saved states. The most recent is now:

```
can take the solid path from B while at  was gone⌄
```

but this also fails: a double quote and a period don't mesh. In fact, the next dozen or so backtracks fail in the same way. It's only when we finally backtrack to

```
can take the solid path from B while at 12:00⌄
```

that the double quote can match. Once done, there is only one path from that box, so no decision needs to be made nor any new state saved. And as it turns out, we have an overall match!

```
And then "Right," said Fred, "at 12:00" and he was gone.
         ←――――――――――――――――――――→
```

Now that we've reached an overall match, we can consider ourselves done. Sure, there are some other saved states that may well also lead to overall matches (actually, there are two others still in there), but since we have a match already, who cares? (Answer: a POSIX engine might, but not Perl).

Thus, we come to the rule:

> *THE FIRST MATCH REACHED WINS.*

Note that this is not "the shortest match" or "the first match I see" or "the match I, as a programmer, am hoping for," but the first match that the regex engine actually reaches.

> The decisions about which path to take at any particular point has a direct influence as to *which* match the regex engine will find first.

Now remember—and I can't stress this enough—that the decisions about which path to take have thus far in this article been randomly chosen off the top of my head and have no necessary relation to any reality. I wanted to explain the mechanics of how backtracking works, and do so without muddying the waters with the (equally important) issue of path selection. Had I happen to write the story such that the regex engine made different decisions, the results could have been different.

For example, had I decided that during the "any byte" loop, as the regex matched up to 'Fred, ₐat' the engine suddenly decided to take the solid path, we would have immediately matched the double quote and then reached the overall match

```
And then "Right," said Fred, "at 12:00" and he was gone.
      <————————————————>
```

Or, as another example, had I written that the solid path was suddenly chosen as the engine came up to 12:00 ₐand, we would have reached the same match as in the story, but in quite a more efficient way. In the original story, we'd matched all the characters of ' and he was gone.' only to have to effectively undo that by backtracking to the final double quote. So this illustrates two different avenues to the same match, one with a lot of what turns out to be extra work and one without.

Options, Options, Options

Before getting into the details about *which* path is chosen, let's look at the various regex constructs that yield multiple choices in the first place. The quick summary is that when something is *optional*, the regex engine needs to decide if it should first attempt to match the optional part, or if it should first try the overall match skipping this optional part. Each choice represents a path, and in either case the choice not taken is remembered for later use if backtracking so dictates. So remember, **something optional means multiple paths.**

The most basic "optional" item is anything governed by ?, such as the /(blah)/ in /(blah)?/. We know that Perl's new ?? means optional as well, and that it is "non-greedy," but what does that really mean? It is directly related to path selection (you'll be able to cast aside any shroud of mystery you might have about this in just a moment), but first I'd like to continue summarizing items that are considered optional.

Items governed by * (and *?) are optional not only once, but repeatedly forever (well, to be pedantic, Perl currently has an internal limit of 32K repeats for parenthetical items). Almost the same, items governed by + and +? are optional only after their first match (the first match being required). Items governed by {*min,max*} and {*min,max*}? are optional once their required min matches have been made, and are only optional until the max has been reached. With {*num*}, nothing is optional (which, as you might realize, is why {*num*}? is always exactly the same as {*num*}—there is no difference whatsoever).

Alternation

Let's not forget about alternation. With something like /moe|fred|shemp/, if /
moe/ is attempted first, it is optional because its failure does not mean the entire
regex necessarily fails, since /fred/ and /shemp/ are still available. If indeed /
moe/ fails and, say, /shemp/ is tried next, it too can be considered optional
because there is still the /fred/ left to try. But if /shemp/ also fails, then /fred/
suddenly becomes required, since its failure results in no more alternates. Thus,
alternates are optional as long as there are other alternates left to try.

When alternation is surrounded by parentheses, this "failure" becomes failure of
the component, not of the entire regex. For example, failure to match any of the
alternates in /(moe|fred|shemp)?/ doesn't mean overall failure since matching
any of the alternates was optional via the ? in the first place.

Character classes

One quick note about character classes. A character class alone does *not* represent anything optional. /[xyz]/, for example, does *not* mean "try to match x, or
match y, or match z" (that would be /x|y|z/). Rather, /[xyz]/ means "let's
check out one byte, and if it is an x, y, or z, we match" It is a subtle distinction in
English, but a huge distinction to the regex engine. It should be apparent that the
character class is much more efficient than the /x|y|z/, which might perform up
to three separate matches rather than the one check required by /[xyz]/.

A negated character class (such as /[^xyz]/) is no more or no less efficient than
a normal one. The meaning of the list of characters is simply toggled from "these
allowed" to "something except these allowed."

All the other regex constructs, from /^/ to /\b/ to /(?!...)/ to /\3/, do not
represent anything optional. They may well become optional when governed by
something mentioned above, but there is nothing intrinsically optional about them.

How the Path Is Chosen

Finally, the last piece of the puzzle! We know about saving states for untried
paths, and we know about using those states to backtrack if needed. Only one
question remains: when faced with multiple paths, which one will the Perl regular
expression engine actually attempt first?

Rephrasing the above in a more human point-of-view, when faced with an
optional item (or with alternation items), will the Perl regular expression engine
first attempt to match the optional item, or will it first attempt to skip the optional
item? (Or in the case of alternation, in which order will the items be tried?)

?, *, +, and {*min*, *max*}, the so-called "greedy" or "maximal matching" metacharacters, will always *attempt an optional item first*. They will skip an optional item only if forced via backtracking.

??, *?, +?, and {*min*, *max*}?, the so-called "ungreedy" or "minimal matching" metacharacters, will always *skip an optional item first*. They will return to try matching the item only if forced via backtracking.

With alternation, Perl always *attempts the alternates in order* (counting from left to right). The first alternate will always be attempted first. The second and subsequent alternates will be attempted (in turn) only if so forced via backtracking.

That's Pretty Much It!

If I were telling about Japanese instead of regular expressions, the point we've reached would be comparable to my having told you 90% of the grammar rules and vocabulary of the Japanese language. Were that the case, I certainly wouldn't expect you to start jabbering away in Japanese—it takes time and experience to internalize the information and to draw out the relevancy to what you already know about human communications or, as the case may be, Perl regular expressions.

So far I've given you motions, but no directions. Words, but no acting. Fred has this funny look on his face, not really sure if he understands why he's been listening for the last hour. Depending on your previous exposure to Perl regular expressions, you might well be thinking "wow, so *that's* why such-and-such turns out that way!" But for most, I think the lessons of this story require a fair amount of real-world context before they sink in completely.

As I noted early on, even Fred knew that /".*"/ would match

```
And then "Right," said Fred, "at 12:00" and he was gone.
```

But rather than "because /.*/ is greedy", I think it would be instructive to carefully run through the match sequence yourself, counting tests, saved states, and backtracks. This will explain in a very tangible way *why* /".*"/ does not match

```
And then "Right," said Fred, "at 12:00" and he was gone.
```

as many new Perl hackers expect. Furthermore, applying the same rigorous step-through to /".*?"/ will clearly show why it *does* match 'Right,'.

Really, please try working through these examples on your own. In the next issue of *TPJ*, I'll focus much more on how to put these mechanics to practical use, but to use them effectively you must understand them completely. Working through these two simple examples is a good start.

Match Statistics

Against the text:

```
And then "Right," said Fred, "at 12:00" and he was gone.
    ⋏
```

with the count starting at the marked position, the match statistics are:

regex	tests (pass/fail)	backtracks	abandoned states
/".*"/	67 (48 / 19)	19	28
/".*?"/	14 (8 / 6)	6	1
/"[^"]*"/	9 (8 / 1)	1	6

Don't let the 67 tests of the first example intimidate you—it's not really as complicated as it might seem. Starting from the first successful match of the leading /"/, we follow with 46 successful matches of /./. It finally fails when attempting to match the nothingness at the end of the text. We backtrack to try skipping this most-recently attempted /./, leading us to attempt the final /"/. This also fails to match the nothingness at the end of the text. So far: 47 successful tests, 2 failures.

Backtracking again (which effectively "unmatches" the /./ having matched the text-ending period), we have another failure as /"/ cannot match it. This backtrack-and-fail cycle continues for a total of 17 times (once for each character in '.enog saw eh dna ') until we finally backtrack to unmatch the final quote, allowing a successful match of /"/.

This leaves us with 1+46+1 = 48 matches, and 2+17 = 19 failures.

As you work through them, keep a tally of how many individual tests are performed (such as "does 'match a double quote' succeed?"), noting how many are successful and how many fail. Keep a count of how many times you have to backtrack, and also note exactly how many states are discarded as no longer needed once the overall match is found. For the purposes of all these counts, start counting with the first successful match of the leading /"/ as test (and match) number 1. Once you feel comfortable that you understand how the matching proceeds, you can check your answers with the chart in the sidebar to the right.

Oh, and as a bonus, it should be quite instructive to do the same work-through with /"[^"]*"/. The associated statistics are also included in the sidebar.

And in the next issue, I'll start to develop some working rules and conclusions from all this (but hopefully you'll be able to make some of your own as you start to re-examine what you already know in this new light).

By the way, I guess I should make one mention about how Perl sometimes optimizes how it deals with regular expressions. Sometimes it might actually perform

fewer tests than what I've described. Or it perhaps does some tests more efficiently than others (for example, `/x*/` is internally optimized such that it is more
efficient than `/(x)*/` or `/(?:x)*/`). Sometimes Perl can even decide that a
regex can *never* match the particular string in question, so will bypass the test
altogether.

These optimizations are interesting, but the base workings are much more important. Once you've got that down pat, you might start to delve into the nitty-gritty
details enough such that you can attempt to incorporate an understanding of
them into your regular expressions.

Oh, and one final item before I close the article. Fred is still asking why on earth
his `/^([0-9]+|::)*$/` was taking so long. In a future column, I'll talk much
more about this issue, which can rear its ugly head in more than just Fred code—
it can be rather common. But until then, I'll let you help Fred. Do the work-
through of applying this regex to the text '12:'. We know it will fail, but the
regex engine doesn't until it tries all the matching and backtracking that this
whole article has been about. Then try the text '123:', and if you still don't get
the picture, try '1234:'. I hope the reason becomes clear and you can explain it
to Fred instead of being *a* Fred.

*Jeffrey Friedl works at Omron Corp (Kyoto, Japan), and spends his copious free
time on a regex book for O'Reilly. He can be reached at* jfriedl@omron.co.jp.

CGI Scripts and Cookies   by Lincoln Stein

In the last installment of this column I promised to talk about MiniSvr, a central
part of the CGI::* modules and an easy way to maintain state within a CGI script.
Unfortunately I've made several changes to my system in the last few weeks
(upgrading to Perl 5.003 and Apache 1.1b4), and MiniSvr broke. At press time, I
still haven't figured out what's gone wrong. So today I'm going to talk about a
sweeter subject, cookies.

What's a cookie? The folks at Netscape came up with the idea for Navigator 1.1.
It's just a `name=value` pair, much like the named parameters used in the CGI
query string. When a Web server or CGI script wants to save some state information, it creates a cookie or two and sends them to the browser inside the HTTP
header. The browser keeps track of all the cookies sent to it by a particular server
and stores them in an on-disk database so that the cookies persist even when the
browser is closed and reopened later. The next time the browser connects to a
Web site, it searches its database for all cookies that belong to that server and
transmits them back to the server within the HTTP header.

Cookies can be permanent or set to expire after a number of hours or days. They can be made site-wide, so that the cookie is available to every URL on your site, or restricted to a partial URL path. You can also set a flag in the cookie so that it's only transmitted over the Internet when the browser and server are communicating by a secure protocol such as SSL. You can even create promiscuous cookies that are sent to every server in a particular Internet domain.

The idea is simple but powerful. If a CGI script needs to save a small amount of state information, such as the user's preferred background color, it can be stored directly in a cookie. If lots of information needs to be stored, you can keep the information in a database on the server's side and use the cookie to record a session key or user ID. Other browsers have begun to adopt cookies (notably Microsoft in its Internet Explorer), and cookies are on their way to becoming a part of the HTTP standard.

So how do you create a cookie? If you use the CGI.pm library it's a piece of cake:

```
0   #!/usr/bin/perl
1
2   use CGI qw(:standard);
3
4   $cookie1 = cookie(-name  => 'regular',
5                     -value => 'chocolate chip');
6   $cookie2 = cookie(-name  => 'high fiber',
7                     -value => 'oatmeal raisin');
8   print header(-cookie => [$cookie1, $cookie2]);
```

Line 2 loads the CGI library and imports the `:standard` set of function calls using a syntax that's new in library versions 2.21 and higher. This syntax allows you to call all of the CGI object's methods without explicitly creating a CGI instance—a default CGI object is created for you behind the scenes. Lines 4 through 7 create two new cookies using the CGI cookie() method. The last step is to incorporate the cookies into the document's HTTP header. We do this in line 8 by printing out the results of the header() method, passing it the `-cookie` parameter along with an array reference containing the two cookies.

When we run this script from the command line, the result is:

```
Set-cookie: regular=chocolate%20chip
Set-cookie: high%20fiber=oatmeal%20raisin
Content-type: text/html
```

As you can see, CGI.pm translates spaces into %20's, as the Netscape cookie specification prohibits whitespace and certain other characters, such as the semicolon. (It also places an upper limit of a few kilobytes on the size of a cookie, so don't try to store the text of Hamlet in one.) When the browser sees these two cookies it squirrels them away and returns them to your script the next time it needs a document from your server.

To retrieve the value of a cookie sent to you by the browser, use cookie()
without a **-value** parameter:

```
0  #!/usr/bin/perl
1
2  use CGI qw(:standard);
3
4  $regular   = cookie('regular');
5  $high_fiber = cookie('high fiber');
6
7  print header(-type => 'text/plain'),
8      "The regular cookie is $regular.\n",
9      "The high fiber cookie is $high_fiber.";
```

In this example, lines 4 and 5 retrieve the two cookies by name. Lines 7 through
9 print out an HTTP header (containing no cookie this time), and two lines of
text. The output of this script, when viewed in a browser, would be

```
The regular cookie is chocolate chip.
The high fiber cookie is oatmeal raisin.
```

The cookie() method is fairly flexible. You can save entire arrays as cookies by
giving the **-value** parameter an array reference:

```
$c = cookie(-name => 'specials',
            -value => ['oatmeal',
                       'chocolate chip','alfalfa']);
```

Or you can save and restore whole associative arrays:

```
$c = cookie(-name => 'prices',
            -value => {        'oatmeal' => '$0.50',
                       'chocolate_chip' => '$1.25',
                              'alfalfa' => 'free'});
```

Later you can recover the two cookies this way:

```
@specials = cookie('specials');
%prices   = cookie('prices');
```

By default, browsers will remember cookies that only until they exit, and will
only send the cookie out to scripts with a URL path that's similar to the script that
generated it. If you want them to remember the cookie for a longer period of
time, pass an **-expires** parameter to cookie() containing the cookie's shelf life.
To change the URL path over which the cookie is valid, pass its value in **-path**:

```
$c = cookie(-name => 'regular',
            -value => 'oatmeal raisin',
             -path => '/cgi-bin/bakery',
          -expires => '+3d');
```

This cookie will expire in three days' time ('+3d'). Other cookie() parameters
allow you to adjust the domain names and URL paths that trigger the browser to

send a cookie, and to turn on cookie secure mode. The -path parameter shown here tells the browser to send the cookie to every program in /cgi-bin/bakery.

The next page shows a CGI script called *configure.cgi*. When you call this script's URL you're presented with the fill-out form shown above. You can change the page's background color, the text size and color, and even customize it with your name. The next time you visit this page (even if you've closed the browser and come back to the page weeks later), it remembers all of these values and builds a page based on them (see Figure B-3).

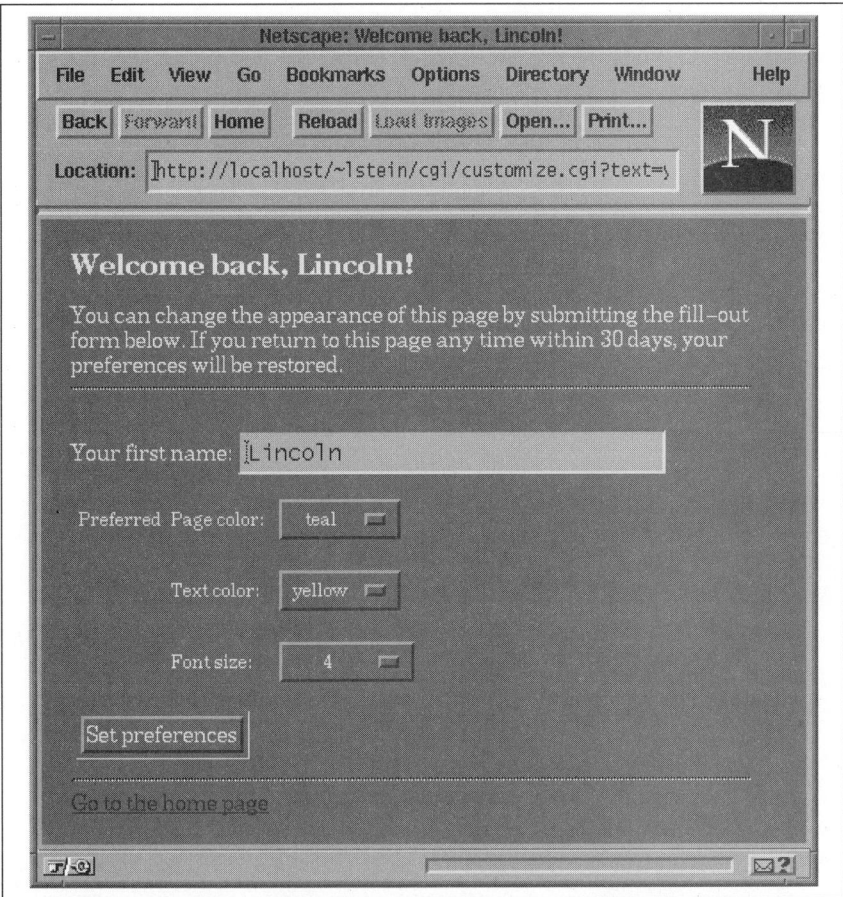

Figure B-3. CGI script configure.cgi in browser

This script recognizes four CGI parameters used to change the configuration:

- **background**: Set the background color.
- **text**: Set the text color.

- `size`: Set the size to the indicated value (1-7).

- `name`: Set the username.

Usually these parameters are sent to the script via the fill out form that it generates, but you could set them from within a URL this way:

```
/cgi-bin/configure.pl?background=silver&text=blue&name=Stein
```

Let's walk through the code. Line 2 imports the CGI library, bringing in both the standard method calls and a number of methods that generate HTML3-specific tags. Next we define a set of background colors and sizes. The choice of colors may seem capricious, but it's not. These are the background colors defined by the newly-released HTML3.2 standard, and they're based on the original colors used by the IBM VGA graphics display.

Line 9 is where we recover the user's previous preferences, if any. We use the cookie() method to fetch a cookie named "preferences," and store its value in a like-named associative array.

In lines 12 through 14, we fetch the CGI parameters named `text`, `background`, `name`, and `size`. If any of them are set, it indicates that the user wants to change the corresponding value saved in the browser's cookie. We store changed parameters in the `%preferences` associative array, replacing the original values.

Line 17 and 18 set the text and background colors to reasonable defaults if they can't be found in either the cookie or the CGI script parameters.

Lines 21 through 25 generate the page's HTTP header. First we use the cookie() method to create the cookie containing the user's preferences. We set the expiration date for the cookie for 30 days in the future so that the cookie will be removed from the browser's database if the user doesn't return to this page within that time. We also set the optional `-path` parameter to /. This makes the cookie valid over our entire site so that it's available to every URL the browser fetches. Although we don't take advantage of this yet, it's useful if we later decide that these preferences should have a site-wide effect. Lastly we emit the HTTP header with the `-cookie` parameter set.

In lines 30 to 36 we begin the HTML page. True to the intent of making it personalizable, we base the page title on the user's name. If it's set, the title and level 1 header both become "Welcome back <name>!" Otherwise, the title becomes an impersonal "Customizable page." Line 32 calls the start_html() method to create the top part of the HTML page. It sets the title, the background color and the text color based on the values in the `%preferences` array. Line 36 sets the text size by calling the basefont() method. This simply generates a `<BASEFONT>` HTML tag with an appropriate SIZE attribute.

Lines 38 and up generate the content of the page. There's a brief introduction to the page, followed by the fill-out form used to change the settings. All the HTML is generated using CGI.pm "shortcuts," in which tags are generated by like-named method calls. For example, the hr() method generates the HTML tag <HR>. As shown in the first column in this series, we start the fill-out form with a call to start_form(), create the various form elements with calls to textfield(), popup_ menu(), and submit(), and close the form with end_form().

When I first wrote this script, the popup menus and popup menus in the form didn't line up well. Because all the elements were slightly different widths, everything was crooked. To fix this problem, I used the common trick of placing the form elements inside an invisible HTML3 table. Assigning each element to its own cell forces the fields to line up. You can see how I did this in lines 52 through 77, where I define a table using a set of CGI.pm shortcuts. An outer call to table() generates the surrounding <TABLE> and </TABLE> tags. Within this are a series of TR() methods, each of which generates a <TR> tag. (In order to avoid conflict with Perl's built-in tr/// operator, this is one instance where CGI.pm uses uppercase rather than lowercase shortcut names.) Within each TR() call, in turn, there are several td() calls that generate the <TD> ("table data") cells of the HTML table.

Fortunately my text editor auto-indents nicely, making it easy to see the HTML structure.

On a real site, of course, you'd want the user's preferences to affect all pages, not just one. This isn't a major undertaking; many modern Web servers now allow you to designate a script that preprocesses all files of a certain type. You can create a variation on the script shown here that takes an HTML document and inserts the appropriate <BASEFONT> and <BODY> tags based on the cookie preferences. Now just configure the server to pass all HTML documents through this script and you're set.

Cringe, Microsoft, cringe!

configure.cgi: a cookie script

```
00  #!/usr/bin/perl
01
02  use CGI qw(:standard :html3);
03
04  # Some constants to use in our form.
05  @colors = qw/aqua black blue fuchsia gray green lime maroon navy olive
               purple red silver teal white yellow/;
06  @sizes = ("<default>", 1..7);
07
08  # recover the "preferences" cookie.
09  %preferences = cookie('preferences');
```

```
10
11  # If the user wants to change the background color or her name, they will
        appear among our CGI parameters.
12  foreach ('text', 'background', 'name', 'size') {
13      $preferences{$_} = param($_) || $preferences{$_};
14  }
15
16  # Set some defaults
17  $preferences{background} = $preferences{background} || 'silver';
18  $preferences{text} = $preferences{text} || 'black';
19
20  # Refresh the cookie so that it doesn't expire.
21  $the_cookie = cookie( -name => 'preferences',
22                        -value=> \%preferences,
23                        -path => '/',
24                      -expires => '+30d');
25  print header(-cookie => $the_cookie);
26
27  # Adjust the title to incorporate the user's name, if provided.
28  $title = $preferences{name} ? "Welcome back, $preferences{name}!" :
            "Customizable Page";
29
30  # Create the HTML page.  We use several of the HTML 3.2 extended tags to
        control the background color
31  # and the font size. It's safe to use these features because cookies don't
        work anywhere else anyway.
32  print start_html(-title => $title,
33                  -bgcolor => $preferences{background},
34                    -text => $preferences{text});
35
36  print basefont({SIZE=>$preferences{size}}) if $preferences{size} > 0;
37
38  print h1($title),<<END;
39  You can change the appearance of this page by submitting
40  the fill-out form below.  If you return to this page any time
41  within 30 days, your preferences will be restored.
42  END
43  ;
44  # Create the form
45  print hr,
46      start_form,
47
48      "Your first name: ",
49      textfield(-name    => 'name',
50                -default => $preferences{name},
51                -size    => 30), br,
52      table(
53        TR(
54            td("Preferred"),
55            td("Page color:"),
56            td(popup_menu(  -name => 'background',
57                          -values => \@colors,
58                          -default => $preferences{background})
59              )
```

```
60            ),
61         TR(
62            td(''),
63            td("Text color:"),
64            td(popup_menu(   -name => 'text',
65                             -values => \@colors,
66                             -default => $preferences{text})
67               )
68            ),
69         TR(
70            td(''),
71            td("Font size:"),
72            td(popup_menu(   -name => 'size',
73                             -values => \@sizes,
74                             -default => $preferences{size})
75               )
76            )
77         ),
78         submit(-label => 'Set preferences'),
79         end_form,
80         hr;
81
82  print a({HREF=>"/"}, 'Go to the home page');
```

To try out this script online, point your browser at:

http://www.genome.wi.mit.edu/ftp/pub/software/WWW/examples/customize.cgi

CGI Programming: The LWP Library
by Lincoln Stein

In previous columns I've focused on the Web from the server's point of view. We've talked about how the CGI protocol works, how to write server scripts, and how to maintain long-running transactions across the Web. But what about the client side of the story? Does Perl offer any support for those of us who wish to write our own Web-creeping robots, remote syntax verifiers, database accessors, or even full-fledged graphical browsers? Naturally it does, and the name of this support is LWP.

LWP (Library for WWW access in Perl), is a collection of modules written by Martijn Koster and Gisle Aas. It derives in part from the Perl 4 libwww-perl library created by Roy Fielding. To understand what LWP can do, consider the tasks your average Web browser is called upon to perform:

- read and parse a URL

- connect to a remote server using the protocol appropriate for the URL (e.g., HTTP, GOPHER, FTP)

- negotiate with the server for the requested document, providing authentication when necessary

- interpret the retrieved document's headers

- parse and display the document's HTML content

The LWP library provides support for all of the tasks listed above, and several others, including handling proxy servers. In its simplest form, you can use LWP to fetch remote URLs from within a Perl script. With more effort, you can write an entirely Perl-based Web browser. In fact, the Perl/Tk library comes complete with a crude but functional graphical browser based on LWP.

The LWP modules are divided along the following categories:

```
URI::*            URL creation and parsing
HTML::*           HTML creation, parsing and formatting
HTTP::*           The HTTP protocol
LWP::UserAgent    Object-oriented interface to the library
LWP::Simple       Procedural interface to the library
LWP::Protocol::*  Interfaces to various protocols
```

To illustrate what you can do with LWP, I've written a Perl script (*get_weather*, shown on the next page) that fetches and prints the current weather report. You could run this script from an hourly cron job and incorporate the result into an HTML page, or use it to produce the text for a scrolling marquee applet (and produce a special effect that does something useful for a change!).

The US National Oceanographic and Atmospherics Service (NOAA) runs a series of Web servers that provide constantly updated weather reports and weather maps. Its servers were designed for human interactive use using fill-out forms; by changing the form, you can select among the cities that the NOAA monitors, and choose among a variety of text and graphical reports. By reverse-engineering its forms, I was able to determine that you can obtain a basic weather report by passing the CGI script

```
http://www.nnic.noaa.gov/CGI-bin/netcast.do-it
```

a query string that looks like this (all one line):

```
state=<state>&city=on&area=Local+Forecast&
match=Strong+Match&html=text+only+format
```

Everything in the string is constant except for the <state> parameter, which despite its name should be one of NOAA's three-letter city abbreviations (e.g. "BOS" for Boston, "NYC" for New York City; you can learn the list of abbreviations by browsing NOAA's site.) When you fetch this URL you'll receive a short HTML page that contains the weather report plus a few graphics and links to NOAA's other pages.

On the next page you'll see the code for *get_weather*, which fetches the current weather report from the NOAA server. You invoke it from the command line with the city code as its argument (default "BOS"). An example of the script's output is shown on the next page.

Thanks to the LWP library, the code is very straightforward. Lines 04-06 load the components of the LWP library that we need. In addition to the LWP::UserAgent module, which provides URL-fetching functionality, we import routines from the HTML::Parse and HTML::FormatText modules. The first provides the ability to create a parse tree from HTML text, and the second turns the parse tree into pretty-printed text.

Lines 08-11 set up various globals for the script. The city is read from the command line, and globals for the server URL and its CGI parameters are defined.

The interesting part begins in lines 13-17, where we connect to the NOAA server, send the query, and retrieve the result. First we create a LWP::UserAgent object, which is essentially a virtual browser. Next we create an HTTP::Request object to hold information about the URL we're requesting. We initialize the request object with the string 'GET' to indicate we want to make a GET request, and with the URL we want to fetch. The actual connection and data transfer occurs in line 15, where we invoke the UserAgent's `request()` method and receive an HTTP::Response object as the result. Lastly we check the transaction's result code by calling the response object's `isSuccess()` method and die with an informative error message if there was a problem.

We now have an HTTP::Response object in hand. It contains the HTTP status code, the various MIME headers that are transmitted along with the document, and the document itself. In lines 19-24 we extract the document, reformat it, and print it out. First we extract the HTML document using the response object's `content()` method, and immediately pass its result to the `parse_html()` function. Next we create a new HTML formatter object. LWP provides several types of formatters, including one that generates PostScript, but we're interested in HTML::FormatText, which creates pretty-printed ASCII text. We then pass the parse tree to the formatter's `format()` method, effectively stripping all HTML tags from the text and returning HTML entity codes to their original characters.

The script isn't quite done, however, because the pretty-printed page still contains cruft such as the links to NOAA's home page that we don't want in the final output. The last part of the script splits the pretty-printed text into an array of lines and extracts all the text between the two rows of hyphens that NOAA uses to delimit the weather report.

This example only gives a taste of what you can do with LWP. The LWP library distribution is itself a good source for ideas. Among the sample application

programs that accompany it is a Web mirror application that can be used to repli-
cate a tree of Web pages, updating the local copies only if they are out of date
with respect to the remote ones. Other parts of the library include the basic
components required to write your own web crawling robots.

LWP is distributed under the Perl Artistic License and can be downloaded from
any CPAN archive. To find an archive near you, visit *http://www.perl.com/CPAN.*

get_weather: a Perl script that fetches the current weather report

```
01 #!/usr/bin/perl
02 # File: get_weather
03
04 use LWP::UserAgent;
05 use HTML::Parse;
06 use HTML::FormatText;
07
08 # options
09 $CITY = shift || 'BOS';
10 $URL = 'http://www.nnic.noaa.gov/cgi-bin/netcast.do-it';
11 $OPTIONS='city=on&area=Local+Forecast&match=Strong+Match&html=text+only+format';
12
13 $agent = new LWP::UserAgent;
14 $request = new HTTP::Request('GET', "$URL?state=$CITY&$OPTIONS");
15 $response = $agent->request($request);
16 die "Couldn't get URL. Status code = ", $response->code
17 unless $response->isSuccess;
18
19 $parse_tree = parse_html($response->content);
20 $formatter = new HTML::FormatText;
21 @lines = split("\n",$formatter->format($parse_tree));
22 foreach (@lines) {
23     print $_, "\n" if /^\s*[-]+\w/../^\s*[-]+$/;
24 }
```

Output from *get_weather*:

```
--------------410 AM EST TUESDAY OCTOBER 29 1996--------------
.Today...sunny...windy and cool. High in the mid 50s. Northwest wind
20 to 30 mph...diminishing late.
.Tonight...clear and cool. Some clouds late. Low 35 to 40. Northwest
wind becoming light and variable.
.Wednesday...becoming cloudy. A 50 percent chance of afternoon showers.
High in the mid 50s.
--------------------------------------------------------------------
```

Index

About the Author

Brian Jepson is a "100-foot-tall nonstudent" who specialized in Social Sabotage as a student at the University of Rhode Island. His now-defunct coffeehouse, Cafe de la Tete, was part of a successful "culture jamming" experiment disguised as a program for mass liberation. Not content to enjoy the relaxed life of a coffeehouse operator and student, Brian made his way to Wall Street, where he remained cleverly disguised as a database programmer for many years. After picking up a copy of *Programming Perl*, he entered a larval stage, and emerged with the realization that Perl's aesthetic and culture would allow him to get back to where he was trying to get to in the first place. Wherever that is...

Colophon

The animal featured on the cover of the *Perl Resource Kit, UNIX Edition*, is a camel (one-hump dromedary). Camels are large ruminant mammals, weighing between 1,000 and 1,600 pounds and standing six to seven feet tall at the shoulders. They are well known for their use as draft and saddle animals in the desert regions, especially in Africa and Asia. Camels can go for days without water. If food is scarce, they will eat anything, even their owner's tent. Camels live up to 50 years.

Ted Meister designed this cover and the packaging for the *Perl Resource Kit*. The layouts were produced using Adobe Photoshop 4 and QuarkXpress 3.32, with Adobe ITC Garamond and Helvetica Condensed fonts. The camel image is from the Dover Pictorial Archive.

The interior layout was designed by Nancy Priest and Edie Freedman, and implemented in FrameMaker 5.0 by Mike Sierra. The text and heading fonts are ITC Garamond Light and ITC Garamond Book, by Adobe. The illustrations were created in Macromedia Freehand 7 by Robert Romano.

Whenever possible, our books use RepKover™, a durable and flexible lay-flat binding. If the page count exceeds RepKover's limit, perfect binding is used.

 # More Titles from O'Reilly

Perl

Perl Resource Kit—UNIX Edition

By Larry Wall, Clay Irving, Nate Patwardhan, Ellen Siever & Brian Jepson
1st Edition November 1997 (est.)
1700 pages (est.)
ISBN 1-56592-370-7

The *Perl Resource Kit* is the most comprehesive collection of documentation and commercially enhanced software tools yet published for Perl programmers. The UNIX edition, the first in a series, is the definitive Perl distribution for webmasters, programmers, and system administrators.

Software tools on the Kit's CD include:

- A Java/Perl back-end to the Perl compiler, written by Larry Wall, creator of Perl

- Snapshot of the freeware Perl archives on CPAN, with an Install program and a web-aware interface for identifying more recent online CPAN tools

This new Java/Perl tool allows programmers to write Java classes with Perl implementations (innards), and run the code through a compiler back-end to produce Java byte-code. Using this new tool, programmers can exploit Java's wide availability on the browser (as well as on the server), while using Perl for the things that it does better than Java (such as string processing).

The Kit also includes four tutorial and reference books that contain systematic documentation for the most important Perl extension modules, as well as documentation for the commercially enhanced and supported tools on the CD. The books in the Kit are not available elsewhere or separatelyand include:

- *Perl Module Programmer's Guide*, by Clay Irving and Nate Patwardhan.
- *Perl Module Reference Manual* (two volumes), compiled and edited by Ellen Siever and David Futato.
- *Perl Utilities*, by Brian Jepson.

The *Perl Resource Kit* is the first comprehensive tutorialand reference documentation for hundreds of essential third-party Perl extension modules used for creating CGI applications and more. It features commercially enhanced Perl utilities specially developed for the Kit by Perl's creator, Larry Wall. And, it is all brought to you by the premier publisher of Perl and UNIX books and documentation, O'Reilly & Associates.

Programming Perl, 2nd Edition

By Larry Wall, Tom Christiansen & Randal L. Schwartz
2nd Edition September 1996
670 pages, ISBN 1-56592-149-6

Programming Perl, second edition, is the authoritative guide to Perl version 5, the scripting utility that has established itself as the programming tool of choice for the World Wide Web, UNIX system administration, and a vast range of other applications. Version 5 of Perl includes object-oriented programming facilities. The book is coauthored by Larry Wall, the creator of Perl.

Perl is a language for easily manipulating text, files, and processes. It provides a more concise and readable way to do many jobs that were formerly accomplished (with difficulty) by programming with C or one of the shells. Perl is likely to be available wherever you choose to work.And if it isn't, you can get it and install it easily and free of charge.

This heavily revised second edition of *Programming Perl* contains a full explanation of the features in Perl version 5.003. Contents include:

- An introduction to Perl
- Explanations of the language and its syntax
- Perl functions
- Perl library modules
- The use of references in Perl
- How to use Perl's object-oriented features
- Invocation options for Perl itself, and also for the utilities that come with Perl

Perl 5 Desktop Reference

By Johan Vromans
1st Edition February 1996
46 pages, ISBN 1-56592-187-9

This is the standard quick-reference guide for the Perl programming language. It provides a complete overview of the language, from variables to input and output, from flow control to regular expressions, from functions to document formats—all packed into a convenient, carry-around booklet. Updated to cover Perl version 5.003.

O'REILLY™

TO ORDER: **800-998-9938** • **order@oreilly.com** • **http://www.oreilly.com/**
OUR PRODUCTS ARE AVAILABLE AT A BOOKSTORE OR SOFTWARE STORE NEAR YOU.
FOR INFORMATION: **800-998-9938** • **707-829-0515** • **info@oreilly.com**

Perl

Learning Perl, 2nd Edition

By Randal L. Schwartz & Tom Christiansen,
Foreword by Larry Wall
2nd Edition July 1997
302 pages, ISBN 1-56592-284-0

In this update of a bestseller, two leading Perl trainers teach you to use the most universal scripting language in the age of the World Wide Web. With a foreword by Larry Wall, the creator of Perl, this smooth, carefully paced book is the "official" guide for both formal (classroom) and informal learning. It is now current for Perl version 5.004.

Learning Perl is a hands-on tutorial designed to get you writing useful Perl scripts as quickly as possible. Exercises (with complete solutions) accompany each chapter. A lengthy, new chapter in this edition introduces you to CGI programming, while touching also on the use of library modules, references, and Perl's object-oriented constructs.

Perl is a language for easily manipulating text, files, and processes. It comes standard on most UNIX platforms and is available free of charge on all other important operating systems. Perl technical support is informally available—often within minutes—from a pool of experts who monitor a USENET newsgroup *(comp.lang.perl.misc)* with tens

of thousands of readers.

Contents include:

- A quick tutorial stroll through Perl basics
- Systematic, topic-by-topic coverage of Perl's broad capabilities
- Lots of brief code examples
- Programming exercises for each topic, with fully worked-out answers
- How to execute system commands from your Perl program
- How to manage DBM databases using Perl
- An introduction to CGI programming for the Web

Advanced Perl Programming

By Sriram Srinivasan
1st Edition August 1997
434 pages, ISBN 1-56592-220-4

This book covers complex techniques for managing production-ready Perl programs and explains methods for manipulating data and objects that may have looked like magic before. It gives you necessary background for dealing with networks, databases, and GUIs, and includes a discussion of internals to help you program more efficiently and embed Perl within C or C within Perl.

Learning Perl on Win32 Systems

By Randal L. Schwartz, Erik Olson &
Tom Christiansen
1st Edition August 1997
306 pages, ISBN 1-56592-324-3

In this carefully paced course, leading Perl trainers and a Windows NT practitioner teach you to program in the language that promises to emerge as the scripting language of choice on NT. Based on the "llama" book, this book features tips for PC users and new, NT-specific examples, along with a foreword by Larry Wall, the creator of Perl, and Dick Hardt, the creator of Perl for Win32.

Mastering Regular Expressions

By Jeffrey E. F. Friedl
1st Edition January 1997
368 pages, ISBN 1-56592-257-3

Regular expressions, a powerful tool for manipulating text and data, are found in scripting languages, editors, programming environments, and specialized tools. In this book, author Jeffrey Friedl leads you through the steps of crafting a regular expression that gets the job done. He examines a variety of tools and uses them in an extensive array of examples, with a major focus on Perl.

Java Programming

Java in a Nutshell, DELUXE EDITION

By David Flanagan, et al.
1st Edition June 1997
628 pages, includes CD-ROM and book,
ISBN 1-56592-304-9

Java in a Nutshell, Deluxe Edition, brings together on CD-ROM five volumes for Java developers and programmers, linking related info across books. *Exploring Java, 2nd Edition*, covers Java basics. *Java Language Reference, 2nd Edition*, *Java Fundamental Classes Reference*, and *Java AWT Reference* provide a definitive set of documentation on the Java language and the Java 1.1 core API. *Java in a Nutshell, 2nd Edition*, our bestselling quick reference, is included both on the CD-ROM and in a companion desktop edition. This deluxe library is an indispensable resource for anyone doing serious programming with Java 1.1.

Exploring Java, Second Edition

By Pat Niemeyer & Josh Peck
2nd Edition September 1997 (est.)
628 pages (est.)
ISBN 1-56592-271-9

Whether you're just migrating to Java or working steadily in the forefront of Java development, this book, fully revised for Java 1.1, gives a clear, systematic overview of the language. It covers the essentials of hot topics like Beans and RMI, as well as writing applets and other applications, such as networking programs, content and protocol handlers, and security managers.

Java Language Reference, Second Edition

By Mark Grand
2nd Edition July 1997
492 pages, ISBN 1-56592-326-X

This book helps you understand the subtle nuances of Java—from the definition of data types to the syntax of expressions and control structures—so you can ensure your programs run exactly as expected. The second edition covers the new language features that have been added in Java 1.1, such as inner classes, class literals, and instance initializers.

Java Fundamental Classes Reference

By Mark Grand &
Jonathan Knudsen
1st Edition May 1997
1114 pages, ISBN 1-56592-241-7

The *Java Fundamental Classes Reference* provides complete reference documentation on the core Java 1.1 classes that comprise the *java.lang, java.io, java.net, java.util, java.text, java.math, java.lang.reflect*, and *java.util.zip* packages. Part of O'Reilly's Java documentation series, this edition describes Version 1.1 of the Java Development Kit. It includes easy-to-use reference material and provides lots of sample code to help you learn by example.

Java AWT Reference

By John Zukowski
1st Edition April 1997
1074 pages, ISBN 1-56592-240-9

The *Java AWT Reference* provides complete reference documentation on the Abstract Window Toolkit (AWT), a large collection of classes for building graphical user interfaces in Java. Part of O'Reilly's Java documentation series, this edition describes both Version 1.0.2 and Version 1.1 of the Java Development Kit, includes easy-to-use reference material on every AWT class, and provides lots of sample code.

Java in a Nutshell, Second Edition

By David Flanagan
2nd Edition May 1997
628 pages, ISBN 1-56592-262-X

The bestselling Java book just got better. Newly updated, it now describes all the classes in the Java 1.1 API, with the exception of the still-evolving Enterprise APIs. And it still has all the great features that have made this the Java book most often recommended on the Internet: practical, real-world examples and compact reference information. It's the only quick reference you'll need.

O'REILLY™

TO ORDER: **800-998-9938** • *order@oreilly.com* • *http://www.oreilly.com/*
OUR PRODUCTS ARE AVAILABLE AT A BOOKSTORE OR SOFTWARE STORE NEAR YOU.
FOR INFORMATION: **800-998-9938** • **707-829-0515** • *info@oreilly.com*

Java Programming *continued*

Java Distributed Computing

By Jim Farley
1st Edition November 1997 (est.)
350 pages (est.), ISBN 1-56592-206-9
Java Distributed Computing offers a general introduction to distributed computing, meaning programs that run on two or more systems. It focuses primarily on how to structure and write distributed applications and, therefore, discusses issues like designing protocols, security, working with databases, and dealing with low bandwidth situations.

Java Examples in a Nutshell

By David Flanagan
1st Edition September 1997 (est.)
400 pages (est.), ISBN 1-56592-371-5
Java Examples in a Nutshell is chock full of practical, real-world Java programming examples. The author of the bestselling *Java in a Nutshell* has created an entire book of example programs that you can learn from and modify for your own use. If you learn best "by example," this companion volume to *Java in a Nutshell* is the book for you.

Netscape IFC in a Nutshell

By Dean Petrich with David Flanagan
1st Edition August 1997
370 pages, ISBN 1-56592-343-X
This desktop quick reference and programmer's guide is all the documentation programmers need to start creating highly customizable graphical user interfaces with the Internet Foundation Classes (IFC), Version 1.1. The IFC is a Java class library freely available from Netscape. It is also bundled with Communicator, making it the preferred development environment for the Navigator 4.0 web browser. Master the IFC now for a head start on the forthcoming Java Foundation Classes (JFC).

Developing Java Beans

By Robert Englander
1st Edition June 1997
316 pages, ISBN 1-56592-289-1
Developing Java Beans is a complete introduction to Java's component architecture. It describes how to write Beans, which are software components that can be used in visual programming environments. This book discusses event adapters, serialization, introspection, property editors, and customizers, and shows how to use Beans within ActiveX controls.

Java Virtual Machine

By Jon Meyer & Troy Downing
1st Edition March 1997
452 pages, includes diskette
ISBN 1-56592-194-1

This book is a comprehensive programming guide for the Java Virtual Machine (JVM). It gives readers a strong overview and reference of the JVM so that they may create their own implementations of the JVM or write their own compilers that create Java object code. A Java assembler is provided with the book, so the examples can all be compiled and executed.

Database Programming with JDBC and Java

By George Reese
1st Edition June 1997
240 pages, ISBN 1-56592-270-0
Database Programming with JDBC and Java describes the standard Java interfaces that make portable, object-oriented access to relational databases possible and offers a robust model for writing applications that are easy to maintain. It introduces the JDBC and RMI packages and includes a set of patterns that separate the functions of the Java application and facilitate the growth and maintenance of your application.

Java Network Programming

By Elliotte Rusty Harold
1st Edition February 1997
442 pages, ISBN 1-56592-227-1
The network is the soul of Java. Most of what is new and exciting about Java centers around the potential for new kinds of dynamic, networked applications. *Java Network Programming* teaches you to work with Sockets, write network clients and servers, and gives you an advanced look at the new areas like multicasting, using the server API, and RMI. Covers Java 1.1.

Java Threads

By Scott Oaks and Henry Wong
1st Edition January 1997
268 pages, ISBN 1-56592-216-6
With this book, you'll learn how to take full advantage of Java's thread facilities: where to use threads to increase efficiency, how to use them effectively, and how to avoid common mistakes like deadlock and race conditions. Covers Java 1.1.

Developing Web Content

WebMaster in a Nutshell, Deluxe Edition

By O'Reilly & Associates, Inc.
1st Edition September 1997 (est.)
356 pages (est.), includes CD-ROM
ISBN 1-56592-305-7

The Deluxe Edition of *WebMaster in a Nutshell* is a complete library for web programmers. The main resource is the Web Developer's Library, a CD-ROM, containing the electronic text of five popular O'Reilly titles: *HTML: The Definitive Guide, 2nd Edition*; *JavaScript: The Definitive Guide, 2nd Edition*; *CGI Programming on the World Wide Web*; *Programming Perl, 2nd Edition*—the classic "camel book," written by Larry Wall (the inventor of Perl) with Tom Christiansen and Randal Schwartz; and *WebMaster in a Nutshell*. The Deluxe Edition also includes a printed copy of *WebMaster in a Nutshell*.

WebMaster in a Nutshell, Deluxe Edition, makes it easy to find the information you need with all of the convenience you'd expect from the Web. You'll have access to information webmasters and programmers use most for development—complete with global searching and a master index to all five volumes—all on a single CD-ROM. It's incredibly portable. Just slip it into your laptop case as you commute or take off on your next trip and you'll find everything at your fingertips with no books to carry.

The CD-ROM is readable on all hardware platforms. All files except Java code example files are in 8.3 file format and, therefore, are readable by older systems. A web browser that supports HTML 3.2 (such as Netscape 3.0 or Internet Explorer 3.0) is required to view the text. The browser must support Java if searching is desired.

The Web Developer's Library is also available by subscription on the World Wide Web. See http://www.ora.com/catalog/webrlw for details.

WebMaster in a Nutshell

By Stephen Spainhour & Valerie Quercia
1st Edition October 1996
374 pages, ISBN 1-56592-229-8

Web content providers and administrators have many sources for information, both in print and online. *WebMaster in a Nutshell* puts it all together in one slim volume for easy desktop access. This quick reference covers HTML, CGI, JavaScript, Perl, HTTP, and server configuration.

HTML: The Definitive Guide, 2nd Edition

By Chuck Musciano & Bill Kennedy
2nd Edition May 1997
552 pages, ISBN 1-56592-235-2

This complete guide is chock full of examples, sample code, and practical, hands-on advice to help you create truly effective web pages and master advanced features. Learn how to insert images and other multimedia elements, create useful links and searchable documents, use Netscape extensions, design great forms, and lots more. The second edition covers the most up-to-date version of the HTML standard (HTML version 3.2), Netscape 4.0 and Internet Explorer 3.0, plus all the common extensions.

JavaScript: The Definitive Guide, 2nd Edition

By David Flanagan
2nd Edition January 1997
664 pages, ISBN 1-56592-234-4

This second edition of the definitive reference guide to JavaScript, the HTML extension that gives web pages programming language capabilities, covers JavaScript as it is used in Netscape 3.0 and 2.0 and in Microsoft Internet Explorer 3.0. Learn how JavaScript really works (and when it doesn't). Use JavaScript to control web browser behavior, add dynamically created text to web pages, interact with users through HTML forms, and even control and interact with Java applets and Navigator plugins. By the author of the bestselling *Java in a Nutshell*.

CGI Programming on the World Wide Web

By Shishir Gundavaram
1st Edition March 1996
450 pages, ISBN: 1-56592-168-2

This book offers a comprehensive explanation of CGI and related techniques for people who hold on to the dream of providing their own information servers on the Web. It starts at the beginning, explaining the value of CGI and how it works, then moves swiftly into the subtle details of programming.

Developing Web Content *continued*

Information Architecture for the World Wide Web

By Louis Rosenfeld & Peter Morville
1st Edition November 1997 (est.)
200 pages (est.), ISBN 1-56592-282-4

Information Architecture for the World Wide Web is about applying the principles of architecture and library science to web site design. With this book, you learn how to design web sites and intranets that support growth, management, and ease of use. This book is for webmasters, designers, and anyone else involved in building a web site.

Learning VBScript

By Paul Lomax
1st Edition July 1997
616 pages, includes CD-ROM
ISBN 1-56592-247-6

This definitive guide shows web developers how to take full advantage of client-side scripting with the VBScript language. In addition to basic language features, it covers the Internet Explorer object model and discusses techniques for client-side scripting, like adding ActiveX controls to a web page or validating data before sending it to the server. Includes CD-ROM with over 170 code samples.

Web Client Programming with Perl

By Clinton Wong
1st Edition March 1997
228 pages, ISBN 1-56592-214-X

Web Client Programming with Perl shows you how to extend scripting skills to the Web. This book teaches you the basics of how browsers communicate with servers and how to write your own customized web clients to automate common tasks. It is intended for those who are motivated to develop software that offers a more flexible and dynamic response than a standard web browser.

Building Your Own WebSite

By Susan B. Peck & Stephen Arrants
1st Edition July 1996
514 pages, ISBN 1-56592-232-8

This is a hands-on reference for Windows® 95 and Windows NT™ users who want to host a site on the Web or on a corporate intranet. This step-by-step guide will have you creating live web pages in minutes. You'll also learn how to connect your web to information in other Windows applications, such as word processing documents and databases. The book is packed with examples and tutorials on every aspect of web management, and it includes the highly acclaimed WebSite™ 1.1 server software on CD-ROM.

Designing for the Web: Getting Started in a New Medium

By Jennifer Niederst
with Edie Freedman
1st Edition April 1996
180 pages, ISBN 1-56592-165-8

Designing for the Web gives you the basics you need to hit the ground running. Although geared toward designers, it covers information and techniques useful to anyone who wants to put graphics online. It explains how to work with HTML documents from a designer's point of view, outlines special problems with presenting information online, and walks through incorporating images into web pages, with emphasis on resolution and improving efficienc

System Administration

Essential System Administration

By Æleen Frisch
2nd Edition September 1995
788 pages, ISBN 1-56592-127-5

Thoroughly revised and updated for all major versions of UNIX, this second edition of *Essential System Administration* provides a compact, manageable introduction to the tasks faced by everyone responsible for a UNIX system. Whether you use a stand-alone UNIX system, routinely provide administrative support for a larger shared system, or just want an understanding of basic administrative functions, this book is for you. Offers expanded sections on networking, electronic mail, security, and kernel configuration.

System Performance Tuning

By Mike Loukides
1st Edition November 1990
336 pages, ISBN 0-937175-60-9

System Performance Tuning answers the fundamental question: How can I get my UNIX-based computer to do more work without buying more hardware? Some performance problems do require you to buy a bigger or faster computer, but many can be solved simply by making better use of the resources you already have.

Using & Managing UUCP

By Ed Ravin, Tim O'Reilly, Dale Dougherty & Grace Todino
1st Edition September 1996
424 pages, ISBN 1-56592-153-4

Using & Managing UUCP describes, in one volume, this popular communications and file transfer program. UUCP is very attractive to computer users with limited resources, a small machine, and a dial-up connection. This book covers Taylor UUCP, the latest versions of HoneyDanBer UUCP, and the specific implementation details of UUCP versions shipped by major UNIX vendors.

termcap & terminfo

By John Strang, Linda Mui &
Tim O'Reilly
3rd Edition April 1988
270 pages, ISBN 0-937175-22-6

For UNIX system administrators and programmers. This handbook provides information on writing and debugging terminal descriptions, as well as terminal initialization, for the two UNIX terminal databases.

Managing NFS and NIS

By Hal Stern
1st Edition June 1991
436 pages, ISBN 0-937175-75-7

Managing NFS and NIS is for system administrators who need to set up or manage a network filesystem installation. NFS (Network Filesystem) is probably running at any site that has two or more UNIX systems. NIS (Network Information System) is a distributed database used to manage a network of computers. The only practical book devoted entirely to these subjects, this guide is a "must-have" for anyone interested in UNIX networking.

Volume 8: X Window System Administrator's Guide

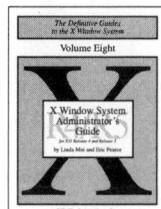

By Linda Mui & Eric Pearce
1st Edition October 1992
372 pages, ISBN 0-937175-83-8

This book focuses on issues of system administration for X and X-based networks—not just for UNIX system administrators, but for anyone faced with the job of administering X (including those running X on stand-alone workstations).

Web Server Administration

UNIX Web Server Administration

By John Leavitt
1st Edition December 1997 (est.)
350 pages (est.), ISBN 1-56592-217-4

The web server is one of the most crucial services a company can offer. *UNIX Web Server Administration* is a book for web administrators. It covers installation, customization, log analysis, multihoming, security, long-term maintenance, and performance tuning of the Apache, NCSA, CERN, and Netscape web servers.

Managing USENET

By David Lawrence & Henry Spencer
1st Edition October 1997 (est.)
400 pages (est.), ISBN 1-56592-198-4

USENET, also called Netnews, is the world's largest discussion forum, and it is doubling in size every year. This book, written by two of the foremost authorities on USENET administration, contains everything you need to know to administer a Netnews system. It covers C News and INN, explains the basics of starting a Netnews system, and offers guidelines to help ensure that your system is capable of handling news volume today—and in the future.

Web Security & Commerce

By Simson Garfinkel with Gene Spafford
1st Edition June 1997
506 pages, ISBN 1-56592-269-7

Learn how to minimize the risks of the Web with this comprehensive guide. It covers browser vulnerabilities, privacy concerns, issues with Java, JavaScript, ActiveX, and plug-ins, digital certificates, cryptography, web server security, blocking software, censorship technology, and relevant civil and criminal issues.

Apache: The Definitive Guide

By Ben Laurie & Peter Laurie
1st Edition March 1997
274 pages, includes CD-ROM
ISBN 1-56592-250-6

Despite all the media attention to Netscape, Apache is far and away the most widely used web server platform in the world. This book, written and reviewed by key members of the Apache Group, is the only complete guide on the market today that describes how to obtain, set up, and secure the Apache software. Includes CD-ROM with Apache sources and demo sites discussed in the book.

Managing Internet Information Services

By Cricket Liu, Jerry Peek, Russ Jones,
Bryan Buus & Adrian Nye
1st Edition December 1994
668 pages, ISBN 1-56592-062-7

This comprehensive guide describes how to set up information services and make them available over the Internet. It discusses why a company would want to offer Internet services, provides complete coverage of all popular services, and tells how to select which ones to provide. Most of the book describes how to set up Gopher, World Wide Web, FTP, and WAIS servers and email services.

O'REILLY™

TO ORDER: **800-998-9938** • **order@oreilly.com** • **http://www.oreilly.com/**
OUR PRODUCTS ARE AVAILABLE AT A BOOKSTORE OR SOFTWARE STORE NEAR YOU.
FOR INFORMATION: **800-998-9938** • **707-829-0515** • **info@oreilly.com**

Linux

Linux in a Nutshell

By Jessica P. Hekman &
the Staff of O'Reilly & Associates
1st Edition January 1997
438 pages, ISBN 1-56592-167-4

Linux in a Nutshell covers the core commands available on common Linux distributions. This isn't a scaled-down quick reference of common commands, but a complete reference containing all user, programming, administration, and networking commands. Also documents a wide range of GNU tools.

Linux Multimedia Guide

By Jeff Tranter
1st Edition September 1996
386 pages, ISBN 1-56592-219-0

Linux is increasingly popular among computer enthusiasts of all types, and one of the applications where it is flourishing is multimedia. This book tells you how to program such popular devices as sound cards, CD-ROMs, and joysticks. It also describes the best free software packages that support manipulation of graphics, audio, and video and offers guidance on fitting the pieces together.

Running Linux, 2nd Edition

By Matt Welsh & Lar Kaufman
2nd Edition August 1996
650 pages, ISBN 1-56592-151-8

Linux is the most exciting development today in the UNIX world—and some would say in the world of the PC-compatible. A complete, UNIX-compatible operating system developed by volunteers on the Internet, Linux is distributed freely in electronic form and for low cost from many vendors. This second edition of *Running Linux* covers everything you need to understand, install, and start using your Linux system, including a comprehensive installation tutorial, complete information on system maintenance, tools for document development and programming, and guidelines for network and web site administration.

Linux Network Administrator's Guide

By Olaf Kirch
1st Edition January 1995
370 pages, ISBN 1-56592-087-2

One of the most successful books to come from the Linux Documentation Project is the *Linux Network Administrator's Guide*. It touches on all the essential networking software included with Linux, plus some hardware considerations. Topics include serial connections, UUCP, routing and DNS, mail and News, SLIP and PPP, NFS, and NIS.

Linux Device Drivers

By Alessandro Rubini
1st Edition November 1997 (est.)
300 pages (est.), ISBN 1-56592-292-1

Linux Device Drivers is for anyone who wants to support computer peripherals under the Linux operating system or who wants to develop new hardware and run it under Linux. This practical guide shows how to write a driver for a wide range of devices, revealing information previously passed by word-of-mouth or in cryptic source code comments.

You don't have to be a kernel hacker to understand and use this book; all you need is a knowledge of C and some background in UNIX system calls. It describes step-by-step how to write a driver for character devices, block devices, and network interfaces, illustrated with full-featured examples that show driver design issues, which you can compile and run without special hardware. For those curious about how an operating system does its job, this book provides insights into address spaces, asynchronous events, and I/O. The book is centered on version 2.0, but also covers 1.2.13 and experimental versions up to 2.1.44. Also discusses how to maximize portability among hardware platforms.

UNIX Basics

Learning the UNIX Operating System

By Grace Todino, John Strang & Jerry Peek
3rd Edition August 1993
108 pages, ISBN 1-56592-060-0

If you are new to UNIX, this concise introduction will tell you just what you need to get started and no more. Why wade through a 600-page book when you can begin working productively in a matter of minutes? It's an ideal primer for Mac and PC users of the Internet who need to know a little bit about UNIX on the systems they visit. This book is the most effective introduction to UNIX in print. The third edition has been updated and expanded to provide increased coverage of window systems and networking. It's a handy book for someone just starting with UNIX, as well as someone who encounters a UNIX system as a "visitor" via remote login over the Internet.

Learning GNU Emacs, 2nd Edition

By Debra Cameron, Bill Rosenblatt & Eric Raymond
2nd Edition September 1996
560 pages, ISBN 1-56592-152-6

Learning GNU Emacs is an introduction to Version 19.30 of the GNU Emacs editor, one of the most widely used and powerful editors available under UNIX. It provides a solid introduction to basic editing, a look at several important "editing modes" (special Emacs features for editing specific types of documents, including email, Usenet News, and the World Wide Web), and a brief introduction to customization and Emacs LISP programming. The book is aimed at new Emacs users, whether or not they are programmers. Includes quick-reference card.

Learning the bash Shell

By Cameron Newham & Bill Rosenblatt
1st Edition October 1995
310 pages, ISBN 1-56592-147-X

Whether you want to use bash for its programming features or its user interface, you'll find Learning the bash Shell a valuable guide. If you're new to shell programming, it provides an excellent introduction, covering everything from the most basic to the most advanced features, like signal handling and command line processing. If you've been writing shell scripts for years, it offers a great way to find out what the new shell offers.

Learning the Korn Shell

By Bill Rosenblatt
1st Edition June 1993
360 pages, ISBN 1-56592-054-6

This Nutshell Handbook is a thorough introduction to the Korn shell, both as a user interface and as a programming language. The Korn shell is a program that interprets UNIX commands. It has many features that aren't found in other shells, including command history. This book provides a clear and concise explanation of the Korn shell's features. It explains ksh string operations, co-processes, signals and signal handling, and command-line interpretation. The book also includes real-life programming examples and a Korn shell debugger called kshdb, the only known implementation of a shell debugger anywhere.

Using csh and tcsh

By Paul DuBois
1st Edition August 1995
242 pages, ISBN 1-56592-132-1

Using csh and tcsh describes from the beginning how to use these shells interactively to get your work done faster with less typing. You'll learn how to make your prompt tell you where you are (no more pwd); use what you've typed before (history); type long command lines with few keystrokes (command and filename completion); remind yourself of filenames when in the middle of typing a command; and edit a botched command without retyping it.

Learning the vi Editor

By Linda Lamb
5th Edition October 1990
192 pages, ISBN 0-937175-67-6

This book is a complete guide to text editing with vi, the editor available on nearly every UNIX system. Early chapters cover the basics; later chapters explain more advanced editing tools, such as ex commands and global search and replacement.

UNIX Basics *(continued)*

sed & awk, 2nd Edition

By Dale Dougherty & Arnold Robbins
2nd Edition Winter 1997
450 pages (est.), ISBN 1-56592-225-5

sed & awk, one of the most popular books in
O'Reilly & Associates' Nutshell series,
describes two text processing programs that
are mainstays of the UNIX programmer's
toolbox. The book lays a foundation for both
programs by describing how they are used and by introducing
the fundamental concepts of regular expressions and text matching. This new edition covers the *sed* and *awk* programs as they
are now mandated by the POSIX standard. It also includes a discussion of the GNU versions of both programs, which have extensions beyond their UNIX counterparts. Many examples are used
throughout the book to illustrate the concepts discussed.

SCO UNIX in a Nutshell

By Ellie Cutler & the staff of O'Reilly & Associates
1st Edition February 1994
590 pages, ISBN 1-56592-037-6

The desktop reference to SCO UNIX and
Open Desktop®, this version of *UNIX in a
Nutshell* shows you what's under the hood of
your SCO system. It isn't a scaled-down
quick reference of common commands, but
a complete reference containing all user,
programming, administration, and networking commands.

UNIX in a Nutshell: System V Edition

By Daniel Gilly &
the staff of O'Reilly & Associates
2nd Edition June 1992
444 pages, ISBN 1-56592-001-5

You may have seen UNIX quick-reference
guides, but you've never seen anything like
UNIX in a Nutshell. Not a scaled-down quick
reference of common commands, *UNIX in a
Nutshell* is a complete reference containing
all commands and options, along with generous descriptions and
examples that put the commands in context. For all but the
thorniest UNIX problems, this one reference should be all the
documentation you need. Covers System V, Releases 3 and 4, and
Solaris 2.0.

What You Need to Know: When You Can't Find Your UNIX System Administrator

By Linda Mui
1st Edition April 1995
156 pages, ISBN 1-56592-104-6

This book is written for UNIX users, who are
often cast adrift in a confusing environment.
It provides the background and practical
solutions you need to solve problems you're
likely to encounter—problems with logging
in, printing, sharing files, running programs, managing space
resources, etc. It also describes the kind of info to gather when
you're asking for a diagnosis from a busy sys admin. And, it gives
you a list of site-specific information that you should know, as
well as a place to write it down.

Volume 3M: X Window System User's Guide, Motif Edition

By Valerie Quercia & Tim O'Reilly
2nd Edition January 1993
956 pages, ISBN 1-56592-015-5

The *X Window System User's Guide, Motif
Edition* orients the new user to window
system concepts and provides detailed
tutorials for many client programs, including the xtermterminal
emulator and the twm, uwm, and
mwmwindow managers. Later chapters explain how to customize
the X environment. Revised for Motif 1.2 and X11 Release 5.

Security

Practical UNIX & Internet Security, 2nd Edition

By Simson Garfinkel & Gene Spafford
2nd Edition April 1996
1004 pages, ISBN 1-56592-148-8

This second edition of the classic *Practical UNIX Security* is a complete rewrite of the original book. It's packed with twice the pages and offers even more practical information for UNIX users and administrators. In it you'll find coverage of features of many types of UNIX systems, including SunOS, Solaris, BSDI, AIX, HP-UX, Digital UNIX, Linux, and others. Contents include UNIX and security basics, system administrator tasks, network security, and appendixes containing checklists and helpful summaries.

Building Internet Firewalls

By D. Brent Chapman &
Elizabeth D. Zwicky
1st Edition September 1995
546 pages, ISBN 1-56592-124-0

Building Internet Firewalls is a practical guide to building firewalls on the Internet. If your site is connected to the Internet, or if you're considering getting connected, you need this book. It describes a variety of firewall approaches and architectures and discusses how you can build packet filtering and proxying solutions at your site. It also contains a full discussion of how to configure Internet services (e.g., FTP, SMTP, Telnet) to work with a firewall, as well as a complete list of resources, including the location of many publicly available firewall construction tools.

PGP: Pretty Good Privacy

By Simson Garfinkel
1st Edition January 1995
430 pages, ISBN 1-56592-098-8

PGP is a freely available encryption program that protects the privacy of files and electronic mail. It uses powerful public key cryptography and works on virtually every platform. This book is both a readable technical user's guide and a fascinating behind-the-scenes look at cryptography and privacy. It describes how to use PGP and provides background on cryptography, *PGP*'s history, battles over public key cryptography patents and U.S. government export restrictions, and public debates about privacy and free speech.

Computer Crime

By David Icove, Karl Seger &
William VonStorch
(Consulting Editor Eugene H. Spafford)
1st Edition August 1995
462 pages, ISBN 1-56592-086-4

This book is for anyone who needs to know what today's computer crimes look like, how to prevent them, and how to detect, investigate, and prosecute them if they do occur. It contains basic computer security information as well as guidelines for investigators, law enforcement, and system administrators. It includes computer-related statutes and laws, a resource summary, detailed papers on computer crime, and a sample search warrant.

Computer Security Basics

By Deborah Russell & G.T. Gangemi, Sr.
1st Edition July 1991
464 pages, ISBN 0-937175-71-4

Computer Security Basics provides a broad introduction to the many areas of computer security and a detailed description of current security standards. This handbook uses simple terms to describe complicated concepts like trusted systems, encryption, and mandatory access control, and it contains a thorough, readable introduction to the "Orange Book."

How to stay in touch with O'Reilly

1. Visit Our Award-Winning Web Site

http://www.oreilly.com/

★ "Top 100 Sites on the Web" —*PC Magazine*
★ "Top 5% Web sites" —*Point Communications*
★ "3-Star site" —*The McKinley Group*

Our web site contains a library of comprehensive product information (including book excerpts and tables of contents), downloadable software, background articles, interviews with technology leaders, links to relevant sites, book cover art, and more. File us in your Bookmarks or Hotlist!

2. Join Our Email Mailing Lists

New Product Releases

To receive automatic email with brief descriptions of all new O'Reilly products as they are released, send email to: **listproc@online.oreilly.com**
Put the following information in the first line of your message (*not* in the Subject field):
subscribe oreilly-news "Your Name" of "Your Organization" (for example: subscribe oreilly-news Kris Webber of Fine Enterprises)

O'Reilly Events

If you'd also like us to send information about trade show events, special promotions, and other O'Reilly events, send email to: **listproc@online.oreilly.com**
Put the following information in the first line of your message (*not* in the Subject field):
subscribe oreilly-events "Your Name" of "Your Organization"

3. Get Examples from Our Books via FTP

There are two ways to access an archive of example files from our books:

Regular FTP
- ftp to:
  ftp.oreilly.com
  (login: anonymous
  password: your email address)
- Point your web browser to:
  ftp://ftp.oreilly.com/

FTPMAIL
- Send an email message to:
  ftpmail@online.oreilly.com
  (Write "help" in the message body)

4. Visit Our Gopher Site

- Connect your gopher to:
  gopher.oreilly.com

- Point your web browser to:
  gopher://gopher.oreilly.com/

- Telnet to:
  gopher.oreilly.com
  login: gopher

5. Contact Us via Email

order@oreilly.com
To place a book or software order online. Good for North American and international customers.

subscriptions@oreilly.com
To place an order for any of our newsletters or periodicals.

books@oreilly.com
General questions about any of our books.

software@oreilly.com
For general questions and product information about our software. Check out O'Reilly Software Online at **http://software.oreilly.com/** for software and technical support information. Registered O'Reilly software users send your questions to: **website-support@oreilly.com**

cs@oreilly.com
For answers to problems regarding your order or our products.

booktech@oreilly.com
For book content technical questions or corrections.

proposals@oreilly.com
To submit new book or software proposals to our editors and product managers.

international@oreilly.com
For information about our international distributors or translation queries. For a list of our distributors outside of North America check out:
http://www.oreilly.com/www/order/country.html

O'Reilly & Associates, Inc.
101 Morris Street, Sebastopol, CA 95472 USA
TEL   707-829-0515 or 800-998-9938
         (6am to 5pm PST)
FAX   707-829-0104

Programming with Perl Modules

Programming with Perl Modules

Nathan Patwardhan
with Clay Irving

O'REILLY™

Cambridge · Köln · Paris · Sebastopol · Tokyo

Programming with Perl Modules

by Nathan Patwardhan with Clay Irving

Copyright © 1997 O'Reilly & Associates, Inc. All rights reserved.
Printed in the United States of America.

Published by O'Reilly & Associates, Inc., 101 Morris Street, Sebastopol, CA 95472.

Editor: Linda Mui

Production Editor: Mary Anne Weeks Mayo

Printing History:

November 1997:　First Edition.

Table of Contents

Preface

This book is a Perl programmer's introduction to using modules. The Perl community is a generous one, and you should take advantage of it. Just as Perl itself is developed and distributed freely, Perl modules are written out of love (or necessity, arguably the same thing) and offered to Perl programmers for little more than appreciation and occasional bug reports.

Perl modules are distributed on the Comprehensive Perl Archive Network (CPAN), a snapshot of which is included on the *Perl Resource Kit* CD. Since Perl makes it easy to develop documentation along with the code itself, most modules are accompanied by their own documentation describing its functionality and usage. But if you're fairly new to Perl modules, you might not be sure what's out there and what it's good for. That's where this book comes in.

Programming with Perl Modules is part tutorial, part demonstrational, part inspirational. We have tried to isolate some of the more essential modules and show how to use them. We don't try to teach you the ins and outs of the Perl language; for that we recommend *Learning Perl* or *Programming Perl*, both published by O'Reilly & Associates. Instead, we teach you how to take advantage of the Perl modules that are available with the standard Perl distribution and on CPAN, the Comprehensive Perl Archive Network.

How to Use This Book

This book has 14 chapters, as follows:

Chapter 1, *Introduction to Perl Modules and CPAN*, explains how modules, references, and packages work in Perl. We also cover the structure of the CPAN hierarchy.

Chapter 2, *Parsing Command-Line Arguments*, shows how to use Getopt::Long to work with options supplied on command-line driven applications.

Chapter 3, *Manipulating Files and Text*, talks about the File and Text utilities. We also cover Convert::UU, for uuencoding and uudecoding files.

Chapter 4, *The Mail and MIME Modules*, covers the modules for sending and reading email.

Chapter 5, *Date and Time*, discusses manipulations with timestamps using the Date modules.

Chapter 6, *Building Graphical Interfaces Using Perl/Tk*, gives a quick introduction to pTk, which can be used to build a GUI under both the X Window System and Microsoft Windows.

Chapter 7, *Graphics and Plotting*, covers GD, PerlMagick, and GIFgraph, which can create and display images.

Chapter 8, *The Database Modules*, gives a conceptual overview of database design and DBI.

Chapter 9, *The Net Modules*, shows how to do rudimentary Internet programming with Perl.

Chapter 10, *News::NNTPClient and News::Newsrc*, explains some of the NNTP protocol and demonstrates how to write an NNTP client in Perl.

Chapter 11, *Web Applications with LWP*, gives a conceptual overview of CGI and shows some examples that use the LWP modules to create HTTP clients and servers.

Chapter 12, *Web Server Efficiency*, discusses several approaches to maximizing the efficiency of the Apache web server.

Chapter 13, *Contributing to CPAN*, walks you though the conception and development of a new module, and submitting it to CPAN.

Chapter 14, *Examples*, contains some extended examples with graphical interfaces.

About the Perl Resource Kit

Until now, Perl has been something that was accessible only to an "in crowd"—much as the Internet itself was a few years ago. Perl is widely available on the Net, but it hasn't had any kind of standard packaged distribution. This has limited its availability both to new users and to many corporate users who must have a supported distribution before they can adopt a product. The *Perl Resource Kit* addresses this need, while providing valuable resources, technical knowledge, and software tools to those members of the in-crowd who already use Perl on a regular basis.

The *Perl Resource Kit*, UNIX Edition, is a definitive Perl distribution, complete with essential documentation, for all Perl users. It contains a collection of Perl software and over 1500 pages of documentation, including the first printed documentation for more than 600 widely used Perl modules. The Kit is for programmers, webmasters, system administrators, and others who use—or want to use—Perl.

The modules documented in the *Perl Resource Kit* were created by members of the Perl freeware community. O'Reilly actively supports the Perl freeware community and has since the publication of our first Perl book, *Programming Perl*. With the *Perl Resource Kit* and our Perl books, Perl conferences, and other efforts, we seek to extend the visibility of Perl and help ensure the healthy growth of Perl and its community.

The *Perl Resource Kit* contains:

- *Programming with Perl Modules*, an introduction to programming with some of the most important Perl modules.

- *Perl Module Reference* (two volumes), a comprehensive reference for significant Perl modules.

- *Perl Utilities Guide*, documentation for Perl software tools contained in the Kit.

- *Perl Resource Kit Software* (on CD-ROM), which includes a Java/Perl tool (JPL) written by Larry Wall, which allows programmers to write Java classes with Perl implementations; a snapshot of the freeware Perl tools on CPAN, with an install program, a search tool, and a web-aware interface for identifying more recent online CPAN tools; and many bits of example code and sample programs.

- The Autumn 1997 issue of *The Perl Journal*, a quarterly magazine devoted to the Perl language.

Conventions Used in This Book

This section lists the conventions we used.

Italic
> is used for URLs, filenames, and email addresses, and new terms when first defined.

`Constant width`
> is used for functions, methods, and other fragments of Perl code in regular text, as well as for blocks of code examples.

Contacting Technical Support

If you've thoroughly investigated other sources for help (see Chapter 1 of the *Perl Utilities Guide* for suggestions) and still need assistance, technical support is available for the *Perl Resource Kit*. Before contacting technical support, make sure you have registered your copy of the kit online at *http://perl.oreilly.com/register.html*. Registering your copy helps us provide better service and keep you up-to-date on what is happening with Perl at O'Reilly.

Support for the *Perl Resource Kit* comes in three flavors:

- Once you register your kit, you have up to 30 days of free initial installation support on Solaris 2.5.* and higher and Linux 2.0.* and higher for the software included on the CD-ROM. This support is available by phone at (707) 829-0515 from 7:00 a.m. to 5:00 p.m. (U.S. Pacific Time), Monday through Friday.

- After the 30 days or for software problems beyond installation, technical support is available for a fee through the Perl Clinic, which you can reach in several ways:
  - — on the Web at *http://www.perlclinic.com/*
  - — by email at *info@perlclinic.com*
  - — by phone in the United States and Canada at (604) 606-4611
  - — by phone in Europe and elsewhere at 44 (0) 1483 424424

- For help and information on the books included in the kit, technical support is available by email at *perltech@oreilly.com*. Please use this email address to ask questions about and/or report errors in the books.

Acknowledgments

I'd like to thank Clay Irving, who contributed materials to Chapters 5 and 8; Brian Jepson, who provided material for Chapter 8, and acted as advisor and reviewer for that chapter; Gina Blaber, product manager for the *Perl Resource Kits*; and Linda Mui, who acted as editor for the book. Also, special thanks to Andy Oram, who gave me some constructive suggestions on rewriting several of the chapters.

While several beta testers of the *Perl Resource Kit* provided some review comments for this book, the most thorough reviews were performed under arduous circumstances while the book was already in production, requiring near-instant turnaround. Those reviewers were Tom Christiansen, Gurusamy Sarathy, and Sriram Srinivasan. I can't thank them enough for their insights and technical contributions.

On the O'Reilly production team, I'd like to thank Mary Anne Weeks Mayo, our very patient production editor and project manager, who endured delay after delay and still churned out a book on schedule. Thanks also to Ellie Fountain Maden and Sheryl Avruch, who assured the book's quality; Mike Sierra, who contributed his FrameMaker tools expertise; Seth Maislin, who wrote the index; and Robert Romano, for excellent image manipulation in Chapter 6. Madeline Newell helped with the production process, and Colleen Miceli lent freelance support.

On the personal side, I'd like to thank all of these special folks in my family: the Patwardhans, the Kiebzaks, the Lusbys, the Hills, the Powerses, and Stella Niagara Education Park. And to friends: brothers Mobius, the Clarks, Joyce Lenz, Al Smooth (play guitar overnight), Pope Dick I, U. Heights "Players," David Coverband, the gang from Banta Integrated Media, Page Hamilton, and Gumby. Finally, without fail, thanks to Larry Wall. Larry, your kind demeanor and openness to contributions and ideas from the group has been quite flattering and appreciated.

1

Introduction to Perl Modules and CPAN

Perl modules are best described as batches of reusable code. Want to send an email message from your Perl program? You could write the code from scratch, or you can just use Net::SMTP. Want to give your script an elegant graphical interface? Take a look at the pTk module, which does just that.

The virtues extolled for Perl programmers are laziness, impatience, and hubris. Together, these admirable characteristics have led to the creation and use of many publicly accessible Perl modules. Because of laziness, programmers would rather write modules than repeat a procedure over and over (and would rather use modules written by other people than write new code from scratch). Because of impatience, programmers write consolidated code that is flexible enough to antici-pate their future needs. And because of hubris, programmers share their triumphs with the rest of the Perl community and continually tweak their modules until they're the best they can be.

Recent Perl distributions include a variety of modules that perform a number of tasks, from parsing command-line arguments using the `Getopt` modules, to timing programs using `Benchmark`.

This chapter offers a conceptual overview of packages and modules in Perl and an introduction to the structure of the Comprehensive Perl Archive Network (CPAN).

If you're interested in writing your own Perl modules, refer to Chapter 13, *Contributing to CPAN*, which details the process of writing Perl modules and how to register with and distribute your contributions through CPAN.

What Are Packages?

Most people consider it rude to enter someone's home without knocking on the door. Even if you're a family member or close friend, you're probably imposing on someone's privacy if you don't alert them when you arrive.

Perl provides a mechanism to separate residents and guests, known as packages. A package can act like the front door to your house; you only invite people you know to come inside; you decide who can enter. People who live in your house extend the same courtesy to your neighbors by knocking before entering those people's homes.

Your residence and property might be compared to a package's namespace: when you buy a property, the mortgage is in your name—"Nathan owns this house."

So, what if I live in a duplex or condominium? The same applies. Although there may be 20 units in your building, each unit has its own address and door.

A package, then, is a namespace implementation that protects packages from affecting variables in other packages.

The extent of the effects of the package statement includes everything from the package declaration through the end of the enclosing block, eval, end of file, or declaration of another package—whichever comes first. A package statement affects only dynamic variables (globals, even when `local()`ized), not lexical variables (declared with `my()`).

So What's in a Name?

As mentioned above, a package starts with a package statement; let's work with a package named BushWhack:

```
package BushWhack;
```

Let's add a subroutine called `lawn_kid()`:

```
sub lawn_kid {
    my $lk = shift;
    print("$lk is a lawn kid.\n");
}
```

The code compiled in package `BushWhack` can access `lawn_kid()` without fully qualifying its name:

```
lawn_kid('Joe'); # or
BushWhack::lawn_kid('Joe\'s sister Sue');
```

Now's let's add package `LawnCare` to the same file:

```
package LawnCare;
```

Bear in mind that it is confusing to have multiple packages in the same file. Look at this:

```
my$asleep = 151;
my $not_paying_attention = 20;
package DUH; print "$not_paying_attention, $asleep\n";
package WAKEUP; print "$not_paying_attention, $asleep\n";
```

Oops. The `$not_paying_attention` is visible in both pieces of code, because a package declaration only affects dynamics (globals), not lexicals (`my()`s). And both packages could have their own global `$not_paying_attention`, both accessing them as `$DUH::not_paying_attention` and `$WAKEUP::not_paying_attention`, respectively. But code compiled in those packages in a different scope (block, eval, file) can't get the lexical `$not_paying_attention` from the scope above. And a lexical can't be qualified with a package namespace.

The `awful_chemical()` subroutine is in package `LawnCare`:

```
sub awful_chemical {
        my $ac = shift;
        print("$ac is a(n) awful chemical.\n");
}
```

This function, however, can't be called from `BushWhack` in the same way. To call `awful_chemical()` from `BushWhack`, give it the package name where the subroutine lives:

```
LawnCare::awful_chemical('Chlorine');
```

Otherwise, you'll get an undefined subroutine error.

You are able to create a `BushWhack::LawnCare` package. Symbols are local to the current package or qualified from the outer package down. In other words, there is no place in `BushWhack` where `$LawnCare::BushWhack::variable` refers to `$BushWhack::variable`.

Packages and Symbol Tables

A package's namespace is a *symbol table*. The name of your package is stored in a hash named after your package with two colons appended to it. If you name a package `BushWhack`, its symbol table name is `%BushWhack::`. Packages are represented as %main:: or %:: in the symbol table by default. Since we're dealing with a hash, each key must have a value. Because keys are identifiers, values are the corresponding typeglob values; globs are pretty efficient because they do the symbol table lookups at compile-time.

In other words, *BushWhack represents the value of %BushWhack::—see the following:

```
local *low_flyer = *BushWhack::variable; # compile time
local *low_flyer = *BushWhack::{"variable"}; # run time
```

You can look up all the keys and variables of a package with this example. You may use undef() on these to clear their memory, and they will be reported as undefined. You shouldn't undefine anything here unless you don't plan to load these packages again. Because the memory has already been filled, it saves time when you load them if you leave them defined:*

```
foreach $symbol_name (sort keys %BushWhack::) {
        local *local_sym = $BushWhack::{$symbol_name};
        print "\$$symbol_name is defined\n"
                if($local_sym);
        print "\@$symbol_name is defined\n"
                if(@local_sym);
        print "\%$symbol_name is defined\n"
                if(%sym);
}
```

Package Constructors and Destructors

The BEGIN and END routines are constructors and destructors. A BEGIN subroutine is executed immediately; it's a way for the compiler to make a call into the interpreter.

Even if you have a subroutine call that appears before BEGIN, BEGIN still executes first:

```
package MakeRoom;
call_me_now();
sub call_me_now { print "I'm gonna be first!\n"; } # umm, no
BEGIN { print "See, told you that I'd be first.\n"; }
END { print "th-th-th-that's all folks.\n"; }
```

and outputs:

```
See, told you that I'd be first.
I'm gonna be first!
th-th-th-that's all folks.
```

---

* Warning: this counterintuitive behavior of defined() on aggregates may be changed, fixed, or broken in a future release of Perl.

Multiple BEGIN blocks are executed in the order they have been defined:

```
package Repetition;
call_me_now();
sub call_me_now {
        # err, no
        print "Hey, I *said* that I was going to be first!\n";
}
BEGIN { print "Yeah, I'm first!\n"; }
BEGIN { print "And I'm next!\n"; }
END { print "Well, you've got nothing to complain about - I'm ",
              "last\n"; }
```

This outputs:

```
Yeah, I'm first!
And I'm next!
Hey, I *said* that I was going to be first!
Well, you've got nothing to complain about - I'm last
```

You can't call BEGIN; it's undefined as soon as it's finished running. Any code it uses returns to Perl's memory pool.

The END subroutine does what it says. Code contained in an END subroutine is executed when the interpreter is exiting; even if the interpreter is exiting because of a die().

A program can have multiple END statements, where the last END is executed until the first END is reached:*

```
END { print "Am I *really* first?\n"; }
$random_file = 'some_file.ext';
open(FOO, $random_file)
    or die("can't open $random_file: $!");
close(FOO);
END { print "Am I *really* second?\n"; }
```

This program outputs:

```
can't open some_file.ext: No such file or directory at myscript line 4.
Am I *really* second?
Am I *really* first?
```

Modules

Unlike languages like C++ or Java, Perl doesn't use an explicit class declaration. A module may work like a class if you implement its subroutines as methods. Packages can derive methods from other packages by including the other package's name in its @ISA array.

---

* ENDs can be circumvented by signals that you have to trap on your own.

So, what's a module? A module is a package stored in a file with the same name; it is intended to be reused. Modules can export symbols into their caller's package. Symbols don't need to be explicitly exported. Class modules can also export their symbols but typically should not.

Regardless of the mechanism you use to write a module or any other goodies, such as exporting symbols or creating objects, Perl modules have a *.pm* extension.*

Since you probably won't be writing your modules to be *pragmas* (compiler directives), you should capitalize module names. Since we must use the package name as its filename, such as Nathan::LastName, we'll use a filename like *Nathan/Last-Name.pm*. In this example, we'll be discussing Some::Module, contributed by Tom Christiansen.

Create a file called *Some/Module.pm*, and insert the following into it:

```
package Some::Module;  # assumes Some/Module.pm
use strict;
BEGIN {
    use Exporter    ();
    use vars        qw($VERSION @ISA @EXPORT @EXPORT_OK %EXPORT_TAGS);
    # set the version for version checking
    $VERSION       = 1.00;
    @ISA           = qw(Exporter);
    @EXPORT        = qw(&func1 &func2 &func3);
    %EXPORT_TAGS = ( );        # eg: TAG => [ qw!name1 name2! ],
    # your exported package globals go here,
    # as well as any optionally exported functions
    @EXPORT_OK     = qw($Var1 %Hashit);
}
use vars        @EXPORT_OK;
# nonexported package globals go here
use vars        qw(@more $stuff);
# initialize package globals, first exported ones
$Var1   = '';
%Hashit = ();
# then the others (which are still accessible as $Some::Module::stuff)
$stuff  = '';
@more   = ();
# all file-scoped lexicals must be created before
# the functions below that use them.
# file-private lexicals go here
my $priv_var    = '';
my %secret_hash = ();
# here's a file-private function as a closure,
# callable as &$priv_func;  it cannot be prototyped.
my $priv_func = sub {
# stuff goes here.
```

---

* A module can also call dynamically linked executables or autoload subroutines associated with the module, but this is transparent to the user.

```
};
# make all your functions, whether exported or not;
# remember to put something interesting in the {} stubs
sub func1      {}      # no prototype
sub func2()    {}      # proto'd void
sub func3($$)  {}      # proto'd to 2 scalars
# this one isn't exported, but could be called!
sub func4(\%)  {}      # proto'd to 1 hash ref
END { }        # module clean-up code here (global destructor)
```

Let's look at this example more closely.

1. After the package declaration and enabling of the **strict** pragma, we use a BEGIN to initialize **@EXPORT_OK**; we'll need to use **vars** **@EXPORT_OK** later.

   ```
   BEGIN {
       use Exporter   ();
   ```

   We use the **Exporter** module as if we're going to import symbols, but we're not importing anything. When you use **use()**, you're telling the package not to import any symbols into your current package. In this case, we're not importing any symbols from **Exporter**, just loading it in at compile-time.

2. Next, we bring in some globals the **Exporter** needs.

   ```
   use vars       qw($VERSION @ISA @EXPORT @EXPORT_OK %EXPORT_TAGS);
   # set the version for version checking
   $VERSION       = 1.00;
   ```

   @ISA tells the interpreter where to look for a method that can't be found in the current package; this is how Perl handles inheritance. One class (package) recursively inherits methods from all classes (packages) listed in its **@ISA** array. **@ISA** contains names of other packages; the packages are searched (depth-first, recursively) for the methods the interpreter is seeking. For example, we'll be using **Exporter** to handle importing.

   ```
   @ISA           = qw(Exporter);
   ```

3. Now, let's tell what we'll be exporting. In this case, it's both functions (**&func1, &func2, &func4**) and exported package globals and/or functions (**$Var1, %Hashit, &func3**).

   ```
   @EXPORT        = qw(&func1 &func2 &func4);
   %EXPORT_TAGS = ( );      # eg: TAG => [ qw!name1 name2! ],
   # your exported package globals go here,
   # as well as any optionally exported functions
   @EXPORT_OK     = qw($Var1 %Hashit &func3);
   }
   ```

4. Finally, it's time to add the nonexported globals, lexicals, and function prototypes, and the global destructor.

   ```
   END { }
   ```

Use Versus Require

The use statement implies a BEGIN block. The library module is loaded and symbols imported as soon as the use statement is compiled (even before the rest of the file). use allows modules to declare subroutines that are visible as list operators to the rest of the file. More important, it also makes visible prototypes from the module subroutines from that point onward. Of course, prototypes are compile-time only, so are ignored on method calls.

In other words, use and require (which is used for reading Perl libraries) are two different things.

You can use Perl modules in your program with:

```
use Module;
use Module LIST;
```

This is not the same as:

```
require "Module";
require "Module.pm";
```

If you use require, you aren't importing anything from the module unless you explicitly make the module accessible. If you choose not to use use, you must do something like the following:

```
BEGIN { require "Module.pm"; import Module; }
```

or:

```
BEGIN { require "Module.pm"; import Module LIST; }
```

Let's say you have a module called TestModule containing the function test_me_ out(). If you choose to use require, you need to make TestModule accessible in order to call its functions and die:

```
require TestModule;
$value = TestModule::test_me_out();
```

You can't employ require with TestModule in this fashion. Doing so results in a function that doesn't exist, main::test_me_out(), being called:

```
require TestModule;
$value = test_me_out(); # wrong!
```

You can use use to import the names from TestModule and then call test_me_ out():

```
use TestModule;
$value = test_me_out();
```

Object-Oriented Programming

Stop me if you've heard this one before:

> [Language name here] is a revolutionary object-oriented programming language...

So?

> It makes your life easier when you're trying to generate a canvas filled with bouncing heads.

What does this have to do with object-oriented programming? And if anything, what does this have to do with Perl?

You can use Perl modules for object-oriented programming (OOP), but this doesn't mean you'll need to write (or even rewrite) your modules with object-oriented methodology in mind. Let's put Perl modules and OOP into perspective:

*   An object is simply a reference that happens to know which class it belongs to.

*   A class is simply a package that happens to provide methods to deal with object references.

*   A method is simply a subroutine that expects an object reference (or a package name, for class methods) as the first argument.

An Object Is Simply a Reference

Unlike C++ or Java, Perl doesn't have a predefined syntax for constructors. Perl constructors must allocate new memory, whereas C++'s constructors are just initializing memory already allocated when they're called. Object-oriented Perl modules use a subroutine that returns a reference to something "blessed" into a class as a constructor—with `bless()`. `bless()` marks a reference with a default package so the interpreter can look there for method definitions.

Here's a minimal case:

```
package FrothyMug;
sub new { bless {} }
```

`{}` returns a reference to a new anonymous hash, an empty one with no key/value pairs. When `{}` is `bless()`ed, it's telling the object it references that it's a `FrothyMug` and returns the reference whatever has been `blessed`. The referenced object is aware that it has been `blessed`.

```
sub new {
    my $self = {};
    bless $self;
    return $self;
}
```

You must use the two-argument form of `bless` if you plan on dealing with inheritance (which you probably will do sooner or later):

```
sub new {
    my $class = shift;
    my $self = {};
    bless $self, $class;
    $self->initialize();
    return $self;
}
```

Remember the package examples we showed before? The function `trolling()` in a package `GoFish` can only be called if it's been fully qualified. Other packages must call this function (if they're allowed) with `GoFish::trolling()`.

The scenario is similar here. A package's methods treat the reference as any other reference. Outside the package, the reference should only be accessed through the package's methods.

A Class Is Simply a Package

C++ and Java use class declarations; Perl does not. You create a class by putting subroutine definitions and a package declaration into a file. Yes, it's that easy.

The interpreter uses `@ISA` (see previous section, "Modules") to search for missing methods. If you change `@ISA` or add new subroutines, Perl needs to look up the method again because the cache has been changed. If Perl still can't find a method in `@ISA`, it does the lookup in UNIVERSAL, but if you have defined an (object's package) AUTOLOAD routine, AUTOLOAD is called instead of the missing method. If Perl can't find an AUTOLOAD routine, it checks (object's `@ISA`) AUTOLOAD. Finally, it checks for the method in UNIVERSAL AUTOLOAD; if this fails, the program exits with an error that the method can't be found.

Perl only does method inheritance, that is, interface inheritance. Access to instance data is left to the class. This isn't a problem because most classes' objects use an anonymous hash, which is very much like the grassy areas in the heartland of the United States—the anonymous hash acts like a grassy field where herds of cattle (other classes) come to graze.

A Method Is Simply a Subroutine

Perl doesn't use any special syntax for method definition; a method is a subroutine. A method's first argument will be the object or package that invokes it:

```
Class->meth();
$obj->meth();
$obj_or_classname->meth();
meth Class;
```

```
meth $obj;
meth $obj_or_clasname;
```

Class and instance methods

Class and object methods could be static and instance methods, except that static is a fighting word in the Perl community. Class methods expect the name of the class as the first argument passed to the method. The constructor is an example of a class method. Class methods may simply ignore the first argument because the package of their caller is irrelevant.

You can also use a class method to look up an object by name:

```
sub find_my_object_by_name {
    my ($class, $name) = @_;
    $objtable{$name};
}
```

An instance method expects an object as its first argument. Typically it shifts the first argument into a **self** or **this** variable, and then uses that as an ordinary reference:

```
sub display_widget {
    my $self = shift;
    my @keys = @_ ? @_ : sort keys %$self;
    foreach $key (@keys) {
        print "\t$key => $self->{$key}\n";
    }
}
```

Method Invocation

There are two ways to invoke a method; we'll cover both of them in this section. Let's say that we have two statements:

```
$object = method Class "Whatever";
method_2 $object 'Param 1', 'Param 2';
```

We can combine these statements into one with a BLOCK in the indirect object slot:

```
method_2 { method Class "Whatever" } 'Param 1', 'Param 2';
```

Those of you who salivate over C++ (or even at `perl -e 'print "\007";'`) will probably like the `->` notation that does the same as the above. You'll need to use parentheses if you'll be passing any arguments:

```
$object = Class->method("Whatever");
$fred->display('Param 1', 'Param 2');
```

Yes, the parentheses are important. Freedom is nice, but it's not always appropriate to let things hang out, particularly when this causes your program to act unreliably. You should probably avoid coding techniques such as:

```
$parrot = Bird->noisy("Shh"), 'be', 'quiet';
$parrot->shoot(times => 5), pain => 'likely';
```

And shamefully I must admit that:

```
m1 $ob->m2;
```

parses as:

```
$ob->m1->m2;
```

not as:

```
$ob->m2->m1;
```

The CPAN Architecture

The Comprehensive Perl Archive Network represents the development interests of a cross-section of the Perl community, including Perl utilities, modules, documentation, and (of course) the Perl distribution itself. CPAN was created by Jarkko Hietaniemi and Andreas Koenig.

The *Perl Resource Kit* contains a complete CPAN distribution, so access to the Perl modules discussed in this book is at your fingertips. See the accompanying *Perl Utilities Guide* for more information on how to install modules from the *Perl Resource Kit CD*.

CPAN Mirrors

The design of CPAN is to support and maintain many identified sites, or *mirrors*, across the globe. This ensures that anyone with an Internet connection can have reliable access to its contents at any time. Since the structure of all CPAN sites are the same, a user searching for the current version of Perl can be sure that the *latest.tar.gz* file is the same on every site.

Users can directly connect to a CPAN site if they know the specific address. However, to facilitate the use of CPAN, site maintainers have also developed a multiplexor to automate the downloading of materials from CPAN sites. If a user visiting a multiplexed site (such as *http://www.perl.com/CPAN/*) selects a file, the multiplexor connects to the CPAN site best suited to the user.

How Is CPAN Organized?

CPAN materials are categorized by Perl modules, distributions, documentation, announcements, ports, scripts, and contributing authors. Each category is linked with related categories. For example, links to a graphing module written by an author appears in both the CPAN modules and author areas.

Most CPAN materials are distributed "tar-gzipped." `tar` and `gzip` are popular UNIX data-archiving formats. Non-UNIX-based users must download software that extracts tar files first. A version of such software for Microsoft Windows 95 is `Winzip`, which is available from *http://www.winzip.com*.

Since CPAN provides the same offerings worldwide, the directory structure has been standardized so files can be located in the same location in the directory hierarchy at all CPAN sites. All CPAN sites use *CPAN* as the root directory, from which the user can select a specific Perl item. The CPAN snapshot that appears on your CD-ROM contains the same directory structure, starting with a *CPAN* directory.

From the *CPAN* directory you have the following choices:

```
Current directory is CPAN
CPAN.html        An HTML formatted CPAN info page
ENDINGS          Describes what the ".tgz" file extensions mean
MIRRORED.BY      A list of sites mirroring CPAN
MIRRORING.FROM   A list of sites mirroring CPAN
README           A brief description of what you'll find on CPAN
README.html      An HTML formatted version of the README file
RECENT           Recent additions to the CPAN site
RECENT.DAY       Recent additions to the CPAN site (daily)
RECENT.html      An HTML formatted list of recent additions
RECENT.WEEK      Recent additions to the CPAN site (weekly)
ROADMAP          What you'll find on CPAN and where
ROADMAP.html     An HTML formatted version of ROADMAP
SITES            An exhaustive list of CPAN sites
SITES.html       An HTML formatted version of SITES
authors          A list of CPAN authors
clpa             An archive of comp.lang.perl.announce
doc              Various Perl documentation, FAQs, etc.
indices          All that is indexed.
latest.tar.gz    The latest Perl distribution sources
misc             Misc Perl stuff like Larry Wall quotes and gifs
modules          Modules for Perl version 5
other-archives   Other things yet uncategorized
ports            Various Perl ports
scripts          Various scripts appearing in Perl books
src              The Perl sources from various versions
```

The directory we're most concerned with is *modules*. It categorizes modules in three ways:

```
by-author    Modules organized by author's registered CPAN name
by-category  Modules categorized by subject matter (see below)
by-module    Modules categorized by namespace (i.e., MIME)
```

In CPAN, Perl modules are currently organized into 21 categories. Each category is linked to contributors and related modules. The modules chosen for discussion in this book fit into many of these categories:

```
02_Perl_Core_Modules
03_Development_Support
04_Operating_System_Interfaces
05_Networking_Devices_Inter_Process
06_Data_Type_Utilities
07_Database_Interfaces
08_User_Interfaces
09_Interfaces_to_Other_Languages
10_File_Names_Systems_Locking
11_String_Processing_Language_Text_Process
12_Option_Argument_Parameter_Processing
13_Internationalization_and_Locale
14_Authentication_Security_Encryption
15_World_Wide_Web_HTML_HTTP_CGI
16_Server_and_Daemon_Utilities
17_Archiving_and_Compression
18_Images_Pixmap_Bitmap_Manipulation
19_Mail_and_Usenet_News
20_Control_Flow_Utilities
21_File_Handle_Input_Output
22_Microsoft_Windows_Modules
23_Miscellaneous_Modules
99_Not_In_Modulelist
```

Once you've chosen the area from which you'd like to download a module, you should tell your `ftp` client to request a directory listing for the area. You'll find a list of files in the directory; tar files have a *.tar.gz* extension and *README* files have a *.readme* extension.

Here's a sample directory listing from a CPAN site:

```
ANDK@                             CGI.pm-2.35.tar.gz@
CGI-Out-96.081401.readme@         CGI.pm-2.36.readme@
CGI-Out-96.081401.tar.gz@         CGI.pm-2.36.tar.gz@
CGI-Response-0.03.readme@         CGI_Imagemap-1.00.readme@
CGI-Response-0.03.tar.gz@         CGI_Imagemap-1.00.tar.gz@
CGI-modules-2.75.readme@          CGI_Lite-1.62.pm.gz@
CGI-modules-2.75.tar.gz@          DOUGM@
CGI-modules-2.76.readme@          LDS@
CGI-modules-2.76.tar.gz@          MGH@
CGI.pm-2.32.readme@               MIKEH@
CGI.pm-2.33.readme@               MUIR@
CGI.pm-2.34.readme@               SHGUN@
CGI.pm-2.35.readme@
cdrom:/.21/perl/CPAN/modules/by-module/CGI>
```

If your `ftp` client supports inline viewing of files on an `ftp` server, select the *.readme* file of the most current archive and review its contents carefully. *README* files often give special instructions about building the module; they obtain other modules needed for proper functioning and they inform you if the module can't be built under certain versions of Perl.

How Do I Install the Module?

Most system administrators install popular software so that it can be executed globally. When you log in to your account, your system administrator might even announce software installations or upgrades in the login message. Perl modules can also follow this pattern. Since many Perl modules are useful to everyone, the modules are installed so they can be used globally, generally in a branch of the lib directory with the rest of the Perl libraries.

If you have *root* privileges or write access to the locations where Perl modules are installed on your system, you can easily follow these steps when installing most modules:

```
perl Makefile.PL
make
make test
make install
```

If you don't have write permission to global areas (e.g., if you have your UNIX account with an ISP), you'll probably have to install your modules locally. You might also install modules locally if you wish to test a module in your home directory before installing for the world at large. To install a module locally, you must pass the PREFIX argument to Perl when generating a Makefile from *Makefile.PL*. The PREFIX argument tells MakeMaker to use the directory following PREFIX as the base directory when installing the module.

For example, to install a module in the directory */home/nvp/Perl/Modules*, the PREFIX argument would look like:

```
perl Makefile.PL PREFIX=/home/nvp/Perl/Modules
```

Then you would follow the same steps as above:

```
make
make test
make install
```

You now have one more step. Since Perl generally looks in systemwide areas for modules, it won't find local modules unless you tell Perl where to find them. Otherwise, you'll receive an error message like the following:

```
Can't locate <ModuleName>.pm in @INC.
BEGIN failed--compilation aborted.
```

For example, if the module has been installed in */home/nvp/Perl/Modules*, you need to tell Perl to look in that location with use lib 'path':

```
#!/usr/local/bin/perl -w
use lib '/home/nvp/Perl/Modules';
use ModuleName;
```

Where Is the Module Documented?

Many of the modules you'll be interested in are covered in this book. However, there is also often documentation that is provided by the module author itself, written in a special format called *pod*. Most of the pod documentation for CPAN modules is printed in the t*he Perl Module Reference, Volumes 1 and 2.*

"Pod" stands for "plain old documentation." If you are familiar with mark-up languages like HTML, you won't have a difficult time understanding pod. Pod-formatted files contain plain text represented by special tags in a Perl module or script that doesn't require an interpreter to be read by humans. Pod tags are not interpreted when the script is executed; programmers may use pod tags as multi-line comments. You'll find several examples of auto-generating pod tags in Chapter 13, *Contributing to CPAN.*

Pod files are installed into a subdirectory of the Perl lib directory, *Pod*, which contains the base manpages included with your Perl distribution. You can view these pages by using the perldoc command or by converting the pod file to the format of your choice by using one of the pod2XXX tools (e.g., pod2text, which converts to plain text; pod2html, which converts to HTML; or pod2man, which converts to standard manpage (n/troff) format).

For the nonstandard modules installed on your system, you can also use the perldoc command. For example:

```
perldoc CGI
```

shows the pod documentation for the CGI.pm module.

Most modules were also distributed with manpages formatted in nroff or troff, in which case you can use the man command. If the man command fails, either the manpages have failed to have been installed or the location of the Perl manpages is not in your MANPATH. If the latter is the case, ask your system administrator to add the location of the Perl manpages to your system's global manpath.

How Do I Know What Modules Are Installed on My System?

Each time a module is installed globally, information gets appended to *perllocal.pod*. This file contains the date, the location, the linktype (dynamic versus static), and the version of the module installed, as well as information about any executables installed with the module. You can parse this file using one of the pod-conversion tools previously mentioned. You can also use the CPAN setup tool discussed in Chapter 2 of the *Perl Utilities Guide.*

2

Parsing Command-Line Arguments

The examples in this book offer several different interfaces: command-line driven programs, programs with X Windows interfaces, and programs with World Wide Web interfaces. In this chapter, we discuss command-line driven interfaces and how to parse command-line arguments. We also introduce the conventions used for the example programs discussed throughout the book.

Most UNIX commands take command-line options (also called *arguments* or *switches*) that affect how the program behaves. For example, the `ls` command with a −1 option behaves differently than `ls` with a −R option, or than `ls` without an option. Imagine how difficult it would be if commands didn't have command-line options and were instead rewritten under different names to perform only slightly different functions?

Parsing command-line arguments plays a role in creating robust, multifunctional programs in Perl. Examples you'll find in this book use intuitive command-line options and output descriptive usage messages when options are incorrect or missing. You'll also notice that the example programs use the `strict` module for error checking and data integrity.

How Are Command-Line Arguments Extracted?

Perl holds command-line arguments in an array called @ARGV. The total number of arguments can be obtained by using `scalar(@ARGV)` or `$length = @ARGV`. Unlike `argv[0]` in a C program, Perl's `$ARGV[0]` represents the first argument passed to the script, not the script name itself; Perl uses a special variable, $0, to represent the program name and path.

Given the script:

```
#!/usr/local/bin/perl -w

use strict;
my($i);

print scalar(@ARGV),"\n"; # number of elements in @ARGV
$i = 0; # will represent the current member of @ARGV
foreach (@ARGV) { print "\$ARGV[$i] is ".$_."\n"; $i++; }
```

in a program executed as follows:

```
scriptname arg1 arg2 arg3
```

the values of $0, `scalar(@ARGV)`, and `@ARGV` are:[*]

```
$0 is scriptname
scalar(@ARGV)is 3 (the number of members in @ARGV)
$ARGV[0] is arg1
$ARGV[1] is arg2
$ARGV[2] is arg3
```

Controlling Command-Line Arguments Without Options

Without parsing any command-line arguments for flags like -F, -t, etc., a user can be required to enter a specific number of arguments. This is done by requiring @ARGV to contain a specific number of items. For example:

```
#!/usr/local/bin/perl -w

# exactly two arguments can be passed to the script
usage() unless scalar(@ARGV) == 2;

# sends both arguments to STDOUT
foreach (@ARGV) { print $_,"\n"; }

sub usage {
    print("Usage: $0 arg1 arg2\n");
    exit(0);
}
```

In the above example, a program usage message is output if the user fails to enter exactly two arguments.

---

[*] @ARGV is not to be confused with $ARGV, which represents the current filename when using the diamond operator (<>) that reads files named on the command line. For example:

```
perl -e 'while(<>) { print $ARGV.": ".$_."\n"; }' file1 file2 fileN
```

Using the Getopt Modules

To retrieve options from the command line, you can examine each value in
@ARGV, but it's much easier to use the Getopt modules. These modules, included
in the standard Perl distribution, extract options from the command line into aptly
named variables.

There are two Getopt modules: Getopt::Std and Getopt::Long. Getopt::Std is for
simple, single-character switches, such as -p or -v. Getopt::Long is for multicharacter options, such as -print or -verbose, in addition to single-character
options.

The Getopt::Long module is more versatile than Getopt::Std, because
Getopt::Long accepts multicharacter options and has implemented a superior
method for determining the data types of options. The GetOptions() function
accepts arguments of mixed types: float, integer, string, and boolean, as well as
optional arguments, where missing arguments won't cause a compiler warning or
Getopt error. Therefore, we'll only be covering Getopt::Long in this book.

The Getopt modules contain several functions that handle argument parsing:
getopt(), getopts(), and GetOptions() for each possible type of option.
These functions define a variable called $opt joined with an underscore and the
name of the switch the variable represents, such as $opt_i for the -i option. The
$opt variables are global variables in the user's namespace that are assigned on
demand. $opt variables not set by one of the Getopt functions or not populated
with a value on the command line are undefined. For example, in a program
executed like:

```
progname -f filename -o outputfile
```

The $opt_f variable is set to filename and the $opt_o variable is set to
outputfile. Other $opt_ variables are undefined.

Programs using the Getopt modules can also take boolean arguments, where variables representing options return 1 if the switch was present. In a program
executed like:

```
progname -f filename -y
```

the $opt_f variable is set to filename; the $opt_y variable is set to 1.

Getopt::Long

Few applications that take command-line arguments are limited to single-character
options. Many have implemented multicharacter options like -name and -exec

when the application's functionality dictates more options than there are letters in the alphabet.

Multicharacter options also allow more descriptive argument passing. For example, a "find" application that takes arguments for the filename and access time would not be well represented as:

```
findprogram -f filename -t time
```

On the other hand,

```
findprogram -name filename -atime time
```

offers more insight about the effect command-line options have on the functionality of the program.

Getopt::Long implements a more complex, getopt-like function called GetOptions() that allows command-line options to be multiple characters instead of single ones. The Getopt::Long module also contains several types for arguments, including string, integer, and real number. The following example takes one string and one float argument such as:

```
programname -rockband "Spinal Tap" -bassists 9.99
```

Here's the code:

```perl
#!/usr/local/bin/perl -w

use Getopt::Long;
use strict; # oy! oy! oy!

my($rockband, $bassists);

GetOptions('rockband=s', \$rockband, 'bassists=s', \$bassists);

usage() unless $rockband && $bassists;
print("Rock band $rockband has consumed $bassists bass players.\n");

sub usage {
    print("Usage: programname -rockband <name> -bassists <rate>\n");
    exit(1);
}
```

Table 2-1 shows a breakdown of the arguments and purposes of the arguments that can be passed to GetOptions():

Table 2-1. Arguments for GetOptions()

Option type	Description	Usage
<none>	The no-options attribute is GetOptions() boolean type that returns 1 if the option is present.	program_name --version

Table 2-1. Arguments for GetOptions() (continued)

Option type	Description	Usage
=s	The =s attribute requires that a mandatory string argument appears along with the option. `GetOptions()` returns an error if the string isn't present.	`program_name --first-name=Nathan`
:s	This option takes an optional string argument and is assigned to the option variable. If omitted, it is assigned "" (an empty string). If the string argument starts with - or --, it is considered an option itself.	
=i	This option takes a mandatory integer argument and is assigned to the option variable. Note that the value may start with - to indicate a negative value.	`program_name --pizzas=12`
:i	This option takes an optional integer argument and is assigned to the option variable. If omitted, the value 0 is assigned. Note that the value may start with - to indicate a negative value.	
=f	This option takes a mandatory real number argument and is assigned to the option variable. Note that the value may start with - to indicate a negative value.	`program_name --pi=3.14`
:f	This option takes an optional real number argument and is assigned to the option variable. If omitted, the value 0 is assigned.	

`GetOptions()` uses several more methods to define options, but the predominant method used in the book examples is:

```
GetOptions('-option=type', \$scalar_representation);
```

which tells `GetOptions()` to assign an `-option` of type `type` to `\$scalar_representation`.

Let's see what happens when we use `GetOptions()` with the following variables:

```
my($employee, $hours, @rate);
GetOptions('employee=s', \$employee, 'hours=i', \$hours, 'rate=f', \@rate);
```

The following command line:

```
program -employee biff -hours 23 -rate 2.3 -rate 1.2
```

assigns the following values:

```
$emp = 'biff';
$hours = 23;
@rate = (2.3, 1.2);
```

Since Getopt::Long implements a set of datatypes for options (see above), it complains if the user supplies an unexpected datatype:

```
program -employee 3.14 -hours "i like cheese" -rate 12 -rate 192
```

In this situation, Perl responds:

```
Value "i like cheese" invalid for option hours (number expected)
3.14
<warning about unassigned variable>
12
192
```

since the variables were assigned as follows:

```
$emp = '3.14';
$hours = i like cheese; # fails because string != integer
@rate = (12, 192);
```

Notice that the program outputs the value 3.14 for -employee, as Getopt::Long assigned $emp='3.14', but wasn't able to assign i like cheese to -hours, which was expecting an integer value. $rate didn't have any problems with 12 and 192 because both values fit into the category of real numbers.

Programs using Getopt::Long can also use optional options. When options are defined in GetOptions(), the : delimiter is used to represent an optional switch, so that:

```
GetOptions('employee=s', \$emp, 'hours:i', \$hours);
```

means a program could be executed as:

```
program -employee string_arg1 -hours intval
```

or

```
program -employee
```

but not like:

```
program -hours intval
```

nor like:

```
program
```

Without the $scalar_representation, GetOptions() assigns the value of options to $opt variables, where a program executed as:

```
program -string "string here" -integer 23 -real 2.34
```

assigns the following $opt values:

```
$opt_string = 'string here';
$opt_integer = 23;
$opt_real = 2.34;
```

GetOptions() also accepts subroutines as arguments that are used as callback functions whenever the user passes a specific option to a program. This is extremely convenient for programs containing internal help messages, which are invoked with a **-help** switch, like:

```
progname -help
```

or

```
progname --help
```

Here's an example that calls a function when the user passes the **-help** option to the program.

```
#!/usr/local/bin/perl -w

use strict;
use Getopt::Long;

# Note: option has <none> required arguments
GetOptions('help', \&usage);

sub usage {
    print "$0 -help\n";
    exit(0);
}
```

Were the program to be invoked as:

```
progname -help
```

GetOptions() would call the **usage()** subroutine, and the program would exit after displaying an instructional message.

3

Manipulating Files and Text

With Perl's strong system-level capabilities, it's easy to write utilities to read, write, search, or create files. Perl provides file and directory functions such as `mkdir()`, `rmdir()`, `unlink()`, `chmod()`, `opendir()`, `readdir()`, and `closedir()`. You might be familiar with these functions if you are familiar with UNIX and/or have done any systems programming.

This chapter doesn't propose that you abandon common utilities in favor of Perl utilities that perform the same function. The focus of this chapter is to encourage you to use a Perl module that implements a utility's functionality without the platform dependence of calling an external program.

find2perl and the File::Find Module

The UNIX `find` command locates files based on name, location, and type, and many other criteria. `find` traverses the directories and performs an action on each filename found. The syntax of the `find` command is:

```
find /path -name "what to find" -action
```

For example, you can show all files in your home directory ending in *.html* using the `find` command, as follows:

```
find /home/nvp -name "*.html" -print
```

Your Perl distribution includes a script called `find2perl`, which translates `find` commands into Perl code. Although `find2perl` doesn't generate Perl code that uses the File::Find module (discussed later in this section), `find2perl` is an excellent starting place when writing any program that finds and operates on files. You can even edit the Perl code generated by `find2perl`.

The code from `find2perl` generates the `find()` and `wanted()` functions. The `find()` function searches for **wanted** files in a certain directory.

Let's apply the command shown above to an example using `find2perl`:

```
find2perl /home/nvp -name "*.html" -print
```

`find2perl` generates the following:

```
#!/usr/local/bin/perl

eval 'exec perl -S $0 ${1+"$@"}'
        if $running_under_some_shell;

require "find.pl";

# Traverse desired filesystems

&find('/home/nvp');

exit;

sub wanted {
    /^.*\.html$/ &&
    print($name."\n");
}
```

The File::Find module works much like `find2perl` but implements two `find` functions: `find()` and `finddepth()`. `finddepth()` is similar to `find()` except that it does depth-first searching. Both the `find()` and `finddepth()` functions take two arguments: the `wanted()` function to call and the directories to search.

File::Find represents the location and filename as `$File::Find::name` and the current found member as `$_`. Let's revise the code generated by `find2perl` to use File::Find:

```
#!/usr/local/bin/perl -w

use File::Find;

# Traverse desired filesystems
find(\&wanted, '/home/nvp');

exit;

sub wanted {
```

```
     /^.*\.html$/ &&
     # show what we've found
     print $_."\n";
}
```

Parse Filenames with File::Basename

Looking at a file's absolute path, three portions of information can be extracted: the location of the file (path), the basename of the file (for example, the basename of *foo.txt* is *foo*), and the extension of the file (the extension of *foo.txt* is *.txt*). File::Basename offers functionality for non-UNIX operating systems, and regular expression file extension matching.

Using the File::Basename module, a revised version of the above example looks like:

```
#!/usr/local/bin/perl -w

use File::Basename;

$dirname = '/home/nvp'; # Base directory

opendir(DIR, $dirname)
    or die("Error opening directory $dirname: $!");

while($file = readdir(DIR)) {

    # don't show cwd or parent
    next if $file eq '.' or $file eq '..';

    # fullname directory/filename
    $file = "$dirname/$file";

    # now, parse the file's full name and send the
    # parsed version to STDOUT
    ($name,$path,$suffix) = fileparse($file);

    print("Filename: $name\n",
          "Location: $path\n",
          "File Type: $suffix\n");

}
closedir(DIR);
```

Create/Delete Directories with File::Path

The File::Path module creates and deletes multiple directories with specified permissions. By creating and removing multiple directory entries, File::Path overcomes mkdir()'s limitation of creating one directory at a time and rmdir()'s limitation of deleting one directory at a time.

File::Path defines two methods, mkpath() and rmtree(). The first argument in mkpath() is the directory name (or directory names). The second argument is a boolean value, where 1 tells mkpath() to output the directory names as they are created. The third argument is the octal value for directory permissions. Here's an example:

```
#!/usr/local/bin/perl -w

use File::Path;

# sets a base directory.  necessary if rmtree() will
# be called on the same directory structure
$basedir = '/tmp/nvp';
$all_dirs = $basedir."/ora/perl/nutshell";

# creates all directories with 0755 permissions
mkpath([$all_dirs], 1, 0755);
```

rmtree() deletes a directory tree, starting from the root directory. The first argument is a directory name. The second argument (with a value of 1) displays the directory names as they are deleted. The third argument leaves nonwriteable (deletable) files untouched. The following code removes a directory tree, like UNIX's rm command with the -r option:

```
#!/usr/local/bin/perl -w

use File::Path;

$basedir = '/tmp/nvp';
rmtree([$basedir], 1, 1);
```

Copy Files and Directories with File::Copy

The File::Copy module distributed with Perl includes the copy() function. The version of File::Copy on CPAN also includes the copydir() function; it replicates UNIX's cp -r, which copies files (including the directories) recursively. The following code shows an example using File::Copy:

```
#!/usr/local/bin/perl -w

use strict;
use File::Copy;

my($file, $dest);
usage() unless scalar(@ARGV) == 2;

($file, $dest) = (@ARGV);
copy($file, $dest);
```

```
sub usage {
    print STDERR "Usage: $0 <original file> <destination>\n";
    exit(1);
}
```

Here's an example using the `copydir()` function:

```
#!/usr/local/bin/perl -w

use File::Copy;
use strict;

my($src, $dest);

usage unless scalar(@ARGV) == 2;

($src, $dest) = (@ARGV);
copydir($src, $dest);

sub usage {
    print STDERR "Usage: $0 <source directory> <destination directory>\n";
    exit(1);
}
```

Manipulate Directory Trees with File::Recurse

The File::Recurse module operates on a directory tree. File::Recurse supports a function called `recurse()` that is used like this:

```
recurse(\&func, $dirname);
```

The basic usage is similar to the *find.pl* library. The function takes two parameters: a function reference and a directory. The function referenced by the first parameter should itself expect to take one parameter: the full path to the file currently being operated on. This function is called once for every file under the directory named by the second parameter.

A directory tree can be copied to another location using File::Recurse:

```
#!/usr/local/bin/perl -w

use File::Basename;
use File::Copy;
use File::Recurse;

$dir = '/home/nvp/Perl';
$dest = '/tmp';

recurse(\&copyfunc, $dir);
```

```
sub copyfunc {
    if(-f $_) {
        ($name, $path, $suffix) = fileparse($_, '\.*');
        print("Copying $_ to $dest/$name.copy\n");
        copy($_, "$dest/$name$suffix.copy");
    }
}
```

File::Tools-A Wrapper for File Modules

File::Tools was written as a wrapper to the File modules, like File::Copy and File::Recurse. File::Tools has no unique functions of its own, but saves you the bother of importing all File modules:

```
#!/usr/local/bin/perl -w

use File::Tools;
use File::Basename;

$dir = '/home/nvp/Perl';
$dest = '/tmp';

# recurse() is part of File::Recurse
recurse(\&copyfunc, $dir);

sub copyfunc {
    if(-f $_) {
        ($name, $path, $suffix) = fileparse($_);
        print("Copying $_ to $dest/$name.copy\n");

        # copy is a part of File::Copy
        copy($_, "$dest/$name.$suffix.new");
    }
}
```

Formatting Text with Text::Wrap and Text::Tabs

Aside from the filesystem modules, CPAN distributes a number of text-formatting and conversion modules, including Text::Wrap and Text::Tabs. Text::Wrap is a lightweight paragraph formatter; given a lengthy paragraph, Text::Wrap breaks the lines into *word boundaries* or segments defined by a columns variable. Text::Wrap uses `wrap()` to break the words into specified lines.

Here's an example using Text::Wrap:

```
#!/usr/local/bin/perl -w

use Text::Wrap;
use strict;
```

```
my($file, @lines, @wrapped);

usage() if scalar(@ARGV) != 1;
($file) = (@ARGV);

open(FILE, $file)
    or die("infile $file error: $!");
@lines = <FILE>;
close(FILE);

my $outfile = $file.".out";
open(OUTFILE, ">".$outfile)
    or die("outfile $outfile error: $!");
@wrapped = wrap("\t", "", @lines);
print OUTFILE @wrapped;
close(OUTFILE);

sub usage {
    print STDERR "Usage: $0 <inputfile>\n";
    exit(1);
}
```

The Text::Tabs module works like the UNIX **expand** and **unexpand** utilities.
Given a line with tabs in it, **expand** replaces the tabs with the appropriate
number of spaces. Given a line with or without tabs in it, **unexpand** adds tabs
when it can save bytes by doing so. Text::Tabs doesn't perform a replacement
that substitutes each tab character for one space character; it assigns a value to
the number of spaces held by a tab character (\t) and replaces a tab character
with the number of spaces corresponding to the number of spaces held by the
tab character. In other words, the contents of the expanded file won't appear any
different from the contents of the input file, but examining the contents (per character) of the output file proves differently.

Here are the contents of the file that will be expanded:

```
This    is      a       file    separated       with    a       number  of
tabs    and     it will be properly    parsed by this    Perl script
where all tabs will     be      replaced    with spaces.
```

The **expand** script is thus:

```
#!/usr/local/bin/perl -w

use Text::Tabs;
use strict;

my($infile, $tabstop);
my(@tabs, @lines);
usage() unless scalar(@ARGV) == 1;

($infile) = (@ARGV);
```

```
open(IN, $infile)
    or die("input file $infile error: $!");
@lines = <IN>;
close(IN);

$tabstop = 4;

my $outfile = $infile.".exp";
open(OUT, ">".$outfile)
    or die("output file $outfile error: $!");
@tabs = expand(@lines);
print OUT @tabs;
close(OUT);

sub usage {
    print("$0 <input file>\n");
    exit(1); # failure
}
```

The contents of the new file after expansion are as follows:

```
This    is      a       file    separated      with     a        number  of
tabs    and     it will be properly      parsed by this     Perl script
where all tabs will     be      replaced   with spaces.
```

"Unexpanding" a file might be compared to a lightweight compression scheme, in that larger numbers of characters (spaces) are converted into smaller numbers of characters (tabs). Here is the **unexpand** script corresponding to the **expand** script above:

```
#!/usr/local/bin/perl -w

use Text::Tabs;
use strict;

my($infile, $tabstop);
my(@tabs, @lines);
usage() unless scalar(@ARGV) == 1;

($infile) = (@ARGV);

open(IN, $infile)
    or die("input file $infile error: $!");
@lines = <IN>;
close(IN);

$tabstop = 4;

my $outfile = $infile.".unx";
open(OUT, ">".$outfile)
    or die("output file $outfile error: $!");
@tabs = unexpand(@lines);
print OUT @tabs;
close(OUT);
```

```
sub usage {
    print("$0 <input file>\n");
    exit(1); # failure
}
```

Uuencoding Files with Convert::UU

If you are familiar with the concepts behind Multipurpose Internet Mail Extensions (MIME), *uuencoding* serves a similar purpose: it transfers binary files over
transmission media that support only 7-bit ASCII (text) data.

The UNIX *uuencode* command reads input from a file, or STDIN, and writes
encoded information to STDOUT (which can be redirected to a file). Uuencoded
files are bounded by a begin line containing the filename (and permissions) and
an end line, denoted by the word "end." The core of the decoded file is the
encoded information. The *uudecode* command translates the encoded information
back to its original form, extracts the filename (and permissions) from the begin
line, and reads until the "end" statement. It ignores leading or trailing spaces after
the begin line or before the end line and doesn't retain the setuid and execute
bits of the original file.

Perl's `pack()` and `unpack()` functions provide easy methods to encode and
decode information, along with `oct()` and `hex()`, which convert characters
between numeric bases. The Convert::UU module includes the `uuencode()` and
`uudecode()` functions, descriptively implemented to uuencode and uudecode
information. The `uuencode()` function takes a scalar (or filehandle reference)
argument, a filename, and a mode (permissions) argument; it returns a scalar,
which is a uuencoded string. The `uudecode()` function takes a string (or filehandle reference) argument; it returns a uudecoded string, filename, and mode
(permissions). Using Convert::UU, uuencoding information is accomplished like
this:

```
#!/usr/local/bin/perl -w

use Convert::UU qw(uudecode uuencode);
use strict;

my($infile, $outfile, $mode, $encoded_line); # scope

usage() unless scalar(@ARGV) == 2;
($infile, $outfile) = (@ARGV);

open(IN, $infile)
    or die("can't open input file $infile: $!");

open(OUT, ">".$outfile)
    or die("can't open output file $outfile: $!");
```

```
$encoded_line = uuencode(\*IN, $infile, $mode);
print OUT $encoded_line;
close(OUT);

close(IN);

sub usage {
    print STDERR "Usage: $0 <inputfile> <outputfile>\n";
    exit(1);
}
```

Conversely, to uudecode information, use this:

```
#!/usr/local/bin/perl -w

use Convert::UU qw(uudecode uuencode);
use strict;

my($infile, $outfile, $mode, $decoded_line); # scope

usage() unless scalar(@ARGV) == 1;
($infile) = (@ARGV); # we only need input filename

open(IN, $infile) or die("input file $infile error: $!");
($decoded_line, $outfile, $mode) = uudecode(\*IN); # uudecode input

open(OUT, ">$outfile") or die("outfile $outfile error: $!");
print OUT $decoded_line; # output uudecoded lines to file
close(OUT);

close(IN);

sub usage {
    print STDERR "Usage: $0 <inputfile>\n";
    exit(1);
}
```

4

*The Mail and
MIME Modules*

Electronic mail is arguably the most essential Internet application. Although there are many different mail clients, standards for mail delivery and retrieval simplify the process of writing a mail client to send and/or retrieve mail.

The Send Mail Transfer Protocol, or SMTP, is responsible for clients negotiating RCPT ("to") and FROM ("from") requests with the SMTP server, then sending data to the SMTP server, followed by an EOF.

The Post Office Protocol Version 3, or POP3, was designed to retrieve electronic mail from a server after a user has authenticated with a username and password. Authenticated users can retrieve any information about their mailboxes, including the number of messages, headers, and message bodies, and specific messages by entering the message number.

You'll find that many of the `Mail` modules satisfy a host of tasks you might have accomplished either with an external program or by writing a socket client (using the `Socket` module) that communicates with the SMTP or POP server. Although the Mail::Mailer and Mail::Send modules interact with external mail programs such as `mail`, `mailx`, or `sendmail`, we'll also introduce you to Net::SMTP, which talks to an SMTP server through a socket.

This chapter covers modules designed for sending and retrieving email, as well as "helper" modules for more rudimentary message handling. We also cover the MIME and encoding modules used to package data for mail transfer and translate data upon receipt.

Send Email with Mail::Mailer

The Mail::Mailer module interacts with external mail programs. When you "use" Mail::Mailer or create a new Mail::Mailer object, you can specify which mail program you want your program to talk to:

```
use Mail::Mailer qw(mail);
```

You can also specify the mail program that sends the mail:

```
use Mail::Mailer;
$type = 'sendmail';
$mailprog = Mail::Mailer->new($type);
```

$type is the mail program you'll be using. Once you've created a new object, you use the open() function to send the message headers to the mail program, where %headers is a hash of key/value pairs that represent the header type and the value of the header:

```
# mail headers to use in the message
%headers = (
    'To' => 'nvp@mail.somename.com',
    'From' => 'nvp@mail.somename.com',
    'Subject' => 'working?'
);
```

This code represents a set of headers where the recipient of the mail message is *nvp@mail.somename.com*, the mail was sent from *nvp@mail.somename.com*, and the subject of the mail message is "working?"

Once %headers or an array of scalars has been defined, this hash or array is passed to open():

```
$mailprog->open(\%headers);
```

The body of the message is then sent to the mail program:

```
print $mailprog "This is the message body.\n";
```

Now, close the program when the message is finished.

```
$mailprog->close;
```

Let's put it all together. A practical example of using Mail::Mailer would be a command-line-driven application that works much like the UNIX mail program, reading STDIN until EOF or mailing a file specified on the command line, like so:

```
mailprogram filename
```

The code for this program might look like:

```
#!/usr/local/bin/perl -w

use Mail::Mailer;
use strict; # or forever hold your peace
```

```
my($mailer, $body);
my(%headers);

# use sendmail for mailing
$mailer = Mail::Mailer->new('sendmail');

# mail headers to use in the message
%headers = (
    'To' => 'nvp@mail.somename.com', # the recipient
    'From' => 'nvp@mail.somename.com', # the sender
    'Subject' => 'working?' # the subject
);

# send headers to the mail program
$mailer->open(\%headers);

# undefine record separator, this is necessary
# to assign <> to a scalar
undef $/;

# read <> for body of message
$body = <>;

# send $body to the mail program
print $mailer $body;

# end session
$mailer->close;
```

Better Header Control with Mail::Send

Mail::Send is built on top of Mail::Mailer, which means that you can also choose the mail program that sends the mail. Mail::Mailer has implemented functions to(), cc(), bcc(), and subject() to replace the %headers hash used in Mail::Mailer.

Mail::Send uses the open() function to open the mail program for output; it is built on Mail::Mailer's new function, so:

```
# Start mailer and output headers
$fh = $msg->open('sendmail');
```

serves the same purpose as:

```
# use sendmail for mailing
$mailer = Mail::Mailer->new('sendmail)';
```

This code tells Mail::Send to use **sendmail** as the mail program. Here's a rewritten example of the above, which takes command-line arguments for subject and recipient, but still reads from <>:

```
mailprogram -t <recipient> -subj <subject> <filename>
```

The program is written as:

```perl
#!/usr/local/bin/perl -w

use strict; # or I'm coming to your house to sell you some knives
use Getopt::Long;
my($recip, $subj, $fh, $msg, $body); # for strict

require Mail::Send;

# $recip is the variable for the -t switch
# $subj is the variable for the -subj switch
# both switches are required or output a usage message
GetOptions('t=s', \$recip, 'subj=s', \$subj);

# we have both switches
if($recip && $subj) {
    $msg = Mail::Send->new();

    # who the message is for
    $msg->to($recip);

    # the subject of the message
    $msg->subject($subj);

    # Start mailer and output headers
    $fh = $msg->open('sendmail');

    # undefine record separator so scalar can be
    # assigned to <> instead of an array
    undef $/;

    # read <>
    $body = <>;

    # send the body of the message to the mailer
    print $fh $body;

    # complete the message and send it
    $fh->close;

# something's missing.  give usage message and exit.
} else {
    &usage();
    exit(0);
}

# the usage message
sub usage {
    print("Usage: $0 -t <recipient> -subj <subject> <filename>\n");
}
```

Mail::Send also provides the **set()** and **add()** functions, which assign a value to a header tag and append a value to a header tag. The **set()** function takes two arguments: a header tag and a value. The **set()** function is used like this:

```
$msg->set($scalar, @array);
```

Therefore, to address a message to *nvp@mail.somename.com*:

```
$msg->set('To', 'nvp@mail.somename.com');
```

The above sets the To header to *nvp@mail.somename.com*; however, the following sets the To header to *postmaster@mail.somename.com* and *nvp@mail.some-name.com*, because they represent an array of values.

```
$msg->set('To', ('nvp@mail.somename.com', 'postmaster@mail.somename.com'));
```

The set() function can't be used to add multiple values to a header value, like:

```
$msg->set('To', 'nvp@mail.somename.com');
$msg->set('To', 'someone@their.mailaddress.com');
```

The set() function doesn't append information from one call to another; the previous case only addresses mail to *someone@their.mailaddress.com*. The add function is used for this purpose. For example:

```
$msg->add('To', 'nvp@mail.somename.com');
$msg->add('To', 'someone@their.mailaddress.com');
```

This example addresses mail to both parties.

Rewriting the Mail::Send example shown above to use set() and add() subject and recipient fields would be represented as follows:

```
# @ recip from GetOptions('t=s', \@recip);
$msg->add('To', @recip);

# $subj from GetOptions('subj=s', \$subj);
$msg->set('Subject', $subj);
```

Putting it all together, mail can be sent to multiple recipients using Mail::Send with the following example:

```
#!/usr/local/bin/perl -w

# strict checking is our friend.  although it's not good
# to use one's friends, it's always good to use strict. :-)
use strict;
use Getopt::Long;
my(@recip, $subj, $fh, $msg, $body); # for strict
require Mail::Send;

# @recip is an array of recipients - at least one recipient
# is required.  $subj is the subject of the message (this is
# also required)
GetOptions('t=s', \@recip, 'subj=s', \$subj);

# both switches have been entered
if((scalar(@recip) > 0) && $subj) {
# new Mail::Send object
$msg = Mail::Send->new();
```

```perl
# Add recipients to the list
$msg->add('To', @recip);

# Set the subject of the message
$msg->set('Subject', $subj);

# Start mailer and output headers;
# in this case, use sendmail.
$fh = $msg->open('sendmail');

# undefine record separator so we can use a scalar
undef $/;

# read <> into $body
$body = <>;

# send the message body to the mailer
print $fh $body;

# complete the message and send it
$fh->close;
} else {
    usage();
}

sub usage {
    print("Usage: $0 -t <recipient> -subj <subject> <filename>\n");
    exit(0);
}
```

Interface to SMTP with Net::SMTP

Net::SMTP, a subclass of Net::Cmd and IO::Socket::INET, was written by Graham Barr (*gbarr@ti.com*) and is included with the libnet distribution. Net::SMTP implements an interface to the SMTP and ESMTP protocols, which send mail by talking to an SMTP server (through a socket) as described in RFC 821.

When would you want to use Net::SMTP instead of sending mail with an external program? Since socket communications through sockets don't involve spawning an external program, your programs won't suffer from the overhead associated with running an extra process. Talking to SMTP is convenient in cases of sending a volume of messages through electronic mail. Naturally, your server must have an SMTP server running or a remote mailhost must allow you to talk to it; otherwise you won't be able to use this module. If your server (or a remote host) doesn't have an SMTP server running, you'll be forced to use an external program to send your email with Mail::Mailer or Mail::Send; such is the case with home computers, which don't generally run their own SMTP server.

The SMTP Protocol and the SMTP Session

The SMTP protocol defines a set of commands a client sends to an SMTP server. The SMTP server is generally bound to port 25 of a mailhost. This section walks you through an SMTP session by showing you how the requests and responses are negotiated between the client and the server.

When a client negotiates an SMTP session with a server, the server tells the client that it's listening:

```
Trying 127.0.0.1 ...
Connected to mailhost.somename.com.
Escape character is '^]'.
220-mailhost.somename.com Spammers Beware Sendmail 8.6.13/8.6.11 ready at
Thu, 11 Sep 1997 21:07:36 -0400
220 ESMTP spoken here
```

The server returns a 220 message if everything is OK. If there is no server running on port 25, you'd receive an error message that your connection to port 25 was refused.

After you've connected to port 25 of the server, you introduce yourself to the server by issuing a HELO command. The HELO command accepts one parameter, your hostname; HELO defaults to your remote hostname if you don't specify a hostname.* Successful HELO commands receive a 250 response. Let's send a HELO command to the server:

```
HELO
250 mail.somename.com Hello some-remote-host.com [127.0.0.1], pleased to
meet you
```

Once you've been greeted by the server, you'll have to tell the server who the sender of the message is by sending the MAIL command. The MAIL command takes the string From: user@hostname as an argument. If the MAIL command is successful, the server sends a 250 response:

```
MAIL From: realuser@realhost.com
250 realuser@realhost.com ... Sender ok
```

Then tell the server who you're sending the message to with RCPT. If the RCPT command is successful, the server sends a 250 response:

```
RCPT To: nospam@rid-spam-now.com
250 nospam@rid-spam-now.com ... Recipient ok
```

---

* Some SMTP servers do name lookups that disconnect requests at port 25 if the remote hostname can't be resolved. This practice is used to thwart evil commercial email programs that send junk mail by disguising themselves as fictitious hosts.

Now you're ready to send the body of your message to the server. The DATA command tells the server that all the data until the . on a line by itself will be received as the body of the email message.

```
DATA
354 Enter mail, end with "." on a line by itself
Subject: Hi, just thought you'd be interested ...

Hi, sorry to bother you, but I figured that you wouldn't mind
sparing a moment of your time to read about something disgusting,
explicit, or downright irritating blah blah blah ...

Please reply to my email address with the Subject: REMOVE so we
know that your email address is valid and can send you more
junk mail in the future.

.
250 VAA09505 Message accepted for delivery
```

Once the message has been accepted for delivery (with a 250 response), you can exit the SMTP session with the QUIT command, which returns 221 on success:

```
QUIT
221 mail.somename.com closing connection
Connection closed by foreign host.
```

The Net::SMTP Interface to SMTP

The Net::SMTP methods are named after the SMTP command they perform. This section introduces you to these methods and walks you through a complete SMTP session using Net::SMTP.

Create a new object with new()

Before you can negotiate an SMTP session with a mailhost, you must create a new object with new(). All SMTP commands are accessed through this object. The new() method takes the hostname of the mail server and options for the SMTP connection (see below) as arguments. The other options are passed to new() as a hash (name/value pairs).

Here are the options that can be passed to new():

Hello

> Sends a HELO command to the SMTP server and requires a string that represents your domain; if not present, Hello guesses your domain.

Timeout

> Time after which the client stops trying to establish a connection with the SMTP server; the program then exits. The default is 120 seconds.

Debug

> Turns on debugging information that tells you what's transpiring with your connection, requests, and responses. The value 1 enables debug mode.

Here's how you'd create a new Net::SMTP object for a mailhost, $mailhost, that times out in 30 seconds if a connection can't be made with the SMTP server and outputs debugging information:

```
$mailhost = 'mail.someplace.com';
$smtp = Net::SMTP->new($mailhost,
            Hello => $mailhost,
            Timeout => 30,
            Debug   => 1,
);
```

The following Net::SMTP methods each return a value if successful, and **undef** otherwise.

domain()

> This method returns the domain of the remote SMTP server.

hello()

> This method sends an EHLO to the mail server or HELO if EHLO fails. This method executes automatically when you create a Net::SMTP object, so you shouldn't have to do it manually.

```
$smtp->hello('my-maildomain-com');
```

mail()

> This method sends a MAIL command to the server. Takes an address as the argument:

```
$smtp->mail('me@my-domain.com');
```

> mail() initiates the message sending process.

recipient()

> The current message should be sent to all the specified recipients. As defined in the RFC, each address is a separate command that is sent to the server.

```
@mailto = ('she@her.com', 'him@his.com');

# send a separate To: line for each recipient
for(@mailto) { $smtp->recipient($_); }
```

to()

> This method is interchangeable with **recipient**.

data()

> This method starts sending the body of the current message. There are a number of ways to send data to the server with Net::SMTP, including a list or a reference to a list. The data must end with a period (.); the function returns **true** if accepted.

datasend()

> This method sends extra header information and the body of the message to the server.

dataend()

> This method sends a `.\r\n` to the server telling it that input has finished and to send the message.

> Here's an example that sends a list to **datasend()**:

```
@list_data = (1..10);

$smtp->data();
$smtp->datasend(@list_data);
$smtp->dataend();
```

help()

> If your server has implemented the HELP command, you can pass a subject to **help** and have the **help** text returned to you.

```
$subject = 'HELO';
$help_text = $smtp->help($subject);
print $help_text."\n" if $help_text;
```

quit()

> This method sends the QUIT command to the remote SMTP server and closes the socket connection.

Let's put it all together. Here's an example that sends a message to the webmaster of your favorite web site called *www.my-favorite-site.com*:

```
#!/usr/local/bin/perl -w

use Net::SMTP;
use strict;
my($mailhost, $sender, $recipient);

# mailhost, sender, and recipient declarations
$mailhost = 'smtp.my-mailhost.com';
$sender = 'me@mail.somesite.com';
$recipient = 'webmaster@www.my-favorite-site.com';

# constructor
$smtp = Net::SMTP->new($mailhost);

# our sender and recipient
$smtp->mail($sender);
$smtp->to($recipient);

# start sending the DATA command to the server
$smtp->data();

# now, send the data to the server
$smtp->datasend(<<END);
```

```
To: $recipient
Subject: how are you enjoying your log?

Mine's pretty woody.

Love,
$sender

END

# stop sending data to the server
$smtp->dataend();

# now, quit the connection
$smtp->quit;
```

Read Email with Mail::POP3Client

Many networks have machines dedicated to sending and receiving electronic mail. Since users might hold accounts on *foo.bar.com*, and mail is sent to *pop-server.bar.com*, there must be a means to transfer this mail from the "post office machine" to the host that the user works on every day. The Post Office Protocol, or POP, negotiates this mail transfer from machine A to machine B.

The machine that runs POP has a server bound to port 109 or 110 (or others) depending on the machine's configuration. When a user wants to retrieve his or her mail, the user's mail client connects to the POP server and authenticates the user with a login name and password. After the user is authenticated, the user can list, read, and delete messages from the POP server.

This section introduces you to the important aspects of Mail::POP3Client and offers some examples using this module in the context of the command line. In Chapter 14, *Examples*, we also show an application using Mail::POP3Client to read electronic mail from a web page.

The Mail::POP3Client module simplifies the process of "talking POP" by implementing a number of functions to login, parse, and read mail messages held on the POP server. POP "vitals," such as login name (required), password (required), POP host, port, and debugging flag are passed to the constructor when a new POP3Client object is created. For example:

```
#!/usr/local/bin/perl -w

use Mail::POP3Client;

$pop = Mail::POP3Client->new("login", # required
                             "password", #required
                             "pophost.your.domain", # not required
                             port, # default is 110
                             debug_flag); # any positive integer
```

Counting Messages

The Count() function represents the number of messages in the mailbox: if authentication fails, Count() returns -1; otherwise, it returns 0 or a positive integer indicating the number of messages in the mailbox. Once authenticated, a user can list the headers of the messages in their mailbox using the Head() function in conjunction with the Count() function, as shown in the following example:

```
#!/usr/local/bin/perl -w

use strict; # i will eat it very quick i will eat it using strict
use Mail::POP3Client;

my($pop, $num_mesg, $i);

$pop = Mail::POP3Client->new("nvp",
                             "xxxxxx",
                             "mail.somename.com",
                             110,
                             1);

        # How many messages do we have?
$num_mesg = $pop->Count;
print("You have ".$num_mesg." new message(s).\n");

        # Now, output the headers for all the messages.
for ($i = 1; $i <= $num_mesg; $i++) {
    print $pop->Head($i), "\n";
}
```

You can also use a regular expression to parse the headers to show wanted information, like sender and/or subject of each mail message:

```
#!/usr/local/bin/perl -w

use strict; # be there or be square
use Mail::POP3Client;

my($pop, $num_mesg, $i);

$pop = Mail::POP3Client->new("nvp", # required
                             "xxxxxx", # required
                             "mail.somename.com", # pop host
                             110, # port (an integer)
                             1); # debug flag (an integer)

$num_mesg = $pop->Count;
print("You have ".$num_mesg." new message(s).\n");

for ($i = 1; $i <= $pop->Count; $i++) {
    foreach ($pop->Head($i)) {
                # output from and subject
```

```
        # if matched by regexp
        print $_." " if /^(From|Subject)/;
    }
        # now, send a trailing \n for grins
    print "\n";
}
```

The above code outputs:

```
~/ORA/PRK/Chapters/Mail/scripts> ./ex1_7.pl
POP3: POPStat at ./ex1_7.pl line 8
You have 1 new message(s).
TOP 1 0
+OK Top of message follows
From: "Nathan V. Patwardhan" <nvp> Subject: pop test
```

Getting and Setting the Host and Port

The Host() function returns or sets the current POP host. For example:

```
$obj->Host;
```

returns the current POP host and sets the new POP host to *new-pop.bar.com.*

```
$new_host = 'new-pop.bar.com';
$obj->Host($new_host);
```

The Port() function works like Host(), returning or setting the current port the POP server is bound to:

```
$obj->Port;
```

This returns the current port the POP server is bound to and sets the new port to 7000.

```
$new_port = 7000;
$obj->Port($new_port);
```

Retrieving the Message Body

Naturally, you'll want to read more than the headers of your mail messages, so Mail::POP3Client contains the Body(), HeadAndBody(), and Retrieve() functions. The Body() function outputs the body of the message, and both HeadAndBody() and Retrieve() output both the head and body of the message. Given the above example, an entire message can be output with the following code:

```
#!/usr/local/bin/perl -w

use strict; # those who are late will not be served fruit cup.
use Mail::POP3Client;

my($pop, $num_mesg, $i);
```

```
$pop = Mail::POP3Client->new("nvp", # required
                             "xxxxxx", # required
                             "mail.somename.com", # pop host
                             110, # port (an integer)
                             0); # debug flag (an integer)

$num_mesg = $pop->Count;
print("You have ".$num_mesg." new message(s).\n");

for ($i = 1; $i <= $pop->Count; $i++) {
    foreach ($pop->Retrieve($i)) { # show the message, $i
        print $_,"\n"; # add a \n to end of each line
    }
    print "\n";
}
```

This example outputs the message:

```
~/ORA/PRK/Chapters/Mail/scripts> ./ex1_8.pl
You have 1 new message(s).
Received: (from nvp@localhost)
        by mail.somename.com (8.8.5/8.8.5) id AAA03248
        for nvp; Mon, 9 Jun 1997 00:11:09 -0500 (EST)
Date: Mon, 9 Jun 1997 00:11:09 -0500 (EST)
From: "Nathan V. Patwardhan" <nvp>
Message-Id: <199706090511.AAA03248@mail.somename.com>
To: nvp
Subject: pop test
Status: RO
this is a pop test
```

Deleting and Undeleting Messages

Messages can be deleted from the POP mailbox with the `Delete()` function. `Delete` temporarily marks messages for deletion until the `QUIT` command is received, at which time the messages are permanently removed. `Delete()` takes one argument, the number of the message to delete:

```
$pop->Delete(1);
```

This deletes the first mail message.

Like most mail programs, Mail::POP3Client can undelete messages marked for deletion before the program is terminated and the changes saved. The `Reset()` function takes one argument, representing the number of the message to undelete:

```
$pop->Reset(1);
```

`Reset()` unmarks the first mail message from pending deletion upon program termination.

Checking the Connection

Most programs that require a user to log in will time out after a given period of time for security and resource reasons. Unattended programs are a welcome find to individuals wanting to cause harm to the system, and they are also taxing on the system, because the program is running idle. The `Alive()` function checks to see if the connection to the POP server is still open; it returns `true` if the connection is good, or `false` if the connection is closed. For example:

```
#!/usr/local/bin/perl -w

use strict; # be there or be square
use Mail::POP3Client;

my($pop, $is_alive);
$pop = Mail::POP3Client->new("nvp", # required
                             "xxxxx", # required
                             "mail.somename.com", # pop host
                             110, # port (an integer)
                             1); # debug flag (an integer)

$is_alive = $pop->Alive; # Alive() returns 1 if connected
if($is_alive == 1) {
    print("You are currently connected to: ".$pop->Host."\n");
} else {
    print("Error: disconnected!\n");
}
```

The above code causes the POP server to respond (if connected):

```
~/ORA/PRK/Chapters/Mail/scripts> ./ex1_10.pl
POP3: POPStat at ./ex1_10.pl line 8
You are currently connected to: mail.somename.com
```

Explicitly Opening and Closing Connections

POP connections can be explicitly opened and closed with `Login()` and `Close()`. `Close()` takes no arguments and closes the connection to the POP server; here's a test using `Close()`:

```
$pop->Close;
if($pop->Alive == 1) {
    print "Connected.\n";
} else {
    print "Not connected.\n";
}
```

Mail Helper Modules

The `Mail` helper modules covered in this chapter are Mail::Folder, Mail::Internet, and Mail::Address. We call them *helper* modules because they perform less complex tasks than core `Mail` modules like Mail::Send or Mail::POP3Client, yet come in quite handy when working with email messages.

Handle Folders with Mail::Folder

Once you've begun downloading and reading your email from a POP server, you might want to save or categorize your messages into folders which allow you to add, delete, save, and move messages easily.

Mail::Folder was written by Kevin Johnson (*kjj@pobox.com*) as an object-oriented, folder-independent interface to email folders that supports `mbox`, `maildir`, `emaul`, and NNTP mailbox formats. Since `mbox` is a standard mailbox format supported by a number of UNIX mail clients, the examples in this section demonstrate Mail::Folder's `mbox` (Mail::Folder::Mbox) capabilities. You can find examples for other mail folder formats in Chapter 19 of the *Module Reference Guide, Volume 2.**

You'll need to create a Mail::Folder object before you can use the module. Mail::Folder uses the `new()` method as a constructor. The `new()` method takes three arguments: the type of the folder you'll be using, the name of the folder, and a list of options described below. If you specify the name of the folder, Mail::Folder automatically opens the folder with the `open()` method.

The options to the `new()` constructor for Mail::Folder are:

`Create`
   The folder is created if it doesn't already exist.

`Content-Length`
   The Content-length header is created or updated by `append_message()` and `update_message()`.

`DotLock`
   Uses *.lock* style folder locking with the proper folder interface (`mbox` is the only interface that currently uses this).

`Flock`
   Uses flock-style folder locking with the proper folder interface (`mbox` is the only interface that currently uses this).

`NFSLock`
   Deals with NFS-style file locking with the proper folder interface and the NFS server in question.

---

* Mail::Folders enables you to read, write, add, save, and delete messages from your existing mail folders reliably as of Mail::Folder Version 0.06 and Perl Version 5.004_01.

Timeout

The folder interface overrides the default value for timing out. This is particularly useful for folder interfaces that involve network communications. Time is specified in seconds.

DefaultFolderType

Auto-detects folder type if AUTODETECT has been set (neat!).

You can create a Mail::Folder object that reads the file */home/nvp/Mail/nvp* in mbox format with the following code:

```
$ftype = 'mbox';
$foldername = '/home/nvp/Mail/nvp';
$fldr_obj = new($ftype, $foldername [, %options]);
```

Let's look at the key methods you'll need to get started with Mail::Folder.

open()

If you haven't specified a folder name in the constructor, you'll need to call the open() method, which takes the folder name as an argument. open() populates the internal data structures with information it gathers from the mail folders. readonly is set if the folder is determined to be read-only.

```
$folder_obj->open($foldername);
```

get_message()

Once you've opened a mail folder, you'll want to read the messages. The get_message() method takes a message number as an argument and returns 0 for failure.

```
$num = 24;
$folder_obj->get_message($num);
```

get_mime_message()

Mail::Folder also parses messages with MIME content (see the section, "The MIME Modules," later in this chapter). The get_mime_message() method calls get_message_file() to get a file to parse, creates a MIME::Parser object, and reads the content into MIME::Entity. get_mime_message() takes the same options as MIME::Entity.

get_message_file()

This method returns a filename instead of a Mail::Internet object reference and works well with the MIME tools package.

```
$num = 2;
$folder_obj->get_message_file($num);
```

get_header()

The get_header() method extracts a message header and takes one argument, the message number.

```
$num = 45;
$folder_obj->get_header($num);
```

get_mime_header()

This method works much like get_header(), but calls MIME::Head instead. It takes one argument, the message number.

```
$num = 392;
$folder_obj->get_mime_header($num);
```

append_message()

The append_message() method adds a message to a folder and takes a reference to a Mail::Internet object as an argument.

```
$folder_obj->append_message($mi_ref);
```

refile()

This method moves messages between folders and takes a message number and folder reference as arguments.

```
$folder_obj->refile($num, $fldr_ref);
```

delete_message()

The delete_message() method takes a list of messages to be marked for deletion. Messages won't actually be deleted until **sync** is called.

```
@all = (1, 2, 3, 5);
$folder_obj->delete(@all);
```

undelete_message()

This method unmarks a list of messages that have been marked for deletion. Like delete_message(), it takes a list as an argument:

```
@unmark(1, 3, 4, 6);
$folder_obj->undelete_message(@unmark);
```

message_list()

This method returns a list of the message numbers in the folder (in no particular order).

```
print $folder_obj->message_list."\n";
```

qty()

This method returns the number of messages in the folder.

```
print "There are ".$folder_obj->qty." messages in your folder\n";
```

Handle Messages with Mail::Internet

Mail::Internet implements a number of helpful functions to manipulate a mail message, including body(), print_header(), and head().

Mail::Internet is built on top of Mail::Header, which parses the header of an electronic mail message. Mail::Internet inherits the Mail::Header constructor style that requires a file descriptor or reference to an array be used. For example:

```
@lines = <STDIN>;
$mi_obj = new Mail::Internet([@lines]);
```

reads a mail message from STDIN (using a reference to an array). The following example reads a mail message from a filehandle, *FILE*.

```
open(FILE, "/home/nvp/Mail/nvp");
$mi_obj = new Mail::Internet(\*FILE);
close(FILE);
```

The `print_header()` function outputs the header of a message to a file descriptor; the default is STDOUT.

```
open(FILE, "/home/nvp/Mail/nvp");
$mi_obj = new Mail::Internet(\*FILE);
close(FILE);
$mi_obj->print_header(\*STDOUT);
```

The above example outputs:

```
From nvp Mon Jun  9 00:11:10 1997
Received: (from nvp@localhost) by mail.somename.com (8.8/8.8) id
    AAA03248 for nvp; Mon, 9 Jun 1997 00:11:09 -0500 (EST)
Date: Mon, 9 Jun 1997 00:11:09 -0500 (EST)
From: "Nathan V. Patwardhan" <nvp>
Message-Id: <199706090511.AAA03248@mail.somename.com>
To: nvp
Subject: pop test
X-Status:
X-Uid: 1
Status: RO
```

where `print_body()` also takes a file descriptor as an argument, but only outputs the body of the message, whereas the `print()` function outputs an entire message.

Parse Email Addresses with Mail::Address

Mail::Address was written by Graham Barr (*gbarr@ti.com*). This module parses RFC 822-compliant email addresses with the form:

```
"Full Name or Phrase" <username@host> (Comment Area)
```

For example, under RFC 822, an address might be represented as:

```
"Nathan V. Patwardhan" <nvp@mail.somename.com> (No Comment)
```

or

```
"Nathan V. Patwardhan" <nvp@mail.somename.com>
```

The Mail::Address constructor parses an email address into three parts based on the categories shown above:

```
$addr = Mail::Address->new("Full Name or Phrase",
                           "username@host",
                           "(Comment Area)");
```

Mail::Address also outputs portions of the email address with the functions
`phrase()`, `address()`, `comment()`, `format()`, `name()`, `host()`, and `user()`.
The `phrase()`, `address()`, and `comment()` functions represent the first, second,
and third entities that were passed to the Mail::Address constructor, where the
`phrase()` function when used as follows:

```
print $addr->phrase();
```

outputs:

```
Nathan V. Patwardhan
```

The `address()` function when used like:

```
print $addr->address();
```

outputs:

```
nvp@mail.somename.com
```

And the `comment()` function when used like:

```
print $addr->comment();
```

outputs:

```
No Comment
```

A real electronic mail address can be "unmangled," or parsed from its *user@some-host.com* format, with the `user()` and `host()` functions. The `user()` function
removes everything after and including @, and `host()` removes everything before
and including @. Using the previous example of *nvp@mail.somename.com*, the
following line:

```
print $addr->user;
```

outputs:

```
nvp
```

And the following line using the `host()` function:

```
print $addr->host;
```

outputs:

```
nvp@mail.somename.com
```

If you create a Perl script called *parsefrom.pl* using MIME::Head and Mail::Address
to parse the `From` line of an incoming mail message, and put a statement like:

```
|/path/parseform.pl your_username
```

in your *.forward* file, your script passes the contents of the `From` line into
Mail::Address, and parses a mail address for each incoming mail message. Here's
an idea of how `parseform.pl` might be written:

```
#!/usr/local/bin/perl -w

use MIME::Head; # used to parse the message header
use Mail::Address; # used to parse the sender's address
use strict; # the hills are alive

my($header, $bar, $foo);

$header = new MIME::Head;
$header->read(\*STDIN); # read message from STDIN
$bar = $header->get('From', 0); # grab the header containing 'From'

# If the address doesn't match the form
# PHRASE ADDRESS (COMMENT), use the first regexp which won't
# try to match (COMMENT).  Otherwise, grab everything.
if(....) {
#match address type 1
} else {
#match address type 2
}
```

Handling MIME Data

Nontext file types like executables, pictures, and file archives can be sent through electronic mail using MIME, or Multipurpose Internet Mail Extensions. MIME messages are sent in multiple parts separated by boundaries, with specific stamps representing the contents of the boundary. (MIME-encoded messages can also be referred to as multipart messages.)

Although many mail readers are able to parse and decode the contents of MIME messages, others, like RMAIL and elm, require an external program to parse and display the contents of a MIME-encoded mail message. There are several different packages that handle MIME message interpretation, but we'll concentrate on the metamail package, and specifically the *mailcap* file. The *mailcap* file is read by metamail to determine how entities of multipart mail messages or nontext attachments are handled.

For more information on sending mail with MIME attachments, see the discussion of Base64-encoding later in this chapter.

Format of the mailcap File

The *mailcap* file is generally found in */etc* or */usr/local/etc*, but can be located anywhere, providing that metamail knows where to find it. The MAILCAPS environment variable can be set to point to the location of the *mailcap* file if it is different than the default.

mailcap entries are divided into four fields, separated by semicolons. The four fields are:

- The Content-type of the entry
- A command to execute when the Content-type is encountered
- An optional flag that is passed to the command if necessary
- An optional entry description, denoted with a description tag

A *mailcap* entry might look like:

```
application/x-perl; ptkat %s; nonummy
```

With a description tag, the above entry could be illustrated like:

```
application/x-perl; ptkat %s; nonummy; \
description="pTk applications that should not be."
```

The above entry represents a valid Content-type as specified in RFC 822, `application/x-perl`. When `metamail` encounters the `application/x-perl` Content-type, `ptkat` executes with one argument as well as the `nonummy` flag, which tells `ptkat` not to suppress anything being sent to STDOUT.

mailcap entries preceded with a # are considered comments and are skipped by `metamail`; blank lines are also ignored. Multiline entries can be written, providing they are denoted with a backslash (\). Many editors automatically insert a backslash at the end of any line that exceeds x characters.

Using the Mail::Cap Module

Mail::Cap follows the convention defined in RFC 1524, pointing to a default *mailcap* file or the one specified in the MAILCAPS environment variable. You can create a new Mail::Cap object with the default *mailcap* file as follows:

```
$mailcap = Mail::Cap->new();
```

You can also create a new Mail::Cap object with a custom, or local, *mailcap* file. For example:

```
# use the mailcap file stored in /path called local_mailcap
$my_mailcap_file = '/path/local_mailcap';
$mailcap = Mail::Cap->new($my_mailcap_file);
```

Mail::Cap has implemented four functions to handle messages being analyzed by the *mailcap* file: `view()`, `compose()`, `edit()`, and `print()`. Each function takes two arguments: a Content-type and the name of a file to be operated on per the directives in the *mailcap* file.

The `view()` function takes the two parameters (Content-type and filename) and executes the external programs specified in the second and third fields of the mailcap file; `edit()`, `compose()`, and `print()` work in a similar fashion.

Here's a simple program that takes a command-line argument and handles the data from `$ARGV[0]`:

```perl
#!/usr/local/bin/perl -w

use Mail::Cap;

$capfile = '/home/nvp/mailcap';
$mcap = Mail::Cap->new($capfile);
$mcap->view('image/jpg', $ARGV[0]);
```

This program spawns the external viewer corresponding to the `image/jpg` Content-type, `xloadimage`. It is extremely limited, however; if the file specified by `$ARGV[0]` isn't of type `image/jpg`, the program fails, and the file won't be displayed.

The mime.types File

Mail readers aren't the only ones that handle MIME data. Web servers such as Apache have the responsibility of telling Web clients what kind of data they are sending, and for that they use an external file, generally called *mime.types*. The *mime.types* file lists Content-types with the file extensions associated with that type of file, such as *.jpeg* or *.jpg* for a JPEG image, or *.html* for an HTML file. An external file is used, because it's easier to add new entries to a file than recompile the program each time an entry is added.

Like the *mailcap* file, the *mime.types* file contains a number of RFC 822-compliant Content-types, but the *mime.types* file generally doesn't contain information about external programs to be executed when a given Content-type is encountered; that decision is made on the browser's end. The *mime.types* file is used to create an association between a file's extension and Content-type. The server conveys the Content-type to the browser, and the browser takes it from there.

Here's a command-line-based program that parses a file's extension (using File::Basename), and searches a *mime.types* file for a matching extension. If an extension is found, the Content-type of the document is returned and passed to the Mail::Cap `view()` function so the document can be viewed correctly.

```perl
#!/usr/local/bin/perl -w

use File::Basename; # for the file's extension
use Getopt::Long; # for the command-line arguments
use Mail::Cap; # to parse the mailcap file
```

```
# you're not leaving this table until you've eaten all of your peas
use strict;

# remember, we're using strict
my($infile, $capfile, $file_ext, $mimetype, $mailcap);

# program must be executed like: programname -file inputfile
# if not, output a usage message
GetOptions('file=s', \$infile);
$infile or usage();

# specific capfile.  without declaring this, and creating an
# object like: $mailcap = new Mail::Cap, Mail::Cap will expect
# that you have an existing mailcap file (in /etc/mailcap or such),
# or have defined an environment variable MAILCAPS
$capfile = 'mailcap';

# From File::Basename, grab the extension of the file (field 2).
# This extension will be passed to lookup_type-by_extension, which
# returns a Content-type if the extension matches an entry in the
# mime.types file
($file_ext) = (fileparse($infile, '\..*'))[2];
$mailcap = Mail::Cap->new($capfile);
$mimetype = lookup_type_by_extension($file_ext);
$mailcap->view($mimetype, $infile);

sub lookup_type_by_extension {
    my($ext) = @_;
    my($ctype, @ftype, @found);
    my($m_types) = 'mime.types';

    open(TFILE, $m_types) or die("error opening $m_types: $!");
    while(<TFILE>) {
        # remove newlines
        chop;

        # get the content-type and extensions (file types) of
        # mime.types entries by splitting each line of the file
        # on the tab character
        ($ctype, @ftype) = split(/\t/, $_, 2);

        # check to see if extension appears in @ftype array
        # yes Virginia, I've been reading perlfaq4  :-)
        my %found = ();
        for(@ftype) { $found{$_} = 1; }

        # if extension exists, there will be an element in @found,
        # so scalar(@found) will be greater than zero. Return the
        # content-type of the mime.types entry
        return $ctype if $found{$ext};
    }
    close(TFILE);

}
sub usage {
```

```
print("Usage: $0 -file <filename>\n");
exit(0); # failure
    }
```

The MIME Modules

This section introduces you to the creation of, mailing, parsing, reading, and decoding multipart MIME messages using the MIME modules. We'll cover:

* MIME:Base64, the heart of the MIME modules, which handles encoding and decoding MIME data

* MIME::Lite, a simple yet powerful module for creating simple MIME attachments

* MIME::Entity, a more robust module for creating MIME attachments

* MIME::Parser, which can parse MIME messages

Encoding and Decoding with MIME::Base64

As described previously, MIME makes it possible to send non-ASCII files via email. The way it performs this magic is via base64 encoding, which is then packed into a maximum of 76-character lines, an appropriate length for email. At the heart of the MIME modules is MIME::Base64, which implements the **encode()** and **decode()** methods that handle streams of information to be base64-encoded or -decoded.

Here's what the base64 algorithm does:

1. Reads data into a variable (in this case, we're using a scalar, $_) and defines an end-of-line character. We'll need to add this to the 76th character of each encoded line.

   ```
   $end_of_line = "\n" unless defined $end_of_line;
   ```

2. Iterates through $_ and encodes lines using **substr()** and **pack()** with the u attribute to uuencode the lines, appending each line to a scalar, **$res**, then chopping the last character from each line.

   ```
   while ($_[0] =~ /(.{1,45})/gs) {
       $encoded .= substr(pack('u', $1), 1);
       chop($res);
   }
   ```

3. After uuencoding all the data, transforms certain characters using **tr///** to comply with the MIME specification. Also adjusts the padding of each line. The **tr** and padding statements represent the actual base64-encoded string.

   ```
   # for 'smart' base64 'uu'encoding
   $encoded =~ tr|` -_|AA-Za-z0-9+/|;
   ```

```
# fix padding at the end
my $padding = (3 - length($_[0]) % 3) % 3;
$encoded =~ s/.{$padding}$/'=' x $padding/e if $padding;
```

4. Now, using a regular expression, breaks the string into lines containing no more than 76 characters.

```
if (length $end_of_line) {
    $encoded =~ s/(.{1,76})/$1$end_of_line/g;
}
```

5. Finally, returns the base64-encoded string.

```
$encoded
```

What results is a file that looks like gibberish when not viewed with software capable of parsing base64-encoded content. MIME and the base64 encoding scheme are an ingenious way of transmitting multiple segments of mixed data between individuals who are using software capable of decoding these messages.

Here's an example using MIME::Base64 that encodes a clear text string.

```
#!/usr/local/bin/perl -w

### Script: test.b64

use MIME::Base64 ();

        ### clear text string
$to_encode = "There once was the good Duke of Earl,\n".
            "who used to sit home and hack Perl.";

        ### output the clear text string
print("Clear String: \n". $to_encode ."\n");

        ### Now, encode the clear text string, $to_encode
$encoded = MIME::Base64::encode($to_encode);

        ### Let's output the encoded string
print("\nEncoded: \n$encoded\n");

        ### decode the clear text string
$decoded = MIME::Base64::decode($encoded);

        ### If all has gone okay, we're right back to where
        ### we started. Output the decoded string.
print("\nDecoded: \n".
            $decoded
            ."\n");
```

Naturally, base64-encoded information can also be decoded from an input file. Here's an example that does just that.

```
#!/usr/local/bin/perl -w

### Script name: test3.b64
```

```
use MIME::Base64 ();

$input = 'output.mime'; ### input file
$output_file = 'from_mime.gif'; ### output file

print("Base64-encoded file: $input\n");
print("Output image: $output_file\n");

open(INPUT, "$input") or die("Input file $input error: $!");
open(OUTPUT, ">$output_file") or die("Output file $output_file error: $!");

        ### Again, DON'T chop() lines from the input file. This will
        ### break the base64-encoding scheme for the input file and
        ### your output file will get corrupted!
while($line = <INPUT>) {
    $decoded = MIME::Base64::decode($line); ### output decoded line
    print OUTPUT $decoded;

}

close(OUTPUT);
close(INPUT);
```

Handling Multipart Mixed Messages

Now that you've been introduced to how information is base64-encoded, you might wonder why we've referred to MIME-encoded messages as multipart or mixed messages. The answer is that each document has a format or type that is considered when sending multipart messages. For example, you might send someone an electronic mail message containing ASCII text and a picture of yourself in GIF format. Since the mail message contains more than one type of content, it's referred to as containing multipart or multipart/mixed content.

When you add content to a multipart message, you're asking your mail program to map a Content-type to the extension of the filename you've included. If your mail program can't determine the Content-type of one of the files you've attached, most programs will use a default Content-type.

So, how's an ordinary mail message different from a multipart mail message?

Normal mail headers contain the following information: From, Date, Subject, and To. If I were to send myself a plaintext (nonencoded) mail message, with the subject "Here's looking at you, Nate," the headers would look like:

```
From nvp Wed Mar  5 20:34:43 1997
Received: (from nvp@localhost) by mail.somename.com (8.7.5/8.7.3) id
UAA00505 for nvp; Wed, 5 Mar 1997 20:34:42 -0500 (EST)
Date: Wed, 5 Mar 1997 20:34:42 -0500 (EST)
From: "Nathan V. Patwardhan" <nvp>
Message-Id: <199703060134.UAA00505@mail.somename.com>
To: nvp
```

```
Subject: Here's looking at you, Nate
Status: RO
```

Multipart messages differentiate between content by using boundaries or dashed
lines and character markers, which represent the type of content appearing
between the boundaries. According to the RFC documents that deal with MIME
messages, electronic mail messages that contain multiple types of content are
bound like the following:

1. First, send a MIME header that announces our version of MIME.

   ```
   MIME-Version: 1.0
   ```

2. Next, send the Content-type and boundary for the document. Since our mail
   message will contain several different types of content, we'll use the multipart/
   mixed Content-type and define a boundary that will separate all the different
   parts we'll attaching to our message. The RFC documents state that a
   message's boundary must be preceded by two dashes for each of the
   message's boundaries, and that the message's ending boundary must also
   contain two trailing dashes, so we'll start with the boundary shown below.

   ```
   Content-Type: multipart/mixed; boundary = "--someboundaryhere"
   ```

3. Now, start adding content to our multipart message, which follows a line of
   text that reads like the following:

   ```
   This is a multipart message in MIME format.
   ```

4. Each section of content that appears in a multipart message is denoted by the
   boundary shown above and formatted with the Content-Type, filename,
   Content-Transfer-Encoding, and Content-Disposition of the attachment included
   in the section.

   ```
   --someboundaryhere
   Content-Type: format/type; name="filenamehere"
   Content-Transfer-Encoding: base64
   Content-Disposition: inline; filename="filenamehere"
   ```

5. Finally, we'll end the multipart message by sending an ending boundary
   denoted by the two trailing slashes described in the RFC.

   ```
   --someboundaryhere--
   ```

Here's some code that assembles a multipart message, including boundaries.
Although its message assembly routine isn't very robust, you'll get an idea of how
to use the MIME modules to construct multipart mail messages.

```
#!/usr/local/bin/perl -w

# we'll need this to check filenames
use File::Basename;
# needed for Base64 encoding
use MIME::Base64;

# the mail program we'll be using for sending
$mailprog = '/usr/lib/sendmail';
```

```perl
# the subject of our mail message
$subject = 'This is a test message in MIME format';

# who'll be receiving our mail message
$recip = 'nvp@ora.com';

# okay, let's generate a boundary for each section
# of the multipart mail message
$bndry = encode_boundary($subject);

open(MAILER, "|".$mailprog." -t ".$recip)
    or die("error opening $mailprog: $!");
print MAILER "To: $recip\n";
print MAILER "X-Mailer: $0/1.0\n";
print MAILER "MIME-Version: 1.0\n";
print MAILER "Content-Type: multipart/mixed;".
         "boundary=\"".$bndry."\"\n\n";
print MAILER "This is a multi-part message in MIME format.\n";

# now, let's do something with each @ARGV member if it's a file
# other entries will be treated as body text in the message
for(@ARGV) {
    # if it's a file, let's encode the contents and
    # send them to the mailer
    if(-e $_) {
        undef $/;
        open(IN, $_) or die("no: $!"); $enc = <IN>; close(IN);
        $encoded = MIME::Base64::encode($enc);
        print $encoded."\n";
        print MAILER<<TYPE;
$bndry
Content-Type: application/octet-stream; name="$_"
Content-Transfer-Encoding: base64
Content-Disposition: inline; filename="$_"

$encoded
TYPE
    } else {
# otherwise, we'll send the contents to
# the mailer as-is
print MAILER<<TEXT;
$bndry
Content-Type: text/plain; charset=us-ascii
Content-Transfer-Encoding: 7bit

$_
TEXT
    }
}

# okay, we're done sending the parts.
# let's send the ending boundary
print MAILER $bndry.'--'."\n\n";
close(MAILER);
```

```
# subroutine to encode a boundary. There are *much* better ways
# to do this, but this subroutine is offered only for illustration
sub encode_boundary {
    my $boundary = shift;
    $boundary =~ s/(\s+)//g;
    $boundary = '------------'.substr(pack('u', $boundary), 0, 24);
    return $boundary;
}


# ok, if the entity name has an extension, we'll attach it as a file
# if it doesn't have an extension, we'll attach it as-is
sub do_part {
    my $part = shift;
    my($ext) = fileparse($part);

    unless(defined($ext)) {
        return undef;
    } else {
        return $ext;
    }
}
```

Although functional, the above example is lengthy and painful in the context of writing code from scratch versus using Perl modules. Thankfully, there are a number of modules that simplify the process of sending mail messages with attachments.

Create Simple Attachments with MIME::Lite

Since the essence of this book has been to write applications with Perl modules instead of reinventing the wheel, the rest of this chapter focuses on some interesting uses of the MIME modules to generate and parse multipart messages. We'll start from the ground up, with MIME::Lite, developed by *eryq@enteract.com.*

Let's start with MIME::Lite because of the lightweight nature of this module and straightforward API details that make it easy to get started writing applications with MIME::Lite. In fact, you can send email with an attachment using MIME::Lite in three steps:

1. Use this module.

   ```
   use MIME::Lite;
   ```

2. Create a MIME::Lite object and pass it the necessary header information so that the file(s) can be included.

   ```
   $object = MIME::Lite->new(
       From    =>'nvp@somemail.com',
       To      =>'recipient@theirdomain.com',
       Cc      =>'do you want to copy anyone?',
       Subject =>'What\'s your favorite subject',
       Type    =>'mime type here',
   ```

```
    Encoding =>'encoding type here - base64 for binaries',
    Path     =>'path and name of file here');
```

3. Send the message. You can represent the message as a string with **as_ string** and send **$show_string** to STDOUT:

```
$show_string = $object->as_string;
print $show_string."\n";
```

Or, send the message through a filehandle:

```
$object->print(\*SENDMAIL);
```

Assuming you're on a UNIX system, you can send the message directly to **sendmail** without using a filehandle:

```
$object->send;
```

As you noticed from the example above, it's not difficult to send an email message containing one attachment with MIME::Lite. But what about multipart messages?

MIME::Lite uses the **attach()** method to add parts to a multipart message. Since you aren't able to add multiple parts to the MIME::Lite constructor, like so,

```
# WRONG! - DON'T DO THIS

$message = MIME::Lite->new(
    From     => 'nvp@somemailhost.com',
    To       => 'recipient@someotherhost.com',
    Subject  => 'Stop hitting me!',
    Type     => 'multipart/mixed',
    Type     => 'image/gif',
    Encoding => 'base64',
    Path     => 'some_useless_animated_and_blinking.gif',
    Type     => 'image/jpeg',
    Encoding => 'base64',
    Path     => 'another_senseless.jpg');
```

you must add a multipart/mixed type to the constructor, then add each part with the **attach()** method. For example, you can create a multipart message with an attached GIF, JPEG, and body text with the following steps.

1. First, tell MIME::Lite that it's going to be adding parts to a message by setting the Content-type to multipart/mixed.

```
$message = MIME::Lite->new(
    From     => 'nvp@somemailhost.com',
    To       => 'recipient@sybil-has-multiple-parts-too.com',
    Subject  => 'GIF and JPEG for you!',
    Type     => 'multipart/mixed');
```

2. Now, use **attach** to add the first attachment to the mail message, a GIF.

```
attach $message
    Type     => 'image/gif',
```

```
Path    => '/the/path/less/traveled',
Filename => 'some_gif_to_add.gif';
```

3. Next, use **attach** to add another attachment to the mail message, a JPEG.

```
attach $message
    Type     =>'image/jpeg',
    Path     =>'/the/path/slightly/less/traveled',
    Filename =>'some_jpeg_to_add.jpg';
```

4. After you've finished adding parts to the message, send the contents of the message to STDOUT. This is helpful if you want to debug the contents of your message before sending it to someone. For example, it would be embarrassing to accidentally send something bawdy to a person who didn't appreciate bawdy content.

```
$check_message_for_smut = $msg->as_string;
print $check_message_for_smut."\n";
```

5. Finally, after you've ensured that your message is syntactically and "morally" correct, you can send it. Since you're probably running a UNIX flavor that supports the **send()** method, we'll use that:

```
$message->send;
```

Other MIME::Lite methods that come in handy when debugging email messages are **header_as_string()** and **body_as_string()**. Like their method names indicate, **header_as_string()** outputs the header of an email message created with MIME::Lite, and **body_as_string()** outputs the body of an email message created with MIME::Lite. Both are used like **as_string()**:

```
# Show us your body
$body_not_bawdy = $message->body_as_string;
print $body_not_bawdy."\n";

# Show us your header
$header_how_are_you = $message->header_as_string;
print $header_how_are_you."\n";
```

Instead of using **as_string()**, **body_as_string()**, or **header_as_string()**, you can use **print(FILEHANDLE)**, **print_body(FILEHANDLE)**, or **print_header(FILEHANDLE)**. For example, if you wanted to output the contents of an email message to a file before sending the email, you could do the following:

```
$outfile = '/path/output_file_name';
open(OUTFILE, ">".$outfile)
    or die("output file $outfile error: $!");
$message->print(\*OUTFILE);
close(OUTFILE);
```

Header Hacking with MIME::Lite

Since you might choose to use MIME::Lite as part of an email application you're developing, you'll want the capability to add and remove items from the headers of messages you'll be sending. Let's review the contents of the object, $message, we've been using for the examples in this section; $message contains:

```
$message = MIME::Lite->new(
    From    => 'nvp@somemailhost.com',
    To      => 'recipient@sybil-has-multiple-parts-too.com',
    Subject => 'GIF and JPEG for you!',
    Type    => 'multipart/mixed');
```

Let's say you realized you wanted to CC this message to other users, but you forgot to do so when you initialized $message. MIME::Lite's add() method allows you to add/modify members of the message hash you initialized when you created the object, $message. The add() method works like this:

```
$object->add(Header-Type => 'value');
```

To add a CC header (for multiple recipients) to $message, type:

```
$message->add(CC => 'user@host1.com, user@host2.com');
```

Bear in mind that hashes use a name/value pair that assigns one value to one name unless you're using hashes of hashes. This means you must be careful with the add() method, as add()ing a header that already exists means you'll over-write the old value with the new. You might opt to use the replace() method instead, where:

```
$object->replace(Header-Type => 'new-header-value');
```

As you might have noticed, there are limitations to what you can do with MIME::Lite (it's light and fluffy, after all). MIME::Lite doesn't handle reading from filehandles, nor can it efficiently parse members of the message headers hash that was populated when you created a new MIME::Lite object.

The remainder of this chapter discusses the modules distributed with the MIME-tools package. The MIME-tools package was also written by Eryq (*eryq@enteract.com*), and features a MIME header parser and multipart message generator similar to that in MIME::Lite. You'll want to use the MIME-tools package for any application you'll write that needs to both parse and create multipart MIME messages as well as manipulate mail header fields and their respective values.

More Robust Attachments with MIME::Entity

The MIME::Entity module works much like MIME::Lite. When you create a new MIME::Entity object, you're creating a hash of header/value pairs as you did in

MIME::Lite. Instead of using **new** for creating a new object, MIME::Entity uses the **build** method that works in a similar fashion.

Remember the **$message** object we used in the MIME::Lite examples? Let's re-write it so it can be used with MIME::Entity.

1. First, you'll notice that **new** has been replaced with **build**. Since we'll be building a multipart message, we'll need the **build** method to get us started. You'll also notice that the message's type (multipart/mixed) doesn't appear as a named parameter like From, To, Subject, and Type. If you don't create your **$message** object properly, you'll get an error message that looks something like the following.

   ```
   can't build entity: no body, and not multipart! at
   /usr/local/lib/perl5/site_perl/MIME/Entity.pm line xxx.
   ```

   Your MIME::Entity constructor should look like this:

   ```
   my $message = MIME::Entity->build(
       Type      =>"multipart/mixed",
       -From     => 'nvp@somemailhost.com',
       -To       => 'recipient@parts-are-parts.com',
       -Subject  => 'GIF and JPEG for you!',
       -Type     => 'multipart/mixed');
   ```

2. Now it's time to attach content to the message. You'll be using the **attach** method as you did with MIME::Lite.

   ```
   attach $message
       Path => '/path/to/content',
       Type => 'whatever/whatever',
       Encoding => 'base64';
   ```

   For example, you could attach a GIF to your message with:

   ```
   attach $message
       Path => '/home/nvp/some_nutty_image.gif',
       Type => 'image/gif',
       Encoding => 'base64';
   ```

3. After you've added the content you wanted, you can send the mail message. Unlike MIME::Lite, MIME::Entity doesn't implement a **send** method, so you'll need to open an external mail program to send your mail. The **print** method takes a filehandle as an argument, so you can open a pipe to your mail program in a filehandle and print the contents of the MIME message using the **print** method.

   ```
   open(MAILER, "|mailprogram params")
       or die("mailer error: $!");
   $message->print(\*MAILER);
   close(MAILER);
   ```

4. Let's put it all together in this example.

```perl
#!/usr/local/bin/perl -w

use MIME::Entity;

# the mail program of choice
$mailprog = '/usr/lib/sendmail';

# who the mail is from, to, and the subject of this message
$from = 'wwwmailer@mimetest.com';
$to = 'nvp@mail.somename.com';
$subject = 'Looks like a runner!';

# files to attach
$text_attach = '/home/nvp/.cshrc';
$img_attach = '/home/nvp/Perl/PRK/MIME/scripts/mygif.gif';

# Text to place at the end of the message (after the other attachments)
$message = 'This is the end of the message.';

# Create the object, and set up the mail headers:
$message = MIME::Entity->build(
    Type      =>"multipart/mixed",
    -From     => "$from",
    -To       => "$to",
    -Subject  => "$subject");

# Attachment #1: a simple text document:
attach $message  Path=>"$text_attach";

# Attachment #2: a GIF file:
attach $message  Path          => "$img_attach",
    Type          => "image/gif",
    Encoding      => "base64";

# Attachment #3: some literal text:
attach $message  Data=>$message;

# Send it!
open(MAIL, "|$mailprog -t $to")
    or die("mail open $mailprog error: $!");
$message->print(\*MAIL);
close(MAIL);
```

Parsing MIME Messages with MIME::Parser

If you don't have a news or mail reader that supports MIME, you can save the MIME-encoded message as is and use MIME::Parser. With MIME::Parser, you create a new MIME::Parser object, a directory where both extracted content and prefixes for the extracted content are deposited. Then you tell MIME::Parser to read from a filehandle and handle the information accordingly. Let's examine the MIME::Parser's methods you'll need to parse multipart messages:

1. The **new()** method, the constructor, is needed to create a MIME::Parser object.

   ```
   $object = new MIME::Parser;
   ```

2. Next, the **output_dir()** method tells MIME::Parser where you'll be depositing the entities you've parsed from the multipart message.

   ```
   $output_to_dir = '/path/to/put/files';
   $object->output_dir($output_to_dir);
   ```

3. Now, use the **output_prefix()** method that tells MIME::Parser to append a certain prefix to the entities it extracts from the multipart message. If you choose not to add a prefix to the output files, the filenames default to the names listed in the boundary sections of the multipart message.

   ```
   $default_prefix = 'entity_oh_my_goodness';
   $object->output_prefix($default_prefix);
   ```

4. You'll need to read an input file containing the multipart message to be parsed. MIME::Parser's **read()** method reads from a filehandle and assigns the data to a scalar.

   ```
   open(INPUT, $input)
       or die("Input $input error: $!");
   my $entity = $object->read(\*INPUT)
       or die "couldn't parse MIME stream";
   close(INPUT);
   ```

5. When you're ready to parse and output entities from the file, you'll need the **output_to_core()** method, which outputs the entities of a MIME message to the filesystem.

   ```
   $object->output_to_core;
   ```

MIME::Parser can run silently. That is, you don't have to read what MIME::Parser tells you has been decoded. Although you should use any and all capabilities to debug your program's output, you don't have to use MIME::Parser's **dump_skeleton()** method that outputs something similar to:

```
Content-type: multipart/mixed
Body-file: NONE
Subject: Mail message with MIME attachment.
Num-parts: 2
--
    Content-type: text/plain
    Body-file: /tmp/get_mime.pl-12113-1.doc
    --
    Content-type: image/gif
    Body-file: /tmp/tiffany.gif
    --
```

Here's an example that decodes a multipart/mixed message containing a GIF and some text:

```perl
#!/usr/local/bin/perl -w

# for our MIME parsing needs
use MIME::Parser;

# for our filename/path parsing needs
use File::Basename;

# please use me - i like it!
use strict;

# where to put the decoded parts
my $output_path = '/tmp';

# derive the base filenames of extracted parts from
# the name of the script. uses basename method of
# File::Basename.yippee.
my ($parsed) = (basename($0))[0];

# our input file, a multipart message
my $input_file = '/tmp/mime.head';

my $parser = MIME::Parser->new();

# output directory for parsed files
$parser->output_dir($output_path);

# Basenames for parsed files
$parser->output_prefix($parsed);

# KEY PART: Now, write the entities (parsed from boundaries)
# to the filesystem
$parser->output_to_core();

# Parse the input file: (which can be @ARGV if you want it to be!)
open(INPUT, "$input_file") or die("Input error: $!");
my $entity = $parser->read(\*INPUT)
    or die "couldn't parse MIME stream";
close(INPUT);

# Tell us about the MIME entities!  You can suppress
# this if you don't want output for the sake of debugging
$entity->dump_skeleton;         # for debugging
```

5

Date and Time

I need to find a bunch of dates fast!

> I'm leaving Thursday and returning on Tuesday in two weeks. I need to pay a bill on the first Friday in August, and the final draft of my book is due five days before September 23rd. What day will I arrive home and will my book be finished?

We're sorry that you might have had a flashback to the scholastic aptitude tests you took throughout your academic career. Thankfully the problem is easily solved with Perl's `Date` modules, which make it simple to handle various forms of dates numerically. The `Date` modules enable you to evaluate and calculate phrases like "Tuesday in two weeks," or "five days before September 23rd" without having to write code that parses the dates for you.

Getting the Date and Time

Although many Perl programmers have been accustomed to obtaining the date and time by capturing the output of the UNIX `date` command using backticks, this method is unnecessary because it spawns an extra process, not to mention the dangers of using backticks to call external programs. Perl's `localtime()` function works like the UNIX `date` command as shown in this program:

```
#!/usr/local/bin/perl -w

$date = localtime;
print $date."\n";
```

which outputs:

```
Sun Jun 8 11:44:00 1997
```

Let's look at what `localtime()` does. This function actually accepts an expression of time in number of seconds since January 1, 1970 (what we commonly refer to as "the Epoch") and returns time in a list or scalar context. For example:

```
#!/usr/local/bin/perl -w
$date = localtime(860000000);
print $date."\n";
```

returns in a scalar context:

```
Wed Apr 2 11:53:20 1997
```

The `localtime()` function takes the number of nonleap seconds since the Epoch as an argument, using the current value of the `time()` function when there is no argument. The following code shows you the current value of `time()`:

```
#!/usr/local/bin/perl -w
$seconds_since_epoch = time;
print $seconds_since_epoch."\n";
```

When I ran it, this program output:

```
868204759
```

The `localtime()` function may be represented in a list context:

```
($sec,$min,$hour,$mday,$mon,$year,$wday,$yday,$isdst) = localtime(time);
```

The elements returned in list context are:

$sec	Seconds
$min	Minutes
$hour	Hour
$mday	Day of the month
$mon	Month number, starting with 0 (Jan = 0, Aug = 7)
$year	Year with 1900 subtracted from it (2002 = 102)
$wday	Day of the week
$yday	Day of the year
$isdst	Is it Daylight Savings Time?

It's important to remember that $mon has the range 0 through 11, and $year has 1900 subtracted from it. Also, by adding 1900 to $year, you're able to output years past 1999. For example:

```
#!/usr/local/bin/perl -w

$mon = (localtime)[4]; # Get the 5th element of the localtime array
```

```
$year = (localtime)[5]; # Get the 6th element of the localtime array

print $mon." ".$year."\n";

$mon++; # Increment the month by 1
$year = $year + 1900; # Add 1900 to the year

print "$mon $year";
```

outputs:

```
5 97 6 1997
```

Getting the Time From a Remote System with Net::Time

Sometimes we need to get the time from a remote system. For example, we might want to check that the times on two systems are synchronized. Net::Time uses two protocols to get the time from remote UNIX systems: `time` (defined by RFC 868: Time Protocol) and `daytime` (RFC 867: Daytime Protocol). `time` returns a machine-readable time (in seconds since midnight on January 1, 1970), and `daytime` returns a human-readable time string. Both subroutines take three arguments: the target hostname, the protocol (TCP or UDP), and a timeout value. The target hostname defaults to localhost. These simple programs illustrate how to use the Net::Time module:

```
#!/usr/local/bin/perl -w

use Net::Time qw(inet_time);

print inet_time() . "\n";
print inet_time('some-random.host.com') . "\n";
print inet_time('localhost', 'tcp') . "\n";
print inet_time('localhost', 'udp') . "\n";
```

The output of `inet_time()` is the time expressed as number of seconds since January 1, 1970:

```
865785783
865785448
865785783
865785783
```

`inet_daytime()` does the same as `inet_time()`, except it provides the date in a human-readable form. For example:

```
#!/usr/local/bin/perl -w

use Net::Time qw(inet_daytime);

print inet_daytime()."\n";
print inet_daytime('some-random-host.com')."\n";
```

```
print inet_daytime('another-random-host.com')."\n";
```

outputs:

```
Mon Jun 23 08:49:45 1997
Mon Jun 23 08:43:58 1997
Mon Jun 23 08:43:42 1997
```

Date and Time Representation

You're probably starting to realize that the date and time can be expressed in many potentially confusing formats. You've been introduced to human-readable formats like "Sun Nov 2" and machine-readable formats like the number of seconds since the Epoch. What is a date written in 865 million seconds good for? I mean, I have a digital wristwatch; I sold the sundial at a garage sale and the hourglass is out of sand.

Contrary to what you might think, a date written in 865 million seconds makes it easier to calculate date and time. For example, let's calculate two weeks from now by using the number of seconds since January 1, 1970, returned by `time()` and adding two weeks of seconds to it:

```
#!/usr/local/bin/perl -w

$today = localtime;

# two weeks is 14 days * 24 hours/day = 3600 seconds/hour
$two_weeks = 14 * 24 * 3600;
$two_weeks_from_now = localtime(time * $two_weeks));

# Now, tell the contestants what they've won - a date on us!
print "Today is: ".$today.".\n";
print "Two weeks from now is: ".$two_weeks_from_now.".\n";
```

This program outputs:

```
Today is: Sun Jul 6 14:03:36 1997.
Two weeks from now is: Sun Jul 30 14:03:36 1997.
```

Standard Representations of Date and Time

There are standard ways to express the date and time. For example, the International Standard, ISO 8601 Date/Time Representations, specifies the numeric representation of date and time. The international standard date notation is:

```
YYYY-MM-DD
```

where YYYY is the year in the usual Gregorian calendar, MM is the month of the year between 01 (January) and 12 (December), and DD is the day of the month between 01 and 31. For example, the seventh day of June 1997 is represented as:

```
1997-06-07
```

There are many other common representations of date including 6/7/97, 7/6/97, 97/6/7, 7.6.1997, 07-JUN-1997, and 7-June-1997. The international standard notation for the time of day is:

```
hh:mm:ss
```

where hh is the number of complete hours that have passed since midnight (00-24), mm is the number of complete minutes that have passed since the start of the hour (00-59), and ss is the number of seconds since the start of the minute (00-59). Without further designation, the time is usually expressed as local time. In order to indicate that a time is measured in Universal Time (UTC), a capital letter Z is appended to the time:

```
07:47:00Z
```

The Z stands for the *zero meridian*, which goes through Greenwich in London and is commonly used in radio communication where it is pronounced "Zulu" (the word for Z in the NATO radio alphabet). The strings:

```
+hh:mm, +hhmm, or +hh
```

can be added to the time to indicate that the used local time zone is hh hours and mm minutes ahead of UTC: for time zones west of the zero meridian, which are behind UTC, the notation:

```
-hh:mm, -hhmm, or -hh
```

is used instead. For example, Central European Time (CET) is +0100 and United States/Canadian Eastern Standard Time (EST) is -0500. It's important to note that there is no international standard to represent the local time zone and its abbreviation.

Since UNIX systems represent the time in seconds since 00:00:00 UTC, January 1, 1970, 1997-06-08 11:03:52 is represented as:

```
865782232
```

What we need are Perl modules to simplify the task of formatting the date and time in so many different formats.

Converting Dates with Date::Format

The Date::Format module converts time to ASCII strings. Date::Format's routines correspond to the C library routines strftime() and ctime(). Two routines, time2str() and strftime(), take a conversion specification (format template) and time() as an argument, and return an ASCII representation of the date. The first routine, time2str(), takes time in a scalar context. The latter, strftime(), takes time in a list context (like that of the array returned by localtime()).

Templates to format the date are built by using the conversion specifications listed in Table 5-1.

Table 5-1. Date Formats

Format	Description	Output
%%	Percent sign	%
%a	Day of the week abbreviation	Sun
%A	Day of the week	Sunday
%b	Month abbreviation	Jun
%B	Month	June
%c	ctime format	06/22/97 16:02:11
%C	ctime format	Sun Jun 22 16:02:11 EDT 1997
%d	Numeric day of the month	22
%e	DD	22
%D	MM/DD/YY	06/22/97
%h	Month abbreviation	Jun
%H	Hour, 24-hour clock, leading 0s)	16
%I	Hour, 12-hour clock, leading 0s)	04
%j	Day of the year	173
%k	Hour	16
%l	Hour, 12-hour clock	4
%m	Month number, starting with 1	06
%M	Minute, leading 0s	02
%n	Newline	
%o	Ordinal day of month: "1st", "2nd", "25th", etc.	22nd
%p	A.M. or P.M.	PM
%r	Time format: 09:05:57 P.M.	04:02:11 PM
%R	Time format: 21:05	16:02
%s	Seconds since the Epoch, UCT	867009731
%S	Seconds, leading 0s	12
%t	Tab	
%T	Time format: HH:MM:SS	16:02:12
%U	Week number, Sunday as first day of week	25
%w	Day of the week, numerically, Sunday = 0	0
%W	Week number, Monday as first day of week	24
%x	Date format: 11/19/94	06/22/97
%X	Time format: 21:05:57	16:02:12

Table 5-1. Date Formats (continued)

Format	Description	Output
%y	Year (two digits)	97
%Y	Year (four digits)	1997
%Z	Time zone in ASCII	EDT
%z	Time zone in format -/+0000	-0400

For example:

```
#!/usr/local/bin/perl -w

use Date::Format;

# define a template: %D = MM/DD/YY, %T = HH:MM:SS
$template = "%D %T\n";
print time2str($template, time)."\n";
```

outputs:

```
05/17/97 14:51:16
```

The other two subroutines provided in the Date::Format module are **ctime** and **asctime**. Both take **time** as an argument and return the time in a format of **%a %b %e %T %Y**. The first function, **ctime**, takes time in a scalar context; the latter, **asctime**, takes time in a list context.

Let's see what we can do with the Date::Format module. Print the day name and the ordinal day number:

```
#!/usr/local/bin/perl -w

use Date::Format;

# An example to print the ordinate day, like the 17th
$ordinate_day = time2str('%o', time);
$month_name = time2str('%B', time);
$day_name = time2str('%A', time);

print "Today is $day_name, the $ordinate_day of $month_name.\n";
```

prints:

```
Today is Saturday, the 17th of May.
```

Time Zones with Time::Zone

Here is a good place to discuss time zones. Time zones are commonly represented as a three-character code like GMT or PST, but there is no international standard to define these three-character time zones. They are defined by local standards, and there may be duplicate time-zone codes. The international stan-

dard that represents time zones is a one-character code (see the World Timezone
Map at *http://tycho.usno.navy.mil/tzonemap.html*). The de facto standard for time
zones on the Internet is found at *ftp://elsie.nci.nih.gov/pub/*.

In the world of Perl, the Time::Zone module provides a hash of time-zone codes
and offsets:

```
#!/usr/local/bin/perl -w
use Time::Zone;

for $num (-12 .. 12) {
    $offset = $num * 3600;
    $tz = $tz_name($offset);
    print $num*00 $tz."\n";
}
```

This program prints:

```
-1200 idlw -1100 nt -1000 cat -900 hdt -800 ydt -700 pdt -600 mdt -500 cdt -
400 edt -300 adt -200 at -100 wat 000 gmt 100 bst 200 mest 300 bt 400 zp4
500 zp5 600 zp6 700 wast 800 wadt 900 jst 1000 east 1100 eadt 1200 nzt 1300
nsdt
```

What's the offset from Greenwich Mean Time?

```
#!/usr/local/bin/perl -w

use Date::Format;

$tz = time2str('%Z', time);
$offset = time2str('%z', time);
print "The timezone is $tz ($offset from GMT)\n";
```

This prints:

```
The timezone is EDT (-400 from GMT)
```

Parsing Dates with Date::Parse

Date::Parse does the reverse of the Date::Format by providing two subroutines to
parse date strings into UNIX time values. The two routines, str2time and strptime, take a date string and optionally a time zone as arguments. The first,
str2time, returns a UNIX time value (the number of seconds since midnight
January 1, 1970), or undef if it fails. The later, strptime, returns an array of
values ($ss, $mm, $hh, $day, $month, $year, $zone) or an empty array if it fails.

Let's use str2time to calculate the number of seconds until the year 2000:

```
#!/usr/local/bin/perl -w

use Date::Parse;

$then = "Jan 1 2000 00:00";
```

```
$seconds_until_then = str2time($then);

# convert to Unix time value
$now = time;

# express as Unix time value
$seconds_left = $seconds_until_then - $now;
print "Only $seconds_left seconds until the year 2000.\n";
```

This code outputs:

```
Only 78484972 seconds until the year 2000.
```

Thankfully, we don't have to trouble ourselves with converting the date into the number of seconds since January 1, 1970 and calculating the number of seconds to some date in the future. To make our lives easier, some kind souls wrote Perl modules to do these calculations and date manipulations.

Calendar Calculations with Date::DateCalc

Date::DateCalc provides more than 20 subroutines for Gregorian Calendar date calculations in compliance with ISO/R 2015-1971 and DIN 1355 standards. For example, the `leap()` function tells you if a year is a leap year or not. The `check_date()` function lets you know if something is a valid date.

Suppose you want to calculate the weekday for July 15th with Date::DateCalc. We'll use three routines to complete this task.

* `decode_month()` takes a string, attempts to decode the month, and returns the corresponding month number. If it can't decode the month from a string, it returns 0.

* `day_name_tab()` takes a weekday number (`Sun=0`, `Mon=1` . . .) and returns the name of the weekday.

* `day_of_month()` takes a string, attempts to decode the month, and returns the corresponding month number. If it can't decode the month from the string, it returns 0.

Let's put these together in a program:

```
#!/usr/local/bin/perl -w

use Date::DateCalc qw(day_name_tab day_of_week decode_month);

$special_day = "Jul 15 1997";
($month, $day, $year) = split(/ /. $special_day);
$mm = decode_month($month);
```

```
print "$year-$mm-$day\n";

$weekday = day_of_week($year, $mm, $day);
$day_name = day_name_tab($weekday);

print "$special_day is $day_name\n";
```

The output produced is:

```
1997-7-15
Jul 15 1997 is Tuesday
```

First, take a string containing the date in U.S. format (MMM DD YYYY) and split the string into components $month, $day, $year. You'll need the numeric representation of the month, too, as an argument to the day_of_week function in order to use the decode_month function to translate the month name string into a month number. Once you have the correct date representation, pass the date as an argument to day_of_week to get a weekday number. Then pass the number to day_name_tab to convert the weekday number to a string name.

Of course, the routines can be nested to shorten the program:

```
#!/usr/local/bin/perl -w

use Date::DateCalc qw(day_name_tab day_of_week decode_month);

$special_day = "Jul 15 1997";
($month, $day, $year) = split(/ /, $special_day);

$mm = decode_month($month);
$day_name = day_name_tab(day_of_week($year, $mm, $day));

print "$special_day is $day_name\n";
```

Another task you may be asked to do is to calculate the number of days between two dates. For example, how many days are there until the year 2000?

```
#!/usr/local/bin/perl -w

use Date::Parse;
use Date::DateCalc qw(dates_difference);

$today = localtime;
($d1, $m1, $y1) = chop_date($today);
$then = "Jan 1 2000 00:00";
($d2, $m2, $y2) = chop_date($then);
$days_left = dates_difference($y1, $m1, $d1, $y2, $m2, $d2);

print "Today is $today\n";
print "There are only $days_left days left until the year 2000!\n";

sub chop_date {
    my $date = shift;
    (undef, undef, undef, $dd, $mm, $yy, undef) = strptime($date);
```

```
    $yy += 1900;
    $mm++;

    return($dd, $mm, $yy);
}
```

First, find today's date using `localtime()`. The year 2000 is represented as a
date string. To calculate the number of days between the two dates with `dates_`
`difference()`, you need to parse the dates into month, day, and year variables.
Once you parse the dates, pass the data to `dates_difference()` to get the
number of days until the year 2000.

Parse Dates with Date::Manip

Like Date::DateCalc, the Date::Manip module provides more than 20 subroutines
that simplify any common date/time manipulation. If you've ever wanted to
convert phrases like "two days before Christmas" or "New Year's Eve" into
numeric dates, then you should use Date::Manip. Also as with Date::DateCalc,
Date::Manip can compare two times and calculate time intervals, but its big advantage is its robust date parser that extracts information from almost any date format.

The subroutine `ParseDate()` takes an array or a string as arguments, parses it to
extract a date, and returns the date. Later, we'll discuss the wide range of strings
`ParseDate()` recognizes. With it, we can do things like:

```
#!/usr/local/bin/perl -w

use Date::Manip;

$today = ParseDate("today");
$tomorrow = ParseDate("tomorrow");

print "Today is $today and tomorrow is $tomorrow\n";
```

The output of this program is:

```
Today is 1997062215:18:30 and tomorrow is 1997062315:18:30
```

Blech! This format is fine for computers, but ugly for humans. By default, **Parse-**
Date() outputs the date in a format of:

```
YYYYMMDDHH:MM:SS
```

Fortunately, we can use another one of the subroutines provided with the
Date::Manip module to format the date string returned by `ParseDate()`. The
`UnixDate()` subroutine takes a date output by `ParseDate()` and formats the

output using the conversion specifications listed in Table 5-1 with the addition of those listed below in Table 5-2.

Table 5-2. More Date Formats

Format	Description	Output
%E	Ordinal day of month: "1st", "2nd", "25th", etc.	22nd
%f	Month of year	6
%F	%A, %B %e, %Y	Sunday, June 22, 1997
%g	%a, %d %b %Y %H:%M:%S %z	Sun, 22 Jun 1997 16:24:26 EDT
%i	Hour, 12-hour clock	4
%l	Date in `ls(1)` format %b $e $H:$M (if within six months) %b %e %Y	Jun 22 16:24
%P	%Y%m%d%H%M%S	1997062216:24:29
%q	%Y%m%d%H%M%S	19970622162427
%Q	%Y%m%d	19970622
%u	%a %b %e %H:%M:%S %z %Y (Same as %C)	Sun Jun 22 16:24:27 EDT 1997
%v	Short weekday abbreviation	S
%V	%m%d%H%M%y	0622162497

For example:

```
#!/usr/local/bin/perl -w

use Date::Manip;

$today = ("today");
$tomorrow = ParseDate("tomorrow");
$today = UnixDate($today, "%F");
$tomorrow= UnixDate($tomorrow, "%F");

print "Today is $today and tomorrow is $tomorrow\n";
```

Now the output looks suitable for humans:

```
Today is Sunday, June 22, 1997 and tomorrow is Monday, June 23, 1997
```

Stylistically, the program is better written:

```
#!/usr/local/bin/perl -w

use Date::Manip;

$today = UnixDate(ParseDate("today"), "%F");
$tomorrow = UnixDate(ParseDate("tomorrow"), "%F");
print "Today is $today and tomorrow is $tomorrow\n";
```

Remember what we had to do to calculate how many days left until January 1st
2000 using the Date::DateCalc module? Let's see how to do a similar calculation
using the Date::Manip module.

```
#!/usr/local/bin/perl -w

use Date::Manip;

$delta = DateCalc(ParseDate("today"), ParseDate("Jan 1st 2000"), $err);
if(! $err) { print $delta . "\n"; }
```

Another nice feature of the Date::Manip module is its ability to do date calculations based on business working days. As installed, the Date::Manip module uses
a configuration file named *.DateManip.cnf* located in your home directory or the
current directory. The location of this file (and other defaults) is defined in the
Manip.pm file in your Perl library:

```
# Location of a the global config file.
# Tilde (~) expansions are allowed.
$Date::Manip::GlobalCnf="";
$Date::Manip::IgnoreGlobalCnf="";

### Date::Manip variables set in the global config file

# Name of a personal config file and the path to search for it.
# Tilde (~) expansions are allowed.
$Date::Manip::PersonalCnf=".DateManip.cnf";
$Date::Manip::PersonalCnfPath=".:~";
```

Let's build a configuration file to specify holidays the module should know:

```
*HOLIDAY

1/1                           = New Year's Day
third Monday in Feb           = Presidents' Day
last Monday in May            = Memorial Day
7/4                           = Independence Day
1st Monday in Sep             = Labor Day
fourth Thu in Nov             = Thanksgiving
fourth Thu in Nov + 1 day     = Day after Thanksgiving
12/25                         = Christmas
12/26                         = Day after Christmas
3rd Monday in Jan             = Martin Luther King Day
```

It's easy to set up a table of holidays because the dates may be entered in any
format the **ParseDate()** subroutine can parse. Now that we have the holiday
schedule built, let's look at a program that uses the schedule:

```
#!/usr/local/bin/perl -w

use Date::Manip;

$today = UnixDate("today", "%m/%d/%y");
```

```
    print "Today is $today\n";

    $err = 0;

    $date = DateCalc("today","+ 45 days",$err);
    if (!($err)) {

      $date = UnixDate($date, "%m/%d/%y");
      print "$date is 45 days from today\n";

    }

    $err = 0;

    $bdate = DateCalc("today","+ 45 business days",$err);
    if (!($err)) {

      $bdate = UnixDate($bdate, "%m/%d/%y");
      print "$bdate is 45 business days from today";
    }
```

outputs:

```
    Today is Sunday, June 22, 1997
    08/06/97 is 45 days from today
    08/26/97 is 45 business days from today
```

Uh oh. The boss just said we have to work on July 4th. Let's modify the holiday schedule and rerun the program. The new holiday schedule is:

```
    *HOLIDAY

    1/1                         = New Year's Day
    third Monday in Feb         = Presidents' Day
    last Monday in May          = Memorial Day
    #7/4                        = Independence Day
    1st Monday in Sep           = Labor Day
    fourth Thu in Nov           = Thanksgiving
    fourth Thu in Nov + 1 day   = Day after Thanksgiving
    12/25                       = Christmas
    12/26                       = Day after Christmas
    3rd Monday in Jan           = Martin Luther King Day
```

The output of the program is now:

```
    Today is Sunday, June 22, 1997
    08/06/97 is 45 days from today
    08/25/97 is 45 business days from today
```

It's worse: now we have to work Saturdays! Instead of modifying the configuration table, just change the definition of the work week in the program by resetting the value of an internal variable called WorkWeekEnd:

```
    #!/usr/local/bin/perl -w
```

```
use Date::Manip;

Date_Init("WorkWeekEnd=06");

$today = UnixDate("today", "%m/%d/%y");
print "Today is $today";

$err = 0;

$date = DateCalc("today","+ 45 days",$err);
if (!($err)) {

  $date = UnixDate($date, "%m/%d/%y");
  print "$date is 45 days from today";
}

$err = 0;

$bdate = DateCalc("today","+ 45 business days",$err);
if (!($err)) {

  $bdate = UnixDate($bdate, "%m/%d/%y");
  print "$bdate is 45 business days from today";
}
```

Now the program outputs:

```
Today is Sunday, June 22, 1997
08/06/97 is 45 days from today
08/15/97 is 45 business days from today
```

Other internal variables that customize Date::Manip are:

PersonalCnf

Personal configuration file.

PersonalCnfPath

Path to the personal configuration file. Tilde (~) expansions may be used; for example: ~nvp.

Language

Language used to parse dates (including French, English, Swedish).

DateFormat

Setting `DateFormat` to US forces the U.S. date format (12/10 is December 10th). Setting `DateFormat` to anything else sets the more common format of 10/12.

TZ

Time zone.

FirstDay

Sets the first day of the week; by default, it's set to Sunday (day 0).

WorkWeekBeg

Sets the beginning of the work week; by default, it's set to Monday (day 1).

WorkWeekEnd

Sets the end of the work week; by default, it's set to Friday (day 5).

WorkDayBeg

Sets the beginning time of the workday.

WorkDayEnd

Sets the ending time of the workday.

6

Building Graphical Interfaces Using Perl/Tk

If you're running a UNIX workstation, you're probably using the X Window System, whose graphical interface offers virtual desktops, windows, menus, and colors. If you are writing for such an environment, you often want to create a graphical interface for your scripts. A convenient way to create these is to use the Tk extension to Perl, also known as pTk.

Tk is a graphical toolkit designed by John Ousterhout for his Tcl language. It was ported to Perl by Nick Ing-Simmons. Although Tk is primarily used on UNIX systems, it has also been ported to Microsoft Windows and is included with Sarathy Gurasamy's port of Perl.

This chapter doesn't propose to be the definitive guide to graphical interface design, nor will it delve into the nuts and bolts of Perl/Tk. There are many on-line resources that serve as comprehensive tutorials on the Tk toolkit and graphical interface design, listed at the end of this chapter.

This chapter does introduce you to Perl/Tk; demonstrate why (and when) you might use it instead of a command-line interface; and describe when you shouldn't use a graphical interface for the sake of good program design and sanity. In Chapter 14, *Examples*, we include several examples that show how a pTk interface enhances the functionality of other modules we cover in this book.

What Is Perl/Tk?

Perl/Tk shouldn't be confused with its predecessor, TkPerl, a Tk interface to Perl version 4 written by Malcolm Beattie. Perl/Tk is a graphical interface to Perl; it's a wedding of sorts between the Tk 4.0 patch-level 3 toolkit and Perl's object-oriented capabilities appearing in Versions 5.0 and after. Examples in this book are based on Tk400.202.

The Tk toolkit contains graphical primitives known as widgets. pTk supports the following primitives (which will be described as they're introduced later on in this chapter):

- Button
- Canvas
- Checkbutton
- Entry
- Frame
- Label
- Listbox
- Menu
- Menubutton
- Message
- Radiobutton
- Scale
- Scrollbar
- Text
- Toplevel

You will see examples using the following primitives in this chapter (and in this book): Button, Entry, Frame, Listbox, Scrollbar, Text, and Toplevel.

If you're already familiar with the Tcl/Tk syntax, a Tcl/Tk program implementing the traditional "Hello, World!" example contains:

```
#!/usr/local/bin/wish
button .b -text "Hello, World!" -command exit
pack .b
```

This behaves the same as a Perl program:

```
#!/usr/local/bin/perl -w
use Tk; MainWindow->new->Button(-text => "Hello, World!",
-command => sub { exit })->pack; MainLoop;
```

Both display the window shown in Figure 6-1.

When or Why Should I Use Perl/Tk?

With a maturing toolkit, and user-contributed extensions to Tk, you'll find that pTk can handle large-scale development projects as well as other toolkits.

Figure 6-1. The ubiquitous "Hello, World!"

If you're already familiar with Tcl/Tk, you'll find that pTk uses the same functions such as `pack`, `text`, `command`, and others in the context of Perl's object-oriented capabilities. Since pTk uses the same OOP interface as other Perl modules, you can easily write a pTk application that implements a GUI to an application using another Perl module, such as a GUI-based mail reader that is a front end to Net::POP3 (and Net::SMTP) or an image viewer that is a front end to Image::Magick.

Graphical interfaces tend to be well suited to programs that don't have adequate interfaces otherwise, such as image viewers, WYSIWYG word processors or drawing programs where the user is best served by seeing what the program outputs. Several pTk examples in Chapter 14 of this book deal with images and graphing, because Tk primitives and functions such as `Frame`, `Canvas`, `Photo`, and `Pixmap` can appropriately be used to show ways to use other modules.

Graphical interfaces aren't well suited for programs that perform minimal, repetitive, or batch-like functions best-suited for a command line interface. Using such a program with a graphical interface would take longer to load than it would take to execute a program (with arguments) from the command line.

Before writing any interfaces, you should size up the project by asking yourself these questions:

* Why should this program have an interface?

* How would this program (or the end user) benefit by having an interface?

* Will this program only have a graphical interface or will there be a command-line interface as well?

Many people have the tendency to attach a GUI to any program for the sake of visual appeal, which causes otherwise simple programs to become cumbersome, ridiculous, and irritating to the end user.

Consider, for example, a GUI that implements a function such as UNIX's `cat`, a program that typically takes one or two command-line arguments. From the command line, the `cat` program executes like this:

```
cat -switch filename
```

or, using Perl, a `cat`-like implementation could be:

```
perl -e 'while(<>) { print $_; }' <filename>
```

but as a GUI, the `cat` program is executed like Figure 6-2.

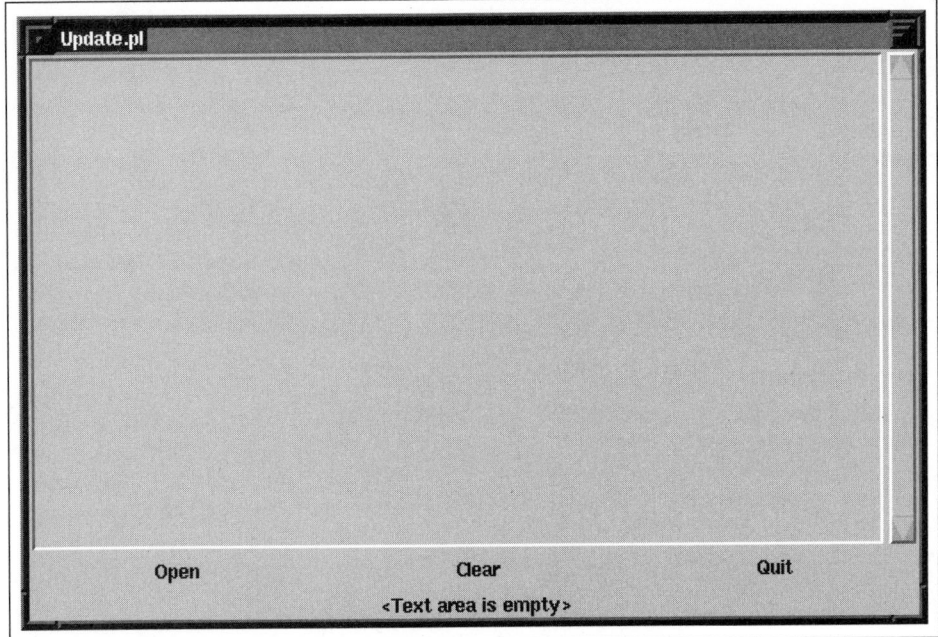

Figure 6-2. ptkat: a Tk version of the cat command

Although the above example is a bit of an exaggeration, many people write need-less interfaces for unsophisticated tasks that don't need them.

Introduction to Perl/Tk Primitives

Returning to our "Hello, World" example:

```
#!/usr/local/bin/perl -w
use strict;
use Tk;

MainWindow->new->Button(-text => "Hello, World!",
                        -command => sub {exit})->pack;
MainLoop;
```

Breaking this example down, after using the all-important `strict` module, the following line:

```
use Tk;
```

tells Perl that your program will use the Tk module.

After you've included the modules, you need to initialize a new **MainWindow**, the primary container your program will use. Although our example initialized a **MainWindow** object like this:

```
MainWindow->new();
```

it's necessary to assign your **MainWindow** to a scalar. In fact, future examples depend on it because you'll need to extract the return values of Tk methods and use these values when building larger interfaces:

```
$main = MainWindow->new();
```

Once you've created a **MainWindow** object, other widgets can be placed, or packed, into the **MainWindow**. In this case, we're adding a **Button** labeled "Hello, World!" to the **MainWindow**. The **Button** function's **-command** parameter tells Tk to execute the "command" when the **Button** is pressed:

```
MainWindow->new->Button(-text => "Hello, World!",
                        -command => sub {exit})->pack;
```

The preferred method is:

```
$main->Button(-text => "Hello, World!",
              -command => sub {exit})->pack;
```

Future examples will use a form like this:

```
$button_1 = $main->Button(-text => "Hello, World!",
                          -command => sub {exit});
$button_1->pack;
```

When your widget is ready to be displayed, use the **MainLoop** function:

```
# The Main Event
MainLoop;
```

The MainWindow Container

For a widget to be displayed, the minimum pTk program must include:

```
use Tk;
MainWindow->new();
MainLoop;
```

MainWindow is the primary container in which widgets and other containers are placed, and **MainLoop** tells pTk to display all widgets. In this case pTk outputs an "empty" window. See Figure 6-3.

Failure to call **MainLoop** prevents your widgets from being displayed.

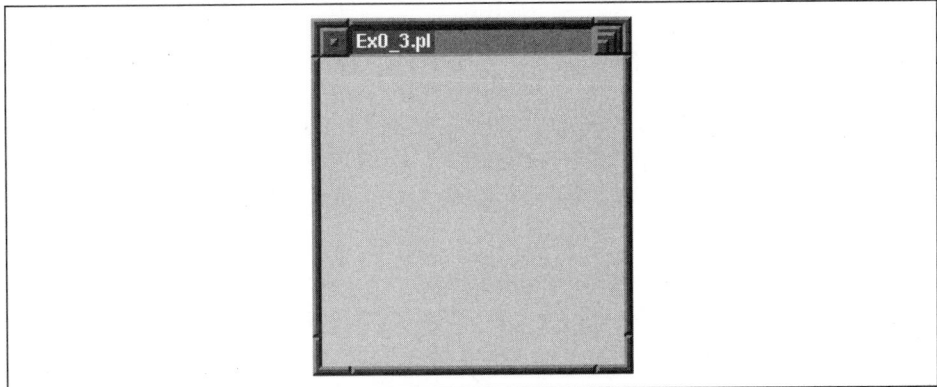

Figure 6-3. An empty window

Setting the Titlebar

By default, pTk uses the program name as the title of the application. A pTk program named `ex0_1.pl` shows `Ex0_1.pl` in the titlebar of the window. The `title()` function replaces the default application name with a title passed to `title()`. `title()` takes one argument, the title of the application, as in the following example:

```
#!/usr/local/bin/perl -w

use Tk;
use strict;

my($main);

$main = MainWindow->new();

# Title the application
$main->title("Ira the Beatmaster Schwartz");

# The Main Event
MainLoop;
```

Packing the Widget

The `pack()` function tells Tk to place a widget in a container; if a widget isn't packed, it isn't given any space on the screen and won't displayed. Going back to our "Hello, World" example, a `Button` is displayed like this:

```
$main->Button(-text => "Hello, World!",
              -command => sub {exit})->pack;
```

A `Button` isn't displayed with this:

```
$main->Button(-text => "Hello, World!",
              -command => sub {exit});
```

The `pack()` function dictates how widgets are placed in a container with the
`-side` attribute. If `pack()` hasn't been passed the `-side` attribute, widgets are
placed in a container in a north-to-south orientation by default. `pack()` tells Tk to
format the placement in relation to other widgets. Revising our example then, if a
second `Button` is added, the buttons are oriented north to south, starting with the
`Button` labeled `"Hello, World!"`:

```
#!/usr/local/bin/perl -w

use strict;
use Tk;

my($main, $button_north, $button_south);

$main = MainWindow->new();

# Add the first button (default orientation: north)
$button_north = $main->Button(-text => "Hello, World!",
                              -command => sub {exit});
$button_north->pack;

# Add the second button (default orientation: south)
$button_south = $main->Button(-text => "Goodbye, World!",
                              -command => sub {exit});
$button_south->pack;

# The Main Event
MainLoop;
```

If you want the `Buttons` packed left to right, pass the `-side` attribute to `pack()`.
So in this example, the first button is packed on the left side of the `MainWindow`,
and the second button is packed on the right side of the `MainWindow`:

```
#!/usr/local/bin/perl -w

use strict;
use Tk;

my($main, $button_left, $button_right);

$main = MainWindow->new();

# Add the first button (packed side is left)
$button_left = $main->Button(-text => "Hello, World!",
                             -command => sub {exit});
$button_left->pack(-side => 'left');

# Add the second button (packed side is right)
$button_right = $main->Button(-text => "Goodbye, World!",
                              -command => sub {exit});
```

```
$button_right->pack(-side => 'right');

# The Main Event
MainLoop;
```

In the book examples, `pack()` uses the following attributes and values:

Attribute	Value
Side	Left, right, bottom
Anchor	Any variation of n, s, e, w (north, south, east, west)
Expand	If the application is enlarged or reduced on the desktop, this attribute defines if the widgets are proportionally resized; takes **yes** or 1 values for (boolean) **true**

The Label Widget

After initializing a new `MainWindow` (object) and placing `MainLoop` at the end of your program, you can start adding primitives like `Buttons` and `Labels` to the main container. Once you've created your object, you can use it to create the widget you'll be using, like a `Label`. Each primitive's function has been written to take parameters, where each parameter represents an attribute of how the primitives are displayed. Some functions, such as `Entry()`, don't need parameters to function properly. As mentioned before, primitives must contain a function name, and they must be packed to appear in the container widget:

```
#!/usr/local/bin/perl -w

use Tk;
use strict;

my($main);

$main = MainWindow->new;

# initialize the Label widget then pack it.
$main->Label(-text => 'Testing')->pack;

# ding ding ding - the main event
MainLoop;
```

The code displays a widget like that in Figure 6-4.

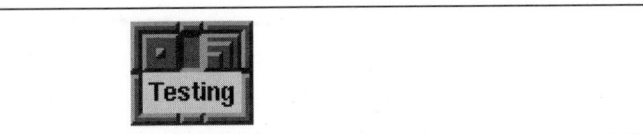

Figure 6-4. A simple label

As shown in the example above, the `Label` primitive takes a text parameter, which defines the text that appears in the `Label`. You can also use variables to represent the text, such as:

```
#!/usr/local/bin/perl -w

use Tk;
use strict;

my($label_val, $main);

$label_val = "Testing";
$main = MainWindow->new();
$main->Label(-text => $label_val)->pack;

# the main event
MainLoop;
```

Widget defaults don't have to be hardcoded. You can use the `Getopt` modules to extract values from the command line and input these to the widget. The following example retrieves the value of the `-labeltext` switch from the command line, and places this value into the `Label`:

```
#!/usr/local/bin/perl -w

use Tk;
use Getopt::Long;
use strict;

my($ltext);

# -labeltext is the switch to use
# $ltext is the value extracted from -labeltext
GetOptions('labeltext=s', \$ltext);

$main = MainWindow->new();

# Now, add the value to Label
$main->Label(-text => $ltext)->pack;

# the main event
MainLoop;
```

The Button Widget

An important pTk primitive is the `Button`, as `Button`s take a `-command` parameter for performing actions. `Button` also takes a text parameter, which can be a variable as illustrated in Figure 6-4.

`Button` is (minimally) used like this:

```
#!/usr/local/bin/perl -w

use Tk;
use strict;

my($main);

$main = MainWindow->new();
$main->Button(-text => 'Test Button')->pack;

# the main event
MainLoop;
```

which displays a `Button` in a container, but the `Button` doesn't perform any function, so the program is useless. To make the `Button` perform, use the `-command` parameter:

```
#!/usr/local/bin/perl -w

use Tk;
use strict;

my($main);

$main = MainWindow->new();
$main->Button(-text => 'Test Button',
              -command => sub {exit})->pack;

# the main event
MainLoop;
```

The `-command` attribute tells the `Button` to call (execute) the associated subroutine. In this case the function causes the program to exit; the `-command` attribute takes a subroutine value or calls an anonymous subroutine:

```
$obj->Primitive(-command => sub {exit});
```

The above calls `exit` by using an anonymous subroutine, but:

```
$obj->Primitive(-command => [\&helper]);
```

This code calls a subroutine called `helper`.

My preference is to use `helper` subroutines where possible, which allows various input types to use the same subroutine. The following example uses a `helper` subroutine called `button_helper()`:

```
#!/usr/local/bin/perl -w

use Tk;
use strict;

my($main, $in);
$main = MainWindow->new();
```

```
# Create a Button which calls button_helper
# Pass button_helper a value, 'bar'.
$main->Button(-text => 'Test Button',
              -command => [\&button_helper])->pack;

# the main event
MainLoop;

# Helper function
sub button_helper {
    print("Did you just come from a bar?\n");
}
```

See Figure 6-5 for an example of this output.

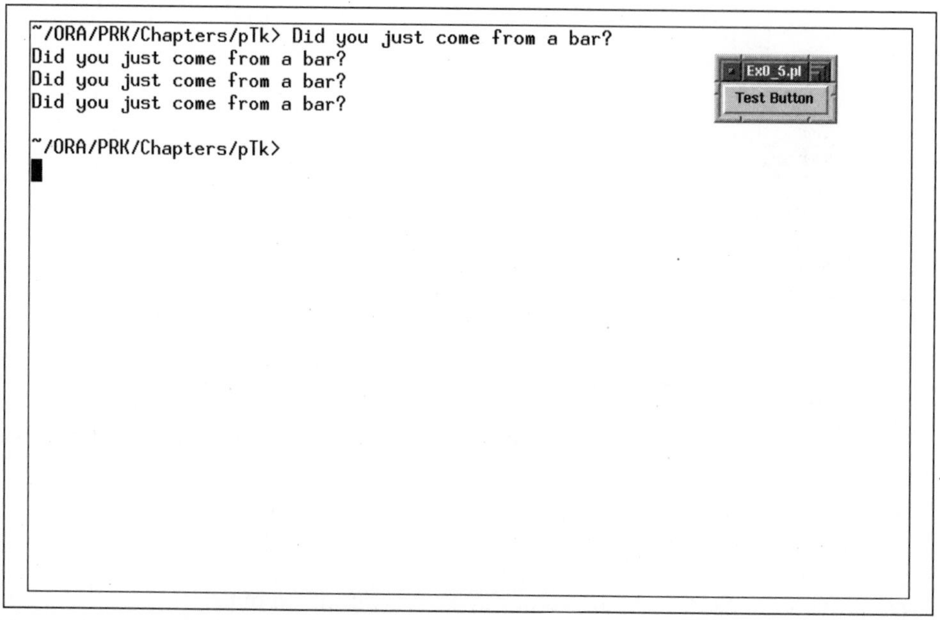

Figure 6-5. A sample button widget

The Entry Widget

The Entry method creates a single line textbox, useful for short pieces of information, where the Entry box can be initialized empty or a default value can be inserted. Entry is useful for short pieces of information like names, addresses, and phone numbers on a fill-out form.

Entry can be assigned to a scalar, as follows:

```
#!/usr/local/bin/perl -w

use Tk;
use strict;
```

```
    my($main, $ety);

    $main = MainWindow->new();

    # Get the return value from entry
    $ety = $main->Entry;
    $ety->pack;

    # the main event
    MainLoop;
```

By assigning a scalar to the return value of an **Entry**, **Entry** values can be extracted using **get()**:

```
    #!/usr/local/bin/perl -w

    use Tk;
    use strict;

    my($main, $ety);

    $main = MainWindow->new();

    $ety = $main->Entry;
    $ety->pack;

    $btn = $main->Button(-text => 'Show Entry Value');
    $btn->configure(-command => [\&get_entry_value]);
    $btn->pack;

    # the main event
    MainLoop;

    # Helper function
    sub get_entry_value {
        my $entryval = shift;
        print("You entered: ".$entryval->get."\n");
    }
```

Entry uses **-textvariable** to insert a default value into an **Entry** box. The **-textvariable** option takes a reference to a scalar as an argument. When the text inside of **$ent** changes, the value of **$default_text** changes:

```
    $default_text = 'Jack D. Ripper';

    # Now, use the reference to the scalar $default_text
    $ent = $main->Entry(-textvariable = \$default_text);
    $ent->pack;
```

The Listbox Widget

A **Listbox** is a widget that holds one entry per line. Unlike **Entry**, multiple items can be selected by clicking Button 1 of the mouse on an item. Default items can be inserted into a `Listbox`, and a `Listbox` can be automatically sized to fit data members by assigning a width and/or height of −1.

In this example, a list of items containing `owl`, `camel`, `larry`, `birdie`, and `num-num` are inserted into a `Listbox`, `$lb`. The `insert()` function takes two arguments, `end` and `$scalar`, where `$scalar` is the item to be inserted into the `Listbox`. All items are appended to the end of the `Listbox` and positioned behind the previous item that was inserted into the `Listbox`.

```perl
#!/usr/local/bin/perl -w

use Tk;
use strict;

my($main, $lb, @items);

# items to insert into the list
@items = ('owl', 'camel', 'larry', 'birdie', 'num-num');
$main = MainWindow->new();

# initialize a list which automatically resizes to fit
# the longest item in the list (in this case: 'num-num')
$lb = $main->Listbox(-width => -1, -height => -1);

# iterate through the list, and insert each item,
# $_, into the Listbox.
for(@items) { $lb->insert('end', $_); }

$lb->pack;

# the main event
MainLoop;
```

In the example above, the `Listbox` is populated as shown in Figure 6-6.

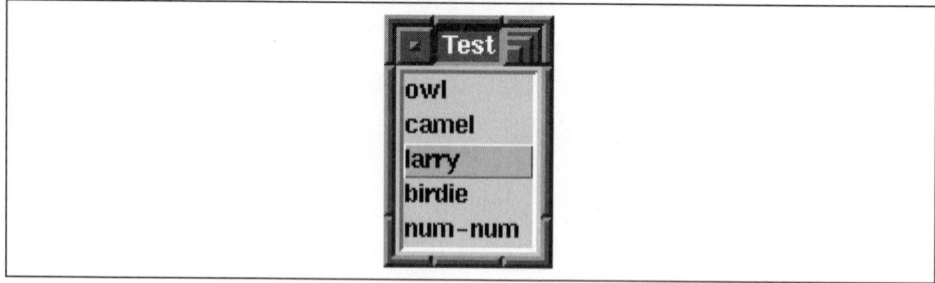

Figure 6-6. A sample listbox with automatic resizing

Without automatic resizing (i.e., removing the width and height parameters), the image would look like that in Figure 6-7.

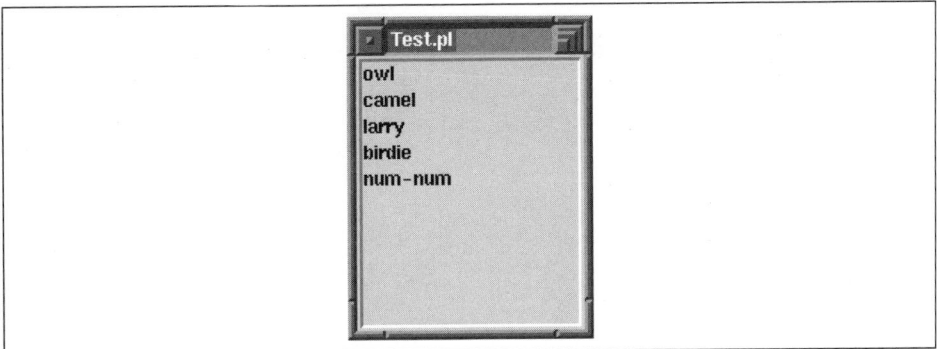

Figure 6-7. A sample listbox without automatic resizing

The Text Widget

The **Text** widget, also known as the Text area, is an editable pane that can have text inserted and new text created. From the **Text** widget, text can be copied and pasted; the **Text** widget also has a movable cursor for navigation through the text in the window. The **Scrollbar** widget is often used with the **Text** widget for better navigation of the area (see the **Scrollbar** example below).

```perl
#!/usr/local/bin/perl -w

use Tk;
use strict;

my($file, $main, $txt);

$file = '/home/nvp/.ctwmrc';
$main = MainWindow->new();

# by default, use a width of 20 characters, and
# a height of 20 characters
$txt = $main->Text(-width => 20, -height => 20);
$txt->pack;

# open a file and insert the contents of the file
# into the Text area, starting from the end.
open(IN, $file) or die("file error: $!");
while(<IN>) {
    $txt->insert('end', $_);
}
close(IN);

# the main event
MainLoop;
```

Adding Scrollbars

The `Scrollbar` aids navigation in a `Listbox` or `Text` widget; it appears on
the x and/or y sides of the widget, packed left, right, or bottom. Going back to
the `Listbox` example, we can add a scrollbar to the y axis of the right side of
the `Listbox`:

```
#!/usr/local/bin/perl -w

use Tk;
use strict;

my($main, $lb, $scroll, @items);

@items = ('owl', 'camel', 'larry', 'birdie', 'num-num');
$main = MainWindow->new();

# size the Listbox and insert items into it
$lb = $main->Listbox(-width => -1, -height => 3);
for(@items) { $lb->insert('end', $_); }

# 1. creating a new scrollbar which will appear vertically
$scroll = $main->Scrollbar(-command => [N$lb]);

# 2. setting the scrollbar to scroll vertically on the Listbox
$lb->configure(-yscrollcommand => [N$scroll]);
$lb->pack(-side => 'left');

# 3. Packing the scrollbar to the right of the Listbox (which
# is packed right)
$scroll->pack(-side => 'right', -fill => 'y');

# the main event
MainLoop;
```

The scrollbar appears like that in Figure 6-8.

Figure 6-8. A listbox with a scrollbar

Frames

As `MainWindow` is the container that holds all of the primitives you'll be packing
into your interface, `Frame` is a primitive that acts like a subcontainer and can hold
any primitives you pack into a `MainWindow`. Frames can be contained inside of

Frames, and other primitives like `Buttons`, `Labels`, etc., can be contained inside of the `Frames` that are themselves contained inside a `Frame`. In other words, `Frames` allow you to create individually controllable panels.

Referring again to our "Hello, World!" example, here's how it would be written using `Frame`. Although it's unnecessary for this example, you'll get an idea of how `Frame` is used:

```
#!/usr/local/bin/perl -w

use Tk;
use strict;

my($main, $ctnr);

$main = MainWindow->new();
$ctnr = $main->Frame;

$ctnr->Label(-text => 'Hello, world!')->pack;
$ctnr->Button(-text => 'Quit', -command => sub{exit})->pack;
$ctnr->pack;

# the main event
MainLoop;
```

When using `Frame`, you create an object from the `MainWindow` object which is, in this example, $main. The `Frame` object then calls functions like you would in the original example, except the `Frame` must be packed before executing `MainLoop` or your program won't work correctly.

You should create the largest container first; this container will hold all the subcontainers you add through the development process. For an example, see Figure 6-9.

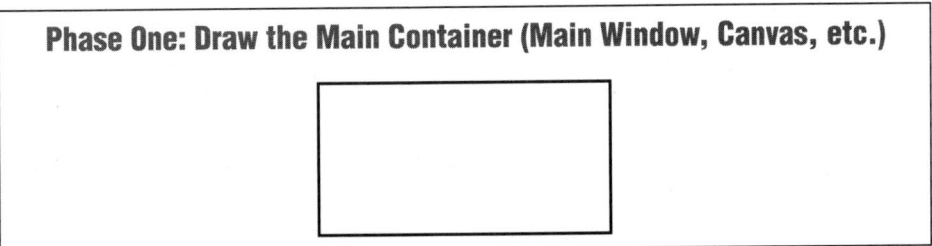

Figure 6-9. Draw the main container

This example uses the code:

```
#!/usr/local/bin/perl -w

use Tk;
use strict;
```

```
my($main, $bigkid, $left, $right, $ctr, ... etc);

$main = MainWindow->new(); # the MainWindow

$bigkid = $main->Frame; # the bigkid of all Frames
$bigkid->pack;

# the main event
MainLoop;
```

You should decide how your container will be divided into the main panels, which will also be **Frames**. Remember, **Frames** can be contained inside of **Frames**. In this case, let's use three panels, which are packed to the left of each other. For an example, see Figure 6-10.

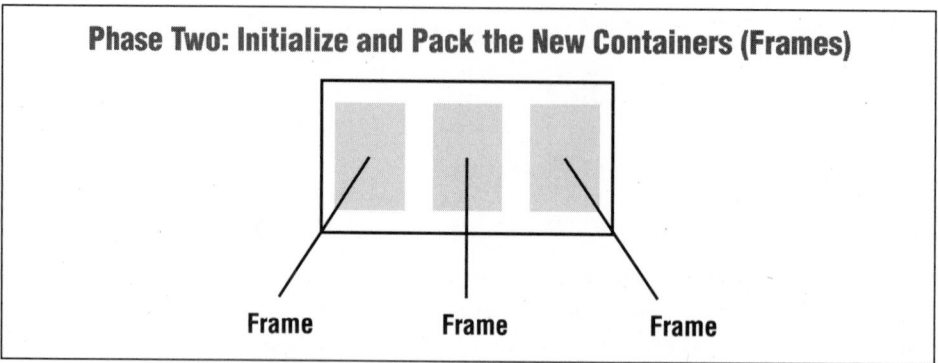

Figure 6-10. Pack the frames

```
$left = $bigkid->Frame;
$left->pack(-side => 'left');

$ctr = $bigkid->Frame;
$ctr->pack(-side => 'left');

$right = $bigkid->Frame;
$right->pack(-side => 'left');
```

The left and right panels contain a **Listbox** on the top and bottom, and a **Button** in the center. The center panel contains three buttons. You don't have to do any special packing in any of the panels because they are oriented north to south by default:

```
# let's do the left side of the container first
$left = $bigkid->Frame;
$lt = $left->Listbox();
$lt->pack;
$lm = $left->Button(-text => 'left middle');
$lm->pack;
$lb = $left->Listbox();
$lb->pack;
```

```
$left->pack(-side => 'left');

# now for the center of panel of the container
$ctr =   $bigkid->Frame;
$ct = $left->Button(-text => 'top center');
$ct->pack;
$cm = $left->Button(-text => 'middle center');
$cm->pack;
$cb = $left->Button(-text => 'bottom center');
$ctr->pack(-side => 'left');

# now for the right side of the container
$right =   $bigkid->Frame;
$rt = $left->Listbox();
$rt->pack;
$rm = $left->Button(-text => 'right middle');
$rm->pack;
$rb = $left->Listbox();
$right->pack(-side => 'left');
```

This code produces a screen like that in Figure 6-11.

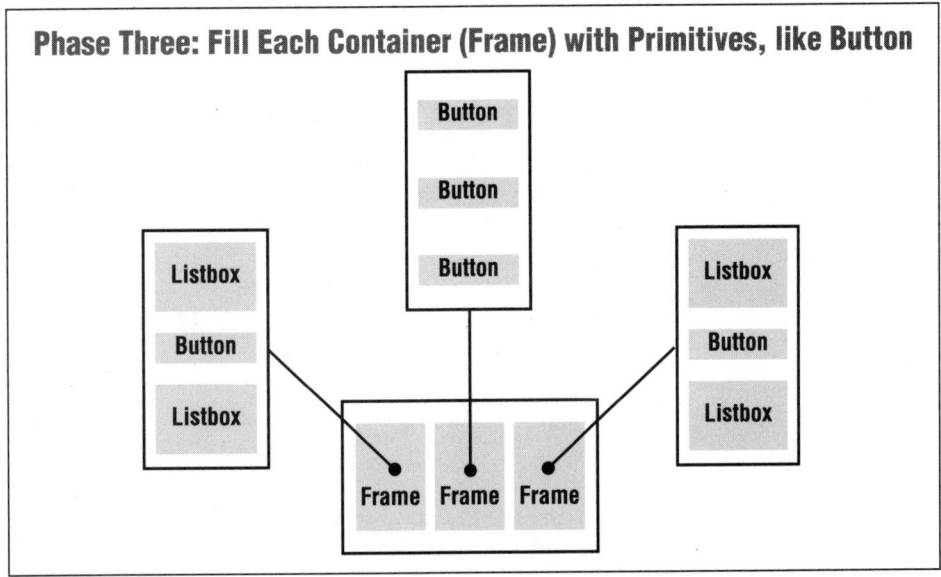

Figure 6-11. Fill each container with primitives

It also could produce a screen like that in Figure 6-12.

The Toplevel Container

Complex GUIs rarely use just one window in their functionality. pTk handles secondary windows using Toplevel. Toplevel is a container like MainWindow

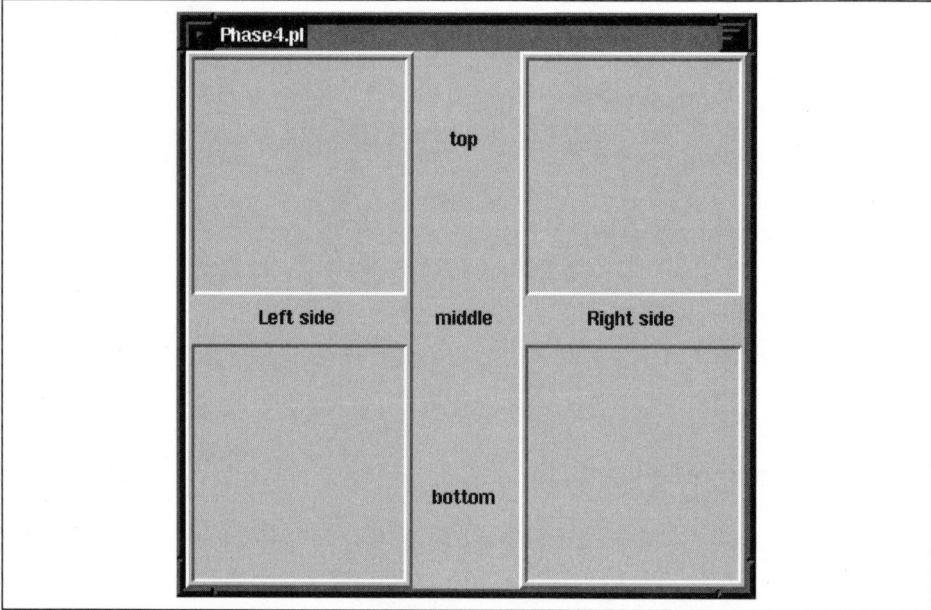

Figure 6-12. A sample widget with multiple frames

that can contain widgets and `Frames` (like `MainWindow`), or can spawn other
`Toplevel` windows.

`Toplevel` is used much like `MainWindow`, although `Toplevel` can't be initialized
as the main container of a widget and can't interact directly with the window
manager. The following code is incorrect.

```
#!/usr/local/bin/perl -w

use Tk;
use strict;

my($main);


# Toplevel can't be used as the main container since it can't talk
# to the window manager
$main = new Toplevel;
$main->Button(-text => 'Toplevel here')->pack;

# The Main event
MainLoop;
```

`Toplevel` can appear to have been created as the main container of the program.
If a `MainWindow` object is created and then creates `Toplevel` window, the `Main-`

`Window` can be withdrawn, so the `Toplevel` window acts like the main container. The correct code would be:

```
#!/usr/local/bin/perl -w

use Tk;
use strict;

my($main, $tl, $butn);

$main = MainWindow->new();

$tl = $main->Toplevel;
$butn = $tl->Button(-text => "I have reached the top level!");
$butn->pack;

$main->withdraw;

# The Main Event
MainLoop;
```

The example above creates a new **MainWindow** object that creates a `Toplevel` window with a `Button` labeled `I have reached the top level!`. The **Main-Window** is then withdrawn. This gives the appearance that the `Toplevel` window created itself, although, given the previous incorrect example, this is not true.

In this next example, each `Button` is bound to a subroutine that creates a new `Toplevel` window containing a `Button`. Each `Button` calls another subroutine, which creates a new `Toplevel` window containing a `Button`. The final subroutine exits the program when the user selects the `Button` labeled `Now we are`.

```
#!/usr/local/bin/perl -w

use Tk;

# woolly bully
use strict;

# m-m-m-my--sharona!
my($main, $lb, $tl, $tl_but, $tl2, $tl2_but);

# the main window
$main = MainWindow->new();

# the first button contains the text 'Press Me'. When pressed,
# an anonymous subroutine is executed and a Toplevel window is created
$lb = $main->Button(-text => 'Press Me!', -command => sub {

    # okay, here's the Toplevel window
    $tl = $main->Toplevel;

    # now, create a second button on the first Toplevel window
    # when this button is pressed, create *another* Toplevel window
    # with *another* button.
```

```
$t1_but = $t1->Button(-text => 'Are we there yet?', -command => sub {

    $t12 = $t1->Toplevel;

    # finally, create a button, which, when pressed
    # exits the program
    # orange you glad I didn't say banana?
    $t12_but = $t12->Button(-text => 'Now we are', -command => sub {exit});
    $t12_but->pack();

    });

    $t1_but->pack();

});

$lb->pack();

# ding ding -- the main event!
MainLoop;
```

Figure 6-13 shows the program output. Pressing the first button creates a second button, pressing the second button creates a third button, and pressing the third exits the program.

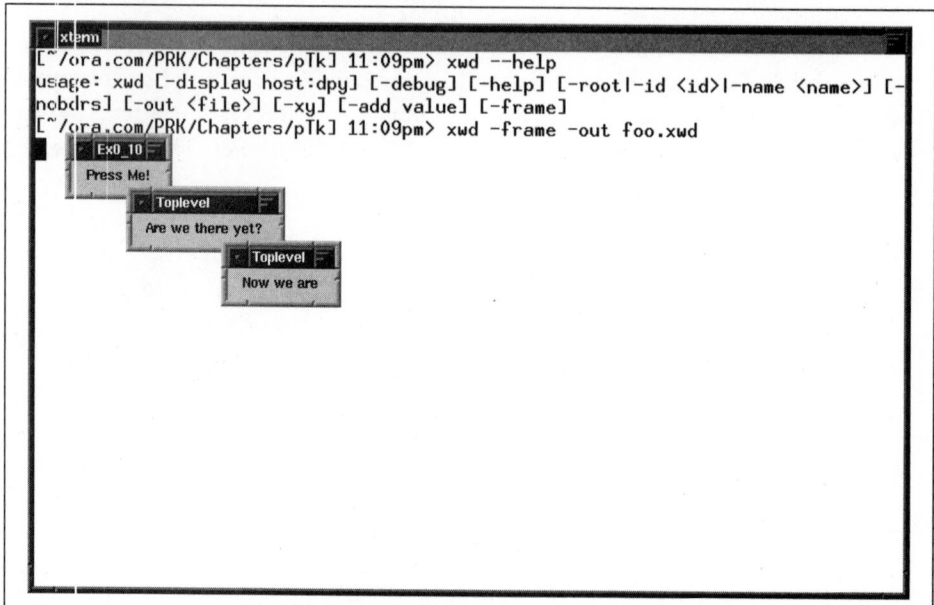

Figure 6-13. Multiple top-level windows

Using the get() Function

A pivotal pTk function is get(). The get() function retrieves user-selected entries from a widget. The program manipulates this data and passes it back into the interface. It can perform back-end work on the data, such as File I/O, or insert the information into a database. Each primitive that accepts input handles get() a little differently. This section covers retrieving input from each widget; see Chapter 14 for examples using get().

Getting Input from an Entry Widget

The simplest widget to retrieve input from is Entry, because Entry's input is limited to one line of text. Unlike other widgets documented in this section, the get() function doesn't require any arguments when extracting input from Entry. This example extracts and outputs the text (to STDOUT) from Entry when the Button labeled What did I enter? is selected by the user.

```
#!/usr/local/bin/perl -w

use Tk;
use strict;

my($main, $ent, $btn, $get_entry);

$main = MainWindow->new();

# Create an Entry widget
$ent = $main->Entry;
$ent->pack;

# Use anonymous subroutine to get the data from Entry,
# which is executed when the Button is pressed.
$btn = $main->Button(-text => 'What did I enter?',
                -command => sub {
                $get_entry = $ent->get; # get entry text
                print "You entered: ",
                        $get_entry,
                            "\n";
                });
$btn->pack;

# the main event
MainLoop;
```

The previous example can be revised to use a helper subroutine that performs the same function. The helper subroutine, get_entry_text() is passed the Entry widget name, $ent, and sends the contents of $ent->get to STDOUT:

```perl
#!/usr/local/bin/perl -w

use Tk;
use strict;

my($main, $ent, $butn);

$main = MainWindow->new();

# Use an Entry widget - call it $ent
$ent = $main->Entry;
$ent->pack();

# The Button calls get_entry_text with the $ent parameter
# when clicked by the user.
$butn = $main->Button(-text => 'What did I Enter?',
                      -command => [\&get_entry_text, \$ent]);
$butn->pack;

# The Main Event
MainLoop;

# Helper functions
sub get_entry_text {

    # Pass in $ent.  $entry_text represents the Entry object
    # which is passed into get_entry_text
    my $entry_text = shift;

    # assign $gotten to $entry_text->get
    my $gotten = $entry_text->get;

    # send user input to STDOUT
    print("You entered: $gotten\n");
}
```

Getting Input from a Listbox

Since a `Listbox` can contain multiple entries, and a user can select multiple entries in a `Listbox`, entries can't be extracted in the same fashion as `Entry`.

The following is incorrect:

```perl
$list_entries = $listbox->get;
print "You selected $list_entries\n";
```

`Listbox` implements a function called `curselection()`, which returns an array of selected values from a `Listbox`. Selected items can be extracted from the array using a `for` loop, where each element is retrieved using `get()`.

The following example extracts a list of selected items from a `Listbox`, `$lb`, and returns the elements to an array `@chosen` using `curselection`. After `@chosen` is populated, each selected item is extracted using `get()` and sent to STDOUT.

```
#!/usr/local/bin/perl -w

use Tk;
use strict;

my($main, $lb, $btn);

$main = MainWindow->new();

# Initialize and pack a Listbox
$lb = $main->Listbox;
$lb->pack();
for(1..10) { $lb->insert('end', $_); }

$btn = $main->Button(-text => 'Your kiss is on my list?',
                     -command => sub {
                     # return selected items to @chosen
                     @chosen = $lb->curselection;
                     # now, iterate through @chosen, and get each
                     # item, $_. send each item to STDOUT.
                     for(@chosen) { print $lb->get($_),"\n"; }
});
$btn->pack;

# The Main Event
MainLoop;
```

Getting Input from a Text Widget

The Text widget doesn't require any intermediate functions like curselection() to extract user input using get(). Instead, the get() function takes two parameters: starting and ending boundaries. The starting boundary appears as a decimal that represents the x, y position of the beginning text. The end boundary is the end tag that tells get() to read until the last character in the Text area.

This example uses get() to retrieve input from a Text area from 0.0 to end.

```
#!/usr/local/bin/perl -w

use Tk;
use strict;

my($main, $txt, $btn);

$main = MainWindow->new();

# initialize and pack the Text widget (height, width = 40)
$txt = $main->Text(-width => 40, -height => 40);
$txt->pack;

$btn = $main->Button(-text => 'Read all about it!',
                     -command => sub {
```

```
                    # anonymous subroutine to get the text from Text
                    # area from 0.0 position to end
                    $gotten = $txt->get('0.0', 'end');


                    });
    $btn->pack;

    # the main event
    MainLoop;
```

Updating Widgets Using Callbacks

Callback functions are always supplied by the user's code, so -command is used
for associating functions with a widget. Callback functions are also executed by
using the -command attribute. The syntactical difference is that callback functions
are arrays containing a reference to the subroutine to be called.

Here's the syntax of a callback function:

```
    $widget = $container->Func(-attribute => 'value',
                               -command => [\&func, \$widget]);
    $widget->pack;
```

A practical application that redraws widgets using a callback function might be a
row of five Buttons packed left to right. Instead of using pack('forget') to
unpack a Button, then using pack to repack a Button, a callback function
simply redraws the Button with new attributes such as -text or -command.

The next example takes a row of five Buttons and updates each Button by
executing callback subroutine cb_func() when the Button is pressed. The callback function calls configure(), which passes the -text attribute back to the
Button, updating it.

```
    #!/usr/local/bin/perl -w

    use Tk;
    use strict;

    my($main, $button1, $button2, $button3, $button4, $button5);

    # Initialize the main container
    $main = MainWindow->new();

    # create the 5 Buttons. each Button calls the
    # cb_func subroutine when the Button is pressed
    # with a reference to the scalar representing the widget

    $button1 = $main->Button(-text => 'Active',
                             -command => [\&cb_func, \$button1]);
    $button1->pack(-side => 'left');

    $button2 = $main->Button(-text => 'Active',
                             -command => [\&cb_func, \$button2]);
```

```
$button2->pack(-side => 'left');

$button3 = $main->Button(-text => 'Active',
                         -command => [\&cb_func, \$button3]);
$button3->pack(-side => 'left');

$button4 = $main->Button(-text => 'Active',
                         -command => [\&cb_func, \$button4]);
$button4->pack(-side => 'left');

$button5 = $main->Button(-text => 'Active',
                         -command => [\&cb_func, \$button5]);
$button5->pack(-side => 'left');

# the Main Event
MainLoop;

sub cb_func {
    # pass in the widget to be updated
    # then configure the new text which will appear
    # in the widget
    my $but = shift;

    $$but->configure(-text => 'Inactive');
}
```

Binding Mouse Keys to Handle Events

In addition to calling event handlers by clicking a button, you can also bind keyboard and/or mouse events to call them. The Listbox example from the pTk FAQ offered one such implementation by binding the left mouse button to a subroutine to delete Listbox items like this:

```
use Tk;

my $m = MainWindow->new();
my $l = $m -> Listbox();

$l -> bind('<Double-1>' => sub{sleepy($l)} );
my @nuts   = qw(Almond Brazil Chestnut Doughnut Elmnut Filbert);

for (@nuts) { $l -> insert('end',$_); }
$l -> pack;
```

The bind() function takes a key or mouse button, denoted by <>, and maps the specified key or button to a subroutine:

```
$init = $obj->Func();
$init->bind('<...>' => sub {call it here});
$init->pack;
```

The following example binds the Return key to the subroutine helper(), which outputs a message and exits the program when the Return key is pressed in the widget and the mouse pointer is on top of the Button marked Press Here.

When the Return key is bound to an event, mouse-clicking is unchanged; you can still click on the Button with your mouse, and the program behaves the same.

```perl
$bbut = $main->Button(-text => 'Press Here');
$bbut->configure(-command => [\&helper]);

# Bind the Return key to the subroutine helper as well
$main->bind('<Return>' => [\&helper]);
$bbut->pack;

sub helper {
    print("Help me, I'm bound for trouble!\n");
    exit;
}
```

The next example contains only an Entry box. When the user fills out the Entry box and hits Return, the get_entry() subroutine is called, and the contents of the Entry box are sent to STDOUT.

```perl
#!/usr/local/bin/perl -w

use Tk;
use strict;

my($main, $label, $ent);

$main = MainWindow->new();

# Place a Label next to the Entry
$label = $main->Label(-text => 'Tell me: ');
$label->pack(-side => 'left');

# Add an Entry box
$ent = $main->Entry;

# Bind the Return key to the get_entry subroutine
$ent->bind('<Return>' => [\&get_entry]);
$ent->pack(-side => 'right');

sub get_entry {
    my $ihave = shift;
    print $ihave->get."\n";
}

# the main event
MainLoop;
```

Tk-Related Reference Materials

Here is a short-form list of Tk (and pTk) web sites as listed in the pTk FAQ:

Main site	*http://w4.lns.cornell.edu/~pvhp/ptk/ptkFAQ.html* *http://w4.lns.cornell.edu/~pvhp/ptk/doc/*
World Wide Web	*http://pubweb.bnl.gov/~ptk/doc/index.html* *http://w4.lns.cornell.edu/~pvhp/ptk/doc/* *http://w4.lns.cornell.edu/~pvhp/ptk/pod/*
The Perl/Tk newsgroup	*news:comp.lang.perl.tk*

In this chapter:
- *The GD Graphics Library and GD.pm*
- *Manipulate Images with PerlMagick*
- *GIFgraph*

Graphics and Plotting

Humans can't live on ASCII alone!

Since it's been proven that the Earth isn't flat and many publications are black, white and read all over, let's put on our rose-colored lenses and take a look at some interesting modules to create graphics: GD, PerlMagick, and GIFGraph.

The GD Graphics Library and GD.pm

GD.pm is a port of Thomas Boutell's GD graphics library, as adapted by Lincoln Stein. GD allows you to create color drawings using a variety of graphics primitives like lines, shapes, and fills. GD supports the popular GIF format as well as the GD format that was developed by Thomas Boutell.

This chapter introduces you to the GD function and implements a number of sample programs where GD fits the bill for producing images dynamically. At the end of these sections dealing with GD, you should be able to write Perl code with GD that adds shapes, fills, colors, and text to an image. The following example draws a rectangle sized to fit the text, fills it red, then draws a black frame around the rectangle and adds text to it.

```perl
#!/usr/local/bin/perl -w

use GD;
use Getopt::Long;
use strict; # can i hear an amen from the congregation

my($im, $outfile, $word_to_gif, $len_word);
my($white, $black, $red, $blue);

$word_to_gif = 'What\'s black and white and red all over?';
$len_word = length($word_to_gif);
```

```perl
GetOptions('out=s', \$outfile);
die("Usage: testgd.pl -out <outfile>\n")
    unless $outfile;

# create a new image - resized x value for x*8 which is
# the x coordinate of the 8x16 font. Just set the y-value
# to 16 since characters no larger than 16 pixels high.
$im = GD::Image->new($len_word*8, 16)
    or die("can't create GD object: $!");

# allocate some colors
$white = $im->colorAllocate(255,255,255);
$black = $im->colorAllocate(0,0,0);
$red = $im->colorAllocate(255,0,0);

# make the background transparent and interlaced
$im->transparent($white);
$im->interlaced('true');

# place a black 'frame' around the filled rectangle
$im->rectangle(0,0,$len_word*8,16,$black);

# fill the rectangle with red
$im->fill(20,20,$red);

# okay, now add the word to the gif
$im->string(gdLargeFont,0,0,$word_to_gif,$white);

# Convert the image to GIF and send it to a file specified
# on the command-line
open(OUT, ">".$outfile)
    or die("can't open output file $outfile: $!");
binmode(OUT); # for you cats out in PC-land
print OUT $im->gif;
close(OUT);
```

GD implements three classes: GD::Image, GD::Font, and GD::Polygon.

- GD::Image is an image class; it holds the image data and graphics primitives methods.

- GD::Font is a font class; it holds the font information for rendering text.

- GD::Polygon is a polygon object used for storing (lists of) vertices before the polygon is rendered as an image.

You always need at least one **Image** in order to use the primitives or create the image. You can also use one or more **Fonts** and **Polygons**, providing that you have initialized at least one **Image** object.

Creating Images with GD::Image

The `Image` constructor, `new()`, takes one or two arguments: the filehandle of an image file that has been opened and/or the dimensions of the image to be output.

To create a new `Image` object where the image will have the dimensions 100 by 100 pixels, use the following code:

```
$image = GD::Image->new(100,100);
```

GD also allows you to open existing images for display to be copied, modified, or output as a separate image. GD::Image contains a number of method calls to open and save images. In this example, we use `GD::Image::newFromGif` to open a GIF from a filehandle:

```
$gifname = 'foo.gif';

open (GIF, $gifname)
    or die("error opening GIF $gifname: $!");
$image = GD::Image->newFromGif(GIF)
    or die("newFromGif error: $!");
close GIF;
```

Defining Colors

After initializing a new object, RGB (red, green, blue) values must be defined for the new image. The `colorAllocate` function takes three arguments, each a value between 0 and 255 that represents an RGB value. An RGB value of 0,0,0 is the color black; 255,255,255 is the color white.

RGB values can be allocated in an array:

```
($white,$black,$red,$blue) =
    (
        $im->colorAllocate(255, 255, 255),
        $im->colorAllocate(0, 0, 0),
        $im->colorAllocate(255, 0, 0),
        $im->colorAllocate(0, 0, 255),
    );
```

or one value per line:

```
$white = $im->colorAllocate(255, 255, 255);
$black = $im->colorAllocate(0, 0, 0);
$red = $im->colorAllocate(255, 0, 0);
$blue = $im->colorAllocate(0, 0, 255);
```

You can use `rgb()` to output the RGB values that represent a specified color:

```
@RGBVAL = $im->rgb($white);
print "The color has the RGB values: ",
    join(" ", @RGBVAL),"\n";
```

This outputs:

```
255 255 255
```

Creating Transparent and Interlaced GIFs

GD supports transparent (GIF89) GIFs and normal (GIF87a) GIFs. If you've ever prepared images to use on the Web, you've probably had to create transparent GIFs that have "show-through" regions, so the background shows through those parts of the image. A single color is marked to be made transparent.

GD's `transparent()` function solves the problem of which color is transparent in the image; it uses one of the values from the RGB table that has already been defined.

Images can also be interlaced with the `interlaced()` function, which takes one parameter, 0 (or `false`) for noninterlaced, or 1 (or `true`) for interlaced GIFs. GIFs that are interlaced have a "venetian blind" effect.

```
$im->transparent($white);
$im->interlaced('true');  # or $im->interlaced(1);
```

Creating Shapes

Using GD's graphics primitives, a number of functions correspond to the shapes that are rendered; the `rectangle()` function draws rectangles; the `arc()` function creates round renderings; the `polygon()` function creates a polygon, etc.

`rectangle()` outputs the outline of a rectangle, or unfilled rectangle; it has five arguments that represent the rectangle's upper and lower bounds and color:

```
$im->rectangle(
    $x1, $y1, # upper left hand coordinates
    $x2, $y2, # lower right hand coordinates
    $color); # color of the rectangle
```

`filledRectangle()` takes the same arguments as `rectangle()`, but outputs a solid-colored rectangle:

```
$im->filledRectangle(
    $x1, $y1, # upper left hand coordinates
    $x2, $y2, # lower right hand coordinates
    $color); # color of the rectangle
```

The `polygon()` function takes two arguments: polygon and color. The `polygon()` function differs from the `rectangle()` function, as polygons can have multiple sides (not less that three sides). `polygon()` works with the `addPt()` function that takes two coordinates:

```
$poly = GD::Polygon->new();
```

```
$poly->addPt(50,0);
$poly->addPt(99,99);
$poly->addPt(0,99);
$im->polygon($poly,$blue);
```

Brush Patterns

Lines and shapes can be rendered with a brush pattern. Brushes are images that enhance the colors and shapes of lines. You can create and manipulate them as you would other images under GD.

You must create and load a brush with **setBrush** before you can use it to create images. Once you've set the brush, you can use **gdBrushed** to draw the lines with the new brush type. Let's walk through the process of creating a brush: in this case we'll be creating a line that runs diagonally northeast.

1. Create a GD object.

   ```
   $diagonal_brush = GD::Image->new(50,50);
   $im = GD::Image->new(50,50);
   ```

2. Allocate the RGB values and define white as the transparent color.

   ```
   $white = $brush_type->colorAllocate(255,255,255);
   $black = $brush_type->colorAllocate(0,0,0);
   $brush_type->transparent($white);
   ```

3. Now, create the line.

   ```
   $diagonal_brush->line(0,4,4,0,$black); # NE diagonal
   ```

4. Now, set the brush and draw a circle using the brush:

   ```
   $im->setBrush($diagonal_brush);
   $im->arc(50,50,25,25,0,360,gdBrushed);
   ```

5. Finally, output the image.

   ```
   binmode(STDOUT); # meow, meow PC-land
   print $im->gif;
   ```

Drawing Lines

The GD primitive for solid line drawings is the **line()** function that takes five arguments:

```
$im->line(0,0,   # origin at x1y1
     150,150,    # destination at x2y2
     gdBrushed); # brushtype
```

The GD primitive for dashed-line drawings is the **dashedLine()** function that takes the same arguments as **line()**.

Outputting the Image

Once you have created the image, you must choose the format in which it will be output. The GIF function sends a GIF to STDOUT (by default); the GD function sends a GD-format image to STDOUT (by default). To send an image to STDOUT as a GIF, you must print the image like this:

```
binmode(STDOUT); # kitty on my foot and I want to touch it
print $im->gif
```

You can redirect this image to a file from the command line like so:

```
perl test.pl > outfile.gif
```

Or you can output `$im->gif` to a filehandle:

```
$output_to_gif = 'outfile.gif';

open(FILE, ">" . $output_to_gif)
    or die("cannot open $output_to_gif for writing: $!");
binmode(FILE); # let me roll up onto the sidewalk and take a look, yes.
print FILE $im->gif;
close(FILE);
```

Obtaining Information About the Image

You can obtain various pieces of information from a preexisting image, such as size and format.

The `getBounds()` function returns an x,y pair of dimensions for the image:

```
$image_to_read = 'myimage.gif';

open(IMG, $image_to_read)
    or die("error reading image $image_to_read: $!");
$info = GD::Image->newFromGif(IMG);
close IMG;

($xval, $yval) = $info->getBounds();
print("Image: $image_to_read measures $xval by $yval pixels.\n");
```

Color (RGB) information can be extracted from each pixel of an image with the `getPixel()` function that takes two arguments, an x and y coordinate, and the `rgb()` function that takes the return of `getPixel()` and outputs a value for r, g, and b. The previous example can be revised to output the RGB values of every pixel in the image from 0,0 to the maximum dimensions obtained using `getBounds()`:

```
$read_image = 'get_my_pixels.gif';

open(IMG, $read_image)
    or die("error reading image $read_image: $!");
$info = GD::Image->newFromGif(IMG);
```

```
close IMG;

($xval, $yval) = $info->getBounds();
print("Image: $image is $xval by $yval pixels.\n");

for ($i=0; $i<=$yval; $i++) {
    $index = $info->getPixel($i, $i);
    ($r, $g, $b) = $info->rgb($index);
    print("RGB for $i  x $i is $r : $g : $b \n");
}
```

The `colorsTotal()` function returns the total number of colors in the object:

```
$total_colors = $image->colorsTotal;
print("The image $imagename is comprised of  $total_colors colors.\n");
```

The `colorExact()` function takes a set of RGB values and returns a positive integer if the color is found in the color table. If the color is not found, `colorExact()` returns −1.

```
$rose = $myImage->colorExact(255,100,80);
die "Color not found!" if $rose == -1;
```

or

```
$white = $myImage->colorExact(255,255,255);
print "The color ",$white," is defined." if $white == 1;
```

Strings and Fonts

Characters (and strings) can be added to images using `string()`. GD currently supports four fonts: `gdLargeFont`, `gdMediumBoldFont`, `gdSmallFont`, and `gdTinyFont`, derived from public fonts 8x16, 7x13, 6x12, and 5x8, respectively.

Given an initialized GD object and RGB allocation, `string()` takes five arguments:

```
font type (gdLargeFont, gdMediumBoldFont, gdSmallFont, gdTinyFont)
x coordinate
y coordinate
character or string to output
$color (as defined in the RGB table)
```

that appear like this:

```
$word_to_image = 'insert this string into the image';
$image_obj->string(font,x,y,$word_to_image,$color);
```

When you initialized a new GD object, you declared its width and height. The image you created must fit into x,y bounds you input to the constructor. If you declared an image with the dimensions (100, 100), and you only output the string "This is a string" in `gdLargeFont` (8x16 pixels), you'd have a lot of unused space in the image (from top to bottom). The string would be truncated (from left to right), as the string ends up longer than the 100-pixel width when using the 8x16 font.

Since the 8x16 font is 8 pixels wide per character, and your string is 19 characters long (including spaces and punctuation), the region occupied by the string written in 8x16 font is 19 (characters) x 8 pixels per character wide = 152 pixels total, which is 52 pixels wider than the dimensions declared in the constructor!

Thankfully, the width and height of the image can be precalculated if the length (or the maximum length) of the string and font to be used is known. Given the above example, the code would look like this:

```
$word_to_image = 'This is the string'; # string to appear in the image
$width = length($word_to_image); # how many characters in the word?
$height = 16; # height for the 8x16 font stays constant

$width*=8; # width*x = correct max width dimensions for gif

$image = GD::Image->new($width,$height); # the constructor
($white,$black) =
(
$im->colorAllocate(255, 255, 255),
$im->colorAllocate(0, 0, 0)
);
$im->transparent($white);    # white background is transparent
$im->interlaced(1);

$im->string(gdLargeFont,0,0,$word_to_image,$black); # output phrase
```

Image::Size and Copying Images

As mentioned previously, the getBounds() function returns an x,y pair representing image dimensions. This information is useful for copying images; obtaining the dimensions for the original image is necessary for duplicating its contents to a second image.

The getBounds() function can generate the WIDTH and HEIGHT attributes of an HTML <IMG> tag:

```
$image_to_open = 'some_interesting_name.gif';

open(IMG, $image_to_open)
    or die("error opening image $image_to_open: $!");
$info = GD::Image->newFromGif(IMG);
close IMG;

($xval, $yval) = $info->getBounds();
print qq/<IMG SRC="$image_to_open" WIDTH="$xval" HEIGHT="$yval">/."\n";
```

While getBounds() is sufficient for GIFs, alternatives exist to do the same for a variety of different image formats.

The Image::Size module extracts image size information for a variety of image formats. It analyzes image sizes by the image's name or when the image name is embedded in an HTML <IMG> tag with WIDTH and HEIGHT attributes. Image::Size also generates width and height attributes for an <IMG> tag (using the html_ imgsize function) to be used in conjunction with another module, like CGI.pm.

Image::Size returns the dimensions of an image, such as in the following example:

```
$image = 'somename.gif';
($x_dim, $y_dim) = imgsize($image)
    or die("error sizing image --  $image: $!");

print("X-dimension: $x_dim\n",
"Y-dimension: $y_dim\n");
```

which outputs:

```
X-dimension: 50
Y-dimension: 51
```

The image can be copied to another image (name and/or type) by using the image's existing dimensions and copying the image using GD::Image::copy() or rescaling the dimensions to resize the image using GD::Image::copy-Resized().

To create a new image twice the size of the original:

1. Extract the dimensions of the original image.

```
($x_dim, $y_dim) = imgsize($image); # get size of the original image
```

2. Compute the dimensions of the new image that are twice the size of the original.

```
$x = $x_dim*2; # rescale height and width
$y = $y_dim*2;
```

3. Plug the parameters into copyResized(), which takes the following arguments.

```
$im->copyResized(source_image, # the source image
    dstX, dstY, # where in the destination image is placed
    srcX, srcY, # upper left corner of the source image
    destW, destH, # destination width and height
    srcW, srcH); # source width and height
```

4. Put the process together.

```
$im->copyResized($gif,0,0,0,0,$x,$y,$x_dim,$y_dim); # now copy the image
binmode(STDOUT); # millions of peaches, peaches for me
print $im->gif; # and send the new image somewhere
```

Image Conversion and Manipulation with GD

GD implements several functions to manipulate existing images, including `GD::Image::setPixel()` and `GD::Image::colorDeallocate()`, which change the colors allocated to a pixel and remove colors allocated in the color table, respectively. This section of the chapter introduces you to the aforementioned functions and implements several programs based on the materials covered in this chapter, including a program to create transparent GIFs from nontransparent GIFs (useful in background images displayed in web pages) and the web hit counter that uses digits generated using GD.

`GD::Image::setPixel()` sets the given x,y coordinate to the specified RGB value (as the color appears in the color table).

```
# This assumes that $blue is already allocated.
$myImage->setPixel(50,50,$blue);
```

`GD::Image::setPixel()` takes three arguments: x, y, and RGB value, and doesn't return a value on failure or success.

Here's a program that replaces all the pixels containing the RGB white value with the RGB red value:

```
$image = 'original.gif';
$outfile = 'recolored.gif';

open(IMG, $image)
    or die("error opening image $image: $!");
$info = GD::Image->newFromGif(IMG);
close IMG;

$red = $info->colorAllocate(255, 0, 0); # allocate the color red
($xval, $yval) = $info->getBounds(); # get the max bounds

# Now, go through the pixels and change each white pixel to red
for ($i=0; $i<=$yval; $i++) {
    for($j=0; $j<=$xval; $j++) {
        $index = $info->getPixel($j, $i);
        ($r, $g, $b) = $info->rgb($index);
        $info->setPixel($j,$i,$red) if $r == 255 && $g == 255 && $b == 255;
}
$outgif = $info->gif; # $output is the new gif (with color substitution)

open(OUT, ">".$output)
    or die("error opening output file $output: $!");
binmode(OUT); # pour your misery down
print OUT $outgif;
close(OUT);
```

`GD::Image::colorDeallocate()` removes a color from the color table so the color can be reallocated. It can be called multiple times to deallocate colors.

```
$im->colorDeallocate($peach);
$peachykeen = $im->colorAllocate(255,210,185);
```

Here's a program that creates a range of images (either letters or numbers); each image represents a number (or letter) in the range. For example, if the user entered **-r aa:ae** on the command line, five GIFs labeled **aa**, **ab**, **ac**, **ad**, and **ae** would be created, containing the corresponding strings. This program is useful for creating single-character images for applications like graphical hit counters seen on web pages.

```perl
#!/usr/local/bin/perl -w

use strict;
use Getopt::Long;
use GD;

my(@range, $r);
GetOptions('r=s', \$r);

if($r) {
    (@range) = split(/:/, $r); # arguments must resemble first:last
    # or output the usage message for error
    if(scalar(@range) == 2) {
        make_image($range[0], $range[1]); # now, output images from first to
last
    } else {
        usage(); # failed
    }
} else {
    usage(); # failed
}

sub make_image {
    my($first, $last) = @_; # pass-in first, last gif numbers
    my($im, $white, $black, $width, $height);

    for ($first .. $last) {

    # Compute the ratio of $width, $height to the font (8x16 - large)
    $width = length($_)*8; # Single digits = 8, double = 16, etc.
    $height = 16; # the height will always be 16 for the large font

    # output all gifs to the Images directory.  Change this per your spec
    open(OUTFILE, ">Images/$_.gif")
        or die("output file error: $!");
    print("Opening: $_.gif for writing.\n");

    $im = GD::Image->new($width, $height);
```

```
        ($white,$black) =
            (
            $im->colorAllocate(255, 255, 255),
            $im->colorAllocate(0, 0, 0)
        );
        $im->transparent($white);      # white color is transparent
        $im->interlaced(1);            # cool venetian blinds effect

        $im->string(gdLargeFont,0,0,$_,$black); # use the 8x16 font

        print OUTFILE $im->gif; # output the image to (FILEHANDLE)
        close(OUTFILE);
        }
    }

sub usage {
    print("Usage: $0 -r <first:last>\n");
    exit(0); # failure
    }
```

Manipulate Images with PerlMagick

Like GD, PerlMagick is a Perl interface to ImageMagick, a package used to read, manipulate, and write images or sequences of images. ImageMagick implements a higher-level interface for image manipulation than GD. It supports an impressive number of graphics formats including GIF, JPEG, TIFF, and PICT as well as its own image format, Magick Interchange Format (MIFF).

Converting images with ImageMagick is ridiculously easy: just enter the input and output filenames, and ImageMagick does the conversion for you.* Use the **read()** method to read images like so:

```
$image_1 = 'first.gif';
$image_2 = 'second.gif';
$image_3 = 'third.gif';

$imgk->read($image_1, $image_2, $image_3);
```

Use the **write()** method to save a new image to the filesystem. **write()** takes at least one argument: the filename, and an optional attribute argument. (See the following section for supported image attributes.)

```
$output = 'send_me_out.jpg';
$imgk->write($output);
```

Here's an example that converts a GIF to a JPEG:

```
#!/usr/local/bin/perl -w
```

---

* You must have ImageMagick (see PerlMagick documentation for required version) installed on your system for PerlMagick to work.

```
use Image::Magick;
use strict; # it takes a very steady hand

my($q, $x, $infile, $outfile);

$infile = 'input_file.gif';
$outfile = 'output_file.jpg';

# create an Image::Magick object
$q = Image::Magick->new;

# read the input file
$x = $q->Read($infile);
    warn "error reading: $infile $x" if "$x";

# read the output file
$x = $q->Write($outfile);
    warn "error writing: $outfile $x" if "$x";
```

Getting Image Attributes with ImageMagick

It's likely that you'll want to get the current image attributes so that they can be manipulated before writing the new image. The attributes listed in Table 7-1 tell you everything you'll need to know about the original image.

For example, here's how we can get the size of the image:

```
($width, $height) = $imgk->Get('width', 'height');
print("Image is $width by $height pixels in size\n");
```

Table 7-1. Image Attributes

Attribute	Value	Purpose
base_columns	Integer	Base image width (before transformations)
base_filename	String	Base image filename (before transformations)
base_rows	Integer	Base image height (before transformations)
class	{DirectClass, PseudoClass}	Image class
columns	Integer	Image width
comment	String	Image comment
depth	Integer	Image depth
filesize	Integer	Number of bytes of the image on disk
gamma	Double	Gamma level of the image
geometry	String	Image geometry
height	Integer	Number of rows or height of an image
label	String	Image label
matte	{true, false}	True if the image has transparency

Table 7-1. Image Attributes (continued)

Attribute	Value	Purpose
mean	Double	Mean error per pixel computed when an image is color-reduced
normalized_max	Double	Normalized maximum error per pixel computed when an image is color-reduced
normalized_mean	Double	Normalized mean error per pixel computed when an image is color-reduced
packets	Integer	Number of length-encoded packets in the image
packetsize	Integer	Number of bytes in each pixel packet
rows	Integer	Number of rows or height of an image
signature	String	MD5 signature associated with the image
text	String	Any text associated with the image
units	{Undefined pixels/ inch, pixels/centimeter}	Units of resolution
width	Integer	Number of columns or width of an image
x_resolution	Integer	x resolution of the image
y_resolution	Integer	y resolution of the image

Setting Image Attributes with ImageMagick

set() sets an image attribute:

```
$imgk->Set(background=>'green');
```

Table 7-2 shows the image attributes that you can set with ImageMagick.

Table 7-2. Settable Image Attributes

Attribute	Usage
adjoin	Adds images into a multiimage file; adjoin takes true and false as attributes
background	Sets the background color; takes a string that represents a background color as an attribute
bordercolor	Sets the image's border color; takes a string that represents the border color as an attribute
colormap[i]	Sets the color at pixel; takes the strings red, green, and blue (for RGB values)
compress	Sets the type of image compression: No, Runlength, Zip
delay	Controls the animation sequence of a GIF (within Netscape)
density	Returns the vertical and horizontal resolution of the image in pixels
dispose	Removes an image; takes image's geometry as an attribute
dither	Applies error diffusion to the image; takes true/false as attributes

Table 7-2. Settable Image Attributes (continued)

Attribute	Usage
filename	Sets the filename represented by `$string`
font	Sets the font when adding text to an image; adds the font specified by `$string`
format	Sets the image format specified by string
geometry	Shortcut for the width and height parameters; it can be specified like `geometry => '106x80'` or `width => 106, height => 80`
interlace	Sets the interlacing scheme; attributes are `None`, `Line`, `Plane`, `Partition`
iterations	Adds a Netscape-specific loop extension to a GIF animation; takes an integer as an attribute
loop	Adds a Netscape-specific loop extension to your GIF animation; takes an integer as an attribute
magick	Sets the image format specified by `$string`
mattecolor	Sets the image matte color specified by `$string`
monochrome	Transforms the image to black and white; attributes are `true` and `false`
number	Sets the preferred number of colors in the image; takes an integer as an attribute
page	Sets the size and location of the PostScript page specified by `$string`
pointsize	Sets the point size of the PostScript font as specified by integer
quality	Sets the quality of the JPEG as specified by integer
size	Sets the width and height of an image as specified by `$string`
texture	Adds a texture to the image's background as specified by `$string`
verbose	Outputs detailed information about the images; attributes are `true` and `false`

Manipulating Images with ImageMagick

ImageMagick's image manipulation functions take the same arguments as its `Set` functions. The following code shows how to manipulate an image:

```
$width = 80;
$height = 100;

# okay, now grab the part of the image that we want
$imgk->Crop(width => $width, height => $height)
```

Table 7-3 displays a list of ImageMagick image-manipulation functions and their meanings.;

Table 7-3. Image Manipulation Functions

Attribute	Purpose	Values
AddNoise	Adds noise or texture to the image	Accepts the attributes: Uniform, Gaussian, Multiplicative, Impulse, Laplacian, Poisson
Blur	Causes an image to lose its sharpness	Takes a percentage as an argument
Border	Adds a border of color to the image	Attributes are geometry, width, height, and color
Charcoal	Simulates a charcoal drawing	Takes a percentage as an argument
Chop	Chops an image	Takes geometry, width, and height as arguments
Clone	Makes a copy of an image	Takes image names as arguments
Colorize	Colorizes the image with the pen color	Takes colorname and pen as arguments
Comment	Adds a comment to an image	String specified by $string
Crop	Extracts a portion of an image	Takes geometry, width, height, and x as arguments
Draw	Adds primitives to an image	Types are point, line, rectangle, fillrectangle, circle, fillcircle, polygon, fillpolygon, color, matte, text, image
Enhance	Adds a filter to a noisy image	true/false
Flip	Creates a mirror image of the original in a vertical direction	Image name
Frame	Adds a decorative border to the image	Takes geometry=>geometry, width=>integer, height=>integer, inner=>integer, outer=>integer, color=>colorname as arguments.
Label	Adds a label to an image represented	By $string
Magnify	Increases the size of an image	By *x*
Minify	Decreases the size of an image	By *x*
Negate	Adds color conversion to the image	true/false
Rotate	Rolls an image vertically or horizontally	degrees=>double, crop=>{true, false}, sharpen=>{true, false}
Sample	Scales an image (with pixel sampling)	geometry=>geometry, width=>integer, height=>integer

Table 7-3. Image Manipulation Functions (continued)

Attribute	Purpose	Values
Scale	Sets an image to specified size	geometry=>geometry, width=>integer, height=>integer
Sharpen	Sharpens an image by x percent	factor=>percentage
Texture	Adds texture to the background of an image	Name of texture
Transparent	Makes x color transparent in the image	color=>colorname
Zoom	Scales an image to the desired size	geometry=>geometry, width=>integer, height=>integer, filter=>{Box, Mitchell, Triangle}

ImageMagick Display Options

ImageMagick allows you to create a montage of images with Montage. Montage creates a composite image that combines several separate images. See Table 7-4 for a list of the display options.

For example:

```
$height = 100;
$width = 100;

$imgk->Montage(width => $width, height => $height, tile => '2x2');
```

Table 7-4. ImageMagick Display Options and Attributes

Attribute	Value	Meaning
background	String	X11 color name
borderwidth	Integer	Image border width
compose	{composite operator, filename, string, name of montage, image}	{Over, In, Out, Atop, Xor, Plus, Minus, Add, Subtract, Difference, Bumpmap, Replace, MatteReplace, Mask, Blend, Displace}
filter	{Box, Mitchell, Triangle}	Uses this filter to resize the image tile
font	String	X11 font name
foreground	String	X11 color name
frame	Geometry	Surrounds the image with an ornamental border
geometry	String	Preferred tile and border size of each tile of the composite image

Table 7-4. ImageMagick Display Options and Attributes (continued)

Attribute	Value	Meaning
gravity	{NorthWest, North, NorthEast, West, Center, East, South-West, South, South-East}	Direction image gravitates to within a tile
label	String	Assigns a label to an image
mode	{Frame, Unframe, Concatenate}	Thumbnail framing options
shadow	{true, false}	Adds a shadow beneath a tile to simulate depth
texture	String	Name of texture to tile onto the image background
tile	Geometry	Number of tiles per row and column
transparent	String	Makes this color transparent within the image

Or suppose you want to convert your color image to grayscale:

```
$q->Set(colorspace=>'gray');
$q->Quantize();
```

Handling Errors with ImageMagick

All PerlMagick routines return **undef** upon success. If any problems occur, the error is returned as a string with an embedded numeric status code. A status code less than 400 is a warning, which means that the operation didn't complete but was recoverable to some degree. A numeric code greater or equal to 400 is an error and indicates the operation failed completely. See Table 7-5 for a list of the error types and their descriptions. Here is how errors are returned for the different methods:

```
$x = $q->Read(...);
warn "$x" if "$x";      # print the error message
$x =~ /(\d+)/;
print $1;               # print the error number
print $x;               # print the number of images read
```

Here is an example error message:

```
Error 400: Memory allocation failed
```

Here's what a program should output if you're using numeric response codes correctly:

```
$image = 'checkme.gif';

$x = $q->Read($image);
```

```
$x =~ /(\d+)/;
die "unable to continue" if ($1 == ResourceLimitError);
```

Table 7-5. ImageMagick Error Codes and Descriptions

Code	Message	Description
0	Success	Method completed without an error or warning
300	ResourceLimitWarning	A program resource is exhausted (e.g., not enough memory)
305	XServerWarning	An X resource is unavailable
310	OptionWarning	A command-line option was malformed
315	PluginWarning	An ImageMagick plug-in returned a warning
320	MissingPluginWarning	The image type can't be read or written because the appropriate plug-in is missing
325	CorruptImageWarning	The image file may be corrupt
330	FileOpenWarning	The image file couldn't be opened
400	ResourceLimitError	A program resource is exhausted (e.g., not enough memory)
405	XServerError	An X resource is unavailable
410	OptionError	A command-line option was malformed

GIFgraph

GIFgraph was written by Martien Verbruggen (*mgjv@comdyn.com.au*) to create a GIF that represents a graph. It needs GD to create the images, so you'll need to have GD installed for GIFgraph to function.

Here's how you'll use GIFgraph:

1. Fill an array of arrays with the *x* values and the values of the data sets. Make sure that every array is the same size.

   ```
   @data = (
       ["1st","2nd","3rd","4th","5th","6th","7th", "8th", "9th"],
       [   1,    2,    5,    6,    3,  1.5,    1,    3,    4]
   );
   ```

2. Create a new **Graph** object by calling the **new** operator on the graph type you want to create (**chart** is **bars**, **lines**, **points**, **linepoints**, **area**, or **pie**).

   ```
   $my_graph = GIFgraph::chart->new();
   ```

3. Set the graph options.

   ```
   $my_graph->set( 'x_label'      => 'X Label',
           'y_label'      => 'Y label',
           'title'        => 'A Simple Line Graph',
           'y_max_value'  => 8,
           'y_tick_number' => 8,
           'y_label_skip'  => 2 );
   ```

4. Output the graph.

```
$my_graph->plot_to_gif( "sample01.gif", \@data );
```

GIFgraph Methods

Each GIFgraph object requires the use of a constructor, **new()**. **new()** takes optional width and height arguments; the default width is 400 and the default height is 300:

```
$width = 600;
$height = 1000;

$some_chart = GIFgraph::chart_type->new($width, $height);
```

You'll need to replace **chart_type** with the type of chart you'll be creating: bars, lines, points, line points, area, or pie. To create a bar chart with a width of 300 and a height of 500, you'll need to do:

```
$width = 300;
$height = 500;

$session_do_bar = GIFgraph::bars->new($width, $height);
```

- **set_text_clr()** sets the text color.

```
$text_color = 'red';
$session_do_bar->set_text_clr($text_color);
```

- **set_title_font()** sets the font used for the chart's title; available types are limited to those supported by GD.

```
$tfont = '8x16';
$session_do_bar->set_title_font($tfont);
```

- **plot()** plots the chart and returns the GIF data.

```
@data = ( ... data here ...);
@plotted_as_gif = plot(\@data);
```

- **plot_to_gif()** plots the chart and writes the GIF data to a specified file.

```
$filename_for_gif = 'graphed_to_here.gif';
@data = ( ... data here ... );

plot_to_gif($filename_for_gif, \@data);
```

- **set_x_label_font()** sets the font type for the labels on the x-axis.

```
$font = '8x16';
$my_graph_obj->set_x_label_font($font);
```

- **set_y_label_font()** sets the font type for the labels on the y-axis.

```
$font = '8x16';
$my_graph_obj->set_y_label_font($font);
```

- **set_x_axis_font()** sets the font we'll use to label the x-axis.

```
$font = '8x16';
$my_graph_obj->set_x_axis_font($font);
```

- set_y_axis_font() sets the font we'll use to label the y-axis.

```
$font = '8x16';
$my_graph_obj->set_y_axis_font($font);
```

Pie Chart Methods

- set_label_font() adds a text label to the pie chart.

```
$font_name = '8x16';
$do_pie_chart->set_label_font($font_name);
```

- set_value_font() sets the font that labels the value(s) represented by the pie chart.

```
$font_name = '8x16';
$do_pie_chart->set_value_font($font_name);
```

GIFGraph Options

Table 7-6, Table 7-7, and Table 7-8 show the graph attribtues. You'll find several examples that use these options in Chapter 14, *Examples*.

Table 7-6. All Graph Types

Attribute	Meaning
bgclr, fgclr, textclr, labelclr, axislabelclr, accentclr	Defines background, foreground, text, label, axis label, and accent colors
gifx, gify	Sets the width and height of the GIF file in pixels; default: 400 x 300
interlaced	The GIF is interlaced with a value of 1
t_margin, b_margin, l_margin, r_margin	Sets margins to be used by the GIF
transparent	The GIF has the (specified) background color marked as transparent with a value of 1

Table 7-7. Graph with Axis (Bars, Lines, Points, Linepoints, and Area)

Attribute	Meaning
axis_space	Represents the size of the blank space between the axis and the text (default is 4)
box_axis	Draws the axes as a box, if 1 (default)
line_width	Sets the width of the line used in lines and line points in pixels (default is 2)
long_ticks, tick_length	If long_ticks are set to 0, the tick_length is represented by the value given to tick_length. Otherwise, long_ticks are the same length as the axis

Table 7-7. Graph with Axis (Bars, Lines, Points, Linepoints, and Area) (continued)

Attribute	Meaning
marker_size	Represents the size of the markers (for points and line points) in pixels (default is 4)
x_label_skip, y_label_skip	Skips every *x*th number under the tick on the specified axis
x_plot_values, y_plot_values	With a value of 1, tick values on the axis are plotted next to the tick
y_tick_number	Represents the number of ticks to print on the y-axis (default is 5)

Table 7-8. Pie Graphs

Attribute	Meaning
3d	Outputs the graph with a 3D look (default is 1)
pie_height	Sets the thickness of the pie (default is: 0.1*GIF's y dimension)
start_angle	Sets the angle at which the first data slice is displayed – 0degrees == 3 o'clock (default is 0)

8

The Database
Modules

In this chapter:
- *Database Design Principles*
- *Elements of the Database*
- *The SQL Language and Using the DBI*
- *qdsql: A Quick and Dirty Interactive SQL Client*

Interfacing with databases is one of the most powerful applications of Perl. But there are many database packages to choose from, and prior to Perl Version 5, there was no way to universalize database support for Perl. You'd have to rebuild the Perl executable itself against libraries that included subroutines for direct access to the database package. For example, `sybperl` and `oraperl` are both packages for building Perl Version 4 with Sybase and Oracle calls embedded, respectively.

However, newer, more mature versions of Perl (Version 5 and later) support binary extension loading at run-time. This means that database support can be added at run-time, which simplifies adding database interfaces to Perl programs while keeping the size of the Perl binary to a minimum.

Support for binary extensions didn't mean that database access has been standardized. There were still a bunch of database extensions to Perl. Each of these had a different API but a strikingly similar purpose: connect to the database, issue queries, fetch results, and disconnect from the database.

However, with Perl, it has become possible to develop a standard set of methods to work with any database. The DBI modules are database-independent modules for Perl. DBI itself is simply a Perl module that defines a collection of methods for database access. With DBI, the same methods can be used for database access regardless of the underlying database engine.

Database Design Principles

Designing and developing a database component almost always represents a departure from typical programming practice. In a relational database environment, information stored in the database doesn't always cleanly map to its representation within your Perl application. For example, imagine the way a customer record might be represented in Perl:

```
my %cust = (
        first_name      => 'Nathan',
        last_name       => 'Patwardhan',
        company         => 'Someplace Attractive',
        invoice_numbers => [10249, 17582, 33678]
);
```

This sort of representation is convenient at the application level, because all of the information is immediately available within the data structure. If you need to pick out an invoice number, or if you need to find the company with which the customer is affiliated, all this information is at your fingertips. However, although Perl's data structures are helpful for data storage and retrieval, this sort of representation isn't always efficient when you're dealing with larger applications; you'll recognize diminished performance when you're dealing with databases that contain a significant number of records.

Most of the time, your application will be concerned with handling one item at a time. For example, your database might contain several records of individuals affiliated with the same company. It is problematic to store the name of the company on each customer record, because human error (in data entry) would leave otherwise similar records unable to be consolidated by company name. Also, since you're storing the company name in each record, you're increasing the amount of storage you'll need for each record.

If you stored the company name elsewhere with a company code, a customer record only needs to store that code. This solves both problems. Each company name and code is stored in a separate location, and the user performing data entry on customers chooses a company name from a list. The customer record is associated with the appropriate record in the list of companies. Also, the amount of storage required by each customer record is diminished, since you don't need to store numerous copies of an arbitrarily long string in each customer record.

Elements of the Database

Information is stored in databases in the forms of columns, rows, and tables. The SQL language effectively handles these storage types. But before we introduce you to SQL, let's examine some Perl data structures that correspond to these SQLisms.

Remember the %cust hash shown in the previous section? This is a Perl-based counterpart to a row. A row is a logical unit of information that corresponds to one item of information being represented. You may sometimes hear the term *record* used simultaneously with the term *row*. A collection of these rows is referred to as a table. This could be represented in Perl as an array of references to each hash. Here's a collection of customer rows:

```perl
my %cust1 = (
        first_name      => 'Maeda',
        last_name       => 'Schwartz',
        company         => 'Frobozz Interactive',
        invoice_numbers => [13249, 10011]
);
my %cust2 = (
        first_name      => 'Nathan',
        last_name       => 'Patwardhan',
        company         => 'Forbozz Interactive',
        invoice_numbers => [10249, 17582, 33678]
);
my %cust3 = (
        first_name      => 'Mr.',
        last_name       => 'Fiction',
        company         => 'Homer, Doh!',
        invoice_numbers => [ ]
);
my @rows = (\%cust1, \%cust2, \%cust3);
```

In database parlance, each hash attribute corresponds to a column. It's important to note that the structure of each row must be the same for each occurrence. Even if there is not a single invoice for a given customer, there must be a place-holder for it, in case one is added. Also, purely relational databases cannot hold multiple values for a single column within a given row, so we'll have to do something different with the invoice numbers.

Table 8-1 shows an approximation of how these three customers might be logically organized within a customer table.

Table 8-1. Logical Organization of Customers in a Table

first_name	last_name	company	invoice_one	invoice_two	invoice_three
Maeda	Schwartz	Frobozz Interactive	13249	10011	NULL
Nathan	Patwardhan	Frobozz Interactive	10249	17582	33678
Mr.	Fiction	Homer, Doh!	NULL	NULL	NULL

Not according to Dr. E. F. Codd, the creator of the relational model. Codd established a theory for data modeling in a paper entitled "A Relational Model of Data for Large Shared Data Banks," which established the canonical guidelines for the processes of data normalization. These processes optimize the way your data is logically organized in tables. Normalization is not concerned with the physical organization of the data, such as where on the disk or tape it is stored, but with the way the data appears from the programmer's viewpoint. Each step in the process of normalization is known as a *normal form.*

The First Normal Form

Databases that adhere to the first normal form may not contain any repeating columns. With this in mind, examine the customer table shown above. Note that for each customer, there are three invoice columns. The structure of the table limits each customer to three invoices. If the customer has more than three, they are out of luck. If they have less than three, the columns are still there, but they have a value of NULL.

About NULL

NULL isn't really a value. Think of it as a game token that you might purchase at a video arcade: it's not legal tender but it works in their video games. NULL columns indicate that there is no value in the column; the column has been defined, but it's empty. NULL is not zero: 0 + 10 = 10, but NULL + 10 = NULL.

For this table to qualify for first normal form, we must create another table to store invoice numbers. This new table, the invoice table, also needs some way of referring to the customer table. For this purpose, a sequential ID is created for the customer table. This is called a *primary key* and no two rows in the customer table may have the same value for their primary key. Primary key values are generated by the database system each time a new customer is added, and the numbers are never reused, even if a customer is deleted. Table 8-2 shows the revised structure of the customer table, and Table 8-3 shows the new invoice table.

Table 8-2. Revised Structure of the Customer Table

first_name	last_name	company	Customer ID
Maeda	Schwartz	Frobozz Interactive	1
Nathan	Patwardhan	Frobozz Interactive	2
Mr.	Fiction	Homer, Doh!	3

Table 8-3. New Structure of the Invoice Table

Customer ID	Invoice Number
1	13249
1	10011
2	10249

Table 8-3. New Structure of the Invoice Table (continued)

Customer ID	Invoice Number
2	17582
2	33678

Natural and Artificial Keys

Unlike the customer table, the invoice table doesn't have a primary key. In the case of the customer table, its primary key is said to be an artificial key, since its value has absolutely nothing to do with the data the table is designed to represent. In the case of the invoice table, the invoice number is the primary key, since it is assumed that an invoice number is unique (otherwise, things could get difficult if you dug up an invoice from several years ago). This key is considered a natural key, since it is derived from the data the table is designed to represent.

In this fictional system, the invoice numbers are derived from the numbers that are printed on the invoice forms and are not generated by the database system. Sure, we could have used the computer to generate the invoice numbers, but we got such a good deal on a warehouse full of prenumbered invoices ten years ago!

Something New

The invoices won't be much use without line items, will they? Table 8-4 shows the line item table, which includes some sample line items. Each line item is linked to an invoice using the invoice number.

Table 8-4. Line Items Linked to Invoices wth Invoice Numbers

Invoice Number	Item	Item Code	Quantity
13249	Task Chair	C038	4
13249	Mouse Pad	M079	3
10011	Large Filing Cabinet	F189	1
10249	Task Chair	C038	8
10249	Copy Stand	H112	4
17582	Mouse Pad	M079	2
33678	2000 BTU Air Conditioner	D100	1

The Second Normal Form

The second normal form goes a bit farther than the first. Although the first normal form manages to eliminate repeating columns and removes the limitations imposed by having one column for each invoice, there are a couple of extra steps that can improve the state of things. The second normal form seeks to eliminate columns that aren't dependent upon the combined attributes of a compound primary key. In the case of the line item table, the primary key is said to be a compound primary key, a combination of the invoice number and the item code. However, the item name repeats for each occurrence of that item, and is only dependent upon the item code, not the invoice number. This is undesirable, since there is a possibility that the names of items may not be spelled consistently, resulting in reporting anomalies. This sort of problem can be eliminated quite easily. It is simply a matter of creating a table called *item* (Table 8-5) and storing nothing but the item name and item code. After this has been done, the *line item* table (Table 8-6) can be reorganized to use the item code rather than the item name.

Table 8-5. Item Table with Names and Codes

Item	Item Code
2000 BTU Air Conditioner	D100
Copy Stand	H112
Large Filing Cabinet	F189
Mouse Pad	M079
Task Chair	C038

Table 8-6. Line Item Table with Codes Only

Invoice Number	Item Code	Quantity
13249	C038	4
13249	M079	3
10011	F189	1
10249	C038	8
10249	H112	4
17582	M079	2
33678	D100	1

The Third Normal Form

The third normal form is similar to the second normal form, but it is concerned with eliminating columns that aren't dependent upon the table's primary key. In contrast, the second normal form sought to eliminate columns not dependent upon part of a compound primary key. In the case of the customer table, the company name is a value that is not dependent upon the customer ID and should be eliminated from that table. In order to maintain the connection between customer and company name, a new table is defined, *company*. The company table will have a company name and a company ID column as shown in Table

8-7. The customer table will be modified to have a company ID in place of the company name, as shown in Table 8-8.

Table 8-7. Customer Table with Name and ID

Company Name	Company ID
Frobozz Interactive	101
Homer, Doh!	103

Table 8-8. Customer Table with with ID Only

first_name	last_name	Company ID	Customer ID
Maeda	Schwartz	101	1
Nathan	Patwardhan	101	2
Mr.	Fiction	103	3

Choosing a Database and Database Driver

The Perl DBI supports a number of SQL database systems, including a number of free or shareware databases. Among the supported commercial databases are Informix, Sybase, Oracle, DB2, and Solid. Free and shareware databases supported by the DBI include mySQL, PostgreSQL, and miniSQL. There are other drivers available; to find the latest list of supported databases, you should visit the DBI pages at *http://www.hermetica.com/technologia/perl/DBI/index.html.*

If you've already got a DBI-supported database server, then you won't need to go through the process of choosing one. Choosing a database system does not have to be a source of complete anxiety; the whole purpose of the DBI is to liberate the Perl programmer from database-specific constraints. For the most part, programs written using the DBI are portable from one database system to another. While this doesn't hold entirely true for complex applications that make use of the server's native dialect of SQL, it is certainly applicable to the sort of simple applications you'd develop as you familiarize yourself with databasing in general. As a result, you can start out with something simple like miniSQL or mySQL, and move up to Sybase, PostgreSQL, Informix, or another higher-end database server if you feel it's necessary. Lightweight engines like miniSQL and mySQL are useful for many tasks, so you may not need to "upsize" at all.

If you don't have a database server installed, but would like to work through this chapter, you may wish to visit one of the home pages listed in Table 8-9. The freeware or shareware database servers are available for download from the URLs shown in the table, and some of the commercial servers offer evaluation copies for download. The DBI is installed like any other Perl module.

You should also choose a database driver (DBD) from Table 8-9

Table 8-9. Database Types and URLs with DBDs

Server	URL	Database Driver (DBD)
DB2	*http://www.software.ibm.com/data/db2/*	DBD::DB2
Empress	*http://www.empress.com/*	DBD::Empress
Fulcrum	*http://www.fulcrum.com*	DBD::Fulcrum
Informix	*http://www.informix.com/*	DBD::Informix
Ingres	*http://www.cai.com/products/ingres.htm http://epoch.cs.berkeley.edu:8000/postgres/ index.html*	DBD::Ingres
miniSQL	*http://www.hughes.com.au/*	DBD::mSQL
MySQL	*http://www.tcx.se/*	DBD::mysql
Oracle	*http://www.oracle.com/*	DBD::Oracle
PostgreSQL	*http://www.postgresql.com/*	DBD::Pg
QuickBase	*http://www.openbase.com/*	DBD::QBase
Solid	*http://www.solidtech.com/*	DBD::Solid
Sybase	*http://www.sybase.com/*	DBD::Sybase

The SQL Language and Using the DBI

SQL was developed to allow programmers to manipulate relational databases. There are many implementations of SQL, and each database server adds nuances that deviate from the standard. Every attempt has been made in this tutorial to use SQL that is portable to a wide variety of database engines.

The examples in this chapter introduce you to SQL commands and their DBI equivalents (where applicable). We've chosen to use mSQL in these examples because it can handle the information we're covering, and mSQL is either free or can be licensed for a relatively low price, depending on who you are and what you plan to do with it. See the mSQL license agreement for more information.

Using the DBI

Before you can open a connection to a database with DBI, you must create the database. Although you can create the database and tables with DBI, you should use `msqladmin` to do so:

```
msqladmin create database-name
```

The DBI provides a consistent, easy-to-learn interface. The `qdsql` utility (discussed later in this chapter) demonstrates some of the commonly used API functions, including connecting, querying, and processing result sets.

In order to make a database connection, you must supply a DBI connection string. This string always starts with dbi:, which is followed by the name of the driver and a ":". For example, a connection string for the mSQL driver always start with dbi:mSQL:. The second colon should be followed by any information required by driver to make the database connection. In the case of mSQL, you must supply a database name (prk in the following example), a hostname (localhost), and the port number of the database server (1114):

```
dbi:mSQL:prk:localhost:1114
```

Before you can make a connection, you must use the DBI module. Then you can invoke the DBI connect() method, supplying the connection string as an argument. If the connection is successful, a database handle is returned. If not, an undefined value is returned, and any error message can be found in $DBI::errstr. Here's a simple example that connects to a database, storing the database handle in the variable $dbh:

```
use DBI;
use strict;
# Attempt to connect to the data source. If this fails, die
# with an error report.
my($db_type, $db_name, $hostname, $port, $dbh, $sth);
# you should change these parameters to suit your
# system and configuration
$db_type = 'mSQL';
$db_name = 'test';
chop($hostname = 'hostname');
$port = 3334;
$dbh = DBI->connect("DBI:$db_type:$db_name:$hostname:$port",
                    undef, undef)
            or die "Could not connect: $DBI::errstr";
```

Using SQL to Create Tables

Before you can get any data out of a database, you need to put some data in it. Before you can put any data in a database, you need to create at least one table to store the data. As a result, you will find the CREATE TABLE statement rather useful. It's used to create an empty table within your database; once you have created a table, you can use the INSERT statement to add data to it. The CREATE TABLE statement follows this syntax:

```
CREATE TABLE tablename
    (column_name column_type [(column_width[, column_precision])]
    [,column_name, column_type [(column_width[, column_precision])]]
    ...)
```

The table name is followed by one or more column definitions. These must include the column name and the data type of the column. While each database server supports a wide variety of data types, two of the most common types are

INT and CHAR. The size of the INT data type is not specified in the CREATE
TABLE statement, but the CHAR data type requires you to specify this. For
example, here is the table definition for the Customer table:

```
CREATE TABLE Customer (
   first_name CHAR(10),
   last_name CHAR(15),
   Company_ID INT,
   Customer_ID INT
)
```

In the case of mSQL, you should become the msqluser/adminstrator (i.e., if you
don't have write permissions in the *msql.acl* file) and use the DBI prepare()
method to send an SQL command to the database server—in this case we'll be
creating a table named Customer. Then, execute() executes the command:

```
$sth = $dbh->prepare(<<END);
CREATE TABLE Customer (
   first_name CHAR(10),
   last_name CHAR(15),
   Company_ID INT,
   Customer_ID INT
)
END
$sth->execute;
$sth->finish;
```

Here are the CREATE TABLE statements for the remaining tables:

```
$sth = $dbh->prepare(<<END);
CREATE TABLE Company (
   Company_Name CHAR(20),
   Company_ID INT
)
END
$sth->execute;
$sth->finish;
$sth = $dbh->prepare(<<END);
CREATE TABLE Item (
   Item CHAR(64),
   Item_Code CHAR(4)
)
END
$sth->execute;
$sth->finish;
$sth = $dbh->prepare(<<END);
CREATE TABLE Line_Item (
   Inv_No INT,
   Item_Code CHAR(4),
   Quantity INT
)
END
$sth->execute;
$sth->finish;
```

```
$sth = $dbh->prepare(<<END);
CREATE TABLE Invoice (
  Inv_No INT,
  Customer_ID INT
)
END
$sth->execute;
$sth->finish;
```

Using SQL to Add Data to Tables

The SQL INSERT statement allows you to add rows to a given table. Here is the form of the INSERT statement:

```
INSERT INTO table-name [(column-identifier [, column-identifier]...)]
   VALUES (insert-value [, insert-value] ...)
```

The INSERT statement requires the name of the table, an optional list of columns, and a list of values. If you specify a list of columns, each value in the list of values must correspond to the columns in the column list. If you choose to omit the column list, you must supply a value for each column in the table, and that value must appear in the list in the same order in which the columns were added to the table when the CREATE TABLE statement was used. As a result, the following two INSERT statements are equivalent:

```
INSERT INTO Company (
  Company_Name,
  Company_ID
)
VALUES ('Someplace Attractive', 101)
INSERT INTO Company
VALUES ('Someplace Attractive', 101)
```

You should use the full version of the INSERT statement, since the explicitly stated column names will save you trouble down the road. If you change the structure of the table, say by adding a new column or transposing old columns, you need to change the old INSERT statements. Also, since all the column names are explicitly stated, the full version of the INSERT statement is self-documenting. The following SQL statements can be used to populate all of the tables created so far.

Here are the INSERT statements for the tables. Note the use of the DELETE statement to remove all rows from the tables prior to the INSERTs; this ensures against placing duplicate rows into the table.

```
DELETE FROM Company
```

You can execute this DELETE command with DBI as follows:

```
$sth->prepare("DELETE FROM Company");
$sth->execute;
$sth->finish;
```

Now, for some insertion:

```
INSERT INTO Company (
  Company_Name,
  Company_ID
)
VALUES ('Someplace Attractive', 101)
```

You can execute this **INSERT** command with DBI:

```
$sth->prepare(<<INSERT);
INSERT INTO Company (
  Company_Name,
  Company_ID
)
VALUES ('Homer, Doh!', 103)
INSERT
$sth->execute;
$sth->finish;
DELETE FROM Customer
INSERT INTO Customer (
  first_name,
  last_name,
  Company_ID,
  Customer_ID
)
VALUES ('Maeda', 'Schwartz', 101, 1)
INSERT INTO Customer (
  first_name,
  last_name,
  Company_ID,
  Customer_ID
)
VALUES ('Nathan', 'Patwardhan', 101, 2)
INSERT INTO Customer (
  first_name,
  last_name,
  Company_ID,
  Customer_ID
)
VALUES ('Mr.', 'Fiction', 103, 3)
DELETE FROM Invoice
INSERT INTO Invoice (
  Customer_ID,
  Inv_No
)
VALUES (1, 13249)
INSERT INTO Invoice (
  Customer_ID,
  Inv_No
)
VALUES (1, 10011)
INSERT INTO Invoice (
  Customer_ID,
  Inv_No
)
```

```
VALUES (2, 10249)
INSERT INTO Invoice (
  Customer_ID,
  Inv_No
)
VALUES (2, 17582)
INSERT INTO Invoice (
  Customer_ID,
  Inv_No
)
VALUES (2, 33678)
DELETE FROM Item
INSERT INTO Item (
  Item,
  Item_Code
)
VALUES ('2000 BTU Air Conditioner', 'D100')
INSERT INTO Item (
  Item,
  Item_Code
)
VALUES ('Copy Stand', 'H112')
INSERT INTO Item (
  Item,
  Item_Code
)
VALUES ('Large Filing Cabinet', 'F189')
INSERT INTO Item (
  Item,
  Item_Code
)
VALUES ('Mouse Pad', 'M079')
INSERT INTO Item (
  Item,
  Item_Code
)
VALUES ('Task Chair', 'C038')
DELETE FROM Line_Item
INSERT INTO Line_Item (
  Inv_No,
  Item_Code,
  Quantity
)
VALUES (13249, 'C038', 4)
INSERT INTO Line_Item (
  Inv_No,
  Item_Code,
  Quantity
)
VALUES (13249, 'M079', 3)
INSERT INTO Line_Item (
  Inv_No,
  Item_Code,
  Quantity
)
```

```
VALUES (10011, 'F189', 1)
INSERT INTO Line_Item (
  Inv_No,
  Item_Code,
  Quantity
)
VALUES (10249, 'C038', 8)
INSERT INTO Line_Item (
  Inv_No,
  Item_Code,
  Quantity
)
VALUES (10249, 'H112', 4)
INSERT INTO Line_Item (
  Inv_No,
  Item_Code,
  Quantity
)
VALUES (17582, 'M079', 2)
INSERT INTO Line_Item (
  Inv_No,
  Item_Code,
  Quantity
)
VALUES (33678, 'D100', 1)
```

The SQL SELECT Statement

The **CREATE TABLE** statement helps create the medium (the table), and the **INSERT** statement allows you to add the message (data). Now that you have a medium and a message, there must be some way to get that message out. The SQL **SELECT** statement is a powerful tool for extracting data. The most basic form of the SQL **SELECT** statement is shown here:

```
SELECT column-list FROM table-list
```

The `column-list` is a comma-delimited list of columns. It can also be replaced by *, which selects all columns in the table or tables. The `table-list` is also separated by commas. This **SELECT** statement retrieves all the names from the company table:

```
SELECT Company_Name
    FROM Company
GO
```

This retrieves all of the company names:

```
+--------------------+
| Someplace Attractive|
| Homer, Doh!        |
+--------------------+
```

When you need to issue a query using the DBI, you must first obtain a *statement handle*, which is obtained by invoking the database handle's **prepare()** method and supplying the SQL query as an argument. The statement handle that is returned by invoking this method is actually a fully *bless*ed reference to an object, and as such, has methods that you can invoke to process the results of the query. The statement handle (**$sth** in the next example) can be obtained as follows:

```
$sth->prepare(<<SLCT);
SELECT Company_Name
    FROM Company
SLCT
if (!$sth->execute) { die "Error:" . $sth->errstr . "\n"; }
```

Once you have a statement handle, you may execute the statement using its **execute()** method. If this method returns a true value, you may begin fetching rows using one of the DBI's fetch methods. In the example shown below, each row is fetched until there are no more to fetch. The **fetchrow_arrayref()** method returns a reference to an array of values corresponding to each column in the row:

```
my $names = $sth->{'NAME'};
my $numFields = $sth->{'NUM_OF_FIELDS'};
for(my $i = 0;  $i < $numFields;  $i++) {
    printf("%s%s", $$names[$i], $i ? "," : "");
}
print "\n";
while (my $ref = $sth->fetchrow_arrayref) {
    for(my $i = 0;  $i < $numFields;  $i++) {
        printf("%s%s", $$ref[$i], $i ? "," : "");
    }
    print "\n";
}
```

The **SELECT** statement pulls data in from multiple tables by specifying one or more *join conditions*. A join condition links two tables together by specifying column names from each table and the conditions by which they are joined. Generally, this would be the equality operator, since it allows you to join the Company and Customer tables together, and then say things like "give me the first and last name of each customer, and throw in the company name, too." If you don't specify a join condition for the two tables, there is no way to correlate the two tables. When you specify more than one table, it can be helpful to prefix each column name with the name of its table followed by a period. Here is a **SELECT** statement that retrieves all of the Customer names along with the name of the Company with which they are affiliated:

```
SELECT Customer.first_name,
        Customer.last_name, Company.Company_Name
FROM Customer, Company
WHERE Customer.Company_ID = Company.Company_ID
GO
```

Notice that the table name prefix is more than a luxury in this example. Without it, the SQL engine would not know which of the two Company_ID columns you are referring to. Here is the output of that SELECT statement:

```
+-------+------------+--------------------+
| Maeda | Schwartz   |Someplace Attractive |
| Nathan| Patwardhan |Someplace Attractive |
| Mr.   | Fiction    |Homer, Doh!         |
+-------+------------+--------------------+
```

Trouble in Whereville

If the **WHERE** clause doesn't specify a join condition for each table, strange things begin to happen. Each row in each table is matched with each row in each other table, producing what is known as a Cartesian product. For example, you may attempt to get a list of customers and companies without a join expression:

```
SELECT Customer.first_name,
       Customer.last_name, Company.Company_Name
FROM Customer, Company
GO
```

If you did that, you get the following results:

```
+-------+------------+--------------------+
| Maeda | Schwartz   |Someplace Attractive |
| Maeda | Schwartz   |Homer, Doh!         |
| Nathan| Patwardhan |Someplace Attractive |
| Nathan| Patwardhan |Homer, Doh!         |
| Mr.   | Fiction    |Someplace Attractive |
| Mr.   | Fiction    |Homer, Doh!         |
+-------+------------+--------------------+
```

Note that there are two rows in the Company table and three rows in the Customer table. Multiply the two together, and you get six. Notice how each name is matched to each company. Without some sort of join condition, it's hard to get useful results.

If you need to combine more than one table, you must use more than one join expression using the **AND** operator. Here is an example that reports customer names, invoice numbers, and each line item. Since the customer name and the invoice number repeat for each row in the result set, it's important to ensure that they are ordered correctly, which prevents data from appearing out of order. This is accomplished with the **ORDER BY** clause, which lists the columns to sort the results by.

```
SELECT Customer.first_name,
       Customer.last_name,
       Invoice.Inv_No,
       Item.Item
FROM Customer, Invoice, Item, Line_Item
```

```
WHERE Customer.Customer_ID = Invoice.Customer_ID
   AND Invoice.Inv_No = Line_Item.Inv_No
   AND Item.Item_Code = Line_Item.Item_Code
ORDER BY Customer.first_name, Customer.last_name, Invoice.Inv_No
GO
```

Here are the results of that query:

```
+-------+------------+-------+-------------------------+
| Nathan| Patwardhan | 10249 | Copy Stand              |
| Nathan| Patwardhan | 10249 | Task Chair              |
| Nathan| Patwardhan | 17582 | Mouse Pad               |
| Nathan| Patwardhan | 33678 | 2000 BTU Air Conditioner |
| Maeda | Schwartz   | 10011 | Large Filing Cabinet    |
| Maeda | Schwartz   | 13249 | Task Chair              |
| Maeda | Schwartz   | 13249 | Mouse Pad               |
+-------+------------+-------+-------------------------+
```

It's okay for a result to violate some or all of the normal forms, as long as the underlying data doesn't do the same. The principle of the normal forms is to find the most efficient storage mechanism for the data, which doesn't always translate to the most convenient organization for reports or user interfaces. You'll find that a lot of report writing involves denormalizing data, as has been done with the customer name, invoice numbers, and line item example.

You can also add expressions to the WHERE clause that filters the data. These are generally specified as arithmetic comparisons between a database variable and a constant value, such as Line_Item.Quantity > 4, or a string comparison, such as Customer.first_name = 'Maeda'. This updated example only retrieves line items that have a quantity of either one or more than four:

```
SELECT Customer.first_name,
       Customer.last_name,
       Invoice.Inv_No,
       Item.Item,
       Line_Item.Quantity
FROM Customer, Invoice, Item, Line_Item
WHERE Customer.Customer_ID = Invoice.Customer_ID
   AND Invoice.Inv_No = Line_Item.Inv_No
   AND Item.Item_Code = Line_Item.Item_Code
   AND (Line_Item.Quantity = 1 OR Line_Item.Quantity > 4)
ORDER BY Customer.first_name, Customer.last_name, Invoice.Inv_No
GO
```

Here are the results of that query:

```
+-------+------------+-------+-------------------------+---+
| Nathan| Patwardhan | 10249 | Task Chair              | 8 |
| Nathan| Patwardhan | 33678 | 2000 BTU Air Conditioner | 1 |
| Maeda | Schwartz   | 10011 | Large Filing Cabinet    | 1 |
+-------+------------+-------+-------------------------+---+
```

The SQL UPDATE Statement

By now, SQL probably looks like a write-only language, since you've only seen the CREATE TABLE, INSERT, and SELECT statements. However, the UPDATE statement can be used to update the data in one or more rows. Unless you wish to perform a mass update on an entire table, you need to employ a WHERE clause, which is similar to the one found in the SELECT statement. The UPDATE statement takes the form:

```
UPDATE table-name
SET column-identifier = expression
[, column-identifier = expression]
[WHERE search-condition]
```

The search condition is optional. Again, if you do not specify a WHERE clause, the entire table is updated. Here's an example that updates the Line_Item table by doubling the quantity of each line item:

```
UPDATE Line_Item
    SET Quantity = Quantity * 2
GO
```

The previous example updates every row in the table. You can also specify a filter condition in the WHERE clause. Here's an SQL UPDATE statement that doubles the quantity only if more than four items are on the invoice:

```
UPDATE Line_Item
    SET Quantity = Quantity * 2
    WHERE Quantity > 4
GO
```

Here's the DBI equivalent to an UPDATE statement:

```
$sth->prepare(<<YE);
UPDATE Line_Item
    SET Quantity = Quantity * 2
    WHERE Quantity > 4
YE
$sth->execute;
$sth->finish;
```

The SQL DELETE Statement

The DELETE statement allows you to delete one or more rows from a table, and it takes the form:

```
DELETE FROM table-name
    [WHERE search-condition]
```

Any of the search conditions shown for the UPDATE statement will work with the DELETE statement. Here's an example which will delete every line item with a Quantity less than 4:

```
DELETE FROM Line_Item
   WHERE Quantity < 4
GO
```

The do Method

The DBI offers a convenient method for issuing SQL statements that are not expected to return results. These are referred to as updates (including, but not limited to the UPDATE statement itself) rather than queries. SQL statements like DELETE, DROP, CREATE, UPDATE, and INSERT all fall into this category. The DBI allows you to prepare and execute these instantaneously with the do() method. There is no mucking about with statement handles, as shown in the next snippet of code:

```
my $sql = qq[INSERT INTO Company (Company_Name, Company_ID) ] .
          qq[VALUES ('Someplace Attractive', 101)];
my $status = $dbh->do($sql);
unless ($status) {
    print "Could not execute the command: $DBI::errstr";
}
```

qdsql: A Quick and Dirty Interactive SQL Client

Many SQL systems ship with an interactive query tool: Sybase has isql, miniSQL has msql, and so forth. These tools are useful for executing queries at the command line and obtaining results that are formatted as ASCII tables. They are often used to run batch queries or for ad hoc interaction with the server. The *Perl Resource Kit* CD-ROM includes qdsql, a quick and dirty SQL client for the Perl DBI. Before you run it, you will need to install the Data::ShowTable module.

The qdsql program also includes support for ReadLine-style command-line editing and history, but only if you have installed the Term::ReadKey and Term::ReadLine::Perl modules. You can install qdsql by copying it to a directory in your path, such as */usr/local/bin*. Also, by typing ./qdsql, you can execute it from within your current directory. Note that the qdsql uses the #! 'shebang' notation to refer to */usr/bin/perl*; if you do not have Perl or a symlink to the real Perl in this location, change the first line of qdsql to point to the correct location of the Perl executable.

Inside qdsql

qdsql is a remarkably simple application. By using the magic of ReadLine extensions and Data::ShowTable, qdsql manages to be a useful tool without being overly complex. The first parameter must be a DBI data source string. If there is no data source supplied, qdsql dies with an error message.

qdsql can operate in one of two modes. If the user supplied a -i switch followed by a filename, qdsql reads all input from that file; if not, it uses the ReadLine extension to allow the user to interactively issue queries. The user may type multiline SQL statements, since the SQL isn't sent to the server until the user types GO followed by a carriage return.

If a query is issued that returns no results, the user is informed of this fact. If the query returns results, the ShowTable() function is invoked to format it. There is a fair amount of preprocessing done on the result set before handing it off to ShowTable(); this is mainly in place to determine the maximum width of each column.

```perl
#!/usr/bin/perl
use DBI;
use Term::ReadLine;
use Data::ShowTable;
# The user should have supplied a DBI data source on the
# command line. If not, explain this to them and terminate
# the script.
my $datasource = $ARGV[0] || die "Usage: qdsql DATASOURCE";
# Attempt to connect to the data source. If this fails, die
# with an error report.
my $dbh = DBI->connect($datasource) || die "Could not connect: $DBI::errstr";
$dbh->{PrintError} = undef;
# Create a new Term::ReadLine object. This will give us a
# simple interactive shell.
#
my $term = new Term::ReadLine 'Quick and Dirty SQL';
$OUT = $term->OUT || STDOUT;
my $sql;
my $cnt = 1;
# If they supplied an input file with the -i parameter, then
# the input should be read from STDIN and not processed
# through readline.
if ($ARGV[1] eq '-i') {
    my $fn = $ARGV[2] || die "Please specify a filename.";
    open (FN, $fn) || die "Could not open $fn: $!";
    while (<FN>) {
        print qq[ $cnt>];
        process_input($_, \$sql, \$cnt);
    }
    close(FN);
} else {
    my $rl_avail =
        defined &Term::ReadLine::Perl::readline
            ? "enabled"
            : "available (get Term::ReadKey and Term::ReadLine::Perl)";
    print qq[qdsql - Quick and Dirty SQL for DBI\n] .
        qq[Readline support $rl_avail\n\n];
```

```
        # Loop until they hit CTRL+D.
        while( defined ($_ = $term->readline("qdsql: $cnt>")) ) {
            process_input($_, \$sql, \$cnt);
        }
    }
$dbh->disconnect;
sub process_input {
        $_  = shift;
        my $sql = shift;
        my $cnt = shift;
        # GO is the query separator. When it's encountered, it
        # signifies that the query is ready to go to the server.
        # If the current line of user input is not "GO", then
        # it's assumed that the line should be appended to the
        # query, and we issue a 'next' to read another line.
        unless (/^\s*GO\s*$/i || /^\s*GO_SHHH\s*$/i) {
            chomp;
            $$sql .= $_;
            $$cnt++;
            next;
        }
        if ($$sql =~ /^\s*$/) {
            next;
        }
        # Send the query to the server.
        my $sth = $dbh->prepare($$sql);
        $$sql = ""; $$cnt = 1;
        unless ($sth->execute) {
            # Don't die if there was an error executing the
            # statement - it's possible that the user typed in
            # gibberish. Don't print an error if the user typed
            # GO_SHHH instead of GO. This is usually used for
            # batch scripts where you type DROP TABLE foo before
            # the CREATE TABLE statement. If the table doesn't
            # exist, you get an error that might alarm users.
            unless (/^\s*GO_SHHH\s*$/i) {
                print "\nStatement failed: " . $sth->errstr . "\n";
            }
        } else {
            # Data::ShowTable likes to know a lot about the data
            # we're formatting. Unfortunately, we don't know a
            # lot about it ourselves :-). The only thing that
            # seems to be ultra-critical is the width of each
            # column. Although we would normally give an
            # anonymous subroutine that fetches rows to the
            # ShowTable method, this bit of code will actually
            # prefetch all the rows, and calculate the maximum
            # width as it goes along. The extra advantage of
            # this is a result set that can scroll backward.
            my (@titles, @types, @widths, $row, @allrows);
            # Fetch each row as a reference to an array.
            while ($row = $sth->fetchrow_arrayref) {
                my @row = @$row;
                # Loop over each column and check its width
```

```
            # against the widths in the @widths array. If we
            # encounter a column that is larger than the
            # maximum width we've stored, then we'll
            # replace the value in the @widths array. For
            # padding, an extra 2 is added to the width.
            my $i;
            for ($i = 0; $i <= $#row; $i++) {
                if (length($row[i]) + 2 > $widths[$i]) {
                    $widths[i] = length($row[i]) + 2;
                }
            }
            # The @allrows array is an array of references
            # to each row.
            push @allrows, \@row;
        }
        if (@allrows) {
            # j is an iterator for the array of rows. The
            # getrow() method will return rows, using $j
            # as an iterator.
            my $j = 0;
            my $code = sub { return getrow(\@allrows, \$j, @_) };

            ShowTable \@titles, \@types, \@widths, $code;
        } else {
            print "\nNo results were returned from this query.\n";
        }
    }
}
sub getrow {
    my $rows      = shift; # a reference to an array of all the rows
    my $index_ref = shift; # a reference to the index variable
    my $rewind    = shift; # flag to tell if we need to rewind the index

    my @rows = @{$rows}; # dereference the array of rows.

    # If ShowTable() passed in a nonzero value for this
    # parameter, then rewind the index and return. This does
    # not return a row.
    if ($rewind) {
        $$index_ref = 0;
        return 1;
    }

    # Return the current row and increment the index.
    return @{$rows[$$index_ref++]};
}
```

Using qdsql

In order to use qdsql, you must supply a DBI data source string on the command line. The syntax of this string varies from driver to driver, so please check the DBI documentation for your driver to determine the correct syntax.

Here is a sample invocation of **qdsql** that uses the DBD::mSQL driver *bash-2.00$ qdsql dbi:mSQL:prk:localhost:1114*

```
qdsql - Quick and Dirty SQL for DBI
Readline support enabled
qdsql: 1>
```

The data source string shown in the previous example connects to the mSQL server listening on port 1114 on the local host. You must have created the **prk** database using the **msqladmin** utility. Procedures for creating databases will vary between database servers, so you should check the server documentation for more information.

The **qdsql: 1>** prompt indicates that **qdsql** is waiting for you to give it some SQL to execute. You can type SQL statements your database server understands and then type GO on a line by itself to execute the SQL and display the results.

9

The Net Modules

Perl has supported networking almost from the beginning, but raw socket programming can be a large task when you want to deal with higher-level services like FTP and Telnet. The Net modules make it almost as easy to deal with common services as to use the command-line interfaces they provide. In this chapter, we'll give you an introduction to using network services in Perl.

In addition to the modules we describe here, there are several other useful ones in the Net hierarchy, but they are already well documented in the pod and are used only in specialized situations, so we haven't bothered to rehash the information here. These modules include Net::DNS, Net::hostent, Net::netent, Net::protoent, Net::servent, Net::Config, Net::DummyInetd, Net::PH, Net::SNPP, Net::Socket, Net::Country, Net::DNS, Net::Gen, Net::Ident, Net::Inet, and Net::UNIX.

Domain Information with Net::Whois

InterNIC is an organization formed to keep records of the Internet domain and administrative controls. InterNIC acts like a phone book or directory listing of the people who are using the Internet.

A domain's whois listing announces a domain's contact information, creation, and last-updated status. Net::Whois::Domain was written by Chip Salzenberg to retrieve and parse a domain's whois information from InterNIC.

A typical whois entry looks like:

```
Some Fictitious Company, Inc.
12C Gucci-gucci-coo St.
Beverly Hills, CA 90210

Domain Name: SOMEFICCOM.COM

Administrative Contact, Technical Contact, Zone Contact:
    Doe, John (JD86) johndoe@someficcom.com
    xxx-xxx-xxxx x xxx
Billing Contact:
    Doe, Jane (JD495) janedoe@someficcom.com
    xxx-xxx-xxxx x xxx

  Record last updated on 27-May-97.
  Record created on 27-May-97.
  Database last updated on 15-Sep-97 04:41:03 EDT.

  Domain servers in listed order:

  NS.SOMEFICCOM.COM               127.0.0.1
```

Net::Whois::server() contacts *whois.internic.net* by default; this can be changed by calling Net::Whois::server with another server name. Here's an example that takes a domain, *someficcom.com*, and outputs as many entries it can from InterNIC's whois listing:

```perl
my $dom = 'someficcom.com';
my $w = Net::Whois::Domain->new($dom)
    or die("Can't find info on $dom\n");

print "Domain: ", $w->domain, "\n";
print "Name: ", $w->name, "\n";
print "Tag: ", $w->tag, "\n";
print "Address:\n", map { "    $_\n" } $w->address;
print "Country: ", $w->country, "\n";
print "Servers:\n", map { "    $$_[0] ($$_[1])\n" } @{$w->servers};

my ($c, $t);
if ($c = $w->contacts) {
    print "Contacts:\n";
    for $t (sort keys %$c) {
        print "   $t:\n";
        print map { "\t$_\n" } @{$$c{$t}};
    }
}

$cur_server = Net::Whois::server;
```

Domain Names and Hostnames with Net::Domain

Net::Domain, part of the *libnet* package by Graham Barr (*gbarr@ti.com*) implements several methods to find the Fully Qualified Domain Name (FQDN) of the current host. Once the FQDN has been found, the hostname and host domain can be derived.

Get the Fully Qualified Domain Name with hostfqdn()

This method identifies and returns the FQDN of the current host. It returns **undef** if the FQDN isn't found. Here's an example of **hostfqdn()** that extracts the FQDN from a machine called *voyager.charred-wreck.com*:

```perl
#!/usr/local/bin/perl -w
use Net::Domain qw(hostfqdn);
use strict;

my $fqdn = hostfqdn();
print "My FQDN is $fqdn\n";
```

If everything works correctly, the program outputs:

```
My FQDN is voyager.charred-wreck.com
```

Get the Hostname with hostname()

This method returns the smallest part of the FQDN that can be used to identify the host. It returns **undef** if the hostname isn't found. Here's an example of **hostname()** that extracts a hostname from a machine called *nervous-tick.chief-inspector.com*:

```perl
#!/usr/local/bin/perl -w
use Net::Domain qw(hostname);
use strict;

my $hname = hostname();
print "My hostname is $hname\n";
```

The program outputs:

```
My hostname is nervous-tick
```

Get the Domain Name with hostdomain()

This method returns the remainder of the FQDN after the hostname has been removed: the domain. It returns **undef** if the host domain isn't found. Here's an example that outputs the domain of a machine called *seven.in-one-blow.com*:

```
#!/usr/local/bin/perl -w
use Net::Domain qw(hostdomain);
use strict;

my $hname = hostdomain();
print "My domain is $hname\n";
```

The program outputs:

```
My domain is in-one-blow.com
```

Net::Ping and Network Connectivity

The `ping` utility has been used on UNIX-based operating systems for many years. `ping` sends out packets of information to other hosts based on specific parameters and reports the status of outside hosts' network connectivity based on success or failure.

When you `ping` a machine on a network, you're testing the machine for reachability. If the machine responds to your `ping`, the machine is possibly available and you can connect to it.

`ping`ing can be accomplished in one of three ways. First, you could try to `ping` a remote host through TCP, where `ping()` tries to connect to the remote machine's echo port; any established connection means that the host can be reached. Next, you can use the `udp` protocol, which tells `ping()` to send a `udp` packet to the remote machine's echo port; if the sent and received packets are identical, the remote host is considered reachable. Finally, you can send an `icmp` echo message to the remote machine; if the remote machine received and returned a correct echoed message, the remote machine is considered to be reachable. You must be *root* (or a program setuid to *root*) to use the `icmp` protocol.

`ping` should be tested on the local machine first, to test the local network interface. On a UNIX-based machine, the syntax of a simple `ping` request would be `ping localhost`, or `ping 127.0.0.1`, or simply `ping 127.1`.

(This is `ping` the utility, not `ping` with Net::Ping.) If successful, `ping` responds with a message like this:

```
PING 127.0.0.1 (127.0.0.1): 56 data bytes
64 bytes from 127.0.0.1: icmp_seq=0 ttl=255 time=1.277 ms
64 bytes from 127.0.0.1: icmp_seq=1 ttl=255 time=0.919 ms
64 bytes from 127.0.0.1: icmp_seq=2 ttl=255 time=0.922 ms
64 bytes from 127.0.0.1: icmp_seq=3 ttl=255 time=0.916 ms
64 bytes from 127.0.0.1: icmp_seq=4 ttl=255 time=0.926 ms
64 bytes from 127.0.0.1: icmp_seq=5 ttl=255 time=0.923 ms

--- 127.0.0.1 ping statistics ---
6 packets transmitted, 6 packets received, 0% packet loss
round-trip min/avg/max = 0.916/0.980/1.277 ms
```

If unsuccessful, `ping` responds with a message like this:

```
PING 128.200.0.0 (128.200.0.0): 56 data bytes
ping: sendto: No route to host
ping: wrote 128.200.0.0 64 chars, ret=-1
ping: sendto: No route to host
ping: wrote 128.200.0.0 64 chars, ret=-1
ping: sendto: No route to host
ping: wrote 128.200.0.0 64 chars, ret=-1


--- 128.200.0.0 ping statistics ---
3 packets transmitted, 0 packets received, 100% packet loss
```

Here's an example using Net::Ping that `pings` a remote host called *www.some-host.com*; the `ping` request doesn't execute an external program to check the remote host and times out after 10 seconds if there is no reply:

```perl
#!/usr/local/bin/perl -w

use Net::Ping;
use strict;

my $host_to_ping = 'www.somehost.com';
my $pinger = Net::Ping->new(Timeout => 10);

if($pinger->ping($host_to_ping)) {
    print $host, " responded.\n";
} else {
    print $host, " is unreachable.  Try again later.\n";
}
```

Simple TCP Interaction with Net::Telnet

Net::Telnet was written by Jay Rogers (*jay@rgrs.com*) for interactive I/O over TCP. It implements the simple I/O methods `print`, `get`, and `getline` and supports timeouts and pattern matching from the input stream (i.e., a system prompt).

The Net::Telnet module is useful to those people who aren't well versed in sockets programming or who are seeking a simple method of interacting with a remote host's TCP services. Many people have tried to use pipes and filehandles to send data to a remote host, which doesn't work (most of the time), like:

```perl
#!/usr/local/bin/perl -w

$tprog = '/usr/bin/telnet';
$hostname = 'myhost.somename.com';
$login = 'joeuser';
$password = 'whatjane';

open(TELNET, "|".$tprog)
        or die("error opening telnet $tprog: $!");
print TELNET $login."\n";
```

```
print TELNET $password."\n";
print TELNET "ls -al\n";
close(TELNET) or die("error closing telnet: $!");
```

If you've ever tried anything like this or you'd like to use a module that can, Net::Telnet is for you.

The Net::Telnet constructor, **new**, takes arguments documented with the complete Net::Telnet API in the *Perl Module Reference*. Specify the session defaults used in the Net::Telnet constructor. In this case, we'll be contacting host *humpy.camel.com* with a 10-second timeout, and will expect to encounter the prompt represented by the regular expression below:

```
$hostname = 'humpy.camel.com';

$np_telnet = Net::Telnet->new(
                    Host => $hostname,
                    Timeout => 10,
                    Prompt => '/[$%#>] $/'
);
```

Net::Telnet uses `login()` to authenticate a user with a remote host. `login()` times out if the prompt (shown above) doesn't match. `login()` requires two arguments: a username and password. Empty or missing arguments lead to failed logins:

```
$username = 'jcamel';
$password = 'noway';

$np_telnet->login($username, $passwd);
```

The `cmd()` method executes a command on the remote system and returns the results to a variable. `cmd()` times out if the prompt (shown above) doesn't match the prompt you wrote in the constructor:

```
$remote_cmd = "/usr/bin/finger";

@response = $np_telnet->cmd($remote_cmd);
for(@response) { print $_; }
```

`waitfor()` is another important Net::Telnet method. It tells Net::Telnet to wait for or expect a certain character or set of characters to come from the input stream. Once the match is found, `print()` your response to the remote host and `waitfor()` another match:

```
$np_telnet->waitfor('/some match here/');
$np_telnet->print("come again?");

$np_telnet->waitfor('/right back at ya!/');
$np_telnet->print("EXIT");
```

Now, close the connection to the remote host:

```
$np_telnet->close;
```

Here's an example that connects you to an archie server, sends a query to the server, and returns a list of matches to your query. In this case we'll search for *latest.tar.gz*, the latest Perl distribution:

```perl
#!/usr/local/bin/perl -w

use strict;
use Net::Telnet;

my $archie_host = 'archie.mcgill.ca';
my $login = 'archie';

my $tel_obj = Net::Telnet->new(Host => $archie_host,
                    Timeout => 20
                    );

# wait for the login prompt, then send the login name: archie. we have to
# do it this way because you don't need a password when logging
# into an archie server with telnet. login() won't work since it's
# expecting a username/pass pair.
$tel_obj->waitfor('/login:.*$/');
$tel_obj->print($login);

# wait for the archie> prompt.
$tel_obj->waitfor('/archie.*$/');

# if we've got the prompt, then send our query.
# when the query is completed, show us what we have.
my @found = $tel_obj->cmd("find latest.tar.gz");
for(@found) { print $_; }
```

File Transfers with Net::FTP

File Transfer Protocol (FTP) is a popular means of transferring files between computers. FTP communication follows the client/server model: the client initiates commands, and the server responds with messages and status codes. Net::FTP, written by Graham Barr (*gbarr@ti.com*), provides a number of wrapper functions to implement the client side of FTP.

The FTP protocol allows for two-way transactions of files, in which files can be sent to or taken from an FTP server. These transactions involve the local file-system (on the client side) and the remote filesystem (on the server side). Net::FTP implements file transfers so that a file on the server is downloaded with the same filename unless a destination filename is specified.

The FTP protocol also specifies various types of files that can be transferred. These types define (among many other things) how end-of-line characters are handled for different types of files.

The following is a list of some commonly used Net::FTP methods.

new()

> new() is the Net::FTP constructor used to create a new Net::FTP object. You must specify a hostname in new():

```
$ftphost = 'ftp.some-neat-anon-site.com';
$my_ftp_session = Net::FTP->new($ftphost);
```

> new() also takes these options that are passed as key/value pairs:

Firewall

> Machine name acting as an FTP firewall. This can be overridden by setting the FTP_FIREWALL environment variable.

Port

> Port number to connect to on the remote machine. (Most FTP servers run on port 21.)

Timeout

> Timeout after *x* seconds. The default is 120 seconds.

Debug

> Debug level sets the maximum number of lines used to show the debugging information.

Passive

> Takes a true or false value. If Passive is set to true, all data transfers are done in passive mode; can be overridden by the FTP_PASSIVE environment variable.

login()

> login() logs into the FTP server with the username and password. Net::FTP defaults to Net::Netrc (see next section) if login() hasn't been given any arguments. Anonymous logins without a specified password default to the user's email address as a password:

```
$username = 'anonymous';
$password = 'getreal@true-fiction.com';

$my_ftp_session->login($username, $password);
```

authorize()

> Connections attempted through a firewall use authorize() to send data. Without arguments, authorize() uses Net::Netrc to conduct lookups.

type()

> type() tells the remote machine what type to use when transferring the data. Net::FTP uses these synonyms for type: ascii, binary, ebcdic, byte.

```
$my_ftp_session->type("I");
```

cwd()

>cwd() tells the remote server to change directories to the argument passed to cwd(). It takes one argument—the directory name:

```
$change_me = '/pub/perl/CPAN/';
$my_ftp_session->cwd($change_me);
```

cdup()

>cdup() changes the directory to the parent of the current remote directory.

pwd()

>pwd() returns the full pathname of the current remote directory.

ls()

>ls() gets a listing of the current directory and takes one argument—the directory name.

```
$dirname = '/pub/ftp/perl/src';
print $my_ftp_session->ls($dirname);
```

dir()

>dir() works like ls(), except dir() gets a directory listing in long format (file sizes, dates, etc). It takes one argument—the directory name.

```
$long_dir = '/pub/hats/man/with/yellow';
print $my_ftp_session($long_dir);
```

get()

>get() grabs a file from the remote host and stores it locally. If a local filename is not specified, the local file inherits the same basename as the file on the server.

```
$get_me = '/pub/ftp/magic/all-magic-files.tar.gz';
$local_file = 'all-magic-files_rev.tar.gz';

$my_ftp_session->get($get_me, $local_file);
```

put()

>put() takes a file from the local filesystem and transfers it to the remote host machine. It can take two arguments: the first for the local file and the second for the remote file. Or it can take one argument, and the remote file will inherit the same basename as the local file:

```
$put_me = 'give_me_up.txt';
$my_ftp_session->put($put_me);
```

quit()

>quit() sends a QUIT command to the FTP server, which closes the socket and ends the session.

Here is an example Net::FTP client that logs into an FTP host anonymously and downloads a file called *TESTFILE*:

```
#!/usr/local/bin/perl -w
```

```
use Net::FTP;

$hostname = 'fictitious.somehost.com';
$username = 'anonymous';
$password = 'rybrdbry@who-needs-celsius.com';
$ftp_home = '/pub';
$filename = 'TESTFILE';

$ftp = Net::FTP->new($hostname);
$ftp->login($username, $password);

# changes the current directory to $home and announces the cwd
print $ftp->cwd($ftp_home),"\n";

# lists and announces the contents of the current directory
print $ftp->ls($home),"\n";

# gets the specified filename
$ftp->get($filename);

# closes the connection to the ftp server
$ftp->quit;
```

FTP Configuration with Net::Netrc

UNIX-based FTP clients use a file called *.netrc*, which the user can configure to simplify access to frequently visited sites. With a properly defined *.netrc* file, you can simply execute the FTP command to a favorite FTP host, and be automatically logged in to the FTP server. Your *.netrc* file contains several tags FTP needs when your login is being authenticated: machine, login, and password. Your specifics are placed after each tag in your *.netrc* file:

```
machine machine-to-login-to login username password yourpassword
```

Net::Netrc was written by Graham Barr (*gbarr@ti.com*) to implement a simple interface to the *.netrc* file. Net::Netrc tells you which hosts you are able to automatically connect to by reading the *.netrc* file. Net::Netrc itself doesn't connect to remote hosts; it's simply used to query your configuration file.

If you think it's a big security risk to enter your user name and password for remote sites in unencrypted form, you're right. Many sites consider *.netrc* files a violation of security policies and do not allow them. If you do use *.netrc* files, we recommend that you only enter anonymous logins there. In addition, most FTP clients require that the *.netrc* file is owned by you, with 0400 or 0600 permissions so no one else can peek; if the permissions aren't correct, the file won't be read. Net::Netrc follows this security convention.

Using Net::Netrc

The Net::Netrc constructor isn't called **new** because it doesn't really create a new object. Instead, it's called `lookup` because Net::Netrc looks up the machine name in the *.netrc* file and defines the following tokens accordingly:

machine

> **machine** searches in your *.netrc* for a machine that matches the name you specified.
>
> ```
> machine some-remote-machine
> ```

name

> **name** denotes the name of the remote machine. Net::Netrc's autologin process searches the *.netrc* for the remote machine specified when you created the Net::Netrc object.
>
> ```
> some-remote-machine
> ```

default

> **default** is the default name that matches any machine name; it gives the user anonymous logins to machines not listed in the *.netrc*.
>
> ```
> default login anonymous password myemail@mysite.address
> ```

login

> This token denotes the user who is logged into the remote machine. The autologin process uses the specified name.

password

> **password** is the password for the user who logs in. The auto-login process uses the specified password if the remote server requires one.

account

> **account** is an additional password for the user who logs in. The autologin process uses the additional password if the remote server requires one.

macdef name

> This token defines a macro that is compatible only with FTP, as implemented in Net::Netrc.

The following methods are defined by Net::Netrc:

lookup()

> This method looks up and returns a reference to the entry for the specified machine:
>
> ```
> $host = 'ftp.please-look-me-up.com';
> $machine = Net::Netrc->lookup($host);
> ```

lookup() optionally takes a login argument. If the login argument isn't supplied, lookup() returns the first entry in the *.netrc* for the machine in question.

lookup() returns a reference to the default entry only if it can't find a matching entry.

login()

This method returns the username (login id) specified by the *.netrc* login token.

```
$login = $machine->login;
print "Found your login: $login in the .netrc file\n"
    if $login;
```

password()

password() returns the password specified by the *.netrc* password token.

```
# be careful with this one
$password = $machine->password;
print "Found your password: $password in the .netrc file\n";
    if $password;
```

account()

This method returns account information specified by the *.netrc* account entry (if any has been given).

```
$account = $machine->account;
print "Account information from .netrc: $account\n"
    if $account;
```

lpa()

lpa() returns a list of login, password, and account information specified by the *.netrc* tokens.

```
(@login_pass_account) = $machine->lpa;
for(@login_pass_account) { print $_."\n"; }
```

10

News::NNTPClient and News::Newsrc

Usenet is a collection of bulletin-board-like groups on the Internet, covering every topic under the sun. If you have a hobby or interest, it's likely you'll find a Usenet newsgroup in which it is discussed by hundreds (or thousands) of other aficionados.

The first incarnation of Usenet appeared in late 1979 as the work of two Duke graduate students who wanted to hook computers together so information could be exchanged between members of the UNIX community. Several years later, in 1984, the volume of information on Usenet had increased, so a mechanism was added to the "B" news software for moderated newsgroups, and in 1986, the "B" news format was extended to include a new naming convention for newsgroups. "C" news software soon followed the change in Usenet naming conventions.

The current implementation of Usenet was shaped by the Network News Transfer Protocol (NNTP), released in March 1986, which transfers information through TCP/IP. Unlike the old Usenet software, NNTP allows a single server to run NNTP software and multiple machines to have reading and posting privileges to the local newsfeed. Overall, NNTP is much faster than its predecessor, UUCP, and machines running NNTP software don't have the load impact that is characteristic of UUCP.

Information is propagated through Usenet by newsfeeds. One site requests a newsfeed from another site, and a third site requests a newsfeed from the second site, etc. Each site running an NNTP server dictates which sites (if any) can receive a newsfeed from the site running NNTP services. When a user is running a news user agent, like rn, their client software talks to the NNTP server and requests are negotiated. When a client posts, or sends information to a worldwide newsgroup hosted by the server, this posting is received by the NNTP server and fed to other servers worldwide. Each server periodically updates newsgroup information and obtains recent news articles. Usenet articles exist (as files) on the NNTP server.

There are a variety of newsgroup distribution types, from local newsgroups to world newsgroups. A local newsgroup was created for users on only one NNTP server. Local newsgroups may often have a greater range of hierarchies than world newsgroups, as the local news administrator may create a newsgroup of any name, providing that the content remains pertinent to their site or region. World newsgroups are world-readable. Whether you post an article to a world-readable or local newsgroup, the NNTP commands and responses are the same.

This chapter explores NNTP commands and responses. It also looks at **NNTP-Client.pm**, which simplifies the process of writing a Perl-based NNTP news client, or user agent. To use this chapter effectively, you must have installed News::NNTPClient and News::Newsrc.

The NNTP Protocol

Like other servers, the NNTP server is bound to a port, listens for incoming connections, and returns appropriate responses depending on a client's request. Most news servers run on port 119, as listed in */etc/services*, which news clients attempt to connect to by default. When a news client connects with an NNTP server or the port on which the NNTP server is running, a message like the following is produced:

```
Trying 0.0.0.0...
Connected to hostname.mydomain.com.
Escape character is '^]'.
200 newshost.mydomain.com InterNetNews NNRP server INN 1.5.1 17-Dec-1996
ready (posting ok).
```

Many NNTP servers understand the `help`, or `HELP,` command. When a client issues a `help` command, servers respond with a list of available commands. We'll explore many of these commands as implemented by News::NNTPClient throughout this chapter.

My server outputs the following with a `help` command:

```
200 news.mydomain.com InterNetNews NNRP server INN 1.5.1 17-Dec-1996 ready
(posting ok).
HELP
100 Legal commands
    authinfo user Name|pass Password|generic <prog> <args>
    article [MessageID|Number]
    body [MessageID|Number]
    date
    group newsgroup
    head [MessageID|Number]
```

```
    help
    ihave
    last
    list
[active|active.times|newsgroups|distributions|distrib.pats|overview.fmt|
    subscriptions]
    listgroup newsgroup
    mode reader
    newgroups yymmdd hhmmss ["GMT"] [<distributions>]
    newnews newsgroups yymmdd hhmmss ["GMT"] [<distributions>]
    next
    post
    slave
    stat [MessageID|Number]
    xgtitle [group_pattern]
    xhdr header [range|MessageID]
    xover [range]
    xpat header range|MessageID pat [morepat...]
    xpath MessageID
Report problems to <usenet@news.mydomain.com>
```

All unrecognized commands receive a 500 **What?** error.

After connecting to the NNTP server (and receiving a 200 message that indicates success), you select a newsgroup with your news client. If you connect directly to *news.mydomain.com*, and select the newsgroup `local.test` with the `group` command, your session might look like this:

```
200 news.mydomain.com InterNetNews NNRP server INN 1.5.1 17-Dec-1996 ready
(posting ok).
group local.test
211 4 1 4 local.test
QUIT
205 .
```

The `211 4 1 4` to the left of `local.test` represents:

- `211` is the success code; if the group had not been found, the server would have returned a 411 error.

- `4` is the total number of articles in `local.test`.

- `1` is the number of the first article in `local.test`.

- `4` is the number of the last article in `local.test`. Executing `list active` shows all of the active newsgroups on the server.

Once the server returns a 211 code, the client can send an article request to the server. The `article` command takes one or two arguments, the first being a message ID, the second an article number. If the `article` command is successful, the server outputs the selected message. If the `article` command is incorrect, the server returns a 501 error with the correct command syntax. If the article does not exist, the server returns a 423 error for "bad article number."

The `xhdr` command returns the selected headers (X-headers) from a certain news-group. An X-header contains all the information about the news article, including the poster's mail address, the subject of the message, the date and time the message was posted, the newsgroup(s) the message appeared in, and the message-ID (among other headers). If you want to see the subjects of articles 1-4 of `local.test`, execute `xhdr subject 1-4`. `xhdr` returns a 221 on success. `xpat` is similar to `xhdr`; it matches patterns of X-headers against the input string. If you execute `xpat subject 1-9 *test*` for `local.test`, NNTP returns:

```
xpat subject 1-9 *test*
221 subject matches follow.
1 testing!
3 TIN test
4 your horse is in my backyard!
5 a rolling stone grows drunker and older
6 to die unsung would really bring you down...
8 ONE MILLION E-MAIL ADDRESSES FOR $19.95!!!!!!!
9 IGPAY ATINLAY ISWAY UNFAY ONTDAY OUYAY INKTHAY?
```

You can also post news articles with NNTP. When you issue the **post** command, the server returns 340 if posting is permitted. If you get an error, such as 501, you can't post articles with this method. Most servers require that your headers include a `Newsgroups`, `Subject`, and `From` header, but allow an empty message body. You receive a 240 reply if your message has been posted without error. Here's an example of posting to `local.test` by using NNTP:

```
200 news.mydomain.com InterNetNews NNRP server INN 1.5.1 17-Dec-1996 ready
(posting ok).
post
340 Ok
Newsgroups: local.test
Subject: talking NNTP
From: nvp@mydomain.com

    As you can see, I speak NNTP!

.
240 Article posted
QUIT
205 .
```

When the article arrived in `local.test`, it looks like:

```
From news.mydomain.com!not-for-mail Sun Mar  9 19:18:37 1997
Path: news.mydomain.com!not-for-mail
From: nvp@mydomain.com
Newsgroups: local.test
Subject: talking NNTP
Date: 10 Mar 1997 00:09:33 GMT
Organization: Unix Perl Resource Kit
Lines: 2
Distribution: local
Message-ID: <5fvjft$k3$2@news.mydomain.com>
```

```
NNTP-Posting-Host: news.mydomain.com
Xref: news.mydomain.com local.test:6
```

```
    This is a test posting.
```

Perl and inews

Another method of posting articles to an NNTP server is `inews`. The `inews` program is distributed with the INN news server package and is considered a front end to an NNTP server. `inews` takes command-line arguments for each attribute of an article's X-header, such as `From`, `Subject`, and `Newsgroups`, but receives the message's body from a file redirected from STDIN.

Here's what `inews` command-line switches do:

-n Name of newsgroup, in this case, `local.test`

-f Who the posting is from, in this case, *nvp@mydomain.com*

-o Name of organization, like O'Reilly and Associates

-t Subject of article, in this case "Test Posting Using Inews"

For example, a file called *testpost.txt* containing, "this is a test posting!" would be posted using `inews`, like:

```
inews -n local.test -f nvp@mydomain.com -o "Your Organization Here" \
   -t "Test Posting Using Inews" < testpost.txt.
```

Here's an example using a filehandle that pipes STDIN into `inews`:

```
#!/usr/local/bin/perl -w

use strict; # watch your mouth, young man!
my($inews_prog, $subject, $from, $org, $ng);

$inews_prog = '/usr/news/bin/inews';
$subject = 'Perl piping to inews';
$from = 'nvp@mydomain.com';
$org = 'Unix Perl Resource Kit';
$ng = 'local.test';

print("[NNTP] Talk to me: ");
chop($quip = <STDIN>);

open(INEWS,
    "|$inews_prog -n $ng -f \"$from\" -o \"$org\" -t \"$subject\"")
       or die("$inews_prog error: $!");
print INEWS "$quip\n";
close(INEWS);
```

News::NNTPClient and Automating NNTP Commands

The NNTPClient modules were written by Rodger Anderson (*rodger@boi.hp.co*) to automate communicating with a news server. News::NNTPClient methods share the same names as commands you'd send to an NNTP server.

To use News::NNTPClient, the first line of your script should be:

```
use News::NNTPClient; or require News::NNTPClient;
```

Then, create a new News object, like:

```
$c = News::NNTPClient new(); # Use default port and hostname
```

or specify the new host you'll be connecting to:

```
$newshost = 'news.mydomain.com';
$c = News::NNTPClient->new($newshost); # Use $newshost with default port 119
```

or specify the new host and port you'll be connecting to:

```
$newshost = 'news.mydomain.com';
$port = 8080;
$c = News::NNTPClient->new($newshost, $port); # Use $newshost and $port
```

Opening a Newsgroup and Printing Articles

NNTPClient has a group() function, which works the same as the NNTP group command. This function is used like so:

```
($art1, $art2) = $c->group('groupname');
```

where $art1 is the first available article, and $art2 is the last available article in the newsgroup. group() can be used with article() to output all the articles in group('groupname').

Putting it all together, you can output all the articles from the newsgroup local.test like:

```
#!/usr/local/bin/perl -w

use News::NNTPClient;
use strict; # yummy!
my($c, $nntpserv, $newsgroup, $first, $last);

$nntpserv = 'news.mydomain.com';
$newsgroup = 'local.test';

$c = News::NNTPClient->new($nntpserv);

($first, $last) = ($c->group($newsgroup));
```

```
print("Newsgroup $newsgroup has ",
        $last-$first, " articles, numbered ",
        "from $first to $last.\n");

for (; $first <= $last; $first++) {
    print $c->article($first);
}
```

Accessing Response Codes

NNTPClient outputs the response code from the news server using the code() function. Here is the above example with code():

```
#!/usr/local/bin/perl -w

use News::NNTPClient;
use strict;
my($nntpserv, $nntpgroup, $c, $first, $last);

$nntpserv = 'news.somenewshost.com';
$newsgroup = 'local.test';

$c = News::NNTPClient->new($nntpserv);

($first, $last) = ($c->group($newsgroup));

print("Newsgroup $newsgroup has ",
        $last-$first, " articles, numbered ",
        "from $first to $last.\n");

for (; $first <= $last; $first++) {
    print $c->article($first);

    # Now, output the server response code.
    print ("Server responded: ",
            $c->code, ".\n");
}
```

Checking for New Articles

Newsgroups can also be checked for new articles received within a specified amount of time. NNTPClient's newnews() function behaves the same way as the newnews command. To find how many articles were posted in the last hour to local.test, do:

```
$newsgroup = 'local.test';
$c->group($newsgroup);
$c->newnews(time() - 3600); # 3600 = number of seconds in the last hour
```

The newnews() function also accepts wildcards, like:

```
# New articles from all of local
$c->newnews("local.*,test.*", time() - 3600);
```

```
# New articles (in all newsgroups) not ending in test
$c->newnews("local.*,!*.test", time() - 3600);
```

Posting Articles

NNTPClient posts articles, using post(). The post() command has three param-
eters, @header, "", and @body, representing X-header, linefeeds, and body text.
Each of these variables can be hardcoded in the script or retrieved from a file or
STDIN.

Here's an example of post() using hardcoded variables.

```
#!/usr/local/bin/perl -w

use News::NNTPClient;
use strict; # or Christiansen will start hollering
my($c, $from, $nntpserv, $newsgroup, @header, @body);
$c = News::NNTPClient->new($nntpserv);

$nntpserv = 'news.mydomain.com';
$newsgroup = 'local.test';
$from = 'nvp@mydomain.com';

@header = ("Newsgroups: $newsgroup", "From: $from",
           "Subject: Test One",
           "Organization: O'Reilly and Associates");
@body = ("Testing Testing One Two Three");

$c->post(@header, "", @body);
```

Here's an example of post() using values retrieved from a file:

```
#!/usr/local/bin/perl -w

use News::NNTPClient;
use strict;
my($c, $nntpserv, $textfile, $header_test, @body, @header);

$c = News::NNTPClient->new($nntpserv);

$nntpserv = 'news.mydomain.com';
$textfile = 'body.txt'; # where body text resides
$header_text = 'header.txt'; # where headers reside

open(NEWSBODY, $body_textfile)
        or die("Body text $body_textfile error: $!");
@body = <NEWSBODY>;
close(NEWSBODY);

open(HEADER, $header_text)
        or die("header $header_text error: $!");
```

```
@header = <HEADER>;
close(HEADER);

$c->post(@header, "", @body);
```

Extracting Header Information

You can also extract newsgroup information using xhdr() and xpat(); both describe the articles of a newsgroup based on X-header information. Using xhdr(), you can extract information about a newsgroup, such as the email addresses of all authors who have posted to the newsgroup.

```
#!/usr/local/bin/perl -w

use News::NNTPClient;
use strict; # birdie num-num
my($c, $newshost, $group, @entries, $author, $first, $last);

$newshost = 'news.mydomain.com';
$group = 'undertow.test';

$c = News::NNTPClient->new($newshost);

($first, $last) = ($c->group($group));

for (; $first <= $last; $first++) {
    push(@entries, $c->xhdr("From", $first));
}

print("Authors who have posted to $group.\n");
    foreach $author (@entries) {
        print $author;
    }
```

The xpat() function is similar to xhdr(), but returns X-header information that matches a text pattern or wildcard (*). Using the above example, xhdr() is replaced with xpat() in the example below, and the text pattern matches author names containing nvp.

```
#!/usr/local/bin/perl -w

use News::NNTPClient;
use strict; # oh well-a well-a well-a
my($newshost, $group, $c);

$newshost = 'news.mydomain.com';
$group = 'local.test';

$c = News::NNTPClient->new($newshost);

($first, $last) = ($c->group($group));
```

```
# match any containing nvp
push(@entries, $c->xpat("From", $first, $last, "*nvp*"));

print("Authors who have posted to $group.\n");
foreach $author (@entries) {
    print $author;
}
```

News::Newsrc and Your News Configuration File

Most UNIX-based newsreaders parse and extract a user's newsgroup information from a *.newsrc* file. The *.newsrc* contains newsgroup names and article totals from 1 to the current article number. When your newsreader connects to an NNTP server and you select a newsgroup, your newsreader (if configured) displays current articles based on the (new) ending article number of the newsgroup minus the (old) ending article number of the newsgroup. When you "catch up" a newsgroup by marking all the articles as read, or exit the newsreader program, your *.newsrc* is updated to indicate recent newsgroup activity.

News::Newsrc parses your *.newsrc* file and performs the same functions a newsreader would, such as adding, deleting, and catching up newsgroups by changing *.newsrc* entries. Note: you must be running at least Perl 5.002, with Exporter and Set::IntSpan 1.01. Table 10-1 displays a list of News::Newsrc functions.

Table 10-1. News::Newsrc Functions

Function	Purpose	Parameters
add_group()	Adds new group to *.newsrc*	Group name as parameter
del_group()	Removes group from *.newsrc*	Group name as parameter
exists()	Returns true if the group exists	Group name
groups()	Returns list of groups in *.newsrc*	None
load()	Loads *.newsrc* file into *.newsrc* object	Default is *$HOME/.newsrc*; can read alternate file
mark()	Adds article to the list for specified group	Group name and article number as parameters
marked()	Returns true if group exists and contains article	Group name and article number
mark_list()	Adds multiple articles to the list for specified group	Group name and list of articles
mark_range()	Adds articles in the specified range to the list	Group name, start and end articles
marked_articles()	Returns the list of articles in the group	Group name

Table 10-1. News::Newsrc Functions (continued)

Function	Purpose	Parameters
save(), save_as()	Save changes to *.newsrc* file or save changes to a new file	save_as() works like save, but outputs information to another file
sub_groups()	Returns list of subscribed groups in *.newsrc*	None
subscribe()	Subscribes to newsgroup in *.newsrc*	If the group doesn't exist, it's created; group name as parameter
subscribed()	Returns true if the group is subscribed	Group name
unmark()	Removes article from the group list	Group name and article number
unmark_list()	Removes list of articles from the group list	Group name and list of articles
unmark_range()	Removes a range of articles from *x* to *y*	Group name, start and end articles
unmarked_articles()	Returns the list of articles from *x* to *y*	Group name, first and last articles
unsub_groups()	Returns list of unsubscribed groups in *.newsrc*	None
unsubscribe()	Unsubscribes to newsgroup in *.newsrc*	If the group doesn't exist, it's created; group name as parameter

The following example reads a specified *.newsrc* file, outputs the existing groups, removes `local.boo`, adds a new newsgroup `local.newtest`, and saves changes to a new *.newsrc* file.

```perl
#!/usr/local/bin/perl -w

use News::Newsrc;
use strict;
my($newsrc, $file, $goner, $newgroup, @groups);

$newsrc = News::Newsrc->new();

# alternate .newsrc
$file = '/home/nvp/ORA/Nutshell/NNTP/scripts/newsrc.test';

# group to remove
$goner = 'local.buh-bye';

# group to add
$newgroup = 'local.newtest';

# open .newsrc
$newsrc->load($file);
```

```
# show initial newsgroups
@groups = $newsrc->groups();
print("You're subscribed to: @groups\n");

# remove newsgroup
$newsrc->del_group($goner);

# show groups after deletion
@groups = $newsrc->groups();
print("Subscribed to: @groups\n");

# add newsgroup
$newsrc->add_group($newgroup);

# show groups after addition
@groups = $newsrc->groups();
print("Subscribed to: @groups\n");

# "save as <new filename>" newsrc
$newsrc->save_as("$file.NEW");
```

Integrating News::NNTPClient and News::Newsrc

Here's an example that integrates News::Newsrc and News::NNTPClient. This example extracts newsgroup information from the *.newsrc* and compares the information to article information from the NNTP server. Each of the newsgroups is checked for new articles since the last update of the *.newsrc* and subtracts the last article listed in the *.newsrc* from the last article listed in the newsgroup, announcing the number of new articles in each newsgroup.

```
#!/usr/local/bin/perl -w

use News::NNTPClient;
use News::Newsrc;
use strict;
my($newshost, $total, $c, $newsrc, $group, $last @groups);

$newshost = 'news.somenewshost.com'; # nntp host
$total = 0; # initialize total to zero

$c = News::NNTPClient->new($newshost);

$newsrc = News::Newsrc->new();

$newsrc->load(); # default .newsrc
@groups = $newsrc->sub_groups(); ### subscribed newsgroups

foreach $group (@groups) {
```

```
    # check each newsgroup containing marked articles
    @articles = $newsrc->marked_articles($group);
    $total = scalar(@articles);

    # number of last article in group
    $last = ($c->group($group))[1];

    # new articles derived from last minus total
    my $current = ($last - $total);

    if ($current <= 0) { # no new articles
        print("Newsgroup $group has no new articles.\n");
    } elseif($current == 1) { # new article, but watch plurals
        print "Newsgroup $group: has $current new article.\n";
    } else { # more than one new article
    print "Newsgroup $group: has $current new articles.\n";
}

}
```

11

Web Applications with LWP

Despite perceptions to the contrary, programming on the World Wide Web doesn't begin and end with CGI. Using a set of modules distributed under the LWP umbrella, you can use Perl to write specialized web clients and servers or develop robot applications that traverse the Web magically.

In this chapter, you'll be introduced to concepts such as maintaining state in a CGI program, HTML tag stripping, and output formatting. We'll also talk about some interesting things you can do with the LWP modules, such as writing your own web server.

An Introduction to CGI

The CGI, or Common Gateway Interface, is the mechanism by which servers execute programs on the server side, enabling dynamic content. CGI programs are like regular programs except for their reliance on the server's environment to receive data and deliver content.

With CGI, users can enter data into their browser window. When the data is submitted, the browser transfers the data to the server while it requests an associated document. When the server discovers that the requested document is a CGI program (either from the document's suffix or the directory it resides in), it transfers the data to the program, and waits while the program executes. The server then transfers any output that the program generates back to the browser.

Suppose the client requests the URL:

```
http://www.ripoff.com/someform.html
```

The HTML for the form might be crudely written as follows:

```
<FORM METHOD="POST" ACTION="/cgi-bin/sucker.pl">
Enter your name:  <INPUT NAME="username">
```

```
Do you want more information on our products?
              <INPUT TYPE="checkbox" NAME="more_info" VALUE="YES" CHECKED>
              <INPUT TYPE="checkbox" NAME="more_info" VALUE="NO">
<INPUT TYPE="submit">
</FORM>
```

The user fills in his data: a textbox with his name and a checkbox for more information.* When he is done, he presses a submit button.

After a (hopefully short) interval, the user sees a new page saying thanks (using his name as submitted) and promising to send loads and loads of junk mail.

In order for this magic to happen, the browser needs to send the user's input to the server, the server needs to process it, and then the server needs to generate a new page. Since it wouldn't make sense to rewrite the server itself every time you wanted to collect spam victims, the server just passes the processing off to an external CGI program.

Request Methods

To understand CGI, you need to know how HTTP works. In every HTTP request, the first line declares the *method* of the request.

Most requests over the Web use the GET method. In its simplest form, GET is used to retrieve a simple file. For example, to retrieve */index.html* on a web site, you could connect to the web server (generally port 80) and enter:

```
GET /index.html HTTP/1.1
```

`HTTP/1.1` defines the version of the HTTP protocol you are using. Note that no actual content is sent from the client to the server with a GET request.

CGI and GET

In addition to retrieving static documents, you can also use the GET method to transfer name/value pairs of data to a CGI program. Any data after a question mark (?) in the URL is taken to be encoded name/value pairs. If the document being requested is a CGI program, the name/value pairs are transferred to the program via an environment variable named QUERY_STRING. (We'll talk more about CGI environment variables later on in this chapter.)

For example, suppose you filled out a form with your name and checked "Yes" on a field asking whether you wanted more information on their products. When you press the "Submit" button on the form, the GET request might read:

```
GET /cgi-bin/sucker.pl?username=Nathan%20Patwardhan&more_info=YES
```

---

* Obviously this is a fictitious example, since you'd think they'd want some way to contact the user!

Although there are some special characters stuck in there, you should be able to make out that the `username` and `more_info` variables are being assigned after the question mark. For GET requests, name/value pairs are separated by ampersands (`&`) and special characters are represented by a percent sign followed by their hexadecimal representation (in this case, `%20` for a space. Alternatively, many browsers and servers use the convention of a plus sign (`+`) representing a space.) This encoding scheme is called *URL encoding*.

When the server receives the request, it calls the `/cgi-bin/sucker.pl` program and assigns environment variables from which the program can retrieve its needed information. From the point of view of the CGI program, when the request method is GET (i.e., when `$ENV{REQUEST_METHOD}` is `"GET"`), you need to retrieve the name/value pairs from `$ENV{QUERY_STRING}` and then parse the encoded information therein.

CGI and POST

While GET requests can be used both for static documents and for CGI, POST requests are used to literally "post" information to the server. Unlike GET requests, POST requests can be accompanied by content. You could post any sort of information, but most applications of POST are for CGI.

The big difference between GET and POST is that instead of appending name/value pairs onto the URL, POST requests used for CGI place name/value pairs into the content area of the request. In addition, the browser sends headers telling the server the Content-type of the incoming data and the length of that content, represented by the environment variables CONTENT_TYPE and CONTENT_LENGTH, respectively.

Using the previous example, if you fill in an HTML form with your name (let's say, `"Nathan Patwardhan"`) and check the box asking for more information, the client sends the server:

```
POST /cgi-bin/sucker.pl HTTP/1.1
Content-type: application/x-www-form-urlencoded
Content-length: 36

name=Nathan+Patwardhan&more_info=YES
```

When the server receives the request, it calls the `/cgi-bin/sucker.pl` program, assigns the REQUEST_METHOD environment variable to POST, assigns the CONTENT_TYPE and CONTENT_LENGTH variables as specified in the headers, and sends the name/value pairs (i.e., the actual content) in standard input (STDIN). From the point of view of the program, when `$ENV{REQUEST_METHOD}` is set to `"POST"`, you need to read `$ENV{CONTENT_LENGTH}` characters from STDIN to retrieve the name/value pairs, and then parse the URL-encoded data as needed.

CGI Environment Variables

Web servers set up a special environment when the CGI program is run. Unlike the normal environment, your CGI program's environment contains only limited information about your system, with several server-defined environment variables.

Some environment variables are static and don't change. Others depend on the conditions under which the CGI program is executed. Table 11-1 shows a list of static environment variables defined when a web server is started.[*]

Table 11-1. Static Variables

Variable	Description
GATEWAY_INTERFACE	The CGI Gateway interface: current (standard) version is 1.1
HOSTNAME	The hostname of the server (a fully qualified domain name)
SERVER_PORT	Port at which requests are received
SERVER_PROTOCOL	Since this server accepts only HTTP requests, we'll follow the current (standard) Version 1.1
SERVER_SOFTWARE	The name and current version of the software

Table 11-2 shows a list of environment variables that change based on which request, client type, or program is executed.

Table 11-2. Variables That Change

Variable	Description
CONTENT_LENGTH	The length of data being sent to the server
CONTENT_TYPE	The content type of documents being requested through POST or PUT
PATH_INFO	Virtual pathname
QUERY_STRING	Information following ? in the URL passed to the script
REMOTE_ADDR	The IP address of the REMOTE_HOST
REMOTE_HOST	Hostname of who's making the request
REQUEST_METHOD	Method with which request was made (GET, POST, PUT, etc.)
SCRIPT_NAME	Virtual path pointing to the script being executed

You can access these environment variables as you would in any Perl program, using the %ENV hash.

---

[*] This depends on the type of web server. Every web server supports a slightly different environment.

CGI Output

As mentioned earlier, the CGI program is responsible for generating output that the web server can then send on to the browser. This means that the output needs to begin with some headers, including, at minimum, a Content-type header.

As touched on in Chapter 4, *The Mail and MIME Modules*, web servers need to know what kind of content they are sending the web client. Generally, the file suffix will imply what kind of data it is. For example, a file with an *.html* suffix is assumed to have the Content-type of `text/html`, a file with a *.gif* suffix is assumed to be Content-type `image/gif`, and so on. The server's *mime.types* file contains a listing of Content-types and their associated suffixes.

The CGI program poses a complication, however, because the files are being created on the fly. Since they are never written to disk, they never have filenames. Without a filename (and thus, without a suffix!), the server has no way to tell what kind of file it is, so the CGI program needs to generate a Content-type header itself. The most common problem for CGI novices is failing to generate a Content-type. Since servers won't send data without a Content-type, the server will simply send the user an error message.

From the CGI programmer's point of view, all this means is that the first line of output that the program generates must declare the Content-type, followed by a blank line. For example:

```
print <<END;
Content-type: text/html

<HTML><HEAD><TITLE>Thanks!</TITLE></HEAD>
<BODY>
<P>
Thanks, Nathan!  And since you've asked for more information on
our products, we'll be sure to send you lots and lots of junk mail!
</BODY>
END
```

CGI.pm and Maintaining State

HTTP is a stateless protocol. The connection to the server is closed after content is delivered to the client. Whether you're browsing HTML documents or executing a CGI program, the request and/or data you've sent to the server disappears after the server handles your request.

Although some browsers have implemented a state-tracking mechanism called *cookies*, which are passed in the HTTP headers, cookies aren't implemented by every browser, and users can sometimes disable cookies on browsers that support them. An alternative way to maintain state between executions of a CGI program is to design the CGI program to remember values of previous selections between invocations of the CGI program.

By passing arguments to functions that handle HTML fill-out form types, `CGI.pm` instantiates the attributes of form input types into HTML. This example creates an HTML page with four radio buttons called `button1`, `button2`, `button3`, and `button4`: `button1` and `button4` are selected by default. When the user selects or deselects one (or more) of the buttons, `CGI.pm` maintains the previous values of the selected buttons:

```
#!/usr/local/bin/perl -w

use CGI ':standard';

print header;
print start_html('Checkbox Example'),
h1('Checkbox Example'),

start_form,
checkbox_group(-name=>'buttons', -values=>
['button1','button2','button3','button4'],
          -defaults=>['button1','button4']),
p,
submit,
end_form,
hr;

if (param()) {
print "The selected buttons are: ",em(join(", ",param('buttons'))),
p,
hr;
}
```

So, how does `CGI.pm` preserve state between executions of a CGI program? Let's look at form data parsed by a CGI program that doesn't use `CGI.pm`. We need to do this to show how basic CGI programs don't maintain state. This CGI program extracts the values of two textboxes (named `box_a` and `box_b`) from an HTML form. The boxes are empty by default.

First, the CGI program outputs a Content-type header and the top of the fill-in form:

```
print("Content-type: text/html\n\n");
print <<HTML_FORM;
<HTML>

    <HEAD>
      <TITLE>fill-in form - hey we aren't saving state!</TITLE>
    </HEAD>

    <BODY>
```

```
<FORM METHOD="POST" ACTION="/cgi-bin/some_script.pl">
<INPUT NAME="box_a">
<INPUT NAME="box_b">
<INPUT TYPE="submit">

<HR NOSHADE>
<BR>

</BODY>

</HTML>

HTML_FORM
```

Now, let's fill out this form and execute the CGI program. What happens to the textboxes after you've executed the CGI program? The boxes are empty again. Why? Because box_a and box_b don't contain any values to be reassigned at each execution of the CGI program.

How do CGI.pm's state-saving methods differ from the CGI program shown above? Since CGI.pm implements a set of functions to represent fill-in form input types, name/value pairs are passed to these functions and stored or retrieved with the param function. Let's take a look at some code to illustrate this. Returning to the example with box_a and box_b, we'll walk you through how the state of the values present in box_a and box_b is preserved by the method calls you'll find in CGI.pm. You'll also notice that box_a and box_b are populated with the new values after the CGI program is executed. Here's the code:

```
#!/usr/local/bin/perl -w

use CGI ':standard';

# Sends the Content-type header (that's all we need in this example)
print header;

# Sends the fill-in form titled 'Box A and Box B'
print start_html('Box A and Box B'),
    h1('Box A and Box B'),
    start_form,
    textfield(-name => 'box_a'),
    "<br>",
    textfield(-name => 'box_b'),
    "<br>",
    submit,
    end_form,
    hr;

# Ahh, param must be populated with something, so let's get
# our values
if(param()) {
    print "Box A: ".param('box_a')."<BR>\n";
    print "Box B: ".param('box_b')."<BR>\n";
}
```

What happened with our input types and their state? In `CGI.pm`, when you call a function that represents an input type, you pass the function arguments. In this case we're using `textfield()` without a default value, so we'll just have to pass a `-name` parameter to `textfield()`:

```
textfield(-name => 'box_a'),
textfield(-name => 'box_b'),
```

`textfield()` checks to see if the parameter is already defined with the `param()` function. The `param()` function returns the value of a named parameter. If invoked in a list context, `param()` returns the entire list; otherwise `param()` returns the first member of the list. In this case, we asked `param()` for the value of the named parameters—box_a and box_b—so we passed one argument to `param()`, the name of the fill-in type. If the parameter already exists but is redefined, the original value is replaced with the new value; the old value is kept as the default if a new value isn't specified.

Therefore, `CGI.pm` preserves state by checking the current values of an input type with `param()` when a function is called, before assigning new values. Old values that aren't reassigned retain their original values, and new values replace the old.

LWP: A Comprehensive Web Package

LWP (Libraries for WWW Access in Perl) is a comprehensive collection of web-related modules, ranging from HTTP request modules to HTML formatting tools. Many individuals have contributed to the LWP modules, and the `libwww` package is regularly updated when an included module changes.

The LWP modules support almost all of the functionality of web client and server applications, from downloading a web page to POSTing to forms on a remote server. Even if you have written your own web modules or standalone programs, you can draw many ideas from LWP. The LWP modules include File, Font, HTML, HTTP, LWP, MIME, URI, and WWW.

In this chapter, we'll show several examples that use LWP to send requests to a web server, download HTML pages, and other functionality you might want to add to your existing web-related programs.

URL Parsing with URI::URL

URLs specify the document a browser wants to access on a web server. LWP's URI::URL module class parses URLs into their respective parts: protocol scheme, host, port, and path/document name. Given the URL:

```
http://www.some-web-host.com:80/path/document.type
```

the parts of the URL are broken into:

Protocol scheme	*http*
Host	*www.some-web-host.com*
Port	*80*
Path/document name	*/path/document.type*

URI::URL implements methods that represent the corresponding parts of a URL. With URI::URL, you can break the URL shown above into parts, as shown in the following example:

```
#!/usr/local/bin/perl -w

use URI::URL;
use strict;

my ($url) = 'http://www.some-web-host.com:80/path/document.type';
my $url_entity = url($url);

# the scheme method parses the protocol scheme - in this case it's http
print "Protocol: $url_entity->scheme\n";

# the host method parses the hostname -
# in this case it's www.some-web host.com
print "Host: $url_entity->host\n";

# the port method parses the port we'd use to connect to
# the HTTP server: this time it's 80
print "Port: $url_entity->port\n";

# the path method parses the path/document name - in this case it's /path/
print "Path: $url_entity->path\n";
```

Client Requests with LWP::Simple and HTTP::Request

The LWP::Simple module provides functions for rudimentary client connections. The head() function returns metainformation about the document, including the type, size, and age. head() is especially useful if you just want to check whether or not a document exists. The following code lets you know if a URL doesn't exist:

```
#!/usr/local/bin/perl -w

use LWP::Simple;

$url = 'http://www.some-overdone-website.com/index.html';
print "Error contacting URL: $url!\n"
    unless head($url);
```

To retrieve a complete document, LWP::Simple provides the get(), getprint(), and getstore() functions. Although you can use the GET script that was installed when you built LWP, here are some other methods to send GET requests to a web server:

- `get()` returns a document passed in a URL.

  ```
  use LWP::Simple;

  $doc = get 'http://www.sn.no/libwww-perl/';
  print "$doc\n";
  ```

- `getprint()` prints the content of a URL to STDOUT.

  ```
  perl -MLWP::Simple -e 'getprint "http://www.perl.com/perl/CPAN/CPAN.html"'
  ```

- `getstore()` retrieves the contents of a remote document and stores it on the local filesystem. It takes two arguments: the URL where the content is locasted and the name of the local file in which to place the the content.

  ```
  perl -MLWP::Simple -e 'getstore \
      "ftp://ftp.somesite.com/pub/magic/ooga-booga.tar.gz",
      "beware-of-voodoo.tar.gz"'
  ```

While LWP::Simple is useful for quick requests, the HTTP::Request module gives you more complete control over handling both the headers sent and the response returned. In addition to HTTP::Request, the following example uses LWP::User-Agent to define the User-agent header for the client:

```
use LWP::UserAgent;
require HTTP::Request;

$url = 'http://www.baba-ganouj.com/eggplant-dishes.html';

$ua = LWP::UserAgent->new();
$ua->agent("$0/0.1");

$req = HTTP::Request->new('GET' => $url);
$req->header('Accept' => 'text/html');

# send the request
$res = $ua->request($req);

# check the outcome
if ($res->is_success) { # request was successful
    print $res->content;
}
```

HTTP::Request also gives you a mechanism for initiating POST requests (although you can also use the POST script that was installed when you built your LWP distribution).

```
use LWP::UserAgent;

$url = 'http://www.blinking-text-haters.com/cgi-bin/Bth_Survey.pl';
$ua = LWP::UserAgent->new();
```

```
my $req = new HTTP::Request 'POST', $url;
$req->content_type('application/x-www-form-urlencoded');
$req->content('user=Nathan+Patwardhan&hateblinking=yes');

my $res = $ua->request($req);
print $res->as_string;
```

Displaying Raw HTML Tags

It's common for HTML documents to need to be converted to another format.
LWP provides several modules for converting HTML documents, including
HTML::Entities, HTML::FormatPS, HTML::FormatText, HTML::HeadParser, and
HTML::LinkExtor. There are many ways to write your own unformat/de-tag/
reformat HTML programs using regular expressions and substitutions, but LWP's
HTML hierarchy contains simple, efficient, and robust modules to complete the
tasks for you.

Suppose you want to display your HTML markup on a web page in its raw (unfor-
matted) form. To get HTML tags to display verbatim, you have to replace all <
and > characters with "<" and ">". Otherwise, the tags are interpreted, and
their markup appears as part of the HTML page.

HTML::Entities opens an HTML file and either encodes or decodes the HTML tags
to their specified ISO-8859/1 characters. Here's an example that translates all the
HTML tags from a file into their respective ISO-8859/1 characters:

```
#!/usr/local/bin/perl -w

use HTML::Entities ();

usage() unless scalar(@ARGV) == 1;
($file) = (@ARGV);

open(HTML, $file)
    or die("error opening input file $file: $!");
while($a = <HTML>) {
    $encoded = HTML::Entities::encode($a);
    print $encoded;
}
close(HTML);

sub usage {
    print("Usage: $0 <filename>\n");
    exit(1);
}
```

Displaying HTML as ASCII or PostScript

If you've ever used a text-based browser like Lynx, you may be familiar with the
–dump option that displays a document as formatted text (i.e., without the HTML

tags). The `parse_html` function in HTML::Parse works much like Lynx's `-dump` option. The following example accesses a page on a web site using the `get()` function from LWP::Simple and displays the page as formatted text.

```
#!/usr/local/bin/perl -w

use LWP::Simple;
use HTML::Parse;

$remote_doc = 'http://www.perl.com/CPAN/CPAN.html';
print parse_html(get $remote_doc)->format;
```

You can also output HTML documents as PostScript using HTML::FormatPS. Although this method doesn't format tables or forms at the moment, it offers interesting potential for the future. Here's an example that uses FormatPS to read an HTML document, covert it, and send PostScript to STDOUT:

```
#!/usr/local/bin/perl -w

use HTML::Parse;
require HTML::FormatPS;

usage() unless scalar(@ARGV) == 1;
($filename) = (@ARGV);

$html = parse_htmlfile($filename);
$formatter = HTML::FormatPS->new(
    FontFamily => 'Helvetica',
    PaperSize  => 'Letter');

# Save for debug
# print $formatter->format($html);

sub usage {
    print("Usage: $0 <filename>\n");
    exit(1);
}
```

Link Extraction

To extract links from an HTML document, you can use HTML::Parse and HTML::Element. In the following example, we show all the links from the specified URLs.

```
#!/usr/local/bin/perl -w

use LWP::Simple;
use HTML::Parse;
use HTML::Element;

# URLs we'll be contacting
@URLS = (
```

```
            "http://www.ora.com/index.html",
            "http://www.acsu.buffalo.edu/index.html"
);

# now, connect to each URL and show us links within
foreach $url (@URLS) {
    print "Contacting: $url\n";
    $response = get $url;
    $parsed_file = HTML::Parse::parse_html($response);
    for(@{ $parsed_file->extract_links() }) {
        $show_link = $_->[0];
        print "$show_link\n";
    }
}
```

Accessing Protected Documents

If you need to access documents that are protected by basic authorization, use the
authorization_basic() function from LWP::UserAgent. The following example
sends a username/password pair to the specified URL:

```
use LWP::UserAgent;

$url = 'http://www.my-intranet.com';
$username = 'biffo';
    #You really shouldn't hardcode passwords.
    #Ask for the password from STDIN or something.
    #Hardcoding $ was used just in this example.
$password = 'bigdogbark';

$ua = LWP::UserAgent->new();

$req = HTTP::Request->new(GET => $url);
$req->authorization_basic($username, $password);
print $ua->request($req)->as_string;
```

Developing a Web Server with LWP

Using the HTTP::Daemon module, you can develop a complete web server that
handles requests from a browser and delivers content accordingly.

The web-server implementation we'll show in the remainder of this chapter,
HTTPerl, handles static documents as well as CGI GET and POST requests. We'll
also show how to write a CGI based on the CGI specification.

Some of the code in this section is a lighter-weight implementation of Kirves, a
maturing web server written in Perl and built on the LWP modules.

Serving Web Pages

The HTTP server's delivery of static pages to the client (web browser) is the smallest component of the HTTP client-server model. When the client issues a GET request to the web server (generally at port 80), the server parses the request information and returns a static page to the client.

For example, if the client issues a GET request for the URL *http://www.some-name.com/index.html*, the server at *www.somename.com* receives the name of requested page, */index.html*. It then determines which file on the filesystem corresponds to that URL by associating it with its *document root*.

The document root is the directory in which the web documents reside. When a page is requested from the server, the server appends the requested pathname to the appropriate directory root. For example, if the document root were */usr/local/httpd/htdocs*, then when the client requests */index.html*, the server returns a set of headers and the contents of the document */usr/local/httpd/htdocs/index.html*.

Let's walk through this process with the URL shown above.

1. Client issues a GET request onto port 80 of *www.somename.com*:

   ```
   GET /index.html HTTP/1.0
   ```

2. The server opens the path */usr/www/apache/htdocs/index.html*.

3. The server returns a set of headers and the contents of the document. (The first line of the response contains the status code of the response, in this instance 200 OK. If it failed to open the document, it would have returned 404 NOT FOUND.)

   ```
   HTTP/1.0 200 OK
   Date: Sun, 17 Aug 1997 23:50:35 GMT
   Server: libwww-perl-daemon/1.13
   Content-Length: 200
   Content-Type: text/html
   Last-Modified: Mon, 03 Mar 1997 22:47:02 GMT
   Client-Date: Sun, 17 Aug 1997 23:50:35 GMT

   <HTML>

   <HEAD><TITLE>Welcome to HTTPerl!</TITLE></HEAD>

   <BODY>

   <I>Welcome to HTTPerl!</I>
   <HR NOSHADE>
   <A HREF="foo.html">So many links --- so little time!</A>

   </BODY>

   </HTML>
   ```

Using HTTP::Daemon

HTTP::Daemon is built with these modules: IO::Socket, IO::Socket::INET, HTTP::Request, HTTP::Response, HTTP::Status, HTTP::Date, URI::URL, and LWP::MediaTypes. These give HTTP::Daemon full access to many of the LWP URL, response, and socket-related utility functions. HTTP::Daemon starts a server that uses your machine's fully qualified domain name and binds the server to a port (default is 80) in the HTTP::Daemon constructor. For example:

```
$http_daemon = HTTP::Daemon->new();
```

The server name you choose must be a valid name in your machine's DNS records; otherwise the server can't start, because the server name you have specified cannot be resolved. You can specify the server's name and default port like this:*

```
$http_daemon = HTTP::Daemon->new(
    LocalAddr => 'www.somefqdn.com',
    LocalPort => 80);
```

HTTP::Daemon accepts incoming connections with the **accept()** method. The following line tells your server to accept connections at the hostname and port specified in the constructor.

```
$connect = $http_daemon->accept;
```

Once your server is running, it needs to process incoming requests and handle the delivery of data accordingly. HTTP::Daemon uses **get_request()** to interpret the request type and **method()** to represent the request type as a string. (Our web server, HTTPerl, only handles GET and POST requests.)

```
$request = $connect->get_request;
$method_as_string = $request->method;

print("I've been asked to ",
    $method_as_string,
    " something.\n");
```

You should also initialize the REQUEST_METHOD environment variable with the following:

```
$request = $connect->get_request;

# now, assign a request method to ENV{'REQUEST_METHOD'}
$ENV{'REQUEST_METHOD'} = $request->method;

print("I've been asked to ",
```

---

* Under UNIX, if you don't have root access, you can't bind the server to port 80 or any other port less than 1000. You must choose a higher-numbered port. Common ports for "renegade" web servers are 8000 and 8080.

```
$ENV{'REQUEST_METHOD'},
" something.\n");
```

If the server is delivering a static document through a GET request, it uses the **send_file_response**() method to send the contents of the requested document to the client:

```
$connect->send_file_response($requested_file);
```

Here's how HTTPerl handles GET requests for static pages. This example is an excerpt of the HTTPerl code that has been revised for the sake of brevity.

1. Declare the variables **ServerRoot**, **ServerName**, and **ServerPort**:

```
$ServerRoot = '/home/nvp/ORA/PRK/Chapters/WWW/WebAdmin/Server';
$ServerName = 'www.somename.com';
$ServerPort = 8080;
```

2. Create a new HTTP::Daemon object:

```
$http_daemon = HTTP::Daemon->new(
    LocalAddr => $ServerName,
    LocalPort => $ServerPort);
```

3. Announce the URL where the server can be contacted:

```
print "Please contact me at: <URL:", $http_daemon->url, ">\n";
```

4. Accept requests (keep the server running):

```
while ($connect = $http_daemon->accept) {
        $req = $connect->get_request;
        if ($req) {
```

5. Assign $ENV{'REQUEST_METHOD'} to $req->method:

```
$ENV{'REQUEST_METHOD'} = $req->method;
```

6. Send the document. You need to send a complete path and filename consisting of **$ServerRoot** and **$ENV{'PATH_INFO'}**. If PATH_INFO is /, as in the case of *http://www.somename.com/*, append *index.html* to PATH_INFO:

```
if ($ENV{'REQUEST_METHOD'} eq 'GET') {
    # open index.html if $document = /
        $filename = $ServerRoot.$document;
    $connect->send_file_response($filename);
} else {
```

7. Send an error if the request method isn't GET. We can't handle this type of thing right now.

```
    $connect->send_error(RC_FORBIDDEN)
}
```

GET and Your CGI

The LWP modules can extract the QUERY_STRING with the **equery()** method.
Given the URL *http://www.somename.com/cgi-bin/script?name=value*, you can
extract the query string and populate $ENV{'QUERY_STRING'} as follows:

```
$ENV{'QUERY_STRING'} = $req->url->equery() if
    $req->url->equery();
```

Once a value has been assigned to QUERY_STRING, your CGI program can go
about its business with name/value parsing as covered in the beginning of this
chapter.

Like an HTML document, a CGI program maps a virtual path to an absolute path
before delivering content to the client. Unlike a static document, a CGI program is
executed, not merely opened and output to the client. If your web server is
sending a CGI program's source code to the client, something has been
misconfigured.

You're probably familiar with pipes and filehandles, where pipes are used to send
data to or read data from an external program. To review, forward pipes send
data to an external program, and after pipes read data from an external program.
You may use your standard Perl distribution's file-handling capabilities (without
modules) to read data from an external program, as illustrated in the following
code segment:

```
# open an external program
open(EXTPROG, "/path/programname |")
        or die("Program error: $!");

# grab output from the external program
@output = <EXTPROG>;

# send the external program's output to STDOUT
for(@output) { print $_; }

# close the external program
close(EXTPROG) or die("error closing external program: $!");
```

Like Kirves, HTTPerl uses IO::File to extract the output from the CGI program, so
the CGI handler can use a typeglob for extraction:

```
# read from the external program - we'll use this for GET only
# this *will not* work for POST (handling POST is covered later)
$cgi_get_proc = IO::File("$cgi_prog |")->new();

# use a typeglob to parse the data and prepare it for output to the client
while (<$cgi_get_proc>) {
    # do something with the output
}
```

Here's one method of handling a GET request for a CGI program with the IO and LWP modules:

1. The client requests a URL from the server.

   ```
   http://www.somename.com/cgi-bin/testscript.pl.
   ```

2. The server parses the URL and appends the script name to `$ServerRoot`.

   ```
   # $e->url->path is /cgi-bin/testscript.pl
   $cgi_program = $ServerRoot.$e->url->path;
   ```

3. The server executes the CGI program and captures the program's output into a variable.

   ```
   $cgi_get_output = IO::File("$cgi_program |")->new();
   ```

4. The server uses a typeglob to parse the output of the program and prepares it for proper delivery to the client.

   ```
   while (<$cgi_get_proc>) {
       # remove line-endings
       tr/\r\n//d;

       # we know we're at the end if there's nothing
       # to read (data has no length)
       last unless length;

       # parse the program's output to grab things
       # that will be output as headers.  Without this parsing
       # routine (borrowed from Kirves), our document and its
       # headers will surely be mangled and we'll cry out in
       # pain that our CGI program is broken.  :-(
       if (/^([^:]+):\s*([^\r\n]+)$/) {
           # prepare the headers and put them into the HTTP::Daemon header hash.
           $http_resp->header("$1" => "$2");
       } else {
           # oops!  something's wrong with the program's output -
           # guess we should give a server error and have the
           # programmer fix the code.
           return $connect->send_error(RC_INTERNAL_SERVER_ERROR);
       }
   }
   ```

5. The server does the same parsing and sends the remaining content to HTTP::Daemon.

   ```
   while(<$cgi_get_proc>) {
       # prepare the rest of the content and append
       # it to the content we've been building
       $http_resp->add_content($_);
   }
   ```

6. Now, send everything to the client.

   ```
   $connect->send_response($http_resp);
   ```

Post Requests and Your CGI

The `content_type()` and `content_length()` functions return the values of the
Content-type and Content-length headers as sent by the client, and the
`content()` function returns the actual body of the request. For processing CGI
requests using the POST method, you need to use these functions to assign the
CONTENT_LENGTH and CONTENT_TYPE environment variables and send the
content as standard input.

Since data is being sent to the server with a POST request, processed, assigned to
environment variables, and returned to STDOUT to be handled by a CGI
program, HTTPerl's POST method must be able to read data from and send data
to the CGI program. Because filehandles can't be bidirectionally piped, we'll have
to use IPC::Open2, which allows us to read from and write to an external
program:

```
use IPC::Open2;

$program = '/path/program_name';
$pid = open2(\*READER, \*WRITER, $program);
```

The `open2()` function takes three arguments. The first argument is the handle
being read from, the second is the handle being written to, and the third is the
name of the program being executed. Although `open2()` allows arguments to be
passed to the program, this isn't applicable to CGI programs.

For example, let's look at a POST request handler that uses IPC::Open2,
IO::Handle, and the LWP modules. This code is based on Kirves' POST
functionality.

Since IPC::Open2's first two arguments are handles, we'll use IO::Handle to create
one handle for input data and another handle for output data:

```
my $data_in  = IO::Handle->new();
my $data_out = IO::Handle->new();
```

Like a GET request, we'll grab the CGI program name and append it to
`$ServerRoot`:

```
$post_program = '/base_directory/cgi-bin/some_secure_script.pl';
```

First, we'll set the environment variables for REQUEST_METHOD, CONTENT_
TYPE, and CONTENT_LENGTH:

```
my $cnt_len = $req->content_length();

$ENV{'REQUEST_METHOD'} = 'POST';
$ENV{'CONTENT_TYPE'}   = $req->content_type();

delete $ENV{'CONTENT_LENGTH'};
$ENV{'CONTENT_LENGTH'} = $cnt_len if $cnt_len;
```

Next, let's start the ball rolling with open2(), the input and output handles, and the CGI program:

```
if ($cgi_result = open2($data_in, $data_out, $post_program)) {
```

Don't forget to flush the output stream:

```
$data_out->autoflush(1);
```

Now, send the content (url-encoded string) to the output stream if the CONTENT_ LENGTH is not zero, and close the output stream:

```
$data_out->print($req->content()) if $clen;
$data_out->close;
```

Like the GET request, we'll need to parse the output of the external program so things won't get truncated due to linefeeds and other unwanted characters:

```
# call parse function here
# parser($this, $that);

$data_in->close();
```

Now, return all the data to the CGI program.

```
$http_res->send_response($res);
return ($res->content_length);
}
```

12

In this chapter:
- *What Is Sfio?*
- *Embedded Perl and mod_perl*

Web Server Efficiency

Following a traditional client-server model, first-generation web servers like NCSA's httpd spawned a single process at startup to handle incoming HTTP requests. Early HTTP servers worked efficiently for small amounts of requests, but exhibited significantly diminished performance when servers were forced to handle a volume of concurrent requests.

The growing popularity of the World Wide Web and the demand for efficient delivery of dynamic content dictated that web servers must handle a large number of concurrent requests (or "hits") without a substantial effect on the performance of the server. A new breed of powerful web servers was developed, including the Apache server that was originally based on NCSA's httpd.* These servers are capable of forking multiple processes (based on a directive in the server's configuration) to handle a large volume of HTTP requests and offer source code modularity for server extensibility.

Running an efficient web site isn't limited to running a web server capable of forking multiple processes, hosting numerous virtual clients, or writing intelligent CGI programs. Effective web sites are a combination of properly configured servers and an understanding of the HTTP protocol so the server can be optimized. The focus of this chapter is preparing your Perl distribution to use Sfio, and optimizing Apache's performance by embedding Perl into the executable.

---

* One of the few vestiges of the NCSA server that remains with Apache is the configuration file syntax; you'd be hard-pressed to find much else.

What Is Sfio?

AT&T's Sfio has superior performance to *stdio.h* in many cases and is extensible by the use of *discipline* modules. Sfio currently builds only on a subset of the UNIX platforms Perl supports. Because the data structures are completely different from `stdio`, Perl extension modules or external libraries may not work. This configuration exists to allow these issues to be worked on.

Sfio is a library of functions for efficient I/O on buffered streams. Each Sfio stream is a file stream, representing a file, or a string stream, representing a memory segment. Sfio also extends the `sfprintf()`/`sfscanf()` family of functions for generalized data formatting using application-defined patterns.

Three standard streams are provided:.

- `sfstdin` for standard input (file descriptor 0 on UNIX systems)
- `sfstdout` for standard output (file descriptor 1)
- `sfstderr` for standard error output (file descriptor 2)

The buffer of a stream is typically a memory segment allocated via `malloc` or supplied by the application (like using the `malloc` that was included with your Perl distribution). File streams may also use memory mapping if that is deemed a more efficient way to do I/O.

Your Perl Distribution and Sfio Support

Before you can use many of the examples in this section, you need to rebuild your Perl executable (Version 5.003_97 or later) with Sfio support.

Since there are a number of steps you'll have to follow to insure that the Sfio library gets installed correctly, we'll document the process in this section.

This section is partially based on the I/O layer and abstraction sections of the *INSTALL* file included with your Perl 5.004_0x distribution. You'll probably need to review these materials before rebuilding your Perl distribution if you haven't had success with the rebuild, or if you need a step in the right direction before proceeding.

Perl and I/O Abstraction

Previous versions of Perl used the standard I/O mechanisms as defined in *stdio.h*. Versions 5.003_02 and later of Perl allow alternate I/O mechanisms like Sfio through "PerlIO" abstraction, but the `stdio` mechanism is still the default and the only supported mechanism.

You can try to build Perl with I/O abstraction by passing the following to `Configure`:

```
sh Configure -Duseperlio
```

or interactively at the appropriate `Configure` prompt.

If you choose to use the PerlIO abstraction layer, there are two (experimental) possibilities for the underlying I/O calls. These have been tested to some extent on some platforms, but are not guaranteed to work everywhere.

How Do I Build a Perl Executable with Sfio Support?

A fairly old version of Sfio is in CPAN, and work is in progress to make it more easily buildable by adding `Configure` support. The CPAN distribution on the Perl Resource Kit CD includes the Sfio distribution, located in */cdrom_mount_point/ CPAN/src/misc/sfio97.src.unix.tar.gz*.

Before building your Perl distribution with Sfio support, you should confirm that your Perl distribution hasn't already been built with Sfio support by running:

```
perl -V | grep sfio
```

If your Perl distribution already supports Sfio, you should see lines like the following:

```
bincompat3=y useperlio=define d_sfio=define
cppflags='-I/usr/local/include/sfio -I/usr/local/include'
ccflags ='-I/usr/local/include/sfio -I/usr/local/include'
ld='ld', ldflags ='-L/usr/local/lib/sfio -L/usr/local/lib'
libpth=/usr/local/lib/sfio /usr/local/lib /usr/lib
libs=-lsfio -lgdbm -lm -lc -lcrypt
cccdlflags='-DPIC -fpic', lddlflags='-Bshareable \
            -L/usr/local/lib/sfio -L/usr/local/lib'
```

If your Perl distribution doesn't support Sfio, you'll have to build the Sfio libraries first, as your Perl distribution needs to be linked against them.

Building the Sfio Libraries

Before you build Sfio, extract *sfio97.src.unix.tar.gz*. Since *sfio97.src.unix.tar.gz* doesn't currently extract its contents into a base directory, it's best to create your own base directory, say `SFIO`, and extract the contents of the archive there. Otherwise, it will be difficult for you to keep track of the number of files and directories that were extracted from the archive.

Once you've extracted the files from the archive, enter the *src* directory. You might need to edit the makefile (named *makefile*) for Sfio to build properly on your system. You should copy the makefile to *makefile.date*[*] or *makefile.orig* so

---

[*] Date is actually `date` or `localtime()`

you can refresh the original if you've made a mistake. Edit the makefile for your system's specifics. When you're convinced that that makefile is correct for your system's attributes, save the new version of the file, and type `make`.

Since the Sfio libraries redefine some of the I/O functions and/or macros present in your system's existing header files (*stdio.h, stat.h, types.h* on some systems), your build might fail for certain BSD-related UNIX systems like FreeBSD or Sun OS 4.x. You might have to redefine (or undefine!) some macros if the build fails. Once you've redefined (or undefined) the conflicting function names or definitions, you should be able to finish building Sfio.

Finally, you must install the Sfio libraries and header files in the correct places. You might have noticed that your Sfio distribution's *include* directory contained a file called *stdio.h*:

```
your_base_directory/include/ast_common.h
your_base_directory/include/stdio.h
your_base_directory/include/sfio.h
your_base_directory/include/sfio_t.h
```

You should not install *stdio.h* in place of your existing *stdio.h* file. This causes many things to break horribly or fail to build correctly. Beware. You should keep these things separated by creating two directories (one for libraries and one for header files) where the Sfio files will reside:

```
/usr/local/include/sfio
/usr/local/lib/sfio
```

When you've copied the files over, these directories should contain the following:

```
/usr/local/include/sfio:
    ast_common.h
    sfhdr.h
    sfio.h
    sfio_t.h
/usr/local/lib/sfio:
    libsfio.a
    libstdio.a
```

Now, you're ready to build your Perl executable with Sfio support.

Linking Perl Against Sfio

To build Perl with Sfio support, run the `Configure` script as follows:

```
sh Configure -Duseperlio -Dusesfio
```

If you have already selected **-Duseperlio**, and if `Configure` detects that you have Sfio, then Sfio is the default suggested by `Configure`. You must remember to tell `Configure` where your Sfio header files are:

```
-I/usr/local/include/sfio
```

and where your libraries are:

```
-L/usr/local/lib/sfio -lsfio
```

Once you've run through `Configure`, or if you've decided to edit *config.sh* manually (or at the end of the `Configure` script before `make depend`), your Sfio entries in *config.sh* should look something like:

```
### Note: sfio is listed first in anything with an
### include (-I) or that will be linked in (-L).
ccflags='-I/usr/local/include/sfio -I/usr/local/include'
cppflags='-I/usr/local/include/sfio -I/usr/local/include'
d_sfio='define'
i_sfio='define'
lddlflags='-Bshareable  -L/usr/local/lib/sfio -L/usr/local/lib'
ldflags='-L/usr/local/lib/sfio -L/usr/local/lib'
libpth='/usr/local/lib/sfio /usr/local/lib /usr/lib'
libs='-lsfio -lgdbm -lm -lc -lcrypt'
libswanted='sfio net socket inet nsl nm ndbm gdbm dbm db dl \
            dld ld sun m c cposix posix ndir dir crypt ucb \
            bsd BSD PW x'
usesfio='true'
```

Note: on some systems, Sfio's *iffe* configuration script fails to detect that you have an `atexit` function (or equivalent). Apparently, this is a problem for some versions of Linux and SunOS 4.

You can test if you have this problem by trying the following shell script:[*]

```
#!/bin/sh
cat > try.c <<'EOCP'
#include <stdio.h>
main() { printf("42\n"); }
EOCP
cc -o try try.c -lsfio
val='./try'
if test X$val = X42; then
echo "Your sfio looks ok"
else
echo "Your sfio has the exit problem."
fi
```

If you have this problem, you can fix it by changing *iffe*'s guess about `atexit` (or whatever your platform uses.[†]) After `make` is complete don't forget to run `make test`. This is essential to confirm that your Perl distribution is working correctly. If any tests fail, don't run `make install`, as this installs a partially broken version of Perl on your system as the default.

---

[*] You will have to add extra cflags and libraries since you might not have changed LD_LIBRARY_PATH or such when you placed the Sfio libraries and header files into their own Sfio directories.

[†] We had no problems running this script under Solaris 2.4, FreeBSD 2.2.2, or Linux 2.0.x with the Sfio build and linking information shown at the beginning of this section.

Embedded Perl and mod_perl

Despite the significant enhancements made to web servers, there are still limitations on the rate at which HTTP requests can be processed by a server on which many CGI programs are executed concurrently. Regardless of state-saving CGI modules like mod_perl, HTTP's stateless nature causes a heavily trafficked server to suffer from poor performance when a CGI program is executed multiple times.

Although forking multiple server processes has proved effective in accepting multiple HTTP GET requests for static HTML pages, executing CGI programs still exhibit a problem with excessive overhead and strain on the server. The solution we'll discuss in the section is to use mod_perl and Apache to run CGI programs with an embedded Perl interpreter instead of spawning a Perl process with each execution of the program.

The modules you'll find in this section are extensions to the Apache web server. These modules have been chosen because of their comprehensive APIs, ease of extensibility, and their importance to the effectiveness of your web server.*

Why Apache?

Although there are a number of web servers for UNIX on the market, we've chosen to document Apache modules. This is because the Apache distribution includes source code, a programming API, and methods for creating modules or extensions using the API. The fact that Apache holds a substantial portion of the market for UNIX web servers (hence, the majority of readers would find this section useful) doesn't hurt, either.

Doug MacEachern (*dougm@osf.org*) wrote mod_perl, which embeds a Perl interpreter into an Apache executable. Documents to be interpreted by the embedded Perl executable are specified between <Perl> and </Perl> directives in the Apache configuration files. When you start Apache, it starts the Perl interpreter.

mod_perl makes it possible to write Apache modules entirely in Perl. By embedding the interpreter in the server, you avoid the overhead of starting an external interpreter and the penalty of Perl start-up (compile) time.

To use mod_perl, you'll need to have CGI.pm and the LWP modules (along with dependencies) installed. Otherwise mod_perl won't be able to build or be tested. It's also expected that you have *root* or *sudo* privileges, as you'll need to edit

---

* If you've successfully built your Perl distribution with Sfio support, you shouldn't have any problem building these modules using your existing Perl distribution. This section provides the necessary details you'll need to build the Apache modules, along with a number of examples you'll find helpful when using these modules.

Apache's configuration files. You won't need to be on a network, but your server must be able to run when it's time to test the examples.

Building Apache Embedded Perl Support

Before you can use **mod_perl**, you must build and install first Apache, and finally **mod_perl** itself. You can obtain the Apache source from *ftp://ftp.apache.org/ apache/dist/apache_1.2.x.tar.gz*. You can obtain **mod_perl** from *http:// www.perl.com/CPAN/modules/Apache/mod_perl-x.tar.gz*.

1. Extract your Apache distribution in the area where you wish to build it. The tar extraction should create a hierarchy of directories:

   ```
   /apache_version/cgi-bin
   /apache_version/conf
   /apache_version/htdocs
   /apache_version/src
   /apache_version/support
   ```

2. Extract your **mod_perl** distribution into the */apache_version/src* directory, so the hierarchy looks something like:

   ```
   /apache_version/cgi-bin
   /apache_version/conf
   /apache_version/htdocs
   /apache_version/src
   /apache_version/src/mod_perl-x.xx
   /apache_version/support
   ```

3. Change directories into the */apache_version/src/mod_perl-x.xx* directory. This is your working directory.

4. Your **mod_perl** distribution should have included *Makefile.PL*. Run it.

   ```
   perl Makefile.PL
   ```

5. According to the **mod_perl** documentation, there are several stages of a request where the Apache API allows a module to step in and do something. The Apache documentation will tell you all about those stages and what your modules can do. By default, these hooks are disabled at compile-time; see the *INSTALL* document for information on enabling these hooks.

   The following configuration directives take one argument, which is the name of the subroutine to call. If the value is not a subroutine name, **mod_perl** assumes it's a package name that implements a handler subroutine.

   ```
   PerlInitHandler
   PerlTransHandler
   PerlAuthenHandler
   PerlAuthzHandler
   PerlAccessHandler
   PerlTypeHandler
   PerlFixupHandler
   ```

```
PerlLogHandler
PerlHeaderParser (requires apache1.2b5 or higher)
PerlCleanupHandler
```

6. You are then asked a series of questions. You will see the following output:

```
ReadLine support enabled
Enter 'q' to stop search
Please tell me where I can find your apache src
 [] /base_directory/src (your entry)
Shall I build 'httpd'? [y] y
<Makefile then checks for LWP, CGI, etc modules and begins
 build if everything is present.  You'll need CGI.pm version
2.32 or higher>
```

7. Once `httpd` has been built (see the **mod_perl** *README* for more information about building the module), you should install it in the correct areas. For the sake of these examples, our Apache web server is installed in the following areas:

```
/usr/sbin/httpd          - the Apache daemon
/usr/www/apache/cgi-bin - the directory aliased to cgi-bin
/usr/www/apache/conf     - the Apache configuration files
/usr/www/apache/htdocs   - the Apache document root
/usr/www/apache/icons    - a directory of images
/usr/www/apache/logs     - the Apache logfiles
```

Using mod_perl as a CGI Replacement

The Apache::Registry module emulates the CGI environment, but Perl CGI programs that use Apache::Registry are quicker than normal CGI programs, because they're using the Perl interpreter you embedded into your Apache executable. CGI programmers can write Perl programs that run under CGI or **mod_perl** without change.

Apache::Registry maintains a cache of all compiled Perl programs. A Perl program is cached the first time it's executed or when the program has been changed (updated on the filesystem).

Once the server starts receiving requests, the embedded interpreter will compile code for each **require** file it has not seen yet, and each new Apache::Registry subroutine that's compiled, along with whatever modules it's **use**ing or **require**ing. Modules that you use are compiled when the server starts, unless they are inside an **eval** block. Your Apache executable will grow just as big as your Perl executable (or a CGI process), depending on your setup.

Since we (and **mod_perl**) presume you're running at least Version 5.004 of Perl (with Sfio support), scripts running under Apache::Registry won't look any different from your other CGI scripts. If you're running an older version or a version that doesn't support Sfio, different exercises with the Apache modules are left up to the reader, based on the documentation that are included with the Apache modules.

This section presumes you've configured *http.conf, srm.conf,* and *access.conf* to your liking and that the only lines you need to add to your configuration files are those that involve `mod_perl`.

Doug MacEachern recommends the following configuration for using Apache::Registry.

1. First, create a directory from which your Perl CGI scripts will be executed (this is not the same directory as your *cgi-bin* directory).

   ```
   mkdir /usr/www/apache/perl
   ```

2. Then, edit your *access.conf* to alias a directory name to the directory that holds the Perl programs that will use Apache::Registry.

   ```
   # access.conf
   Alias /perl-bin/  /usr/www/apache/perl
   ```

3. Since `mod_perl` doesn't send any headers by itself, you may want to use this directive:

   ```
   PerlSendHeader On
   ```

4. Since `PerlSendHeader` won't send a terminating newline, your script must send that itself.

   ```
   print "Content-type: text/html\n\n";
   ```

5. Finally, add the following lines to your *srm.conf* file. Note: there is a limit of 10 Perl modules used in your `Location` directives. (You can use more than 10 if one module pulls in many other modules. Also, see the discussion of the PerlScript directive later in this chapter.)

   ```
   # srm.conf
   <Location /perl-bin>
   SetHandler  perl-script
   PerlHandler Apache::Registry
   Options ExecCGI
   </Location>
   ```

Let's look at the directives we've added to *srm.conf.* You'll notice that the `<Location /perl-bin>` entry is similar to your `/cgi-bin` entry, except for the `mod_perl`-specific entries. As was the case in the other `<Location>` tags you added to *srm.conf,* the `Location /perl-bin` directive tells Apache to do something with the `/perl-bin` alias. The `SetHandler`, `PerlHandler`, and `Options` directives:

- Tell Apache to execute all files in */perl-bin* as Perl scripts that use Apache::Registry as their handler.

- Call Apache::Registry's `handler` method.

- Allow Apache to execute CGI programs residing in */perl-bin*.

Like regular CGI programs, the file must exist and be executable.

Here's a `mod_perl` CGI program that's executed when the URL *http://www.some-name.com/perl-bin/test_ar.pl* is called:

```
# no shebang is needed - we're running embedded,
# and using the correct directives.  :-)
print("Content-type: text/html\n\n");
foreach (keys %ENV) { print $_." => ".$ENV{$_}."<BR>\n"; }
```

Without a doubt you've seen the program above a million times. We're showing you this example again because there are several environment variables that have changed when you run this program using Apache::Registry, instead of Apache's normal CGI Gateway:

```
SERVER_SOFTWARE => Apache/1.2.1 mod_perl/1.00
GATEWAY_INTERFACE => CGI-Perl/1.1
SCRIPT_NAME => /perl-bin/test_ar.pl
```

First, you'll notice that Apache announces it's running with `mod_perl` support. Then, you'll notice that the `GATEWAY_INTERFACE` is no longer CGI 1.1. Last, you'll recognize that the `SCRIPT_NAME` is `/perl-bin/scripname`, not `/cgi-bin/scriptname`. If you caught the comment in the above code, you don't have to use the shebang (`#!`) path when executing CGI scripts that use Apache::Registry.

You can also tell `mod_perl` to execute scripts in any location, provided these scripts have a specific extension:

```
<Files *.extension>
SetHandler perl-script
PerlHandler Apache::Registry
Options ExecCGI
</Files>
```

The PerlScript Directive

With the 10-module-per-directive limit, you'll have to employ other methods when you want to use more than 10 modules. The PerlScript directive tells `mod_perl` to start up a given script when the Apache is launched:

```
PerlScript /usr/www/apache/perl/start_me_up.pl
```

The script contains the following (from the `mod_perl` distribution):

```
use strict;
use CGI::Switch ();
my $q = new CGI::Switch;
$q->print(
   $q->header,
```

```
    $q->start_html(),
    "Can you tell if I've been run under CGI or Apache::Registry?<p>",
    $q->start_form(),
    $q->textfield(-name => "textfield"),
    $q->submit(-value => "Submit"),
    $q->end_form,
    "<p>textfield = ", $q->param("textfield"),
    $q->dump,
    "<hr><pre>",
    (map { "$_ = $ENV{$_}\n" } keys %ENV),
    "</pre>",
    $q->end_html,
);
```

Configuring the Server with Perl Sections

`Perl` directives are referred to in the `mod_perl` instructions as *Perl sections*. You can configure your server entirely in Perl with Perl sections. However, Perl sections won't work if you haven't defined PerlScript.

Add the following to *httpd.conf*:

```
#httpd.conf
<Perl>
@PerlModule = qw(Mail::Send Devel::Peek);
#run the server as whoever starts it
$User  = getpwuid($>) || $>;
$Group = getgrgid($)) || $);
$ServerAdmin = $User;
</Perl>
```

This is equivalent to:

```
# httpd.conf
User nobody
Group nogroup
ServerAdmin webmaster@someplace.com
# access.conf
<Location /perl>
PerlModule Mail::Send Devel::Peek
</Location>
```

`Location` directives populate a hash, called `Location`:

```
$Location{"/directory_name/"} = {
AuthUserFile => '/path/htpasswd',
AuthType => 'Basic',
AuthName => 'coolstuff',
DirectoryIndex => [qw(index.html index.htm)],
Limit => {
  METHODS => 'GET POST',
  require => 'user nvp',
},
};
```

If you choose to mix Perl code with normal directives in *httpd.conf,* or you write
your entire `httpd` configuration in Perl (brave soul), your Perl sections should
look like the following:

```
<Perl>
#!/path/perl
... your code ...
__END__
</Perl>
```

Use `perl -cx httpd.conf` to check the syntax of the `Perl` sections in *httpd.conf*
before starting your server with the *httpd.conf* file.

Using Server-Side Includes with mod_perl

Like many web servers, Apache supports server-side includes. A *server-side
include* is a tag written into HTML that directs the server to display a special variable, to execute a script, or to include the contents of a file into a static HTML
page. Server-side includes can add dynamic content to web pages (without using
CGI programs), although they can pose large security holes if not used properly.

Under most servers without embedded Perl support, the syntax of server-side
includes is:

```
<!--#server_side_include_type="attribute"-->
```

Server-side includes under Apache with embedded Perl support and the
Apache::Include module use anonymous subroutine or some generic
package::handler calls (instead of regular server-side includes that use types and
attributes):

```
<!--#perl sub="sub { ... Perl stuff here ... }" -->
```

For example:

```
Page accessed <!--#perl sub="sub {print ++$count }" --> times.
```

Although you can also use *virtual includes* to include Apache::Registry scripts,
using `#perl` saves the overhead of making Apache go through the motions of
subrequest creation and destruction. Therefore, it's preferred that you use
Apache::Registry and `mod_include`.

```
<!--#perl sub="Apache::Include" arg="/scripts/script.pl" -->
```

13

Contributing to CPAN

Until this point, the role of the module developer has purposely been placed in the background. We decided to place a developer-oriented chapter toward the end of the book so the would-be Perl module developer could review some existing modules before proposing and/or developing a module that had already been implemented.

This chapter presumes that you have a working knowledge of Perl and modules; if you haven't already done so, please read and review Chapter 1, *Introduction to Perl Modules and CPAN*. We'll describe the steps you should take when you choose to contribute your work to CPAN, assist with new versions or extend an existing module, or even mirror a CPAN site from your own server. You'll also be given some direction about writing clean modules that pay close attention to namespace, method names, and writing tidy code.

With the number of comprehensive modules you've been introduced to throughout this kit, you might have been inspired to contribute your own. Great! The success and life of CPAN depends on the dedication and contributions of the Perl community; willing individuals with time, resources, and knowledge are always welcome.

The Developer Side of CPAN

The most important part of your contribution to CPAN is your relationship with the Perl community as a developer. This chapter takes you from "the drawing board" where you develop your ideas and share them with CPAN administrators, to the uploading and propagation of your contribution to hundreds of CPAN mirrors worldwide

The Drawing Board

With the hundreds of modules available on CPAN, the largest hurdle you'll need to cross is proposing a module with subject matter that has not already been implemented by another module developer.

Before registering with CPAN, you should mail your proposal to *modules@franz.ww.TU-Berlin.DE* so you can get feedback from CPAN administrators regarding the relevance of your proposal. Although you may be granted a CPAN developer account (see the next section) without proposing any modules to CPAN administrators, it is preferred that you share ideas and have them approved before registering with CPAN.

For example, you've been working on some Perl code that parses input from an HTML form and is capable of encoding a normal string to be sent to another HTML form. You've proposed that your module should be called `CGI_Helper` with an extension CGI_Helper::CGI_Encode.

Since there are two existing modules that handle HTML form input (`CGI.pm` and `CGI_Lite.pm`), your proposal is denied on the grounds that the subject matter of your module has already been implemented in existing modules. The CPAN administrators suggest that you pursue another facet of the subject matter you're hoping to develop.

Your CPAN Account

Before you upload any materials to hundreds of mirror sites worldwide, you must follow a series of steps to ensure that this process adheres to the CPAN guidelines and will appear seamless to the end user who use your contributions. You must introduce yourself to CPAN maintainers and be granted privileges to upload your materials to begin your relationship with the Perl community as a developer.

Unlike an account with an Internet service provider, your CPAN account doesn't entitle you to shell access to a remote host. Access to CPAN is limited to anonymous FTP and HTTP (WWW). When you upload your contributions to CPAN using the Web, you'll be using a logging system called PAUSE, short for Perl Authors Upload Server.

To set up your CPAN developer account, you must follow these steps. After noting each step, you will be shown what kinds of responses to expect from the CPAN maintainers and administrative bots.

1. Mail the following information to the CPAN modules list:

   — Your full name.

   — An encrypted password. You must generate an encrypted password using
   PGP (preferred), Perl's `crypt()` function, base64, or uuencode. Please
   don't send clear text passwords.

   — Your electronic mail address.

   — The URL of your homepage.

   — A description of module(s) you intend to upload to PAUSE.

   — A description of the status of each module (development stage, language
   used, API, and a maximum 45-character description).

   — Where the (proposed) modules might have been discussed or might be
   discussed, such as in a newsgroup (*comp.lang.perl.modules*), in a book
   (like an upcoming publication), in an essay on a homepage, etc.

   When I (Nathan) registered with CPAN, my mail message contained:

   ```
   To: modules@franz.ww.TU-Berlin.DE
   Subject: CPAN author registration
   Name: Nathan V. Patwardhan
   Password: <encrypted password>
   Email: sender@sorry-charlie.com
   Homepage: none
   Module: Proposed module name here
   Level: Will this be a release?  Alpha?  Beta?
   Description: What will this module do?  What is the namespace
   this module will use?
   ```

2. The initial confirmation message from CPAN. You'll receive this message after
   your first mail to *modules@franz.ww.TU-Berlin.DE*:

   ```
   Welcome Nathan V. Patwardhan,
   PAUSE, the Perl Authors Upload Server, has a userid for you:
         NVPAT
   Once you've gone through the procedure of password approval
   with the CPAN admin (see
   http://www.perl.com/CPAN/modules/04pause.html), this
   userid--as it stands, case-sensitive--will be the User-ID that
   you can use to upload your work and eventually correct your
   credentials in the PAUSE database.
   These are in the database now:
     Name:        Nathan V. Patwardhan
     email:       sender@sorry-charlie.com
     homepage:
     enteredby:   Andreas Koenig
   As already mentioned: see CPAN/modules/04pause.html for
   details of how to proceed next.
   Virtually Yours,
   Id: add_user,v 1.29 1997/01/16 06:04:46 k Exp k
   P.S.: Please be patient with the PAUSE admin. He may have
   ```

```
set up your account but may have no time to follow up this
message. Let him know if you have any questions. Thank You!
```

3. The final confirmation message. After the PAUSE administrator has set up your account, you'll receive the following message. If everything has gone smoothly, you can begin uploading your materials to CPAN.

```
Return-Path: <nobody@franz.ww.TU-Berlin.DE>
Date: Sun, 2 Mar 1997 18:28:01 +0100 (CET)
Subject: User update
To: "Nathan V. Patwardhan" <sender@ora.com>,
        modules@franz.ww.TU-Berlin.DE
Record update in users database:
     userid: [NVPAT]
   fullname: [Nathan V. Patwardhan]
      email: [sender@ora.com]
   homepage: []
           Entered by Nathan V. Patwardhan at Sun Mar  2 17:27:59
             1997 GMT


Virtually Yours,
The edit_me Program
```

You are now able to upload further materials to CPAN using anonymous FTP:

```
ftp://franz.ww.TU-Berlin.DE/incoming (preferred)
ftp://ftp.cis.ufl.edu/incoming
```

If you have been assigned a username and have cleared a password with CPAN administrators, you can use the WWW interface:

```
http://franz.ww.TU-Berlin.DE/perl/user/add_uri
```

4. What if this failed?

Occasionally the CPAN administrators deem a certain proposal to be unacceptable or in need of revisions before granting an account to a developer. Although unfortunate, this happens, but it can be remedied by revising, solidifying, or specifying your ideas so CPAN administrators have a clearer idea of the concept you're hoping to illustrate. Often, CPAN administrators will suggest that new developers work with current module authors to extend existing modules so new versions of the module include both developers' functionality, but preserve the module's namespace and don't reimplement attributes present in an existing module.

Don't hesitate to approach existing module authors. Most authors are interested in listening to members of the Perl community when it comes to developing a module many people will use.

Your Module

Say that CPAN administrators disapprove your idea to write a CGI module, and now you decide you'd like to write a module dealing with various types of speech and words, including a Morse code generator, pig latin converter, and other word coding/encoding schemes. CPAN administrators like this idea and suggest you use the `SpeakWord` namespace for any modules you'll be submitting to CPAN dealing with words, codes, or dialects.

The rest of this chapter follows the path of `SpeakWord` from the drawing board to distribution through CPAN. Although there is no existing `SpeakWord` module, you'll be introduced to many details about creating, documenting, and extending a module conforming to the standards proposed by CPAN administrators through examples illustrating `SpeakWord`'s development cycle.

Introducing SpeakWord

Once you've been given the go-ahead for module development by CPAN administrators, you should begin by outlining the contents of your module in terms of namespace and API. Focus on your module's base functionality and how you might choose to extend or expand on your module later.

The key to writing a good module is to start with small, robust pieces of code that work under different situations. You'll find that your module's development cycle makes the code grow over time. "Featureitis" only hinders your efforts in the early stages of your module, because the code becomes bloated and difficult to expand or extend without making significant changes. End users shouldn't have to change their code with each version you release.

Returning to `SpeakWord`, let's name the methods found in the `SpeakWord` module. Each of these methods should be appropriate for what the method is designed to accomplish:

`new()`
> The constructor.

`ReadWordOrSentence()`
> Reads a word (or sentence) passed as a string or from STDIN; returns an array of tokens, or single words.

`WriteWord()`
> Outputs a word (or sentence) passed as an array; sends output to STDOUT.

In the `SpeakWord` namespace, the `SpeakWord` module contains helper methods used by other modules, like `PigLatin` and `MorseCode`. Can you see why `Speak-Word` contains only a simple set of core functions? If `SpeakWord` contains too many functions that perform too many dissimilar tasks, it becomes difficult to modularize the code between different modules.

Creating the Module

Although you can create directories and skeletal modules by hand or from your own homespun templates, you should use **h2xs** (which was included with your Perl distribution), to generate the Makefiles since the modules you'll be submitting to CPAN must adhere to the CPAN guidelines. In addition, these guidelines specify that your module must use ExtUtils::MakeMaker, and there are also other requirements, as you'll see. If you have already reviewed the **perltoc**, **perlmod**, **perltoot**, and/or **perlxstut** manpages, you've probably noticed several ways **h2xs** can be used.

Executing **h2xs** without any arguments outputs the following help message:

```
Must supply header file or module name
h2xs [-AOPXcfh] [-v version] [-n module_name]
          [headerfile [extra_libraries]]
version: 1.16
    -f  Force creation of the extension even if the C header
        does not exist.
    -n  Specify a name to use for the extension (recommended).
    -c  Omit the constant() function and specialised AUTOLOAD
        from the XS file.
    -A  Omit all autoloading facilities (implies -c).
    -O  Allow overwriting of a pre-existing extension directory.
    -P  Omit the stub POD section.
    -X  Omit the XS portion.
    -v  Specify a version number for this extension.
    -h  Display this help message
    extra_libraries
    are any libraries that might be needed for loading the
    extension, e.g. -lm would try to link in the math library.
```

Since you won't be using language extensions or glue at this juncture, you shouldn't need to use **XS**, so you should create your module's namespace and skeletal files with the following:

```
h2xs -X -n namespace
```

This tells **h2xs** to create the skeletons for a module (**-n**) namespace without generating the stubs needed by **XS**.

For **SpeakWord**, you would do this:

```
h2xs -X -n SpeakWord
```

This tells **h2xs** to create the skeletons for a module (**-n**) **SpeakWord** without generating the stubs needed by **XS**. You'll know things have worked correctly if **h2xs** outputs:

```
Writing SpeakWord/SpeakWord.pm
Writing SpeakWord/Makefile.PL
Writing SpeakWord/test.pl
```

```
Writing SpeakWord/Changes
Writing SpeakWord/MANIFEST
```

Here's what was generated by **h2xs**:

SpeakWord.pm

The core module file; you'll be adding your core methods to this file.

Makefile.PL

The file that uses ExtUtils::MakeMaker to generate a Makefile when executed like Perl *Makefile.PL.*

test.pl

A script where you'll add any test functions. **test.pl** is executed with **make test** and ensures that your module works correctly for those who use the module.

Changes

Tells users what has changed between numbered revisions of your module.

MANIFEST

The contents (files) of everything included in your module's distribution (generally in a tarball). If something is present in the directory but missing in the **MANIFEST**, MakeMaker complains. You need to hand-edit this file if you add files to your distribution.

So why was a **SpeakWord** directory created when you executed **h2xs**? When you pass the **-n** flag to **h2xs**, you are telling **h2xs** to use the **SpeakWord** namespace. In Perl, modules residing in a certain directory inherit the name of the directory as their namespace. Looking at your Perl distribution, the *lib* directory containing your base modules contains a subdirectory, *File*. The *File* directory contains **Base-name.pm**, **CheckTree.pm**, **Copy.pm**, **Find.pm**, and **Path.pm**; each module in the *File* directory can be used like so:

```
File::Basename (package File::Basename)
File::CheckTree (package File::CheckTree)
File::Copy (package File::Copy)
File::Find (package File::Find)
File::Path (package File::Path)
```

Adding Methods to SpeakWord.pm

Let's examine the contents of **SpeakWord.pm**, which was generated by **h2xs**. You'll notice that **h2xs** created **SpeakWord.pm** with all the components needed by the **SpeakWord** module, like **package**, **ISA**, **EXPORT**, etc., but didn't include any methods or method names. You'll be adding these when you edit **SpeakWord.pm**.

The skeletal **SpeakWord.pm** starts with a package declaration.

```
package SpeakWord;
```

Good module writers always use strict checking. Your module is an embarrassing hack if you don't.

```
use strict;
```

Next, we include global declarations used by the module.

```
use vars qw($VERSION @ISA @EXPORT);
```

We require the **Exporter** module. This is necessary if we ever want to extend this module or export methods to other modules. See **perlmod** for details.

```
require Exporter;
require AutoLoader;
@ISA = qw(Exporter AutoLoader);
# Items to export into caller's namespace by default. Note: do
# not export names by default without a very good reason. Use
# EXPORT_OK instead. Do not simply export all your public
# functions/methods/constants.
@EXPORT = qw(

);
```

Always include the current version of the module (more about this in the section later entitled "Writing Intelligent Modules").

```
$VERSION = '0.01';
# Preloaded methods go here.
```

Since we're not doing any dynamic loading, this is where we're going to put our methods.

```
# Autoload methods go after =cut, and are processed by the
# autosplit program.
```

We won't be using any autoloading, so this section remains empty for now.

```
# Always return true for modules and libraries!
1;
__END__
# Below is the stub of documentation for your module. You
# better edit it!
```

Oh look, pod skeletons! Just in case you would have been sneaky and omitted it, the ExtUtils::MakeMaker authors offer a pleasant reminder. Please remember to add good documentation; it's helpful to end users and other developers who are working with your module. See the section, "Writing Intelligent Modules" for more details.

```
=head1 NAME
SpeakWord - Perl extension for blah blah blah

=head1 SYNOPSIS
use SpeakWord;
  blah blah blah
```

```
=head1 DESCRIPTION
Stub documentation for SpeakWord was created by h2xs. It looks
like the author of the extension was negligent enough to leave
the stub unedited.
Blah blah blah.

=head1 AUTHOR
A. U. Thor, a.u.thor@a.galaxy.far.far.away

=head1 SEE ALSO
perl(1).

=cut
```

Now, let's add implementations of these methods to `SpeakWord.pm`:

```
new
ReadWordOrSentence
WriteWord
```

Here's how these methods look when implemented for `SpeakWord.pm`:

```perl
# the constructor - we'll use this to initialize an object
sub new {
    my $type = {};
    bless $type;
    return $type;
}

sub ReadWordOrSentence {
    my $type = shift;
    my($word) = @_;

    my(@tokens);
    (@tokens) = split(/\s+/, $word);
    return(@tokens);
}

sub WriteWord {
    my $type = shift;
    my(@input_word) = @_;

    print join(" ", @input_word);
}
```

Once you've added the methods to `SpeakWord.pm`, it's time to test your module. Create a file called *mod_test.pl* and add the following to it:

```perl
#!/usr/local/bin/perl -w

use lib '.'; # add current directory to @INC
use SpeakWord; # use the SpeakWord module

# now, create a new SpeakWord object
$senderobj = SpeakWord->new();
```

```
# here are the words / sentence to test
$testwords = "this is a test";

# now, read the words into ReadWordOrSentence
@words = $senderobj->ReadWordOrSentence($testwords);
die("Sentence seems to be empty... exiting!")
    if scalar(@words) == 0;

# send the words to STDOUT
$senderobj->WriteWord(@words);

# send an extra \n to STDOUT for output cleanliness
print "\n";
```

When $testwords is passed to ReadWordOrSentence(), the spaces are removed because the sentence has been split into words. If you were to output the return of ReadWordOrSentence(), it would look like:

```
thisisatest
```

WriteWord() beautifies the output by joining words with spaces and sends the tokens to STDOUT with:

```
print join(" ", @array_of_tokens);
```

Your test program (and SpeakWord.pm) are working correctly if the following is output:

```
this is a test
```

Extending SpeakWord

When you extend a module, you have added functionality to an existing module by adding methods that can be called from the same namespace. With this arrangement, you can use multiple modules together by importing and exporting desired parts of different modules.

Now, let's extend the SpeakWord namespace to include the TokenReverse module that contains the ReverseWord() method. ReverseWord() takes one argument, an array of characters, and returns a scalar of reversed tokens.

For example, passing:

```
this is a sentence
```

to ReverseWord() outputs:

```
sentence a is this
```

Here are the contents of TokenReverse.pm:

```
package TokenReverse;

# always use strict checking!
```

```
use strict;

# globals
use vars qw($VERSION @ISA @EXPORT);

require AutoLoader;
require Exporter;

# Import SpeakWord AutoLoader and Exporter
@ISA = qw(SpeakWord AutoLoader Exporter);

# Items to export into caller's namespace by default. Note: do
# not export names by default without a very good reason. Use
# EXPORT_OK instead.
# Do not simply export all your public functions/methods
# constants. See the perlmod manpage for explanation.
@EXPORT = qw();

# version of the module
$VERSION = '0.01';

# Preloaded methods go here.

# ReverseWord method is passed an array and returns
# a scalar containing reversed characters.
sub ReverseWord {
    my $word = shift;
    my(@input_word) = @_;
    my $reversed = join(" ", reverse(@input_word));
    return($reversed);
}

# Autoload methods go after =cut, and are processed by the
# autosplit program.
# Return true for all modules and libraries.
1;
__END__
```

```
# The POD skeletons have been snipped for the time being.
```

With the addition of TokenReverse.pm, you must add the following line to the
beginning of SpeakWord.pm so you can use the ReverseWord() method from
TokenReverse.pm in programs using SpeakWord.pm. You should place this line
before the @ISA inclusion:

```
require TokenReverse;
```

After you've added this line to SpeakWord.pm, the beginning of SpeakWord.pm
should look like:

```
package SpeakWord;

use strict;
use vars qw($VERSION @ISA @EXPORT);
```

```
require Exporter;
require AutoLoader;
require TokenReverse;
```

Now let's test this extension to **SpeakWord.pm**. Create a file called *mod_test2.pl* that contains:

```perl
#!/usr/local/bin/perl -w


# use strict checking
use strict;

# use the SpeakWord module
use SpeakWord;

# create a new SpeakWord object
my $sw_obj = SpeakWord->new();

# read and output tokens
my $test_sent = "this is a test";
my @words = $sw_obj->ReadWordOrSentence($test_sent);

$sw_obj->WriteWord(@words);
print "\n";

# now, call the TokenReverse::Reverse() method
# and output its return, $bk
my $bk = $sw_obj->ReverseWord(@words);
print $bk."\n";
print "\n";
```

If your program is working correctly, it should output:

```
this is a test
test a is this
```

Writing Intelligent Modules

Do you think the **SpeakWord** and **TokenReverse** modules were well-developed? Do you think they were poorly developed? If you think them poorly developed or in need of some enhancements, you're right. Although Perl offers a number of different methods to solve various tasks, it can't stop you from shooting yourself in the foot once in a while.

SpeakWord and **TokenReverse** give you an idea about writing your own modules, but neither would fare well through a long-term development cycle because they will require serious revisions once they are no longer easily extended.

This section deals with writing intelligent modules that conform to the CPAN guidelines; after reviewing this section you'll have a better grasp of writing solid modules to distribute through CPAN.

The continuity and stability of your modules is essential. Don't forget that a contribution of this magnitude should be useful and straightforward to developers worldwide. Your module introduces you and your software development skills to thousands of other Perl programmers around the world. The developers who are relying on your module to fulfill their programming tasks view you as an expert programmer.

CPAN Guidelines

All modules released to CPAN should use `strict` checking for data integrity; anything not using `strict` checking is a hack.

Module Style Guide

Use underscores to separate words. It's easier to read `$var_names_like_this` than `$VarNamesLikeThis`, especially for nonnative speakers of English. It's also a simple rule that works consistently with `$VAR_NAMES_LIKE_THIS`.

Package/module names are an exception to this rule. Perl informally reserves lowercase module names for `pragma` modules like `integer` and `strict`. Other modules normally begin with a capital letter and use mixed case with no underscores (the names need to be short and portable).

You may find it helpful to use letter case to indicate the scope or nature of a variable. For example:

`$ALL_CAPS_HERE`
    Not recommended because of clashes with Perl variables

`$Some_Caps_Here`
    Use for package-wide global/static variables

`$no_caps_here`
    Use as function scope (`my()` or `local()`) variables

Function and method names seem to work best as all lowercase. For example, `$obj->as_string()`.

You can use a leading underscore to indicate that a variable or function should not be used outside the package that defined it.

For method calls, use either:

```
$object = new ModuleName $arg1, $arg2; # no parentheses
$object = ModuleName->new($arg1, $arg2);
```

but avoid the ambiguous form that looks like a function call:

```
$object = new ModuleName($arg1, $arg2);
```

On how to report constructor failure, Larry Wall said:

> I tend to see it as exceptional enough that I'll throw a real Perl exception (die) if I can't construct an object. This has a couple of advantages right off the bat. First, you don't have to check the return value of every constructor. Just say:

```
$scraps = new Doggie;
```

> and presume it succeeded. This leads to clearer code in most cases.

> Second, if it does fail, you get a better diagnostic than just the undefinedness of the return value. In fact, the exception it throws may be quite rich in "stacked" error messages, if it's rethrowing an exception caught further in.

> If, on the other hand, you expect your constructor to fail a goodly part of the time, then you shouldn't use exceptions, but you should document the interface so that people will know to check the return value. You don't need to use `defined()`, since a constructor would only return a **true** reference or a **false** **undef**. So good Perl style for checking a return value would simply say

```
$conn = new Connection $addr or die "Couldn't create Connection";
```

> In general, make as many things meaningful in a boolean context as you can. This leads to straightforward code. Never write anything like:

```
if (do_your_thing() == OK)
```

> in Perl. That's just asking for logic errors and domain errors. Just write:

```
if (do_your_thing())
```

> Perl is designed to help you eschew obfuscation, if that's your thing.

Selecting What to Export

This section was drawn from the `modlist` document distributed through CPAN. The `modlist` files are maintained by Tim Bunce and Andreas Koenig.

Don't export method names! Don't export anything else by default without a good reason!

Exports pollute the namespace of the module user. If you must export, try to use `@EXPORT_OK` in preference to `@EXPORT`, and avoid short or common names to reduce the risk of name clashes.

Generally anything not exported is still accessible from outside the module using the *ModuleName::item_name* (or `$blessed_ref->method`) syntax. By convention you can use a leading underscore on names to informally indicate they are internal and not for public use.

As a general rule, if the module is trying to be object oriented, then export nothing. If it's just a collection of functions, then @EXPORT_OK anything, but use @EXPORT with caution.

Using Named Parameters

Complex modules often contain methods taking multiple parameters. Although you, the programmer, understand how your module and methods work, another programmer might have a difficult time following a method that takes four parameters for four distinct purposes.

For example, suppose you've written a method that takes four parameters: name, date, age, and employer. These parameters can only be in one order, and all four parameters must be present. When another programmer uses your module, they are forced to do:

```
$object->method("name", "date", "age", "employer");
```

Although the method could check for missing parameters, it would be rather difficult to differentiate between parameters if the method had been called like so:

```
$object->method("date", "employer", "age", "name");
```

An excellent way of parameter-tracking is to use *named parameters*. Named parameters use a HASH to hold the contents of name/value pairs extracted from @_. You would populate a hash like so:

```
%HASH = (
        name1 => value1,
        name2 => value2,
        name3 => value3
);
```

Here's how a hash (representing named parameters) is populated:

```
#!/usr/local/bin/perl -w

sub show_named_parameters {
    my(%NAMED) = @_;

    foreach (keys(%NAMED)) {
        print "$_ has been assigned $NAMED{$_}\n";
    }
}

show_named_parameters(name1 => value1,
                      name2 => value2,
                      name3 => value3);
```

The named-parameters model works well if you provide a name/value pair for parameter-name/parameter-value. Before operating on parameters passed to the method, you should check HASH entries and confirm that no hash member is undefined.

Module authors Lincoln Stein (CGI.pm) and Nick Ing-Simmons (Perl/Tk) use a more robust version of naming parameters than the example above. Both authors have implemented methods to pass named parameters, so:

```
$return_value = $object->method(-param1 => value1,
                                -param2 => value2);
```

is equivalent to:

```
$return_value = $object->method(param1 => value1,
                                param2 => value2);
```

Methods can also be called like:

```
$return_value = $object->method(value1, value2);
```

Using CGI.pm's `header()` method, named parameters are passed like:

```
print $query->header(-type => 'text/html');
```

After `@_` is returned to the calling method, the parameters are rearranged, so the order they are passed to the method doesn't matter.

```
print $query->header(-type=>'text/html',
                     -nph=>1);
```

is equivalent to:

```
print $query->header(-nph=>1,
                     -type=>'text/html);
```

Documenting Your Module

Perl includes an internal documentation mechanism known as *pod*, short for "plain old documentation." If you are familiar with the UNIX manpage format, you already know what to expect from pod. UNIX manpages are generally written for nroff or troff, two UNIX text-formatting utilities; these documents are basically illegible if not viewed through an nroff or troff interpreter. Pod, on the other hand, is plain text enclosed within special tags in a Perl module or script. Pod tags are not interpreted as Perl statements when a script is executed.

Earlier in the chapter, we generated the SpeakWord module using:

```
h2xs -X -n SpeakWord
```

SpeakWord.pm contained pod skeletons for you to add your own documentation to the SpeakWord module. Since many programmers around the world will use your module, it's expected that your module will be well documented so others can use it to its maximum potential. Since h2xs created the pod skeletons for you, it's pretty simple to add your own documentation to the module.

Well-documented modules should always include:

- Module name

- Author name and email address

- Purpose of the module

- Synopsis: a short program that shows how the module can be used

- Method/API descriptions, including return types and values

- Sample programs showing how the module would be used under various conditions

- Known bugs

Copyrighting Your Module

This section was extracted from the modlist document distributed through CPAN. The modlist files are maintained by Tim Bunce and Andreas Koenig.

How you choose to license your work is a personal decision. The general mechanism is to assert your copyright and then make a declaration of how others may copy, use, or modify your work.

Perl, for example, is supplied with two types of license: the GNU GPL and the Artistic License (see the files *README, Copying,* and *Artistic*). Larry Wall has good reasons for not just using the GNU GPL. My personal recommendation, out of respect for Larry, Perl, and the Perl community at large, is to simply state something like this:

```
Copyright (c) 1997 Your Name. All rights reserved.
This program is free software; you can redistribute it and/or
modify it under the same terms as Perl itself.
```

This statement should at least appear in the *README* file. You may also wish to include it in a *Copying* file and your source files. Remember to include the other words in addition to the copyright.

The Intelligent SpeakWord

Now, let's use the suggestions on how to write better modules found in the "Writing Intelligent Modules" section to prepare SpeakWord Version 0.01 for distribution to CPAN.

You've probably noticed that earlier examples of **SpeakWord** contained a number of the problems we explicitly warned about earlier. Before releasing **Speakword** Version 0.01 to CPAN, these inconsistencies should be worked out so the module is reliable. Let's walk through this process together.

Planning the Directory Tree for Your Distribution

Most modules you download and install from CPAN extract from the tarball (like *latest.tar.gz*) into their own directory, which represents ModuleName-ModuleVersion. Each subdirectory represents a portion of the namespace and contains an appropriately named module. With the changes that will be made to **SpeakWord**, the directory tree looks like:

```
SpeakWord-0.01/
SpeakWord-0.01/Makefile.PL
SpeakWord-0.01/SpeakWord.pm
SpeakWord-0.01/SpeakWord/MainFunc.pm
SpeakWord-0.01/SpeakWord/TokenReverse.pm
```

This directory structure and naming convention is important, because users will want to know the version of a module they're downloading from CPAN. Once the module has been downloaded, the user may choose to install different versions of a module in different areas; thus, there should be a different base directory name for each version of a module, representing the contents and version of it.

File Placement

Once you've decided on your directory structure, you can start placing files where they belong in the tree. To get everything started, create the base directory and *cd* into it:

```
mkdir SpeakWord-0.01
cd SpeakWord-0.01
```

Now you should be in the base directory. You must run **h2xs** to generate *Makefile.PL*, the **MANIFEST**, and *.pm* files:

```
h2xs -X -n SpeakWord
```

The *SpeakWord-0.01* directory should now contain:

```
Changes
MANIFEST
Makefile.PL
SpeakWord.pm
test.pl
```

Since you're going to be extending **SpeakWord** into SpeakWord::MainFunc and SpeakWord::TokenReverse, you'll need to create a *SpeakWord* directory:

```
mkdir SpeakWord
```

The *SpeakWord-0.*01 directory should now contain:

```
Changes
MANIFEST
Makefile.PL
SpeakWord (directory)
SpeakWord.pm
test.pl
```

You'll need to redo the method names, because they don't conform to the guidelines found in the "Writing Intelligent Modules" section. The original SpeakWord module contained these methods:

```
new
ReadWordOrSentence
WriteWord
ReverseWord
```

Let's rename these methods:

```
new
read_word_or_sentence
write_word
reverse_word
```

Recoding the SpeakWord Module

SpeakWord.pm originally contained ReadWordOrSentence() and WriteWord(), and TokenReverse.pm originally contained ReverseWord(). This isn't exactly the case now. *SpeakWord-0.01* added two new files: MainFunc.pm and TokenReverse.pm. SpeakWord.pm now only contains a constructor and documentation. SpeakWord.pm now acts as a wrapper for the methods found in MainFunc.pm and TokenReverse.pm by importing the methods.

Let's examine the contents of SpeakWord.pm:

```
package SpeakWord;

use strict;
use vars qw($VERSION @ISA @EXPORT);

require AutoLoader;
require Exporter;

# we'll need to use these modules and certain functions
# found in each module
use SpeakWord::MainFunc qw(read_word_or_sentence write_word);
use SpeakWord::TokenReverse qw(reverse_word);

@ISA = qw(Exporter AutoLoader);
# Items to export into callers namespace by default. Note: do
# not export names by default without a very good reason. Use
# EXPORT_OK instead. Do not simply export all your public
```

```
# functions/methods/constants.
@EXPORT = qw();

# *Always* remember to use the correct version
$VERSION = '0.01';

# Preloaded methods go here.

# constructor
sub new {
    my $type = {};
    bless $type;
    return $type;
}

# Autoload methods go after =cut, and are processed by the
# autosplit program.
# always return true for modules
1;
__END__
# Below is the stub of documentation for your module. You
# better edit it [SNIPPED]!
```

As you noticed, **SpeakWord.pm** only imports method names into its namespace; it hasn't implemented any functions except the constructor.

Here are the contents of **MainFunc.pm**. SpeakWord::MainFunc implements the **read_word_or_sentence()** and **write_word()** methods.

```
package SpeakWord::MainFunc;

use strict;
use vars qw($VERSION @ISA @EXPORT);

require Exporter;
@ISA = qw(Exporter);

# Items to export into callers namespace by default. Note: do
# not export names by default without a very good reason. Use
# EXPORT_OK instead. Do not simply export all your public
# functions/methods/constants.
@EXPORT = qw(ReadWordOrSentence WriteWord);

$VERSION = '0.01';
# Preloaded methods go here.

# Pass in a word or sentence and split into single words
# or tokens returns an array of tokens
sub read_word_or_sentence {
    my $type = shift;
    my($word) = @_;
    my(@tokens);
    (@tokens) = split(/\s+/, $word);
```

```
        return(@tokens);
    }


    # output an array of tokens joined by spaces
    sub write_word {
        my $type = shift;
        my(@input_word) = @_;
        print join(" ", @input_word);
    }


    # Autoload methods go after =cut, and are processed by the
    # autosplit program.
    # modules and libraries return true
    1;
    __END__
```

Here are the contents of **TokenReverse.pm**, which implements Speak-
Word::TokenReverse and **reverse_word( )**:

```
    package SpeakWord::TokenReverse;

    require Exporter;

    use strict;
    use vars qw($VERSION @ISA @EXPORT);

    @ISA = qw(Exporter);

    # Items to export into caller's namespace by default. Note: do
    # not export names by default without a very good reason. Use
    # EXPORT_OK instead. Do not simply export all your public
    # functions/methods/constants.
    @EXPORT = qw(ReverseWord);

    $VERSION = '0.01';

    # Preloaded methods go here.

    # returns a reversed set of tokens
    sub reverse_word {
        my $word = shift;
        my(@input_word) = @_;
        my $reversed = join(" ", reverse(@input_word));
        return($reversed);
    }

    # Autoload methods go after =cut, and are processed by the
    # autosplit program.
    1;
    __END__
```

Manifest Density

Okay. Do we have it all? We've generated `Makefile.PL`, edited `SpeakWord.pm`, and created `MainFunc.pm` and `TokenReverse.pm`. No, we don't. Never forget to edit the `MANIFEST` file that was generated by `h2xs`; the `MANIFEST` file contains the names of all files and directories included with your module's distribution. Failure to do so prevents the module from building properly (or maybe at all!).

Here's the `MANIFEST` for *SpeakWord-0.01*:

```
Changes
MANIFEST
Makefile.PL
SpeakWord/MainFunc.pm
SpeakWord/TokenReverse.pm
test.pl
```

Once you think you have everything, let's run a test program using the **Speak-Word** modules we've created:

```
#!/usr/local/bin/perl -w

use SpeakWord;

$senderobj = new SpeakWord;
@words = $senderobj->ReadWordOrSentence("this is a test");
$senderobj->WriteWord(@words);

print "\n";

$bk = $senderobj->ReverseWord(@words);
print $bk."\n";
```

If *SpeakWord-0.01* is working correctly, the program should output:

```
this is a test
test a is this
```

Now, add your pod documentation to the module (not shown) and create a *README* file in the SpeakWord-0.01 directory. The *README* file is extracted by CPAN administrators when your tarball is extracted from your upload area and placed in the directory where your module is distributed. Your *README* file should contain the name and version of the module, and information about building/installing the module. Don't forget to add *README* to the `MANIFEST`.

The Version for CPAN

It's time to archive your module into a tarfile and upload it to CPAN. When **taring** your module, please remember to keep the base directory name intact and to name the tarball with the same convention you named the base directory.

Bear in mind that some versions of `tar` don't allow a trailing slash in the name of the directory being `tar`'d.*

```
tar cvf SpeakWord-0.01.tar SpeakWord-0.01/
```

Now, `gzip` the file:

```
gzip SpeakWord-0.01.tar
```

Then, follow the instructions given to you by the CPAN administrators to get your module propagated through CPAN. Congratulations!

How to Become a CPAN Mirror

CPAN mirror sites are always welcome. It's a painless process to mirror CPAN on your own machine. If you have at least 260 MB of available disk space, and maintain a reliable Internet connection (ISDN, cable modem, T1, etc.), you are an excellent candidate for a CPAN mirror. After you have spec'd your system, you should obtain the file *MIRRORED.BY* from your preferred CPAN site, and review the CPAN sites available in your area. If your area is already well equipped with CPAN sites, it's possible you won't be able to mirror a CPAN site for the moment. When you are ready to apply for your mirror, contact the CPAN administrators at the mail address shown earlier in this chapter. Once you have reached the phase of mirroring a CPAN site, you should download *mirror-2.8.tar.gz* (version subject to change) from CPAN. *mirror-2.8.tar.gz* is fully documented and requires `chat2.pl` and `lchat.pl` to be installed with the software.

Private/Local Mirroring

If you want a private/local CPAN mirror that's not advertised, there's no need to contact the CPAN administrators. You need to review the CPAN site that offers the best bandwidth for file transfer, and contact the CPAN administrator (*dst_contact*) listed in the *MIRRORED.BY* file for information about acceptable times you can mirror their CPAN site. A list of registered CPAN sites follows.

Table 13-1. Registered CPAN Sites

Continent	Country/State	Site
Africa	South Africa	*ftp://ftp.is.co.za*
Asia	Hong Kong	*ftp://ftp.bkstar.com*
	Japan	*ftp://ftp.jaist.ac.jp*
		ftp://ftp.lab.kdd.co.jp

---

* Depending on your version of `tar`, you might be able to automatically `gzip` your tarfile with the `z` option. For example, *tar zcvf filename.tar.gz* creates a `gzip`'d tarfile.

Table 13-1. Registered CPAN Sites (continued)

Continent	Country/State	Site
	South Korea	*ftp://ftp.nuri.net*
	Taiwan	*ftp://dongpo.math.ncu.edu.tw* *ftp://ftp.wownet.net*
Australia		*ftp://ftp.netinfo.com.au*
	New Zealand	*ftp://ftp.tekotago.ac.nz*
Europe	Austria	*ftp://ftp.tuwien.ac.at*
	Belgium	*ftp://ftp.kulnet.kuleuven.ac.be*
	Czech Republic	*ftp://sunsite.mff.cuni.cz*
	Denmark	*ftp://sunsite.auc.dk/pub/languages/perl/CPAN/*
	Finland	*ftp://ftp.funet.fi*
	France	*ftp://ftp.ibp.fr* *ftp://ftp.pasteur.fr*
	Germany	*ftp://ftp.gmd.de* *ftp://ftp.leo.org* *ftp://ftp.rz.ruhr-uni-bochum.de* *ftp://ftp.uni-erlangen.de* *ftp://ftp.uni-hamburg.de*
	Greece	*ftp://ftp.ntua.gr*
	Hungary	*ftp://ftp.kfki.hu*
	Italy	*ftp://cis.utovrm.it*
	the Netherlands	*ftp://ftp.EU.net*
	Norway	*ftp://ftp.uit.no*
	Poland	*ftp://ftp.pk.edu.pl* *ftp://sunsite.icm.edu.pl*
	Portugal	*ftp://ftp.ci.uminho.pt* *ftp://ftp.telepac.pt*
	Russia	*ftp://ftp.sai.msu.su*
	Slovenia	*ftp://ftp.arnes.si*
	Spain	*ftp://ftp.etse.urv.es* *ftp://ftp.rediris.es*
	Sweden	*ftp://ftp.sunet.se*
	Switzerland	*ftp://sunsite.cnlab-switch.ch/mirror/CPAN/*
	United Kingdom	*ftp://ftp.demon.co.uk* *ftp://sunsite.doc.ic.ac.uk* *ftp://unix.hensa.ac.uk*
North America	Ontario	*ftp://ftp.utilis.com* *ftp://enterprise.ic.gc.ca*
	Manitoba	*ftp://theory.uwinnipeg.ca*
	California	*ftp://ftp.digital.com* *ftp://ftp.cdrom.com*

Table 13-1. Registered CPAN Sites (continued)

Continent	Country/State	Site
	Colorado	*ftp://ftp.cs.colorado.edu*
	Florida	*ftp://ftp.cis.ufl.edu*
	Illinois	*ftp://uiarchive.cso.uiuc.edu*
	Massachusetts	*ftp://ftp.iguide.com*
	North Carolina	*ftp://ftp.duke.edu*
	Oklahoma	*ftp://ftp.ou.edu*
	Oregon	*ftp://ftp.orst.edu*
	Pennsylvania	*ftp://ftp.epix.net*
	Texas	*ftp://ftp.sedl.org* *ftp://ftp.metronet.com*
	Washington	*ftp://ftp.spu.edu*
South America	Chile	*ftp://sunsite.dcc.uchile.cl*

In this chapter:
- *A Web-Based Newsreader*
- *A Graphical Mail Reader*
- *A Graphical FTP Client*
- *An Image Viewer*
- *An Image Generator*

14

Examples

In writing this book, we developed some extended examples that were too involved to leave in the chapters themselves, but which we wanted to include anyway. This chapter includes the following five examples:

- A web-based newsreader using News::NNTPClient and `CGI.pm`. It uses HTML frames to show the subject and author in the top frame and the article itself in the bottom frame.

- A graphical mail reader that uses Getopt::Long, Mail::POP3Client, and pTk to provide an interface for reading and deleting mail messages.

- A graphical FTP client that uses Net::FTP and pTk. It allows you to transfer files and navigate through both the local and remote file systems.

- An image viewer that uses pTk and Getopt::Long. To view an image, you can either run it from the command line or use the `Open` button on the GUI.

- An image generator that uses GD and Getopt::Std.

A Web-Based Newsreader

```
#!/usr/local/bin/perl -w

# This script uses CGI.pm's frameset functionality to deliver news
# articles in separate frames. You might want to review the PATH_INFO
# environment variable, if you are unfamiliar with its meaning.

# By default, the top frame of the HTML page shows the newsgroups you
# can read, and the bottom frame gives a message that it cannot find any
# subject headers.

# print_prompt() outputs the default screen for NNTP-WWW2, the newsgroup
# list.  When POSTED to, CGI.pm's output is redirected to the top frame,
```

```
# until an article is selected; the article then appears in the bottom
# frame.

use CGI;

$newshost = 'news.somenews.com';
$query = CGI->new(); # new CGI object

print $query->header;

$path_info = $query->path_info;
if (!$path_info) {
    print_frameset();
    exit 0;
}

print_html_header(); # top of HTML page
# not posting, load default page
print_prompt($query) if $path_info=~/query/;
print_response($query) if $path_info=~/lower/; # posting, so handle events
print_end(); # bottom of html page

# Create the frameset with noresize attributes (keeps things tidy)
# The top frame is 10% smaller than the bottom frame.
sub print_frameset {
    $script_name = $query->script_name;
    print <<EOF;
<html><head><title>NNTP-WWW: A WWW-based Usenet Reader</title></head>
<frameset rows="40,60">
<frame src="$script_name/query" name="query" noresize>
<frame src="$script_name/lower" name="lower" noresize>
</frameset>
EOF
    ;
    exit 0;
}

sub print_html_header {
    print
        $query->start_html("NNTP WWW - A World Wide Web-based Usenet
Reader");
}

sub print_end {

    print <<END;
    <HR NOSHADE>
        <ADDRESS>Nathan V. Patwardhan</ADDRESS><BR>
            [<A HREF="http://www.somenews.com/cgi-bin/nntp_www2.pl" TARGET="_
top">Return Home</A>]
            <BR>
            [<A HREF="http://www.somenews.com/cgi-bin/nntp_www2.pl?new_
group=yes" TARGET="_top">Choose New Newsgroup</A>]
END
    print $query->end_html;
}
```

```
sub print_prompt {

    my($query) = @_; # pass in $query->param();

    $script_name = $query->script_name;

    # output <FORM> with target attribute.
    print $query->startform(-action=>"$script_name/lower",
                            -TARGET=>"query");

    # List available newsgroups in multiple select.
    print "<P><EM>Available Newsgroups</EM>  ";
    print $query->scrolling_list(
                            -name=>'newsgroups',
                            -values=>[show_active_ng()],
                            -size=>3,
                            -multiple=>'');

    print "<P>",$query->reset;
    print $query->submit('Send News Request'); # send news request button
    print $query->endform;

}

sub print_response {

    # print_response() is passed $query->param(), and handles events based
    # on input type. If the input is not a subject, or newsgroup choice,
    # a "No articles selected" message will appear.

    my($query) = @_; # pass in $query->param
    my(@values,$key);

    $script_name = $query->script_name;

    if ($query->param('newsgroups') eq '' && $query->param('subjects') eq
'') {
        print "<H2>Current Settings</H2>";
        print "<b>No articles selected.</b>";
    }


    if($query->param('new_group')) { # if chosen, return to the main page.
        print_prompt($query);
        return;
    }

    if($query->param('subjects')) {

        # A subject has been chosen. Pass subject (article number) and
        # newsgroup to show_article_as_html() so article can be output
        # as an HTML page in bottom frame.
```

```perl
        print "<P><EM>Reading Article ", $query->param('subjects'),".</EM>
";

        show_article_as_html($query->param('subjects'),
                              $query->param('newsgroups'));
         # blow away existing newsgroups variable
         # since it was reassigned as a hidden.
        $query->delete('newsgroups');

        return;
    }

    if($query->param('newsgroups')) {

        # Newsgroup has been chosen, so output list of subjects
        # to upper frame. The list of subjects is targeted to the
        # lower frame, for split-screen feel.

        print $query->startform(-action=>"$script_name/lower",
                                -TARGET=>"lower");
        print "<P><EM>Subjects for ", $query->param('newsgroups')," </EM>  ";
        show_subjects_from_active($query->param('newsgroups'));
        print "<P>",$query->reset;

        # reassign newsgroups to a hidden field, or it will
        # disappear at next POST.
        print $query->hidden(-name=>'newsgroups',
                             -default=>[$query->param('newsgroups')]);

        print $query->submit('Select Article');
        print $query->endform;

        return;
    }
}

### Helper functions

sub show_active_ng {

    # Basically the same function as NNTP-WWW.PL, but
    # empty newsgroups are no longer displayed in the main select box.

    use News::NNTPClient;

    $c = News::NNTPClient->new($newshost);

    @newsgroups = $c->list("active.times"),"\n";
    foreach (@newsgroups) {
        # remove unwanted newsgroup information
        ($groupname, $vol, $active, $owner) = split(/\s/, $_);
        undef $vol; undef $active; undef $owner; # reclaim

        ($last) = ($c->group($groupname))[1];
```

```
            if($last > 0) { # don't show empty newsgroups
                push(@groups, $groupname);
            }
        }

        return(sort(@groups)); # return active newsgroups - sorted
    }

    sub show_subjects_from_active {

        # Same function as first example

        my($newsgroup) = @_; # pass in newsgroup

        use News::NNTPClient;

        $c = News::NNTPClient->new($newshost);

        $sel_mult = "<SELECT NAME=\"subjects\" SIZE=6>\n";
        push(@articles, $sel_mult);

        for ($c->xover($c->group($newsgroup))) {
            ($article, $subject) = split /\t/;
            if($subject =~ /Re:/) {
                $subject = "<OPTION VALUE=\"$article\">".$subject."\n";
            } else {
                $subject = "<OPTION VALUE=\"$article\">"."Re: ".$subject."\n";
            }
            push(@articles, $subject);
        }

        $sel_mult = "</SELECT>\n";
        push(@articles, $sel_mult);

        print(@articles,"\n");

    }

    sub show_article_as_html {

        # same as example one.
        # pass in article number
        # and newsgroup
        my($article_number, $newsgroup) = @_;

        use News::NNTPClient;

        $c = News::NNTPClient->new($newshost);

        $c->group($newsgroup);
        @lines = $c->article($article_number);

        print("<HR NOSHADE>\n");
```

```
    foreach $line (@lines) {
        $line =~ s/\n/<BR>\n/g;
        print $line;
    }
}
```

A Graphical Mail Reader

```perl
#!/usr/local/bin/perl -w

use Getopt::Long;                    # for command line options
use Mail::POP3Client;                # for POP functions
use Tk;                              # for primitives.
use Tk::Dialog;                      # for dialog box

# $host is assigned to 'hostname' (if -host $host is undefined)
# -help switch shows program usage message; program exits

GetOptions('host:s', \$host, 'help:s', \&usage);
chop($host = 'hostname') unless $host;

$main = MainWindow->new;                    # the main container

# Top frame of ptk_mailer

$top = $main->Frame;

$sv = $top->Button(-text => 'Save', -relief => 'raised',
                   -borderwidth => 2,
                   -command => [\&save_message_to_file])->pack();
$sv->pack(-side=>'left');

$dm = $top->Button(-text => 'Delete', -command => [\&delete_message],
                   -relief => 'raised', -borderwidth => 2)->pack();
$dm->pack(-side=>'left');

$ex = $top->Button(-text => 'Exit', -command => sub{exit},
                   -relief => 'raised', -borderwidth => 2)->pack();
$ex->pack(-side=>'left');

$li = $top->Button(-text => 'Login', -relief => 'raised',
                   -command => [\&popup_auth_window]},
                   -borderwidth => 2)->pack();
$li->pack(-side=>'left');
$top->pack(-fill => 'both', -expand => 'yes');

# Middle frame of ptk_mailer

$middle = $main->Frame;
$msg_area = $middle->Listbox(-relief => 'sunken', -borderwidth => 3,
                             -width => 80, -height => 10, -setgrid => 'yes');
$msg_area->bind('<Double-1>', \&show_message_body);
$lst_scrl = $middle->Scrollbar(-command => [N$msg_area]);
```

```perl
$msg_area->configure(-yscrollcommand => [N$lst_scrl]);
$msg_area->pack(-side => 'left', -fill => 'both', -expand => 'yes');
$lst_scrl->pack(-side => 'right', -fill => 'y', -expand => 'yes');
$middle->pack(-fill => 'both', -expand => 'yes');

# Bottom frame of ptk_mailer

$bottom = $main->Frame;
$msg_text = $bottom->Text(-width => 80, -height => 40,
                          -relief => 'sunken', -borderwidth => 3);
$bdy_scrl = $bottom->Scrollbar(-command => [N$msg_text]);
$msg_text->configure(-yscrollcommand => [N$bdy_scrl]);
$msg_text->pack(-side => 'left', -fill => 'both', -expand => 'yes');
$bdy_scrl->pack(-side => 'right', -fill => 'y', -expand => 'yes');
$bottom->pack(-fill => 'both', -expand => 'yes');


# THE MAIN EVENT
MainLoop;

### Helper Functions

sub popup_auth_window {

    $tl = $main->Toplevel;
    $lw = $tl->Frame;
    $lw->Label(-text => 'Username: ')->pack(-side => 'left');
    $un = $lw->Entry(-relief => 'sunken', -borderwidth => 2);
    $un->pack(-side => 'left');
    $lw->Label(-text => 'Password: ')->pack(-side => 'left');
    $pa = $lw->Entry(-relief => 'sunken', -borderwidth => 2,
                     -show => 'x');
    $pa->pack(-side => 'left');
    $lw->pack;

    $bt = $tl->Frame;
    $bt->Button(-text => 'Login', -relief => 'raised',
                -borderwidth => 2,
                -command => [\&user_auth])->pack(-side=>'left');
    $bt->Button(-text => 'Cancel', -relief => 'raised', -borderwidth => 2,
                -command => sub{$tl->withdraw})->pack(-side=>'left');
    $bt->Button(-text => 'Exit', -relief => 'raised', -borderwidth => 2,
                -command => sub{exit})->pack(-side => 'left');
    $bt->pack;

}

sub user_auth {
    $pop = new Mail::POP3Client($un->get, $pa->get, $host);
    if(pop_login() == 1) {
        $tl->withdraw;
        $li->pack('forget');
        $li = $top->Button(-text => 'Logout',
                           -relief => 'raised',
```

```
                            -borderwidth => 2,
                            -command => [\&logout_user]);
          $li->pack(-side => 'left');
          for ($i = 1; $i <= $pop->Count; $i++) {
              foreach ($pop->Head($i)) {
                  /^(From): / and $frm eq $_;
                  /^(Subject): / and $subj eq $_;
              }
              $frm = $i.". ".$frm." ".$subj;
              $msg_area->insert('end', $frm);
          }
      } else {
          $tl->withdraw;
          $err_text = "Login Failed, or host not running POP.  Try again?";
          $err_dlg = $main->Dialog(
                                  -title => 'Login Failed.',
                                  -text  => $err_text,
                                  -default_button => 'Exit',
                                  -buttons       => ['Retry', 'Exit']);
          $choice = $err_dlg->Show;
          if($choice eq 'Yes') {
              &popup_auth_window();
          } else {
              exit;
          }
      }
  }


sub pop_login {
    if($pop->Count != -1) {
        return 1;
    } else {
        return 0;
    }
}


sub show_message_body {
    my @message = $msg_area->curselection;
    for(@message) {
        $get_msg = $msg_area->get($_);
        $get_msg =~ /\d\.\sFrom:/; $get_msg = $&; $get_msg =~ s/\D//g;
        @lines = $pop->Retrieve($get_msg);
        $msg_text->delete('0.0', 'end');
        $txt = join("\n", @lines); $txt =~ s/\r//g;
        $msg_text->insert('0.0', $txt);
    }
}


sub save_message_to_file {
    $savewin = $main->Toplevel;

    $save_top = $savewin->Frame;
    $save_txt = $save_top->Label(-text => 'Filename:');
    $save_txt->pack(-side => 'left');
```

```
        $save_nm = $save_top->Entry;
        $save_nm->pack;
        $save_top->pack;

        $save_btm = $savewin->Frame;
        $save_cncl = $savewin->Button(-text => 'Cancel Save',
                                      -command => sub{$savewin->withdraw});
        $save_cncl->pack(-side => 'left');
        $save_ok = $savewin->Button(-text => 'Save As', -command => sub{
            if(-e $save_nm->get) {
                # file exists, confirm overwrite
            } else {
                open(OUT, ">>".$save_nm->get)
                    or die("Cannot open file $save_nm->get for writing: $!");
                print OUT $msg_text->get('0.0', 'end');
                close(OUT);
                $savewin->withdraw;
            }
        });
        $save_ok->pack(-side => 'left');
        $save_btm->pack;
}

sub delete_message {
    my @message = $msg_area->curselection;
    for(@message) {
        $get_msg = $msg_area->get($_);
        $get_msg =~ /\d\.\sFrom:/; $get_msg = $&; $get_msg =~ s/\D//g;
        $pop->Delete($get_msg);
        $msg_area->delete('active');
        $msg_area->update;
        $msg_text->delete('0.0', 'end');
    }
}

sub logout_user {
    $pop->Close;
    $li->pack('forget');
    $li = $top->Button(-text => 'Login', -relief => 'raised',
                       -command => [\&popup_auth_window]},
                       -borderwidth => 2)->pack();
    $li->pack(-side=>'left');
    $msg_area->delete(0, 'end');
    $msg_text->delete('0.0', 'end');
}

### Program Usage
sub usage {
    print("Usage: $0 -host <pop host>\n");
    exit(1);
}
```

A Graphical FTP Client

```perl
#!/usr/local/bin/perl -w

require 5.002;
use English;

use Tk;
use Tk::Dialog;
use Net::FTP;

$top = MainWindow->new;
$top->Label(-text => 'Perl/Tk FTP Client')->pack(-fill => 'both', -expand =>
1);
$tl = $top->Frame();

$local_list = $tl->Frame(-relief => 'raised', -borderwidth => '2');
$ll = $local_list->Label(-text => 'Local Filesystem');
$ll->pack(-fill => 'both', -expand => 1);
$local_list->pack(-fill => 'both', -expand => 1, -side => 'left');

# LOCAL FILESYSTEM - Left Side
$left_top = $local_list->Frame();
my $localdir = $left_top->Listbox(
    -exportselection => 0,
    -relief => 'sunken',
    -width => 30,
    -height => 10,
    -setgrid => 'yes',
    -relief => 'sunken',
    -borderwidth => '2'
);
my $scroll2 = $left_top->Scrollbar(-command => [N$localdir],
                                   -relief => 'sunken',
                                   -borderwidth => '2',
                                   );
$localdir->configure(-yscrollcommand => [N$scroll2]);

# Bind left button to double-click local directory
$localdir -> bind('<Double-1>' => sub{change_local_directory()});

$scroll2->pack(-side => 'right', -fill => 'y');

$localdir->pack(-side => 'left',
                -fill => 'both',
                -expand => 1);

foreach (1..10) {
    $localdir->insert('end', "");
}

$left_top->pack(-side => 'top');

my $ld_button = $local_list->Button(-text => 'Open Local Filesystem',
```

```
                    -relief => 'raised', -borderwidth => '2',
            -command => [\&open_local_filesystem]})->
                        pack(-fill => 'both', -expand => 1);
my $ld_button = $local_list->Button(-text => 'Close Local Filesystem',
    -relief => 'raised', -borderwidth => '2',
    -command => [\&close_local_filesystem])->pack(-fill => 'both',
                                            -expand => 1);
$left_bottom = $local_list->Frame();
my $localfile = $left_bottom->Listbox(
    -selectmode => 'multiple',
    -exportselection => 0,
    -relief => 'sunken',
    -width => 30,
    -height => 10,
    -setgrid => 'yes',
    -relief => 'sunken',
    -borderwidth => '2'
);
my $scroll2 = $left_bottom->Scrollbar(-command => [N$localfile],
                                    -relief => 'sunken',
                                    -borderwidth => '2',
                                    );
$localfile->configure(-yscrollcommand => [N$scroll2]);
$scroll2->pack(-side => 'right', -fill => 'y');

$localfile->pack(-side => 'left',
                -fill => 'both',
                -expand => 1);

foreach (1..10) {
    $localfile->insert('end', "");
}

$left_bottom->pack(-side => 'bottom');


# BUTTONS - packed left of remote filesystem (north down)
$buttons = $tl->Frame();
my $button_left = $buttons->Button(-text => '<--', -relief => 'raised',
                                -borderwidth => '2',
                                -command => [\&download_file]},
                                -anchor => 'n')->pack(-fill => 'both',
                                                    -expand => 1);
my $button_quit = $buttons->Button(-text => 'Quit', -relief => 'raised',
                                -borderwidth => '2',
                                -command => sub{exit})->pack(-fill =>
'both', -expand => 1);
my $button_right = $buttons->Button(-text => '-->', -relief => 'raised',
                                -borderwidth => '2',
                                -command => [\&upload_file])->pack(-fill
=> 'both', -expand => 1);
$buttons->pack(-fill => 'both', -expand => 1, -side => 'left');


# REMOTE FILESYSTEM - Right Side
```

```perl
$remote_list = $tl->Frame(-relief => 'raised', -borderwidth => '2');
$12 = $remote_list->Label(-text => 'Remote FileSystem');
$12->pack(-fill => 'both', -expand => 1);
$remote_list->pack(-fill => 'both', -expand => 1, -side => 'right');

$tl->pack(-fill => 'both', -expand => 1);

$right_top = $remote_list->Frame();
my $remotedir = $right_top->Listbox(
    -exportselection => 0,
    -relief => 'sunken',
    -width => 30,
    -height => 10,
    -setgrid => 'yes',
    -relief => 'sunken',
    -borderwidth => '2'
);
my $scroll2 = $right_top->Scrollbar(-command => [N$remotedir],
                                    -relief => 'sunken',
                                    -borderwidth => '2',
                                    );
$remotedir->configure(-yscrollcommand => [N$scroll2]);
$scroll2->pack(-fill => 'both', -expand => 1,
               -side => 'right', -fill => 'y');

# Bind left button to double-click local directory
$remotedir -> bind('<Double-1>' => sub{open_ftp_connection('',
                                                            '',
                                                            '',
                                                            'cwd')});

$remotedir->pack(-side => 'right',
                 -fill => 'both',
                 -expand => 1);
$right_top->pack(-fill => 'both', -expand => 1, -side => 'top');

$ld_button = $remote_list->Button(-text => 'Open Remote Filesystem',
                                  -relief => 'raised',
                                   -borderwidth => '2',
                                  -command => [\&auth_info])->pack(-fill =>
'both', -expand => 1);
$ld_button = $remote_list->Button(-text => 'Close Remote Filesystem',
                                  -relief => 'raised',
                                   -borderwidth => '2',
                                  -command => sub {&open_ftp_connection('',
                                                                         '',
                                                                         '',
                                                                         'quit')
                                            })->pack(-fill => 'both',
                                                     -expand => 1);

$right_bottom = $remote_list->Frame();
my $remotefile = $right_bottom->Listbox(
    -selectmode => 'multiple',
```

```
                -exportselection => 0,
                -relief => 'sunken',
                -width => 30,
                -height => 10,
                -setgrid => 'yes',
                -relief => 'sunken',
                -borderwidth => '2'
    );
    my $scroll2 = $right_bottom->Scrollbar(-command => [N$remotefile],
                                           -relief => 'sunken',
                                           -borderwidth => '2',
                                           );
    $remotefile->configure(-yscrollcommand => [N$scroll2]);
    $scroll2->pack(-fill => 'both', -expand => 1, -side => 'right', -fill =>
    'y');

    $remotefile->pack(-fill => 'both',
                      -expand => 1);
    $right_bottom->pack(-fill => 'both', -expand => 1, -side => 'bottom');

    # THE MAIN EVENT
    MainLoop;

    # Toplevel Windows

    sub auth_info {

        $pane = $top->Toplevel(-title => 'Login to FTP Server');
        $auth_form = $pane->Frame;
        $auth_form->pack;

        $tophalf = $auth_form->Frame();

        $first = $tophalf->Frame(-relief => 'raised', -borderwidth => '2');
        $first->Label(-text => 'Username: ')->pack(-side => 'left');
        $username = $first->Entry(-width => 30,
                                  -relief => 'sunken')->pack(-side => 'left');
        $first->pack(-side => 'left');

        $second = $tophalf->Frame(-relief => 'raised', -borderwidth => '2');
        $second->Label(-text => 'Password: ')->pack(-side => 'left');
        $password = $second->Entry(-width => 30, -relief => 'sunken',
                                   -show => '*')->pack(-side => 'left');
        $second->pack(-side => 'left');

        $third = $tophalf->Frame(-relief => 'raised', -borderwidth => '2');
        $third->Label(-text => 'FTP Host: ')->pack(-side => 'left');
        $ftp_host = $third->Entry(-width => 30,
                                  -relief => 'sunken')->pack(-side => 'left');
        $third->pack(-side => 'right');

        $tophalf->pack(-side => 'top');

        $bottomhalf = $auth_form->Frame();
```

```
        $button_1 = $bottomhalf->Button(-text => 'Login',
                    -command => sub {open_ftp_connection($username, $password,
                                    $ftp_host, '')});
        $button_1->pack(-side => 'left');
        $button_2 = $bottomhalf->Button(-text => 'Clear Entries',
                                        -command => [\&clear_auth_form]);
        $button_2->pack(-side => 'left');

        $button_3 = $bottomhalf->Button(-text => 'Exit Authorization',
                                        -command => [$pane => 'withdraw'],
                                        -anchor => 'center');
        $button_3->pack(-side => 'left');
        $button_4 = $bottomhalf->Button(-text => 'Quit Program',
                                        -command => sub {exit});
        $button_4->pack(-side => 'left');
        $bottomhalf->pack(-side => 'bottom');


}


# Helper functions

sub clear_auth_form {

    $username->delete(0, 'end');
    $password->delete(0, 'end');


}

sub open_local_filesystem {

    # first, cleanup
    $localdir->delete(0, 'end');
    $localfile->delete(0, 'end');

    foreach (file_type($ENV{'HOME'},'dir')) {
        $localdir->insert('end', $_);
    }

    foreach (file_type($ENV{'HOME'},'file')) {
        $localfile->insert('end', $_);
    }


}

sub change_local_directory {

    $prevdir = '' unless $prevdir;

    @local_dir = $localdir->curselection;
    for(@local_dir) { $newdir = $localdir->get($_);};
    chdir($newdir);

    if($prevdir eq '') {
        $todir = $ENV{'HOME'}."/".$newdir."/";
```

```
        } else {
                $prevdir .= $newdir."/";
                $todir = $prevdir;
        }
        $prevdir = $todir;

        # Reset ../ if current dir is the same as ../../foo/../../bar
        if((stat($todir))[1] eq (stat($ENV{'HOME'}))[1]) {
            $todir = $ENV{'HOME'};
            $newdir = '';
            $prevdir = '';
        }

        # first, cleanup
        $localdir->delete(0, 'end');
        $localfile->delete(0, 'end');

        # then, open it up
        foreach (file_type($todir,'dir')) {
            $localdir->insert('end', $_);
        }

        foreach (file_type($todir,'file')) {
            $localfile->insert('end', $_);
        }

}

sub close_local_filesystem {

    # clear out both panes
    $localdir->delete(0, 'end');
    $localfile->delete(0, 'end');

}

sub open_ftp_connection {

    my($user, $pass, $host, $cmd) = @_;
    my($login, $password, $ftp_host);

    if($cmd eq '' && $user ne '' && $pass ne '' && $host ne '') {
        # we're not quitting
        # first, cleanup
        $remotedir->delete(0, 'end');
        $remotefile->delete(0, 'end');

        $login = $user->get();
        $password = $pass->get();
        $ftp_host = $host->get();

        $ftp = Net::FTP->new($ftp_host, Debug=>2000);
        $ftp->login($login, $password);
```

```
        @entries = $ftp->dir('-al');
        foreach (@entries) {
            (@foo) = split(/\s+/, $_);
            next if $foo[8] eq '';
            if($foo[0] =~ /d(.+)/ || $foo[0] =~ /l(.+)/) {
                print "DIR: ",$foo[8],"\n";
                $remotedir->insert('end', $foo[8]);
            } else {
                print "File: ",$foo[8],"\n";
                $remotefile->insert('end', $foo[8]);
            }
        }
    } elsif($cmd eq 'quit' && $user eq ''
            && $pass eq '' && $host eq '') {
        # send (ftp) quit
        $ftp->quit;
    } elsif ($cmd eq 'cwd' && $user eq ''
                && $pass eq '' && $host eq '') {
        @dir = $remotedir->curselection;
        for(@dir) { print $remotedir->get($_),"\n";
                    $ftp->cwd($remotedir->get($_)); }

        $remotedir->delete(0, 'end');
        $remotefile->delete(0, 'end');

        @entries = $ftp->dir('-al');
        foreach (@entries) {
            (@foo) = split(/\s+/, $_);
            next if $foo[8] eq '';
            if($foo[0] =~ /d(.+)/ || $foo[0] =~ /l(.+)/) {
                print "DIR: ",$foo[8],"\n";
                $remotedir->insert('end', $foo[8]);
            } else {
                print "File: ",$foo[8],"\n";
                $remotefile->insert('end', $foo[8]);
            }
        }
    } else {
        print("Nothing matches.\nBailing out...\n");
        $ftp->quit;
    }

}

sub download_file {

    my(@files);

    @files = $remotefile->curselection;
    @tolocal = $localdir->curselection;

    for(@tolocal) { $todir = $localdir->get($_); }

    for(@files) {
```

```perl
            print "Getting --> ",$remotefile->get($_),"\n";
            $ftp->get($remotefile->get($_),
                    $todir."/".$remotefile->get($_));
    }

}

sub upload_file {

    my(@files);

    @files = $localfile->curselection;
    for(@files) {
        print "Putting --> ",$localfile->get($_),"\n";
        $ftp->put($localfile->get($_));
    }

}

sub close_remote_fs {

    # clear out both panes
    $remotedir->delete(0, 'end');
    $remotefile->delete(0, 'end');

}

sub file_type {

    my($dirname, $type) = @_;
    my (@files, @dirs);

    chdir($dirname);

    opendir(DIR, $dirname) or die("dir $dirname open error: $!");
    while($entry = readdir(DIR)) {
        if(-f $dirname."/".$entry) {
            push(@files, $entry);
        } else {
            push(@dirs, $entry);
        }
    }
    closedir(DIR);

    if($type eq 'file') {
        return(@files);
    } elsif($type eq 'dir') {
        return(@dirs);
    }

}
```

An Image Viewer

```perl
#!/usr/local/bin/perl -w

use strict;
use Tk;
use Tk::JPEG;
use Getopt::Long;

my($main, $left, $right);
my($image, $im_l, $im_type, $image_file);
my($i_name);
my($file_sel, $top, $text, $fname, $btm);
my($b1, $b2, $b3);

# Default image that gets loaded when there is not a command line argument
my $earth = '/usr/local/lib/perl5/site_perl/Tk/demos/images/earth.gif';

# Get the command line arguments.
# Switches: image, help.  Image takes one argument - help calls sub help
GetOptions('image:s', \$i_name, 'help:s', \&help);

$main = MainWindow->new;

$left = $main->Frame(-relief => 'sunken', -borderwidth => 3);

if($i_name) {
    $i_name =~ /(.+)\.(.+)/;
    if(($im_type = check_image_format($2)) eq '') {
        print("Image format not supported.\n");
        exit(1);
    }
    $image = $left->Photo('-format' => $im_type,
                          -file => $i_name);
} else {
    $image = $left->Photo('-format' => $im_type,
                          -file => $earth);
}
    $im_l = $left->Label('-image' => $image);
    $im_l->pack(-expand => 1, -fill => 'both');

$left->pack(-expand => 1, -fill => 'both', -side => 'left');

$right = $main->Frame();
$right->Button(-text => 'Open Image', -command => sub {

    $file_sel = $main->Toplevel(-title => 'Select a file');
    $top = $file_sel->Frame();
    $text = $top->Label(-text => 'Filename: ');
    $text->pack(-expand => 1, -fill => 'both', -side => 'left');
    $fname = $top->Entry();
    $fname->pack(-expand => 1, -fill => 'both', -side => 'left');
    $top->pack(-expand => 1, -fill => 'both');
```

```
        $btm = $file_sel->Frame();
        $b1 = $btm->Button(-text => 'Open', -command => sub {
            $image_file = $fname->get;
            if(-f $image_file) {
                print("Loading: $image_file\n");
                $image->delete;
                $im_l->pack('forget');

                $image_file =~ /(.+)\.(.+)/;
                if(($im_type = check_image_format($2)) eq '') {
                    print("Image format not supported.\n");
                    exit(1);
                }
                $image = $left->Photo('-format' => $im_type,
                                       -file => $image_file);
                $im_l = $left->Label('-image' => $image);
                $im_l->pack(-expand => 1, -fill => 'both');

                $file_sel->withdraw;
            } else {
                # Error, man.
                print("Cannot load file.\n");
            }
        });
        $b1->pack(-side => 'left');
        $b2 = $btm->Button(-text => 'Cancel',
                           -command => [$file_sel=>'withdraw']);
        $b2->pack(-side => 'left');
        $b3 = $btm->Button(-text => 'Quit', -command => sub{exit});
        $b3->pack(-side => 'left');
        $btm->pack(-expand => 1, -fill => 'both');
})->pack(-expand => 1, -fill => 'both');

$right->Button(-text => 'Close Image',
            -command => sub { $image->delete; })->pack(-expand => 1,
                                                  -fill => 'both');
$right->Button(-text => 'Exit Program',
            -command => sub{$image->delete; exit})->pack(-expand => 1,
                                                  -fill => 'both');
$right->pack(-expand => 1, -fill => 'both', -side => 'right');

# THE MAIN EVENT
MainLoop;

# Helper functions

sub help {
    print("Usage: showimage.pl -image <imagename>\n");
    print("                    -help\n");
    print("                    <none> (default)\n");
    exit(1);
}

sub check_image_format {
```

```perl
    my($ext) = @_;
    my(%TYPES) = ();

    %TYPES = ( 'jpg' => 'jpeg', 'gif' => 'gif');

    foreach (keys %TYPES) {
        if($ext eq $_) { return($TYPES{$_}); }
    }
}
```

An Image Generator

```perl
#!/usr/local/bin/perl

use strict;
use vars qw($opt_r);
use Getopt::Std;
use GD;

my(@range);

getopt('r'); # one argument for range

if($opt_r) {
    (@range) = split(/:/, $opt_r); # arguments must resemble first:last
                                   # or output the usage message for error
    if(scalar(@range) == 2) {
        make_image($range[0], $range[1]); # now, output images from
                                           # first to last
    } else {
        usage(); # fail-case.  output usage message
    }
} else {
    usage(); # fail-case.  output usage message
}

sub make_image {

    my($first, $last) = @_; # pass-in first, last gif numbers
    my($im, $white, $black, $width, $height);

    for ($first .. $last) {

        # Compute the ratio of $width, $height to the font (8x16 - large)
        $width = length($_)*8; # Single digits = 8, double = 16, etc.
        $height = 16; # the height will always be 16 for the large font

        # output all gifs to the Images directory.  Change this per your spec
        open(OUTFILE, ">Images/$_.gif")
            or die("output file $_.gif error: $!");
        print("Opening: $_.gif for writing.\n");

        $im = GD::Image->new($width, $height);
```

```
        ($white,$black) =
            (
            $im->colorAllocate(255, 255, 255),
            $im->colorAllocate(0, 0, 0)
            );
        $im->transparent($white);      # white color is transparent
        $im->interlaced(1);            # cool venetian blinds effect

        $im->string(gdLargeFont,0,0,$_,$black); # use the 8x16 font

        print OUTFILE $im->gif; # output the image to (FILEHANDLE)
        close(OUTFILE);
    }
}

sub usage {
    print("Usage: $0 -r <first:last>\n");
    exit(1); # failure
}
```

Index

international standard date/time
     notation, 75–76
InterNIC, 161
invoking methods, 11–12
IO modules
     IO::File, 202–203
     IO::Handle, 204
IPC::Open2 module, 204
@ISA array, 7
iterations attribute, 130

J

Johnson, Kevin, 50
join conditions, 152–154

K

keyboard events, 113–114
keys
     artificial, 142
     compound primary, 143
     natural, 142
     primary, 141
Koenig, Andreas, 234

L

Label( ), 131
label attribute, 128, 133
Label widgets, 95–96
Language variable (Date::Manip), 86
leap( ), 80
Libraries for WWW Access in Perl, 193–205
libraries, Sfio, 208–209
line( ), 120
lines, drawing, 120
links, extracting from HTML, 197–198
Listbox widgets, 99–100
     getting input from, 110–111
load( ), 182
local CPAN mirroring, 240–242
localtime( ), 72–74
Location directives, 216
locking email message folders, 50
Login( ), login( )
     Mail::POP3Client, 49
     Net::FTP, 168
     Net::Netrc, 172
     Net::Telnet, 166

lookup( ), 171
loop attribute, 130
lpa( ), 172
ls( ), 169
LWP package, 193–205
     developing Web server with, 198–205
     LWP::Agent module, 195
     LWP::Simple module, 194–195
     LWP::UserAgent module, 198

M

MacEachern, Doug, 211
magick attribute, 130
Magnify( ), 131
mail (see email)
mail( ), 43
MAIL command (SMTP), 41
Mail modules
     Mail::Address, 53–55
     Mail::Cap, 56
     Mail::Folder, 50–52
     Mail::Header, 52
     Mail::Internet, 52
     Mail::Mailer, 36–37
     Mail::POP3Client, 45–49
     Mail::Send, 37–40
mailcap file, 55–57
MainLoop procedure (pTk), 92
MainWindow container (pTk), 92
MANIFEST file, 239
manipulating (see editing)
manpages, 233
manpages for modules, 16
mark( ), 182
mark_list( ), 182
mark_range( ), 182
marked( ), 182
marked_articles( ), 182
matte attribute, 128
mattecolor attribute, 130
mean attribute, 129
message_list( ), 52
messages, mail (see email)
method( ), 200
methods, 10
     adding to modules, 224–227
     invoking, 11–12
     (see also subroutines)

About the Authors

Prior to joining O'Reilly & Associates as UNIX system administrator, **Nathan Patwardhan** was a software developer and system administrator for Banta Integrated Media in Cambridge, MA. When not hacking Perl or advocating FreeBSD and Linux to his friends, coworkers, relatives, and other folks who don't know UNIX from Munich, Nathan is an avid music collector.

By day, **Clay Irving** is the MIS director of Skechers USA, Inc. Away from the office, he maintains several popular web sites including the Perl Reference section of *www.perl.com*, Newton Reference, New York City Reference, and New York City Beer Guide. Clay is an amateur radio operator and is actively involved in emergency communications.

Colophon

The animal featured on the cover of the *Perl Resource Kit*, UNIX Edition, is a camel (one-hump dromedary). Camels are large ruminant mammals, weighing between 1,000 and 1,600 pounds and standing six to seven feet tall at the shoulders. They are well known for their use as draft and saddle animals in the desert regions, especially in Africa and Asia. Camels can go for days without water. If food is scarce, they will eat anything, even their owner's tent. Camels live up to 50 years.

Ted Meister designed this cover and the packaging for the *Perl Resource Kit*. The layouts were produced with Adobe Photoshop 4 and QuarkXpress 3.32, using Adobe ITC Garamond and Helvetica Condensed fonts. The camel image is from the Dover Pictorial Archive.

The interior layout was designed by Nancy Priest and Edie Freedman, and implemented in FrameMaker 5.0 by Mike Sierra. The text and heading fonts are ITC Garamond Light and ITC Garamond Book, by Adobe. The illustrations were created in Macromedia Freehand 7 by Robert Romano.

Whenever possible, our books use RepKover™, a durable and flexible lay-flat binding. If the page count exceeds RepKover's limit, perfect binding is used.

Register Your Copy of the

Perl

Resource Kit Today

O'REILLY & ASSOCIATES, INC. SOFTWARE LICENSE AGREEMENT